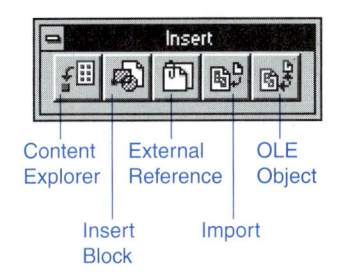

Insert

- Content Explorer
- External Reference
- OLE Object
- Insert Block
- Import

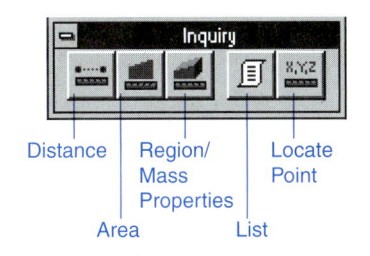

Inquiry

- Distance
- Region/Mass Properties
- Locate Point
- Area
- List

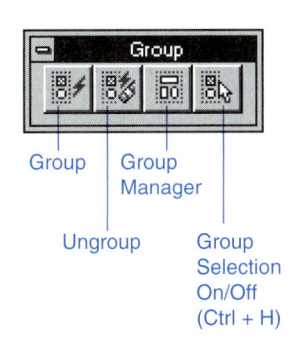

Group

- Group
- Group Manager
- Ungroup
- Group Selection On/Off (Ctrl + H)

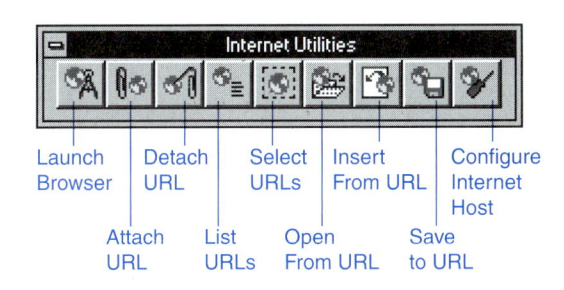

Internet Utilities

- Launch Browser
- Detach URL
- Select URLs
- Insert From URL
- Configure Internet Host
- Attach URL
- List URLs
- Open From URL
- Save to URL

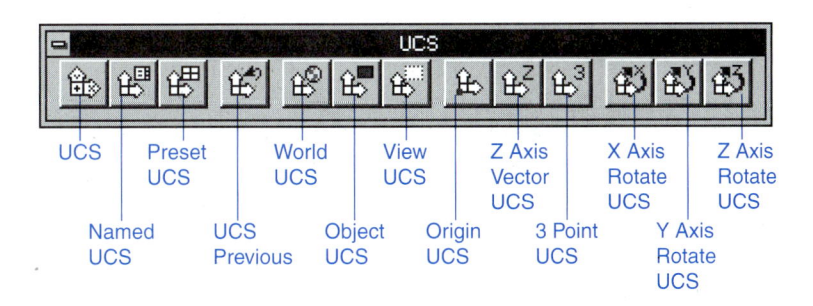

UCS

- UCS
- Preset UCS
- World UCS
- View UCS
- Z Axis Vector UCS
- X Axis Rotate UCS
- Z Axis Rotate UCS
- Named UCS
- UCS Previous
- Object UCS
- Origin UCS
- 3 Point UCS
- Y Axis Rotate UCS

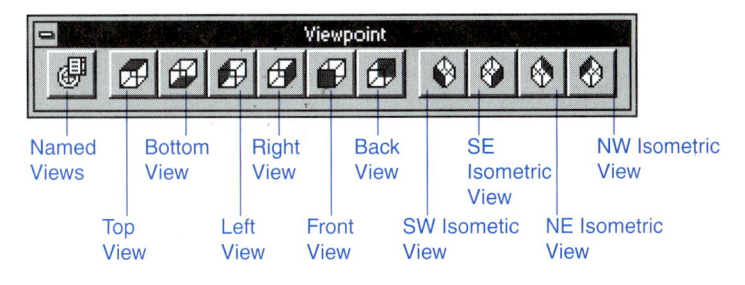

Viewpoint

- Named Views
- Bottom View
- Right View
- Back View
- SE Isometric View
- NW Isometric View
- Top View
- Left View
- Front View
- SW Isometric View
- NE Isometric View

AutoCAD LT®98

Basics Through Advanced

AutoCAD LT®98

Basics Through Advanced

David A. Madsen
Chairman
Drafting Technology
Autodesk Premier Training Center

Clackamas Community College
Oregon City, OR

Former Board of Directors
American Design Drafting Association

Rod Rawls
Autodesk Certified Instructor
Drafting Technology
Autodesk Premier Training Center

Clackamas Community College
Oregon City, OR

PRENTICE HALL
Upper Saddle River, New Jersey ||| Columbus, Ohio

Library of Congress Cataloging-in-Publication Data

Madsen, David A.
    Autocad LT 98: basics through advanced / David A. Madsen, Rod Rawls.
      p.   cm.
    ISBN 0-13-085100-0
    1. Computer graphics.   2. AutoCAD LT for Windows.   I. Rawls, Rod R.   II. Title.
    T385.M323   2000
    604.2′0285′5369—dc21
                                                   99-31018
                                                      CIP

Cover art: © Jason Moore
Editor: Stephen Helba
Production Editor: Louise N. Sette
Production Supervision: Karen Fortgang, bookworks
Design Coordinator: Karrie Converse-Jones
Cover Designer: Jason Moore
Production Manager: Deidra M. Schwartz
Marketing Manager: Chris Bracken

This book was set in Times Roman by STELLARViSIONs and was printed and bound by Courier/Kendallville, Inc. The cover was printed by Phoenix Color Corp.

© 2000 by Prentice-Hall, Inc.
Pearson Education
Upper Saddle River, New Jersey 07458

All rights reserved. No part of this book may be reproduced, in any form or by any means, without permission in writing from the publisher.

AutoCAD LT®98 is a trademark of Autodesk, Inc.

Printed in the United States of America

10 9 8 7 6 5 4 3 2 1

ISBN: 0-13-085100-0

Prentice-Hall International (UK) Limited, *London*
Prentice-Hall of Australia Pty. Limited, *Sydney*
Prentice-Hall of Canada, Inc., *Toronto*
Prentice-Hall Hispanoamericana, S. A., *Mexico*
Prentice-Hall of India Private Limited, *New Delhi*
Prentice-Hall of Japan, Inc., *Tokyo*
Prentice-Hall (Singapore) Pte. Ltd., *Singapore*
Editora Prentice-Hall do Brasil, Ltda., *Rio de Janeiro*

A message to students and teachers: please let us know how we can make this text better, and please send us drawing projects that you would like to be considered for the next edition of this text.

—David Madsen

I would like to express my sincere thanks to you, the reader, for making it all worthwhile – and to my loving and patient family for making it all possible.

—Rod Rawls

Preface

AutoCAD LT®98: Basics Through Advanced is a text and workbook that provides complete coverage of AutoCAD LT. This text provides the beginning student and the drafting or engineering professional with a complete understanding of every AutoCAD LT command using professional drafting methods and techniques. All software commands are presented in a manner that shows each prompt with examples of the exact input you should use. This text also contains a variety of valuable features that help make learning AutoCAD LT easy for you:

- It is easy to read, use, and understand.
- Learning Goals are provided at the beginning of each chapter to identify what you will learn as a result of completing the chapter.
- The text includes Microsoft Windows® 95, Windows98, and Windows NT applications.
- Commands are presented in a manner that shows every prompt with the exact input you should use.
- Field Notes explain special applications, tricks, and professional tips for using AutoCAD LT.
- Through the Window ... is a unique feature that shares Windows95, Windows98, and Windows NT applications.
- Exercises are provided throughout for you to practice as you learn AutoCAD LT.
- Learning Checkpoints are questions that are placed throughout the text following each major topic discussion. Answering these questions provides you with an excellent way to review the previous information and check your knowledge and understanding.
- Multiple choice tests, matching exercises, and word scrambles are provided with each chapter to help you learn and have fun with AutoCAD LT.
- Multidisciplinary projects allow you to learn how to use AutoCAD LT in your drafting, engineering, or architectural field.
- The Instructor's Resource Manual contains project solutions and multiple choice, matching, and word scramble solutions. The Instructor's Resource Manual also has additional multiple choice tests, crosswords, word finds, and fill-in-the-blank activities related to each chapter in the text. Answers and solutions are also provided for these tests and activities.

Format of Text

The format of this text helps you learn how to use AutoCAD LT both by example and complete explanations of each feature.

Command Access Mapping

Every AutoCAD LT command discussion begins with a display of the available options for accessing that command. For example, the toolbar button that starts the LINE command is displayed at the top of the graphic image in the margin next to this paragraph. Also included is the name of the toolbar and the tooltip — for easier recognition. The second area shows the name and option used to access the command from the pull-down menu system. The command name and any default command shortcuts (aliases) or accelerator keystrokes are shown last.

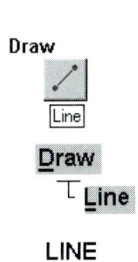

Draw

Line

Draw

Line

LINE
L

Accessing AutoCAD LT Commands

In addition to the quick reference mapping of available command selection methods, all options are further described within the text. For example, the LINE command can be accessed by picking Line from the Draw pull-down menu, by picking Line in the Draw toolbar, or by typing **L** or **LINE** at the Command: prompt. The keyboard letter used to access the menu and the command is shown underlined just as it is in the AutoCAD LT menu system.

When a command sequence is discussed, examples of the command are presented as if you are typing at the keyboard, or as it appears when you pick the command from the toolbar or pull-down menu. When the command is presented as if it is typed at the keyboard, any available keyboard shortcut is always given before the full command name. One goal of this book is for you to see all of the methods of using AutoCAD LT commands and to decide which methods work best for you.

Understanding the Command Format Presented in This Text

When a command is issued at the keyboard, the command shortcut and full name are displayed in bold full caps and the return arrow symbol (↵) shows you when to press the Enter key. This is an example of how a command is displayed when entered at the keyboard:

Command: **L** or **LINE**↵

When the command prompts are answered by typing a value, the typed information is also presented in bold. For example, the following LINE command prompts are answered with coordinate values followed by pressing the Enter key:

Command: **L** or **LINE**↵
From point: **4.5, 2.5**↵
To point: **7.5, 8.5**↵
To point: ↵
Command:

When you pick a point or use a technique other than typing, the prompt is followed by the suggested method presented in italics and angle brackets:

Command: **L** or **LINE**↵
From point: ⟨*pick a point*⟩
To point: ⟨*pick a point*⟩
To point: ↵
Command:

After you have learned the different ways to respond to AutoCAD LT prompts, you can use the method that works best for you. For example, if the prompt reads

From point: ⟨*pick a point*⟩

you can pick a point, as suggested, enter coordinate values, or use any other input method you prefer.

Presenting Command Options

When a prompt asks you to select a command option, the capitalized letter or letters within the option name must be entered at the keyboard. If a letter in more than one word is capitalized, you can enter either letter. The polyline command options are used in the following example:

Command: **PL** or **PLINE**↵
From point: ⟨*pick a point*⟩
Arc/Close/Halfwidth/Length/Undo/Width/<Endpoint of line>: **W**↵

If you are given a prompt with a value in brackets <>, you can enter a new value or press Enter to accept the value in the brackets like this:

PREFACE ix

```
Command: PL or PLINE↵
From point: ⟨pick a point⟩
Arc/Close/Halfwidth/Length/Undo/Width/<Endpoint of line>: W↵
Starting width <0.0000>: .25↵
Ending width <0.2500>: ↵
```

Identifying Key Words

Key words are *bold italic* for your ease in identification. These words relate to AutoCAD LT terminology and professional applications. These words are defined in the content of the text and in the glossary. Key words are an important part of your AutoCAD LT learning process, because they are part of the world of computer-aided drafting, drafting standards, and AutoCAD LT communication.

Special Features

AutoCAD LT 98: Basics Through Advanced contains several special features that help you learn and use AutoCAD LT, Windows95, Windows98, and Windows NT as explained in the following paragraphs. Most features are shown here as they appear in the book.

- ☐ Learning Goals
- ☐ Use AutoCAD LT to prepare drawings in your field of interest or in a variety of disciplines.
- ☐ Answer questions related to AutoCAD LT.
- ☐ Use AutoCAD LT and drafting related terminology.
- ☐ Do exercises as you learn AutoCAD LT.
- ☐ Use matching, multiple choice, word scramble, and projects activities to learn AutoCAD LT and for fun.

Exercise P.1

1. An exercise is provided after each AutoCAD LT topic or command lesson.
2. The exercises allow you to practice what you have just learned. Practicing AutoCAD LT applications is one of the most important keys to learning the program effectively.
3. Exercises should be completed at a computer while using AutoCAD LT to reinforce what you have just studied.
4. Exercises are saved to disk and can be used only as practice or as classroom assignments.

✓ LEARNING CHECKPOINT

- ☐ A Learning Checkpoint is provided after every major AutoCAD LT learning section in each chapter.
- ☐ Learning Checkpoints are questions that relate to the previous content of the chapter.
- ☐ These questions are key to what you should learn about AutoCAD LT.
- ☐ Learning Checkpoint questions can be used as review or as mini-tests for checking your progress.

Through the Window...

Through the Window . . . is a special feature that provides you with instructions and applications, plus insightful tips and tricks for using Windows95, Windows98, and Windows NT effectively with AutoCAD LT.

Windows95/Windows98/Windows NT 4.0

The screen images used in *AutoCAD LT®98: Basics Through Advanced* show the Windows NT operating system being used, but all AutoCAD commands and functions work exactly the same whether you are using Windows95, Windows98, or Windows NT.

> ### ✏️ Field Notes
>
> Field Notes are another special feature of *AutoCAD LT®98: Basics Through Advanced*. Field Notes are placed throughout the text to provide you with any one or more of the following advantages:
>
> - Professional tips and applications
> - Special features of AutoCAD LT
> - Advanced applications
> - Additional instruction about how certain features work

Multiple Choice Test

There is a multiple choice test at the end of each chapter. The multiple choice tests can be used to check your understanding of the chapter content or they can be used as review. The multiple choice tests allow you to quickly determine your knowledge and they are easy for you or your instructor to evaluate. Expanded comprehensive multiple choice tests are provided in the Instructor's Resource Manual and correlated with every chapter of the text.

Matching Exercises

At the end of every chapter there is a matching exercise that provides a word list and chapter-related statements. You match the word to the statement. This is a convenient way to review the key terminology related to the current chapter.

Word Scramble

Each chapter has a word scramble. These puzzles provide you with a fun way to review key words and commands that are important in the current chapter.

Projects

Drafting projects are one of the most important ways to complete and solidify your learning and understanding of AutoCAD LT. It has been said many times, in terms of learning AutoCAD, that if you do not practice you will forget. The projects allow you to put to practice what you have just learned. The projects are different from the exercises, because they combine a variety of commands that are used in the current chapter and in past chapters. Exercises focus only on using the currently discussed command. The projects at the end of every chapter are designed to provide AutoCAD LT practice for a variety of drafting fields. You or your instructor can select the projects that relate directly to the type of drafting you are doing. Projects are identified with the following icons that correlate to the related drafting field. This makes it easier for you to target the desired projects.

This icon identifies projects that are designed to develop AutoCAD LT skills in the area of mechanical drawing for the machine manufacturing industry.

This icon represents projects that are based on the architectural drafting and building construction industry.

This icon is used to identify projects that are designed to relate to the electrical and electronics drafting industry.

This icon is used to describe projects that relate to the industrial pipe drafting, plumbing, or the fluid power industry.

This icon is used to identify drawings that are done in the graphics industry. These projects include signs, logos, charts, graphs, and art-related topics.

Appendices

The appendices for this text are designed to help you use AutoCAD LT in the architectural, engineering, and drafting environments. The appendices contain the following valuable information:

- Installing AutoCAD LT 98
- Drafting Standards
- Standard Support Libraries

Instructor's Resource Manual

The Instructor's Resource Manual for this text provides the following items:

- Introduction: How to Use this Text
- Chapter Learning Checkpoint Answers
- Chapter Multiple Choice Test Answers
- Chapter Matching Answers
- Chapter Word Scramble Answers
- Chapter Exercise Solutions
- Chapter Project Solutions
- Suggested Course Syllabi
- Handouts
- Companion Website Information

The Instructor's Resource Manual also contains for additional fun and training with AutoCAD LT:

- Comprehensive multiple choice tests and solutions
- Crossword puzzles and solutions for each chapter
- Word finds and solutions for each chapter
- Fill-in-the-blank questions and solutions for each chapter

Companion Website
http://www.prenhall.com/madsen/

The Companion Website is a valuable instructional aid that benefits students and instructors alike. On the website you will find materials such as objective listings for each chapter, additional tests that can be taken on-line and e-mailed directly to the instructor, and current course syllabi (provided by your instructor). More than a simple evaluation method, these tests provide hints and, upon completion, immediate feedback to the student — transforming the Companion Website into a powerful learning tool.

Acknowledgments

We would also like to express our appreciation to the reviewers of this text: Gerald Bacza, Fairmont State College; Thomas Hester, California Polytechnic University, Pomona; Scott MacKenzie; and Graham Walker, Manhattan College.

Warning and Disclaimer

This book is designed to provide tutorial information about the AutoCAD LT®98 computer program. Every effort has been made to make this book complete and as accurate as possible, but no warranty or fitness is implied.

The information is provided on an "as-is" basis. The author and Prentice-Hall, Inc. shall have neither liability nor responsibility to any person or entity with respect to any loss or damage in connection with or arising from information contained in this book.

Contents

Chapter 1
An Introduction to AutoCAD LT — 1

About Computer-Aided Drafting   1
Computer Equipment and Terminology   2
    Computer,   2
    Monitor,   3
    Keyboard,   3
    Pointing Devices,   4
    Data Storage Devices,   6
    Printers and Plotters,   6
    Computer Networks,   7
    Operating Systems,   9
    Ergonomics in the Workplace,   9
    Accessibility Options,   10
About AutoCAD LT   11
    Starting AutoCAD LT   11
    Using Dialog Boxes,   12
    Accessing AutoCAD LT Commands and Features,   16
    Canceling an AutoCAD LT Command,   18
    Using Pull-Down Menus in AutoCAD LT,   18
    Accelerator Keys,   19
AutoCAD LT Toolbars and Toolbar Buttons,   20
    The AutoCAD LT Command Window and the Text Screen,   22
    Sizing and Positioning the AutoCAD LT Window,   24
    Sizing and Moving Other Windows Components,   27
    Starting a Drawing Session,   28
    Ending a Drawing Session,   30
Using On-Line Help in AutoCAD LT,   31
    Browsing the Help Contents,   31
    Help Information Display Controls,   33
    Using the Index,   34
    Searching the Help System,   34
    Context-Sensitive Help,   35

Multiple Choice   36
Matching   37
Word Scramble   37

Chapter 2

Introduction to Drafting with AutoCAD LT — 39

Drafting with AutoCAD LT   39
The AutoCAD LT Drawing Setup Options   39
    Using the Quick Setup,   39
    Setting Units of Measure,   40
    Setting the Drawing Size,   41
    More About Drawing Limits,   43
    Introduction to Model Space and Paper Space,   43
Introduction to the AutoCAD LT Drawing Aids   44
    Setting the Grid and Snap,   44
    Things to Consider When Setting Drawing Aids,   45
Drawing Lines with AutoCAD LT   46
    Drawing Lines by Picking Points,   47
    Save Your First Drawing,   48
    Open a Saved Drawing,   50
    Drawing Lines by Entering Distances, Angles, and Coordinates,   51
    Coordinate Entry Options,   51
    Using Absolute Coordinates,   52
    Using Relative Coordinates,   53
    Using Polar Coordinates,   54
    Closing a Polygon,   55
    Repeating the Previous Command Quickly,   56
    Combining Coordinate Methods,   57
    Entering Units in AutoCAD LT,   58
More AutoCAD LT Drawing Aids   59
    Using Ortho,   59
    An Introduction to Transparent Commands,   60
    Marks on the Screen,   61
    Cleaning Up the Screen,   61
Erasing Objects   62
    Selecting Objects to Erase,   62
    Entering the ERASE Command Before Selecting the Objects,   62
    Picking Objects,   62
    Erasing the Last Object Drawn,   63
    Selecting Objects with a Window,   63
    Erasing Objects with a Crossing Box,   64
    Removing Selected Objects from the Selection Set,   65
    Noun/Verb Selection and an Introduction to Grips,   66
    Using the OOPS Command,   68
    Changing the Pick Box Size,   68
    Undoing and Redoing,   69
Printing Your First Drawing   71
    Introduction to the Print/Plot Configuration Dialog Box,   71

CONTENTS xv

Multiple Choice   77
Matching   78
Word Scramble   79
Projects   79

Chapter 3
Drawing Basic Objects   85

Additional AutoCAD LT Setup Options   85
    Using the Advanced Setup Option,   85
    More about Model Space and Paper Space,   91
    Starting from Scratch,   92
    Using an AutoCAD LT Template,   93
    Setting Units and Limits Outside of the AutoCAD LT Setup,   93
Using Template Drawings   96
    Customizing Existing Template Drawings,   96
Drawing Curved Objects   99
    Drawing Circles,   100
    Drawing Arcs,   103
    Drawing Ellipses,   108
    Drawing Elliptical Arcs,   109
Drawing Polygons   112
    Drawing Polygons Based on a Circle,   112
    Drawing a Polygon Using the Edge Option,   113
    Drawing Rectangles,   114
Drawing Filled Objects   116
    Drawing Donuts,   116
    Drawing Solids,   117
Multiple Choice   119
Matching   120
Word Scramble   121
Projects   122

Chapter 4
Drawing Display Control   127

Changing Your View of the Drawing   127
Using the ZOOM Command Options   127
    Using the Zoom In Option,   128
    Using the Zoom Out Tool,   129
    Using the Zoom Scale Tool,   129
    Using the Zoom Window Tool,   130
    Using the Zoom All Tool,   130
    Using the Zoom Extents Tool,   133
    Using the Zoom Center Tool,   133
    Using the Zoom Previous Tool,   135
    Using the Real-Time Zoom Tool,   135
    Zooming with the IntelliMouse,   137

Using the PAN Command Options and Scrolling   137
  Using the Real-Time Pan Tool,   137
  Using the Pan Point Tool,   138
  Using the Scroll Bars,   139
How to Zoom Transparently   140
Using the Aerial View Window   141
  Zooming with Aerial View,   142
  Panning with Aerial View,   143
  Adjusting the Aerial View Window Display,   143
  Controlling the Updating of the Aerial View Window,   143
Creating Named Views   144
  Defining Named Views,   145
  Getting Named View Descriptions,   146
  Restoring Named Views,   146
  Deleting Named Views,   146
  Managing Views Transparently,   146
Multiple Choice   147
Matching   148
Word Scramble   149
Projects   149

Chapter 5
Using Layers, Linetypes, and Colors   151

An Introduction to AutoCAD LT Layers   151
Managing Drawing Layers   151
  Creating Layers,   152
  Making a Layer Current,   160
  Controlling Layer Visibility,   162
  Locking and Unlocking Layers,   162
Layer and Linetype Control at the Command Line   163
Overriding Layer Settings   166
  Overriding Layer Color,   167
  Overriding Layer Linetype,   168
Modifying Layers   168
  Renaming Layers and Linetypes,   169
  Changing an Object's Layer,   170
  Changing Layer, Linetype, and Color of Grip-selected Objects,   171
  Adjusting Layer Listings,   171
  Adjusting Linetype Listings,   174
Plotting Line Widths Assigned to Layer Colors   174
Multiple Choice   176
Matching   177
Word Scramble   178
Projects   179

Chapter 6
Precision Drafting Tools 181

AutoCAD LT's Precision Drafting Tools 181

Object Snaps 181
    Snap to an Endpoint, 183
    Snap to the Middle of an Object, 184
    Snap to an Intersection, 185
    Snap Perpendicular to an Object, 186
    Snap to the Center, 187
    Snap to a Quadrant, 188
    Snap to a Tangent Point, 189
    Snap to the Insertion Point, 191
    Snap to a Node, 191
    Snap to the Nearest Point, 191
    Disabling Object Snap, 191
    Using Running Object Snaps, 191
    Adjusting the Aperture Size, 193
    Changing Your AutoSnap Settings, 193

Reference Points and Other Point Objects 196
    Measuring and Dividing Objects, 197

Using the From Option to Establish a Point from an Existing Point 198

Using Point Filters 200

Using Direct Distance Entry 200

Tracking Points with AutoCAD LT 201

Using PolarSnaps 204

Drawing Inquiry Tools and Making Calculations 206
    Identifying Points, 206
    Calculating Distances and Angles, 207
    Calculating Areas, 207
    Listing Object Properties, 209
    Getting Information about Drawing Time, 209

Advanced Drawing Inquiries, 210
    Using the Union Command, 211
    Using the Subtract Command, 211
    Using the Intersect Command, 212
    Listing Physical Properties of Regions, 212

An Introduction to Drawing Construction Lines 214
    Drawing Construction Lines with the XLINE Command, 214
    Drawing Rays, 219

Adjusting Snap Angle and Origin 220

Multiple Choice 222

Matching 224

Word Scramble 225

Projects 226

Chapter 7
Editing Your Drawing   233

Object Selection Methods   233
    The Window and Crossing Polygon Selection Options,   234
    The Fence Selection Option,   235
    Selecting Objects That Are Very Close Together or Stacked,   236
    Using the SELECT Command,   237
    Customizing Selection Options,   238
    Selecting with GRIPS,   240

Copying Objects   242
    Using the COPY Command,   242
    Making Parallel Copies with the OFFSET Command,   243
    Creating Mirror Images,   244

Creating an Array of Objects   246
    Creating a Rectangular Array,   246
    Creating a Polar Array,   248

Changing an Object,   249
    Moving Objects,   249
    Rotating Objects,   250
    Scaling Objects,   253
    Lengthening Objects,   255
    Stretching Objects,   259

Editing with Grips   261
    Stretching with Grips,   262
    Moving with Grips,   264
    Rotating with Grips,   266
    Scaling with Grips,   267
    Mirroring with Grips,   268
    Changing the Properties of an Object with Grips,   270

Trimming and Extending Objects   271
    Removing a Portion from an Object,   271
    Trimming Objects,   273
    Extending Objects,   278

Drawing Fillets and Chamfers   279
    Drawing Fillets,   279
    Drawing Chamfers,   282

Using a Dialog Box to Edit Objects   284

Using the Windows Clipboard   285
    Cutting Objects,   285
    Copying Objects,   286
    Pasting AutoCAD LT Drawings,   286

Copying an Object's Properties   287

Multiple Choice   289

Matching   290

Word Scramble   291

Projects   292

Chapter 8
Drawing and Editing Polylines and Double Lines — 299

Introduction to Polylines and Double Lines   299
Drawing Polylines   299
    Using the PLINE Command Options,   300
Editing Polylines   305
    Using the PEDIT Command Options,   306
    Drawing Fillets and Chamfers on Polylines,   316
Drawing and Editing Spline Curves   318
    Displaying the Spline Frame,   319
    Converting Spline Polylines to True Splines,   320
    Closing a Spline,   320
    Adjusting the Fit Tolerance of a Spline,   321
    Editing Splines,   322
Drawing Double Lines   328
    Using the DLINE Command,   328
Drawing Revision Clouds   334
Multiple Choice   335
Matching   336
Word Scramble   337
Projects   337

Chapter 9
Placing Text on a Drawing — 341

Introduction to Drawing Text   341
Creating Single-Line Text   341
    Using the DTEXT and TEXT Commands,   342
    Text Alignment Options,   344
Creating and Using Text Styles   347
    Setting and Creating Text Styles,   348
    Steps in Creating a Text Style,   352
    Customizing Text Styles,   353
    Defining Text Styles at the Command: Prompt,   354
Creating Multiline Text   355
    Adjusting Multiline Text Properties,   360
    Finding and Replacing Multiline Text Items,   362
    Placing Paragraph Text at the Prompt Line,   364
Additional Line and Paragraph Text Applications   364
    Using Special Characters and Symbols,   364
    Pasting Text from the Clipboard,   366
Editing Existing Text   367
    Using the DDEDIT Command,   367
    Using the DDMODIFY Command,   369
    Using the CHANGE Command on Text,   372
Mirroring Objects with Text   373
Making Quick Text   374

Checking Your Spelling   374
    Changing, Using, and Creating Dictionaries,   376
Multiple Choice   379
Matching   380
Word Scramble   381
Projects   381

Chapter 10

Drawing Patterns and Section Lines   383

Introduction to Drawing Patterns and Section Lines   383
Using the BHATCH Command   384
    Selecting a Pattern Type,   384
    Changing Pattern Properties,   386
    Accessing the ISO Pattern Types,   388
    The Other Pattern Type List Options,   388
    Drawing a Hatch Pattern,   389
    Using the Additional Features of the Boundary Hatch Dialog Box,   391
Drag-and-Drop Hatching with the Content Explorer,   400
    Accessing Hatch Patterns in the Content Explorer,   400
    Setting Up Hatch Pattern Defaults in the Content Explorer,   402
Using the HATCH Command   404
    Hatching Objects Solid,   405
    Drawing User-Defined Hatch Patterns with the HATCH Command,   406
    Using Direct Hatching with the HATCH Command,   407
    Drawing a Hatch Pattern with Individual Elements,   408
Hatching around Text   409
Editing Hatch Patterns and Using the HATCHEDIT Command   411
Multiple Choice   413
Matching   414
Word Scramble   414
Projects   415

Chapter 11

Dimensioning a Drawing   423

Creating Dimensions   425
    Drawing Linear Dimensions,   425
    Drawing Chain and Datum Dimensions,   429
    Drawing Dimensions Aligned with an Angled Object,   431
    Dimensioning Angles,   432
    Dimensioning Circles and Arcs,   433
    Creating Ordinate Dimensions,   435
    Creating Oblique Dimensions,   437
Managing Dimension Styles   438
    Creating New Dimension Styles,   438

CONTENTS

Changing Dimension Variables   440
    Changing Dimension Style Geometry,   440
    Changing the Dimension Format,   446
    Changing the Dimension Text,   453

Drawing Leader Lines and Notes   462

Drawing Geometric Tolerancing Symbols without a Leader   465

Creating a Dimension Style for Use with Mechanical Drafting Symbols   466

Editing Existing Dimensions   468
    Making Other Changes to Existing Dimensions,   469
    Changing the Variables of Existing Dimensions,   470

Dimensioning at the Command Line   473

Multiple Choice   475

Matching   476

Word Scramble   477

Projects   478

Chapter 12

Designing and Using Your Own Symbols   481

Grouping Objects   481
    The Group Manager,   481
    The Group Toolbar,   484

Using Drafting Symbols in AutoCAD LT   485

Creating and Inserting Blocks in a Drawing   486
    Creating Blocks,   486
    Inserting Blocks,   491
    Other Insertion Scale Factor Options,   495
    Presetting Block Insertion Parameters,   496
    Using the Content Explorer to Insert Blocks,   498

Working with Blocks   500
    Editing a Block,   501
    Exploding a Block,   502
    Inserting an Exploded Block,   502
    Redefining a Locally Defined Block,   503
    Renaming a Block,   505
    Nesting Blocks,   505
    Blocks and Layers,   507
    Block References and Layer Controls,   508
    Creating and Managing a Symbol Library,   509
    Saving a Block as a Separate Drawing File,   510
    Using the WBLOCK Command,   511
    Inserting a Drawing File,   513
    Inserting a Drawing File Using the Content Explorer,   514
    Defining or Redefining Block Definitions from the Symbol Library,   516
    Using the Content Explorer to Create and Manage Symbol Libraries,   517
    Changing the View in the Content Explorer,   518

Using Block Attributes   519
    Defining Attributes,   520
    Automating Drawing Procedures Using Attributes,   524

CONTENTS

Modifying Attribute Definitions, 524
Editing Attribute Values in a Single Block Reference, 525
Suppressing Attribute Prompts, 528
Extracting Attribute Values from a Drawing, 528
Special Extract File Formats, 535

Using Clip Art   536

Multiple Choice   538

Matching   539

Word Scramble   540

Projects   540

Chapter 13

External References and Multiview Drawing Layout   543

Externally Referenced Drawings   543
    Attaching an External Reference, 544
    Using the Content Explorer to Attach an External Reference, 546
    Dependent Symbols, 546
    Overlaying an External Reference, 548
    Detaching an External Reference, 550
    External References and Demand Loading, 550
    Updating an External Reference, 551
    The External Reference Directory Path, 551
    Unloading External References, 552
    Obtaining Information About External References, 552
    Using the Xref Log File, 553
    Binding Xrefs, 555
    Binding Dependent Symbols, 556

Multiview Drawing Layout   558
    Model Space Concepts, 558
    Paper Space Concepts, 559
    Switching to Paper Space, 560
    Floating Model Space Viewports, 560

Working with Floating Model Space Viewports   565
    Changing the Scale of a Viewport, 565
    Changing Layer Visibility in a Floating Model Space Viewport, 567
    Using Tiled Model Space, 572
    Plotting a Multiview Layout, 573

Multiple Choice   574

Matching   575

Word Scramble   576

Projects   577

Chapter 14

3-D Drafting with AutoCAD LT   579

3-D Drafting   579
    Using X, Y, Z Point Coordinates, 580
    The Right-Hand Rule, 582

CONTENTS

3-D Polar Coordinate Entry, 582
Applying 3-D Coordinates, 584

Customizing the User Coordinate System 585
Controlling the UCS Icon, 586
Relocating the UCS, 587
Displaying the Current UCS, 590
Working with Named UCSs, 590
UCS Presets, 592

Setting Up 3-D Viewing Angles 594
Using the Rotate Option, 596
3-D Viewpoint Presets, 597
Giving Objects Thickness, 598
Using Elevation, 600

Simulating 3-D Surfaces 601
Removing Hidden Lines, 601
Adding Color to Surfaces, 604
Dynamic 3-D Viewing Options, 606
Using the CAmera Option, 608
Using the TArget Option, 609
Using the Distance Option, 609
Using the POints Option, 610
Using the PAn Option, 610
Using the Zoom Option, 611
Using the TWist Option, 611
Using the CLip Option, 612
Using the Hide Option, 612
Using the Off Option, 612
Using the Undo Option, 613
Exiting the DVIEW Command, 613

Tiled Viewports and 3-D Drawings 613

Creating Isometric Drawings 616
Drawing Isometric Circles and Arcs, 617
Isometric Text, 618
Isometric Arrowheads, 619

Multiple Choice 621

Matching 622

Word Scramble 623

Projects 624

Chapter 15

File Management and Data Exchange   627

AutoCAD LT Files 627
Managing Drawing File Size, 627

Removing Unused Data from a Drawing 628
Using the PURGE Command, 628
Purging Selectively, 629
Purging All Unused Data, 629
The Power Purge, 630

Networked Environments and File Sharing 631

Exchanging Drawing Information with Other Applications 631
    Exchanging Drawing Files, 631
    Importing Drawing Interchange File Information, 632
    Creating DXF Files, 633
    Exchanging Windows MetaFiles, 635
    Using the WMFIN Command, 636
    Using the WMFOPTS Command, 636
    Using the WMFOUT Command, 636
    Exchanging Bitmap Files, 637
    Exporting PostScript Files, 637
    Plotting to a File, 639

Using Object Linking and Embedding 639
    Embedding Objects in AutoCAD LT Drawings, 640
    Embedding AutoCAD LT Drawings in Other Applications, 642
    Linking Objects in AutoCAD LT Drawings Using the Clipboard, 642
    Linking Objects in AutoCAD LT Drawings Using Data Files, 645
    Linking AutoCAD LT Drawings in Other Applications, 647
    Managing Links in AutoCAD LT, 647
    Working with Slide Files, 649
    Creating a Slide Library, 650

Multiple Choice 651

Matching 652

Word Scramble 653

Projects 653

Chapter 16

AutoCAD LT and the Internet   655

The Internet Connection 655

Accessing Web Resources 656
    The Internet Utilities, 660
    Sending Drawings as E-mail Attachments, 660
    The Internet Utilities Toolbar, 661
    Saving a Drawing to a URL, 661
    Opening a Drawing from a URL, 663
    Inserting a Drawing from a URL, 663
    Working with Drawing Web Format Files, 663
    Using HyperLinks in DWG and DWF Files, 665
    Removing a Link in a Drawing, 666
    Locating Links in a Drawing, 666
    Listing Link Information, 666

Multiple Choice 667

Matching 668

Word Scramble 669

Chapter 17
Customizing AutoCAD LT — 671

Why Customize? 671
Creating Your Own Command Aliases 671
Automating AutoCAD LT Using Command Scripts 674
Customizing Toolbars and Toolbar Buttons 677
    The Customize Dialog Box, 679
    Creating a New Toolbar, 680
    Adding Buttons to a Toolbar, 680
    Working with Toolbar Buttons, 683
    Creating Toolbar Flyouts, 691
Customizing the AutoCAD LT Menu System 693
    Menus in the Workplace, 694
    Menu Sections, 694
    MENU GROUP Names and Partial Menus, 695
    Loading the Menu, 696
    Working with Buttons Menus, 699
    Customizing Pull-Down Menus, 701
    Creating Cascading Submenus, 705
    Working with Image Tile Menus, 706
    Defining Help Strings, 709
    Defining Custom Accelerator Keys, 710
    Customizing Tablet Menus, 714
An Introduction to DIESEL Code 714
Creating Custom Linetypes 718
Defining Custom Hatch Patterns 722
Multiple Choice 727
Matching 728
Word Scramble 729
Projects 730

Appendix A
Installing AutoCAD LT 98 — 731

Appendix B
Drafting Standards — 741

Appendix C
Standard Support Libraries — 759

Appendix D
Accessibility Options — 767

Glossary — 775

Index — 783

AutoCAD LT®98

Basics Through Advanced

CHAPTER 1

An Introduction to AutoCAD LT

LEARNING GOALS
- Describe two principal computer-aided drafting concepts.
- Identify computer equipment and terminology.
- Start AutoCAD LT.
- Use the AutoCAD LT interface.

About Computer-Aided Drafting

The personal computer, or PC, is rapidly changing the way most things are done both in industry and at home. Today's PCs have the capability of storing, processing, and retrieving huge amounts of information very quickly. Its versatility and affordability have helped the PC to become the primary tool used by most industries for creating drawings and calculating engineering data. *Computer-aided design and drafting* (CADD) is the term that describes this growing technology. CADD technology provides many powerful engineering tools for the creation and analysis of precision technical drawings. Many of these drawings can be used as a source of information for creating computer-generated models. Analyzing such models helps the designer to find design flaws or potential failure points long before the first part is ever built. Industries using CADD can increase efficiency and speed up the process of bringing a product to market.

The area of CADD that is associated with the creation and editing of technical drawings is known as CAD, or *computer-aided drafting.* The use of a computer for drafting, rather than pencils, scales, and templates, has many benefits. One of the main benefits is accuracy. Modern CAD software programs provide a virtually unlimited drawing area, in which most objects can be drawn actual size regardless of how large or small they are. Your display can be changed quickly to show any area of the drawing. This means that, like a camera lens, you can zoom out or zoom in, allowing you to get very close to work with small features of your drawing, or to back off so you can see the whole picture. Computer-aided drafting programs can provide up to 16 decimal places of accuracy, with tools that allow you to use this precision easily in your drawings.

The greatest benefit to productivity within a drafting department comes from the fact that, with CAD, objects need only be drawn once, after which they can be used over and over again. For example, electronic schematic diagrams use symbols for resistors, transistors, capacitors, and other electronic components. Using CAD software, you can draw such a symbol once and then copy it to every location in your drawing where you need that symbol. It can even be saved permanently to a symbol library and used in other drawings. Companies using CAD benefit from these symbol libraries in their day-to-day drafting tasks.

Revisions to existing drawings can be done quickly and efficiently using CAD. After the required changes have been made, a new drawing can be produced within minutes using modern printers.

After a CAD drawing has been created, it can be transferred almost anywhere in the world within minutes using telephone communication lines. This feature plus PC affordability has made it possible for designers and drafters to operate their own businesses out of the home.

These and many other benefits have made PC CAD applications the primary tools for modern drafters.

☑ LEARNING CHECKPOINT

- What are the advantages of using computer-aided drafting?
- What is the greatest benefit to productivity from using CAD?

Computer Equipment and Terminology

As you learn to use AutoCAD LT, you need to become familiar with the equipment used to run the program. Physical computer equipment is referred to as *hardware,* and the programs that the computer runs are called *software.* The central component of a personal computer system is the microcomputer, and the input and output devices are known as *peripherals.* A personal computer that is set up for work applications is commonly referred to as a *workstation.* Many possible combinations of equipment can be used in a PC system. The most common components are discussed here. The typical components of a PC-based CAD system are shown in Figure 1.1.

FIGURE 1.1 Typical components of a PC-based AutoCAD LT workstation.

Computer

The personal computer belongs to a class of computers known as *microcomputers.* The most commonly used microcomputer systems for CAD applications are IBM systems and systems made by other manufacturers that are referred to as IBM *compatibles* or *clones.* The particular brand name of the computer you are using does not matter, but the available resources such as memory and disk storage space are very important.

The primary component of your computer system is the *central processing unit,* or *CPU.* This is housed in a rectangular metal box along with your disk drives and other equipment necessary for your computer to function properly. The CPU does all of the actual data processing and numeric calculations required to run your software applications. IBM-compatible processors are sometimes described as the $x86$ family of processors. The oldest processor that can run AutoCAD LT 98 is the 486, but you get much better performance from the newer Intel Pentium® family of processors.

Another very important feature of your computer is the amount of installed *memory.* Your system's memory is actually composed of several computer chips that can be used to store data temporarily while programs are running. Generally speaking, the more memory your computer has, the better off you are. Memory size is measured in *bytes.* One byte is the approximate space required by the computer to store one text character. Computer terminology uses the metric-style prefixes, so that one *kilo*byte is about one thousand bytes and a *mega*byte (MB) is about one million bytes.

Modern computers are typically sold with 16 to 32 MB of installed memory. The operating system you are using determines the minimum amount of memory required by your computer (operating systems are discussed later). The AutoCAD LT documentation recommends 32 MB of memory be installed to run this software, but it can actually run with only 16 MB installed. Note that running the software with less than the recommended amount of memory may slow down performance.

Additional components include printed circuit boards, often called *cards,* that plug into the larger main system board. Some of these cards merely provide a way for your computer to communicate with various peripheral devices such as your display monitor, pointing device, or printer. Other cards may control disk drives, provide the basis for a sound system, or give you network or telephone line access.

Monitor

The display device for your computer is called a ***monitor.*** Desktop-style workstations usually use CRT (cathode-ray tube) monitors, similar to televisions. Laptop and portable computers often use LCD (liquid crystal diode) display systems.

The screen display is actually composed of many tiny rectangles called ***pixels.*** The term *pixel* is an acronym for *picture elements*. Display quality is measured by the total number of pixels that can be displayed on screen and the number of colors that can be used. The term used to indicate display quality is ***resolution.*** A typical resolution might be 800 × 600. This mean that the display is divided into 800 pixels horizontally and 600 vertically. Higher resolutions, such as 1280 × 1024, use smaller pixels and make the text and images appear smoother. The most common resolutions used on CAD systems provide 1024 × 768 × 256 or better. The last number (256) in this specification indicates how many colors can be displayed.

The resolutions available on your system are related not only to the monitor, but also to your ***video adapter card*** (also referred to as a *graphics card*). This is one of the printed circuit boards mentioned earlier that plugs into your computer to allow it to communicate with peripheral devices. The monitor is a peripheral device and requires an adapter card.

AutoCAD LT requires that you have a VGA (video graphics array) card or better in your system. It is recommended that your display be set to 800 × 600 × 256 or better for AutoCAD LT 97. Your display looks much better if you have an SVGA (super VGA) or a graphics accelerator card.

Keyboard

The ***keyboard*** is one of the primary tools for communicating with your computer. If you have learned to touch-type then you have a strong advantage when learning to use AutoCAD LT. Although many of your CAD tools can be found through using the menu system, all of the tools are available by typing the proper command name or option using your keyboard. Experienced professionals often tell you that the keyboard is the fastest way to use your CAD application. Although it is not necessary in order to learn AutoCAD LT, regular practice or a course in typing may be helpful.

Many styles of keyboards are available in today's marketplace. Which keyboard you use is an important consideration. The old standard is the 101-key flat keyboard, as shown in Figure 1.2A. If you use one of these keyboards, you should follow certain guidelines to protect yourself from injury. Frequent typing with your wrists bent can cause unnecessary strain and may result in carpal tunnel syndrome or tendinitis. Most computer stores sell wrist pads that are placed in front of the keyboard to keep your wrists elevated and straight to reduce the risk of injury.

FIGURE 1.2 Keyboards used at a CAD workstation. (A) A 101-key flat keyboard. (Courtesy of IBM) (B) A 104-key ergonomic keyboard. (Courtesy of Microsoft Corporation)

Modern keyboards are designed with the normal positions of your hands taken into consideration. These are often referred to as ergonomic keyboards, as shown in Figure 1.2B. These keyboards have features such as built-in wrist pads and contoured key positioning and are angled at the center to allow you to position the keyboard at the proper angle to match the normal position of your hands and to keep your wrists straight.

Pointing Devices

A pointing device is a very important part of your CAD system. Many of the features of your computer software are accessed by an onscreen symbol of an arrow, called a ***cursor.*** Within some applications, a vertical and horizontal line combination called ***crosshairs*** is used. The pointing device is used to move the screen cursor or crosshairs to the desired location. Many styles of pointing devices are available depending on your particular needs or preferences.

The most common device used for this purpose is the ***mouse*** (see Figure 1.3A). This is because the mouse is inexpensive and yet versatile enough to meet the needs of many different software applications. The most commonly used mouse is the mechanical mouse. This device contains a small ball on the underside that rolls when the mouse is moved across a flat surface. Sensors inside the mouse report the motion to your soft-

FIGURE 1.3 Popular CAD system pointing devices. (A) Mechanical mouse. (B) Puck. (C) The wheel on a "wheel mouse" offers special functionality in AutoCAD LT 98 (A: courtesy of IBM. B: courtesy of Ford Motor Company, Detroit.)

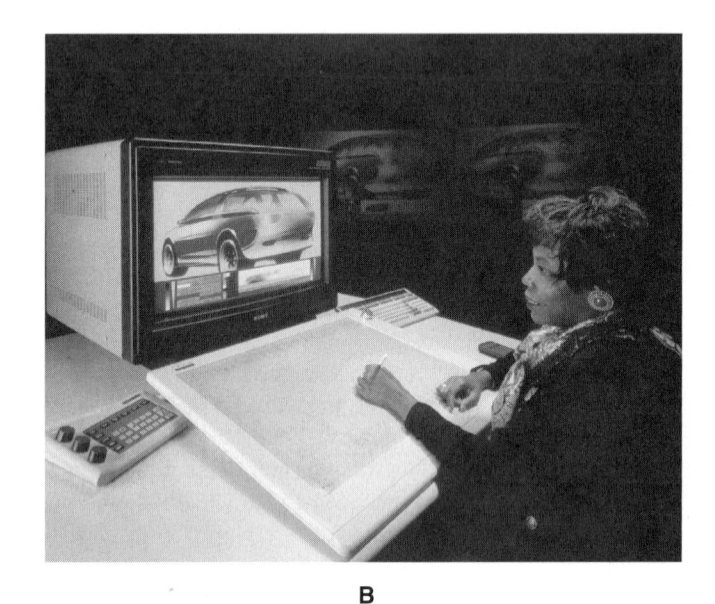

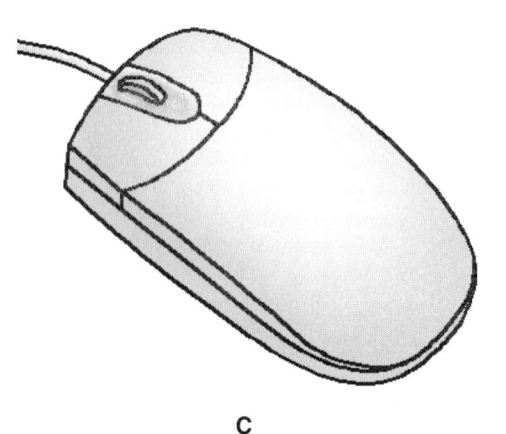

CHAPTER 1 ||| An Introduction to AutoCAD LT

ware application and the screen cursor is moved appropriately. Once the cursor is in the desired position, the ***pick button*** can be pressed to cause an action. This action might be selection of a menu item or specification of an object location. A mouse typically has two or three buttons. The purpose of the additional buttons is often determined by your operating system.

Autodesk recommends the use of the Microsoft™ IntelliMouse® with the AutoCAD LT 98 software. This mouse provides special functionality in the form of a small device between the two primary buttons that acts as both a wheel and a button. The wheel can be rolled, or pressing on it allows it to act as a button. The IntelliMouse is discussed in each area where it applies within this text.

Another style of mouse is the optical mouse. This mouse utilizes a reflective pad with nonreflective grid lines and a light and light sensor. In essence, the light "blinks" each time a grid line is crossed, and each "blink" represents a certain distance moved. This type of mouse cannot be used without the special reflective pad.

The trackball is also a popular pointing device. It works much like a mechanical mouse turned upside down. Rather than moving the device itself, the ball is rolled in place. Rolling the ball causes your screen cursor to change position. If you have difficulty using a mouse, the trackball is an excellent alternative.

More specialized types of pointing devices are also available. Two that are often used in CAD applications are the ***puck*** and the ***stylus.*** These two devices must be attached to a ***digitizer tablet.*** The digitizer tablet tracks the position of the pointing device on its surface. This makes it an excellent tool for digitizing existing drawings, or tracing them into the computer. Some tablets are very large to aid in tracing maps and other large drawings.

The puck, which looks somewhat like a mouse but only works on the surface of the digitizer tablet, is shown in Figure 1.3B and 1.4A. These devices usually have between 4 and 16 buttons. Each of the buttons on the puck can be assigned to a specific function.

The stylus is shaped like a pen (see Figure 1.4A). It is often used for more precise digitizing tasks, because it can be controlled much more accurately than a puck. A stylus is typically equipped with one or two buttons, one of which is the pick button.

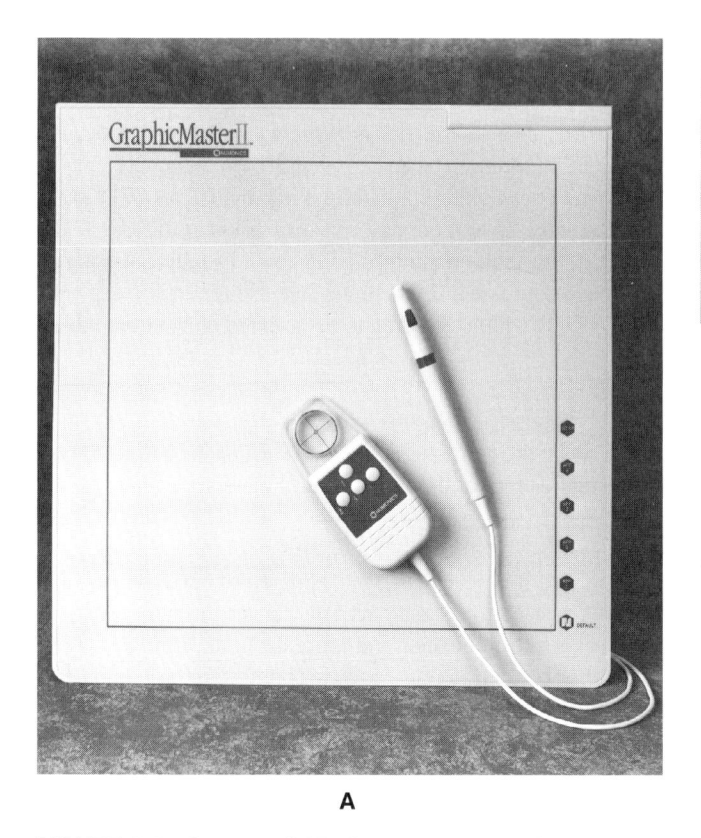

FIGURE 1.4 Common CAD digitizing devices. (Courtesy of Numonics) (A) Digitizer puck; stylus. (B) Desktop digitizer tablet; large table digitizer.

A menu template can be placed on the digitizer tablet to give you access to commonly used menu picks for your AutoCAD LT software. A menu template placed on a digitizer is shown in Figure 1.4B. Many companies create custom templates designed to fit their specific needs.

> ✏️ Field Notes
>
> Although a Microsoft™ IntelliMouse® is officially recommended by AutoDesk, many other mouse manufacturers now offer a model with a wheel button. If you decide to purchase an alternative brand, be certain that the mouse has 100% Microsoft wheel functionality. This information should be indicated on the product packaging.

Data Storage Devices

A typical CAD system has one or two disk drives that use floppy diskettes. These removable disks are most commonly used for transferring data to or from your computer. The current industry standard is the high-density 3½-in. diskette, which stores up to 1.44 MB of data files. For compatibility with older systems, your computer may also have a high-density 5¼-in. drive. These diskettes are less durable and less reliable than the 3½-inch style, and they cannot store as much data. Additionally, the 3½-in. diskette is enclosed in a hard protective case, which makes it very convenient to transport.

To be able to permanently store the program files required to run your software applications, personal computers typically use what are called **hard disks** or **nonremovable drives.** These drives come in many sizes, but as a rule you cannot have too much hard disk space. With the price of magnetic disks continuing to decrease, today's computers are often sold with 1 *giga*byte (one billion bytes) or more of storage space available. This may seem like a lot of space, but you can use up to 100 MB or more of disk space just between the operating system and the AutoCAD LT software. Depending on what software packages you are using, you may use 20% to 30% or more of a gigabyte just to store your original software program files. Then when you consider the space needed to store your drawings and documents, you may need to add an additional disk drive.

Optical disk drives (commonly known as compact disk or CD) are a popular storage device as well. These drives use disks that can store up to 4 GB or more on a single disk. Some of these disks are *rewritable,* meaning that just like a magnetic drive, you can store, erase, and replace files as needed.

Another type of optical disk is the CD-ROM. The **ROM** stands for **read-only memory.** This means that the disk can be read, but none of the files can be changed and no additional data can be stored on them. CDs are often used by software companies to deliver their programs. For example, AutoCAD LT is provided on a CD-ROM disk. The entire program fits on a single CD, but it would take 25 or more of the 3½-in. diskettes to store all the files required by AutoCAD LT 98. (Refer to Appendix A for additional information about installing AutoCAD LT.) A CD-ROM drive is very useful not only for easy and convenient installations, but also for conserving your hard disk space. Many applications can run just off of the CD without needing to be installed on your hard disk.

Printers and Plotters

A *printer* or *plotter* allows you to take a drawing that is on the computer and place it on paper, referred to as *hardcopy.* Printers are typically used for producing smaller format drawings, and plotters are used to create larger format drawings.

Many different styles of printers are available. The most commonly used printers in industry today are *laser printers* and *ink-jet printers.* Laser printers produce high-quality images using up to 600 dots per inch (dpi) resolution (see Figure 1.5A). The term *resolution* is used for printers and plotters in the same way it is used for your display system. Higher resolution values result in cleaner and more accurate printed images. Today's ink-jet printers provide up to 720-dpi or higher resolution and can print photographic-quality images. Ink-jet printers, shown in Figure 1.5B and 1.5C, generally print much slower than laser printers. *Dot matrix printers* can also be used for check prints, but because of lower quality images (as low as 180 dpi) they are seldom used for final drawings.

Printers are less expensive than plotters and, as a rule, they produce an image much faster than a plotter. For this reason, they are often used to produce check prints. But printers are typically limited to small sizes, such as A size (8.5 × 11 in.) or B size (11 × 17 in.), with some printers producing up to C size (17 × 22 in.) prints. Larger sizes are often produced using plotters.

CHAPTER 1 ||| An Introduction to AutoCAD LT

A

B

C

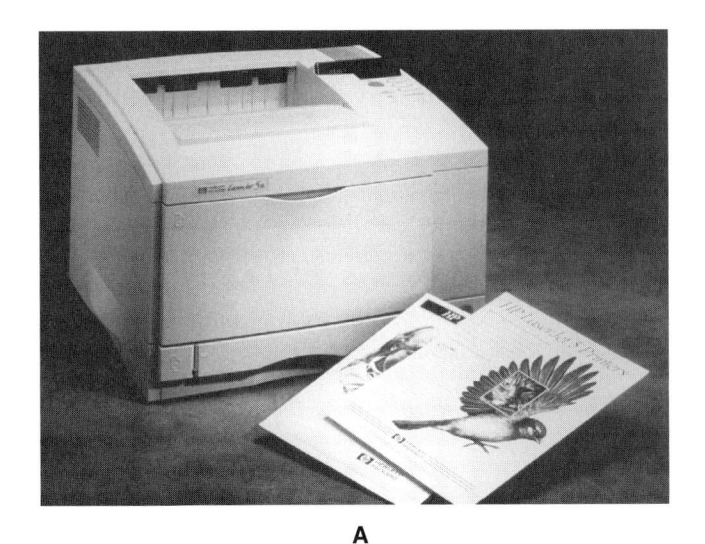

FIGURE 1.5 Printers are often used to produce check prints. (Photos courtesy of Hewlett-Packard Company)

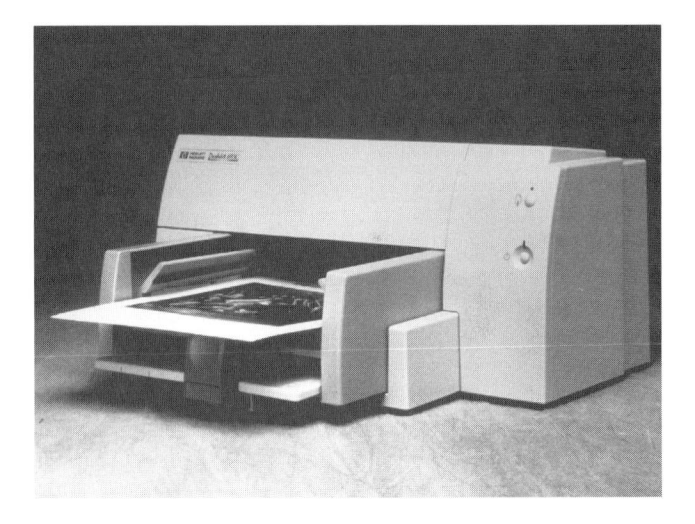

Plotters are often used in industry to produce high-quality final prints. A large-format plotter can produce any size drawing from A size to E size (34 × 44 in.) or larger. Some plotters are small enough to go on a desktop and produce only A size or B size drawings.

Pen plotters and ***pencil plotters*** produce the highest quality drawings, but a complex drawing can sometimes take up to an hour or more to complete. Ink-jet plotters can complete a high-quality large-format drawing in a few minutes. This, combined with low cost, has made ink-jet plotters very popular in industry. ***Electrophotographic plotters*** and ***thermal plotters*** are extremely fast and use 300- to 600-dpi resolution to produce a drawing. Many modern plotters can be loaded with an entire roll of paper for unattended plotting. Two styles of plotters are shown in Figure 1.6.

Computer Networks

In an engineering or drafting department where there is more than one workstation, it can be difficult to maintain drawing file control. This refers to ensuring that as a drawing is *edited,* or changed, only the latest revision of the drawing is used by the various people who need to access it. Problems can occur if two or more

FIGURE 1.6 Plotters can produce high-quality final prints in large or small format. (A and B: courtesy of Hewlett-Packard Company; C: courtesy of CalComp Technology, Inc.)

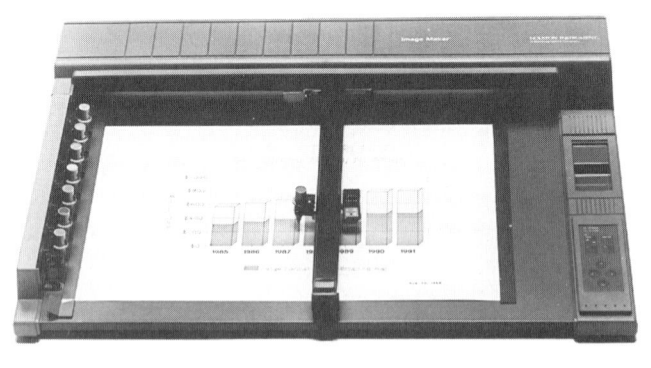

workstations have a copy of the same drawing file, because separate editing can occur in each location, which can result in inconsistent versions of the same drawing being available.

Connecting all of your computer systems in a local-area network (LAN) can help to avoid this and many other possible problems. A typical CAD network uses one computer with a large amount of storage space as a *file server*. This file server provides a central location for all of the company's or school's drawing files so only one working copy of each file exists. All of the other computers can be connected with a cable to this file server to provide access to the stored files. Networks provide various degrees of security for files, and can be set up so that they do not allow more than one person to work on the file at one time.

In addition to drawing file control, networks provide communication capabilities through the use of *e-mail* (electronic mail), security for sensitive data files, and accurate logs of time spent on projects.

CHAPTER 1 ||| An Introduction to AutoCAD LT

Operating Systems

The software that controls your computer system, such as MS DOS or Windows (95/98/NT), is known as an *operating system.* AutoCAD LT 98 can be run under Windows95, Windows98, or Windows NT operating systems. Both operating systems provide the same style of interface, and AutoCAD LT works exactly the same in each operating system. Figure 1.7 shows an example of the Windows operating system desktop. The term *desktop* refers to the layout of icons and features on the operating system screen.

FIGURE 1.7 The Windows desktop.

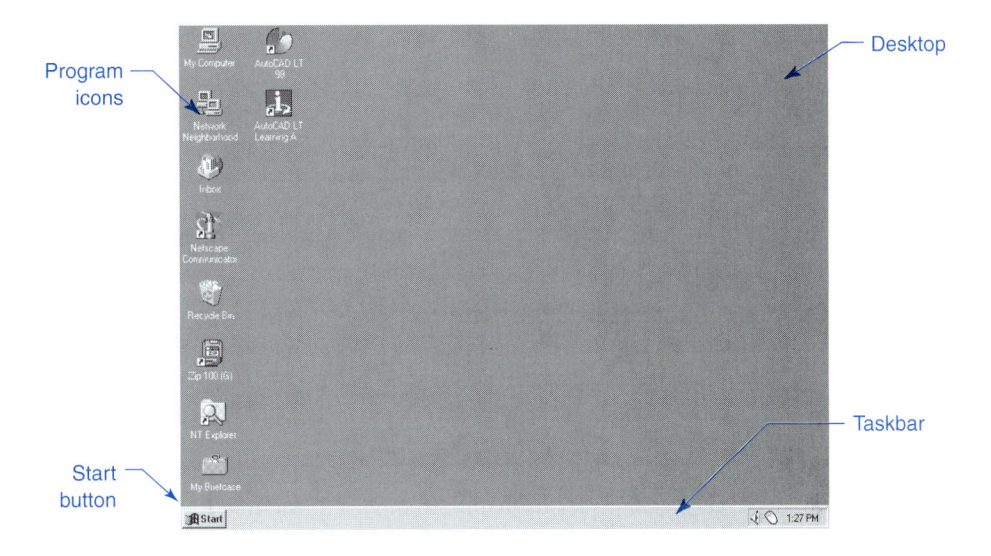

Ergonomics in the Workplace

On-the-job injuries related to computer usage are very common today. Most of these injuries are due to what is called *repetitive stress.* This has to do with making the same movements over and over again, such as typing at the keyboard or using a mouse. One of the most well-known repetitive stress injuries is known as *carpal tunnel syndrome. Tendinitis* is another common problem that can occur while working with computers. Both of these disorders can cause pain in your arms, wrists, and hands and can make movement difficult. Other common computer-related problems include neck, back, or leg pain and eye strain.

Many of these problems can be prevented by designing your workstation ergonomically (see Figure 1.8). The term *ergonomic* in this sense refers to the science of adapting your workstation to fit your body comfortably. Many types of ergonomic equipment can be purchased for your workstation, but there are also many things you can do to your workstation and for yourself to help prevent this type of injury. The following is a listing of considerations and practices to help avoid various types of injuries and disorders:

FIGURE 1.8 An ergonomic workstation.

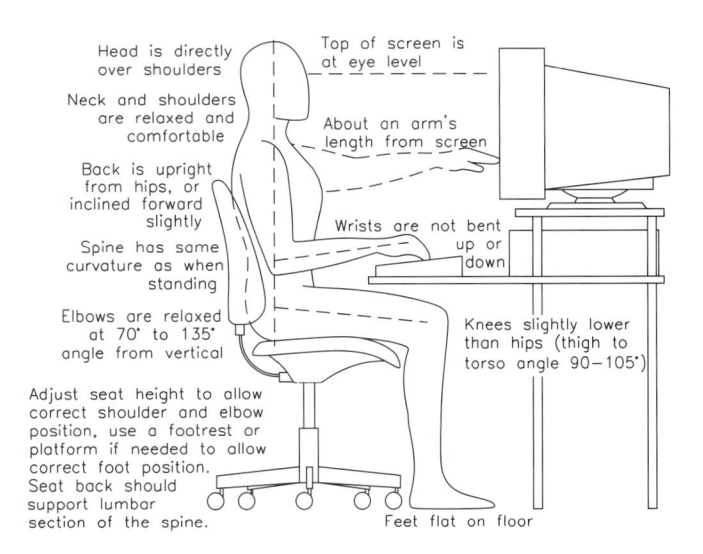

Wrists and Arms
- Use an ergonomically designed keyboard and pointing device. These devices should fit your hands comfortably and keep your wrists straight while you are using them.
- If you rest your wrists while typing, be sure to use a wrist support pad to keep them straight. The best practice is to not rest your wrists while typing.
- Practice periodic stretching and exercising of shoulders, arms, and wrists.

Neck
- Place your monitor so the top of the screen is at eye level. This keeps you from having to tilt your head either up or down to view your screen.

Back
- Use a comfortable chair with good back support. Your chair should be adjustable for height and tilt and should have armrests.
- Maintain a good sitting posture.
- Take frequent breaks. Stand up and do stretches frequently throughout the day.

Legs
- Adjust the height of the chair so that your feet can rest flat on the floor.
- Use a tilted footrest under the desk to relieve the pressure on your legs while working.
- When possible, take a walk during breaks to stretch and exercise your legs.

Eyes
- The ideal distance from the monitor to your eyes is 18 to 30 inches.
- Keep your screen angled for minimum glare from lighting. If necessary, use a glare screen.
- At least once every 15 min, look away from the screen for a minute or two and focus your eyes on an object at least 20 ft away.

Working every day at the computer is a sedentary job. The only things that really receive regular exercise are your brain and your fingers, so it is important that you participate in sports or other physical activities as appropriate to maintain a healthy heart and lungs. Remember to check with your doctor before beginning a new exercise program.

Accessibility Options

Working at a computer workstation can provide special challenges for people with disabilities. Most of today's computer software applications provide options to adjust the size and colors of features on the screen to improve visibility, as well as alternative methods of entering commands or options. Many computer hardware options are available also, such as specialized pointing devices for users with varied levels of mobility and dexterity. Appendix D provides additional information on accessibility options.

> ### Exercise 1.1
>
> 1. Write down a list of the equipment currently at your CAD workstation (home, school, or work) with a short description of each piece of equipment. Include settings such as display resolution, memory and hard disk sizes, etc.
> 2. Adjust your workstation to be as ergonomic as possible. Create a list of additional adjustments that could be made to reduce your risk of injury and increase your comfort while working.

☑ LEARNING CHECKPOINT

☐ What are the primary components of a typical CAD workstation?
☐ How much memory is recommended for running AutoCAD LT?
☐ What is *resolution*? What is a good resolution for a CAD system?
☐ What two types of devices are used for creating hardcopy drawings?
☐ What is the most commonly used pointing device? Why?
☐ How can a network help you maintain drawing control?
☐ Why should your workstation be designed ergonomically?
☐ Why are breaks, stretching, and exercises an important part of each day?

About AutoCAD LT

AutoCAD LT 98 software is a full-featured CAD package. This means that it provides many powerful drawing tools and is suitable for use by engineers, architects, drafters, and other design professionals. With more than 250,000 users worldwide, AutoCAD LT is the leading two-dimensional computer-aided drafting program.

The popularity of this software is due to several factors. It provides a full-featured CAD tool set and yet is relatively inexpensive when compared to other packages. Additionally, AutoCAD LT 98 can directly share drawings with AutoCAD Release 14. For companies that are not yet using solid modeling or other advanced features in their design process, AutoCAD LT represents an inexpensive alternative to AutoCAD. In fact, the two packages look and work much the same except for some of the advanced features in AutoCAD that are not present in AutoCAD LT. These missing items include solid modeling and photorealistic rendering, AutoLISP programming, and a few other items that are not required for most conventional two-dimensional drafting tasks.

AutoCAD LT is easy to learn, provides on-line help, and can be an ideal starting package for companies and individuals converting from manual to CAD drafting. Many design professionals who use AutoCAD at work have installed AutoCAD LT at home to enable them to work at home as well. Many drafting and engineering students also use AutoCAD LT because it so closely resembles AutoCAD, yet it costs much less.

In addition to its powerful tool set, AutoCAD LT provides an optional extensive library of predrawn drafting symbols and clip art. These tools can help you get started producing professional-quality drawings right away.

Starting AutoCAD LT

To start AutoCAD LT, the program must first be installed on the hard disk of your computer. The installation process makes copies of the program files on your hard disk. If you have not yet installed the software, refer to Appendix A for installation information.

During installation a new folder is placed in the Programs section of your Start menu. One way to start AutoCAD LT is to pick the Start button, pick Programs, pick the AutoCAD LT 98 program folder, and then pick the AutoCAD LT 98 program selection. This menu pick is shown in Figure 1.9. Another way to start AutoCAD LT in Windows NT is to double-click on the AutoCAD LT 98 shortcut icon. The term ***double-click*** means to press the mouse pick button twice very quickly. If it does not work the first time, try it again a little faster. The AutoCAD LT shortcut icon is placed on your desktop during the installation process. The icon is shown in Figure 1.10.

When you start to load the program, your cursor changes into an hourglass shape. This means that the Windows system is busy and that you must wait while the program loads into memory. After a moment or two, an AutoCAD LT logo screen appears in the center of your screen.

The logo screen then disappears and is replaced by the AutoCAD LT program window. You are now ready to begin to explore the AutoCAD LT interface. The term ***interface*** is used to describe the methods by which you communicate with a computer program.

FIGURE 1.9 Starting AutoCAD LT.

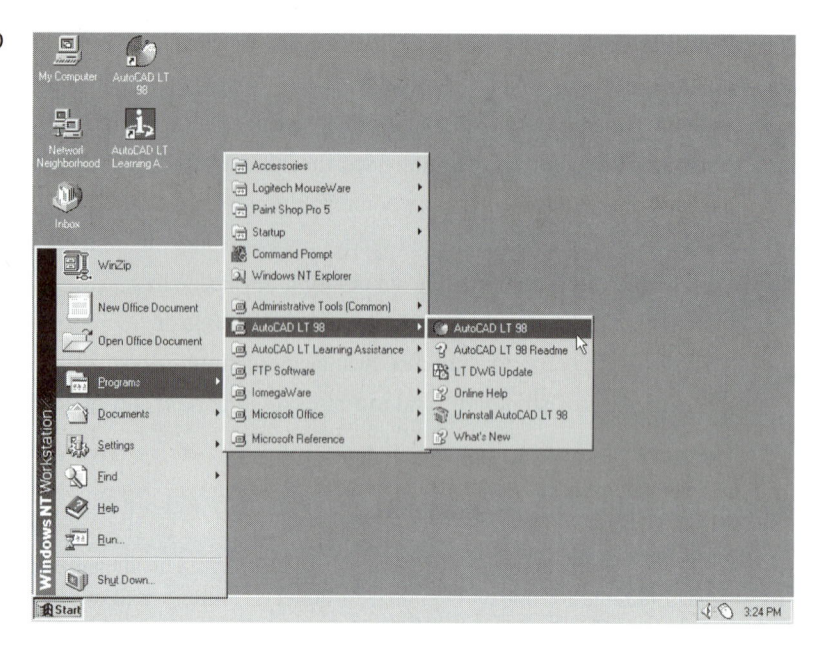

FIGURE 1.10 The AutoCAD LT 98 shortcut icon.

Through the Window...

If you are a new Windows user and have not yet mastered the double-click, you can change the Windows settings to accept a slower double-click. Here's how: Pick the Start button, then select Settings followed by Control Panel. Point at the Mouse icon and right-click (press the *right* mouse button), then pick Open. The Mouse Properties dialog box allows you to adjust and test the double-click speed. If you are using a Microsoft IntelliMouse, picking the Mouse icon launches the configuration software for the IntelliMouse, which can be used to specify your desired mouse settings.

Exercise 1.2

1. If AutoCAD LT is not yet installed on your system, refer to Appendix A and follow the described installation procedures. If you are using a school or work computer, ask your instructor or system administrator for guidance.
2. Use the appropriate method to start AutoCAD LT. When the AutoCAD LT program window appears, do not do anything else yet. Continue to read this text for a tour of the AutoCAD LT interface.

Using Dialog Boxes

The first thing AutoCAD LT does once it is running is display the Start Up ***dialog box.*** A dialog box looks somewhat like a program window with a title bar but no border. The purpose of a dialog box is to provide a means for you to enter instructions or settings for a software program with what is referred to as an ***intuitive interface.*** This means that the options are presented in a way to make them clear and easily recognizable. Additionally, dialog boxes require a minimum of typing. Many choices are made simply by moving your cursor to the desired selection and pressing the pick button. Most dialog boxes also provide what is known as ***on-line help.*** The term *on-line* used in this sense means "while you are working." Help is usually available without the need to exit the dialog box you are using, so it does not require an interruption of your work to get guidance or additional information.

Dialog boxes in AutoCAD LT have standard features that accept information in a specific way. It is important to understand how to enter or change information using these various features and how to get help when you need it. The following descriptions give you an introduction to dialog box components and familiarize you with how they work.

Buttons

Dialog box buttons appear as slightly raised rectangular buttons. Buttons are most often used to start an action of some type. Every dialog box has at least one button that exits the dialog box. The OK and Cancel buttons are the two most common exit buttons. If you pick the OK button, all of the settings or changes you made in the dialog box are accepted; if you press Cancel, then any changes you made are discarded. Many dialog boxes also have a Help button that displays a help screen regarding the dialog box you are using. Figure 1.11 shows an OK, Cancel, and Help button arrangement as encountered in many dialog boxes. Note the bold outline around the OK button; this indicates that it is the default option, which is the option that will be selected if you press the Enter key on your keyboard.

FIGURE 1.11 The OK, Cancel, and Help buttons are found at the bottom of many of the AutoCAD LT dialog boxes.

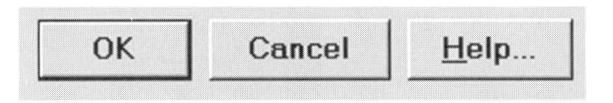

Buttons that cause specific actions have a unique style of text label. For example, the *ellipses* (three periods: …) behind the word Help … in Figure 1.11 indicates that a ***subdialog box*** will be displayed after you pick this button. A subdialog box is displayed and made active without hiding or ending the previous dialog box. When you finish working in the subdialog box, the previous dialog box is again made active.

When a button label is followed by the less than symbol (<), which resembles a left-facing arrow, then picking that button temporarily hides the current dialog box and allows you to provide input by picking an object or a location in the drawing.

List Boxes

When several options are available to you, they are often presented in the form of a list in a ***list box.*** A selection can be made by pointing to it and pressing the pick button on your mouse. If more options are available than can be displayed at once, a scroll bar and arrows are placed on the side of the list. You can use the scroll bar and arrows to move up or down in the list and display additional choices. In some lists, more than one selection can be made at one time. An example of a list box is shown in Figure 1.12.

FIGURE 1.12 A list box can present several options.

Popup List Boxes

A popup list is similar to a list box, except that it must first be expanded to see the available selections. On the right side of a popup list is a button with a down arrow. Picking this button displays the options contained in the list. Another difference between popup lists and list boxes is that you can make only one selection at a time in a popup list. As with the list boxes, if more options are available than can be displayed at once in the list, a scroll bar and arrows are placed on the side of the list. The current selection is displayed when the list is collapsed. Figure 1.13 shows the same popup list in a collapsed and an expanded state.

FIGURE 1.13 Picking a popup list expands it to display available options.

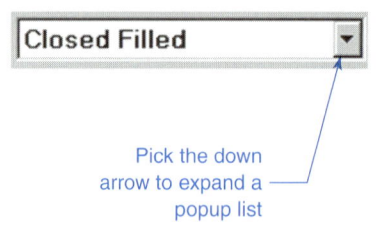

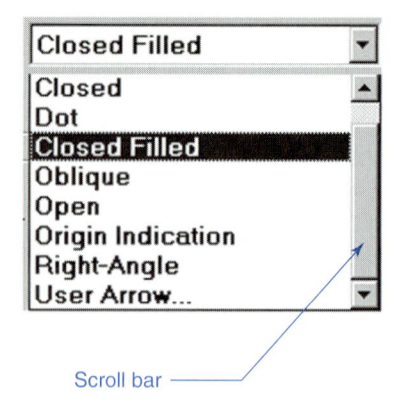

Pick the down arrow to expand a popup list

Scroll bar

Radio Buttons

Radio buttons typically present a number of options, allowing only one item to be selected. Radio buttons are named after the buttons on a car radio. By pressing one of the buttons, you switch to a new setting and turn off the button that was previously selected. The same is true of radio buttons in a dialog box. A set of radio buttons is shown in Figure 1.14.

FIGURE 1.14 A set of radio buttons allows only one selection.

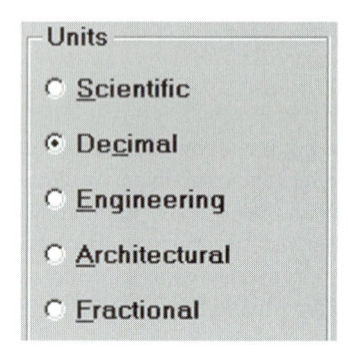

Edit Boxes

An *edit box* provides a means of entering text or number values into the dialog box. Edit boxes are sometimes referred to as *text boxes*. Some edit boxes allow only a limited number of characters to be entered, while others scroll from side to side to provide additional room for text. Edit boxes typically provide a text label that describes what type of information should be entered. Figure 1.15 shows an example of an edit box.

FIGURE 1.15 Edit boxes are used for entering text or number values.

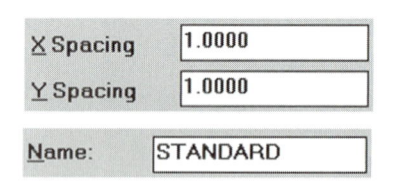

Field Notes

When using edit boxes, you can edit the text using some of the tools available in most Windows text editing programs. These techniques can save you time and make your editing much easier:

- Use your arrow keys on the keyboard to move the cursor location.
- The Home key moves the cursor to the beginning of a line of text. The End key moves it to the end of the text.
- The Ctrl and Shift keys can be used in combination with the arrow keys for faster movement and highlighting text.
- Typing while all or part of the text is highlighted automatically replaces the highlighted text.
- Double-clicking in an edit box highlights the entire contents.
- The Delete key and Backspace key can be used to remove text as needed.
- Ctrl+C copies the highlighted text, Ctrl+V can be used to paste, and Ctrl+X cuts the text.

CHAPTER 1 ||| An Introduction to AutoCAD LT 15

Images and Image Buttons
Dialog boxes often provide images within the dialog box that show the current settings. Some of these images are buttons, allowing you to pick an image directly and toggle through the available settings until you get the desired image. Other types of images include simple square color swatches that show color settings. Images help to make items in dialog boxes instantly recognizable. An example of an image button that controls the appearance of arrowheads is shown in Figure 1.16.

FIGURE 1.16 Some images are also buttons that can be selected directly.

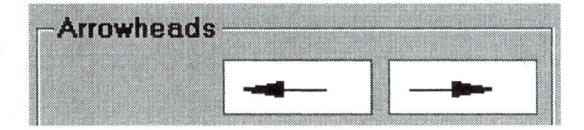

Toggles
A *toggle,* like an electric light switch, turns a feature on or off. Each toggle, or *checkbox,* consists of a small square box and a label describing a feature. If the feature is on or active, a check mark or an X appears in the box. If the box is empty, the feature is turned off. Picking the label or the box switches the setting. Figure 1.17 shows an example of toggles.

FIGURE 1.17 Picking a toggle turns it either on or off, depending on the current value.

Sliders
Sliders are used to change values interactively. A slider can be adjusted by picking the arrows at either end, which moves the slider in small steps. Larger steps can be taken by picking the background area of the slider bar itself. You can also point to the elevator button, press, and hold your pick button and move the slider interactively. Releasing the pick button places the elevator button in its current location. The slider shown in Figure 1.18 changes the size of the square in the image to the right.

FIGURE 1.18 Sliders provide an interactive way to adjust values.

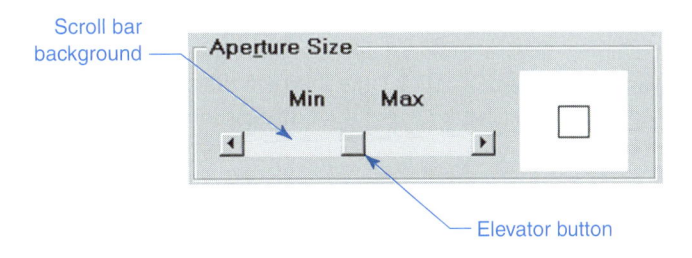

Dialog Box Error Messages
If a required value is omitted, or a value is entered incorrectly, most dialog boxes display an error message. Messages regarding simple errors are usually displayed in the lower left corner of the dialog box. Figure 1.19A shows the appearance of this type of error message.

More serious errors or warnings are often displayed in an ***alert box*** (see Figure 1.19B). An alert box requires that you pick a button, usually an OK button, before you can proceed. It is important to read these messages, because sometimes the warnings are to prepare you for what might otherwise be unexpected results in your drawing efforts.

A Dialog box error message   **B** Alert box

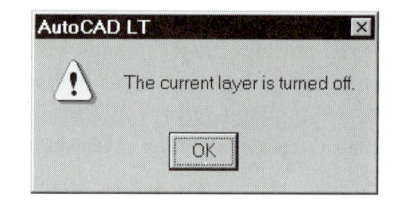

FIGURE 1.19 Some error messages are displayed in the lower left corner of the dialog; others may be displayed in alert boxes. (A) Dialog box error message. (B) Alert box.

Keyboard Shortcuts

Many of the labels on a dialog box show one character underlined. This provides you with the ability to access dialog box features using your keyboard. To access an item displaying an underscored character, press the Alt key in combination with the underscored character. For example, to access the Help button displayed in Figure 1.19, you press Alt+H.

When an item has keyboard focus (when it is highlighted), the value can be changed by typing a new value. Toggle values can be changed by pressing the spacebar; radio buttons can be cycled through using the arrow keys. In most cases, however, using your cursor is the easiest way to use a dialog box.

☑ LEARNING CHECKPOINT

- ☐ How is AutoCAD LT 98 started?
- ☐ What are the advantages of a dialog-style interface?
- ☐ Describe the usage of buttons, lists, radio buttons, toggles, and sliders.
- ☐ Where are the two primary locations for error messages in a dialog session?
- ☐ How can dialog box features be accessed with the keyboard?

Accessing AutoCAD LT Commands and Features

AutoCAD LT provides several ways to access its commands and features. This adds versatility to the program and allows you to use the method that works best for you. Becoming familiar with the layout of the AutoCAD LT screen and how to access commands quickly is an important part of mastering the use of AutoCAD LT 98.

The primary means of accessing AutoCAD LT commands and features is through the ***menu*** system. Like a menu at a restaurant, a menu in AutoCAD LT offers you a list of available options and commands from which to choose. This section introduces you to the techniques for using AutoCAD LT's menu system.

When you first start AutoCAD LT the Start Up dialog box is displayed (see Figure 1.20). This dialog box is discussed in detail in Chapter 2. For now, dismiss this dialog box without making any changes by picking the Cancel button.

FIGURE 1.20 The Start Up dialog box is displayed when you start AutoCAD LT.

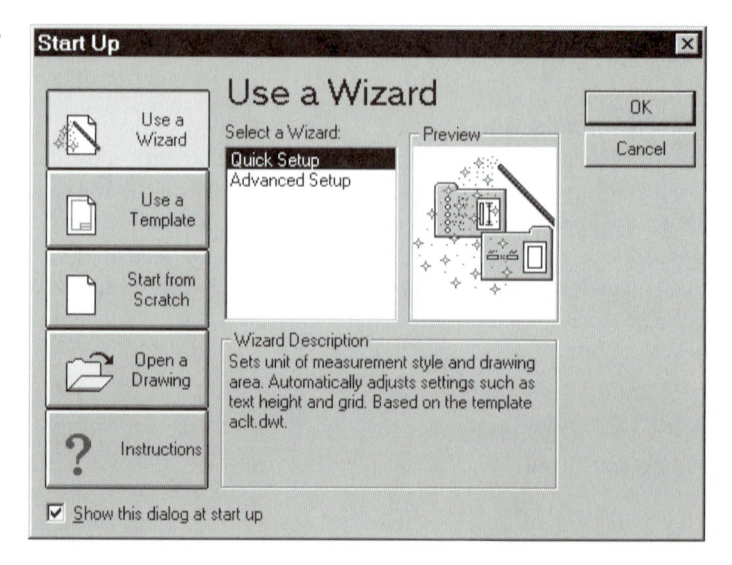

CHAPTER 1 ||| An Introduction to AutoCAD LT   17

After dismissing the Start Up dialog box, the AutoCAD LT graphics screen is completely visible. AutoCAD LT has three screens. The graphics screen is used for drawing and editing objects, and the text screen is used for obtaining text-based information about the drawing. The third screen is the Content Explorer, which is started by default when you first start AutoCAD LT 98. The Content Explorer is a secondary window that provides easy ways to find, preview, and access hatch patterns, symbols and drawing files. The Content Explorer is discussed later in the text. For now, this window can be closed or simply ignored. If this window is on top of the AutoCAD LT 98 drawing window, simply pick within the drawing window to bring it to the top. The text screen is not visible at this time. The graphics screen layout is detailed in Figure 1.21. Study this figure along with the descriptions that follow. Note that in the Windows operating system, your task bar may be displayed at the bottom, depending on how you have your desktop configured.

FIGURE 1.21 The AutoCAD LT graphics screen layout.

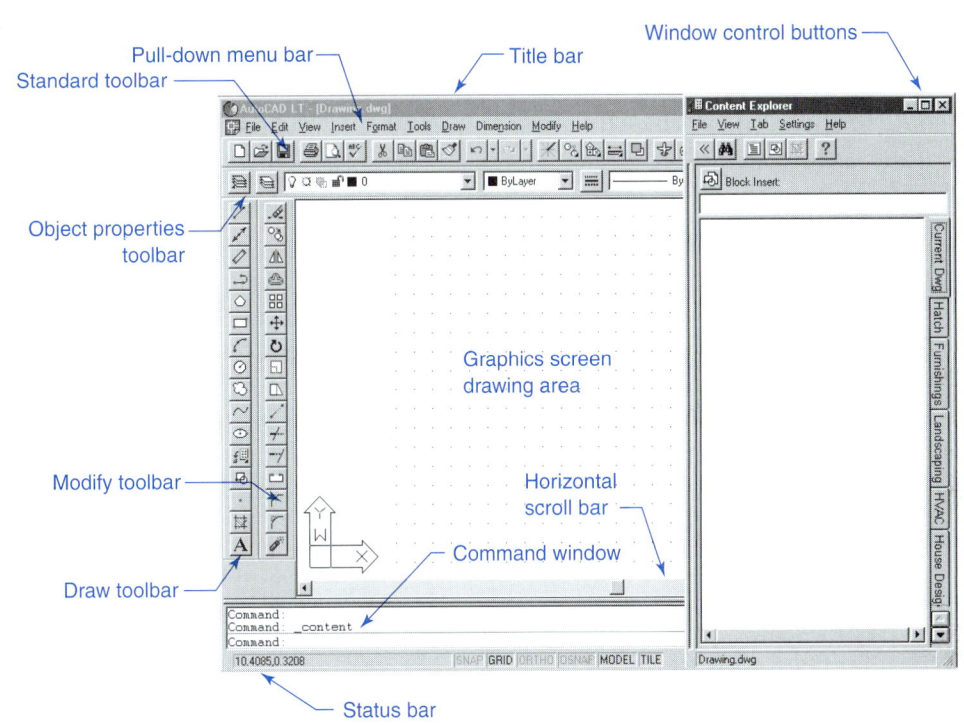

Brief descriptions of each of the AutoCAD LT graphics screen components are given here. Their usage is detailed in the sections that follow.

- *Title bar:* The title bar of the AutoCAD LT screen is a standard feature of all program windows. In AutoCAD, the title bar reports the name of the application and displays the name of the current drawing in square brackets. If you have not yet given the current drawing a name, the name *Drawing.dwg* appears in the brackets.
- *Window control buttons:* These buttons appear at the top of all program windows. They provide a simple means to adjust the size of the AutoCAD LT window.
- *Pull-down menu bar:* Each of the names on this menu bar is associated with a pull-down menu. Picking the menu name displays the associated menu.
- *Standard toolbar:* Each of the buttons on this toolbar starts a command or performs a function in AutoCAD LT. The toolbar buttons grouped in this toolbar include those for standard Windows tools, along with a selection of commonly used AutoCAD LT commands.
- *Object Properties toolbar:* This toolbar presents a set of tools that control the appearance and various properties of the objects in your drawing.
- *Draw toolbar:* The most commonly used drawing options are presented in this toolbar.
- *Modify toolbar:* This toolbar provides access to the most frequently used object modification options in AutoCAD LT.
- *Graphics screen drawing area:* This is where the current view of your drawing is displayed. As you work in your drawing, this is where you will most commonly interact with your drawing.
- *Horizontal and vertical scroll bars:* These scroll bars provide a convenient means to change the drawing display area to show another area of your drawing.

- *Command window:* This is where commands typed in will appear, along with prompts from AutoCAD LT requesting information from you.
- *Command window scroll bars:* These allow you to scroll up, down, right, or left as needed to view information not currently visible in the command window.
- *Status bar:* The status bar displays information about your drawing and the current settings for various features of AutoCAD LT. When you point at a toolbar button or menu item, a help string is displayed on the status bar.

Canceling an AutoCAD LT Command

Any instruction you give to AutoCAD LT is referred to as a ***command***. AutoCAD LT has many commands available, some for creating drawing objects and others for modifying drawing objects. Frequently, after starting a command, you may decide that you want to stop the command without completing it. Most commands, even if they are currently in progress, can be canceled by pressing the Esc (Escape) key on your keyboard. The Esc key is found at the upper left corner of most keyboards. Pressing the Esc key once or twice returns AutoCAD LT to a ready state so another command can be entered, or even the same command using different options.

Using Pull-Down Menus in AutoCAD LT

The primary text-based menu structure in AutoCAD LT is the ***pull-down menu*** system. The pull-down menu bar shown in Figure 1.21 displays several options that can be picked to display a pull-down menu. To see how these menus work, point to the File option and press the pick button. The menu displayed appears to be pulled down from the menu bar (see Figure 1.22). As you move your cursor up and down the menu, the item you are currently pointing at appears highlighted. Another area to watch as you scroll through the menu choices is the lower left area of the screen. The status line is temporarily hidden and a ***help string*** is displayed in its place. A help string is a brief description that expresses the effect of the command associated with the menu selection at which you are pointing. The description ends with a colon (:), followed by the name of the command associated with that menu selection. Pressing the pick button selects the currently highlighted item and starts the associated command. As you point at the New … command in the File menu, note the help string message: *Creates a new drawing file: new.*

The underlined character in the menu bar titles and each of the menu options is referred to as a ***menu access key.*** These provide keyboard access to the pull-down menus. For example, to access the New … option from the File menu, first press an Alt+F keystroke to display the File menu. Then, press the N key to access the New … option.

If you have selected a menu that does not contain the option that you are looking for, simply pick another menu name. The previous menu is hidden and the new menu is then displayed. If you want to dismiss the currently displayed menu without making another selection, you can press the Esc key.

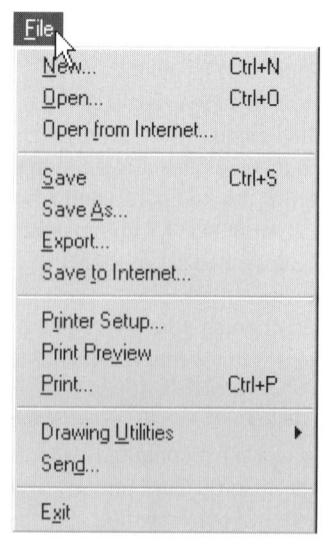

FIGURE 1.22 The File pull-down menu.

Many pull-down menu choices display a ***cascading submenu,*** also known as a *walking* or *hierarchical menu,* that presents a group of related commands. This allows a single pull-down menu to provide access to many more options without increasing the size of the menu. Menu selections that have a cascading submenu display an arrow on the right edge of the menu. When you select one of these options, the cascade is automatically displayed. Then you can pick the desired menu selection. Figure 1.23 shows the cascading submenu for the Drawing Utilites option on the File pull-down menu.

FIGURE 1.23 Cascading submenus display additional choices.

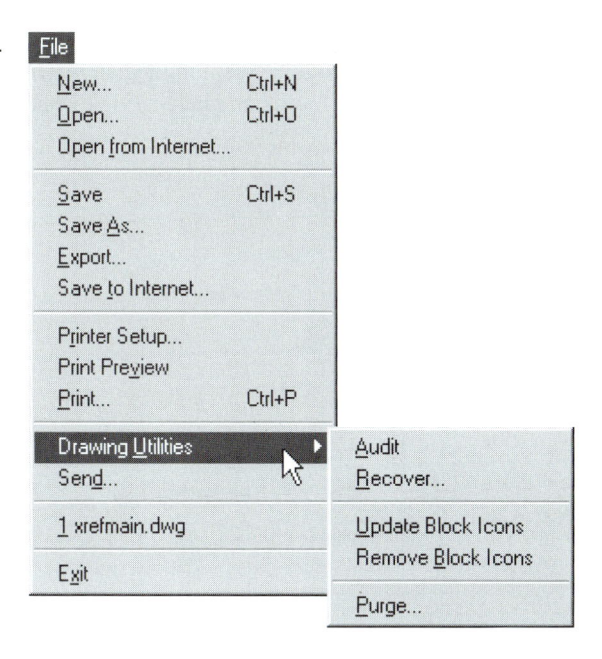

Accelerator Keys

On the File and Edit pull-down menus, some of the selections show a description of a keystroke combination that is referred to as an ***accelerator key.*** An accelerator key is an option provided for easy access to commonly used functions and commands. As an example, rather than picking the New … command in the File menu, you could instead use the Ctrl+N keystroke to start the NEW command. To perform a Ctrl+N keystroke, press and hold the Ctrl button on your keyboard. Next, press the N key and then release both keys.

AutoCAD LT is said to be *Microsoft Office 97 compatible,* meaning that the toolbars, menus, and accelerator keys are similar to those available in Microsoft Office applications, such as Word, Access, and Excel. If you currently use any of these applications, you may already be familiar with many of the accelerator keys available in AutoCAD LT 98.

Field Notes

There are actually two completely different methods for using pull-down menus with your mouse. The first method requires making two or more individual picks. For example, to select the New … command from the File menu:

1. Point to the menu bar and pick File by pressing and immediately releasing the pick button.
2. Point to the New … command and press and release the pick button.

The second method is done by picking only once:

1. Point to the menu bar and pick File by pressing and continuing to hold the pick button.
2. Move the cursor to the New … command and release the pick button.

Either method produces the same results. Use the method that you are most comfortable with.

AutoCAD LT Toolbars and Toolbar Buttons

The key features of the AutoCAD LT interface are the toolbars and toolbar buttons. These are typically preferred to the use of pull-down menus, because a toolbar button usually requires only one pick to start a command. Each toolbar displays a variety of buttons that start AutoCAD LT commands or functions. By default, the first time you start AutoCAD LT, only four toolbars are visible: the Standard toolbar, the Object Properties toolbar, the Draw toolbar, and the Modify toolbar. Figure 1.24 shows the Draw and Modify toolbars. There are many different buttons on these toolbars, each with its own unique image. In a short time most of these will be familiar to you and you will recognize them immediately. One of the primary features of AutoCAD LT that will help you in this area is the tooltip and help string displayed by each button.

FIGURE 1.24 The Draw and Modify toolbars.

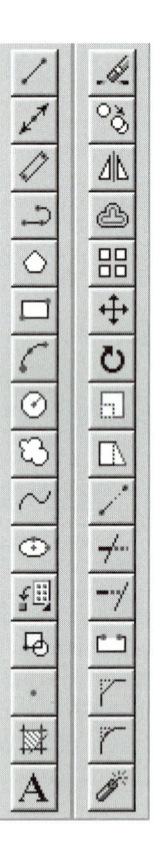

When you point at a toolbar button with your cursor and leave it there for about a half of a second or so, a small text box is displayed next to the cursor that gives the name of the button—this is called a ***tooltip***. When a tooltip is displayed, a help string also appears on the status line in the lower left area of the AutoCAD LT window. The tooltip most often serves as a reminder of what the graphic image on the button means. Using this feature you can quickly familiarize yourself with the appearance of the buttons you use frequently. The help strings for toolbar buttons are the same as described earlier regarding pull-down menu selections. For example, in Figure 1.25, note the tooltip for the New button and the help string displayed on the status line. The tooltip reminds you that the graphic image represents the NEW command. If you need to know more about the NEW command, read the description on the status line. This button displays the message: *Creates a new drawing file: new.* The help string for a command typically remains constant regardless of the method used to pick the command. If you need more information than is displayed in the help string, you can use AutoCAD LT's Help facility, which is discussed later in this chapter. Pointing to a toolbar button and picking it activates its command.

FIGURE 1.25 Tooltips and help strings help you to recognize toolbar buttons quickly.

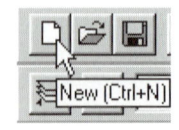

Tooltip

Help string

CHAPTER 1 ||| An Introduction to AutoCAD LT

Some of the toolbar buttons display an arrow in the lower right corner of the image. This type of button is known as a *flyout.* A flyout is a special type of button that is like a toolbar within a toolbar. To access the currently displayed button on the flyout, point to it and pick just as you would with any other button. The tooltip and help string for a flyout are displayed in the same manner as other toolbar buttons. To see how a flyout is different, point to it, press, and hold down the pick button.

A flyout will typically display a group of related commands. After displaying the flyout, move the cursor to the additional buttons. Continue to hold the pick button in until you are ready to make your choice. Note that you can display tooltips and help strings for each of the buttons on the flyout as well. Once you have made your decision, point to the desired button and release the pick button on the mouse. The command you are pointing to when you release the pick button is activated.

For example, in Figure 1.26, the flyout for the Zoom button on the Standard toolbar is shown. Note that the tooltip for the Zoom In button is visible. Releasing the pick button while pointing to the Zoom In button activates the appropriate command for changing the display. This command is covered in Chapter 4.

FIGURE 1.26 The Zoom flyout. Flyouts display additional related commands.

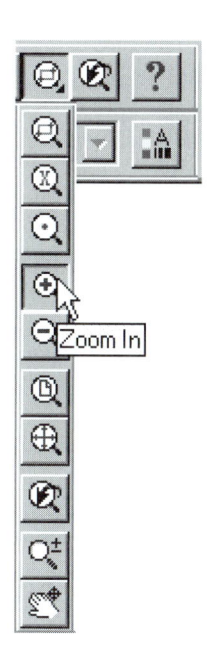

When you select an option from a flyout, the image for the most recent button selected from the flyout is displayed on the top-level button. The button displayed when the rest of the flyout is not visible is considered the top-level button.

After making a selection as shown in Figure 1.26, the Zoom In button becomes the top-level button. See the change in the Standard toolbar shown in Figure 1.27. If you need to access a different zooming option, you must display the flyout as you did to select the Zoom In button and use the same method to select the new option.

FIGURE 1.27 The most recently selected button becomes the top-level button on a flyout.

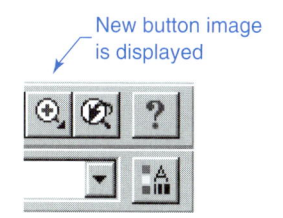

New button image is displayed

Field Notes

One common problem for new AutoCAD LT users comes from accidentally hiding a floating toolbar. Hiding a toolbar makes it unusable until it is again made visible. In Windows, a floating toolbar is hidden by picking the button in the upper right corner. By default, your toolbars are docked in the initial view. Floating and docking toolbars are covered later in this chapter.

If you do accidentally hide a toolbar, it is easy to make it visible again. Here's how:

1. Pick the View pull-down menu.
2. Select the Toolbars ... option to display the Toolbars dialog box.
3. Place a checkmark in the box next to the toolbar name (for example: Draw) by picking it.
4. Pick the OK button to return to your drawing.

The AutoCAD LT Command Window and the Text Screen

One of the primary areas to watch on the AutoCAD LT screen is the Command window (see Figure 1.28). If the command you are using does not use a dialog box, this is where AutoCAD LT communicates with you. Options for commands are listed in this area, and AutoCAD LT's requests for information, warnings, and error messages are found here as well. For example, if you start a LINE command, the prompt *From point:* appears in the command window. The term ***prompt*** refers to a request by AutoCAD LT for input.

FIGURE 1.28 Watch the Command window carefully to see what type of input is required.

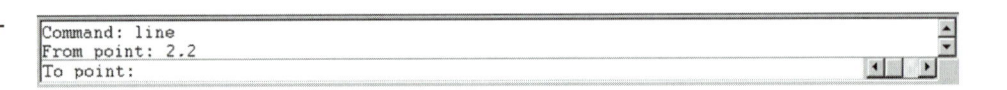

```
Command: line
From point: 2.2
To point:
```

You can also enter commands directly into the Command window using the keyboard. When you type a command or option at the command line, you must follow the command with an Enter keystroke. If you watch the Command window while picking a command using a toolbar button or a menu selection, you see the command entered in the Command window automatically. If you do type commands, you can type the full command name or for some commands you can type what is known as a ***command alias.*** A command alias is a shortened version of a command name made to boost your speed for Command window entries. As commands are discussed in this text, if a command alias exists it will be listed as well.

By default, the current line and the two previous lines of information are displayed in the Command window. To the right of the Command window are a vertical and a horizontal scroll bar. These can be used to view lines of text that have scrolled up and are no longer visible. In some cases, on lower resolution screens, some command option lines or messages may be too wide to be displayed in the Command window. Use the horizontal scroll bar to scroll right if you need to see the rest of the text.

It is very important to pay close attention to the Command window. If AutoCAD LT is currently prompting you with a Command: prompt, then it is awaiting entry of a command. The term *Command: prompt* is used to indicate a prompt on the bottom line of the command window that reads simply *Command:*. If a Command: prompt is not visible, then a command is already active. When a command is active, an ***option line*** is often displayed. An option line presents the available options for the currently active command.

Even so, some messages may scroll off of the Command window before you can completely read them. Or you may wish to check to see if you entered something incorrectly. You can view as many as 200 lines of text that have scrolled off of the Command window by opening AutoCAD LT's Text window.

Press the F2 function key on your keyboard to toggle back and forth between the graphics and text window. Figure 1.29 shows the appearance of the AutoCAD LT Text window. The scroll bars can be used if you need to review more information than is displayed currently in the Text window.

FIGURE 1.29 The Text window can be used to view text that has scrolled off of the Command window.

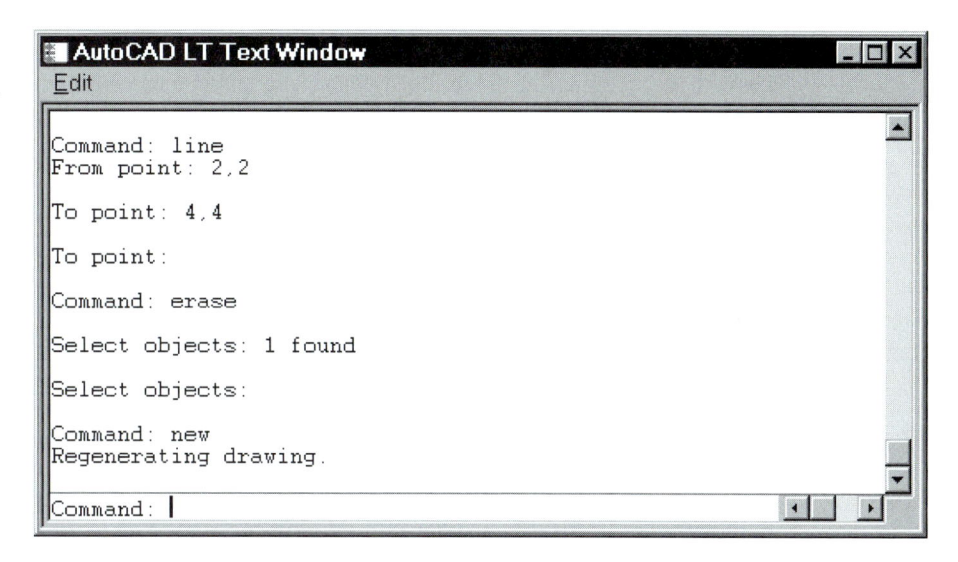

```
AutoCAD LT Text Window
Edit

Command: line
From point: 2,2
To point: 4,4
To point:
Command: erase
Select objects: 1 found
Select objects:
Command: new
Regenerating drawing.
Command:
```

Exercise 1.3

1. Open the AutoCAD LT program.
2. In the Start Up dialog box, press each of the buttons on the left side. Note the changes in the dialog box content. Pick the Cancel button to dismiss the dialog box.
3. Use your mouse to explore the pull-down menus and toolbar buttons, reading the tooltips and help strings as you do so. If you accidentally start a command, press the Esc key to cancel it.
4. Use your mouse to pick the New ... option from the File pull-down menu. When the Create New Drawing dialog box appears, press the Esc key to cancel.
5. Use your keyboard to access the New ... option from the File pull-down menu. When the Create New Drawing dialog box appears, pick the Cancel button to cancel it.
6. Pick the New toolbar button from the Standard toolbar. When the Create New Drawing dialog box appears, pick the Close button at the upper right corner of the dialog box to cancel it.
7. Type **NEW** in at the Command: prompt and press Enter. Again, cancel the Create New Drawing dialog box.
8. Use the accelerator keystroke Ctrl+N to enter the NEW command and cancel the Create New Drawing dialog box.
9. Think about the many ways available to enter or to cancel an AutoCAD LT command. Consider the advantages and disadvantages of each method.

✓ LEARNING CHECKPOINT

☐ What is the primary means of accessing AutoCAD LT commands?
☐ Name the primary text-based menu system in AutoCAD LT.
☐ What is a menu access key and how is it used?
☐ What are cascading submenus?
☐ List the four toolbars visible the first time you start AutoCAD LT.
☐ What are tooltips and help strings and how can they help you?
☐ How is a flyout used?
☐ What are accelerator keys and where are they listed?
☐ What is the Command: prompt?
☐ Why is it important to watch the Command window very carefully?
☐ What is the AutoCAD LT text screen and how can it be displayed?

Sizing and Positioning the AutoCAD LT Window

In Windows, programs that you run are displayed within a rectangular border known as a ***window.*** The program windows provide a great deal of flexibility, allowing you to move and size the windows as needed. Program windows in both operating systems provide the same capabilities, but provide different ways of doing things.

The reason for needing to size and move your program windows has to do with the capability in Windows operating systems of running more than one program at a time. This even applies to AutoCAD LT 97, meaning that you can run more than one drawing session at a time. This gives you the capability of sharing drawing data by copying objects from one drawing into another. Professional drafters are often able to reuse symbols or geometry from drawings created previously. Being able to open more than one drawing at a time makes it easy to copy things from one drawing to the other and can save a lot of time.

Whether you are running multiple sessions of AutoCAD LT, running other applications, or just working in a single application, it is important to understand how to work with program windows.

In both operating systems, the ***title bar*** is the location of the controls for most of the window functions. The title bar is the area across the top of a program window that lists the program and the name of the currently opened file. The Windows operating system uses icons, or pictures, rather than text wherever possible. Figure 1.30A shows the AutoCAD LT 98 title bar displayed in Windows and lists the features. In Figure 1.30B, note that the icon image associated with AutoCAD LT is displayed in the upper left corner. Picking this icon displays a menu. A menu is a listing of tasks or options that can be started simply by pointing to the desired item and pressing the pick button.

FIGURE 1.30 AutoCAD LT program window title bars.

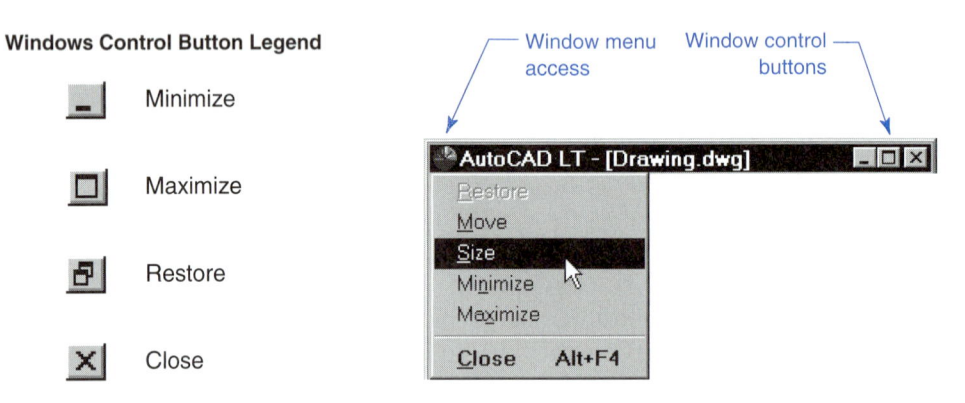

The standard program window menus for both operating systems are shown in Figure 1.30. Items that are available to you are printed distinctly, and items that are not currently available appear to be somewhat transparent, or "grayed out." The options are described here:

- Restore: Only available when the program window is either maximized or minimized, this option restores the window to the last floating position.
- Move: Only available on floating windows, this option changes the cursor to a four-way arrow and allows you to move the window. Point to the title bar, press and hold the pick button, and move your mouse. Release the pick button to drop the window and leave it in its new position. Note that you can do the same task without picking Move first. Just point to the title bar with your standard cursor, press and hold pick, and move the window in the same way.
- Size: Only available on floating windows, this option changes the cursor to a four-way arrow and allows you to change the size of the window. Point to the border on the edge of the window and the cursor changes shape to show you whether your resizing operation is horizontal, vertical, or diagonal. Note that you can do the same task without picking Size first. Just point to the border with your standard cursor, press and hold pick, and size the window in the same way.
- Minimize: This option reduces the program window to a task bar button. To return to the program window after minimizing, pick the task bar button or double-click the program icon.
- Maximize: Picking Maximize increases the size of the program window to fill the entire screen. This can also be done by double-clicking on the title bar of a floating window.
- Close: This option closes the application contained in the window. Basically, this is an off switch for the program running within the window.

CHAPTER 1 ||| An Introduction to AutoCAD LT   **25**

To make the AutoCAD LT window as large as it can be on your screen, *maximize* it. This fills the screen with the AutoCAD LT program window. Any other program windows that are also open are hidden behind the AutoCAD LT window.

When you are using more than one program at a time and need to be able to see two or more applications at once, your windows should be floating. The term *floating* applies to a window that is neither maximized nor minimized. A floating window can be temporarily sized and positioned as needed. Floating windows can also be arranged so that multiple windows are visible at the same time. An example of a situation where you would want to use more than one program at a time might be if you are producing technical documentation in a word processor that uses drawings in the document.

If you need to work in another application for a period of time, but plan to return to AutoCAD LT and continue the work you are doing there, *minimize* the AutoCAD LT window. When you minimize the AutoCAD LT window it is not usable until it is restored to a floating or maximized position. In Windows, a minimized application is displayed as a button on the task bar.

Working with floating windows affords you the greatest flexibility in terms of window sizing and positioning capabilities. As mentioned previously, you do not need to select the Move or Size options in the window control menu in order to move or resize a window.

Through the Window...

> If you need to work in more than one program at a time, but need your applications to be maximized, you can have each of the windows maximized and still easily switch from one application to another. Here's how: For each program you need to run, pick the Start button, start the application, and maximize each window by picking the maximize button or using the window control menu. Now, when you need to switch from one application to another, press and hold the Alt key on your keyboard. Press and release the Tab key while still holding the Alt key. A small window appears in the center of the screen with icons representing each of the applications that are currently running. Press and release the Tab key until the application you need is outlined. To select an application, release the Alt key.

To move the AutoCAD LT window when it is floating, move the cursor to the title bar area then press and hold the pick button. Move the cursor while continuing to hold the pick button down. Depending on your operating system and display configuration, you may see an outline representation of the window as it is moved (see Figure 1.31). When it is in the desired location, drop the window into position by releasing the pick button.

A program window can be sized in three different ways as described previously. The window can be resized horizontally, vertically, or diagonally. When sizing the window diagonally, you are actually sizing it

FIGURE 1.31 Moving a floating AutoCAD LT program window.

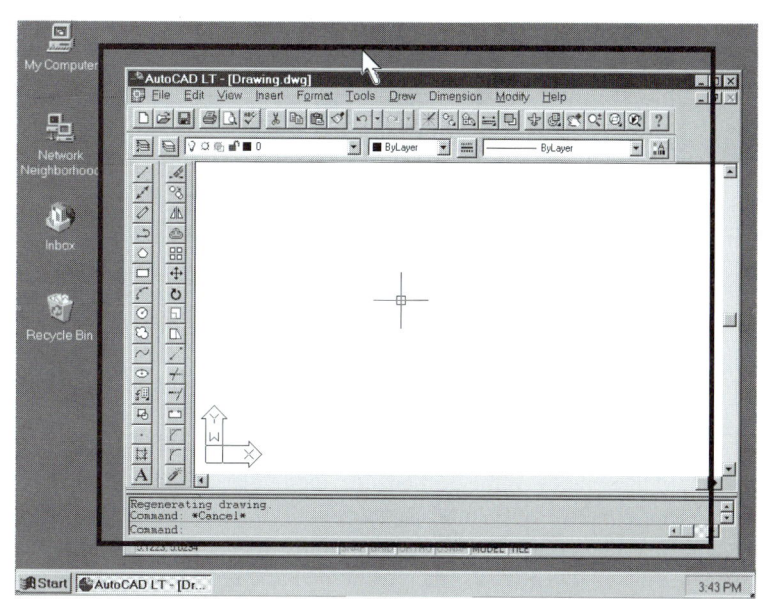

both horizontally and vertically at the same time. To size a window horizontally, move the cursor to either the left or right vertical edge of the window until it changes its shape into a left and right arrow. Press and hold the pick button, and move your pointing device. Your movement is reflected by the program window. Figure 1.32 shows the AutoCAD LT program window being sized horizontally. When the window is the desired size, release the pick button.

FIGURE 1.32 Sizing the AutoCAD LT window horizontally.

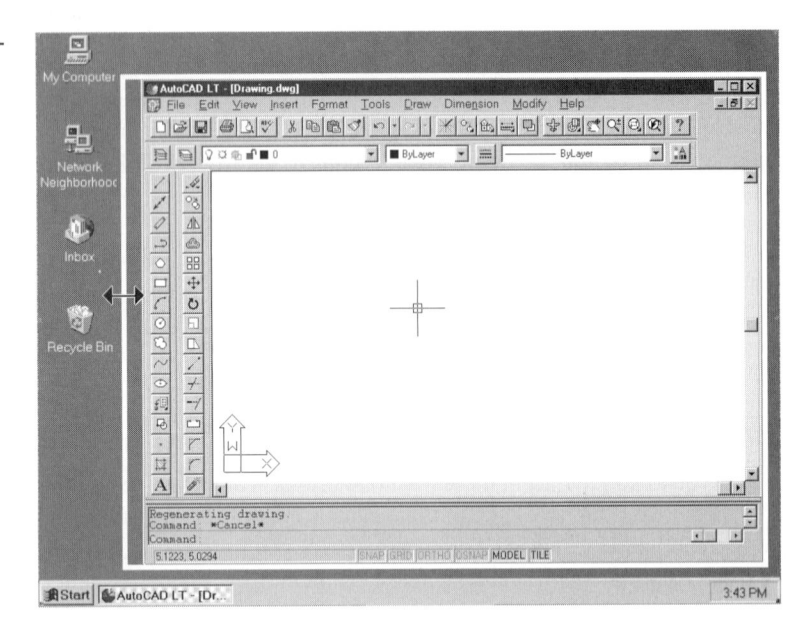

Figure 1.33 shows a vertical sizing operation. This is done in the same way as the horizontal sizing, except that you must initially point to either the top or the bottom edge of the window, and the movement cursor is an up and down arrow.

FIGURE 1.33 Sizing the program window vertically.

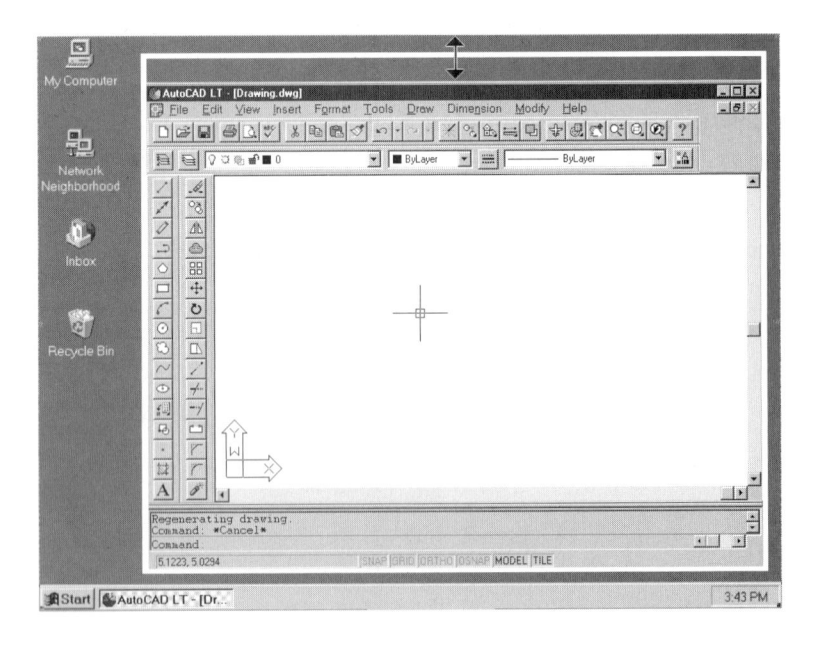

Resizing the window diagonally allows you to change both the height and the width of the window at the same time. This requires that you point to one of the four corners of the window then press and hold the pick button. This is shown in Figure 1.34; note the shape of the diagonal sizing cursor. As before, move the cursor until the window is the desired size; then release the pick button.

One of the most powerful features of the Windows operating systems is the capability to run more than one application at a time. In addition to running different programs at once, you can even run more than one session of AutoCAD LT. Using the positioning and sizing capabilities discussed previously, you can arrange

CHAPTER 1 ||| An Introduction to AutoCAD LT

FIGURE 1.34 Sizing the window diagonally changes both horizontal and vertical size.

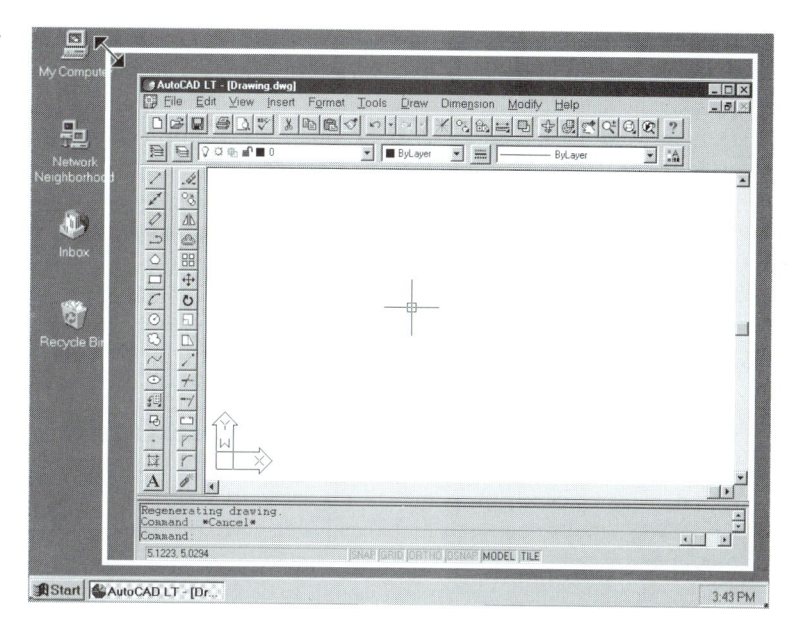

your desktop as needed. In Figure 1.35, AutoCAD LT and a word processing application are both visible on the desktop. This gives you great flexibility in working with your applications. Such an arrangement may not be possible on systems with lower display resolution capabilities. For more information on adjusting your display resolution, see Appendix A.

FIGURE 1.35 Two different program windows can be displayed at once.

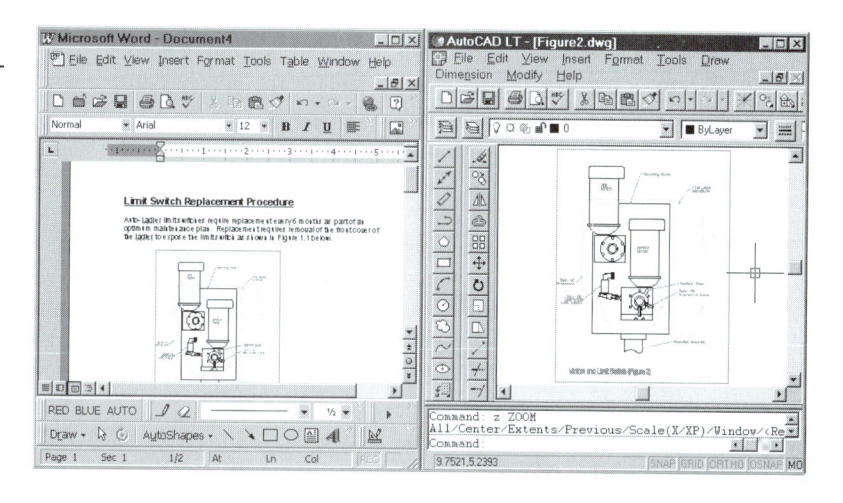

Through the Window...

When you need to display two or more program windows at once on your desktop, there is an easier way than manually sizing and positioning each window. Here's how: Point to the task bar (avoid any buttons) and press the right mouse button. The menu that is displayed provides options for arranging windows currently floating on your desktop. Cascade displays the windows overlapped. Pick the one you want and it comes to the top. Tile Horizontally or Tile Vertically displays your windows without overlapping them, sizing each window equally. This menu provides an option to Undo the last option, in case you do not like the results of the selected arrangement.

Sizing and Moving Other Windows Components

AutoCAD LT's toolbars can be moved and resized in much the same way as program windows. Pointing to the top, bottom, left, and right edges produces the resizing cursor. With toolbars, you cannot resize diagonally. To move a toolbar, point to the title bar, press and hold the cursor button and move the mouse—just as you would with program windows.

Toolbars can also be attached, or *docked,* at the edges of the AutoCAD LT window. Docking a toolbar removes the title bar and embeds it in the program window. The Standard toolbar and Object Properties toolbar are docked by default at the top of the screen (refer to Figure 1.21). To return a docked toolbar to a floating state, point to the background area of the toolbar, carefully avoiding selecting a button. Press and hold the pick button and move the toolbar to the new location.

If you are trying to move the toolbar close to the edge, but do not want it docked, press the Ctrl key while you are moving the toolbar. This prevents docking. More information on working with toolbars is found in Chapter 17.

Field Notes

Any command or option specified at the command line in AutoCAD LT must be followed with an ENTER keystroke. You can execute the ENTER keystroke by pressing the **Enter** key or the space bar, or by right-clicking your mouse. If you right-click when you are pointing at an object or screen feature, a popup cursor menu may be displayed. If you are pointing at a toolbar button when you right-click, a toolbar customization menu is displayed. This menu allows you to control the visibility settings of the toolbars and offers an option to customize the toolbar buttons. Use this menu if you accidentally hide a toolbar and want it to be made visible again, but you should not select the Customize option until after you have reviewed the information in Chapter 17.

Exercise 1.4

1. Open the AutoCAD LT program.
2. Pick the Cancel button to dismiss the Start Up dialog box.
3. Use the window control buttons found in the upper right corner of the program window to minimize the AutoCAD LT application.
4. Double-click on the Task Bar button to maximize the window.
5. Pick the Restore button to change to a floating window.
6. Use your cursor to resize the floating window horizontally, vertically, and diagonally.
7. Reposition the AutoCAD LT window into a new location on the screen.
8. Select the maximize button again.
9. Try steps 3 through 8 using selections from the window control menu in the upper left corner instead of the buttons.

✓ LEARNING CHECKPOINT

- ☐ What is the primary reason for needing to size and move program windows?
- ☐ Where are most of the program window controls found?
- ☐ Name each of the available window control options.
- ☐ What reason might you have for needing two windows visible at once?
- ☐ Describe each of the alternate cursors used to move and size windows.
- ☐ What is the easiest way to close a program window?

Standard
New (Ctrl+N)

File
New...

NEW
N
Ctrl+N

Starting a Drawing Session

When you start a drawing session with AutoCAD LT, you either begin a new drawing or open an existing drawing to continue your work from a previous session. The Start Up dialog box is displayed when you first start AutoCAD LT, and this gives you the option of opening an existing drawing or starting a new drawing using a variety of formats. The Start Up dialog box is discussed in detail in Chapter 2.

If you have already been working in AutoCAD LT and you wish to either start a new drawing or open an existing one, you need to enter the appropriate command to do so. The command to start a new drawing is NEW.

To enter the NEW command, press the New button on the Standard toolbar. You may also enter this command by picking the New ... option from the File pull-down menu, by pressing Ctrl+N, or by typing **NEW** at the Command: prompt. The NEW command displays the Create New Drawing dialog box. This is the same as the Start Up dialog box, except it does not provide an option for opening an existing drawing. The optional formats for starting your new drawing are discussed in detail in Chapter 2. To start your first new drawing, enter the NEW command by any of the methods described. When you get to the Create New Drawing dialog box, pick the Start from Scratch button as shown in Figure 1.36. This starts a drawing with the default options. In this example, the term *default* indicates that no custom settings have been made.

FIGURE 1.36 The NEW command displays the Create New Drawing dialog box.

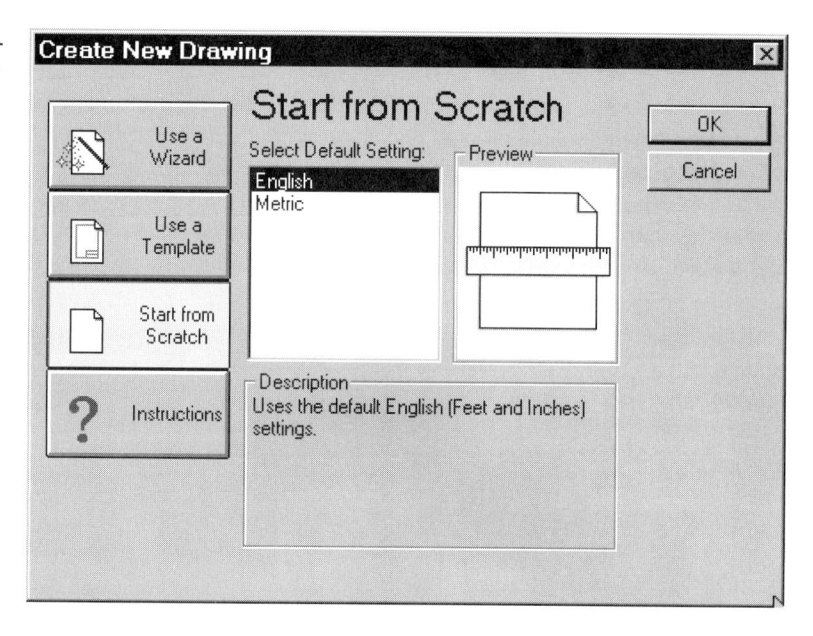

After selecting Start from Scratch, pick the OK button and you are returned to the AutoCAD LT drawing editor. After starting a new drawing using this method, the title bar for the AutoCAD LT window displays the name *[unnamed]*. This indicates that the current drawing does not yet have a name. A name is assigned to a drawing when the drawing file is written to your disk drive using the Save Drawing As dialog box. This feature is also discussed further in Chapter 2.

If you want to open a drawing you have worked on previously, you can use the OPEN command.

The OPEN command opens a drawing file from your disk drive. Pick the Open button from the Standard toolbar to start this command. You can also pick the Open … option from the File … pull-down menu, use the Ctrl+O accelerator key, or type **OPEN** at the Command: prompt.

When you start the OPEN command, the Select File dialog box is displayed (Figure 1.37). In the upper left corner of the window is the File name: edit box. This shows the currently highlighted drawing name. When you first see this dialog box, no file name is yet selected and the edit box contents are "*.dwg." This is because AutoCAD LT drawing files are saved with a file extension of ".dwg." The list box directly below the Look in: dropdown list is the file list. This list shows the names of the drawings that are found in the current directory folder. In Figure 1.37, the current directory folder is C:\Program Files\AutoCAD LT 98, as shown in the Look in: window.

Standard

Open (Ctrl+O)

File
  Open…

OPEN
OP
Ctrl+O

FIGURE 1.37 The Select File dialog box is displayed when you enter the OPEN command.

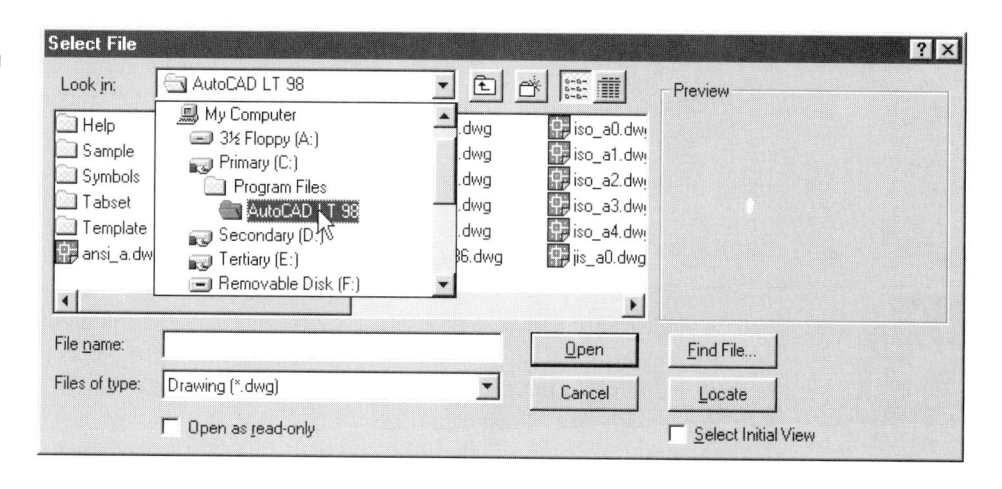

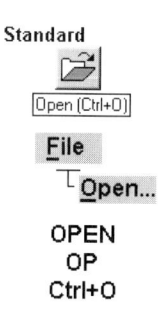

To look in another directory folder, double-click on the new folder. For example, to look in the sample folder, point to the folder and double-click. Now the contents of this folder are displayed in the file list. To move back to the AutoCAD LT 98 directory, double-click on that folder again. If you need to look on another disk drive or folder, pick the Look in: dropdown list and select the new destination. If you are connected to a network, the available network drives are also displayed in this list.

The Files of type: popup list contains the specification Drawing (*.dwg), DXF (*.dxf), and Drawing Template File (*.dwt), because AutoCAD LT opens only these types of files directly. Some other types of files can be imported; this option is covered in Chapter 15.

The Preview box displays an image of the currently selected file. This can be very helpful when you are looking for a file but cannot remember its name. To use this feature, point to one of the drawings in the file list and press the pick button once. The name of the highlighted file is then displayed in the File name edit box and an image of the file is shown in the Preview image tile. Figure 1.38 shows the drawing named ansi_b.dwg selected, and its image is displayed in the Preview image tile. Picking the OK button will open the drawing currently highlighted, or you can double-click on the file name. To find out more about any feature of this dialog box, pick the question mark button on the title bar and then pick the feature.

FIGURE 1.38 The Preview image tile displays an image of the currently selected drawing file.

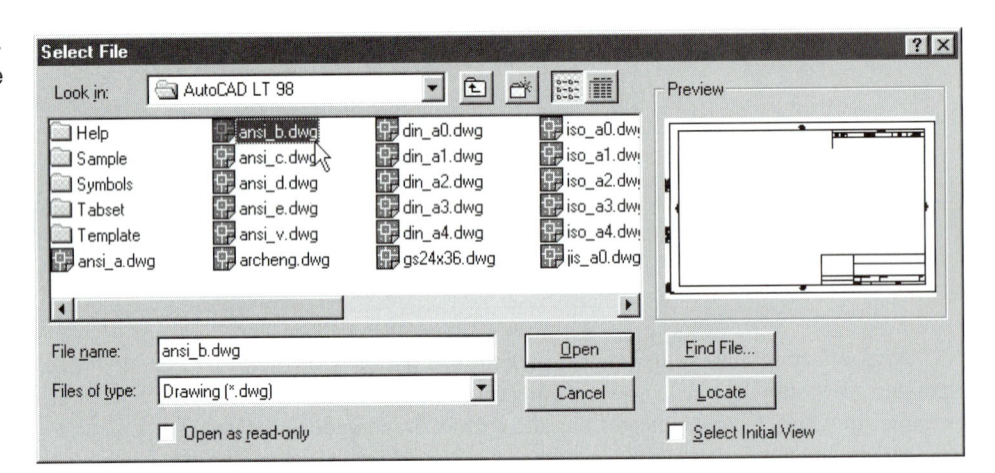

Through the Window...

When AutoCAD LT is installed on your computer, it registers the AutoCAD drawing file extension with Windows. This means that Windows associates files with the extension .dwg with the AutoCAD LT program and can automatically start the AutoCAD LT program with the requested file preloaded. Here's how:

In Windows Explorer, or My Computer, navigate to the appropriate disk drive and directory folder and find the desired drawing name. Point to the file icon with the cursor and double-click.

In the Windows environment, almost any file dialog box can be used to perform basic file-maintenance tasks, such as copying, renaming, moving, or even deleting files. To display a menu of your options, point at a file name in the file list area and right-click your mouse. Right click in a blank area, where no filename is highlighted, to display a menu of options for the list itself. These features are discussed in Chapter 15.

Ending a Drawing Session

After you complete your work in AutoCAD LT, you can exit the program most easily by pointing to the program window Close button. As discussed earlier, this is the button with the X found in the upper right corner of every program window (see Figure 1.30). Picking this button enters the QUIT command at the Command: prompt. The QUIT command can be typed at the Command: prompt as either QUIT or EXIT, or you can pick Exit from the File pull-down menu.

CHAPTER 1 ||| An Introduction to AutoCAD LT

If you have made no changes to the drawing that is currently open, AutoCAD LT is closed with no further prompts. When the drawing has unsaved changes, you will see a dialog box asking you if you want to save these changes. Figure 1.39 shows this warning dialog box as it appears when the current drawing has not been named. If the drawing has been named, its name appears in place of *Drawing.dwg*.

If you are finished working in the current drawing, but need to either open or begin another drawing, do not use the QUIT command. It is not necessary to close AutoCAD LT in order to exit the current drawing. Enter the OPEN or the NEW command as described previously; if the current drawing has unsaved changes, the dialog box shown in Figure 1.39 is displayed.

FIGURE 1.39 Select Yes to save changes, No to discard changes, or Cancel to remain in the drawing.

Exercise 1.5

1. Open the AutoCAD LT program.
2. Pick the Cancel button to dismiss the Start Up dialog box.
3. Pick the File menu and point to the Exit option. Look on the status bar at the helpstring; you will see that QUIT is listed as the command name used.
4. Select the Exit option to close AutoCAD LT.

✓ LEARNING CHECKPOINT

- ☐ What command is used to start a new drawing session?
- ☐ How is an existing drawing opened for further editing?
- ☐ How can the drawing preview feature be used to your advantage?
- ☐ How can double-clicks be used in a Select File dialog box?
- ☐ What are three different ways to exit AutoCAD LT?

Using On-Line Help in AutoCAD LT

AutoCAD LT provides a comprehensive help system for getting fast answers or guidance while you are working. You can access the help system at any time—even while another command is active. The on-line help in AutoCAD LT 98 is started using the HELP command. If no command is currently active, you can type **HELP** or enter a question mark (**?**) at the Command: prompt. Optimally, you can press the F1 function key on your keyboard, pick the Help button on the Standard toolbar, or select AutoCAD LT Help Topics from the Help pull-down menu. Figure 1.40 shows the AutoCAD LT 98 Help System window, with the Contents tab active.

The AutoCAD LT 98 Help System window displays navigation buttons, similar to those used in a web browser, along the top. The help system information is divided into a left and a right frame. The left frame, also called the *Contents Window*, is for navigation and searching. It has three tabs that display the table of **Contents**, the **Index**, and the **Search** tools. The frame on the right displays the actual help information. For many topics, this frame also displays three tabs used to control the type of information displayed. The **Concepts** tab provides conceptual information relevant to the selected topic. The **Procedures** tab shows step-by-step procedural information, and the **Reference** tab provides links to related information.

Browsing the Help Contents

When you enter the HELP command at the Command: prompt, the AutoCAD LT 98 Help System window appears as shown in Figure 1.40. You can browse through the help system information using the Contents tab. The icons displayed in the Contents tab are illustrated and described here:

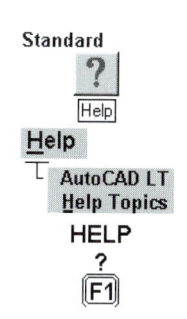

FIGURE 1.40 The Contents tab is active by default in the AutoCAD LT 98 Help System window.

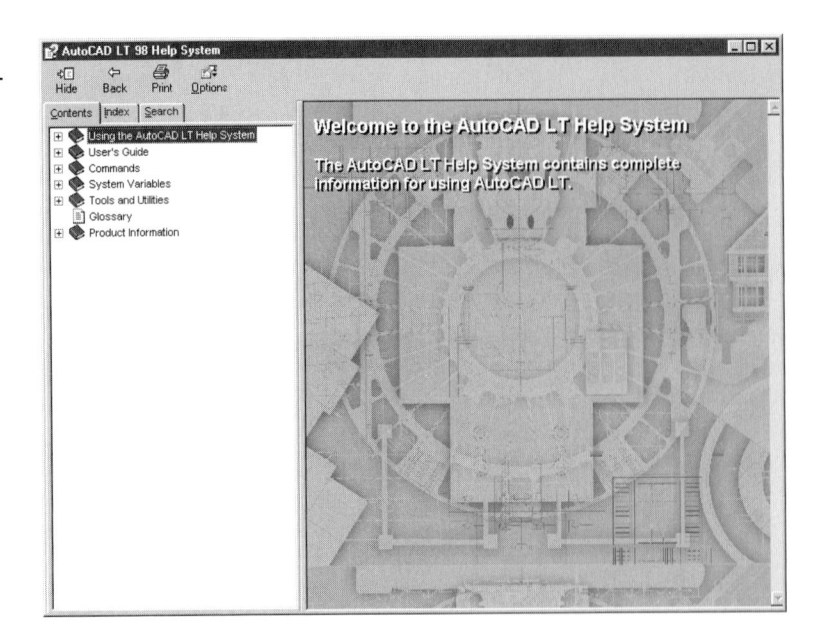

| | Represents an unopened grouping of informational topics, such as Book, Chapter, or Section. Picking a book icon displays information in the frame to the right. Double-click on this icon (or pick the Plus Sign icon) to open it and display its contents. |

Represents an opened grouping of informational topics. Double-click on this icon (or pick the Minus Sign icon) to close it and hide its contents.

📄 or ❓ Both of these icons represent a page of information. Picking one displays the topical information in the frame to the right. To hide page icons, close the book in which they are contained.

➕ A closed book displays a Plus Sign icon. Picking the plus sign, similar to double-clicking an unopened book, displays additional contents. Using the Plus Sign icons allows faster navigation because the book you open is not selected, so its information is not displayed.

➖ An open book displays a Minus Sign icon. Picking the minus sign closes the book and hides its contents.

The categories found under the Contents tab are divided into several categories, and where appropriate, these categories are further subdivided. The primary categories are as follows:

- **Using the AutoCAD Help System** Contains information about using the help system.
- **User's Guide** Provides conceptual and procedural information, with links to associated commands.
- **Command Reference** Lists detailed information on all commands available in AutoCAD LT 98, plus any available command options.
- **System Variables** Provides detailed information on available settings within AutoCAD LT 98 and their effects.
- **Tools and Utilities** Details the use of special tools available in AutoCAD LT 98, along with available external utility programs.
- **Glossary** Lists definitions for terms associated with AutoCAD LT 98.
- **Product Information** Contains copyright and compatibility information.

In the Contents tab, the shortcut menu displays three general options. Right-click anywhere in the Contents tab to display this menu. See Figure 1.41. The Open all selection expands all branches of the help file so that all books are opened and all available topics are visible in the Contents tab. Be careful—using this op-

FIGURE 1.41 Right-clicking in the Contents tab area displays this shortcut menu.

tion may make it more difficult to find what you are looking for. The Close all option provides a convenient method for immediately closing all branches.

You can also print out help file information by picking the Print… option. This option displays a subsequent dialog box, as shown in Figure 1.42. Use only the first option: *Print the current page*. If you use the *Print everything contained in the current heading*, all information within the current top level heading is sent to the printer. With some categories, this may print 60 pages or more.

FIGURE 1.42 It is best to use the *Print the current page* option to avoid printing errors and huge print jobs.

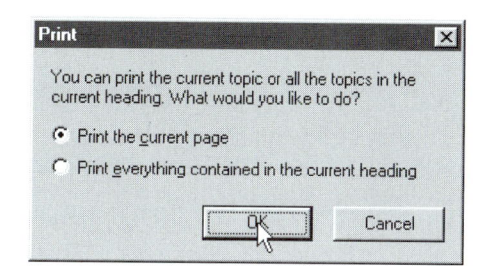

Field Notes

Caution! Using the *Print everything contained in the current heading* for either the *Using the AutoCAD LT Help System* or *User's Guide* sections produces several error messages indicating that needed files cannot be found, and you will have to pick OK several times to continue. *In the User's Guide section, this produces literally **hundreds** of error messages, and you must pick the OK button for each individual message before you can return to the help system.* After picking OK for each error message, if you select OK in the Print dialog box the printed pages contain no useful information.

Once you have found the category of information you are looking for, you can hide the Contents window to reduce the amount of screen space required by the AutoCAD LT 98 Help System window. Use the Show and Hide buttons found on the navigation bar to control the visibility of the Contents window. Figure 1.43 shows these two buttons. You can now arrange the Help System window to allow you to see the AutoCAD LT program window again. You can make the AutoCAD LT program window current by pointing to it and pressing the pick button on your mouse. The Help System window will stay "on top," meaning you will be able to see both windows at the same time. This feature allows you to view relevant help information while you work in AutoCAD LT.

To exit the help system completely, pick the X button in the upper right corner of the Help System window.

FIGURE 1.43 Use the Show and Hide buttons to control the visibility of the Contents window.

Help Information Display Controls

Many of the help information pages display three tabs at the top, as indicated earlier in this discussion. Use these tabs to specify the type of information you are looking for. The Concepts tab gives conceptual information, providing a foundation and appropriate context for learning about the current topic. The Procedures tab provides the "how to" information and links to associated pages of information. A *link*, often called a *hyperlink*, is blue underlined text that is linked to another document in the help system. To use a link, simply point your cursor to the text and pick it. The linked document is then displayed. If you have used another Windows-based help system, or if you have used a Web browser such as Netscape or Internet Explorer, you may already be familiar with the use of links. The third tab, the Reference tab, contains brief listings and links to related command and system variable help pages.

If you want to return to previously viewed information, one option is to select the Back button found on the navigation bar at the top of the Help System window. Optimally, you can right-click in the frame on the right and select Back from the short-cut menu.

Using the Index

Like any other reference manual, the AutoCAD LT 98 Help System provides a comprehensive index to allow you to search an alphabetical list for a desired topic. To use the index, select the Index tab. In the edit box at the top of the Index area, type the entry you are looking for. As you type, the help system automatically displays the first index entry that matches the text you are entering, as shown in Figure 1.44. To display the information for any index entry, double-click on it. Some entries may have more than one relevant help page. Double-clicking on an entry that has more than one associated help topic displays the Topics Found dialog box, where you can specify which topic is of interest to you. Figure 1.45 shows the Topics Found dialog box.

FIGURE 1.44 The Index tab displays topics that match your text entry. Double-click on an entry to see the help information.

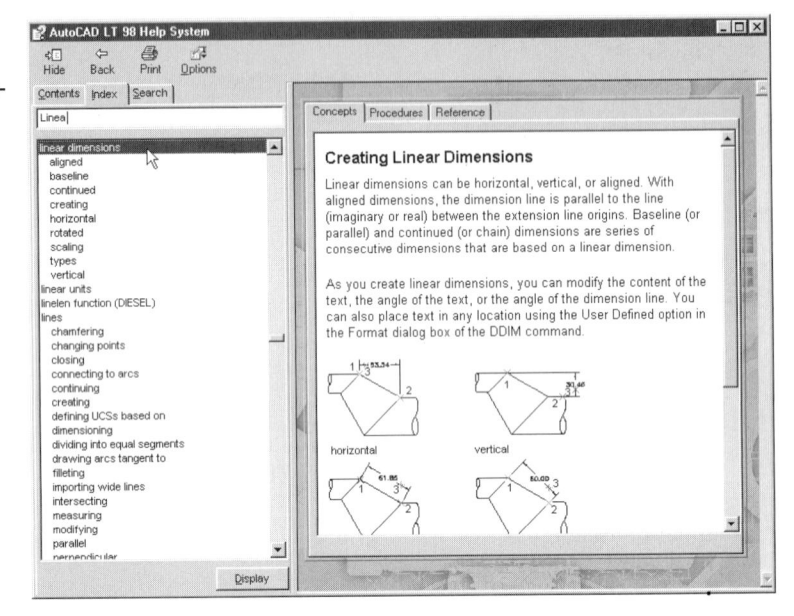

FIGURE 1.45 The Topics Found dialog box is displayed when more than one associated topic is available for an entry.

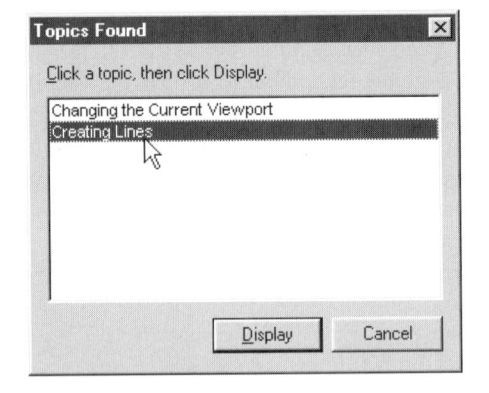

To print a topic found in the Index, select the Print button from the navigation bar at the top of the Help System window. Note that once you display the contents of a topic found in the Index, selecting the Contents tab then displays the page location in the table of contents, along with adjacent topics from which you can select.

Searching the Help System

In many cases, the fastest and most convenient method for finding information you need is by searching the help system. The Search tab allows you to specify a keyword and find all topics containing that word. First, enter a keyword pertaining to the topic you are interested in, then select the List Topics button. Now, double-click on the topic to see the associated help information. An example search is shown in Figure 1.46.

Using a keyword like *line* may produce undesirable results because well over 400 topics are found. You can use multiple words to narrow your search. If you type more than one keyword, only the topics that contain all the keywords are displayed. For example, if you enter the words *creating lines*, all the topics displayed contain both of these words, but, again, too many topics are displayed and many that have absolutely nothing to do with creating lines. To specify an exact phrase that you want to find, enclose it in quotation marks. Specifying a keyword as *"creating lines"* displays only nine topics, and because they contain the exact phrase "creating lines," most of the topics contain useful information. Avoid phrases that are too specific, such as *"creating a single line segment,"* because the wording in the help file may not contain this exact phrase, and your search produces no results.

When you view a topic, the keywords entered are highlighted to make them easy to find. Highlighting can be turned off from the Options menu. To print a topic found in the Search tab, select the Print button on the navigation bar at the top of the Help System window.

FIGURE 1.46 The Search tab provides a convenient way to search the help files for specific information.

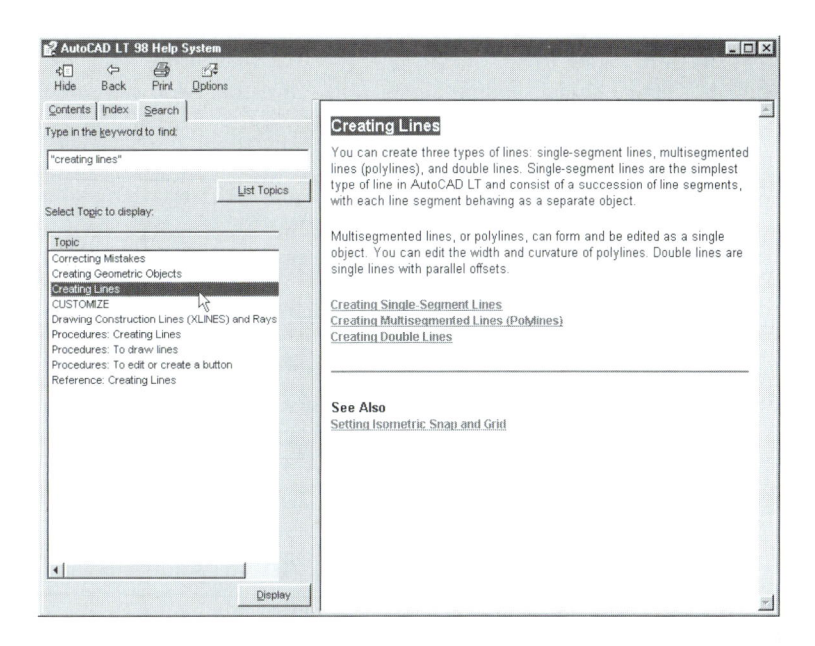

Context-Sensitive Help

The single most useful feature of the AutoCAD LT 98 Help System is *context-sensitive help*, which provides help on the currently active command. For example, if you are trying to use a command such as LINE, and you need assistance, just start the LINE command and then press F1. Alternatively you can pick the Help button, which appears on the Standard Toolbar as a question mark. When you do this, the help system is started and information on how to use the currently active command is automatically displayed.

Exercise 1.6

1. Start the AutoCAD LT 98 Help System by typing HELP. Use the Content tab to find information on the LINE command. Exit the help system.
2. Start the AutoCAD LT 98 Help System by picking the Help button from the Standard Toolbar. Use the Index tab to find information on the LINE command. Exit the help system.
3. Start the AutoCAD LT 98 Help System by picking the AutoCAD LT Help Topics selection from the Help pull-down menu. Use the Search tab to find information on the LINE command. Exit the help system.
4. Type **LINE** at the Command: prompt and press Enter. At the From point: prompt, press the F1 key.
5. Right-click in the Contents tab area and select Close all.
6. Open the *User's Guide* category, then open *Creating Geometric Objects* and *Creating Lines*.
7. Display the topic labeled *Creating Single-Segment Lines*.
8. Review the Concepts page, and then pick the Procedures tab. From the Procedures page, pick the LINE link at the bottom of this page.
9. Return to the previous topic by selecting the Back button. Pick the Reference tab.
10. In the Reference tab, pick the XLINE link.
11. Exit the help system.

MULTIPLE CHOICE

Circle the choice or enter your response on an answer sheet by selecting the option that most accurately completes or answers the given statements.

1. AutoCAD LT documentation recommends _____ of memory be installed.
   - a. 16 megabytes
   - b. 256 megabytes
   - c. 64 kilobytes
   - d. 32 megabytes

2. Frequent typing with your wrists bent can result in:
   - a. eye strain
   - b. carpal tunnel syndrome
   - c. backache
   - d. foot odor

3. When the label of a dialog button is followed by this symbol, it means that picking the button opens a subdialog box:
   - a. <
   - b. ...
   - c. >
   - d. ?

4. To access a dialog box item with the keyboard, press the _____ key and the underscored character at the same time.
   - a. Ctrl
   - b. Enter
   - c. Alt
   - d. Esc

5. The key that cancels an operation in AutoCAD LT is:
   - a. Ctrl
   - b. Enter
   - c. Alt
   - d. Esc

6. The AutoCAD LT text screen can be viewed by pressing:
   - a. F1
   - b. F3
   - c. F2
   - d. F4

7. The NEW command *cannot* be started doing this:
   - a. Ctrl+N
   - b. Pick the New toolbar button.
   - c. Pick New… from the File pull-down.
   - d. Alt+N

8. A shortened version of a command name that you can type in at the Command: prompt is called a:
   - a. command alias
   - b. dialog box
   - c. menu access key
   - d. cancel

9. A toolbar that is attached to the edge of the AutoCAD LT program window is referred to as being:
   - a. docked
   - b. minimized
   - c. floating
   - d. maximized

10. The accelerator keystroke Ctrl+O starts the _____ command.
    - a. NEW
    - b. OPEN
    - c. QUIT
    - d. CLOSE

CHAPTER 1 ||| An Introduction to AutoCAD LT

MATCHING

Match each term to the correct description by writing the appropriate number in each box at the left.

☐ Dialog box
☐ Tooltip
☐ Help string
☐ Radio button
☐ Edit box
☐ List box
☐ Toggle
☐ Image
☐ Exit button
☐ Close button
☐ Popup list
☐ Interface
☐ Menu access key
☐ Help
☐ Accelerator key

1. General term describing the way you communicate with the computer.
2. Turns something on or off.
3. Help located at the cursor.
4. Text is entered using this.
5. A combination keystroke to access a command quickly.
6. A button with an X located in the upper right corner.
7. A graphic element of a dialog box.
8. Pick this button to get assistance.
9. Used to present a listing of options in a dialog.
10. A button that allows only one selection.
11. Information on the status bar.
12. This list allows only one selection.
13. Provides an intuitive interface.
14. Usually OK or Cancel.
15. Provides keyboard access to pull-down menu items.

WORD SCRAMBLE

Unscramble the six scrambled words below, one letter to each square, to form six AutoCAD LT–related words:

NIDWOW

KETROWN

RORCUS

ROMINTO

CAPEES

NUME

Unscramble the circled letters to form the special answer, as suggested by the illustration.

CHAPTER 2

Introduction to Drafting with AutoCAD LT

LEARNING GOALS

- Set up a quick AutoCAD LT drawing.
- Establish the drawing limits and set the units style.
- Use Grid and Snap to assist in making a drawing.
- Draw lines by picking points.
- Draw lines by entering distances, angles, and coordinates.
- Use the ORTHO command to assist in drawing lines.
- Use the REDRAW command to remove Blips from the screen.
- Erase objects by picking, windowing, and crossing.
- Use the ERASE command before or after selecting objects.
- Remove objects from a selection set.
- Use the OOPS, U, and REDO commands.
- Print or plot a drawing.

Drafting with AutoCAD LT

The first step in any drawing is to set up the drawing environment. The term *drawing environment* refers to the settings your drawing uses, such as the overall drawing size and the units of measurement. AutoCAD LT allows you to specify units in several different formats, such as feet and inches or decimal style units. The drawing area can be set up for creating very small mechanical parts or designing an entire office complex. This chapter discusses methods of setting up drawings and introduces the fundamentals of creating, editing, and printing drawings.

The AutoCAD LT Drawing Setup Options

AutoCAD LT provides several methods for setting up your drawing, including *Wizards*, which you may have used in other Windows applications. A Wizard is an automated process that prompts you for information about how you want your document to be set up and then makes all the specific settings for you. The AutoCAD LT Wizards automatically adjust many drawing settings to match the size and type of your drawing. You can choose a Quick Setup, or for a more detailed setup process, you can use the Advanced Setup Wizard.

Using the Quick Setup

When you open AutoCAD LT, you get the Start Up dialog box shown in Figure 2.1. You can start a similar dialog box by picking New… in the File pull-down menu, but it is called the Create New Drawing dialog box and it does not offer the Open a Drawing option.

The Use a Wizard button lets you select Quick Setup or Advanced Setup. Quick Setup is the default when you do the initial AutoCAD LT Start Up. Whatever is selected in the Start Up or Create New Drawing dialog box becomes the default for the next session. You may also pick the Use a Template, Start from Scratch, or Instructions buttons. Pick Use a Wizard to access the setup options. A description of the setup option that is highlighted is provided in the Wizard Description compartment (see Figure 2.1). To do a quick setup, double-click the Quick Setup Wizard or pick Quick Setup and pick the OK button or press Enter. Now you get the Quick Setup dialog box shown

Standard
New (Ctrl+N)
File
 New...
NEW
N
Ctrl+N

FIGURE 2.1 The Start Up dialog box. Notice the Wizard Description of the Quick Setup option.

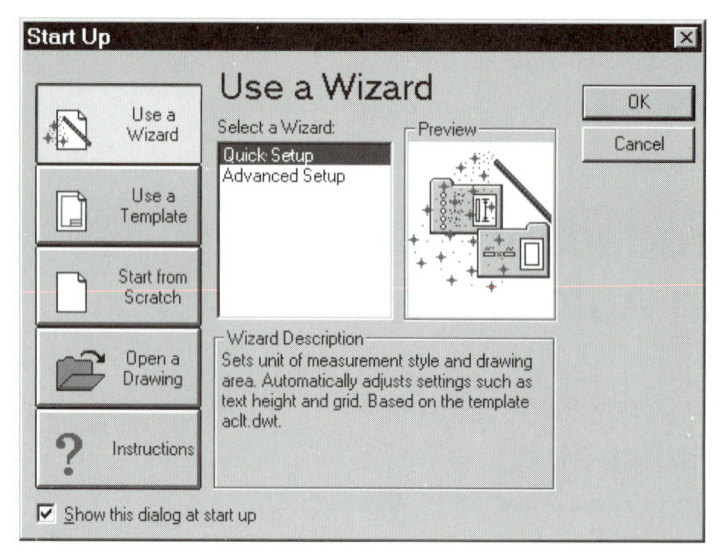

in Figure 2.2. The Quick Setup dialog box allows you to set the drawing units and area to your specifications. AutoCAD LT then sets up the drawing area and changes settings such as text height to an appropriate scale based on the settings you make in this dialog box. Using Quick Setup is a fast way for you to get started using AutoCAD LT.

Setting Units of Measure

The Quick Setup dialog box gives you several options for setting your drawing units in the Units tab. AutoCAD LT calls this Step 1 of the Quick Setup. Step 1 instructions are given in the Units tab. The initial setting is Decimal units and there is an example of a typical decimal units display at the right, under Sample Units (see Figure 2.2A). Select the units option that matches your drawing. When you pick a units option, the selected option becomes active and an example is displayed at the right. Figure 2.2B through E shows the selection and example displayed for each of the unit options. The following types of units are available:

- *Decimal:* This is the default setting and is the most versatile option. Decimal units are the best choice unless you prefer a specific format for specifying drawing information, such as feet and inches, or scientific units. In AutoCAD LT, decimal units can represent whatever your application requires. For example, if you are drawing a small mechanical part, drawing units may represent inches or millimeters. In larger drawing applications, such as maps, units may represent miles or kilometers. Figure 2.2A shows decimal units selected.
- *Engineering:* Drawing in engineering units is generally used in mapping and civil drafting projects such as dam and bridge construction, plot plans, and topography. This selection is shown in Figure 2.2B.
- *Architectural:* This units setting is used when you draw in feet, inches, and fractional inches for architectural drawings such as plans, sections, elevations, and details (see Figure 2.2C).
- *Fractional:* Fractional units are used when you are making a drawing that contains fractional parts of any common unit of measure. Look at Figure 2.2D.
- *Scientific:* These units of measure are used when very large or small values are required. The applications occur in businesses such as chemical engineering or astronomy. The example in Figure 2.2E displays 1.5500E+01. The E refers to an exponent value and the +01 is the exponent 10 to the first power.

Exercise 2.1

1. Open AutoCAD LT and look at the Start Up dialog box. Pick New from the File pull-down menu to access the Create New Drawing dialog box if AutoCAD LT is already running.
2. Double-click on Quick Setup in the Select a Wizard box, or highlight Quick Setup and press Enter. Now you should see the Quick Setup dialog box.
3. Decimal units is the default unit of measure. Look at the Sample Units.
4. Pick each of the unit options and notice how the Sample Units display changes to represent each type of unit.
5. Pick the Done button.

CHAPTER 2 ||| Introduction to Drafting with AutoCAD LT   41

FIGURE 2.2 Step 1 of the Quick Setup dialog box.

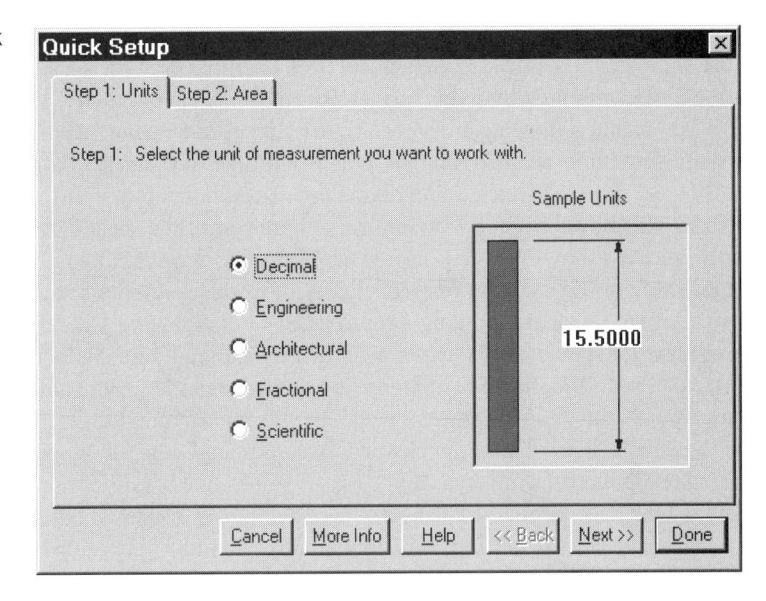

A   Decimal units is the default setting.

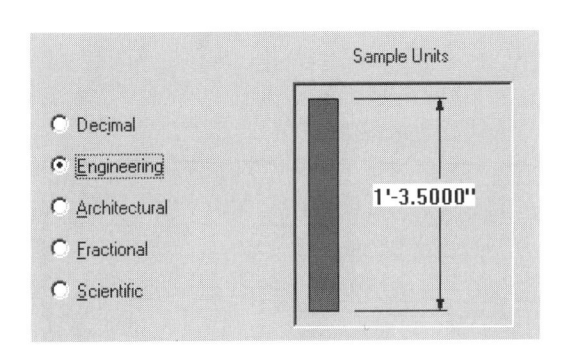

B   Engineering units.

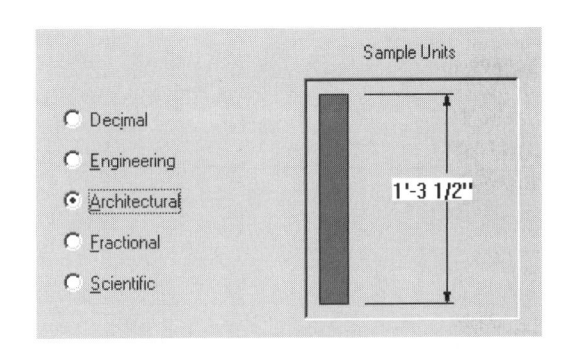

C   Architectural units.

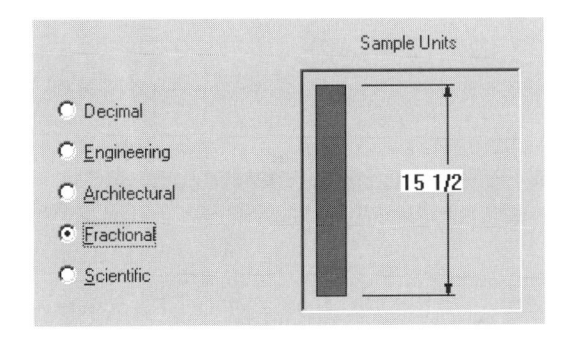

D   Fractional units.

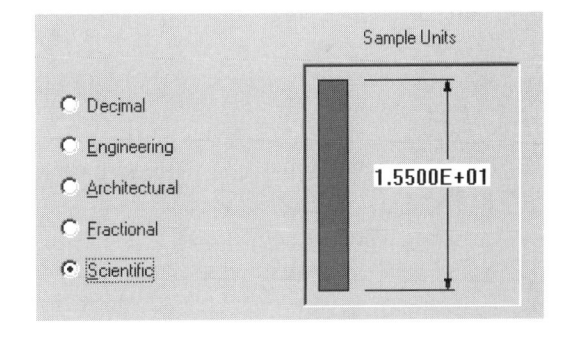

E   Scientific units.

Setting the Drawing Size

AutoCAD LT provides a virtually unlimited amount of space in which you can create your drawing. When you use a Wizard, part of the setup procedure asks you to specify the dimensions of the area that your drawing will occupy. All objects created in AutoCAD LT are drawn at full scale, meaning that they are drawn at their actual size. When setting up your drawing space, make the area large enough to hold all necessary views of your drawing plus any required dimensions.

The drawing area can be very small if you are drawing small objects, or it can be large enough for a building, a residential development, a state map, or even larger if necessary. You can control how much of the drawing is displayed on your screen and specify the scale at which the drawing is to be printed. You can also change the size of the drawing area at any time later in a drawing session.

The drawing area that you specify is referred to as the model space drawing **limits**. Model space is where you create a drawing in AutoCAD LT. In several listings in the AutoCAD LT Help System, model space drawing limits are also referred to as **world size**. You can set the model space drawing limits using the Step 2: Area tab in the Quick Setup dialog box. Keep in mind that this area indicates the amount of space required by the objects you are drawing and not the size of the sheet on which you will be printing.

Figure 2.3 shows the Step 2: Area tab of the Quick Setup dialog box with its default settings. Use your cursor to pick inside the text boxes labeled Width: and Length: to specify the size of your drawing area. Use the style of units you are working with to indicate the drawing size. If you are using architectural units, be sure to place the foot symbol (') after a number indicating a value in feet or it is interpreted as inches. A drawing size of 17 × 11 is specified in Figure 2.4. Notice that the width value is the horizontal dimension, and the length value is the vertical dimension. When you specify the drawing size, AutoCAD LT automatically adjusts the default sizes of text, dimensions, linetypes, and other drawing features that need to be scaled based on the size of your drawing area. If you prefer values that are different from those AutoCAD LT has set, you can adjust them as necessary. Changing these settings is discussed later in the text.

If you are new to drafting, then drawing in real units might seem like a good idea. However, if you have used manual drafting in the past, you may be wondering about the drawing scale. It is best to forget about

FIGURE 2.3 The Step 2: Area folder in the Quick Setup dialog box. Notice the Sample Area image.

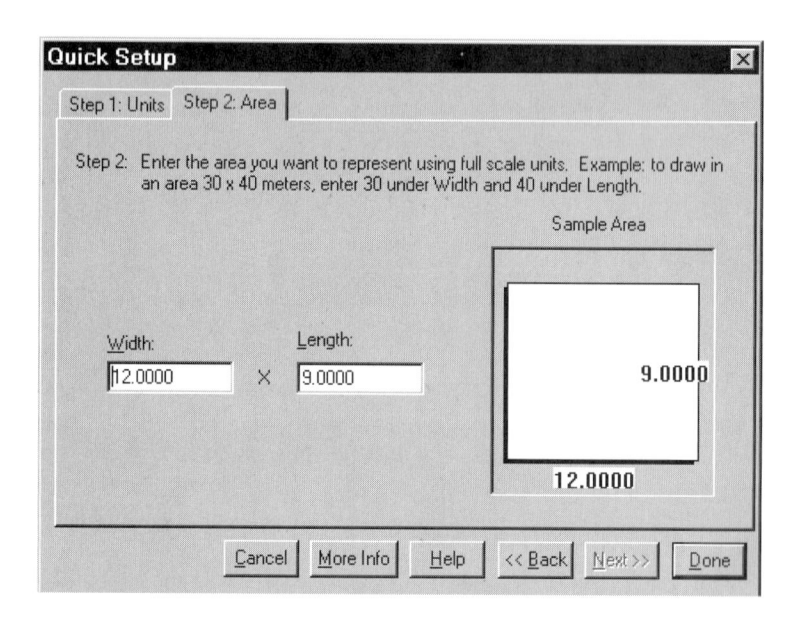

FIGURE 2.4 Changing the drawing area.

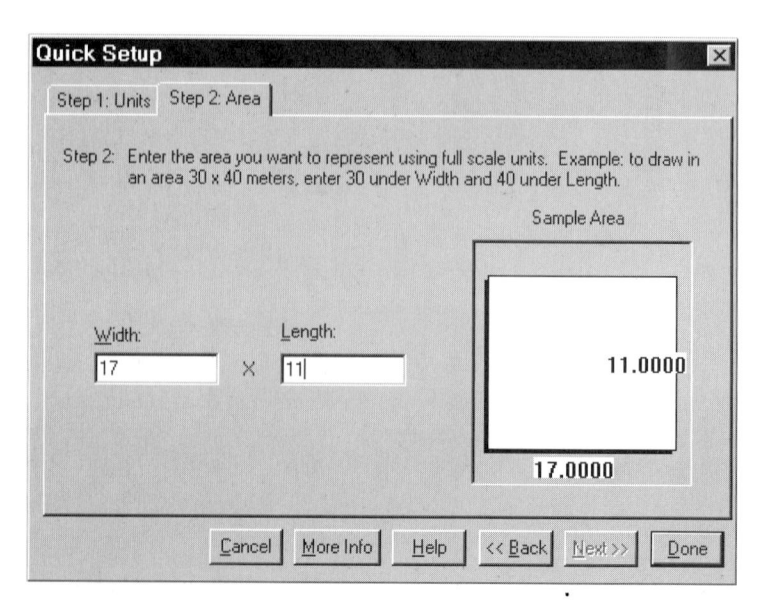

drawing scale for now and think about drawing everything actual or full size. If drawing scales need to be set, this is done during the drawing layout process, which is discussed in the Multiview Drawing Layout section in Chapter 13.

> ✎ Field Notes
>
> Remember, when entering a new value in a text box, all you have to do is double-click on the current value to highlight it. Then just type the new value. It is not necessary to press the Backspace or Delete key first. The highlighted text is automatically replaced by the text you type.

More about Drawing Limits

The initial model space drawing limits are set up in the Step 2: Area tab of the Quick Setup dialog box. Regardless of the settings you specify, the limits are turned off by default. When turned off, the limits have little effect on the drawing process. In addition, the limits setting can be changed at any time. Changing the limits setting and turning limits on or off are discussed in Chapter 3. The effects of the drawing limits are as follows:

- Sets the initially displayed drawing area.
- Specifies where the drawing grid is displayed (Chapter 3)
- Provides an easy display change option for displaying the entire drawing area. (Chapter 4)

The model space drawing limits are not related in any way to the final printed sheet size. The basic rule for determining the most appropriate initial limits setting is to specify an area that will contain your entire drawing. In a multiview drawing application, use your standard drawing layout guidelines based on school or company standards to calculate the required area. If you are drawing a floor plan, use the largest horizontal and vertical dimensions of the building and add enough area to contain dimensions or other required drawing data. You can always adjust the limits later if needed.

Introduction to Model Space and Paper Space

AutoCAD LT provides two drawing areas: **model space** and **paper space**. Model space is the primary area of the drawing. This is where your model (drawing) is created. All drawings are created in model space at actual size without consideration of the final layout or printed size and scale. When your drawing is complete, you then complete your drawing layout in paper space.

When using the Quick Setup wizard, you automatically begin your drawing session in model space. In later chapters, you will learn to use model space to create drawing layouts for industry-standard sheet sizes and print your drawings at industry-standard drawing scales.

Exercise 2.2

1. Open AutoCAD LT if it is not already open. Use the Start Up or Create Drawing dialog box and select Quick Setup.
2. Pick the Step 2: Area tab.
3. Read the Step 2 instructions in the folder.
4. The default limits are Width 12 and Length 9. Change the Width to 17 and the Length to 11.
5. Change the Width to 8.5 and notice the difference in the Sample Area.
6. Pick the Done button.

✓ LEARNING CHECKPOINT

☐ What information is given by the Wizard about Quick Setup?
☐ Name and give an example of each of the five types of units in AutoCAD LT.

- What is meant by world size?
- What is the purpose of the Limits setting?
- What are some of the advantages of an unlimited drawing area?

Introduction to the AutoCAD LT Drawing Aids

AutoCAD LT provides you with drawing aids that help make drawing easy and accurate. Two of the drawing aids that you set up before beginning a drawing are called Grid and Snap. *Grid* is a pattern of dots displayed on the screen at any desired increment that you establish. *Snap* is an invisible grid that forces the screen cursor to move in exact increments. The idea behind these drawing aids is to give you a grid on the screen that matches units of measure on your drawing. This is similar to doing a pencil drawing on graph paper. The lines on the graph paper give you something to follow when making a sketch or drawing. The grid dots on the screen work the same way, and the snap spacing forces the screen cursor to follow the dots exactly as you move the pointing device. The Quick Setup automatically establishes equal grid and snap settings based on the units and drawing area you select.

Setting the Grid and Snap

Tools
└ **Drawing Aids...**

DDRMODES
RM

To set or change the grid and snap, you need to access the Drawing Aids dialog box. To get this dialog box, pick Drawing Aids … in the Tools pull-down menu, or type **DDRMODES** at the command prompt and press Enter. The Drawing Aids dialog box is shown in Figure 2.5. Turn the Snap and Grid options on by picking the On toggle for each. Set the Snap and Grid values by entering the desired X Spacing and Y Spacing in the text boxes. In Figure 2.5, the X and Y Spacing is set to .5 for both Snap and Grid. When you set the X Spacing, the Y Spacing automatically defaults to the same value. You can set different values if you wish, but equal values are common for many applications. A drafter, however, often sets the Grid and Snap spacing to different values, so they complement each other. For example, the Grid might be set at .5 as a general drawing aid, whereas the Snap value is set smaller than the Grid, such as .125, for more precise cursor movement. This is discussed in detail later. A check in each On box turns the Snap and Grid options on. You can individually set the Snap and Grid X and Y Spacing. Pick the OK button when you have the Drawing Aids set the way you want them. Now, the AutoCAD LT drawing window is displayed with the grid dots and the screen cursor ready for you to draw, as shown in Figure 2.6.

Status Bar
[GRID]

GRID
CTRL+G
[F7]

You can change the Snap and Grid values or turn Snap and Grid on or off anytime during your drawing session by using the Drawing Aids dialog box, or more easily by double-clicking SNAP or GRID on the status bar, or by pressing the F7 key for Grid or the F9 key for Snap.

Status Bar
[SNAP]

SNAP
CTRL+B
[F9]

You can also type the GRID and SNAP commands at the Command: prompt. The command sequence for each looks like this:

Command: **GRID**↵
Grid spacing (X) or ON/OFF/Snap/Aspect⟨0.500⟩: **.25**↵
Command: **SNAP**↵
Snap spacing (X) or ON/OFF/Snap/Aspect⟨0.500⟩: **.125**↵
Command:

FIGURE 2.5 The Drawing Aids dialog box.

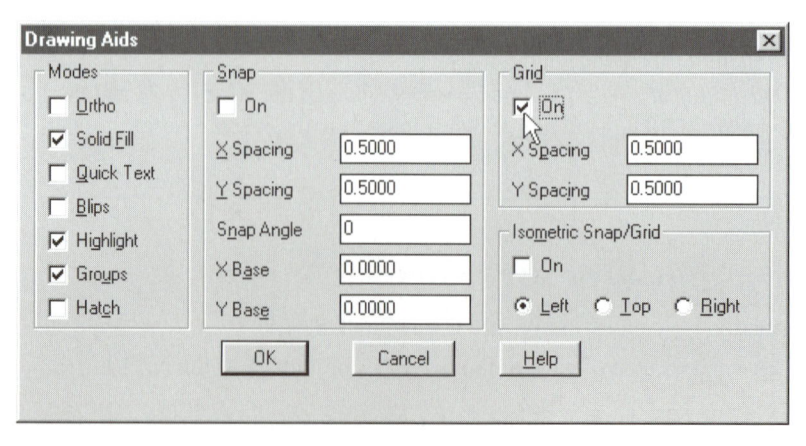

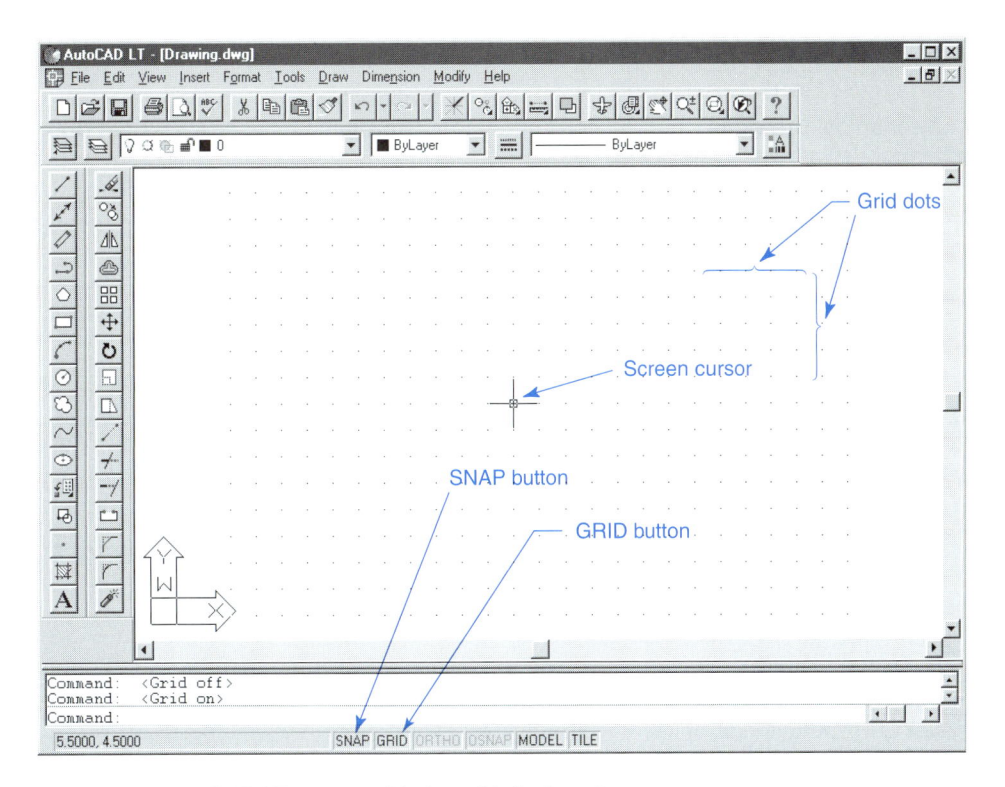

CHAPTER 2 ||| Introduction to Drafting with AutoCAD LT

FIGURE 2.6 The AutoCAD LT screen with the grid displayed.

The shortcut key for toggling the GRID is CTRL + G; CTRL + B toggles SNAP. You can also turn Grid and Snap on or off at the keyboard by typing **GRID** or **SNAP** and entering ON or OFF as needed. Other Drawing Aids dialog box and Grid and Snap options are discussed later.

Things to Consider When Setting Drawing Aids

The Grid dots and Snap settings are usually spaced at some convenient unit of measure that matches units on your drawing. For example, you may be drawing an object in inches with a variety of measurements including .25, .50, .75, and 1.50 in. Then you might want to set the grid and snap spacing to the smallest measurement of .25. Now, when you move the screen cursor it automatically moves in .25-in. increments. Metric drawings might use 1-mm or 10-cm increments, depending on the drawing size. This makes it easy for you to draw the objects by picking points that match the measurements on the drawing. Another example might be for an architectural drawing with a variety of dimensions, including 6″, 1′0″, 1′6″, 4′0″, and 6′6″, for example. In this case, you may want to set the grid and snap spacing to 6″ because this makes it easy for you to draw the exact features that are found on the architectural drawing.

The Grid and Snap settings can be the same as with the AutoCAD LT Quick Setup default, or they can be set to different values. This is up to you. You will see the advantages of different settings as you begin to draw with AutoCAD LT. Here is an example of why you might choose different Grid and Snap settings: If the smallest increment on the drawing is .125 in., then setting the grid at this value places the grid dots very close together. The grid dots basically become useless, and, in some cases, may be too close for AutoCAD LT to display. If they are too close, the message "Grid too dense to display" is given in the Command window. The grid should be a general guide to assist your drawing, but the snap spacing should be very accurate. If the smallest dimension is .125 in., then a snap spacing of .125 and a grid spacing of .5 might be an option to consider. This allows the screen cursor to snap to the exact .125 measurement, and there are four snap increments between each set of grid dots. This forces the screen cursor to snap directly on the grid dots at every fourth snap. Whatever Grid and Snap settings you use, the snap and grid should be equal, or the snap should be a multiple of the grid setting. Some examples are given in Table 2.1. The exact snap and grid increments that you choose depend totally on the requirements for the particular drawing.

TABLE 2.1 Various snap and grid settings

Mechanical Drawings				Architectural Drawings		Civil Drawings	
Snap	Grid	Snap	Grid	Snap	Grid	Snap	Grid
.0625	.125	1 mm	5 mm	4	12	1′	2′
.125	.25	2	10	6	12	1′	5′
.25	.5	5	20	6	24	2′	10′

Exercise 2.3

1. Open AutoCAD LT and access the Quick Setup dialog box.
2. Set Decimal units and 8.5 × 11 limits.
3. Pick the Done button. Notice the pattern of grid dots on the screen; however, the snap should be off at this time.
4. Access the Drawing Aids dialog box.
5. Turn on Snap. Grid should already be on.
6. Notice 0.5000 X and Y Spacing in the Grid and Snap text boxes.
7. Pick the OK button.
8. Notice the pattern of dots on the screen.
9. Move the screen cursor and notice how it automatically "snaps" to the Grid dots.
10. Access the Drawing Aids dialog box again.
11. Set the Snap X and Y Spacing to .25 and the Grid X and Y Spacing to .5.
12. Pick the OK button.
13. Move the screen cursor and notice how it snaps between grid dots.
14. Set the Snap X and Y Spacing to .125 and the Grid X and Y Spacing to .5.
15. Pick the OK button.
16. Move the screen cursor and see the results.
17. Enter **GRID** and **SNAP** at the command prompt to set the Snap X and Y Spacing to .0625 and the Grid X and Y Spacing to .25.
18. Move the screen cursor and see the results.
19. Turn the Grid and Snap options off and on using each of the SNAP and GRID status bar items, the F7 and F9 keys, and the CTRL +G and CTRL+B keystrokes.
20. Access the Drawing Aids dialog box.
21. Set the Snap X and Y Spacing to .25 and the Grid X and Y Spacing to .5.
22. Pick the OK button.

✓ LEARNING CHECKPOINT

- Why does AutoCAD LT provide you with drawing aids?
- Describe *grid* and *snap*.
- Identify at least two things to consider when setting the Grid and Snap options.

Drawing Lines with AutoCAD LT

Lines are used in drafting to communicate an idea. Some drafting fields such as mechanical drafting recommend strict standards for line presentation. Line standards for these drawings are provided in the ASME Y14.2M document. Other drafting fields, such as architectural, piping, and electrical, also have recommended line standards that are commonly used. Standard line examples that are commonly used in industry are displayed in Appendix B.

CHAPTER 2 ||| Introduction to Drafting with AutoCAD LT 47

Drawing Lines by Picking Points

When drawing lines with AutoCAD LT, you use the LINE command. This command can be accessed in any of these ways:

- Pick Line from the Draw pull-down menu.
- Pick the Line button in the Draw toolbar.
- Type **L** or **LINE** at the Command: prompt.

When you enter the LINE command, you get this message at the prompt line:

Command: **L** or **LINE**↵
From point:

Draw
Line

Draw
Line

LINE
L

From point: means that AutoCAD LT is ready for you to enter the first point to begin drawing a line. If Grid and Snap are on, the screen cursor snaps to Snap points as you move the mouse. Also, as you move the screen cursor, the ***coordinate display*** indicates where the cursor is in relation to the drawing origin. The coordinate display may be turned on or off or changed from absolute coordinate to polar coordinate values using the F6 key or by double-clicking on the coordinate display on the status bar. Absolute and polar coordinates are discussed later. The ***drawing origin,*** or *origin,* is in the lower left corner of the screen when you begin an AutoCAD LT drawing with the Quick Setup. Look at Figure 2.7. The drawing origin has a coordinate display of 0.0000,0.0000. As you move the mouse, the coordinate display changes to represent how far you have moved to the right and up from the origin. The coordinate display of 4.5000,4.5000 shown in Figure 2.7 means that the screen cursor is 4.5 units to the right and 4.5 units up from the origin.

Now, use the left mouse button to pick the point. The prompt reads:

Command: **L** or **LINE**↵
From point: ⟨*pick where the coordinates read 4.5000,4.5000*⟩
To point:

The *To point:* prompt tells you to pick another point of the line. As you move the screen cursor, the coordinate display continues to tell you the distance to the right and up from the origin. At the same time, a temporary line is displayed between the first point you picked and the cursor location. This is called a ***rubberband line.*** As you move the mouse, the rubberband line also moves and shows you where the line would be if you picked the next point. Figure 2.8 shows coordinates 6.5000,6.5000 selected as the next point. You may continue drawing as many connected line segments as you wish, because AutoCAD LT continues to give you

FIGURE 2.7 Pick the point at coordinates 4.5000,4.5000. Notice the origin, command line, and coordinate display.

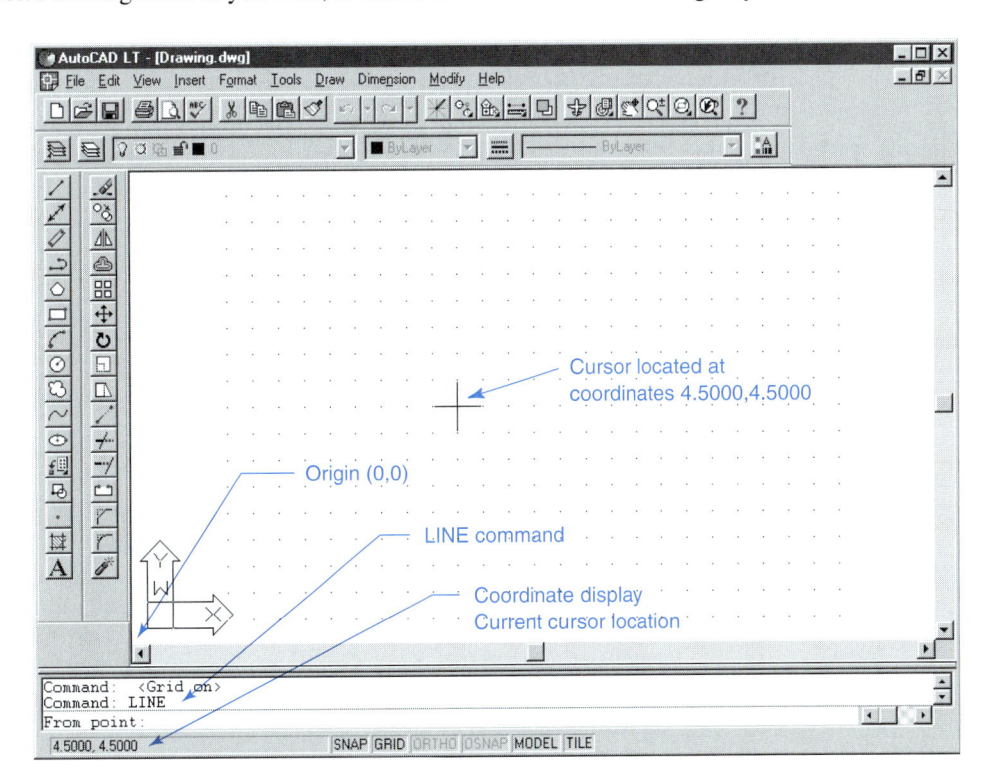

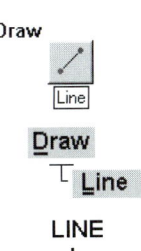

the To point: prompt until you cancel the LINE command. Exit the LINE command by pressing the Esc or Enter key or the space bar:

Command: **L** or **LINE**↵
From point: ⟨*pick where the coordinates read 4.5000,4.5000*⟩
To point: ⟨*pick where the coordinates read 6.5000,6.5000*⟩
To point: *Cancel*
Command:

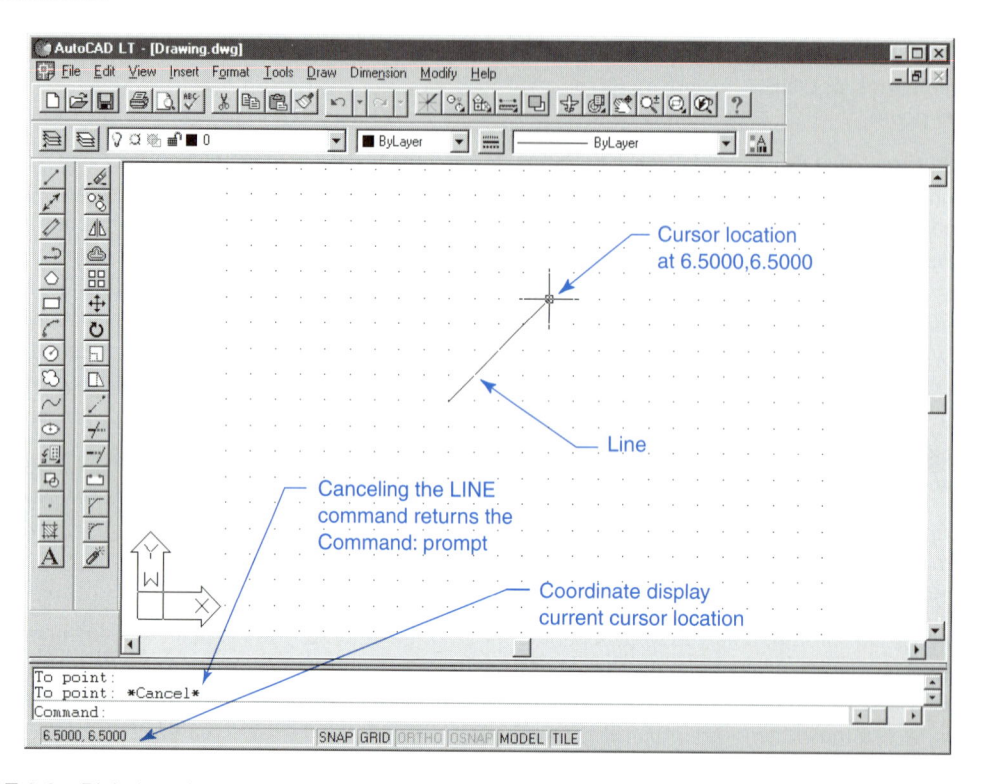

FIGURE 2.8 Pick the other end at coordinates 6.5000,6.5000.

Field Notes

This text shows typed commands in bold print to show you what must be entered at the command line. When you pick a command from a menu or a toolbar, it is entered by AutoCAD LT in a slightly different way at the Command: prompt. Commands accessed in this manner are preceded by an underscore character and the first prompt at the Command: line is automatically entered. For example,

Command: _line From point:

It can be typed this way as well, but the underscore is unnecessary, so it is not commonly used.

Save Your First Drawing

You are asked to save the drawing in the next exercise. A drawing is saved so the work that you have done is protected and you can access it later. Before saving the drawing you need to think of a name. For example, the next exercise asks you to save the drawing as EX2.4, where *EX* stands for exercise and *2.4* is Chapter 2, exercise number 4. Other drawing names may be selected to describe the type of drawing or project, such as FLOOR PLAN, or PART A-100.

When you open AutoCAD LT, the drawing name is specified in brackets in the upper left corner title bar. The title bar displays the default drawing name like this: AutoCAD LT—[Drawing]. This drawing is identified as Drawing because you have not given it a name yet. To save your drawing, go to the File pull-down menu and pick Save As …, or type **SAVEAS** at the Command: prompt. After picking Save As …, the Save Drawing As dialog box is displayed, and the current drawing name is listed in the File name: edit box. Type the desired file name, such as EX2.4, as shown in Figure 2.9. Pick the Save button or press the Enter

Standard
Save (Ctrl+S)

File
 Save

SAVE
SA
CTRL+S

key to save the drawing with the specified name. The SAVEAS command always prompts for a file name, even if the drawing has previously been saved. This allows you to open an existing drawing and make any desired modifications, then save it under a new name. You can also save each revision of a drawing project in a separate file to maintain a complete revision history.

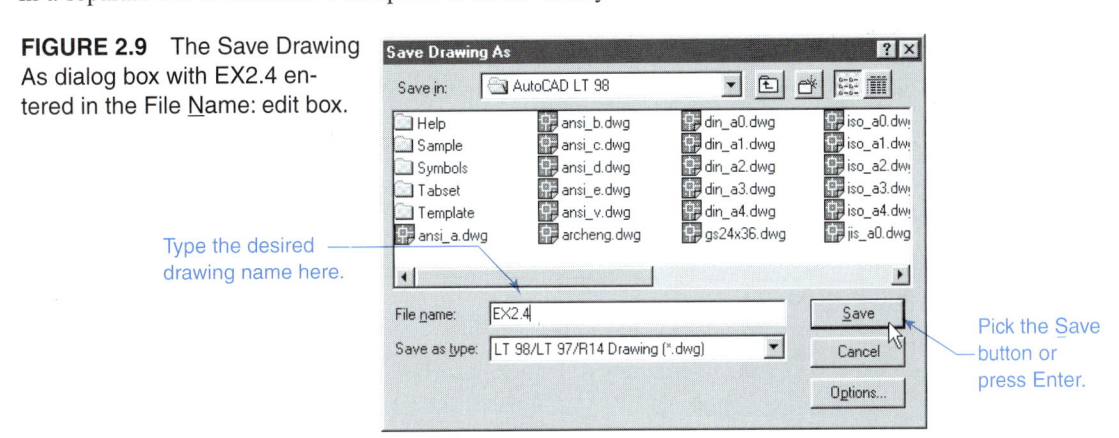

FIGURE 2.9 The Save Drawing As dialog box with EX2.4 entered in the File Name: edit box.

Type the desired drawing name here.

Pick the Save button or press Enter.

It is best to use the SAVEAS command shortly after starting a drawing, because this saves your work in a drawing file with the name you assign. Then, use the SAVE command to save your work as you continue to make progress on the drawing. The SAVE command periodically updates the drawing file with the part of the drawing that you have created since it was previously saved using either the SAVEAS or SAVE commands. If you have not yet saved the current drawing, the SAVE command works exactly like the SAVEAS command and displays the Save Drawing As dialog box. The AutoCAD LT command QSAVE is functionally identical with the SAVE command. When you pick Save from the File menu in a drawing that has previously been saved, you will see the _qsave command in the floating command window. You should save the drawing every *10 to 15 min*. This is wise, because if there is a power failure or some other serious problem with the computer, all of the work done since the last save is lost. It is better to lose 10 minutes' worth of work than 2 hours'. Most people learn this the hard way. The SAVE command is accessed by picking Save in the File pull-down menu, using Ctrl+S, picking the Save toolbar button, or typing **SAVE.** When you are finished with a drawing, you can exit AutoCAD LT by picking Exit in the File pull-down menu or typing **EXIT.** You can start a new drawing by picking New in the File pull-down menu, using Ctrl+N, or typing **NEW.** This accesses the Create New Drawing dialog box discussed earlier. If you have unsaved additions or changes to the current drawing, when you exit AutoCAD LT or start a new drawing session, you are asked if you want to save the changes. If you pick Yes, the SAVE command is activated. Picking No discards any changes you made. If you pick Cancel, then you are returned to the current drawing session.

Through the Window...

AutoCAD LT file names always have a .dwg file extension, but the naming system provides great flexibility. The file name can be up to 256 characters long and can include printable characters such as spaces, dashes, periods, commas, and underscores. This can help you to keep organized by using descriptive file names to tell you what the file contains. Here's how:

- Ensure that long file names are enabled by selecting Preferences ... from the Tools pull-down menu. Pick the File System tab, and be sure that a check mark is placed in the Use Long File Names toggle. Pick the OK button to return to your drawing session.
- Begin the SAVEAS command. In the file name box, type a description that is 256 characters or less. Use punctuation as desired. Here are a few examples of the possibilities:

    Remodeling plan.dwg

    Guest House. 60% complete, needs electrical and plumbing details.dwg

    Allen project, phase 1.dwg

Note that some characters cannot be used in file names, including forward slashes (/), backslashes (\), equals signs (=), question marks (?), and asterisks (*).

Exercise 2.4

1. Continue from Exercise 2.3 or open AutoCAD LT and use the Quick Setup with Decimal measurement, default limits, and turn on the GRID and SNAP commands.
2. Enter the LINE command using the pull-down menu. Cancel the command and enter the LINE command by picking the toolbar button. Cancel the command and type the **LINE** command followed by pressing the Enter key or the space bar. Think about which method you like the best. You should now have a From point: prompt.
3. Move the screen cursor and watch the coordinate display values change.
4. Move the screen cursor until you get coordinate values of 4.5000,4.5000, just like Figure 2.7.
5. Pick this point. You should now have a To point: prompt.
6. Move the screen cursor and watch the rubberband cursor adjust to different line lengths as you move.
7. Move the screen cursor until you get coordinate values of 6.5000,6.5000, just like Figure 2.8.
8. Pick this point.
9. Watch the rubberband cursor again as you move the mouse.
10. Pick some more points and cancel the LINE command when you are done.
11. Save as EX2.4.

Open a Saved Drawing

Standard
Open (Ctrl+O)

File
  Open...

OPEN
OP
CTRL+O

When starting AutoCAD LT, you can pick the Open a Drawing button in the Start Up dialog box. The last four files that were opened in AutoCAD LT are shown in the Select a File: list. Selecting one of these provides a Preview image of the drawing. Double-click on the desired file or highlight it and pick OK to open. Double-click on More files … in the Select a File: list to access the dialog box shown in Figure 2.10. Use the OPEN command if you need to work on an existing drawing without using the Start Up dialog box. To do this, pick Open … in the File pull-down menu, use Ctrl+O, pick the Open toolbar button, or type **OP** or **OPEN.** This displays the Select File dialog box, shown in Figure 2.10. If you want to open EX2.4 to work on it some more, search through the file list until you find EX2.4 and pick it. EX2.4.dwg becomes highlighted and is displayed in the File Name: edit box. An image of the drawing is shown in the Preview box to help you confirm the selection (see Figure 2.10). Pick OK to open the drawing when you are ready.

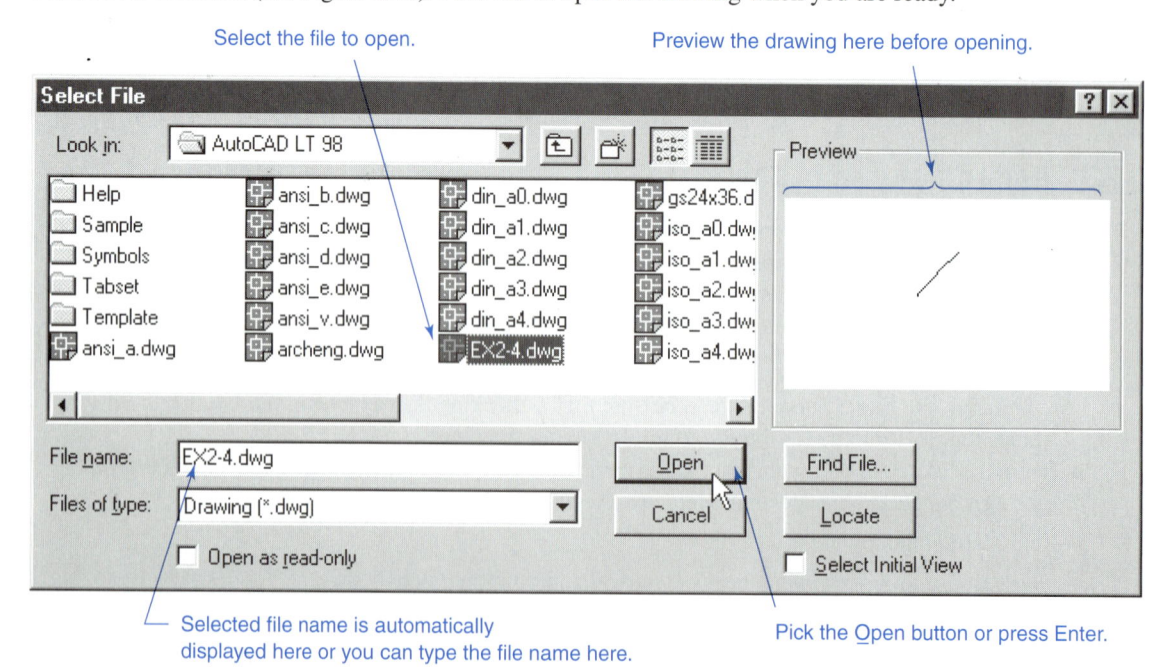

FIGURE 2.10 Open a drawing using the Select File dialog box. Notice the Preview image on the right.

Drawing Lines by Entering Distances, Angles, and Coordinates

In many situations, you can draw lines by picking points as you have just seen. This works if the Grid and Snap settings match the measurements on the object you plan to draw. There are also situations when picking points does not give you the accuracy or flexibility that you need. To give you this advantage, AutoCAD LT uses what is known as the Cartesian coordinate system. The ***Cartesian coordinate system*** relates to numbers that are used to locate points relative to two intersecting axes lines. There is a two-dimensional (2-D) system that relates to an X and Y axis and a three-dimensional (3-D) system that uses an additional Z axis. The 3-D system is discussed in Chapter 14. Points are located from the intersection of the X and Y axes, which is called the *origin*. This origin is the same as the drawing origin that was discussed earlier. When using this system, measurements along the X axis are either right (positive) or left (negative) from the origin, and distances along the Y axis are up (positive) or down (negative) from the origin. Points are always assigned two numbers, such as 5,4. These numbers are called ***coordinates.*** The first coordinate (5) is the X value and the second (4) is the Y value. Look at Figure 2.11.

Generally when you are drawing, the origin is in the lower left corner of the screen. This makes all the X and Y coordinates positive, which is usually easier to use while drawing. Figure 2.12 shows how some sample coordinates read if the origin is the lower left corner of the screen.

FIGURE 2.11 The Cartesian coordinate system.

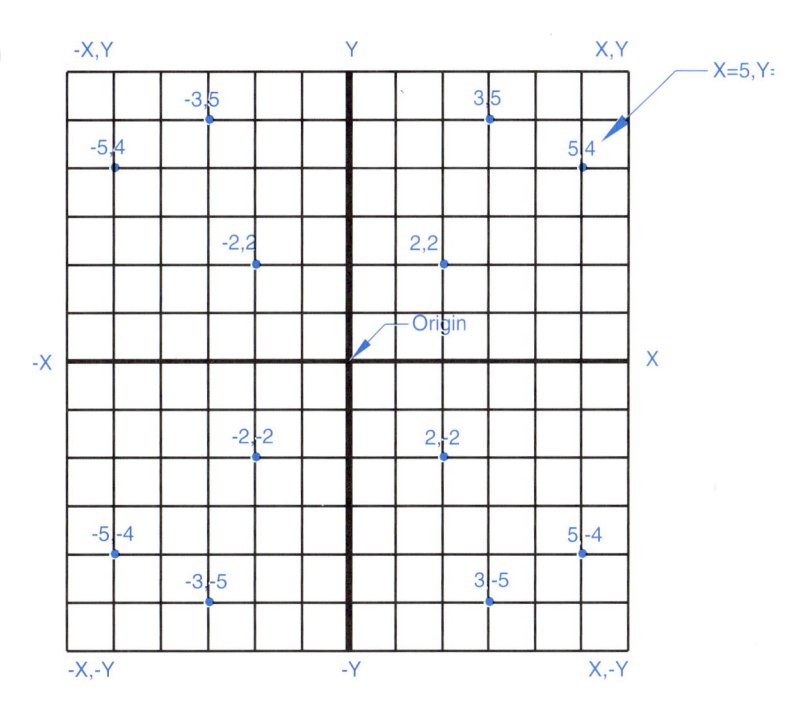

FIGURE 2.12 Coordinates with the origin in the lower left corner.

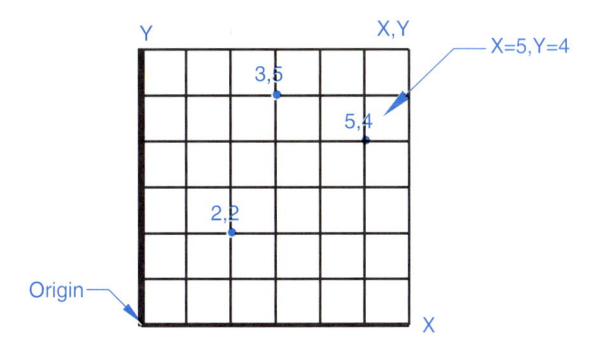

Coordinate Entry Options

The previous discussion introduced you to the Cartesian coordinate system. When you are working with AutoCAD LT, you have the option of entering coordinates to locate points using one of four coordinate entry options. These options are picking points (as you have already learned), absolute, relative, and polar coordinates.

Using Absolute Coordinates

Absolute coordinates are X and Y points that are always established based on their distance from the origin. The origin is coordinate 0,0. This works well in a situation where you know the location of points from the origin. If you want to draw a line from the point coordinate 2,2 to the point coordinate 7.5,6.25, you would use the following command sequence, as shown in Figure 2.13:

Command: **L** or **LINE**↵
From point: **2,2**↵
To point: **7.5,6.25**↵
To point: ↵
Command:

FIGURE 2.13 Drawing a line using absolute coordinates.

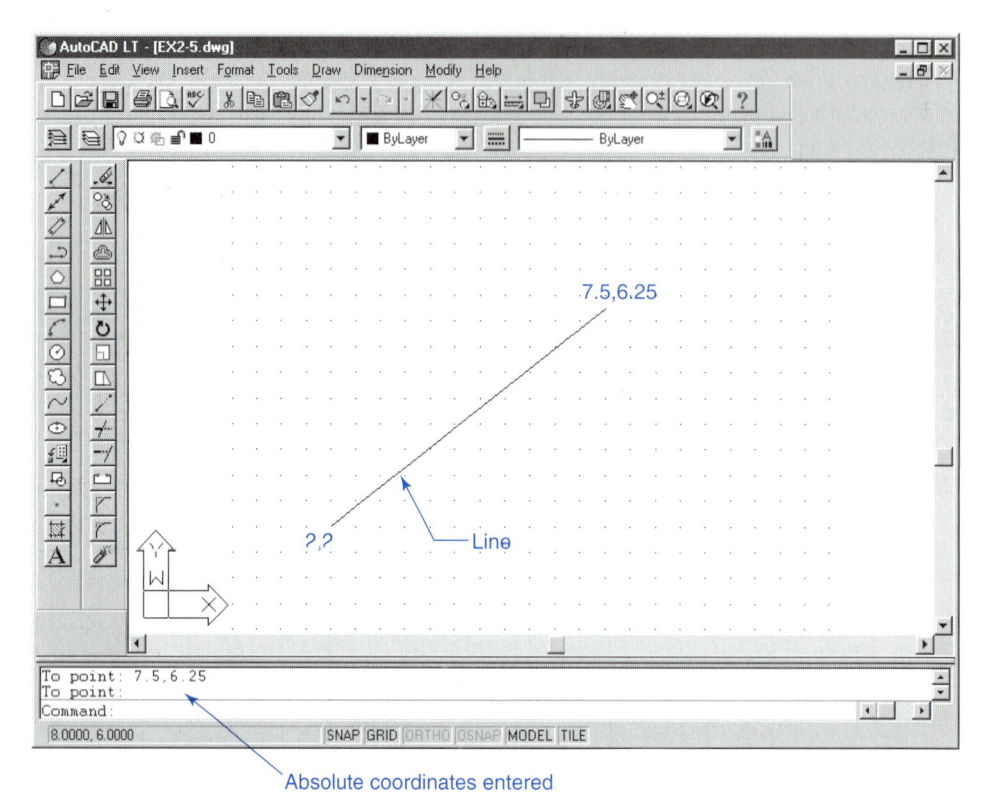

Exercise 2.5

1. Open AutoCAD LT or pick New in the File pull-down menu if it is already open and use the Quick Setup with Decimal measurements, limits of 11 and 8.5, and turn on the GRID command.
2. Use the LINE command to make a drawing with the following absolute coordinates:

    Point 1   2,2

    Point 2   3.5,2

    Point 3   3.5,2.8125

    Point 4   5.875,2.8125

    Point 5   5.875,2

    Point 6   7.375,2

    Point 7   6.25,3.5

    Point 8   3.125,3.5

    Point 9   2,2

3. Cancel the LINE command.
4. Save as EX2.5.

CHAPTER 2 ||| Introduction to Drafting with AutoCAD LT   53

Using Relative Coordinates

Relative coordinates are used when you want to establish a point based on an X axis and a Y axis distance from a previous point. Think of it as locating a point "relative" to another point. The first point of a line may be selected by picking or with absolute coordinates, and the next point is drawn relative to the first using X and Y values, as shown in Figure 2.14. The X,Y prompt for a relative coordinate must be preceded by the "@" symbol like this:

Command: **L** or **LINE**↵
From point: **2,2**↵
To point: **@5,4**↵
To point: ↵
Command:

Figure 2.15 shows the results of this command sequence.

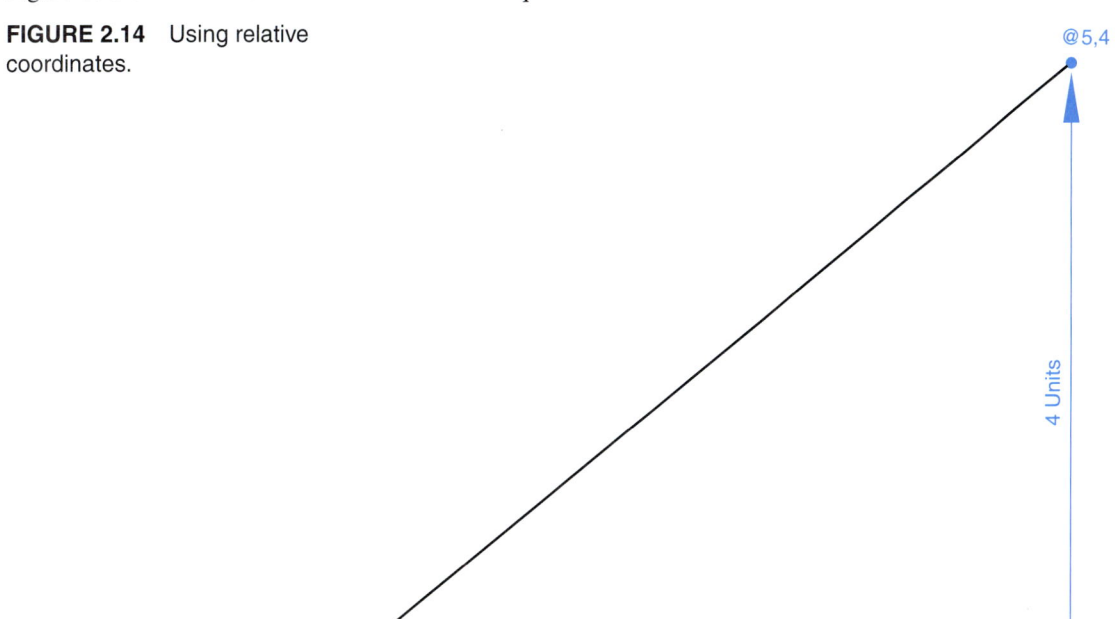

FIGURE 2.14   Using relative coordinates.

Exercise 2.6

1. Open AutoCAD LT or pick New in the File pull-down menu if it is already open and use the Quick Setup with Decimal measurements, limits of 8.5 and 11, and turn on the Grid.
2. Use the LINE command to start a drawing with the following absolute coordinate:

   Point 1   3,4

3. Continue drawing a series of lines with the following relative coordinates:

   Point 2   @1.75,−1.5
   Point 3   @.5,1.125
   Point 4   @1.75,0
   Point 5   @0,.75
   Point 6   @−1.75,0
   Point 7   @−.5,1.125
   Point 8   @−1.75,−1.5

4. Cancel the LINE command.
5. Save as EX2.6.

FIGURE 2.15 Drawing a line using relative coordinates.

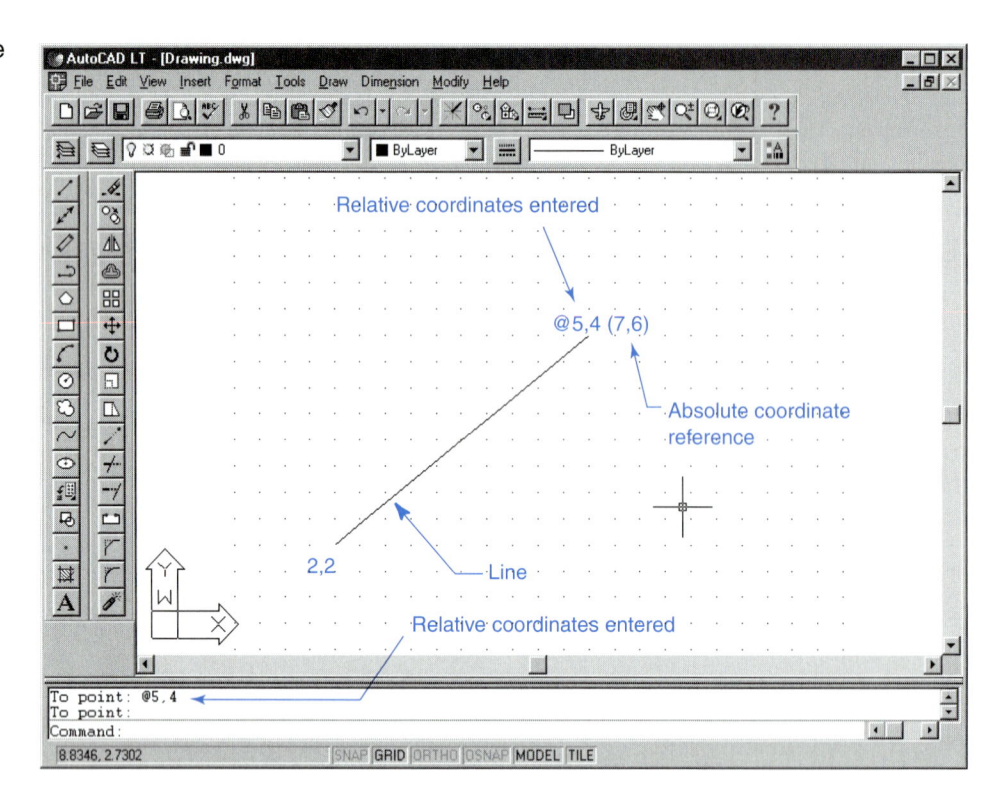

Using Polar Coordinates

Polar coordinates are used when you want to establish a point based on a distance and an angle from a previous point. The angle from the previous point may be positive if measured in a counterclockwise direction or negative if measured in a clockwise direction. The angles are based on the degrees in a circle. There are 360° in a circle with each quarter of the circle being called a *quadrant.* Each quadrant is 90°, as shown in Figure 2.16.

FIGURE 2.16 The quadrants of a circle and a polar coordinate measurement.

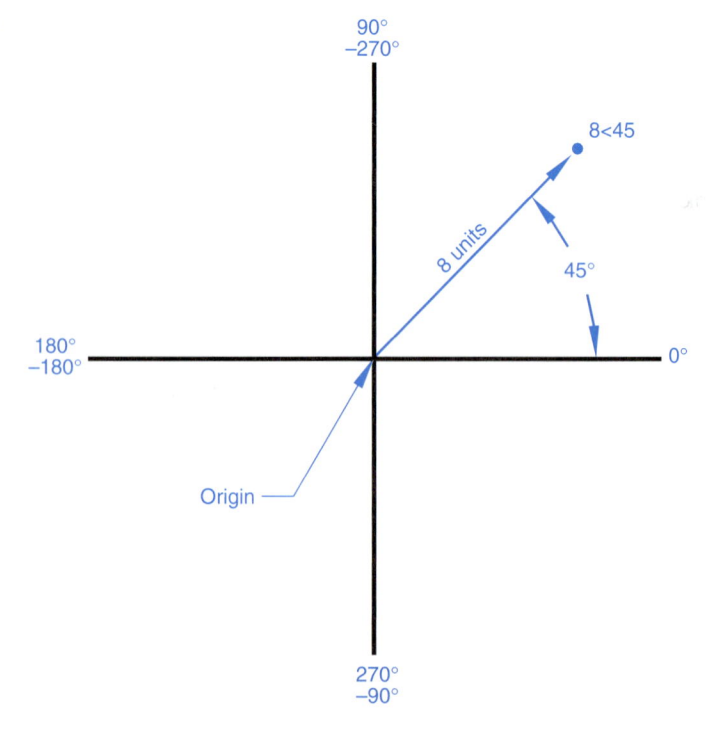

CHAPTER 2 ||| Introduction to Drafting with AutoCAD LT

When you enter a polar coordinate, you enter the distance followed by the angle using a less than (<) symbol. For example, if you want a point that is 8 units at a 45° angle from the origin (0,0), enter 8<45. The results are shown in Figure 2.16. The first point of a line may be selected by picking or with absolute coordinates and the next point drawn from the first using a unit distance and an angle. A polar coordinate must be preceded by the "@" symbol when drawing a line from a previous point. The following command sequence draws the object shown in Figure 2.17:

Command: **L** or **LINE**↵
From point: **3,4**↵
To point: **@2<45**↵
To point: **@2<315** or **@2<−45**↵
To point: **@1.5<270** or **@1.5<−90**↵
To point: **@2.8284<180**↵
To point: **@1.5<90**↵
To point: ↵
Command:

FIGURE 2.17 Using polar coordinates.

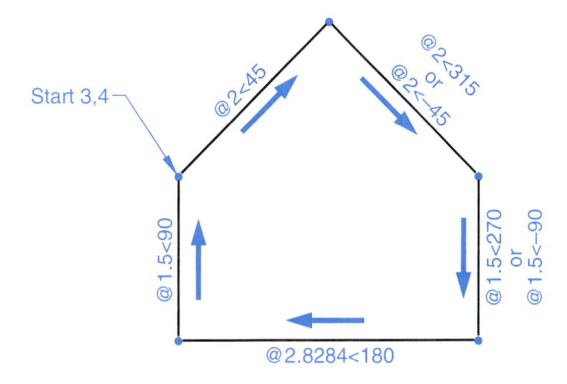

Field Notes

Press the F6 key to turn the coordinate display on or off or to change the display from absolute coordinate to polar coordinate values. The coordinate display may also be toggled using CTRL+D or by double-clicking on the display itself. When the coordinate display is turned off, it updates only when you pick a point. This means that it displays the location of the last point picked.

An absolute coordinate display looks like this: 6.50, 4.75

A polar coordinate display looks like this: 3.75<90

When the display is turned off, it looks like this: 4.50, 3.00

Closing a Polygon

A *polygon* is a closed plane figure with straight sides. The object in Figure 2.17 is an example of a polygon. When drawing a polygon, the last line ends where the first line began. This can be done by entering the same coordinates for the end of the last line that were used for the start of the first line, as was done in the previous command sequence. An easier way to do this is to type **C** for Close at the To point: prompt for the last line, like this:

> Command: **L** or **LINE**↵
> From point: **3,4**↵
> To point: **@2<45**↵
> To point: **@2<315** or **@2<−45**↵
> To point: **@1.5<270** or **@1.5<−90**↵
> To point: **@2.8284<180**↵
> To point: **C**↵
> Command:

Doing this automatically closes the polygon and returns the Command: prompt (see Figure 2.18).

FIGURE 2.18 Using the Close option to close a polygon.

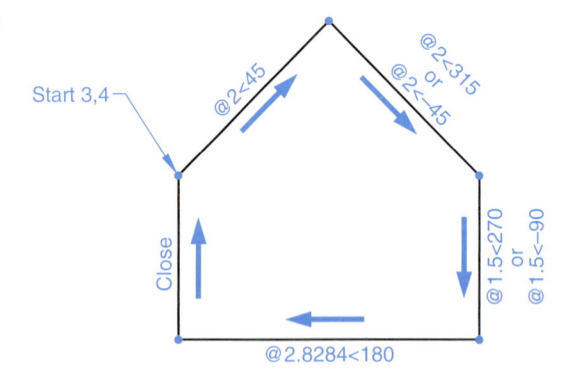

Repeating the Previous Command Quickly

You can easily repeat the previously used command by pressing the Enter key or the space bar. When you are not working with text, pressing the space bar has the same effect as pressing Enter. This practice saves time when compared to accessing the command in another manner. The following command sequence shows how this works:

> Command: **L** or **LINE**↵
> From point: ⟨*pick a point*⟩
> To point: ⟨*pick another point*⟩
> To point: ⟨*pick another point*⟩
> To point: **C**↵
> Command: ⟨*press the Enter key or space bar*⟩
> LINE From point: ⟨*pick a point*⟩
> To point: ⟨*pick another point*⟩
> To point: **Cancel**
> Command:

✎ Field Notes

> The previously used command can also be accessed by pressing the right mouse button to open the cursor menu. The first item in the menu repeats the previous command. For example, if the previous command was LINE, then the cursor menu item is Repeat LINE. Select this to repeat the LINE command.

CHAPTER 2 ||| Introduction to Drafting with AutoCAD LT   57

> **Exercise 2.7**
>
> 1. Open AutoCAD LT or pick New in the File pull-down menu if it is already open and use the Quick Setup with Decimal measurements and limits of 8.5 and 11.
> 2. Use the LINE command to start a drawing with the following absolute coordinate:
>
>   Point 1   3,4
>
> 3. Continue drawing a series of lines with the following polar coordinates:
>
>   Point 2   @1.5<30
>
>   Point 3   @1.5<150
>
>   Point 4   @.75<90
>
>   Point 5   @2.5<0
>
>   Point 6   @3<270
>
>   Point 7   @2.5<180
>
>   Close
>
> 4. Press the Enter key or the space bar to quickly access the LINE command again and draw with these coordinates:
>
>   Point 1   5.25,3.75 (absolute)
>
> 5. Continue with these polar coordinates:
>
>   Point 2   @2<90
>
>   Point 3   @.75<180
>
>   Point 4   @2<270
>
> 6. Close.
> 7. Save as EX2.7.

Combining Coordinate Methods

All the available coordinate entry methods may cause some confusion for the beginning AutoCAD LT user. The best thing to do is practice using all the point entry methods until you become familiar with the way they work. You will then be able to select the entry method that works best for your specific situation. You can use any entry method at any point prompt as desired. For example, it may be easier to pick one point or use the absolute coordinate and then enter relative or polar coordinates for the next point.

When you are planning a drawing, it is usually best to sketch the object and establish the line endpoint coordinates on graph paper. This early planning saves a lot of time when you get ready to draw with Auto-CAD LT. An example is shown with the electronic circuit speaker symbol laid out in Figure 2.19A. This layout shows the length of each line and the angle of lines where needed. The drafter made the sketch in Figure 2.19B displaying the planned point entries for each corner of the object. With this preliminary work done, all you have to do is enter the coordinates:

Command: **L** or **LINE**↵
From point: **3,4**↵
To point: **@.75,0**↵
To point: **@.75<−45**↵
To point: **@0,1.75**↵
To point: **@.75<225**↵
To point: **@.75<180**↵
To point: **C**↵
Command:

Other solutions to the problem may have worked just as well. Your goal is to select AutoCAD LT tools that help you create the drawing as quickly and accurately as possible.

FIGURE 2.19 Using a combination of coordinate entry methods. (A) The engineering layout. (B) The coordinates entries used to draw the speaker symbol.

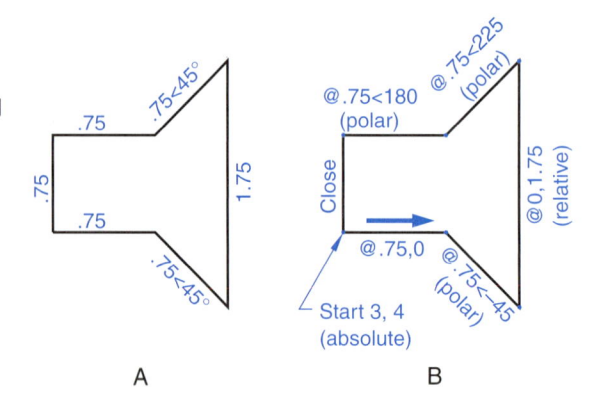

Exercise 2.8

1. Open AutoCAD LT or pick New in the File pull-down menu if it is already open and use the Quick Setup with Decimal measurements and limits of 8.5 and 11.
2. Use the LINE command to make a drawing with the combination of coordinate entry methods displayed in Figure 2.19.
3. Save as EX2.8.

Entering Units in AutoCAD LT

All the examples and exercises that you have studied so far have used generic decimal units for distance specifications. Many of your drawing applications may require a more specialized format for specifying distances. The rules of entry for each available linear unit format are as follows:

Decimal and Fractional Units

- Whole numbers do not require a decimal point.
  Example: 1 14 -22
- Numbers less than 1 do not require a leading zero.
  Example: .5 .0625 -.8477
- Large numbers do not require commas.
  Example: 1024 2844366.0122 -43771
- Trailing zeros do not increase accuracy. The numbers 1.5 and 1.500 give the exact same results.
- Unit specifications are not given for decimal units. For example, if your units represent inches or millimeters, do not include an inch symbol (″) or metric unit callout (mm) with your numeric entry.
- Either fractions or decimals may be used for linear units, but fractions must be separated from the whole number by a hyphen.
  Example: 1/2 2-1/16

Architectural and Engineering Units

- Numbers entered without a unit specification are interpreted as inches. A numeric entry of 3 is interpreted as 3″.
- Numbers intended to represent distances measured in feet must have the foot symbol (′).
  Example: 32′ 142′ -15′
- Foot and inch combinations can be entered with or without a hyphen.
  Example: 1′3 1′-3 1′-3″ -2′4″ -2′-4″
- Decimal or fractional foot and inch values are accepted.
  Example: 1.5′ -2.25′ 4.5 -3.875 1′3.5″ 1/2′
- Fractions of inches must be separated from the whole-inch value with a hyphen.
  Example: 1′3-1/2 1′3-1/2″ 1′-3-1/2″

Scientific Units

- Numbers can be entered as simple decimal values, without scientific notation.
  Example: 1.5   -3.61   377
- Scientific notation expresses a change in the decimal point location. A positive value indicates the decimal moves to the right, negative values mean the decimal point moves to the left.
  Example: 1.5E+3 is equivalent to 1500   1.5E-3 is equivalent to .0015
- Fractions cannot be used.

Field Notes

Coordinate entry is very versatile and accepts many variations of polarity (+ or –) and units style. For example, when drawing a line from an existing base point that extends vertically two units, you can use any of the following *polar* coordinate entries:

@2<90   @2<–270   @–2<270   @–2<–90

Some of these are unlikely applications, but this versatility gives you several added options when specifying coordinate point locations. Remember that when you are using polar coordinates, making either the distance or the angle negative reverses the direction.

LEARNING CHECKPOINT

- Identify three ways to access the LINE command in AutoCAD LT.
- What are the four coordinate entry options?
- What is the symbol @ used for?
- Why is it helpful to combine coordinate entry methods?
- How are feet, inches, and fractional inches specified in AutoCAD LT?
- How can you conveniently close the last segment of a polygon?
- What is the fastest way to repeat the previous command?

More AutoCAD LT Drawing Aids

Earlier in this chapter you were introduced to the Grid and Snap drawing aids. Two other drawing aids are Ortho and Blips. When the Ortho option is on, your pointing device allows only horizontal or vertical movement during drawing and editing operations. **Blips** are temporary screen marks that are displayed when you pick a point.

Using Ortho

Ortho is referred to as a mode. A *mode* is a setting or operating condition that you control. Ortho is a toggle setting, meaning that it can be either on or off. When Ortho is on, the pointing device is allowed only horizontal or vertical movement while drawing. If Ortho is off, then the pointing device may be moved at any angle. Ortho is off by default. An advantage of having Ortho on is seen when you need to draw an object made up of horizontal and vertical lines. Having Ortho on ensures that the lines you draw are exactly horizontal or vertical as needed. Ortho may be quickly turned on or off by double-clicking the ORTHO status bar box or pressing the F8 key. If Ortho is off and you toggle it on, you get this status display at the Command: prompt:

Status Bar
[ORTHO]
ORTHO
OR
CTRL+L
[F8]

Command: <Ortho on>

You can also turn Ortho on by picking Drawing Aids ... in the Tools pull-down menu or by typing **DDRMODES** to access the Drawing Aids dialog box shown in Figure 2.5. Ortho is one of the items in the Modes area. Turn Ortho on by picking the check box. Turn Ortho on at the Command: prompt by typing:

Command: **ORTHO**↵
ON/OFF<Off>: **ON**↵

Now, practice drawing lines with Ortho on and off to notice the big difference in the way the cursor controls the lines you are drawing. Figure 2.20 shows the difference between drawing a line with Ortho on and off.

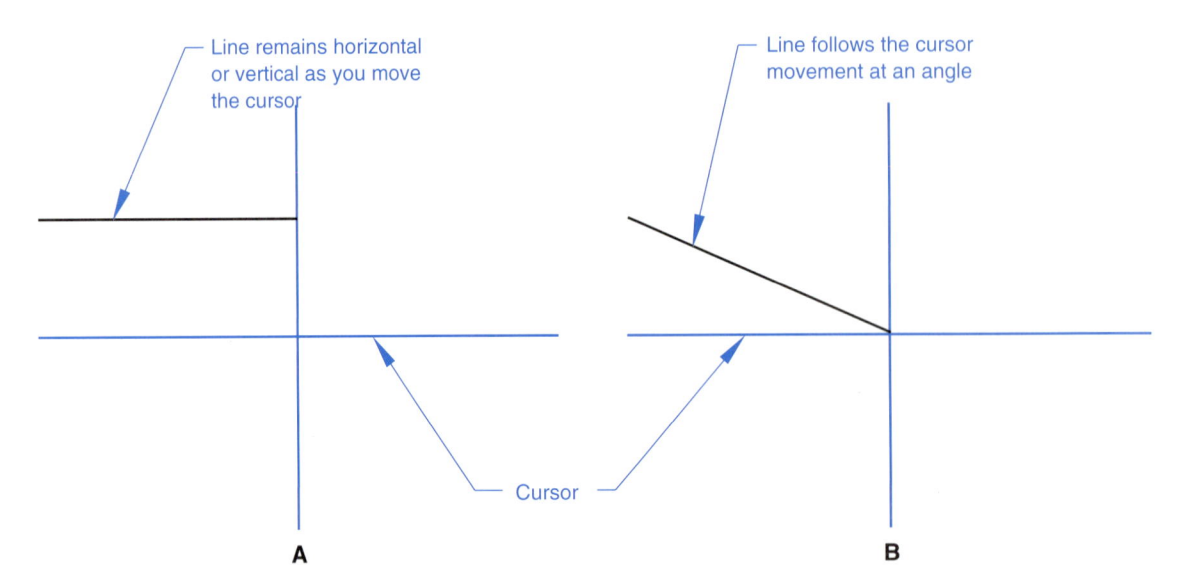

FIGURE 2.20 The difference between drawing a line with (A) Ortho on and (B) Ortho off.

Field Notes

The Ortho setting affects only points entered by picking with the pointing device. A typed coordinate entry, whether absolute, relative, or polar, is not affected by Ortho settings. The Snap settings, however, cannot override the Ortho control.

Another thing to remember about Ortho (and other toggles) is that the status is displayed on the command line when the toggle is activated. This means that if you begin to type a command, it appears after the status display. In the following example, Ortho is toggled on and Snap is toggled off prior to entering a line command:

Command: <Ortho on> <Snap off> **LINE**↵

A toggle status display appears between greater than and less than symbols (<>) and does not interfere with command entry.

An Introduction to Transparent Commands

A *transparent command* is a command that can be started while another command is in progress. Commands that are not transparent must be entered when you have a Command: prompt. A transparent command can be accessed by selection from a pull-down menu, status line button, or toolbar button or by typing the command name preceded by an apostrophe ('). DDRMODES, GRID, SNAP, and ORTHO are transparent commands that you have learned so far. Double-click the ORTHO status line button or type **'ORTHO** (note the apostrophe) if you want to enter the ORTHO command transparently while inside of the LINE command:

Command: **L** or **LINE**↵
From point: ⟨*pick a point or enter coordinates*⟩
To point: **'ORTHO**↵
>>ON/OFF <Off>: **ON**↵
Resuming LINE command.
To point: ⟨*pick a point or enter coordinates*⟩
To point: ⟨*enter another point or Cancel*⟩
Command:

AutoCAD LT lets you know that a transparent command prompt is being issued by showing a double greater than (>>) symbol in front of the prompt as shown in the previous command sequence. After you use the transparent command, AutoCAD LT tells you that you are resuming the command in progress.

Exercise 2.9

1. Open AutoCAD LT or pick New in the File pull-down menu if it is already open and use the Quick Setup with Decimal measurements, limits of 8.5 and 11, and turn on the Grid and Snap.
2. With the Ortho default setting off, use the LINE command to make a rectangle at a size of your own choosing.
3. Turn Ortho on and draw another rectangle. Notice the difference in the control of the vertical and horizontal lines.
4. Turn Ortho on and off using the status bar button, F8 key, and at the command prompt to determine the method that works best for you.
5. Save as EX2.9.

Marks on the Screen

The locations where you pick points to draw lines and other things can be displayed by temporary marks called blips. The blips are helpful in allowing you to visualize selected points more clearly. Blips are turned off, or not displayed, in AutoCAD LT by default. They can be turned on or off in the Drawing Aids dialog box. See the Blips check box in Figure 2.5. You can also enter the following at the command prompt:

Command: **BM** or **BLIPMODE**↵
ON/OFF <On>: **OFF**↵
Command:

Exercise 2.10

1. Open AutoCAD LT or pick New in the File pull-down menu if it is already open and use the Quick Setup with Decimal measurements, limits of 8.5 and 11, and turn on the Grid and Snap.
2. Turn the blips on using the BLIPMODE command.
3. Draw several lines of your own design and notice the Blips.
4. Turn the blips off using the Drawing Aids dialog box.
5. Draw several more lines and notice the difference.
6. Save as EX2.10.

Cleaning up the Screen

After you have done some drafting with blipmode turned on, the blips may become distracting. This is especially true after you have done some erasing, because blips remain even after lines are erased. Blips are easily removed from the screen with the REDRAW command. Access the REDRAW command by picking Redraw in the View pull-down menu, or type **R** or **REDRAW**:

Command: **R** or **REDRAW**↵
Command:

REDRAW is a transparent command. Use it at any time to clean up the screen by typing **'REDRAW** while inside a command, or pick Redraw from the View pull-down menu.

When you learn about erasing, next in this chapter, you will more clearly see the benefits of using REDRAW.

View
└ Redraw
REDRAW
R

Exercise 2.11

1. Open AutoCAD LT or pick New in the File pull-down menu if it is already open and use the Quick Setup with Decimal measurements, limits of 8.5 and 11, and turn on the Grid and Snap.
2. With Blipmode on, draw several lines of your own design.
3. Pick Redraw in the View pull-down menu and notice what happens to the blips.
4. Draw several more lines and then enter R at the command prompt followed by pressing the Enter key or the space bar.
5. Save as EX2.11.

✓ LEARNING CHECKPOINT

- ☐ What is the purpose of Ortho?
- ☐ When should you use Ortho, and when should it not be used?
- ☐ What is the purpose of blips?
- ☐ How do you remove blips from the screen?

Erasing Objects

Modify
Erase
Modify
Erase
ERASE
E
DEL

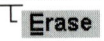

Any time you are changing a drawing by erasing, moving, copying, or altering objects in any way, it is referred to as *editing.* Erasing objects is a very common editing practice. Just as when you are drawing with pencil, you often need to erase. Throughout this book, you will learn that objects may be selected and then an editing task performed, or you may enter an editing command and then select objects to be edited. When you select objects for editing, the objects you choose are called a *selection set.* Although there are many ways to select objects, the following discussion introduces you to the basics.

Selecting Objects to Erase

Objects may be selected to erase by picking, by requesting the last object drawn, by placing a window around the object, or by placing a window partly across an object. Other selection methods are available, but these basic techniques are explained in the following discussion.

Entering the ERASE Command Before Selecting the Objects

You may enter an editing command and then select the objects to be edited, or you can select the objects and then enter the command. The first part of this explanation shows you how to enter the command before selecting objects.

Picking Objects

The ERASE command is accessed by picking Clear from the Edit pull-down menu, by picking the Erase toolbar button, or by typing **E** or **ERASE** at the Command: prompt like this:

Command: **E** or **ERASE** ↵
Select objects:

Now you get the *Select objects:* prompt, and the screen cursor changes to a small box called a *pick box.* Move the pick box to an object, such as a line, and pick it, as shown in Figure 2.21A, by pressing the pick button on the mouse. The object becomes highlighted when you pick it (see Figure 2.21B). You then get another Select objects: prompt. AutoCAD LT allows you to continue picking objects or to press Enter to end the selection process and have the object erased. The complete command sequence works like this and is displayed in Figure 2.21C:

CHAPTER 2 ||| Introduction to Drafting with AutoCAD LT 63

```
Command: E or ERASE↵
Select objects: ⟨pick an object or objects⟩
Select objects: ⟨pick more objects or press Enter⟩
Select objects: ↵
Command:
```

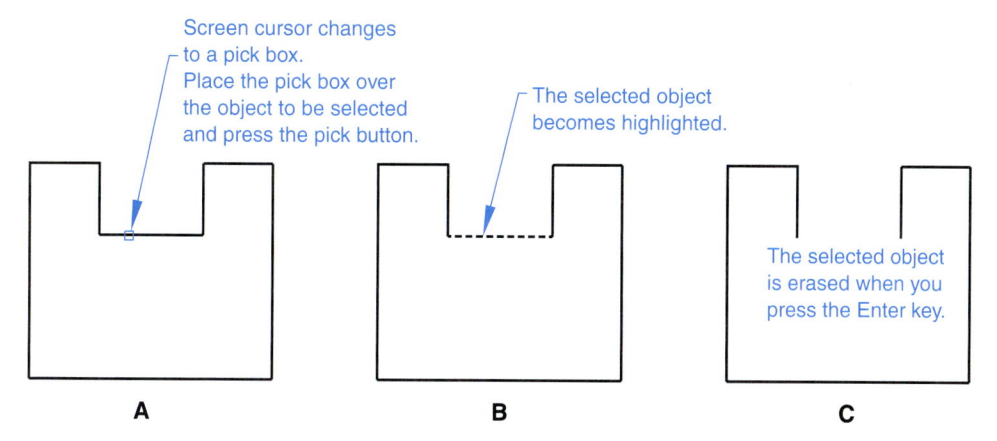

FIGURE 2.21 Picking an object to erase.

Erasing the Last Object Drawn

A handy way to erase the last object you drew is to enter **L** for *last* at the Select objects: prompt. This method erases only the last object that you created and it works like this:

```
Command: E or ERASE↵
Select objects: L↵
Select objects: ⟨pick more objects or press Enter⟩
Select objects: ↵
Command:
```

Exercise 2.12

1. Open AutoCAD LT or pick New in the File pull-down menu if it is already open and use the Quick Setup with Decimal measurements, limits of 8.5 and 11, and turn on the Grid and Snap.
2. Draw an object similar to Figure 2.21A.
3. Enter the ERASE command and pick a line to erase similar to Figure 2.21.
4. Draw a line anywhere and at any desired length.
5. Type **ERASE** and enter **L** at the Select objects: prompt followed by pressing the Enter key to erase the line you just drew.
6. Save as EX2.12.

Selecting Objects with a Window

AutoCAD LT lets you automatically place a window around one or more objects to select by the way you pick and move the mouse. This is referred to as ***implied windowing*** and is accomplished by first picking a point on the screen where no object is found. Next, move the cursor and a dynamic rectangle is formed. If you move the cursor to the *right* of the pick point, the lines of the rectangle are solid and it is called a *window*. By surrounding objects with this window, they can be selected for editing operations. Note that a window must totally surround the object or objects to be selected. To erase objects with a window selection, use the following approach:

- First enter the ERASE command:

  Command: **E** or **ERASE** ↵
  Select objects: ⟨*continue with the following steps*⟩

- Move the cursor to a place at the lower (or upper) left of the object and pick. Refer to the window shown in Figure 2.22A. The cursor becomes a solid outline window as you move the mouse to the right.
- Move the mouse to the right until the window totally surrounds all of the objects to be erased and pick the other corner as shown in Figure 2.22A.
- The selected objects become highlighted as shown in Figure 2.22B.
- Press the Enter key or space bar at the Select objects: prompt and the selected objects are erased, as in Figure 2.22C.

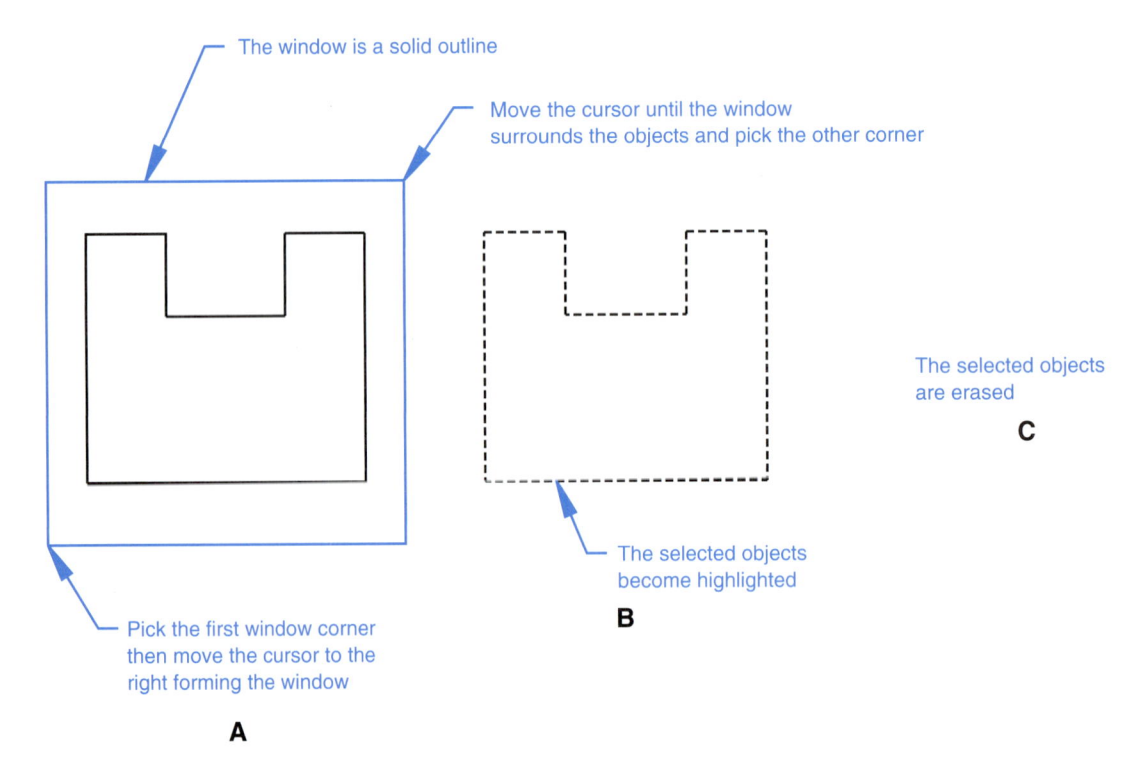

FIGURE 2.22 Selecting objects using a window.

Exercise 2.13

1. Open AutoCAD LT or pick New in the File pull-down menu if it is already open and use the Quick Setup with Decimal measurements, limits of 8.5 and 11, and turn on the Grid and Snap.
2. Using the LINE command, create a drawing similar to Figure 2.22A.
3. Enter the ERASE command and use the window to erase the objects as shown in Figures 2.22B and C.
4. Save as EX2.13.

Erasing Objects with a Crossing Box

A crossing box is formed at an object selection prompt in the same way as a window is formed, except that the rectangle is dragged to the *left* rather than the right. Where the window must totally surround the entire object to be erased, the crossing box selects not only objects it surrounds, but also any objects that it touches, or *crosses*. Windows and crossing boxes each have their own advantages for specific selection needs. As you work in AutoCAD LT, you will find many situations where one or the other better suits your needs. To see a

CHAPTER 2 ||| Introduction to Drafting with AutoCAD LT   65

clear example of the difference between a window and a crossing box, do the following, and compare the results with those shown in Figure 2.22:

- First enter the ERASE command:

    Command: **E** or **ERASE**↵
    Select objects: ⟨*continue with the following steps*⟩

- Move the cursor to a place at the lower (or upper) *right* of the object and pick. Look at Figure 2.23A. The cursor becomes a dashed outline crossing box as you move the mouse to the left.
- Move the mouse to the left until the crossing box totally surrounds or crosses through the objects to be erased and pick the other corner as shown in Figure 2.23A.
- The selected objects become highlighted as shown in Figure 2.23B.
- Press the Enter key at the Select objects: prompt, and the selected objects are erased as in Figure 2.23C.

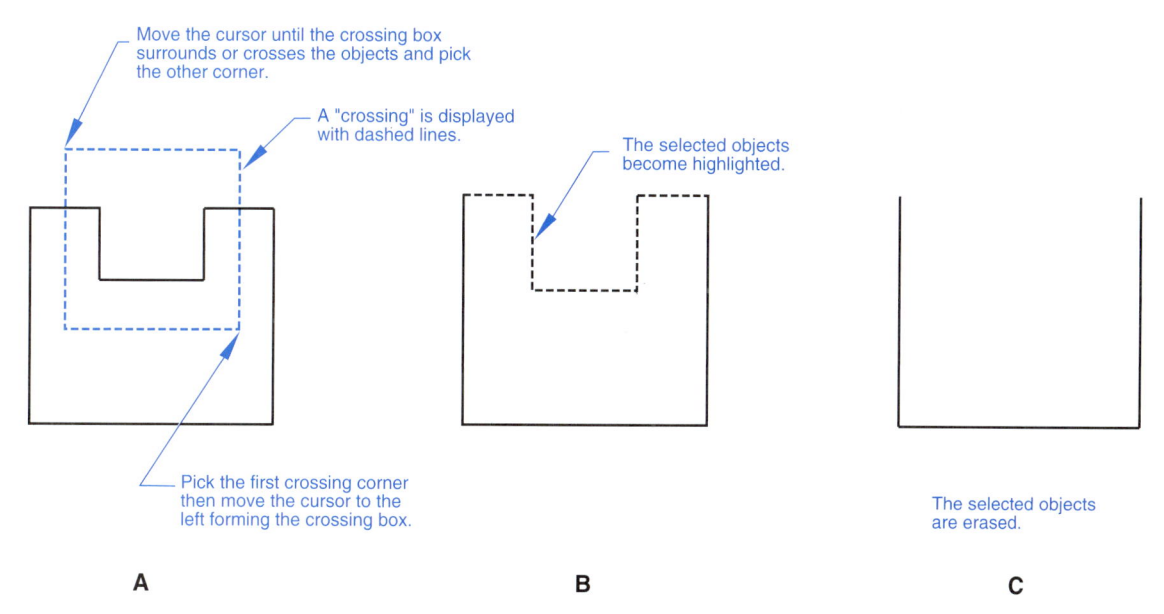

FIGURE 2.23 Selecting objects with a crossing box.

The window is formed by moving the cursor to the *right* of the pick point and a crossing box by moving to the *left*. You can immediately tell the difference between the window and crossing selections because the window is a solid rectangle and the crossing is a dashed rectangle.

Field Notes

In some cases, the geometry of your drawing may be too dense or crowded to be able to pick in the desired location without picking an object. This can make implied windowing difficult or impossible to use. To use a window or a crossing box in such a situation, type **W** for window or **C** for crossing at an object selection prompt. The pick box will turn into crosshairs, allowing very accurate pointing, and will not pick any objects until your window or crossing box is completed.

Also, if you use this method, it does not matter from which direction you form the rectangle. For example, if you enter a **W** for a window, you can form the window by moving to either the left or the right of the pick point.

Removing Selected Objects from the Selection Set

It is common to select a group of objects for editing and then decide that you want one or more of the objects removed from the selection set. This is easy to do by using the Remove option. The Remove option is used by typing **R** at the Select objects: prompt and pressing the Enter key. When you get the Remove objects:

prompt, use pick, window, or the crossing box to select objects to be removed from the selection set:

Command: **E** or **ERASE**↵
Select objects: ⟨*pick an object, use a window or crossing*⟩
Select objects: ⟨*pick more objects or press Enter*⟩
Select objects: **R**↵
Remove objects: ⟨*select the objects*⟩
Remove objects: ⟨*select more objects to remove or press Enter*⟩
removed
Command:

When objects are removed from the selection set, they are no longer highlighted, and AutoCAD LT tells you how many objects were removed. Objects removed from a selection set are not affected by the editing command being used. AutoCAD LT also lets you change your mind again if you select objects to be removed and then want them added back to the selection set. To add objects back, use the Add option by typing **A** at the Remove objects: prompt. This returns the Select objects: prompt so you can select more objects:

Command: **E** or **ERASE**↵
Select objects: ⟨*pick an object, use a window or crossing*⟩
Select objects: **R**↵
Remove objects: ⟨*select the objects to be removed*⟩
Remove objects: **A**↵
Select objects: ⟨*pick an object, use a window or crossing*⟩
Select objects: ↵
Command:

Field Notes

You can also remove objects from a selection quickly and conveniently by pressing the Shift key while you pick a previously selected object. This way, you do not have to type **R** and then **A** to begin selecting again. To add new objects to the selection set, simply release the Shift key and continue to pick.

Pressing Shift to remove also works when you are using a window or a crossing box generated with implied windowing. Press the Shift key while you make the first pick to remove the selected objects from the selection set. Note that using Shift to remove does not work when you type **W** or **C** to begin a window or crossing box.

Exercise 2.14

1. Open AutoCAD LT or pick <u>N</u>ew in the <u>F</u>ile pull-down menu if it is already open and use the Quick Setup with Decimal measurements, limits of 8.5 and 11, and turn on the Grid and Snap.
2. Draw an object similar to Figure 2.23A.
3. Enter the ERASE command and use the crossing box to erase the objects similar to Figure 2.23.
4. Enter the ERASE command and pick the left vertical line to erase and then remove it from the selection. Use the Add option to reselect the same line and then remove it again.
5. Your drawing should still look like Figure 2.23C.
6. Select and deselect objects using the Shift key while picking. Try this with the window and crossing options as well.
7. Save as EX2.14.

Noun/Verb Selection and an Introduction to Grips

In the previous discussion, you learned how to enter the ERASE command and then select the objects to erase. You can also select the objects before you enter the command. This is called *noun/verb selection,* because the object is specified first, then the action. You can use several of the selection methods that were explained earlier, such as picking, windowing, or crossing. The pick box is displayed at the crosshair intersection when no command is active. The available selection methods work just as they did in the previous discussion. This pick box is here just for the purpose of picking objects and it works the same as the standard pick box. The big difference is in what happens to the objects you select. For example, move the screen cursor to a line and pick it as shown in Figure 2.24. Notice the squares that are automatically displayed on the line. There is one square on each end and one in the middle. These squares are called *grips*. Many editing tasks can be performed with grips, as discussed in detail later in this book. What is important for now is that you can select objects and then enter an editing command, such as ERASE. These are the steps:

- Select the objects by picking, window, or crossing.
- Enter the erase command:

Command: **E** or **ERASE**↵
ERASE 4 found
Command:

AutoCAD LT automatically erases the objects, tells you how many objects were found to erase, and returns the Command: prompt. Note that only picking and implied windowing can be used for this type of object selection. An object or objects can be erased quickly after being selected by pressing the Delete key.

FIGURE 2.24 Selecting an object before entering the ERASE command. Notice the grips.

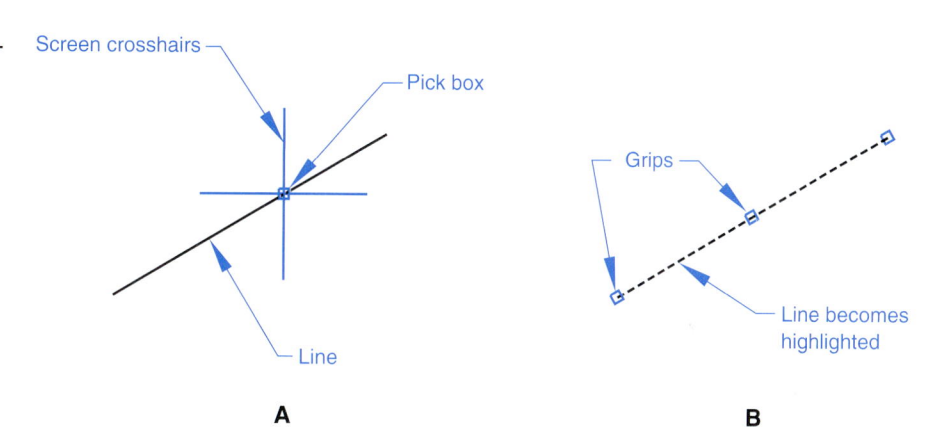

Field Notes

New users of AutoCAD LT may experience some initial difficulty in trying to get used to working with grips. These pointers will help you to get through some of the more common problems with grips:

- Not all editing commands allow objects to be preselected.
- If you accidentally pick objects, and you want to *un*select them, press the Esc key twice.
- When you accidentally start a selection window or crossing, press Esc once to abort the selection process.
- If the objects you select are automatically *un*selected when you enter an editing command and a Select objects: prompt is issued, change the value of the PICKFIRST system variable to 1 as follows:

Command: **PICKFIRST**↵
New value for PICKFIRST <0>: **1**↵

Another method to set this variable is by setting the check box labeled Noun/Verb Selection in the Object Selection Settings dialog box. This is displayed by picking <u>S</u>election in the O<u>p</u>tions pull-down menu.

Using the OOPS Command

If you erase something and then decide that you want it back, you can use the OOPS command. This is an easy command name to remember, because "Oops!" is a common word to say when you accidentally erase objects that you still need. The OOPS command may be used to bring back the most recent objects that you erased like this:

Command: **OOPS**↵
Command:

Note that OOPS brings back only those objects removed by the last ERASE command.

Changing the Pick Box Size

The pick box size is preset by AutoCAD LT, but you can change it if you wish. The default pick box size is 3 pixels. (Pixels are the tiny dots that make up what is displayed on the computer screen, as discussed in Chapter 1.) Look at the pick box that is provided by AutoCAD LT at the intersection of the crosshairs. It is displayed anytime the Command: prompt is present without an active command. This pick box is the same size as the pick box displayed at a Select objects: prompt. You may want to make the pick box size bigger for ease in selecting objects. Or you might need to make the pick box smaller if you are trying to pick objects in a very complex drawing where objects are close together.

Change the pick box size by choosing Sele*c*tion ... in the *T*ools pull-down menu. This accesses the Object Selection Settings dialog box shown in Figure 2.25. More about this dialog box is covered in Chapter 6, but for now, look at the Pickbox *S*ize area. Use the slider bar arrows to increase or decrease the pick box size one pixel at a time or move the elevator button to quickly enlarge or reduce the pick box size. The image at the right shows the pick box size as you make adjustments. Pick the OK button when ready.

You can also change the pick box size using the PICKBOX system variable at the Command: prompt by typing the number of desired pixels:

Command: **PICKBOX**↵
New value for PICKBOX <3>: **6**↵
Command:

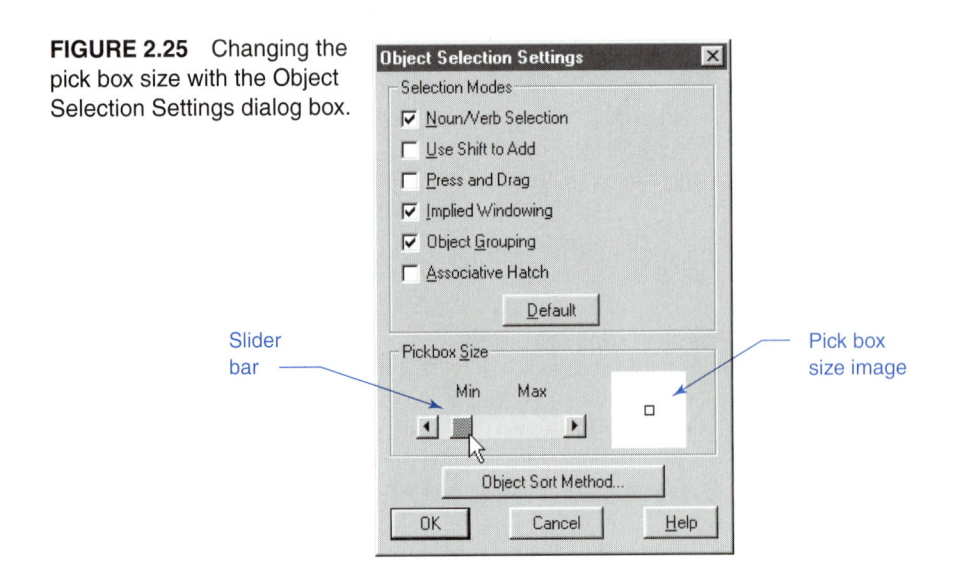

FIGURE 2.25 Changing the pick box size with the Object Selection Settings dialog box.

CHAPTER 2 ||| Introduction to Drafting with AutoCAD LT 69

> **Exercise 2.15**
>
> 1. Open AutoCAD LT or pick New in the File pull-down menu if it is already open and use the Quick Setup with Decimal measurements, limits of 8.5 and 11, and turn on the Grid and Snap.
> 2. Draw a line similar to Figure 2.24A.
> 3. Pick the line.
> 4. Notice the grips displayed on the line and that the line is highlighted.
> 5. Type the **ERASE** command and press the Enter key.
> 6. The line is automatically erased.
> 7. Draw an object similar to the one shown in Figure 2.22A.
> 8. Select the entire object with a window and notice the grips.
> 9. Press the Delete key to erase the object.
> 10. Type the **OOPS** command and press Enter.
> 11. The previously erased object returns.
> 12. Experiment by increasing the pick box size larger than the default.
> 13. Pick a line on the drawing to erase.
> 14. Use OOPS to bring the line back.
> 15. Decrease the pick box size smaller than the default.
> 16. Pick a line on the drawing to erase.
> 17. Use OOPS to bring the line back.
> 18. Change the pick box size back to the default value.
> 19. Think about how changing the pick box size affected your ability to pick objects.
> 20. Save as EX2.15.

✓ LEARNING CHECKPOINT

- What does the term *editing* refer to in an AutoCAD LT drawing?
- What is a selection set?
- Can you name three ways to access the ERASE command?
- What is the square selection cursor called?
- What are the differences between a selection window and a crossing box?
- How can you remove or add objects to a selection set?
- What are grips?
- How is noun/verb selection different from standard selection?
- In what way can altering the pick box size help your selection process?

Undoing and Redoing

There are many times when a command or series of commands does not give you the desired results. You can remove the effects of the last command entered by using the **U** command:

```
Command: E or ERASE↵
Select objects: L↵
1 found
Select objects: ↵
Command: U↵
ERASE
```

Standard
[Undo icon]
Edit
Undo
U
CTRL+Z

The name of the command that was undone is displayed at the command line. You can undo any number of commands one at a time using this method. Alternatively, you can press CTRL+Z, or select the Undo command from the Edit menu. The name of the command to be undone is displayed on this menu.

An undo button and list is available on the Standard tool bar. Picking the Undo button has the same effect as using the U command. By picking the Undo list, as shown in Figure 2.26A, you can undo a number of commands at the same time.

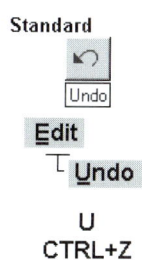

Standard

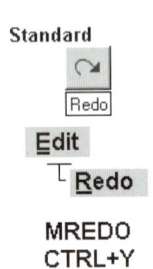

[Redo icon]

Edit

Redo

MREDO
CTRL+Y

If you undo a previous command and then decide you did not want to undo it after all, you can redo the command. To redo a command, select Redo from the Edit pull-down menu, press CTRL+Y or select the Redo button or list from the Standard toolbar; or type MREDO at the Command: prompt.

Command: **MREDO**↵
All/Last/<Number>:

You can specify the number of commands to redo, redo just the last undone command, or redo all undone commands. When you need to redo multiple commands, it is usually easier to do so using the Redo list button on the Standard toolbar, as shown in Figure 2.26B.

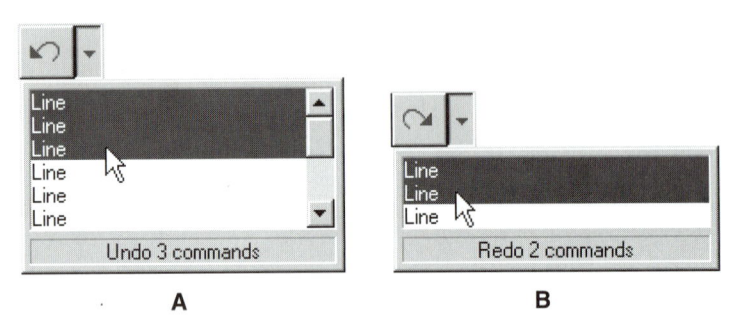

FIGURE 2.26 The Undo and Redo lists can be used to undo or redo several commands at the same time.

Field Notes

Earlier versions of AutoCAD LT had only the REDO command. This limited predecessor to the MREDO command is still present in AutoCAD LT 98. The REDO command reverses the effects of the last U or UNDO command (UNDO is discussed in Chapter 7). The REDO command, however, can be used only *immediately* after the U (or UNDO) command. If you undo a command and then use another command, such as LINE, you can no longer redo what was undone using the REDO command. This also means that REDO cannot be used several times in a row to redo more than one command.

Exercise 2.16

1. Open EX2.15.
2. Use the ERASE command to erase all of the objects.
3. Pick the Undo toolbar icon. The previously erased objects return.
4. Repeat the first two steps, but this time enter the U command by typing **U** or picking Undo from the Edit pull-down menu. Decide which method works best for you.
5. Use the ERASE command to erase all of the objects.
6. Use the LINE command to draw a new line anywhere in the drawing.
7. Enter the U command, the line disappears.
8. Use the U command again. The erased objects return.
9. Enter the REDO command. The objects are erased again.
10. Use the REDO command again. Nothing happens.
11. Use the U command again. The erased objects return.
12. Erase the objects once again and draw a new line anywhere in the drawing.
13. Enter the OOPS command. Erased objects return and the new line remains as well.
14. Think about how this worked. OOPS is often a better option for returning erased objects, but U will undo the effects of almost any command.
15. Save as EX2.16.

CHAPTER 2 ||| Introduction to Drafting with AutoCAD LT   71

☑ LEARNING CHECKPOINT

- What are three ways to undo the results of a command?
- How can you restore a command that has been undone?
- What is the limitation of the REDO command?
- Why is OOPS often a better option for restoring erased objects?

Printing Your First Drawing

When you create a CAD drawing, the drawing exists only as an electronic file and can be viewed only at a computer workstation unless you produce a hardcopy of the drawing using a printer or plotter. Producing a hardcopy is called *printing* or *plotting*. Plotting (or printing) a drawing serves several purposes in the design process. Most obviously, when a drawing project is completed, plotted drawings allow you to communicate design details to others. Plots (or prints) are required at remote locations, on the shop floors, or at any location where a computer workstation is not available. Other applications for printing include creating *check prints* for checking your drawing. Because the display monitor has a limited area and resolution, it is very common to find mistakes on larger printed copies that were not noticed on the computer screen.

This introduction to printing covers the fundamentals of printing drawings from model space. Printing from paper space and producing industry-standard drawing layouts are discussed in later chapters.

Standard
Print (Ctrl+P)
File
  Print...
PLOT
PRINT
CTRL+P

Introduction to the Print/Plot Configuration Dialog Box

Prints and plots are made using the PLOT command. The PLOT command can be accessed by picking the Print toolbar button from the Standard toolbar, picking Print ... from the File pull-down menu, using CTRL+P, or by typing either **PRINT** or **PLOT** at the Command: prompt.

Look at Figure 2.27 or bring the Print/Plot Configuration dialog box up on your screen as you read the following general description and instructions for the use of each area in the dialog box.

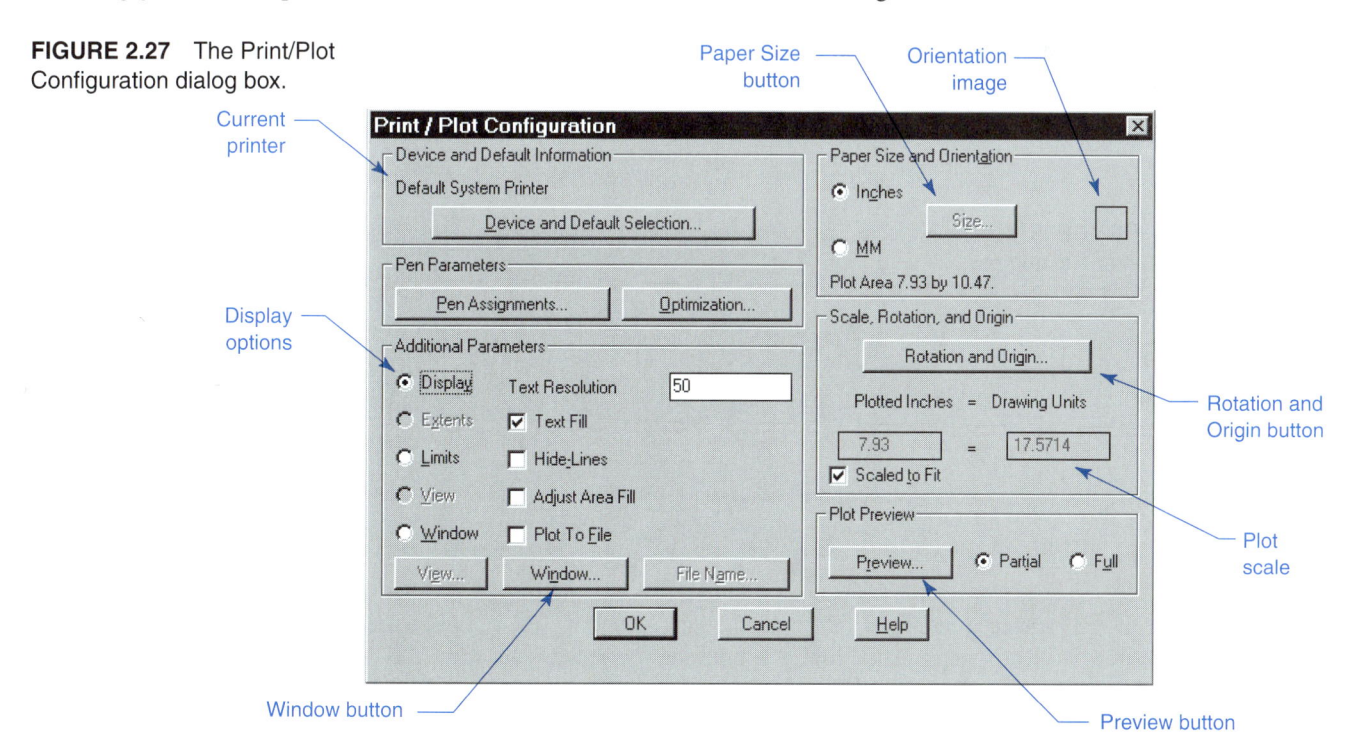

FIGURE 2.27 The Print/Plot Configuration dialog box.

Setup and Default Information
This selection identifies the printer or plotter that you are using and provides a Device and Default Selection ... button where you can access additional printer or plotter setup options. Your instructor or system administrator should have this properly set for you at this time.

Pen Parameters

This area allows you to assign different line widths to different colors and linetypes. Your instructor or system administrator should have this properly set for you at this time.

Paper Size and Orientation

In this area you can select In*c*hes or *M*M (millimeters) as the units for the print or plot. There is a Siz*e* ... button available that accesses the Paper Size dialog box, where you can select different paper sizes. If this button is active, your printer accepts different paper sizes. A paper image tile that shows the paper orientation is displayed at the right. Paper orientation is dependent on your printing or plotting device.

Additional Parameters

The Additional Parameters area has several options. Items of importance for now are Displa*y*, E*x*tents, *L*imits, and *W*indow. The option is described as follows:

- **Displa*y*:** Pick this option to print or plot the screen display. What you see on the screen is what will be printed.
- **E*x*tents:** Select this button to print or plot the drawing extents. *Drawing extents* is the smallest rectangle that contains all of the objects in the drawing. This concept is explained in Chapter 4.
- ***L*imits:** This option allows you to print or plot the drawing limits. Drawing limits is a familiar concept and is a good option for you to use at this time in your training.
- ***V*iew:** This option allows you to plot a view that was saved using the VIEW command. Pick the Vi*e*w ... button if you want to choose a view from the View name dialog box. Creating and using named views is discussed with drawing display control in Chapter 4.
- ***W*indow:** Pick this option if you want to print or plot everything within a window that you define. If the *W*indow option is active, then you pick the Wi*n*dow ... button to access the Window Selection dialog box shown in Figure 2.28. This option works just like the window selection method that you learned earlier. The idea is to put a window around the area you want to print. You can window the entire drawing or you can window just a small portion of the drawing to display a detailed area. Making a Window print is an option that you may want to consider at this time in your training. The Window Selection works as follows:

Enter the X and Y coordinates of the *F*irst Corner and the *O*ther Corner in the text boxes provided. Then pick OK. For example, if you want to print an area 8.5 × 11, enter the first corner as X = 0.00 and Y = 0.00. Then enter the other corner as X = 8.50 and Y = 11.00, as shown in Figure 2.28.

FIGURE 2.28 The Window Selection dialog box.

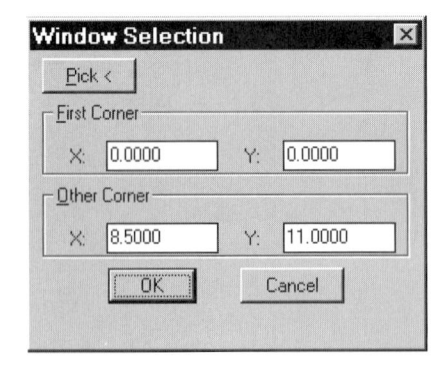

If you need more flexibility, use the *P*ick < button. The screen returns. Move the crosshairs to the desired first corner and pick. Now, a window is formed as you move the cursor. Move the cursor until the window surrounds the area to be printed and pick the other corner. Pick the OK button when the Window Selection dialog box returns.

- **Text Resolution:** This text box allows you to increase or decrease the dots per inch used to print or plot True Type fonts. Higher values increase resolution, but they decrease printing and plotting speed. True Type text fonts are explained in Chapter 9.

CHAPTER 2 ||| Introduction to Drafting with AutoCAD LT

- **Text Fill:** This check box is on by default; it prints and plots True Type fonts as filled text. If you turn this off, the True Type fonts are printed or plotted as outlines of the text shape.
- **Hide-Lines:** This is off by default, which plots hidden lines in model space views. The concept of hidden lines is discussed later in the text.
- **Adjust Area Fill:** This check box is off by default. This option allows you to adjust the pen width when plotting wide polylines or filled solids. This option should be on when plotting these types of objects to ensure the best accuracy. Polylines are covered in Chapter 8.
- **Plot to File:** This check box is off by default. Check this box if you want to send your plot to a file rather than to a printer or plotter. When you do this, AutoCAD LT uses the drawing name with a .plt file extension. Pick the File Name ... button to access the Create Plot File dialog box and give your plot file another name, if you wish. You can include a file extension other than .plt if you type it as needed. You should check the printer or plotter manual for applications that work for your specific machine.

Scale, Rotation, and Origin

This area accesses the following plot features:

- **Rotation and Origin ...:** Pick this button to get the Plot Rotation and Origin dialog box shown in Figure 2.29. This dialog box gives you four plot rotation options. The option you pick determines how the drawing is positioned on the paper. An example of each of the plot rotation options is shown in Figure 2.30. The Plot Origin option allows you to enter X and Y coordinates to establish where the plot begins in relation to the paper. A 0,0 origin is common, but some plotters need a little extra space in the margin for rollers. The plot origin might be 0.5,0.5 for these plotters.
- **Plotted Inches = Drawing Units:** These are edit boxes where you can enter a desired plotting scale. Notice the Scaled to Fit check box. If this is checked, AutoCAD LT automatically scales your drawing to fit the sheet. If this box is not checked, AutoCAD LT sets the scale at 1=1. Some examples of scale options are shown in Table 2.2.

FIGURE 2.29 The Plot Rotation and Origin dialog box.

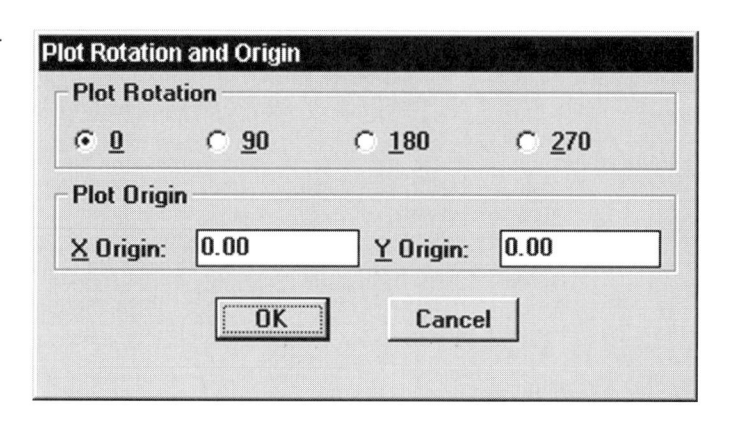

FIGURE 2.30 Plot rotation results.

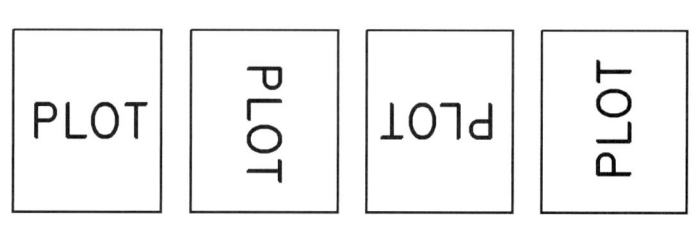

Plot Rotation: 0 90 180 270

TABLE 2.2 Various scaling options

Scale	Plotted Inches	Drawing Units
Full (1:1)	1	1
Half (1:2)	.5	1
Quarter (1:4)	.25	1
Double (2:1)	2	1

Plot Preview

When you have everything set up and you think it is time to plot the drawing, use the Plot Preview to make sure. Plots take time and material to make. The Plot Preview lets you see what the plot looks like before you make it. There are two options, Partial and Full preview. Select the type of preview you want and pick the Preview … button.

- **Partial:** This accesses the Preview Effective Plotting Area dialog box. A partial preview is fast, but it shows only the outline of the paper and the plotting area. AutoCAD LT specifies the size of each area and gives any warnings that you should consider. Notice the Paper size and Effective area options in Figure 2.31. Pick OK when you are done looking at the preview. As you look at Figure 2.31, notice the little triangle in the lower left corner of the area display. This is the rotation image, which displays the drawing rotation. Figure 2.32 shows how this image looks for each of the rotation options.

FIGURE 2.31 A partial preview displays the Preview Effective Plotting Area dialog box.

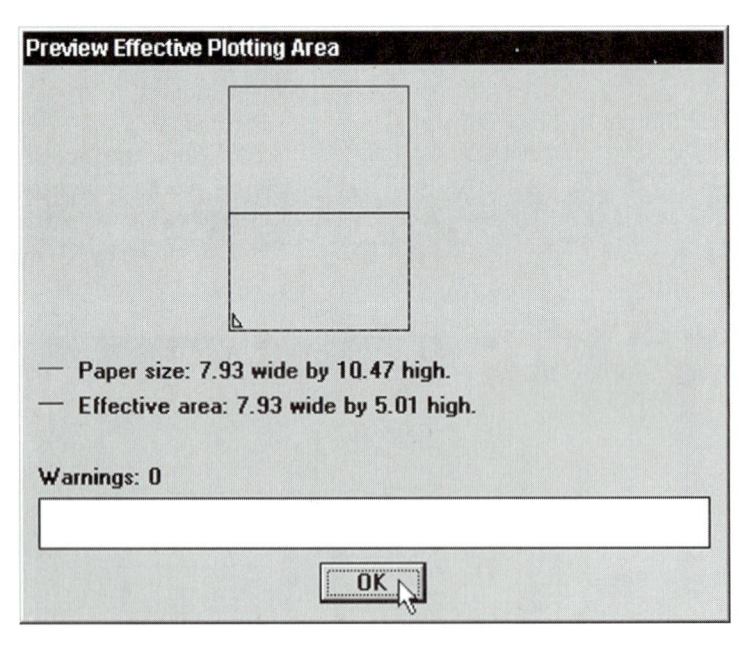

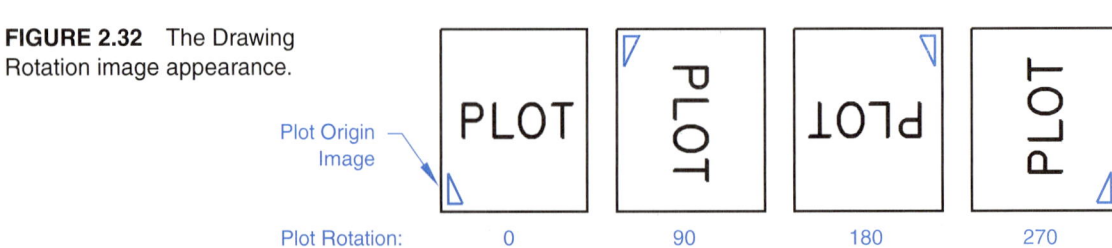

FIGURE 2.32 The Drawing Rotation image appearance.

CHAPTER 2 ||| Introduction to Drafting with AutoCAD LT 75

> ### Through the Window...
>
> Your paper size and orientation are affected by the orientation of your printer. The orientation refers to whether it is printing portrait or landscape style. Portrait means the paper is taller than it is wide, and landscape means that it is wider than it is tall. You can use a Plot Rotation angle to counter the effects of the printer orientation, or you can easily adjust it. Here's how.
>
> #### Windows95/98/NT 4.0
> Double-click on the My Computer icon to display the My Computer window. Now double-click on the Printers folder, and double-click on the icon for the current printer to open the printer control window. Pick Properties from the Printer menu and select the tab marked Paper. Here, you should find an area labeled Orientation with a selection for Portrait and Landscape. Select the appropriate option and pick the Apply button. Use the Close button in the upper right corner to close each of the windows you have opened and return to AutoCAD LT.

- **Full:** The full preview takes more time to display than the partial preview, but it shows the actual drawing displayed within the paper area, as shown in Figure 2.33. The full plot preview has a magnifying glass cursor with a plus/minus symbol. Press the right mouse button to get a popup menu with the options Exit, Pan, Zoom, Zoom Window, and Zoom Previous. The use of these items is explained in Chapter 13.

FIGURE 2.33 The Full plot preview image and the magnifying glass cursor.

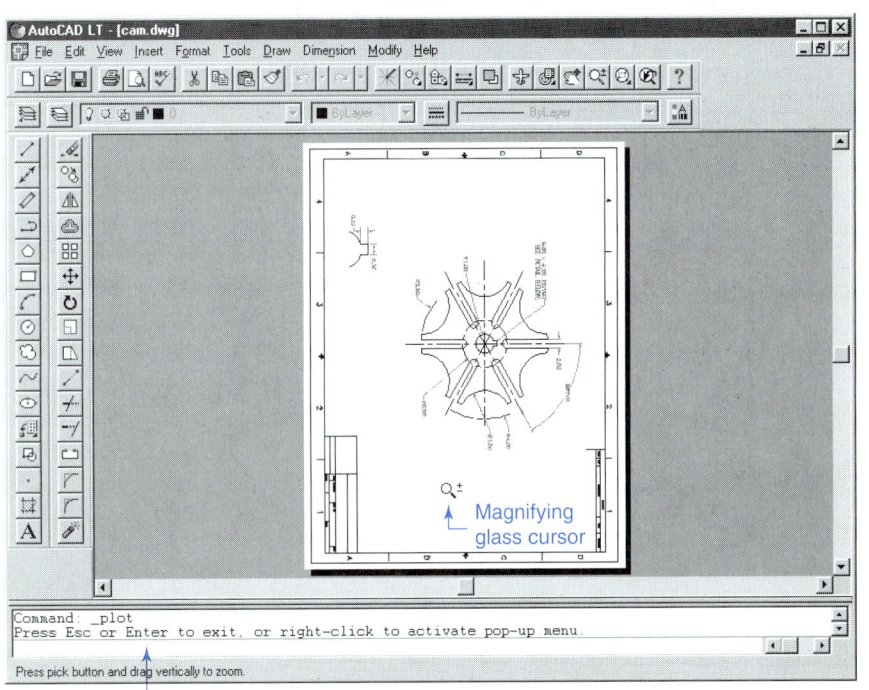

Press the Escape key or pick Exit in the cursor menu to return to the Print/Plot Configuration dialog box. Now you can make changes to the plot configuration and look at another preview or accept the plot configuration. Pick the OK button when you are ready to send the drawing to the printer or plotter. Watch the prompt line after picking OK. AutoCAD LT specifies the effective plotting area and gives you a "Plot complete" message before returning the Command: prompt.

Field Notes

When you are getting ready to do a plot, be sure the printer or plotter is turned on and paper is loaded. If you experience difficulty getting the desired results from your printer or plotter, review the pertinent material in this chapter. If you are still having difficulty, do not spend a lot of time working at it. It makes much more sense to go directly to your instructor or system administrator for assistance.

This is true for all of the subject matter in this text. When you cannot locate an answer to a question in the text in a reasonable amount of time, get immediate assistance whenever possible. Your instructor, system administrator, or an experienced coworker can often help you find a fast solution so that you can continue. This will keep you productive in your learning process and help to avoid unnecessary frustration.

Exercise 2.17

1. Open EX2.15 and prepare to make a print or plot, if approved by your instructor or supervisor. (Refer to the earlier discussion about opening a drawing if you need a review.)
2. Enter the PLOT command to access the Plot Configuration dialog box.
3. Pick the Display radio button.
4. Pick the Partial radio button (it is the default) and pick the Preview ... button.
5. Observe the Preview Effective Plotting Area dialog box and pick OK.
6. Pick the Full radio button and pick the Preview ... button.
7. Observe the full preview and press the Escape key.
8. Pick the Rotation and Origin ... button. 0 is default. Pick the 90 radio button.
9. Pick the Full radio button and pick the Preview ... button.
10. Observe the difference between the 0° and 90° rotation angle.
11. Experiment by setting the 180 and 270 plot rotations and do a full preview to see the results of each.
12. Change the plot rotation to 0.
13. Pick the Extents radio button and check the results with a Partial and Full preview.
14. Pick the Limits radio button and check the results with a Partial and Full preview.
15. Pick the Window ... button and then the Pick< button in the Window Selection box. When the drawing is displayed, place a window around any part of the drawing that you desire. Pick the OK button. Check the results with a Partial and Full preview.
16. Pick the Window ... button again and this time enter 0 in the First Corner X: and Y: text boxes. In the Other Corner text boxes, type 8.5 for X: and 11 for Y:. Pick the OK button. Check the results with a Full preview.
17. Use the options that you feel fit your needs best, and make a print or plot of the drawing.
18. Save as EX2.17.

✓ LEARNING CHECKPOINT

- ☐ What are the four ways to start the PLOT command?
- ☐ What is the difference between the Display, Extents, Limits, and Window Plot Configuration options?
- ☐ How does the rotation angle affect the way the plot looks?
- ☐ What are the results and advantages of using partial or full plot previews?

CHAPTER 2 ||| Introduction to Drafting with AutoCAD LT

MULTIPLE CHOICE

Circle the choice or enter your response on an answer sheet by selecting the option that most closely completes or answers the given statements.

1. Step 1 of the Quick Setup dialog box allows you to set:
   a. drawing aids
   b. limits
   c. units
   d. grid

2. When you make a drawing in AutoCAD LT, you make the drawing actual size. AutoCAD LT refers to actual size as:
   a. full size
   b. true size
   c. scale
   d. world size

3. A pattern of dots that is displayed on the screen at any desired interval:
   a. blips
   b. snap
   c. grid
   d. dots

4. An imaginary pattern that forces the screen cursor to move in exact increments:
   a. blips
   b. snap
   c. grid
   d. dots

5. Allows the pointing device only horizontal and vertical movement:
   a. snap
   b. grid
   c. ortho
   d. blip

6. Clean the screen of unwanted marks with this command:
   a. CLEAN
   b. REDRAW
   c. BLIPMODE
   d. VIEW

7. Changing a drawing by erasing, moving, copying, or altering objects in any way is referred to as:
   a. editing
   b. changing
   c. correcting
   d. modifying

8. When you enter the ERASE command and get the Select objects: prompt, the screen cursor changes to:
   a. crosshairs
   b. box
   c. dashed line
   d. pick box

9. Use this command as many times as you want to remove one or more previous commands:
   a. REMOVE
   b. OOPS
   c. U
   d. R

10. Use this command to save a new drawing for the first time:
    a. SAVE
    b. SAVEAS
    c. NEW
    d. OPEN

MATCHING

Match each term to the correct description by writing the appropriate number in each box at the left.

☐ Absolute	☐ Limits	☐ Polygon
☐ Architectural	☐ Mode	☐ Quadrant
☐ Blips	☐ Model	☐ Relative
☐ Cartesian	☐ Open	☐ REMOVE
☐ Coordinate	☐ OOPS	☐ SAVE
☐ Crossing	☐ Ortho	☐ SAVEAS
☐ Decimal	☐ Paper	☐ Selection
☐ Editing	☐ Pick	☐ Transparent
☐ Engineering	☐ Pixels	☐ Window
☐ Grid	☐ PLOT	☐ World

1. These units are used to specify distances in inches or millimeters.
2. Drawing in these units is generally used in mapping and civil drafting projects such as dams and bridges, plot plans, and topography.
3. These units are used when drawing in feet and inches and fractional inches.
4. AutoCAD LT refers to actual size as this size.
5. This sets your drawing area.
6. The space in which you create your drawing.
7. AutoCAD LT provides you with this space where the drawing is organized and scaled as needed for the end product.
8. This is a pattern of dots that is displayed on the screen at any desired increment you establish.
9. As you move the screen cursor, this display indicates where the cursor is in relation to the drawing origin.
10. Use this command to save your drawing the first time.
11. Use this command to save your work in progress.
12. Use this command if you want to work on a previous drawing.
13. This coordinate system relates to numbers that are used to locate points relative to two intersecting axes.
14. These coordinates are always established based on their X and Y distance from the origin.
15. These coordinates are used when you want to establish a point based on a distance from a previous point.
16. A quarter of a circle.
17. This is a closed plane figure with straight sides.
18. This is a setting or operating condition that you control.
19. These are temporary screen marks that are displayed when you pick a point.
20. With this on, the pointing device allows only horizontal and vertical movement.
21. This is a command that can be started while another command is in progress.
22. AutoCAD LT refers to changing a drawing as this process.
23. When you select objects with AutoCAD LT, the objects are referred to as this kind of a set.
24. When you get a Select objects: prompt, the screen cursor changes to this kind of a box.
25. A box that must totally surround an object to be erased.
26. A box that may either surround or cross through an object to erase it.
27. AutoCAD LT allows you to remove objects from a selection set by using this option.
28. If you erase something and then decide you want it back, you can use this command.
29. These are tiny dots that make up what is seen on the computer screen.
30. Prints are made using this command.

WORD SCRAMBLE

Unscramble the seven scrambled words below, one letter to each square, to form seven AutoCAD LT–related words:

- LOARP
- SIMTIL
- NIROCADTOE
- LOBASETU
- LETAVIRE
- PLIB
- NOWDWI

Unscramble the circled letters above to form the special answer, as suggested by the illustration.

PROJECTS

Draw Projects 2.1–2.5 using the Quick Setup and these settings:

- Decimal units
- 8.5 × 11 limits

2.1 Use the LINE command to draw a graphic design using the following absolute coordinates:

- 1.5,5.75
- 3.25,5.75
- 3.25,4.5
- 5,6.375
- 3.25,8.25
- 3.25,7
- 1.5,7
- 2.125,6.375
- 1.5,5.75
    - Cancel the line command.
    - Save as P2.1.
    - Print the drawing.

2.2 Use the LINE command to draw the sheet metal part using the following relative coordinates after the initial absolute coordinate:

- 2,2 (absolute)
- @3.25,0
- @0,1.875
- @−.875,0
- @0,.75
- @1.75,0
- @0,3.125
- @−.5,.5
- @−1.5,0
- @−.75,−.75
- @−.75,.75
- @−.25,0
- @0,−2
- @.25,0
- @0,−3.5
- @−.25,−.25
- @−.375,0
- Close
  - Save as P2.2.
  - Print the drawing.

2.3 Use the LINE command to draw the latch plate using the following polar coordinates after the initial absolute coordinate:

- 3,4 (absolute)
- @.5<0
- @.625<90
- @2.5<0
- @2.375<90
- @.75<180
- @1.5<270
- @2.25<180
- @.375<270
- Close
  - Save as P2.3.
  - Print the drawing.

2.4 Use the LINE command to draw the trophy base using the following combination of coordinates:

- 1.5,3 (absolute)
- @5,0 (relative)
- @1<90 (polar)
- @5<180 (polar)
- Close.
- Press Enter or the space bar.
- 2.25,4 (absolute)
- @4.5<90 (polar)
- @1.75,1.75 (relative)
- @1.75,−1.75 (relative)
- @4.5<270 (polar)
- Cancel.
- Press Enter or the space bar.
- 2.75,4.75 (absolute)
- @2.5,0 (relative)

- @3.5<90 (polar)
- @2.5<180 (polar)
- Close.
  - Save as P2.4.
  - Print the drawing.

2.5 Use the LINE command to draw the picture frame using the following combination of coordinates:

- Point 1. 1,1 (absolute)
- Point 2. @6.5,0 (relative)
- Point 3. @9<90 (polar)
- Point 4. @−6.5,0 (relative)
- Close.
- Press Enter or the space bar.
- Point 5. 1.5,1.5 (absolute)
- Point 6. @5.5,0 (relative)
- Point 7. @8<90 (polar)
- Point 8. @5.5<180 (polar)
- Close.
- Set Grid to .5.
- Set Snap to .25 and turn Snap on.
- Enter the LINE command and do the following:
  - Pick point 1. *(Note: The point numbers refer to the points established by the previously numbered coordinate entries.)*
  - Pick point 5.
- Cancel.
- Press Enter or the space bar.
  - Pick point 2.
  - Pick point 6.
- Cancel.
- Press Enter or the space bar.
  - Pick point 3.
  - Pick point 7.
- Cancel.
- Press Enter or the space bar.
  - Pick point 4.
  - Pick point 8.
- Cancel.
  - Save as P2.5.
  - Print the drawing.

Draw Projects 2.6–2.14 using the Quick Setup and these settings:

- Units should correlate with the problem
- 8.5 × 11 limits
- .25 Grid
- .125 Snap

Use the LINE command by using the point entry methods that best fit each situation in each problem. It is suggested that you use sketches to determine a planned procedure and coordinates.

Make your drawings proportional to the given product. Dimensions (if any) are given to establish the size of the main feature. Sizes and locations of features that are not dimensioned may be determined to your own specifications. Do not include dimensions or notes on your drawing. Save each drawing as related to the project number, such as P2.6. Make a print or plot as specified by your instructor or supervisor.

2.6 Electrical Drawing: Shock Resistor

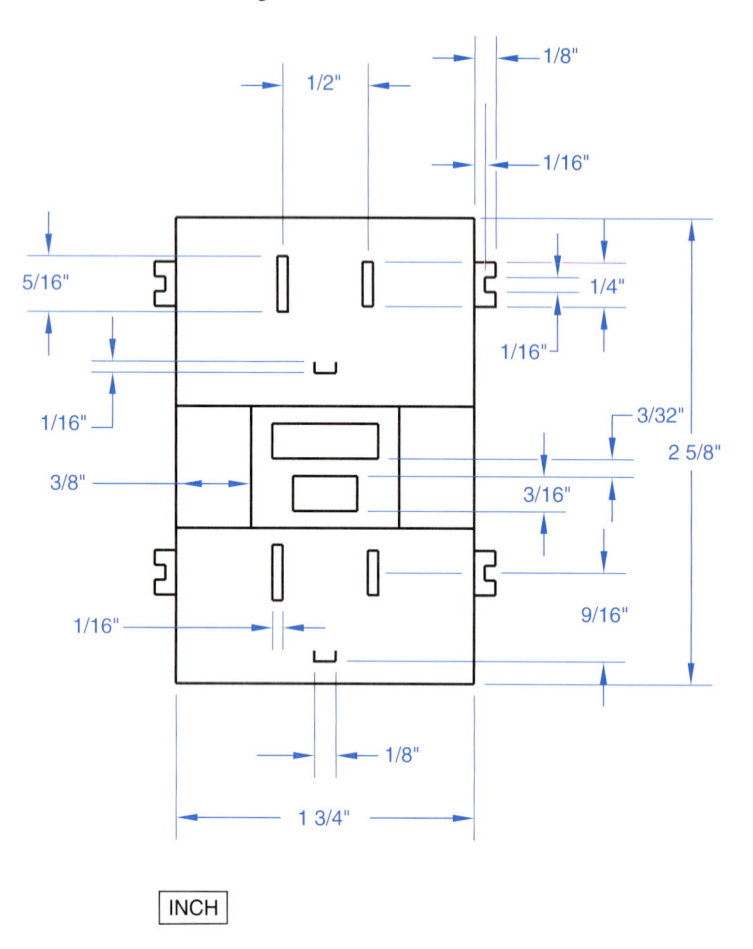

2.7 Mechanical Drawing: Clock Base

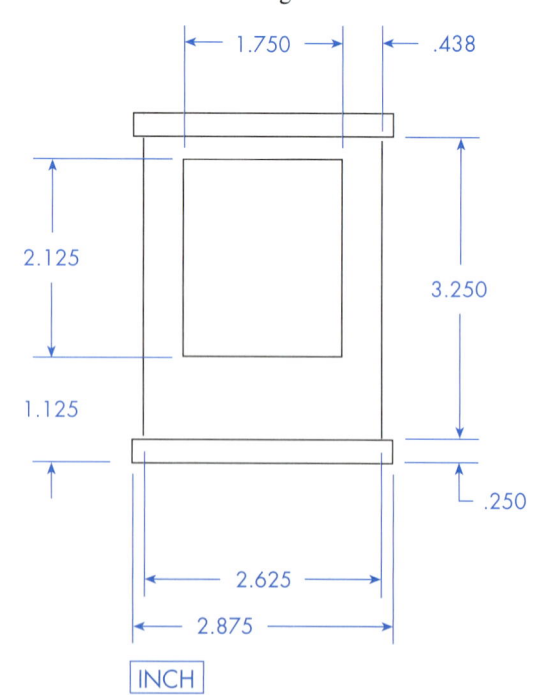

CHAPTER 2 ||| Introduction to Drafting with AutoCAD LT

2.8 Architectural Drawing: Footing Detail

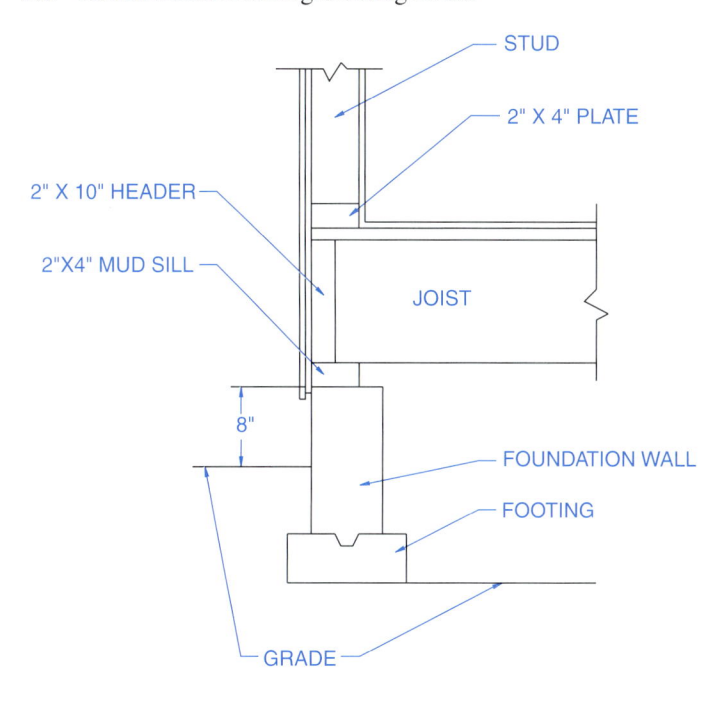

2.9 Electrical Drawing: Baseboard Heater Circuit

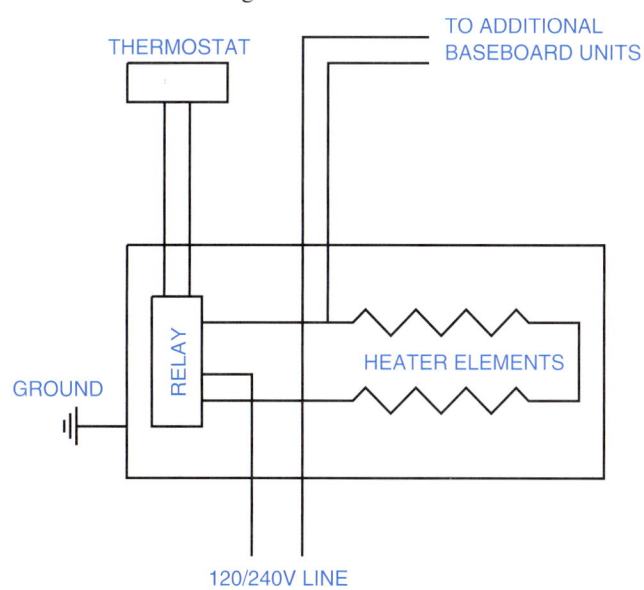

2.10 Pipe Drawing: Pipe Assembly

CHAPTER 3

Drawing Basic Objects

LEARNING GOALS

- Use the AutoCAD LT Advanced Setup option.
- Use an AutoCAD LT template.
- Create a template drawing.
- Customize existing template drawings.
- Draw circles, arcs, ellipses, and elliptical arcs.
- Draw regular polygons and rectangles.
- Use the DONUT command to draw filled rings and circles.
- Draw filled objects with the SOLID command.
- Turn the fill on and off to create different designs.

In Chapter 2 you learned how to quickly set up an AutoCAD LT drawing and practiced fundamental applications of drawing and erasing lines. This chapter provides you with additional setup options, including setting up your own custom drawing formats. Additionally, you will learn to draw basic shapes such as circles, arcs, polygons, and filled shapes.

Additional AutoCAD LT Setup Options

When you open AutoCAD LT, you get the Start Up dialog box and when using the NEW command, the Create New Drawing dialog box is displayed. These dialog boxes were introduced in Chapter 2 with the Quick Setup option. You also have a choice of these options: Advanced Setup, Use a Template, or Start from Scratch.

Using the Advanced Setup Option

The Advanced Setup option is one of the Wizards found in the Start Up and Create New Drawing dialog boxes. The Quick Setup Wizard was introduced in Chapter 2. The Advanced Setup Wizard provides additional flexibility. In the Set Up or Create New Drawing dialog boxes, double-click on Advanced Setup or highlight Advanced Setup and pick the OK button. This displays the Advanced Setup dialog box found in Figure 3.1. This dialog box contains tabs labeled Step 1 through Step 7. Use the tabs in progressive order or as needed to set up your drawing as follows.

Step 1: Units
This tab is the same as the Units tab discussed with the Quick Setup Wizard in Chapter 2. This option allows you to select one of five different units of measure for your drawing. Refer to Setting Units of Measure in Chapter 2. The Precision: drop-down list shown in Figure 3.1 is a feature of the Advanced Setup tabs. Access this list to select the number of digits beyond the decimal point for the numeric display. The Sample Units image changes to match your choice.

FIGURE 3.1 The Advanced Setup dialog box. Notice the seven available tabs.

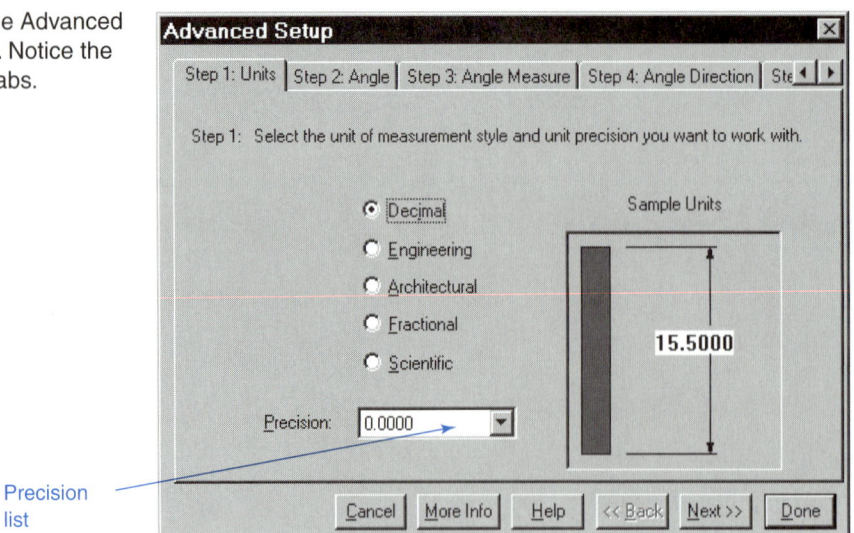

Field Notes

Picking the More Info button at the bottom of the Advanced Setup dialog box provides you with additional information about where to access the items in the specific tab where the button is active.

Step 2: Angle

Pick this tab to choose angular units and the display accuracy of angles you draw (see Figure 3.2). The angle measurement options are explained in the following list:

- **Decimal Degrees** — Decimal degrees is the default normally used in mechanical drafting where degrees and decimal parts of a degree are commonly used. Look at the Sample Angle area in Figure 3.2. Pick the Precision down arrow to access the drop-down list. Pick the desired angle precision. Notice how the Sample Angle image changes to reflect the display precision you select.
- **Deg/Min/Sec** — The Degrees/Minutes/Seconds option is used in mechanical, architectural, structural, and civil drafting when it is necessary for angular measurements to contain accuracy related to minutes and seconds. Notice the Sample Angle area in Figure 3.3. There are 60 minutes in one degree and 60 seconds in one minute. Access the Precision drop-down list to establish the display accuracy of seconds.

FIGURE 3.2 The Advanced Setup dialog box, Step 2: Angle tab. Decimal Degrees is the default. Notice the Sample Angle image shown at the right.

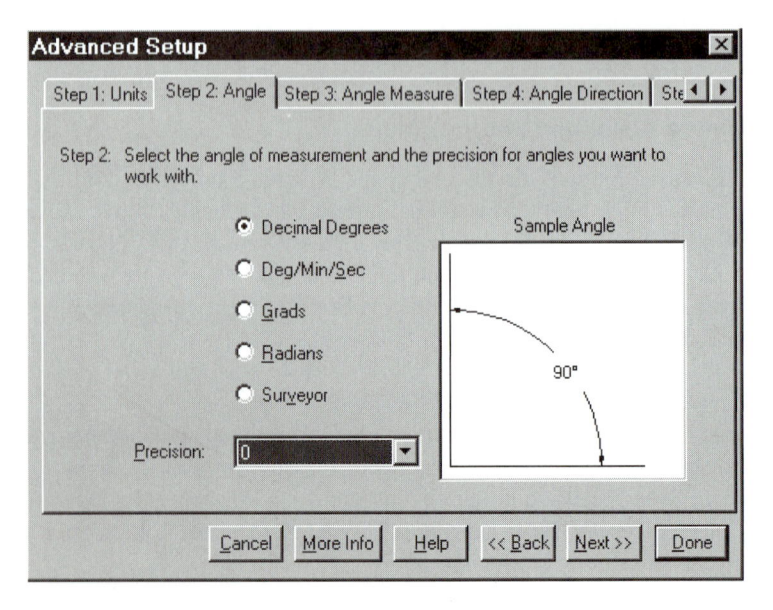

CHAPTER 3 ||| Drawing Basic Objects

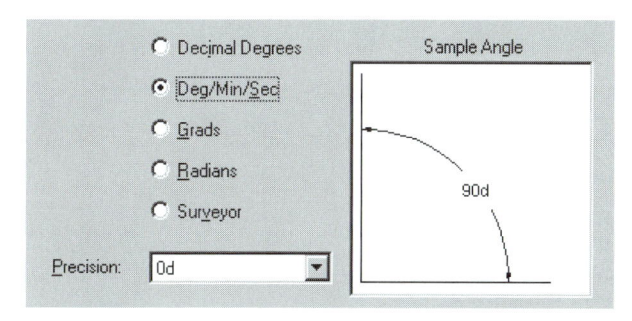

FIGURE 3.3 The Deg/Min/Sec (Degree/Minute/Second) angle option.

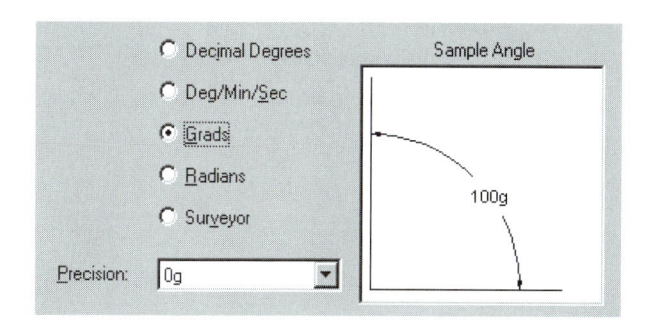

FIGURE 3.4 The Grads angle option.

- **Grads** — This refers to the abbreviation of *gradient,* which is a unit of angular measure. The angular value is followed by a "g," as shown in the Sample Angle area in Figure 3.4. This is based on one-quarter of a circle having 100 grads. A full circle has 400 grads. A 45° angle, for example, has 50 grads. Use the Precision drop-down list to change the display number of decimal grads used.

- **Radians** — The *radian* is an angular unit, arc, or rotational measure where π radians = 180°. A 90° angle, for example, has π/2 radians and an arc length of π/2. Notice the Sample Angle shown in Figure 3.5, which is displayed when Radians is active, and observe the results when you adjust the display precision.

- **Surveyor** — Surveyor angles are measured using bearings. The *bearing* of a line is its direction with respect to one of the quadrants of a compass. Bearings are measured clockwise or counterclockwise depending on the quadrant and beginning from either North or South. Bearings are measured in degrees, minutes, and seconds. An angle measured 45°30′15″ from north toward east is expressed as N45°30′15″E. Figure 3.6 shows the Advanced Setup Surveyor selection and the Sample Angle, and sample bearings represented in relation to the quadrants of a compass. The Precision settings determine decimal display accuracy of the minutes settings.

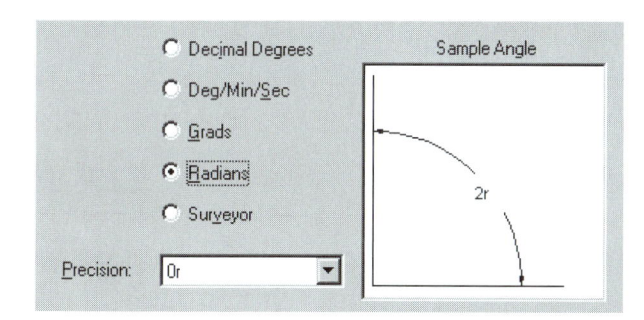

FIGURE 3.5 The Radians angle option.

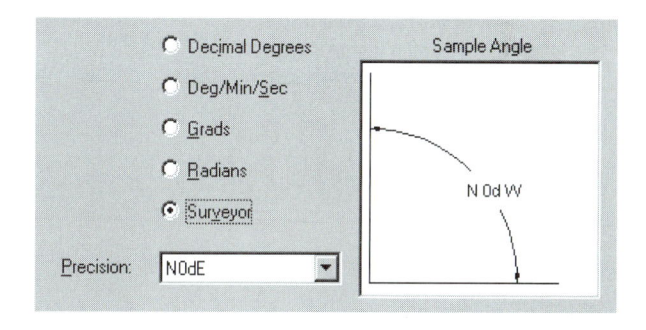

FIGURE 3.6 The Surveyor angle option and sample bearing example.

Field Notes

The precision level affects coordinate displays but does not affect the accuracy of your drawing. Precise entries can be made regardless of the display precision.

Step 3: Angle Measure

This tab lets you choose the compass position from which angles are measured. The AutoCAD LT default has angles measured in a counterclockwise direction beginning at 0° East on the right side of your screen. Notice the Angle Zero Direction image in Figure 3.7 that displays the 0° East (E) compass orientation. The orientation of the compass directions is the same as when you look at a map, with North at the top of your screen. This setting de-

FIGURE 3.7 The Advanced Setup dialog box, Step 3: Angle Measure tab.

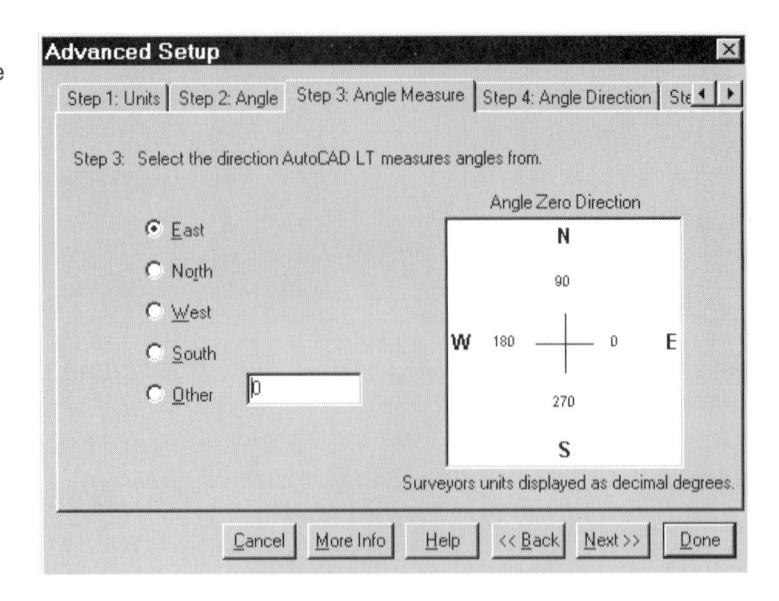

termines which direction is used as angle 0° (or 0r, 0g, etc.). The other options are North, West, South, and Other. The Other option requires that you type a desired starting angle. Use your computer to pick each of the options and notice the change in the Angle Zero Direction image with each selection. When surveyors units are selected in Step 2, a message is displayed below the image tile indicating that the image uses decimal degrees (see Figure 3.7).

Step 4: Angle Direction

The Angle Direction tab allows you to select Counter-Clockwise or Clockwise angle direction. The angle direction originates from the compass position that you used in Step 3. Figure 3.8 shows the Step 4: Angle Direction folder and the default Counter-Clockwise angle direction selection and related Angle Direction image. The default Counter-Clockwise setting is recommended in most applications.

FIGURE 3.8 The Advanced Setup dialog box, Step 4: Angle Direction tab. Notice the counterclockwise example in the Angle Direction image.

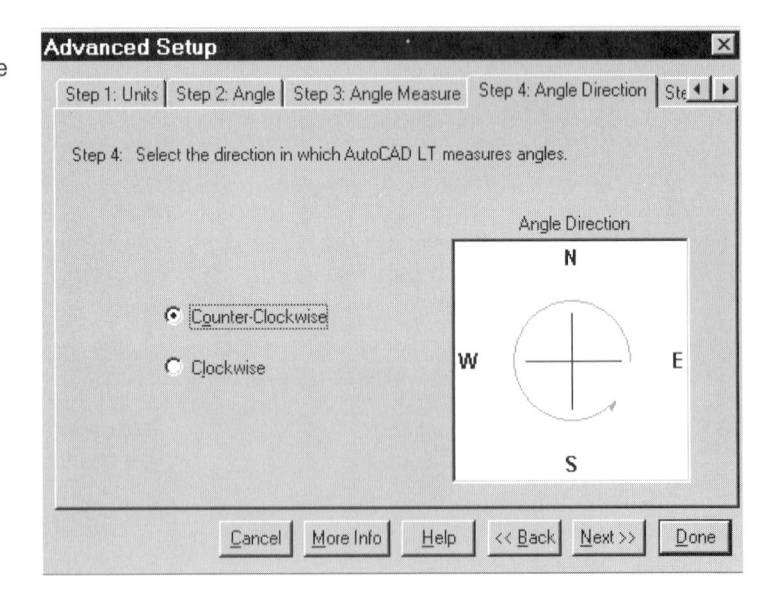

Step 5: Area

The Area tab works the same way as the Quick Setup discussion in Chapter 2. Refer to Setting the Drawing Size in Chapter 2 for a review.

Step 6: Title Block

AutoCAD LT allows you to select one of many standard title block and border formats by picking the Step 6: Title Blocks tab. The initial settings in the Title Block Description and Title Block File Name boxes are *No title block* and *None*. Pick either down arrow to access the drop-down list with a variety of inch, metric, generic, and

CHAPTER 3 ||| Drawing Basic Objects

architectural title block and border options. The choices are related to inch and metric sheet sizes. See Appendix B for a display of standard sheet sizes. Inch sheet sizes are referred to as ANSI A through V, Arch/Eng, and Generic. *ANSI* refers to the American National Standards Institute. Metric sheet sizes are DIN, ISO, and JIS A0 through A4. *DIN* refers to the German standard Deutsches Institüt Für Normung that is established by the German Institute for Standardization. *ISO* is the International Organization for Standardization, and *JIS* is the Japanese Industrial Standard. When you pick a sheet format such as ANSI B (in.), the selection is identified in both text boxes and an example is displayed in the Sample Title Block image as shown in Figure 3.9. AutoCAD LT places the border and title block in paper space. ***Paper space*** is the view in which AutoCAD LT provides you with a place for creating the finished layout for printing or plotting. Paper space is fully discussed in Chapter 13.

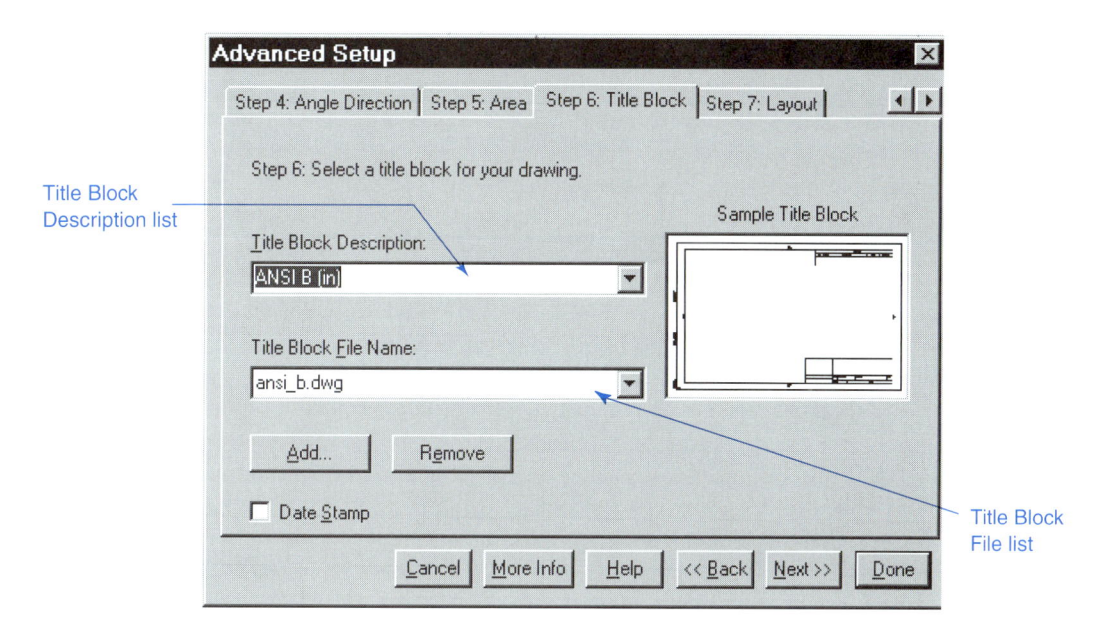

FIGURE 3.9 The Advanced Setup dialog box, Step 6: Title Block tab. Notice the selection ANSI B (in.) and the Sample Title Block image.

In the lower left corner of the Step 6: Title Block tab screen are the Add ... and Remove buttons and the Date Stamp toggle. These features are active when you select a title block from the list. The Add ... button accesses the Select Title Block dialog box where you can pick a desired title block format and give it a description. This allows you to place school or company standard title blocks in the list. The Remove button removes a highlighted title block from the list. Use this button with caution. Check the Date Stamp toggle to have the current date set for the creation of this title block.

Field Notes

- The date stamp feature places your login information (name and company or institution), along with the date, time, and current file name along the left side or at the top of the title block. If the combination of your name and company name is longer than 20 characters, it may overlap the date and time text. To reposition these items, you can use the ATTEDIT command, which is discussed in Chapter 12.

  Because your drawing has not yet been named when it receives the date stamp, the name is specified as *Drawing.dwg*. This also can be changed, using ATTEDIT or DDATTE (Chapter 12).
- ISO and DIN style title blocks do not support the date stamp feature.

Step 7: Layout
This tab allows you to choose the manner in which you work on a drawing relative to the sheet layout. AutoCAD LT refers to your drawing as a ***model*** and you work on the model in ***model space.*** The Layout tab provides a very brief description of model space and paper space by picking the What is paper space? button (see Figure 3.10A,B). You have the option of using advanced layout capabilities in paper space by picking Yes or

FIGURE 3.10 (A) The Step 7: Layout tab of the Advanced Setup dialog box. Pick the **W**hat is paper space? button to get examples and definitions of model space and paper space shown in the Information: Paper Space box displayed in Figure 3.10B. Pick the **D**one button when you are ready. (C) The selected sample title block and border with a single viewport displayed.

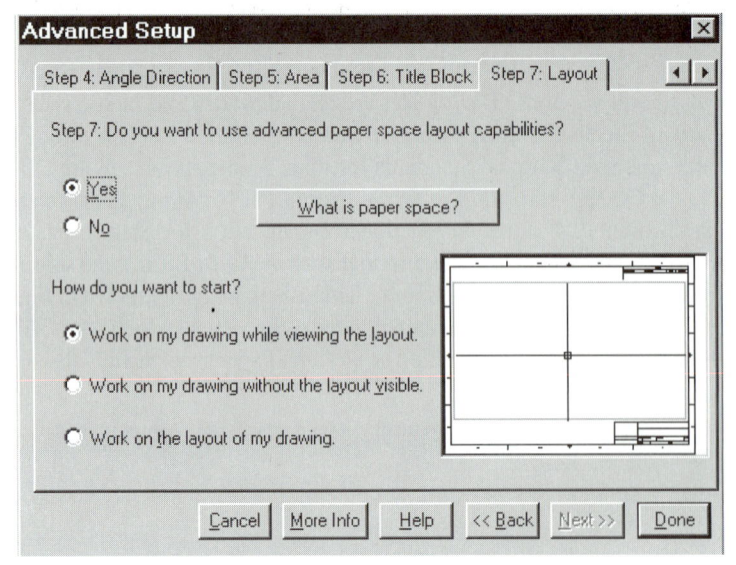

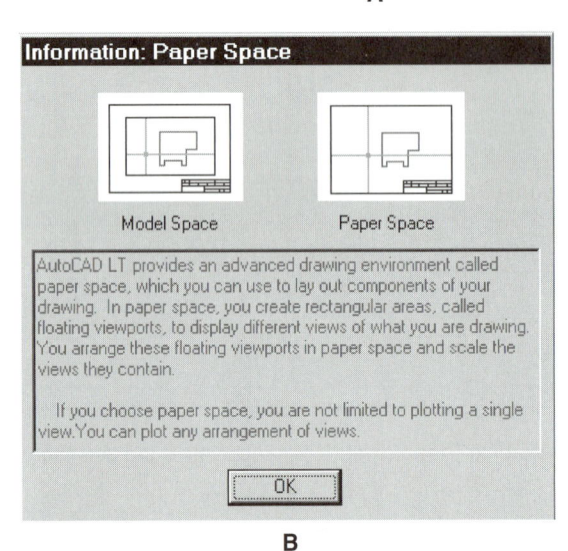

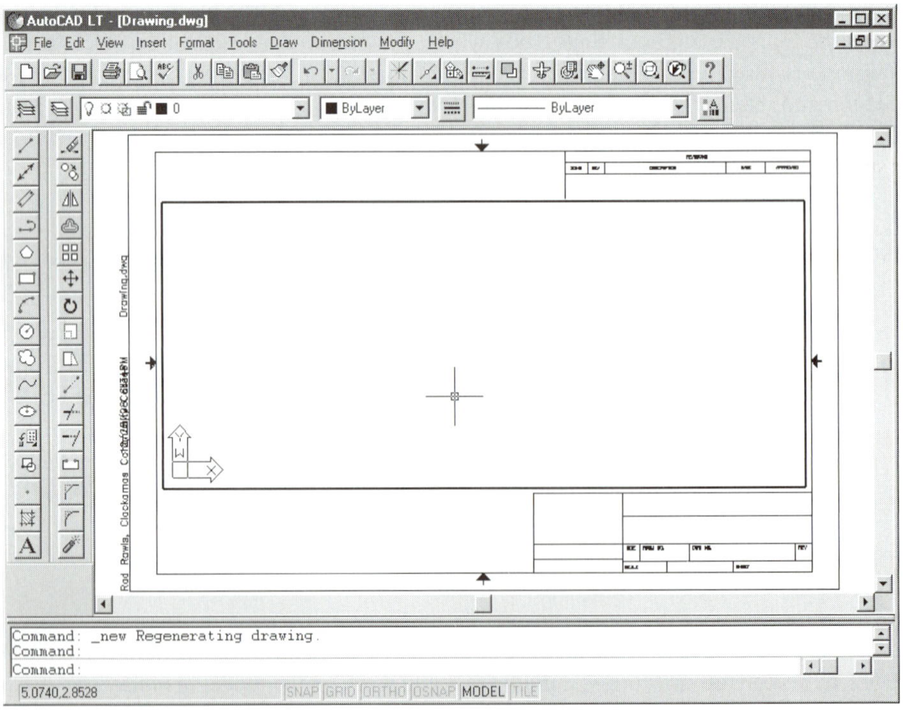

CHAPTER 3 ||| Drawing Basic Objects

No. In paper space, you can create viewports. ***Viewports*** are like windows that display the model space of a drawing in paper space.

Three following options are listed under How do you want to start?:

- Work on my drawing while viewing the layout.: This allows you to work on the drawing with the border and title block displayed. Notice the image in Figure 3.10C, which displays a single viewport inside the border and title block.
- Work on my drawing without the layout visible.: This lets you work on a drawing without the border and title block shown. If you pick this, only the screen cursor is displayed.
- Work on the layout of my drawing.: Pick this option to work on the layout without affecting the drawing in model space. You can add information to the title block or add general notes that are typically displayed with the drawing.

More about Model Space and Paper Space

When the final product of a drawing project requires a formal presentation in a title block and border, you should always use both model space and paper space for your drawing. As indicated previously, the actual drawing (the model) is created in model space. The title block and layout are created in paper space. As you learn more about AutoCAD LT, it will become easy to create custom layouts for specific needs. For now, while you are still learning basic drawing and editing skills, you may wish to use the Wizards to set up the paper space component of your drawing. You can add your own title blocks to the listing and allow AutoCAD LT to insert them into paper space.

If your drawing project does not require a formal presentation, you may wish to indicate that you do not want to use the advanced paper space layout capabilities, or you can use a different setup option.

The topic of paper and model space usage is discussed more extensively later in the text. For now, in the event you are using the Advanced Setup Wizard, you need to understand some fundamental concepts and learn how to use some basic controls.

It is best to think of paper space as a simple sheet of paper that overlays your drawing (model space). The sheet of paper holds items such as the title block and general notes. In order to see your drawing through the paper, one or more rectangular "holes" are cut in the paper. These "holes" are called ***floating model space viewports***. The Advanced Setup Wizard creates a single viewport for you to work with. Depending on the "How do you want to start?" option you select, you will be:

- in model space with paper space visible
- in model space without paper space visible
- in paper space

The primary controls you will need at this time are to switch the active space and control whether paper space is visible. The currently active space is indicated on the status bar as either Model or Paper. Double-click on Model to switch to paper space, or on Paper to switch to model space. If the word Tile (also on the status bar) is gray, then paper space is visible even when model space is active. Double-click on Tile to hide paper space and increase the usable display space on your screen. Double-click on Tile again to make paper space visible. Other controls are discussed later.

`MODEL TILE`

Exercise 3.1

1. Open AutoCAD LT if it is not already open. Use the Start Up dialog box or if AutoCAD LT is open, use the NEW command to access the Create New Drawing dialog box and select Advanced Setup.
2. Notice the Sample Units image displayed for the decimal units default. As a review from Chapter 2, pick each of the other four unit options and observe the Sample Units image for each. Pick the Decimal option and set the precision to 0.000 before going on.
3. Open the Step 2: Angle tab. Change the Precision to a couple of different settings and look at the Sample Angle image as you pick each of the angle unit options. Select Decimal Degrees and set the precision to 0.00 before you go on.
4. Select Step 3: Angle Measure and pick each of the four compass orientation options. Notice how the Angle Zero Direction image changes with each selection. Pick the East option before going on.
5. Access the Step 4: Angle Direction tab and notice the Angle Direction image for the Counter-Clockwise default. Pick the Clockwise option and see the difference in the image representation. Pick Counter-Clockwise before going on.
6. Pick the Step 5: Area tab and change the Width to 17 and the Length to 11.
7. Open the Step 6: Title Block folder. Access the Title Block Description drop-down list and pick several different title block formats while looking at the Sample Title Block image for each. Select ANSI B (in.) before going on.
8. Access the Step 7: Layout tab. Pick the What is paper space? button and read the Information: Paper Space dialog box. Pick OK. Notice how the image changes as you pick each of the How do you want to start? radio buttons. Pick Work on my drawing while viewing the layout. Pick Done and see the viewport displayed within the title block and border you selected.
9. Set Grid at .5 and Snap at .25. Draw a simple line object of your own design.
10. Use the Model, Paper, and Tile buttons on the status bar to switch the current space and view of paper space. Consider the potential applications for each option.
11. Save the drawing as EX3.1.

Starting from Scratch

The AutoCAD LT Start Up and Create New Drawing dialog boxes have a Start from Scratch button. Select this option if you want to set up a drawing with your own options. When you pick Start from Scratch, AutoCAD LT lets you choose either English or Metric default settings (see Figure 3.11). Starting from scratch

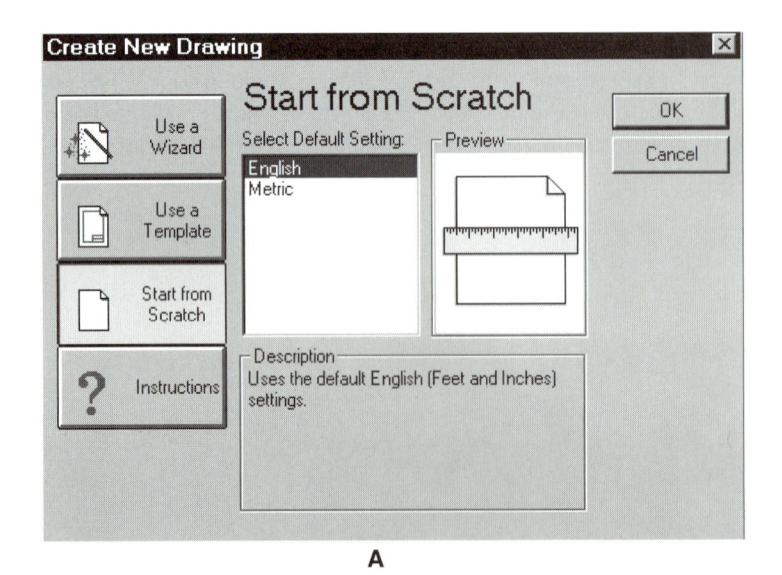

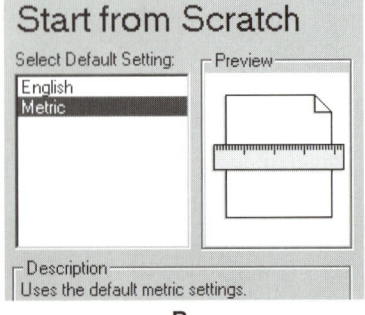

FIGURE 3.11 The AutoCAD LT Start from Scratch option allows you to select either (A) English (feet and inch) or (B) Metric default settings.

CHAPTER 3 ||| Drawing Basic Objects

may not be the best choice for new AutoCAD LT users, because it requires you to set up all your layout conditions on your own. This option always places you in model space.

Using an AutoCAD LT Template

AutoCAD LT provides you with many standard border and title block formats such as ANSI, ISO, DIN, JIS, and architectural, as discussed earlier with the Advanced Setup options. AutoCAD LT refers to these standard settings as a *template.* Another name for a template is a *prototype.* A prototype, or template, is a drawing file with preestablished settings. A discussion about creating and using prototypes is given later in this chapter. To use one of these templates, pick the Use a Template option in the Start Up or Create New Drawing dialog box. Choose the desired template from the Select a Template list as shown in Figure 3.12. The template that you select is displayed in the Preview image box and a Template Description is provided. In the Select a Template list, the aclt.dwt option allows you to start a drawing using feet and inch settings, whereas the acltiso.dwt choice is for metric settings. These options do not have title blocks. The .dwt file extension is for drawing templates.

FIGURE 3.12 In the AutoCAD LT Use a Template option, pick the desired template from the Select a Template list. Notice the selected template is displayed in the Preview box and a report is provided under the Template Description.

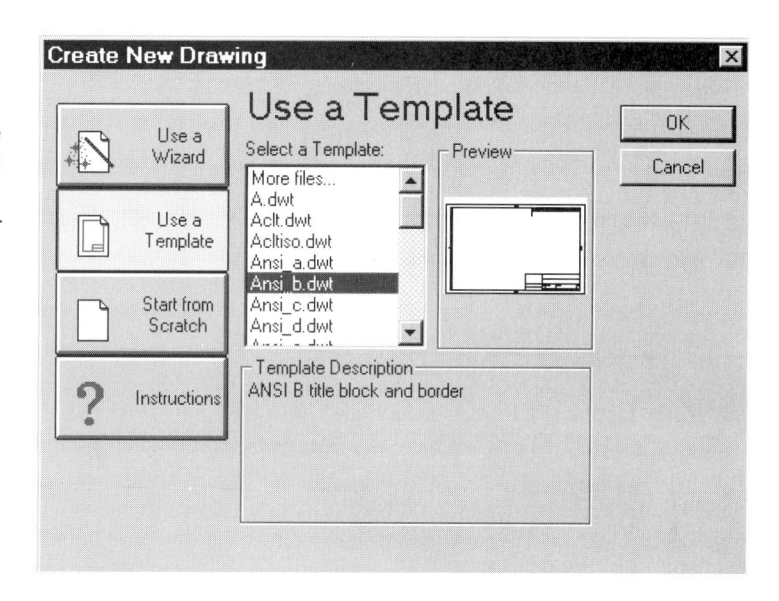

Setting Units and Limits Outside of the AutoCAD LT Setup

You have now seen how to set up an AutoCAD LT drawing using the Quick Setup and Advanced Setup options. Although this is a convenient way to set the drawing units and limits, you may need to change these settings during your drawing session, or you may just want additional flexibility. The drawing units may be changed at any time with the UNITS or DDUNITS commands. Using the UNITS command opens the AutoCAD LT Text Window where information and examples are given and your input is requested at the prompt line. Each prompt line contains a value in angle brackets such as <2>. Access the units command by typing -UN (hyphen UN) or UNITS at the Command: prompt. This represents the default value. The following example sets decimal units for a mechanical drawing:

UNITS
-UN

    Command: **-UN** or **UNITS** ↵
    Report formats: (Examples)

    1. Scientific   1.55E+01
    2. Decimal   15.50
    3. Engineering   1'-3.50"
    4. Architectural   1'-3 1/2"
    5. Fractional   15 1/2

    With the exception of Engineering and Architectural formats, these formats can be used with any basic unit of measurement. For example, Decimal mode is perfect for metric units as well as decimal English units.

    Enter choice, 1 to 5 <2>: ↵
    Number of digits to the right of decimal point (0 to 8) <4>: **3**↵

Systems of angular measure: (Examples)

1. Decimal degrees   45.0000
2. Degrees/minutes/seconds   45d0'0"
3. Grads   50.0000g
4. Radians   0.7854r
5. Surveyor's units   N 45d0'0" E

Enter choice, 1 to 5 <1>: ↵
Number of fractional places for display of angles (0 to 8) <4>: **2**↵

Direction for angle 0.00:
East   3 o'clock = 0.00
North   12 o'clock = 90.00
West   9 o'clock = 180.00
South   6 o'clock = 270.00
Enter direction for angle 0.00 <0.00>: ↵

Do you want angles measured clockwise? <N>: ↵
Command:

If you type 4 for Architectural or 5 for Fractional units, the next prompt is different from the previous example because you are asked to decide the denominator of the smallest fraction. The original default is 16. This specifies the smallest fractional increments to 1/16-in. units. Select the default by pressing Enter or type one of the other options followed by pressing Enter:

Enter choice, 1 to 5 <2>: **4** or **5**↵
Denominator of smallest fraction to display
(1, 2, 4, 8, 16, 32, 64, 128, or 256) <16>: ↵

When finished, press the F2 key or pick the Close button to close the AutoCAD LT Text Window.

Using the DDUNITS command is a faster way to set the units and angles because the Units Control dialog box is displayed for easy control of the settings. This command may be accessed by typing UN or DDUNITS or by picking Units … in the Format pull-down menu (see Figure 3.13A). Use the Units Control dialog box to pick one of the five buttons to select the desired Units format and one of the five buttons to choose the desired Angles format. Access the Precision: drop-down list in the Units compartment to set the

Format
  Units...

DDUNITS
  UN

FIGURE 3.13 (A) Use the DDUNITS command to access the Units Control dialog box. (B) Pick the Direction … button in the Units Control dialog box to get the Direction Control dialog box.

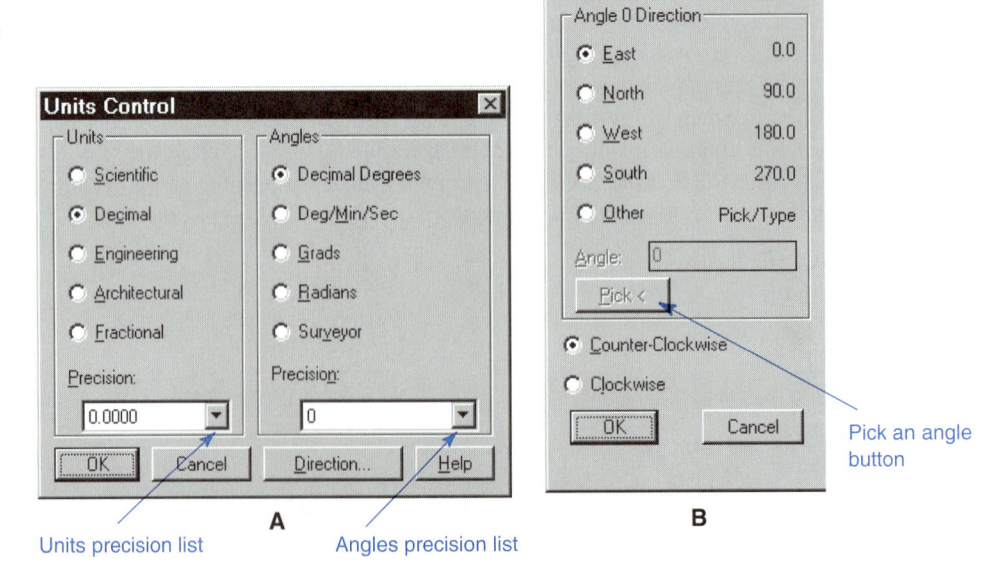

number of digits to the right of the decimal point. Pick the Precision down arrow in the Angles compartment to get the options for the number of fractional places for the display of angles.

Look at Figure 3.13A and notice the Direction ... button. Pick this button to access the Direction Control dialog box shown in Figure 3.13B. This dialog box has the standard East, North, West, and South options. You can also pick Other to activate the Angle text box and the Pick< button. The Angle text box allows you to specify the angle that you want to be the angle zero direction. Select the Pick < button to pick two points on the screen that establish the angle zero direction. The Direction Control dialog box also contains selections for either Counter-Clockwise or Clockwise angle measurements.

Setting the sheet size may also be done using the LIMITS command by typing **LM** or **LIMITS** or by picking Drawing Limits in the Format pull-down menu. The LIMITS command asks you to specify the coordinates of the lower left corner and the upper right corner of the drawing area. The lower left corner is usually 0,0 but you can specify something else (0,0 is the drawing default so press Enter to accept this coordinate). The upper right corner usually identifies the upper right corner of the drawing area. If you want a 17 × 11 drawing area, then the upper right corner is 17,11. The command works like this:

Command: **LM** or **LIMITS** ↵
Reset Model space limits:
ON/OFF/⟨Lower left corner⟩ <0.0000,0.0000>: ↵
Upper right corner <12.0000,9.0000>: **17,11**↵
Command:

The LIMITS command also provides an ON and an OFF option. Turning limits on has the effect of restricting the coordinates you can enter when drawing objects to the rectangular area defined by the limits settings. In the following example the limits are set to 0,0 and 17,11, and limits are turned on:

Command: LINE↵
From point: 10,7.25↵
To point: 18,7.25↵
**Outside limits

To point: @8<0↵
**Outside limits

To point: *Cancel*

Notice that the coordinate entry method does not matter. If the result is drawing an object that goes outside the limits, an error message is displayed and no object is drawn. Relatively few applications require limits to be turned on, so limits are off by default.

Field Notes

When you set the limits manually using the LIMITS command, the currently displayed area of your drawing does not change from the previous limits setting. To display your current limits, select the View pull-down menu, then pick the All option from the Zoom cascade. Additional display change commands and options are covered in Chapter 4.

> **Exercise 3.2**
>
> 1. Open AutoCAD LT if it is not already open. Use the Start Up or Create New Drawing dialog box.
> 2. Pick Start from Scratch. Notice the Select Default Setting: that is highlighted. Look at the related Preview image and Description box.
> 3. If English is highlighted, pick Metric, or if Metric is highlighted, pick English. Now, look at the related Preview image and Description box to see the difference.
> 4. Pick the Use a Template button. Notice the list of Select a Template: options. Pick one of each type of template formats from the list, such as ansi_b.dwt, archeng.dwt, din_a2.dwt, iso_a2.dwt, and jis_a2.dwt. Look at the Preview image and read the description as you make each selection.
> 5. Go to the Select a Template option that looked most interesting to you during Step 4 and double-click on that option. The AutoCAD LT screen displays the border and title block that you selected. As always, the screen cursor is available for you to make a drawing.
> 6. Turn the limits on and try to draw a line that extends beyond the limits area. While still at the To point: prompt, enter the limits command transparently by typing **'LM** and turn limits off. Try again to draw the same line.
> 7. Draw a few lines of your own design and then print it if a printer is available.
> 8. Save the drawing as EX3.2.

Using Template Drawings

As you learned earlier, templates are drawing files that contain established standards and settings. When you begin a new drawing with the Use a Template option, you are starting with a group of settings that are already set up and saved in the template file. When you begin a new drawing with the Quick Setup, Advanced Setup, or Start from Scratch options, you are working with a series of settings that you establish combined with standard AutoCAD LT settings. Every type of drawing you make should have a set of standards that you use. For example, there are different standards for mechanical, architectural, and electrical drawings. Templates typically contain correctly preset values for common drawing features, including:

- Standard limits with a border and title block
- Grid and snap settings
- Units and angle values
- Text standards and typical notes (Chapter 9)
- Dimensioning standards (Chapter 11)

Customizing Existing Template Drawings

As previously discussed, AutoCAD LT has many templates available for you to use for the prototypes of your drawings. The Use a Template option lets you move directly into a border and title block format in a drawing where some or all the available settings are already configured for the type and size of drawing you are creating. However, the templates provided with AutoCAD LT 98 have very generic settings and may need to be adjusted. After entering the desired format, you can establish additional drawing settings that are considered common for the type of drawing you are making. The following list shows basic settings that might be used for a drawing in the mechanical and architectural drafting fields:

	Mechanical	*Architectural*
Select a Template:	ansi_c.dwt	archeng.dwt
Grid	.5	12
Snap	.125	2

A template of this type is very fundamental. Additional settings such as text and dimension styles are discussed later in this text. You need to save your drawing as a template for later use after entering each of the specific desired settings. Follow these steps to save the template for future use:

CHAPTER 3 ||| Drawing Basic Objects

1. Enter the SAVEAS command. This opens the Save Drawing As dialog box shown in Figure 3.14A.
2. Access the Drawing Template File (*.dwt) type in the Save as type: list, as shown in Figure 3.14B. The .dwt extension is a drawing template file.
3. Type a name for your drawing template in the File name: text box and then pick Save, as shown in Figure 3.14C. Give your template a name that correlates with the type of drawing you are creating. For example, choose something such as MECHANICAL_IN_B for a drawing to be done using ANSI standards, inch dimensions, and a B size (11 × 17-in.) sheet. Enter a name such as MECHANICAL_MM_A3 for a drawing to be done using ANSI or ISO standards, metric dimensions, and an A3 size (420 × 297-mm) sheet. Use a name such as ARCHIT_C for an architectural drawing done on a C size (18 × 24-in.) sheet.
4. The Template Description dialog box is automatically displayed. Type a description of your template in the Description text box, as shown in Figure 3.14D. A good description helps you identify the template later when you pick it from the Start Up or Create New Drawing dialog box. Use a description such as "Mechanical drawings using ANSI/IN. with B size sheet and title block" or "Architectural drawing with C size sheet and title block."
5. While still in the Template Description dialog box, pick the desired unit style, English (inch) or Metric, in the Measurement drop-down list. Pick OK when you are finished.

FIGURE 3.14 Naming, describing, and saving your template-drawing. (A) The Save Drawing As dialog box. (B) Access the Drawing Template File [*.dwt] in the Save as type: list. (C) Type the template name in the File name: text box and pick the Save button. (D) Type the description of your template in the Description text box and enter the desired units, inch or metric, in the Measurement text box. Pick OK when ready.

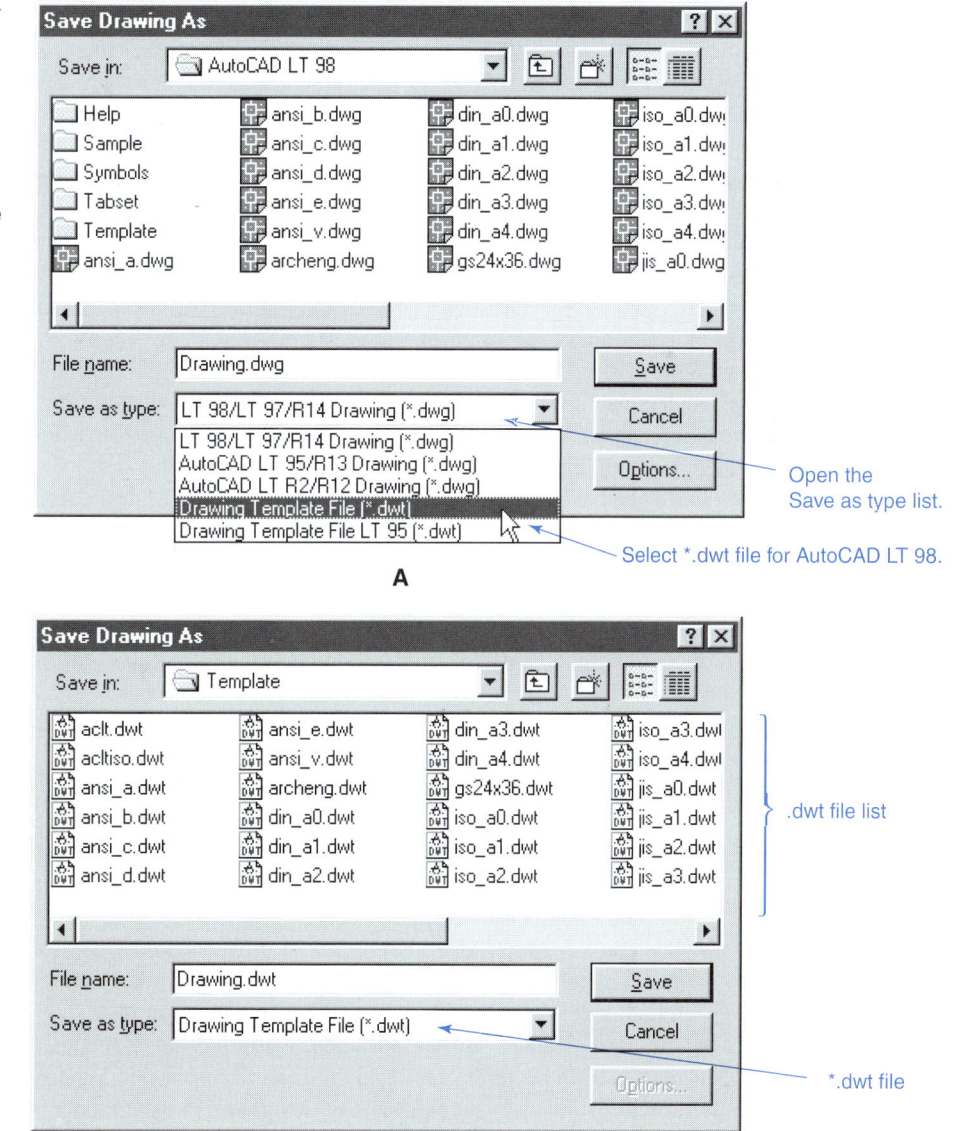

FIGURE 3.14 continued

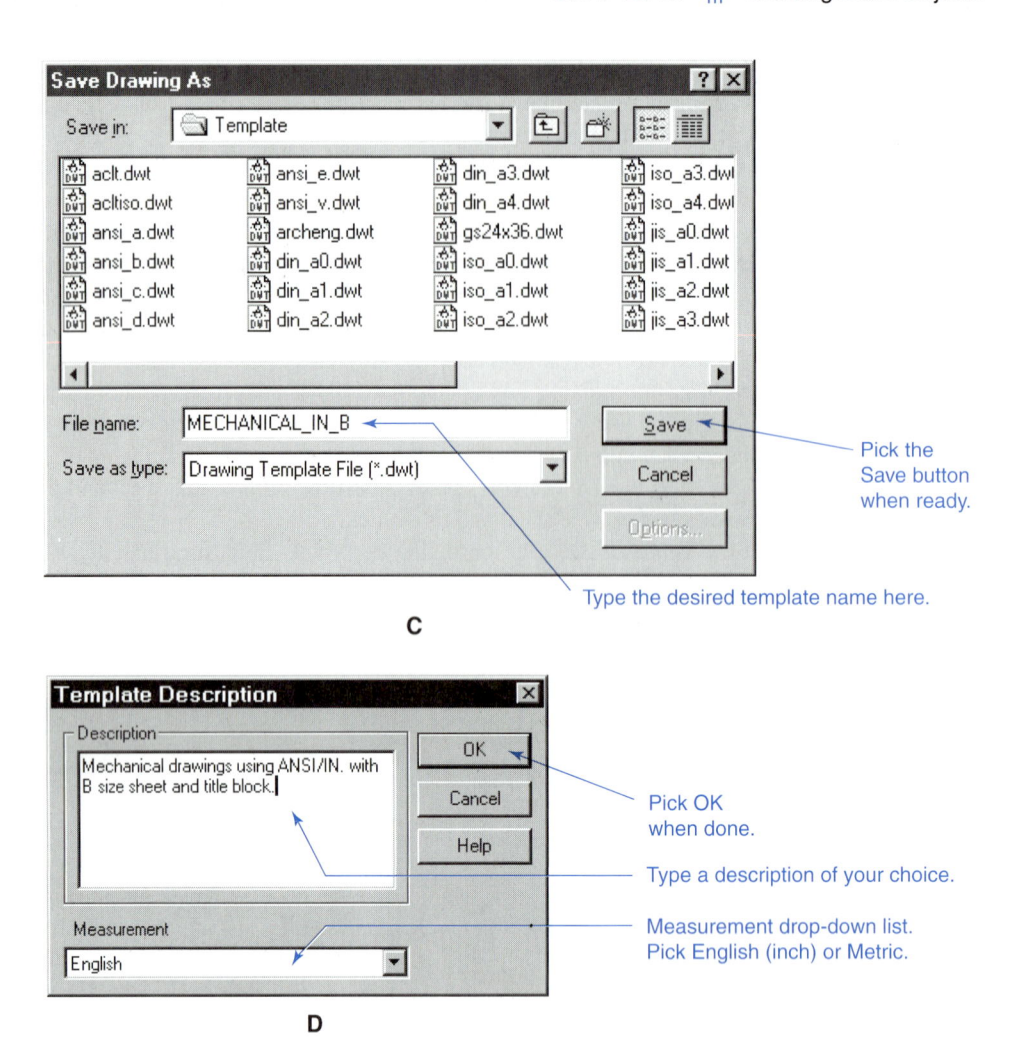

C

Pick the Save button when ready.

Type the desired template name here.

D

Pick OK when done.

Type a description of your choice.

Measurement drop-down list. Pick English (inch) or Metric.

The new template file is saved in the Template folder with the .dwt extension. Now you can access the template any time you want it in the Select a Template: list of the Use a Template option in the Start Up or Create New Drawing dialog box.

Once you have a template established, you can use it as the beginning basis for each drawing of its type such as mechanical, architectural, or electrical, for example. Use the template to prepare the desired drawing and then use the SAVEAS command to save the drawing with a file name that describes the specific drawing. This leaves the template unchanged for use each time you want it. Drawing names, for example, might relate to a part number or product in mechanical drawing, to a project name and drawing type such as a floor plan in architectural drawing, or to a product schematic in electronic drafting.

Field Notes

- When you save a new template file, you are automatically moved to the AutoCAD LT 98\Template folder. By default, this is where AutoCAD LT looks to determine what templates are available, so only those files saved in this folder are displayed in the list of available templates. To look in other folders, pick More files ... from the list.
- You can tell AutoCAD LT to look in a different folder by selecting Preferences ... from the Tools menu. In the Preferences dialog box, pick the Files tab and change the folder name found under the *Template Drawing File Location* setting.
- AutoCAD LT also can use normal drawing files as templates. In the template list, pick More files ... from the template list. In the Select Template dialog box, pick the Files of type: list and specify Drawing (*.dwg) files. A drawing used in this manner is not opened, it is just used as a model for the creation of your new drawing.

CHAPTER 3 ||| Drawing Basic Objects

Through the Window...

Your file selection dialog boxes may display only file names and not the file extension. You can turn the display of file extensions on or off as desired. This is a function of the operating system, not AutoCAD LT. Here's how:

1. Pick the Start button from the task bar, select Programs and then Windows (95/98/NT) Explorer.
2. Select Options... from the View menu.
3. On the View tab of the Options dialog box, either place or remove the check mark next to Hide file extensions for known file types.
4. The change will take effect the next time you start AutoCAD LT 98.

Exercise 3.3

1. Open AutoCAD LT if it is not already open. Use the Start Up or Create Drawing dialog box.
2. Pick Use a Template.
3. Access a template of your choice in the Select a Template: list. If you are interested in mechanical drafting, pick a template such as ansi_b.dwt for an inch drawing or iso_a2.dwt for a metric drawing. If you are working in architectural drafting, try the archeng.dwt template. Double-click or highlight the desired template and pick OK.
4. The template of your choice is now displayed on the screen. You can modify it in any way to suit your drafting needs. For a very fundamental custom template, enter the settings that may be used for a drawing in the mechanical or architectural drafting fields as you desire:

	Mechanical	Architectural
Grid	.5	12
Snap	.125	2

5. Enter the SAVEAS command and pick Drawing Template in the Save File as Type: file list.
6. Type a desired template name in the File Name: text box. Use a name of your choice or as described in the previous discussion.
7. Type a description of your template in the Template Description box. Select or type the desired units in the Measurement box. Pick the OK button.
8. Enter the NEW command and look through the Select a Template: list of the Create New Drawing dialog box until you find the name of the template you just created. Access the new template.
9. Make a simple drawing of your choice.
10. Save the drawing as EX3.3.

✓ LEARNING CHECKPOINT

☐ Where is the Advanced Setup option found?
☐ Write an example of decimal degrees and degrees/minutes/seconds.
☐ Make a sketch of the surveyor's angle N45°W.
☐ Name at least four standard border and title block formats provided by AutoCAD LT.
☐ Describe model space and paper space.
☐ What advantage is provided by using templates?

Drawing Curved Objects

In Chapter 2 you learned how to draw lines and how to edit your drawing by erasing. The rest of the discussion in this chapter teaches you how to draw circles, arcs, ellipses, rectangles, polygons, and filled objects. As you go through this discussion, keep in mind that prompts answered with ⟨pick a point⟩ in the examples can also use absolute, polar, or relative coordinate entry.

Drawing Circles

Circles are drawn using the CIRCLE command, which is found by accessing the Circle cascade in the Draw pull-down menu, by picking the Circle button in the Draw toolbar, or by typing **C** or **CIRCLE** at the Command: prompt. Four options can be used to draw a circle. These options are based on features related to the circle and are discussed next.

Drawing a Circle with the Center and Radius

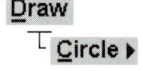

You can draw a circle by selecting a center point and then either picking or typing a radius value. The *radius* is the distance from the center to the circumference of the circle. To do this, go to the Draw pull-down menu and pick the Circle cascade followed by Center, Radius, or pick the Circle toolbar button, or type **C** or **Circle** at the Command: prompt. The Command: prompt asks you to pick a center point. After you select a center point, move the cursor to drag the circle to a desired radius and pick or type a specific radius value. If you pick a point, the distance between the center point and the next point you pick is used as the radius value (see Figure 3.15). The Command: looks like this as you draw a circle:

Command: **C** or **CIRCLE**↵
3P/2P/TTR/<Center point>: ⟨pick a center point⟩
Diameter/<Radius>: ⟨type a radius value or pick the radius⟩
Command:

FIGURE 3.15 Drawing a circle using the Center, Radius option.

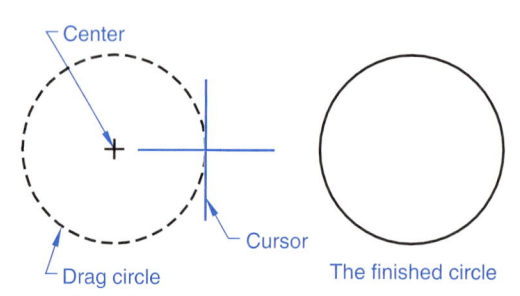

Pick the center point and drag the circle and pick the radius or type a radius

Field Notes

When you are finished drawing a circle, you can press Enter or the space bar at the Command: prompt to immediately start the **CIRCLE** command again. The previously used radius value is displayed in angle brackets <>. The brackets are not visible for the first circle drawn in any drawing session. You can press Enter to accept this value or type a new value.

Drawing a Circle with the Center and Diameter

A circle can also be drawn by selecting a center point and then either picking or typing a diameter value. *Diameter* is the distance across the circle and passing through the center. To do this, go to the Draw pull-down menu and pick Circle followed by Center, Diameter. The Command: prompt asks you to pick a center point. After you select a center point, move the cursor to drag the circle to a desired diameter and pick or type a specific diameter value. When you use the Center, Diameter option, the screen cursor extends beyond the circle a distance equal to the radius. This process shows you the diameter as the distance between the center and the cursor (see Figure 3.16).

Command: _circle 3P/2P/TTR/<Center point>: ⟨pick a center point⟩
Diameter/<Radius>_d Diameter: ⟨type a diameter value or pick the diameter⟩
Command:

Additionally, you can type **C** or **CIRCLE** at the Command: prompt and use the Diameter option. When using the Diameter option at the keyboard, you need to type **D** at the Diameter/<Radius>: prompt like this:

CHAPTER 3 ||| Drawing Basic Objects   **101**

    Command: **C** or **CIRCLE**↵
    3P/2P/TTR/<Center point>: ⟨*pick a center point*⟩
    Diameter/<Radius>: **D**↵
    Diameter: ⟨*type a diameter value or pick the diameter*⟩
    Command:

If the Center, Diameter option is picked from the pull-down menu, the diameter option is automatically used. When you use the Diameter option, the screen cursor extends beyond the circle a distance equal to the radius.

FIGURE 3.16 Drawing a circle using the Center, Diameter option.

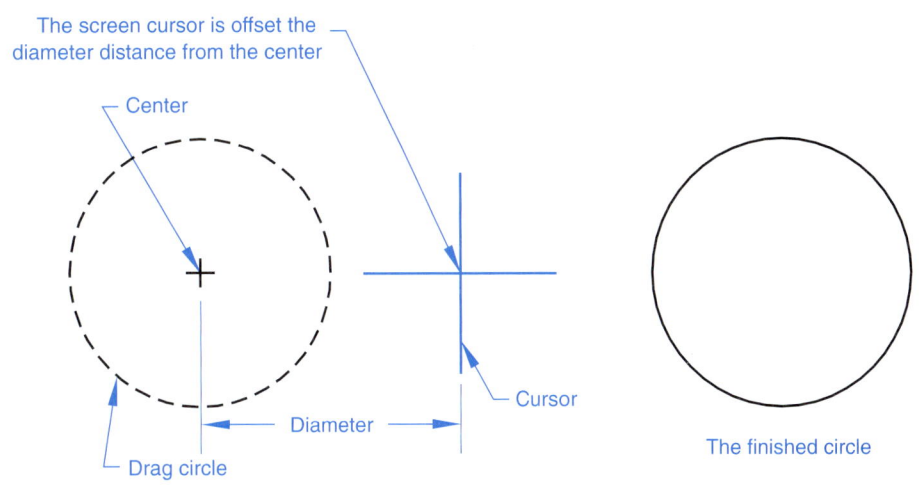

The screen cursor is offset the diameter distance from the center

Center

Drag circle

Diameter

Cursor

The finished circle

Pick the center point and then type the diameter value or drag the circle to a desired diameter and pick

Drawing a Circle with the 2 Points Option

A circle can be defined by specifying two points on the diameter of the circle. The points can be picked freehand or entered from the keyboard using any standard coordinate entry method. You can pick Circle from the Draw pull-down menu and select 2 Points, or use the 2P option at the command line (see Figure 3.17). The prompt sequence is as follows:

    Command: Circle↵
    3P/2P/TTR/<Center point>: 2P↵
    First point on diameter: ⟨*pick the first point*⟩
    Second point on diameter: ⟨*pick the second point*⟩
    Command:

FIGURE 3.17 Drawing a circle using the 2 Points option.

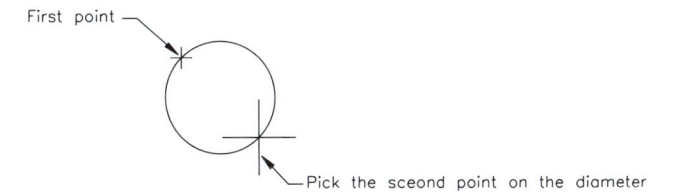

First point

Pick the sceond point on the diameter

Drawing a Circle with the 3 Points Option

You can draw a circle by picking three points on the circumference. The ***circumference*** is the perimeter line of the circle. To do this, pick Circle and then 3 Points in the Draw pull-down menu or use the **3P** option at the command line. AutoCAD LT asks you to select the First point, Second point, and Third point. When using the pull-down menu, AutoCAD LT automatically asks for the points. After you pick the second point, AutoCAD LT drags the circle to the place where you pick the third point (see Figure 3.18). When using the keyboard, type **3P** like this:

    Command: **C** or **CIRCLE**↵
    3P/2P/TTR/<Center point>: **3P**↵
    First point: ⟨*pick the first point*⟩
    Second point: ⟨*pick the second point*⟩
    Third point: ⟨*pick the third point*⟩
    Command:

FIGURE 3.18 Drawing a circle with the 3 Points option.

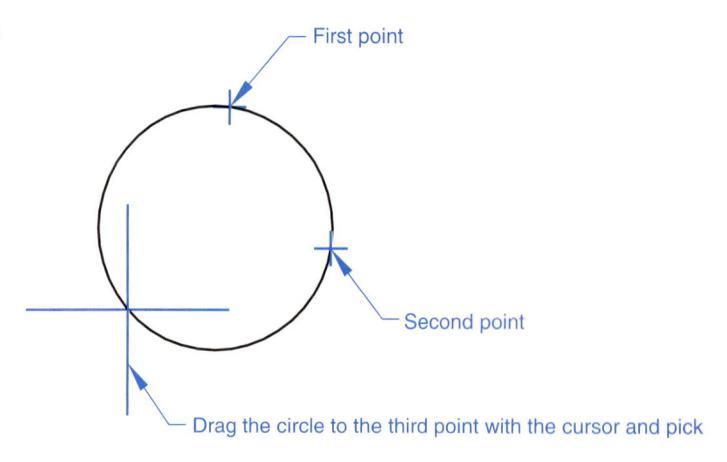

Drawing a Circle Tangent to Two Objects

AutoCAD LT lets you easily draw a circle tangent to two other objects such as lines, arcs, and circles. ***Tangent*** means that the circle touches the objects at only one point without intersecting or crossing the objects. Draw a circle tangent to objects by picking Circle and then Tan, Tan, Radius in the Draw pull-down menu, or type the **TTR** option at the prompt line. When using this option, AutoCAD LT asks you to pick the object with which the circle is to be tangent, and then enter the radius of the circle. Figure 3.19 shows examples of drawing a circle tangent to two lines, to a line and a circle, and to two circles. When you select Tan, Tan, Radius from the pull-down menu, AutoCAD LT automatically issues the TTR option. After entering the TTR option, AutoCAD LT asks you for the Tangent spec. ***Spec*** is the abbreviation for specification. The tangent specifications are the objects to which your circle will be tangent. Enter **TTR** at the keyboard like this:

Command: **C** or **CIRCLE**↵
3P/2P/TTR/<Center point>: **TTR**↵
Enter Tangent spec: ⟨*pick the first object*⟩
Enter second Tangent spec: ⟨*pick the second object*⟩
Radius <default>: ⟨*type the desired radius* ↵⟩
Command:

FIGURE 3.19 Drawing a circle using the Tangent, Tangent, Radius option.

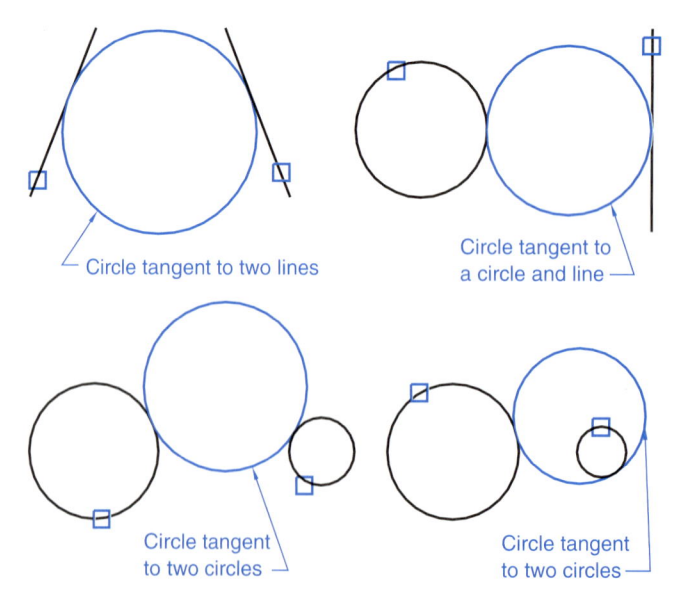

□ This symbol represents the tangent specs (pick points)

CHAPTER 3 ||| Drawing Basic Objects   103

Field Notes

- When you point to an object to use for a tangency specification, a marker will appear at the cursor location. If you stop your cursor movement while the marker is visible, a tool tip–like feature called a *SnapTip* appears at the cursor location. These items are part of an important feature in AutoCAD LT called *AutoSnap*. In this application, the SnapTip reads Deferred Tangent… and it indicates that AutoCAD LT will attempt to find a location where tangency occurs, based on subsequent input. The AutoSnap feature is covered in detail in Chapter 6.
- If you are drawing a circle tangent to two angled line segments and the radius is too large, the circle is automatically placed beyond the lines. If the radius of the circle that you want tangent to two objects is too small, AutoCAD LT gives you the message "Circle does not exist."

Exercise 3.4

1. Open AutoCAD LT if it is not already open. Use the setup option of your choice. A border and title block are not required.
2. Set limits at 8.5,11.
3. Draw the objects shown using the CIRCLE command options specified. The exact sizes are up to you, except for the objects where specific dimensions are given. Do not draw dimensions.
4. Save as EX3.4.

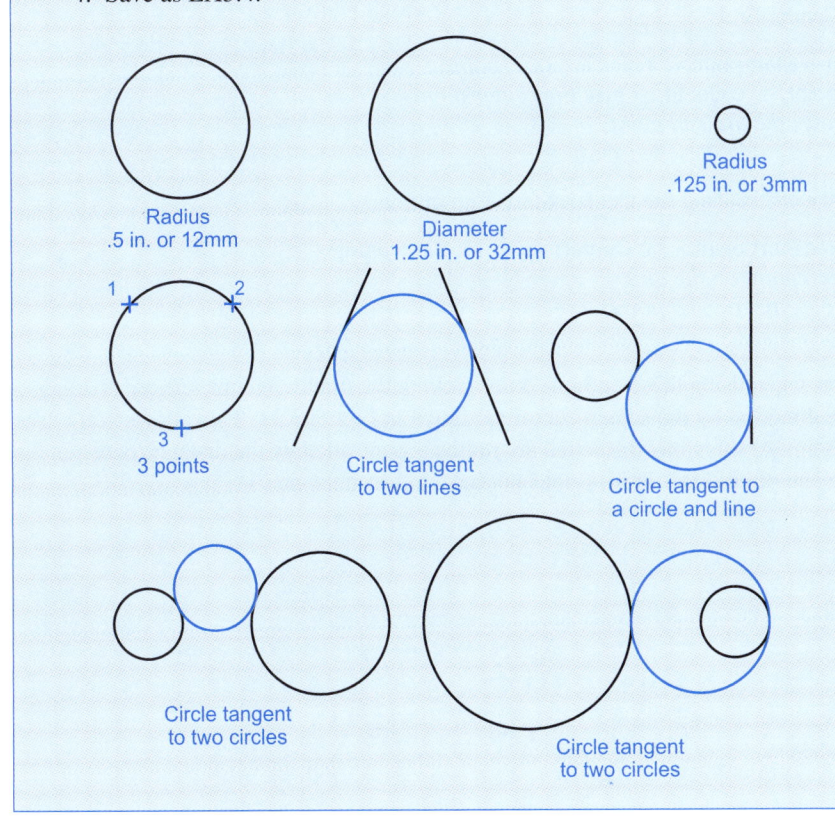

Radius
.5 in. or 12mm

Diameter
1.25 in. or 32mm

Radius
.125 in. or 3mm

3 points

Circle tangent
to two lines

Circle tangent to
a circle and line

Circle tangent
to two circles

Circle tangent
to two circles

Drawing Arcs

AutoCAD LT provides several methods for drawing arcs. The variety of options gives you maximum flexibility when drawing arcs. The ARC command is found in the Draw pull-down menu and in the Draw toolbar, or you can type **A** or **ARC** at the Command: prompt.

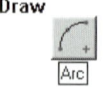

Drawing Arcs by Specifying Three Points

When the ARC command is entered at the keyboard, the default is an arc drawn by picking three points on the arc. The three-point method is also available by selecting Arc and then 3 Points in the Draw pull-down menu, or by picking the Arc toolbar button. AutoCAD LT asks for three points along the arc:

Command: **A** or **ARC**↵
Center/<Start point>: ⟨*pick the first point on the arc*⟩
Center/End/<Second point>: ⟨*pick the second point on the arc*⟩
End point: ⟨*pick the third point on the arc*⟩
Command:

After picking the second point, the arc is dragged into place as you decide where to place the third point. Figure 3.20 shows arcs drawn with the three-point option.

FIGURE 3.20 Drawing arcs using the 3 Points option.

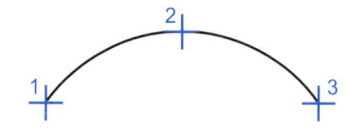

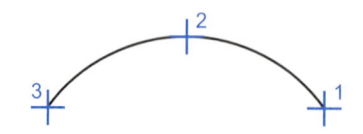

Drawing Arcs Using the Start, Center, End Options

In some situations, you may know the location of the start point, the center of the arc, and the arc end point, or you may know the center location, the start, and the end. These options are found in the Draw pull-down menu by picking Arc followed by Start, Center, End or Center, Start, End in the cascading submenu. AutoCAD LT automatically answers the option prompts when you use the pull-down menu. This is the command sequence when using Start, Center, End:

Command: _arc Center/<Start point>: ⟨*pick the start point*⟩
Center/End/<Second point>: _c Center: ⟨*pick the center point*⟩
Angle/<End point>: ⟨*pick the arc end point*⟩
Command:

This is what AutoCAD LT asks when using the Center, Start, End option:

Command: _arc Center/<Start point>: _c Center: ⟨*pick the start point*⟩
Start point: ⟨*pick the first point on the arc*⟩
Angle/<End point>: ⟨*pick the arc end point*⟩
Command:

Something interesting happens when using these options. After picking the first two items, the arc is dragged in a default counterclockwise direction by the screen cursor as shown in Figure 3.21. This allows you to see the arc as you select the end point. At this time, the actual arc radius is controlled by the distance between the first point and the center. The end point that you pick does not have to be on the arc.

FIGURE 3.21 Drawing arcs using the Start, Center, and End options.

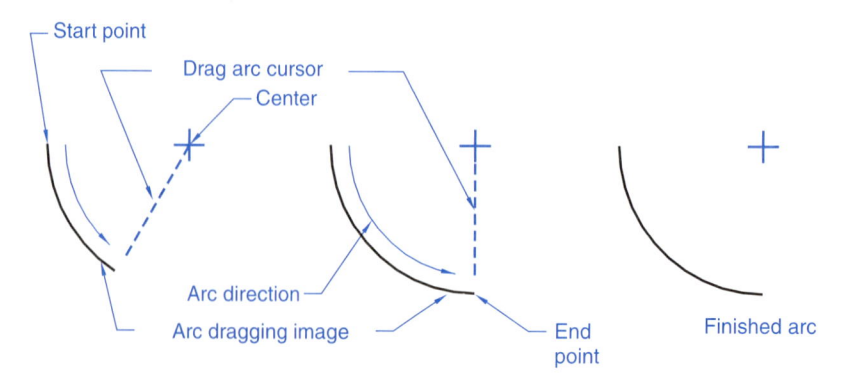

When entering these options at the keyboard, you need to type the capitalized letter of the desired option at the prompt line. The Start point option is the default at the first prompt, or you can begin with the Center option like this:

CHAPTER 3 ||| Drawing Basic Objects

Command: **A** or **ARC**↵
Center/<Start point>: **C**↵
Start point: ⟨*pick the arc start point*⟩
Angle/<End point>: ⟨*pick the arc end point*⟩
Command:

Drawing Arcs Using the Angle Options
AutoCAD LT lets you draw arcs using a combination of the start point, end point, center, and included angle. The included angle specifies degrees in a counterclockwise direction. A negative angle can be used to draw the arc in a clockwise direction. An ***included angle*** is the angle formed between the start point, end point, and center of the arc as shown in Figure 3.22. These options are found in the Draw pull-down menu as Start, Center, Angle; Start, End, Angle; and Center, Start, Angle.

FIGURE 3.22 Drawing arcs using the Included Angle option.

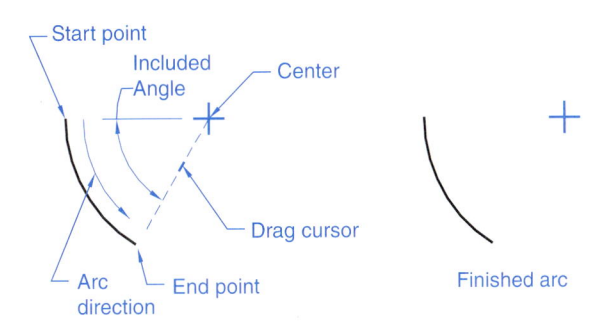

When you select the desired option from the Draw pull-down menu, AutoCAD LT automatically issues the prompts based on the option chosen. This is an example of the prompts and responses when using the Start, Center, Angle option:

Command: _arc Center/<Start point>: ⟨*pick a start point*⟩
Center/End/<Second point>: _c enter: ⟨*pick a center point*⟩
Angle/<End point>: _a Included angle: ⟨*type an angle value such as* **45**⟩
Command:

If you want to enter the ARC command using the Angle option at the keyboard, just enter **A** at the prompt. For example, use the Center, Start, Angle option like this:

Command: **A** or **ARC**↵
Center/<Start point>: **C**↵
Center: ⟨*pick the center point*⟩
Start point : ⟨*pick the start point*⟩
Angle/<End point>: **A**↵
Included angle: ⟨*type an angle such as* **60**⟩
Command:

Drawing Arcs Using the Length of Chord Option
A chord is defined as a line that connects two points on a curve. AutoCAD LT allows the definition of an arc based on the start point, center point, and the length of the chord. If the specified chord length is positive, the minor arc is drawn counterclockwise from the start point. If the length is negative the major arc is drawn counterclockwise. Figure 3.23 illustrates the creation of an arc using this method. The prompt sequence is shown here:

Command: **ARC**↵
Center/<Start point>: ⟨*pick a point*⟩
Center/End/<Second point>: **C**↵
Center: ⟨*pick a point*⟩
Angle/Length of chord/<End point>: **L**↵
Length of chord: **1.5**↵

FIGURE 3.23 Drawing arcs using the Length of Chord option.

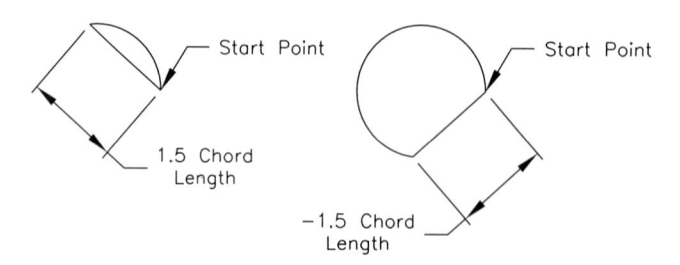

Drawing Arcs Using the Radius Option

The Radius option is used with the start and end points specified to define an arc. When a positive radius value is used, the minor arc is drawn. If the radius entry is negative, the major arc is drawn. Figure 3.24 illustrates the use of this option. The prompt sequence is as follows:

Command: **ARC**↵
Center/<Start point>: ⟨*pick a point*⟩
Center/End/<Second point>: **E**↵
End point: ⟨*pick a point*⟩
Angle/Direction/Radius/<Center point>: **R**↵
Radius: **1**↵

FIGURE 3.24 Drawing arcs using the Radius option.

Drawing Arcs Using the Direction Option

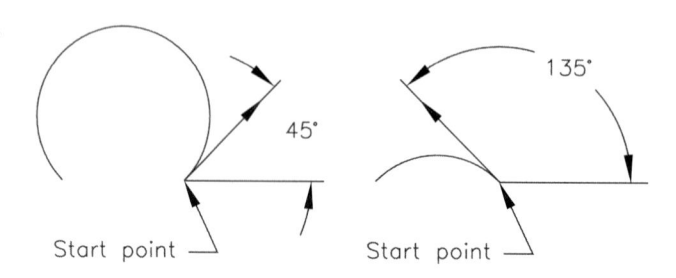

Using the Direction option, you can specify the direction of travel for an arc at its start point based on a specified start and end point. Because this option allows you to specify the direction of travel for the arc from its start point, it may not always be drawn counterclockwise. Figure 3.25 shows this option in use. The prompt sequence looks like this:

Command: **ARC**↵
Center/<Start point>: ⟨*pick a point*⟩
Center/End/<Second point>: **E**↵
End point: ⟨*pick a point*⟩
Angle/Direction/Radius/<Center point>: **D**↵
Direction from start point: **45**↵

FIGURE 3.25 Drawing arcs using the Direction option.

Drawing an Arc from a Previously Drawn Line or Arc

It is easy to draw an arc tangent to the end of a previously drawn line or arc. To do this, enter the ARC command immediately after drawing the line or arc that you plan to connect. After entering the ARC command, at the first prompt, press the Enter key or the space bar. Doing this automatically makes the end point of the previously drawn line or arc the start point of the new arc as shown in Figure 3.26. You can also use the Draw pull-down menu by selecting Arc followed by Continue. The command sequence looks like this:

CHAPTER 3 ||| Drawing Basic Objects 107

Command: **A** or **ARC**⏎
Center/<Start point>: ⏎
End point: ⟨*pick the arc end point*⟩
Command:

You can connect a series of tangent arcs by continuing this process until all of the desired arcs have been connected.

FIGURE 3.26 Drawing arcs continued from previous lines or arcs.

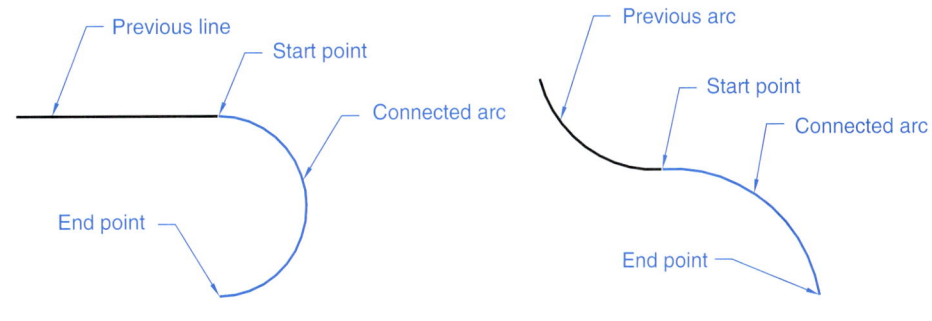

Connecting an arc to a previously drawn line

Connecting an arc to a previously drawn arc

Field Notes

You can also draw a line from a previously drawn arc or line by using the Continue option previously described. To do this, draw a desired arc and then enter the LINE command. Press the Enter key or space bar at the From point: prompt like this:

Command: **L** or **LINE**⏎
From point: ⏎
To point: ⟨*pick the line end point*⟩
To point: ⏎
Command:

Exercise 3.5

1. Open AutoCAD LT if it is not already open. Use the setup option of your choice. A border and title block are not required.
2. Set limits at 8.5,11.
3. Draw the objects shown using the ARC command options specified. The exact sizes are up to you.
4. Save as EX3.5.

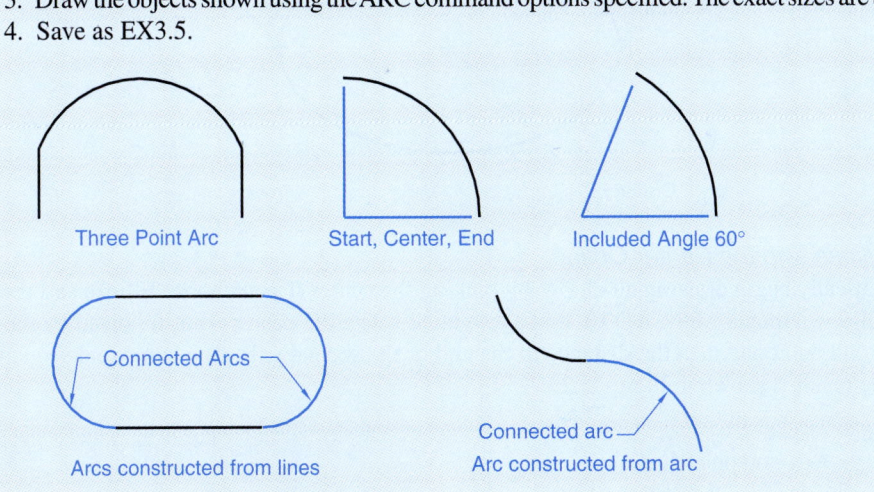

Three Point Arc   Start, Center, End   Included Angle 60°

Arcs constructed from lines

Arc constructed from arc

Drawing Ellipses

Draw
 [Ellipse]

Draw
 └ Ellipse▸

ELLIPSE
EL

An *ellipse* is commonly referred to as an oval, but the technical definition is an object that is drawn by a curve that has a constant value equal to the sum of its distance from two fixed points. One of the primary uses of an ellipse is for showing a circle on an inclined surface. The length of an ellipse is called the ***major axis*** and the width is the ***minor axis.*** The parts of an ellipse are shown in Figure 3.27. AutoCAD LT allows you to draw an ellipse by establishing the length of the major and minor axes, by selecting the center and the axial lengths, or by providing the length of an axis and a rotation angle. You can also draw an elliptical arc.

FIGURE 3.27 The parts of an ellipse.

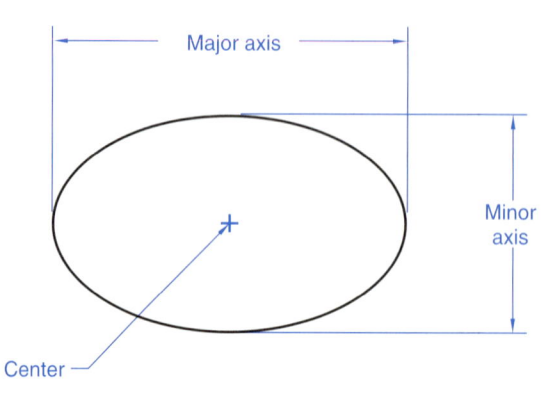

Drawing an Ellipse with the Axis End Points Option

You can draw an ellipse by establishing the axis end points. To do this select Ellipse and then Axis, End from the Draw pull-down menu, pick the Ellipse button on the Draw toolbar, or type **EL** or **ELLIPSE** at the Command:prompt. AutoCAD LT asks you for the first axis end points and then requests a distance from the center to the end of the other axis as shown in Figure 3.28. This is the command sequence:

Command: **EL** or **ELLIPSE**↵
Arc/Center/<Axis end point 1>: ⟨*pick the first axis end point*⟩
Axis end point 2: ⟨*pick the second end point of the first axis*⟩
<Other axis distance>/Rotation: ⟨*pick the end point of the second axis or type a distance from the center to the end point*⟩
Command:

FIGURE 3.28 Drawing an ellipse using the Axis, End point option.

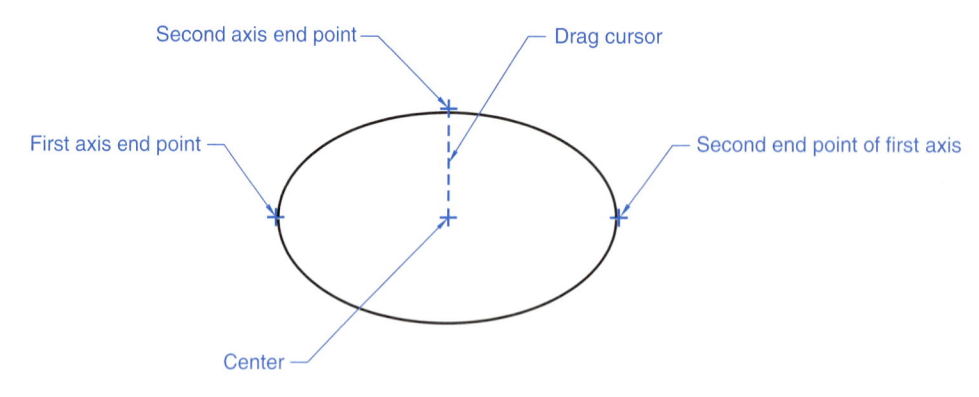

Drawing an Ellipse with the Center Option

You can automatically begin drawing an ellipse by picking the center if you choose Ellipse and then Center in the Draw pull-down menu. AutoCAD LT first asks you to select the center point followed by the distance to the first axis end point and then the distance to the end of the second axis. The command sequence looks like this, and the result is shown in Figure 3.29.

Command: _ellipse
Arc/Center/<Axis end point 1>: _c
Center of ellipse: ⟨*pick the center point*⟩
Axis end point: ⟨*pick or type the distance to the first axis end point*⟩
<Other axis distance>/Rotation: ⟨*pick or type the distance to the second axis end point*⟩
Command:

CHAPTER 3 ||| Drawing Basic Objects   **109**

If you use the keyboard to enter the ELLIPSE command, you need to enter **C** at the following prompt to use the Center option:

    Command: **EL** or **ELLIPSE**↵
    Arc/Center/<Axis end point 1>: **C**↵

The command continues as previously shown.

FIGURE 3.29 Drawing an ellipse using the Center option.

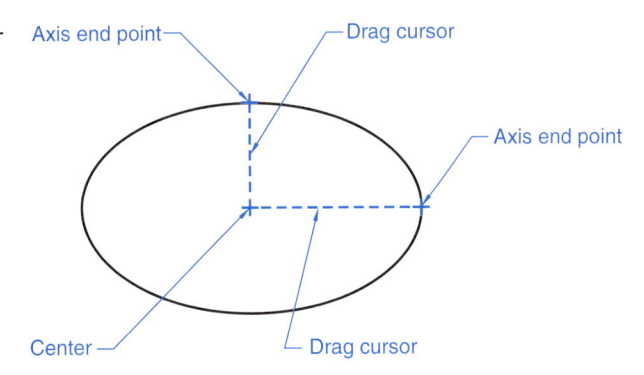

Drawing an Ellipse by Using the Rotation Angle

You can draw an ellipse by typing or picking a desired rotation angle. You can visualize this by holding a coin. The coin looks like a circle when you look at the flat surface. Then, as you rotate the coin, it begins to look like an ellipse. The more you rotate the coin, the flatter it gets. The amount that you rotate the coin is called the rotation angle. AutoCAD LT allows you to enter a rotation angle from 0 to 89.4°. A rotation angle of 0 creates a circle, whereas 89.4 is nearly a straight line. Figure 3.30 shows ellipses drawn using a variety of rotation angles. The ELLIPSE command may be accessed by any of the previously described means. The Rotation option is then accessed at the keyboard by typing **R** and then an exact rotation angle is usually typed for the best accuracy, like this:

    Command: **EL** or **ELLIPSE**↵
    Arc/Center/<Axis end point 1>: ⟨*pick the first axis end point*⟩
    Axis end point 2: ⟨*pick the second end point of the first axis*⟩
    <Other axis distance>/Rotation: **R**↵
    Rotation around major axis: ⟨*type a rotation angle such as* **45**↵⟩
    Command:

FIGURE 3.30 Various ellipse rotation angles.

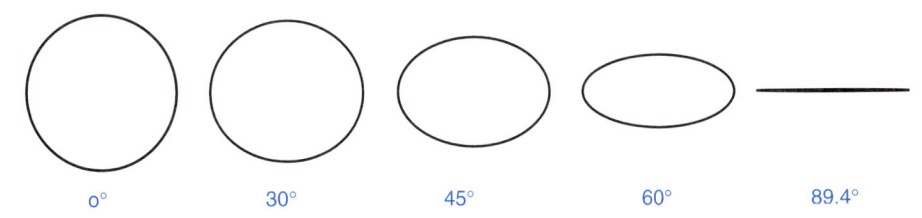

Drawing Elliptical Arcs

An elliptical arc is part of a full ellipse. An elliptical arc is drawn by accessing Ellipse and then Arc in the Draw pull-down menu or by entering the ELLIPSE command and then typing **A** to get the Arc option at the keyboard. Elliptical arcs are created by first drawing an ellipse using one of the methods previously explained. Look at Figure 3.31A. You then have three options for creating the arc. You can select the start and end angles of the arc, the start angle and the included angle, or the arc parameters.

Drawing an Elliptical Arc with the Start and End Angles

The elliptical arc default asks you for a start and end angle. The start and end angles are measured from the first end point of the first axis. You can either pick desired angles or type a specific angle value at the keyboard. The angles are measured in a counterclockwise direction by default as shown in Figure 3.31B. The command looks like this when entered at the keyboard (see Figure 3.31):

Command: **EL** or **ELLIPSE**↵
Arc/Center/<Axis end point 1>: **A**↵
<Axis end point 1>/Center: ⟨*pick the first axis end point*⟩
Axis end point 2: ⟨*pick the second end point of the first axis*⟩
<Other axis distance>/Rotation: ⟨*pick the second axis end point*⟩
Parameter/<start angle>: ⟨*enter an angle <u>measured from the first end point of the first axis</u>, such as* **90**↵⟩
Parameter/Included/<end angle>: ⟨*enter an angle measured from the first end point of the first axis, such as* **270**↵⟩
Command:

FIGURE 3.31 Drawing an elliptical arc using the Start and End Angle option.

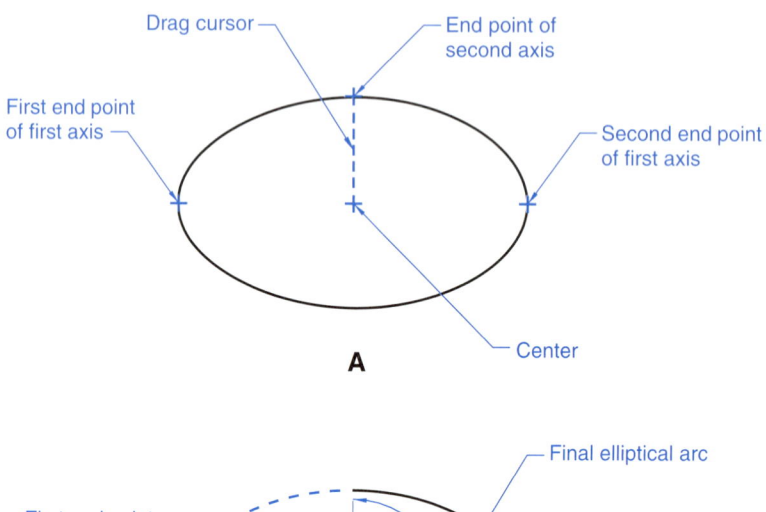

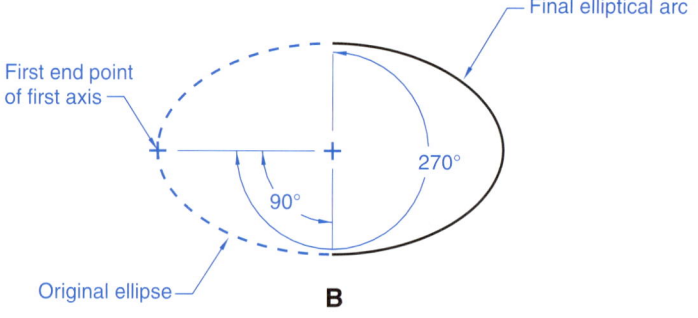

Field Notes

An elliptical arc is affected by the direction and base for angular measure. Elliptical arcs are still drawn counterclockwise, but the input angles are different.

Drawing an Elliptical Arc Using the Included Angles

An elliptical arc can also be drawn by entering a start angle followed by an included angle. The included angle is measured from the start angle as shown in Figure 3.32. After the initial ellipse is drawn, the prompts continue like this:

Parameter/<start angle>: ⟨*enter an angle measured from the first end point of the first axis, such as* **90**↵⟩
Parameter/Included/<end angle>: **I**↵
Included angle<previous>: ⟨*enter an angle measured from the start angle, such as* **270**↵⟩
Command:

CHAPTER 3 ||| Drawing Basic Objects

FIGURE 3.32 Drawing an elliptical angle using the Included Angle option.

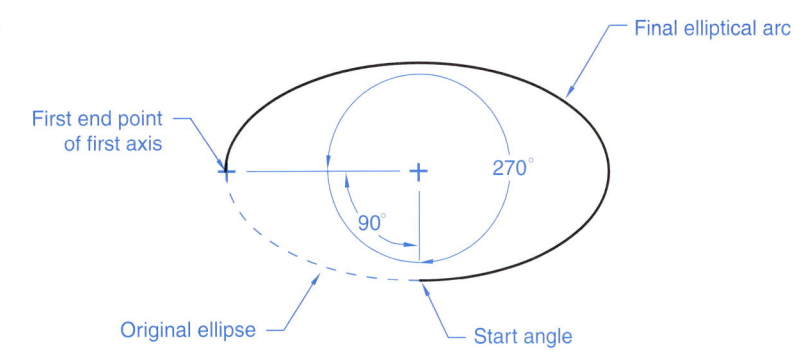

Drawing an Elliptical Arc Using Parameters

The Parameter option uses the same basic input as the Start angle/End angle option but calculates the arc based on a parametric vector equation. The equation is $p(u) = c + a* \cos(u) + b* \sin(u)$, where c is the center of the ellipse, a is the major axis, and b is the minor axis. Some applications of this option may produce the same results as the angle specifications, whereas other applications may produce quite different results. For example, a start of 0 and end of 90 produces the same results whether the values are specified as angles or parameters. The following sequence of commands was used to produce the two ellipses in Figure 3.33: ellipse A using the Angle options, ellipse B using the Parameter options. The input for both options is the same, as follows:

    Command: **ELLIPSE**↵
    Arc/Center/<Axis endpoint 1>: **A**↵
    <Axis endpoint 1>/Center: **4,4**↵
    Axis endpoint 2: **2,4**↵
    <Other axis distance>/Rotation: **1**↵
    Parameter/<start angle>: **30**↵
    Parameter/Included/<end angle>: **45**↵

    Command: **ELLIPSE**↵
    Arc/Center/<Axis endpoint 1>: **A**↵
    <Axis endpoint 1>/Center: **4,4**↵
    Axis endpoint 2: **2,4**↵
    <Other axis distance>/Rotation: **1**↵
    Parameter/<start angle>: **P**↵
    Angle/<start parameter>: **30**↵
    Angle/Included/<end parameter>: **45**↵

FIGURE 3.33 These two elliptical arcs were created using the same input: elliptical arc A using the Angle options, and elliptical arc B using the Parameter options.

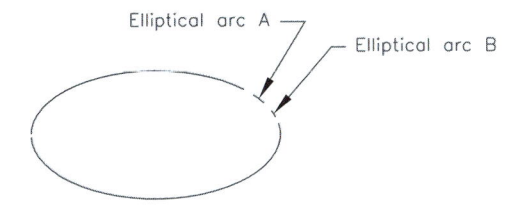

Exercise 3.6

1. Open AutoCAD LT if it is not already open. Use the setup option of your choice. A border and title block are not required. Dimensions and notes are not needed.
2. Set limits at 8.5,11.
3. Draw an ellipse similar to the following:
   - Figure 3.28 with the Axis and End point option.
   - Figure 3.29 with the Center option.
   - Figure 3.30 with the Rotation option.
4. Draw elliptical arcs similar to the following:
   - Figure 3.31 with the Start and End Angle option.
   - Figure 3.32 with the Included Angle option.
   - Figure 3.33 with both the angle and the Parameter options.
5. Save as EX3-6.

✓ LEARNING CHECKPOINT

- ☐ Describe at least four ways to draw a circle.
- ☐ How do you make a circle tangent to two objects?
- ☐ What is the shortest way to enter the CIRCLE command at the keyboard?
- ☐ Identify at least three ways to draw an arc.
- ☐ How do you draw an arc from a previously drawn line or arc?
- ☐ Describe at least three ways to draw an ellipse.
- ☐ What is the difference between the Start and End Angle methods when compared with the Included Angle option for drawing elliptical arcs?
- ☐ How do you draw an elliptical arc with the Parameter option?

Drawing Polygons

A *polygon* is a planar geometric object with three or more sides. ***Regular polygons*** have equal length sides. AutoCAD LT lets you easily draw any regular polygon with between 3 and 1024 equal-length sides. Polygons with many sides are usually not practical and they begin to look like circles. AutoCAD LT can also be used to create rectangles. ***Rectangles*** are geometric figures with four sides and four right (90°) angles.

Drawing Polygons Based on a Circle

The POLYGON command is accessed by typing **PG** or **POLYGON** at the Command: prompt, by picking the Polygon toolbar button, or by picking Polygon from the Draw pull-down menu. You are asked for the number of sides and a center point for placement of the polygon, which is the center point for the imaginary circle AutoCAD LT uses in defining a polygon. The next prompt asks if the polygon is to be *inscribed in circle or circumscribed about circle.* Inscribed means *drawn inside,* and circumscribed means *drawn around.* Your choice depends on how you are defining the polygon.

If you know the distance across the flats of the polygon, enter a **C** for circumscribed about circle. This means that a regular polygon with the specified number of sides will be drawn around the circle you define. Note that a circle is not actually drawn; rather, its definition is used to create the polygon. The following sequence draws a six-sided figure (hexagon) that measures 2 units across the flats:

Command: **PG** or **POLYGON**↵
Number of sides <4>: **6**↵
Edge/<Center of polygon>: **4,4**↵
Inscribed in circle/Circumscribed about circle (I/C) <I>: **C**↵
Radius of circle: **1**↵

CHAPTER 3 ||| Drawing Basic Objects 113

Notice that the radius is specified as 1 unit. This is because the radius is half the distance across the circle being used to define the polygon. The result of this command sequence is illustrated in Figure 3.34. Notice that the polygon is drawn around the defining circle.

FIGURE 3.34 Using the *circumscribed* option defines a polygon by the distance across its flats.

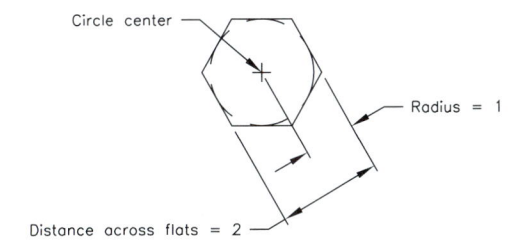

If you are creating a polygon based on the distance across its points, you must use the Inscribed option. The following sequence creates the polygon shown in Figure 3.35, which is defined as being 2 units across its points.

Command: **PG**↵
POLYGON Number of sides <6>: ↵
Edge/<Center of polygon>: **4,4**↵
Inscribed in circle/Circumscribed about circle (I/C) <C>: **I**↵
Radius of circle: **1**↵

FIGURE 3.35 Using the *Inscribed* option defines a polygon by the distance across its points.

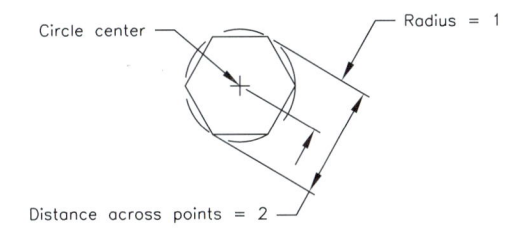

Drawing a Polygon Using the Edge Option

In some situations, you may know the length of the polygon edges. AutoCAD LT lets you use this information to easily draw the desired polygon. Figure 3.36 shows how to draw a hexagon with the Edge option. Use the Edge option by typing **E** at the prompt line to draw an octagon (a regular polygon with eight sides):

Command: **PG** or **POLYGON**↵
Number of sides <6>: **8**↵
Edge/<Center of polygon>: **E**↵
Inscribed in circle/Circumscribed about circle (I/C) <I>:
First end point of edge: ⟨*pick the first point of the edge*⟩
Second end point of edge: ⟨*pick the second edge point*⟩
Command:

FIGURE 3.36 Drawing a regular polygon (octagon) using the Edge option.

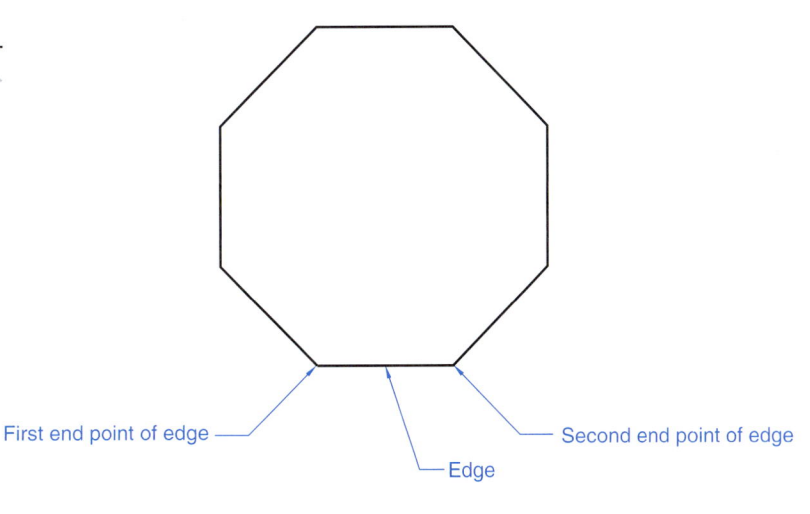

Drawing Rectangles

Draw
Rectangle

Draw
Rectangle

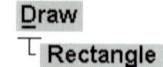

RECTANG
REC

Rectangles can be drawn by picking Rectangle from the Draw pull-down menu, picking the Rectangle toolbar button, or typing **REC** or **RECTANG** at the Command: prompt. AutoCAD LT asks you to select the first corner of the rectangle. The cursor then turns into a rectangle as you drag to the right or left. Pick the opposite corner of the rectangle when the desired shape is established as shown in Figure 3.37. The command works like this:

Command: **REC** or **RECTANG**.↵
Chamfer/Elevation/Fillet/Thickness/Width/〈First corner〉: 〈*pick the first rectangle corner*〉
Other corner: 〈*pick the opposite corner of the rectangle*〉
Command:

FIGURE 3.37 Drawing a rectangle using the RECTANG command.

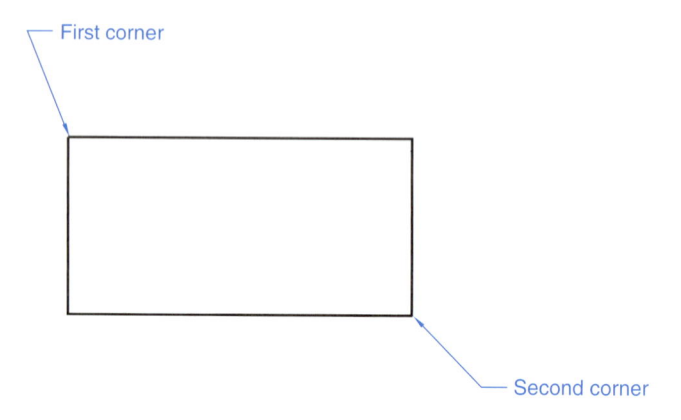

— First corner

— Second corner

Field Notes

An easy way to draw an accurately sized rectangle is to specify the first corner as you would normally, then enter a relative coordinate at the Other corner: prompt. For example, if you wanted to create a rectangle that was 6 units wide and 4 units tall, the command sequence would look like this:

Command: _rectang
Chamfer/Elevation/Fillet/Thickness/Width/〈First corner〉: 〈*pick first corner*〉
Other corner: **@6,4**↵

Notice in addition to the default <First corner> prompt, the RECTANG command has several other options:

Chamfer/Elevation/Fillet/Thickness/Width/〈First corner〉:

These other options are explained in the following:

- Chamfer: This option allows you to draw a rectangle with angled corners. The word ***chamfer*** comes from mechanical drafting and manufacturing as a reference to angled corners on an object, but chamfers on a rectangle can be used in any drafting field to make angled corners on a rectangular object. When you enter **C** to get the Chamfer option, AutoCAD LT asks you for the chamfer distances. The first chamfer distance you type is automatically set for the second chamfer distance. You can accept the second chamfer distance by pressing Enter or you can type another value. Equal chamfer distances make 45° corners on the rectangle, as shown in Figure 3.38A. This is the command sequence used to draw Figure 3.38A:

Command: **REC** or **RECTANG** ↵
Chamfer/Elevation/Fillet/Thickness/Width/〈First corner〉: **C** ↵
First chamfer distance for rectangles <0.0000>: **.25** ↵
Second chamfer distance for rectangles <0.2500>: ↵
Chamfer/Elevation/Fillet/Thickness/Width/〈First corner〉: *pick the first corner*
Other corner: *pick the second corner*
Command:

CHAPTER 3 ||| Drawing Basic Objects

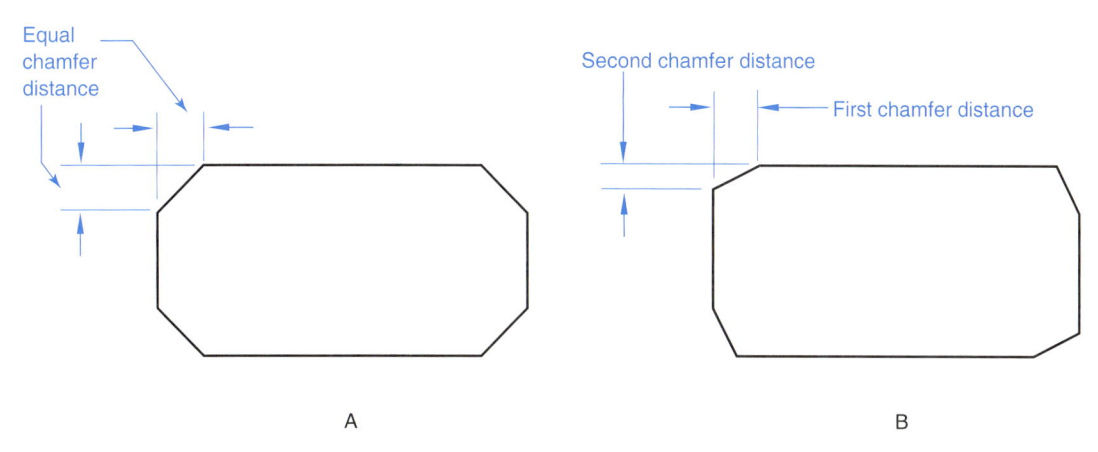

FIGURE 3.38 (A) A rectangle drawn with equal chamfer distances. (B) A rectangle drawn with different chamfer distances.

When you start AutoCAD LT, the initial default chamfer distance is 0.0000, which draws square corners. When you set a chamfer distance, such as .25, it remains in effect until changed. Figure 3.38B shows different chamfer distances drawn on a rectangle using these prompts:

Chamfer/Elevation/Fillet/Thickness/Width/⟨First corner⟩: **C** ↵
First chamfer distance for rectangles <0.0000>: **.25** ↵
Second chamfer distance for rectangles <0.2500>: **.125** ↵
Chamfer/Elevation/Fillet/Thickness/Width/⟨First corner⟩: *pick the first corner*
Other corner: *pick the second corner*

- Elevation: This option allows you to enter a value for the Z coordinate location when drawing in 3-D. 3-D drafting with AutoCAD LT is covered in Chapter 14.

- Fillet: This option allows you to draw a rectangle with arced corners. The word *fillet* comes from mechanical drafting and manufacturing as a reference to inside curved corners on an object, but fillets in AutoCAD LT can be inside or outside arced corners. Fillets on a rectangle can be used in any drafting field to make arced corners on a rectangular object. When you enter **F** to get the Fillet option, AutoCAD LT asks you for the fillet radius. When you start AutoCAD LT, the initial default Fillet radius is 0.0000, which draws square corners. When you set a Fillet radius, such as .25, it remains in effect for chamfers and fillets until changed. A previously set Chamfer distance also becomes the default Fillet radius. Figure 3.39 shows fillets drawn on a rectangle using these prompts:

Command: **REC** or **RECTANG**↵
Chamfer/Elevation/Fillet/Thickness/Width/⟨First corner⟩: **F** ↵
Fillet radius for rectangles <0.0000>: **.25** ↵
Chamfer/Elevation/Fillet/Thickness/Width/<First corner>: *pick the first corner*
Other corner: *pick the second corner*
Command:

FIGURE 3.39 Using the RECTANG command's fillet option to draw rounded corners on a rectangle.

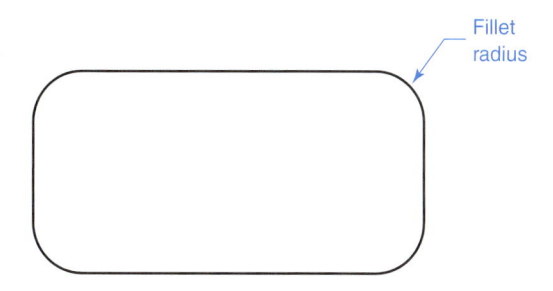

- Thickness: This option is also use in AutoCAD LT 3-D applications. The thickness controls Z axis dimensions. See Chapter 14.

- Width: By default, the line used to create your rectangles has a width of zero. This option allows you to set a specific pen width for the line. Figure 3.40 shows a 6 × 4 rectangle with a .5 radius fillet and a line width of .125.

FIGURE 3.40 The Width option allows you to set a pen width for the lines of a rectangle.

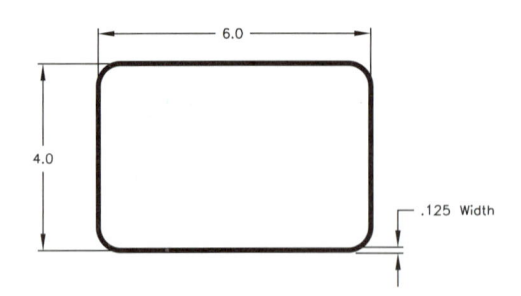

Field Notes

- AutoCAD LT remembers the settings specified for the last rectangle you created and defaults to the same values. Even if you exit the current drawing and start a new drawing, the settings default to those used in the last rectangle you created.
- If you try to draw a rectangle and instead get a big blob on your screen, chances are that your width setting is too big for the size of rectangle you are drawing.

Exercise 3.7

1. Open AutoCAD LT if it is not already open. Use the setup option of your choice. A border and title block are not required. The placement of the objects is up to you.
2. Set limits at 8.5,11.
3. Draw the following regular polygons, each circumscribed around a .5-in. radius:
   - Square
   - Pentagon (five sides)
   - Hexagon
   - Octagon
4. Draw a hexagon with a horizontal edge measuring 1 in.
5. Draw a rectangle that is 4 in. (horizontal) × 2 in.
6. Save as EX3.7.

Drawing Filled Objects

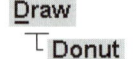

AutoCAD LT provides you with commands that can be used to create a variety of filled shapes. Filled circles, rings, and square or rectangular shapes are common, but other more creative shapes are possible. These shapes may be used for certain drafting practices such as the creation of symbols or used in a graphic design for custom artwork. The DONUT command is used for filled circular objects and SOLID for other shapes. In Chapter 10, you will learn how to fill any closed shape or object with a solid pattern.

Drawing Donuts

AutoCAD LT refers to filled circles and rings as *doughnuts,* or **donuts** for short, and they are drawn with the DONUT command. The DONUT command is found in the Draw pull-down menu by picking Donut, picking the Donut button in the Draw toolbar, or typing **DO** or **DONUT** or **DOUGHNUT** at the Command: prompt. The DONUT command asks you to create a solid ring or circle by giving the inside diameter and the outside diameter followed by the center point. Figure 3.41 shows the parts of a donut and donuts drawn with different specifications. The command continues to ask you to select the center of additional donuts. You can draw as many donuts as you wish and press Enter when finished:

Command: **DO** or **DONUT**↵
Inside diameter <0.50>: ↵ ⟨*or type any desired value such as* **.75**↵⟩
Outside diameter <1.00>: ↵ ⟨*or type any desired value such as* **1.5**↵⟩

CHAPTER 3 ||| Drawing Basic Objects

Center of doughnut: ⟨*pick the center*⟩
Center of doughnut: ⟨*pick the center*⟩
Center of doughnut: ↵
Command:

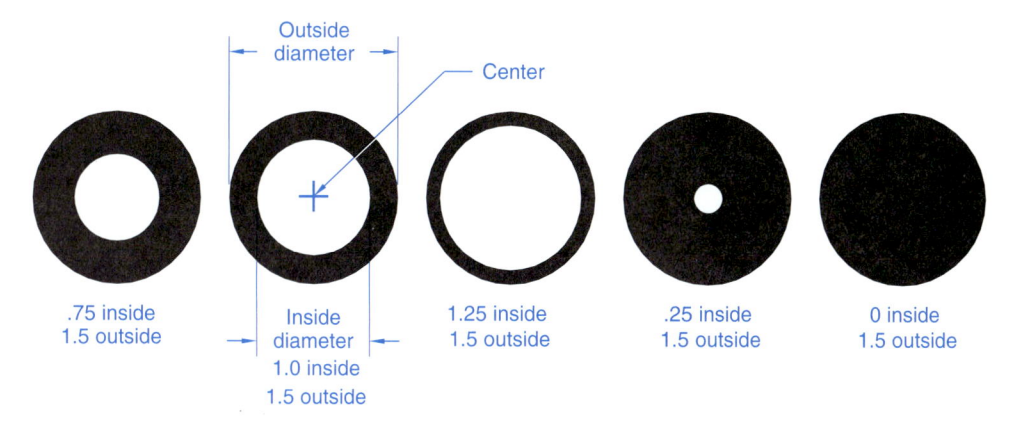

FIGURE 3.41 A variety of donuts with different specifications and the parts of a donut. Notice the solid circle at the right is a donut with 0 (zero) inside diameter.

Field Notes

A solid circle is a donut with a 0 (zero) inside diameter as shown in Figure 3.41. The original AutoCAD LT donut defaults are 0.50 inside diameter and 0.75 outside diameter. The previously set inside and outside diameters are given in brackets. These default values remain the same in the current drawing session until you change them.

Drawing Solids

A variety of filled objects can be drawn using the SOLID command. This command is accessed by typing **SO** or **SOLID** at the Command: prompt. When you enter the SOLID command, AutoCAD LT asks you to pick up to four points. If you pick three points and press Enter, you get a solid triangle as shown in Figure 3.42A. Press Enter again to exit the command. If you pick four points, you get a shape that varies depending on the order and position of the points. If you want a solid square or rectangle, you need to pick the corners in an order similar to the example in Figure 3.42B. Notice the object and order of points shown in Figure 3.42C. After picking four points, AutoCAD LT asks you to pick another third point and then another fourth point. You can press Enter at any time to end the point requests or keep picking points to create an infinite number of possibilities. Figure 3.42D shows an example of an object drawn by picking additional third and fourth points. This is the command sequence used to draw the object shown in Figure 3.42D:

Command: **SO** or **SOLID**↵
First point: ⟨*pick the first point*⟩
Second point: ⟨*pick the second point*⟩
Third point: ⟨*pick the third point*⟩
Fourth point: ⟨*pick the fourth point*⟩
Third point: ⟨*pick the fifth point*⟩
Fourth point: ⟨*pick the sixth point*⟩
Third point: ↵
Command:

SOLID
SO

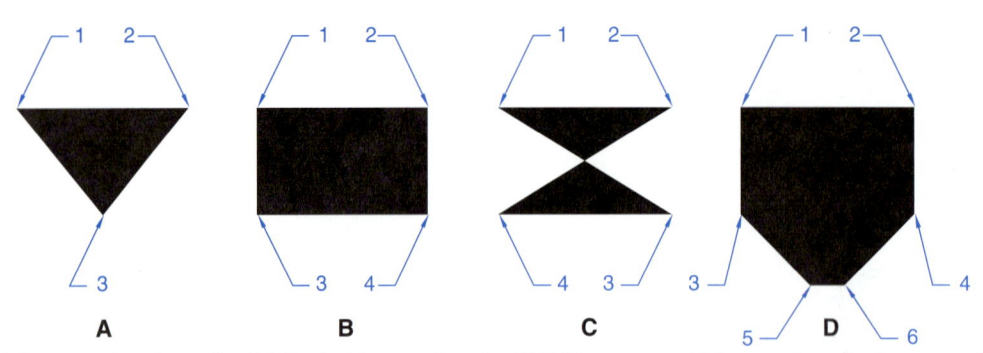

FIGURE 3.42 A variety of solid filled objects using the SOLID command. The numbers in the examples are the order in which points were picked.

Removing the Fill from Solid Objects

There may be a number of reasons why you might want to remove the fill from a solid object or donut. Removing the fill may create a desired design, speed up display changes, or reduce plotting time for a check plot. Whatever the reason, you can remove the fill using the FILL command. FILL is either on or off. FILL is on by default, but you can turn it off like this:

   Command: **FILL**↵
   ON/OFF <ON>: **OFF**↵
   Command:

If you have a solid filled object on the screen, turning FILL off does not automatically remove the fill from the object. Before you can see the difference, you need to update the drawing's screen display. AutoCAD LT refers to this as *regenerating.* You can regenerate the screen by using the REGEN command:

   Command: **RE** or **REGEN**↵
   Regenerating drawing
   Command:

AutoCAD LT gives you the message "Regenerating drawing" and automatically returns the Command: prompt. If you want to turn FILL back on, enter the FILL command, use the On option, and then use the REGEN command to update the screen display. Figure 3.43 shows the same objects that were in Figures 3.41 and 3.42 with the FILL turned off.

FIGURE 3.43 The same donuts and solids shown in Figures 3.41 and 3.42 with FILL turned off.

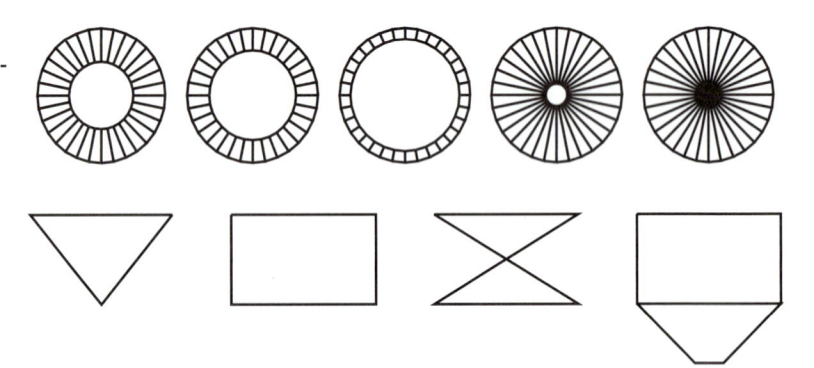

Exercise 3.8

1. Open AutoCAD LT if it is not already open. Use the setup option of your choice. A border and title block are not required. The placement of the objects is up to you.
2. Set limits at 8.5,11.
3. Draw the donuts shown in Figure 3.41.
4. Draw solid shapes similar to those shown in Figure 3.42.
5. Turn the FILL off and then use the REGEN command. Notice the difference.
6. Turn the FILL back on and then use the REGEN command. Notice the difference again.
7. Save as EX3.8.

CHAPTER 3 ||| Drawing Basic Objects 119

✓ LEARNING CHECKPOINT

☐ Identify two ways to draw regular polygons.
☐ Name the command used to draw rectangles.
☐ What command is used to draw filled rings?
☐ How do you draw a filled circle?
☐ Make a sketch of a filled rectangle with the corners numbered so as to identify the order in which points were picked.
☐ Explain what happens to solid filled objects when you turn FILL off.
☐ What is the purpose of the REGEN command with regard to turning FILL off and on?

MULTIPLE CHOICE

Circle the choice or enter your response on an answer sheet by selecting the option that most closely completes or answers the given statements.

1. When using the Advanced Setup, AutoCAD LT provides you with a place for creating the finished layout for printing or plotting. This is referred to as the:
   a. layout
   b. paper space
   c. model space
   d. title block

2. When using AutoCAD LT, you work on your drawing in what view?
   a. layout
   b. paper space
   c. model space
   d. title block

3. A drawing file with preestablished settings:
   a. prototype
   b. settings
   c. format
   d. layout

4. After drawing a circle, you can automatically enter the CIRCLE command again by:
   a. pressing the space bar
   b. pressing the Enter key
   c. either a or b
   d. neither a nor b

5. Do this to automatically make the endpoint of the previously drawn line or arc the start point of the new arc:
   a. press the space bar
   b. press the Enter key
   c. either a or b
   d. neither a nor b

6. AutoCAD LT does not ask for this information when creating a polygon:
   a. center of polygon
   b. radius of circle
   c. number of sides
   d. none of the above

7. Filled circles and rings are drawn with AutoCAD LT by using this command:
   a. DOUGHNUTS
   b. FILL
   c. SOLID
   d. DONUT

8. A variety of filled objects may be drawn using this command:
   a. SOLIDS
   b. FILL
   c. SOLID
   d. DONUT

9. This command allows you to set or change the sheet size at any time during your drawing session:
   a. LIMIT
   b. LIMITS
   c. FORMAT
   d. UNITS

10. This command allows you to change the drawing units in the Units Control dialog box:
    a. UNITS
    b. UNIT
    c. DDUNITS
    d. DDUNIT

MATCHING

Match each term to the correct description by writing the appropriate number in each box at the left.

- [ ] Bearing
- [ ] Counterclockwise
- [ ] Diameter
- [ ] Donut
- [ ] Enter
- [ ] Major
- [ ] Minor
- [ ] Polygon
- [ ] Template
- [ ] Radius
- [ ] Rectangle
- [ ] Solid
- [ ] Surveyor
- [ ] Tangent

1. These angles are measured using bearings.
2. This term refers to the angle of a line with its direction in respect to one of the quadrants of a compass.
3. The AutoCAD LT default has angles measured in this direction beginning at 0° East.
4. Using one of these to begin a drawing saves time.
5. This is the distance from the center to the circumference of the circle.
6. When you are finished drawing an object, you can press this or the space bar at the Command: prompt to get the same command again.
7. This is the distance across the circle passing through the center.
8. This means that the circle touches an object at only one point without intersecting or crossing the object.
9. The length of an ellipse is along this axis.
10. The width of an ellipse is along this axis.
11. A hexagon is drawn using this command.
12. This is drawn by picking the first corner and then moving the cursor to pick the other corner.
13. AutoCAD LT refers to filled circles and rings as this.
14. A filled rectangular shape may be drawn using this command.

CHAPTER 3 ||| Drawing Basic Objects   **121**

WORD SCRAMBLE

Unscramble the seven scrambled words below, one letter to each square, to form seven AutoCAD LT–related words:

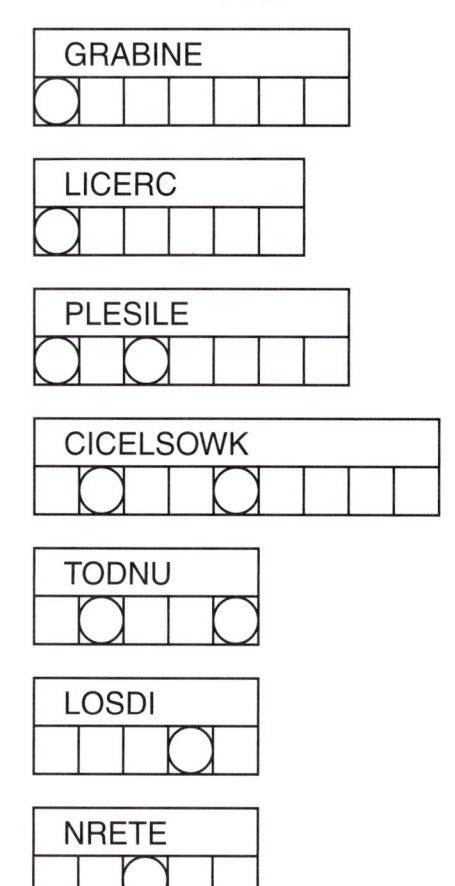

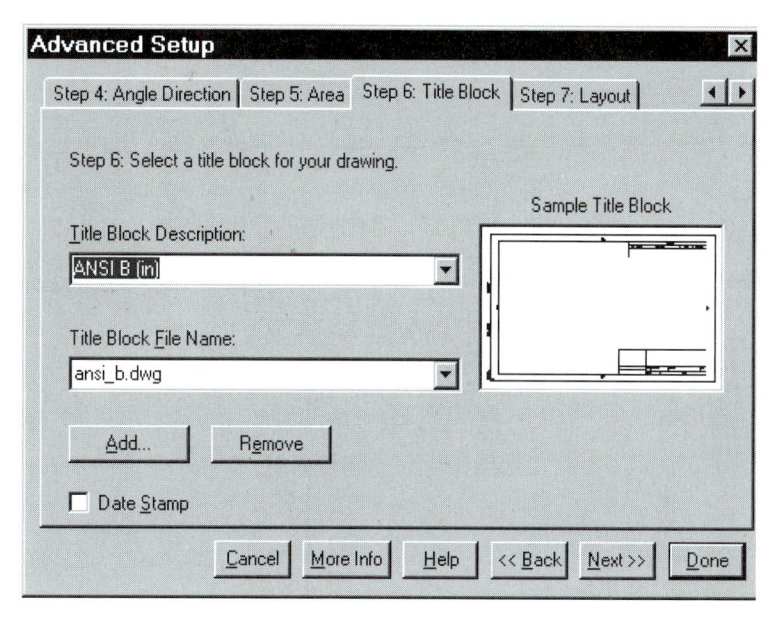

GRABINE

LICERC

PLESILE

CICELSOWK

TODNU

LOSDI

NRETE

Unscramble the circled letters above to form the special answer, as suggested by the illustration.

PROJECTS

3.1 Porch Light
Design a porch light with features, sizes, and proportions similar to the one shown below. Save as P3.1.

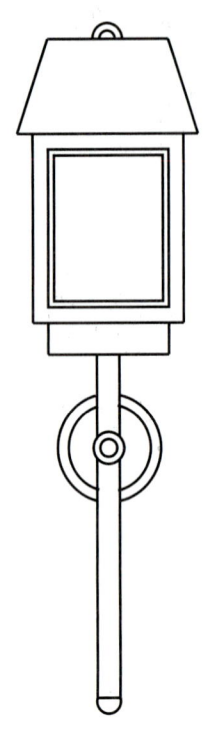

3.2 Duplex Convenience Outlet
Open P2.6 and make the changes shown below. Do not draw dimensions. Save as P3.2.

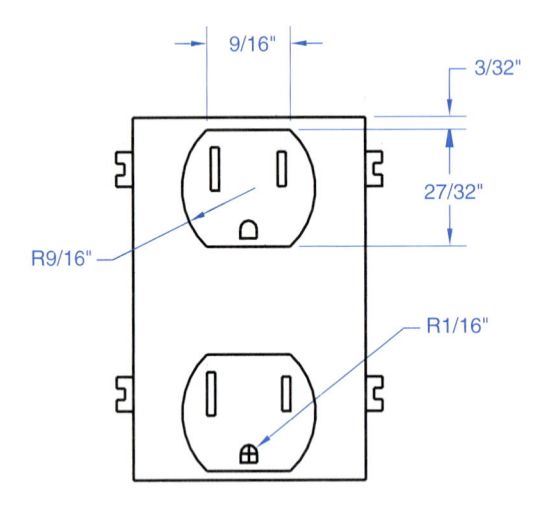

CHAPTER 3 ||| Drawing Basic Objects   123

3.3 Clock
Open P2.7 and add the circles and ellipse shown below. Do not draw dimensions. Save as P3.3.

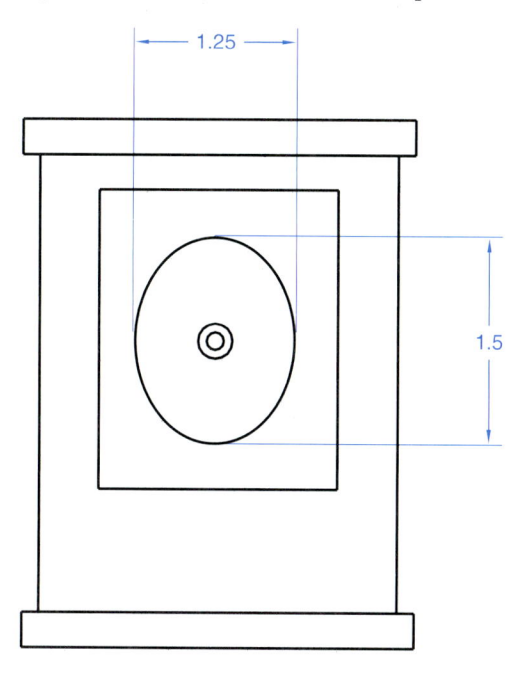

3.4 Cover Plate
Draw the object shown below without center lines or dimensions. Save as P3.4.

INCH

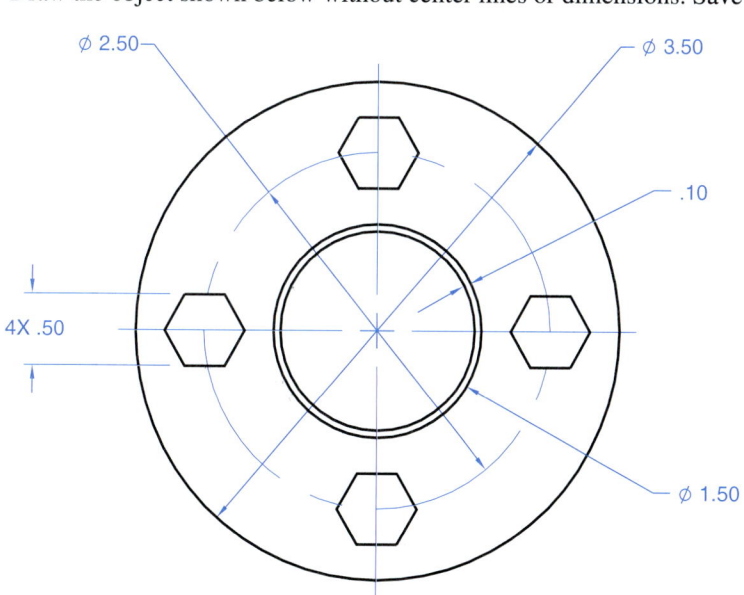

3.5 Cover Plate
Draw the object shown below without center lines or dimensions. Save as P3.5.

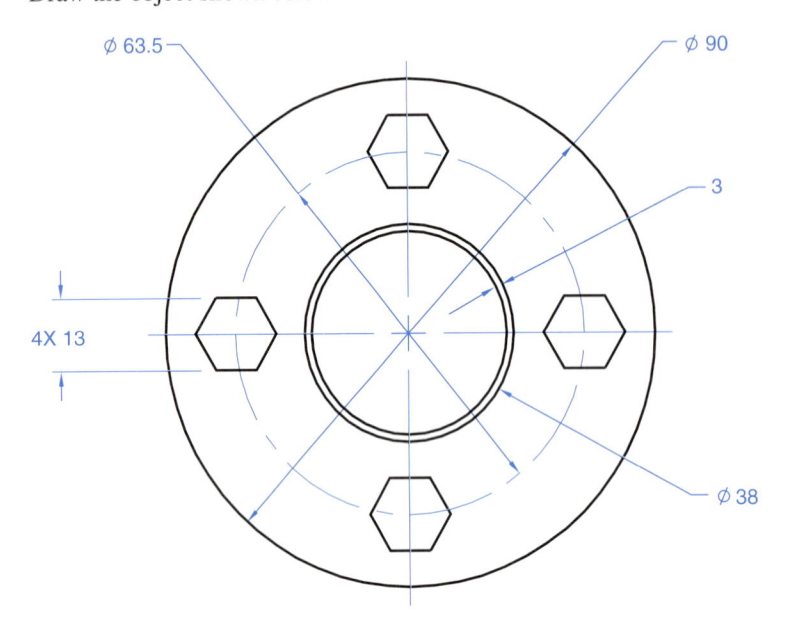

3.6 Gasket
Draw the object shown below without center lines or dimensions. Save as P3.6.

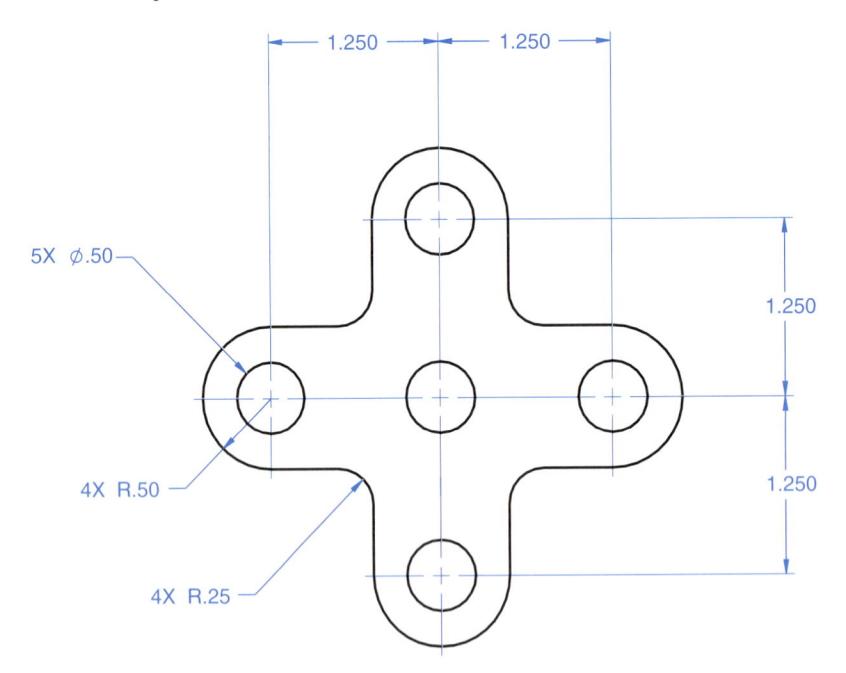

CHAPTER 3 ||| Drawing Basic Objects

125

3.7 Gasket
Draw the object shown below without center lines or dimensions. Save as P3.7.

METRIC

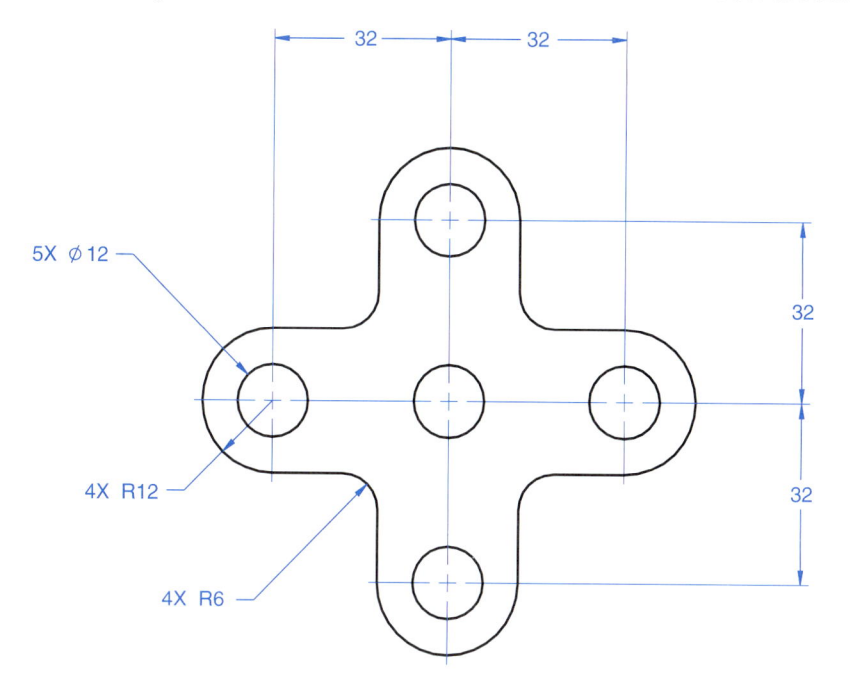

5X ⌀12

4X R12

4X R6

32 32

32

32

3.8 Gazebo
Draw a floor plan of the gazebo shown below. Draw the 8X ⌀4″ POSTS as circles. Do not draw dimensions or notes. Save as P3.8. (Drawing courtesy of Mike W. Hehr.)

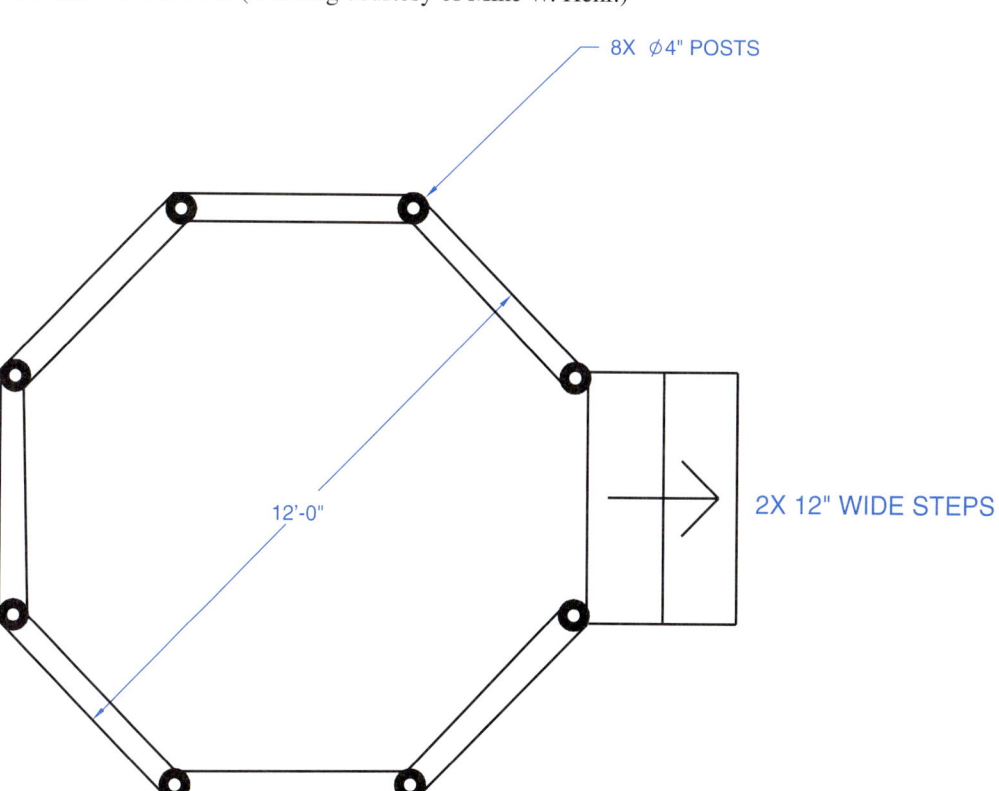

8X ⌀4″ POSTS

12′-0″

2X 12″ WIDE STEPS

3.9 Clothes Dryer Circuit
Draw the schematic shown below. Do not draw dimensions or notes. Save as P3.9.

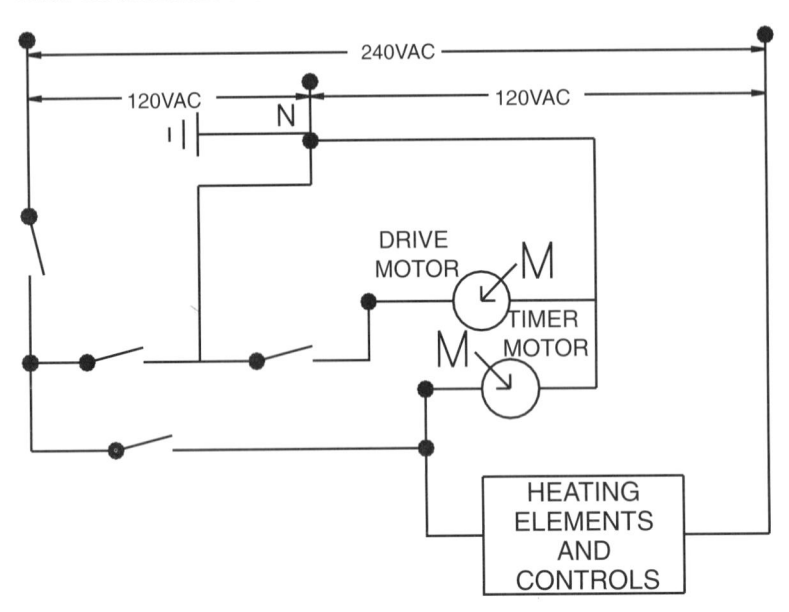

CLOTHES DRYER CIRCUIT

3.10 Piping Symbols
Draw the piping symbols shown below. Save as P3.10.

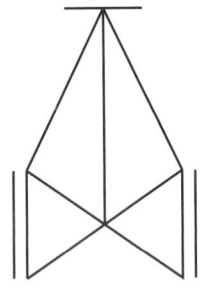

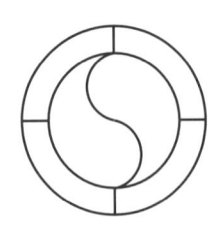

CHAPTER 4

Drawing Display Control

LEARNING GOALS

- Change the display area to magnify small details or reduce large areas.
- Display any area of the drawing on your screen.
- Use the Aerial View window to change the display area.
- Optimize display settings and options to speed your work.
- Create and manage named viewing areas in your drawing.

Changing Your View of the Drawing

Your computer monitor provides a small area in which you can display a drawing. An average 17-in. monitor actually provides a drawing area that is about 12 in. wide by 8 in. high, depending on your screen resolution and window arrangement. Unless your drawing layout is for an 8½ × 11-in. sheet you cannot view the entire drawing at full size. Your CAD drawings may often have smaller details that are difficult or even impossible to see without changing the drawing display area.

AutoCAD LT provides a number of tools for changing the drawing display. Many of these display tools work in the same manner as a camera. With a camera, to *zoom* is to change the apparent size of the objects you are viewing. Changing the area that is displayed does not change the actual size of the objects, it merely changes the way in which you view them—this is the same for AutoCAD LT. To view something that appears small on your display, you *zoom in;* to increase the area displayed by shrinking the apparent size of the objects, you *zoom out.* Also similar to a camera, to view something outside of the current viewing area without changing the apparent size of the objects displayed, you can pan up, down, left, or right. The term *pan* indicates changing the location of the view without changing the magnification. If you think of your drawing display control as being like a camera, it makes the display change tools much easier to master. This first section covers the options for the ZOOM and PAN commands.

Using the ZOOM Command Options

The ZOOM command has several different options to help you view any area of the drawing you need to see at virtually any magnification level. Entering the ZOOM command manually displays each of these options in the Command Window and allows you to specify the option you want to use:

ZOOM
Z

    Command: **Z** or **ZOOM**↵
    ZOOM All/Center/Extents/Previous/Scale(X/XP)/Window/<Realtime>: ⟨*enter an option*⟩

You can type the full command name if desired, but it is quicker and easier to use the shorter command alias (keyboard shortcut) by typing **Z**↵ instead. The option listing for any command presents the required entry in uppercase, meaning that most options can be accessed by typing only the first letter. Even so, the pull-down menu and toolbar button selections can be easier to use for some of the zooming options because of the automated command line input. The available zooming tools are explained in the following subsections.

Using the Zoom In Option

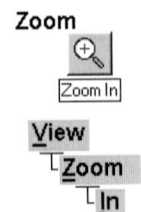

A direct way to double the apparent size of the objects on the screen is to use the Zoom In option. You can pick the toolbar button from the Zoom flyout found on the Standard toolbar or pick the In option from the Zoom cascade on the View pull-down menu. If you look closely at the command line when using this option, you will notice that a 'ZOOM command is automatically entered by AutoCAD LT, followed by a 2X option. This is one way to use the Zoom Scale option. Entered at the keyboard, the command sequence looks like this:

Command: **Z** or **ZOOM**↵
ZOOM All/Center/Extents/Previous/Scale (X/XP)/Window/<Realtime>: **2X**↵

The scale option allows you to change the zoom factor relative to the current display. For example, the 2X (or 2 times) option zooms in closer to the drawing so that the objects appear twice (or two times) as large as they were (see Figure 4.1A). Notice that the center of the view remains the same. This is like adjusting your camera zoom lens to zoom in without moving the camera.

FIGURE 4.1 (A) Zoom 2X makes the objects on screen appear twice (2×) as large. (B) Zoom .5X makes the objects on screen appear half (0.5×) as large.

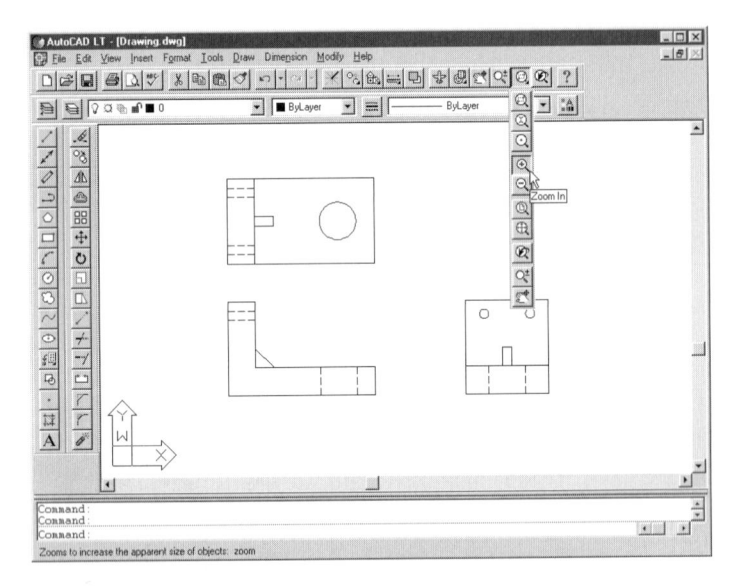

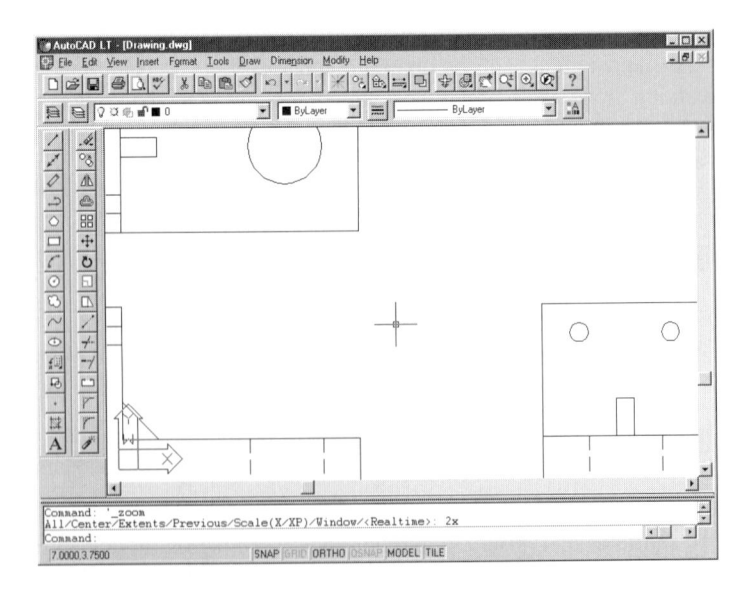

A

FIGURE 4.1 (continued)

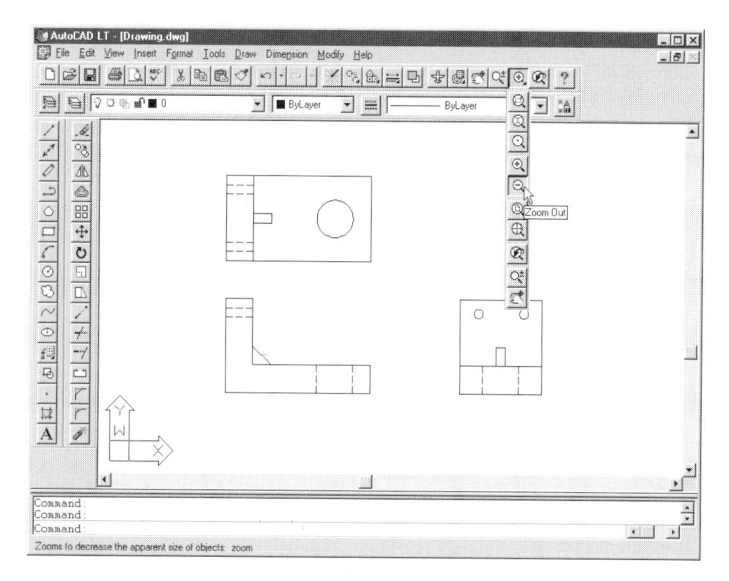

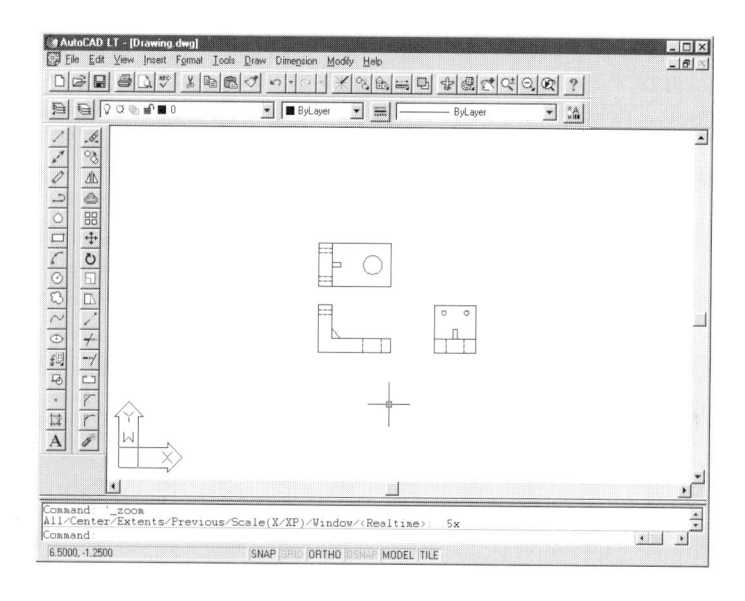

B

Using the Zoom Out Tool

The Zoom Out tool is used to reduce the apparent size of the drawing to half its current size. Pick the Zoom Out button from the Zoom flyout on the Standard toolbar or select Out from the Zoom cascade on the View pull-down menu. This option changes the display so that the objects on screen appear to be one-half (0.5X) the size they appear in the current display (see Figure 4.1B). At the command line, the option is used like this:

Command: **Z** or **ZOOM**↵
ZOOM All/Center/Extents/Previous/Scale (X/XP)/Window/<Realtime>: **.5X.**↵

Using the Zoom Scale Tool

The Zoom Scale tool allows greater flexibility than the Zoom In and Zoom Out tools. You can pick the Zoom Scale tool from the Zoom flyout found on the Standard toolbar, or you can pick Scale from the Zoom cascade on the View menu.

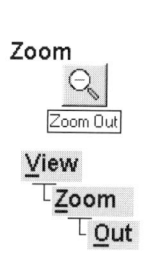

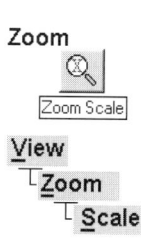

The Zoom Scale tool activates the same Zoom command option used by Zoom In and Zoom Out, but prompts you to enter a zoom scale value. You can specify any number followed by an **X** (or **x**). This number serves as a multiplier for the apparent size of objects on the screen. The Zoom In tool, discussed earlier, automatically specifies a 2X value to double the apparent size of the objects. The Zoom Out tool automatically specifies .5X to decrease the apparent size of objects to one-half that of the current display. The Zoom Scale tool allows you to specify any desired magnification value using the keyboard.

To reduce the apparent size of the objects in the current view using this option, specify a decimal number greater than zero and less than one. For example, to reduce the zoom factor to one-fourth of the current view, enter **.25X** as the scale value:

    Command: **Z** or **ZOOM.↵**
    ZOOM All/Center/Extents/Previous/Scale (X/XP)/Window/<Realtime>: **.25X.↵**

If you want to get closer to your work, specify a number greater than one. For example, to increase the apparent size of the objects on screen by four times, use a 4X option:

    Command: **Z** or **ZOOM.↵**
    ZOOM All/Center/Extents/Previous/Scale (X/XP)/Window/<Realtime>: **4X.↵**

Exercise 4.1

1. Open a drawing from one of the exercises in Chapter 3.
2. Use the Zoom In and Zoom Out tools to enlarge and reduce the view size.
3. Use the Zoom Scale tool to try values that enlarge the display and then enter values to reduce the magnification.
4. Return the drawing to the original view and save it as EX4.1.

Using the Zoom Window Tool

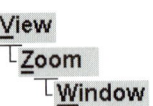

The Zoom Window tool is probably one of the most commonly used zooming options in AutoCAD LT. While the Zoom Scale tool can be used to zoom in or out incrementally, the fact that it keeps the center of the screen the same can be limiting when the feature you want to see closer is not at the center of the current view.

You can select the Zoom Window tool from the Zoom flyout on the Standard toolbar, pick Window from the Zoom cascade on the View menu, or enter the ZOOM command from the keyboard and specify the Window option.

When Zoom Window is selected, you are then prompted to select the First corner and the Other corner. This is similar to when you are selecting objects to edit using the Window selection mode:

    Command: **Z** or **ZOOM.↵**
    ZOOM All/Center/Extents/Previous/Scale (X/XP)/Window/<Realtime>: **W.↵**
    First corner: ⟨*pick the first corner*⟩
    Other corner: ⟨*move the cursor and pick the other corner*⟩

The window you draw at the First corner: and Other corner: prompts can be of any ratio of height to width, but the resulting view change is displayed at the same proportion as the drawing area. This is because the shape of the drawing area in the AutoCAD LT window cannot change to match the shape of the window you draw. The new display shows *all the area contained in the window you define, centered on the screen.* Study the Zoom Window operations shown in Figures 4.2, 4.3, and 4.4 and compare the resulting display.

At the ZOOM command prompt line, it is not necessary to press **W.↵** to start the Window option. Instead, at the prompt, simply pick the first point with your cursor. It is understood that you are using the Window option, and AutoCAD LT then prompts you for the other corner of the window.

Using the Zoom All Tool

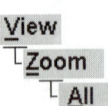

The Zoom All tool lets you see the entire drawing. This tool zooms to display the limits of your drawing on the screen. If you have drawn objects outside of the limits, the view is expanded to include these objects as well. You can select Zoom All from the Zoom flyout on the Standard toolbar, pick All from the Zoom cascade of the View menu, or you can type it at the Command: prompt:

    Command: **Z** or **ZOOM.↵**
    ZOOM All/Center/Extents/Previous/Scale (X/XP)/Window/<Realtime>: **A.↵**
    Regenerating drawing.

CHAPTER 4 ||| Drawing Display Control

FIGURE 4.2 (A) The top view of the part fills the window specified for the zoom operation. (B) The resulting display shows everything that was in the window, centered in the display.

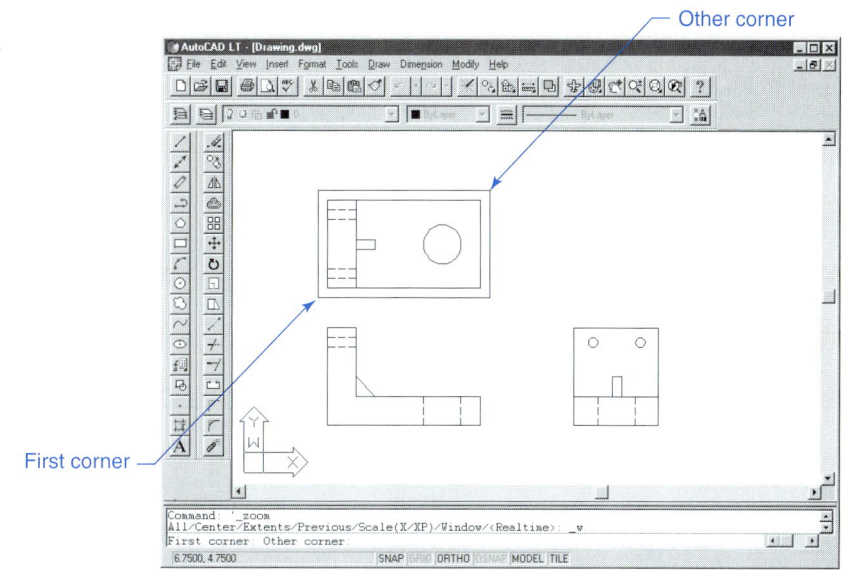

A

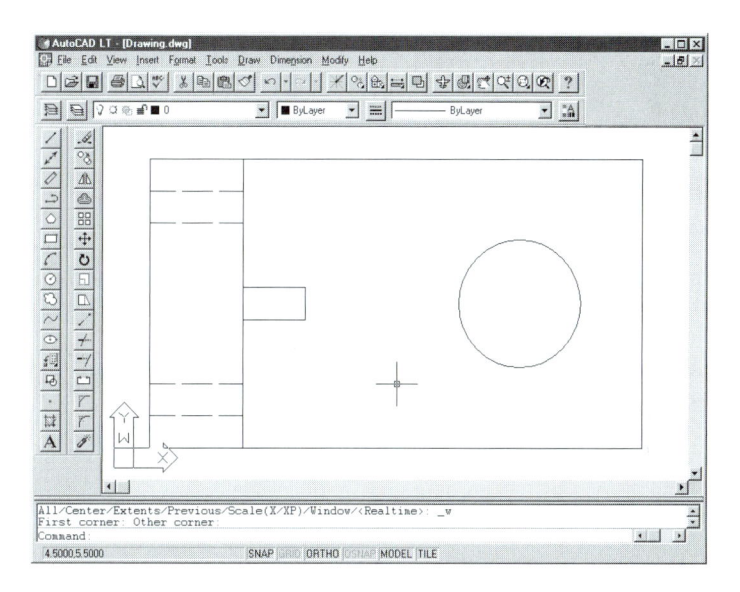

B

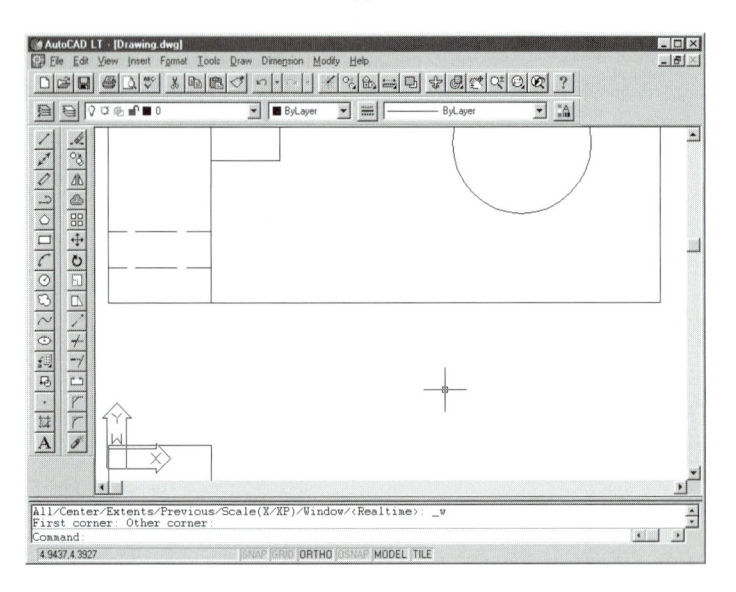

FIGURE 4.3 (A) The window picked is as wide as the part, but very short vertically. (B) The resulting display shows all that was windowed centered on the screen.

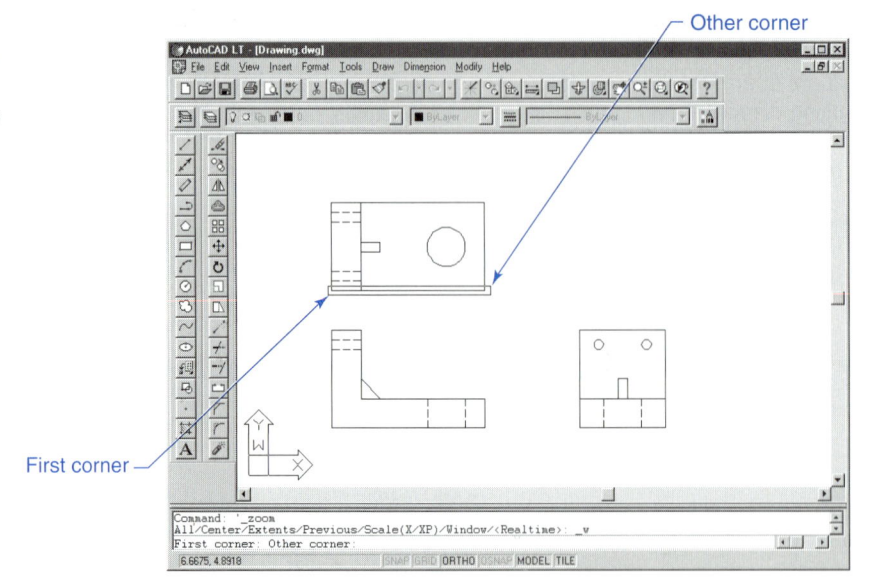

A

B

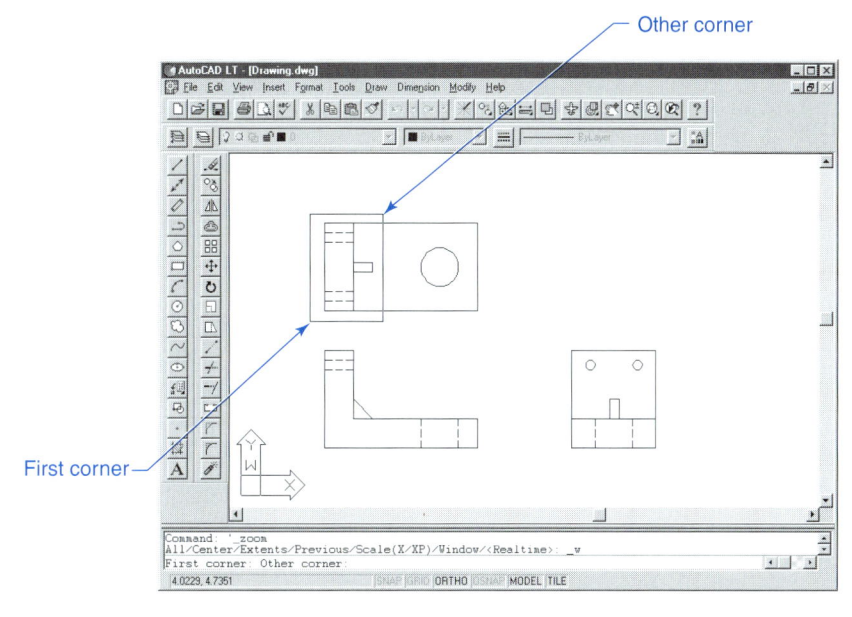

CHAPTER 4 ||| Drawing Display Control   **133**

FIGURE 4.4 (A) The window picked is as tall as the part, but very short horizontally. (B) The resulting display shows the windowed area centered on the screen.

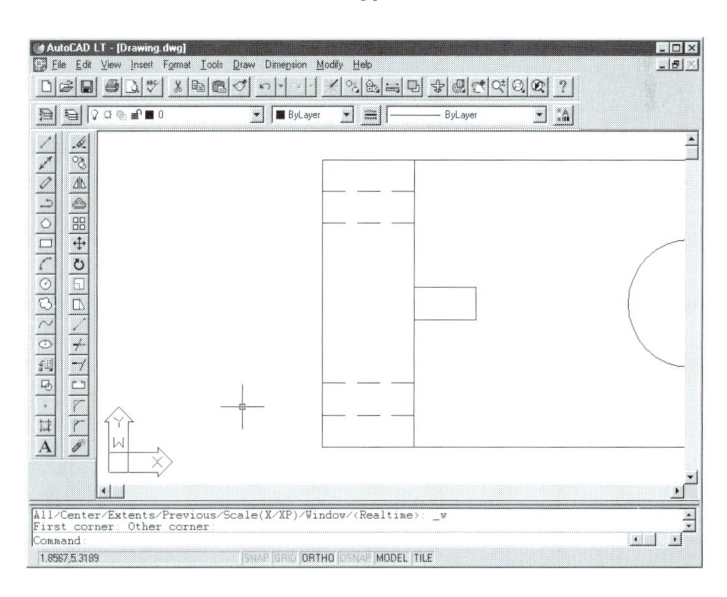

A

B

Using the Zoom Extents Tool

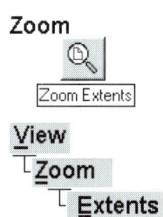

The Zoom Extents tool displays all of the objects in your drawing on screen at once, centered on the screen. The objects are shown as large as possible while still displaying all of the objects. Zoom Extents can be selected from the Zoom flyout on the Standard toolbar or you can pick Extents from the Zoom cascade of the View menu or type it:

Command: **Z** or **ZOOM.**↵
ZOOM All/Center/Extents/Previous/Scale (X/XP)/Window/<Realtime>: **E.**↵
Regenerating drawing.

Using the Zoom Center Tool

The Zoom Center tool allows you to change the display to be centered on a new point and specify the relative magnification or size of the area displayed. AutoCAD LT first prompts you to specify the point co-

Zoom

Zoom Center

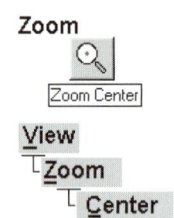

View
  Zoom
    Center

ordinate that is to be displayed at the center of the screen. You can type a coordinate or pick a point on the screen.

Zoom Center can be selected from the Zoom flyout on the Standard toolbar or you can pick <u>C</u>enter from the <u>Z</u>oom cascade of the <u>V</u>iew menu or type it. This first example shows a point being picked and the magnification is doubled.

Command: **Z** or **ZOOM**↵
ZOOM All/Center/Extents/Previous/Scale (X/XP)/Window/<Realtime>: **C**↵
Center point: ⟨*pick a point*⟩
Magnification or Height <9.0000>: **2X**↵

The magnification works the same as the Zoom Scale option: A number greater than one followed by an X zooms closer to your work and a number less than one zooms out. The magnification number is relative to the current display size shown in the default brackets. In the preceding example, the current display shows nine drawing units vertically, so 9.0000 is the default height. If you omit the X from the number you enter, AutoCAD LT considers the entry an absolute screen height. The absolute screen height indicates how many drawing units are displayed vertically in the drawing display area. In the example shown in Figure 4.5, the result-

FIGURE 4.5 (A) The Zoom Center tool allows you to locate the center of the display area. (B) The resulting display shows four drawing units vertically in the display area and is centered on the point 3.25,6.0.

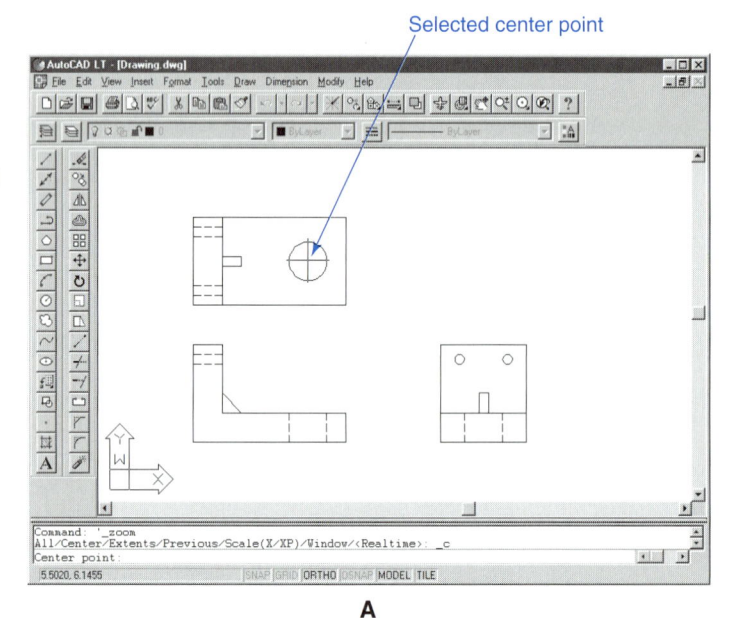

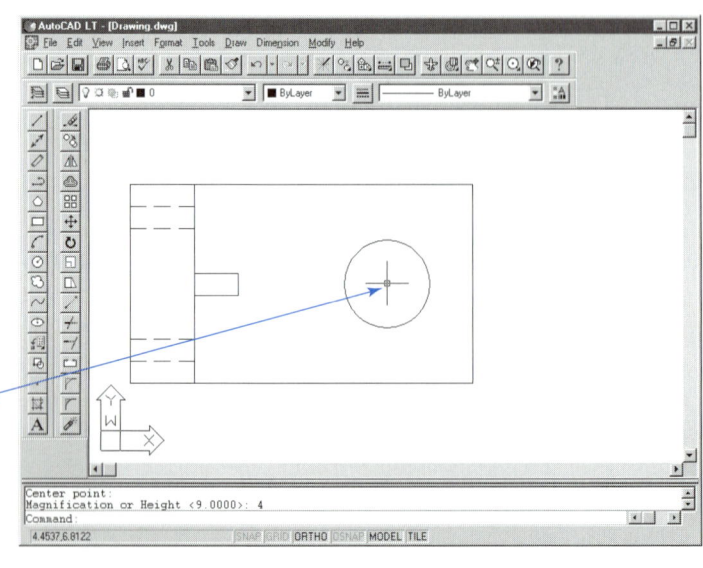

ing display shows four drawing units vertically, and the point 3.25,6.0 (the center of the circle) is at the center of the screen:

> Command: **Z** or **ZOOM**↵
> ZOOM All/Center/Extents/Previous/Scale (X/XP)/Window/<Realtime>: **C**↵
> Center point: **3.25,6**↵
> Magnification or Height ⟨9.0000⟩: **4**↵

Using the Zoom Previous Tool

The Zoom Previous tool is likely to be the single most frequently used zooming option. The view that was displayed previously to the current view is displayed again when you select Zoom Previous. This makes it easy to get back to where you were before you zoomed to the current view. AutoCAD LT keeps the last 10 display areas available so that you can back up through a series of display changes to return to a desired view.

As with all display changes, returning to the previous view has no effect on the objects in the drawing. Although using the U command will undo a display change, using Zoom Previous does not undo any drawing or editing commands. You can pick the Zoom Previous toolbar button from the Standard Toolbar, pick Previous from the Zoom cascade of the View pull-down menu, or type the command at the Command: prompt:

> Command: **Z** or **ZOOM**↵
> ZOOM All/Center/Extents/Previous/Scale (X/XP)/Window/<Realtime>: **P**↵

Exercise 4.2

1. Open a drawing from one of the exercises in Chapter 3.
2. Use the Zoom Window and Zoom Previous tools to zoom in on various features of the drawing and then return to the previous display.
3. Try the Zoom All and Zoom Extents tools and note the differences. Draw an object outside of your limits and then try both of these tools again.
4. Use the Zoom Center tool to change the magnification of your display. Try setting an absolute screen height with this option.
5. Save the drawing as EX4.2.

Using the Real-Time Zoom Tool

The Real-Time Zoom tool provides an interactive Zoom Scale process. This feature allows you to zoom in or out without having to enter a numeric value. Instead, moving your pointing device changes the display size as you watch, allowing you to decide when the display size fits your needs. The continuous feedback provided while you are adjusting the display makes this an *interactive* process. The Real-Time Zoom tool is available on the Standard toolbar, Real-Time can be picked from the Zoom cascade of the View pull-down menu, or it is the default option of the Zoom command prompt:

> Command: **Z** or **ZOOM**↵
> ZOOM All/Center/Extents/Previous/Scale (X/XP)/Window/<Realtime>: ↵
> Press Esc or Enter to exit, or right-click to activate popup menu.

Notice that the cursor now changes shape to appear as a magnifying glass with a plus and a minus sign to the right, similar to the image on the toolbar button. To begin the interactive zooming process, press and hold the pick button. While holding the pick button down, move your cursor up to increase magnification or down to decrease magnification. You can continue this process, zooming in and out as needed, until your display appears the way you want it.

When you are zooming in or out, your cursor may reach the edge of the screen and not allow you to go any further. If this happens, release the pick button and reposition the cursor on screen. Then you can press and hold the pick button again and continue your zooming operation. Once the display appears the way you want it to, press either the Enter key or the Esc (Escape) key.

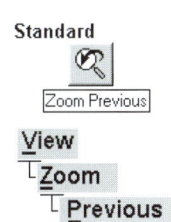

To display the real-time popup menu, press the right mouse button while in the real-time zoom command. The popup menu appears at the cursor location and presents the real-time display change options. See Figure 4.6.

FIGURE 4.6 The real-time popup menu appears at the cursor location when you right-click and presents the available real-time display change options.

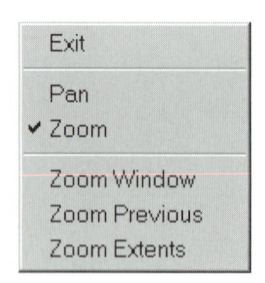

```
Exit
Pan
✓ Zoom
Zoom Window
Zoom Previous
Zoom Extents
```

The options on this menu are as follows:

Exit: Exits the real-time zoom or pan command.

Pan: Toggles the display change tool to Pan (Pan is covered later in this chapter).

Zoom: Toggles the display change command to Zoom.

Zoom Window: Changes to a Window mode for zooming. This option requires that you *press and hold* the pick button, drag the mouse to form a window, and then release the pick button to accept the defined window.

Zoom Previous: Returns the display to the state it was in when you started the real-time display change command.

Zoom Extents: Same as the regular Zoom extents option; shows the whole drawing.

Note that the real-time zooming option can be used only within the limits of what is called the logical extents. **Logical extents** refers to the area of the drawing that AutoCAD LT 98 is currently keeping within video memory. This means that display changes outside this area require AutoCAD LT to regenerate the drawing. The topic of drawing regeneration is discussed later in this chapter. When you have zoomed in as far as possible without regenerating the drawing, the + sign disappears from your real-time zooming cursor. Likewise, when you have zoomed out as far as possible, the − sign disappears.

> ### Field Notes
>
> - If a display change does not occur as you expected and you want to try again, the quickest way to get back to where you were is to use the Zoom Previous tool.
> - In a drawing where you have drawn several objects and Zoom All or Zoom Extents causes the objects to disappear, you may have accidentally created objects that are *very* far apart. If the objects are far enough apart, they may be too small to display properly and instead appear as small dots in opposing corners of the drawing. To check for this condition, after you zoom, check your coordinate display on the status bar as you move your cursor. If the coordinate numbers are much larger than your intended drawing area, this may be the case. If not, try a Zoom 0.9X to see if your objects are simply pushed up against the edges of the drawing area. Either way, a Zoom Previous takes you back to where you were.
> - In earlier versions, entering RTZOOM activates the Real-Time Zoom command. AutoCAD LT 98 still recognizes this command, but it is easier just to type **Z** and press Enter at the prompt.

✓ LEARNING CHECKPOINT

☐ Which ZOOM command option is used by the Zoom In and Zoom Out tools?

☐ What is the primary limitation of the Zoom Scale option?

☐ Describe the use of the Zoom Window tool.

- What is the easiest way to return to the previously displayed view?
- What is the difference between Zoom All and Zoom Extents?
- Name the interactive zooming option and describe its use.

Zooming with the IntelliMouse

Autodesk recommends the use of the Microsoft IntelliMouse with AutoCAD LT 98. There are many different brands of "wheel mouse" products on the market. Before you purchase an alternative product, be sure that it is 100% Intellimouse compatible. If you have the IntelliMouse, you can zoom and pan transparently using the Intellimouse wheel. The real-time zooming and panning features are subject to the same limitation as the actual commands, but the wheel provides an easier way to access these options.

To perform a real-time zoom, roll the wheel button without pressing it down. When you roll the wheel forward, the display is zoomed in, or made larger. When you roll the wheel backward, the display is zoomed out. Because it is a transparent function, it can be used within other commands. The zoom factor using the IntelliMouse is set in the Pointing Device Input area of the System tab on the Preferences dialog box. The Preferences dialog box can be accessed by typing **PR** or **PREFERENCES**.

Pressing the wheel button down accesses the real-time panning feature. Then, just move your mouse to change the location of the display. The original location of your cursor is shown as four arrows with a dot in the center. Your cursor then becomes an arrow as well, and your display moves in the direction of the arrow. The display moves slowly when the cursor is close to the point of origin and faster as you move the cursor further away. Note that the real-time panning feature works only if the button assignment for the wheel button is set to "default." This setting is adjusted in Mouse Properties under the Control Panel.

The AutoCAD LT 98 *Readme* file indicates some instances of certain difficulties when using real-time panning while the Aerial View window is open. View the Readme file for more information. This file is accessed by picking Programs from your Start menu on the Task Bar and then picking AutoCAD LT 98 and AutoCAD LT 98 Readme.

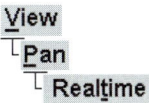

Using the PAN Command Options and Scrolling

The PAN command changes your view of the drawing without changing the magnification. This is very useful when you zoom into an area of the drawing and you need to see something that lies just outside of the currently visible area. Two Pan tools are available in AutoCAD LT: Real-Time Pan and Pan Point, or you can use the drawing area scroll bars.

Using Real-Time Pan Tool

The Real-Time Pan tool is the most convenient Pan option. It is an interactive display change tool similar to real-time zoom. Select the Real-Time Pan button from the Standard toolbar, pick Realtime from the Pan cascade of the View pull-down menu, or type **P** or **PAN** at the Command: prompt to use this tool.

Command: **P** or **PAN**↵
Press pick button and move cursor to pan [Enter or Esc to exit]:

When this command is entered, your cursor changes to a small hand with a four-way arrow to the right similar to the image on the toolbar button. To use this option, press and hold the pick button, then move your cursor to slide the drawing around. You can release the pick button if you need to reposition the cursor and continue to pan the drawing in much the same way as the real-time zoom option.

Although this command appears to slide the drawing around, nothing in the drawing actually changes position—the only thing that changes is your view of the drawing. If a line was drawn from the point coordinate 2,2 to 4,4 and you slide the drawing six units to the right, the coordinates for the endpoints of the line are still 2,2 and 4,4.

Right-clicking while using the Real-Time Pan option displays the same popup menu as when using the Real-Time Zoom option. This menu was discussed in the previous section. Also, the Real-Time Pan option can be used only within the logical extents of the drawing. When you have reached the logical extent on the top, bottom, left, or right, the cursor displays a bar to show that you can go no further in that direction.

-PAN
-P

Using the Pan Point Tool

The Pan Point tool also allows you to slide the drawing display, but it is not interactive. Instead, with this option you can enter an X and Y displacement value or you can specify two points on the screen that describe how you want the drawing display to move.

To enter X and Y displacement values, type an **X,Y** value at the Displacement: prompt and press Enter at the Second point: prompt. For example, move the display so the drawing appears to be four units to the right and two units above its current location:

Command: **-P** or **-PAN.↵**
PAN Displacement: **4,2.↵**
Second point: ↵

The other way to use this option is to specify a point coordinate at each prompt. The points can be selected with your cursor or entered from the keyboard using absolute, relative, or polar coordinates. AutoCAD LT measures the distance between the two points on both the X and Y axes and pans the display accordingly. For example:

Command: **-P** or **-PAN.↵**
PAN Displacement: **4,2.↵**
Second point: **6,3.↵**

This example moves the display so the drawing appears to be two units to the right and one unit above where it was previously. Figures 4.7 and 4.8 show the resulting display for these examples of the Pan Point tool. On

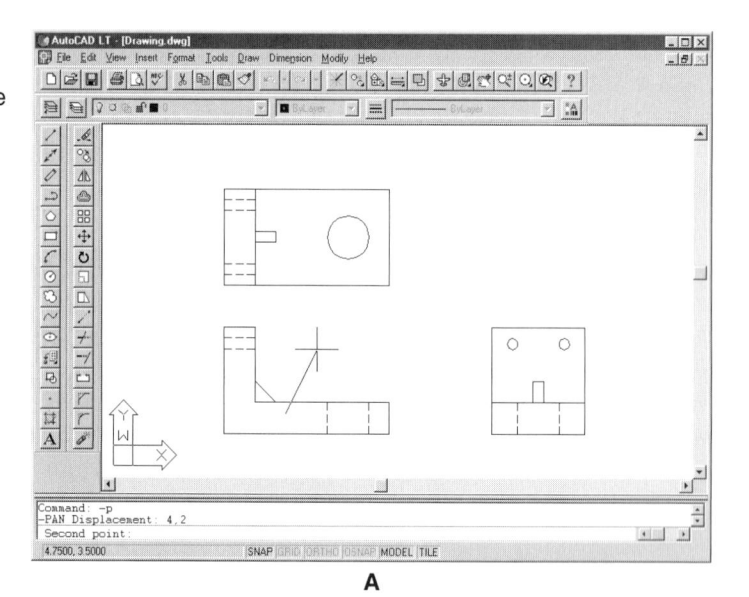

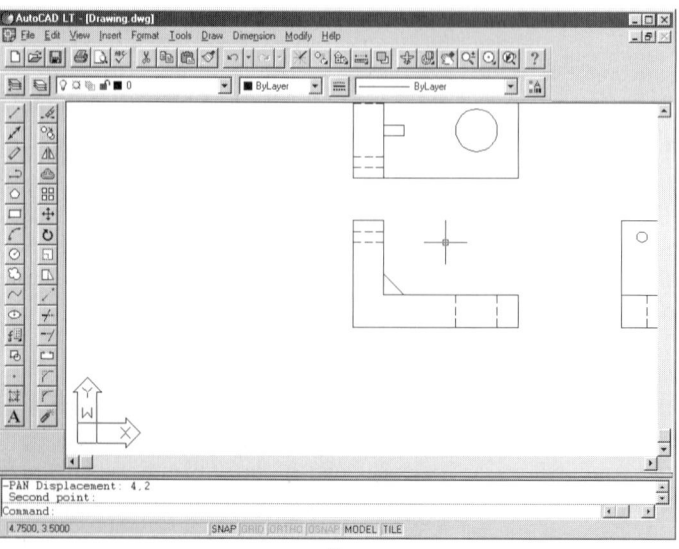

FIGURE 4.7 (A) The resulting display after entering a pan displacement value of 4 units on the X axis and 2 on the Y axis. (B) Pressing the Enter key at the Second point: prompt causes AutoCAD LT to use the value as an absolute displacement.

A

B

FIGURE 4.8 (A) The resulting display after entering a pan base point of 4,2 as the X,Y coordinate. (B) Enter a second point coordinate at the Second point: prompt and AutoCAD LT measures the distance and angle between the two points to use as the pan displacement value.

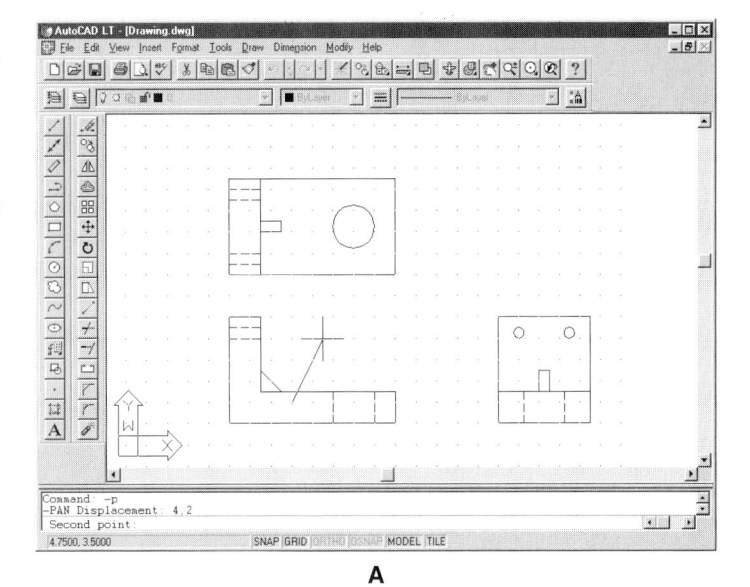

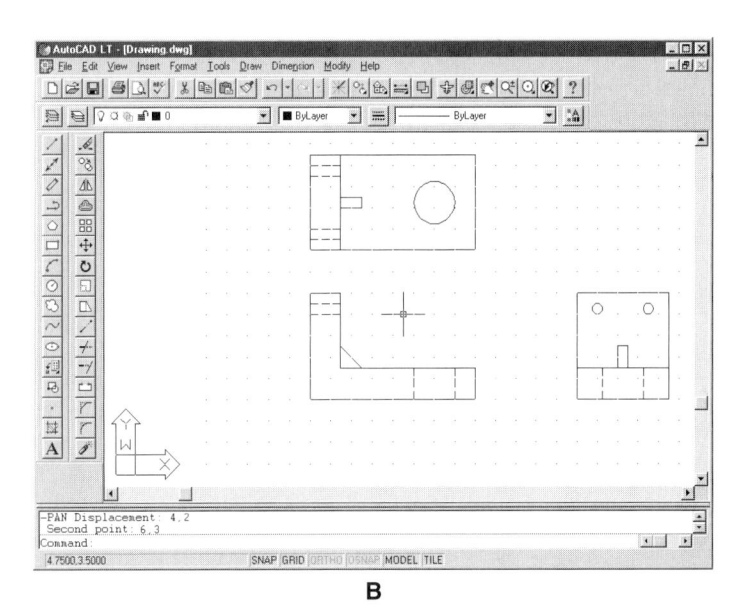

the Pan cascade of the View menu, AutoCAD LT presents four other options, Left, Right, Up, and Down. Selecting one of these options pans the display in the specified direction a distance equal to 20% of the current display height.

Using the Scroll Bars

The drawing area scroll bars are a quick and easy way to adjust the position of your drawing display. By default, AutoCAD LT displays scroll bars on the bottom and the right side of the drawing area. These are used like the scroll bars in any other Windows-based application.

At each end of a scroll bar is an arrow button. Picking this button moves the viewing area 10% in the direction indicated. You can move the display 80% by picking in the scroll bar background area; the side of the slider you point to when you pick is the direction the display is moved.

You can also point to the slider button, press and hold the pick button, and move the slider to a new position. The position of the slider relative to the scroll bar indicates where your current view is centered relative to the extents of the drawing. The ***drawing extents*** is the area of your drawing that contains objects, or the area that is displayed when you use the Zoom Extents tool. If you are not zoomed in too close, you can scroll freely through the extents of your drawing using the slider.

> ✏️ **Field Notes**
>
> If scroll bars are not visible in your AutoCAD LT window, you can turn them on by using the <u>P</u>references ... option found in the <u>T</u>ools pull-down menu. On the Work Space page of the Preferences dialog box, place a check mark in the <u>D</u>isplay scrollbars toggle. This toggle is located in the upper left area of the dialog box. Pick the OK button to exit the dialog box and return to the drawing editor.

☑ LEARNING CHECKPOINT

☐ Describe the use and advantages of the Real-Time Pan tool.
☐ What two methods can be used with the Pan Point tool?
☐ What are the three different ways the scroll bars can be used?

How to Zoom Transparently

In Chapter 2 you were introduced to transparent commands. A ***transparent*** command can be used without interrupting a currently active command—as long as it does not require a drawing regeneration and it does not change the drawing database. The term ***drawing database*** refers to the information that AutoCAD LT stores to define the objects in a drawing file. Drawing and editing commands cannot be used transparently because they make direct changes to the drawing database.

AutoCAD LT maintains a certain area of the current drawing in memory, so you can quickly change the display area without the need to read the drawing file from your hard disk. This area is called the ***logical extents.*** If the requested display change shows an area that lies outside of the current logical extents, then AutoCAD LT must first regenerate your drawing. The term ***regenerate*** means that AutoCAD LT reads the current drawing database and redefines the virtual screen area. All of the objects in the new logical extents are loaded into memory from the current drawing database. Your drawing must also be regenerated if a display change shows an area that is extremely small in relationship to the current logical extents.

To increase your flexibility while drawing and editing, the zoom options can be used transparently as long as the results can be displayed using the current logical extents. The Pan tools and the scroll bars can also be used transparently under these same conditions.

When a display change option is selected from the menu, AutoCAD LT automatically checks to see if it can be done without a drawing regeneration. If so, the command is entered transparently. When entered at the Command: prompt, a transparent command behaves no differently than normal. However, entering a transparent command while another command is active temporarily stops the currently active command while the transparent command is processed. The following example shows the first point for a line object being picked. A zoom operation is done transparently to magnify part of the drawing and a second point is picked, then the previous display is returned to transparently:

```
Command: LINE↵
From point: ⟨pick a point⟩
To point: 'Z or 'ZOOM↵
>>All/Center/Extents/Previous/Scale (X/XP)/Window/<Realtime>: W↵
>>First corner: ⟨pick first corner⟩
>>Other corner: ⟨pick other corner⟩
Resuming LINE command.
To point: ⟨pick a point⟩
To point: 'Z or 'ZOOM↵
>>All/Center/Extents/Previous/Scale (X/XP)/Window/<Realtime>: P↵
Resuming LINE command.
To point:
```

As shown in the example, a transparent command has an apostrophe preceding the command name. The >> characters before the prompt indicate that you are working transparently while another command is active.

CHAPTER 4 ||| Drawing Display Control   141

Also in the previous example, notice that the W and the P are not preceded by an apostrophe. Command options entered for a transparent command do not require an apostrophe. When the transparent command is finished, a message is issued indicating that the active command is being resumed.

In the next example, the requested display change cannot be completed without a drawing regeneration. AutoCAD LT issues an appropriate message and resumes the active command:

Command: **LINE**↵
From point: ⟨*pick a point*⟩
To point: **'Z** or **'ZOOM**↵
>>All/Center/Extents/Previous/Scale (X/XP)/Window/<Realtime>: **W**↵
>>First corner: ⟨*pick first corner*⟩
>>Other corner: ⟨*pick other corner*⟩
**Requires a regen, cannot be transparent.
Resuming LINE command.
To point:

If the display change is required for you to continue, press the Esc key to cancel the currently active command and return to the Command: prompt. Now you can enter the display change option. You may notice that display changes requiring regenerations are somewhat slower than other display changes. This display speed difference is even more significant when working with larger drawings.

Exercise 4.3

1. Open a drawing from one of the exercises in Chapter 3.
2. Zoom in and out with the Real-Time Zoom tool. See how far in and how far out you can zoom. Try Real-Time Pan, Pan Point, and panning using the scroll bars. Note the advantages and disadvantages of each method.
3. Start a drawing or editing command and use some of your display change tools transparently. Try entering a transparent display change using the keyboard.
4. On a piece of paper, write down the names of each of the display change tools. Indicate which ones can be used transparently and which cannot.
5. Save the drawing as EX4.3.

✓ LEARNING CHECKPOINT

☐ How can display change commands be used transparently?
☐ What types of commands cannot be used transparently?
☐ Which two Zoom options cannot be used transparently?
☐ What character precedes prompts to indicate the command is transparent?

Using the Aerial View Window

The Aerial View window provides a powerful set of display management tools. This tool opens up a separate window where your entire drawing is displayed, and a number of display change options are available. The Aerial View window starts out as a small window initially displayed in the lower right area of the AutoCAD LT window, but can be moved and resized as needed. Figure 4.9 shows the Aerial View window.

The Aerial View window display is toggled by picking the Aerial View toolbar button from the Standard toolbar, by picking Aerial Vie<u>w</u> from the <u>V</u>iew pull-down menu, or by typing **DS** or **DSVIEWER** at the Command: prompt. The DSVIEWER command is a toggle, meaning that if the Aerial View window is currently hidden, it will be displayed, and if it is currently visible, then this option hides it.

The Aerial View window toolbar and pull-down menus provide tooltips, and like any other window in a Windows environment, it can be resized or moved as desired.

Refer to Figure 4.10 for a map of the Aerial View window features.

Standard
Aerial View

View
Aerial Vie<u>w</u>

DSVIEWER
DS

FIGURE 4.9 The Aerial View Window appears in the lower right area of the AutoCAD LT window by default but can be moved as desired.

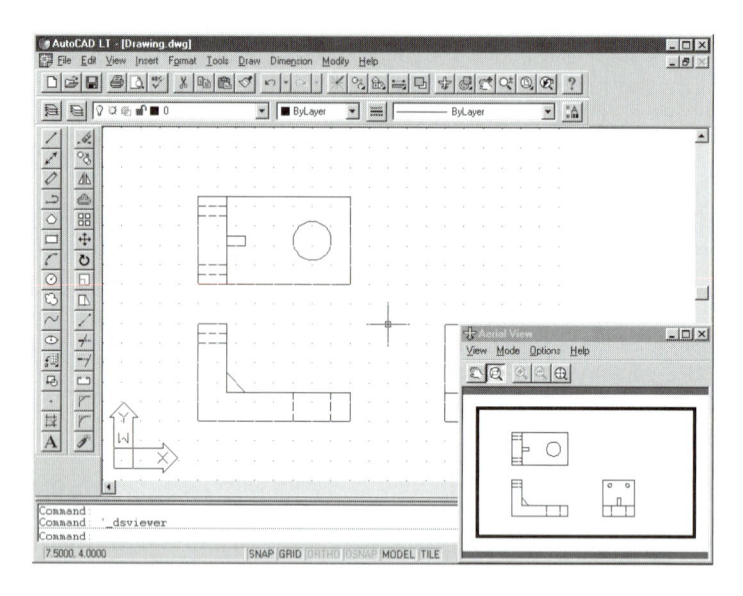

FIGURE 4.10 The features of the Aerial View window: Pull-down menu bar, Pan button, Zoom button, Zoom In button, Zoom Out button, Global button, Current View box.

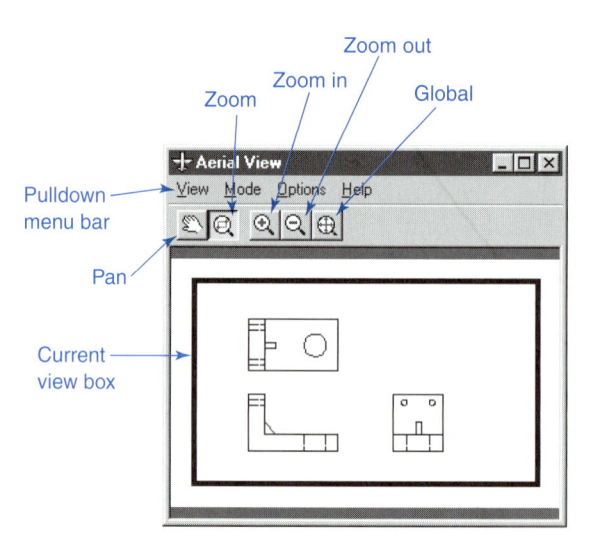

Zooming with Aerial View

When you first start the Aerial View window, the Zoom button should appear depressed, indicating the Zoom mode is active. The entire drawing should be visible in the Aerial View window drawing display area. Notice that in order to use the zooming feature, Zoom mode must be active. If it is not, pick the Zoom toolbar button or pick Zoom from the Mode pull-down menu in the Aerial View window.

The zoom mode allows you to draw a window in the Aerial View window to define the new display area. As you move the cursor over the Aerial View window from the AutoCAD LT window, the cursor changes to a system cursor (the arrow cursor). The first pick inside this window makes the Aerial View window current, the next two picks are just like using the Zoom Window tool. Move the crosshairs to pick the two corners of the area to be displayed. Once you have selected two corners, the AutoCAD LT drawing display is changed accordingly.

One of the remarkable features of the Aerial View window is that even if the current view in the AutoCAD LT drawing display area is greatly magnified, the entire drawing still appears in the Aerial View window. This means that you can return to the Aerial View window to zoom to another window that is not even visible in the AutoCAD LT drawing display area.

CHAPTER 4 ||| Drawing Display Control 143

When you are finished with the zooming operation and ready to begin or continue your drawing or editing tasks in the AutoCAD LT window again, move your cursor into the AutoCAD LT window and press the pick button to make AutoCAD LT the active window again.

Field Notes

- All Aerial View window display changes are entered transparently. If you attempt to make a display change that would require a regeneration, the request is ignored.
- You can return to a previous view using the Zoom Previous tool even when Aerial View was used to change the display.
- The U command has no effect on the DSVIEWER command, but will undo display changes made via the Aerial View window.

Exercise 4.4

1. Open a drawing from one of the exercises in Chapter 3.
2. Zoom in and out using the Aerial View window.
3. Pan using the Aerial View window.
4. Start a drawing or editing command and make a few transparent display changes using the Aerial View window.
5. Compare the use of the Aerial View window to other zooming options. Which display change tools are more convenient to use?
6. Save the drawing as EX4.4.

Panning with Aerial View

To activate Pan mode in the Aerial View window press the Pan toolbar button, pick Pan from the Mode pull-down menu in the Aerial View window, or right-click in the aerial viewer window. Now, rather than crosshairs, your cursor appears as a rectangle that shows the current view size. Remember that when panning, the view size does not change. Move the rectangle to the desired position and press the pick button. The AutoCAD LT drawing display is updated to show the new display area. To toggle back to zoom mode, right-click again.

Aerial View

Pan

Field Notes

The Aerial View window is meant to supplement the standard display change options available in AutoCAD LT, not replace them. Use all the available display change options to the best of your advantage.

Adjusting the Aerial View Window Display

If you are working in a small area within a large drawing, you may wish to change the size of the image displayed in the Aerial View window to make the display changes easier. The Aerial View Zoom In tool increases the apparent size of the objects in the Aerial View window by 2X, and the Zoom Out tool reduces the apparent size by one-half. The Global tool is used to display the entire drawing. Each of these tools is available as toolbar buttons in the Aerial View window or on the View pull-down menu. Adjusting the size of the image displayed in the Aerial View window has no effect on the drawing display.

Aerial View

Zoom In

Zoom Out

Global

Controlling the Updating of the Aerial View Window

By default, the Aerial View window is updated dynamically. This means that when you make a change to your drawing, such as adding a new object or modifying an existing object, the changes are reflected in the

Aerial View window immediately. In small drawings, this is not likely to affect your system performance. In larger drawings this can affect your editing speed significantly if you have to wait on the Aerial View window to update each time you make a change.

You can turn off the dynamic update feature by picking Dynamic Update from the Options menu in the Aerial View window. When you pick this menu, a check mark is displayed by the menu selection if it is active. Picking the item toggles its current state.

If you turn off the dynamic update feature, the image is only updated when you move the cursor into the Aerial View window.

The AutoViewport selection on the Options menu controls whether the Aerial View window is automatically updated to display the contents of the current tiled viewport. This is discussed further in Chapter 13.

Through the Window...

Using the Alt+Tab keystroke enables you to switch easily from one application window to another in Windows. However, this will not work for switching between the AutoCAD LT and Aerial View windows. This is because the Aerial View window is considered a *child* process of AutoCAD LT and not a separate application.

Since Aerial View is a child process of AutoCAD LT, if you minimize AutoCAD LT then Aerial View is minimized also, but it does not display its own icon or taskbar button.

Exercise 4.5

1. Open a drawing from one of the exercises in Chapter 3.
2. Start the Aerial View window.
3. Use the Zoom and Pan modes to change your drawing display.
4. Use the Zoom In and Zoom Out options to adjust the image displayed in the Aerial View window. Use the Global tool to reset the image to include the entire drawing.
5. Use the Locator tool. Adjust the magnification level and use the Locator again.
6. Add some new objects to your drawing and edit existing objects. Watch the Aerial View window as you do so and note the automatic updates.
7. Turn the Dynamic Update feature off. Again, add some new objects to your drawing and edit existing objects. Force an update by moving your cursor into the Aerial View window.
8. Save the drawing as EX4.5.

LEARNING CHECKPOINT

- What command starts the Aerial View window?
- What advantages are there to using the Aerial View options?
- Describe the options for updating the Aerial View window.

Creating Named Views

When working in AutoCAD LT, you may find yourself frequently zooming to one or more specific views of the drawing. You can use the standard display change tools and the Aerial Viewer to zoom in and out as necessary. For greater speed and convenience you can assign names to the views and return directly to the named views from anywhere in the drawing. The Named Views tool allows you to create, manage, and restore named views in the drawing. Using named views can increase productivity by making display changes fast and accurate.

To display the View Control dialog box, select Named Views from the View flyout on the Standard toolbar, pick Named Views ... from the View pull-down menu, or type **DDVIEW** or **V** at the Command: prompt. The View Control dialog box is shown in Figure 4.11.

FIGURE 4.11 The View Control dialog box.

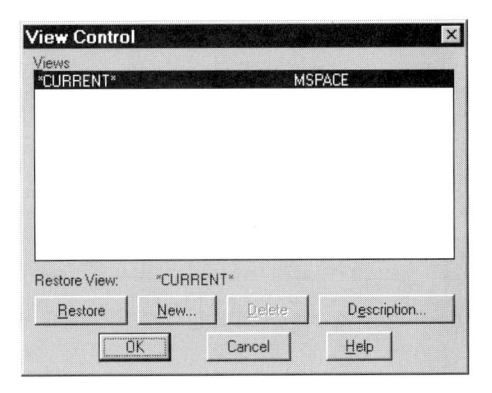

Defining Names Views

The View Control dialog box displays the names of each defined view in the current drawing and indicates whether they are in model space or paper space. The view named *CURRENT* is always present in this dialog box. It is not actually a specific view, but a reference to whatever is the currently visible view of your drawing. To define your own named view, first pick the New ... button to display the Define New View dialog box (see Figure 4.12).

FIGURE 4.12 The Define New View dialog box.

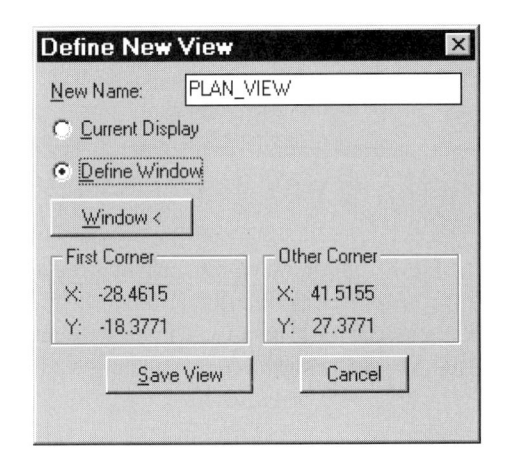

It is usually a good idea to keep view names simple and descriptive so that it is easy to remember what area of the drawing each one displays. AutoCAD LT allows you to name a view using up to 32 characters. A view name can contain alphanumeric characters (letters and numbers) but cannot have spaces or asterisks. Some nonalphanumeric characters can be used as well, such as dollar signs ($), hyphens (-), and underscores (_).

When defining a new view, you have a choice of assigning the view name to the Current Display or you can select Define Window. The Current Display option assigns the view name to the area that is currently displayed in the AutoCAD LT drawing display area.

The Define Window option assigns the view name to the display area described by the X and Y axes values listed in the First Corner and Other Corner areas of the dialog box. To change these coordinates, pick the Window < button. You are then prompted, on the command line, to specify the two corners. You can pick the points or type the point coordinates using the keyboard. When defining the window, you can use transparent display change tools as needed to zoom in or out or pan the drawing.

Once you have defined the display area for the new view name, pick the Save View button to save the view and return to the View Control dialog box.

Field Notes

- While using the View Control dialog box to define new views, if you select the Cancel button rather than the OK button, all of the views you have defined in this session of the View Control dialog will be discarded.
- If you pick the Window < button to define a window, pressing the Esc key at the First Corner or the Other Corner prompt cancels the View Control dialog session and discards all of your changes and additions. If you don't like the first pick point, pick any other points in the drawing and then when you return to the Define New View dialog, pick the Window < button again. This way you do not lose the changes.

If you define a named view and later want to change the definition, pick the New ... button in the View Control dialog box. Define the view with the desired changes and name it the same as the view you want to redefine. When you pick the Save View button, an Alert box is displayed with a warning that the view name already exists and asks if you want to redefine it (see Figure 4.13). If you do want to redefine it, pick the Redefine button; otherwise select Cancel and when you return to the Define New View dialog box you can change the name.

FIGURE 4.13 The view redefinition Alert box issues a warning if you are about to overwrite an existing view definition.

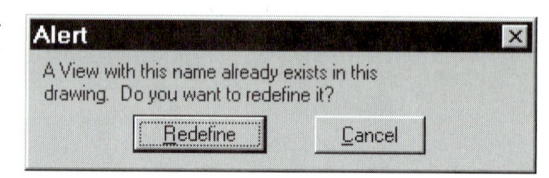

Getting Named View Descriptions

The Description ... button in the View Control dialog box provides the defining information for the currently highlighted view displayed in the View Description dialog box. Much of the information displayed applies only to 3-D drawing, which is discussed in Chapter 13. The View Name, Width, Height, and Center (WCS) show you the name, location, and size of the view.

Restoring Named Views

To restore a named view, start the View Control dialog box by entering the DDVIEW command. Highlight the desired view, press the Restore button, and pick OK. The selected view is displayed when the dialog box disappears.

Deleting Named Views

When a named view is no longer needed, it can be removed from the Views list in the View Control dialog box. To delete a named view, highlight the view name in the list and pick the Delete button.

There is no further prompt when you pick the Delete button, the view is simply removed from the list. If you accidentally delete a view that you need, pick the Cancel button to discard all changes. If you do pick the OK button, you can use the U command to undo the changes made in the View Control dialog box.

Managing Views Transparently

VIEW
-V

The DDVIEW command cannot be used transparently, but much of the real value of named views comes from transparent use. To manage named views transparently, use the 'VIEW command or type '-V. This example shows the 'VIEW command being used to restore a previously defined view during a LINE command sequence:

Command: **LINE**↵
From point: ⟨*pick a point*⟩
To point: **'-V** or **'VIEW**↵

```
>>?/Delete/Restore/Save/Window: R↵
View name to restore: PLAN-VIEW↵
Resuming LINE command.
To point:
```

The options of the VIEW command are almost the same as the options of the DDVIEW command, but they are entered at the command line instead of in a dialog box. To save the current display as a named view, use the Save option. The Window option allows you to draw a window to describe a view and assign a name to it. The question mark, ?, gives you a listing of the currently defined views, and Delete removes named view definitions. Probably the most commonly used 'VIEW command option is Restore.

Field Notes

- If you use the VIEW command frequently, you will want to keep view names short. If you use 32-character view names, it may be faster to use the zooming and panning tools instead—especially if you are not a fast and accurate typist.
- Establishing a standard set of named views for all of your drawings can boost productivity. One way of doing this is to create an appropriate series of named views in each of your prototype drawings.

Exercise 4.6

1. Open a drawing from one of the exercises in Chapter 3.
2. Start the View Control dialog box.
3. Create one named view that shows your entire drawing; name it ALL.
4. Create three or more views of different areas of your drawing and name them appropriately.
5. Use the Restore button in the View Control dialog box to restore each view.
6. Use the VIEW command to list the available views.
7. Draw a line that starts in one of your smaller views, then transparently restore another view and finish the line.
8. Save the drawing as EX4.6.

LEARNING CHECKPOINT

- ☐ What are the four ways of starting the DDVIEW command?
- ☐ How can using named views increase your productivity?
- ☐ Why should you avoid pressing Esc when defining a window in DDVIEW?
- ☐ How can named views be restored transparently?

MULTIPLE CHOICE

Circle the choice or enter your response on an answer sheet by selecting the option that most accurately completes or answers the given statements.

1. To increase the apparent size of the objects on your screen, you should:
   - **a.** zoom out
   - **b.** wear glasses
   - **c.** zoom in
   - **d.** zoom extents

2. A Zoom Scale specification that would bring you closer to your work:
   - **a.** 1X
   - **b.** 1/2X
   - **c.** .5X
   - **d.** 2X

3. The Real-Time Zoom tool allows you to:
   a. zoom out
   b. zoom interactively
   c. zoom in
   d. all of the above

4. The zooming option that displays the drawing limits or extents, whichever is greater:
   a. Zoom All
   b. Zoom Out
   c. Zoom Extents
   d. Zoom Limits

5. A command that is issued while another command is active is a:
   a. hidden command
   b. transparent command
   c. error
   d. cancel

6. If you enter a coordinate at the first prompt of the PAN command and press Enter at the second prompt, the coordinate is considered to be:
   a. an exact value
   b. an incorrect value
   c. an error value
   d. a displacement value

7. To issue a command transparently, precede the command name with:
   a. Esc
   b. Alt
   c. an asterisk
   d. an apostrophe

8. Some commands can be used transparently if they do not require:
   a. user input
   b. a menu pick
   c. a regeneration
   d. a display change

9. The command that starts the Aerial View window is:
   a. DSVIEWER
   b. AVIEWER
   c. AV
   d. AERIAL

10. Named Views can be managed using the:
    a. Aerial View window
    b. REDRAW command
    c. View Control dialog box
    d. ZOOM command

MATCHING

Match each term to the correct description by writing the appropriate number in each box at the left.

☐ Zoom Window
☐ Zoom Extents
☐ Zoom All
☐ Zoom Previous
☐ Zoom Scale
☐ Real-Time Zoom
☐ Pan Point
☐ Real-Time Pan
☐ Scroll bars
☐ Arrow button
☐ Scroll bar background
☐ View Restore
☐ View Save
☐ View Window
☐ View Delete

1. Interactive panning tool.
2. Returns to the previously displayed view.
3. Interactive zooming tool.
4. A convenient means of sliding the drawing vertically or horizontally.
5. Displays the selected named view.
6. Pans the drawing display 80%.
7. Used to draw a window describing your display change.
8. Saves the current display area as a named view.
9. Magnifies or reduces the drawing display by a specified scale.
10. Saves a windowed area as a named view.
11. Shows all objects in your drawing.
12. Deletes a named view.
13. Pans the drawing display 10%.
14. Zooms to the limits or extents, whichever is greater.
15. Slides the drawing display by picking two points.

CHAPTER 4 ||| Drawing Display Control

WORD SCRAMBLE

Unscramble the six scrambled words below, one letter to each square, to form six AutoCAD LT–related words:

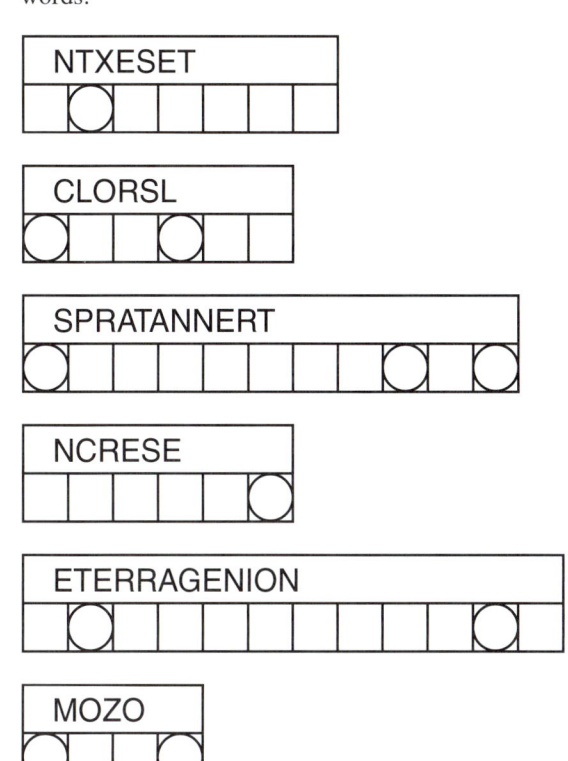

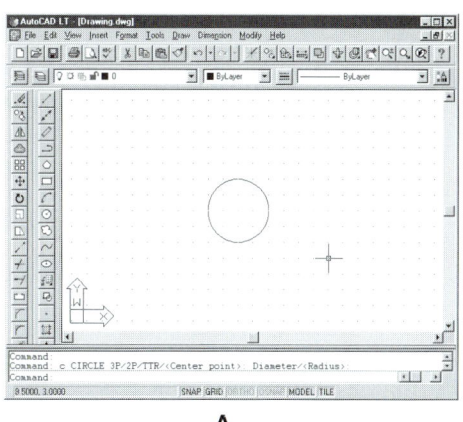

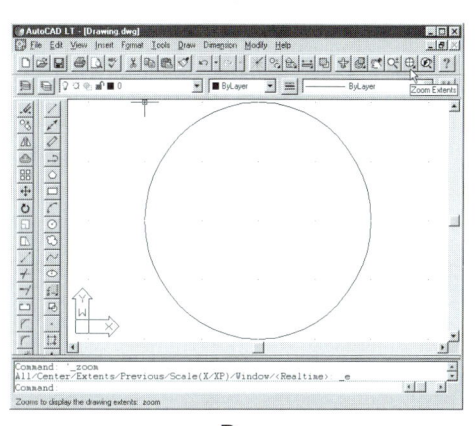

NTXESET

CLORSL

SPRATANNERT

NCRESE

ETERRAGENION

MOZO

A

B

Unscramble the circled letters above to form the special answer, as suggested by the illustration.

PROJECTS

4.1 Open drawing P3.1 for editing. Create four named views as follows: HOOD, GLASS, MOUNT, ALL. The named views should show the appropriate area of the drawing. Save the drawing as P4.1.

4.2 Open drawing P3.2 for editing. Create three named views as follows: TOP-PLUG, BTM-PLUG, ALL. The named views should show the appropriate area of the drawing. Save the drawing as P4.2.

4.3 Open drawing P3.3 for editing. Create two named views as follows: ELLIPSE, ALL. The named views should show the appropriate area of the drawing. Save the drawing as P4.3.

4.4 Open drawing P3.4 for editing. Create five named views as follows: TOP-HEX, RGT-HEX, LFT-HEX, BTM-HEX, PLATE. The named views should show the appropriate area of the drawing. Save the drawing as P4.4.

4.5 Open drawing P3.5 for editing. Create five named views as follows: TOP-HEX, RGT-HEX, LFT-HEX, BTM-HEX, PLATE. The named views should show the appropriate area of the drawing. Save the drawing as P4.5.

4.6 Open drawing P3.6 for editing. Create six named views as follows: TOP, RGT, LFT, BTM, CTR, GASKET. The named views should show the appropriate area of the drawing. Save the drawing as P4.6.

4.7 Open drawing P3.7 for editing. Create six named views as follows: TOP, RGT, LFT, BTM, CTR, GASKET. The named views should show the appropriate area of the drawing. Save the drawing as P4.7.

4.8 Open drawing P3.8 for editing. Create two named views as follows: STAIRS, ALL. The named views should show the appropriate area of the drawing. Save the drawing as P4.8.

4.9 Open drawing P3.9 for editing. Create four named views as follows: DRIVE, TIMER, CONTROLS, CIRCUIT. The named views should show the appropriate area of the drawing. Save the drawing as P4.9.

CHAPTER 5

Using Layers, Linetypes, and Colors

LEARNING GOALS

- Explain the importance of layers and good layer management.
- Create layers by name, color, and linetype.
- Draw objects on different layers.
- Adjust the linetype scale.
- Control layer visibility.
- Explain the difference between a frozen and a locked layer.
- Discuss why caution should be used when overriding layers.
- Change the objects layer.
- Filter layers.
- Plot line widths assigned to layer colors.

An Introduction to AutoCAD LT Layers

A *layer* is defined by AutoCAD LT as a logical grouping of data, like transparent overlays on a manual drawing. Try to envision these overlays as clear sheets, each with its own specific type of drawing information. As you stack these clear sheets together, you can see through each sheet to the drawings on the sheets below. You can view overlays or layers individually or in combination. Layers might be considered as a series of drawing overlays. In architectural drafting, layers may be made up of several overlays including border and title block, floor plan, dimensions, notes, electrical, plumbing, and structural. Each layer can be displayed in its own color and plotted in color if a color plotter is available. Each layer can be displayed and plotted individually or together in any desired combination. Figure 5.1 provides a pictorial example of how layers work.

Layers for a mechanical drawing might be set up based on linetype. For example, you might create one layer each for object lines, hidden lines, center lines, and dimensions. The layers for each linetype may be set up using individual colors, which makes each linetype stand out clearly on the computer screen. During the plotting or printing process, each layer's color can be assigned a specific pen width. In this manner, line widths can be varied, with thick lines plotted 0.6 mm wide and thin lines plotted 0.3 mm wide to conform to ASME standards. These different widths provide line contrast even if the plot contains only black lines. Appendix B displays the recommended ASME linetypes and widths.

Managing Drawing Layers

A good layer management system and record keeping are very important. Layers may be managed by name or number, or by the project, or based on company or national standards. Layer names should be recorded in a procedures manual or drawing log with information about the content. The manual should provide the layer name, color, linetype, and specific information about the layer content and use. A good example of a layer management system is published in *CAD Layer Guidelines,* by the American Institute of Architects (AIA) Press, 1735 New York Avenue, N.W., Washington, D.C. 20006. In this format, layer names are based on abbreviations that are easy to recognize. Layer names are based on a logical grouping of objects in a drawing, such as A-DOOR for architectural doors or E-LITE for electrical lighting. AutoCAD LT lists layers alpha-

FIGURE 5.1 A pictorial representation of a CAD layering system showing how information is shared among drawings. (Drawing courtesy of Carl Backstrom.)

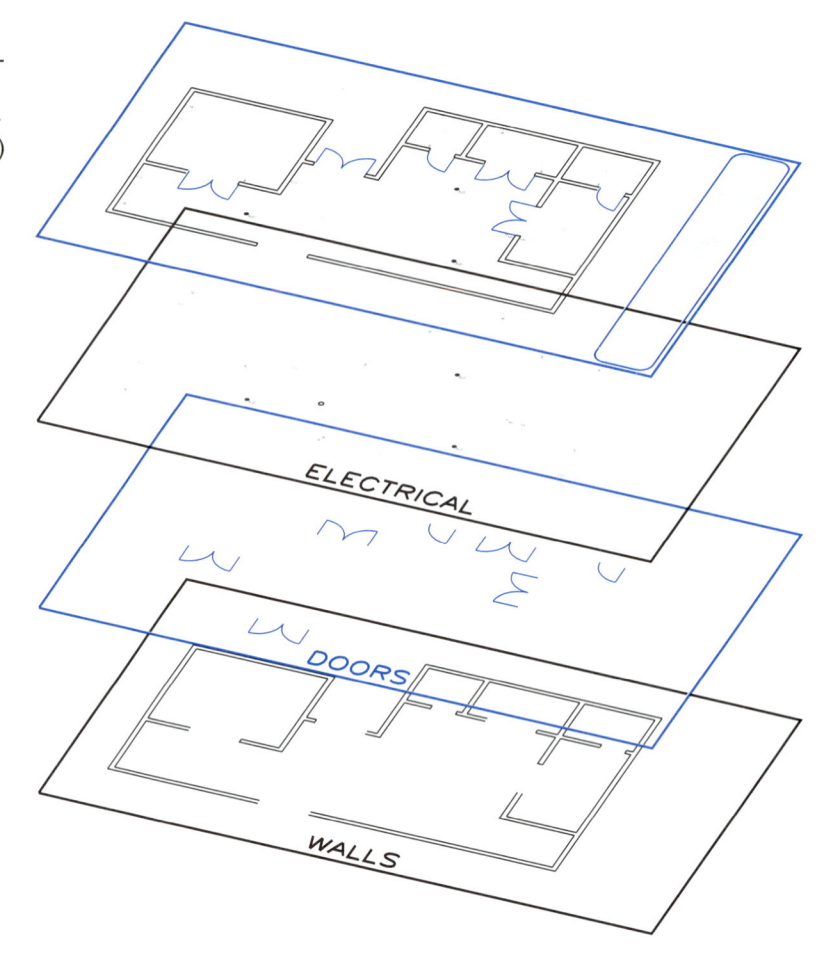

betically by name for ease of location. Use of a common prefix for all similar layers helps when you are trying to locate or sort layers. The AIA has established eight major groups of layer prefixes:

A	Architectural, interiors, and facility management
S	Structural
M	Mechanical
P	Plumbing
F	Fire protection
E	Electrical
C	Civil engineering and site work
L	Landscape architecture

You should determine if company, school, or national standards are available to follow when designing your layer names and content. If not, set up your layer naming system based on the information found in the drawing. Information regarding the CAD Layer Guidelines document can also be found at the AIA Online Network Web site. The URL is http://www.aia.org/

Creating Layers

Layers are created in the Layer & Linetype Properties dialog box. Access this dialog box by picking Layer … in the Format pull-down menu, pick the Layer button in the Object Properties toolbar, or type **Layer**, **LA,** or **DDLMODES**. The Layer & Linetype Properties dialog box contains information about your layers. It also allows you to add or delete layers or to perform other layer management activities. When you start an AutoCAD LT drawing from scratch or with Quick Setup, the only layer listed is the default layer 0 (zero), as shown in Figure 5.2A. If you start an AutoCAD LT drawing from a template, additional layers may be listed. For example, look at Figure 5.2B and notice the list including Layer Name, State, Color, and Linetype. The 0 layer is listed with Tb and Title_block. Pick the New button to add new layer names to the layer list. A new

CHAPTER 5 ||| Using Layers, Linetypes, and Colors   153

FIGURE 5.2 (A) The Layer & Linetype Properties dialog box shows the AutoCAD LT default layers when starting from scratch or using Quick Setup. The 0 layer is the default for all starting options. (B) Additional layers automatically added when starting with a template.

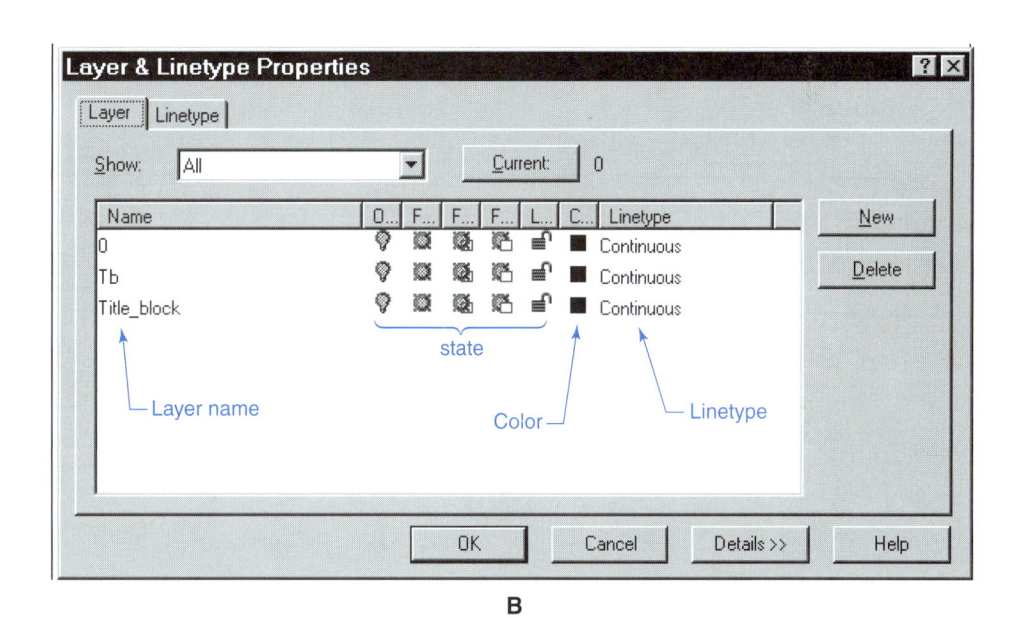

default layer named Layer1 is added to the list and highlighted when you pick the New button, as shown in Figure 5.3. New layers have the default state, color, and linetype. These features are discussed later. You can add default layers named Layer2, Layer3, etc., each time you pick the New button. The default layer names might work for some applications, but they usually are not descriptive enough for professional use.

When you pick the New button, the default Layer1 name is highlighted inside a text box. This allows you to immediately type a new layer name, such as Object, as shown in Figure 5.4. The Object layer might be used for drawing the object lines on a mechanical drawing. You can press Enter twice, after typing the desired layer name, to create another new layer. This is easier than pressing the New button. Then all you have to do is type another layer name in place of the default Layer name. An easy way to enter several layer names at the same time is to type each name, followed by a comma. Typing the comma drops the layer list to the next line, with the Layer1 name highlighted for you to type another new layer name. Figure 5.5 shows the layer names Center, Dimension, Hidden, and Section added to the list in this manner. These layers are used for displaying the type of line associated with the name. For example, the Center layer is used for centerlines and the Dimension layer is used for dimensions. You do not have to use capital letters when typing layer names. AutoCAD LT automatically capitalizes the first letter of the layer name display, but layer names are not case sensitive. This means that you can type layer names using either caps or lowercase letters. Picking

FIGURE 5.3 Pick the New button in the Layer & Linetype Properties dialog box to add a new layer. The default layer is named Layer1.

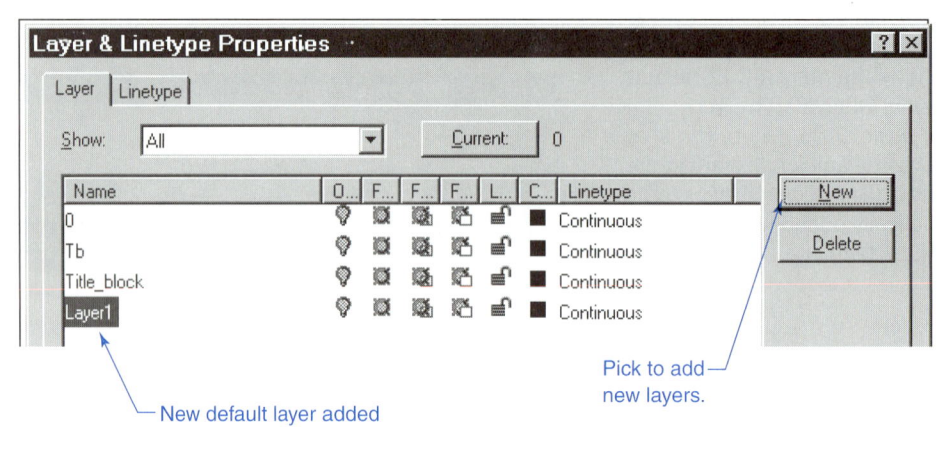

FIGURE 5.4 Type the desired layer name in the text box.

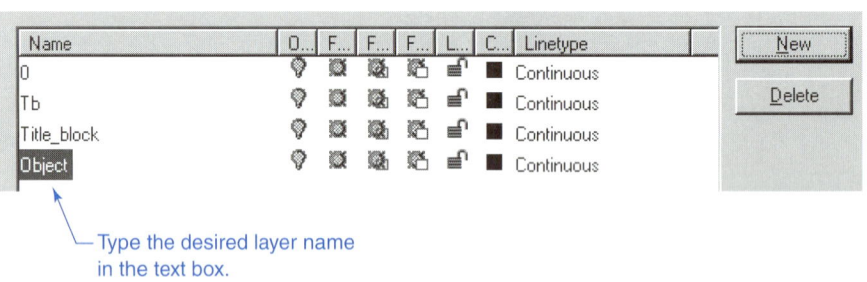

FIGURE 5.5 Type a comma after each layer name to have AutoCAD LT automatically go to the next line.

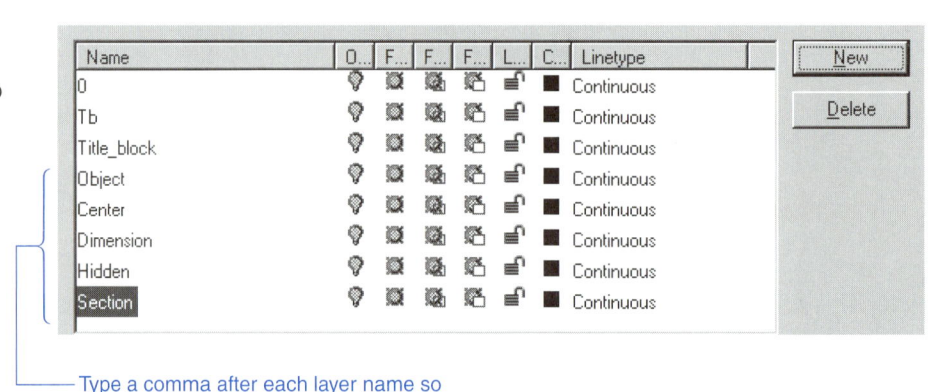

the Cancel button discards all changes and layers made during this dialog session. Pick the OK button to close the Layer & Linetype Properties dialog box when you are done working with layers.

Open the Layer & Linetype Properties dialog box again and you will see that AutoCAD LT has automatically arranged the layer names in alphabetical order, as shown in Figure 5.6. Every new layer has the default status, color, and linetype.

FIGURE 5.6 AutoCAD LT automatically lists layer names in alphabetical order.

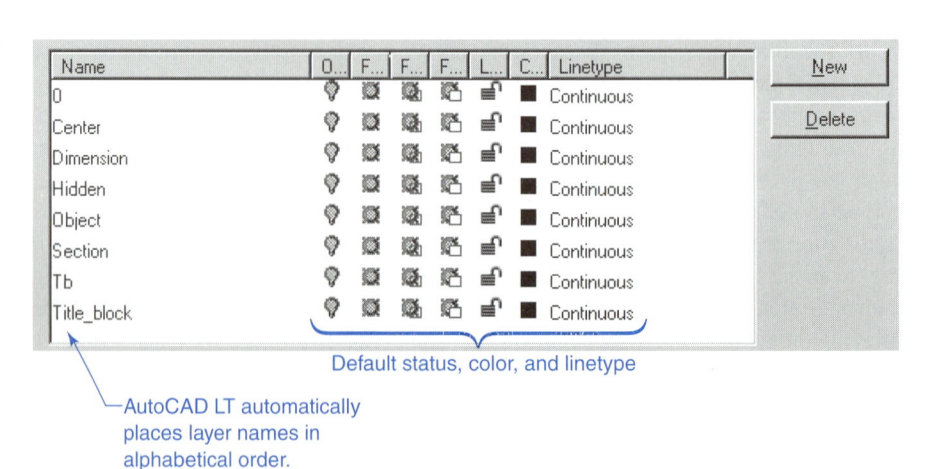

CHAPTER 5 ||| Using Layers, Linetypes, and Colors

The following describes several ways to work with layers in the Name list:

- Pick a layer name to highlight it and then pick again to have a text box placed around the layer name. Now you can type a different layer name, if desired.

- Pick a layer name and then hold the Shift key to have every layer name highlighted between the first pick and the second.

- Hold the Ctrl key while picking layer names to highlight multiple layer names when the names are not adjacent.

- Pick to highlight one or more layer names and then pick the Delete button to have the highlighted layers removed from the list. A layer cannot be removed if it is current or it contains objects.

- Move the cursor inside the layer list box and press the right mouse button. This displays the Select All and Clear All cursor menu shown in Figure 5.7. Pick Select All to highlight all layers in the list, or pick Clear All to have all of the highlighted layers cleared. Notice when you move the cursor to a layer name, AutoCAD LT gives you the following tool tip: Layers; right click for menu.

Layer names can have up to 31 characters and you can use letters, numbers, and special characters such as underscores (_), hyphens (-), and dollar signs ($). Layer names cannot have blank spaces.

FIGURE 5.7 Move the cursor inside the layer list box and click on the right mouse button to get the cursor menu.

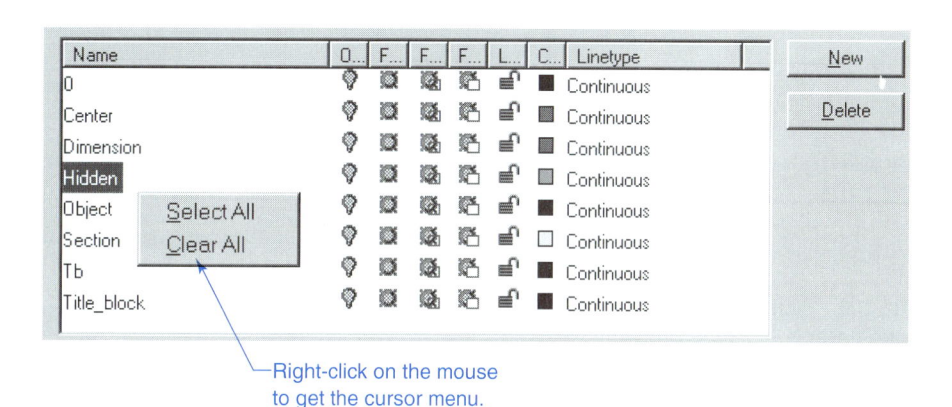

Right-click on the mouse to get the cursor menu.

Using Layer Colors

As with many lists in Windows, the label at the top of each column in the layer list is actually a button. By default, the color column is labeled **C...** and displays just a color swatch showing the color assigned to that layer. If you want to see the entire label, point to either vertical edge of the button, and the resizing cursor is displayed. Press and hold the pick button and move the cursor to resize the button and the column below it. When the color column is expanded, the color name or number is displayed to the right of the square color swatch.

Notice in Figure 5.6 that all of the listed layers are shown with the color white. The color white is white on a black display screen or it is black on a white display screen. Having all of the lines displayed with the color white is an option, but a better application is to assign each layer its own color. The standard AutoCAD LT colors are recognized by name and by color number. The following is a list of standard colors by name and number:

Color	Number
RED	1
YELLOW	2
GREEN	3
CYAN	4
BLUE	5
MAGENTA	6
WHITE	7

Colors beyond the basic colors are identified only by numbers. The total color range runs from number 1 through 255.

To change a layer color, pick the color swatch associated with that layer. When you point to a color swatch, AutoCAD LT gives you a "color" tooltip. You can pick as many layers as you want to highlight and then pick any of the color swatches. When you pick the color swatch of a highlighted layer or layers, the Select Color dialog box is displayed. See Figure 5.8. The current color is displayed in the Color: text box. Move the cursor to a desired color, such as green, and pick. The color you pick is displayed in the Color: text box. Pick the OK button when you are ready. Colors can be picked in this manner or you can enter the color number in the text box. Change the layer color for all of the desired layers. Note that the selected color is assigned to all the currently highlighted layers. Figure 5.9 shows the selected layer colors for the previously named layers.

FIGURE 5.8 Pick the color swatch of the highlighted layer or layers to access the Select Color dialog box.

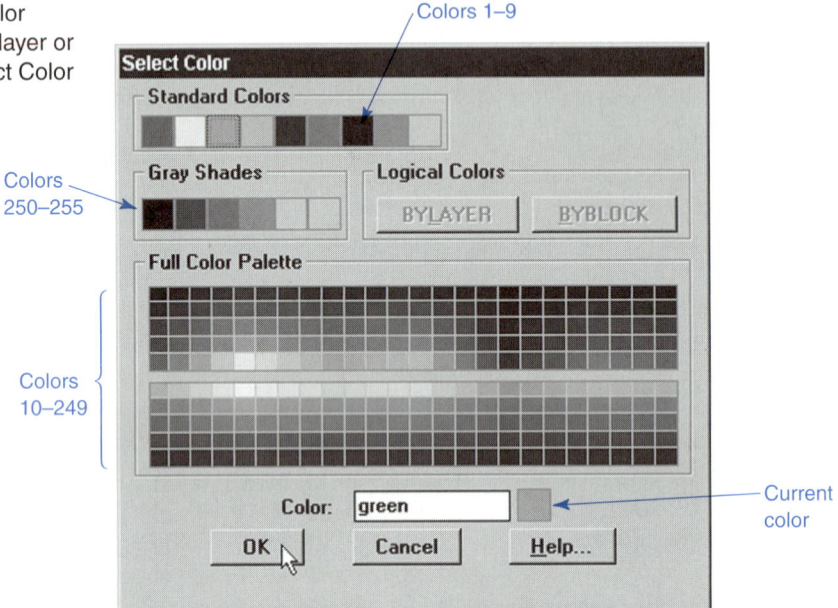

FIGURE 5.9 Pick the OK button in the Layer & Linetype Properties dialog box to accept the colors that were assigned to each layer.

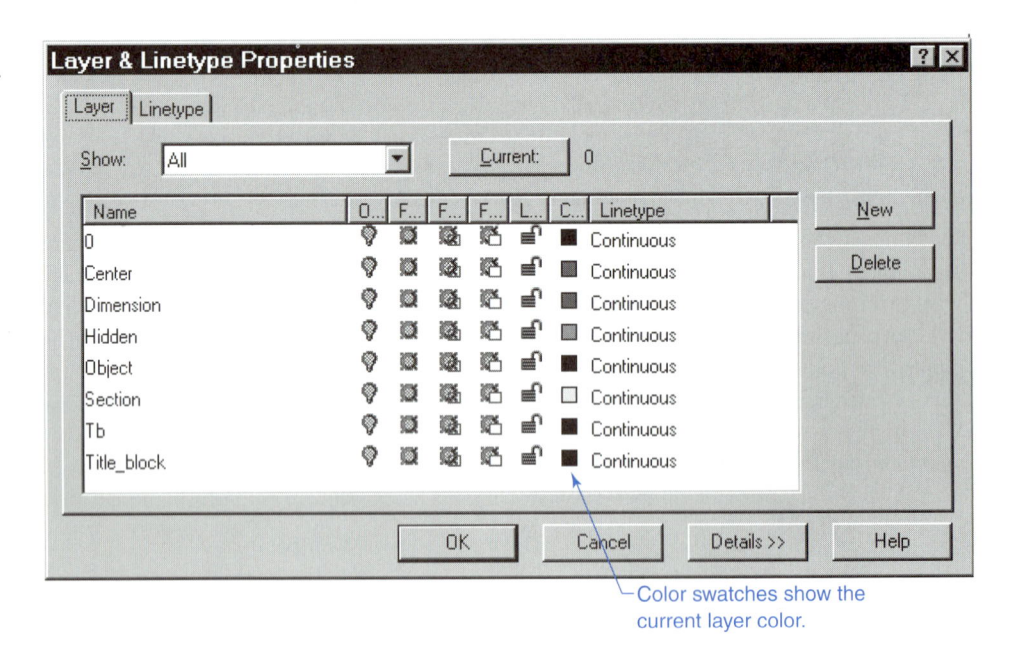

Field Notes

Look at the Select Color dialog box in Figure 5.8. The Full Color Palette compartment displays colors 10 through 249. The Gray Shades compartment shows color options 250 through 255.

Using Layer Linetypes

The term *linetype* is AutoCAD LT's way of referring to types of drafting lines. Recommended linetypes are identified in the American National Standards Institute document *Line Conventions and Lettering* (ASME Y14.2M). These lines are shown in Appendix B. If needed, refer to the examples in that appendix for a review of drafting standards and practices.

When you initially name a new layer, the listed linetype is Continuous. Continuous linetypes are solid lines (without dashes). A Continuous linetype setting is used for object lines, section lines, and dimension lines, which should all be solid lines. However, for drawing lines to proper standards, you want to set lines in layers such as center, hidden, and phantom to their proper linetype representation. To do this, open the Layer & Linetype Properties dialog box, move the cursor to the linetype name of the desired layer, and pick. AutoCAD LT gives you a "Linetype" tool tip to let you know that you have moved the cursor to a linetype. The Select Linetype dialog box shown in Figure 5.10 is displayed when you pick the desired linetype. The Select Linetype dialog box lists the available linetype name, shows what the line looks like, and gives a short description of the line. The only linetype listed when you start AutoCAD LT is Continuous. You must load additional linetypes before they can be used with your layers. To load more linetypes, pick the Load ... button to get the Load or Reload Linetypes dialog box shown in Figure 5.11. The aclt.lin file contains ISO (International Organization for Standardization) inch linetypes with dots and dashes, standard ASME inch linetypes with dots and dashes, and complex linetypes with shapes and text. Use the down arrow or the scroll bar to access available linetypes. Pick to highlight the desired linetypes and then pick the OK button to have them loaded into the Select Linetype dialog box. Figure 5.12 shows the Center, Hidden, and Phantom linetypes loaded along with the Continuous default linetype. Now, pick the desired linetype that matches the layer you chose and pick the OK button, or double-click on the linetype to automatically return the Layer & Linetype Properties dialog box. Figure 5.13 shows the linetypes changed for the Center, Hidden, and a newly created Phantom layer. Pick the OK button in the Layer & Linetype Properties dialog box to have the layer linetype changes accepted by AutoCAD LT. Appendix C displays the aclt.lin linetypes.

The Show: drop-down list, the Current: button, and the Details>> button are explained later in this chapter.

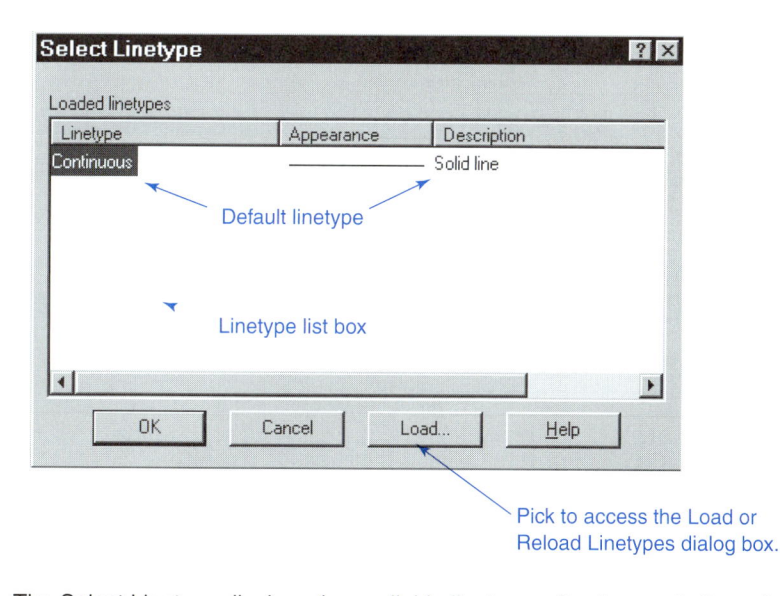

FIGURE 5.10 The Select Linetype displays the available linetypes. Continuous is the only linetype listed when you start AutoCAD LT. Pick the Load ... button to open the Load or Reload Linetypes dialog box where you can load additional linetypes.

Field Notes

> The list of available linetypes is very long in the Load or Reload Linetypes dialog box. You can use the scroll bar or elevator button to locate the desired linetype, but this takes time. A quick way to find a linetype is to pick inside the Linetype window and then type the first letter of the linetype name. For example, if you type h, the list automatically advances and highlights the Hidden linetype. If you type p, the Phantom linetype is quickly highlighted.

FIGURE 5.11 Pick the Load … button in the Select Linetype dialog box to open the Load or Reload Linetypes dialog box.

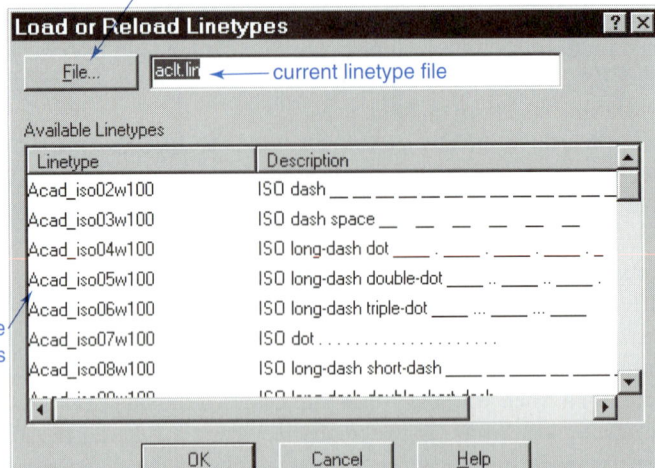

FIGURE 5.12 Linetypes loaded into the Select Linetype dialog box from the Load or Reload Linetypes dialog box.

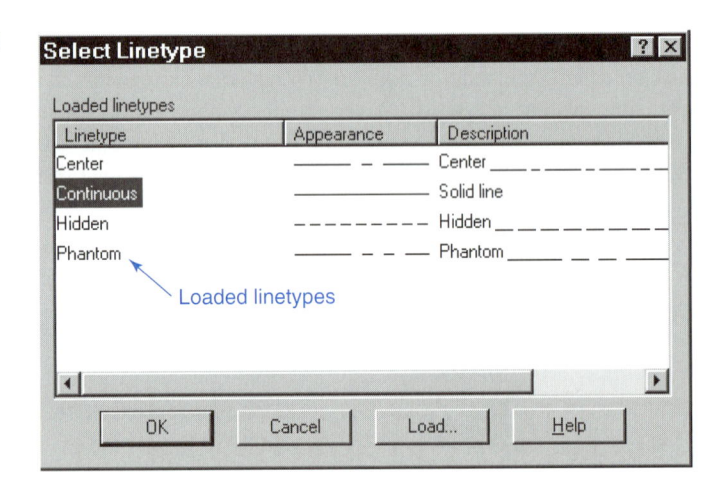

FIGURE 5.13 The desired linetypes are applied to their layers.

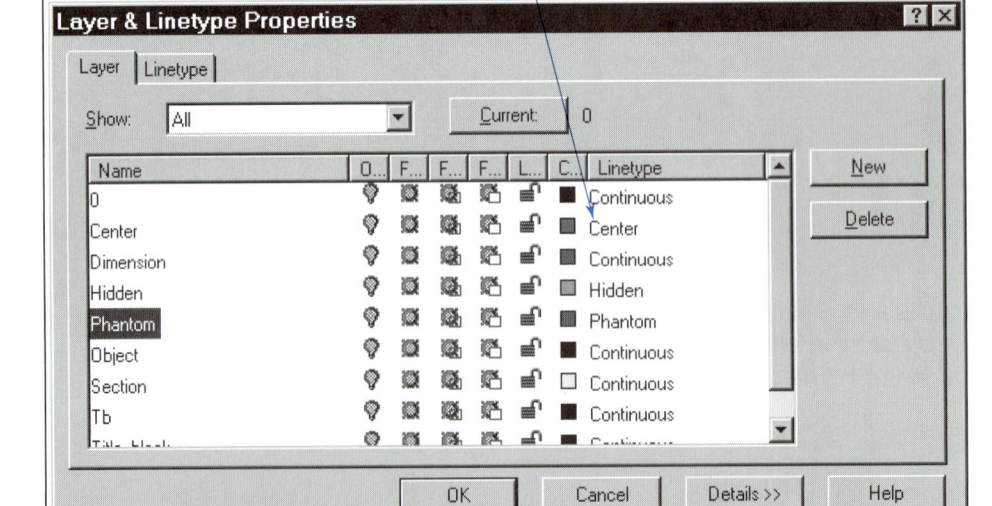

CHAPTER 5 ||| Using Layers, Linetypes, and Colors

Field Notes

Notice the File ... button in Figure 5.11. Pick this button to access the Select Linetype File dialog box shown in Figure 5.14. There are two AutoCAD LT linetype files:

aclt.lin — These are the standard and complex linetypes for inch drawings.

acltiso.lin — These are the standard and complex linetypes for metric drawings.

Access the linetype file that contains the linetypes needed for your drawing and pick the OK button. These linetypes are now available in the Load or Reload Linetypes dialog box. Load the desired linetypes as previously explained.

FIGURE 5.14 The Select Linetype File dialog box. Notice the two AutoCAD LT linetype LIN files: aclt and acltiso.

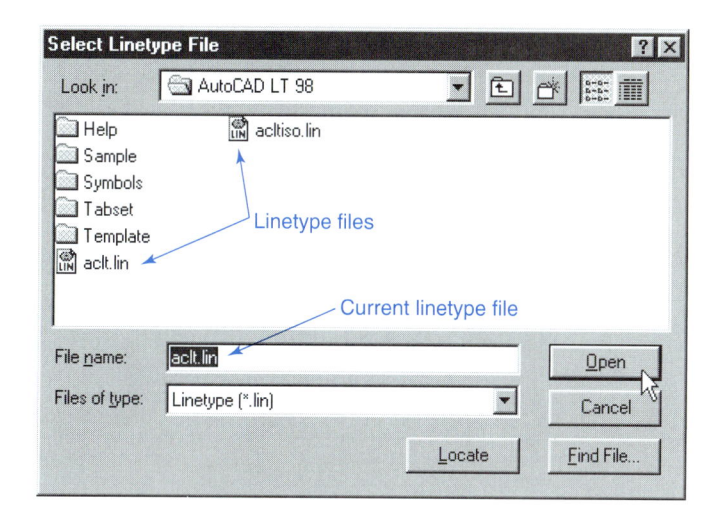

You can also find and load linetypes by picking the Linetype tab in the Layer & Linetype Properties dialog box. You can have the Layer & Linetype Properties dialog box with the Linetype tab open and displayed automatically by picking the Linetype button in the Object Properties toolbar, by picking Linetype ... in the Format pull-down menu, or by typing LT, LINETYPE, or DDLTYPE. The Linetype tab is shown in Figure 5.15 with the previously loaded linetypes displayed. The Load ... button acts as previously discussed by opening the Load or

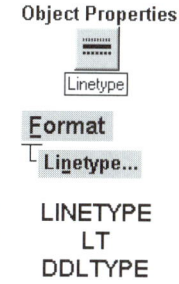

FIGURE 5.15 The Linetype tab of the Layer & Linetype Properties dialog box displays the previously loaded linetypes.

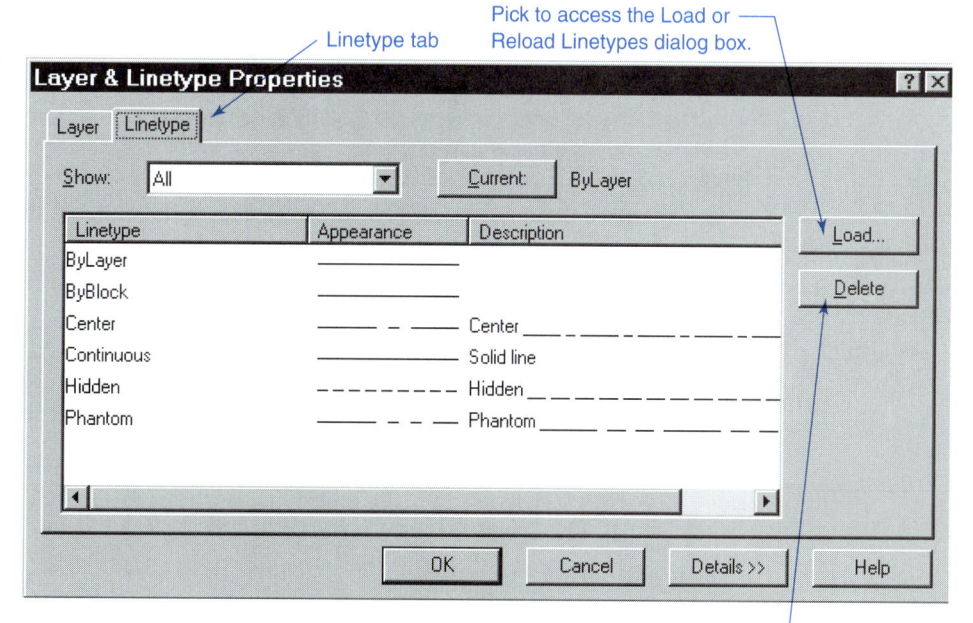

Reload Linetypes dialog box. The Delete button is used to remove any highlighted linetypes from the list. Use of the Show: drop-down list, the Current: button, and the Details>> button are explained later in this chapter.

> **Exercise 5.1**
>
> 1. Open AutoCAD LT if it is not already open. Use the setup option of your choice, open an exercise from a previous chapter, or open a prototype.
> 2. A border and title block are optional.
> 3. Set limits at 8.5,11 unless your prototype contains other limits settings and is approved by your instructor or supervisor.
> 4. Establish the following layers by Name, Color, and Linetype:
>
> | Layer Name | Color | Linetype |
> |---|---|---|
> | CENTER | green | CENTER |
> | CONSTRUCTION | red | CONTINUOUS |
> | DIMENSION | blue | CONTINUOUS |
> | HIDDEN | magenta | HIDDEN |
> | OBJECT | white | CONTINUOUS |
> | PHANTOM | yellow | PHANTOM |
> | SECTION | cyan | CONTINUOUS |
>
> 5. Open the Load or Reload Linetypes dialog box and pick the File ... button. This opens the Select Linetype File dialog box. The default aclt.lin file should be active. Pick the acltiso.lin file and then pick OK. Look at the available linetypes displayed in the Load or Reload Linetypes dialog box. Return to the aclt.lin file.
> 6. Save the drawing as EX5.1.

Making a Layer Current

All objects drawn in AutoCAD LT are automatically placed on the currently active layer, typically referred to as the *current layer*. By default, the objects you draw automatically take on the properties assigned to that layer. For example, if the CENTER layer is current, its color is set to green and linetype to CENTER, then the objects you draw are displayed using green centerlines. A layer can be made current by using the Layer & Linetype Properties dialog box or by picking the Layer Control drop-down list.

In the Layer & Linetype Properties dialog box, pick the desired layer to highlight it and then pick the Current: button. The selected layer name is displayed to the right of the Current: button. Pick the OK button, shown in Figure 5.16, when ready. The current layer with its color and linetype are displayed in the list boxes found in the Object Properties toolbar. (Figure 5.17). The term *ByLayer* in the layer color and linetype list boxes means that the objects drawn on a specific layer use the color and linetype assigned to that layer.

A layer can be made current faster by accessing the Layer Control list box in the Object Properties toolbar. When the list box is displayed, pick the desired layer to make it current automatically, as shown in Figure 5.18. The current layer with its color and linetype are then displayed as shown in Figure 5.17.

You can also make the layer of an existing object on the drawing current. To do this, pick the Make Object's Layer Current button at the far left end of the Object Properties toolbar. AutoCAD LT then asks you to select an object. AutoCAD LT gives you a message indicating the layer of the object you selected is now current:

Object Properties

Make Object's Layer Current

AI_MOLC

Command: ⟨pick the Make Object's Layer Current button⟩
Select object whose layer will become current: ⟨pick the desired object⟩
CENTER is now the current layer.
Command:

CHAPTER 5 ||| Using Layers, Linetypes, and Colors   161

FIGURE 5.16 Highlight the desired layer and pick the <u>C</u>urrent: button. The selected layer name is displayed to the right of the <u>C</u>urrent: button.

1. Highlight the desired layer.

2. Pick the <u>C</u>urrent: button.

Displays the selected layer name

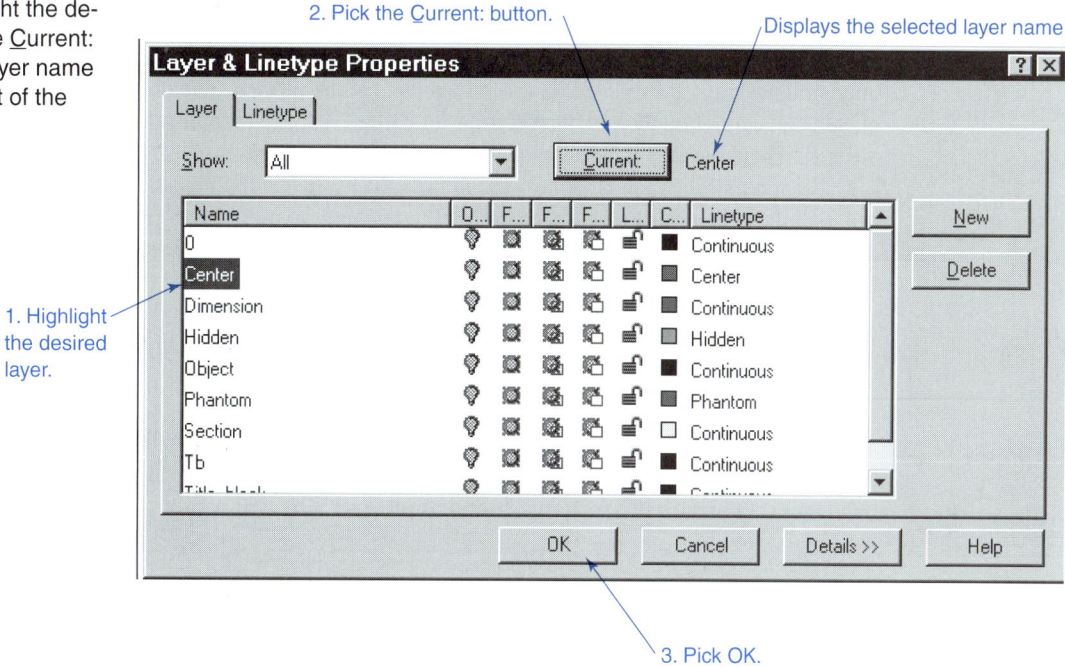

3. Pick OK.

FIGURE 5.17 The current layer color and linetype are displayed in the list boxes found in the Object Properties toolbar.

Current layer name
Current layer color
Current layer color
Current layer linetype

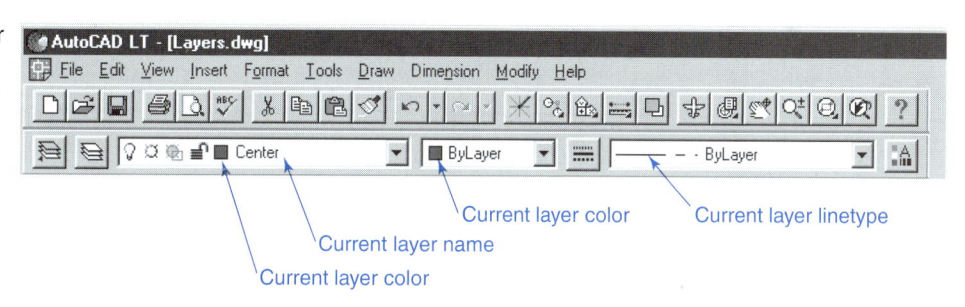

FIGURE 5.18 Open the Layer Control list box and select a layer to automatically make it current.

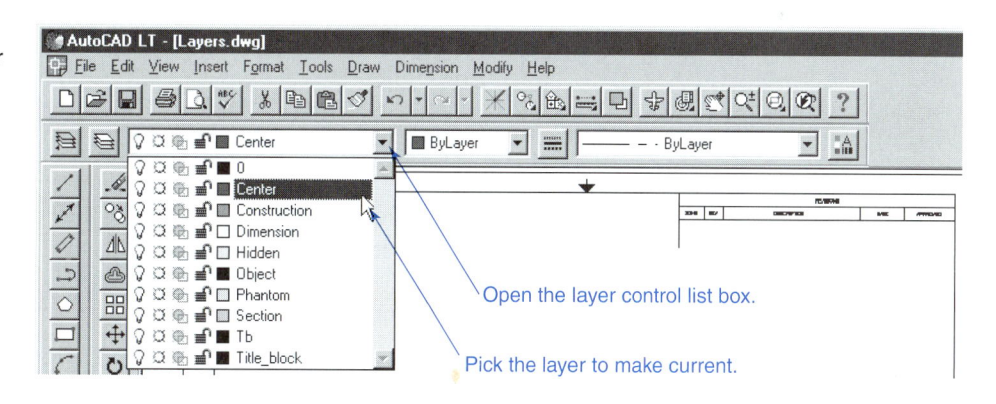

Open the layer control list box.
Pick the layer to make current.

Field Notes

Use the scroll bar to access additional layers when more layers exist in the Layer & Linetype Properties dialog box or the Layer Control list box than can be displayed in the list.

Controlling Layer Visibility

Layer visibility determines if the objects that have been drawn on a layer are visible or invisible. The objects on visible layers are displayed on the screen and can be plotted. The objects on nonvisible layers are not displayed and cannot be plotted. One reason for using layers is the ability to make the information on a specific layer visible if it needs to be seen or invisible if it is not in use.

Layer visibility can be controlled in the Layer & Linetype Properties dialog box and in the Layer Control list box. A layer name becomes highlighted when you pick one or more of the visibility options. The visibility options are displayed using symbolic icons in the Layer & Linetype Properties dialog box and in the Layer Control list box. A tooltip tells you the function when you move the cursor to one of these symbols. All you have to do to change the visibility of a specific layer is pick the desired symbol. The appearance of the symbol changes to represent the visibility status. The following displays the visibility symbols, their associated tooltips, and what happens when they are used:

ON/OFF

When a layer is on, it is visible and available for use. When a layer is off, objects on the layer are invisible and do not plot. You can turn off the current layer, but AutoCAD LT gives you a warning box that says, The current layer is turned off. If you turn off the current layer, you will not see the objects on the layer or any new objects you create.

FREEZE/THAW IN ALL VIEWPORTS

When a layer is frozen, objects on the layer are invisible and cannot be plotted. A frozen layer does not regenerate when you change a view in the visible layers. Freezing layers can help speed up ZOOM, PAN, and decrease regeneration time for complex drawings. If you try to freeze the current layer, AutoCAD LT gives you this warning: Cannot freeze the current layer.

FREEZE/THAW IN CURRENT VIEWPORT

Pick this symbol to freeze or thaw selected layers in the current viewport without affecting layer visibility in other viewports. A *viewport* is a window or windows in which the model space of a drawing is displayed in paper space. Viewports were introduced in Chapter 3 and are fully explained in Chapter 14.

FREEZE/THAW IN NEW VIEWPOINT

Pick this symbol to freeze or thaw selected layers in newly created viewports without affecting layer visibility in current viewports.

> **Field Notes**
>
> Turning off a layer rather than freezing it can slow down drawing time, because AutoCAD LT redraws the objects on that layer. If you often change layers between visible and invisible, turning layers off and on saves time. However, if layers are invisible for long periods of time, freezing and thawing speeds drawing time.

Locking and Unlocking Layers

LOCK/UNLOCK

A layer can be locked to keep you from accidentally editing it or to keep others from tampering with the contents of the layer. You cannot edit a locked layer, but you can look at it, you can add objects, and you can use inquiry commands. You can also freeze and thaw a locked layer and change its color and linetype setting. Layers can be quickly locked or unlocked in the Layer & Linetype Properties dialog box and in the Layer Control list box at the top of the screen. Click on the lock symbol to either open or close the lock. The lock and unlock symbols with related tooltip looks like the example in the margin:

CHAPTER 5 ||| Using Layers, Linetypes, and Colors   163

Exercise 5.2

1. Open AutoCAD LT if it is not already open and then open EX5.1.
2. Draw the schematic shown using the designated layers that were established in Exercise 5.1. The actual size is up to you. Do not include notes.

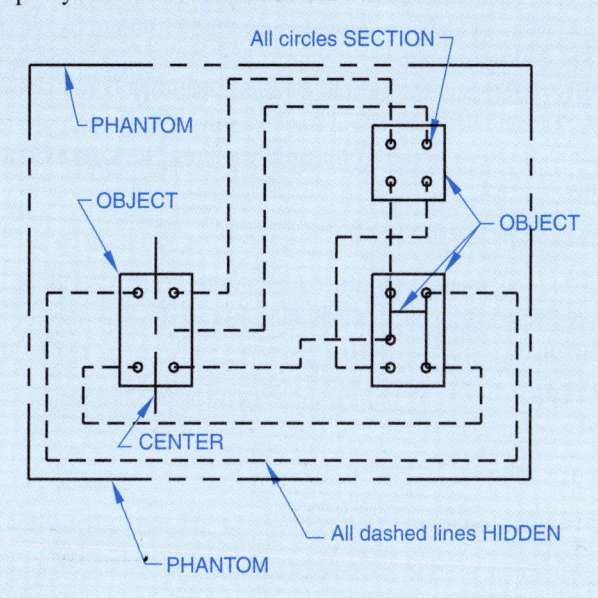

3. Adjust the linetype scale so each line clearly represents the proper linetype. Try a linetype scale of .5.
4. Turn off the PHANTOM layer and observe the results.
5. Freeze the HIDDEN layer and observe the results.
6. Right-click to open the cursor menu and then pick the Select All option in the Layer & Linetype Properties dialog box to turn on and thaw all layers.
7. Save the drawing as EX5.2.

Layer and Linetype Control at the Command Line

Using the dialog box and the drop-down list is the easiest way to manage layers. You can also do these things, with the -LAYER command, at the keyboard if you like to type commands. To access the Layer command at the keyboard, type -LA or -LAYER. There is a hyphen (-) in front of the command name. The -LAYER command looks like this:

-LAYER
-LA

Command: **-LA** or **-LAYER**↵
?/Make/Set/New/ON/OFF/Color/Ltype/Freeze/Thaw/LOck/Unlock:

The options match the features you have already used in the previous discussions. Some of the options are self-explanatory, such as Freeze and Thaw. The following provides brief information about the other options:

- **?** Type a question mark (?) to get a list of available layers.

- **Make** Type **M** for the Make option to create a new layer and automatically make it current. If the layer you make already exists, it is simply made current.

- **Set** Type **S** for the Set option to set a new current layer.

- **New** Type **N** for the New option to create a new layer without changing the status of the current layer.

- **Ltype** Allows you to change the linetype setting for a layer. Linetypes are loaded as needed, if they are found in the currently referenced linetype file.

> ✏️ **Field Notes**
>
> - If you are not creating a new layer or changing a layer's associated color, the Linetype Control drop-down list is the quickest and most convenient means of adjusting layer settings. For creating new layers or changing colors, you will find that the Layer & Linetype Properties dialog box provides a more convenient and intuitive interface than is offered by the -LAYER command.
> - The Layer Control dialog box can be used transparently by picking the Layers toolbar button or by typing **'DDLMODES** at the current prompt. Visibility settings, linetypes, and colors are the only changes that actually take effect transparently. Other changes, such as Current Layer, are updated when you return to the Command: prompt. The Layer Control list box cannot be used transparently.

-LINETYPE
-LT

Linetypes can also be loaded and set at the command line, but it is not as convenient as using the dialog box. To do this, type -LINETYPE, which is a hyphen (-) typed before the command name. Typing -LINETYPE gives you these options:

Command: **-LINETYPE**↵
?/Create/Load/Set:

The options are described as follows:

- **?**   Type a question mark (?) to get a list of the currently loaded linetypes.
- **Create**   This option is used to create custom linetypes and is explained in Chapter 16.
- **Load**   Type **L** for the Load option if you want to load linetypes. The Load option asks you which linetypes you want to load. You can type one or more desired linetype names, separated by a comma; for example:

?/Create/Load/Set: **L**↵
Linetype(s) to load: **HIDDEN,CENTER,PHANTOM**↵

           The Select Linetype File dialog box is now displayed. You select one of the linetype files as previously explained. The Set option works like this:

- **Set**   Type **S** for the Set option if you want to set linetypes for use in the current drawing. This sets the current linetype. The default is BYLAYER, which means that linetypes are set based on layer controls.

Adjusting Linetype Scale

The ***linetype scale*** determines the length of dashes in linetypes such as hidden and centerlines. Setting a linetype scale confirms that the lines you draw are represented properly on the screen or when the drawing is plotted. Linetype scales also allow you to control the appearance of very short lines. When you draw a short center line, for example, AutoCAD LT does not display the dashes if there is not enough room. So, rather than getting a center line symbol, you may get a solid line. If this is not acceptable, you can reduce the linetype scale in an attempt to get the display you want. You can change the linetype scale for each line depending on the requirements or length of the line. Normally, however, it is not necessary to change the linetype scale except for special conditions.

> ✏️ **Field Notes**
>
> When you use a Wizard in the Drawing Setup dialog box, the Linetype Scale factor is preset based on the area you specify. At the default of 12 × 9, LTSCALE is preset to 1. If you set a drawing area of 120 × 90, for example, the LTSCALE is preset to 10. Even though the linetype scale is preset in the Wizard, you can change it if needed.

CHAPTER 5 ||| Using Layers, Linetypes, and Colors   165

The linetype scale can also be set to match the scale factor of the drawing or for individual objects. Setting the linetype scale for the entire drawing is referred to as a global scale factor. *Global* means that the setting affects everything on the entire drawing. If the linetype scale is set for drawing-specific objects, it is referred to as an individual object linetype scale factor. The term *individual* means that the setting affects only individually drawn objects without changing the entire drawing. The *scale factor* determines the final size of things such as text height, dimension characteristics, and linetype appearance when your drawing is plotted. For a full-scale (1:1) mechanical drawing, the scale factor is 1.0, which is the AutoCAD LT default. If the scale is half (1:2), the scale factor is 1/2, or 0.5. If you are making an architectural drawing that you plan to plot at 1/4″ = 1′0″, then the scale factor is 48. This is calculated as follows:

$$1/4 = 12$$
$$1 = 12 \times 4$$
$$1 = 48$$

You can change the linetype scale for the entire drawing or for new objects by using the Details<< button in the Linetype tab of the Layer & Linetype Properties dialog box. Pick the Linetype button in the Object Properties toolbar, pick Linetype ... in the Format pull-down menu, or type LT, LINETYPE, or DDLTYPE at the Command: prompt to display this dialog box. Then highlight the desired linetype and pick the Details<< button at the bottom of the dialog box. Picking the Details<< button expands the dialog box, as shown in Figure 5.19. The following identifies the features of the Details area:

- The Name: text box can be used to change the linetype name.

- The Description: text box can be used to change the linetype description.

- The Global scale factor: text box is where you change the linetype scale factor for the entire drawing. This feature is also controlled by LTSCALE, which is explained next.

- The Current object scale: text box is where you can set the linetype scale of new lines only. This change does not affect existing lines. The current object linetype scale is also controlled by the CELTSCALE system variable, where you can enter a scale factor at the prompt line.

- The Use paper space units for scaling check box is on by default. This scales linetypes the same for model space and paper space. This is also controlled at the prompt line using the PSLTSCALE system variable.

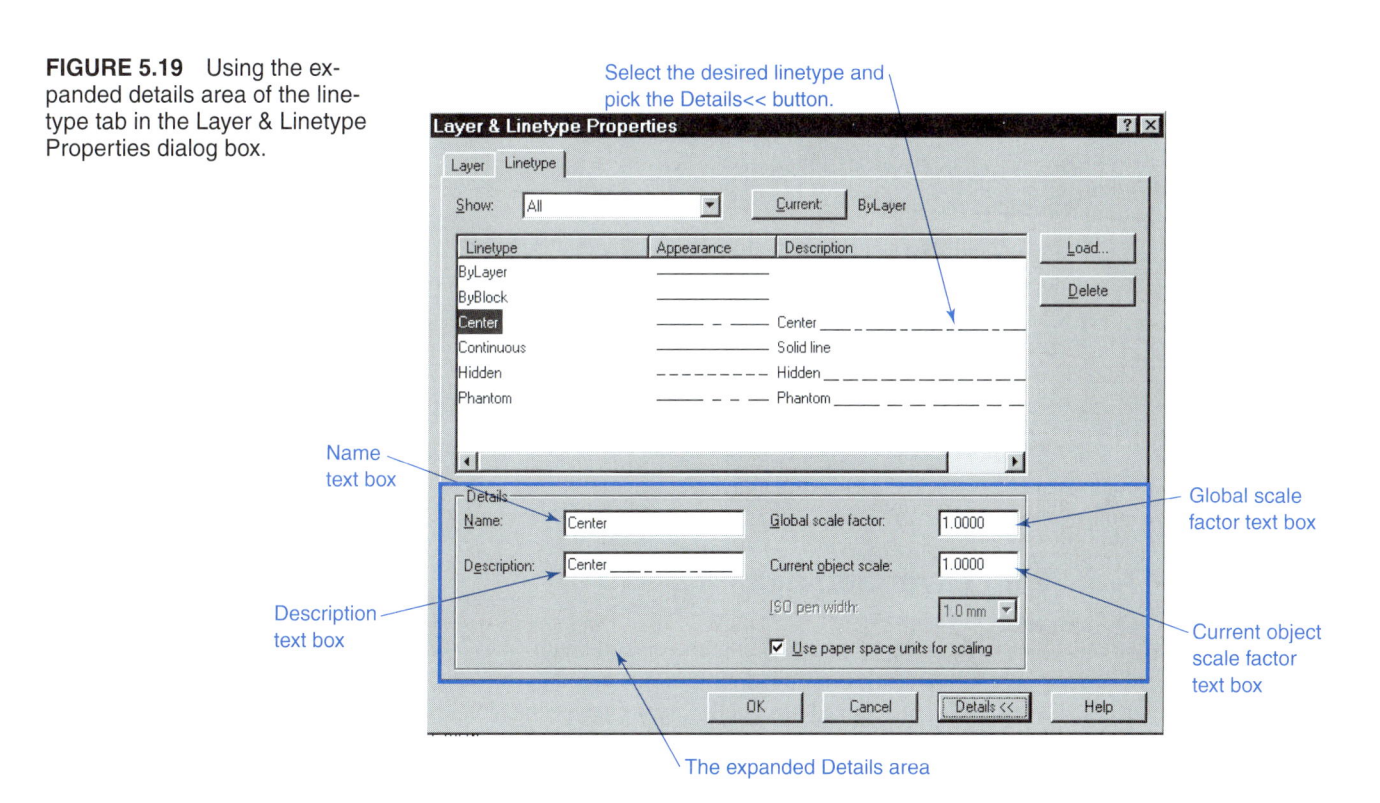

FIGURE 5.19 Using the expanded details area of the linetype tab in the Layer & Linetype Properties dialog box.

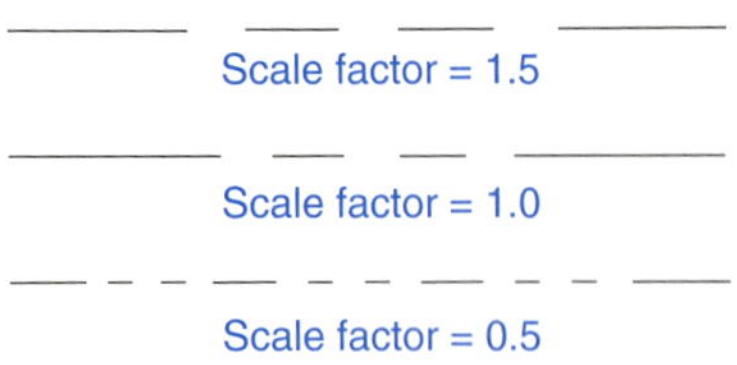

FIGURE 5.20 A comparison of different linetype scale settings.

Scale factor = 1.5

Scale factor = 1.0

Scale factor = 0.5

- The ISO pen width: list box is inactive unless you select an ISO linetype that allows for pen width adjustment.

Pick the Details<< button again to return to the original Linetype tab format. Pick the OK button when you are finished. Figure 5.20 gives you an example of using different linetype scales on a phantom line.

You can change the global linetype scale at the keyboard using the LTS or LTSCALE command. Making linetype scale changes in this manner alters the scale of every linetype on the drawing to match the specification you request. The command sequence looks like this:

Command: **LTS** or **LTSCALE**↵
New scale factor <1.000>: **.5**↵
Regenerating drawing.
Command:

Field Notes

Sometimes you need to adjust the scale factor for linetypes in small increments and look at the display after each adjustment until the desired appearance is achieved. The dash length you select should match American Society of Mechanical Engineers (ASME) or other standards you are using. Sample ASME standard lines are shown in Appendix B. If you choose a Linetype scale that is too big, some lines with dashes will appear solid.

LEARNING CHECKPOINT

- ☐ Briefly explain why layers are important.
- ☐ Why is a good layer naming system needed?
- ☐ How do you create a new layer in the Layer Control dialog box that is named HIDDEN, is assigned the color green, and is for the HIDDEN linetype?
- ☐ What is a CONTINUOUS linetype?
- ☐ Define linetype scale.
- ☐ Explain the difference between global and individual settings.
- ☐ What is the linetype scale of a drawing to be plotted at HALF (1:2) scale?
- ☐ What is the linetype scale of a drawing to be plotted at 1/4″ = 1′0″ scale?
- ☐ Describe two ways to make a layer current.
- ☐ With regard to layer visibility, what is the difference between Off and Freeze?
- ☐ How do you activate a frozen layer so it can be seen and used again?
- ☐ What is the purpose of locking a layer?

Overriding Layer Settings

Layers are very important when designing and drafting with AutoCAD LT. When you see the term *ByLayer* in a dialog box or in a display of any kind, it means that the AutoCAD LT ByLayer feature is available on a specific layer. Objects are created using a ByLayer linetype and color by default in AutoCAD LT, and this indicates that the newly drawn objects take on the color and linetype properties as assigned to the layer that is current when they are created. In some cases you might want new objects to be on the same layer as others that they are associated with—yet use different colors or linetypes. This can be done with direct color and linetype settings.

Caution should be exercised when overriding layers. Overriding layers happens, for example, when you set an object color or linetype during a drawing session without using the Layer & Linetype Properties dialog box, drop-down list, or -LAYER command. An example of this situation is when you are drawing lines and decide to just change the color without regard to the color setting of the current layer. There may be some uses for this practice, but caution should be used because mixing colors and linetypes outside of layer control can result in a confusing drawing.

Overriding Layer Color

All objects are drawn in the current color. If the current color is ByLayer, the objects reference the current layer for their color value. If a color is specified, then the object is still created on the current layer, but the object is displayed in the current color rather than the color assigned to the current layer. The DDCOLOR and COLOR commands allow you to change the color of any individual objects you are drawing.

The Select Color dialog box is accessed by typing **COL** or **DDCOLOR** and is entered automatically when you pick Other ... in the Color Control drop-down list or Color ... from the Format pull-down menu. Refer to Figure 5.7 for a review of the Select Color dialog box. Notice that the Logical Colors compartment contains the BYLAYER and BYBLOCK buttons. Picking one of these buttons assigns the colors ByLayer or BYBLOCK as appropriate. BYBLOCK is explained in Chapter 12. Picking one of the colors sets a specific color for the objects to be drawn.

A quick way to change the current color is by using the Color Control list box located near the center of the Object Properties toolbar. The default color is set ByLayer, but you can change the color by opening the list and selecting the desired color, as shown in Figure 5.21. The last option in the Color Control list is Other ..., which opens the Select Color dialog box, where you can access additional colors.

Change the drawing color at the Command: prompt by typing **COLOR** like this:

Command: **COLOR↵**
New object color <BYLAYER>: ⟨*type a color name or number such as* **RED↵**⟩
Command:

Notice that ByLayer is the default in the above command. Ignore the ByLayer default by typing a desired color name or number, or press Enter to accept the BYLAYER default. Type **BYLAYER** here later if you want to return to the layer control. The color for newly drawn objects can also be changed using the CECOLOR system variable.

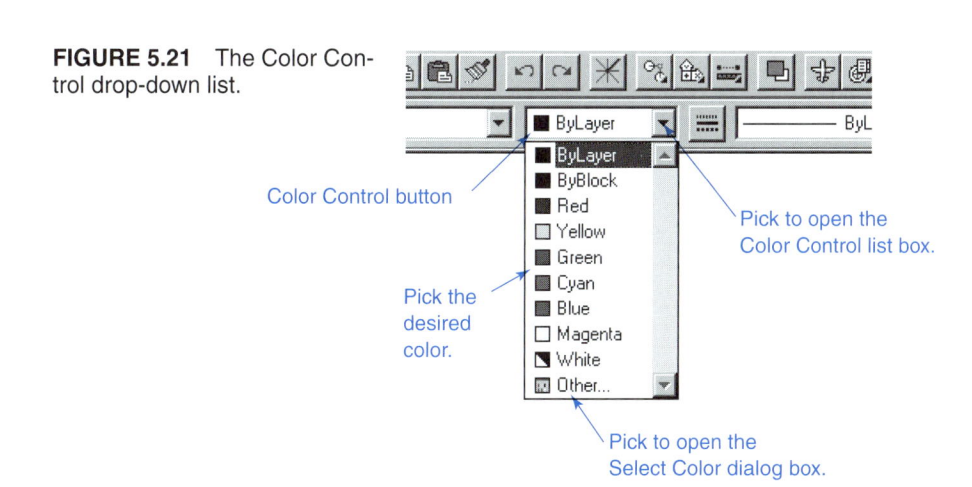

FIGURE 5.21 The Color Control drop-down list.

> ✏️ **Field Notes**
>
> The DDCOLOR command can be used transparently by picking <u>C</u>olor … from the F<u>o</u>rmat menu or by typing **'CO, 'COL,** or **'DDCOLOR** at the current prompt. Although the setting can be changed transparently, the setting will not take effect transparently during all commands. After finishing the command you will notice that the Color Control button is updated to show the new setting. However, if you change the color setting while drawing line segments, the segments drawn before the change stay in the original color and the segments drawn after are in the new color.

Overriding Layer Linetype

All objects are drawn with the current linetype. If the current linetype is ByLayer, then the current layer is referenced for the linetype value. If a specific linetype is used, then the object is still created on the current layer, but the object is displayed with the specific linetype rather than the linetype assigned to the current layer. You can change the linetype of any objects you are drawing by accessing the Linetype tab of the Layer & Linetype Properties dialog box as previously discussed.

A quick way to change the current linetype is by using the Linetype Control list box located to the right of the Color Control list box in the Object Properties toolbar. The default linetype is set ByLayer, but you can change the linetype by opening the list and selecting the desired linetype, as shown in Figure 5.22. Linetypes must have been previously loaded before they are displayed in the Linetype Control drop-down list. Loading linetypes was explained earlier.

The -LINETYPE command can also be used to access a specific linetype. This command was previously discussed with regard to loading linetypes at the keyboard. The -LINETYPE command's Set option automatically loads a linetype if it is not already loaded, as long as the desired linetype is found in the currently referenced linetype file. Supportive information regarding the currently referenced linetype file was discussed previously with the loading linetypes explanation. Using the Set option in the -LINETYPE command to set a current linetype overrides the layer control. The set option sets a current linetype like this:

   ?/Create/Load/Set: **S**↵
   New object linetype (or ?) <BYLAYER>: **HIDDEN**↵
   ?/Create/Load/Set: ↵
   Command:

The options of the -LINETYPE command were explained previously.

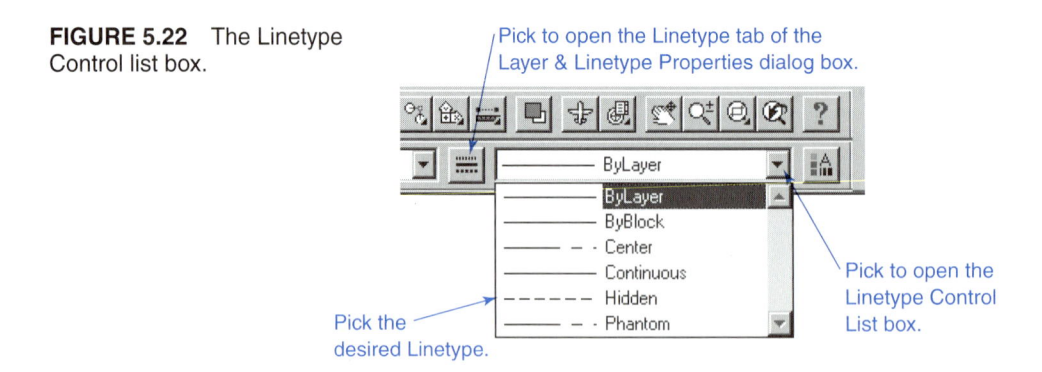

FIGURE 5.22 The Linetype Control list box.

Modifying Layers

Situations may occur that require you to change features within layers. You can change an object's layer, linetype, and color. You can also rename layers or control which layers are displayed in the layer name listing in the Layer & Linetype Properties dialog box.

Renaming Layers and Linetypes

It is easy to rename an existing layer using any one of three ways. One method uses the Layer & Linetype Properties dialog box. The second method opens the Rename dialog box with the DDRENAME command. The third method uses the RENAME command at the keyboard.

To rename a layer in the Layer & Linetype Properties dialog box, double-click on the name of the layer you want to change. The name of the highlighted layer is displayed in the text box. Use the cursor and keyboard to change the name as desired. Pick the OK button. The layer name is now changed. This was demonstrated earlier. You can also change a layer name in the Name: text box by picking the Details>> button of the layer or Linetype tab in the Layer & Linetype Properties dialog box, which is explained later.

The Rename dialog box is a powerful tool that can be used to rename layers, linetypes, and other named features in your drawing. The Rename dialog box, shown in Figure 5.23A, can be accessed by picking Rename … from the Format pull-down menu, or by typing **REN** or **DDRENAME** at the Command: prompt. A list of Named Objects is shown. Notice that Layer is the highlighted object. A list of the Items found in the named object is also displayed. Change a layer name by picking the desired layer name. OBJECT is selected in Figure 5.23A. The selected layer name is displayed in the Old Name: text box. Type a new name, such as **OBJECT-LINES,** in the Rename To: text box and pick the Rename To: button. The new layer name is now displayed in the Items list as shown in Figure 5.23B. Now, pick the OK button. Use the Rename dialog box to change a linetype name in the same manner.

A convenient way to rename layers or change color and linetype is to pick the Details>> button of the Layer tab in the Layer & Linetype Properties dialog box. Picking the Details>> button expands the Layer tab, as shown in Figure 5.24. The layer name can be changed in the Name: text box. The changed name is automatically displayed in the layer list. Change the layer color as needed by picking a desired color in the drop-down list at the Color: box. Change the layer linetype by picking a previously loaded linetype from the Linetype: drop-down list. Notice the right side of the Details area also has layer visibility check boxes. The displayed layer visibility options can be turned on and off as needed here. The Retain changes to xref-dependent layers check box is in the lower left corner. This is on by default. Xrefs are completely explained in Chapter 13.

You can also use the RENAME command to change a layer name at the Command: line. Change a layer name with the keyboard like this:

Command: **-REN** or **RENAME**↵
Block/Dimstyle/LAyer/LType/Style/Ucs/VIew/VPort: **LA.**↵
Old layer name: **OBJECT.**↵
New Layer name: **OBJECT-LINES.**↵
Command:

Use the LType option of the RENAME command to rename a linetype in the same manner. When renaming a linetype, it is renamed only in the current drawing and the original definition in the linetype file is not affected.

Format
  Rename...
DDRENAME
REN

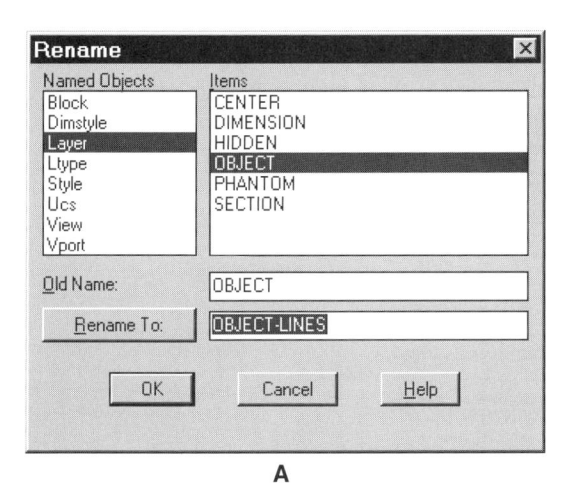

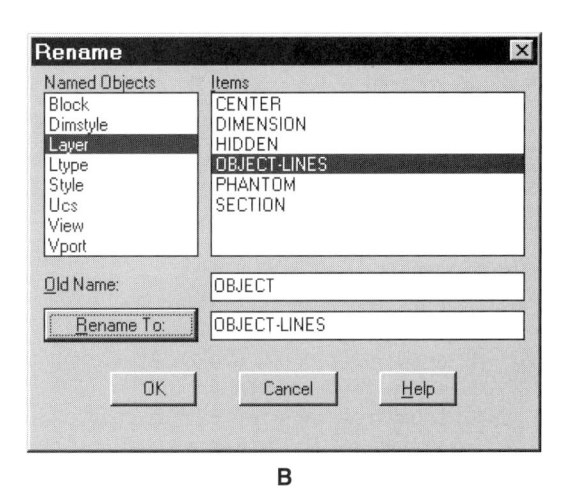

FIGURE 5.23 Using the Rename dialog box to rename a layer. (A) Pick Layer from the list of Named Objects. Pick the layer name to be changed from the Items list. Type a new name in the Rename To: text box and then pick the Rename To: button. (B) The new layer name is now displayed in the Items list.

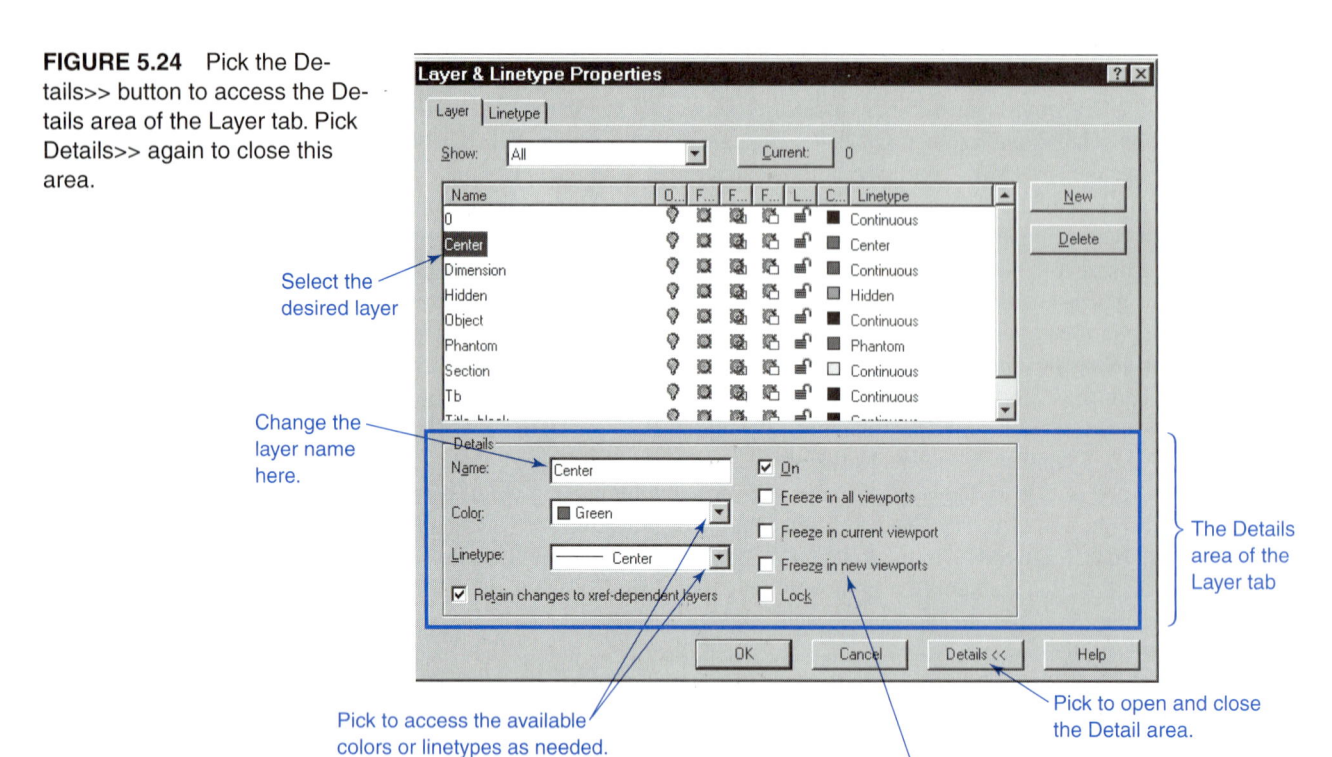

FIGURE 5.24 Pick the Details>> button to access the Details area of the Layer tab. Pick Details>> again to close this area.

Changing an Object's Layer

During creation of a drawing, you may discover that you forgot to change the layer before creating an object. If this happens, it is easy to change the objects to the correct layer. Changing an object's layer also changes the object to the color and linetype that is assigned to that layer if it was created using ByLayer settings. To do this, pick Properties ... from the Modify pull-down menu, pick the Properties toolbar button, or type **CH** or **DDCHPROP** at the Command: line. When you access the DDCHPROP command, AutoCAD LT asks you to select objects. Choose the objects you want changed and press Enter. If you select more than one object, this displays the Change Properties dialog box shown in Figure 5.25. Pick the Layer ... button to access the Select Layer dialog box. Pick the desired layer and then pick OK. The Change Properties dialog box returns with the changed layer, linetype, and color displayed. Pick the OK button.

If you select only a single object such as a line, for example, you get the Modify Line dialog box. Selecting a single circle displays the Modify Circle dialog box, and selecting an arc results in the Modify Arc dialog box. AutoCAD LT automatically checks to see what type of object you selected and displays the appropriate dialog box. Properties is the top compartment of this dialog box. Pick the Layer ... button to access the Select Layer dialog box. Pick the desired layer and then pick OK. The Modify Line dialog box returns with the new current layer, linetype, and color displayed. Pick the OK button when you are satisfied. Select the Color ... or Linetype ... buttons to change the color or linetype.

You can also select a single object to change by typing **MO** or the **DDMODIFY** command at the keyboard.

A layer, color, and linetype can be changed using the keyboard, but it is more work. To use this method, you need to enter the desired layer name, linetype, and color. Type the **CHPROP** command and follow this sequence:

Command: **CHPROP**↵
Select objects: ⟨select the objects⟩
Select objects: ↵
Change what property (Color/LAyer/LType/ltScale/Thickness) ? **LA**↵
New layer <0>: **HIDDEN**↵
Change what property (Color/LAyer/LType/ltScale/Thickness) ? **LT**↵
New linetype <BYLAYER>: ↵
Change what property (Color/LAyer/LType/ltScale/Thickness) ? **C**↵
New color <BYLAYER>: ↵
Change what property (Color/LAyer/LType/ltScale/Thickness) ? ↵
Command:

FIGURE 5.25 The Change Properties dialog box. Pick the Layer button to change layers.

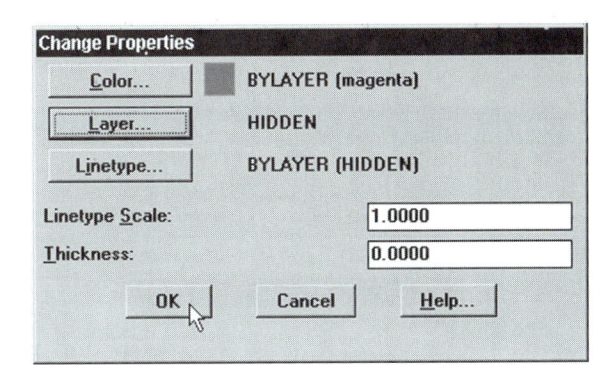

Field Notes

If you have accessed an option of the CHPROP command such as Color or Linetype and the desired value is already present in the default brackets <>, pressing Enter accepts the default setting. The default always reflects the current setting. In the preceding example, the ByLayer setting was desired for linetype and color, so pressing Enter at the prompts preserved the default, which was <ByLayer>.

Changing Layer, Linetype, and Color of Grip-selected Objects

Grips were introduced in Chapter 2, and they are fully explained in Chapter 7. A quick way to change the layer, linetype, and color of an object or objects is to select the objects. When objects are selected, the grips are displayed. Then you can use the Object Properties toolbar Layer list to change the layer of the selected objects. Use the Color list to select a different color for the selected objects, or access a different linetype from the Linetype list. After you have changed the object layer, color, or linetype as desired, press the Esc key twice to remove the grips.

Exercise 5.3

1. Open AutoCAD LT if it is not already open and then open EX5.2.
2. Change the dashed lines to the CENTER layer.
3. Change the phantom lines to the HIDDEN layer.
4. Change the center line to the PHANTOM layer.
5. Change everything back to the condition found in the final drawing for Exercise 5.2.
6. Make the OBJECT layer current.
7. Load the TRACKS linetype from the aclt.lin linetype file.
8. Override the current layer color with red and the current layer linetype with TRACKS.
9. Use the LINE command to draw a line 0.5 in. away from and all around the current phantom line border. This line should be red and represented by the TRACKS linetype.
10. Override the current linetype scale with a setting of 2.
11. Use the LINE command to draw a line .5 in. away from and all around the current TRACKS line.
12. Change all settings back to the original ByLayer format and linetype scale.
13. Save the drawing as EX5.3.

Adjusting Layer Listings

The Layer tab of the Layer & Linetype Properties dialog box has several options for specifying which layers are displayed in the layer name list. These options are found in the Show: drop-down list displayed in Figure 5.26. The following explains each of the options:

FIGURE 5.26 The Show: list of the Layer tab allows you to determine which layers are displayed in the layer name list.

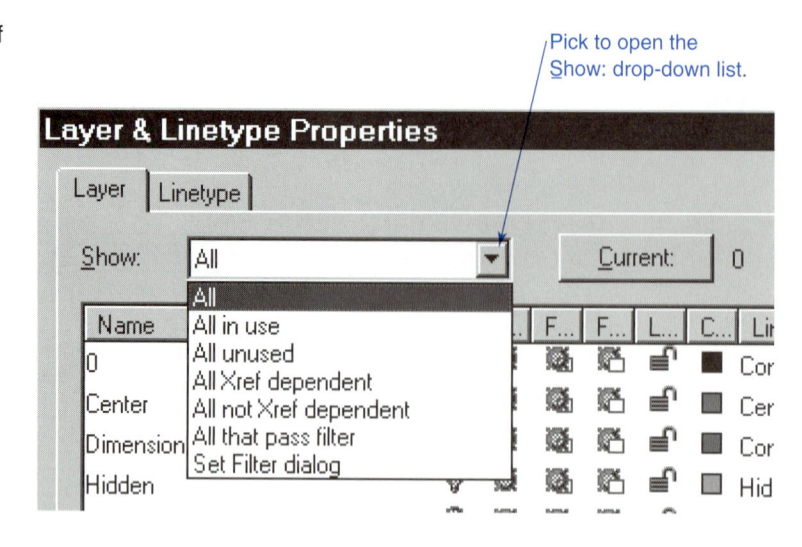

- **All:** This is the default, which displays all layer names available in the drawing.

- **All in Use:** This option displays all of the layer names that are currently in use in the drawing. For example, you may have created 10 layers, but you have drawn objects on only 5 of the layers. The 5 layers that have been used in the drawing are displayed.

- **All unused:** This option allows you to list the layer names that are not in use.

- **All xref dependent:** Xref stands for external reference. *External references* are a source outside of the current drawing. Chapter 13 covers xrefs in detail. This option lists layer names that are xref-dependent.

- **All not xref dependent:** This option lists layer names that are not xref-dependent.

- **All that pass filter:** This option displays all layer names that match the settings made in the Select Layer Filter dialog box, which is explained next.

- **Set Filter dialog box:** This option displays the Set Filter dialog box. The next discussion explains how to use the Set Layer Filters dialog box for layers control.

Using the Set Layer Filters Dialog Box

If you have many layers established, you can decide which to display in the layer name list of the Layer & Linetype Properties dialog box. This works well if you are working on a large drawing with many layers, but you are only using a few key layers. Filtering the unneeded layers makes it easier for you to access the needed layers. You can filter layers based on names, color, linetype, visibility, or locked versus unlocked status. When you filter layers, you are choosing the characteristics of layers that will be listed. Pick Set Filter dialog in the Show: drop-down list of the Layer tab. See Figure 5.26. This opens the Set Layer Filters dialog box shown in Figure 5.27. The filter options allow you to filter by visibility or selection settings, or by name, color, or linetype.

The settings in the Set Layer Filters dialog box are cumulative. This means that you can look for layers that are both Off and Locked, or On, Frozen, and Red, for example. The options for layers filtered by visibility or selection settings are described as follows:

- **On/Off** Pick the arrow to access the list shown in Figure 5.27B. The options include Both, which is the default. This filters layers by both on and off. In other words, all layers that are on and off are displayed. Pick On to filter layers that are turned on. This means that layers that are turned on are listed but layers that are turned off are not listed. Pick Off to filter layers that are turned off.

CHAPTER 5 ||| Using Layers, Linetypes, and Colors

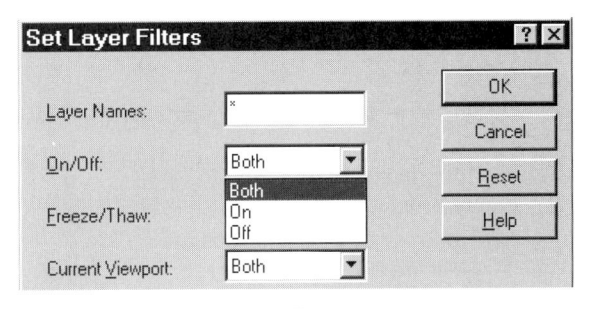

FIGURE 5.27 (A) Using the Set Layer Filters dialog box to filter layers. (B) Pick the down arrow to access the list.

- **Freeze/Thaw**　　　　　　　　Filter layers that are frozen or thawed by picking Both, On, or Off.

- **Lock/Unlock**　　　　　　　　Filter layers that are locked or unlocked by picking Both, On, or Off.

- **Current Viewport and New Viewport**　　Filter layers that are frozen or thawed in the current and new viewports by selecting Both, On, or Off. Viewports are explained in Chapter 13.

The options for layers filtered by name, color, and linetype are as follows:

- **Layer Names**　　There is a text box for this filtering application. The asterisk (*) shown is the default. The asterisk symbol is referred to as a wild card. A ***wild card*** allows you to match anything that is similar. For example, if you have several layers that begin with the name ELEC-, you can filter only those layers by entering ELEC-*. Now, only the ELEC- layers are listed. You can also remove the asterisk and type a desired layer name. You can also identify layers using question marks (?). For example, to find all layers that have E as the third letter, enter **??E***. Another example might be one in which you want to find all layers that are related to the electrical plan on the fourth floor and the layer names look like ELEC-SW-4 and ELEC-WR-4. These could be found with the entry **ELEC-??-4.**

- **Colors**　　This allows you to filter layers by color names using the asterisk wild card or by individual color; or multiple criteria can be specified, separated by commas.

- **Ltypes**　　This allows you to filter layers by linetype using the asterisk wild card or by individual linetype; or multiple criteria can be specified, separated by commas.

You can pick the Reset button in the Set Layer Filters dialog box to reset all values back to the default settings. The Apply this filter to the Layer control on the Object Properties toolbar check box is on by default. This allows you to see the effect of layer filtering displayed in the Layer Control List box.

Pick the OK button to accept the layer filters that you have set. The layer filter settings are now available for use. If no matching layer names are found, no layer names are displayed and you get a message in the lower left corner of the Layer Control dialog box that states: "No layers matching filter criteria."

Adjusting Linetype Listings

The Linetype tab of the Layer & Linetype Properties dialog box has several options for specifying which linetypes are displayed in the linetype list. These options are found in the Show: drop-down list displayed in Figure 5.28. The following explains each of the options:

- **All:** This is the default option, which displays all the loaded linetypes in the Linetype list.

- **All in use:** This option displays all the loaded linetypes that are currently in use in the drawing. Linetypes that are not being used are not listed.

- **All Xref dependent:** This option displays all xref-dependent linetypes that are loaded in the current drawing.

- **All not Xref dependent:** This option displays all loaded linetypes that are not xref-dependent.

FIGURE 5.28 The Show: list of the Linetype tab allows you to determine which linetypes are displayed in the linetype list.

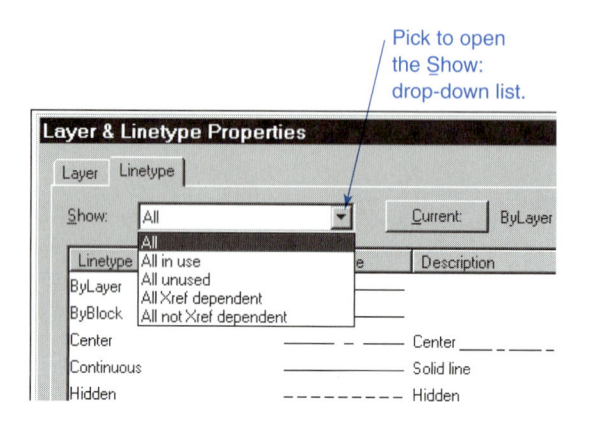

Plotting Line Widths Assigned to Layer Colors

Remember, to print or plot a drawing, pick the Print toolbar button, pick Print ... in the File pull-down menu, press Ctrl+P, or type **PLOT**. Any of these actions accesses the Plot Configuration dialog box discussed in Chapter 2 (more explanation is given in Chapter 13). The Plot Configuration dialog box contains a compartment titled Pen Parameters shown in Figure 5.29. Pick the Pen Assignments ... button to access the Pen Assignments dialog box. You can use this dialog box to set pen widths for plotting if your plotter or printer supports different line widths. Appendix B shows recommended ASME standard line widths for mechanical drafting. Different disciplines may use other line width recommendations.

FIGURE 5.29 Pick the Pen Assignments . . . button in the Pen Parameters area of the Plot Configuration dialog box to access the Pen Assignments dialog box.

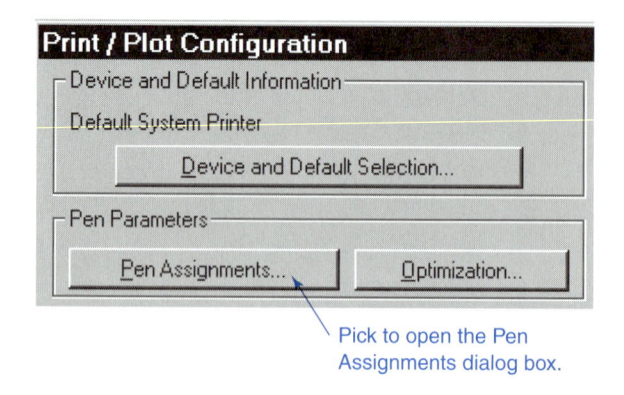

To change a line width specification, pick the desired color or colors. You can change more than one pen width at a time if you wish. If you have object lines set to color 7 (white), then pick the color 7, as shown in Figure 5.30A, for example. Notice that the Color: 7 (white), Pen: 7, and Width: 0.010 (default) are displayed in the Modify Values compartment. Use the Modify Values compartment to change the Width to .025 in. (0.6 mm) for object lines and pick the OK button as shown in Figure 5.30B. Now, when you make a print or plot, the lines that are assigned to color 7 and pen number 7 (for plotters) are printed or plotted .025 in.

CHAPTER 5 ||| Using Layers, Linetypes, and Colors   **175**

Pick one or more colors to change pen width.

A Pen width text box **B**

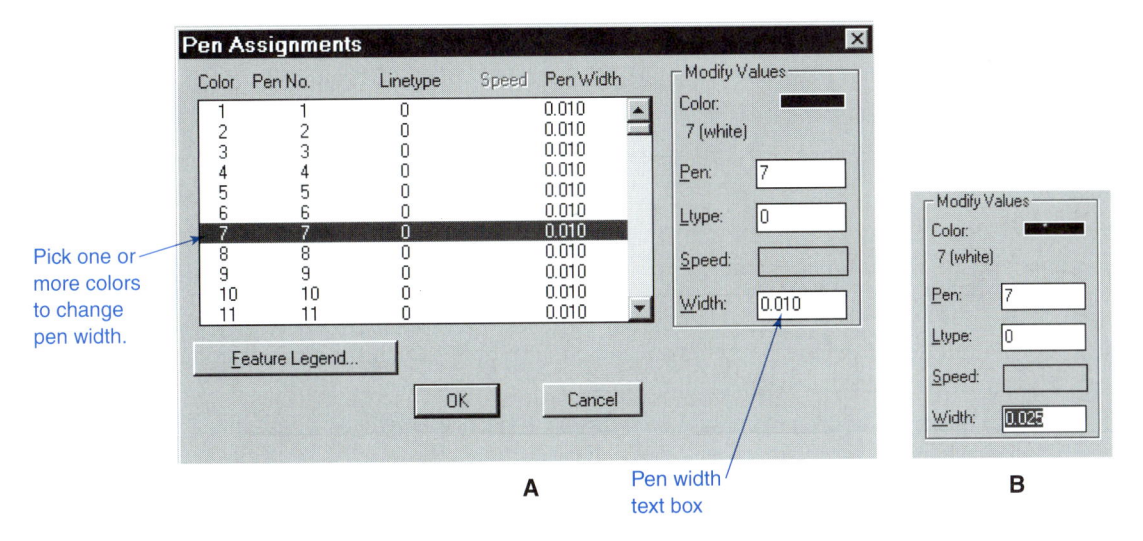

FIGURE 5.30 (A) Using the Pen Assignments dialog box to set pen width. Pick the Pen Width that you want to change. (B) Use the Modify Values compartment to change the pen width in the Width: text box and then pick the OK button.

thick. This allows you to set line contrast to make your drawing match the drafting standards you are using. Be sure to change the pen assignments for each plot if the line width specifications change.

Field Notes

Some hardcopy drivers may not provide a pen width option. For example, you cannot specify pen widths when you are using a pen plotter. The pen width is dependent on how you set up the carousel—you merely specify which pen numbers to use.

Exercise 5.4

1. Open AutoCAD LT if it is not already open and then open EX5.2.
2. Use the Plot Configuration dialog box to change the Pen Assignments of the OBJECT layer lines to .025 width and the SECTION layer lines to .12 width.
3. Make a print or plot of the drawing displaying these line widths.
4. Experiment with layer filters by doing this:
   - Enter the Layer Control dialog box and pick Set ... in the Filters compartment.
   - In the Set Layer Filters dialog box, set the On/Off: option to On, and pick OK.
   - Now, back in the Layer Control dialog box, turn Off at least two of your layers and see what happens—they should disappear from the layer list.
   - Pick the On button in the Filters compartment to remove the check and see what happens—the layers should reappear on the layer list.
5. Turn the layers back On that you turned Off.
6. Save the drawing as EX5.4.

LEARNING CHECKPOINT

- What does the term *ByLayer* mean?
- Why should caution be used when overriding layers?
- How do you rename a layer in the Layer & Linetype Properties dialog box?
- How do you access the Rename dialog box?

- Describe the process for changing the layer of a group of objects using the DDCHPROP command.
- Explain the difference between the DDCHPROP and DDMODIFY commands.
- Why would you want to filter layers?
- Provide a brief explanation covering how to set a specific layer to be plotted with wider lines than the other layers.

MULTIPLE CHOICE

Circle the choice or enter your response on an answer sheet by selecting the option that most closely completes or answers the given statements.

1. A logical grouping of data, like transparent overlays on a drawing:
   a. transparencies
   b. overlays
   c. layers
   d. sheets

2. The DDLMODES command accesses this dialog box:
   a. Layer & Linetype Properties
   b. Select Color
   c. Select Linetype
   d. Change Properties

3. This is the AutoCAD LT default linetype:
   a. SOLID
   b. CONTINUOUS
   c. OBJECTS
   d. none of the above

4. This command or dialog box changes the linetype scale of every object on the drawing:
   a. LTSCALE
   b. Select Linetype dialog box
   c. SCALE
   d. DDLMODES

5. A layer is in this state when objects on the layer are invisible, and regenerations can occur when you change a view in the visible layers:
   a. On
   b. Off
   c. Lock
   d. Freeze

6. A layer is in this state if you want to keep people from accidentally editing or tampering with the layer contents:
   a. On
   b. Off
   c. Lock
   d. Freeze

7. Use this command to change the layer of several objects at one time:
   a. DDRENAME
   b. DDCHPROP
   c. DDMODIFY
   d. DDLAYER

8. This means that the setting affects everything on the entire drawing:
   a. individual
   b. specific
   c. all
   d. global

9. Adjust the linetype scale of individual objects using this command:
   a. LAYER
   b. LTSCALE
   c. DDLTYPE
   d. SELECTLT

10. There are three standard AutoCAD LT linetype files: aclt.lin, acltiso.lin, and ltypeshp.lin. These are accessed through this dialog box:
    a. Select Linetype
    b. Linetype File
    c. Layer & Linetype Properties
    d. Select Linetype File

MATCHING

Match each term to the correct description by writing the appropriate number in each box at the left.

- ☐ Continuous
- ☐ Current
- ☐ DDCHPROP
- ☐ DDLMODES
- ☐ DDMODIFY
- ☐ Filtering
- ☐ Freeze
- ☐ Layer
- ☐ Lock
- ☐ Off
- ☐ Scale Factor

1. Defined by AutoCAD LT as a logical grouping of data, like transparent overlays on a drawing.
2. Access the Layer & Linetype Properties dialog box with this command.
3. What is the default linetype when you initially name a new layer?
4. This determines the final size of things such as text height, dimension characteristics, and linetype appearance.
5. A layer is in this state when it is active and ready for use.
6. A layer is in this state when objects on the layer are invisible and regenerations happen when a view is changed in visible layers.
7. A layer is in this state when objects on the layer are invisible and regenerations do not happen when a view is changed in visible layers.
8. Layers are in this state to keep people from tampering with the contents of the layer.
9. This command allows you to change the layer of several objects.
10. This command lets you change the layer of a single object.
11. If you have a drawing with many layers but you are working with only a few layers, you can use this to have the unneeded layers removed from the layer list.

WORD SCRAMBLE

Unscramble the seven scrambled words below, one letter to each square, to form seven AutoCAD LT–related words:

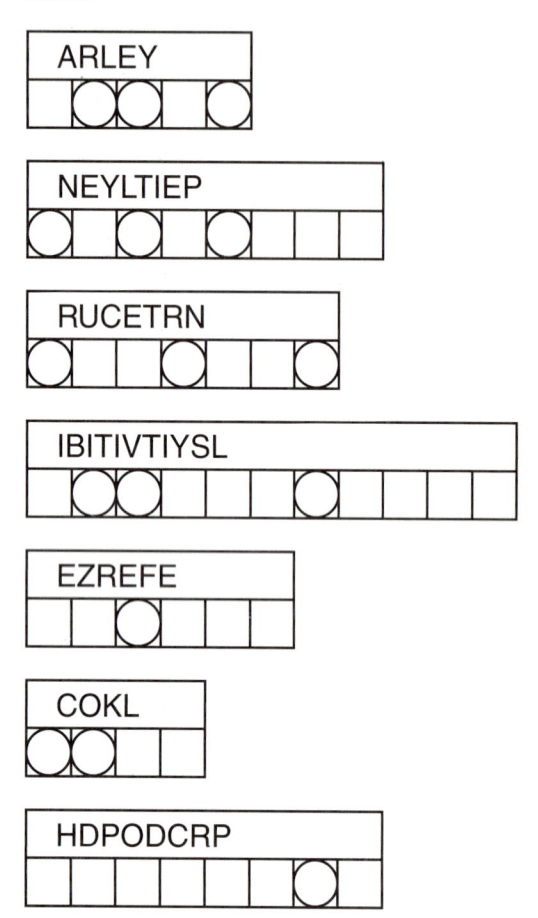

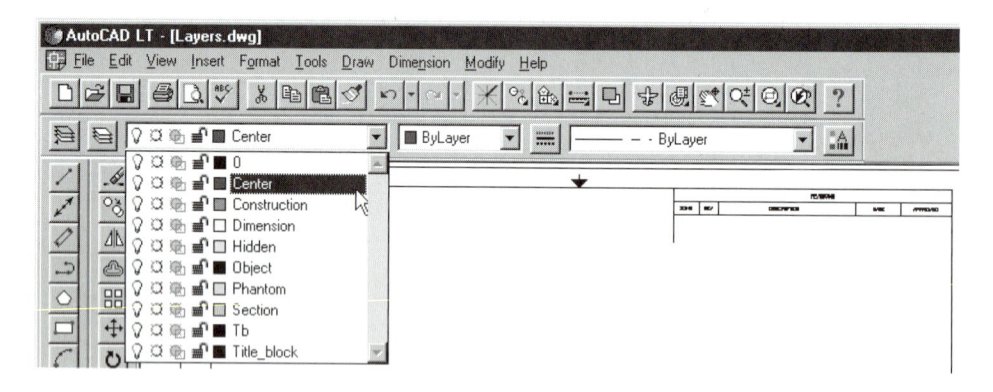

ARLEY

NEYLTIEP

RUCETRN

IBITIVTIYSL

EZREFE

COKL

HDPODCRP

Unscramble the circled letters above to form the special answer, as suggested by the illustration.

CHAPTER 5 ||| Using Layers, Linetypes, and Colors   **179**

PROJECTS

Set up the following drawing projects with layers that relate to the type of drawing as outlined and discussed in this chapter.

5.1 Amplifier Schematic
Draw the schematic shown below. Do not place text or connections that are shown as solid circles. Save as P5.1.

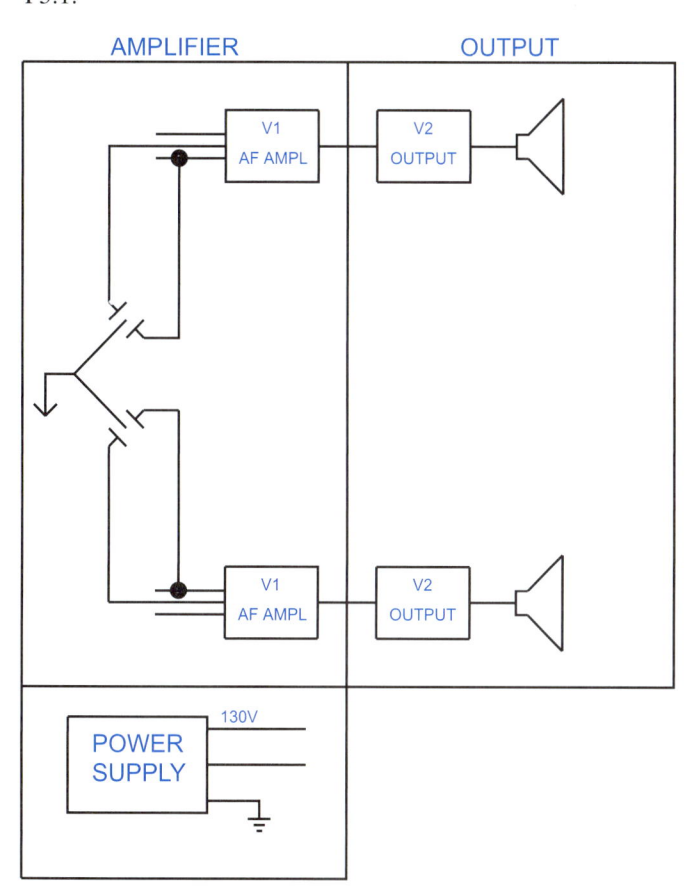

5.2 Hex Head Bolt
Draw the fastener shown below. Do not draw dimensions or notes. Save as P5.2.

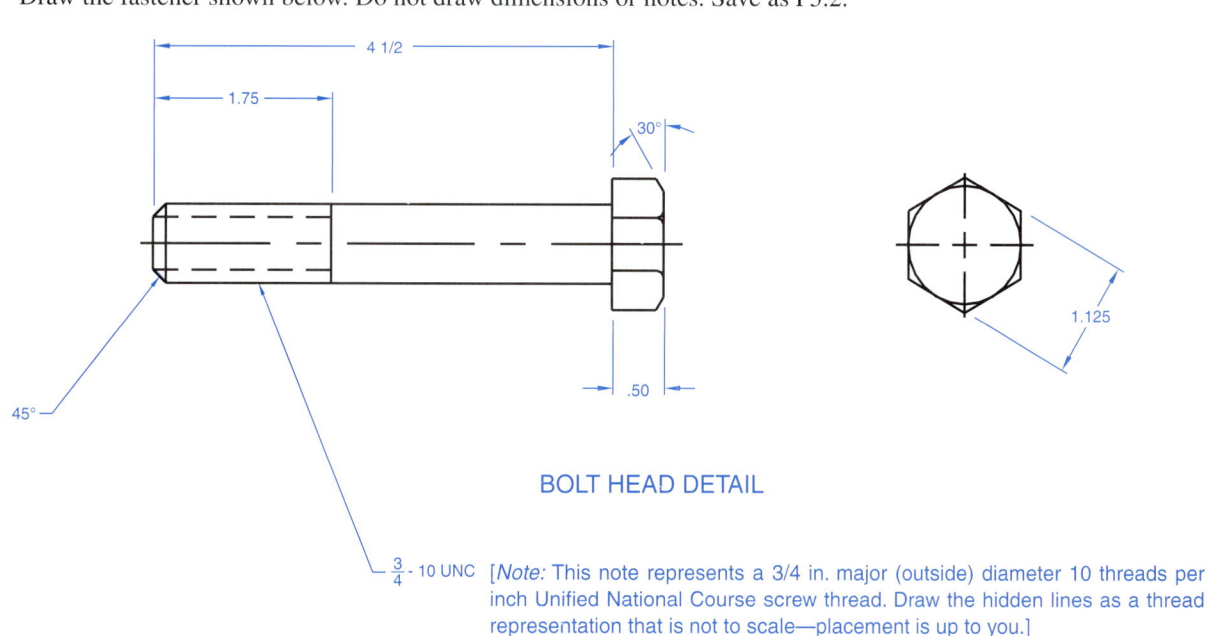

BOLT HEAD DETAIL

$\frac{3}{4}$ - 10 UNC [*Note:* This note represents a 3/4 in. major (outside) diameter 10 threads per inch Unified National Course screw thread. Draw the hidden lines as a thread representation that is not to scale—placement is up to you.]

5.3 Kitchen Floor Plan

Draw the plan shown below without notes or dimensions. Save as P5.3.

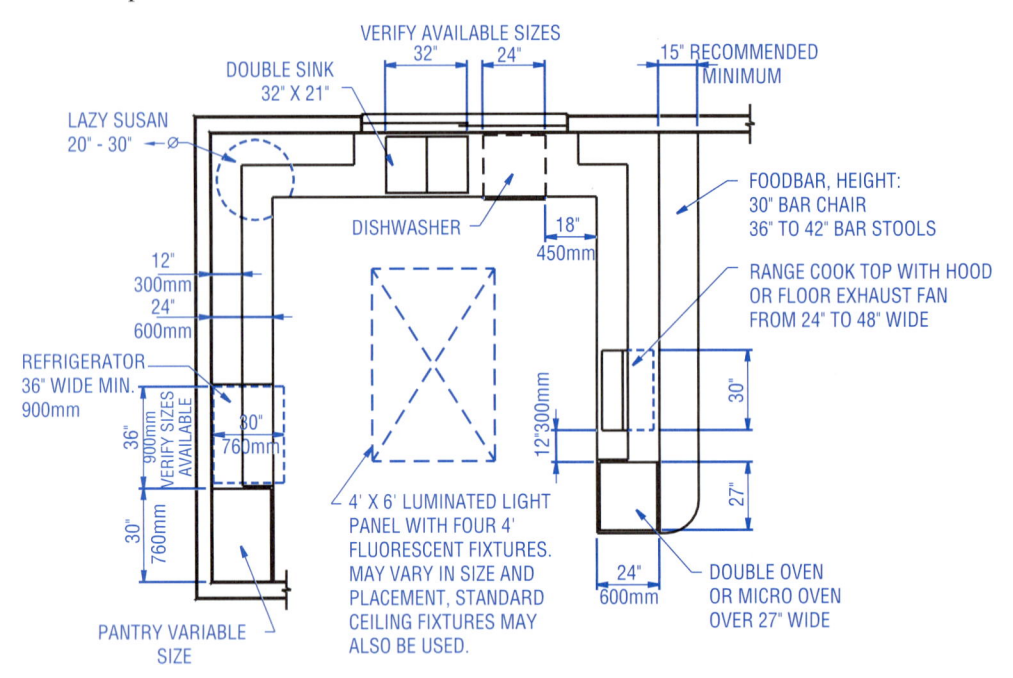

CHAPTER 6

Precision Drafting Tools

LEARNING GOALS

- Use AutoSnap features to place points quickly and accurately.
- Use the From option to establish a point from an existing point.
- Set and clear running object snaps.
- Control the AutoSnap settings.
- Draw a variety of point styles and sizes.
- Divide objects into equal lengths.
- Establish equally spaced segments on an object.
- Use point filters to establish a point.
- Use the From option to draw objects using direct distance entry.
- Use tracking to determine a new point location from a series of directions and distances.
- Identify the coordinates of an existing point.
- Calculate distances, angles, and areas.
- Use the 2D Region Modeler to determine physical properties of shapes and areas.
- List object properties.
- Use the built-in timer features.
- Draw construction lines using the XLINE command options and the RAY command.
- Adjust the Snap Angle and Origin options.
- Use the Polar Snap feature to create specific angle and distance measurements.

AutoCAD LT's Precision Drafting Tools

Learning to use the many precision drafting tools in AutoCAD LT 98 allows you to create and use highly accurate drawings. Rather than trying to point accurately with the mouse, you can force AutoCAD LT to find exact points in your drawing with greater than eight decimal places of accuracy. Powerful inquiry tools allow you to extract manufacturing and engineering data from your drawing-including point locations, surface area calculations, centroids, moments of inertia, and more. AutoCAD LT even provides construction tools that let you use existing geometry to define new objects in your drawing.

The tools and commands discussed in this chapter will help you draw faster and more accurately and increase the usefulness of the drawings you create.

Object Snaps

Object snaps allow you to quickly pick exact locations on an object without having to be directly at the desired location. Object snaps are available for almost any need. Object snaps can be used any time AutoCAD LT asks you to select a point. When using object snaps, an AutoSnap marker is displayed at the snap location when you move the cursor to a related object or snap point. AutoSnap gives you a visual symbol, known as a marker, that lets you know which snap is being used. Also, if you pause just for a moment when you see the AutoSnap marker, a SnapTip is provided that tells you the name of the object snap being used. AutoSnap is on by default.

Object snaps can be accessed from the Object Snap toolbar, from the Object Snap cursor menu, or by typing the desired object snap abbreviation. Object snaps can be used at any point prompt or select objects prompt. Display the Object Snap toolbar by picking Toolbars ... in the View pull-down menu. This opens the Customize dialog box, with the Toolbars tab selected, as shown in Figure 6.1A. Pick the Object Snap option in the Toolbars list and then pick the Close button. Another method for toggling the toolbars display is to right-click on an existing toolbar button to get a popup cursor menu. See Figure 6.1B. A check by the toolbar name indicates that it is currently displayed. Picking any toolbar name toggles its display either on or off. Picking the Customize... option at the bottom displays the Customize dialog box shown in Figure 6.1A. The Object Snap toolbar is shown in Figure 6.2 with each button name provided. The toolbar can be located where you want it on the screen or "docked" below the Object Properties toolbar or above the Command window. Refer to Chapter 1 for a review. When typed on the keyboard, each object snap uses the first three letters or more of the name, as shown in Figure 6.2.

FIGURE 6.1 Selecting Object Snap in the Toolbars dialog box.

Pick to display the Object Snap toolbar.

Pick this button to display buttons in a large format.

ToolTips are on by default.

Pick when done.

A   B

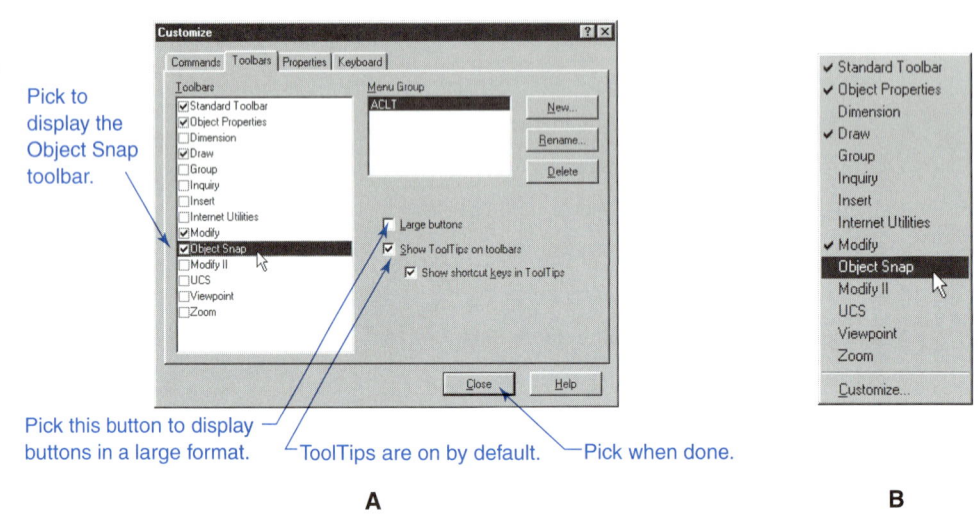

FIGURE 6.2 The Object Snap toolbar with each toolbar button labeled. The three-letter abbreviation in parentheses by each object snap name is what you type when entering object snaps on the keyboard.

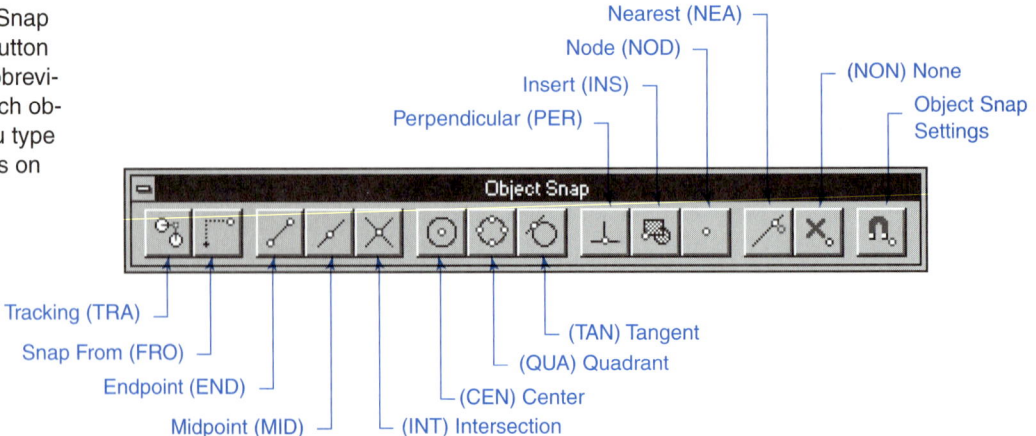

Nearest (NEA)
Node (NOD)
(NON) None
Insert (INS)
Object Snap Settings
Perpendicular (PER)

Tracking (TRA)
Snap From (FRO)
(TAN) Tangent
Endpoint (END)
(QUA) Quadrant
(CEN) Center
Midpoint (MID)
(INT) Intersection

There is also a cursor menu that contains the Object Snap options, as shown in Figure 6.3. The cursor menu is displayed where the cursor is located on the screen when you hold down the Shift key and press the right mouse button. The cursor menu disappears as soon as you pick the desired option. When the cursor menu is displayed, move the cursor arrow down the list of Object Snap options and pick the desired one.

The AutoSnap markers and the related SnapTips are displayed in Figure 6.4.

CHAPTER 6 ∭ Precision Drafting Tools

FIGURE 6.3 The Object Snap cursor menu is opened at the cursor location by pressing the Shift key and pressing the right mouse button.

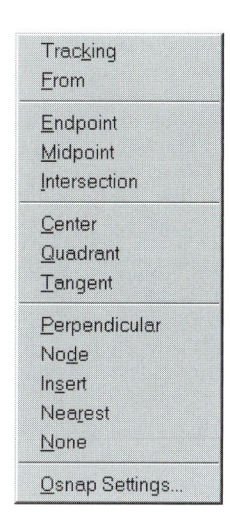

FIGURE 6.4 The AutoSnap markers and related SnapTips.

AutoSnap markers	SnapTip	AutoSnap markers	SnapTip
□	Endpoint	⌐⌐	Insert
△	Midpoint	⌐	Perpendicular
○	Center	○	Tangent
◇	Quadrant	⊠	Nearest
×	Intersection	⊗	Node

Snap to an Endpoint

The Endpoint object snap is convenient for accurately picking the endpoint of an object such as a line or arc. For example, if you want to draw a line from the endpoint of an existing line, pick the Snap to Endpoint toolbar button, select Endpoint from the popup menu, or type **END** at the From point: prompt. Next, AutoCAD LT gives you the "of" prompt. This means that AutoCAD LT wants you to pick the object that you want to select the endpoint "of." If you want the endpoint of a line, move the crosshairs to anywhere "near" the end, and past the middle, of the desired line and pick on the object as shown in Figure 6.5. Notice the AutoSnap marker and SnapTip that provides you with visual identification that you have selected the correct point. The complete command sequence looks like this:

Object Snap

ENDpoint

Command: **L** or **LINE**↵
From point: **END**↵
of ⟨*move the cursor near the endpoint and pick*⟩
To point: ⟨*pick the next point*⟩
To point: ↵
Command:

The object snap is no longer active after the object is picked. Each object snap is active only for the next point selection, whether or not it is successful. An object snap is only successful if you pick a point where the cursor touches a visible object and the object has the requested feature. If, for example, you specify an Endpoint object snap and pick a point on a circle, no point is found. Also, the object snap you picked is deactivated and your point prompt is repeated. If you pick a point where the cursor does not touch any objects, again no point is found, the object snap is deactivated, and the point prompt is repeated. This is where the AutoSnap marker offers a great advantage, because you know the object is successfully picked when the marker is displayed at the desired location.

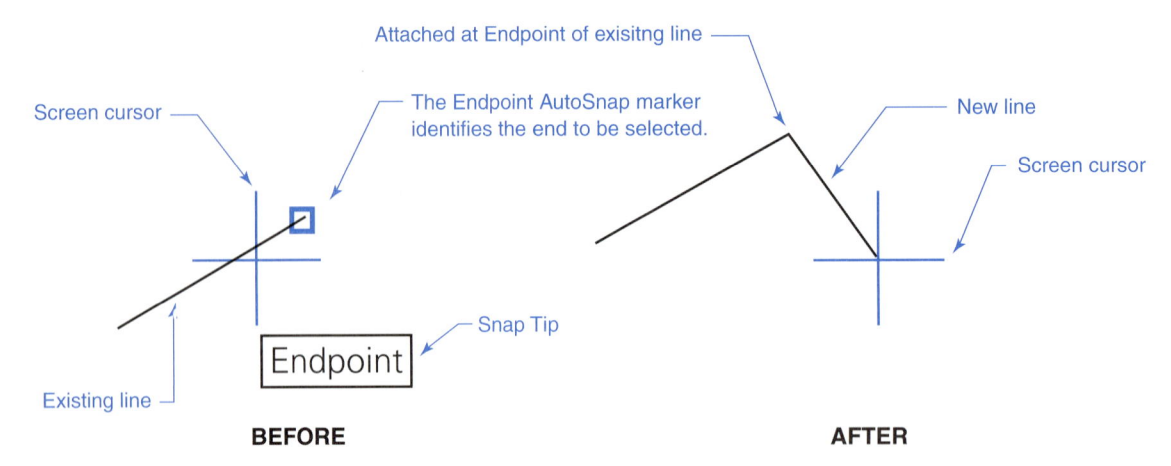

FIGURE 6.5 The object snap ENDpoint option finds the endpoint closest to the center of the screen cursor.

> ### Field Notes
>
> Notice that when you pick an Endpoint object snap from the menu that the entry at the prompt is _endp, and not _end. The reason for this is that END is also a command name in previous AutoCAD LT releases. If you were to accidentally enter END at a Command: prompt instead of a point selection prompt, your drawing would be automatically saved and AutoCAD LT would close. This could be very dangerous if you made changes that you did not want to save. Even if you were going to save the changes anyway, you would still experience the inconvenience of having to wait while exiting AutoCAD LT and then restarting it. It is strongly recommended that if you use the keyboard to enter your object snaps in previous AutoCAD LT releases, you should always type **ENDP** when you need Endpoint. However, the END command was discontinued in AutoCAD LT 97. This allows you to type END when using the Endpoint object snap on the keyboard.

Snap to the Middle of an Object

You can easily snap exactly to the middle of an object such as a line or arc. When you get a point prompt, select the Snap to Middle toolbar button, pick Midpoint in the cursor menu, or type **MID.** Move the cursor to any place on the line or arc and pick. Look at Figure 6.6 as you follow this command sequence:

Command: **L** or **LINE**↵
From point: ⟨*pick the desired midpoint of the new line*⟩
To point: **MID**↵
of ⟨*pick the original line*⟩
To point: ↵
Command:

FIGURE 6.6 Using the object snap MIDpoint option.

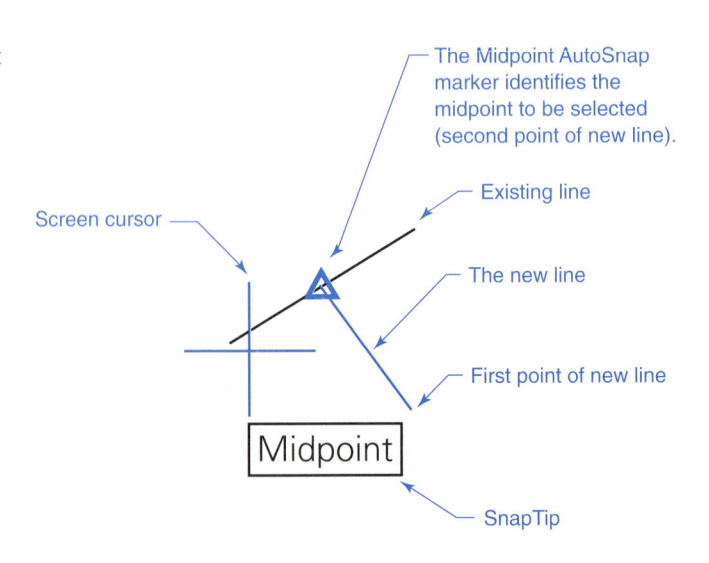

CHAPTER 6 ⋯ Precision Drafting Tools

Snap to an Intersection

It is a common drafting practice to connect a line to the intersection of other lines or objects. The Intersection object snap allows you to snap automatically to the intersection of objects such as lines, corners, arcs, and circles. Use this object snap by picking the Snap to Intersection toolbar button, selecting Intersection in the cursor menu, or typing **INT** when needed. Then move the cursor on or near the desired intersection or corner and pick. The following command sequence is shown in Figure 6.7A:

Object Snap

INTersection

Command: **L** or **LINE**↵
From point: ⟨*pick the desired endpoint of the new line*⟩
To point: **INT**↵
of ⟨*move the cursor on or near the desired intersection and pick*⟩
To point: ↵
Command:

In some cases it may be inconvenient or even impossible to place the cursor on or very near the actual intersection. If this is the case, you can pick both objects individually and AutoCAD LT will find the point where they intersect. When you do this, you get the Extended Intersection AutoSnap marker and related SnapTip shown in Figure 6.7B when you pick the first object. You get the regular Intersection marker when you pick the second object.

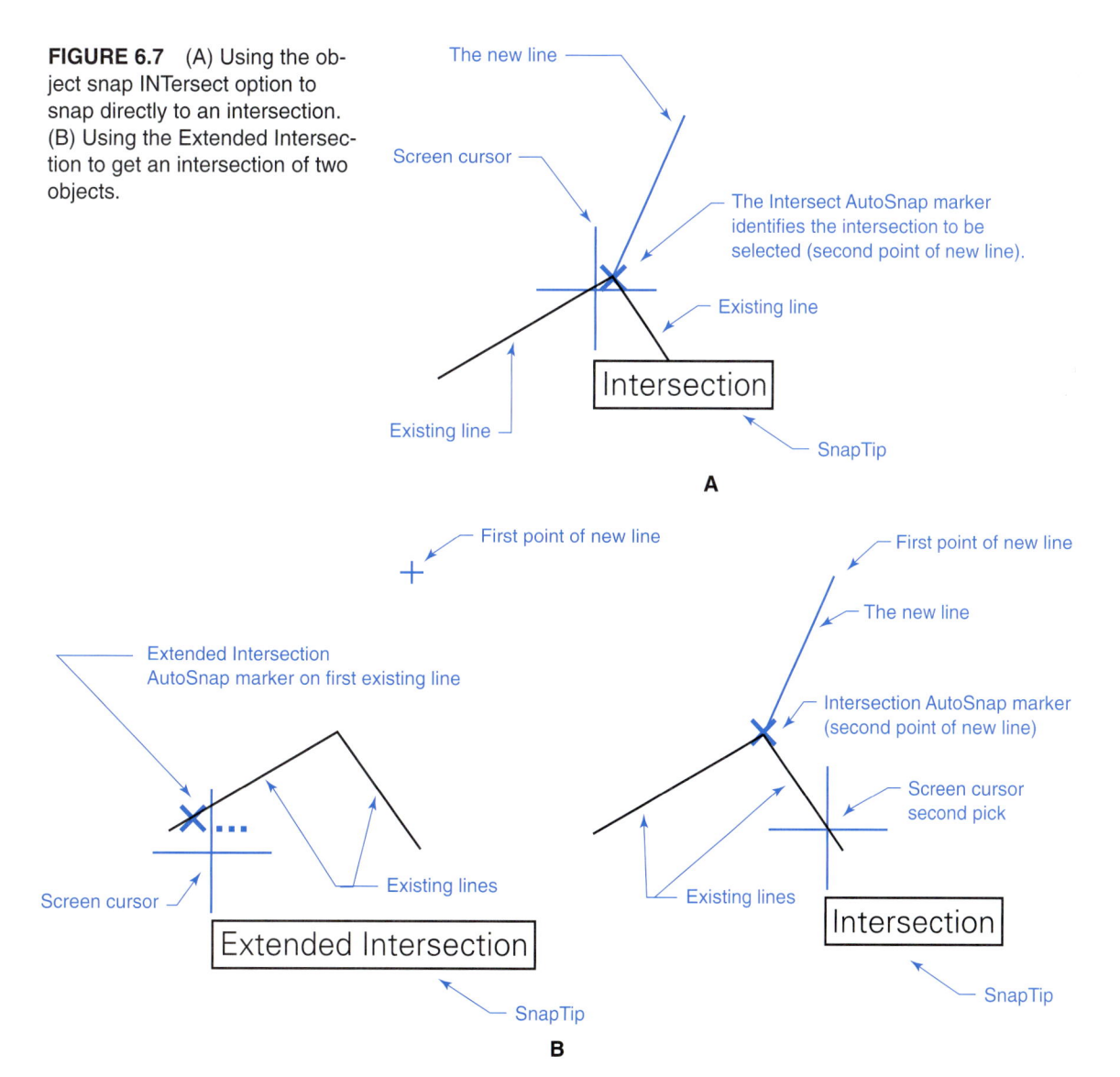

FIGURE 6.7 (A) Using the object snap INTersect option to snap directly to an intersection. (B) Using the Extended Intersection to get an intersection of two objects.

> **Field Notes**
> - As long as the objects you are picking are visible, the intersection can occur off screen and it will still be found.
> - If the objects do not actually physically intersect, the point where they would intersect (if they were extended far enough) is found. This is true even for arcs, which are extended along their radius.

Snap Perpendicular to an Object

Object Snap

PERpendicular

The Perpendicular object snap allows you to snap easily to an object perpendicular to another object. The term *perpendicular* means at right (90°) angles. To use the Perpendicular object snap, pick the Snap to Perpendicular toolbar button, select the Perpendicular option in the cursor menu, or type **PER**. Look at Figure 6.8 while you follow this command sequence:

Command: **L** or **LINE**↵
From point: ⟨*pick the desired endpoint of the new line*⟩
To point: **PER**↵
of ⟨*move the cursor to the original line and pick*⟩
To point: ↵
Command:

FIGURE 6.8 Using the object snap PERpendicular option.

In some situations, you may want to draw a line perpendicular to an existing object by selecting the existing object first, followed by selecting a point away from the object. When you do this, AutoCAD LT gives you the Deferred Perpendicular AutoSnap marker and related SnapTip. Deferred Perpendicular means that AutoCAD LT will establish the perpendicularity after waiting for you to pick the next point. Figure 6.9 shows how Deferred Perpendicular works.

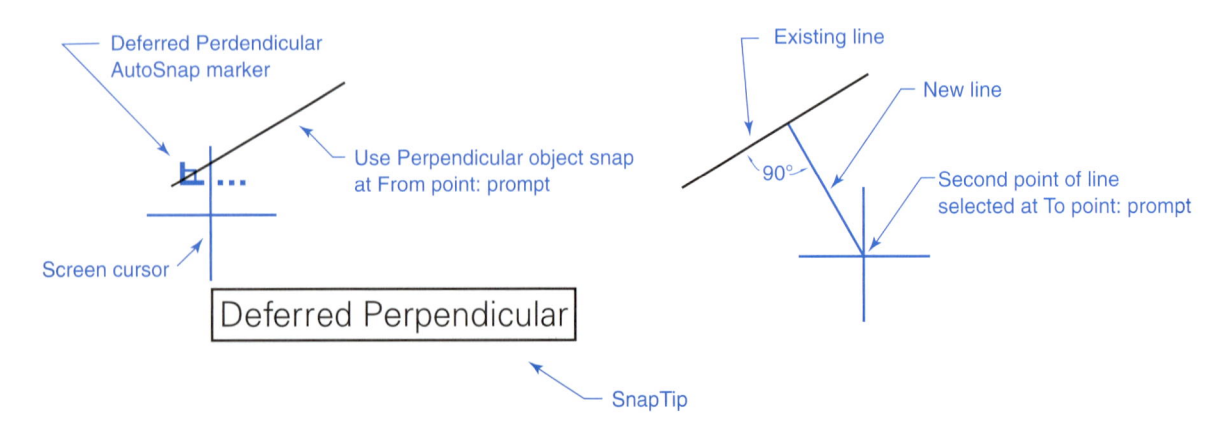

FIGURE 6.9 Using the Deferred Perpendicular object snap feature.

CHAPTER 6 ■ Precision Drafting Tools

Field Notes

A common difficulty that you may encounter when using object snaps is accidentally picking the wrong menu item and activating an object snap other than the one you really need. If you do pick the wrong object snap and need to cancel it, here's how: Remember that simply picking any point deactivates the object snap whether or not the pick was successful, and if you pick a point where no object exists, then no point is found and the point prompt is reissued. You can use this feature to your advantage. When an incorrect object snap is selected, simply pick a point onscreen where no objects are found. The object snap is deactivated and the point prompt is reissued. Now you can select the correct object snap and continue working.

Exercise 6.1

1. Open AutoCAD LT if it is not already open. Use the setup option of your choice. A border and title block are not required. Dimensions and notes are not needed.
2. Set limits at 8.5,11.
3. Draw the object shown below using the steps given and suggested object snaps for accuracy.
4. Save the drawing as EX6.1.

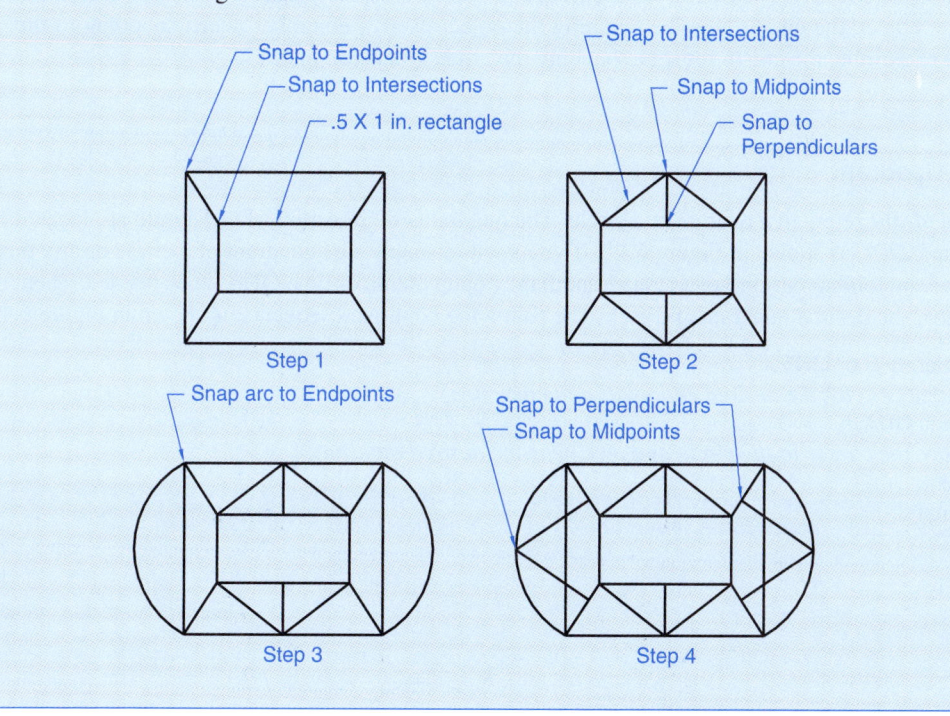

Step 1 — Snap to Endpoints, Snap to Intersections, .5 X 1 in. rectangle

Step 2 — Snap to Intersections, Snap to Midpoints, Snap to Perpendiculars

Step 3 — Snap arc to Endpoints

Step 4 — Snap to Perpendiculars, Snap to Midpoints

Snap to the Center

Snap an object to the center of a circle, arc, or ellipse by picking the Snap to Center toolbar button, selecting the Center option in the cursor menu, or typing **CEN** at the desired point prompt. Figure 6.10 shows a line drawn to the exact center of a circle by using the Center object snap. Move the cursor to anywhere on the circle and pick. Follow this command sequence:

Command: **L** or **LINE**↵
From point: ⟨*pick the desired endpoint of the new line*⟩
To point: **CEN**↵
of ⟨*move the cursor to the circle and pick*⟩
To point: ↵
Command:

Object Snap

CENter

FIGURE 6.10 Using the object snap CENter option.

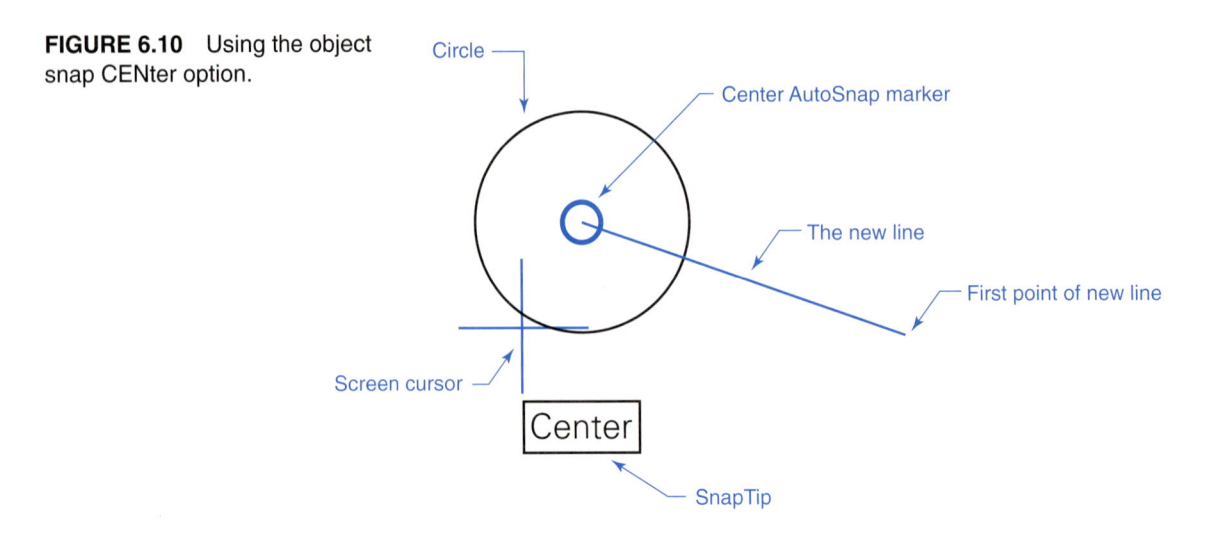

> ### Field Notes
>
> One common mistake when learning to use the CENter object snap is trying to pick a point at the center of the circle. This does not work because in order for object snap to find a point associated with an object, the cursor must be touching the object itself. Remember, when snapping to the center of a circle, the cursor must be touching the circle when you pick.

Snap to a Quadrant

Object Snap

QUAdrant

The term *quadrant* refers to a quarter of a circle. The quadrants of an AutoCAD LT circle are located at 0°, 90°, 180°, and 270°, as shown in Figure 6.11. If you want to snap to the quadrant of a circle or arc, pick the Snap to Quadrant toolbar button, select Quadrant in the popup menu, or type **QUA** when needed. Then, move the cursor near the desired quadrant and pick. The following command sequence is shown in Figure 6.12:

Command: **L** or **LINE**↵
From point: ⟨*pick the desired endpoint of the new line*⟩
To point: **QUA**↵
of ⟨*move the cursor to the circle and pick near the desired quadrant*⟩
To point: ↵
Command:

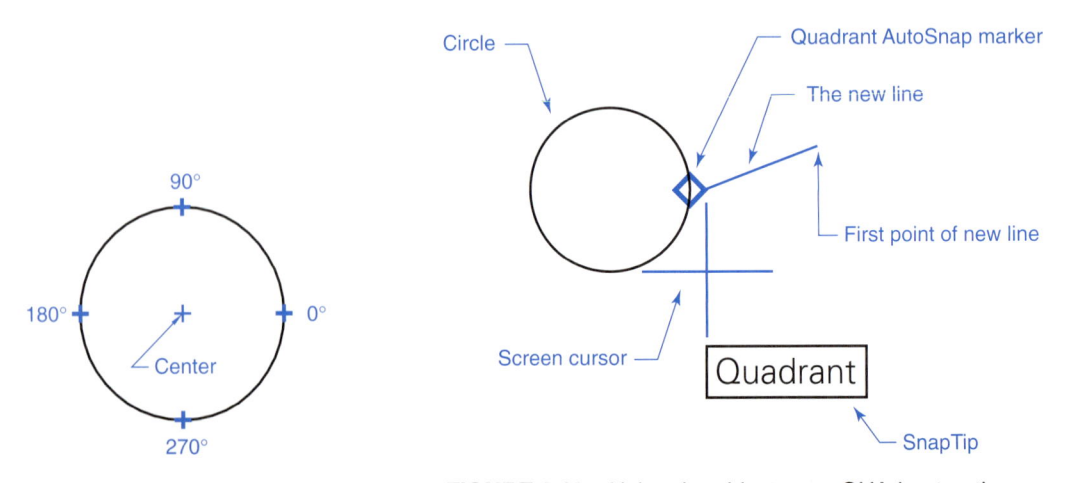

FIGURE 6.11 The quadrants of a circle.

FIGURE 6.12 Using the object snap QUAdrant option.

CHAPTER 6 ‖‖ Precision Drafting Tools 189

Snap to a Tangent Point

The Tangent object snap is used to snap accurately to the point of tangency of a curved object such as a circle, arc, or ellipse. Tangent means that a line, arc, circle, or ellipse touches another arc, circle, or ellipse at only one point, without crossing. To use this object snap option, pick the Snap to Tangent toolbar button, pick Tangent in the cursor menu, or type **TAN.** Move the cursor to a place on the circle near the intended point of tangency. Figure 6.13 shows a line drawn to the point of tangency of a circle. This is the command sequence:

> Command: **L** or **LINE**↵
> From point: ⟨*pick the desired endpoint of the new line*⟩
> To point: **TAN**↵
> to ⟨*move the cursor to the circle and pick near the desired tangency*⟩
> To point: ↵
> Command:

FIGURE 6.13 Using the object snap TANgent option.

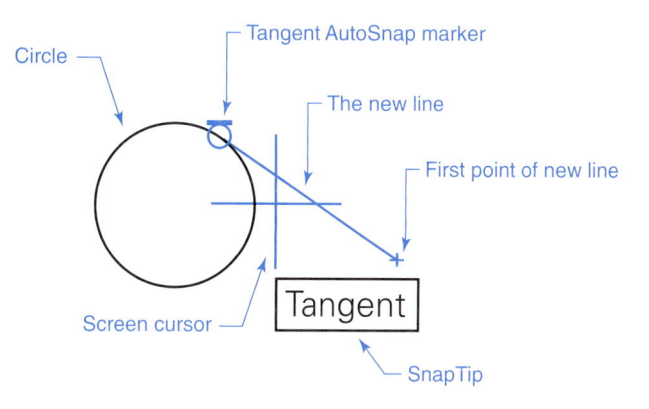

In some situations, you may need to pick the tangent point first and then pick the second point. In this case, AutoCAD LT gives you the Deferred Tangent AutoSnap marker and related SnapTip. The Deferred Tangent AutoSnap marker looks like the Tangent marker with three dots following. Deferred Tangent means that AutoCAD LT will establish the actual point of tangency after waiting for you to pick the next point. The command sequence looks like this:

> Command: **L** or **LINE**↵
> From point: **TAN**↵
> to ⟨*pick the circle or arc near the desired point of tangency*⟩
> To point: ⟨*pick the endpoint of the line*⟩
> To point: ↵
> Command:

You can also draw circles and arcs tangent using the Three Point options. For example, you can draw a circle tangent to the three given circles in Figure 6.14 if you use the CIRCLE command's 3 Points option with each point tangent to a different circle. The command works like this:

> Command: **C** or **CIRCLE**↵
> 3P/TTR/⟨Center point⟩: **3P**↵
> First point: **TAN**↵
> to ⟨*move the cursor to the first circle and pick*⟩
> Second point: **TAN**↵
> to ⟨*move the cursor to the second circle and pick*⟩
> Third point: **TAN**↵
> to ⟨*move the cursor to the third circle and pick*⟩
> Command:

You can also draw a circle tangent to one other circle by using the CIRCLE command's Radius option if TANgent is used at the Radius prompt.

FIGURE 6.14 Using the CIRCLE command's Three Point option and the TANgent object snap to draw a circle tangent to three existing circles. *Note:* The AutoSnap markers and SnapTips are left off for clarity.

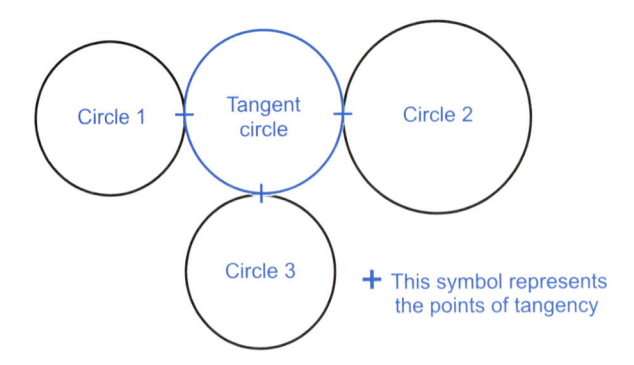

Field Notes

When picking T<u>a</u>n, Tan, Tan from the <u>C</u>ircle cascade on the <u>D</u>raw pull-down menu, the TANgent entries are automatic, but if you pick where no object exists you will see an "invalid" 2D point message. To continue this command, you will need to restart the Tangent object snap mode. You can pick it from the menu, the tool bar, or enter it manually at the keyboard.

Exercise 6.2

1. Open AutoCAD LT if it is not already open. Use the setup option of your choice. A border and title block are not required. Notes are not needed.
2. Set limits at 8.5,11.
3. Draw the object shown below using the steps given and suggested object snaps for accuracy. The exact size is up to you.
4. Save the drawing as EX6.2.

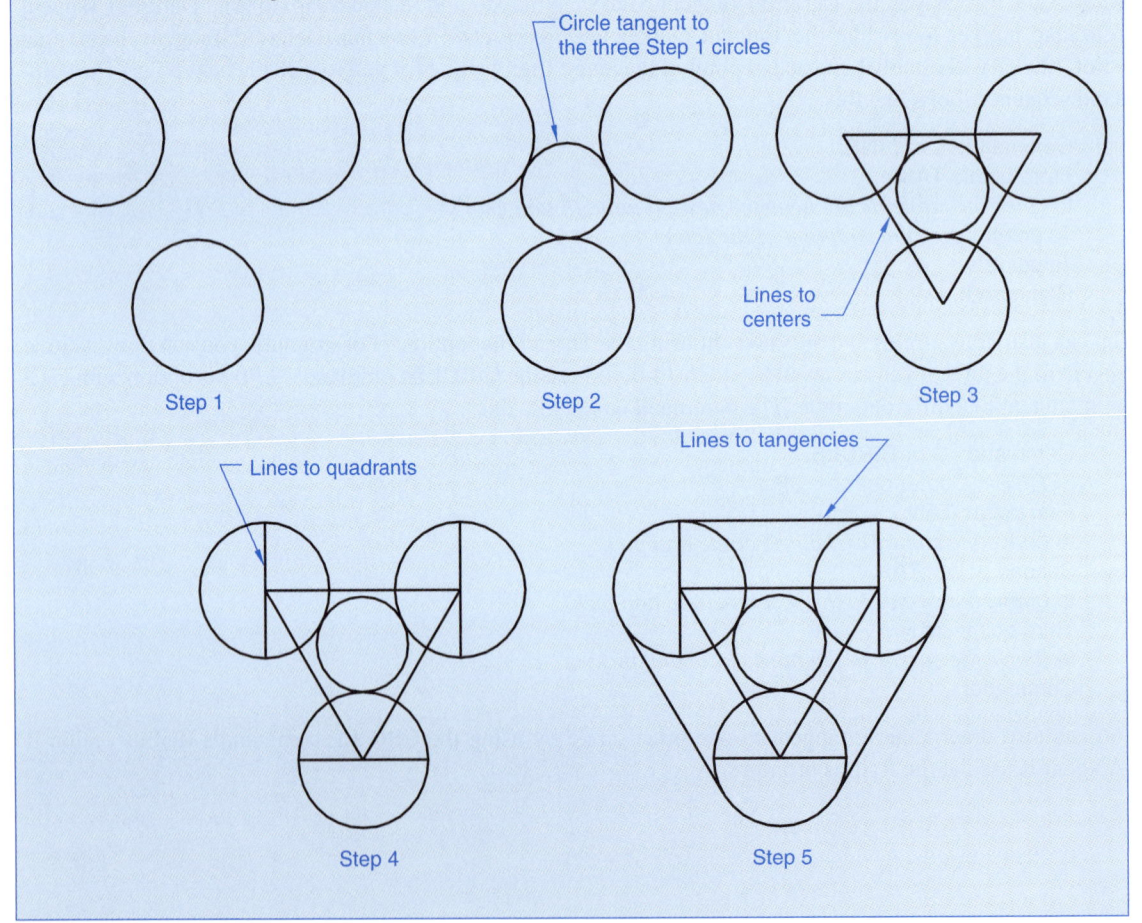

Snap to the Insertion Point

You will not use the Insert object snap until Chapters 9 and 12, but it is introduced here with the other object snap options. The Insert object snap is used to snap to the insertion point of text objects, blocks, attributes, and attribute definitions. ***Text*** is the AutoCAD LT term for letters and numbers. Text is explained in Chapter 9. The word ***block*** refers to an object, a group of objects, a drawing, or a symbol that is created as one object, generally for multiple use. An ***attribute*** contains information about a block. For example, an attribute might be a description or text within a block. An ***attribute definition*** describes the characteristics of the attribute. Blocks, attributes, and attribute definitions are explained in Chapter 12. Snap to an insertion point by picking the Snap to Insert toolbar button, selecting Insert in the cursor menu, or typing **INS**. When you snap to an insertion point, you get the Insert AutoSnap marker and SnapTip. Figure 6.15 shows an example of a text and block insertion point.

FIGURE 6.15 Using the object snap INSertion option.

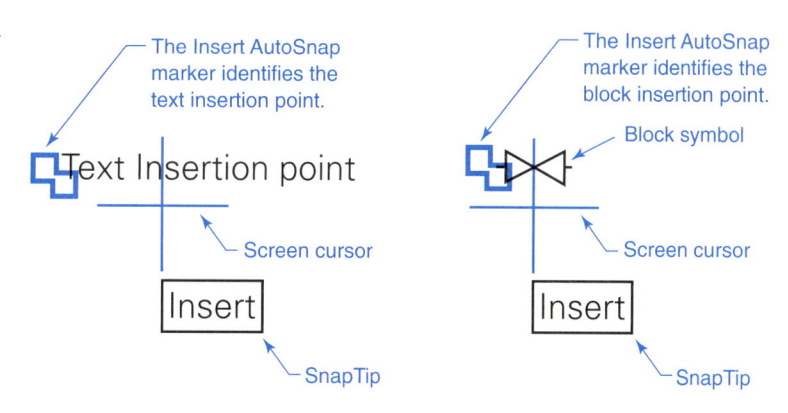

Snap to a Node

A ***node*** is a point object. Point objects are drawn using the POINT command, which is discussed later in this chapter. Snap to a node by picking the Snap to Node toolbar button, picking Node in the cursor menu, or typing **NOD** at the keyboard at a point prompt. When you snap to a point, you get the Node AutoSnap marker and SnapTip if AutoSnap is on.

Snap to the Nearest Point

Oftentimes you may want to snap to an object, but the exact location of the point is not critical. The Nearest object snap allows you to snap to an object at a point that is closest to the cursor location. To access this object snap, pick the Snap to Nearest toolbar button, select Nearest in the cursor menu, or type **NEA**. Move the cursor as close as possible to the desired point and pick. When you use the Nearest object snap, you get the Nearest AutoSnap marker and SnapTip.

Disabling Object Snap

The None object snap option allows you to disable object snaps. This is most effective when you have a running object snap that you do not want to use for a specific application. (Running object snaps are explained later in this chapter.) When used during a command sequence, the None object snap allows only point entry without object snaps for the individual point when it is used. The None option needs to be used every time you want to temporarily disable a running object snap. To use this option, type **NON**, select None at the bottom of the cursor menu, or pick the Snap to None toolbar button.

Using Running Object Snaps

The term ***running object snap*** means that an object snap option or group of options can be set to run continuously. Running object snaps remain active until you change them or turn them off. Running object snaps are useful when you know that the drawing requires several of the same type of object snaps to be used. This saves a lot of time because the object snap that you set is automatically active when needed. You can set one or more object snaps to be active. If you set more than one running object snap, AutoCAD LT automatically uses the most appropriate object snap for the object you select. If two or more different possible object snap selections can be found, AutoCAD LT snaps to the selection that is closest to the cursor crossing. Running object snaps can be set in the Osnap Settings dialog box or at the prompt line. Using the dialog box is most convenient.

Access the dialog box by selecting Object S*n*ap Settings ... from the *T*ools pull-down menu, pick the Object Snap Settings toolbar button, double-click on OSNAP on the status line, or type **O**, **OS**, **OSNAP**, or **DDOSNAP** at the Command: prompt. The OSNAP display on the status line only starts DDOSNAP if no object snap modes are currently running. The default Osnap Settings dialog box shown in Figure 6.16A displays all the object snap options as toggles that are turned off. Turn on one or more desired running object snaps by picking the appropriate toggle. Figure 6.16B shows the *E*ndpoint, *C*enter, and *I*ntersection running object snaps turned on. Pick the OK button when ready.

Entering running object snaps at the Command: line is more time consuming and is done by using the -OS or -OSNAP command. When you are asked to enter the desired object snap modes, type the abbreviated name of the object snap or group of object snaps. If you enter more than one object snap name, separate each name by a comma. Do this to set the Endpoint, Center, and Intersection running object snaps at the keyboard:

Command: **-O** or **-OSNAP**↵
Object snap modes: **END,CEN,INT**↵
Command:

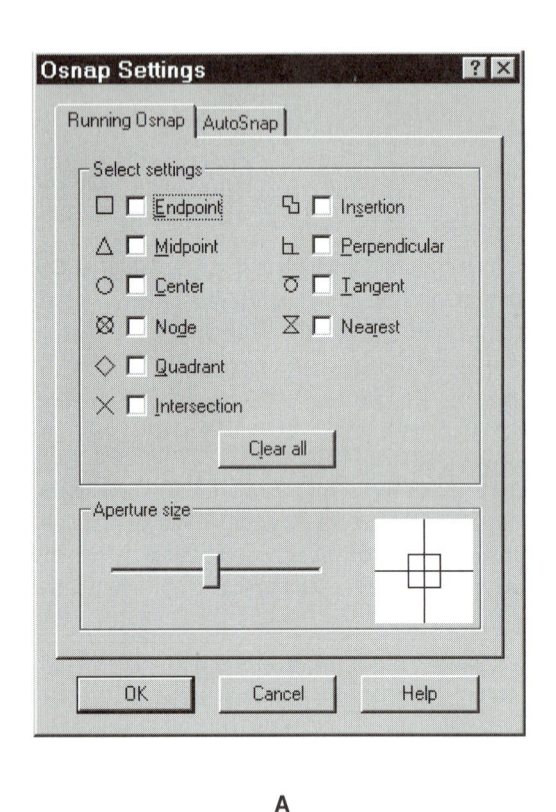

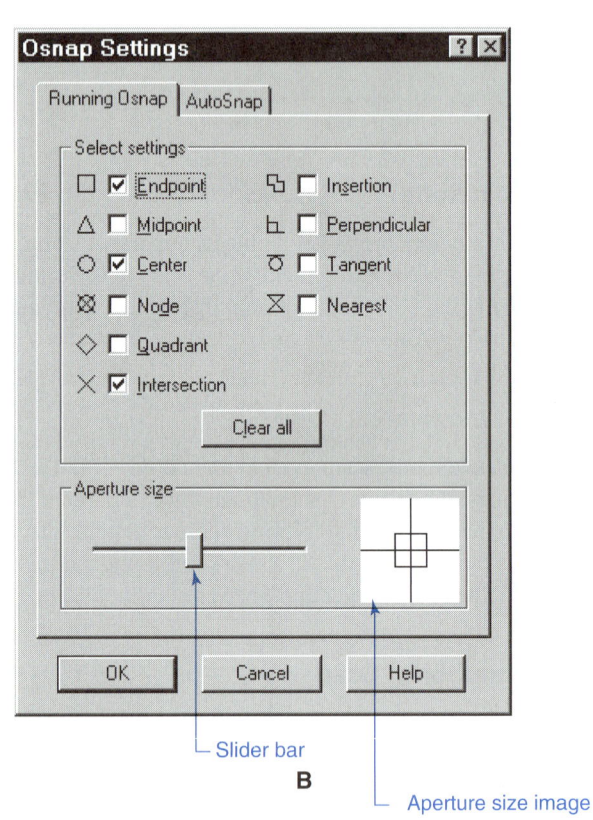

FIGURE 6.16 (A) The Osnap Settings dialog box. (B) Setting the *E*ndpoint, *C*enter, and *I*ntersection running object snaps. Adjust the Ape*r*ture Size in the Osnap Settings dialog box by moving the slider bar.

Turn off specific or all running object snaps if they are not needed. Double-clicking on OSNAP on the status line temporarily turns off the running object snaps. Double-click again if you want to turn them back on. To turn running object snaps totally off, go back to the Osnap Settings dialog box and pick the C*l*ear All button or toggle individual running object snaps as needed. You can also enter the OSNAP command and either press Enter, type **OFF,** or type **NONE.**

This OSNAP toggle feature only works when there are object snap modes currently running. Setting running object snap modes automatically turns on the OSNAP text on the button. Now the currently running object snap modes can be temporarily suspended by double-clicking on OSNAP, which grays out the OSNAP text. Double-clicking again resets the temporarily suspended running object snap modes and restores the OSNAP text. This is a very convenient tool because you do not have to use the OSNAP or DDOSNAP command to restore the previous settings.

Field Notes

- Double-clicking on OSNAP on the status line is very convenient to temporarily turn running object snaps on and off. Another option is to press Ctrl + F. There are times when you may want the running object snaps active and other times when they distract from your drawing performance.
- The one drawback to running object snaps comes when you forget to turn them off. If you are unaware of a running object snap mode, you may get very unexpected results while working in your drawing. There are two ways to recognize that a running object snap mode is active. First, at all point prompts, the aperture will appear, and AutoSnap markers and snap tips will appear on SnapTips. Second, the OSNAP text in the status line will be active. A quick double-click on OSNAP immediately disables the running object snap modes.

Adjusting the Aperture Size

The AutoCAD LT default aperture size is fine for most uses. However, you may want to make the aperture smaller to work on a very crowded drawing or make it bigger for construction in large areas. The aperture size is measured in pixels. *Pixels* (short for *picture elements*) are the tiny dots that make up what is displayed on the computer screen. Review Chapter 1 for a full discussion of pixels. The AutoCAD LT default setting is 10 pixels. AutoCAD LT allows you to change the setting from 1 to 50 pixels. You can set pixel size using the APERTURE command or move the slider bar of the Aperture size compartment of the Osnap Settings dialog box shown in Figure 6.16. When moving the slider, the image to the right shows the current aperture setting at actual size. When changing the aperture size at the command prompt, do this:

Command: **AP** or **APERTURE**↵
Object snap target height (1-50 pixels) <10>: **20**↵
Command:

Field Notes

- Changing the aperture size in the Osnap Settings dialog is quick and easy. You can also see the size of the aperture, displayed in the image tile, as you move the slider bar.
- Aperture size can be adjusted as needed to fit any situation. Increasing the size of the aperture helps you to pick object snap points quickly and easily because you do not have to point so carefully. In a situation where there are many objects in your drawing and a large aperture is not accurate enough, reduce the size and you will be able to pick objects in a crowded area more accurately.

Changing Your AutoSnap Settings

You can make adjustments to your AutoSnap settings in the Osnap Settings dialog box. Access this dialog box as previously discussed and then pick the AutoSnap tab, as shown in Figure 6.17. The AutoSnap tab has these available Select settings options:

- Marker: The marker is on by default. Pick this check box and remove the check to turn it off.
- Magnet: The magnet feature forces the aperture box onto the snap point where the AutoSnap marker is located. This is on by default.

FIGURE 6.17 The AutoSnap tab is where you set AutoSnap options, change the marker size, or change the marker color.

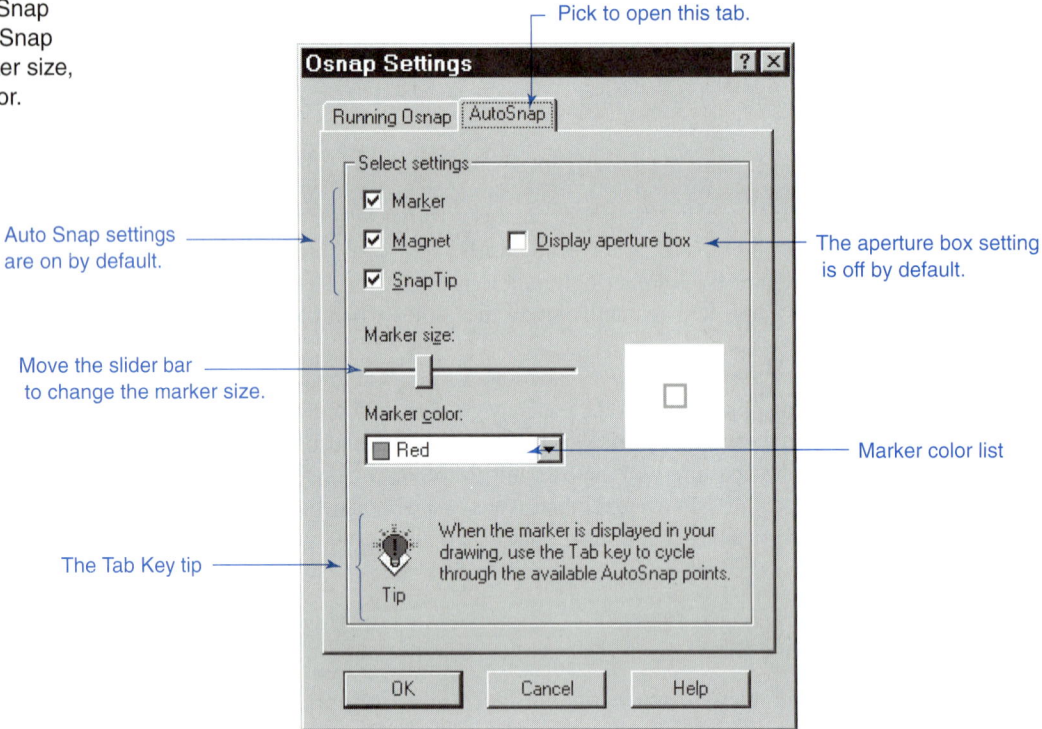

- Auto Snap settings are on by default.
- Move the slider bar to change the marker size.
- The Tab Key tip
- Pick to open this tab.
- The aperture box setting is off by default.
- Marker color list

- <u>S</u>napTip: This is also on by default. This check box allows you to turn the SnapTip on or off.

- <u>D</u>isplay aperture box: The aperture box is located at the intersection of the screen cursor crosshairs when you snap to an object and when this check box is on. This option is off by default. The <u>D</u>isplay aperture box is highlighted only when at least one of the Mar<u>k</u>er, <u>M</u>agnet or <u>S</u>napTip options are on.

The Marker si<u>z</u>e: area has a slider bar that allows you to change the size of the AutoSnap markers. The image tile at the right represents the marker size as you move the slider bar.

The Marker <u>c</u>olor: list box allows you to change the AutoSnap marker color to one of the seven standard colors, as desired.

✏ Field Notes

When you use an object snap to select a point on an object, you can press the Tab key to cycle through all of the available locations that match the current object snap setting on the drawing. If you have more than one running object snap set, pressing the Tab key allows you to cycle through the available running object snaps that match related features on the drawing. This Field Note refers to the tip found at the bottom of the AutoSnap tab in Figure 6.17.

CHAPTER 6　III　Precision Drafting Tools

Exercise 6.3

1. Open AutoCAD LT if it is not already open. Use the setup option of your choice. A border and title block are not required. Notes and dimensions are not needed.
2. Set limits at 8.5,11.
3. Draw the object shown below using the steps given. Use Endpoint, Center, Intersect, and Tangent as running object snaps. The exact size is up to you.
4. Adjust the aperture size to help you make object snap selections.
5. Save the drawing as EX6.3.

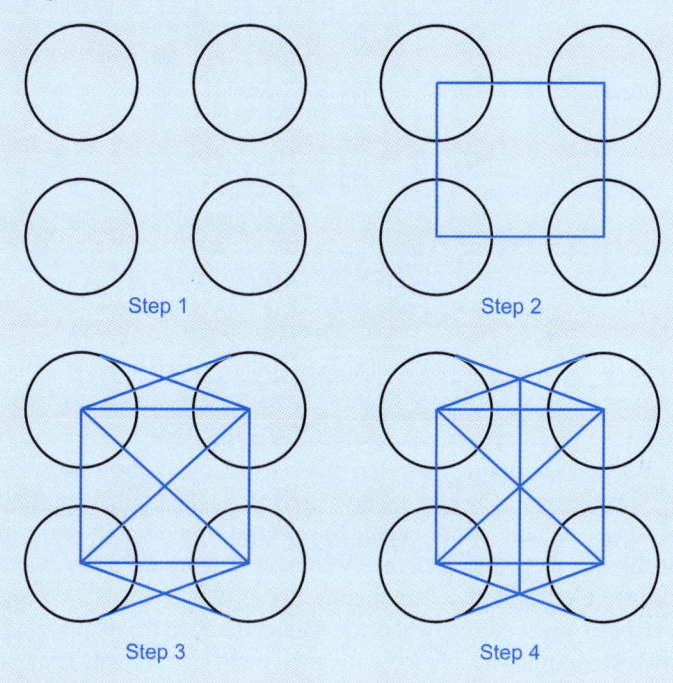

Step 1　　Step 2

Step 3　　Step 4

✓ LEARNING CHECKPOINT

☐ Describe the purpose of object snaps.
☐ How do you display the object snap cursor menu?
☐ Explain when and how object snaps are entered at the keyboard.
☐ List the names of at least 10 object snap options.
☐ Explain the function of the AutoSnap markers and SnapTips.
☐ Define a running object snap.
☐ Identify at least four ways to access the Osnap Settings dialog box.
☐ How are multiple running object snaps entered at the keyboard?
☐ How do you temporarily turn off or on running object snaps?
☐ Describe at least five ways to turn running object snaps off totally.
☐ How do you change the aperture size at the keyboard?
☐ Why is it desirable to change the aperture size using the Running Object Snap dialog box?

Reference Points and Other Point Objects

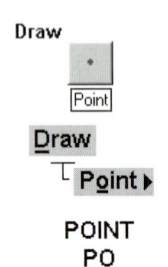

Points can be drawn using AutoCAD LT. The points you draw can look just like a grid dot, or a variety of point styles and sizes are available. Points can be placed on a drawing for reference, as markers, for design, or for snapping with the Node object snap option. The Point Style dialog box shown in Figure 6.18 contains the different point shapes and allows you to change the point size.

FIGURE 6.18 The Point Style dialog box.

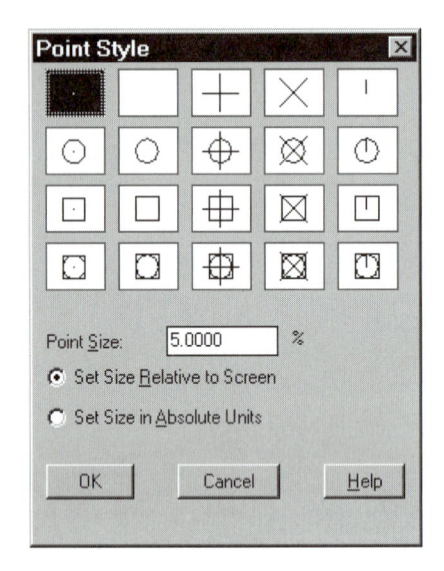

Access the Point Style dialog box by picking Point Style ... in the Format pull-down menu or by typing **DDPTYPE**. The AutoCAD LT default point is a dot. To select a different point style, move the arrow cursor to the desired symbol image and pick; then pick the OK button. Among the many available options, you will notice that the second image tile from the left in the top row is blank. This style suppresses the display of points in your drawing and can be set current when you want to remove the points from your display, but not from your drawing. Two options are available for setting the point size format. The options are activated by picking one of the following radio buttons:

- Set Size Relative to Screen: This is the AutoCAD LT default. Pick this option if you want to set the point size as a percentage of the screen size. This kind of a point display changes when using the ZOOM command, but if you use the REGEN command, the point size returns to its correct size ratio to the screen. When this option is active, there is a percent (%) symbol next to the Point Size text box. Alter the size percentage by changing the value in the text box.
- Set Size in Absolute Units: Use this option if you want to set the point size in units that are specified in the Point Size text box. Points drawn using this format get larger or smaller when using the ZOOM command. When this option is active, Units is specified next to the Point Size text box. The units value you set is the same as your drawing units. For example, a setting of .25 is one-quarter of an inch on an inch drawing.

After using the Point Style dialog box to set the desired point style and size, you are ready to draw a point. To draw a single point, select Point and then Single Point from the Draw pull-down menu, pick the Point button in the Draw toolbar, or type **PO** or **POINT** at the Command: prompt. This command asks you for a point:

Command: **PO** or **POINT**↵
Point: ⟨*pick a point or enter point coordinates*⟩
Command:

You can draw several points by picking Point and then Multiple Point in the Draw pull-down menu. The POINT command remains active for you to draw as many points as needed until you press Esc, Enter, or the space bar to exit the command.

CHAPTER 6 ⅠⅠⅠ Precision Drafting Tools   197

> ✎ Field Notes
>
> You can draw several different point styles and sizes. However, when the drawing is regenerated, AutoCAD LT changes every point style and size to the same representation as the last point style and size drawn. So, in real practice, you can only have one currently active point style and size.

Exercise 6.4

1. Open AutoCAD LT if it is not already open. Use the setup option of your choice. A border and title block are not required.
2. Set limits at 8.5,11.
3. Open the Point Style dialog box, pick a point style of your own choosing, and draw it using the default size and format.
4. Do this again with a different point style.
5. Use the Point Style dialog box to select a different point style and set the size to 20%. Draw the point and notice the difference.
6. Use the Point Style dialog box to select a different point style and set the size to .25 units. Draw the point and notice the difference.
7. Use the Point Style dialog box to select a different point style and set the size to .50 units. Draw the point and notice the difference.
8. With all of the points that you just drew displayed on the screen, type REGEN at the Command: prompt and press Enter. Observe what happens.
9. Save the drawing as EX6.4.

Measuring and Dividing Objects

Now that you know how to control the display of points, AutoCAD LT provides two commands that let you place points at specified distances along an object. These commands are DIVIDE and MEASURE. Before using the DIVIDE or MEASURE commands, you need to decide what you want the points to look like. To do this, use the Point Style dialog box to pick a point style and size. The default point style is a dot. The dot does not show when placed on an object, but it is there and can be snapped to using the Node object snap. If you want the point symbol to display clearly, then use one of the point styles that has a distinct shape. If the points are to be placed on the drawing for construction purposes, you might consider placing them on a construction layer so they can be frozen when not in use.

Using the Divide Command

The DIVIDE command is used to place evenly spaced points or blocks along the length, circumference, or perimeter of an object. Blocks are objects that are grouped together to make a single object or symbol. Blocks are explained in Chapter 12. To make evenly spaced divisions on an object, select Point and then Divide in the Draw pull-down menu or type **DIV** or **DIVIDE**. AutoCAD LT asks for a number of segments, for which you can enter between 2 and 32,767 divisions. Figure 6.19 shows how a line, a circle, and a rectangle are divided into eight segments using this command sequence:

Command: **DIV** or **DIVIDE**.↵
Select object to divide: ⟨*pick the object*⟩
<Number of segments>/Block: **8**↵
Command:

Draw
/n
Divide

Draw
└ P<u>o</u>int ▶

DIVIDE
DIV

FIGURE 6.19 Using the DIVIDE command to make eight equally spaced divisions on three different objects.

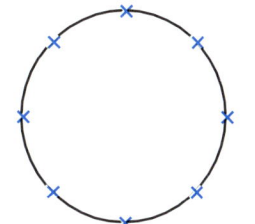

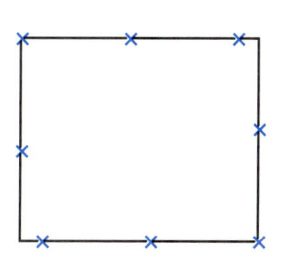

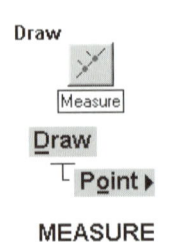

Using the Measure Command

The MEASURE command is used to place points or blocks a measured incremental distance along the length, circumference, or perimeter of an object. To place points a specified distance apart on an object, select Point and then Measure in the Draw pull-down menu or type **ME** or **MEASURE**. AutoCAD LT asks you for a segment length, which is the specified distance between points. The last segment length may be shorter than the specified length if the distance to the end of the object does not allow for a full length. Figure 6.20 shows the results of this command sequence:

Command: **ME** or **MEASURE**↵
Select object to measure: ⟨*pick the object*⟩
<Segment length>/Block: **.25**↵
Command:

FIGURE 6.20 Using the MEASURE command to mark three different objects with specific segment lengths.

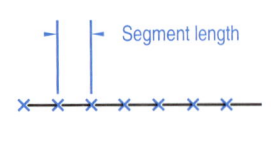

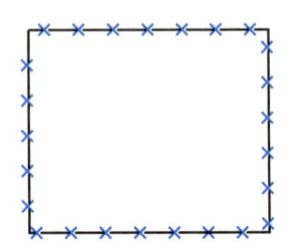

Exercise 6.5

1. Open AutoCAD LT if it is not already open. Use the setup option of your choice. A border and title block are not required.
2. Set limits at 8.5,11.
3. Open the Point Style dialog box. Pick the "X" point style and a size of 2%.
4. Draw a line, circle, and rectangle similar to those shown in Figure 6.19. Use the DIVIDE command to divide each object into eight equal parts.
5. Draw a line, circle, and rectangle similar to those shown in Figure 6.20. Use the MEASURE command to draw .25-in.-long segments on each object.
6. Save the drawing as EX6.5.

Using the From Option to Establish a Point from an Existing Point

With object snaps, you snap to a specific point associated with an object. Yet, there are many situations when you may want to snap to a point that can be located using a specific point of reference. In this situation, you can use the From option. The From option allows you to specify a point, using relative or polar coordinates (or direct distance entry as discussed later), that is at a specified location from a given point. The temporary reference point can be any point on an object such as an endpoint, midpoint, center, or any other known point in the drawing. One application might be when you want to draw a circle with its center a given X and Y distance from the corner of an object. It is easy to do this with the From option, which is accessed by picking the Snap From in the Object Snap toolbar button, selecting From in the Object Snap cursor menu, or typing **FRO**. Follow this command sequence, as you look at the steps in Figure 6.21, to draw a 0.25 circle with its center located .875,.625 from the corner of a plate:

Command: **C** or **CIRCLE**↵
3P/TTR/<Center point>: **FROM**↵
Base point: **INT**↵
of ⟨*pick the corner*⟩ <Offset>: **@.875,.625**↵
Diameter/<Radius>: **D**↵
Diameter: **.25**↵
Command:

The following items are defined from the previous command sequence:

- **Base point**   This is the point from which the From point is established. In this operation, the Base point is the corner of the rectangular plate in Figure 6.21.

CHAPTER 6 ■ Precision Drafting Tools

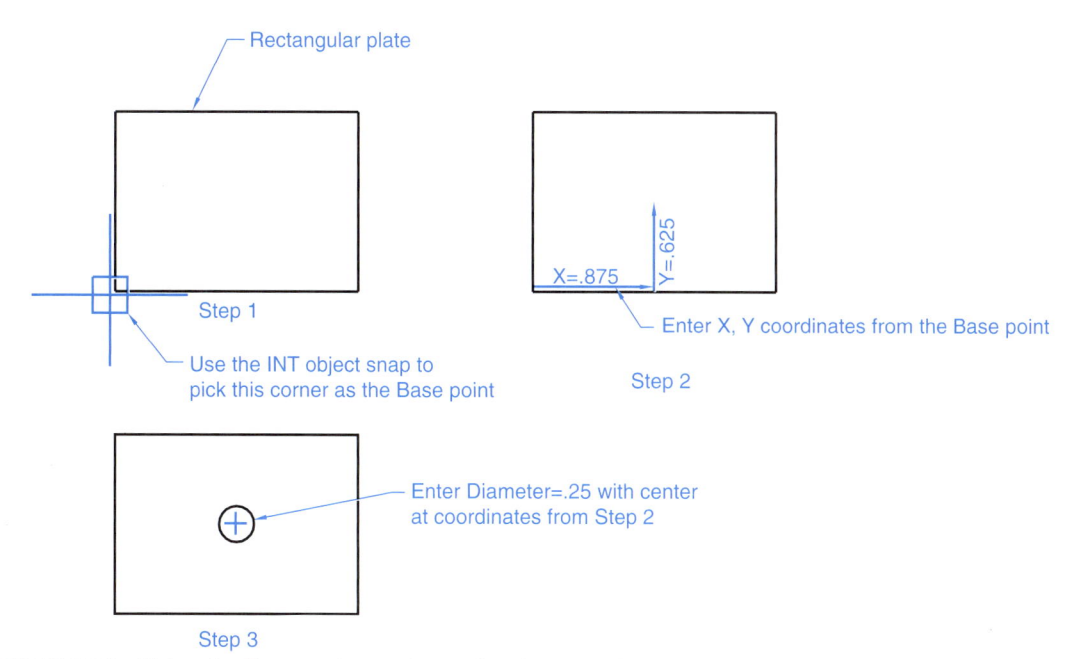

FIGURE 6.21 Using the From option to draw a line from a point perpendicular to a line.

- **Offset** This is the distance in relative or polar coordinates from the Base point. The Offset in the example is relative coordinates @.875,.625 from the Base point.

Any variety of operations may be performed using the From option. The possibilities depend on your specific application. Another example might have been to draw a circle a certain distance from the center of another circle or from the midpoint of a line.

Exercise 6.6

1. Open AutoCAD LT if it is not already open. Use the setup option of your choice. A border and title block are not required. Notes and dimensions are not needed.
2. Set limits at 8.5,11.
3. Draw the rectangular plate with four holes shown below using the From option to locate the holes from the corner of the rectangular plate. Do not draw dimensions and notes.
4. Save the drawing as EX6.6.

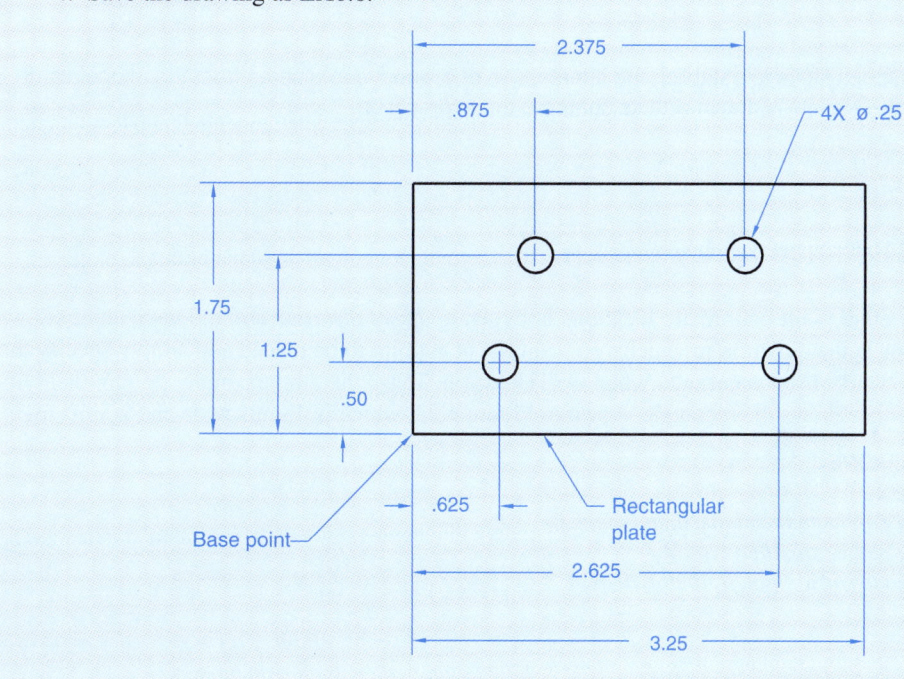

Using Point Filters

The term *filter* means to extract or remove certain information from something in order to create something else. ***Point filters*** are used to extract the X, Y, and Z coordinate values from individual points in order to create a new combined point. Point filters are also called ***coordinate filters.***

Using an X point filter works like drawing an imaginary horizontal line and a Y point filter establishes an imaginary vertical line. Z point filters are used for 3-D applications. Enter point filters by typing **.X** or **.Y** when AutoCAD LT asks you for point entry. Point filters work best when combined with object snaps to improve accuracy. An example of using point filters might be if you need to draw a circle with the center of its X and Y coordinates from the midpoint of the sides of the rectangular plate in Figure 6.22A. To do this, use the X and Y filters and the Midpoint object snaps as follows:

Command: **C** or **CIRCLE**↵
3P/TTR/<Center point>: **.X**↵
of **MID**
of ⟨move the aperture to the bottom horizontal line and pick⟩
of (need YZ): **MID**↵
of ⟨move the aperture to the left vertical line and pick⟩

The center of the circle automatically snaps to the intersection of the X and Y coordinates connected from the midpoints of the sides as shown in Figure 6.22B. Continue the CIRCLE command:

Diameter/<Radius> <>: **.5**↵
Command:

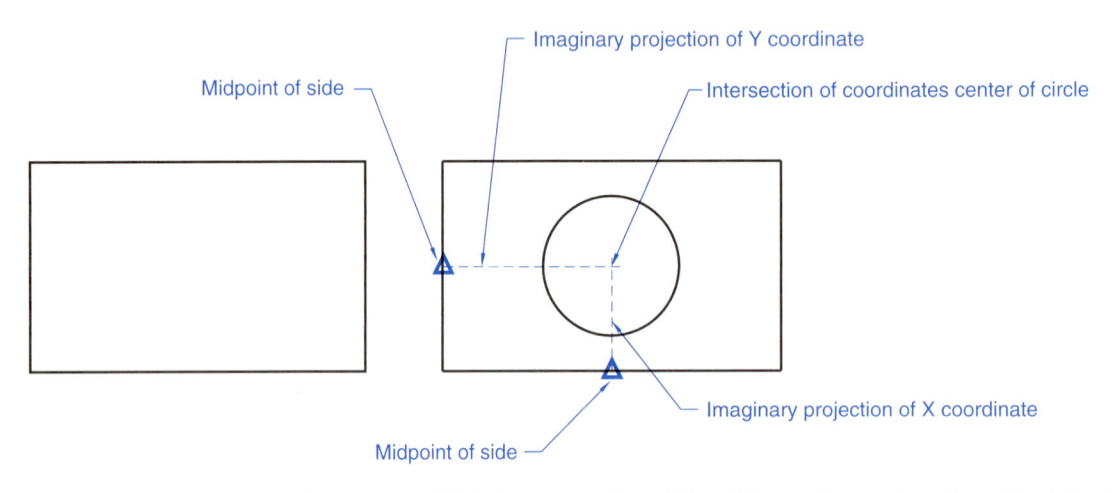

FIGURE 6.22 Using point filters to establish the intersection of X and Y coordinates from the midpoints of the sides of a rectangle. A circle is drawn with its center at the intersection.

Using Direct Distance Entry

A convenient way to enter point coordinate locations is by using ***direct distance entry.*** This feature allows you to point the cursor in the direction in which you want the next point to be placed and simply specify the distance. This feature works most accurately when ORTHO is on. To try this first example, be sure that ORTHO is on. This sequence draws the rectangle shown in Figure 6.23, which is 4 units wide and 2 units high:

Command: **L** or **LINE**↵
From point: **2,2**↵
To point: ⟨drag cursor to the right, then type **4**↵⟩
To point: ⟨drag cursor up, then type **2**↵⟩
To point: ⟨drag cursor to the left, then type **4**↵⟩
To point: **C**↵
Command:

CHAPTER 6 ▪ Precision Drafting Tools 201

FIGURE 6.23 Using direct distance entry to draw a rectangle.

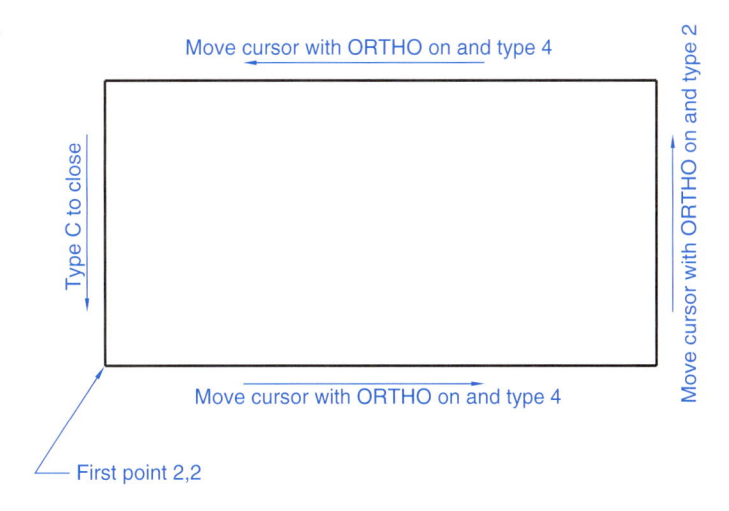

- Move cursor with ORTHO on and type 4
- Move cursor with ORTHO on and type 2
- Type C to close
- Move cursor with ORTHO on and type 4
- First point 2,2

Field Notes

The idea of direct distance entry is to be able to find points quickly and easily with a minimum amount of input. Direct distance entry works very well for drawing perpendicular lines with the ORTHO or SNAP options on. Use polar coordinate entry if freehand pointing does not provide enough accuracy. Direct distance entry can be used anywhere that AutoCAD LT expects a point coordinate value, including both drawing and editing commands. It is also possible to use direct distance entry at the *first* point prompt, such as the From point: prompt of the LINE command. Typing in a single number finds a point that is at the same angle as the cursor in relationship to the LASTPOINT variable, at the specified distance.

Exercise 6.7

1. Open AutoCAD LT if it is not already open. Use the setup option of your choice. A border and title block are not required.
2. Set limits at 8.5,11.
3. In the top portion of the drawing area, draw a rectangle similar to the one shown in Figure 6.22A.
4. Use point filters to draw a circle with the exact center at the X and Y intersection of a projection from the midpoints of the side and bottom of the rectangle. Use Figure 6.22B as an example.
5. Use Figure 6.23 as an example and follow the command sequence provided in the discussion about direct distance entry to draw a 4 × 2 rectangle. It is helpful to have ORTHO on when doing this part of the exercise.
6. Save the drawing as EX6.7.

Tracking Points with AutoCAD LT

Tracking is a way to locate a point relative to other points on the drawing. AutoCAD LT tracks a series of temporary points that you establish. Each point is found from the previous point. This allows you to determine a new point location from a series of directions and distances. The use of direct distance entry and object snaps assists in accurate tracking. Tracking can be used anytime AutoCAD LT asks for a point. The use of tracking is an easy way to find a point located at the imaginary intersection between two sides of an object. This example is similar to the illustration used in Figure 6.22 with the point filter discussion. Access tracking at any point prompt by picking the Tracking button in the Object Snap toolbar, picking Trac*k*ing in the Object Snap cursor menu, or typing **TK** or **TRA.** Press the Enter key to end tracking. Follow this command se-

Object Snap

TRAcking
TK

quence while you look at Figure 6.24 to use tracking to draw a circle at the intersection of the X and Y projection between two points:

> Command: **C** or **CIRCLE**↵
> 3P/TTR/<Center point>: **TK**↵
> First tracking point: **MID**↵
> of ⟨*move the cursor to the bottom horizontal line and pick with the cursor in the direction of the desired center*⟩
> Next point (Press ENTER to end tracking): **MID**↵
> of ⟨*move the cursor to the left vertical line and pick with the cursor in the direction of the desired center*⟩
> Next point (Press ENTER to end tracking): ↵
> Diameter/<Radius> <>: **.5**↵
> Command:

FIGURE 6.24 Using point tracking to establish an intersection from the midpoints of the sides of a rectangle. A circle is drawn with its center at the intersection.

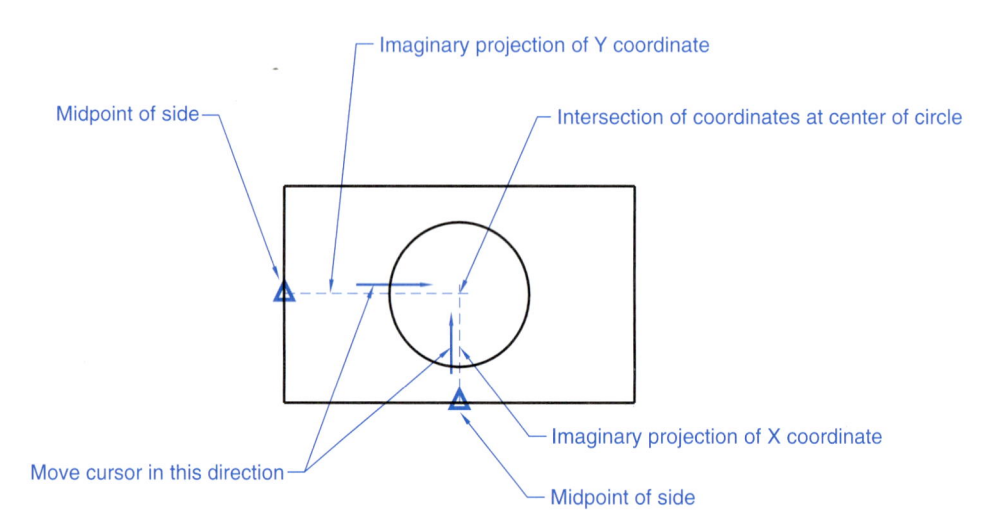

Another application for tracking is the placement of objects, such as holes, a given distance from the corner of a rectangular object. The following command sequence, shown in Figure 6.25, draws 0.125 circles placed .8125 in. each way from two corners:

> Command: **C** or **CIRCLE** ↵
> CIRCLE 3P/TTR/<Center point>: **TK** ↵
> First tracking point: **END** ↵
> of <pick the lower left corner>
> Next point (Press ENTER to end tracking): **@.8125,0** ↵
> Next point (Press ENTER to end tracking): **@0,.8125** ↵
> Next point (Press ENTER to end tracking): ↵
> Diameter/<Radius> <0.0000>: **.125** ↵
> Command: ↵
> CIRCLE 3P/TTR/<Center point>: **TK** ↵
> First tracking point: **END** ↵
> of <pick the lower right corner>
> Next point (Press ENTER to end tracking): **@−.8125,0** ↵
> Next point (Press ENTER to end tracking): **@0,.8125** ↵
> Next point (Press ENTER to end tracking): ↵
> Diameter/<Radius> <0.1250>: ↵
> Command:

CHAPTER 6 ▍▍▍ Precision Drafting Tools   **203**

FIGURE 6.25 Using tracking to locate holes a given distance and coordinates from the corners of a rectangular object.

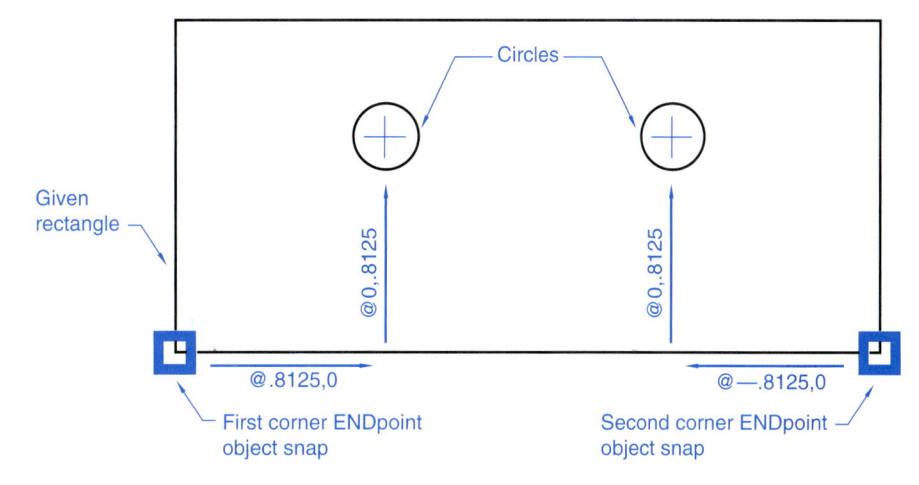

Field Notes

When tracking from one point to the next, be sure that you move the cursor in the desired direction, otherwise unexpected results may occur. Press the Esc key and start again if something you dislike happens. AutoCAD LT continues to ask you for tracking points until you press Enter to turn tracking off.

Exercise 6.8

1. Open AutoCAD LT if it is not already open. Use the setup option of your choice. A border and title block are not required.
2. Set limits at 8.5,11.
3. Draw the rectangle object shown below.
4. Use point tracking to draw a circle with the exact center at the X and Y intersection of a projection from the midpoints of the side and bottom of the rectangle. Use Figure 6.24 as an example.
5. Use tracking to draw the other four circles from their adjacent corners. Use Figure 6.25 as an example.
6. Do not draw dimensions.
7. Save the drawing as EX6.8.

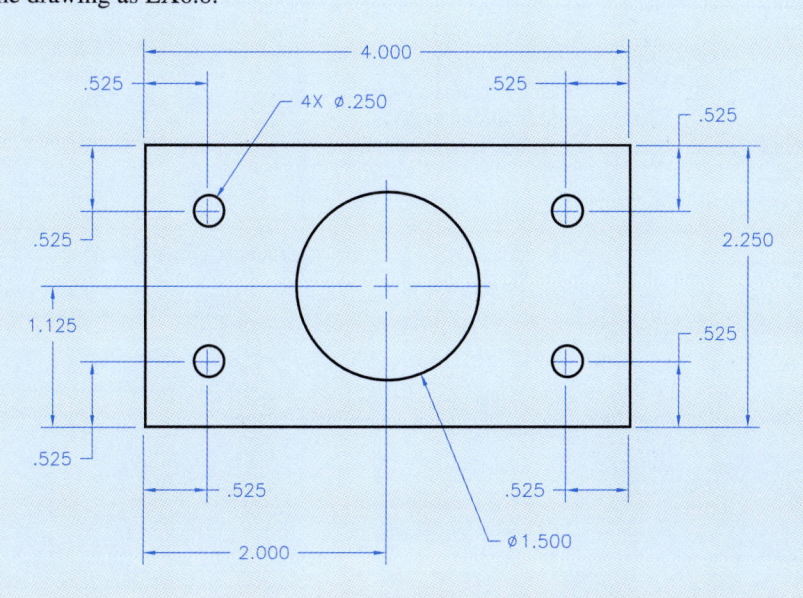

Using PolarSnaps

Standard
PolarSnap Settings
Tools
Polar Snap...

POLAR

PolarSnap settings allow you to draw or edit objects using angle and distance specifications without entering values at the keyboard. The desired values are entered in a dialog box before you start drawing with this application. You can snap from a point using specified distances, angles, or both distances and angles. For example, when you pick the first point of a line, the next point of the line is dragged by the cursor at a specified angle and distance if both angle and distance PolarSnap settings are on. In addition to the drag line provided to show your work in progress, AutoCAD LT gives you a Polar ToolTip that tells you the distance and angle being entered.

The first step in using this AutoCAD LT tool is to establish your PolarSnap settings. This is done in the Ortho/Polar Settings dialog box. This dialog box is opened by picking the PolarSnap Settings button in the Standard toolbar, by picking PolarSnap Settings... in the Tools pull-down menu, or by typing POLAR at the Command: prompt. The PolarSnap settings are off by default. This makes all features of the dialog box inactive. Figure 6.26 shows all the features activated by placing a check in the On check box and by picking the Polar: Angle & Distance Snap radio button. Only one radio button can be on. The following describes each of the features in the Ortho/Polar Settings dialog box:

- **On:** Use this to turn PolarSnap settings and Ortho on and off.

- **Ortho:** Pick this button to turn Ortho on. Remember from Chapter 2 that Ortho can also be turned on and off by typing ORTHO, pressing the F8 key, or double-clicking on the ORTHO button on the status bar. You can also turn Ortho on and off in the Drawing Aids dialog box by typing DDRMODES or by picking Drawing Aids... in the Tools pull-down menu. Everything else is off when Ortho is on.

- **Polar: Angle Snap:** This option lets you set the cursor movement to specific angular increments from the last point. When this option is on, the Angle text box in the PolarSnap Settings area is also on.

- **Polar: Distance Snap:** This option lets you set the cursor movement to specific distance increments from the last point. When this option is on, the Distance text box in the PolarSnap Settings area is also on.

- **Polar: Angle & Distance Snap:** This option lets you set the cursor movement to specific angular and distance increments from the last point. When this option is on, the Angle and Distance text boxes in the PolarSnap Settings area are also on.

FIGURE 6.26 The Ortho/Polar Settings dialog box.

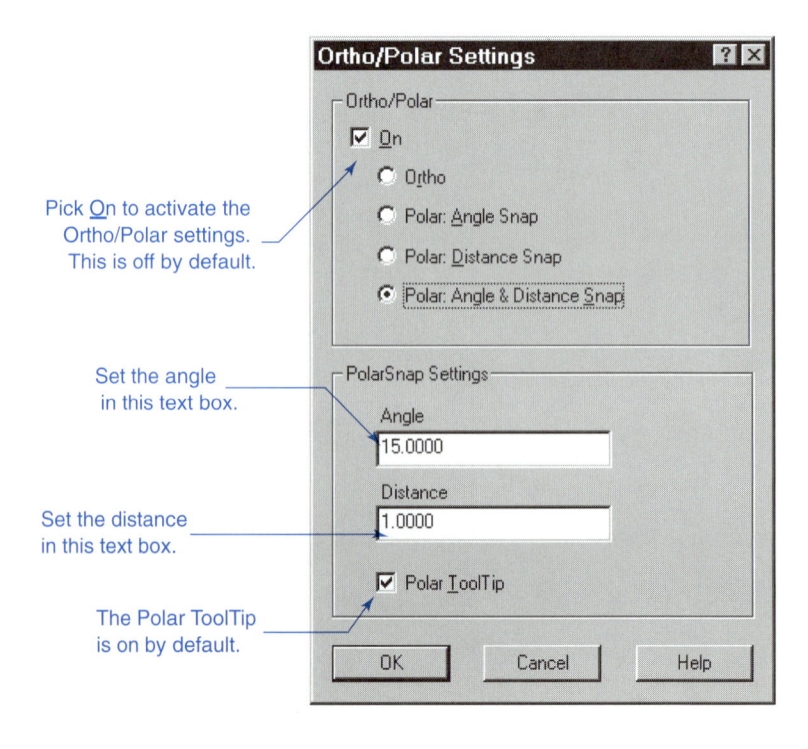

CHAPTER 6 ■ Precision Drafting Tools

205

- Angle: Use this text box to set the angular increments for PolarSnap. The default angle is 15°, but what you set remains in effect until changed in the current drawing. This is also controlled by the POLARANG system variable.

- Distance: Use this text box to set the distance increment for PolarSnap. The default distance is 1.0000, but the value you set remains in effect until changed in the current drawing. This is also controlled by the POLARDIST system variable.

- Polar ToolTip: This option is on by default and displays a ToolTip when you move the cursor to a set location.

Use the following steps to use the Polar: Angle & Distance Snap, for example:

- Open the Ortho/Polar Settings dialog box and pick the On button.
- Pick the Polar: Angle & Distance Snap radio button.
- Set the value in the Angle text box to 30.
- Set the value in the Distance text box to 1.25.
- Keep the Polar ToolTip on.
- Pick the OK button.
- Draw the lines shown in Figure 6.27.

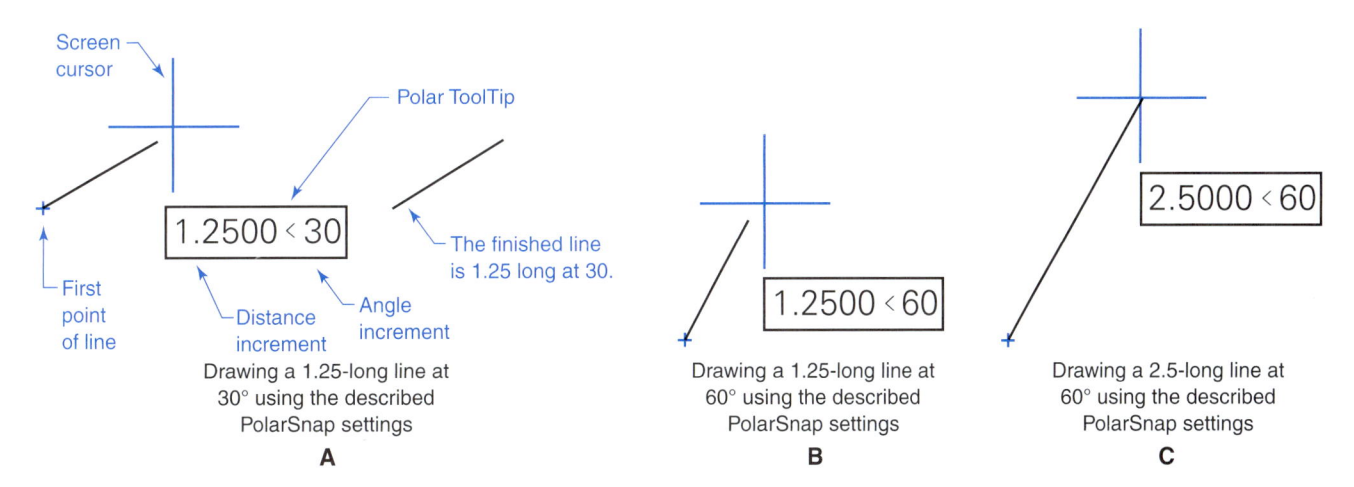

FIGURE 6.27 Using PolarSnap settings to draw lines that are at 1.25 increments in length and 30° angular increments. (A) The line is 1.25 at 30°. (B) The line is 1.25 at 60° (60° is two 30° increments). (C) The line is 2.50 (2.50 is two 1.25 increments) at 60°.

Field Notes

Be sure to turn PolarSnaps off before trying to draw objects that are not confined to specific angle and distance increments. When turning PolarSnap off, pick the Ortho radio button before turning off the On button. This is important because any following use of Ortho automatically uses the active Ortho/Polar Settings dialog box setting.

Exercise 6.9

1. Open AutoCAD LT if it is not already open. Use the setup option of your choice. A border and title block are not required.
2. Set limits at 8.5,11.
3. Set PolarSnaps to your advantage for drawing the object shown below.
4. Do not draw dimensions.
5. Save the drawing as EX6.9.

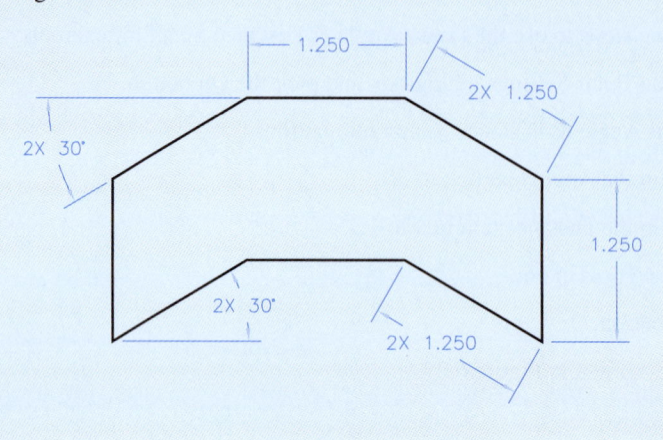

Drawing Inquiry Tools and Making Calculations

You can use AutoCAD LT to help you identify the location of points or to calculate distances, angles, and areas. You can also have AutoCAD LT list object properties and provide drawing information.

Identifying Points

AutoCAD LT lets you determine the coordinates of a specific point and allows you to find a point by entering its coordinates. These tasks are done using a feature called ID Point. Access this feature by picking the Locate Point button from the inquiry flyout on the standard toolbar, pick ID Point from the Inquiry flyout of the Tools pull-down menu, or by typing **ID** at the Command: prompt. Use the command as follows when you want to identify a known point:

Command: **ID**↵
Point: ⟨*pick the point to identify*⟩

AutoCAD LT automatically gives you a listing of the X, Y, and Z coordinates of the point at the prompt line. For example, the point coordinates for the ID command might look like this:

X = 4.5000   Y = 7.0000   Z = 0.00000
Command:

Field Notes

- Obtaining the ID of a point without the aid of snap or object snap will give a reasonable estimate of the coordinate location, but for best results, use your available precision tools.

- The Inquiry flyout on the Standard toolbar is not labeled Inquiry when the toolbar is docked. This flyout contains the four buttons Distance, Area, List, and Locate Point. The Distance button is visible by default when you start AutoCAD LT. Like all flyouts, this one will display the most recently selected button.

CHAPTER 6 ▎▎▎ Precision Drafting Tools   **207**

Calculating Distances and Angles

Two-dimensional and three-dimensional distances and angles are easily calculated with AutoCAD LT. This discussion explains how to find 2-D distances and angles. Finding 3-D distances and angles is covered in Chapter 13. To find the distance and angle between two points, pick the Distance button on the inquiry flyout of the standard toolbar, pick Inquiry and Distance in the Tools pull-down menu, or type **DI** or **DIST.** Next, pick the two points and AutoCAD LT automatically gives you information on the command line. An example looks like this:

> Command: **DI** or **DIST**↵
> First point: ⟨*pick the first point*⟩
> Second point: ⟨*pick the second point*⟩
> Distance = 1.7678   Angle in XY Plane = 45   Angle from XY Plane = 0
> Delta X = 1.2500,   Delta Y = 1.2500,   Delta Z = 0.0000
> Command:

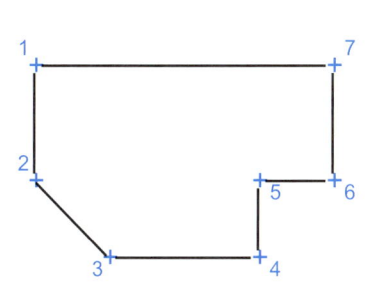

Inquiry

Tools
Inquiry ▶

DIST
DI

The Distance and Angle in the XY plane are shown in Figure 6.28. The Angle from the XY plane is a 3-D angle and is shown in Chapter 13. The term *Delta* in the preceding AutoCAD LT message is a mathematical word meaning a change in distance. In the previous example, the X and Y axis values were each increased by 1.25.

FIGURE 6.28 The distance and angle in the XY plane.

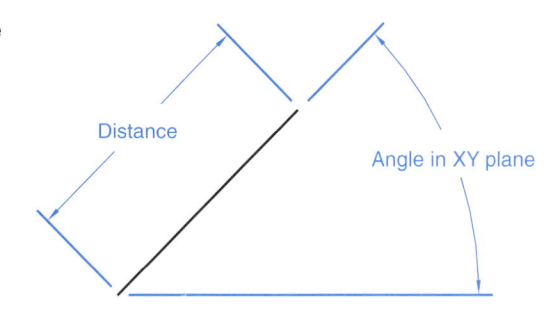

Calculating Areas

AutoCAD LT allows you to calculate the area and perimeter of a feature by picking a series of points to define the object or by directly selecting certain objects. You can calculate a total area by adding and subtracting individual areas. To use this feature, pick the Area button from the standard toolbar, pick Inquiry and Area in the Tools pull-down menu, or type **AA** or **AREA.** The AREA command default option allows you to select a series of points enclosing the desired area. You start at one point and keep picking points around the object to the last point. To keep your area calculations accurate, always use object snap if possible. AutoCAD LT automatically closes the distance between the first point and the last point and displays the Area and Perimeter calculations. The following command calculates the area and perimeter of the object shown in Figure 6.29:

Inquiry

Tools
Inquiry ▶

AREA
AA

> Command: **AA** or **AREA**↵
> <First point>/Object/Add/Subtract: ⟨*pick point 1*⟩
> Next point: ⟨*pick point 2*⟩
> Next point: ⟨*pick point 3*⟩
> Next point: ⟨*pick point 4*⟩
> Next point: ⟨*pick point 5*⟩
> Next point: ⟨*pick point 6*⟩
> Next point: ⟨*pick point 7*⟩
> Next point: ↵
> Area = 2.1250,   Perimeter = 6.2071
> Command:

FIGURE 6.29 Defining a series of points to establish the area of an object.

If you have a closed area such as a circle, ellipse, or regular polygon, AutoCAD LT automatically calculates the area, and perimeter or circumference, using the Object option of the AREA command. You can also calculate the area and perimeter of open and closed polylines. A ***polyline*** is an AutoCAD LT object that is made up of one or more connecting segments that are treated as a single object. Chapter 8 is dedicated to explaining polylines. The circle shown in Figure 6.30 is calculated individually using the following Object option:

Command: **AA** or **AREA**↵
<First point>/Object/Add/Subtract: **O**↵
Select objects: ⟨*pick the circle*⟩
Area = 0.7854,   Circumference = 3.1416
Command:

FIGURE 6.30 Calculating the area of a circle, ellipse, and hexagon.

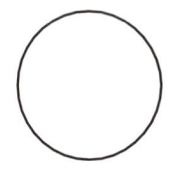

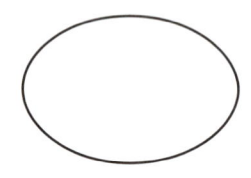

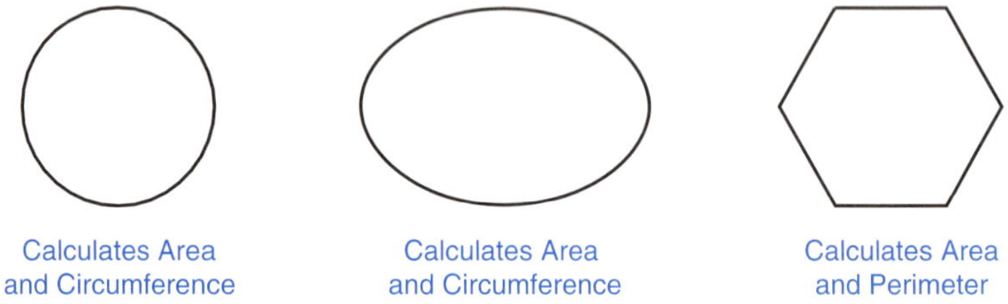

Calculates Area and Circumference

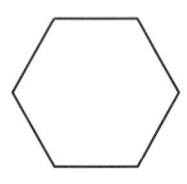

Calculates Area and Circumference

Calculates Area and Perimeter

Many objects contain features that may need to be added or subtracted from the total area. The AREA command provides the Add and Subtract options to help you with this task. Look at the gasket object shown in Figure 6.31. The gasket contains five holes. We want to use the Add and Subtract options to calculate the area of the gasket without the holes. Begin with the Add option to calculate the area of the outside circle forming the entire gasket, and then Subtract the internal holes like this:

Command: **AA** or **AREA**↵
<First point>/Object/Add/Subtract: **A**↵
<First point>/Object/Subtract: **O**↵
(ADD mode) Select objects: ⟨*pick the outside circle*⟩
Area = 3.1416, Circumference = 6.2832
Total area = 3.1416
(ADD mode) Select objects: ↵
<First point>/Object/Subtract: **S**↵
<First point>/Object/Add: **O**↵
(SUBTRACT mode) Select objects: ⟨*pick circle 1*⟩
Area = 0.0491, Circumference = 0.7854
Total area = 3.0925
(SUBTRACT mode) Select objects: ⟨*pick circle 2*⟩
Area = 0.0491, Circumference = 0.7854
Total area = 3.0434
(SUBTRACT mode) Select objects: ⟨*pick circle 3*⟩
Area = 0.0491, Circumference = 0.7854
Total area = 2.9943
(SUBTRACT mode) Select objects: ⟨*pick circle 4*⟩
Area = 0.0491, Circumference = 0.7854
Total area = 2.9452
(SUBTRACT mode) Select objects: ⟨*pick circle 5*⟩
Area = 0.0491, Circumference = 0.7854
Total area = 2.8348
(SUBTRACT mode) Select objects: ↵
<First point>/Object/Add: ↵
Command:

CHAPTER 6 ▬ Precision Drafting Tools   **209**

FIGURE 6.31 Using the Add and Subtract options of the AREA command to calculate the area of gasket material.

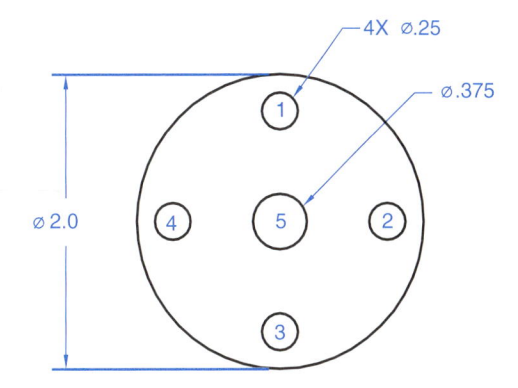

Listing Object Properties

AutoCAD LT provides information about your drawing or about objects in the drawing. The given information is displayed in the command area and in the AutoCAD LT text window. To list information about an object, pick the List button in the standard toolbar, pick Inquiry and List in the Tools pull-down menu, or type **LS** or **LIST**. The command works like this:

    Command: **LS** or **LIST**↵
    Select objects: ⟨pick the object or objects desired⟩
    Select objects: ↵
    Command:

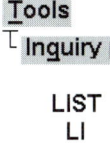

Inquiry

Tools
  Inquiry ▶
    LIST
    LI

The information is displayed. Press the F2 key or pick the close button to remove the AutoCAD LT Text Window.

Field Notes

> The AutoCAD LT Text Window displays object information one page at a time; it waits for the user before proceeding. If you have selected many objects to list, the information may require several pages to be displayed. You will see a message at the bottom of each page that says "Press RETURN to continue." Pressing the Enter key displays the next page of information. If you want to see information that has already scrolled off of the screen, you can use the scroll bars in the text window to scroll the text back down as needed.

Getting Information about Drawing Time

The TIME command provides information about key times and dates in the life of a drawing project. The TIME command is accessed by selecting Time from the Inquiry cascade on the Tools menu, or by typing TI or TIME at the Command: prompt. The current time, the time that the current drawing was created and last updated, plus the total editing time are displayed.

Tools
  Inquiry ▶
    TIME
    TI

    Command: **TIME**↵
    Current time: Saturday, July 24, 1999 at 8:20:08:890 PM
    Times for this drawing:
    Created: Friday, July 23, 1999 at 2:43:27:745 PM
    Last updated: Saturday, January 02, 1999 at 4:21:53:665 PM
    Total editing time: 1 days 05:36:41.145
    Elapsed timer (on): 1 days 05:36:41.145
    Next automatic save in: 0 days 00:45:48.790

    Display/ON/OFF/Reset:

In addition, the TIME command provides a timer that can be used to time specific phases of a drawing for project tracking and control, or even for billing purposes. Before starting the timer, you will probably need to reset it to zero. Enter R for Reset at the prompt line. Next, use the ON option to start the timer running.

Display/ON/OFF/Reset: **R**↵
Timer reset.
Display/ON/OFF/Reset: **ON**↵
Timer on.
Display/ON/OFF/Reset:

When you have completed the task you are timing, view your results using the TIME command again. You can continue, turn the timer off, or reset it and enter the next phase of your project.

Current time: Saturday, July 24, 1999 at 8:35:22:884 PM
Times for this drawing:
Created: Friday, July 23, 1999 at 2:43:27:745 PM
Last updated: Saturday, January 02, 1999 at 4:21:53:665 PM
Total editing time: 1 days 05:51:55.139
Elapsed timer (on): 0 days 00:03:53.215
Next automatic save in: 0 days 00:30:34.796

Display/ON/OFF/Reset: OFF
Timer off.

Advanced Drawing Inquiries

The AREA command, discussed previously, provides the capability to determine the total area of a closed shape such as an ellipse, circle, or polygon. Even complex shapes composed of line segments can be checked for surface area. However, the AREA command does not provide an easy way to check a complex shape composed of irregular line and arc segments. For this purpose, AutoCAD LT provides a 2D region modeler. A region is a complex-shaped two-dimensional object created by any combination of lines, polylines, arcs, circles, ellipses, and splines that form a closed shape. Some of these object types are discussed in later chapters.

To create a region, you must first draw an enclosed shape. Then, to model the region, you use the REGION command, which you can access by picking Region from the Draw pull-down menu or by typing REG or REGION at the Command: prompt. The following sequence was used to create a region from the objects shown in Figure 6.32. Notice that the two closed shapes are made into separate regions even when selected together.

Command: REGION

Using the AREA command on the large region in Figure 6.32 gives the following information:

Command: **AA** or **AREA**↵
<First point>/Object/Add/Subtract: **A**↵
<First point>/Object/Add/Subtract: **O**↵
(ADD mode) Select objects: *<select large region>*
Area = 25.3608, Perimeter = 26.9942
Total area = 25.3608
(ADD mode) Select objects: ↵

You can use the Subtract option to get an overall surface area value:

<First point>/Object/Subtract: **S**↵
<First point>/Object/Add: **O**↵
(SUBTRACT mode) Select objects: *<select small region>*
Area = 2.8475, Perimeter = 9.3763
Total area = 22.5133

Separate regions can be combined into single regions to provide even more flexibility. The methods of combining regions are referred to as *Boolean* operations. The three Boolean functions in AutoCAD LT 98 are *union*, *subtract*, and *intersect*.

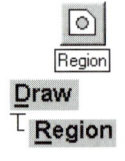

Draw
└ Region

REGION
REG

CHAPTER 6 ⅠⅠⅠ Precision Drafting Tools

FIGURE 6.32 Complex shapes made of many different objects can be combined into a single object called a *region*.

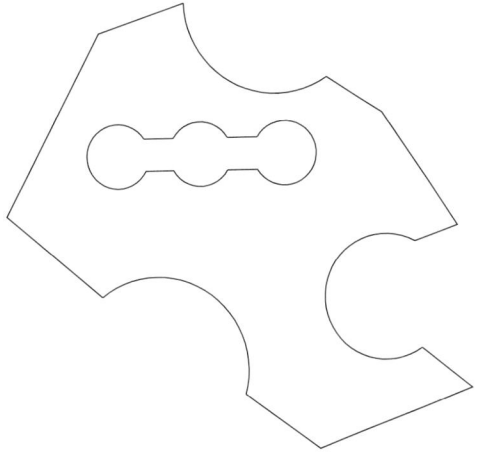

Using the Union Command

The UNION command makes two or more separate regions into a single region by joining them together. You can access this command by picking Union from the Regio*n* cascade on the *M*odify pull-down menu, by picking the Union button on the Modify II toolbar, or by typing **UNI** or **UNION** at the Command: prompt. Figure 6.33 shows three regions being joined using UNION.

```
Command: UNI or UNION↵
Select objects: Other corner: 3 found
Select objects: ↵
```

Modify II

Union

Modify
  Region ▶

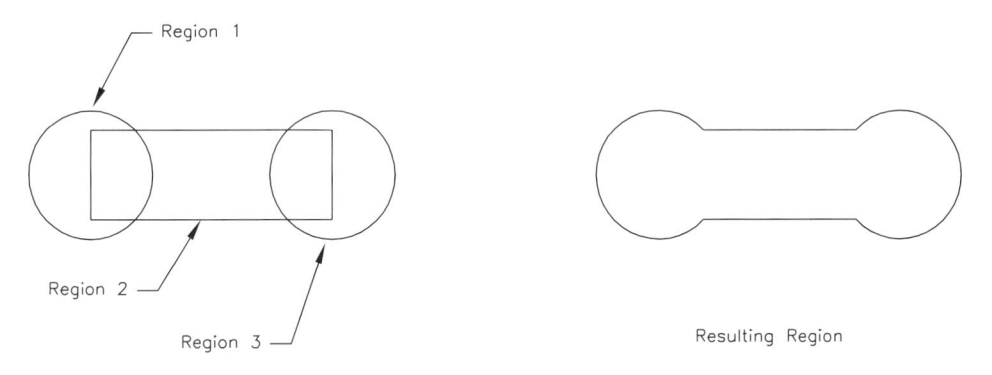

UNION
UNI

FIGURE 6.33 Separate regions can be joined using the UNION command.

Using the SUBTRACT Command

SUBTRACT creates a single region by subtracting a set of one or more regions from another set of one or more regions. You can access this command by picking *S*ubtract from the Regio*n* cascade on the Modify pull-down menu, by picking the Subtract button on the Modify II toolbar, or by typing **SU** or **SUBTRACT** at the Command: prompt. The following sequence was used to perform the subtraction illustrated in Figure 6.34:

```
Command: SU or SUBTRACT↵
Select solids and regions to subtract from...
Select objects: <select first region>
1 found
Select objects: ↵
Select solids and regions to subtract...
Select objects: 1 found
Select objects: 1 found
Select objects: ↵
```

Modify II

Subtract

Modify
  Region ▶

SUBTRACT
SU

FIGURE 6.34 The SUBTRACT command combines regions by subtraction.

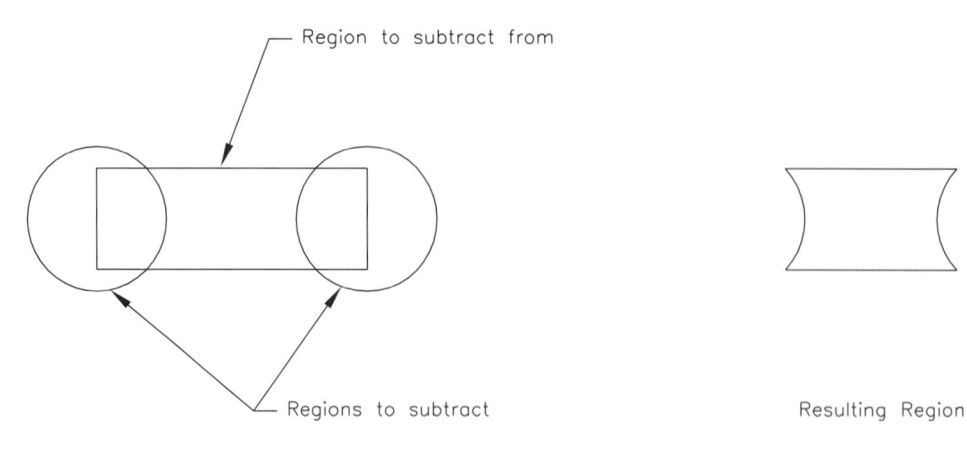

Region to subtract from

Regions to subtract

Resulting Region

Using the INTERSECT Command

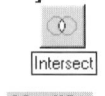

Modify II
[Intersect]

Modify
└ Region ▶
INTERSECT
IN

Intersect creates a single region from the shared area of two or more regions. The INTERSECT command is accessed by picking Intersect from the Region cascade on the Modify pull-down menu, picking the Intersect button from the Modify II toolbar, or by typing **IN** or **INTERSECT** at the Command: prompt. Figure 6.35 illustrates the use of the INTERSECT command.

Command: **INTERSECT**↵
Select objects: Other corner: 2 found
Select objects: ↵

FIGURE 6.35 The INTERSECT command creates a region from the shared area of two or more selected regions.

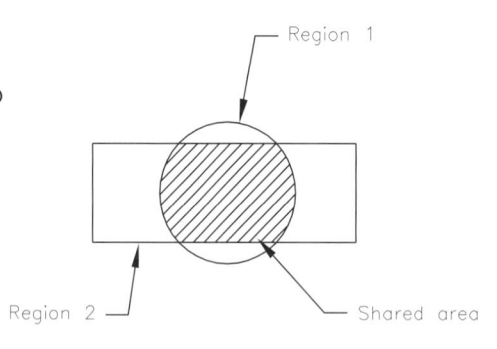

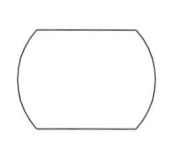

Region 1

Region 2

Shared area

Resulting Region

Listing Physical Properties of Regions

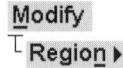

Modify II
[Region/Mass Properties]

Modify
└ Region ▶
MASSPROP

Regions also have physical properties that can be useful in engineering processes. A region can be used to find information such as the centroid (center of mass) and moments and products of inertia. The command used to determine these mass properties is **MASSPROP**. Here is the result of using the MASSPROP command on the large region in Figure 6.32:

Command: **MASSPROP**↵
Select objects:
1 found
Select objects: ↵

          REGIONS
Area: 25.3608
Perimeter: 26.9942
Bounding box: X: 2.1712 − 9.7647
                      Y: 0.6379 − 7.6894
Centroid: X: 5.9103
                      Y: 4.3649
Moments of inertia: X: 545.9712
                      Y: 962.3279
Product of inertia: XY: 625.5470
Radii of gyration: X: 4.6398
                      Y: 6.1600

CHAPTER 6   III   Precision Drafting Tools

Principal moments and X-Y directions about centroid:
    I: 40.0942 along [0.7845 -0.6201]
    J: 99.1152 along [0.6201 0.7845]
Write to a file? <N>:

You have the option of writing the output to a text file that you can reference later or print if needed. If you accept the default answer of no, you are returned to the Command: prompt.

Field Notes

- Regions that do not touch can be joined by the UNION command. The result is a single region object composed of any number of separate areas. Similarly, the SUBTRACT command can result in a single region composed of areas that do not touch one another.
- The INTERSECT command cannot be used on objects that do not touch, because there is no common area, or intersection, from which to make a resulting region.
- Even though the SUBTRACT command asks for *solids* or regions to be selected, these commands cannot be used on 3DSOLID objects created in the full version of AutoCAD.

Exercise 6.10

1. Open AutoCAD LT if it is not already open. Use the setup option of your choice. A border and title block are not required.
2. Set limits at 8.5,11.
3. Write the answer for each of the following requests on a separate sheet of paper.
4. Draw an object similar to the one shown in Figure 6.29. Do not draw the numbers. Calculate the area using the point method.
5. Draw a circle, ellipse, and a hexagon similar to the objects shown in Figure 6.30. Do not place the text. Calculate the area of each object.
6. Draw the gasket shown in Figure 6.31 using the dimensions given. Do not draw dimensions or numbers. The exact hole locations are not important, but the diameters are important. Make your drawing similar to the example in every other manner.
7. Use the ID command to get the coordinates at the center of each 0.25 hole.
8. Use the DIST command to determine the distance from the center of one 0.25 hole to the center of the opposite 0.25 hole.
9. Calculate the area of the gasket material.
10. Use the LIST command to get information about the outside circle.
11. Use the TIME command to see what is displayed.
12. Draw two shapes similar to those in Figure 6.32. Use the REGION command to make each into a region. Subtract the small region from the large one. Use the MASSPROP command to list the mass properties of the resulting region. Write the output to a file named EX6.9.TXT.
13. Save the drawing as EX6.9.

✓ LEARNING CHECKPOINT

☐   Name at least three ways to access the Point Style dialog box.
☐   Describe two ways of setting point size.
☐   Explain the difference between the DIVIDE and the MEASURE commands.
☐   Discuss the purpose of the From option.
☐   Discuss the use of point filters.

- ☐ Explain how direct distance entry works.
- ☐ Define tracking.
- ☐ Describe the basic fundamentals of how PolarSnaps are set up and their functions.
- ☐ Name the command that is used to determine the coordinates of a point.
- ☐ How do you easily calculate the distance between two points?
- ☐ Identify two ways to calculate the area of objects.
- ☐ Name the command that keeps a running total of area calculations as you add and subtract individual areas of an object.
- ☐ What command allows you to get information about your drawing or about objects in the drawing?
- ☐ How do you use AutoCAD LT to get the current time?
- ☐ What is the best way to find the area of a complex closed shape made of different objects?
- ☐ Describe the four commands associated with regions.

An Introduction to Drawing Construction Lines

Construction lines have been used throughout the history of drafting. As the name implies, these lines are used as aids for the purpose of constructing parts of a drawing. Construction lines are generally removed when the drawing is finished. AutoCAD LT provides both construction lines (xlines) and rays. Xlines are infinite-length lines, and rays are semi-infinite in length. The difference is that construction lines extend in two directions from the origin and rays extend only in one direction from the origin. Some practical uses for construction lines might include the following:

- Making geometric constructions, such as bisecting angles or finding the center of a triangle.
- Projecting features from one view to the next in an orthographic projection for multiview drawings in mechanical drafting.
- Projecting between elevations in an architectural drawing.
- Establishing the projection of a bearing wall or partition in an architectural or structural layout.
- Creating temporary intersections for the use of object snaps.

Construction lines should be placed on a layer and in a color that clearly represents drawing development. A company or school practice might be to draw red construction lines on a CONSTRUCTION layer. When the drawing is completed, the CONSTRUCTION layer may be frozen or turned off, because the construction lines are no longer needed. Construction lines are usually not needed on the final plot. However, in some cases, they may be desirable on a check plot to help the checker determine how certain drawing features were established.

Drawing Construction Lines with the XLINE Command

AutoCAD LT gives you a lot of flexibility when drawing construction lines using the XLINE command. You can draw them between two points, from one point horizontally or vertically, at a designated angle, as the bisector of an angle, or offset from a given object. When construction lines are drawn, they extend into infinity, yet they do not alter the total drawing area or affect zooming operations. Construction lines are drawn by picking Construction Line from the Draw toolbar, by choosing Constr__u__ction Line in the __D__raw pull-down menu, or by typing **XL** or **XLINE** at the Command: prompt.

Drawing Construction Lines between Two Points
The default construction line asks for two points. Look at the structural drawing example in Figure 6.36, which uses construction lines to establish the location of a gusset from the corners of an existing gusset using the following command sequence:

```
Command: XL or XLINE↵
Hor/Ver/Ang/Bisect/Offset/<From point>: ⟨pick point 1⟩
Through point: ⟨pick point 2⟩
Through point: ↵
Command:
```

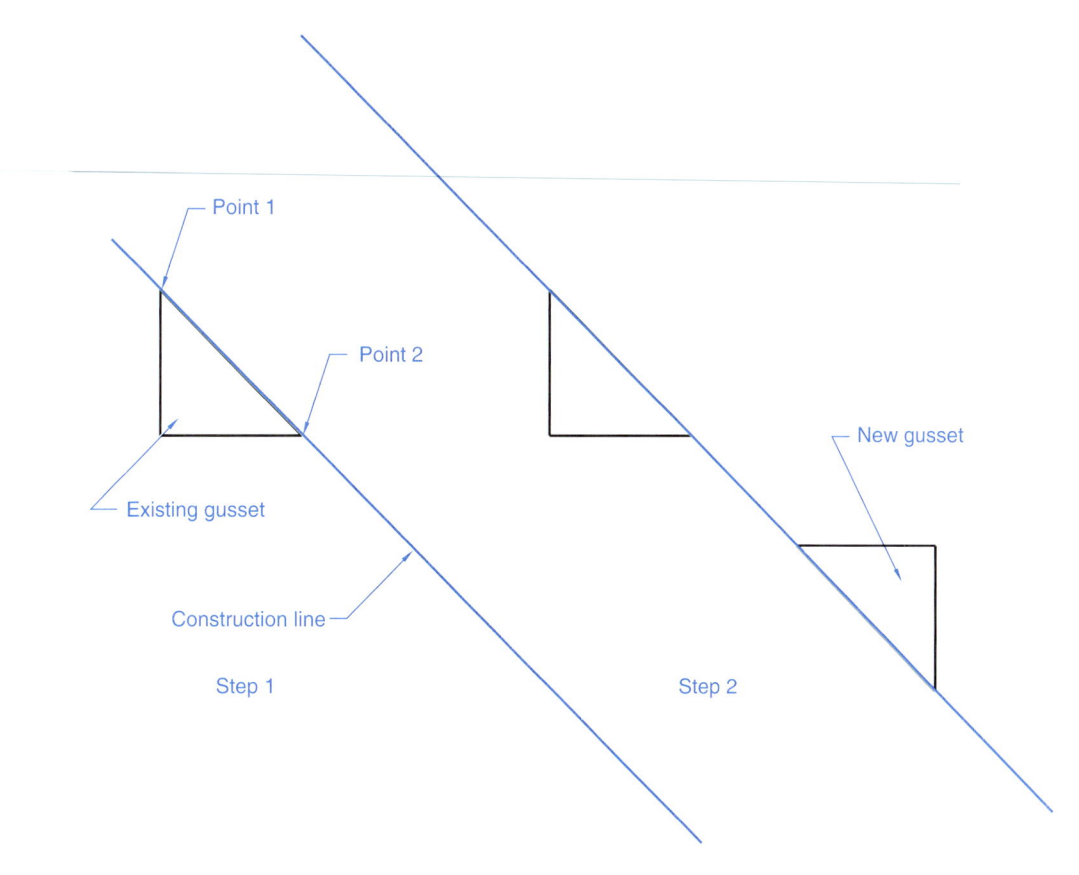

FIGURE 6.36 Using the XLINE command to draw a construction line between two points.

After drawing the first construction line, you keep getting the Through point: prompt, which allows you to draw additional construction lines from the first point. Press Enter to get back to the Command: prompt.

Drawing Horizontal and Vertical Construction Lines
Use the Horizontal option to draw a horizontal construction line from one point or the Vertical option to draw a vertical construction line from one point. Figures 6.37 and 6.38 show the horizontal and vertical projection to find the top and right side views from the front view of a mechanical drawing. This is the command sequence for drawing the horizontal construction lines:

Command: **XL** or **XLINE**↵
Hor/Ver/Ang/Bisect/Offset/<From point>: **H**↵
Through point: ⟨*pick point 1*⟩
Through point: ⟨*pick point 2*⟩
Through point: ⟨*pick point 3*⟩
Through point: ↵
Command:

This is the command sequence for drawing the vertical construction lines:

Command: **XL** or **XLINE**↵
Hor/Ver/Ang/Bisect/Offset/<From point>: **V**↵
Through point: ⟨*pick point 1*⟩
Through point: ⟨*pick point 2*⟩
Through point: ⟨*pick point 3*⟩
Through point: ↵
Command:

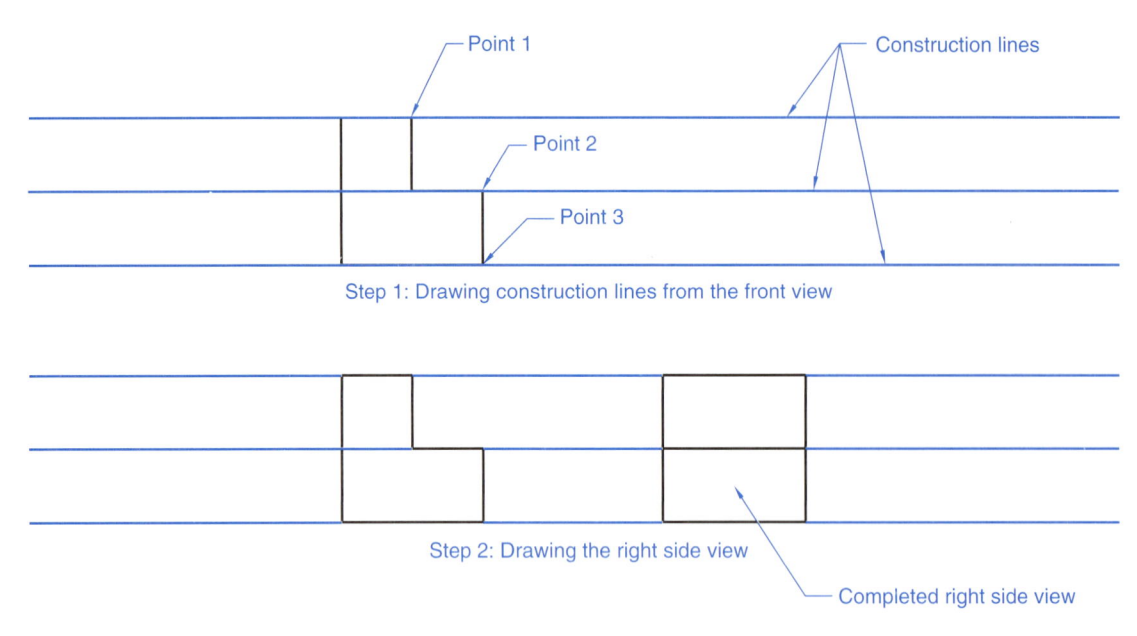

FIGURE 6.37 Using the XLINE command and the Horizontal option to draw construction lines.

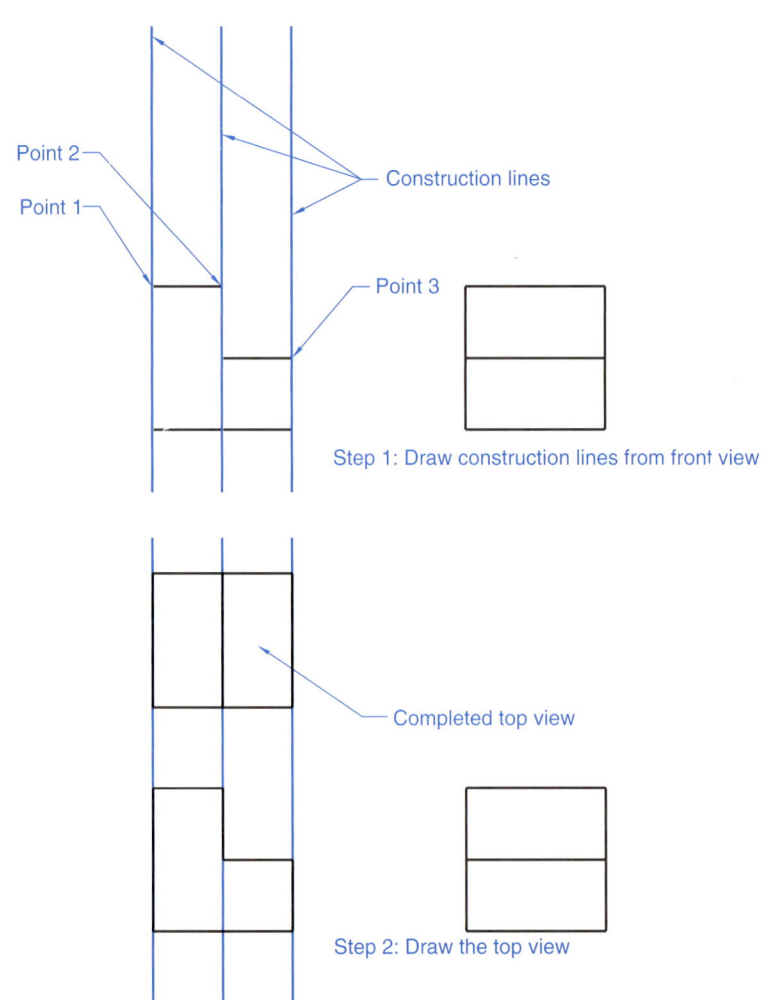

Point 1
Point 2
Point 3
Construction lines
Step 1: Drawing construction lines from the front view

Step 2: Drawing the right side view
Completed right side view

FIGURE 6.38 Using the XLINE command and the Vertical option to draw construction lines.

Point 2
Point 1
Point 3
Construction lines
Step 1: Draw construction lines from front view

Completed top view
Step 2: Draw the top view

CHAPTER 6 ▓ Precision Drafting Tools

Exercise 6.11

1. Open AutoCAD LT if it is not already open. Use the setup option of your choice. A border and title block are not required.
2. Set limits at 8.5,11.
3. Create a layer named CONSTRUCTION with a continuous linetype and red color for drawing the construction lines only.
4. Draw an existing gusset similar to the example in step 1 of Figure 6.36.
5. Draw the new gusset similar to the example in step 2 of Figure 6.36.
6. Draw a front view similar to the example in step 1 of Figure 6.37.

8. Freeze the CONSTRUCTION layer.
9. Save the drawing as EX6.11.

Drawing Construction Lines at an Angle

Drawing construction lines at an angle is valuable for a number of practical applications, for example, constructing the slope of a roof or establishing an auxiliary view. The default of the Angle option asks you for an angle from horizontal. This might be used to draw a roof slope at 22.5° as shown in this command sequence and demonstrated in Figure 6.39:

Command: **XL** or **XLINE**.↵
Hor/Ver/Ang/Bisect/Offset/<From point>: **A**↵
Reference/<Enter angle (0)>: **22.5**↵
Through point: ⟨pick point 1⟩
Through point:
Command:

FIGURE 6.39 Using the XLINE command and the Angle option from horizontal to draw a construction line.

Construction line (22.5° from horizontal)

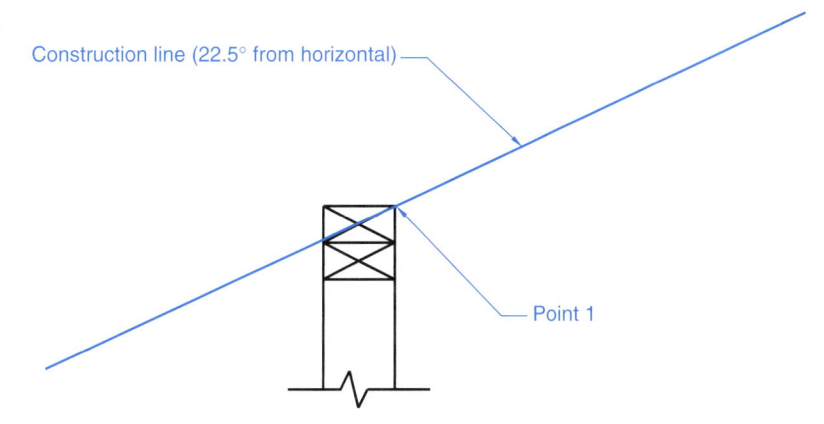

Point 1

The Angle option also has a Reference suboption, which may be handy when creating an auxiliary view for a mechanical drawing project. To use this option, select a reference line and designate an angle for the construction line to be drawn from the reference line. The following command sequence is shown in Figure 6.40:

Command: **XL** or **XLINE**↵
Hor/Ver/Ang/Bisect/Offset/<From point>: **A**↵
Reference/<Enter angle (0)>: **R**↵
Enter angle<0>: **90**↵
Select a line object: ⟨pick the edge view of the slope surface in step 1⟩
Through point: ⟨pick point 1⟩
Through point: ⟨pick point 2⟩
Through point: ⟨pick point 3⟩
Through point: ↵
Command:

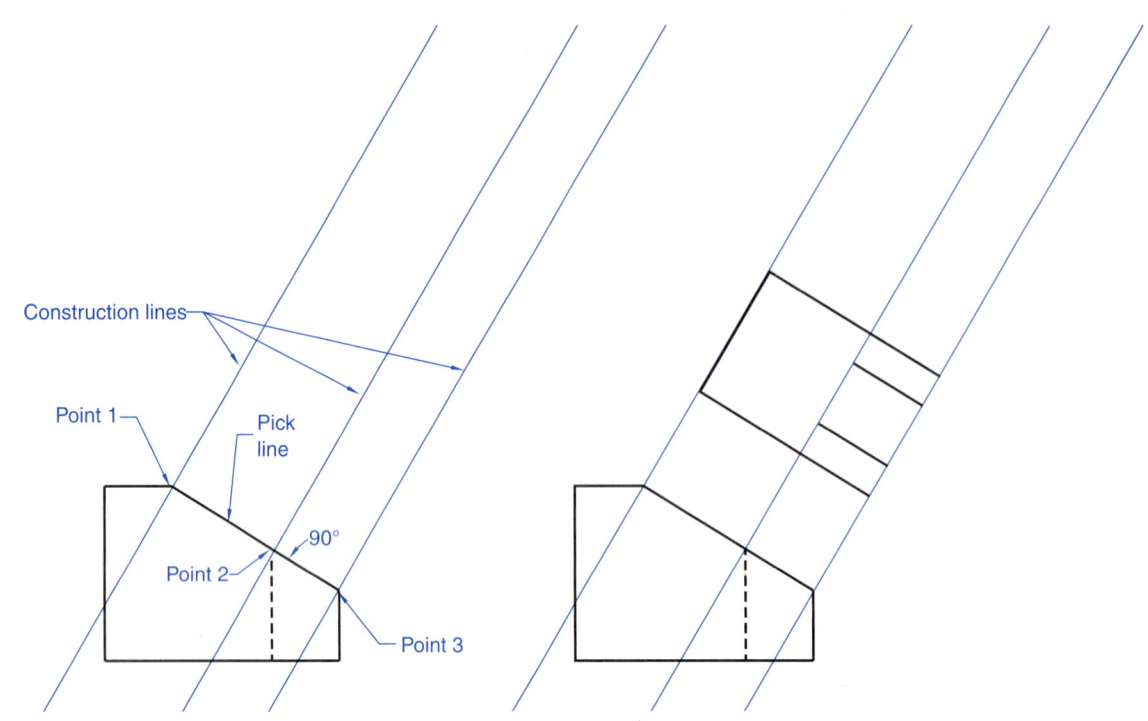

FIGURE 6.40 Using the XLINE command and the Angle option to draw construction lines from a reference line.

> ### Exercise 6.12
>
> 1. Open AutoCAD LT if it is not already open. Use the setup option of your choice. A border and title block are not required.
> 2. Set limits at 8.5,11.
> 3. Open EX6.11 and erase the objects to begin this drawing. If you did not do Exercise 6.11, create a layer named CONSTRUCTION with a continuous linetype and red color for drawing the construction lines only.
> 4. Use construction lines to help you when drawing a front view and auxiliary view that are approximately the same as those of Figure 6.40.
> 5. Freeze the CONSTRUCTION layer.
> 6. Save the drawing as EX6.12.

Drawing the Bisector of an Angle
One of the XLINE command options allows you to draw the bisector of an existing angle. The bisector of an angle splits the angle in two equal parts. Look at Figure 6.41 as you follow this command sequence:

Command: **XL** or **XLINE**↵
Hor/Ver/Ang/Bisect/Offset/<From point>: **B**↵
Angle vertex point: ⟨*pick the vertex*⟩
Angle start point: ⟨*pick one of the sides*⟩
Angle end point: ⟨*pick the other side*⟩
Angle end point: ↵
Command:

Drawing a Construction Line Offset from Another Line
Many situations happen in which you need to draw a construction line to establish a feature parallel to an existing object. You can do this with the construction line Offset option. To do this, you determine the offset distance or pick a point, select the line, and specify the side of the line for the offset construction to be drawn. Figure 6.42 shows the construction of an outside rafter line parallel to the inside line that was drawn previously. This is the command sequence:

Command: **XL** or **XLINE**↵
Hor/Ver/Ang/Bisect/Offset/<From point>: **O**↵
Offset distance or Through <Through>: **.75**↵

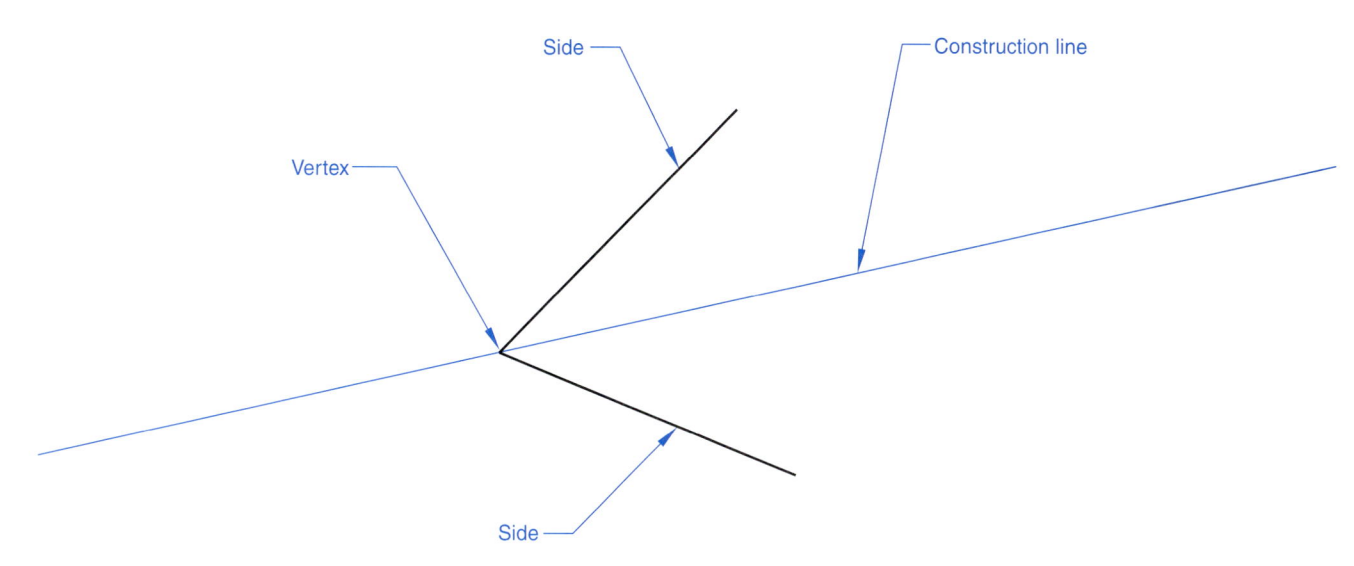

FIGURE 6.41 Using the XLINE command and the Bisect option to draw a construction line.

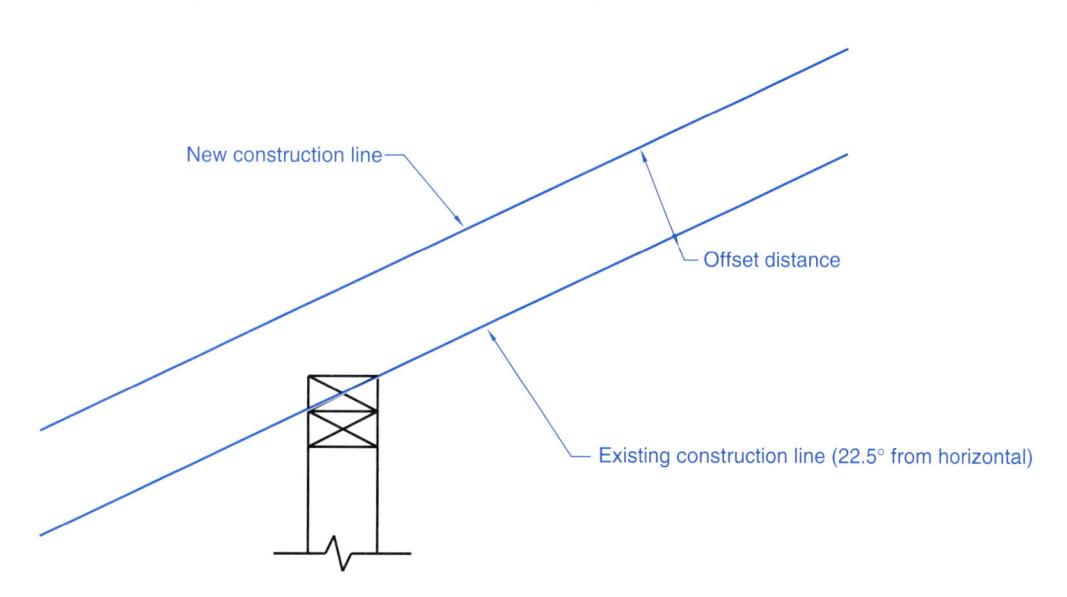

FIGURE 6.42 Using the XLINE command and the Offset option to draw a construction line parallel to an existing line.

"Through" refers to a point you pick through which the construction line goes. You can pick a point for the construction line to go through, or you can specify a distance from the selected object for the construction line to go through. The command continues:

Select a line object: ⟨*pick the existing line*⟩
Side to offset? ⟨*move the cursor to the side where you want the construction line and pick*⟩
Select a line object: ↵
Command:

Drawing Rays

Rays are also construction lines, but they are different from construction lines drawn with the XLINE command. XLINE construction lines extend in two directions from the point you pick, whereas rays extend in only one direction. The advantage of rays is that they go only in one direction and can provide less confusion on the drawing. Rays are drawn using the RAY command. The disadvantage of rays is that the RAY command only has one option, whereas the XLINE command has many options. Rays are drawn by typing **RAY**. The command asks you for the first point and then the point through which you want the ray to pass. This is much like the two-point method of the XLINE command except the ray goes in only one direction from the first point. The RAY command works like this:

Command: **RAY**↵
From point: ⟨*pick the first point to start the ray*⟩
Through point: ⟨*pick the second point for the ray to pass through*⟩
Through point: ⟨*more rays can be drawn from the first point or press Enter*⟩
Through point: ↵
Command:

Field Notes

Although xlines and rays can be used simply as guides and then frozen or deleted when you are finished, they can also be much more versatile. Editing commands discussed in Chapter 7 will show you how to break and trim existing drawing objects to suit your needs. When an xline is trimmed, it now has one endpoint—and is therefore transformed into a ray object. When you trim the infinite end of a ray, it has two endpoints—meaning it becomes a line object. Using these features allows your construction lines to be directly transformed into final geometry, reducing your drawing and editing time.

Exercise 6.13

1. Open AutoCAD LT if it is not already open. Use the setup option of your choice. A border and title block are not required.
2. Set limits at 8.5,11.
3. Open EX6.11 and erase the objects to begin this drawing. If you did not do Exercise 6.11, create a layer named CONSTRUCTION with a continuous linetype and red color for drawing the construction lines only.
4. Draw a double top plate and partial stud detail with a construction line 22.5° from horizontal similar to that shown in Figure 6.39. The scale and size are not important.
5. Draw the outside edge of the rafter using the Offset construction line option. Your drawing should look similar to Figure 6.42.
6. Draw an angle with a Bisector construction line similar to the example in Figure 6.41.
7. Save the drawing as EX6.13.

Adjusting Snap Angle and Origin

You have been using Grid and Snap to make drawing easy and accurate. The Grid and Snap format you use places the grid dots in a horizontal and vertical pattern on the screen. The screen cursor also moves horizontally and vertically to match the grid. This works well for drawing horizontally and vertically oriented objects. When an object has features that are at an angle, it would be helpful if the Grid could be rotated to match the angle. AutoCAD LT has thought about this and allows you to adjust the Snap to any desired angle. When you do this, the Grid angle and the screen cursor also follow the same angle. The Snap angle is changed in the Drawing Aids dialog box. Pick Drawing A̲ids ... in the T̲ools pull-down menu to access the Drawing Aids dialog box. To change the Snap Angle to 30°, for example, type **30** in the S̲nap Angle text box as shown in Figure 6.43 and pick OK. To return to the standard snap orientation, open the Drawing Aids dialog box again and change the angle back to zero.

The Snap origin, also known as the base point, is at the center point of the snap angle rotation by default. Look at Figure 6.43 and notice that the default X B̲ase and Y Bas̲e settings are 0.0000. If you want to move the X and Y base points, enter the desired values in the text boxes.

In the discussion with Figure 6.40 you learned how to draw auxiliary views with constructions lines using the Angle option set at 90°. This method works well, although another technique is to rotate the snap and

CHAPTER 6 ▬ Precision Drafting Tools **221**

FIGURE 6.43 Changing the Snap Angle to 30° in the Drawing Aids dialog box.

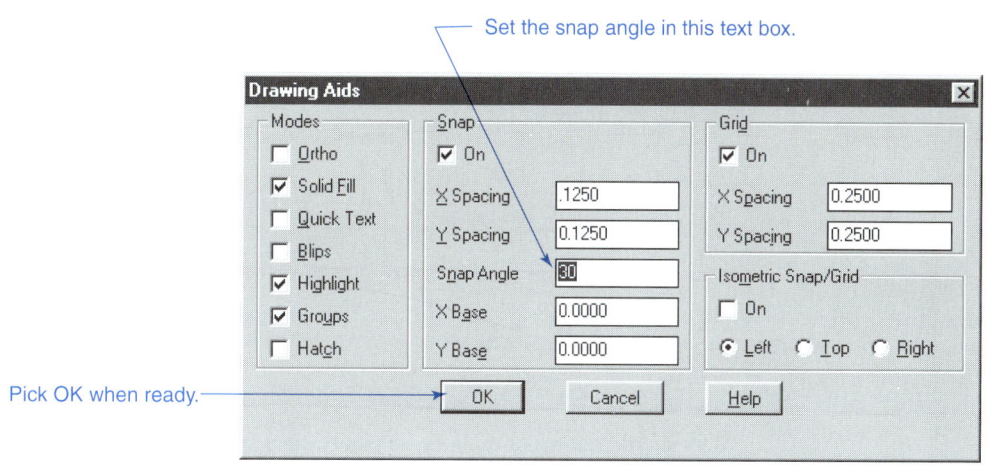

Set the snap angle in this text box.

Pick OK when ready.

grid to match the angle of the slanted surface. This allows you to draw lines at right angles directly from the slanted surface. If you know the angle of the slanted surface, then enter that value in the Snap Angle text box of the Drawing Aids dialog box shown in Figure 6.43. If you do not know the angle, use the LIST command and select the line of the slanted surface. For example, if the LIST command is used on the slanted surface in Figure 6.40, AutoCAD LT reports back Angle in XY Plane = 329. Use this value in the Snap Angle text box and pick the OK button. Figure 6.44 shows the resulting Snap and Grid aligned with the slanted surface. Now, you can use a variety of the methods that you learned in this chapter to help you draw the auxiliary view.

1. Turn Ortho on.
2. Draw projection lines from the ends of the slanted surface. Place these lines on a Construction layer so they can be frozen later.
3. Use the DIST command to determine the exact length of the slanted line in the front view and the length from the lower end of the slanted line to the intersection of the hidden line.
4. Use the LINE command and direct distance entry to complete the perimeter of the auxiliary view, beginning at the end of one of the projection lines.
5. Use the Close option to complete the last line back to the start.

FIGURE 6.44 The Snap and Grid are aligned with the slanted surface to assist in drawing an auxiliary view.

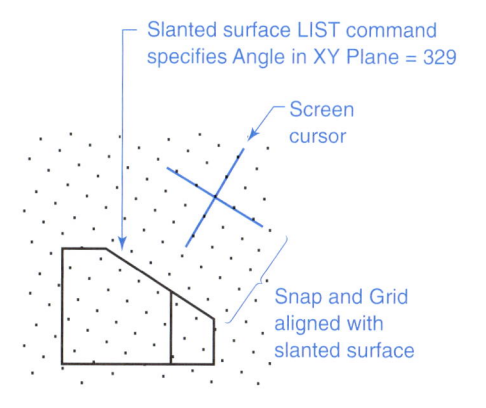

Slanted surface LIST command specifies Angle in XY Plane = 329

Screen cursor

Snap and Grid aligned with slanted surface

Exercise 6.14

1. Open EX6.12.
2. Erase the auxiliary view.
3. Set the snap and grid aligned with the slanted surface.
4. Use the steps described with Figure 6.45 to redraw the auxiliary view.
5. Save the drawing as EX6.14.

FIGURE 6.45 Projecting from the slanted surface to assist in creating an auxiliary view. Follow the steps outlined in the text.

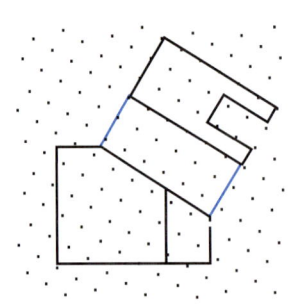

✓ LEARNING CHECKPOINT

- ☐ Why should construction lines be placed on a special layer?
- ☐ Describe the difference between making construction lines with the XLINE command compared with the RAY command.
- ☐ Use short statements to describe the function of the Horizontal, Vertical, Angle, Bisect, and Offset XLINE options.
- ☐ Discuss an advantage of changing the snap angle from the zero-degree default.

||||||||||| MULTIPLE CHOICE

Circle the choice or enter your response on an answer sheet by selecting the option that most closely completes or answers the given statements.

1. The object snap cursor menu is displayed when you perform this action:
    a. Hold down the Ctrl key and press the left mouse button.
    b. Hold down the Shift key and press the right mouse button.
    c. Hold down the Shift key and press the left mouse button.
    d. Hold down the Enter key and press the right mouse button.

2. When object snaps are used, AutoCAD LT gives you this at the object snap location when you move the cursor to indicate the desired object or snap point:
    a. cursor box   c. pick box
    b. marker   d. aperture

3. This term refers to an object snap or group of object snap options that is set to run continuously:
    a. continuous object snap   c. running object snap
    b. DDOSNAP   d. OSNAP

4. This command is used to divide an object into a series of segmented lengths:
    a. DIVIDE   b. MEASURE

5. This AutoCAD LT term means to extract or remove certain information from something in order to create something else:
    a. extract   c. remove
    b. separate   d. filter

6. This is a convenient way to enter point coordinate locations by pointing the cursor in the desired direction and specifying a distance:
    a. point filters   c. tracking
    b. From   d. direct distance entry

7. This command may be used to find the circumference of a circle:
    a. DIST   c. AREA
    b. LIST   d. OBJECT

8. This command allows you to get information about your drawing or about objects on the drawing:
    a. DIST   c. AREA
    b. LIST   d. OBJECT

CHAPTER 6 ▌ Precision Drafting Tools

9. Construction lines that extend an infinite distance in two directions from the pick point are drawn with this command:
   a. XLINE
   b. RAY
10. Double-clicking on this is a very convenient way to turn a running object snap on and off:
    a. OSNAP on the status line
    b. Running Object Snap toolbar button
    c. Running Object Snap on the cursor menu
    d. none of the above

MATCHING

Match each term to the correct description by writing the appropriate number in each box at the left.

- ☐ Area
- ☐ AutoSnap
- ☐ Bisect
- ☐ Center
- ☐ Ddtype
- ☐ Direct
- ☐ Dist
- ☐ Divide
- ☐ Endpoint
- ☐ Filters
- ☐ From
- ☐ Id
- ☐ Intersection
- ☐ List
- ☐ Marker
- ☐ Measure
- ☐ Midpoint
- ☐ Object
- ☐ Object snaps
- ☐ Node
- ☐ None
- ☐ Perpendicular
- ☐ Pixels
- ☐ Point
- ☐ PolarSnaps
- ☐ Quadrant
- ☐ Ray
- ☐ Running
- ☐ Tangent
- ☐ Time
- ☐ Tracking
- ☐ Xline

1. These allow you to quickly pick exact locations on an object without having to be located directly at the desired location.
2. These are used to remove or combine certain values to create a new value.
3. This object snap is convenient for accurately picking the endpoint of a line or arc.
4. When you use an object snap, AutoCAD LT gives you this at the object snap location when you move the cursor to the object.
5. You can easily snap to the middle of an object with this Object Snap option.
6. This object snap allows you to snap easily to the intersection of objects.
7. This term means at right angles.
8. Snap to the center of an object such as a circle, arc, or ellipse with this Object Snap option.
9. Pick this object snap to snap to a quarter of a circle.
10. Use this object snap for a line to touch a circle or arc at one point without intersecting.
11. Snap to a point with this object snap.
12. Disable object snap with this option.
13. This option allows you to specify a point that is at a specified location from a given point.
14. This object snap term means that an Object Snap option or group of options can be set to run continuously.
15. The aperture size is measured in these units.
16. Access the Point Style dialog box using this command.
17. This command is used to place evenly spaced points or blocks along the length, circumference, or perimeter of an object.
18. This command is used to place points or blocks a specified distance along the length, circumference, or perimeter of an object.
19. These filters are used to remove X, Y, and Z values from individual points in order to create a new combined point.
20. This distance entry feature allows you to point the cursor in the direction you want the next point and specify a distance from that point.
21. This allows you to determine a new point location from a series of directions and distances.
22. This command can be used to determine the coordinates of a point.
23. This command can be used to determine the distance and angle between two points.
24. This command can be used to calculate the perimeter of an object.

CHAPTER 6 ‖ Precision Drafting Tools

25. AutoCAD LT automatically calculates the circumference of a circle using this option.
26. Use this command to get information about an object.
27. This command provides information about drawing time.
28. This command draws construction lines that run in two directions from the pick point.
29. This command draws construction lines that run in one direction from the pick point.
30. Divide an angle into two equal angles using this construction line option.
31. Works with object snaps to display a marker when the cursor is near a snap point.
32. Allow you to drag angle and distance increments without entering values at the keyboard.

WORD SCRAMBLE

Unscramble the six scrambled words below, one letter to each square, to form six AutoCAD LT–related words:

RATEPUER

AGTENTN

ODNSPAD

EUSAMER

KGATNCIR

TNOCTUNORCIS

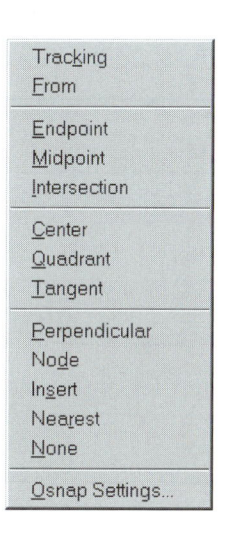

Unscramble the circled letters above to form the special answer, as suggested by the illustration.

PROJECTS

Set up the following drawing projects with layers that relate to the type of drawing as outlined and discussed in Chapter 5.

6.1 Piping Schematic
Draw the schematic shown below. Save as P6.1.

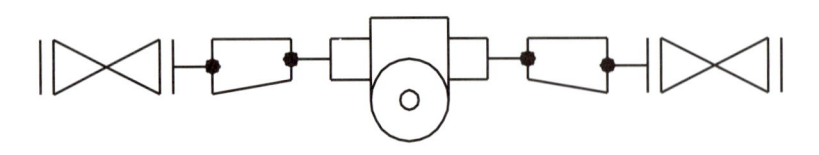

6.2 Doorbell Circuit
Draw the schematic shown below without text. Save as P6.2.

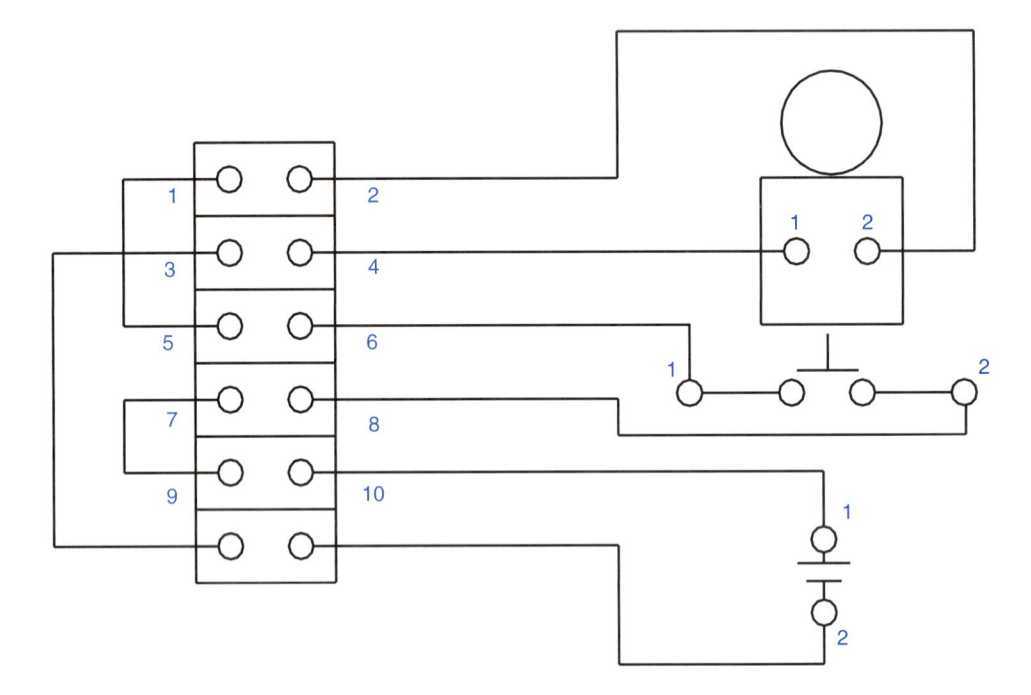

CHAPTER 6 ▌▌▌ Precision Drafting Tools   **227**

6.3 Eave Detail
Draw the detail shown below. Do not draw notes or dimensions. Save as P6.3.

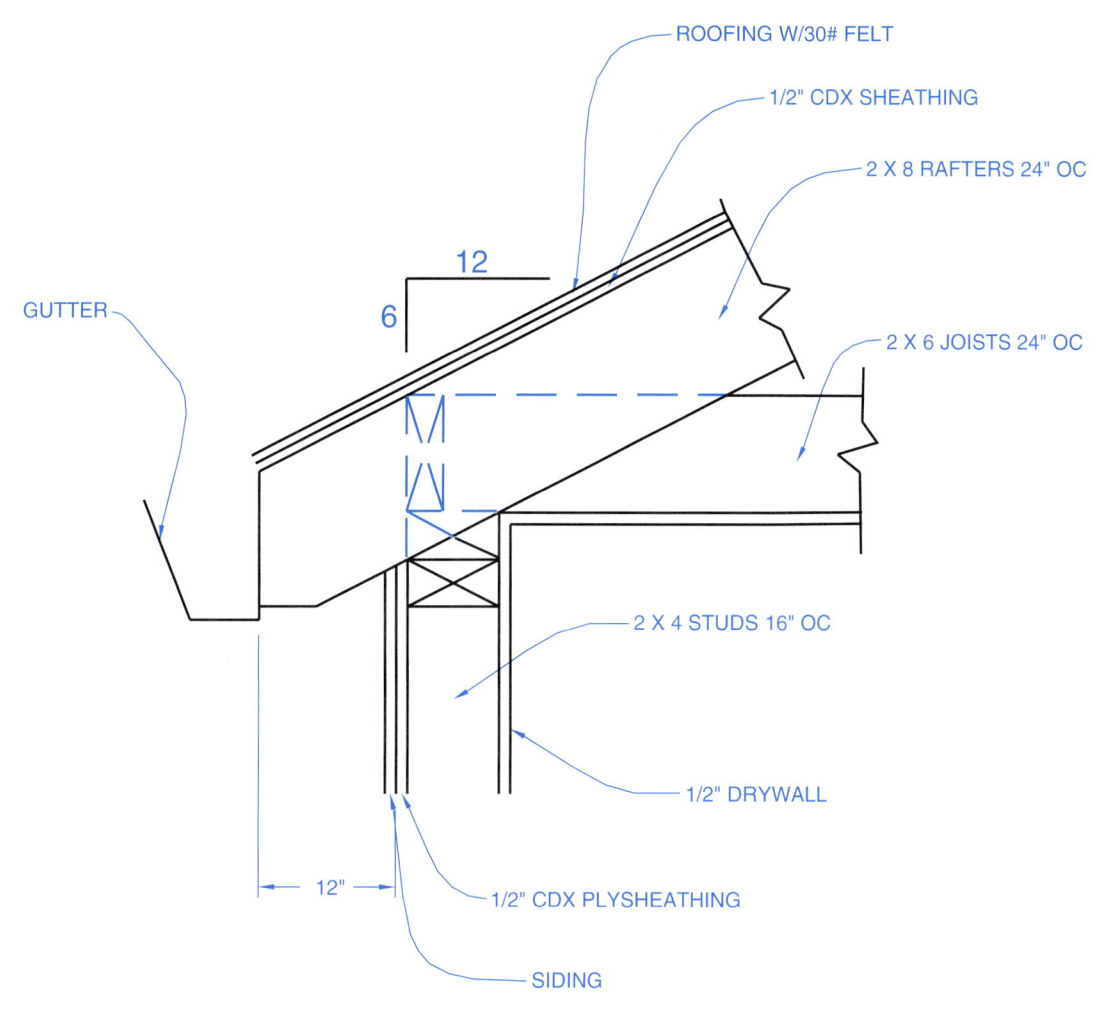

6.4 Rocker Arm
Draw the object shown below without notes or dimensions. Use construction lines to draw the initial layout and then draw arcs as needed. Save as P6.4.

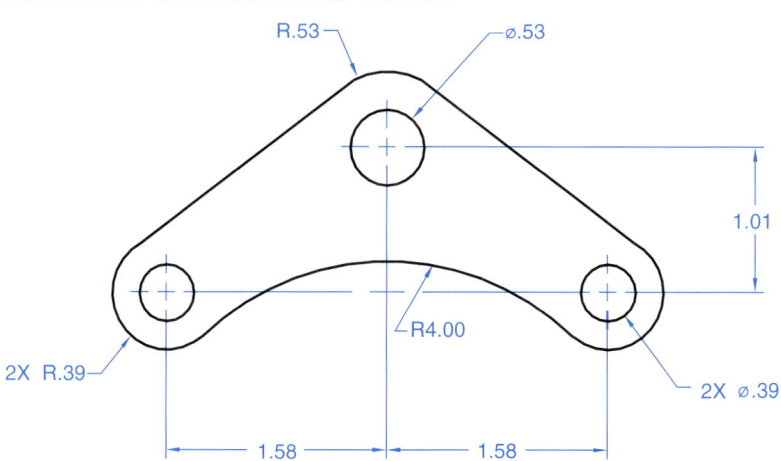

INCH

6.5 Rocker Arm

Draw the object shown below without notes or dimensions. Use construction lines to draw the initial layout and then draw arcs as needed. Save as P6.5.

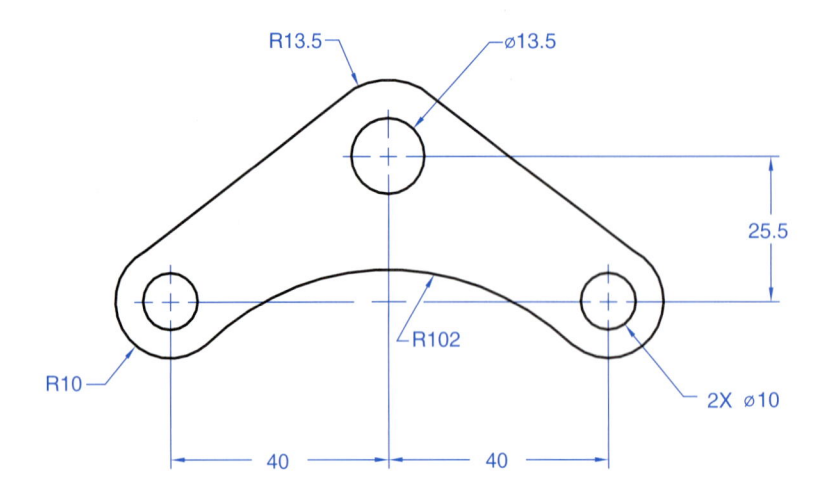

METRIC

6.6 Boss Plate

Draw the object shown below without notes or dimensions. The phantom lines are shown for construction purposes and may be frozen on a construction layer after use. Save as P6.6.

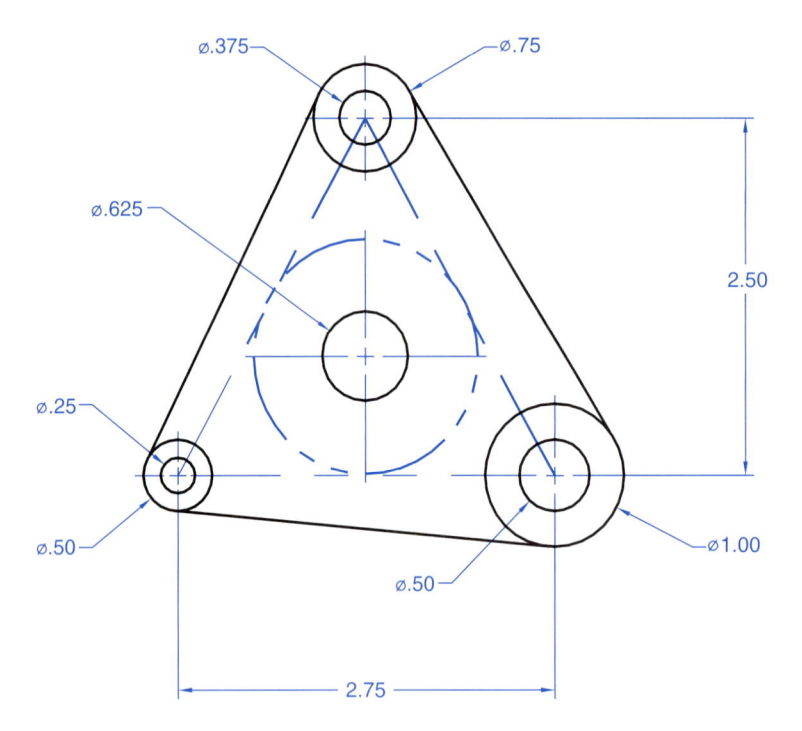

6.7 Ridge Gusset
Use PolarSnaps to assist you in drawing the following object. Do not draw dimensions. Save the drawing as P6.7.

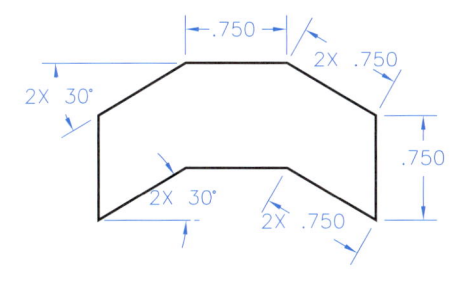

6.8 Angled Brace
Use PolarSnaps and direct distance entry to assist you in drawing the following object. Do not draw dimensions. Save the drawing as P6.8.

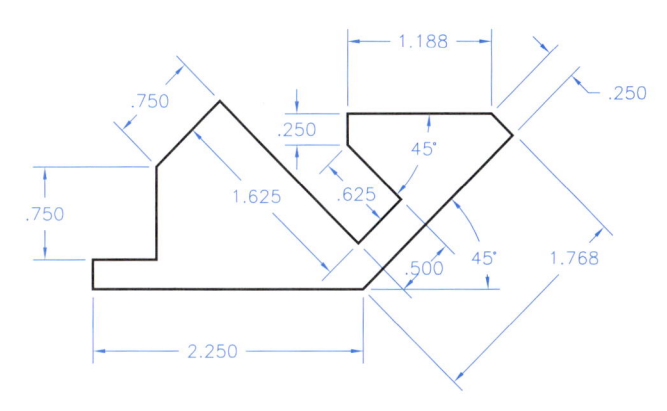

6.9 Step Block
Draw three views of the object shown below without notes or dimensions. Use construction lines as needed to establish the right side view. Save as P6.9.

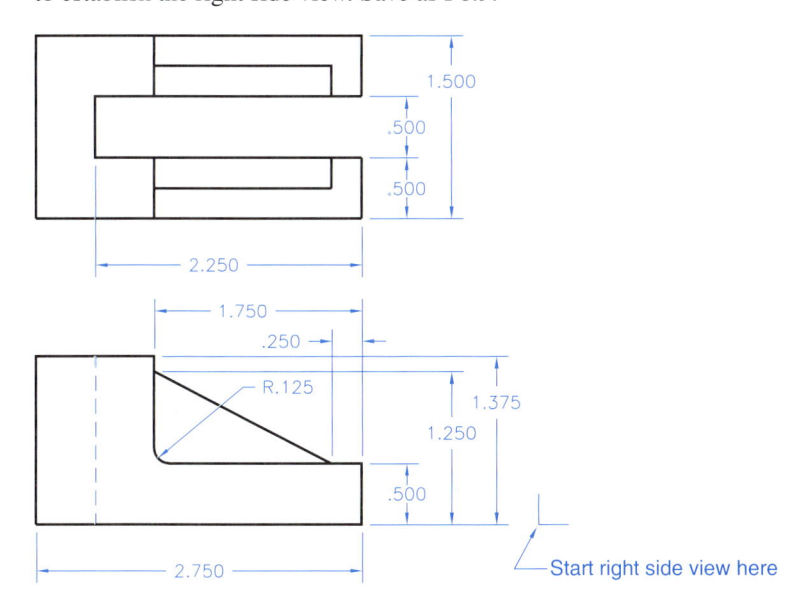

6.10 Slide Stop

Draw at least three views of the object shown below without notes or dimensions. Use construction lines as needed to align the views. Save as P6.10.

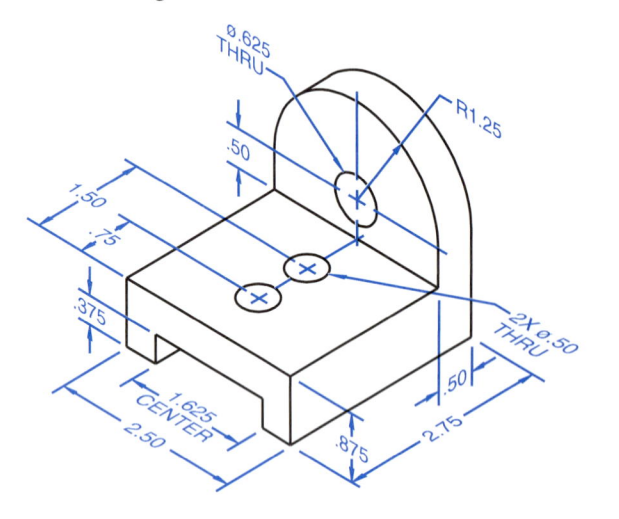

6.11 Angle Bracket

Draw at least three views (one view is an auxiliary view) of the object shown below without notes or dimensions. Use construction lines as needed to align the views. Save as P6.11.

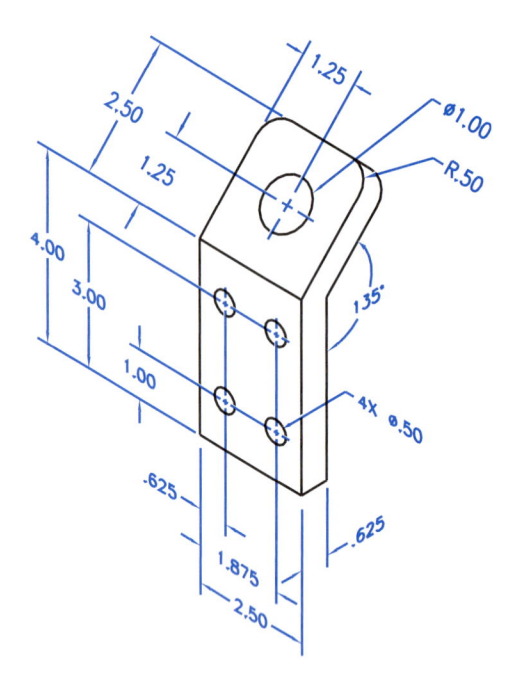

CHAPTER 6 ⅠⅠⅠ Precision Drafting Tools

6.12 Spring
Draw at least three views (two views are needed as auxiliary views) of the object shown below without notes or dimensions. Use construction lines as needed to align the views. Save as P6.12.

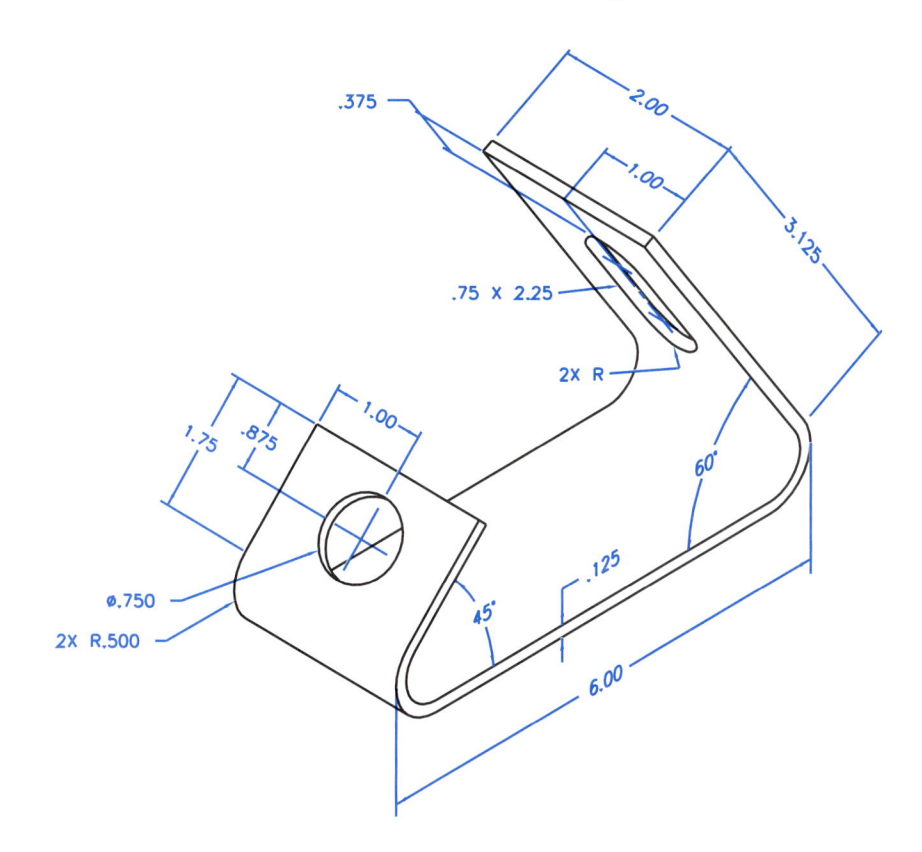

CHAPTER 7

Editing Your Drawing

LEARNING GOALS

- Use the Window Polygon, Crossing Polygon, and Fence selection options.
- Select stacked objects.
- Use the SELECT command and use the selected objects with the Previous option.
- Customize your selection options.
- Copy objects using the COPY, OFFSET, MIRROR, and ARRAY commands.
- Change objects using the MOVE, ROTATE, SCALE, LENGTHEN, and STRETCH commands.
- Select objects before entering commands.
- Use the grip STRETCH, MOVE, ROTATE, SCALE, and MIRROR commands.
- Break a portion out of objects.
- Trim and extend objects.
- Draw fillets and chamfers.
- Use the DDMODIFY to quickly change individual objects.
- Use the Windows Clipboard.

In Chapter 2 you learned to do some basic editing with the ERASE command. You also used OOPS, Undo, and REDO. You were introduced to selecting objects by picking and to use the Window and Crossing boxes. You discovered that commands can be entered before selecting the objects, or you can select the objects to activate grips before the command is entered. This chapter covers additional object selection options and the wide variety of AutoCAD LT editing commands.

Editing commands are far more powerful than drawing commands. Duplicating existing geometry and quickly editing it to meet your needs is far more productive than drawing each object from scratch. For example, consider how much faster it is to offset an existing line and then trim or extend it to meet your needs, rather than using a line command to create a completely new line. Also, the ability to copy and use arrays with objects represents an incredible time savings. Additionally, selecting objects before entering commands provides instant command line access to the more commonly used editing commands using GRIPS.

Object Selection Methods

When editing, you can select one object or a group of objects. The objects you select are called a selection set. AutoCAD LT defines a *selection set* as one or more objects that are specified for processing as a unit. The Window and Crossing selection options allow you to place a box around or through objects to be selected. This discussion explains the use of Window and Crossing Polygons and Fences to provide additional flexibility when selecting objects. You can select objects that are under other objects by cycling through the objects until you find the one you want. You can customize selection methods. You will also use grips for the ease of being able to issue several editing commands quickly after the objects have been selected.

In this section, the object selection methods that are discussed need to be entered at a *Select objects:* prompt. This prompt is issued whenever an editing command is entered. To work through the discussion topics in this section, use the ERASE command to activate the Select objects: prompt. To return the erased objects to the screen and proceed with each new topic, you can enter the OOPS command.

The Window and Crossing Polygon Selection Options

The Select Window and Crossing Polygon options work similar to the Window and Crossing boxes. Remember from Chapter 2 that a Window box must totally surround the objects to be selected, and a Crossing box may surround or cross through the objects to be selected. The Window and Crossing Polygon selection methods give you additional flexibility.

The Window Polygon selection option allows you to place a polygon of your own design around (totally enclosing) an object or group of objects that you want to select. The polygon may have three or more sides of any desired length and angle but may not touch or cross itself. The Window Polygon can be used by typing **WP** at the Select objects: prompt. Follow this Window Polygon sequence as you look at Figure 7.1:

Select objects: **WP**↵
First polygon point: ⟨*pick the first point*⟩
Undo/<Endpoint of line>: ⟨*pick point 2*⟩
Undo/<Endpoint of line>: ⟨*pick point 3*⟩
Undo/<Endpoint of line>: ⟨*pick point 4*⟩
Undo/<Endpoint of line>: ⟨*pick point 5*⟩
Undo/<Endpoint of line>: ⟨*pick point 6*⟩
Undo/<Endpoint of line>: ↵
8 found
Select objects: ↵

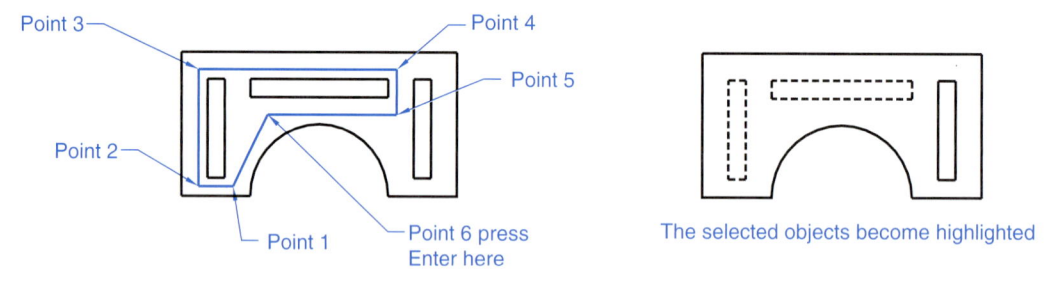

FIGURE 7.1 Use the Window Polygon to select objects that are enclosed within the polygon.

AutoCAD LT provides a solid cursor line to form the Window Polygon as you pick points. Press Enter after picking the last point. AutoCAD LT tells you how many objects were found and returns the Select objects: prompt. Press Enter again when you are satisfied with the polygon that you created. The selected objects become highlighted. When creating the sides of the Window Polygon, if you do not like where you placed one of the polygon sides, use the Undo option at any time:

Undo/<Endpoint of line>: ⟨*pick point 3*⟩
Undo/<Endpoint of line>: **U**↵
Undo/<Endpoint of line>: ⟨*pick a new point 3*⟩
Undo/<Endpoint of line>:

This removes the last polygon line and allows you to pick a new point.

The Crossing Polygon works just like the Window Polygon, except the cursor line is dashed and everything inside or crossing the polygon lines is selected. The Crossing Polygon can be used by typing **CP** at the Select objects: prompt. Follow this sequence as you look at Figure 7.2:

Select Objects: **CP**↵
First polygon point: ⟨*pick the first point*⟩
Undo/<Endpoint of line>: ⟨*pick point 2*⟩
Undo/<Endpoint of line>: ⟨*pick point 3*⟩
Undo/<Endpoint of line>: ⟨*pick point 4*⟩

CHAPTER 7 ||| Editing Your Drawing

Undo/<Endpoint of line>: ⟨*pick point 5*⟩
Undo/<Endpoint of line>: ⟨*pick point 6*⟩
Undo/<Endpoint of line>: ↵
10 found
Select objects: ↵

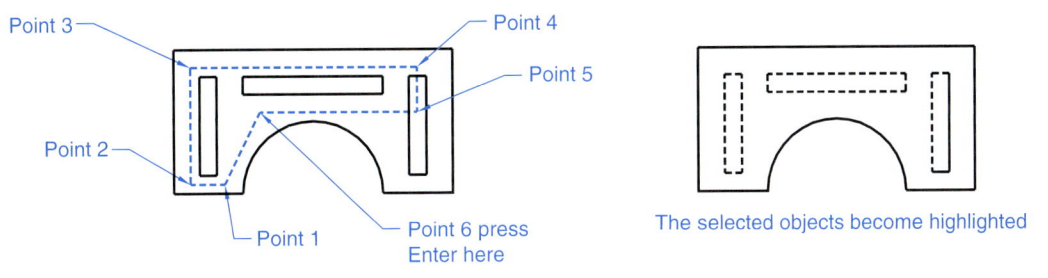

FIGURE 7.2 Use the Crossing Polygon to select objects that are enclosed within and cross the polygon.

Exercise 7.1

1. Begin a new drawing.
2. Draw an object similar to the original object shown in Figure 7.1.
3. Use the ERASE command and the Window Polygon option to select the same objects that are selected in Figure 7.1.
4. Enter OOPS to undo the previous command.
5. Use the ERASE command and the Crossing Polygon option to select the same objects that are selected in Figure 7.2.
6. Enter OOPS to undo the previous command.
7. Save the drawing as EX7.1.

The Fence Selection Option

In some situations, it might be easier to place a selection line through objects to be selected rather than using a box or polygon. The Fence selection option draws a line that selects any object that it crosses. The Fence can be used by typing **F** at the Select objects: prompt. A Fence selection is shown in Figure 7.3 using this sequence:

Select Objects: **F**↵
First fence point: ⟨*pick the first point*⟩
Undo/<Endpoint of line>: ⟨*pick point 2*⟩
Undo/<Endpoint of line>: ⟨*pick point 3*⟩
Undo/<Endpoint of line>: ↵
3 found
Select objects: ↵

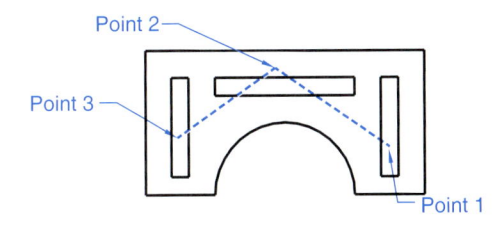

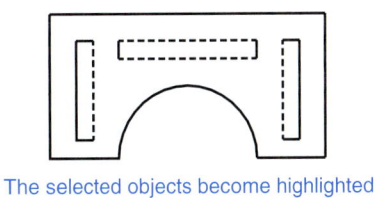

FIGURE 7.3 Use the Fence option to select objects that cross the fence line.

> ### ✎ Field Notes
>
> - If you press the right mouse button at the Command: prompt, a popup menu with editing and display options is provided. The first option in this menu always repeats the previously used command.
> - The Add and Remove options were discussed in Chapter 2. Remember, if you select objects and then decide that you do not want one or more of them in the selection set, use the Remove option. Use the Add option to place more objects in the selection set after using Remove. A more convenient option is to press the Shift key while selecting objects to remove the specified objects from the selection set.

Exercise 7.2

1. Open EX7.1.
2. Use the ERASE command and the Fence option to select the same objects that are selected in Figure 7.3.
3. Use OOPS to undo the previous command.
4. Save the drawing as EX7.2.

Selecting Objects that Are Very Close Together or Stacked

A drawing often contains objects that are very close together or on top of other objects. When objects are on top of other objects, they are referred to as being **stacked**. This may make it difficult to pick only the desired object. If the pick box touches multiple objects, AutoCAD LT selects the one that was created most recently, which may or may not be the one you want—which can be a frustrating experience. You can set the Pickbox variable to a very small value or use the ZOOM command when selecting objects that are very close together, but this does not solve the problem when objects are stacked. It is easy to overcome the problem of picking stacked objects by using what AutoCAD LT calls **cycling**. It is difficult to demonstrate cycling through stacked objects, because stacked objects appear to be one object, but Figure 7.4 makes the attempt. In this figure, the intersecting lines are stacked at the point of intersection. While it would be easy to simply move the pick box to the desired line and pick, this would not show how cycling works. If you pick at the intersection, as shown in Figure 7.4A, you may not select the line you want. To use cycling, press and hold the Ctrl key while you pick, and then release the Ctrl key. One of the objects becomes highlighted as shown in Figure 7.4B. Press the pick button again and the next eligible object becomes highlighted as shown in Figure 7.4C. Pick again to highlight another object as in Figure 7.4D. Press Enter to select the currently highlighted object. AutoCAD LT tells you when cycling is on and off like this:

Select objects: ⟨*press the Ctrl key and pick*⟩ <Cycle on>
⟨*the first object becomes highlighted*⟩
⟨*pick again; the second object becomes highlighted*⟩
⟨*pick again; the third object becomes highlighted*⟩
⟨*press Enter to select the highlighted object*⟩
<Cycle off> 1 found
Select objects: ↵

FIGURE 7.4 Cycling through objects for selection by picking while pressing the Ctrl key.

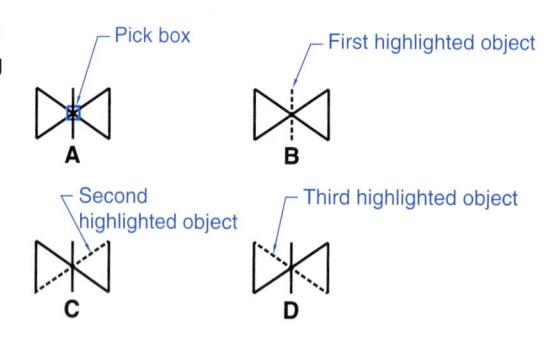

CHAPTER 7 ||| Editing Your Drawing

AutoCAD LT also has a Multiple option that allows you to select two or more stacked objects. This works by typing **M** and pressing Enter at the Select objects: prompt. You then pick at the same point as many times as it takes to select all of the stacked objects. Press Enter when you are done. AutoCAD LT tells you how many objects are selected and returns the Select objects: prompt. The Multiple selection option is different from object cycling, which picks only a single object, and from a crossing, which selects all of the stacked objects.

Using the SELECT Command

The SELECT command allows you to create a selection set with any of the typical selection options and then later use it in an editing application. The objects that are selected using the SELECT command are placed in an AutoCAD LT selection set called *previous*. You can access them when needed at a Select objects: prompt by typing **P** for previous. Type **SELECT** at the Command: prompt to use this command:

Command: **SELECT**↵
Select objects: ⟨*use any selection method*⟩
number found
Select objects: ↵
Command:

Select <u>A</u>ll can be picked from the <u>E</u>dit pull-down menu or by pressing Ctrl + A. This option selects all the objects in the drawing. The Select <u>A</u>ll option highlights all objects when you are at the Select objects: prompt or uses GRIP selection if you are at the Command: prompt.

Field Notes

> Sometimes, the selection of a specific group of objects requires a complex and difficult selection process. Using the Previous option helps when you are performing two or more sequential editing operations on a selection set. If, however, you need to edit a different group of objects before continuing with the current selection set, you would not be able to continue to use the Previous selection option.
>
> A simple feature of AutoCAD LT that can help to keep your Previous selection option available is found in the fact that any objects returned to the screen using the OOPS command immediately become the Previous selection set. So, this means that you can erase your complex selection set, edit the other group of objects, and then use the OOPS command to return the objects to the screen as your Previous selection set, as long as you *do not* use ERASE!
>
> This can be unreliable if you erase another selection set, or if OOPS is used to return the objects and then the Undo option is used to undo the OOPS command. Either of these situations require you to undo all the way back to where the objects were erased.

Exercise 7.3

1. Begin a new drawing.
2. Draw an object similar to the one shown in Figure 7.4A. Do not draw the pick box or the note.
3. Enter the ERASE command and use cycling to cycle through the objects as shown in Figure 7.4B, C, and D.
4. Press Enter when you have seen each object being cycled.
5. Press the Esc key at the Select objects: prompt.
6. Use the SELECT command to select the drawing and return to the Command: prompt.
7. Enter the ERASE command and type **P** at the Select objects: prompt. All of the objects that were selected with the previous SELECT command should be erased.
8. Use OOPS to undo the previous command.
9. Save the drawing as EX7.3.

Customizing Selection Options

Tools
Selection...

DDSELECT
SE

AutoCAD LT allows you to control how object selections are made. A group of system variables is available that can be used individually at the keyboard to control object selection methods. These are also accessed in the Object Selection Settings dialog box by picking Selection … in the Tools pull-down menu or by typing **SE** or **DDSELECT** at the Command: line prompt. The Object Selection Settings dialog box with the default settings is shown in Figure 7.5. Pick the Default button to return to default settings. The discussions and examples in this text use the default settings. The Selection Modes are described as follows:

Noun/Verb Selection	A check in this box allows you to select objects before entering a command. This option is turned on by default and allows you to pick objects first and then start an editing command using the preselected objects. If this option is off, then starting an editing command ignores any grip-selected objects and displays a Select objects: prompt.
Use Shift to Add	Check this box if you want the convenience of pressing the Shift key to add objects to a selection set. Off by default this requires that the Shift key be held down in order to add items to the current selection. This means that if you pick an object at the Select objects: prompt, it is highlighted as normal. However, picking another object at the subsequent Select objects: prompt selects this object and removes any other currently selected items from the selection set. To add additional items to the selection set, you must hold the Shift key down while selecting.
Press and Drag	This option is off by default. When it is on, it changes the way that windows are drawn during object selections. Normally, you press and release the pick button at each desired corner. This option requires that you press and hold the pick button at the first corner, move the cursor to the other corner, and then release the pick button.
Implied Windowing	When set at its default setting of on, this option automatically places you in a Window/Crossing selection mode if a pick is made at a location where the pick box does not touch an object. If this option is off, the same pick simply reports no objects found.
Object Grouping	On by default, this means that all members of a group are selected when you select a single member. Object Groups are discussed in Chapter 12.
Associative Hatch	This option is off by default. Turning it on means that selecting an associative hatch pattern also selects the boundary objects. Hatching is discussed in Chapter 10.

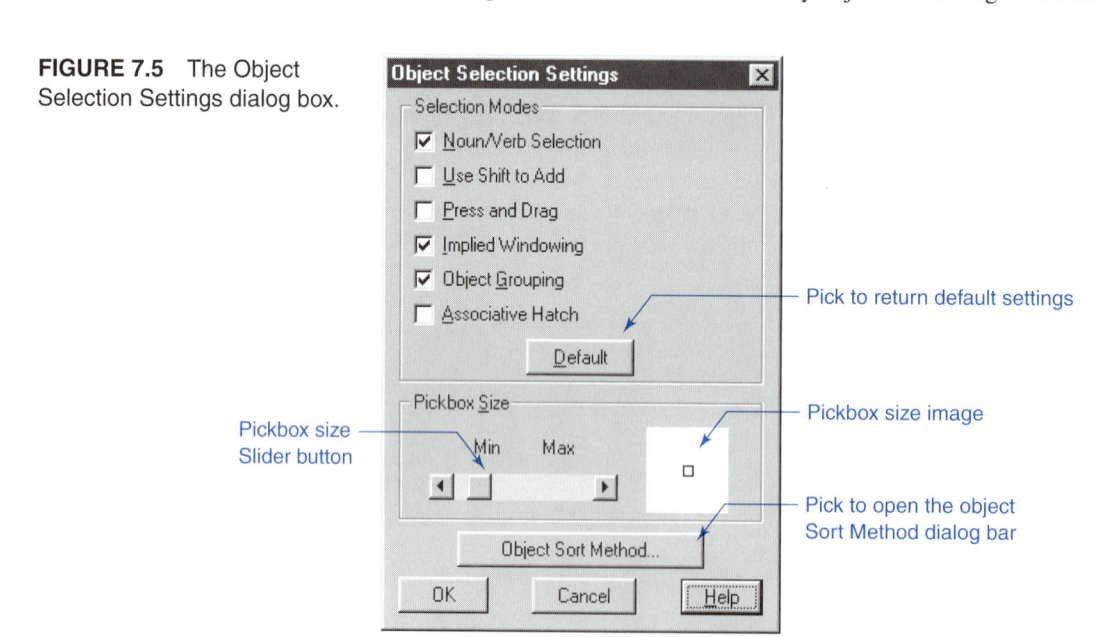

FIGURE 7.5 The Object Selection Settings dialog box.

Field Notes

- Press and Drag or Implied Windowing must be on to automatically use a window or crossing box. If both are on, Implied Windowing does not work.
- Even with the Use Shift to Add option active, if you hold the Shift key and select objects that have already been selected, they are removed from the selection set as they would be normally.

With regard to Implied Windowing, if you are placed in the Window/Crossing selection mode, the setting of Press and Drag still affects the method by which the window must be drawn.

The Pickbox Size compartment allows you to move the slider button to get a desired pick box size. When moving the slider, the image to the right shows the current pick box setting at actual size. A smaller selection box can be used to pick within areas where objects are crowded close together, but if the pick box is too small, then general picking procedures are more difficult because more accuracy is required—this makes it easier to miss your target object. Larger pick boxes make general picking faster and easier, but cannot be used effectively in crowded areas. Finding a pick box size that is not too big or too small can help you be more productive. The pick box can also be sized by specifying the desired number of pixels using the PICKBOX command. Change from the default pixels of 3 like this:

Command: **PICKBOX** ↵
New value for PICKBOX <3>: 6 ↵
Command:

Field Notes

- The DDSELECT command can be used transparently ('**SE** or '**DDSELECT**) to change your selection modes.
- Also, using '**PICKBOX** at any Select objects: prompt is a fast and convenient way to adjust the size of the pick box while working on your drawing.

Pick the Object Sort Method … button to access the Object Sort Method dialog box with the default settings shown in Figure 7.6. The object sort methods can be specified if the order in which the objects were created is important in your drawing or application. These options should not be set unless necessary, because object sorting requires additional processing time. In large or complex drawings, object sorting can result in decreased system performance. The following list explains the object sorting for each of the available options:

Object Selection   When on, objects selected with a window style selection option are added to the selection set in the reverse order in which they were created. When off, the selection order is less predictable, but typically objects are added to the selection set in the order of proximity to the 0,0 coordinate point.

FIGURE 7.6 The Object Sort Method dialog box.

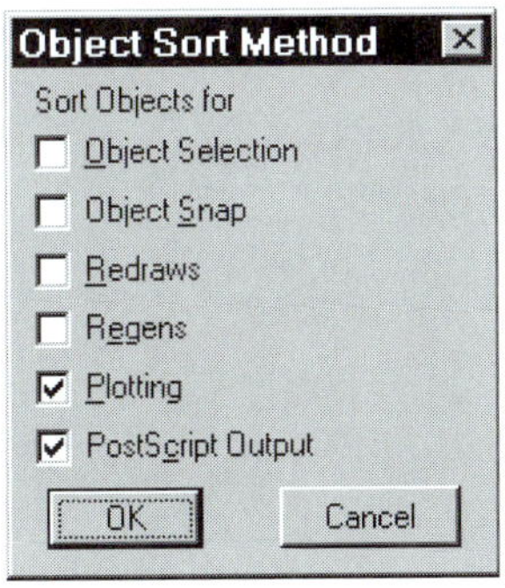

Object Snap	When on, if two qualifying objects are found in the aperture and the specified object snap point is the exact same distance from the picked point, the point referencing the most recently created object is used. When off, the results may not always be predictable.
Redraws	When on, the REDRAW command draws objects in the reverse order in which they were created. When off, the objects are drawn according to their order in the display list managed by the display driver. With the speed of the display on most systems, you may not be able to see any difference between these settings.
Slide Creation	When on, objects in slide files created using MSLIDE are saved in the order in which they are encountered in the drawing database, from last to first. This controls how the slide is displayed later when using VSLIDE. Both MSLIDE and VSLIDE are discussed in Chapter 15.
Regens	When on, the REGEN command regenerates objects in the drawing in the reverse order in which they were created. When off, the order is less predictable—typically starting in the lower left corner of the current view and working up and to the right.
Plotting	When on, the PLOT command processes objects in the order in which they are found in the drawing database, from last to first. This has little value unless you are using a pen-style plotter and want to observe the plot as it is being generated.
PostScript Output	When on, objects written to encapsulated PostScript files created using PSOUT are added to the file in the reverse order in which the objects were created. The PSOUT command is discussed in Chapter 15.

Selecting with Grips

Tools
⌐ Grips...

DDGRIPS
GR

AutoCAD LT places grips on an object when you select objects before entering a command. A brief introduction to grips was provided in Chapter 2. *Grips* are small squares that appear on objects you select while no command is active. The grips can be picked and dragged with the cursor to perform editing operations. Grips are displayed differently depending on the type of object. For example, grips are placed at the quadrants and center of a circle and at the ends and midpoint of a line. Figure 7.7 shows the location of grips on different objects. You can perform editing operations very quickly with grips. When you first select an object, the grips are blue boxes by default. These are called *unselected grips*. Press the Esc key twice to remove the grips from the object. The screen cursor snaps directly to a grip when it is moved over the grip. This allows you to easily use the grips for editing purposes. When you move the screen cursor to a grip and pick, the grip becomes solid red by default. These are called *selected grips*. The grip color may be changed if you wish. Press the Esc key once to return the solid red grip to the blue outline status. When you pick a grip and make it solid red, this grip is called the *base grip*. The base grip is the point from which the editing process occurs. Editing with grips is explained later in this chapter.

FIGURE 7.7 Grips displayed on a variety of objects.

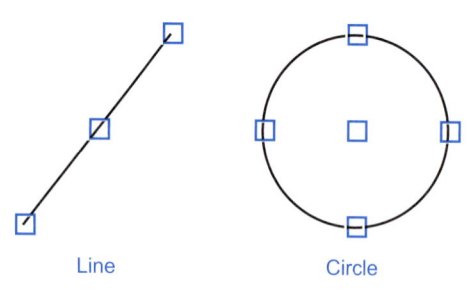

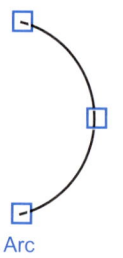

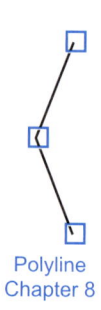

CHAPTER 7 ||| Editing Your Drawing 241

Grips are controlled by using the Grips dialog box shown in Figure 7.8. Access the Grips dialog box by picking G_rips ... in the T_ools pull-down menu or by typing **GR** or **DDGRIPS** at the Command: line prompt. The Grips dialog box has two options in the Select Settings compartment. Grips are enabled by default. Turn grips off by picking to remove the check in the E_nable Grips check box. Grips are shown at the insertion point of a block as in Figure 7.7 by default. You can have grips displayed on every object within a block by picking the Enable Grips Within B_locks check box. Blocks are explained in Chapter 12. You can change grip color in the Grip Colors compartment. Pick the U_nselected ... button to get the Select Color dialog box where you can pick a new color for unselected grips. Pick the S_elected ... button to change the color of selected grips. Use the G_rip Size compartment to change the grip size as needed. Move the slider button to get a desired grip size. When moving the slider, the image to the right shows the current grip setting at actual size.

FIGURE 7.8 The Grips dialog box.

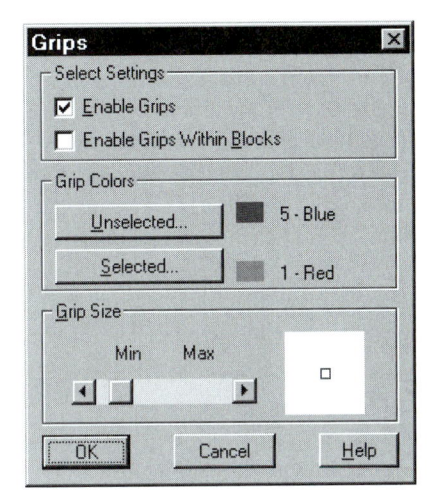

Exercise 7.4

1. Begin a new drawing.
2. Draw a line, a circle, and an arc.
3. Select the line and observe the unselected grips. Pick one of the grips to make it a selected grip. Observe the results. Press the Esc key twice to remove the grips.
4. Do the same thing individually with the circle and arc.
5. Save the drawing as EX7.4.

✓ LEARNING CHECKPOINT

- ☐ Define the term *selection set*.
- ☐ Explain the difference between WP and CP.
- ☐ How does the F selection option work?
- ☐ What is the purpose of cycling?
- ☐ Describe how the SELECT command works.
- ☐ What is Noun/Verb Selection?
- ☐ How does Press and Drag work?
- ☐ What is Implied Windowing?
- ☐ What is the main purpose of using sorting methods?
- ☐ How do you remove grips?
- ☐ Where are grips found on a circle?
- ☐ What happens to an unselected grip when you select it?

Copying Objects

AutoCAD LT supplies a group of commands that allow you to copy objects. These commands are useful for a variety of editing tasks that provide individual and multiple copies of objects in different arrangements. These commands include COPY, OFFSET, MIRROR, and ARRAY.

Using the COPY Command

Modify
Copy Object
Modify
Copy

COPY
CO
CP

Many projects contain features that are duplicated throughout the drawing. Once an object has been drawn, it can be copied as many times as needed. When copying objects, pick the Copy Object button from the Modify toolbar, pick Copy in the Modify pull-down menu, or type **CP** or **COPY** at the Command: prompt. The COPY command asks you to select the objects you want to copy and then asks for a base point. The *base point* is any specific reference point that has a meaningful relationship with the object. For example, circular features in a technical drawing are often located by dimensioning the center point of the circular profile. If you draw a hole in a part that is placed in several locations, the easiest way to locate the new copies accurately is to place them using the center of the circle as the reference point (i.e., the base point). Or, as shown in Figure 7.9, any specific point that can be used to locate the copy can be selected as a base point. The illustration shows a simplified piping symbol for a valve that is connected to the endpoint of a pipe. To copy this valve and place the copy at the endpoint of another pipe, a good base point selection is the MIDpoint of the line at the left side of the valve. The *Second point of displacement* label in Figure 7.9 specifies the new location of the base point in relation to the new copy of the valve. Specifying the ENDPoint of the second pipe accurately places the copy of the valve in the correct location. The COPY command works like this:

Command: **CP** or **COPY**↵
Select objects: ⟨*select the objects to be copied*⟩
Select objects: ↵
<Base point or displacement>/Multiple: ⟨*pick a base point*⟩
Second point of displacement: ⟨*pick a place for the copy*⟩
Command:

FIGURE 7.9 Selecting a base point and using the COPY command.

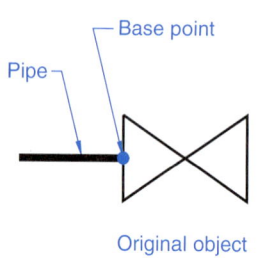

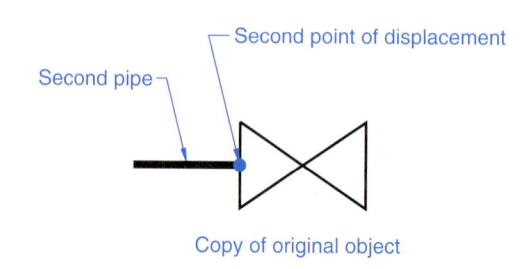

Base point — Pipe — Original object

Second point of displacement — Second pipe — Copy of original object

The previous example allows you to make one copy of the desired objects. You can also make multiple copies by using the Multiple option. Follow this command sequence to make several copies of the same object:

Command: **CP** or **COPY**↵
Select objects: ⟨*select the objects to be copied*⟩
Select objects: ↵
<Base point or displacement>/Multiple: **M**↵
Base point: ⟨*pick a base point*⟩
Second point of displacement: ⟨*pick a place for the first copy*⟩
Second point of displacement: ⟨*pick a place for the second copy*⟩
Second point of displacement: ⟨*pick a place for the third copy*⟩
Second point of displacement: ↵
Command:

The displacement option is used when you enter a coordinate at the "<Base point or displacement>/Multiple:" prompt and press Enter at the "Second point of displacement:" prompt. The copies are then placed at a location that is the specified X and Y distances from the original. Also, this can be done by picking the first point and pressing Enter at the second prompt: the picked point is then used as the X and Y values for displacement.

CHAPTER 7 ||| Editing Your Drawing   243

> ### Field Notes
>
> - The displacement option can be a problem if you pick the first point and accidentally press Enter at the second point prompt—the copies are often made beyond the visible area of the drawing. For example, if you pick the point 11,8, then the copies are made 11 units over on the X axis and 8 units up on the Y axis. If the copies do not appear on screen, use Undo and try again, unless you want to copy off the screen.
> - When objects are grip selected, Copy and Cut options are displayed on the popup cursor menu. Do not use these options to copy objects within a drawing yet. These options start the COPYCLIP and CUTCLIP commands, which use the Windows clipboard to copy objects. Trying to paste the copied objects into your drawing using the Paste option creates a block object. The COPYCLIP, CUTCLIP, and PASTECLIP commands are discussed later in this chapter.

Exercise 7.5

1. Open EX7.3.
2. Use the COPY command's Multiple option to make three duplicates of the original object.
3. Save the drawing as EX7.5.

Making Parallel Copies with the OFFSET Command

The OFFSET command can be used to create parallel copies of objects at a specified offset distance. Many objects can be offset, including lines, arcs, circles, polylines, construction lines, elliptical arcs, and ellipses. When offsetting a line, you create a duplicate line at a specified place parallel to the original line. Circles are offset by concentric placement either larger or smaller than the original circle. Create an offset copy by picking the Offset button from the Modify toolbar, by picking Offset in the Modify pull-down menu, or by typing **OF** or **OFFSET** at the Command: line prompt. The command asks you to specify an offset distance, select an object to offset, and choose which side of the original object you want to offset. Follow this command sequence as you refer to Figure 7.10:

Modify

[Offset icon]

Modify
└ Off**s**et

OFFSET
O

    Command: **OF** or **OFFSET**↵
    Offset distance or Through <Through>: ⟨*offset distance,* **.25** *for example*⟩
    Select object to offset: ⟨*pick the original object*⟩
    Side to offset? ⟨*pick a point on the side to offset*⟩

FIGURE 7.10 Using the OFFSET command.

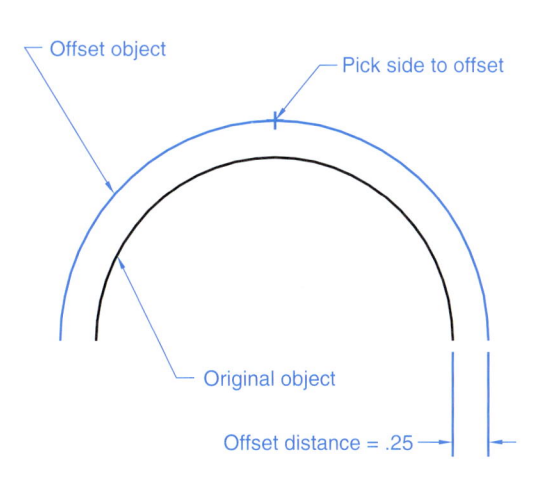

AutoCAD LT continues to ask you to select an object to offset. This allows you to draw as many offsets, using the same distance, as desired:

    Select object to offset: ⟨*select another object or press Enter*↵⟩
    Command:

The OFFSET command allows you to pick a point through which the offset object is drawn. You can also pick two points in a drawing to specify a distance for the Through option. Consider using object snaps to your advantage when offsetting an object through a feature on an object. Use the Through option and follow this command sequence as you look at Figure 7.11:

Command: **OF** or **OFFSET**↵
Offset distance or Through <Through>: **T**↵
Select object to offset: ⟨*pick the original object*⟩
Through point: ⟨*pick a point for the offset to pass through*⟩
Select object to offset: ⟨*select another object or press Enter*↵⟩
Command:

FIGURE 7.11 Using the OFFSET command's Through option.

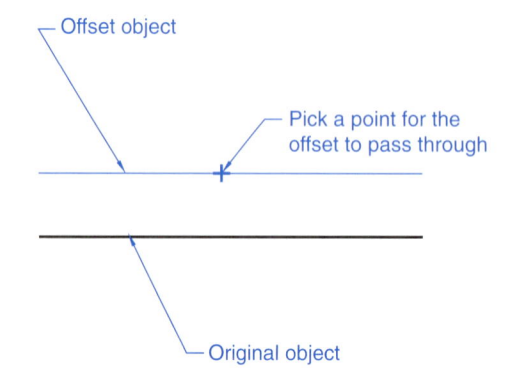

Field Notes

- Some drafting productivity advantages result from the use of the OFFSET command. For example, when drawing a front view of an ortho drawing of a rectangularly shaped part, to get the right side view, use OFFSET Through to pick a location for one of the vertical lines in the right view and then use OFFSET with the distance being the width of the right side view. Horizontal lines can be handled in a similar manner. For example, draw a front view offset upward once using Through, and then the second time using the height of the top view as the distance.
- When using OFFSET to offset several features at varied offset values, a fast and easy way to change the offset distance for the next operation is to quickly press the space bar or Enter key twice. The first Enter ends the current OFFSET command and displays the Command: prompt. The second Enter restarts the OFFSET command and places you at the "Offset distance or Through <default>:" prompt. When you enter the new distance you can continue offsetting objects as before, using the new distance.

Exercise 7.6

1. Begin a new drawing.
2. Draw an arc similar to the original object shown in Figure 7.10.
3. Offset a distance of 0.25 outside of the original arc. The results should be similar to those shown in Figure 7.10.
4. Draw a line similar to the original object shown in Figure 7.11.
5. Use the OFFSET command's Through option to pick a point for the offset to pass through.
6. Save the drawing as EX7.6.

Creating Mirror Images

A mirror image of an object can be made and the original object can remain or it can be deleted. When you have a symmetrical object, you can draw half and then simply mirror the other half into position. Mirror images are drawn by picking the Mirror button on the Modify toolbar, by picking Mirror in the Modify pull-

CHAPTER 7 ||| Editing Your Drawing

down menu, or by typing **MI** or **MIRROR** at the Command: prompt. The MIRROR command asks you to select the objects to mirror, establish a mirror line, and then decide if you want to keep or delete the old objects. The *mirror line* is an imaginary line across which the original object is mirrored. You are asked to pick the first and second point of the mirror line as shown in Figure 7.12. The mirror line may be located next to the original object or away from the original object. The distance between the mirror line and the original object is the same distance to the mirror image. The command sequence works like this:

Command: **MI** or **MIRROR**↵
Select objects: ⟨select the objects to mirror⟩
Select objects: ↵
First point of mirror line: ⟨pick the first endpoint of the mirror line⟩
Second point: ⟨pick the second endpoint of the mirror line⟩
Delete old objects? ⟨N⟩ ↵
Command:

Modify

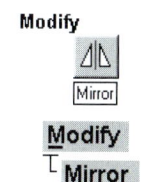

Mirror

Modify
   Mirror

MIRROR
MI

FIGURE 7.12 Using the MIRROR command. (A) The original object remaining after the command. (B) The second example deletes the original object while mirroring.

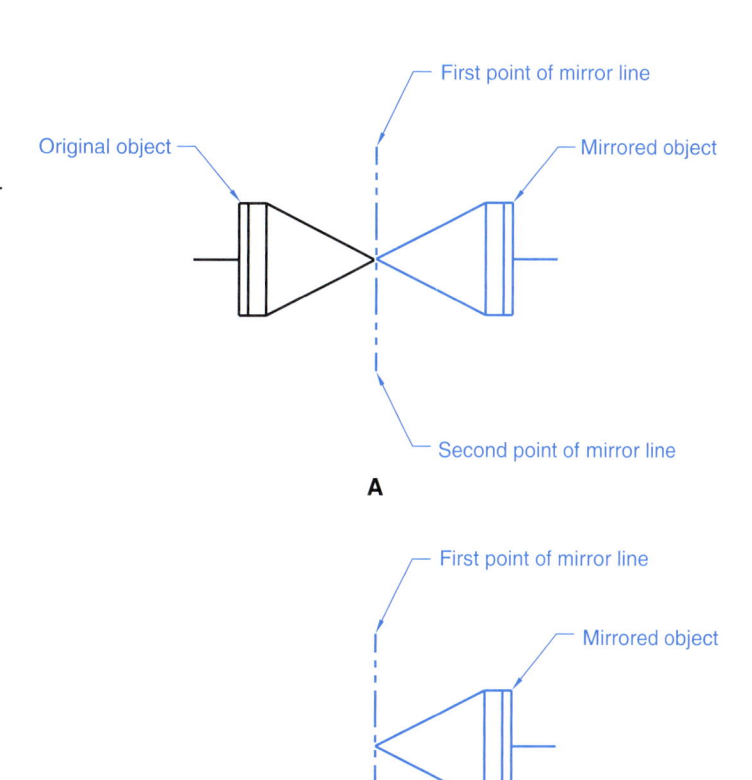

Field Notes

It is easy to create a vertical or horizontal mirror line if you have ORTHO on.

Exercise 7.7

1. Begin a new drawing.
2. Draw an object similar to the original object shown in Figure 7.12.
3. Use the COPY command to duplicate the object directly below its current position.
4. Mirror the first object without deleting the original object, similar to Figure 7.12A.
5. Mirror the second object and delete its mate, similar to Figure 7.12B.
6. Save the drawing as EX7.7.

Creating an Array of Objects

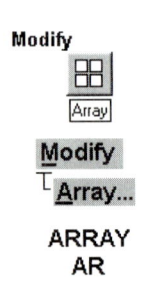

Modify
[Array]

Modify
└ Array...

ARRAY
AR

An **array** is a number of objects arranged in a pattern. The ARRAY command allows you to duplicate existing objects and place the new objects in a defined pattern. You can define rectangular patterns of rows and columns, or circular patterns. Before using the ARRAY command, you must create the original objects from which the pattern is to be made. The ARRAY command is accessed by picking Array … from the Modify pull-down menu, by picking the Array button from the Modify toolbar, or by typing **AR** or **ARRAY** at the Command: prompt. The ARRAY command displays the Array dialog box, where you define the pattern to create. Figure 7.13 shows the Array dialog box.

FIGURE 7.13 The Array dialog box is used to define a pattern of duplicated objects.

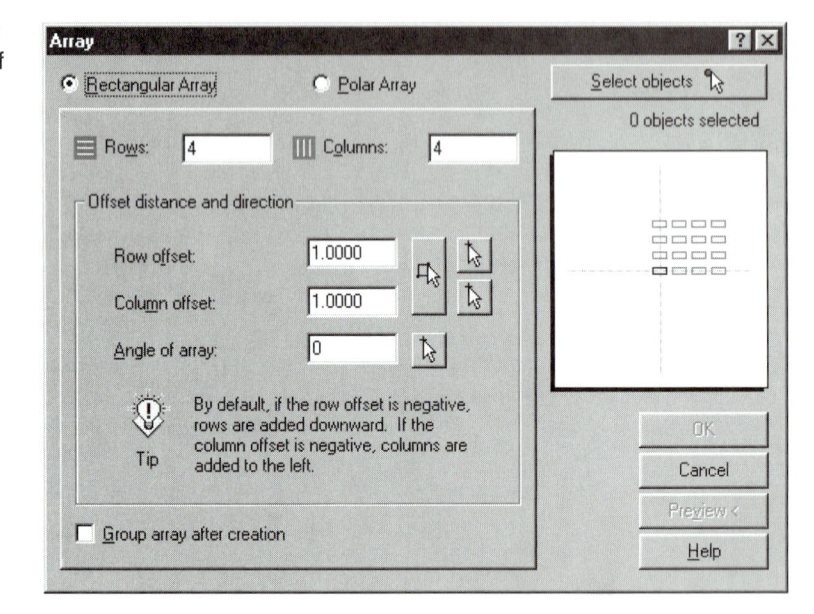

Creating a Rectangular Array

To create a rectangular array, select the radio button at the top of the dialog box labeled Rectangular array. This displays the options for controlling the size and appearance of a rectangular array. At the top right corner is the Select objects button. Unlike most buttons that temporarily hide a dialog box, this and other buttons on this dialog box do not display the "<" symbol. Picking this button does hide the dialog box and allows you to select objects through any standard selection method. When you return to the Array dialog box, the number of objects you selected appears below this button. If you pick the Select objects button again, the previous selection set is discarded, and you must select all the objects to be used in the array.

The Rows: and Columns: settings allow you to control how many rows and columns will be created. A *row* is a horizontal arrangement of objects, and a *column* is a vertical arrangement. The offset values control the distance from one pattern element to the next. The offset values behave exactly like coordinates: positive values move upward (rows) and to the right (columns), and negative values move downward and to the left. Figure 7.14 illustrates these features. The default angle of the rows is 0°, or you can adjust this value in the Angle of array: box. With each adjustment, the preview image is updated to show the results of your current settings.

You can enter the row and column values, distances and angles by typing numbers in the text boxes, or you can pick the values directly on-screen. Figure 7.15 shows the function of each of the selection buttons. When picking a point on-screen, you can use any standard point specification method and apply any appropriate object snap modes.

To get a full preview of the results before accepting the settings, pick the Preview < button. This temporarily hides the dialog box and shows your drawing as it will appear after the currently defined array pattern is created. The dialog box that is displayed prompts you to accept, modify, or cancel the pattern. Picking Accept returns you immediately to the Command: prompt and implements the array settings as they are. Picking Modify returns you to the Array dialog box, and picking Cancel returns you to the Command: prompt after canceling the array command.

CHAPTER 7 ||| Editing Your Drawing   247

FIGURE 7.14 The elements of a rectangular array.

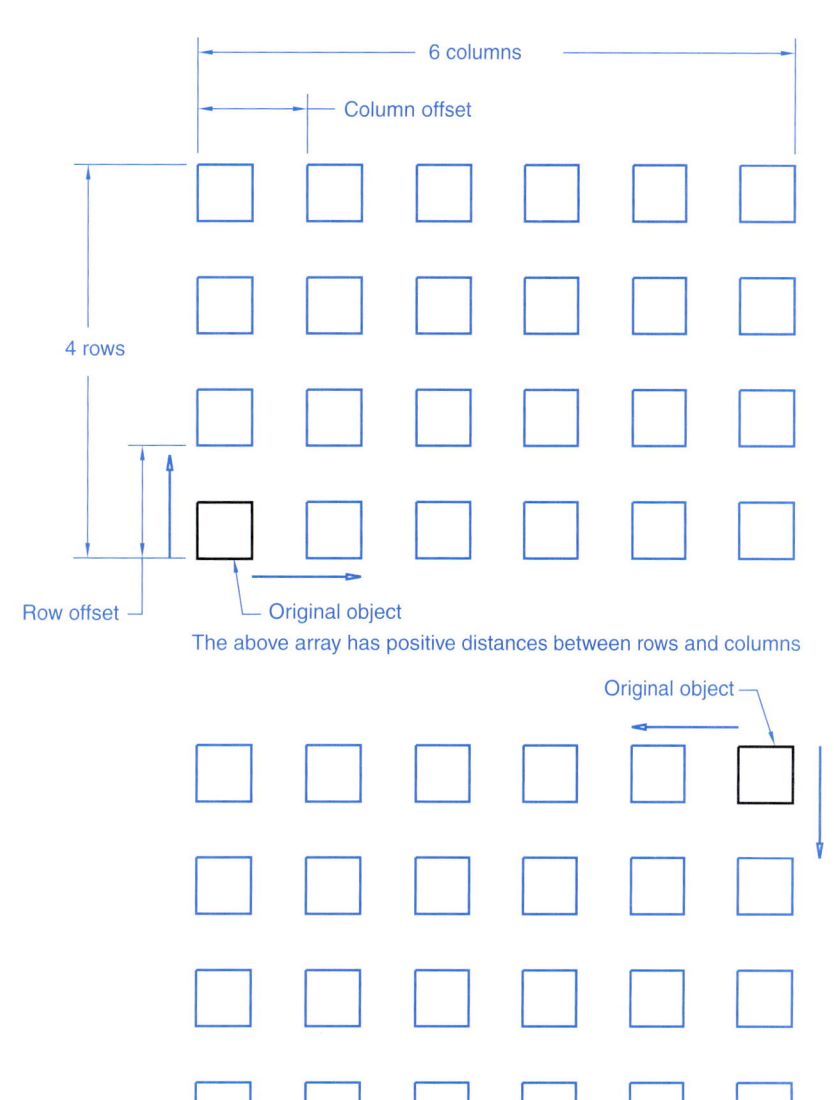

The above array has positive distances between rows and columns

The above array has negative distances between rows and columns

FIGURE 7.15 Values can be typed or picked directly from the screen.

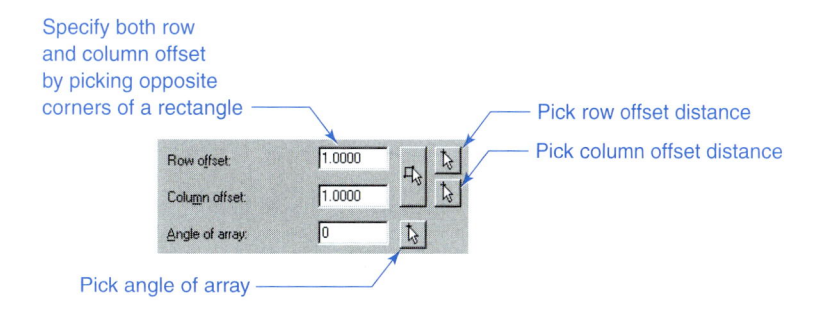

> ### Field Notes
>
> - If you undo a rectangular array, the angle specified for the angle of array becomes the current snap angle. Rotating the snap angle was discussed in Chapter 6. To restore the correct snap angle, undo one more time or use the DDRMODES command to reset it.
> - An option at the bottom of the Array dialog box allows you to group the objects in the array pattern. Grouping objects allows them to be selected and edited as though they were a single object. The GROUP command and working with groups is detailed in Chapter 12. It would be best to review the discussion of groups prior to using this option.

Creating a Polar Array

The polar array creates a circular pattern of objects. See Figure 7.16. Select the Polar array radio button at the top of the Array dialog box to display the polar pattern options. As with the rectangular array, you must select the objects used to create the array pattern. The Center point: is established by typing X and Y values or by picking a point on-screen.

In the *Method and values* area, specify the method for defining the array and the values to use. The available methods are as follows:

- **Total number of items & Angle to fill** — This option allows you to specify how many items, including the original, are to be created. They are equally spaced along a circle defined by the center point and the position of the original. The angle between items is automatically calculated.

- **Total number of items** — Again, you specify the total number of items in the pattern.

- **Angle to fill:** — This option automatically calculates the number of items. You indicate the total included angle of the pattern.

- **Angle between items:** — The included angle between items you indicate in the pattern.

FIGURE 7.16 The Polar array option is used to define a circular pattern of copies.

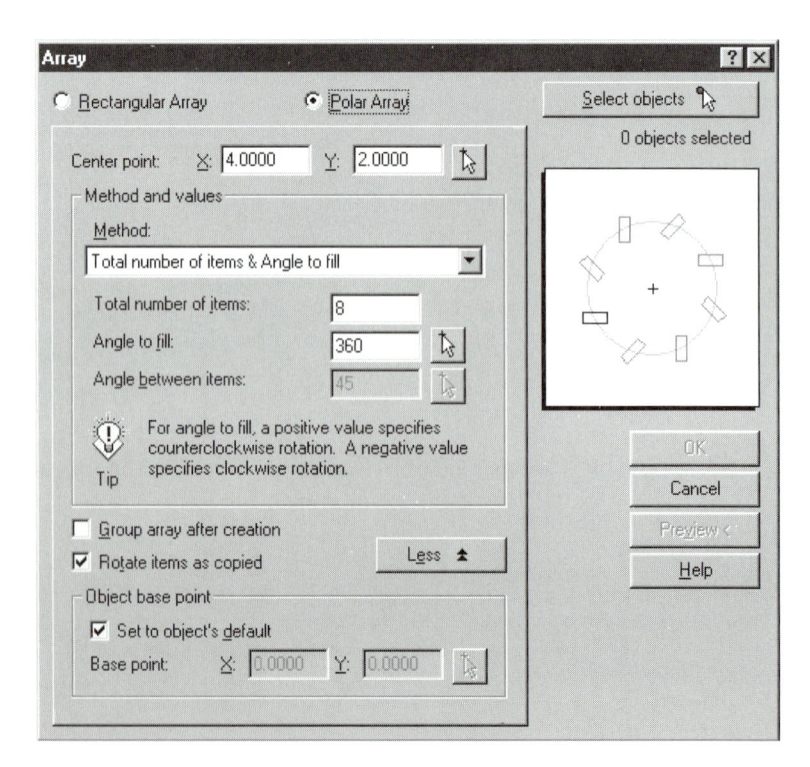

CHAPTER 7 ||| Editing Your Drawing

The three fields in this area are enabled or disabled based on the method you specify. If a positive value is indicated for the Angle to fill: field, the array expansion is counterclockwise. A negative value expands the pattern in a clockwise direction. An easy way to become familiar with the options in this dialog box is to change values and view the preview image to see the effects of the changes you make.

At the bottom of the dialog box, an option is provided for specifying whether the objects are rotated as they are placed around the polar array pattern. When you pick this toggle, the preview image is updated to show the effects on the pattern.

The More button turns to a Less button when selected. It also displays additional options. By default, AutoCAD LT uses object reference points based on the type of objects selected. The last object selected is used for calculation of the array rotation. The rotation is determined by the distance between the array center point and the object base point. The default object base points are as follows:

- Arcs, circles and ellipses—center point
- Polygons and rectangles—first corner
- Donuts, lines, polylines, rays and splines—starting point
- Blocks and text objects—insertion point
- Construction lines—midpoint
- Regions—grip point

If you need to use a different base point, remove the check mark next to Set to object's default. This enables the Base point: settings so they can be changed.

Exercise 7.8

1. Begin a new drawing.
2. Draw an object similar to the original object shown in Figure 7.14.
3. Copy the object into a rectangular array with six columns, four rows, 0.75 units between rows and columns.
4. Copy the original object to a location below the rectangular array that you just made. Leave enough room for a polar array.
5. Use the object that you just copied as the original object for a 360° polar array with a distance of 0.875 units from the center of the object to the center point of the array. Make a total of six copies. Do not rotate the objects.
6. Make another copy of the original object with enough room for a polar array, using the same specifications given in instruction 5. This time rotate the objects to see the difference.
7. Make another copy of the original object with enough room for another polar array. Use the previous specifications but use an angle of 30° between objects.
8. Save the drawing as EX7.8.

Changing an Object

AutoCAD LT provides a group of commands that allow you to change objects in relation to the original placement, position, size, or shape. These commands include MOVE, ROTATE, SCALE, and STRETCH.

Moving Objects

AutoCAD LT provides you with an easy ability to move objects by picking the Move button from the Modify toolbar, by picking Move in the Modify pull-down menu, or by typing **M** or **MOVE** at the Command: prompt. The MOVE command asks for a base point and second point of displacement just like the COPY command. However, the MOVE command places the original object in a new location. Look at Figure 7.17 as you follow this command sequence:

Modify

MOVE
M

```
Command: M or MOVE↵
Select objects: ⟨select the objects to move⟩
Select objects: ↵
Base point or displacement: ⟨pick a base point on the object to be moved⟩
Second point of displacement: ⟨pick a point for the new location⟩
Command:
```

FIGURE 7.17 Using the MOVE command.

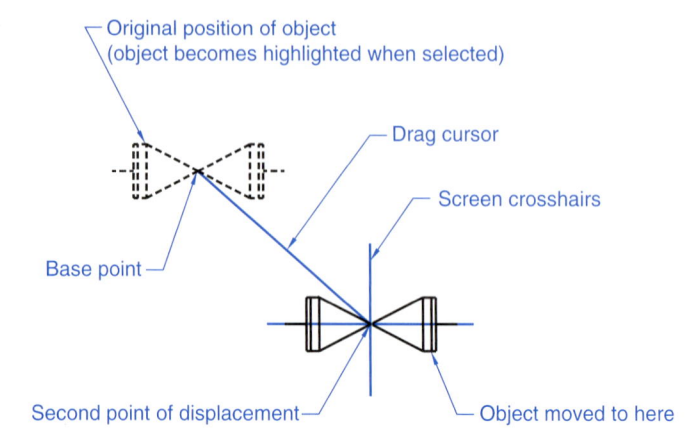

Field Notes

Refer to the earlier discussion covering the COPY command for a review of using and selecting the base point.

The displacement option is used when you enter a coordinate at the "<Base point or displacement>:" prompt and press Enter at the "Second point of displacement:" prompt. The copies are then placed at a location that is the specified X and Y distances from the original. This can also be done by picking the first point and pressing Enter at the second prompt. The picked point is then used as the X and Y values for displacement.

Exercise 7.9

1. Begin a new drawing.
2. Draw an object similar to the original object shown in Figure 7.17.
3. Move the object to a new position similar to the example given in Figure 7.17.
4. Save the drawing as EX7.9.

Rotating Objects

Modify

ROTATE
RO

The ability to rotate objects can be very useful. For example, the rotation of a house on the plot plan gives you the flexibility to determine the best solar orientation in relation to the property lines. In some drawings, such as an assembly drawing or auxiliary view, it may be easier to draw an object in a horizontal or vertical orientation and then rotate it into its correct position. AutoCAD provides two rotation options. You can rotate relative to the existing position of the object, or you can rotate an object with reference to a new angle. Rotate an object by picking the Rotate toolbar button, by picking Rotate in the Modify pull-down menu, or by typing **RO** or **ROTATE** at the Command: line prompt.

CHAPTER 7 ||| Editing Your Drawing

Rotating with a Relative Angle

Rotating objects using a relative angle means that the rotation angle is relative to the current angle of rotation, whatever that might be. For example, if a line object drawn at 0° is rotated with a relative angle of 45°, the new angle is 45°. However, a line drawn at 15° from horizontal that is rotated 45° is placed at a new angle of 60°, which is the result of 15° + 45°. When rotating objects using a relative angle, AutoCAD LT asks for a base point and a rotation angle. The rotation angle can be positive for a counterclockwise rotation or negative for a clockwise rotation. Zero degrees is at the right unless you changed it during setup. After picking the base point, the objects can be rotated dynamically by moving the cursor. You can manually rotate the object in this manner and pick the desired position. Look at Figure 7.18 as you follow this command sequence:

Command: **RO** or **ROTATE**↵
Select objects: ⟨*select the objects to rotate*⟩
Select objects: ↵
Base point: ⟨*pick a base point*⟩
<Rotation angle>/Reference: **45**↵
Command:

FIGURE 7.18 Using the ROTATE command with the Rotation angle option.

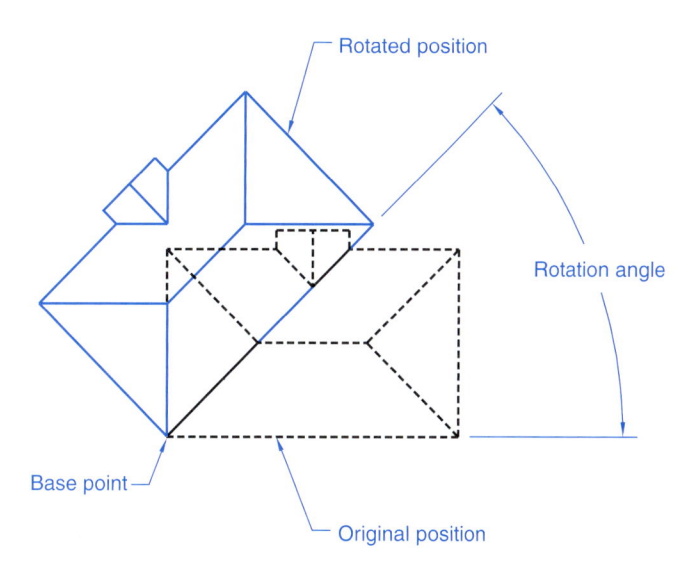

Field Notes

The previous discussion mentioned that counterclockwise angles are positive and clockwise angles are negative. Keep in mind that every negative angle has a positive counterpart. For example, −45° = +315°, −90° = +270°, −180° = +180°, and −270° = +90°.

Rotating with a Reference Angle

A reference angle allows you to rotate an object with reference to the angle of another object. To do this, pick two points on the existing object and then pick a reference point on the other object. You can also specify the angle of the existing object and then enter a new angle. Both the reference angle and the new angle are established from 0° horizontal. Keep in mind that 0° horizontal is relative to the settings of the current drawing and may not be horizontal if the settings were changed. The following command sequence is demonstrated in Figure 7.19:

Command: **RO** or **ROTATE**↵
Select objects: ⟨*select the objects to rotate*⟩
Select objects: ↵
Base point: ⟨*pick a base point*⟩
<Rotation angle>/Reference: **R**↵
Reference angle <0>: **45**↵
New angle: **90**↵
Command:

FIGURE 7.19 Using the ROTATE command with the Reference option.

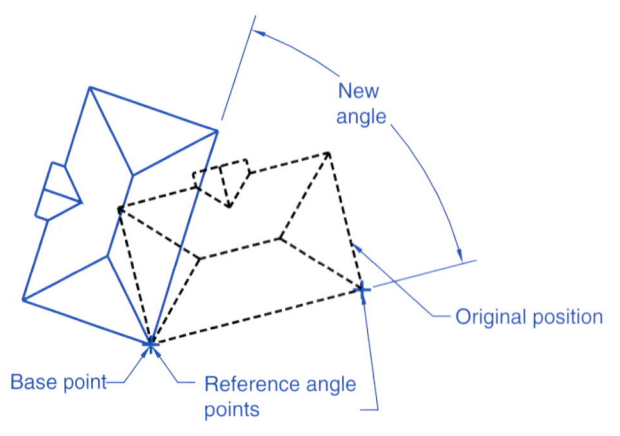

Defining the Reference angle by picking two points and typing the New angle

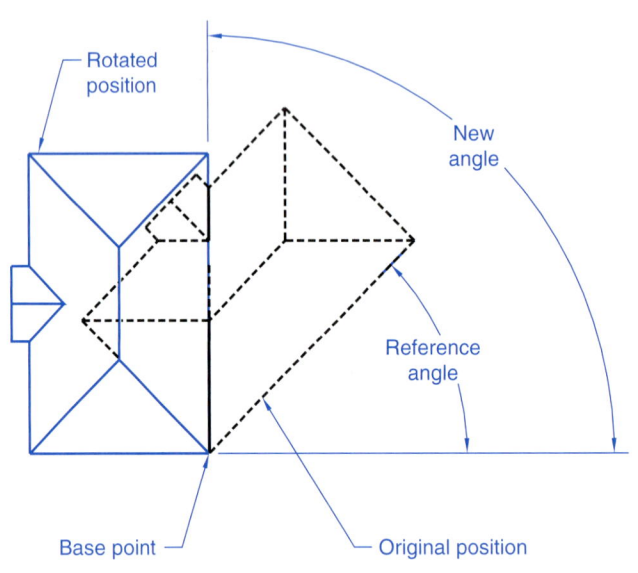

Defining the Reference angle and the New angle by typing the values at the keyboard

Field Notes

The following provides practical examples of how to use the Reference option.

- When an object to be rotated is at a known angle and the new angle is also known, but the difference between the angles requires use of a calculator, the known reference angle and the new angle can be entered numerically using the keyboard.
- When a destination angle is known but the current angle is not, the reference angle can be picked using any appropriate object snap mode and the new angle typed.
- A third option is to use either a picked or numerically entered reference angle followed by picking a point that defines the new angle from the specified base point, with accuracy requirements dictating the use of object snap or other precision drawing aids.

CHAPTER 7 ||| Editing Your Drawing   253

> **Exercise 7.10**
>
> 1. Begin a new drawing.
> 2. Draw an object similar to the roof plan shown in its original position in Figure 7.18.
> 3. Make two copies of the roof.
> 4. Rotate one of the roofs using a rotation angle of 45°. Rotate the object from its current position to a new angle of 90°.
> 5. Rotate another one of the roofs using a rotation angle of 45°. Rotate the object from its current position to a new angle of 217°.
> 6. Rotate the third roof visually using a relative rotation by picking any unknown angle simply by pointing and picking with the cursor. Now, rotate the roof again so it is at 90° by using the Reference option and picking the endpoints of the base line as the reference angle and 90° as the new angle.
> 7. Save the drawing as EX7.10.

Scaling Objects

Existing objects in an AutoCAD LT drawing can be scaled up or scaled down using the SCALE command. When you *scale* an object, it means you are making the object larger or smaller as required. In some cases you may need to scale one or more features of a drawing due to a design change. Another common use for scaling is when similar features exist in a drawing that are different sizes. Rather than duplicate your efforts by drawing the objects again at the new size, it is easier to copy the existing objects and then scale the new copy to the correct size. To access the SCALE command, pick the Scale button from the Modify toolbar, pick Scale from the Modify pull-down menu, or type **SC** or **SCALE** at the Command: prompt.

Modify

Scale

Modify
⌞ Scale

SCALE
SC

Scaling can be used to either reduce or enlarge the size of objects. AutoCAD LT allows you to scale objects by specifying a scale factor or a reference dimension. The original size has a scale factor of 1. A scale factor of less than 1 is used to reduce the size of the object, and a scale factor of more than 1 enlarges the object. Scaling with a reference dimension is done by establishing an existing dimension and then a new desired specification.

Using a Scale Factor to Scale Objects

When scaling objects, AutoCAD LT asks you to select the objects, pick a base point, and type a scale factor. The specified scale factor is used as a multiplier for the size and relative positions of the objects being resized. Negative and zero scale factors are not allowed. Figure 7.20 shows how the SCALE command works and the results of using various scale factors. This is the command sequence:

Command: **SC** or **SCALE**↵
Select objects: ⟨*select the objects to scale*⟩
Select objects: ↵
Base point: ⟨*pick a base point*⟩
<Scale factor>/Reference: **2**↵
Command:

As with many numeric value prompts in AutoCAD LT, an alternative method of entry is to pick points in your drawing rather than entering them at the prompts. When asked for the scale factor, you can move the cursor to see the objects change in size and relative position. If you pick a point, the distance from the base point to the final cursor location is measured and used as the scale factor. For example, if the distance is 2.51 units, a scale factor of 2.51 is used.

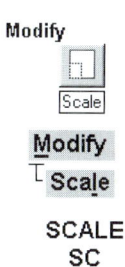

FIGURE 7.20 Using the SCALE command with the Scale factor option.

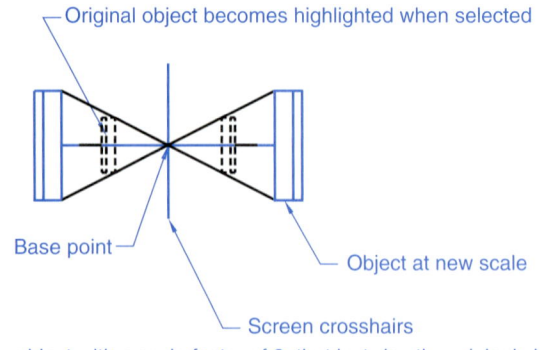

Scaling an object with a scale factor of 2, that is, twice the original size

Half size
scale factor = .5

Original size
scale factor = 1

One and one-half size
scale factor = 1.5

Using the Reference Option to Scale Objects

When using the Reference option to scale objects, you need to specify the reference length, which is the current length. The reference length can be 1, it can be the actual length of the object, or it can be established by picking two points on the object. You then specify a new length, which is either shorter or longer than the reference length. The new length can be the exact length that you want for the scaled object, or you can pick a point to where the object is to be scaled. The new length can also be established by dynamically dragging the object to the desired scale. The object is then scaled to match the new length. Refer to Figure 7.21 as you follow this command sequence:

```
Command: SC or SCALE↵
Select objects: ⟨select the objects to scale⟩
Select objects: ↵
Base point: ⟨pick a base point⟩
<Scale factor>//Reference: R↵
Reference length ⟨1⟩: .875↵
New length: 1.75↵
Command:
```

FIGURE 7.21 Using the SCALE command with the Reference option.

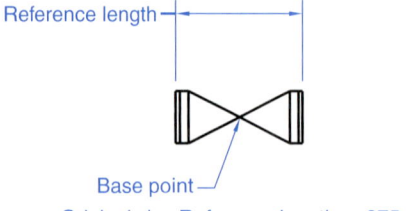

Original size Reference length = .875

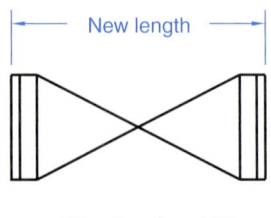

New length = 1.75

CHAPTER 7 ||| Editing Your Drawing

> ✎ Field Notes
>
> The following provides practical applications of the scaling Reference option:
>
> - One example is when an object to be scaled is at a known size and the new size is also known, but determination of the actual required scale factor requires use of a calculator. To deal with this situation, enter the known reference size and the new size numerically using the keyboard.
> - Another example is when a desired size is known but the current size is not. Now the reference length can be picked using any appropriate object snap mode and the new length typed.
> - A third example is using either a picked or numerically entered reference length followed by picking a point that defines the new size as the distance from the specified base point to the picked point, with accuracy, using object snap or other precision drawing aids.

Exercise 7.11

1. Open EX7.9.
2. Make six copies of the object with three above and three below.
3. Scale the top left object with a scale factor of .5.
4. Scale the top right object with a scale factor of 2.
5. Scale the bottom left object with a new length of .4375.
6. Scale the bottom right object with a scale factor of 1.75.
7. The middle objects in both rows remain at the original size for comparison.
8. Save the drawing as EX7.11.

Lengthening Objects

The LENGTHEN command is provided in AutoCAD LT to change the length of objects and the included angle of arcs. An *included angle* is the angle formed between the start point, endpoint, and center of the arc as shown in Figure 3.22 (Chapter 3). The LENGTHEN command does not work on closed objects or objects that have no length definition. When asked to select an object to lengthen, the end of the object closest to the pick point is the end that gets changed. Access this command by picking the Lengthen button from the Modify toolbar, by picking Lengthen from the Modify pull-down menu, or by typing **LEN** or **LENGTHEN** at the Command: prompt. Several options become available when this command is entered:

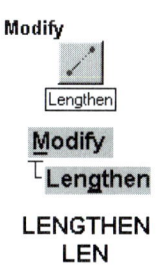

   Command: **LEN** or **LENGTHEN**↵
   DElta/Percent/Total/DYnamic/<Select object>:

Modify

Lengthen

Modify
⌐Lengthen

LENGTHEN
LEN

Using the Select Object Option
The Select object: option of the LENGTHEN command is the default and is simply used to give the length of an object and the included angle of an arc. Just pick any linear object or arc on the drawing and AutoCAD LT gives the length, and the included angle if the object is an arc. The object must have length definition. Objects that have length definition include lines, open or closed polylines, open or closed splines, arcs, circles, and ellipses. Several of these objects have limitations when using other lengthen options, but you can list the length of any of these object types.

Using the Delta Option
The Delta option of the LENGTHEN command is used to change the length of an object by a specified increment. Specify a positive increment to increase the length of a line or arc or a negative increment to decrease the length. Increase the length of an arc with a positive angle, or decrease an arc length with a negative angle. Note, however, that no object can be shortened to a zero length, and arcs cannot be lengthened to a full 360°. Several examples of the use of the Delta option are shown in Figure 7.22. The Delta option works like this:

```
Command: LEN or LENGTHEN↵
DElta/Percent/Total/DYnamic/<Select object>: DE↵
Angle/<Enter delta length (0.000)>: .5↵
<Select object to change>/Undo: ⟨pick the object to change⟩
```

The command continues with the option to pick another object to change, type **U** to undo the last change, or press Enter to exit the command:

```
<Select object to change>/Undo: ↵
Command:
```

The Angle suboption allows you to lengthen an arc by a positive included angle or shorten an arc with a negative included angle, as shown in Figure 7.22:

```
Angle/<Enter delta length (0.000)>: A↵
Enter delta angle <0.000>: 30↵
<Select object to change>/Undo: ⟨pick the arc⟩
<Select object to change>/Undo: ↵
Command:
```

FIGURE 7.22 Using the LENGTHEN command's Delta option.

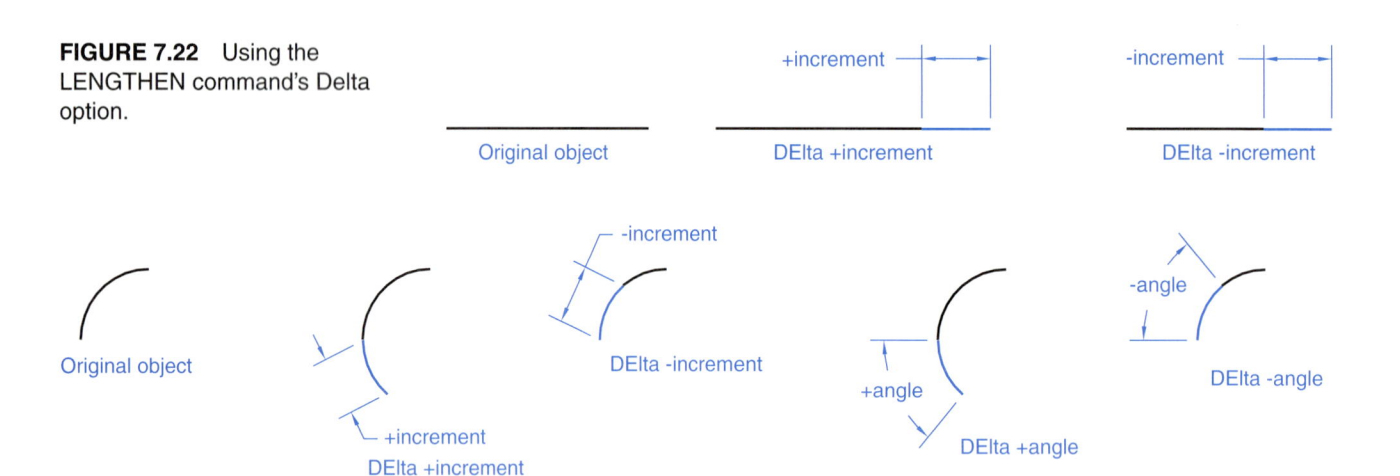

Using the Percent Option

The LENGTHEN command's Percent option is used to change the length of an object or the included angle of an arc by a specified percentage of the current length or included angle. The percentage is calculated according to the current length or included angle of the object selected at the time it is picked, and the percentage indicates total new length—not additional length. This means, for example, that if a percentage of 200% is specified, and a 1 unit long line is picked, it becomes 2 units long. Picking the same line again makes it 4 units long. A value of 100% has no effect, because 100% of anything is still the original value. Any changes made to the length of the line are made at the end nearest the pick point. Specify less than 100% to shorten an object or reduce the included angle, or indicate more than 100% to increase the length or included angle (see Figure 7.23). The following command sequence is used to increase the length of an object by 150%:

```
Command: LEN or LENGTHEN↵
DElta/Percent/Total/DYnamic/<Select object>: P↵
Enter percent length <100>: 150↵
<Select object to change>/Undo: ⟨select the object⟩
<Select object to change>/Undo: ↵
Command:
```

FIGURE 7.23 Using the LENGTHEN command's Percent option.

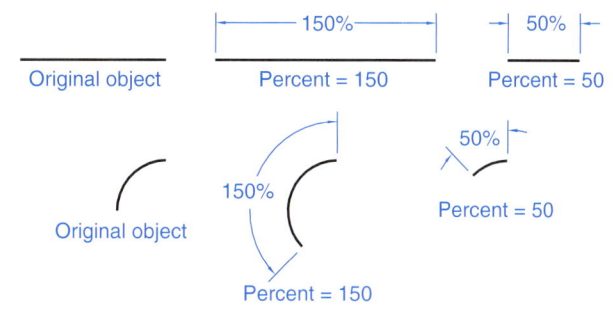

Field Notes

One common mistake users make when learning to use the percentage option is that they try to use decimal values instead of the intended percentage. For example, consider a user who is trying to reduce an object's length by one-half and specifies value of 0.5 as the percentage. Unfortunately, this is actually 0.5%, or one-half of 1%, and results in a *very* short object. The percentage specified to reduce an object length by one-half is 50%.

Using the Total Option

The LENGTHEN command's Total option is used to change the length of an object or the included angle of an arc to a specified total length or included angle. The shortening or lengthening required to change the total length of the object to the new specification is performed on the end nearest to the pick point. Therefore, the total length is actually measured from the opposite end, which remains fixed. This option makes it easy to specify an exact length or included angle. Figure 7.24 demonstrates this command sequence:

Command: **LEN** or **LENGTHEN**↵
DElta/Percent/Total/DYnamic/<Select object>: **T**↵
Angle/<Enter total length (1.00)>: **1.25**↵
<Select object to change>/Undo: ⟨*select the object*⟩
<Select object to change>/Undo: ↵
Command:

FIGURE 7.24 Using the LENGTHEN command's Total option.

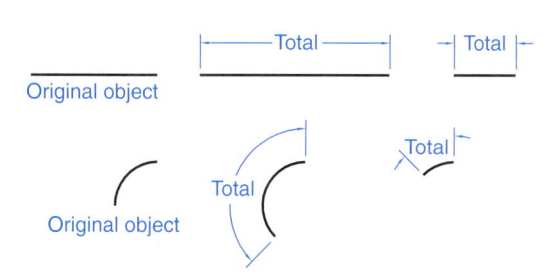

The Angle suboption asks you to enter the total included angle of an arc. Virtually any total value can be specified, but the smallest length value that AutoCAD LT uses is about 0.000001 units. When specifying angles for an arc, acceptable angles must be greater than 0.00005° and less than 360°.

Using the Dynamic Option

The LENGTHEN command's Dynamic option allows you to visually change the length of an object or the included angle of an arc by dragging one of the endpoints to the desired length. When dynamically lengthening an object such as a line, the new length is indicated by the distance between the fixed opposite end and the current cursor location. This can be used in combination with object snap, especially a PERpendicular mode, to accurately place the new location of the selected end. When using the Dynamic option on an arc, the true effects of your cursor movements may not be so obvious. A dragline connects the cursor to the original position of the selected arc endpoint, and moving your cursor either lengthens or shortens the arc. This is not a result of the current length of the dragline, as with a line object. What is actually happening is that the Dynamic option adjusts the included angle to match the absolute angle from the *arc center* to the *current cursor location*. This is used as a total value and is not relative to any current angle. Complex objects such as polylines and splines cannot be lengthened using the Dynamic option. This is the command sequence:

Command: **LEN** or **LENGTHEN.**↵
DElta/Percent/Total/DYnamic/<Select object>: **DY**↵
Specify new endpoint.
<Select object to change>/Undo: ⟨*select the object and drag from the desired endpoint*⟩
<Select object to change>/Undo: ↵
Command:

> ### Field Notes
>
> The Delta and Total options of the LENGTHEN command allow the value to be specified either by typing a numeric value or by picking two points on screen. However, one aspect of the Delta option can cause unexpected results when specifying the value by picking points. If the current delta value is positive, a picked distance is interpreted as a positive distance. When the current delta value is negative, any picked distance is automatically interpreted as a negative value. Therefore, if the current delta value is negative and you pick two points to describe a positive value of 4 units, for example, then the new delta value is −4.0 regardless of the direction of the pick or any other factors.

Exercise 7.12

1. Begin a new drawing.
2. Draw a line 1.5 in. long and a quarter circle arc with a .5-in. radius similar to the original objects shown in Figure 7.22.
3. Make 7 copies (8 total) of the line and 9 copies (10 total) of the arc.
4. Do the following to each line:
   - \+ increment
   - − increment
   - 150%
   - 50%
   - 2.25 total
   - .5 total
   - \+ dynamic
   - − dynamic
5. Do the following to each arc:
   - \+ increment
   - − increment
   - Delta + angle
   - Delta − angle
   - 150%
   - 50%
   - 2.25 total
   - .5 total
   - \+ dynamic
   - − dynamic
6. Save the drawing as EX7.12.

CHAPTER 7 ||| Editing Your Drawing

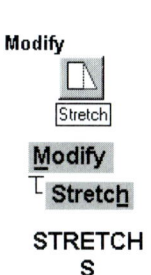

Stretching Objects

The STRETCH command is used to change the location of the defining points for one or more objects in a drawing. Depending on the object type, all or just some of the defining points can be relocated using STRETCH. For example, either one or both of the endpoints of a line can be relocated. If both points are moved the same relative distance, the effect is the same as a MOVE command. If only one of the endpoints is moved, the other remains fixed and the final effect is that the line is stretched to a new length, in a new direction, or both.

The points to be moved by a STRETCH command must be surrounded by a selection window option: Window, Crossing, Window Polygon, or Crossing Polygon. If you specify one window and then another, only the points surrounded by the last window are affected; any previous window specifications are discarded. Also, only the objects selected are affected, whether or not their defining points are surrounded. It is often easiest to use one of the crossing options because the desired points are surrounded and all of the needed objects are selected.

To access the STRETCH command, pick the Stretch button from the Modify toolbar, pick Stretch from the Modify pull-down menu, or type **S** or **STRETCH** at the Command: prompt. To learn the use of this command through an easy approach, start with selecting using a crossing box. Study the use and effects of the STRETCH command in Figure 7.25. The following command sequence is shown in Figure 7.25:

Command: **S** or **STRETCH**↵
Select objects to stretch by crossing-window or -polygon ...
Select objects: ⟨*use a crossing window or polygon to select the objects*⟩
Select objects: ↵
Base point or displacement: ⟨*pick a base point*⟩
Second point of displacement: ⟨*pick the second point of displacement*⟩
Command:

Modify

STRETCH
S

FIGURE 7.25 Using the STRETCH command.

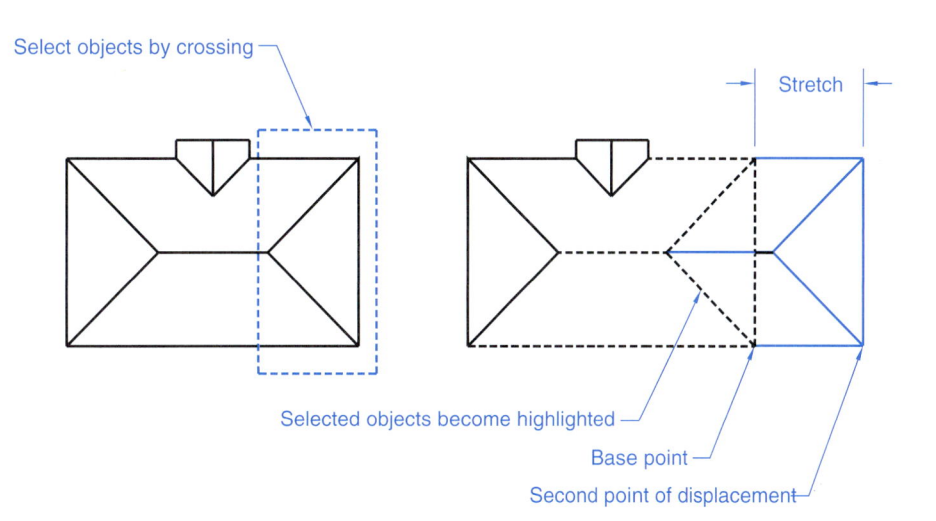

The example in Figure 7.25 can be selected easily by a crossing box. Notice that the three horizontal lines are stretched out, but the vertical line and angled lines are actually just moved. This is because the other ends of the horizontal lines were not surrounded by the selection window option, so they remain fixed. Both of the endpoints of the vertical line were surrounded and therefore both ends were moved the same distance.

This STRETCH command has a variety of uses and is very powerful when understood properly. The following examples help explain the effect of stretch on different object types and how different objects must be selected with the window specification to be affected:

- Circles are unaffected unless the center is surrounded.
- Arcs and lines must have one or both endpoints surrounded.
- Only surrounded vertices on polylines and splines are affected. Polylines are discussed in Chapter 8.
- A Crossing Polygon should be used for complex stretching needs.
- Use the Remove option to remove objects from the selection set with individual picks.
- The Window and Window Polygon options can be used, but their results may be undesirable.

FIGURE 7.26 Moving objects with the STRETCH command.

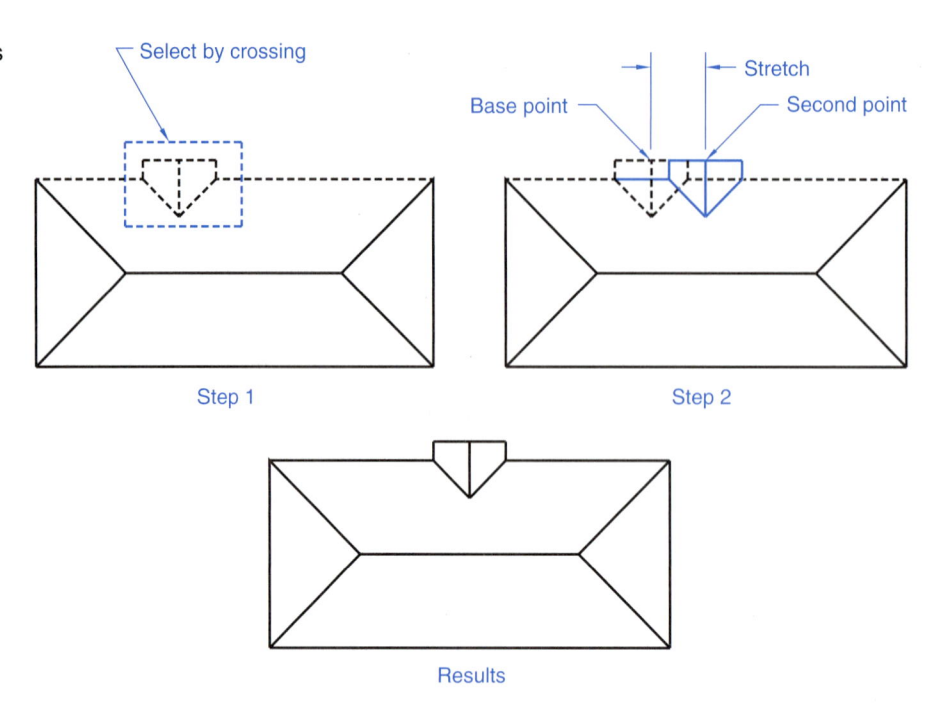

- Objects to be stretched that are not selected by the Window options can be picked individually.
- You can use the pick box to pick a line or the Window option to surround a line, and you stretch the endpoint just as if you had selected using a Crossing box.
- The idea behind using the Crossing options is to select everything inside and crossing the box or polygon. These options are often a convenient selection method.

The STRETCH command can be used with a variety of selection options for different results, as shown in Figure 7.26.

Field Notes

- Consider using ORTHO in conjunction with STRETCH to conveniently stretch the object horizontally or vertically.
- If you specify one window, and then another, only the points surrounded by the last window are affected; any previous window specifications are discarded.

Exercise 7.13

1. Begin a new drawing.
2. Draw a house roof plan similar to the original (left side) shown in Figure 7.25.
3. Stretch the roof similar to the operation shown in Figure 7.25.
4. Move the dormer to the center of the building by stretching and perform other stretching operations, as was done in Figure 7.26.
5. Save the drawing as EX7.13.

LEARNING CHECKPOINT

- Identify at least five ways to enter the COPY command.
- What is the base point and what are commonly selected base points?
- What is the second point of displacement?

- Name the command that is used to make parallel copies.
- Describe the purpose of the mirror line.
- Define an array.
- What are two types of arrays?
- Explain the difference between the COPY and MOVE commands.
- Name the command that allows you to pivot objects at a base point to a desired angle.
- Describe the difference between the SCALE command's scale factor and reference options.
- What is the purpose of the LENGTHEN command?
- Discuss the primary difference between the LENGTHEN and STRETCH commands.

Editing with Grips

As explained earlier, grips are displayed if you select objects before entering a command. In Chapter 2 you learned that you can select an object and then enter the ERASE command to have the object removed. This is the simplest form of selecting an object before entering the command. Grips allow you to perform several key editing operations quickly and conveniently, because you select objects and enter the command at the same time. To see how to use the grip commands, select a line object and then select the grip at the end of the line. The selected grip becomes solid red by default and the command line reads like this:

```
Command:
**STRETCH**
<Stretch to point>/Base point/Copy/Undo/eXit:
```

STRETCH is the first command that is activated when you select a grip. Every time you press the space bar or Enter key, you get another command. The grip commands include STRETCH, MOVE, ROTATE, SCALE, and MIRROR. AutoCAD LT cycles through each of these commands as you press the space bar or Enter key. Keep cycling until you get the desired command like this:

```
Command:
**STRETCH**
<Stretch to point>/Base point/Copy/Undo/eXit: ↵
**MOVE**
<Move to point>/Base point/Copy/Undo/eXit: ↵
**ROTATE**
<Rotation angle>/Base point/Copy/Undo/Reference/eXit: ↵
**SCALE**
<Scale factor>/Base point/Copy/Undo/Reference/eXit: ↵
**MIRROR**
<Second point>/Base point/Copy/Undo/eXit: ↵
**STRETCH**
<Stretch to point>/Base point/Copy/Undo/eXit:
```

The options associated with these commands should look familiar from the previous discussions. Exit the grip mode by typing **X** for exit or press the Esc key. Press Esc twice to remove the grips from the display. The first Esc keystroke deselects the highlighted object and the second hides the grips.

> ### ✏️ Field Notes
>
> - You can press the space bar or Enter key to cycle through the grip editing commands or you can use the keyboard shortcut to go directly to the desired editing command. The keyboard shortcuts are ST for STRETCH, MO for MOVE, RO for ROTATE, SC for SCALE, MI for MIRROR.
> - Another way to access the grip editing commands is to select a grip and then press the right mouse button. This displays the Grips popup menu. The menu has the editing options Move, Mirror, Rotate, Scale and Stretch. It also has the options Base Point, Copy, Reference, Undo, and Exit. The first selection in this menu is Properties ..., which is explained later.
> - The Base point option in each of the grip commands is used to pick a new base point. This does not change the selected grip, it just changes the base point. To use the Base point option, type **B** and press Enter. You then get the Base point: prompt. Now, pick a new base point.

Stretching with Grips

When you select a grip, the first command issued is STRETCH. This allows you to move the selected grip to a new location and stretch the object along with it. Figure 7.27 shows a line being stretched with grips following these steps:

Pick the line.
Pick a grip to select and get this command:
Command:
STRETCH
<Stretch to point>/Base point/Copy/Undo/eXit: ⟨*move the selected grip to a desired location and pick—the line is now stretched as shown in Figure 7.27.*⟩

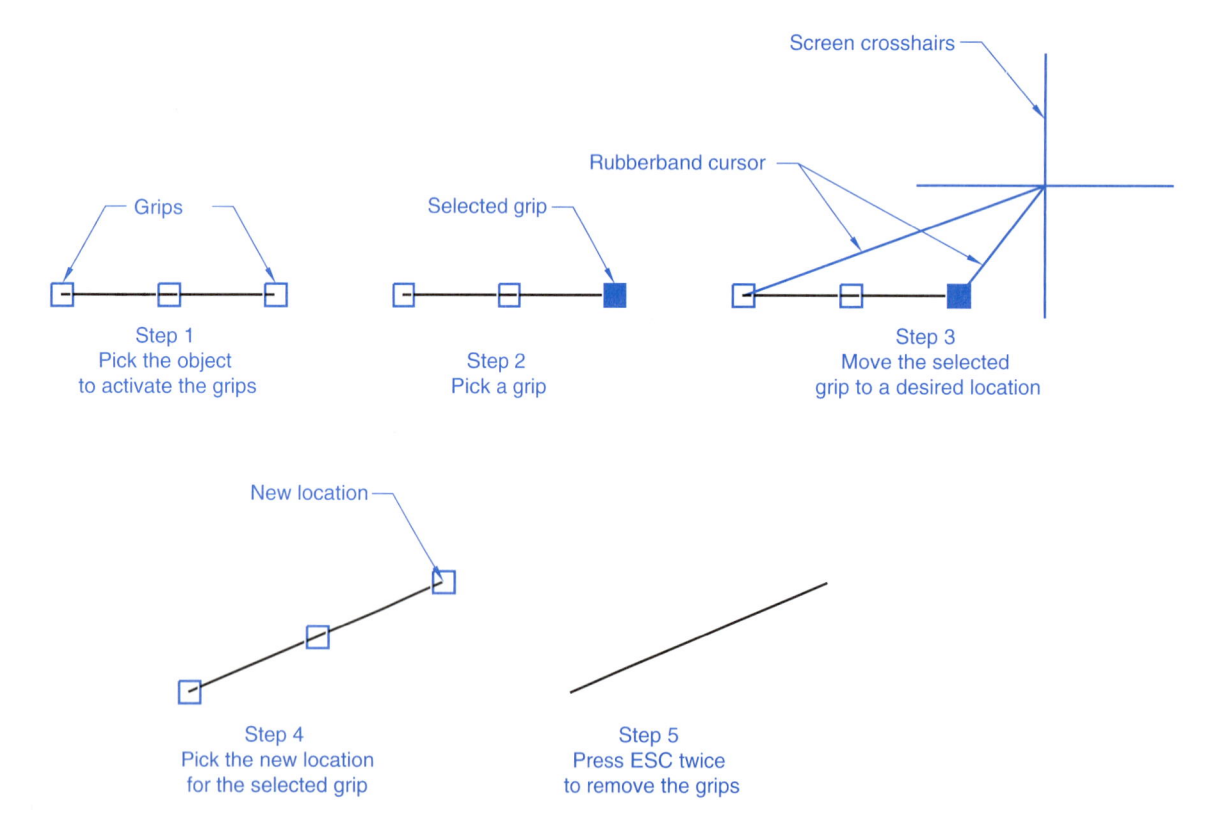

FIGURE 7.27 A line being stretched with grips.

CHAPTER 7 ||| Editing Your Drawing

If you have more than one object to stretch at the same time, you can select two or more grips to edit by holding down the Shift key and picking the desired grips. Release the Shift key after the grips are selected and then pick one of the selected grips as the base point. Figure 7.28 shows how to stretch two lines by selecting two grips, and how to stretch a roof by selecting three grips. One selected grip in each example is picked as the base point. Follow these steps to stretch each of the examples separately:

Select the objects. In the roof example, use a crossing box to select only the lines that will be stretched.
Hold down the Shift key and select the grips—two for the parallel line example and three for the roof example.
Release the Shift key and pick a selected grip to act as a base point.
Command:
STRETCH
<Stretch to point>/Base point/Copy/Undo/eXit: ⟨*move the selected grip to a desired location and pick—the objects are stretched separately as shown in Figure 7.28*⟩

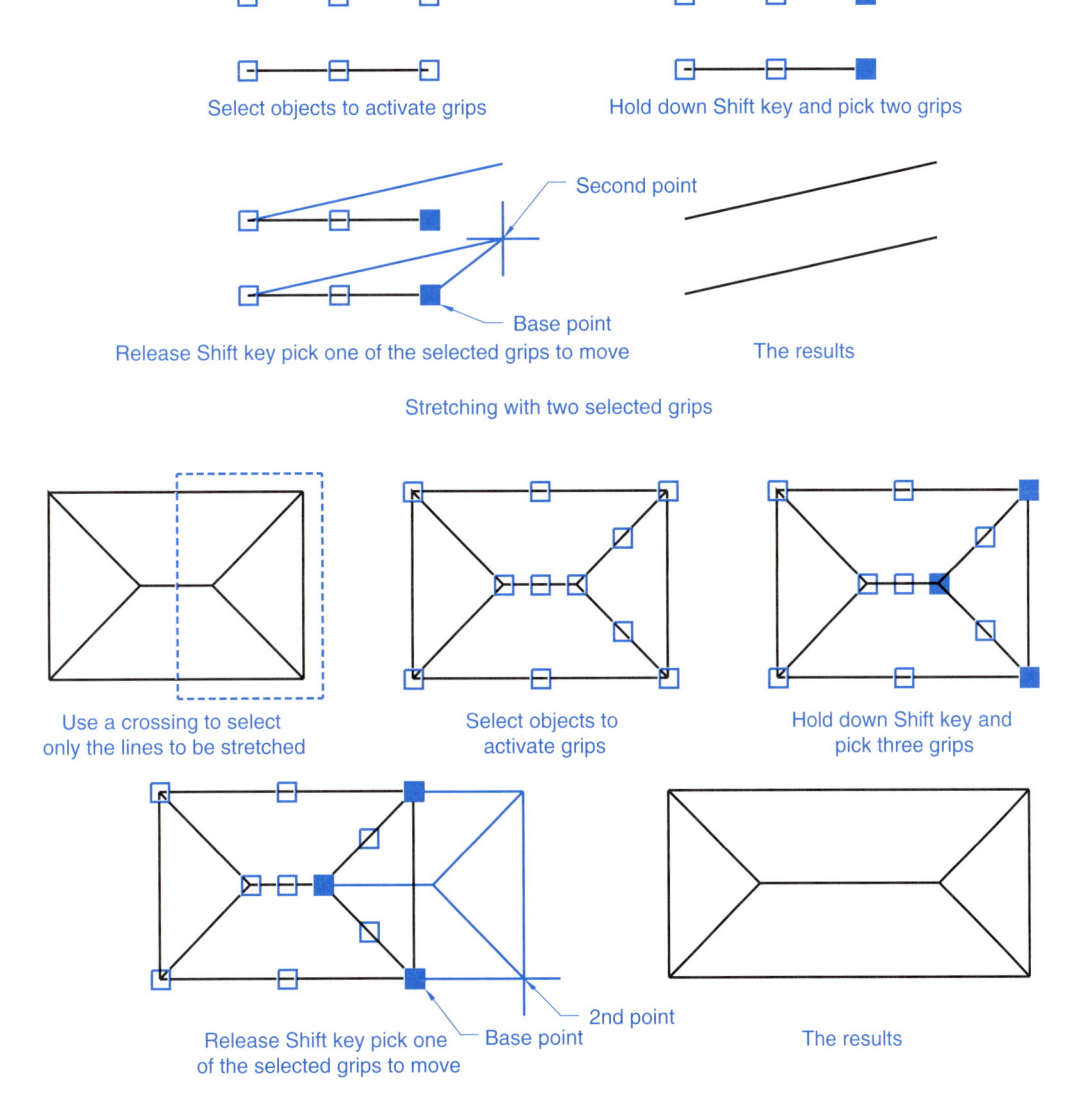

FIGURE 7.28 Stretching with more than one grip selected.

Copying with the Grips STRETCH Command

The grips STRETCH command also has a Copy option that allows you to make multiple stretches of the object. Access this option by typing **C** like this:

> *Select the objects.*
> *Pick a grip to select and get this command:*
> Command:
> **STRETCH**
> <Stretch to point>/Base point/Copy/Undo/eXit: **C**↵
> **STRETCH (multiple)**
> <Stretch to point>/Base point/Copy/Undo/eXit: ⟨*move the cursor to a desired location and pick*⟩
> **STRETCH (multiple)**
> <Stretch to point>/Base point/Copy/Undo/eXit: ⟨*move the cursor to a desired location and pick*⟩
> **STRETCH (multiple)**
> <Stretch to point>/Base point/Copy/Undo/eXit: ⟨*press Enter or type X for exit when done*⟩
> Command:

> ### Field Notes
>
> - If you hold down the Shift key while making the first pick and then release, each new pick creates a new copy at a freely picked point.
> - If you hold down the Shift key while picking the new points, the copies are placed at an offset point based on the first two selected points.
> - The selection process using grips is the same as normal selections. To remove objects from the selection set, press the Shift key while picking a single object, a window, or a crossing. Picking an object a second time in this manner hides its grips.
> - When you are picking multiple grips to edit, you must press the Shift key while selecting each of the grips. If you accidentally miss the grip and pick a point on the selected object, it is then unselected. You can release the Shift key and pick it again to bring it back into the selection set.
> - You can use the grips STRETCH command to move objects when you select a grip at the midpoint of a line, center of a circle, insertion point of text or a block, or on a point object.
> - While inside a grip command, you can type **B** to establish a new base point together with the Copy option to make multiple copies at different base points.

> ### Exercise 7.14
>
> 1. Begin a new drawing.
> 2. Draw a line similar to the one shown in Step 1 in Figure 7.27.
> 3. Use grips to stretch the line as shown in Figure 7.27.
> 4. Draw two parallel lines and use grips to stretch them as shown in the first example in Figure 7.28.
> 5. Draw a house roof plan similar to the second example shown in Figure 7.28.
> 6. Stretch the roof similar to the operation in the second example shown in Figure 7.28.
> 7. Save the drawing as EX7.14.

Moving with Grips

To move objects using grips, all you have to do is select the objects, select a grip to be the base point, and then move to the desired location and pick. The MOVE command works like this:

> *Select the objects as shown in Figure 7.29.*
> *Select a grip and then press the space bar or Enter key until you get this grip command, select* <u>M</u>*ove*
>   *from the popup menu, or type MO:*
> **MOVE**
> <Move to point>/Base point/Copy/Undo/eXit: ↵
> *Move the cursor and pick a new location for the objects.*

FIGURE 7.29 Moving an object with grips.

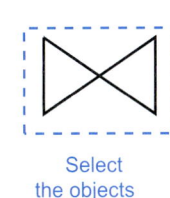

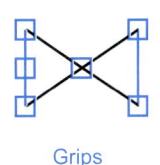

Select the objects   Grips are displayed   Select a grip   Move to the new place

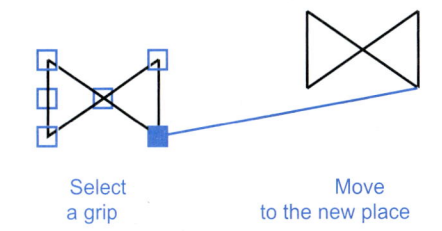

> ### Field Notes
> - All grip selected objects are moved, regardless of whether any other grips are selected.
> - A new base point can be specified at *any time* for both single move operations or multiple copy operations.

Copying with the Grips MOVE Command

The grips MOVE command has a Copy option that allows you to copy objects. The Copy option can be used to pick the locations for copies, or you can use snap locations. The Copy option works like this to pick copy locations:

Select the objects as shown in Figure 7.30.
Select a grip and then select Copy from the popup menu, or press the space bar or Enter key until you get this grip command and type C:
MOVE
<Move to point>/Base point/Copy/Undo/eXit: **C↵**
MOVE (multiple)
<Move to point>/Base point/Copy/Undo/eXit:
The MOVE (multiple) command actually makes copies. Move the cursor and pick location for as many copies as desired. Press Enter when done.

You can also place multiple copies at regularly spaced intervals with offset snap locations. **Offset snap locations** are established by the distance between the selected object and the location of the first copy. All other copies are then placed at an offset distance equal to the first distance. Figure 7.30A displays this application and allows you to see the difference between picking the copies in Figure 7.30B. The following sequence is used to demonstrate this process:

Select the objects as shown in Figure 7.30B.
Select a grip and then select Copy from the popup menu, or press the space bar or Enter key, or type MO to get this grip command and then type C:
MOVE
<Move to point>/Base point/Copy/Undo/eXit: **C↵**
MOVE (multiple)
<Move to point>/Base point/Copy/Undo/eXit:

- *Move the cursor and pick location for the first copy. The distance between the selected object and the first copy is the offset snap distance.*
- *Hold down the Shift key and place additional copies. The additional copies are automatically placed at the same offset snap distance.*
- *Press Enter when done.*

FIGURE 7.30 Copying an object with grips. (A) Making copies with the offset snap location method. (B) Picking the location of multiple copies.

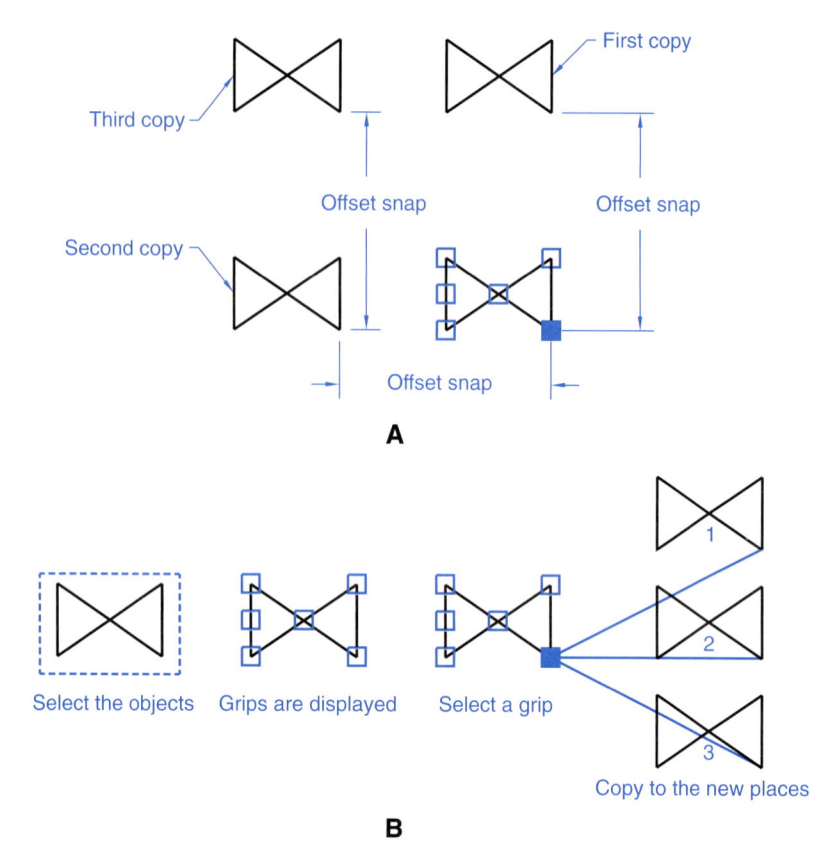

Exercise 7.15

1. Begin a new drawing.
2. Draw an object similar to the original object shown in Figure 7.29.
3. Use grips to move the object as shown in Figure 7.29.
4. Use grips and the MOVE Copy option to make copies of the objects shown in Figures 7.30A and B.
5. Save the drawing as EX7.15.

Rotating with Grips

You can use the ROTATE grip command to rotate objects by selecting a grip as a base point and then either rotating and picking the desired position or entering a rotation angle. The grip ROTATE command works like this:

Select the objects as shown in Figure 7.31.
Select a grip and then press the space bar or Enter key until you get this grip command, select Rotate from the popup menu, or type RO:
ROTATE
<Rotation angle>/Base point/Copy/Undo/Reference/eXit: ⟨*rotate by dragging and pick or type an angle such as* **45** *and press Enter*⟩

FIGURE 7.31 Rotating an object with grips.

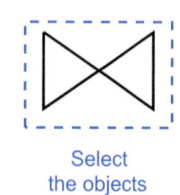

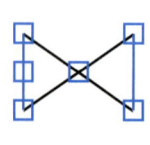

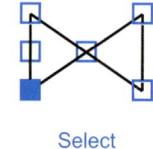

CHAPTER 7 ||| Editing Your Drawing   **267**

> ✎ Field Notes
>
> The ability to change the base point while determining a rotation specification, even between individual copies when using the multiple copy option, gives you maximum flexibility.

Making Multiple Rotations

The grip ROTATE command, as previously discussed, makes a single rotation unless you enter the Copy option. The Copy option lets you make multiple rotations. Enter the ROTATE Copy option like this:

Select the objects.
Select a grip and then press the space bar or Enter key until you get this grip command, select Rotate
   from the popup menu, or type RO:
ROTATE
<Rotation angle>/Base point/Copy/Undo/Reference/eXit: **C**↵
ROTATE (multiple)
<Rotation angle>/Base point/Copy/Undo/Reference/eXit: 〈*drag the objects and pick the desired*
   rotations or type angles and press Enter after each; press Enter when done.〉

Using the Grip Rotation Reference Option

The grip ROTATE command's Reference option works just like the ROTATE command Reference option discussed earlier in this chapter. Follow these steps:

Select the objects.
Select a grip and then press the space bar or Enter key until you get this grip command, select Rotate
   from the popup menu, or type RO:
ROTATE
<Rotation angle>/Base point/Copy/Undo/Reference/eXit: **R**↵
Reference angle <0>: 〈*enter a reference angle of pick points*〉
ROTATE
<New angle>/Base point/Copy/Undo/Reference/eXit: 〈*type a new angle or pick points*〉

Exercise 7.16

1. Open EX7.15.
2. Select one of the objects.
3. Use grips to rotate the object as shown in Figure 7.31.
4. Select another one of the objects.
5. Use grips and the ROTATE command's Copy option to make three rotated copies of the object.
6. Save the drawing as EX7.16.

Scaling with Grips

You can resize objects by using the grips SCALE command. This command allows you to select a grip and then scale the objects by moving the cursor to dynamically drag the objects to the desired scale, or you can type a scale factor and press Enter. You can also use the Reference option, which works the same way as previously described when using the Reference option to scale objects. Follow these steps when scaling objects with grips (see Figure 7.32):

Select the objects.
Select a grip and then press the space bar or Enter key until you get this grip command, select Scale
   from the popup menu, or type SC:
SCALE
<Scale factor>/Base point/Copy/Undo/Reference/eXit: 〈*move the cursor to size the object or type a*
   scale factor such as **.5** *to scale down or* **1.5** *to scale up and press Enter* ↵〉

FIGURE 7.32 Using the Scale factor option to scale objects with grips.

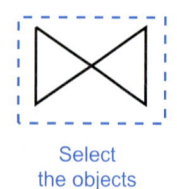

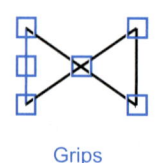

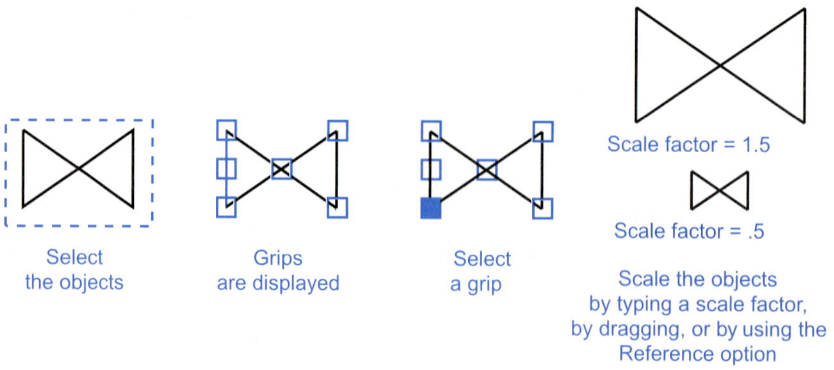

Select the objects | Grips are displayed | Select a grip | Scale factor = 1.5 / Scale factor = .5 / Scale the objects by typing a scale factor, by dragging, or by using the Reference option

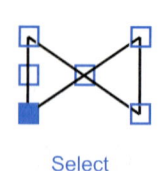

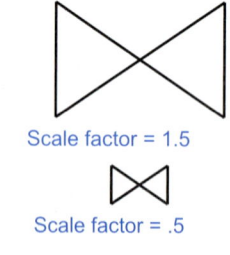

> **Field Notes**
>
> The ability to change the base point while determining a scale factor, even between individual copies when using the multiple copy option, gives you maximum flexibility.

Exercise 7.17

1. Open EX7.16.
2. Select one of the objects.
3. Use grips to scale the object with a 0.5 scale factor.
4. Select another one of the objects and use the grips to scale the object with a 1.5 scale factor.
5. Save the drawing as EX7.17.

Mirroring with Grips

You can easily mirror objects with grips by selecting the objects, selecting a grip, and then accessing the grip MIRROR command. The grip you select automatically becomes the first point of the mirror line. Now, move the cursor and pick the second point of the mirror line. Having ORTHO on helps establish a vertical or horizontal mirror line. Use the Base point option if you want to select another point to be the first mirror line point. The MIRROR command automatically removes the original object, as shown in Figure 7.33.

> **Field Notes**
>
> The base point for the mirror line need not be a grip point. It can be picked anywhere, typed with coordinates, or picked using object snap or any other valid point entry method. This is true for all of the grip command options.

CHAPTER 7 ||| Editing Your Drawing

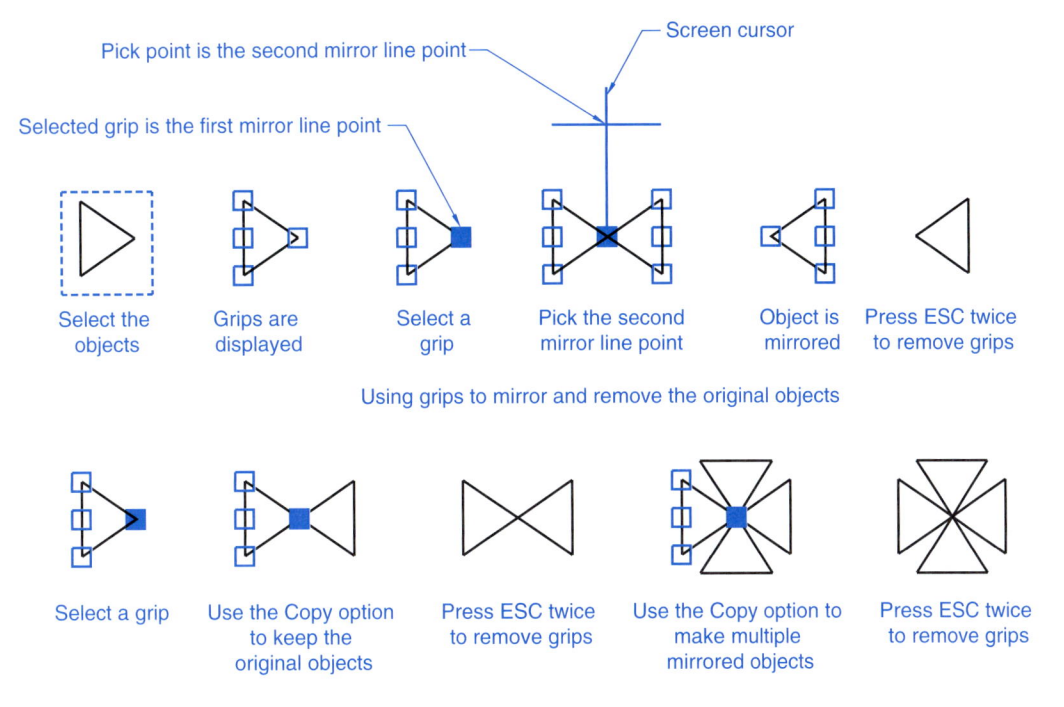

FIGURE 7.33 Mirroring objects with grips.

Use the Copy option or hold down the Shift key when picking the second point of the mirror line. This activates the multiple MIRROR command and keeps the original object while allowing you to mirror more than one of the objects if needed. Press Enter or type **X** for exit to get back to the Command: prompt. Use the Base point and Copy options together to change base points while making one or more mirrored objects (see Figure 7.33). The grips MIRROR command works like this:

Select the objects as shown in Figure 7.33.
Select a grip and then press the space bar or Enter key until you get this grip command, select Mirror from the popup menu, or type MI:
MIRROR
<Second point>/Base point/Copy/Undo/eXit: ⟨*pick the second point of the mirror line*⟩
Command:

Exercise 7.18

1. Begin a new drawing.
2. Draw an object similar to the original object shown in the upper left corner of Figure 7.33.
3. Copy the object to two other locations.
4. Use grips to mirror one of the objects without keeping the original object. Use an object that is similar to the top example in Figure 7.33.
5. Use grips to mirror another one of the objects while keeping the object being mirrored. Use an object that is similar to the lower left example in Figure 7.33.
6. Select another one of the objects and make multiple mirrored objects. Use an object that is similar to the lower right example in Figure 7.33.
7. Save the drawing as EX7.18.

Changing the Properties of an Object with Grips

If you pick an object to activate the grips and then select a grip to make it hot, you can press the right mouse button to get the Grips popup menu shown in Figure 7.34A. This popup menu is connected to the screen cursor drag line when you pick the right mouse button. The first option in this menu is Properties .... The other options are the grip editing commands and related functions that were explained earlier. Picking the Properties ... button opens a "Modify" dialog box that relates to the type of object you selected. For example, you get the Modify Line dialog box if you are editing a line, the Modify Arc dialog box for an arc object, and the Modify Circle dialog box when editing a circle object. The Modify Line dialog box is shown in Figure 7.32B as an example. Each of the dialog boxes has a Properties area, where you can change the color, Layer, Linetype, Thickness for 3D applications, and Linetype Scale. The rest of the dialog box has features that allow you to modify the specific type of object you selected and provides some key information about the object. The following gives you the modify options available when selecting a line, arc, and circle:

Line: Look at Figure 7.34B. Change the From Point and To Point X, Y, and Z values by typing a new coordinate in the desired text box. Use the Pick Point< button for either the From Point or To Point to pick a new point on the screen. The lower right area gives you X, Y, Z, Length, and Angle information about the current line.

Arc: A Center area allows you to either pick a new center or enter a new center location in X, Y, Z text boxes. There are also text boxes provided for you to change the Radius, Start Angle, and End Angle.

Circle: The Center area allows you to either pick a new center or enter a new center location in X, Y, Z text boxes. There is also a text box in which you change the Radius.

Exercise 7.19

1. Begin a new drawing.
2. Draw a line, a circle, and an arc based on your own design and specifications.
3. Pick each of the objects individually to activate the grips. Select a grip to make it hot, followed by pressing the right mouse button. This opens the "Modify" dialog box related to the selected object. Make changes to each object using its related "Modify" dialog box. Observe the speed and convenience available in changing objects in this manner.
4. Save the drawing as EX7.19.

FIGURE 7.34 (A) The Grips pop-up menu is opened by pressing the right mouse button after selecting a grip. Then pick the Properties ... option to open a "Modify" dialog box related to the type of object you are editing. The Modify Line dialog box is shown in B.

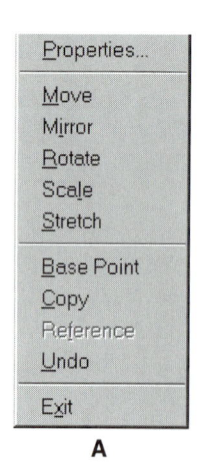

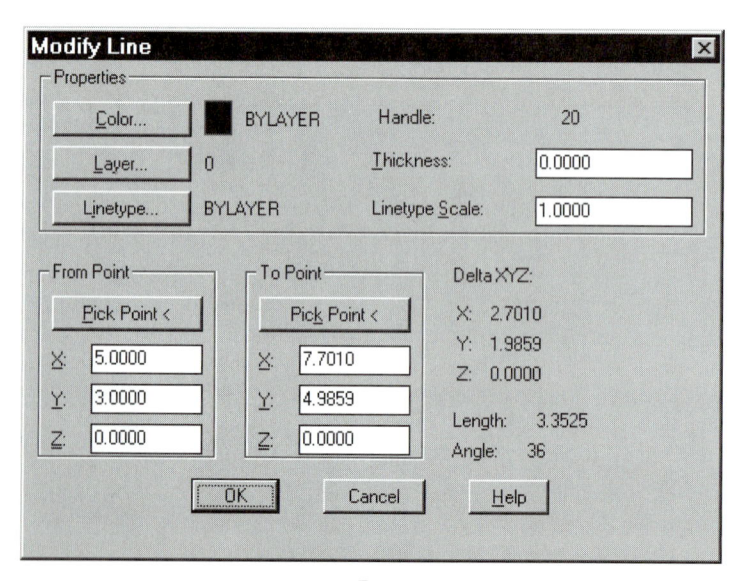

✓ LEARNING CHECKPOINT

- ☐ Identify at least one advantage of editing with grips.
- ☐ What happens to a grip when you select it?
- ☐ List the grip edit commands.
- ☐ How do you cycle through the grip edit commands?
- ☐ What do you do if you want to access a specific grip command without cycling through the grip commands?
- ☐ How do you select multiple grips?
- ☐ How do you copy with grips?

Trimming and Extending Objects

AutoCAD LT provides you with commands that can be used to remove a portion of an object, trim objects to create clean intersections, or extend objects to meet other objects.

Removing a Portion from an Object

The BREAK command is used to remove a portion of an object or to provide a break at one point to create two separate objects. This command can be used in a number of different ways that are determined by how you enter the command. The BREAK command can be accessed by picking Brea_k_ in the _M_odify pull-down menu, by picking the Break button in the Modify toolbar, or by typing **BR** or **BREAK** at the Command: prompt.

Breaking an Object at One Point

An object can be broken at one point when you want to split a single object into two objects. The object is broken at one point, yet it still looks like the original object, but it is now two objects connected at the break point. When you enter the BREAK command, you are asked to select an object. If you select an object by picking, the point you pick becomes the first break point. AutoCAD LT then asks you to Enter the second point. You can pick the second point exactly at the first point by entering the @ symbol and then pressing Enter. The object is now broken at one point. The command sequence looks like this:

Command: **BR** or **BREAK** ↵
Select object: ⟨*pick the object at a point where you want it broken*⟩
Enter second point (or F for first point): **@** ↵
Command:

After selecting an object to break, you decide that you want to break the object at a single point that is different from the selected point; you can use the F option. The F option allows you to select a new first point like this:

Command: **BR** or **BREAK** ↵
Select object: ⟨*pick the object*⟩
Enter second point (or F for first point): **F** ↵
Enter first point: ⟨*pick the object at a point where you want it broken*⟩
Enter second point: **@** ↵
Command:

Modify

Break

Modify
| Break

BREAK
BR

✏ Field Notes

> The reason AutoCAD LT provides the BREAK command's "F" option is to allow an object snap point to be chosen that results in more accurate break point specification.

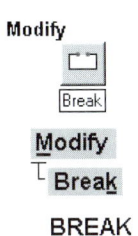

Breaking an Object at Two Points

An object can be broken at two points by picking an object to break. The point of selection becomes the first break point, and then you pick a second break point, as shown in Figure 7.35. The command looks like this:

Command: **BR** or **BREAK**↵
Select object: ⟨*pick the object at the desired break point*⟩
Enter second point (or F for first point): ⟨*pick the second point*⟩
Command:

If you select an object to break and then decide that you want to pick another first break point, you can use the F option. Doing this allows you to select another first break point like this:

Command: **BR** or **BREAK**↵
Select object: ⟨*pick the object at the desired break point*⟩
Enter second point (or F for first point): **F**↵
Enter first point: ⟨*pick the first point*⟩
Enter second point: ⟨*pick the second point*⟩
Command:

FIGURE 7.35 Breaking a line object between two points.

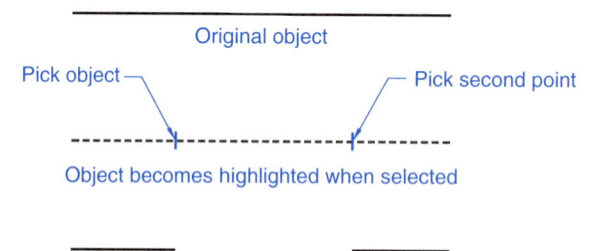

Field Notes

The break happens in a counterclockwise direction when breaking a portion out of a circle, arc, ellipse, or closed spline object. Splines are discussed in Chapter 8. Figure 7.36 demonstrates what happens when breaking a circle depending on how you pick the points.

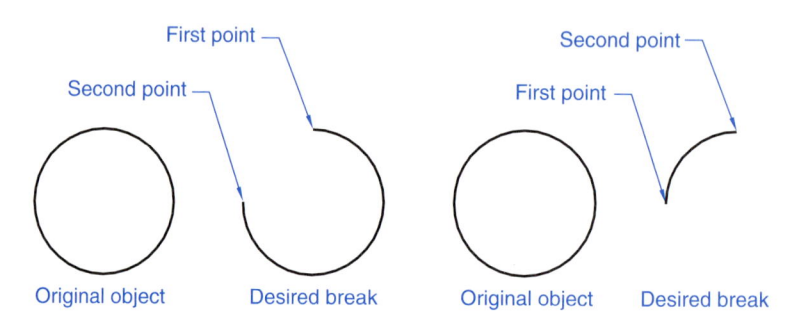

FIGURE 7.36 Breaking a circle between two points. Notice how the break points are selected.

Exercise 7.20

1. Begin a new drawing.
2. Draw a line and break it similar to Figure 7.35.
3. Draw a circle and make a copy of it.
4. Break the first circle by picking points in a counterclockwise direction similar to the example shown on the left in Figure 7.36.
5. Break the second circle by picking points in a clockwise direction similar to the example shown on the right in Figure 7.36.
6. Save the drawing as EX7.20.

Trimming Objects

The TRIM command is a useful tool when you need to trim objects to meet other objects. The command is accessed by picking the Trim toolbar button, by picking Trim in the Modify pull-down menu, or by typing **TR** or **TRIM** at the Command: prompt. When you enter this command, AutoCAD LT asks you to select the cutting edges. *Cutting edges* are objects selected that specify the point where a trimmed object is to be trimmed back to. This point is located at the intersection of the cutting edge object and the object to be trimmed. You can think of the cutting edge objects as the blades used to cut the object being trimmed. Most normal drawing objects having an edge definition that can be used as cutting edges. These edges include lines, arcs, circles, polylines, splines, ellipses, text, xlines, and rays. Objects with no edge definitions cannot be used, such as solids, point objects, and blocks. After selecting the cutting edges, you are asked to select the objects to trim. Look at Figure 7.37 as you follow this command:

```
Command: TR or TRIM↵
Select cutting edges: (Projmode = UCS, Edgemode = No extend)
Select objects: ⟨select the cutting edges⟩
Select objects: ↵
<Select object to trim>/Project/Edge/Undo: ⟨select the object to trim⟩
<Select object to trim>/Project/Edge/Undo: ↵
Command:
```

FIGURE 7.37 Using the TRIM command.

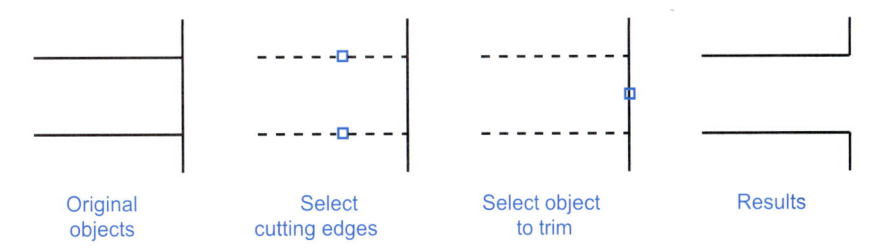

Original objects | Select cutting edges | Select object to trim | Results

□ This symbol represents the pick point.

In some applications, the cutting edges and the objects to trim are the same. Objects that have been specified as cutting edges can be trimmed just like any other object if they intersect a cutting edge. An example is the keyway that needs to be drawn in the hub shown in Figure 7.38. Notice the selection of cutting edges and objects to trim.

The cutting edge determines where an object is trimmed; the point that you pick when specifying the object to trim determines which side is removed and which side stays. The side that is picked is trimmed, and the remaining portion of the object is left on the other side of the cutting edge. When using a wide polyline cutting edge, the actual trim location is at its center line. Polylines are explained in Chapter 8.

To be able to be trimmed, an object must have a portion remaining on the other side of the cutting edge after the trim is complete. To understand why, it helps to visualize the cutting edge again as a blade and the line segment as the material being cut. The material has been brought up to the edge of the blade but does not actually cross the blade's path. If it does not cross the cut path, then the blade cannot cut it. To remove such a line segment, use the ERASE command. Attempting to trim an object that does not cross the cutting edge produces the message:

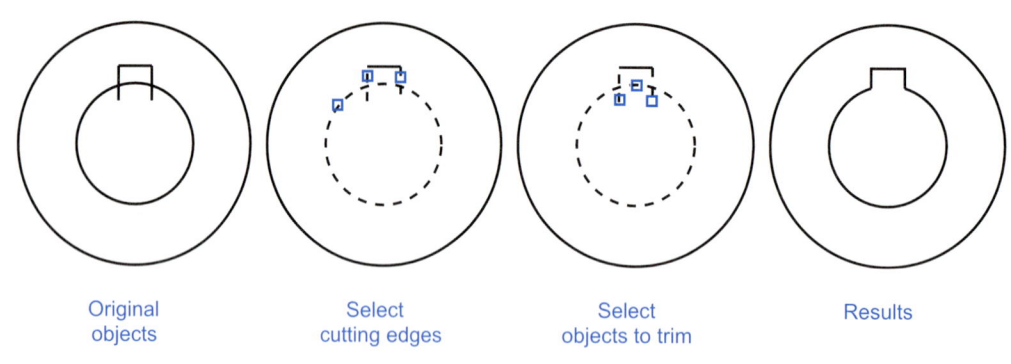

| Original | Select | Select | Results |
| objects | cutting edges | objects to trim | |

▫ This symbol represents the pick point.

FIGURE 7.38 Using the TRIM command.

Object does not intersect an edge.

Some closed objects, such as circles, ellipses, and closed splines must intersect a cutting edge in more than one location. If a line intersects only one cutting edge, the section from the cutting edge to the end is trimmed. A circle has no end to trim off. So, if the circle intersects only one cutting edge and only in one location, both ends of the trim section are at the same point and there is nothing to trim. Such an attempt produces the message:

Circle must intersect twice.

If you try to trim an object that cannot be trimmed, such as text or a block, the following message is displayed:

Cannot TRIM this object.

If the trim operation that you are trying to do comes up with unexpected results, use the Undo option within the TRIM command and try again.

Trimming Multiple Objects

Many situations happen that require you to trim several objects at the same time. This is common, as shown in the example of Figure 7.39A, where a series of lines must be trimmed back to another line. In this example, the Fence selection option is used to conveniently pick all the lines to be trimmed. The command sequence works like this, and the results are demonstrated in Figure 7.39:

Command: **TR** or **TRIM** ↵
Select cutting edges: (Projmode = UCS, Edgemode = No extend)
Select objects: ⟨pick the cutting edge⟩
Select objects: ↵
<Select object to trim>/Project/Edge/Undo: **F** ↵
First fence point: ⟨pick the first fence point⟩
Undo/<Endpoint of line>: ⟨pick the second fence point⟩
Undo/<Endpoint of line>: ↵
<Select object to trim>/Project/Edge/Undo: ↵
Command:

CHAPTER 7 ||| Editing Your Drawing

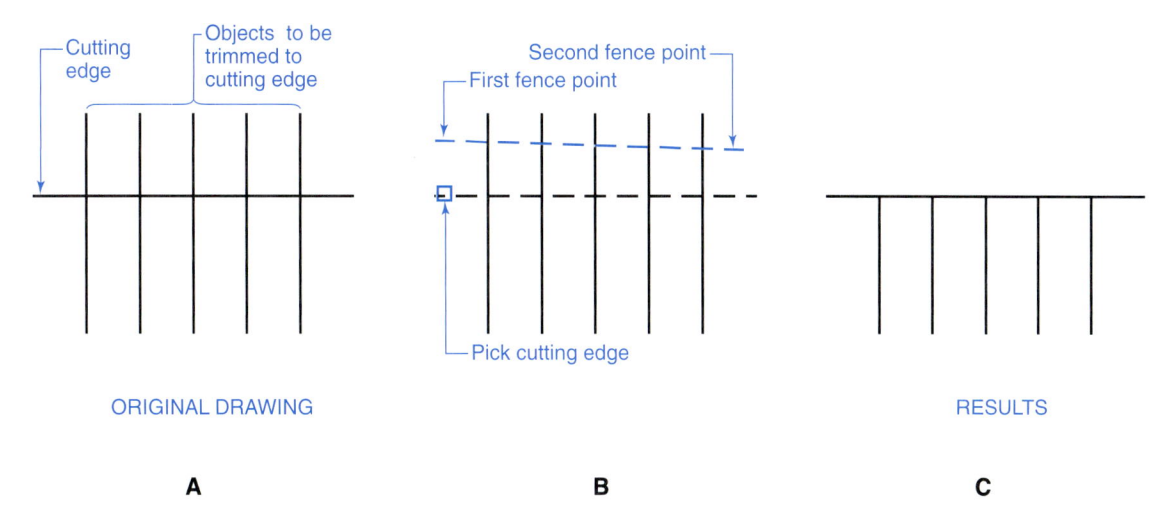

FIGURE 7.39 Trimming several objects back to a cutting edge with the Fence selection option.

Trimming to an Extended Intersection

The TRIM command can be used in a way that does not require a specified cutting edge to actually touch the object being trimmed. Instead, if an extended intersection exists, it can be used as the trim point. The term *extended intersection* describes the point at which one object would intersect another if both objects were extended far enough along their natural paths of extension. For example, an arc being checked for extended intersection is extended along its natural radius path.

To trim to an extended intersection, the Edge option of the TRIM command must first be set properly. If you look back to previous examples of TRIM, you will see in the initial status report that "Edgemode = No extend." This means that extended intersections are not checked for and only cutting edges that physically intersect the object being trimmed are used. The following command sequence sets the Edgemode to Extend and continues to trim the line as shown in Figure 7.40:

Command: **TR** or **TRIM**↵
Select cutting edges: (Projmode = UCS, Edgemode = No extend)
Select objects: ⟨*select the cutting edges*⟩
Select objects: ↵
<Select object to trim>/Project/Edge/Undo: **E**↵
Extend/No extend <No extend>: **E**↵
<Select object to trim>/Project/Edge/Undo: ⟨*select the object to trim*↵⟩
<Select object to trim>/Project/Edge/Undo: ↵
Command:

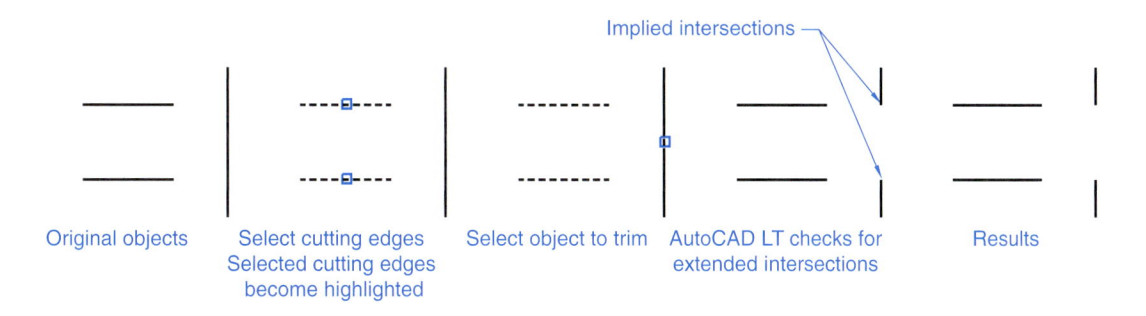

□ This symbol represents the pick point.

FIGURE 7.40 Using the TRIM command with an implied intersection.

Notice that the TRIM command now reports the changed status of Edgemode:

Command: **TR** or **TRIM**↵
Select cutting edges: (Projmode = UCS, Edgemode = Extend)
Select objects:

EDGEMODE is a system variable that can be set in either the TRIM or EXTEND commands. If EDGEMODE is set in TRIM then it also has the same setting for the use of EXTEND, which is discussed next in this chapter. Previously, you saw the Edge option set during the TRIM command. The Edge option can also be set with EDGEMODE. No extend is a 0 (zero) setting, while Extend is a 1 setting. EDGEMODE works like this:

Command: **EDGEMODE**↵
New value for EDGEMODE (0): **1**↵
Command:

Using AutoCAD LT Smart Trimming

AutoCAD LT is smart enough to look for the closest intersecting object or extended intersecting object in the direction of your pick. This object is then used as the cutting edge. This feature is called the *smart* mode. To activate the smart mode, press Enter when you are asked to Select cutting edges. The selected object is automatically trimmed using the following sequence:

Command: **TR** or **TRIM**↵
Select cutting edges: (Projmode = UCS, Edgemode = No extend)
Select objects: ↵
⟨Select object to trim⟩/Project/Edge/Undo: ⟨*pick the object for automatic trimming*⟩
⟨Select object to trim⟩/Project/Edge/Undo: ↵
Command:

The smart mode has the following conditions:

- The EDGEMODE setting for an extended intersection affects the smart mode.
- AutoCAD LT uses an actual intersection if found before an extendied intersection.
- The object must be visible on the screen and cannot be a block or xref object. Blocks and xrefs are explained in Chapter 12.
- Trimming cannot be done between one actual and one extended intersection, but it can be done between two actual intersections, or two extended intersections.

CHAPTER 7 ||| Editing Your Drawing

> **Field Notes**
>
> A common architectural application of the TRIM command is the clean up of intersecting walls similar to the example shown in Figure 7.41A. All four wall lines are selected as cutting edges and then the short internal line segments are selected as the objects to trim. This is an excellent application of the smart mode. With the smart mode, there is no need to select cutting edges, just pick the locations to be trimmed as shown in Figure 7.41B.
>
> Walls to be trimmed — Select cutting edges — Select objects to be trimmed — Results
>
> **A**
>
> Walls to be trimmed — Select objects to be trimmed — Results
>
> **B**
>
> ▫ This symbol represents the pick point.
>
> **FIGURE 7.41** Using the TRIM command on intersecting lines. (A) Selecting objects to be trimmed and selecting the cutting edges. (B) Using the smart mode.

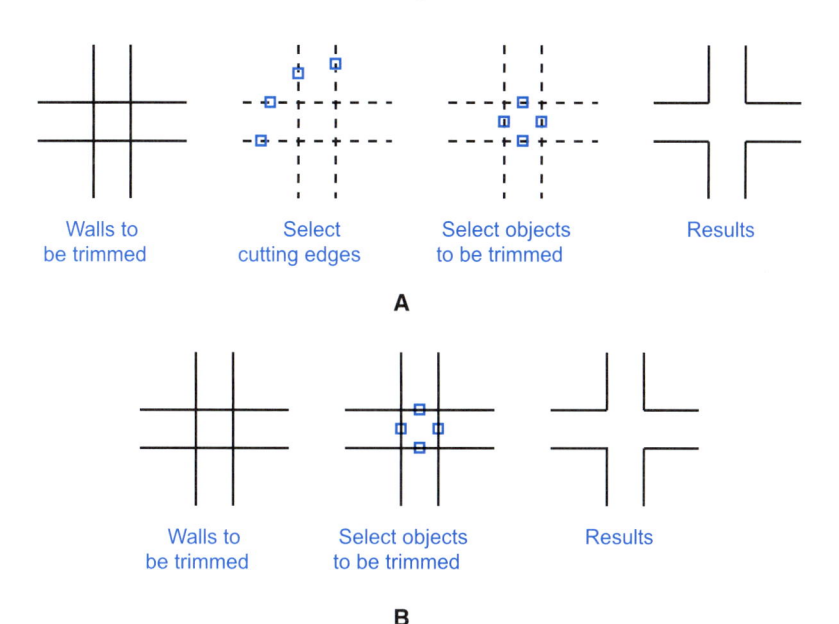

Exercise 7.21

1. Begin a new drawing.
2. Make a drawing similar to the original objects shown in Figure 7.37.
3. Trim the vertical line similar to the results shown in Figure 7.37.
4. Draw two concentric circles and the start of a keyway similar to the original objects shown in Figure 7.38.
5. Trim the keyway similar to the results shown in Figure 7.38.
6. Make a drawing similar to Figure 7.39A and use the Fence selection option to help trim the line extensions back to the cutting edge, as in Figure 7.39C.
7. Make a drawing similar to the original objects shown in Figure 7.40.
8. Trim the vertical line to the implied intersection with the horizontal lines similar to the results shown in Figure 7.40.
9. Draw two intersecting walls similar to the walls to be trimmed in Figure 7.41A.
10. Use the TRIM command to remove the lines inside the walls as was done in Figure 7.41A.
11. Draw two intersecting walls similar to the walls to be trimmed in Figure 7.41B.
12. Use the TRIM command in the smart mode to trim the lines inside the walls as was done in Figure 7.41B.
13. Save the drawing as EX7.21.

Extending Objects

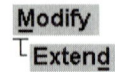

Modify
Extend
EXTEND
EX

The EXTEND command provides the opposite function of the TRIM command. EXTEND allows you to extend objects to meet other objects. The objects that you extend to are called the ***boundary edges.*** AutoCAD LT asks you to select the boundary edges and then select the objects to extend. For example, extending lines to circles is easy with the EXTEND command. The spokes of the wheel in Figure 7.42 are extended to the wheel and the hub with convenience and accuracy. This command is accessed by picking Exten_d_ from the _M_odify pull-down menu, by selecting the Extend button from the Modify toolbar, or by typing **EX** or **EXTEND** at the Command: prompt. Follow this command sequence to extend the spokes in Figure 7.42:

Command: **EX** or **EXTEND**↵
Select boundary edges: (Projmode = UCS, Edgemode = No extend)
Select objects: ⟨*select the boundary edges shown as highlighted*⟩
Select objects: ↵
<Select object to extend>/Project/Edge/Undo: ⟨*pick close to the end of each spoke line—this prompt is repeated for you to pick each line to extend to the hub and wheel*⟩
⟨Select object to extend⟩/Project/Edge/Undo: ↵
Command:

FIGURE 7.42 Using the EXTEND command.

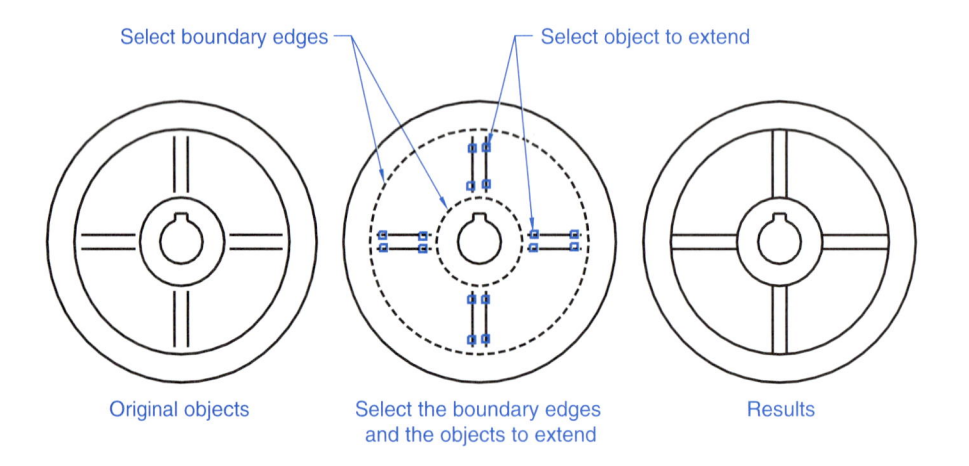

Select boundary edges — Select object to extend

Original objects — Select the boundary edges and the objects to extend — Results

Field Notes

- The Edge option in the EXTEND command is used for extending objects to an implied intersection. The edge option works the same as in the TRIM command but rather than trimming at an implied intersection, the EXTEND command's Edge option extends the selected object. Remember from an earlier discussion that the EDGEMODE system variable also affects the EXTEND command's use with implied intersections.
- The Project option in the TRIM and EXTEND commands is used for trimming and extending objects in 3-D applications and is discussed in Chapter 14.
- The Undo option is available in these editing commands to let you undo the previous selection in case you make a mistake or change your mind.
- Attempting to extend an object that does not cross the boundary edge produces the message:

    No edge in that direction.

If you try to extend an object that cannot be extended, such as text or a block, the following message is displayed:

    Cannot EXTEND this object.

Using AutoCAD LT Smart Extending

The smart mode was explained earlier in the discussion of the TRIM command. Smart mode can also be used with the EXTEND command by automatically looking for the closest intersecting object or extended intersecting object in the direction of your pick. This object is then used as the boundary edge. To activate the

CHAPTER 7 ||| Editing Your Drawing   279

smart mode, press Enter when you are asked to select boundary edges. The selected object is automatically extended using the following sequence:

> Command: **EX** or **EXTEND**↵
> Select boundary edges: (Projmode = UCS, Edgemode = No extend)
> Select objects: ↵
> <Select object to extend>/Project/Edge/Undo: ⟨*pick the object for automatic trimming*⟩
> <Select object to extend>/Project/Edge/Undo: ↵
> Command:

Trim and Extend are two of the default options on the popup cursor menu when you right-click at the Command: prompt. When selected this way, these commands are automatically put into "smart" mode.

Exercise 7.22

1. Begin a new drawing.
2. Make a drawing similar to the original objects shown in Figure 7.42.
3. Make a copy of this drawing.
4. Use one drawing to extend the spoke lines to meet the hub and wheel similar to the results shown in Figure 7.42.
5. Use the other drawing to extend the spoke lines to meet the hub and wheel using the smart mode. The task is easier, but the results are similar to the results shown in Figure 7.42.
6. Save the drawing as EX7.22.

Drawing Fillets and Chamfers

AutoCAD LT allows you to easily draw rounded corners called *fillets* and angled corners called *chamfers*. In mechanical drafting for the manufacturing industry, fillets are rounded inside corners and rounds are rounded outside corners, but AutoCAD LT treats them all as fillets. Chamfers in mechanical drafting are slightly angled corners. AutoCAD LT lets you make rounded and angled corners to any desired specification and for any drafting field by using the FILLET and CHAMFER commands. Draw rounded corners by picking Fillet in the Modify pull-down menu, by picking the Fillet button in the Modify toolbar, or by typing **F** or **FILLET**. Draw angled corners by picking Chamfer in the Modify pull-down menu, by picking the Chamfer toolbar button, or by typing **CHA** or **CHAMFER** at the Command: prompt.

Drawing Fillets

Fillets are drawn by specifying a radius and then selecting the objects to be filleted. The objects can be intersecting or nonintersecting. If objects do not intersect, the FILLET command extends the objects to where they would meet the radius or trims them, as needed, after applying a fillet. You can fillet lines, xlines, rays, circles, arcs, and true ellipses. You can also fillet all of the corners of a rectangle and polyline at one time. For the corners of a rectangle to all be filleted at one time, the rectangle must have been drawn with the RECTANG command. Polylines are explained in Chapter 8. Fillets are drawn on the current layer, in the current color, and with the current linetype. Be sure to properly set the current layer if you want the fillet to match the layer of the connecting objects.

If the objects being filleted are on the same layer, the fillet radius is created on that layer. If the objects are on different layers the radius is created on the current layer. This is also true of color and linetype—if the objects are the same color/linetype then that color/linetype is used, otherwise the current color/linetype is used.

Setting the Fillet Radius
Before drawing fillets, you need to consider the fillet radius. The initial default fillet radius is 0.5 and once it has been changed, the default is the same as the previous setting. The fillet radius is set by entering the Radius option and then typing a radius value like this:

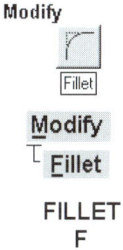

Modify
Fillet

Modify
└ Fillet

FILLET
F

Command: **F** or **FILLET**↵
(TRIM mode) Current fillet radius = 0.5
Polyline/Radius/Trim/<Select first object>: **R**↵
Enter fillet radius <0.5>: **.25**↵
Command:

The Command: prompt returns, but you can press the Enter key or space bar to immediately reenter the FILLET command and select objects to fillet. Figure 7.43 shows fillets drawn on several different objects and situations. This is the command sequence:

Command:
(TRIM mode) Current fillet radius = 0.5
Polyline/Radius/Trim/<Select first object>: ⟨*pick the first object*⟩
Select second object: ⟨*pick the second object*⟩
Command:

FIGURE 7.43 The results of applying the FILLET command to different objects.

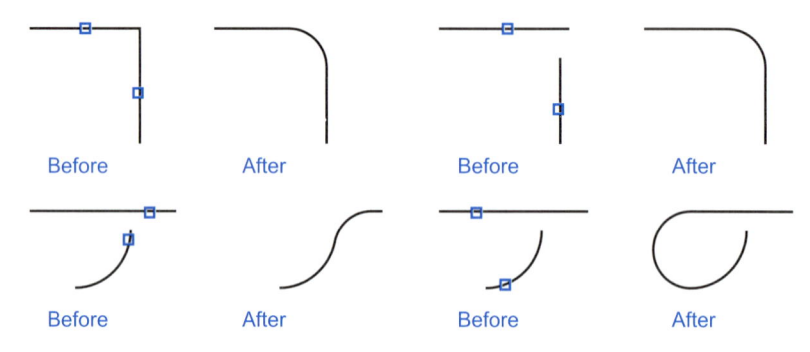

The following points represent some very important applications and practices when drawing fillets:

- Look at Figure 7.43 and notice the pick point associated with drawing fillets to the line and arc objects. The original objects are the same, but the results are different depending on where you pick the original objects.
- A fillet radius of 0 (zero) can be used to connect two nonintersecting objects or to remove a fillet from a polyline as shown in Figure 7.44. This option is commonly used in drafting and is a convenient way for cleaning up corner intersections. If the rounded corner is where two line objects intersect with a fillet, the result of applying a 0 (zero) FILLET Radius is a corner, but the rounded fillet remains.
- The Polyline option is used to fillet the corners of a polyline. If the polyline is closed, the Close option must have been used to close the last segment for all of the corners to be filleted or chamfered. Use this option by typing **P** and then picking the polyline. Polylines are discussed in Chapter 8. If a line and adjacent polyline are filleted, the line becomes part of the polyline.

FIGURE 7.44 The results of applying a 0 (zero) FILLET Radius to different objects.

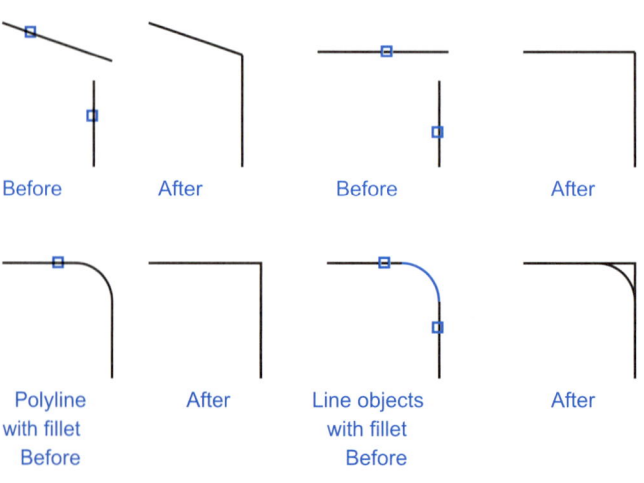

CHAPTER 7 ||| Editing Your Drawing

Using the FILLET Command's Trim Option

Fillets are usually set with a specified radius to use for rounding corners. The Trim option of the FILLET command allows you to decide if you want to keep or remove the original corner during the filleting process. The corner is trimmed by the initial default. The default then changes to the current setting. Figure 7.45 shows the difference between Trim and No trim. If you want to keep the corner, enter the Trim option like this and type **N** for No trim:

Command: **F** or **FILLET**↵
(TRIM mode) Current fillet radius = 0.5
Polyline/Radius/Trim/<Select first object>: **T**↵
Trim/No trim <Trim>: **N**↵
Polyline/Radius/Trim/<Select first object>: ⟨*pick the first object*⟩
Select second object: ⟨*pick the second object*⟩
Command:

FIGURE 7.45 A comparison between the FILLET command's Trim and No trim options.

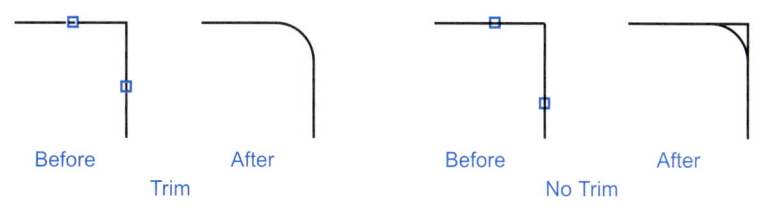

Before   After
Trim

Before   After
No Trim

▫ This symbol represents the pick point

Field Notes

The current setting of the Trim option in the FILLET command is the same for the CHAMFER command, which is discussed next. Trim set in either the FILLET command or the CHAMFER command affects both commands. The Trim can be set within the command as previously shown or set using the TRIMMODE system variable. When TRIMMODE is 0 (zero), the Trim option is active. When TRIMMODE is 1, the No trim option is active. The TRIMMODE variable works like this:

Command: **TRIMMODE**↵
New value for TRIMMODE <1>: **0**↵

Filleting Parallel Lines

The FILLET command can be used to make a rounded connection between two parallel objects such as lines, xlines, and rays. When you select two parallel lines for filleting, AutoCAD LT ignores the current fillet radius setting and automatically draws a round with a diameter that is equal to the distance between lines, as shown in Figure 7.46. If the parallel lines are unequal in length and you pick the longest line, the shortest line is extended to meet the radius. If you pick the shortest line, the longest line is automatically trimmed to meet the radius. This application is controlled by the current TRIMMODE setting.

FIGURE 7.46 Filleting parallel lines.

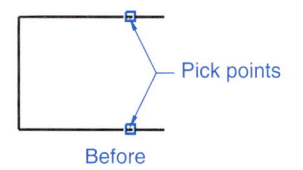

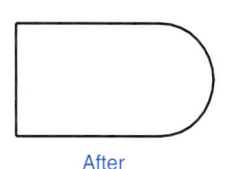

Pick points

Before   After

Exercise 7.23

1. Open EX7.22.
2. Use a 0.125 fillet radius to fillet where the spokes intersect the wheel and hub.
3. Make drawings similar to the before objects shown in Figure 7.43.
4. Set a desired fillet radius and fillet the objects as shown in the results in Figure 7.43.
5. Make drawings similar to the before objects shown in Figure 7.44.
6. Set a 0 (zero) fillet radius and fillet the objects as shown in the results in Figure 7.44.
7. Make drawings similar to the before objects shown in Figure 7.45.
8. Set a desired fillet radius and fillet the objects as shown in the results in Figure 7.45. One object has Trim on and the other has No trim.
9. Make a drawing similar to the before object shown in Figure 7.46.
10. Pick the objects for filleting to get the results shown in Figure 7.46.
11. Save the drawing as EX7.23.

Drawing Chamfers

Modify
Chamfer

Modify
Chamfer

CHAMFER
CHA

AutoCAD LT provides you with a variety of options for drawing chamfers to intersecting or nonintersecting lines, polylines, xlines, and rays. The CHAMFER command lets you specify a distance for the chamfer lengths, which is referred to as the *Distance method.* You can also specify an angle and distance to establish the chamfer. This is called the *Angle method.* You can switch between methods when using the CHAMFER command by using the Method option and then typing either **D** for Distance or **A** for Angle like this:

Command: **CHA** or **CHAMFER**↵
(TRIM mode) Current chamfer Dist1 = 0.5, Dist2 = 0.5
Polyline/Distance/Angle/Trim/Method/<Select first line>: **M**↵
Distance/Angle ⟨Distance⟩: ⟨*type* **D** *or* **A** *or press Enter for the default*⟩
Polyline/Distance/Angle/Trim/Method/<Select first line>:

Drawing Chamfers with Distances

You can specify equal or different horizontal and vertical chamfer distances with the Distance option. Equal chamfer distances result in a chamfer that is at a 45° angle. The value that you set for the first chamfer distance is automatically set as the default for the second chamfer distance. Accept this default by pressing Enter or type a new value and press Enter:

Command: **CHA** or **CHAMFER**↵
(TRIM mode) Current chamfer Dist1 = 0.5, Dist2 = 0.5
Polyline/Distance/Angle/Trim/Method/<Select first line>: **D**↵
Enter first chamfer distance <>: **.75**↵
Enter second chamfer distance <0.75>: **.5**↵
Command:

Now, press the space bar or the Enter key to begin the CHAMFER command again to draw a chamfer with the distance setting that you just made. Look at Figure 7.47 as you follow this command sequence:

Command:
(TRIM mode) Current chamfer Dist1 = 0.5, Dist2 = 0.5
Polyline/Distance/Angle/Trim/Method/<Select first line>: ⟨*pick the first line*⟩
Select second line: ⟨*pick the second line*⟩
Command:

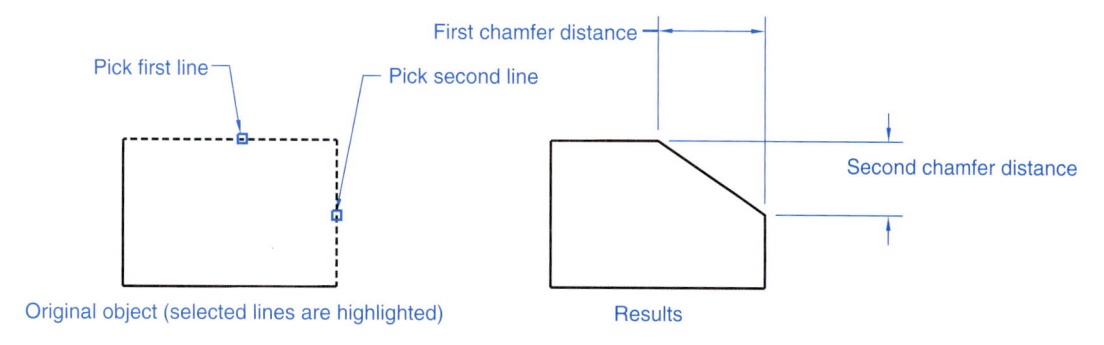

FIGURE 7.47 Using the CHAMFER command to draw a chamfer with distances.

> ### Field Notes
>
> - The chamfering process extends lines or trims lines as needed to create the chamfer in the same manner that this happens with the FILLET command as previously shown.
> - If you set both chamfer distances to 0 (zero), the CHAMFER command extends or trims lines as needed to create a corner, but no chamfer is drawn.
> - The Polyline option is used to chamfer the corners of polylines in the same manner as discussed with the FILLET command. Polylines are covered in Chapter 8.

Drawing Chamfers with the Distance and Angle Option

In some cases, you may know a chamfer distance and the angle. Use the Angle option to draw a chamfer in this manner. Enter the Angle option to set the chamfer distance and angle line like this:

Command: **CHA** or **CHAMFER**↵
(TRIM mode) Current chamfer Dist1 = 0.5, Dist2 = 0.5
Polyline/Distance/Angle/Trim/Method/<Select first line>: **A**↵
Enter chamfer length on the first line <0>: **.75**↵
Enter chamfer angle from the first line <0>: **30**↵
Command:

Enter the CHAMFER command again and set the Method to the Angle option if it was previously set to the Distance option, and then draw the desired chamfer as shown in Figure 7.48:

Command:
(TRIM mode) Current chamfer Dist1 = 0.5, Dist2 = 0.5
Polyline/Distance/Angle/Trim/Method/<Select first line>: **M**↵
Distance/Angle <Distance>: **A**↵
Polyline/Distance/Angle/Trim/Method/<Select first line>: ⟨*pick the first line*⟩
Select second line: ⟨*pick the second line*⟩
Command:

FIGURE 7.48 Using the CHAMFER command to draw a chamfer with distance and angle.

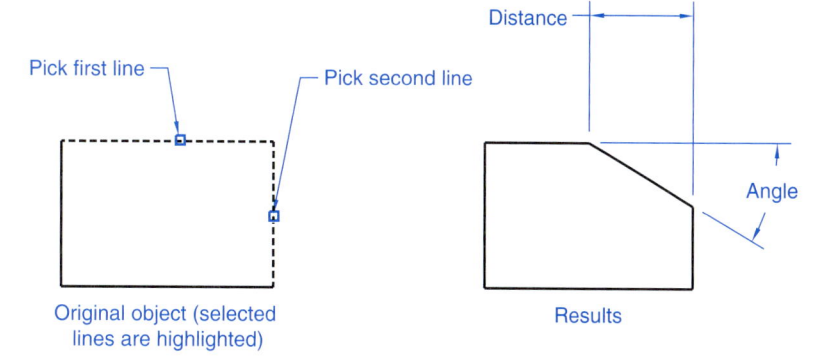

Using the Trim Option

The CHAMFER command's Trim option works just like the Trim option in the Fillet command. The options are Trim and No trim. With Trim on, the original corner is trimmed or extended as necessary. If No trim is active, the original corners are not extended or trimmed.

Exercise 7.24

1. Begin a new drawing.
2. Make a drawing similar to the original object shown in Figure 7.47.
3. Set the chamfer distances to 0.75 and 0.5 and then use the Distance option to draw a chamfer similar to the results shown in Figure 7.47.
4. Make a drawing similar to the original object shown in Figure 7.48.
5. Set the chamfer distances to 0.75 and the angle to 30° and then use the Angle option to draw a chamfer similar to the results shown in Figure 7.48.
6. Save the drawing as EX7.24.

Using a Dialog Box to Edit Objects

Object Properties

Properties

Modify
└ Properties...

DDMODIFY
MO

The DDMODIFY command was briefly introduced in Chapter 5 with regard to changing an object's color, layer, linetype, and linetype scale. This command is also handy for making quick changes to a specific object. The DDMODIFY command asks you to select an object to modify. The name of the dialog box depends on the type of object you select. For example, if you select a circle, the dialog box is called Modify Circle, or if you pick a line the dialog box is called Modify Line. This was introduced to you earlier in this chapter when you picked Preferences ... from the Grips popup menu to open the related "Modify," dialog box. See Figure 7.34. The easiest way to start this command is by picking the Properties button from the Object Properties toolbar, or you can type **MO** or **DDMODIFY** at the Command: prompt. After entering the DDMODIFY command, pick a circle on your drawing using this command to get the Modify Circle dialog box shown in Figure 7.49:

Command: **MO** or **DDMODIFY**↵
Select object to modify: ⟨*pick the circle to get the Modify Circle dialog box*⟩

FIGURE 7.49 The Modify Circle dialog box.

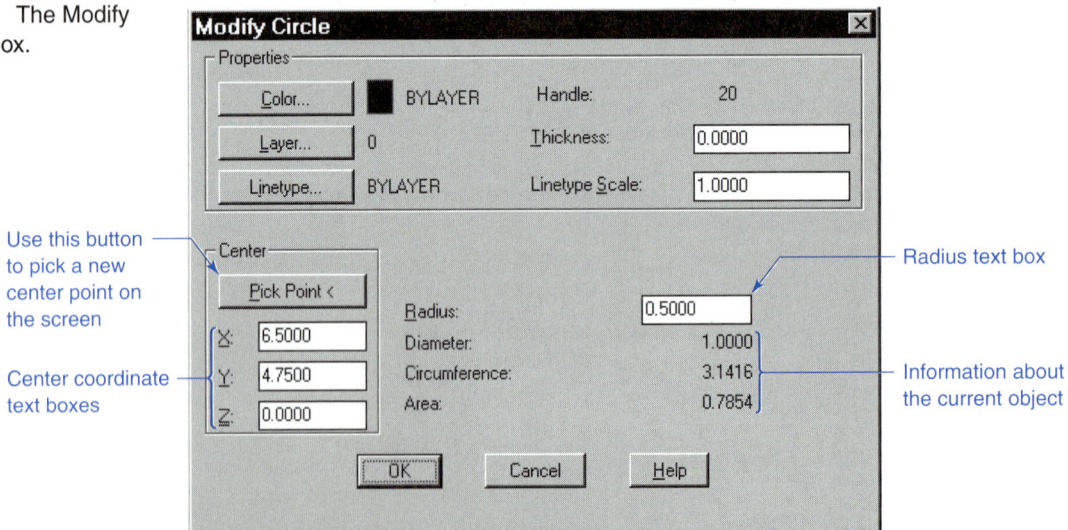

Look at the Modify Circle dialog box in Figure 7.49 as you consider these features:

Properties   The Properties compartment was discussed in Chapter 5. This is where you can conveniently change the object properties that are displayed.

Center   This compartment allows you to change the location of the circle by picking or specifying new coordinates. Pick the Pick Point⟨ button to have the dialog box temporarily removed

CHAPTER 7 ||| Editing Your Drawing 285

	and the cursor available for you to pick a new center point. Type new values in the X:, Y:, or Z: (for 3D) text boxes to change the center point by adjusting the coordinates.
Radius	Enter a new value in this text box to revise the radius of the circle. Information about the circle, such as the Diameter, Circumference, and Area, is also provided.

Pick the OK button when you have made the desired changes.

You get slightly different editing options when you select different types of objects. For example, if you use the DDMODIFY command and pick a line, you get these features in addition to the Properties compartment:

From Point	A Pick Point⟨ button and X:, Y:, Z: text boxes for adjusting the first point of the line.
To Point	A Pick Point⟨ button and X:, Y:, Z: text boxes for adjusting the last point of the line.

Exercise 7.25

1. Begin a new drawing.
2. Draw a .5-in.-diameter circle.
3. Use the Modify Circle dialog box to change the location of the circle and change the diameter to 1.5.
4. Draw a line 1 in. long.
5. Use the Modify Line dialog box to change the length of the line to 2.5 in.
6. Use the Arc Center option to draw an arc with a .75-in. radius with the start point at 0° and the endpoint at 90°.
7. Use the Modify Arc dialog box to change the start angle to 90° and the end angle to 180°. Change the radius to 1.5.
8. Save the drawing as EX7.25.

Using the Windows Clipboard

You can use all or part of an AutoCAD LT drawing in other AutoCAD LT drawings or in applications such as in a Windows document. To do this, you can either cut or copy the desired objects to the Windows Clipboard. The ***Clipboard*** is a place where objects are temporarily stored. AutoCAD LT objects are placed on the Clipboard by using the CUTCLIP or COPYCLIP commands. The CUTCLIP command removes the objects from the drawing and stores them on the Clipboard. The COPYCLIP command copies the objects from the drawing and stores them on the Clipboard. The objects that you place on the Clipboard stay there until you use the CUTCLIP or COPYCLIP commands again because each time you use one of these commands, the newly selected objects replace the objects that were there before. When the objects are on the Clipboard, they are available to be pasted into other Windows applications or into other AutoCAD LT drawings. The objects are transferred to other applications using the PASTECLIP command.

Cutting Objects

Objects can be cut from an AutoCAD LT drawing by picking Cut from the Edit pull-down menu, by picking the Cut to Clipboard button from the Standard toolbar, by pressing the Ctrl key and the X key (Ctrl+X), or by typing CUTCLIP. The command works like this:

Standard

Cut to Clipboard (Ctrl+X)

Edit
⌐ Cut

CUTCLIP
CTRL+X

    Command: **CUTCLIP**↵
    Select objects: ⟨use any selection method⟩
    Select objects: ↵
    Command:

Caution is advised when using the CUTCLIP command, because the objects are removed from the drawing. The OOPS command can be used to bring the objects back, or you can undo the CUTCLIP command. Note that undoing this command in AutoCAD LT does not affect the contents of the Clipboard, so the cut items are still there.

Copying Objects

Standard

[Copy to Clipboard (Ctrl+C)]

Edit
Copy

COPYCLIP
CTRL+C

The COPYCLIP command works just like the CUTCLIP command except that the objects that are copied to the Clipboard remain in the drawing. This command is accessed by picking Copy from the Edit pull-down menu, by picking the Copy to Clipboard button from the Standard toolbar, by pressing the Ctrl key and the C key (Ctrl+C), or by typing COPYCLIP. The COPYCLIP command works like this:

Command: **COPYCLIP**↵
Select objects: ⟨use any selection method⟩
Select objects: ↵
Command:

The objects are copied in vector format. A *vector* is a mathematical object with exact direction and length but without specific location. The objects you copy to the Clipboard are stored there as WMF files (Windows metafiles). However, AutoCAD LT can transfer objects to other applications using a variety of formats.

Pasting AutoCAD LT Drawings

Standard

[Paste from Clipboard]

Edit
Paste

PASTECLIP
CTRL+V

Pasting is the function of taking objects that are stored on the Clipboard and inserting them into a Windows application or into an AutoCAD LT drawing. Objects that are pasted from the Clipboard into an AutoCAD LT drawing are automatically inserted in the format that keeps most of the information intact. You can also specify the desired format. For example, you can paste the objects using an AutoCAD LT format, which is the easiest format for you to use when editing the pasted objects.

Objects must have been placed on the Clipboard before they can be pasted. The command used to paste objects to an AutoCAD LT drawing is PASTECLIP. This command is inactive until an object is placed on the Clipboard. To access this command, pick Paste from the Clipboard button in the Standard toolbar, type **PASTECLIP** at the Command: prompt, pick Paste from the Edit pull-down menu, or press the Ctrl key and the V key (Ctrl+V). This command asks for an insertion point. This is a point at the lower left corner of the object you selected. The objects are dynamically dragged with the screen cursor so you can see the image for placement. Pick the insertion point or enter desired coordinates. AutoCAD LT then asks you for X and Y coordinate scale factors. This allows you to change the X and Y coordinate scales of the objects before insertion, or you can press Enter to accept the X default of a one-to-one or full-size insertion. The Y coordinate default is the same as the value you enter for the X coordinate. If you want to scale down, enter a value of less than one; to scale up, enter a value of more than one. You can also rotate the object while inserting. After objects are on the Clipboard, the PASTECLIP command works like this:

Command: **PASTECLIP**↵
Insertion point: ⟨pick an insertion point⟩
X scale factor <1>/Corner/XYZ: ↵
Y scale factor (default = X): ↵
Rotation angle <0>: ↵
Command:

Modify

[Explode]

Modify
Explode

EXPLODE
X

The pasted objects are inserted as a block. This means that the individual characteristics that existed when you copied the objects to the Clipboard are now combined into one object. Any editing you do affects the entire object. You need to use the EXPLODE command if you want to convert the objects to the individual components. Access this command by picking Explode in the Modify pull-down menu, by picking the Explode button in the Modify toolbar, or by typing **X** or **EXPLODE** at the Command: prompt. The EXPLODE command asks you to select the objects. A single pick highlights the objects, and the objects are converted to their original condition when you press Enter.

The following is a sequence to use when transferring information from one AutoCAD LT drawing to another:

1. Open the AutoCAD LT drawing that contains the desired information.
2. Use the COPYCLIP or CUTCLIP command to select the desired objects for placement on the Clipboard.
3. Open the AutoCAD LT drawing where you want the objects inserted. Multiple drawings can be opened at once with Windows.
4. Use the PASTECLIP command to insert the contents of the Clipboard into the desired drawing.
5. EXPLODE the inserted objects if needed.
6. Save the changes.

CHAPTER 7 ||| Editing Your Drawing   287

> ### Exercise 7.26
>
> 1. Open EX7.22.
> 2. Copy (COPYCLIP) the wheel with spokes and hub to the Clipboard.
> 3. Exit the drawing and save the changes upon exiting.
> 4. Start a new drawing.
> 5. Paste the contents of the Clipboard into this drawing at a 1:1 scale.
> 6. Paste the contents of the Clipboard again at a half scale (0.5 for X and Y).
> 7. Save the drawing as EX7.26.

☑ LEARNING CHECKPOINT

- ☐ Name the command that is used to remove a portion from an object or create two objects from one object.
- ☐ What command is used to remove a portion from an object back to another object?
- ☐ Define a cutting edge.
- ☐ What is an implied intersection?
- ☐ How do you activate the smart mode and what does it do?
- ☐ Name the command that lets you lengthen an object to meet another object.
- ☐ Define boundary edges.
- ☐ Name the command used to make rounded corners.
- ☐ What command is used to draw angled corners?
- ☐ Name the command that allows you to edit a single object using a dialog box.
- ☐ Define Clipboard.
- ☐ What command is used to place an object on the Clipboard without removing it from the drawing?
- ☐ Define pasting.
- ☐ Name the command that is used to place an object from the Clipboard into a drawing.

Copying an Object's Properties

In the editing process, it is much faster to copy an existing object than to create a new object from scratch. When you are editing the properties of an object, it is often much faster to simply copy the properties of an existing object in your drawing by using the *Property Painter*. The command used for the Property Painter is PAINTER. You can access this command by picking the Property Painter button from the Standard toolbar or by typing **PAINTER** at the Command: prompt. You are prompted to select the *source object*. The source object is the object whose properties are to be copied. You can select any single object at this prompt. When you pick an object, AutoCAD LT reports the "currently active settings," which indicates the properties that are to be copied. By default, all properties are active.

Standard

PAINTER

```
Command: PAINTER↵
Select Source Object:
Current active settings = color layer ltype ltscale thickness text dim hatch
Settings/<Select Destination Object(s)>: S↵
Current active settings = color ltype text dim hatch
Settings/<Select Destination Object(s)>: <pick one or more objects>
1 found
Settings/<Select Destination Object(s)>: <pick one or more objects>
1 found
Settings/<Select Destination Object(s)>: ↵
Command:
```

The Settings option displays the currently active properties in the Property Settings dialog box shown in Figure 7.50. Here, you can select which properties will be applied to the destination objects. The effect of each of these settings is as follows:

- **Color** — Applies the color setting of the source object to the destination objects.
- **Layer** — Moves destination objects to the same layer as the source object.
- **Linetype** — Applies the linetype setting of the source object to the destination objects.
- **Linetype Scale** — Applies the object linetype scale of the source object to the destination objects.
- **Thickness** — Applies the 3D thickness setting of the source object to the destination objects.
- **Dimension** — Applies the dimension style of the source object to all selected dimension, leader, and tolerance objects.
- **Text** — Changes the text style of the destination text objects to that of the source object.
- **Hatch** — Applies the associative hatch pattern properties of the source object to selected associative hatch patterns.

FIGURE 7.50 The Property Settings dialog box controls which properties are applied to the destination objects.

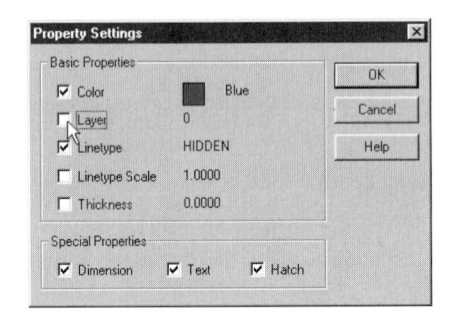

Figure 7.51 shows the color and linetype of the source object being applied to two other objects. One distinct advantage of using the Property Painter is that you can change multiple properties at the same time. Another advantage is that you do not need to know the values to which you want to set them—you can simply match an object that already has the correct settings.

FIGURE 7.51 The color and linetype properties of the source object are applied to the destination objects in the example.

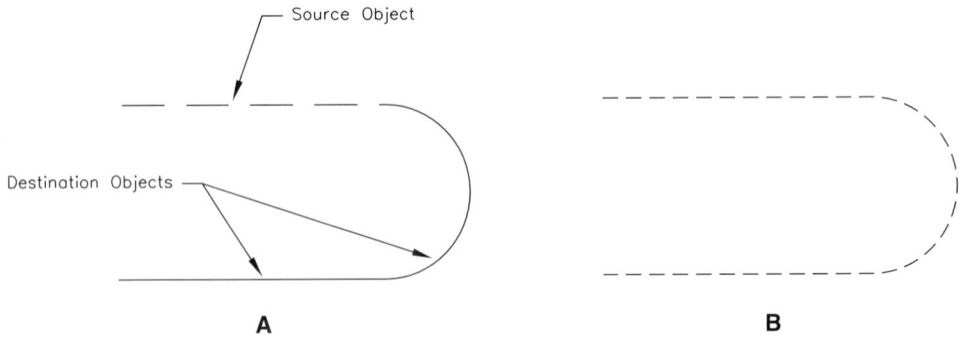

CHAPTER 7 ||| Editing Your Drawing   289

> **Exercise 7.27**
>
> 1. Start a new drawing session from scratch using Metric settings.
> 2. Define two new layers, and assign color and linetype settings of your own design.
> 3. Draw a 40-mm-diameter circle on each of the new layers, using BYLAYER color and linetypes.
> 4. Draw two more circles on these layers using specific colors and linetypes that override layer settings.
> 5. Draw four rectangles on layer 0 with BYLAYER settings.
> 6. Using the Property Painter, assign all the properties of one circle to one of the rectangles. Repeat this procedure for the remaining circles and rectangles.
> 7. Use the Property Painter to assign BYLAYER colors to the objects in your drawing that currently override layer settings.
> 8. Save this drawing as EX7.27.

☑ LEARNING CHECKPOINT

- ☐ Name the command that starts the Property Painter.
- ☐ What are the advantages of using the Property Painter?

MULTIPLE CHOICE

Circle the choice or enter your response on an answer sheet by selecting the option that most closely completes or answers the given statements.

1. One or more objects that are specified for processing as a unit is called a:
   a. selection
   b. selection set
   c. processing unit
   d. group

2. Make a selection by placing a polygon of your own design totally around an object or group of objects using a:
   a. window
   b. crossing
   c. window polygon
   d. window crossing

3. This option allows you to automatically create a window or crossing box by picking the first and second corners:
   a. Noun/Verb Selection
   b. Press and Drag
   c. Use Shift to Add
   d. Implied Windowing

4. Small squares that appear on objects you select are called:
   a. pick boxes
   b. pixels
   c. grips
   d. aperture

5. Create the other half of a symmetrical object with this command:
   a. COPY
   b. OFFSET
   c. MIRROR
   d. ARRAY

6. Make multiple copies of objects in a pattern with this command:
   a. COPY
   b. OFFSET
   c. MIRROR
   d. ARRAY

7. This command allows you to place objects in a new location:
   a. MOVE
   b. SCALE
   c. ROTATE
   d. STRETCH

8. The grip MIRROR command automatically does this to the original object:
   a. keeps
   b. asks to remove or keep
   c. removes
   d. none of the above

9. The size of the arc for the FILLET command is established with a:
   a. diameter
   b. radius
   c. center
   d. endpoints

10. The AutoCAD LT command that allows you to move objects that have been placed in temporary storage to an AutoCAD LT drawing or other Windows application is called:
    a. COPY
    b. COPYCLIP
    c. CUTCLIP
    d. PASTECLIP

MATCHING

Match each term to the correct description by writing the appropriate number in each box at the left.

- ☐ ARRAY
- ☐ BREAK
- ☐ CHAMFER
- ☐ Clipboard
- ☐ COPY
- ☐ DDMODIFY
- ☐ EXTEND
- ☐ Fence
- ☐ FILLET
- ☐ Grips
- ☐ LENGTHEN
- ☐ MIRROR
- ☐ MOVE
- ☐ OFFSET
- ☐ PASTECLIP
- ☐ ROTATE
- ☐ SCALE
- ☐ STRETCH
- ☐ TRIM
- ☐ WP

1. Edit objects so they are longer to meet other objects.
2. Place objects in a new location.
3. Edit objects so they are shorter to meet other objects.
4. Remove a portion from an object.
5. Lengthen or shorten objects.
6. Make duplicates of objects for placement anywhere on a drawing.
7. Copy objects into a specific pattern.
8. Use this command to place an object onto a drawing from the Clipboard.
9. Use this selection option to totally surround objects with a polygon of your design.
10. Use this command to lengthen or shorten closed objects.
11. Draw a corner.
12. Edit objects with these after selecting.
13. Use this to select objects and then access them later with the Previous option.
14. Use this selection option to place a line through objects to select.
15. Move objects to a desired angle.
16. Rounded corners.
17. Make an object bigger or smaller.
18. Make symmetrical copies.
19. Make parallel copies of objects.
20. Edit single objects in a dialog box.
21. Copy objects to here for temporary storage.

CHAPTER 7 ||| Editing Your Drawing

WORD SCRAMBLE

Unscramble the seven scrambled words below, one letter to each square, to form seven AutoCAD LT–related words:

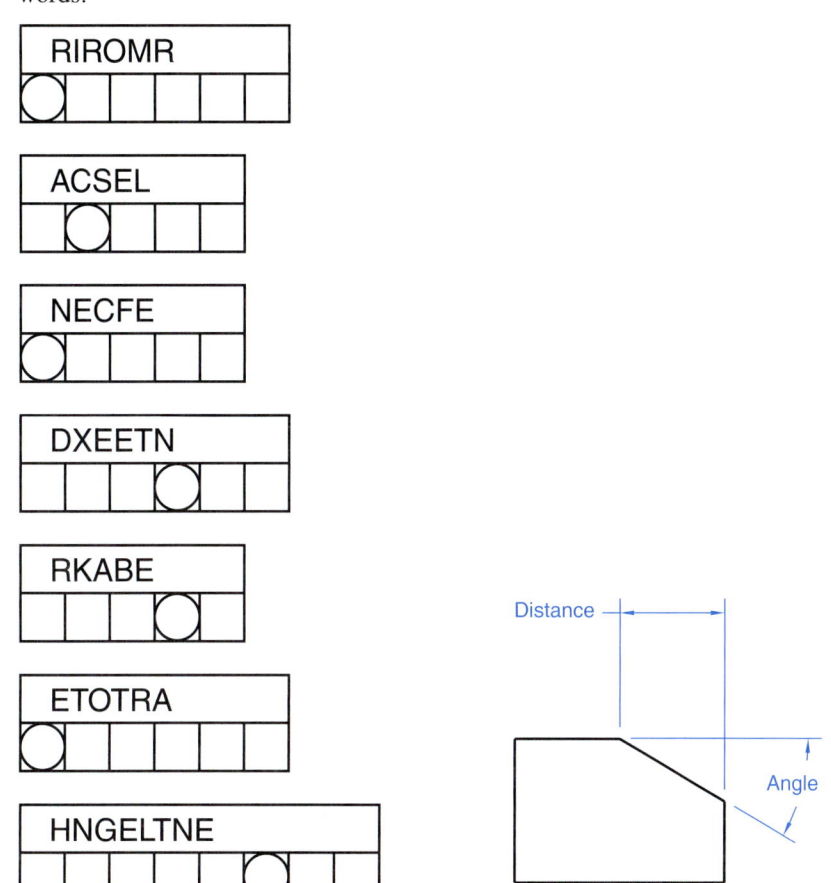

RIROMR

ACSEL

NECFE

DXEETN

RKABE

ETOTRA

HNGELTNE

Unscramble the circled letters above to form the special answer, as suggested by the illustration.

PROJECTS

Set up the following drawing projects with layers that relate to the type of drawing as outlined and discussed in Chapter 5.

7.1 Clock

Open P3.3 and add the fillets to the clock, as shown below. Save as P7.1.

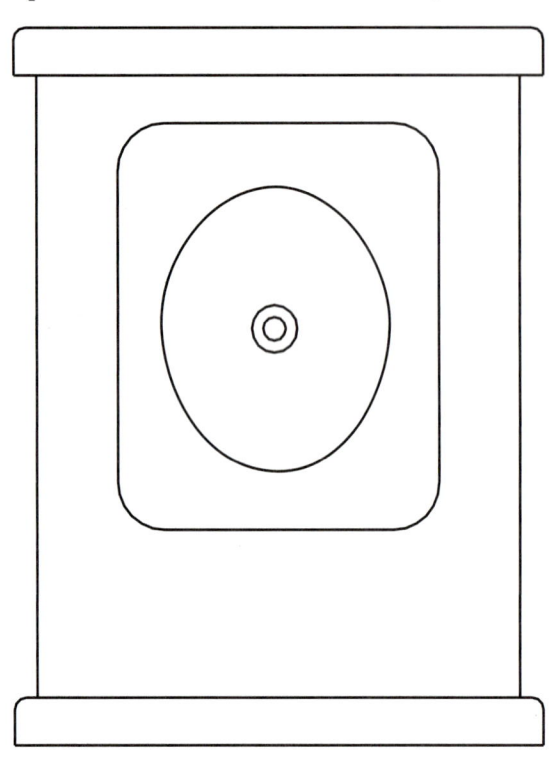

7.2 Piping Drawing

Open P3.10 and edit the symbols as needed to create the drawing shown below. Save as P7.2.

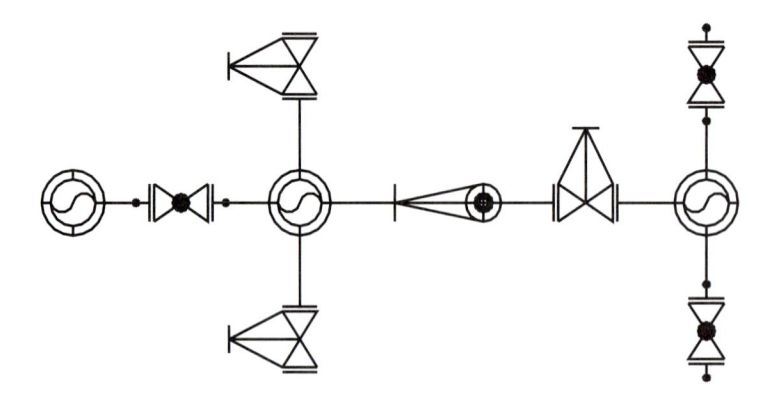

CHAPTER 7 ||| Editing Your Drawing   293

7.3 Chassis Divider
Draw the view shown below. Do not draw dimensions. Save as P7.3.

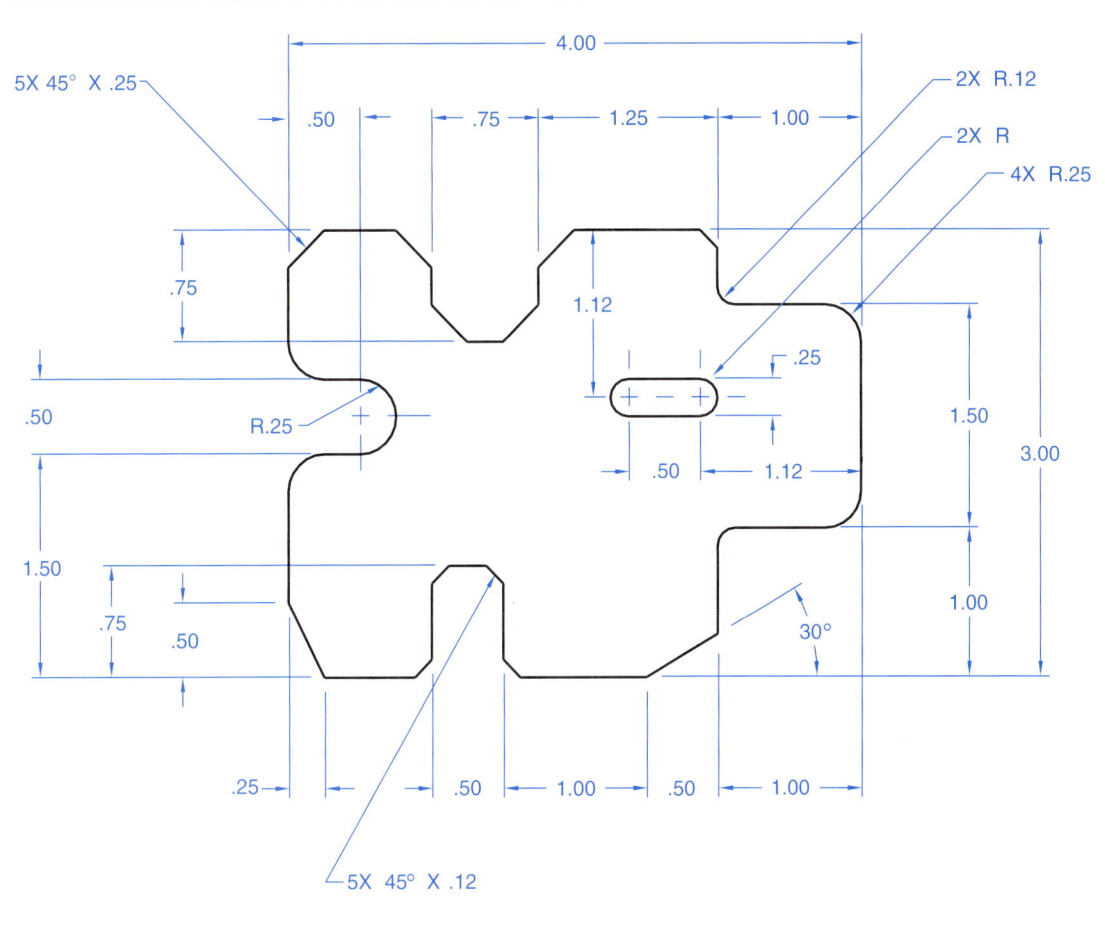

7.4 GFCI Schematic
Paste P2.6 and P3.2 into the drawing to create the schematic shown below without text. Save as P7.4.

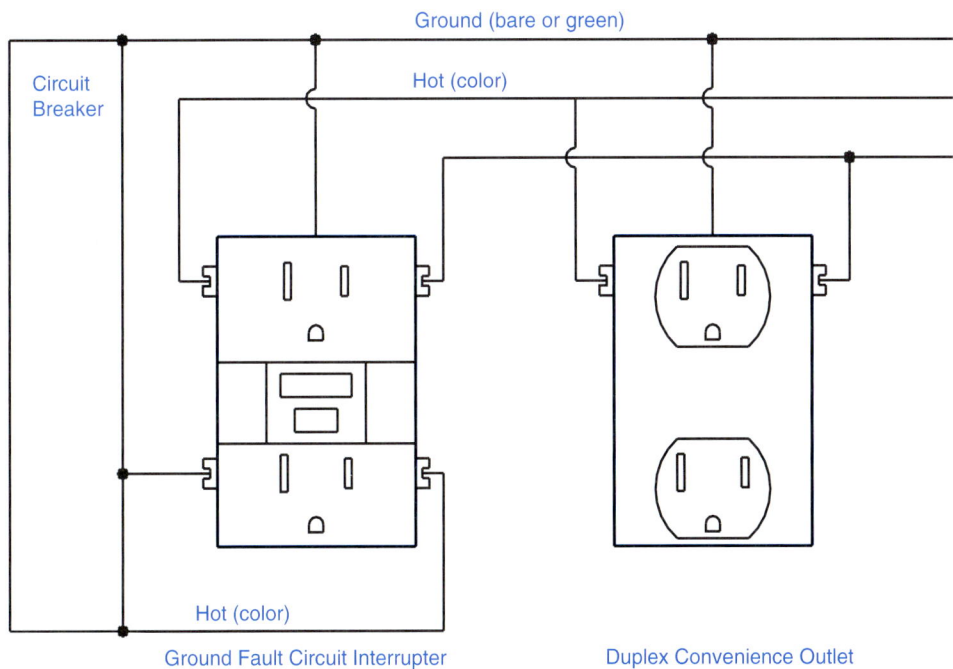

7.5 Integrated Circuit Schematic
Draw the schematic shown below without text. Save as P7.5.

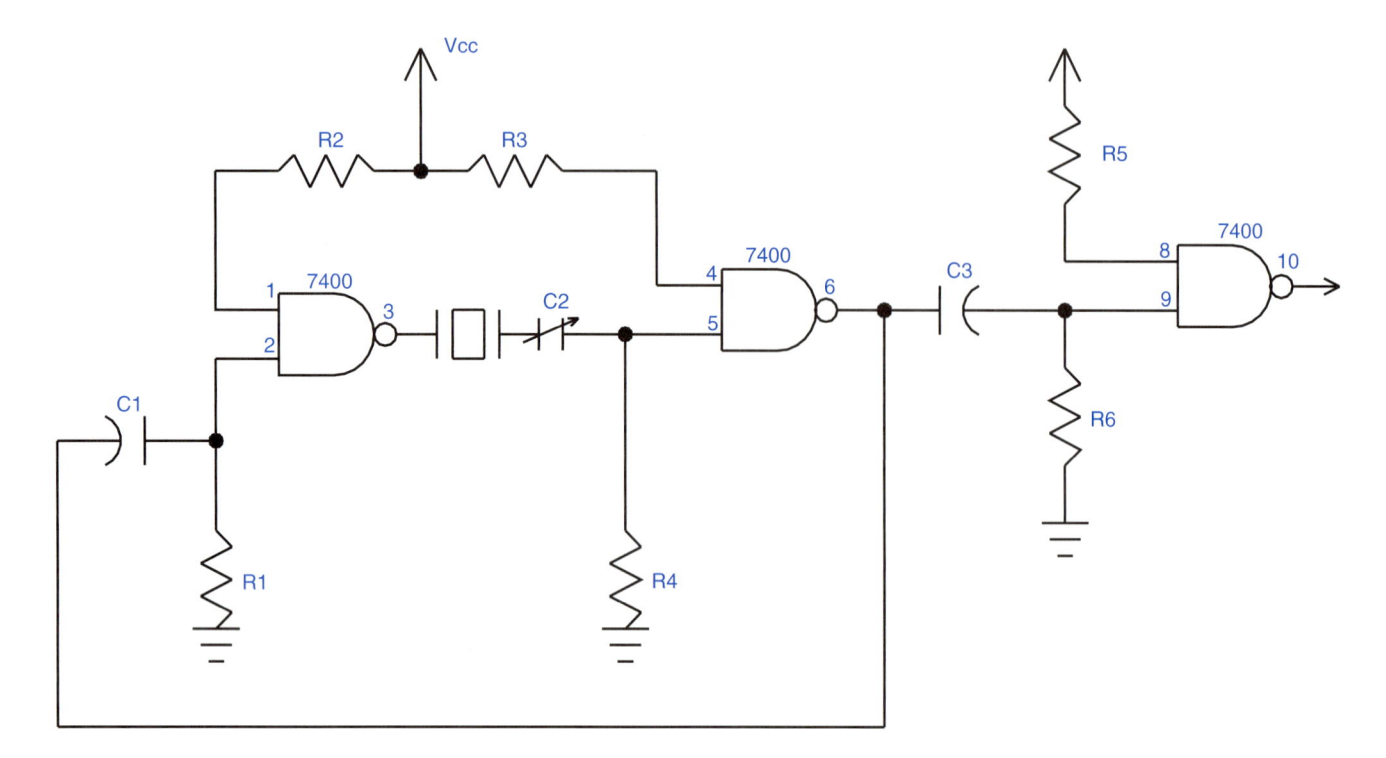

CHAPTER 7 ||| Editing Your Drawing **295**

7.6 Electrical One-Line Diagram
Draw the diagram shown below without text or connectors. Draw the dimensioned examples first and then use the editing commands as needed to complete the diagram. Do not draw dimensions. Save as P7.6.

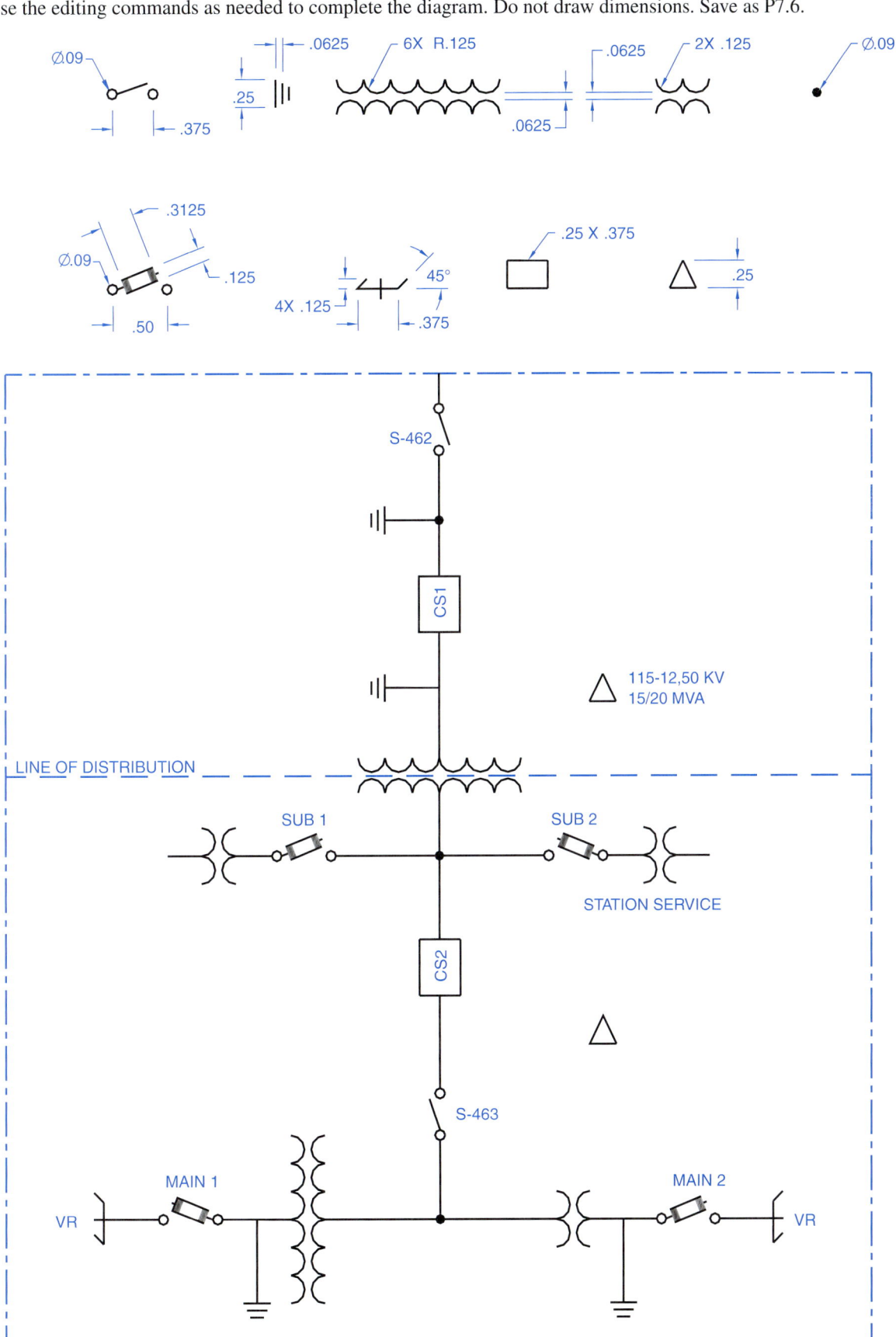

7.7 Gasket

Draw the half view shown below. Mirror along the symmetrical center line to create the other half. Do not draw notes or dimensions. Save as P7.7.

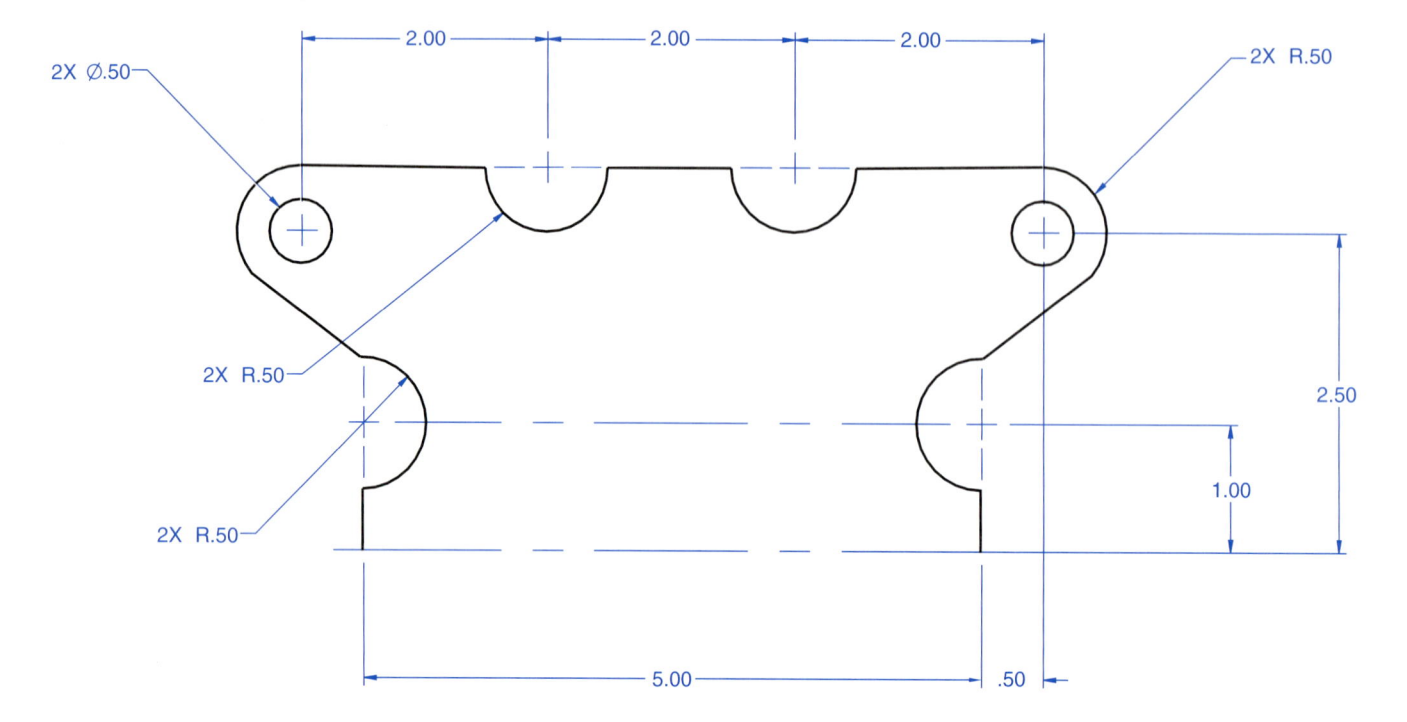

7.8 Wheel
Draw the object shown below without notes or dimensions. Save as P7.8.

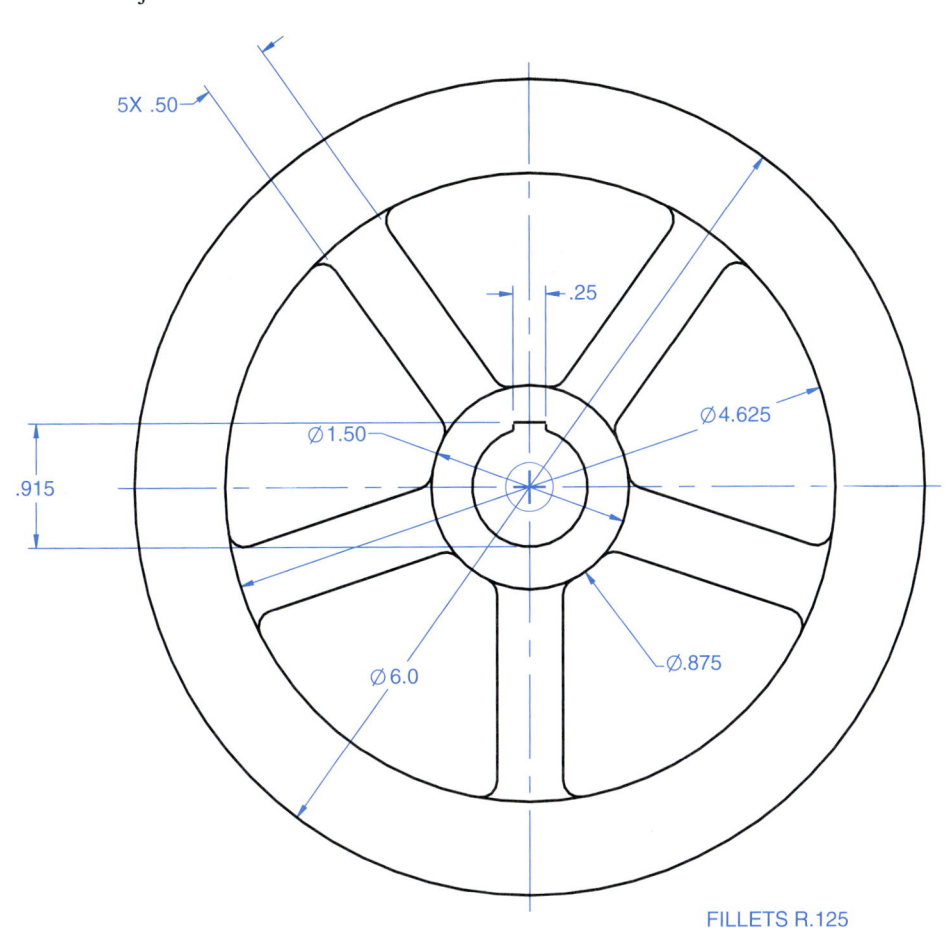

7.9 Drift Boat
Draw the views shown below to your own specifications. Save as P7.9.

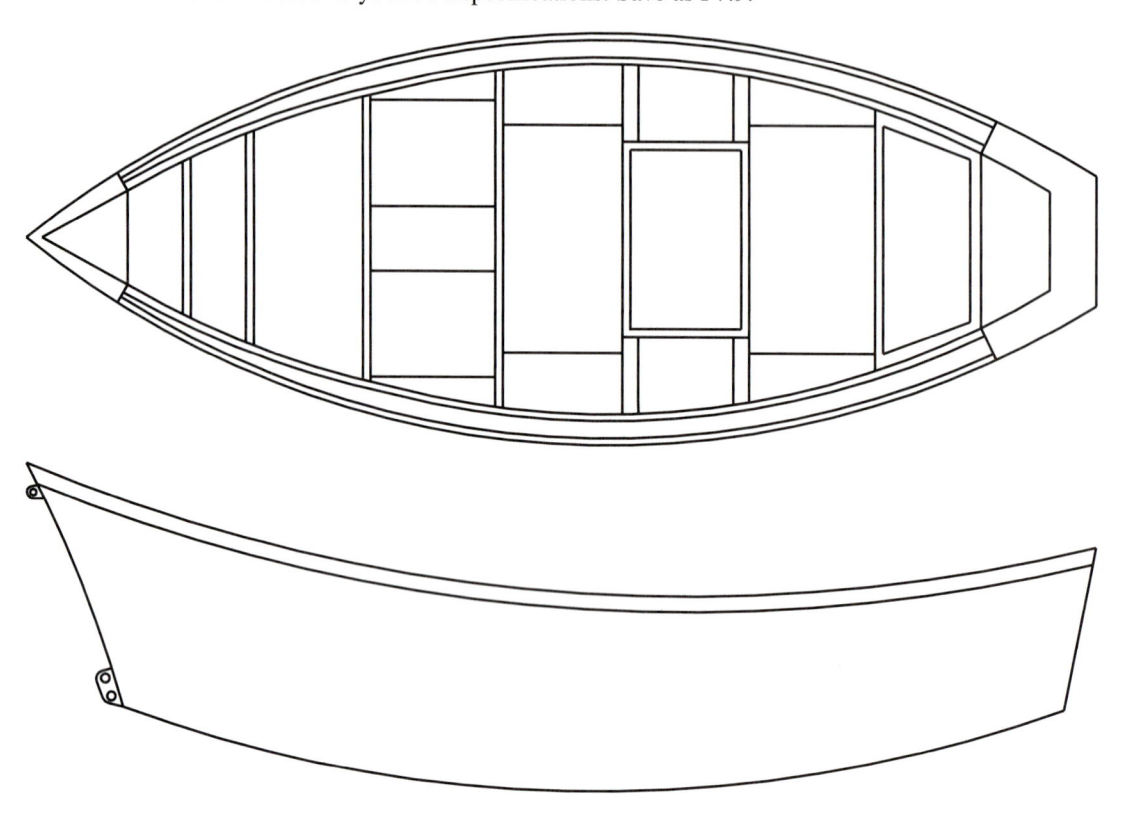

7.10 Plot Plan
Draw the plot plan shown below without dimensions. Save as P7.10.

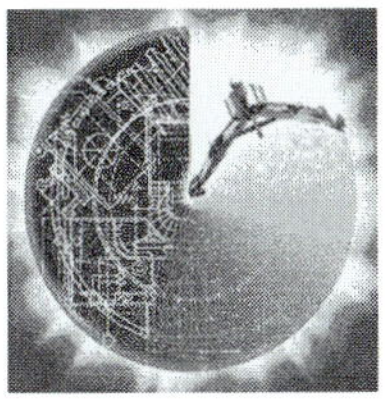

CHAPTER 8

Drawing and Editing Polylines and Double Lines

LEARNING GOALS

- Use the PLINE command options to draw a variety of polyline shapes and designs.
- Use the PEDIT command options to perform several polyline editing operations.
- Explain how to calculate the area of a closed polyline object.
- Make curves out of straight polyline segments.
- Draw fillets and chamfers on polylines.
- Explode a polyline.
- Draw and edit spline curves.
- Use the DLINE command to draw double lines with several design options.
- Set up and draw Revision Clouds.

Introduction to Polylines and Double Lines

AutoCAD LT provides you with the flexibility of creating interconnected line or line and arc segments in any width and of any desired design. These objects are called polylines. AutoCAD LT defines *polylines* as objects composed of one or more line segments or circular arcs that are treated as a single object. Polylines are also called *plines* (pronounced "p-lines") because they are drawn using the PLINE command. Polylines allow you to create objects that are limited only by your imagination, or you can simply use them to trace the boundary of a group of objects for the convenience of making area calculations. The REVCLOUD command uses polylines to construct revision clouds within your drawings. Revision clouds are cloudlike shapes in a drawing used to call attention to revised areas of a drawing.

You can also draw double lines. The format of the lines can be of any width and design you select, including straight and arc double lines. For example, you can draw double lines spaced as needed for the walls of an architectural floor plan. AutoCAD LT calls these *double lines,* and they are drawn using the DLINE command.

Drawing Polylines

Each segment in a series of connected lines or connected lines and arcs is a single object when you draw using the LINE and ARC commands. The PLINE command, however, allows you to draw connected line and arc segments that together form a single object. These polylines offer you some editing flexibility that is not available with individual line and arc segments. For example, in Chapter 7 you learned how to draw fillets and chamfers by selecting two objects. The FILLET and CHAMFER commands have a Polyline option that allows you to pick a polyline and automatically have all of the corners filleted or chamfered as needed. Additionally, polylines offer you unlimited design opportunities by making thick or tapered line and arc objects.

Polylines are drawn by picking the Polyline button in the Draw toolbar, by picking Polyline in the Draw pull-down menu, or by typing **PL** or **PLINE** at the Command: prompt.

Draw
Polyline

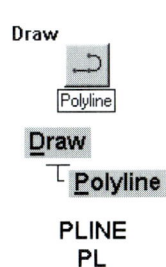

Draw
Polyline

PLINE
PL

299

Using the PLINE Command Options

The initial prompt of the PLINE command is just like the LINE command. You are asked for the From point:, which is the first point of the polyline segment. You are then given several options, but the default asks for the endpoint of the line. The default width of a polyline is 0 (zero). The following command sequence draws the polyline shown in Figure 8.1:

Command: **PL** or **PLINE**.↵
From point: ⟨*pick a point*⟩
Current line-width is 0.0000
Arc/Close/Halfwidth/Length/Undo/Width/<Endpoint of line>: ⟨*pick the endpoint*⟩
Arc/Close/Halfwidth/Length/Undo/Width/<Endpoint of line>: ⟨*pick the endpoint*⟩
Arc/Close/Halfwidth/Length/Undo/Width/<Endpoint of line>: ↵
Command:

FIGURE 8.1 Drawing a two-straight-segment polyline.

Although the object in Figure 8.1 looks like two line segments, it is really one object. All you have to do to erase the whole thing is to pick any place on the polyline at the Select objects: prompt of the ERASE command.

Closing and Undoing Polylines

The Close option in the PLINE command works just like the Close option for the LINE command. The Close option connects the last segment drawn with the start point of the first segment as shown in Figure 8.2. If you are drawing a polyline that you know is going to be closed, just use the Close option to automatically have the last segment closed to the beginning of the first segment like this:

Command: **PL** or **PLINE**.↵
From point: ⟨*pick a point*⟩
Current line-width is 0.0000
Arc/Close/Halfwidth/Length/Undo/Width/<Endpoint of line>: ⟨*pick the endpoint*⟩
Arc/Close/Halfwidth/Length/Undo/Width/<Endpoint of line>: ⟨*pick the endpoint*⟩
Arc/Close/Halfwidth/Length/Undo/Width/<Endpoint of line>: **C**↵
Command:

FIGURE 8.2 Closing a polyline with the Close option.

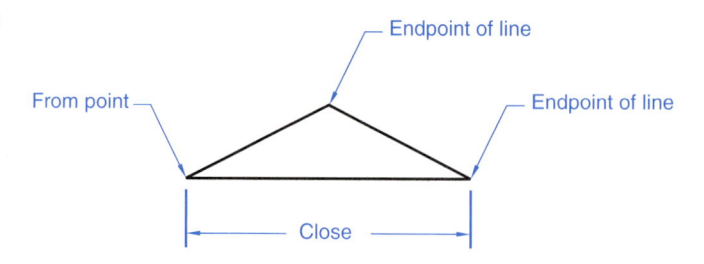

The Undo option is used within the PLINE command to undo the previously drawn polyline segment. This provides you with the convenience of undoing as many previously drawn polyline segments as needed without leaving the PLINE command. To do this, type **U** and press Enter at this PLINE prompt:

Arc/Close/Halfwidth/Length/Undo/Width/<Endpoint of line>: **U**↵

Once you have left the polyline command, you can undo all of the segments drawn in the previous PLINE command by typing **U** at the Command: prompt and pressing Enter.

CHAPTER 8 ||| Drawing and Editing Polylines and Double Lines

> ### Exercise 8.1
> 1. Start a new drawing.
> 2. Draw two straight polyline segments like those shown in Figure 8.1.
> 3. Draw a closed polyline like that in Figure 8.2.
> 4. Save the drawing as EX8.1.

Drawing Polyline Arcs

The PLINE command's Arc option can be used at any time while you are in the PLINE command to draw an arc segment connected to the previous straight or arc polyline segment. After you enter the PLINE command and pick the first point, you can enter the Arc option like this:

Command: **PL** or **PLINE**⏎
From point: ⟨*pick a point*⟩
Current line-width is 0.0000
Arc/Close/Halfwidth/Length/Undo/Width/<Endpoint of line>: **A**⏎
Angle/CEnter/CLose/Direction/Halfwidth/Line/Radius/Second pt/Undo/Width/<Endpoint of arc>:
　⟨*pick arc endpoint*⟩
Angle/CEnter/CLose/Direction/Halfwidth/Line/Radius/Second pt/Undo/Width/<Endpoint of arc>: ⏎
Command:

As you can see, there are many suboptions. The default allows you to move the cursor and pick or type the coordinates of an endpoint of the arc. The coordinates can be entered as absolute, relative, or polar coordinates, or by using direct distance entry, if desired. Notice in Figure 8.3 that the direction in which the arc is drawn depends on which way you move the cursor after picking the first point. In a new drawing, if the cursor is dragged upward, the arc is drawn counterclockwise. If the cursor is dragged downward, the arc is drawn clockwise.

FIGURE 8.3 The direction in which the polyline arc is drawn depends on the direction you move the cursor after picking the first point.

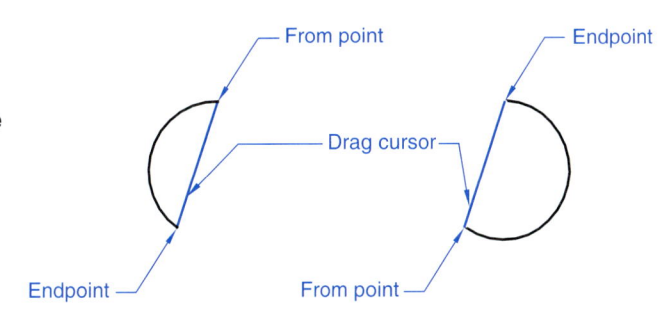

A series of connecting arcs can be drawn if you continue to move the cursor and pick additional arc endpoints. You can also draw polyline arcs connected to straight segments by entering the Arc option and the Line option as needed. The arcs and lines are automatically drawn tangent to each other. The results of the following command sequence are displayed in Figure 8.4. This sequence draws a straight segment followed by two arcs and then another straight segment:

Command: **PL** or **PLINE**⏎
From point: ⟨*pick a point*⟩
Current line-width is 0.0000
Arc/Close/Halfwidth/Length/Undo/Width/<Endpoint of line>: ⟨*pick the endpoint*⟩
Arc/Close/Halfwidth/Length/Undo/Width/<Endpoint of line>: **A**⏎
Angle/CEnter/CLose/Direction/Halfwidth/Line/Radius/Second pt/Undo/Width/<Endpoint of arc>:
　⟨*pick arc endpoint*⟩
Angle/CEnter/CLose/Direction/Halfwidth/Line/Radius/Second pt/Undo/Width/<Endpoint of arc>:
　⟨*pick arc endpoint*⟩
Angle/CEnter/CLose/Direction/Halfwidth/Line/Radius/Second pt/Undo/Width/<Endpoint of arc>: **L**⏎
Arc/Close/Halfwidth/Length/Undo/Width/<Endpoint of line>: ⟨*pick the line endpoint*⟩
Arc/Close/Halfwidth/Length/Undo/Width/<Endpoint of line>: ⏎
Command:

FIGURE 8.4 Drawing a polyline with a straight segment followed by two arc segments and then another straight segment.

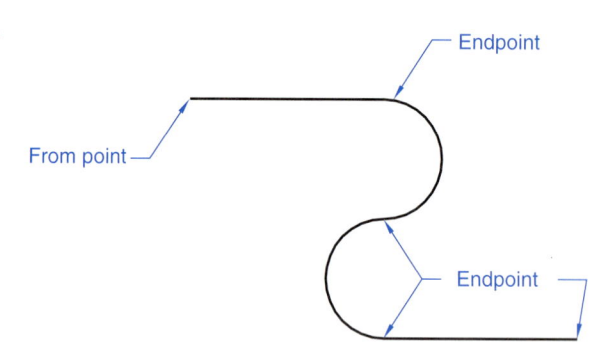

Field Notes

Remember to use ORTHO to your advantage when drawing horizontal and vertical straight polyline segments. Use Polar Snap to assist with angled segments.

The other Arc suboptions that provide you with added flexibility when drawing polyline arcs are similar to the ARC command options that were discussed in Chapter 3. Figure 8.5 shows the results of each of the Arc suboptions. These suboptions are briefly described as follows:

Angle: Type **A** and press Enter to get an Included angle: prompt. Type or pick the desired included angle and then select the arc endpoint or use the Center or Radius option. The prompts work like this:

Angle/CEnter/CLose/Direction/Halfwidth/Line/Radius/Second pt/Undo/Width/<Endpoint of arc>: **A**↵
Included angle: ⟨*type an included angle*⟩
Center/Radius/<Endpoint>: ⟨*pick an endpoint or type* **C** *or* **R**⟩

CEnter: Type **CE** to have the option to pick the arc's center point. You are then asked to pick an endpoint, or use either the Angle or Length option:

Angle/CEnter/CLose/Direction/Halfwidth/Line/Radius/Second pt/Undo/Width/<Endpoint of arc>: **CE**↵

FIGURE 8.5 The results of using the PLINE Arc options.

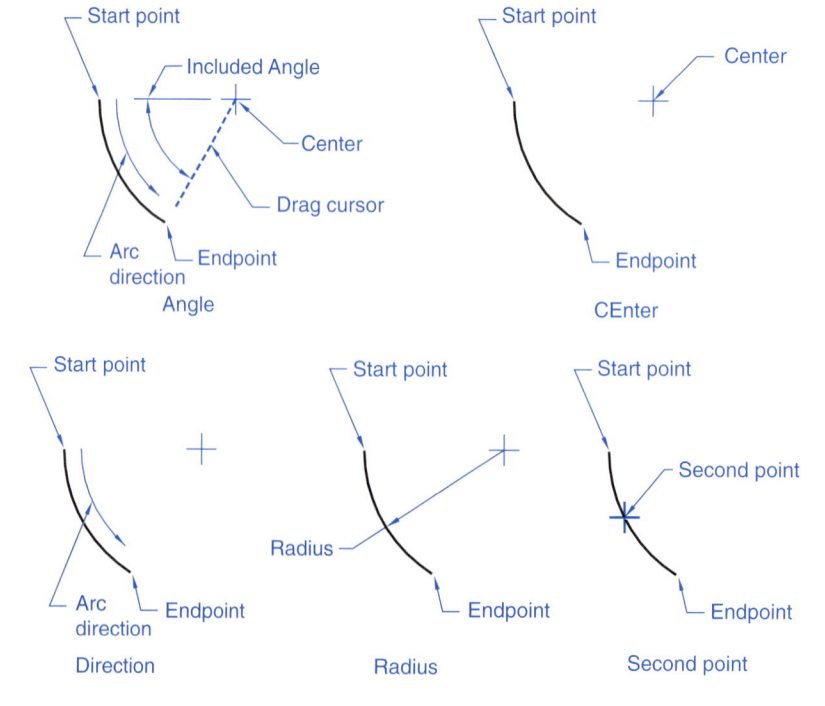

CHAPTER 8 ||| Drawing and Editing Polylines and Double Lines

Center point: ⟨*pick the center point*⟩
Angle/Length/<End point>: ⟨*pick an endpoint or type* **A** *or* **L**⟩

The results of the CEnter option may not create an arc that is tangent to the previous arc.

Direction: Type **D** to be asked for the arc direction followed by the endpoint:

Angle/CEnter/CLose/Direction/Halfwidth/Line/Radius/Second pt/Undo/Width/<Endpoint of arc>: **D.⏎**
Direction from start point: ⟨*pick or type an angle for the arc direction*⟩
Endpoint: ⟨*pick the endpoint*⟩

Radius: Type **R** to be asked to enter the arc radius followed by picking the endpoint or using the angle option:

Angle/CEnter/CLose/Direction/Halfwidth/Line/Radius/Second pt/Undo/Width/<Endpoint of arc>: **R.⏎**
Radius: ⟨*type a radius value*⟩
Angle/<Endpoint>:

Second pt: Type **S** to get the Second point: prompt followed by the Endpoint: prompt:

Angle/CEnter/CLose/Direction/Halfwidth/Line/Radius/Second pt/Undo/Width/<Endpoint of arc>: **S.⏎**
Second point: ⟨*pick the second arc point*⟩
Endpoint: ⟨*pick the arc endpoint*⟩

The results of this option may not provide tangent arcs.

The Arc option also contains the CLose and Undo options that were explained earlier. However, this CLose option requires that you type **CL**. The previous Close option used only a **C**. The remaining Arc options are explained in the next few subsections.

Field Notes

Keep in mind that you type the capitalized letter or letters of the option name.

Exercise 8.2

1. Start a new drawing.
2. Draw connecting straight and arc polyline segments similar to those shown in Figure 8.4.
3. Save the drawing as EX8.2.

Adjusting Polyline Width

The initial polyline width is 0 (zero), which makes a thin line or arc. When you change the polyline width, the new value becomes the default until it is changed again. The PLINE Width option allows you to draw polylines with any desired starting and ending widths. For example, follow this command sequence to draw the .25-in.-wide polyline shown in Figure 8.6:

Command: **PL** or **PLINE.⏎**
From point: ⟨*pick a point*⟩
Current line-width is 0.0000
Arc/Close/Halfwidth/Length/Undo/Width/<Endpoint of line>: **W.⏎**
Starting width <0>: **.25.⏎**
Ending width <0.25>: ⏎
Arc/Close/Halfwidth/Length/Undo/Width/<Endpoint of line>: ⟨*pick the endpoint*⟩
Arc/Close/Halfwidth/Length/Undo/Width/<Endpoint of line>: ⏎
Command:

FIGURE 8.6 The elements of a wide polyline.

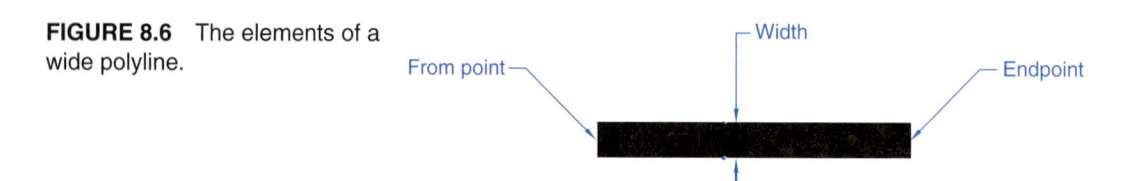

Field Notes

> Notice in the Width option command sequence that the default value for the ending width is automatically the same as the value you entered for the starting width. All you have to do is press Enter to accept the default. Also look at Figure 8.6 and notice that the points you pick to establish the length are at the center of the wide polyline.

The width you set applies to the polyline arcs just as it does for the straight segments. If you want to draw a tapered polyline, enter a different starting and ending width. If you want to draw a polyline with a sharp point, such as an arrow, use 0 (zero) for the starting width and some other value for the ending width. You can also change the polyline width at the beginning of each segment to create a variety of effects. Figure 8.7 shows the results of some different polyline width applications.

FIGURE 8.7 The results of some different polyline width applications.

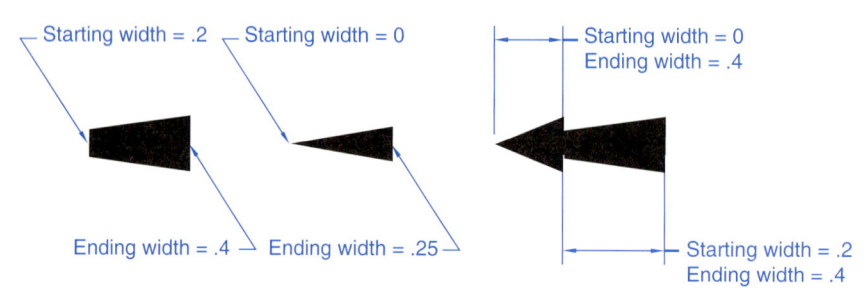

The PLINE command also has a Halfwidth option for drawing wide polylines that are measured from the center to the outside edge. A halfwidth polyline is shown in Figure 8.8 and drawn using this command sequence:

Command: **PL** or **PLINE**↵
From point: ⟨*pick a point*⟩
Current line-width is 0.0000
Arc/Close/Halfwidth/Length/Undo/Width/<Endpoint of line>: **H**↵
Starting half-width <0>: **.25**↵
Ending half-width <.25>: **.5**↵
Arc/Close/Halfwidth/Length/Undo/Width/<Endpoint of line>: ⟨*pick the endpoint*⟩
Arc/Close/Halfwidth/Length/Undo/Width/<Endpoint of line>: ↵
Command:

FIGURE 8.8 Using the PLINE Halfwidth option.

Using the PLINE Length Option

The PLINE command's Length option is used to draw a polyline segment connected to or parallel to and in the same direction as the previously drawn polyline segment, polyline arc, line, or arc. The Length option asks you to type a desired length after picking the endpoint of the line. The Length option works like this:

CHAPTER 8 ||| Drawing and Editing Polylines and Double Lines   305

```
Command: PL or PLINE↵
From point: ⟨pick a point⟩
Current line-width is 0.0000
Arc/Close/Halfwidth/Length/Undo/Width/<Endpoint of line>: L↵
Length of line: 2.5↵
Arc/Close/Halfwidth/Length/Undo/Width/<Endpoint of line>: ↵
Command:
```

You can continue drawing additional polyline or polyline arc segments or press Enter to return to the Command: prompt. If you want to connect a polyline segment to the end of a previously drawn polyline segment or polyline arc, use the @ option at the From point: prompt like this:

```
Command: PL or PLINE↵
From point: @↵
Current line-width is 0.0000
Arc/Close/Halfwidth/Length/Undo/Width/<Endpoint of line>: L↵
Length of line: 2.5↵
Arc/Close/Halfwidth/Length/Undo/Width/<Endpoint of line>: ↵
Command:
```

Exercise 8.3

1. Start a new drawing.
2. Draw a straight polyline segment with a 0.25 starting and ending width similar to that shown in Figure 8.6.
3. Draw three different polyline objects using a variety of width options, as was done in Figure 8.7.
4. Draw a halfwidth object similar to Figure 8.8.
5. Draw a polyline segment and then reenter the PLINE command. Pick a point when you get the From point: prompt. Use the Length option to draw a 2.5-in.-long polyline segment parallel to the previous polyline segment.
6. Reenter the PLINE command again. This time, use the @ option to connect the start of the new polyline to the end of the previous polyline segment. Use the Length option to draw a 2.5-in.-long polyline segment that is connected to the previous polyline segment.
7. Save the drawing as EX8.3.

✓ LEARNING CHECKPOINT

- ☐ What is the default polyline width?
- ☐ How do you draw a polyline arc connected to a straight pline segment?
- ☐ After drawing a polyline arc, how do you draw a connecting pline straight segment?
- ☐ How do you automatically set the same polyline starting and ending widths?
- ☐ Explain how to draw a polyline that looks like an arrowhead.
- ☐ Describe the results of the PLINE Halfwidth option.
- ☐ How do you draw a polyline segment connected to and in the same direction as the previously drawn polyline segment?

Editing Polylines

AutoCAD LT provides several options for editing polylines. For example, you can change the width of polyline segments or of the entire polyline object. You can open or close polyline shapes. Straight polyline segments can be made into polyline curves. If polyline objects and nonpolyline objects meet at the endpoints, they can be joined as one polyline object. You can change the vertices of polylines. The *vertices* are the points at which polyline segments meet; a single instance is called a *vertex.* The editing you can do at vertices includes moving and deleting vertices and straightening between vertices. Polylines are edited with the PEDIT command. To start this command, type **PE** or **PEDIT** at the Command: prompt or pick Polyline in the Object cascade of the Modify pull-down menu.

Using the PEDIT Command Options

When you enter the PEDIT command, you get the following prompt, which asks you to select a polyline:

Command: **PE** or **PEDIT**↵
Select polyline: ⟨*pick the polyline*⟩
Close/Join/Width/Edit vertex/Fit/Spline/Decurve/Ltype gen/Undo/eXit <X>:

The Undo option allows you to undo the previous polyline edits while you are still inside of the PEDIT command. Type **U** and press Enter to use the Undo option. Exit the PEDIT command by pressing Enter to accept the exit default or type **X** and press Enter. The other PEDIT options are explained in the following discussion.

Closing and Opening Polylines
The Close option of the PEDIT command lets you close an open polyline by drawing a segment from the end of the last segment to the beginning of the first segment. After using the Close option, the prompt changes to Open. Type **O** and press Enter if you want to automatically open the polyline you just closed, as shown in Figure 8.9. The command sequence looks like this:

Command: **PE** or **PEDIT**↵
Select polyline: ⟨*pick the polyline*⟩
Close/Join/Width/Edit vertex/Fit/Spline/Decurve/Ltype gen/Undo/eXit <X>: **C**↵
Open/Join/Width/Edit vertex/Fit/Spline/Decurve/Ltype gen/Undo/eXit <X>: **O**↵
Close/Join/Width/Edit vertex/Fit/Spline/Decurve/Ltype gen/Undo/eXit <X>: ↵
Command:

FIGURE 8.9 Closing an open polyline and then opening a closed polyline with the PEDIT command.

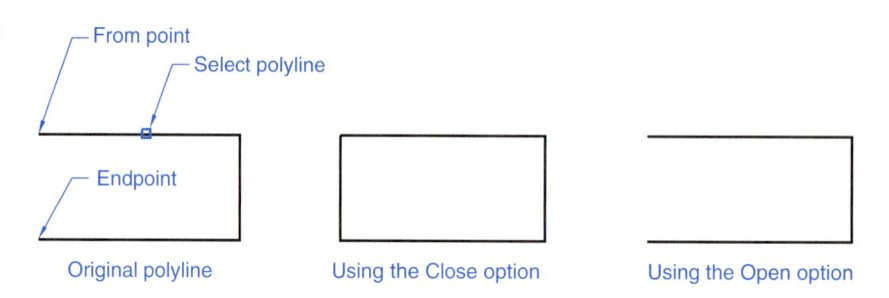

Joining Objects to a Polyline
The Join option of the PEDIT command allows you to join lines, arcs, or other polylines to a polyline if they touch at the endpoints. The Join option removes the curve fitting from a polyline. Curve fitting is discussed later in this chapter. When an object is joined with a polyline, the object and the polyline become one object and the object being joined takes on the same width characteristics as the polyline. Any joined objects are made part of the first selected polyline. Also, the color, layer, and linetype of the first polyline are inherited by the joined objects. The joined polyline objects do not change in width. The prompts work as follows and the result is shown in Figure 8.10:

Command: **PE** or **PEDIT**↵
Select polyline: ⟨*pick the polyline*⟩
Close/Join/Width/Edit vertex/Fit/Spline/Decurve/Ltype gen/Undo/eXit <X>: **J**↵
Select objects: ⟨*pick the object to join*⟩
Select objects: ↵
1 segments added to polyline
Close/Join/Width/Edit vertex/Fit/Spline/Decurve/Ltype gen/Undo/eXit <X>: ↵
Command:

FIGURE 8.10 Using the PEDIT Join option to connect an object to a polyline and have the object take on the characteristics of the polyline.

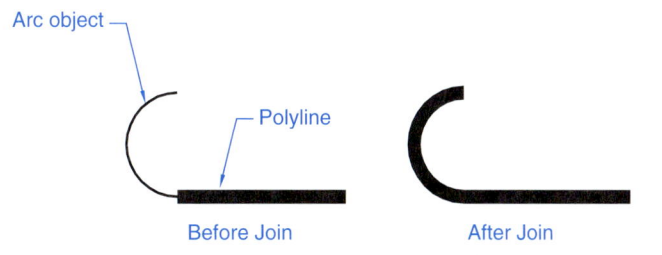

Before Join   After Join

Changing Connected Line and Arc Segments to a Polyline and Calculating the Area of a Closed Polyline

In Chapter 6 you learned about calculating the area of objects that were drawn using the LINE command and commands that created closed objects such as circles and polygons. However, you were unable to calculate the area of an object that was made up of connected lines and arcs. To calculate the area of objects like this, you can do one of three things. You can draw the original object using polyline lines and arcs, creating an outline of the object which is a continuous closed polyline. If the object is already drawn using line and arc segments, you can trace the outline of the object using the PLINE command and its options.

If the object is already drawn using line and arc segments, you can change these segments to a continuous polyline. Do this using the PEDIT command. When the PEDIT command asks you to Select polyline:, pick one of the line or arc objects. AutoCAD LT then tells you that "Object selected is not a polyline—Do you want to turn it into one?" After answering yes to this question, AutoCAD LT turns the selected line or arc into a polyline and then gives you the typical PEDIT options. Now, use the Join option to connect the other arc and line segments to the new polyline segment followed by using the AREA command like this:

Command: **PE** or **PEDIT**↵
Select polyline: ⟨*pick one of the line or arc segments*⟩
Object selected is not a polyline
Do you want to turn it into one? <Y>: ↵
Close/Join/Width/Edit vertex/Fit/Spline/Decurve/Ltype gen/Undo/eXit <X>: **J**↵
Select objects: ⟨*select the remaining line or arc segments*⟩
Select objects: ↵
3 segments added to polyline
Close/Join/Width/Edit vertex/Fit/Spline/Decurve/Ltype gen/Undo/eXit <X>: ↵
Command: **AREA**↵
<First point>/Object/Add/Subtract: **O**↵
Select objects: ↵
Area = 11.2044, Perimeter = 13.4270

Changing Polyline Width

The PEDIT Width option allows you to change the entire width of a polyline to a uniform value that you specify. Look at Figure 8.11 as you follow this command sequence:

Command: **PE** or **PEDIT**↵
Select polyline: ⟨*pick the polyline*⟩
Close/Join/Width/Edit vertex/Fit/Spline/Decurve/Ltype gen/Undo/eXit <X>: **W**↵
Enter new polyline width for all segments: **.1**↵
Close/Join/Width/Edit vertex/Fit/Spline/Decurve/Ltype gen/Undo/eXit <X>: ↵
Command:

FIGURE 8.11 Using the PEDIT Width option to uniformly change the width of an entire polyline.

Before Width change   After Width change

Exercise 8.4

1. Start a new drawing.
2. Draw an open polyline similar to the original polyline in Figure 8.9; close the polyline; and then open it using the process shown in Figure 8.9.
3. Draw an arc connected to a polyline similar to that shown in Figure 8.10 and then join the arc to the polyline.
4. Draw a polyline similar to the before width change example shown in Figure 8.11 and then perform a width change similar to that in Figure 8.11.
5. Save the drawing as EX8.4.

Editing Polyline Vertices

The Edit vertex option of the PEDIT command allows you to make several different changes to polyline vertices. When you enter the Edit vertex option, AutoCAD LT places an X at the first point of the polyline. You can move the X to another vertex by using the Next or Previous suboptions. This lets you edit the vertex where the X is located. The Next suboption is the initial default and then the default changes to the current application of Next or Previous. Figure 8.12 shows the X located at the vertices of a polyline. The command sequence works like this:

Command: **PE** or **PEDIT**↵
Select polyline: ⟨*pick the polyline*⟩
Close/Join/Width/Edit vertex/Fit/Spline/Decurve/Ltype gen/Undo/eXit <X>: **E**↵
Next/Previous/Break/Insert/Move/Regen/Straighten/Tangent/Width/eXit <N>: ↵
Next/Previous/Break/Insert/Move/Regen/Straighten/Tangent/Width/eXit <N>: **P**↵
Next/Previous/Break/Insert/Move/Regen/Straighten/Tangent/Width/eXit <P>: ↵
Next/Previous/Break/Insert/Move/Regen/Straighten/Tangent/Width/eXit <P>:

FIGURE 8.12 Using the Edit vertex (A) Next and (B) Previous options.

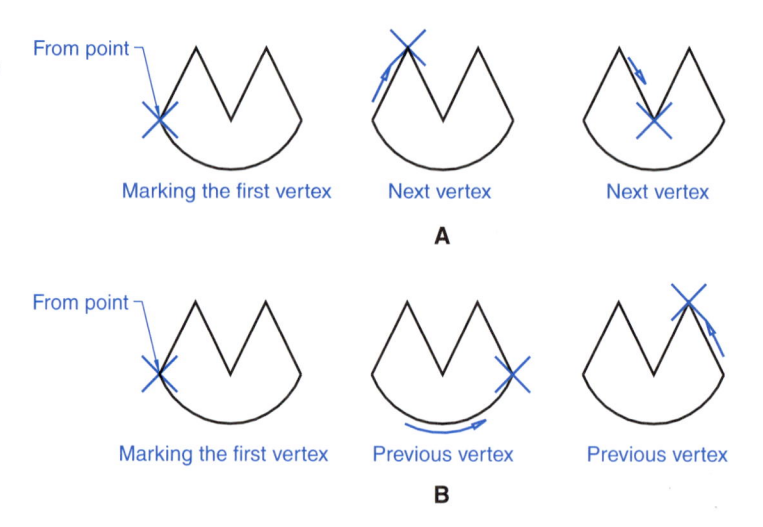

Locating the X at the desired vertex allows you to perform one or more of the Edit vertex options. The remaining Edit vertex options are explained in the following list:

Break: Type a **B** and press Enter to use this option. The Break option places a break in the polyline between the vertices you specify. First, use the Next or Previous option to move the marker to the vertex where you want the break to begin. Then enter the Break option. The Break option allows you to move the X marker to the Next or Previous vertex until you get to the vertex where you want the break to end. Use the Go option to make the break between where you placed the initial X marker and where you moved the X marker before entering Go. The marker then snaps back to the vertex where you started the break as shown in Figure 8.13. Use the Go option by typing **G** and pressing Enter like this:

CHAPTER 8 ||| Drawing and Editing Polylines and Double Lines

Command: **PE** or **PEDIT**↵
Select polyline: ⟨*pick the polyline*⟩
Close/Join/Width/Edit vertex/Fit/Spline/Decurve/Ltype gen/Undo/eXit <X>: **E**↵
Next/Previous/Break/Insert/Move/Regen/Straighten/Tangent/Width/eXit <N>: ↵
Next/Previous/Break/Insert/Move/Regen/Straighten/Tangent/Width/eXit <N>: **B**↵
Next/Previous/Go/eXit <N>: ↵
Next/Previous/Go/eXit <N>: ↵
Next/Previous/Go/eXit <N>: **G**↵
Next/Previous/Break/Insert/None/Regen/Straighten/Tangent/Width/eXit <N>:

FIGURE 8.13 Using the PEDIT Break option.

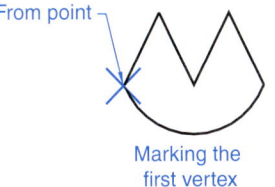

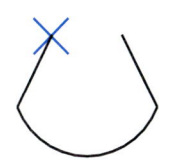

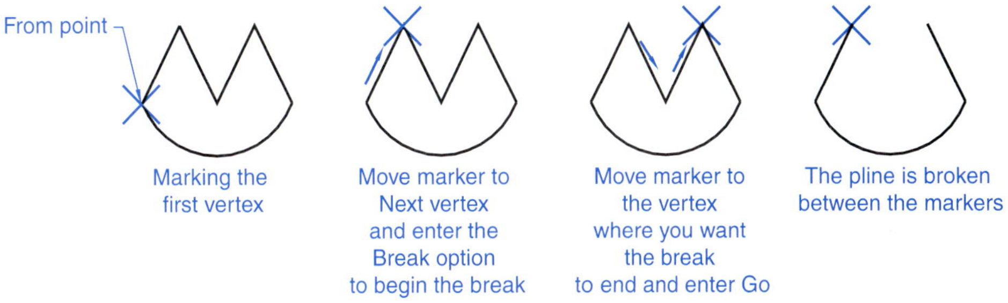

Marking the first vertex

Move marker to Next vertex and enter the Break option to begin the break

Move marker to the vertex where you want the break to end and enter Go

The pline is broken between the markers

The Break option can also be used to break at a specific vertex without removing any segments if Break is used and Go is specified without moving the vertex marker. When Break is used, the polyline is made into two separate polylines—even closed polylines are affected this way.

Insert: This Edit vertex option allows you to insert a new vertex. To do this, move the marker to the vertex next to where you want the new vertex and then type **I** and press Enter for the Insert option. You are then asked to enter the location of the new vertex. A rubber-band cursor is connected to the screen crosshairs to assist you in placing the new vertex. A polar or relative coordinate or direct distance entry uses the current vertex as a base point. The new vertex is connected between the vertex at the marker location and the next vertex as shown in Figure 8.14:

Command: **PE** or **PEDIT**↵
Select polyline: ⟨*pick the polyline*⟩
Close/Join/Width/Edit vertex/Fit/Spline/Decurve/Ltype gen/Undo/eXit <X>: **E**↵
Next/Previous/Break/Insert/Move/Regen/Straighten/Tangent/Width/eXit <N>: ↵
Next/Previous/Break/Insert/Move/Regen/Straighten/Tangent/Width/eXit <N>: **I**↵
Enter location of new vertex: ⟨*pick a new vertex location*⟩
Next/Previous/Break/Insert/Move/Regen/Straighten/Tangent/Width/eXit <N>:

FIGURE 8.14 Using the PEDIT Insert option to insert a new vertex.

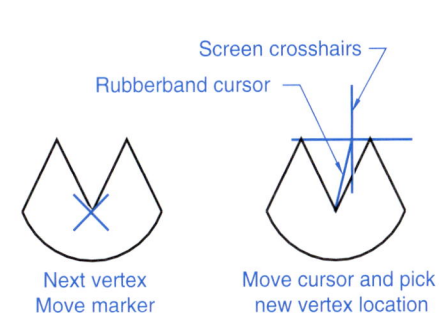

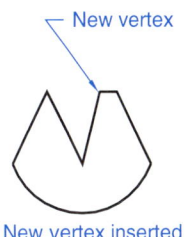

Next vertex Move marker next to desired new vertex location

Move cursor and pick new vertex location

New vertex inserted

Move: This Edit vertex option allows you to move a vertex from where the marker is located to a new position as shown in Figure 8.15. A polar, relative, or absolute coordinate can be entered, or direct distance entry, a pick, or an object snap can be used to indicate the new location. This is the command sequence:

Command: **PE** or **PEDIT**↵
Select polyline: ⟨*pick the polyline*⟩
Close/Join/Width/Edit vertex/Fit/Spline/Decurve/Ltype gen/Undo/eXit <X>: **E**↵

Next/Previous/Break/Insert/Move/Regen/Straighten/Tangent/Width/eXit <N>: ↵
Next/Previous/Break/Insert/Move/Regen/Straighten/Tangent/Width/eXit <N>: **M**↵
Enter new location: ⟨*pick a new vertex location*⟩
Next/Previous/Break/Insert/Move/Regen/Straighten/Tangent/Width/eXit <N>:

FIGURE 8.15 Using the PEDIT Move option to move a vertex.

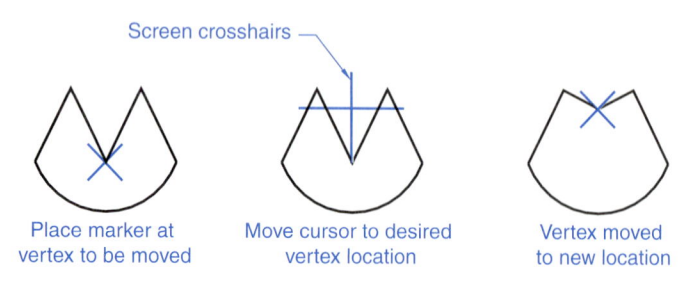

Place marker at vertex to be moved — Move cursor to desired vertex location — Vertex moved to new location

Regen: This Edit vertex option regenerates the computer screen and recomputes the screen coordinates for the vertices that you have edited. This option is very useful for vertext editing options that are not immediately displayed, such as segment width changes.

Straighten: The Straighten option removes the vertices of a polyline between the vertices you specify. First, use the Next or Previous option to move the marker to the vertex where you want the straightening to begin. Then enter the Straighten option. The Straighten option allows you to move the X marker to the Next or Previous vertex until you get to the vertex where you want the straightening to end. Use the Go option to make the break between where you placed the X marker after entering the Straighten option and where you moved the X marker before entering Go. The marker then snaps back to the vertex where you started the straightening process as shown in Figure 8.16. Use the Go option by typing **G** and pressing Enter like this:

Command: **PE** or **PEDIT**↵
Select polyline: ⟨*pick the polyline*⟩
Close/Join/Width/Edit vertex/Fit/Spline/Decurve/Ltype gen/Undo/eXit <X>: **E**↵
Next/Previous/Break/Insert/Move/Regen/Straighten/Tangent/Width/eXit <N>: ↵
Next/Previous/Break/Insert/Move/Regen/Straighten/Tangent/Width/eXit <N>: **S**↵
Next/Previous/Go/eXit <N>: ↵
Next/Previous/Go/eXit <N>: ↵
Next/Previous/Go/eXit <N>: **G**↵
Next/Previous/Break/Insert/None/Regen/Straighten/Tangent/Width/eXit <N>:

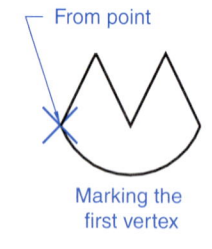

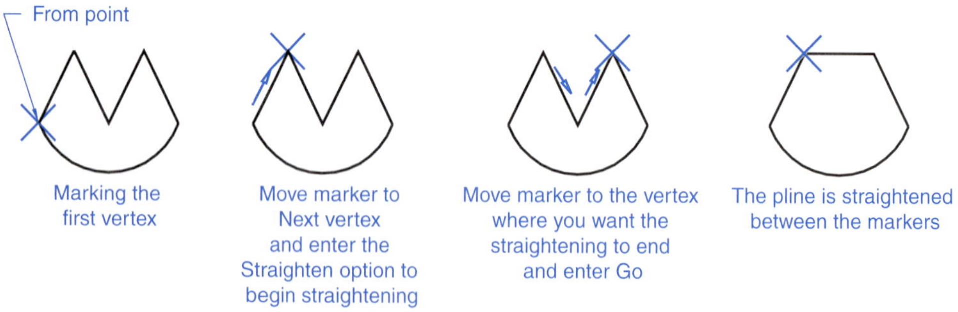

From point

Marking the first vertex — Move marker to Next vertex and enter the Straighten option to begin straightening — Move marker to the vertex where you want the straightening to end and enter Go — The pline is straightened between the markers

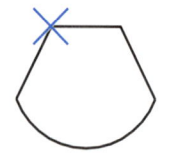

FIGURE 8.16 Using the PEDIT Straighten option.

Tangent: This Edit vertex allows you to attach a tangent direction to the current vertex for later use in curve fitting. The tangency direction can be specified numerically or by picking on screen. If picked, the angle from the vertex to the cursor location is used, as shown in Figure 8.17. This is the command sequence:

Command: **PE** or **PEDIT**↵
Select polyline: ⟨*pick the polyline*⟩
Close/Join/Width/Edit vertex/Fit/Spline/Decurve/Ltype gen/Undo/eXit <X>: **E**↵

CHAPTER 8 ||| Drawing and Editing Polylines and Double Lines 311

Next/Previous/Break/Insert/Move/Regen/Straighten/Tangent/Width/eXit <N>: ↵
Next/Previous/Break/Insert/Move/Regen/Straighten/Tangent/Width/eXit <N>: **T**↵

FIGURE 8.17 Moving the marker to identify the tangency of an arc with the Tangent option.

Move marker to polyline arc

Enter the Tangent option to have the tangent direction shown

Width: The Edit vertex Width option allows you to change the width of each polyline segment. To do this, move the marker to the end of the polyline segment where you want the width change to begin and then enter the width option. Specify the beginning and ending widths. The beginning width is where you first place the marker before entering the Width option. The ending width is where you move the marker after entering width values. Exit the Edit vertex option or use the Regen suboption of the Edit vertex option to have the width change take effect. The following command sequence shows how to change the width of the two polyline segments shown in Figure 8.18:

Command: **PE** or **PEDIT**↵
Select polyline: ⟨*pick the polyline*⟩
Close/Join/Width/Edit vertex/Fit/Spline/Decurve/Ltype gen/Undo/eXit <X>: **E**↵
Next/Previous/Break/Insert/Move/Regen/Straighten/Tangent/Width/eXit <N>: ↵
Next/Previous/Break/Insert/Move/Regen/Straighten/Tangent/Width/eXit <N>: **W**↵
Enter starting width <0>: ↵
Enter ending width <0>: **.1**↵
Next/Previous/Break/Insert/Move/Regen/Straighten/Tangent/Width/eXit <N>: ↵
Next/Previous/Break/Insert/Move/Regen/Straighten/Tangent/Width/eXit <N>: **W**↵
Enter starting width <0>: **.1**↵
Enter ending width <.1>: **0**↵
Next/Previous/Break/Insert/Move/Regen/Straighten/Tangent/Width/eXit <N>: ↵
Next/Previous/Break/Insert/Move/Regen/Straighten/Tangent/Width/eXit <N>: **X**↵

FIGURE 8.18 Using the Edit vertex Width option to change the widths of polyline segments.

Place marker where width change begins

Change width at each segment if needed

Place marker where width change ends and eXit

Exercise 8.5

1. Start a new drawing.
2. Draw a polyline similar to the upper left object shown in Figure 8.12. Use the Direction option to make the last arc segment.
3. Make five copies of the object. You should have a total of six objects.
4. Enter the PEDIT command, select one of the objects, and move the marker around on the object as was done in Figure 8.12.
5. Break the polyline similar to the results in Figure 8.13.
6. Select another one of the objects and establish a new vertex similar to that shown in Figure 8.14.
7. Select another one of the objects and move a vertex to obtain results like those shown in Figure 8.15.
8. Select another one of the objects and straighten a section as was done in Figure 8.16.
9. Select another one of the objects and move the marker to the polyline arc and then enter the Tangent option to display the tangent direction as was done in Figure 8.17.
10. Select another one of the objects and change the width of two segments as shown in Figure 8.18.
11. Save the drawing as EX8.5.

Fitting Curves to Polyline Vertices

The PEDIT command has a Fit option that allows you to make curves out of straight polyline segments. The Fit option creates smooth curves that pass through the vertices of the polyline segments with tangent directions that you specify. A Fit curve operation is performed on a polyline in Figure 8.19 using this command sequence:

Command: **PE** or **PEDIT**↵
Select polyline: ⟨*pick the polyline*⟩
Close/Join/Width/Edit vertex/Fit/Spline/Decurve/Ltype gen/Undo/eXit <X>: **F**↵
Close/Join/Width/Edit vertex/Fit/Spline/Decurve/Ltype gen/Undo/eXit <X>: ↵
Command:

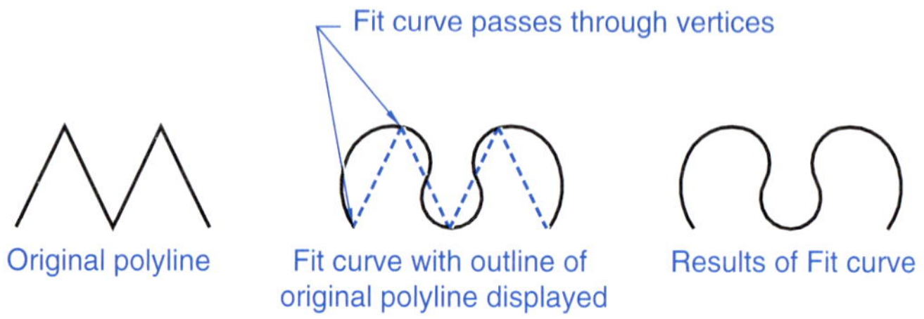

FIGURE 8.19 Using the PEDIT Fit option to make curves out of polyline segments. The Fit curve passes through the polyline vertices.

Original polyline   Fit curve with outline of original polyline displayed   Results of Fit curve

Fit curve passes through vertices

Field Notes

- The Fit option works well when you need to smooth the line between the points of a graph or sheet metal pattern layout that is originally created by connecting points with straight polyline segments, as shown in Figure 8.20.

  FIGURE 8.20 The PEDIT Fit option works well to smooth the polyline segments that are used to connect the points of a graph.

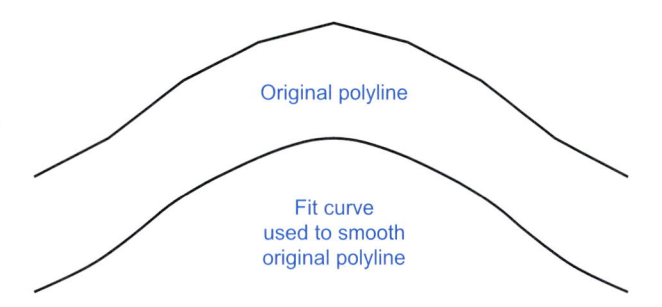

- The curve segment generated for each pline segment is created from two arcs tangent at the endpoints. The default tangency directions are calculated by AutoCAD LT to maintain tangency between each arc from start to end, using the least possible amount of "bulge" on the arcs. If you use the Edit vertex option to alter the tangency direction of any of the vertex points, the fit curve path is generated so the tangency of the arcs intersecting that vertex are in the specified direction.

  If a polyline that has already had a curve fitted to it is edited with the PLINE Edit vertex option and the tangency direction is changed, you must again use the Fit option to reflect the new changes. If a fit curve does not appear as desired, the Edit vertex options can be used to refine its appearance by adjusting tangency directions or by inserting, moving, and deleting vertices as needed. Then reuse the Fit option to update the polyline.

  If a tangency direction is set to be the same angle as an adjoining straight pline segment, that segment remains straight when a fit curve is applied.

- The polyline data are removed when you EXPLODE a curve-fit polyline, but the shape remains the same. You can use the PEDIT command to turn the object back into a polyline.
- The STRETCH, TRIM, and EXTEND commands affect a curve-fit polyline. For example, stretching a curve-fit pline does not cause a refit and may leave arcs no longer tangent to each other. Trimming or breaking a curve-fit pline makes the curve fitting permanent. This means that the curves are converted to actual pline arc segments, so the temporary vertices inserted by curve fitting are incorporated into the pline definition. You can still use the decurve option. However, a decurve reveals new vertex locations that were not used in the initial pline definition.

Creating Spline Curves

The Spline option of the PEDIT command also smoothes polyline segments. This option produces a spline approximation, called a B-spline. This type of spline curve is not as accurate as a true spline, which is created with the SPLINE command (discussed later). The difference between the Fit curve and the Spline curve is that the Fit curve passes through the vertices and the Spline curve uses the vertices as a frame for the curve development. The Spline curve only passes through the first and last vertices, and is pulled toward the others but does not necessarily pass through them. A comparison between the Fit and Spline curve options is shown in Figure 8.21. The Spline curve option works like this:

Command: **PE** or **PEDIT**↵
Select polyline: ⟨*pick the polyline*⟩
Close/Join/Width/Edit vertex/Fit/Spline/Decurve/Ltype gen/Undo/eXit <X>: **S**↵
Close/Join/Width/Edit vertex/Fit/Spline/Decurve/Ltype gen/Undo/eXit <X>: ↵
Command:

FIGURE 8.21 Using the PEDIT Spline option to make curves out of polyline segments. The Spline curve does not pass through the polyline vertices.

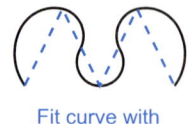

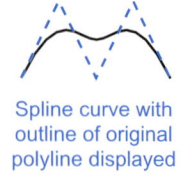

Original polyline   Fit curve with outline of original polyline displayed   Spline curve with outline of original polyline displayed

Additional Curve Options

There are two B-spline curve options that are accessed using the SPLINETYPE system variable. The default setting of 6 creates a ***cubic curve*** when using the PEDIT Spline option. If you change the SPLINETYPE setting to 5, you get a ***quadratic curve.*** The cubic curve default is smoother than the quadratic curve. Change the SPLINETYPE like this:

Command: **SPLINETYPE.┘**
New value for SPLINETYPE <6>: **5.┘**
Command:

You can also adjust the number of segments that are used to create a spline curve. The number of segments is established with the SPLINESEGS variable. The default number of segments is 8, which produces a smooth curve that requires little regeneration time and file size. If you increase the number of segments, you get a smoother curve, but you also increase file size and regeneration time. The SPLINESEGS variable is changed like this:

Command: **SPLINESEGS.┘**
New value for SPLINESEGS <8>: **12.┘**
Command:

Field Notes

Editing commands behave in the following different ways when used on spline-fit plines:

- The STRETCH command stretches the frame such that the spline is recalculated and a new curve is produced.
- OFFSET produces a spline-fit pline with no frame.
- DIVIDE, MEASURE, AREA Object, HATCH, FILLET, and CHAMFER see only the spline, not the frame.
- PEDIT's Join option automatically decurves spline fits for all plines being joined.
- PEDIT's Edit vertex option subcommands move the vertex marker (X) only to the vertices of the frame, whether visible or not. Edit vertex option effects include the following: Break will discard the spline; Insert, Move, Straighten, and Width cause an automatic refit (Width behaves as usual, displaying only if Regen is used when exiting the Edit vertex mode); Tangent specifications on vertices have no effect on a spline-fit curve.
- Object snap sees the spline, not the frame. To snap to control points, do a grip selection or decurve the spline.
- EXTEND adds a new vertex at the intersection of the frame with the boundary geometry.
- You can also edit with grips by selecting the spline-fit curve. The grips are displayed at the vertices. Use any of the desired grip edit commands to change the spline-fit curve accordingly.

Removing the Curve from a Fit or Spline Curve

The PEDIT command Decurve option allows you to remove the curve of a polyline that was edited with the Fit or Spline options. This process changes the curved object back to its original polyline segments. The command sequence is provided in the following and an example is displayed in Figure 8.22:

Command: **PE** or **PEDIT.┘**
Select polyline: ⟨*pick the polyline*⟩
Close/Join/Width/Edit vertex/Fit/Spline/Decurve/Ltype gen/Undo/eXit <X>: **D.┘**

FIGURE 8.22 Using the PEDIT Decurve option.

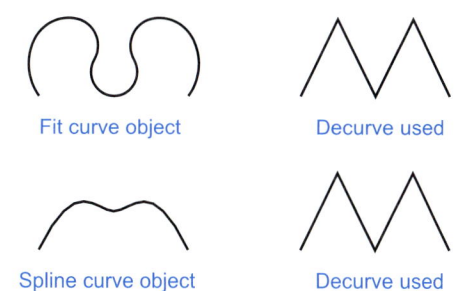

Fit curve object   Decurve used

Spline curve object   Decurve used

Field Notes

- The arc is straightened when the Decurve option is used on curved segments that were created using the Arc option of the PLINE command.
- User assigned tangencies are not lost by decurving. They remain intact and are used by any future curve-fitting operations.
- If a spline-fit polyline is edited using commands such as BREAK and TRIM, the spline frame is lost and any future attempt to decurve the spline back to its original frame has no effect. Also, since the spline no longer has an associated frame, the curve is now generated using standard polyline arc segments, resulting in many new vertices being inserted.

Exercise 8.6

1. Start a new drawing.
2. Draw an open polyline similar to the original polyline shown in Figure 8.19.
3. Make two copies of the polyline.
4. Use the PEDIT Fit option on one of the polylines. You should have results similar to Figure 8.19.
5. Use the PEDIT Spline option on one of the other polylines. You should have results similar to Figure 8.20.
6. Use the Fit option on the third polyline and then use the Decurve option to remove the curve.
7. Save the drawing as EX8.6.

Controlling the Appearance of Polyline Linetypes

The Ltype gen option in the PEDIT command lets you control the way patterned linetypes are drawn in relationship to the vertices of the polyline. The Ltype gen option has ON and OFF settings. OFF is the initial default, which draws linetypes starting and ending with a dash at each vertex. The dashes are placed uniformly with the vertices. When Ltype gen is ON, the linetype is drawn with the dashes uniformly spaced without regard to the vertices. An example of a polyline edited with Ltype gen OFF and ON is shown in Figure 8.23. This is the command sequence:

Command: **PE** or **PEDIT**↵
Select polyline: ⟨*pick the polyline*⟩
Close/Join/Width/Edit vertex/Fit/Spline/Decurve/Ltype gen/Undo/eXit <X>: **L**↵
Full PLINE linetype ON/OFF <Off>: **ON**↵
Close/Join/Width/Edit vertex/Fit/Spline/Decurve/Ltype gen/Undo/eXit <X>: ↵
Command:

FIGURE 8.23 A comparison of the PEDIT Ltype gen options.

Ltype gen OFF   Ltype gen ON

> **Field Notes**
>
> When Ltype gen is ON, short segments display a dashed line, but a corner may not be visible if the corner lines up with a gap.

Drawing Fillets and Chamfers on Polylines

Drawing fillets and chamfers were discussed in Chapter 7 with a brief mention of the Polyline option in the FILLET and CHAMFER commands. The Polyline option allows you to pick a polyline and automatically have all of the corners either filleted or chamfered with the current FILLET or CHAMFER settings. For all of the corners of a closed polyline to be filleted or chamfered, the last segment must have been closed using the Close option. Figure 8.24 shows the difference between drawing fillets and chamfers on closed polylines with and without using the Close option on the last segment. The Fillet command's Polyline option works like this:

Command: **F** or **FILLET**↵
(TRIM mode) Current fillet radius = 0.125
Polyline/Radius/Trim/<Select first object>: **P**↵
Select 2D polyline: ⟨*pick the polyline*⟩
4 lines were filleted
Command:

FIGURE 8.24 Using the FILLET command to round the corners of a polyline. The Close option must have been used to connect the last polyline line segment in order for all corners to be rounded.

Original polyline — Polyline fillet — Last segment not closed with the Close option

Original polyline — Polyline fillet — Last segment closed with the Close option

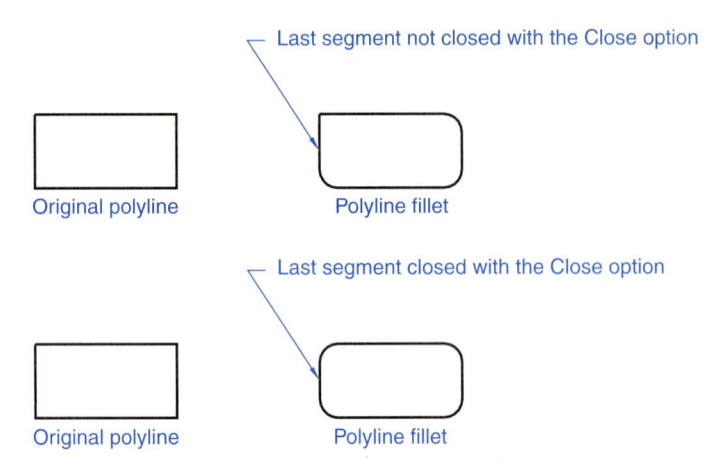

If you want to fillet or chamfer only one corner of a closed polyline, for example, use the Select first object: and Select second object: prompts just as you would when dealing with line objects.

> **Field Notes**
>
> When an object such as a line is filleted or chamfered with a polyline, the result is a desired fillet or chamfer and the line becomes part of the polyline.

Modify
[Explode]
Modify
└ **E**xplode
EXPLODE
X

Exploding Polylines

Polylines segments can be changed to individual lines and arcs by using the EXPLODE command. If you explode a thick polyline, as shown in Figure 8.25, the result is a series of individual thin lines and arcs that follow along the center of the original thick polyline. Access this command by picking the Explode button in the Modify toolbar, by picking E*x*plode in the *M*odify pull-down menu, or by typing **EXPLODE** at the Command: prompt. This is how the EXPLODE command works:

CHAPTER 8 ||| Drawing and Editing Polylines and Double Lines

```
Command: EXPLODE↵
Select objects: ⟨pick the polyline⟩
Select objects: ↵
Exploding this polyline has lost width information
The UNDO command will restore it.
Command:
```

FIGURE 8.25 Using the EXPLODE command to remove the polyline data.

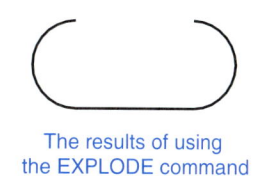

Original polyline

The results of using the EXPLODE command

If the polyline you are exploding has width or tangency specifications, AutoCAD LT warns you about the loss of width information when using the EXPLODE command. You are also reminded that using the UNDO command restores the polyline to its original condition.

Exercise 8.7

1. Open a new drawing.
2. Draw a polyline using a phantom linetype similar to the example at left in Figure 8.23 and then make a copy of the polyline.
3. Use the PEDIT command, select the second polyline, and turn the Ltype gen option ON. Observe the difference between the polylines. The first polyline has Ltype gen OFF by default.
4. Draw a rectangular polyline without using the Close option on the last segment and then fillet the polyline corners as was done to the top example in Figure 8.24.
5. Draw a rectangular polyline using the Close option on the last segment and then fillet the polyline corners as was done to the bottom example in Figure 8.24.
6. Draw an object similar to the original polyline in Figure 8.25 and then use the EXPLODE command to remove the polyline data.
7. Save the drawing as EX8.7.

✓ LEARNING CHECKPOINT

- ☐ How do you exit the PEDIT command?
- ☐ Describe the results of using the PEDIT Join option.
- ☐ Identify at least three ways to calculate the area of objects made up of line and arc segments.
- ☐ Name the PEDIT option that is used to change the entire width of a polyline to a uniform value.
- ☐ How do you select the desired polyline vertex when using the PEDIT command?
- ☐ Name the Edit vertex option that allows you to change the width of individual polyline segments.
- ☐ What is the difference between the Edit vertex Insert and Move options?
- ☐ Describe the difference between a Fit and a Spline curve.
- ☐ What is the effect of Ltype gen ON and OFF?
- ☐ How must a closed polyline be constructed to automatically have all corners rounded with the FILLET command?
- ☐ What is the result of exploding a polyline?

Drawing and Editing Spline Curves

Draw
Spline

Draw
└ Spline

SPLINE
SPL

Earlier, you learned how to create a spline curve from an existing polyline by using the Spline option of the PEDIT command. You can draw true spline curves of your own design using the SPLINE command. A true spline curve passes through the vertices. The spline curve created by AutoCAD LT is called a *nonuniform rational B-spline,* commonly referred to as NURBS. The smoothed polylines that you created with the Fit and Spline options of the PEDIT command are referred to as ***spline-fit curves.*** The differences between NURBS and spline-fit curves are as follows:

- NURBS are true spline curves that pass through the control points.
- Spline-fit polylines are a linear approximation of a true spline.
- NURBS create curved objects more accurately than spline-fit curves.
- True spline curves can be edited with several options using the SPLINEDIT command to be discussed later. Spline-fit curves are converted to splines when edited with the SPLINEDIT command.
- When a true spline and spline-fit curve have about the same shape, the true spline takes up less disk space.
- Both true splines and spline-fit curves can be edited with grips, but the true spline maintains its definition.

Access the SPLINE command by picking the Spline button in the Draw toolbar, by picking Spline in the Draw pull-down menu, or by typing **SPL** or **SPLINE** at the Command: prompt. When you enter the SPLINE command, you are asked to enter a series of two or more points. When you have picked the desired number of points and pressed Enter, the cursor moves back to the start point and you are asked to enter the start tangent. The start tangent determines how the beginning of the spline looks. You can pick a start tangent in any direction. After picking a start tangent, the cursor moves back to the end of the spline and you are asked to enter an end tangent. The end tangent controls the appearance of the spline end. You can press Enter at the tangent requests to have AutoCAD LT use the default tangency directions or you can enter specific tangent directions. Figure 8.26 shows the results of a spline drawn with different tangent endings. The SPLINE command works like this:

Command: **SPL** or **SPLINE**.↵
Object/⟨Enter first point⟩: ⟨*pick a point*⟩
Enter point: ⟨*pick another point*⟩
Close/Fit Tolerance/<Enter point>: ⟨*pick another point*⟩
Close/Fit Tolerance/<Enter point>: ⟨*pick another point*⟩
Close/Fit Tolerance/<Enter point>: ⟨*pick another point*⟩
Close/Fit Tolerance/<Enter point>: ⟨*pick another point*⟩
Enter start tangent: ⟨*pick the start tangent or press Enter*⟩
Enter end tangent: ⟨*pick the end tangent or press Enter*⟩
Command:

FIGURE 8.26 Several different Spline curve starting and ending tangency options on open splines.

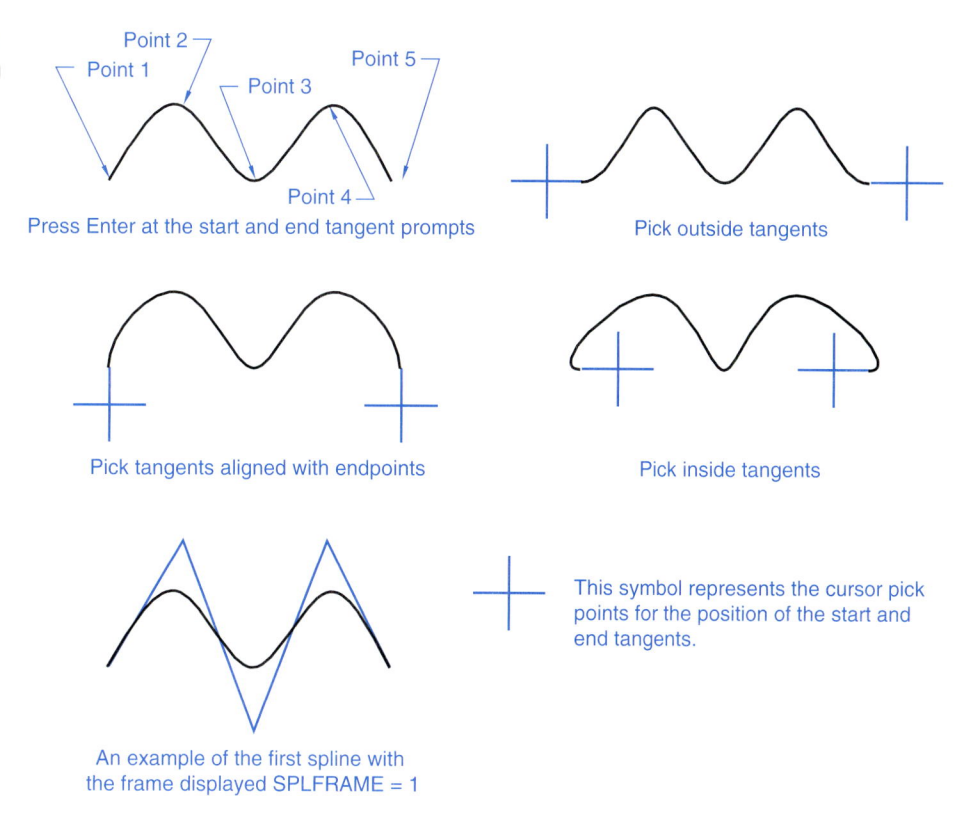

Press Enter at the start and end tangent prompts

Pick outside tangents

Pick tangents aligned with endpoints

Pick inside tangents

This symbol represents the cursor pick points for the position of the start and end tangents.

An example of the first spline with the frame displayed SPLFRAME = 1

Displaying the Spline Frame

The spline frame is a display of the original polyline frame that is used to create either spline-fit or true spline curves. The spline frame is not displayed by default, but it can be displayed using the SPLFRAME system variable. The initial setting of SPLFRAME is 0 (zero), which means the spline frame is turned off. To show the spline frame, set the value to 1 (on) like this:

Command: **SPLFRAME**↵
New value for SPLFRAME <0>: **1**↵
Command:

When SPLFRAME is on, the spline frame is automatically displayed when you create a true spline with the SPLINE command, or when you use PEDIT, on a polyline, to create a spline curve with the Spline option. If you turn SPLFRAME on after drawing spline curves, the spline frame is not immediately displayed. You need to type REGEN at the Command: prompt and press Enter to have the frame shown. Figures 8.26 and 8.27 show examples of the spline frame when displayed.

Field Notes

The SPLFRAME variable affects all spline objects, but the SPLINESEGS and SPLINETYPE variables only affect spline-fit polylines.

> **Exercise 8.8**
>
> 1. Open a new drawing.
> 2. Turn SPLFRAME on.
> 3. Draw four spline curves each with different ending tangents similar to the four examples shown in Figure 8.26.
> 4. Notice the spline frame display with the spline curves you create.
> 5. Turn SPLFRAME off.
> 6. Type REGEN at the Command: prompt and press Enter.
> 7. Notice that the spline frames are gone.
> 8. Save the drawing as EX8.8.

Converting Spline Polylines to True Splines

You can convert a spline polyline into a true spline using the Object option of the SPLINE command. This works on curves that are created using the PEDIT Spline option but not on curves made using the PEDIT Fit option. AutoCAD LT asks you to select the objects:

    Command: **SPL** or **SPLINE**↵
    Object/<Enter first point>: **O**↵
    Select objects to convert to splines.
    Select objects: ⟨select the objects to convert to splines⟩
    Select objects: ↵
    Command:

Only a spline that still has an associated frame can be converted. If a spline-fit polyline has lost its frame, the PEDIT Spline option can be used again to restore the frame. Then the resulting polyline object can be successfully converted into a SPLINE object.

The DELOBJ system variable is used to show or delete objects that are used to create other objects, such as the spline frame. If DELOBJ is ON (1) the original spline-fit pline is deleted when the spline object is created. When OFF (0), the original object is retained. DELOBJ is ON by default.

> **Field Notes**
>
> Keep in mind that **U** can be typed at the SPLINE prompt, followed by pressing ENTER, to undo as many of the drawn segments as necessary—even though the option does not appear in the prompt.

Closing a Spline

The Spline command's Close option allows you to close the spline between the endpoint and the first point. After using the Close option, you are asked to enter a single tangent direction. This is because the start and end are a single point in a closed spline. The tangent you select affects the results of the closed spline in a variety of ways, as shown in Figure 8.27. This is the command sequence:

    Command: **SPL** or **SPLINE**↵
    Object/<Enter first point>: ⟨pick a point⟩
    Enter point: ⟨pick another point⟩
    Close/Fit Tolerance/<Enter point>: ⟨pick another point⟩
    Close/Fit Tolerance/<Enter point>: ⟨pick another point⟩
    Close/Fit Tolerance/<Enter point>: **C**↵
    Enter tangent: ⟨pick a tangent point or press Enter⟩
    Command:

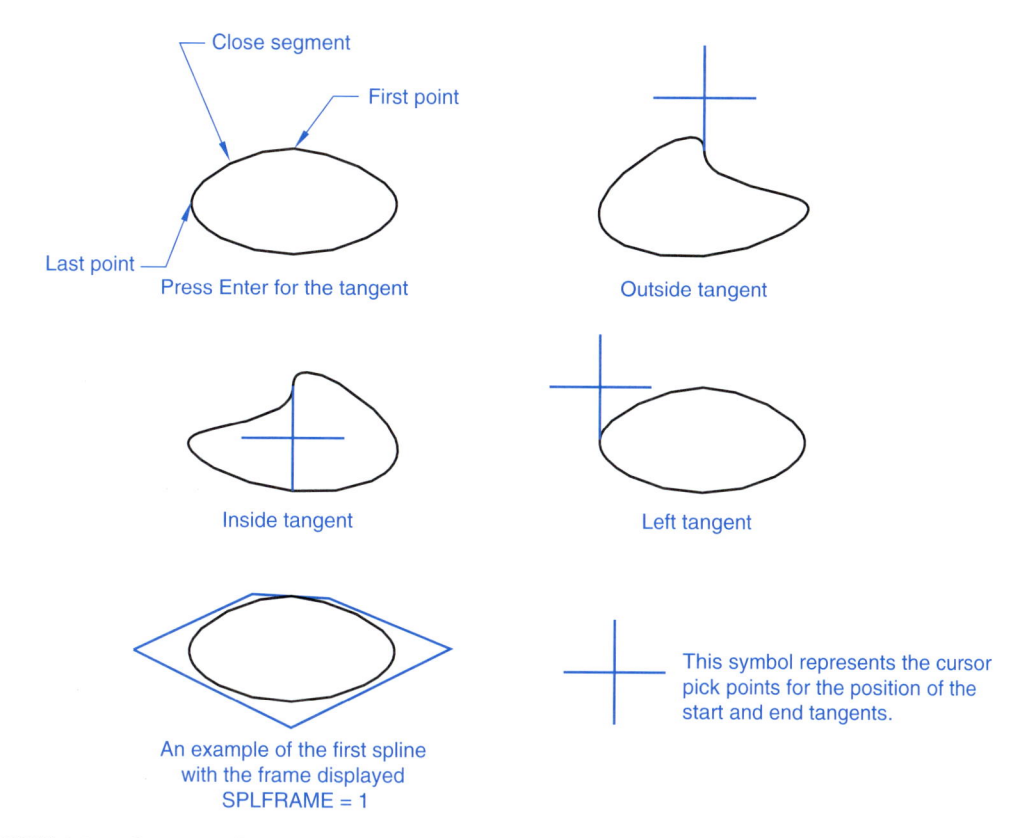

CHAPTER 8 ||| Drawing and Editing Polylines and Double Lines

FIGURE 8.27 Several different Spline curve starting and ending tangency options on closed splines.

Exercise 8.9

1. Open a new drawing.
2. Draw four spline curves using the Close option. Each polyline should have different ending tangents similar to the four examples shown in Figure 8.27.
3. Save the drawing as EX8.9.

Adjusting the Fit Tolerance of a Spline

The SPLINE command has a Fit Tolerance option that allows you to control how close the spline curve comes to the pick points. The default fit tolerance is 0 (zero). This forces the curve to be drawn so it passes directly through the pick points. Values greater than zero create different results and force the curve away from the pick points. The Fit Tolerance value is a proportional value, meaning that the value must be increased to affect larger splines in the same way. The results of different fit tolerances are shown in Figure 8.28 and the option works like this:

Command: **SPL** or **SPLINE**↵
Object/<Enter first point>: ⟨*pick a point*⟩
Enter point: ⟨*pick another point*⟩
Close/Fit Tolerance/<Enter point>: **F**↵
Enter Fit tolerance <0>: **1**↵
Close/Fit Tolerance/<Enter point>: ⟨*pick another point*⟩
Close/Fit Tolerance/<Enter point>: ⟨*pick another point*⟩
Enter start tangent: ↵
Enter end tangent: ↵
Command:

FIGURE 8.28 The results of different Fit Tolerance settings.

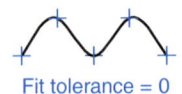

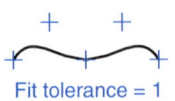

Fit tolerance = 0   Fit tolerance = 1

+ This symbol identifies the pick points.

Field Notes

- The spline shown in Figure 8.28 is drawn using a 1 × 1 snap grid so each pick point is 1 unit away from the next on each axis. If this same fit tolerance of 1.0 were used on a spline whose pick points were 20 units or so from each other, there would be no visible effect.
- You can type either **F** or **T** to access the Fit Tolerance option.
- Although the Fit Tolerance is displayed at each prompt and can be changed at any time, the value is not local to the current vertex; instead, it affects the entire spline.

Exercise 8.10

1. Open a new drawing.
2. Draw two spline curves each with different Fit Tolerance settings that are similar to the examples shown in Figure 8.28.
3. Save the drawing as EX8.10.

Editing Splines

Modify II
[Edit Spline]
Modify
└ Object
  └ Spline
SPLINEDIT
SPE

AutoCAD LT provides you with several ways to edit spline curves. For example, you can reduce or increase the number of fit points of a spline. More fit points increase the accuracy. You can move fit points to change the shape of the spline. Spline curves are edited by picking S̲pline in the O̲bject cascade of the M̲odify pull-down menu or by typing **SPLINEDIT** at the Command: prompt. Selecting a spline-fit pline with SPLINEDIT automatically converts the pline object into a SPLINE object and the command continues as it normally would. After entering the command and selecting a spline, grips are displayed at the control points. The spline edit options follow:

Command: **SPLINEDIT**↵
Select spline: ⟨*pick a spline*⟩
Fit Data/Close/Move Vertex/Refine/rEverse/Undo/eXit <X>:

The Undo and eXit options function as previously discussed.

Field Notes

There are two types of fit points. One type is called an ***interpolation point,*** which is a point through which a curve or surface passes to define the curve or surface. The other is an ***approximation point,*** which is a point that a curve or surface follows, but might not pass through.

Changing the Spline-Fit Data

Fit data include specific information about a spline such as the fit points, the fit tolerance, and all tangents associated with splines created using the SPLINE command. Spline-fit polylines converted into spline objects have no fit data. Also, some options of the SPLINEDIT command result in the loss of fit data, which somewhat reduces your flexibility for editing that spline. The Fit Data option of the SPLINEDIT command allows you to perform several editing tasks with the fit points. The Fit Data options are available when you type **F** and press Enter as follows:

Command: **SPLINEDIT**↵
Select spline: ⟨*pick a spline*⟩
Fit Data/Close/Move Vertex/Refine/rEverse/Undo/eXit <X>: **F**↵
Add/Close/Delete/Move/Purge/Tangents/toLerance/eXit <X>:

CHAPTER 8 ||| Drawing and Editing Polylines and Double Lines   323

The Fit Data options are explained next.

Add: This option allows you to add one or more fit points to the spline curve. To do this, select a grip as shown in Figure 8.29 and follow these prompts:

    Fit Data/Close/Move Vertex/Refine/rEverse/Undo/eXit <X>: **F**↵
    Add/Close/Delete/Move/Purge/Tangents/toLerance/eXit <X>: **A**↵
    Select a point: ⟨*select a grip*⟩
    Enter new point: ⟨*pick a new point*⟩
    Enter new point: ↵
    Select point: ⟨*select another point or press Enter*↵⟩
    Add/Close/Delete/Move/Purge/Tangents/toLerance/eXit <X>:

FIGURE 8.29 Adding a fit point with the SPLINEDIT Fit Data Add option.

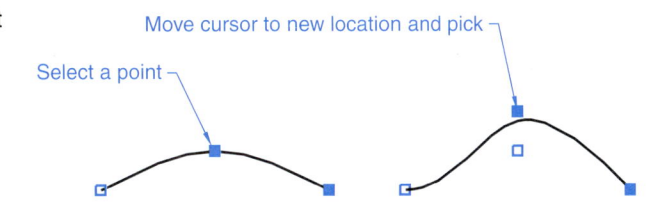

Field Notes

- When the option contains two capitalized words, you can type either capitalized letter. For example, with the option Fit Data, you can enter either **F** or **D**.
- The examples used to demonstrate editing splines show the new points being picked. Remember that you can also use coordinate or direct distance entry.

Close: The Close option lets you close an open spline. If the spline you select for editing is already closed, then the Fit Data option is Open, which allows you to open a closed spline. Using the Close suboption of Fit Data preserves the fit data after closing the spline. This is different from the Close option presented at the initial prompt, which removes fit data when it closes the spline.

Delete: This Fit Data option lets you delete a fit point by selecting it. If there are only three fit points in the spline, and you delete one, the result is a straight segment between the two remaining points. You can select a control point by targeting it with the crosshairs and picking. When control points are deleted, the curve is recalculated using the remaining points and fit data.

Field Notes

The result of a straight line only occurs when the default tangency directions are used. If tangents other than the default are used, the resulting spline is still a curve, even when all fit points are removed. If you delete all of the control points except for the last two, the following message is issued:

    Cannot delete beyond this.

Move: Use this option to move a fit point to a new location. When you select a spline and enter this option, you get Next and Previous prompts that allow you to progressively select different points along the spline until you get to the desired point. The cursor is connected to the selected point and the spline changes shape as you move the cursor. Look at Figure 8.30 as you follow these prompts:

    Fit Data/Close/Move Vertex/Refine/rEverse/Undo/eXit <X>: **F**↵
    Add/Close/Delete/Move/Purge/Tangents/toLerance/eXit <X>: **M**↵
    Next/Previous/Select Point/eXit/<Enter new location>: <N>: ↵
    Next/Previous/Select Point/eXit/<Enter new location>: <N>: ⟨*pick a new location*⟩
    Next/Previous/Select Point/eXit/<Enter new location>: <N>: **X**↵
    Close/Move Vertex/Refine/rEverse/Undo/eXit <X>: ↵
    Command:

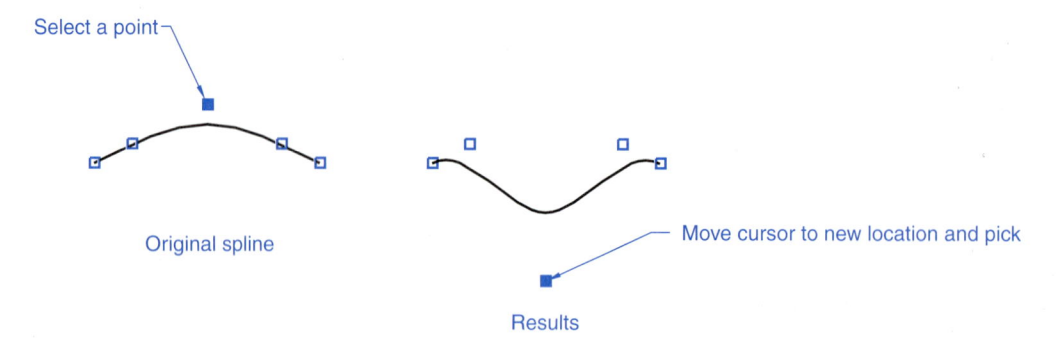

FIGURE 8.30 Moving a fit point with the SPLINEDIT Move Vertex option.

You can also use the Select Point option by typing **S** and pressing Enter. This lets you move the cursor to a desired point and pick it:

Next/Previous/Select Point/eXit/<Enter new location>: <N>: **S**↵
Select point: ⟨select a grip⟩

Purge: This Fit Data option simplifies spline curves by removing fit data. Once Purge has been used, the spline can no longer be edited with the Fit Data option. The Purge option can be used to reduce the file size of very large drawings by simplifying the splines. The Undo option in the next prompt can be used to restore the Fit data.

Tangents: This option allows you to change the start and end tangents of an open spline or edit the tangency of points in a closed spline. The results can affect the spline in a manner that is similar to the tangency displayed in Figures 8.26 and 8.27. When you select a spline and use the Tangents option, the first tangent point is automatically selected for editing. After changing the first tangent point, the cursor switches to the second tangent point for editing. Use of the Tangents option gives the following command sequence:

Fit Data/Close/Move Vertex/Refine/rEverse/Undo/eXit <X>: **F**↵
Add/Close/Delete/Move/Purge/Tangents/toLerance/eXit <X>: **T**↵
System Default/<Enter start tangent>: ⟨edit the first tangent⟩
System Default/<Enter start tangent>: ⟨edit the second tangent⟩
Add/Close/Delete/Move/Purge/Tangents/toLerance/eXit <X>:

If you do not want to change the tangent points to your own specifications, you can accept the System Default option by typing **S** or **D** and pressing Enter:

Fit Data/Close/Move Vertex/Refine/rEverse/Undo/eXit <X>: **F**↵
Add/Close/Delete/Move/Purge/Tangents/toLerance/eXit <X>: **T**↵
System Default/<Enter start tangent>: **S**↵
System Default/<Enter start tangent>: **S**↵
Add/Close/Delete/Move/Purge/Tangents/toLerance/eXit <X>:

toLerance: Use this option to change the fit tolerance data. The prompt asks you to enter a new value for the fit tolerance. Adjusting the fit tolerance was discussed earlier and shown in Figure 8.28.

Exercise 8.11

1. Open a new drawing.
2. Draw a spline curve similar to the original spline shown in Figure 8.29.
3. Make three copies of the spline.
4. Use the SPLINEDIT Fit Data Add option to add a fit point to one of the spline curves similar to those shown in Figure 8.29.
5. Use the Fit Data Move option to move a fit point on one of the spline curves similar to those shown in Figure 8.29.
6. Use the Fit Data Delete option to delete one of the fit points on one of the splines.
7. Use the Fit Data Close option to close one of the splines.
8. Save the drawing as EX8.11.

CHAPTER 8 ||| Drawing and Editing Polylines and Double Lines 325

Using the SPLINEDIT Close/Open Option
If you use the SPLINEDIT command and select an open spline, you get the Close option with the other options. If you select a closed spline, you automatically get the Open option listed. These options perform the operations implied by their names. After closing an open spline, the option changes from Close to Open. Using either of these options removes all fit data from the spline.

Moving a Spline Vertex
The SPLINEDIT's Move Vertex option allows you to move any spline control point to a new location. When you select a spline and enter this option, you get Next and Previous prompts that allow you to progressively select different points along the spline until you get to the desired point. The cursor is connected to the selected point and the spline changes shape as you move the cursor. Look at Figure 8.30 as you follow these prompts:

>   Fit Data/Close/Move Vertex/Refine/rEverse/Undo/eXit <X>: **M.↵**
>   Next/Previous/Select Point/eXit/<Enter new location>: <N>: ↵
>   Next/Previous/Select Point/eXit/<Enter new location>: <N>: ⟨ *pick a new location* ⟩
>   Next/Previous/Select Point/eXit/<Enter new location>: <N>: **X.↵**
>   Close/Move Vertex/Refine/rEverse/Undo/eXit <X>: ↵
>   Command:

You can also use the Select Point option by typing **S** and pressing Enter. This lets you move the cursor to a desired point and pick it.

>   Next/Previous/Select Point/eXit/<Enter new location>: <N>: **S.↵**
>   Select point: ⟨*select a grip*⟩

Refining Spline Curves
The SPLINEDIT command's Refine option is used to modify a spline shape by increasing the number of control points in a portion of the spline. You can change a spline's order. When you increase a spline's order, you increase the number of control points. You can also change the weight of a control point. Changing the weight of a control point forces the spline curve either further from or closer to the point where the change occurs. The options look like this:

>   Command: **SPLINEDIT.↵**
>   Select spline: ⟨*pick a spline*⟩
>   Fit Data/Close/Move Vertex/Refine/rEverse/Undo/eXit <X>: **R.↵**
>   Add control point/Elevate Order/Weight/eXit <X>:

The SPLINEDIT Refine options are explained next.

Add control point: Use this option to add new control points to an existing spline. Each time you pick or enter a point coordinate, a new control point is added between the two points that control the portion of the spline closest to the specified location. The new control points are positioned as close to your pick point as possible without changing the current appearance of the spline curve. The reason for adding new points is to allow tighter control and greater flexibility for further editing procedures, such as moving vertices. You can add as many control points as you wish, but you should avoid doing so unnecessarily. This option also removes fit data. Figure 8.31 shows two control points added using this sequence:

>   Fit Data/Close/Move Vertex/Refine/rEverse/Undo/eXit <X>: **R.↵**
>   Add control point/Elevate Order/Weight/eXit <X>: **A.↵**
>   Select a point on the spline: ⟨*pick a point*⟩
>   Select a point on the spline: ⟨*pick a point*⟩
>   Select a point on the spline: ↵
>   Add control point/Elevate Order/Weight/eXit <X>:

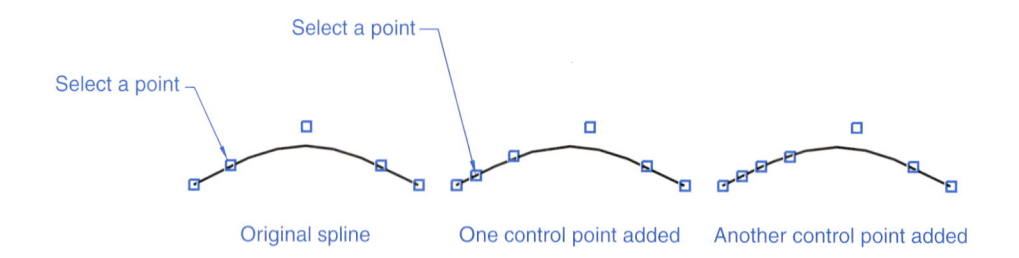

FIGURE 8.31 Adding control points with the SPLINEDIT Add control point option.

Elevate order: Elevating the order of a spline increases the number of control points for greater control uniformly across the spline. The default setting for the order is 4, which allows for four total control points on a one-segment spline, one at the start, one at the end, and two curve control points. AutoCAD LT supports settings of up to 26 for the order of the spline. A single-segment spline with an order of 26 has 24 curve control points, and 26 total control points. When the spline has multiple segments, each segment shares control points with the adjacent segments, which means that a spline initially defined using two segments and elevated in order to 26 will not have 52 total control points. Such a spline would have only 49 control points because 3 of the points belong to both segments. Since it would require AutoCAD LT to arbitrarily remove control points, the order of a spline cannot be reduced after it has been elevated. Because there is no easy way to lower the order of the spline, it is advised that you elevate the order only when necessary. Also, elevating the order of a spline removes all fit data. Figure 8.32 shows a spline with an order of 4 and then the elevated order of 10 as done with this SPLINEDIT command sequence:

> Fit Data/Close/Move Vertex/Refine/rEverse/Undo/eXit <X>: **R.↵**
> Add control point/Elevate Order/Weight/eXit <X>: **E.↵**
> Enter new order <4>: **10.↵**
> Add control point/Elevate Order/Weight/eXit <X>:

FIGURE 8.32 Elevating the order of control points.

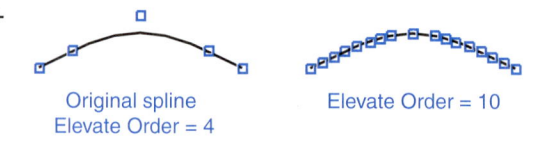

Notice that the resulting spline shows 17 total control points. The original spline definition used two segments, and the order is then elevated to 10. Each segment now has 10 total control points, with 3 being shared, making a total of 17.

Field Notes

- The order of a spline is defined as the degree of the spline polynomial plus 1. What this actually refers to is the equation used to calculate the curve of the spline. A cubic spline is calculated using a third-degree polynomial, so the order of a cubic spline is 4. The curve calculated using a third-degree polynomial has either two or no turning points. This can be easily demonstrated by first generating a spline with just two points, a start and an end (use the default tangencies). The result is a straight spline with no turning points. If you grip select the spline, you see that two control points appear on the spline. Use the GRIP Stretch option to move each of these grips. Now the spline has two turning points. Next, use the SPLINEDIT Refine–Elevate Order option to elevate the order to 5 and return to the Command: prompt. The resulting curve is now calculated using a fourth-degree polynomial, and so the degree of the polynomial plus 1 is equal to 5. When you grip select the spline this time you see an extra control point on the spline. Using your GRIP Stretch option you can now produce 3 turning points on the spline segment.
- When you elevate the order of a spline by 1, you are adding a single new control point on each segment of the spline. Elevating the order by 3 adds three new points on each segment and so on.

CHAPTER 8 ||| Drawing and Editing Polylines and Double Lines   327

Weight: The weight of a fit point determines how much pull the point has on the spline curve. When all control points have the same weight, they all maintain the same amount of control over the spline. The default weight is 1. If you increase the weight of one or more fit points, you force the spline to pull closer to those points. The Weight prompts allow you to move to the next or previous fit points or use the Select Point option to pick the desired point. Adjusting the weight to higher values can cause the curve to pass through the control point regardless of the fit tolerance. Also, adjusting the weight removes fit data. The following sequence selects the desired point and increases the weight, as demonstrated in Figure 8.33:

    Fit Data/Close/Move Vertex/Refine/rEverse/Undo/eXit <X>: R↵
    Add control point/Elevate Order/Weight/eXit <X>: W↵
    Spline is not rational. Will make it so.
    Next/Previous/Select Point/eXit/<Enter new weight> <1.0>: <N>: S↵
    Select point: ⟨pick the point⟩
    Next/Previous/Select Point/eXit/<Enter new weight> <1.0>: <N>: 4↵
    Next/Previous/Select Point/eXit/<Enter new weight> <1.0>: <N>: X↵
    Add control point/Elevate Order/Weight/eXit <X>:

FIGURE 8.33 Using the SPLINEDIT Weight option.

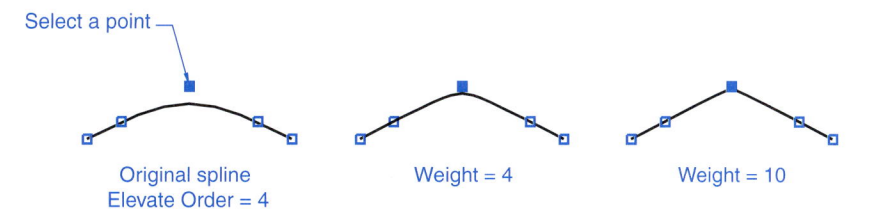

Select a point

Original spline
Elevate Order = 4

Weight = 4

Weight = 10

Exercise 8.12

1. Open a new drawing.
2. Draw a spline curve similar to the original spline shown in Figure 8.31.
3. Make two copies of the spline.
4. Use the SPLINEDIT Refine Add option to add two fit points to one of the splines as was done in Figure 8.31.
5. Use the Refine Elevate Order option to increase the order of one of the splines to 10 as was done in Figure 8.32.
6. Use the Fit Data Delete option to delete one of the fit points on one of the splines.
7. Use the Refine Weight option to increase the weight of one of the spline's control points to 10 as was done in Figure 8.33.
8. Save the drawing as EX8.12.

Using the rEverse Option of the SPLINEDIT Command

This makes the existing endpoint into the start point and reverses the direction of movement when using options that offer a Next and Previous option for selecting control points. If you want to reverse the order of the spline curve control points, type **E** and press Enter to access the rEverse option.

Field Notes

To make fine adjustments to a spline, it is sometimes quicker and easier to use the GRIP Stretch option to move individual fit data points and adjust the curve as needed. If no previous operation has removed the fit data, when you grip select the spline, the fit data points are also available for adjustment. However, if you move one of the control points, the fit data are lost. To be sure which grips are fit points and which are control points, you need to observe the fit-point locations before selecting the splines.

328 CHAPTER 8 ||| Drawing and Editing Polylines and Double Lines

☑ LEARNING CHECKPOINT

- ☐ Name the command that allows you to draw spline curves of your own design.
- ☐ What is the function of the Fit Tolerance option?
- ☐ Explain the purpose of the SPLINEDIT Fit Data Purge option.
- ☐ Describe two ways to select a desired fit point when using the SPLINEDIT Move Vertex option.
- ☐ What is the purpose of the Elevate Order option?
- ☐ Describe the results of increasing the weight of a control point.

Drawing Double Lines

Draw
  Double Line
Draw
  Double Line
DLINE
DL

AutoCAD LT provides you with an excellent tool for drawing pairs of parallel lines and arcs that may be used for drawing the walls of architectural floor and foundation plans. Double lines can be drawn any desired width apart. They can be capped and they can be edited to break where they meet so they look like properly drawn wall intersections. Double lines are drawn using the DLINE command, which is accessed by picking Double Line in the Draw pull-down menu, by picking the Double Line button in the Draw toolbar, or by typing **DL** or **DLINE** at the Command: prompt.

✏ Field Notes

There is no actual "double line" object type. The result of using the DLINE command is a sequence of LINE and ARC segments. Although the command creates *double lines*, after they are created they are just *lines*.

Using the DLINE Command

Double lines are drawn in a manner similar to that used to draw lines. In addition to a number of options, you are asked to pick a start point and the next point. The DLINE command is demonstrated in Figure 8.34 and works like this:

Command: **DL** or **DLINE**↵
Break/Caps/Dragline/Offset/Snap/Undo/Width/<start point>: ⟨*pick a start point*⟩
Arc/Break/CAps/CLose/Dragline/Snap/Undo/Width/<next point>: ⟨*pick another point*⟩
Arc/Break/CAps/CLose/Dragline/Snap/Undo/Width/<next point>: ⟨*pick another point*⟩
Arc/Break/CAps/CLose/Dragline/Snap/Undo/Width/<next point>: ↵
Command:

FIGURE 8.34 The elements of a double line.

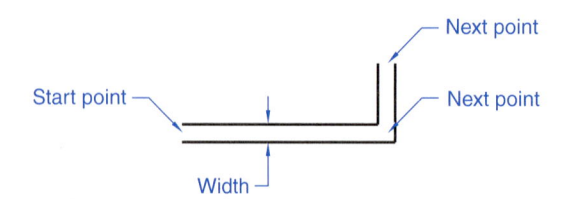

The DLINE command has the Undo and Close options that work just as they do with other applications. The Close option allows you to have AutoCAD LT automatically close the end of the last double line segment with the start of the first segment. The Undo option works while you are inside of the DLINE command to undo the previously drawn double line segments. Use Undo as many times as you need to undo consecutive previous segments.

Setting the Double Line Width
The double line width is one of the first options that you may want to set. This establishes the distance between the two parallel lines. If you are working on an architectural floor plan, you probably want to set the width to 6 in. for exterior walls and 5 in. for interior walls. The initial default width is 0.05. Figure 8.34 shows the double line width. This is how you set the width:

CHAPTER 8 ||| Drawing and Editing Polylines and Double Lines

Command: **DL** or **DLINE**↵
Break/Caps/Dragline/Offset/Snap/Undo/Width/<start point>: **W**↵
New DLINE width <0.05>: **6**↵
Break/Caps/Dragline/Offset/Snap/Undo/Width/<start point>:

Field Notes

Be sure that the displayed drawing area is large enough prior to trying to draw 6-in.-wide walls. If not, drawing in a small area may produce unexpected results. The width of the double lines depends on the type and size of the drawing.

Setting the Dragline

After you set the width, you probably want to set how the double line is drawn. As you pick the points to draw the double line, a rubber-band cursor guides the placement of the double line to your pick points. AutoCAD LT refers to this as the *dragline*. The Dragline option has three settings. Set the Left option like this:

Command: **DL** or **DLINE**↵
Break/Caps/Dragline/Offset/Snap/Undo/Width/<start point>: **D**↵
Set dragline position to Left/Center/Right/<Offset from center = 0>: **L**↵
Break/Caps/Dragline/Offset/Snap/Undo/Width/<start point>:

FIGURE 8.35 The DLINE Dragline options.

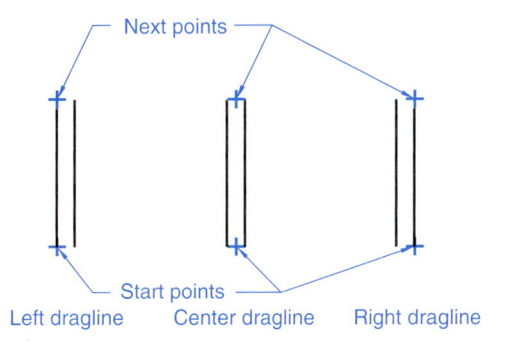

Figure 8.35 shows the difference between the Dragline options, which are explained in the following list:

Center: The initial AutoCAD LT default setting draws double lines placed with your pick points in the center of the two lines. The Dragline setting remains the same until you change it. If you change to another setting, go back to the Center option by typing **C** and pressing Enter. When the Center option is used, the Offset from center = 0 prompt is issued. When the setting is Center, the resulting lines are drawn offset parallel to the dragline half of the width setting in each direction.

Left: The Left option is accessed by typing **L** and pressing Enter. This places the dragline on the left side of the double line as you go from the start point to the next point. The Offset from center prompt gives a negative value when the left option is used. The value is half the distance from the center to the dragline. When the setting is left, the offset is the full width to the right.

Right: The Right option is accessed by typing **R** and pressing Enter. This places the dragline on the right side of the double line as you go from the start point to the next point. When the setting is right, the offset is the full width to the left.

Field Notes

- The Left and Right options are based on a line drawn at 90° upward.
- When drawn counterclockwise, the Left option offsets outward and the right option offsets inward. When drawn clockwise, the Right option offsets outward and the Left option offsets inward.
- When using double lines for the walls in an architectural floor plan, the exterior walls are drawn using either the left or right option with the total wall width inside. This is because dimensions are normally made to the face of exterior studs. The interior walls and partitions are usually drawn using the center option because these walls are normally dimensioned to their centers.

Exercise 8.13

1. Begin a new drawing.
2. Set double line width to .25.
3. Draw three double line segments with each of the dragline options, similar to the segments shown in Figure 8.35.
4. Save the drawing as EX8.13.

Placing Caps on Double Lines

AutoCAD LT allows you to place caps on the ends of double lines. Caps are line segments that connect the ends of double lines. You have the choice of drawing double lines without caps, with caps on both ends, or with a cap on either the beginning or ending. You can change the way caps are placed at any time while drawing double lines. The initial option is Caps, which is accessed by typing **C** and pressing Enter. After picking the start point, the option changes to CAps, which requires you to type **CA** and press Enter to get the Caps option. The Caps option works like this:

Command: **DL** or **DLINE**↵
Break/Caps/Dragline/Offset/Snap/Undo/Width/<start point>: **C**↵
Draw which endcaps? Both/End/None/Start/<Auto>: **B**↵
Break/Caps/Dragline/Offset/Snap/Undo/Width/<start point>: ⟨*pick a point*⟩
Arc/Break/CAps/CLose/Dragline/Snap/Undo/Width/<next point>: **CA**↵
Draw which endcaps? Both/End/None/Start/<Auto>:

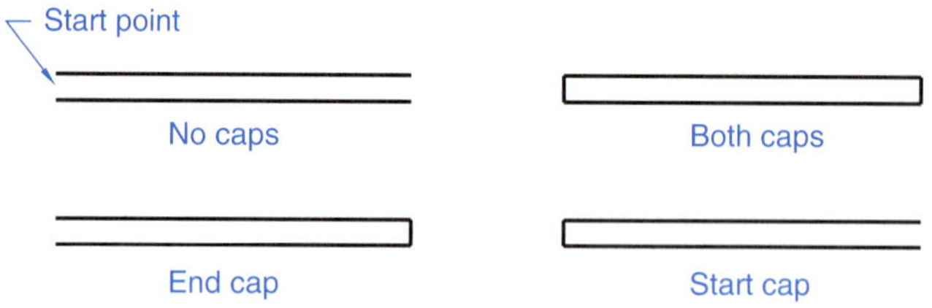

FIGURE 8.36 The DLINE Caps options.

The caps options are shown in Figure 8.36 and explained in the following discussion:

Both: This option places a cap at the start and end of open double lines.

End: Use this option to place a cap only at the end of a double line.

None: This option is used to place no end caps on a double line.

Start: This option places a cap at the start of a double line.

Auto: Use the Auto option if you want AutoCAD LT to automatically place a cap at the ends of double lines except when snapping to other objects. Snapping to other objects is explained later.

Exercise 8.14

1. Begin a new drawing.
2. Set double line width to .25.
3. Draw four double line segments with each of the cap options, similar to the segments shown in Figure 8.36.
4. Save the drawing as EX8.14.

Offsetting the Start of a Double Line

The DLINE's Offset option is used to begin a double line at a specified distance and angle from a known point. This is convenient for drawing a door opening in a floor plan, for example. When you enter the Offset option, AutoCAD LT issues the Offset from: prompt so that you can pick the point where you want the offset

CHAPTER 8 ||| Drawing and Editing Polylines and Double Lines

to begin. You are then asked to pick the direction "toward" the beginning of the double line. Finally, enter the offset distance. The default value is the same as the distance between the "from" point and the "toward" point. Press Enter to accept this distance or type a new value such as 48 for a 48-in. doorway in an architectural floor plan. Draw the first double line with an end cap to establish the first part of the doorway. Use the Caps option to place a start cap at the other side of the doorway. Look at Figure 8.37 as you follow this command sequence:

Command: **DL** or **DLINE.**⏎
Break/Caps/Dragline/Offset/Snap/Undo/Width/<start point>: **C.**⏎
Draw which endcaps? Both/End/None/Start/<Auto>: **S.**⏎
Break/Caps/Dragline/Offset/Snap/Undo/Width/<start point>: **O.**⏎
Offset from: ⟨*pick the start of the offset*⟩
Offset toward: ⟨*move the cursor in the direction of the offset and pick*⟩
Enter the offset distance <48>: ⟨*accept the default distance you picked or type a new distance and press Enter.*⏎⟩
Arc/Break/CAps/CLose/Dragline/Snap/Undo/Width/<next point>: ⟨*pick the next point*⟩
Arc/Break/CAps/CLose/Dragline/Snap/Undo/Width/<next point>: ⏎
Command:

FIGURE 8.37 Using the DLINE Offset option.

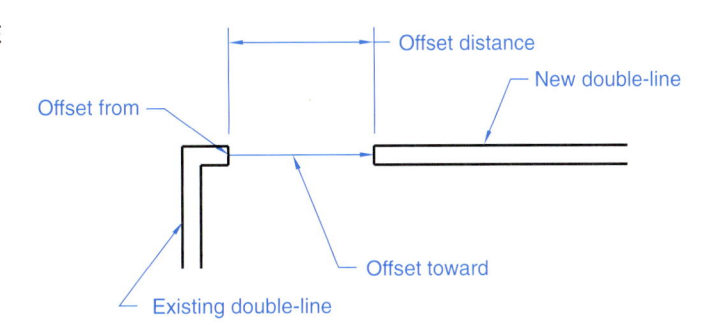

Exercise 8.15

1. Begin a new drawing.
2. Set double line width to .25.
3. Draw a double line with an end cap similar to the existing double line shown in Figure 8.37.
4. Set the end cap to start and use the Offset option to offset the beginning of the next double line a distance of 1.25 from the endpoint of the previous double line, as was done in Figure 8.37.
5. Save the drawing as EX8.15.

Drawing Double Line Arcs

The DLINE command allows you to draw double line separate arcs or arcs connected to straight double line segments. The Arc option is entered after picking the start point. The Arc option allows you to draw a double line arc by picking three points by default, or by typing **CE** to enter the CEnter option. The CEnter option is used to specify the center of the double line arc radius. You can also use the Endpoint option by picking an arc endpoint or by specifying the included angle. After entering the Arc option, the next prompt replaces the Arc option with the Line option. The Line option is used if you want to continue drawing a straight double line segment at the end of a double line arc segment. The following command sequence draws the closed double line with an arc segment that is displayed in Figure 8.38:

Command: **DL** or **DLINE.**⏎
Break/Caps/Dragline/Offset/Snap/Undo/Width/<start point>: ⟨*pick a point*⟩
Arc/Break/CAps/CLose/Dragline/Snap/Undo/Width/<next point>: ⟨*pick the next point*⟩
Arc/Break/CAps/CLose/Dragline/Snap/Undo/Width/<next point>: **A.**⏎
Break/Caps/CEnter/CLose/Dragline/Endpoint/Line/Snap/Undo/Width/<second point>: ⟨*pick a point or use the CEnter or Endpoint option*⟩
Endpoint: ⟨*pick the endpoint*⟩

Break/Caps/CEnter/CLose/Dragline/Endpoint/Line/Snap/Undo/Width/<second point>: **L**↵
Arc/Break/CAps/CLose/Dragline/Snap/Undo/Width/<next point>: ⟨*pick a point*⟩
Arc/Break/CAps/CLose/Dragline/Snap/Undo/Width/<next point>: **CL**↵
Command:

FIGURE 8.38 Drawing a closed double line with an arc segment.

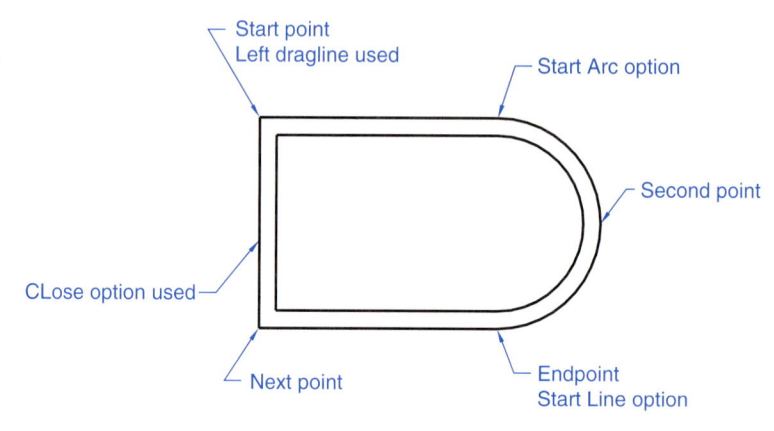

- Start point / Left dragline used
- Start Arc option
- Second point
- CLose option used
- Next point
- Endpoint / Start Line option

The CEnter suboption of the Arc option can be used if you want to draw the double line arc by first picking the start point followed by the center and then either picking the arc endpoint or using the Angle option to specify the included angle. The prompts work like this:

Command: **DL** or **DLINE**↵
Break/Caps/Dragline/Offset/Snap/Undo/Width/<start point>: ⟨*pick a point*⟩
Arc/Break/CAps/CLose/Dragline/Snap/Undo/Width/<next point>: **A**↵
Break/Caps/CEnter/CLose/Dragline/Endpoint/Line/Snap/Undo/Width/<second point>: **CE**↵
Center point: ⟨*pick the center point*⟩
Angle/<Endpoint>: ⟨*press Enter for Endpoint or type* **A** *for Angle*↵⟩
Endpoint: ⟨*pick the endpoint*⟩
Break/Caps/Dragline/Offset/Snap/Undo/Width/<start point>: ↵
Command:

You can make sequential arcs using the CEnter option or by picking a second point and endpoint of the next continuous arc.

Exercise 8.16

1. Begin a new drawing.
2. Set double line width to .25 and Dragline to Left.
3. Draw a double line similar to the one shown in Figure 8.38.
4. Save the drawing as EX8.16.

Snapping a Double Line to Other Objects

A double line can be connected to another double line or to other objects by using the Snap option. You can use this option to either start or end a double line at another object. When using the Snap option, AutoCAD LT automatically trims or extends the ends of the double line to meet exactly with the desired object. The Snap option has a **search area** where AutoCAD LT looks for the object to which the double line will snap. No connection happens if the object is outside of the search area. The size of the search area is set in pixels. The available Snap options include turning Snap ON or OFF or setting the Size, which refers to the search area. The default size is 3 pixels. You can set the Size from 1 to 10 pixels. Set the search area to 5 pixels as follows:

Command: **DL** or **DLINE**↵
Break/Caps/Dragline/Offset/Snap/Undo/Width/<start point>: ⟨*pick a point*⟩
Arc/Break/CAps/CLose/Dragline/Snap/Undo/Width/<next point>: **S**↵
Set snap size or snap On/Off: Size/OFF/<ON>: **S**↵

CHAPTER 8 ||| Drawing and Editing Polylines and Double Lines

New snap size (1-10) <3>: **5**↵
Arc/Break/CAps/CLose/Dragline/Snap/Undo/Width/<next point>: ⟨*pick the next point*⟩
Command:

Setting the Snap Size also turns Snap on for the next point. Turn snap on for each desired connection to an object. The result of the previous command is shown in Figure 8.39.

FIGURE 8.39 Using the DLINE Snap option to connect a double line with another object.

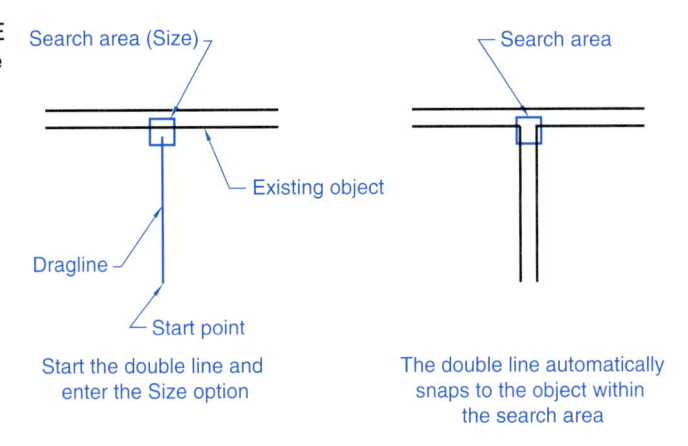

Field Notes

- To give you a clear picture of how big the search area is, set your pick box size using the PB (or PICKBOX) command and specify the desired number. The search area is square like the pick box, meaning that the diagonal search distance is greater than either the horizontal or vertical distance.
- When you start the DLINE command, any running object snap modes are temporarily suspended, but you can still use object snap overrides as desired.

Breaking an Object Where the Double Line Meets

When you snap a double line to an object, you can have the object broken or unbroken where the endpoints of the double line meet the object. Having the object break at the double line is convenient for architectural applications where walls meet. Set the Break option like this:

Command: **DL** or **DLINE**↵
Break/Caps/Dragline/Offset/Snap/Undo/Width/<start point>: **B**↵
Break Dline's at start and end points? OFF/<ON>: ↵
Break/Caps/Dragline/Offset/Snap/Undo/Width/<start point>:

Break is on by default. Figure 8.40 shows the difference between Break ON and OFF.

FIGURE 8.40 A comparison between using the DLINE Snap option with the Break option ON and OFF.

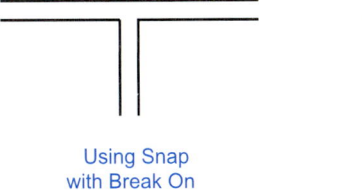

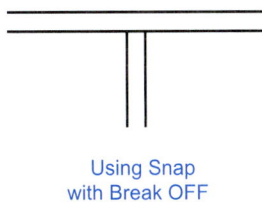

334 CHAPTER 8 ||| Drawing and Editing Polylines and Double Lines

> ### Exercise 8.17
>
> 1. Begin a new drawing.
> 2. Set the double line width to .25.
> 3. Draw a horizontal double line with the Dragline set to Left similar to the existing object shown in Figure 8.39.
> 4. Be sure Break is ON.
> 5. Draw a double line with a Center Dragline and with the Snap option ON to connect the Existing object, as was done in Figure 8.39.
> 6. Save the drawing as EX8.17.

☑ LEARNING CHECKPOINT

- ☐ Where is the double line width measured?
- ☐ Explain how the Dragline option works.
- ☐ Discuss the results obtained when using the DLINE Caps option.
- ☐ Explain how the DLINE Offset option works.
- ☐ How do you draw a double line arc connected to a straight double line segment and followed by a straight segment?
- ☐ What is the Snap option search area?
- ☐ When snapping a double line to an existing object, how can you be sure the object will break at the snap location?

Drawing Revision Clouds

Draw
Revcloud
Tools
└ Revision Cloud
REVCLOUD
RC

Revision clouds are often used in a drawing to draw attention to a revised area of a drawing. Revision clouds consist of connected arc segments created from a polyline object. The REVCLOUD command is accessed by picking the Revcloud button from the Draw toolbar, selecting Revision Cloud from the Tools menu, or typing **RC** or **REVCLOUD** on the keyboard. The REVCLOUD command issues the following prompt:

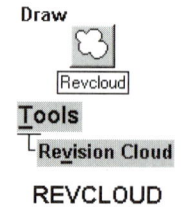

    Command: **RC** or **REVCLOUD**.↵
    Current arc length = 0.5000
    Arc length/<Pick cloud start point>:

Enter an arc length that is appropriate for your drawing. Let us say, for example, you are drawing a floor plan that is to be printed at a scale of ¼"=1', and you want the length of the arcs to be ½" on the print. A scale of ¼"=1' equals a scale factor of 1/48. To adjust drawing feature sizes to match this scale take the reciprocal of the fraction, that is, 48/1 or 48. Multiply the desired arc length by this number to find the correct length, which in this case is 24" (48 x 0.5 = 24). If you have already set an appropriate Dimensioning Scale (DimScale) for your drawing, the specified arc length is automatically multiplied by the set scale. Setting the DIMSCALE is discussed in Chapter 11.

    Arc length/<Pick cloud start point>: **A**.↵
    Specify arc length <0.5000>: **24**.↵
    Pick cloud start point: <pick a point on screen>
    Guide crosshairs along cloud path...
    <Move the cursor along the desired path of the revision cloud>
    Revision cloud finished.

After specifying the starting point, it is not necessary to use the pick button again. Using the pick button specifies the endpoints of new arc segments, but these will be shorter than the specified arc length and will result in a less uniform cloud. Any running object snap modes are temporarily disabled while you draw the revision cloud. Move the crosshairs along the desired path of the revision cloud. The arcs are drawn as you move your cursor. To finish the revision cloud, move the cursor back to the start point. When your cursor comes within the specified arc length of the start point, the revision cloud is closed and you are returned to the Command: prompt. Figure 8.41 shows the creation of a revision cloud.

FIGURE 8.41 The REVCLOUD command automatically draws arc segments along the path that you move your cursor.

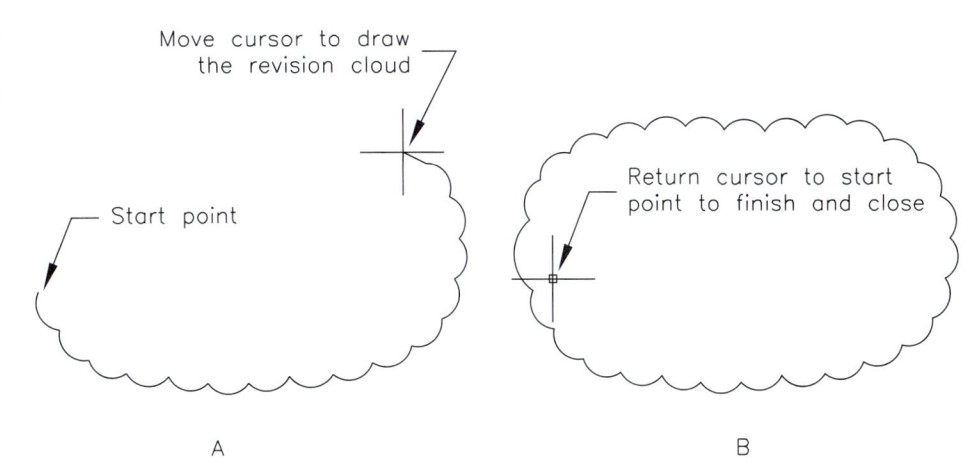

Field Notes

- You cannot undo individual arc segments within the REVCLOUD command. If you make a mistake while drawing a revision cloud, you can press the Esc key to stop the command, then the space bar to restart it.
- The REVCLOUD command can accurately track the cursor movements only when the cursor is visible in the drawing area of the AutoCAD LT window. If you are drawing a revision cloud near the edge of the screen and your cursor moves out of the drawing area, the next arc segment will be drawn to the point where your cursor reenters the drawing area.
- The REVCLOUD command creates a Polyline object that can be edited using the PEDIT command discussed earlier in this chapter. Minor adjustments can also be made using grips (see Chapter 7).

MULTIPLE CHOICE

Circle the choice or enter your response on an answer sheet by selecting the option that most closely completes or answers the given statements.

1. Objects composed of one or more segments treated as a single object are called a:
   a. line
   b. polyline
   c. double line
   d. arc

2. The initial polyline width default is:
   a. 0
   b. 0.05
   c. none
   d. 1

3. If you want to draw a polyline that looks like an arrow with a point at one end and a width of .25 at the other end, use these settings:
   a. start 0, end .25
   b. start .25, end 0
   c. either a or b
   d. neither a nor b

4. Use this PEDIT option to join an object with a polyline and have the joined object take on the same characteristics as the polyline:
   a. Fit
   b. Edit vertex
   c. Join
   d. Undo

5. Use this PEDIT option to change the width of an entire polyline to a new uniform value:
   a. Width
   b. Join
   c. Edit vertex
   d. Fit

6. This Edit vertex option allows you to change the width of different polyline segments as desired:
   a. Fit
   b. Spline
   c. Width
   d. Starting width

7. You must do this if you want a closed polyline to have all corners automatically chamfered using the CHAMFER command:
   a. Close the last segment with the Close option.
   b. Manually close the last segment.

8. Change a polyline to individual line and arc segments using this command:
   a. X
   b. Pick the Explode toolbar button.
   c. EXPLODE
   d. all of the above

9. When drawing a .25-in.-wide double line with the Left Dragline option, the Offset from center prompt reads:
   a. .125
   b. −.125
   c. .25
   d. −.25

10. A spline drawn between two points results in a:
    a. curve between the points
    b. straight segment between the two points
    c. cannot draw a spline between two points
    d. none of the above

MATCHING

Match each term to the correct description by writing the appropriate number in each box at the left.

- ☐ Caps
- ☐ Close
- ☐ Edit vertex
- ☐ EXPLODE
- ☐ Fit
- ☐ Join
- ☐ Offset
- ☐ PEDIT
- ☐ PLINE
- ☐ Polyline
- ☐ Snap
- ☐ Spline
- ☐ Weight

1. Allows you to connect a double line exactly to another object.
2. Used to make one or more changes to polyline vertices.
3. Changes polyline segments to individual lines and arcs.
4. Used to draw a double line from a known point.
5. An object composed of one or more segments that are treated as one.
6. Lines that connect the endpoints of double lines.
7. This uses the polyline vertices as a frame for curve development.
8. The command used to draw polylines.
9. Used to connect the last point with the first point.
10. Used to edit polylines.
11. Used to create smooth curves that pass through polyline vertices.
12. This option forces a spline to pull closer or farther from the control points.
13. Used to connect an object to a polyline and make it part of the polyline.

CHAPTER 8 ||| Drawing and Editing Polylines and Double Lines **337**

WORD SCRAMBLE

Unscramble the five scrambled words below, one letter to each square, to form five AutoCAD LT–related words:

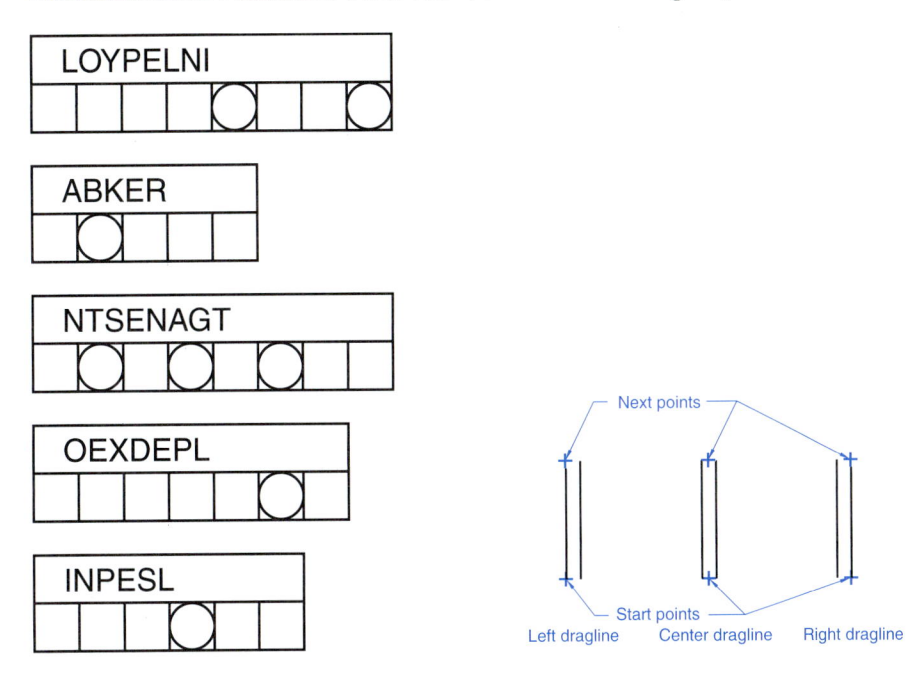

LOYPELNI

ABKER

NTSENAGT

OEXDEPL

INPESL

Unscramble the circled letters above to form the special answer, as suggested by the illustration.

PROJECTS

Set up the following drawing projects with layers that relate to the type of drawing as outlined and discussed in Chapter 5.

8.1 Arrow
Draw the arrow shown below without dimensions. Save as P8.1.

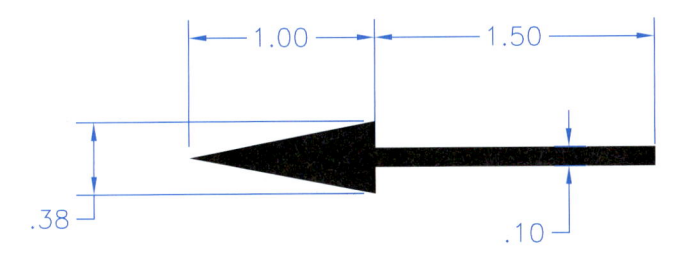

8.2 Graphic Symbol
Draw the symbol shown at the left below without dimensions. Use the ARC command to draw the ends and the PLINE command to draw .1 wide straight polyline segments connecting the arcs. Then use the PEDIT command's Join option to create the symbol shown at the right. Save as P8.2.

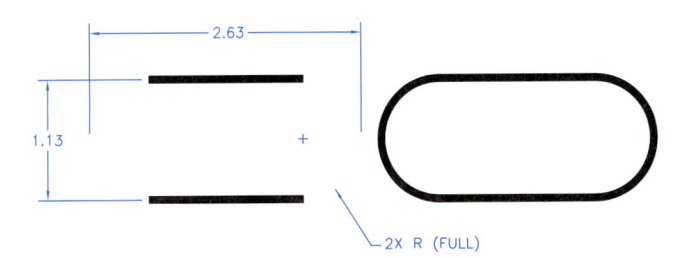

8.3 Graphic Symbol
Draw the symbol shown below without dimensions. Save as P8.3.

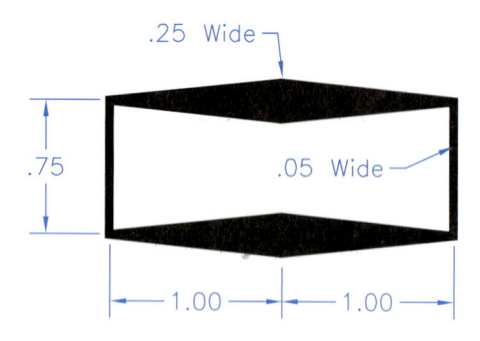

8.4 Graphic Symbol
Draw the symbol shown below without dimensions. Save as P8.4.

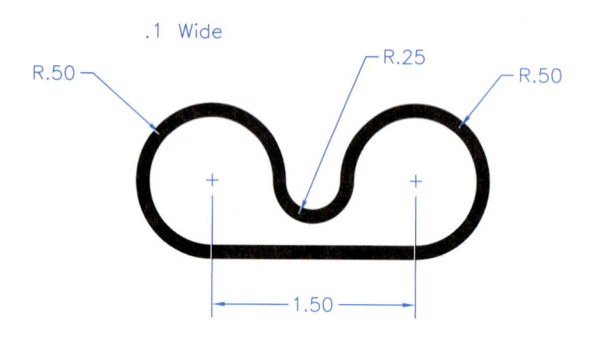

8.5 Arrow
Draw an arrow similar to the one shown below. Save as P8.5.

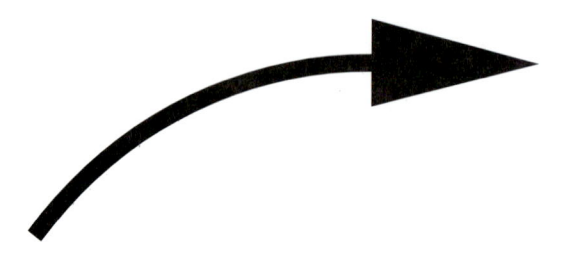

8.6 Graph
Draw two representations of the graph shown below without dimensions as follows:
Set up the graph grid on a blue layer and the graph line on a red layer. Draw one graph by connecting the grid intersection points with continuous straight polyline segments and then use the PEDIT Fit option to create the smooth curve. Draw the other graph using the SPLINE command. Save as P8.6.

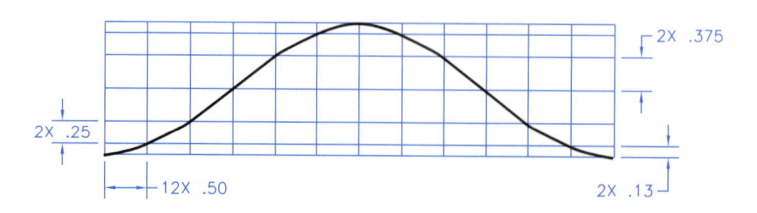

CHAPTER 8 ||| Drawing and Editing Polylines and Double Lines 339

8.7 Clock
Open P7.1 and add the clock hands as shown below. Save as P8.7.

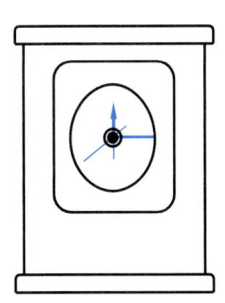

8.8 Star
Draw an object similar to the one shown below. Save as P8.8.

8.9 Floor Plan
Draw the partial floor plan below to your own specifications using double lines. Do not draw text. Save as P8.9.

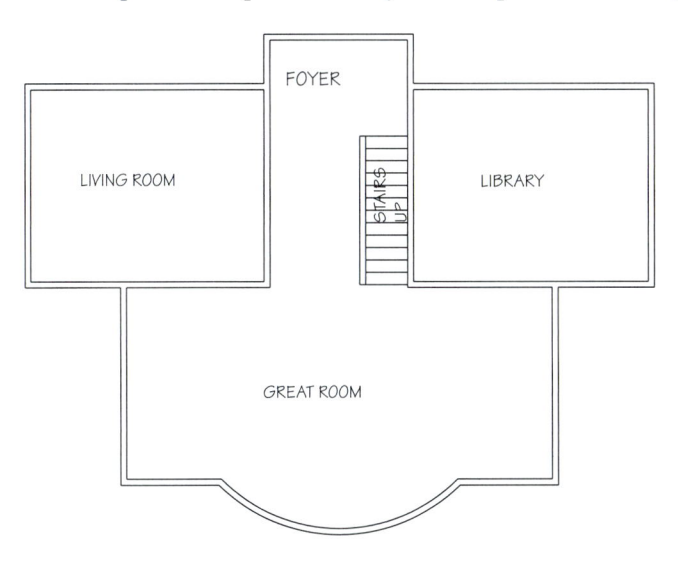

8.10 Floor Plan
Draw the floor plan below to your own specifications using double lines. Place doors, windows, and other objects using your own design. Do not draw text. Save as P8.10.

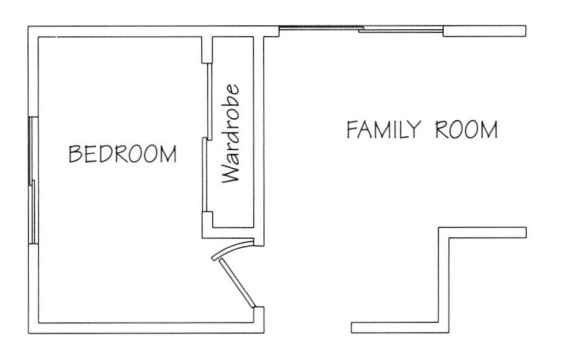

8.11 Revision Cloud

Open the drawing from problem P8.10 for editing. Use the REVCLOUD command to create a revision cloud that surrounds the Wardrobe in the existing drawing. Be sure that the arc length is appropriate to the scale of the drawing. Save as P8.11.

CHAPTER 9

Placing Text on a Drawing

LEARNING GOALS

- Use the TEXT and DTEXT commands to draw single-line text.
- Use the MTEXT command to draw paragraph text.
- Place text with different alignments.
- Create and use text styles.
- Draw special characters and symbols with text.
- Paste text from the Clipboard.
- Drag and drop text into AutoCAD LT.
- Edit text with the DDEDIT, DDMODIFY, and CHANGE commands.
- Mirror text so it is readable.
- Use quick text.
- Check your spelling.
- Create a custom dictionary.

Introduction to Drawing Text

The letters and numbers you place in an AutoCAD LT drawing are referred to as *text.* When manual drafting is used, text is called lettering. Manual lettering on drawings has traditionally been a tedious and time-consuming process. Many professional drafters are able to create quality hand lettering that looks consistent between drawings, but it is often difficult for drafters to match the lettering of others. With AutoCAD LT, the practice of lettering becomes very easy. AutoCAD LT text not only looks the same on every drawing, it can be customized for application on different types of drawings. For example, the smooth uniform appearance of vertical Gothic lettering on mechanical drawings or the artistic look of lettering on architectural drawings can be easily accomplished.

AutoCAD LT provides a wide variety of text styles and options. Text can be prepared as single line or multiline. Every line of single-line text can be edited individually, whereas multiline text can be entered and edited in paragraph form. AutoCAD LT also allows you to check the spelling of words you place on the drawing.

Creating Single-Line Text

AutoCAD LT allows you to create ***single-line text*** that is referred to as ***line text.*** Line text is usually used for short text entries of one or more lines. Each line of line text is an individual object that can be edited separately from the other line text. Line text is drawn with the TEXT or DTEXT commands.

AutoCAD LT provides a variety of text fonts that can be used to create custom text styles. A ***text font*** is a complete set of characters, including letters, numbers, marks, and symbols, that is of unique proportion and design. A ***text style*** is defined as settings that determine the appearance of text characters. The AutoCAD LT text styles can be modified to suit your drafting practices. For example, you can slant, stretch, or compress the text styles for specific applications. Text styles can be defined to duplicate traditional smooth letters and numbers for mechanical drawing or present an artistic style that closely matches architectural hand lettering.

Using the DTEXT and TEXT Commands

Draw
Single Line Text
DTEXT
DT

TEXT
TX

Line text is created using the DTEXT and TEXT commands. Both commands work in a similar manner, except that DTEXT allows you to see the text on the screen as you type and the TEXT command only displays the text being typed at the prompt line. The DTEXT command can be accessed by picking Single Line Text in the Draw pull-down menu or by typing **DT** or **DTEXT** at the Command: prompt. The TEXT command can be entered by typing **TX** or **TEXT** at the Command: prompt. The DTEXT and TEXT commands work much the same, but the DTEXT command is used in the following examples because it displays the text on the screen while you type. When entering these commands, you are asked for a Start point. The Start point is the point where the text is entered on the screen. The Start point is also called the insertion point. Other options include Justify and Style. The Justify option determines how lines of text are aligned. The Justify options are explained later. The Style option is used to change text fonts. The Style option is also discussed later in this chapter.

After you enter the command and pick the Start point, you are asked for the text Height and Rotation angle. The text height should be set to match the desired height of letters and numbers on your drawing or for the specific application. Standard drawing text height is .125 in. or 3 mm. Other text heights such as 5/32 in. (4 mm) can be used depending on your company or school practices. Titles are often drawn .188 (5 mm) or .25 in. (6 mm) high. The initial AutoCAD LT text height depends on the setup or template used. If you use the Wizards, the text height is on the value entered for Length: on the Area page of the Quick or Advanced Setup dialog box. The Start from Scratch option sets the text height at 0.200. The templates set the text height at varied values depending on the size of the sheet and the number system used.

The rotation angle determines the angle the text is placed at in relation to horizontal. The initial rotation angle default is 0, which makes all text horizontal. After you pick the Start point and enter the Height and Rotation angle, you get a Text: prompt and a cursor box is displayed on the screen. The cursor box is equal in size to the height specified for the text, with the width approximating an uppercase "W" in the current style. This cursor moves as you type the desired text. After you type a line of text, press Enter to get the Text: prompt again. Press Enter every time you want to type a new line of text. This causes the cursor to drop down one line and be placed directly below the justification point. Pressing Enter on a blank line ends the DTEXT command. At the end of the last line of text, you can press Enter twice to return to the Command: prompt. Figure 9.1 shows the elements of AutoCAD LT text using the DTEXT command's Start point option:

Command: **DT** or **DTEXT**↵
Justify/Style/<Start point>: ⟨pick a start point⟩
Height <0.2>: **.25**↵
Rotation angle <0>: ↵
Text: **AutoCAD LT text is easy to draw and provides.**↵
Text: **you with a variety of fonts and styles.**↵
Text: ↵
Command:

While the DTEXT cursor is visible, you can pick any new location on the drawing and continue entering new lines of text as desired. You can also use the Backspace key to clear entered text and reenter as needed. Also, during the DTEXT command, any number of previously typed lines can be backspaced through. If you use the Backspace key to remove text from the current entry, you cannot retrieve it. The removed text must be retyped if you decide you need it after all.

CHAPTER 9 ||| Placing Text on a Drawing   **343**

FIGURE 9.1 (A) The steps in drawing AutoCAD LT text using the DTEXT command. (B) A variety of text rotation angle examples.

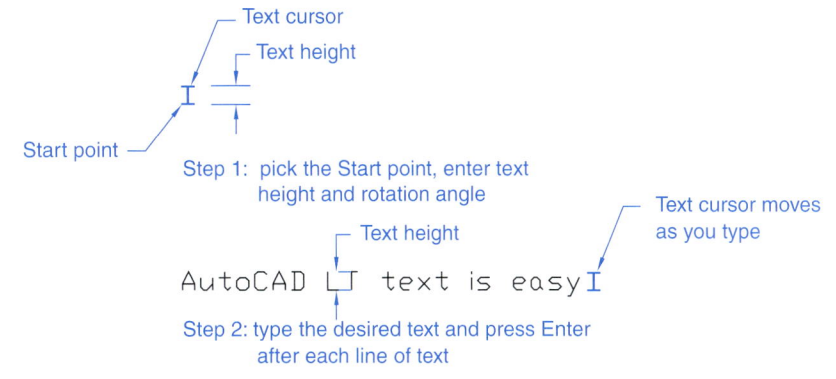

Text cursor
Text height
Start point

Step 1: pick the Start point, enter text height and rotation angle

Text height
Text cursor moves as you type

AutoCAD LT text is easy

Step 2: type the desired text and press Enter after each line of text

AutoCAD LT text is easy to draw and provides you with a variety of fonts and styles.

Step 3: press Enter twice to exit the DTEXT command

A Steps used to draw AutoCAD LT text with the DTEXT command

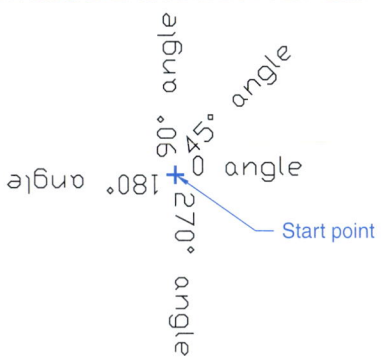

90° angle
45° angle
0 angle
180° angle
270° angle
Start point

B A variety of Rotation angle examples

Field Notes

- The Start point option justifies lines of text along a left edge. This is referred to as left-justified text, as shown in Figure 9.1.
- If you enter the DTEXT command and press Enter at the Start point prompt, AutoCAD LT automatically places the text cursor one line below the last line of text. This is true even if the last line of text has been moved. The new line of text uses the same justification method as the previous line, just as if the text is created during the same DTEXT command.
- Be careful when using the Esc key to exit the DTEXT command because all lines of text that are entered in the canceled DTEXT command are lost.

Exercise 9.1

1. Begin a new drawing.
2. Make the text height .125 in. and the rotation angle 0 for all applications.
3. Use the DTEXT command's Start point option to type the text shown in Figure 9.1A.
4. Use the DTEXT command's Start point option and test the variety of rotation angles shown in Figure 9.1B. Use the same Start point for each line of text.
5. Save the drawing as EX9.1.

Text Alignment Options

Text *justification* determines how text is aligned with the insertion point. AutoCAD LT provides you with several justification options that are available when you enter the TEXT or DTEXT command's Justify option. The default option, Start point, creates text that is justified along the left side, and the bottom left corner of the first line is located at the specified insertion point. The other justification options are accessed like this:

Command: **T**, **DT**, or **DTEXT**↵
Justify/Style/<Start point>: **J**↵
Align/Fit/Center/Middle/Right/TL/TC/TR/ML/MC/MR/BL/BC/BR:

The following discussion explains how each Justify option works and the results:

Align: This option is used to specify two points that control the beginning and ending of the lines of text. The text you enter is placed within the points and the text height is adjusted between the points. Each line of text is automatically adjusted between the two initial points. When typing, the text appears to go beyond or fall short of the second point until you press Enter twice to complete the command. The text being typed is adjusted to the justification method after all text has been entered and you return to the Command: prompt. You need to keep track of the two points so you do not end up with more text between the points than you desire. The result of too much text between the points is very small text; too little text between the points results in big text. The points you pick also control the rotation angle of the text. Also, picking an endpoint that is to the left of the start point results in upside-down text. The following prompts are issued and demonstrated in Figure 9.2:

Command: **T**, **DT**, or **DTEXT**↵
Justify/Style/<Start point>: **J**↵
Align/Fit/Center/Middle/Right/TL/TC/TR/ML/MC/MR/BL/BC/BR: **A**↵
First text line point: ⟨*pick the beginning point*⟩
Second text line point: ⟨*pick the ending point*⟩
Text: **The Align option allows you to pick.**↵
Text: **the beginning and end of the line of.**↵
Text: **text. The text height and width are.**↵
Text: **adjusted between the points..**↵
Text: ↵
Command:

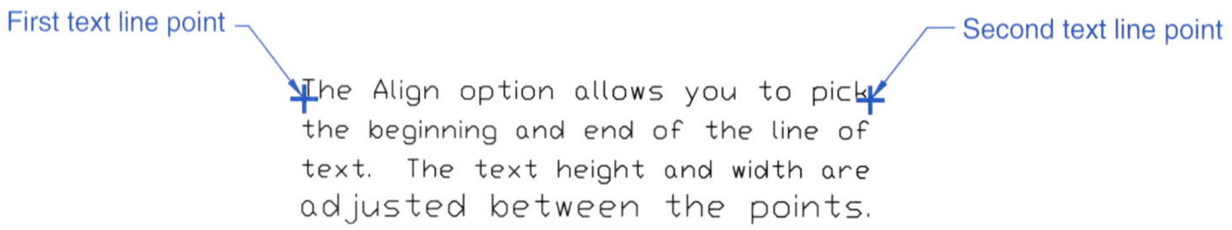

FIGURE 9.2 Using the Align option of the DTEXT Justify option. Notice how the height and width of the text varies depending on how much text is typed between the selected points.

First text line point — Second text line point

The Align option allows you to pick
the beginning and end of the line of
text. The text height and width are
adjusted between the points.

Fit: The Fit option is similar to the Align option, because you pick two points to control the length of the lines of text. However, the Fit option also asks for the text height. The text height remains the same as the value you specify, but the text width varies depending on how much you type between the points. The points you pick control the rotation angle of the text. Look at Figure 9.3 as you follow these prompts:

Align/Fit/Center/Middle/Right/TL/TC/TR/ML/MC/MR/BL/BC/BR: **F**↵
First text line point: ⟨*pick the beginning point*⟩
Second text line point: ⟨*pick the ending point*⟩
Height <0.2>: **.125**↵
Text: **The Fit option allows you to pick.**↵
Text: **the beginning and end of the line of.**↵
Text: **text and also control the text height..**↵
Text: **The text width is adjusted between the points..**↵
Text: ↵
Command:

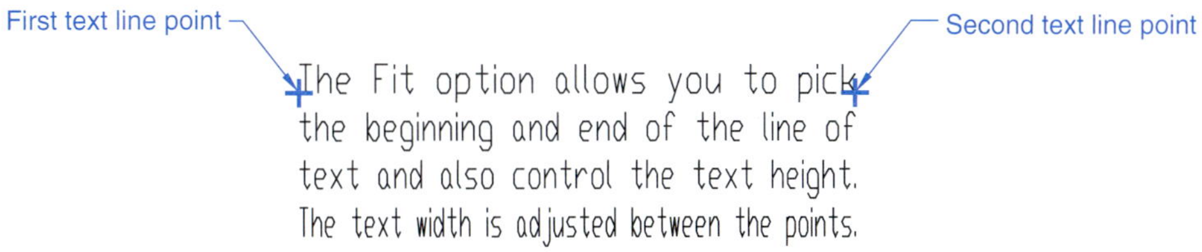

FIGURE 9.3 Using the Fit option of the DTEXT Justify option. Notice how the width of the text varies depending on how much text is typed between the selected points, while the text height remains the same as the value you specify.

First text line point — The Fit option allows you to pick the beginning and end of the line of text and also control the text height. The text width is adjusted between the points. — Second text line point

Field Notes

The Fit text option comes in handy when a line of text is a little too long to fit in a desired area, such as in a title block, bill of materials, parts list, or schedule. Use the Fit option to squeeze the text into these limited areas rather than lowering the text height.

Center: This Justify option allows you to place text by specifying the center. The center is located along the baseline of the text and centered on each line of text you type. When you begin the Center option, the text cursor and the text you type move to the right of the pick point. Do not let this alarm you, because the text is automatically centered when you press Enter twice and leave the command. Figure 9.4 shows the result of the following Center option:

Align/Fit/Center/Middle/Right/TL/TC/TR/ML/MC/MR/BL/BC/BR: **C.↵**
Center point: ⟨*pick the center point*⟩
Height <0.2>: **.125↵**
Rotation angle <0>: ↵
Text: **The Center option allows you to pick.↵**
Text: **the center point of the line or lines of text..↵**
Text: ↵
Command:

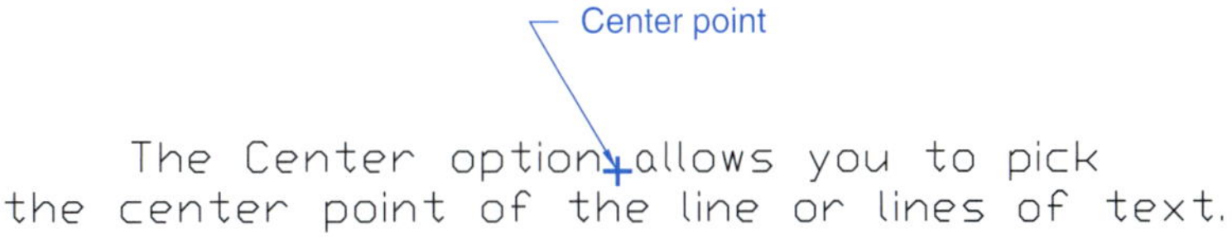

FIGURE 9.4 Using the Center Justify option of the DTEXT command.

Center point — The Center option allows you to pick the center point of the line or lines of text.

Middle: This option allows you to specify the middle of a line of text. The middle is located in the middle of the text height and centered on each line of text you type. When you begin the Middle option, the text cursor and the text you type move to the right of the pick point, just like the Center option. Figure 9.5 shows the result of using the following Middle option:

Align/Fit/Center/Middle/Right/TL/TC/TR/ML/MC/MR/BL/BC/BR: **M.↵**
Center point: ⟨*pick the center point*⟩
Height <0.2>: **.125↵**
Rotation angle <0>: ↵
Text: **The Middle option allows you to pick.↵**
Text: **the midpoint of the line or lines of text.↵**
Text: **and centers the text at that point..↵**
Text: ↵
Command:

FIGURE 9.5 Using the Middle Justify option of the DTEXT command.

```
                                        ─ Middle point
        The Middle option ⊕llows you to pick
     the midpoint of the line or lines of text
       and centers the text at that point.
```

Right: The Right option justifies lines of text along a right edge as shown in Figure 9.6. The prompts work like this:

    Align/Fit/Center/Middle/Right/TL/TC/TR/ML/MC/MR/BL/BC/BR: **R**↵
    Center point: ⟨*pick the center point*⟩
    Height <0.2>: **.125**↵
    Rotation angle <0>: ↵
    Text: **The Right option aligns text.**↵
    Text: **along a right edge.**↵
    Text: **This results in random length lines at the left.**↵
    Text: ↵
    Command:

FIGURE 9.6 Using the Right Justify option of the DTEXT command.

```
                                                     Right point ─
            The Right option aligns text
                    along a right   margin.
        This results in random length lines at the left.
```

In addition to the basic alignment options, AutoCAD LT offers nine more specialized alignment options. The justification points include Top Left, Top Center, Top Right, Middle Left, Middle Center, Middle Right, Bottom Left, Bottom Center, and Bottom Right. Figure 9.7 illustrates these justification points.

When specifying an alignment method, it is not necessary to first type the **J** for Justify at the first prompt. Use this option whenever you need a reminder of what the available options are. If you already know what option you need, simply type the option at the Start point: prompt, as shown here:

    Command: **DT** or **DTEXT**↵
    Justify/Style/<Start point>: **TR**↵
    Top/right point:

FIGURE 9.7 Justification options available for single-line text.

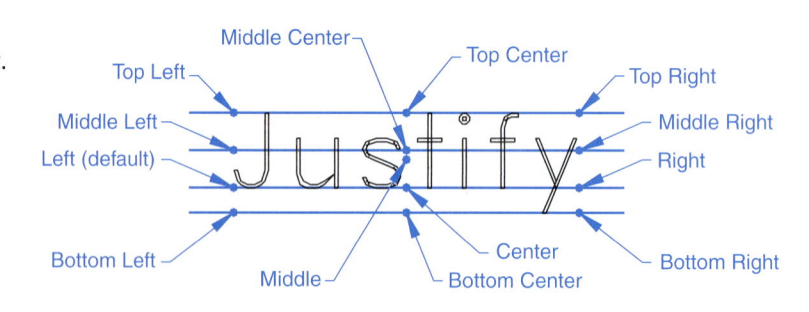

✎ Field Notes

- The INSert object snap mode accesses the justification point specified when creating the text. The INSert point of Fit or Aligned text is the bottom-left point.

Exercise 9.2

1. Begin a new drawing.
2. Make the text height .125 in. and the rotation angle 0 for all applications.
3. Use the DTEXT command's Align option to type the text shown in Figure 9.2.
4. Use the DTEXT command's Fit option to type the text shown in Figure 9.3.
5. Use the DTEXT command's Center option to type the text shown in Figure 9.4.
6. Use the DTEXT command's Middle option to type the text shown in Figure 9.5.
7. Use the DTEXT command's Right option to type the text shown in Figure 9.6.
8. Create one line of text using each of the available specialized justification options. The text height should be .2 units. Type the justification description for the text content (Top/Left, Top/Center, etc.).
9. Draw a donut object, using an inside diameter of 0 and an outside of .1, at the INSert point of each text object in this drawing.
10. Save the drawing as EX9.2.

Creating and Using Text Styles

There are two important AutoCAD LT terms that relate to the use of text. These terms are font file and text style. A general definition was provided earlier in this chapter. Further clarification will help you understand the following discussion. A ***font file*** is a font definition resource where a complete font is available for your use. A ***text style*** is a definition, within a drawing, of a particular application of text that includes the name of the font file along with any specific properties that you assign. A font file can be used by more than one text style. For example, your company may have text standards that are used on drawings. These standards are probably text styles that use font files in different manners. A text style is defined by you or your company to contain the desired text characteristics. In the process of defining a text style, you often load a font file to use as the basis for creating the text style.

The TEXT, DTEXT, and MTEXT commands all have a Style option. The MTEXT command is for drawing multiline text and is discussed later. The Style option is used to set the text style. The AutoCAD LT default style is called STANDARD, which uses the TXT.SHX font file. This is the font that has been used in the previous examples in this chapter. The STANDARD style is also referred to as a ***fast font*** because it is drawn and regenerated very quickly, but it does not look very good for most applications.

Field Notes

Other default text styles may be provided when you use a template, depending on which template you use.

AutoCAD LT provides you with a wide variety of standard text and symbol fonts defined in font files. The standard text and symbol font files have an .SHX extension. For example, the file ROMANS.SHX defines a Roman Simplex font. This font has smooth characters and is commonly used on drawings. Complex fonts such as COMPLEX.SHX provide you with characters that have serifs. ***Serifs*** are fine artistic lines projecting from, generally, the top and bottom of a letter. Gothic fonts such as GOTHICE.SHX are an old English style. The symbol fonts are used for applications such as mapping and math and can produce symbols not found on the keyboard. These fonts substitute symbols for standard keyboard characters. The mapping symbol font is called SYMAP.SHX.

Field Notes

> The names of .SHX files have specific meaning. For example, ROMANS = Roman Simplex, ROMANC = Roman Complex, ROMAND = Roman Duplex, and ROMANT = Roman Triplex. The characteristics of each font are established by the number of lines in the characters. The Simplex has one line, Duplex has two lines, and Triplex has three lines. This standard is maintained across many different .SHX font files.

AutoCAD LT provides True Type fonts that provide greater detail than the standard fonts. You may want to use the City Blueprint, Country Blueprint, or Stylus BT font for your architectural drawings because they closely resemble the artistic hand lettering used by architectural drafters.

Setting and Creating Text Styles

Format
  Text Style...
  DDSTYLE
  STYLE
  ST

The Style option found in the TEXT, DTEXT, and MTEXT commands is used to set a text style. You set a text style by typing the name after entering the Style option. However, before a text style can be used with one of these commands, the style must be defined. If you try to use the Style option and enter a text style, such as ROMANS, before it has been defined, AutoCAD LT gives you this message:

Command: **DT** or **DTEXT**↵
Justify/Style/<Start point>: **S**↵
Style name (or ?) <STANDARD>: **ROMANS**↵
Unknown or invalid text style name.

To solve this problem, you need to define the ROMANS text style. Text styles are defined using the DDSTYLE command. This command is accessed by picking Text Style ... in the Format pull-down menu or by typing **ST**, **STYLE**, or **DDSTYLE** at the Command: prompt. The DDSTYLE command opens the Text Style dialog box shown in Figure 9.8.

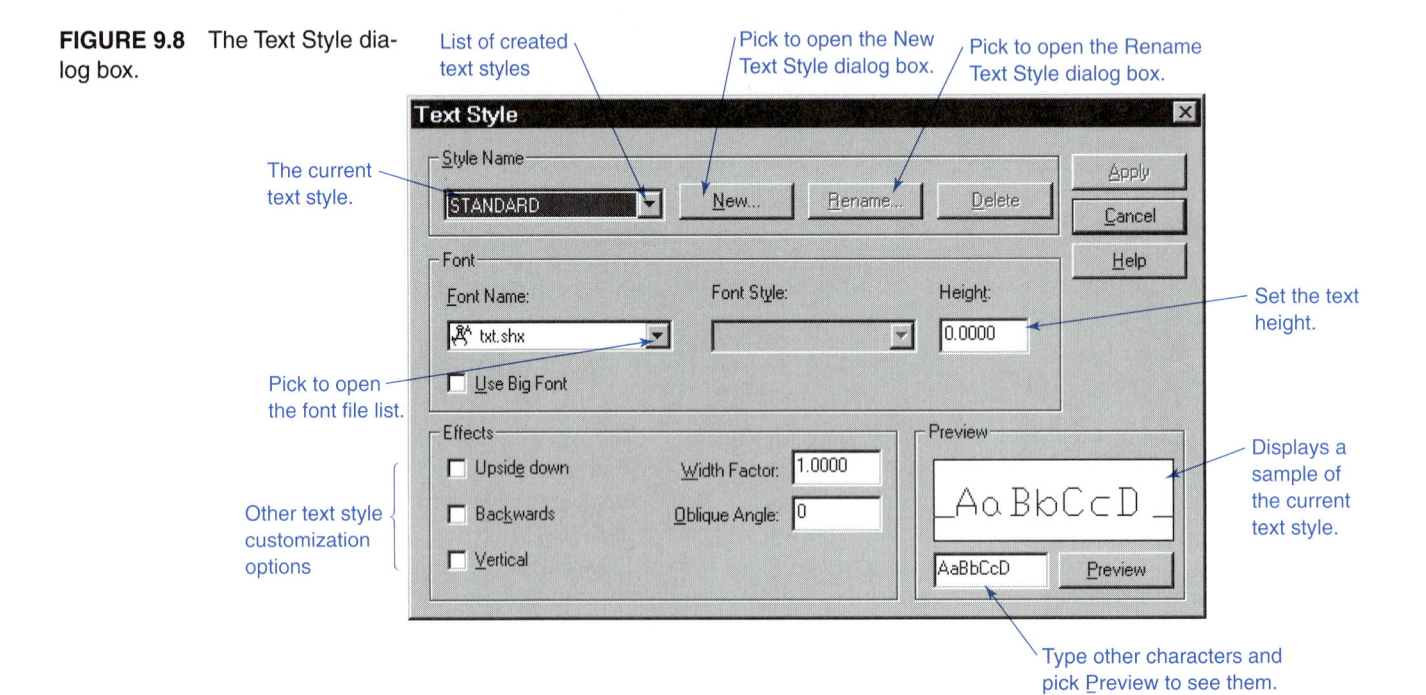

FIGURE 9.8 The Text Style dialog box.

The following provides a brief description of the Text Style dialog box:

Style Name: This area is where the names of existing text styles are listed. You can modify, rename, or delete a listed text style.

The New ... button is used to create a new text style. Picking the New ... button opens the New Text Style dialog box shown in Figure 9.9. By default, STYLE1 is automatically displayed in the Style Name: text box. If you pick the OK button, a new style named STYLE1 is added to the list. Any future picks under the same conditions produce incrementally named styles, such as STYLE2 and STYLE3. It is very convenient to type a desired style name and then pick the OK button. You can type a style name that relates to your drawing, such as MECHANICAL for mechanical drawings or ARCHITECTURAL for architectural drawings. If a style named STYLE1 is created, you can use the Rename ... button to change the name if you wish.

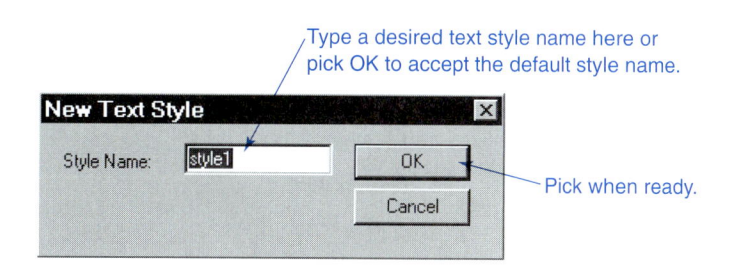

FIGURE 9.9 The New Text Style dialog box.

Type a desired text style name here or pick OK to accept the default style name.

Pick when ready.

The Rename ... button is used to rename a current text style. To use this option, highlight a text style in the list to make it current and then pick the Rename ... button. This opens the Rename Text Style dialog box shown in Figure 9.10. Type a new text style name and pick OK. The current text style takes on the revised name.

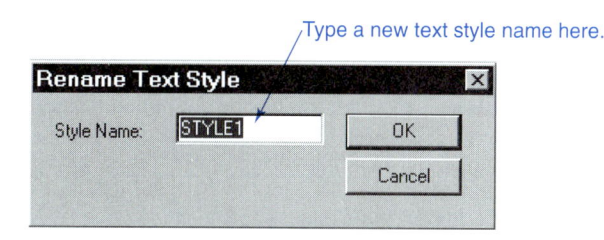

FIGURE 9.10 The Rename Text Style dialog box.

Type a new text style name here.

The Delete button is used to remove a current text style from the list. Notice in Figure 9.8 that the Rename ... and Delete buttons are not active. This is because the only text style listed is the AutoCAD LT STANDARD font, which you cannot rename or delete. When you pick the Delete button, Auto CAD LT issues an ACAD Alert, which gives you a chance to change your mind.

Field Notes

- If you try to rename the STANDARD style name, the Text Style dialog box tells you that you cannot do this. However, the STANDARD text style can be renamed using the DDRENAME command. Even if the STANDARD style is renamed, it cannot be deleted from the Text Style dialog box.
- The ? option of the DTEXT command can be used to list the defined style names. Just type "?" at the Style name (or ?) <>: prompt and press Enter to get a list of the defined style names.

Font: The Font area of the Text Style dialog box is where you select the font you want to use in a text style. Open the Font Name: list to find the available fonts. The romans font is commonly used on mechanical drawings because it closely duplicates the traditional style recommended by ASME. So, if you named the text style MECHANICAL, find the romans.shx file and pick it, as shown in Figure 9.11.

FIGURE 9.11 The Font Name: list in the Text Style dialog box.

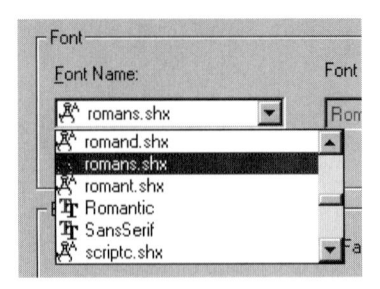

The Font Style: list is active only when you pick a font name that has its own style options. The romans.shx font has no additional style options. If you pick a font name such as SansSerif, the Font Style: list provides options that can be used to change the appearance of the font. See Figure 9.12.

FIGURE 9.12 The Font Style: list is available for some True-Type fonts. This provides different characteristics for the specified font.

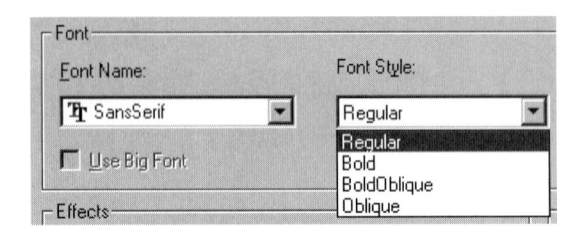

The Height: text box is where you specify the desired text height. The default text height value is 0 (zero). A zero text height entered here allows you to specify the text height every time you enter the TEXT, DTEXT, or MTEXT commands. This provides you with the flexibility to change the text height when you use these commands or simply press Enter to accept the current default. If you specify a value other than zero in the Height: text box, then this height becomes fixed for every time you use this text style. Specifying a fixed height is an advantage when you know that the height for a particular text style is not going to change. However, this can cause unexpected results when a fixed height is specified for a style you need to use at different heights in a drawing. If you are creating text and no prompt is issued for height, it is because a fixed height has been applied to the style. If you find that a style has a fixed height, and you want it to be variable, you can redefine the style using a 0 height. This does not affect any previously drawn text, but any future uses of this style provide the text height prompt.

The Use Big Font check box is off by default and is active only with .shx fonts. Asian and other large-format fonts are called ***big fonts***. The big font is used as a supplement to define many symbols not available in normal font files. The Big Font: list replaces the Font Style: list when you pick the Use Big Font check box. An example of the effects of a big font can be seen by loading a normal font file and a big font file to be used as a text style.

Effects: The Effects area of the Text Style dialog box is where you can choose options for customizing a text font. You have several customization options, which include making text upside down, backwards, or vertical. You can also specify different heights, widths, and character slant. These options are designed into the text style by using the Effects area of the Text Style dialog box. First define a text style, as previously discussed. Next, change the effects as desired before picking the Apply button and closing the dialog box. You can change the effects individually and see the changes displayed immediately in the Character Preview image for any effect caused by a toggle, except the Vertical option. This allows you to view the effects of the design before making a decision to use it. The different elements of the Effects compartment in the Text Style dialog box are explained and demonstrated in the following list:

Upside down — Pick this toggle to have the text placed upside down as shown in Figure 9.13.

FIGURE 9.13 Setting the style as upside-down text.

Backwards — Check this toggle to have text drawn backwards, as shown in Figure 9.14. Backwards text is placed at a 180° angle relative to the specified rotation angle. Backwards text is very useful for plastic and metal cast part tools, where the text must be backwards on the tool for it to be forward on the part.

CHAPTER 9 ||| Placing Text on a Drawing   351

FIGURE 9.14 Setting the style as backwards text.   This is Backward text.

Vertical   This option places text vertically, as shown in Figure 9.15. A 0° rotation angle produced downward text.

FIGURE 9.15 Setting the text style as vertical text.

```
T  V  t
h  e  e
i  r  x
s  t  t
.  i
i  c
s  a
   l
```

Width Factor   This text box allows you to change the width of text characters. The default width is 1. A width of less than 1 compresses the characters, and a width greater than 1 expands the characters. Figure 9.16 displays a variety of different text width specifications.

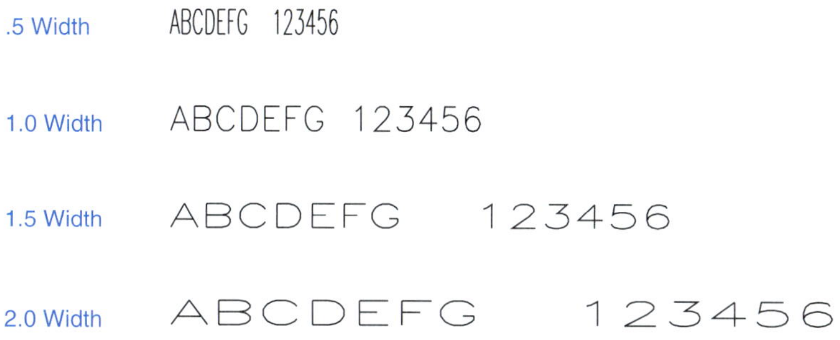

FIGURE 9.16 Examples of different text width settings.

.5 Width   ABCDEFG 123456

1.0 Width   ABCDEFG 123456

1.5 Width   ABCDEFG   123456

2.0 Width   ABCDEFG   123456

Obliquing Angle   The obliquing angle establishes the slant of the characters. A positive obliquing angle slants the text to the right, and a negative angle slants text to the left. Text without any slant has an obliquing angle of 0 (zero). Some drafting fields such as structural or rivers shown on maps use text that is slanted to the right, usually at 15°. Few applications exist that go beyond ±30°. AutoCAD LT limits the obliquing angle to between ±85°. Figure 9.17 shows the results of changing the text obliquing angle.

FIGURE 9.17 Examples of different text obliquing angle settings.

0 Obliquing Angle   ABCDEFG 123456

15° Obliquing Angle   ABCDEFG 123456

30° Obliquing Angle   ABCDEFG 123456

-15° Obliquing Angle   ABCDEFG 123456

-30° Obliquing Angle   ABCDEFG 123456

Preview: This area displays several characters of the current text font. This is a good way to see what the text style looks like before you select it for use in a drawing. The preview image automatically shows the first few characters of a font. You can look at different characters by typing them in the text box to the left of the Preview button. For example, the image in Figure 9.8 displays an upper- and lowercase example of ABC. If you want to see what the numbers for this font look like, type them in the text box and pick the Preview button.

<dl>
<dt>Apply</dt>
<dd>Pick this button to apply the selected style or style changes to all of the text in the current drawings.</dd>
<dt>Close</dt>
<dd>Pick this button to close the Text Style dialog box.</dd>
</dl>

Steps in Creating a Text Style

The previous discussion explained how to create a text style using the Text Style dialog box. The following provides you with a quick step-by-step sequence to use when creating your first text style:

1. Think about the name for your text style. You can name the text style anything you want, but the name normally identifies its use. For example, you can have a text style named MECHANICAL for the general information found on your mechanical drawings. You can have a specific name for titles, such as MECHANICAL-TITLES. You can use similar style names for your architectural drawings, such as ARCH-TITLES. Use abbreviations, if you wish. You can also name a text style with the font name. For example, you can pick a text style name of ROMANS to be used with romans font on your mechanical drawings. Good fonts to use on architectural drawings are StylusBT, CityBlueprint, and CountryBlueprint.

> **Field Notes**
>
> It is best to keep a log of the text styles you create. You can refer to the log as a reminder of the text style characteristics used with the text style name.

2. Open the Text Style dialog box using one of the ways to access the DDSTYLE command.
3. Pick the New... button to open the New Text Style dialog box. Type the desired text style name, such as MECHANICAL, in the Style Name: text box. Pick OK.
4. Open the Font Name: list and pick romans.shx.
5. Leave the Height: as 0 so you can specify the desired text height when you are drawing text.
6. Leave all other options at their default settings, because the romans font named MECHANICAL with flexible text height is what you want at this time.
7. Pick the Apply button.
8. Pick the Close button.

Exercise 9.3

1. Open EX9.2.
2. Use the DDSTYLE command to define romans as a new text style using the romans font file.
3. Make the romans style the current text style in this drawing by picking Apply, and Close the dialog box.
4. Use the romans text style and type the upper- and lowercase alphabet and numbers 1 through 10 with .125-in.-high characters.
5. Notice the difference between the STANDARD style from the previous exercise and the romans style.
6. Save the drawing as EX9.3.

CHAPTER 9 ||| Placing Text on a Drawing

Field Notes

If you use the Text Style dialog box to make a change to an existing text style and then close before creating a new name for that text style, AutoCAD LT gives you this message:

The current style has been modified.
Do you want to save your changes?

If you answer Yes, the changes are saved to the current text style. Pick No to return to the Command: prompt with no changes made.

Exercise 9.4

1. Open EX9.3.
2. Erase the drawing.
3. Use the Text Style dialog box to set upside-down text and then use the DTEXT command to enter the text shown in Figure 9.12.
4. Use the Text Style dialog box to remove the previous effect and set backward text. Use the DTEXT command to enter the text shown in Figure 9.13.
5. Use the Text Style dialog box to remove the previous effect and set vertical text. Use the DTEXT command to enter the text shown in Figure 9.14.
6. Use the Text Style dialog box to remove the previous effect and set the width factor to a variety of values similar to those shown in Figure 9.15. Use the DTEXT command to enter the text after each setting.
7. Use the Text Style dialog box to remove the previous effect and set the obliquing angle to a variety of values similar to those shown in Figure 9.16. Use the DTEXT command to enter the text after each setting.
8. Save the drawing as EX9.4.

Customizing Text Styles

Working with AutoCAD LT text becomes an easy task if you customize the text styles for the drawings you create and have them available in a prototype. Commonly customized text styles might include a variety such as those shown in Table 9.1.

TABLE 9.1 Common customized text styles

Mechanical Drawings

Name	Use	Font	Height	Width	Angle
MECH	Drawing field	ROMANS	0.125	0	0
MECH-TITLES	View titles	ROMAND	0.25	1.5	0
MECH-PLANES	Cutting planes	ROMANS	0.25	0	0

Architectural Drawings

Name	Use	Font	Height	Width	Angle
ARCH	Drawing field	StylusBT	0.125	0	0
ARCH-TITLES	Drawing titles	StylusBT	0.25	1.5	0

Exercise 9.5

1. Begin a new drawing, or a previously developed mechanical or architectural template as appropriate.
2. Use the DDSTYLE command to customize the following text styles for use in either your mechanical drawings or your architectural drawings, whichever you prefer:

Mechanical Drawings

Name	Font	Height	Width	Angle
MECH	ROMANS	0.125	0	0
MECH-TITLES	ROMAND	0.25	1.5	0
MECH-PLANES	ROMANS	0.25	0	0

Architectural Drawings

Name	Font	Height	Width	Angle
ARCH	StylusBT	0.125	0	0
ARCH-TITLES	StylusBT	0.25	1.5	0

3. Save the drawing as EX9.5.

Defining Text Styles at the Command: Prompt

The -STYLE command can be used to create text styles at the keyboard. There is a hyphen (-) typed before the STYLE command name. The features of the -STYLE command are the same as the DDSTYLE command except entries are made at the prompt line. The following command sequence is used to create the TITLES style:

```
Command: -STYLE↵
Text style name (or ?) <STANDARD>: TITLES↵
New style.
Specify full font name or font filename <txt>: ROMAND↵
Height <0>: .25↵
Width factor <1>: 1.5↵
Obliquing angle [0>: ↵
Backwards? <N>: ↵
Upside-down? <N>: ↵
Vertical? <N>: ↵
TITLES is now the current text style.
Command:
```

Although using the Text Style dialog box is convenient and provides better visual aids than the -STYLE command, some people like using the keyboard approach.

✓ LEARNING CHECKPOINT

- ☐ What is line text?
- ☐ Define the term *text font*.
- ☐ Explain the difference between the TEXT and DTEXT commands.
- ☐ What does the Justify option do?
- ☐ Describe the DTEXT Justify options: Start point, Align, Fit, Center, Middle, and Right. Be sure to explain the main difference between Align and Fit.
- ☐ How do you access the Text Style dialog box?
- ☐ Explain how to see different characters for the currently displayed font in the Preview image.

- How do you display a new font image in the Preview box?
- Discuss the effects of changing the text width factor and obliquing angle.
- Outline at least six steps used to customize a text style called TITLES with ROMAND font, 0.25 height, and 1.5 width.

Creating Multiline Text

Multiline text is also referred to as paragraph text. AutoCAD LT defines ***paragraph text*** as consisting of any number of text lines or paragraphs that fit within a width you specify. Each set of lines or paragraphs is one object. This is very different from the previously discussed line text. With line text, every line of text is an individual object. All of the same parameters that affect line text, such as height, width, obliquing angle, and justification options, also work with paragraph text. Paragraph text is much more flexible than line text, allowing individual portions of the text to have varying properties. Multiline text is drawn by picking the Multiline Text button in the Draw toolbar, by picking Paragraph Text… in the Draw pull-down menu, or by typing **T**, **MT**, or **MTEXT**:

Command: **T**, **MT** or **MTEXT** ↵
Current text style: ROMANS. Text height: 0.2000
Specify first corner: ⟨*pick the first corner of the text boundary*⟩
Specify opposite corner or [Height/Justify/Rotation/Style/Width]: ⟨*pick the opposite corner of the text boundary*⟩

The Specify first corner prompt is issued for you to pick the first corner of a box. The Specify opposite corner prompt asks you to move the cursor to form a box that is approximately equal in size to the area where you want the paragraph text to be placed. You can move the cursor in any direction from the first corner. Pick the opposite corner of the box when you have the desired size. In Figure 9.18, note that the box is the text boundary. The ***text boundary*** establishes the width of the paragraph of text. It is important that the text boundary width you establish accurately defines the width of the desired paragraph. The actual width of the paragraph may not be exactly the same as the width you specify, due to word length and wrapping. ***Word wrapping*** is the process by which the words that exceed the boundary width are automatically placed or "wrapped" to the next line. Some lines of text may be wider than others, but none is wider than the defined boundary. If a single word exceeds the defined paragraph width, the text is not wrapped, but is allowed to extend beyond the boundary. In this case, the paragraph width is not changed and all other text is wrapped as usual.

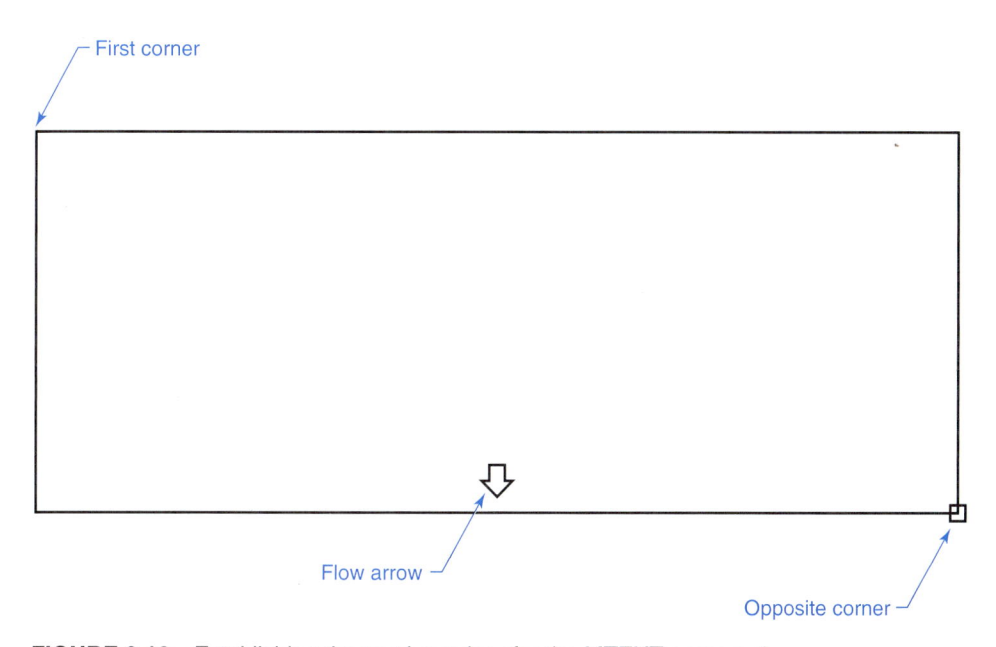

FIGURE 9.18 Establishing the text boundary for the MTEXT paragraph.

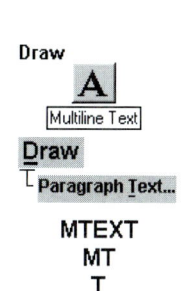

The height of the text boundary does not have to be exact, because AutoCAD LT automatically adjusts the text boundary to match the actual height of the paragraph you type. The flow arrow in Figure 9.18 gives you a reference for the direction the text will flow when it is entered in the boundary. This is related to the multiline text justification, which is discussed later. This flow arrow points down for any top-justified text, up for bottom-justification, or up and down for center-justified text.

The Height, Justify, Rotation, and Style options work as they do with the DTEXT command that was discussed earlier. These options are explained again later in this chapter with the information about the Multiline Text Editor.

The Width option is used by typing **W** and then pressing Enter. The Width option allows you to establish the width of the text boundary. A rubber-band cursor then connects the first point to the next point you pick to establish the width. The prompts are as follows:

Command: **T**, **MT** or **MTEXT** ↵
Current text style: ROMANS. Text height: 0.2000
Specify first corner: ⟨*pick the first point of the text boundary width*⟩
Specify opposite corner or [Height/Justify/Rotation/Style/Width]: **W** ↵
Specify width: ⟨*pick the second point to define the text boundary width*⟩

You can also enter a numeric value at the keyboard. If you enter a 0 (zero), the multiline text continues on the same line until you press Enter. Used with a 0 width, no boundary is attached to the paragraph, and no automatic word wrapping occurs. Also, later grip editing of the width is not possible, although positioning can still be changed with grips.

Immediately after you specify the text boundary width, AutoCAD LT opens the Multiline Text Editor shown in Figure 9.19A. The text cursor is available for you to begin typing the paragraph. The lines of text you type automatically end at the text boundary and continue on the next line. (Remember, this is referred to as ***word wrapping.***) You can move the text cursor to any desired place within the text boundary. Pick where you want the text cursor placed, and then backspace to move the cursor back or press the space bar to move it forward. Backspace to remove text or pick and hold while moving the cursor to highlight text. Press the backspace key or space bar to have highlighted text removed. Type more text as needed. You can press the Enter key at any time to go to the next line. The Multiline Text Editor works just like a word processor. The following list shows additional keystroke options that can be used when working in the Edit MText dialog box:

Keystroke	Results
Ctrl+→	Moves the cursor one word in the direction indicated. (Note: The "+" symbol
Ctrl+←	means that you press the keys before and after the + at the same time.)
Arrow keys	Moves the cursor through the text one position in the direction of the arrow key used.
Home	Moves the cursor to the start of the current line.
End	Moves the cursor to the end of the current line.
Delete	Removes the character directly to the right of the cursor.
Ctrl+Delete	Removes the word directly to the right of the cursor.
← Backspace	The Backspace key removes one character to the left as it moves.
Ctrl+C	Copies the selected text to the Clipboard.
Ctrl+V	Pastes the Clipboard contents to the cursor position.
Ctrl+Shift+Space	Inserts nonbreaking space, keeping the words on either side on one line.
Ctrl + Backspace	Removes the word to the left of the cursor.
Ctrl+X	Cuts the highlighted selection to the Clipboard.
Ctrl+Z	Undoes the previous operation.
Ctrl+Space	Inserts a nonbreaking space. Used to keep text from wrapping to the next line.
Page Up	Moves the cursor to the beginning of the paragraph.
Page Down	Moves the cursor to the end of the paragraph.
Ctrl+Page Up	Moves the cursor to the beginning of the currently visible page.
Ctrl+Page Down	Moves the cursor to the end of the currently visible page.
Ctrl+Home	Moves the cursor to Line 1, Column 1.
Ctrl+End	Moves the cursor to the end of the text.
Ctrl+A	Selects and highlights all of the text.
Shift + →	Highlights text one character at a time in the arrow direction.
Shift + ←	

CHAPTER 9 ||| Placing Text on a Drawing 357

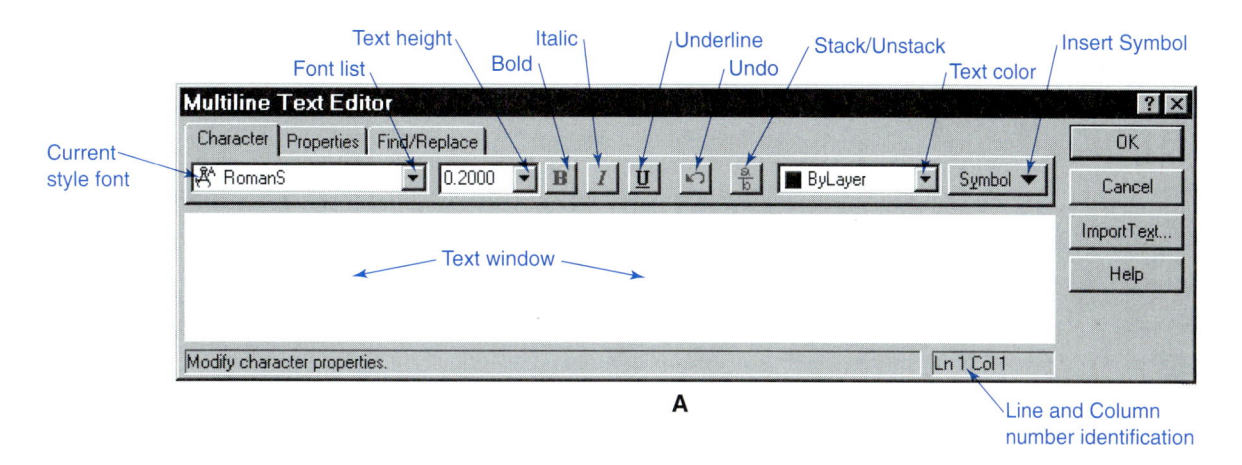

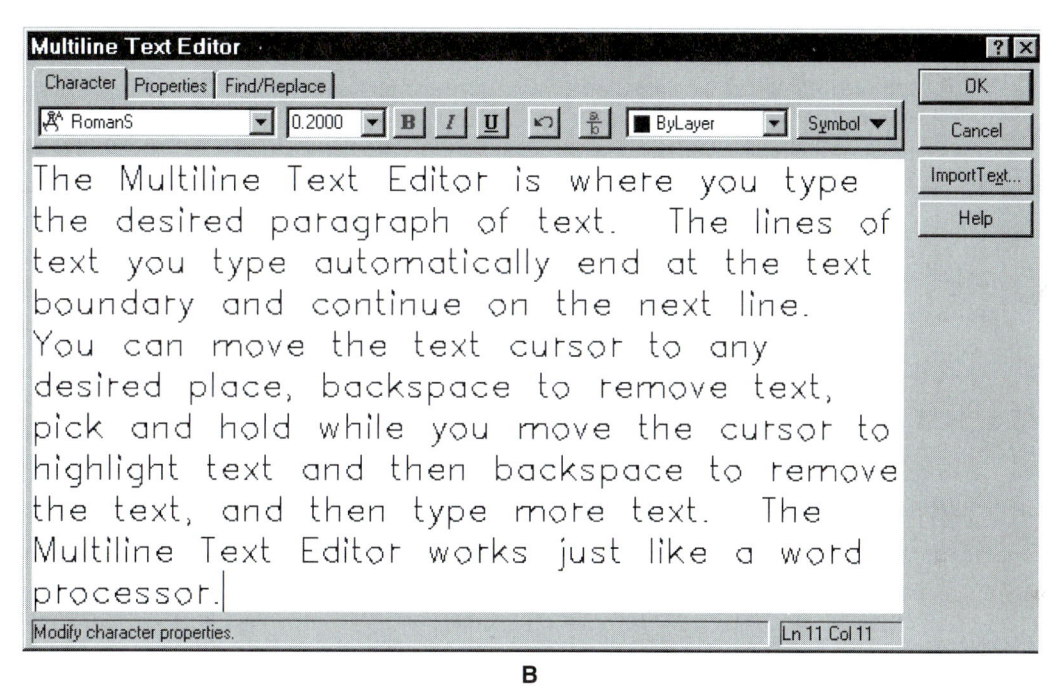

FIGURE 9.19 (A) The Multiline Text Editor. Text is typed—just as if you are using a word processor. (B) A paragraph of text is typed in the Multiline Text Editor.

Shift + ↑   Highlights the line of text in front of and above the cursor.
Shift + ↓   Highlights the line of text behind and below the cursor.
Esc   Closes the Multiline Text Editor (you loose any entries made).

In addition to the key strokes used to help you edit text, there is an Edit Text popup menu. The menu shown in Figure 9.20 is opened by moving the screen cursor inside the text window and picking the right mouse button. You can use the popup menu to do the following things:

Undo: Pick this option to undo the last multiline text activity.

Cut: This option cuts highlighted text from the paragraph and places it on the Clipboard.

Copy: Pick this to copy highlighted text to the Clipboard.

Paste: This option is used to paste items from the Clipboard into the text window at the text cursor location.

Select All: Pick this option to select and highlight all the text in the current document.

Look at the paragraph that has been typed in Figure 9.19.B

FIGURE 9.20 The Edit Text popup menu is available when you move the screen cursor inside the text window and pick the right mouse button.

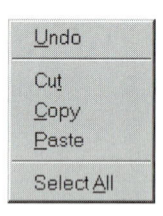

When you have typed and edited the desired paragraph of text, pick the OK button to have the text placed on the screen in the location where you located the text boundary. Figure 9.21 shows the text that was typed in the Multiline Text Editor dialog box in Figure 9.19. You can use the MOVE command if you want to place the paragraph in a new location, or you can grip select the insertion point and use the GRIP Stretch or Move option.

> **Field Notes**
>
> - The final appearance of the text can be different than the display in the Multiline Text Editor. Differences can happen depending on the type of font and the available space on each line. If the font width in the MTEXT editor is not proportionate to the width displayed in the editor, the resulting word wrap may be different with the onscreen text.
> - Grip selection of paragraph text displays the four grips that represent the paragraph text boundary. These grips can be used to make adjustments to the width of the paragraph, but they do not affect the height.

As you look at Figure 9.19, notice that the Multiline Text Editor has three tabs, the Character, Properties, and Find/Replace tabs. The Character tab is open when the editor initially appears. This is where you type in the text window, as previously shown. The other features of the Character tab are explained in the following:

Font: The current style font is displayed when you enter the Multiline Text Editor. You can open the Font list to use a different font for text typed at the cursor location. You can also pick a font from the list to have it used in highlighted text within the paragraph.

Font height: The value specified is the height of the current text style. You can change the value for text typed at the cursor location or for highlighted text within the paragraph.

Bold: Pick this button to have highlighted text become bold or to change bold text back to regular text. This does not work on .shx text but is active for some TrueType fonts.

Italic: Pick this button to have highlighted text become italicized or to change bold text back to regular text. This does not work on .shx text but is active for some TrueType fonts.

The Multiline Text Editor is where you type the desired paragraph of text. The lines of text you type automatically end at the text boundary and continue on the next line. You can move the text cursor to any desired place, backspace to remove text, pick and hold while you move the cursor to highlight text and then backspace to remove the text, and then type more text. The Multiline Text Editor works just like a word processor.

FIGURE 9.21 The result of the text that was entered in the Multiline Text Editor dialog box in Figure 9.18B using the MTEXT command.

FIGURE 9.22 The Insert Symbol drop-down menu found in the Character tab of the Multiline Text Editor.

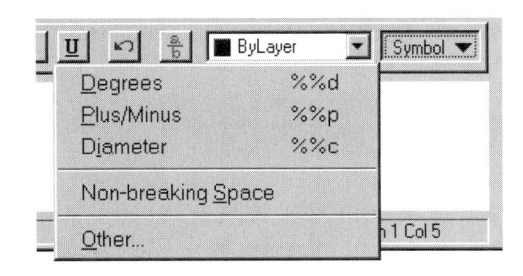

Underline: Pick this button to underline highlighted text or to change underlined text back to regular text.

Undo: Pick this button to undo the previous action.

Stack/Unstack: This button is used to stack text, such as fractions, or to unstack stacked text. Before using this button, a forward slash (/) needs to be typed between the text characters to be stacked. Then highlight the characters and pick the button. Use a caret symbol (^) between characters to stack without a dividing bar between.

Text Color: The current text color is set ByLayer, but you can change the color for new text or for highlighted text.

Insert Symbol: This drop-down menu, shown in Figure 9.22, provides commonly used symbols and a selection for Non-breaking Space, which keeps two words together when at the end of a line of text. Place a symbol at the cursor location by picking the desired item from the list. Pick Other... to open the Unicode Character Map shown in Figure 9.23. This provides you with many additional symbols to use in your text. Insert a symbol from the Unicode Character Map dialog box using the following features:

Font: This provides a list of available font character maps.

Subset: This list gives optional characteristics for the current font.

Next and Previous: These buttons allow you to quickly switch between the next and previous subset items.

Select: When a character or symbol in the Unicode Character map window is picked, it is framed within its compartment. The following steps can be used to insert the symbol or characters into your document:

1. Pick the Select button. This displays the selected character or symbol in the Characters to Copy box. You can continue in this manner to display as many items in the Characters to Copy box as you wish. Items can be removed from the Characters to Copy box by picking and highlighting the desired characters and then picking the Select button.

2. When you have the desired items in the Characters to Copy box, pick the Copy button to have them copied to the Clipboard.

3. Pick the Close button to close the Unicode Character Map dialog box.

4. Now you are back in the Multiline Text Editor. Move the text cursor to where you want the symbol placed.

FIGURE 9.23 The Unicode Character Map dialog box is opened when you pick Other ... from the Insert Symbol drop-down menu.

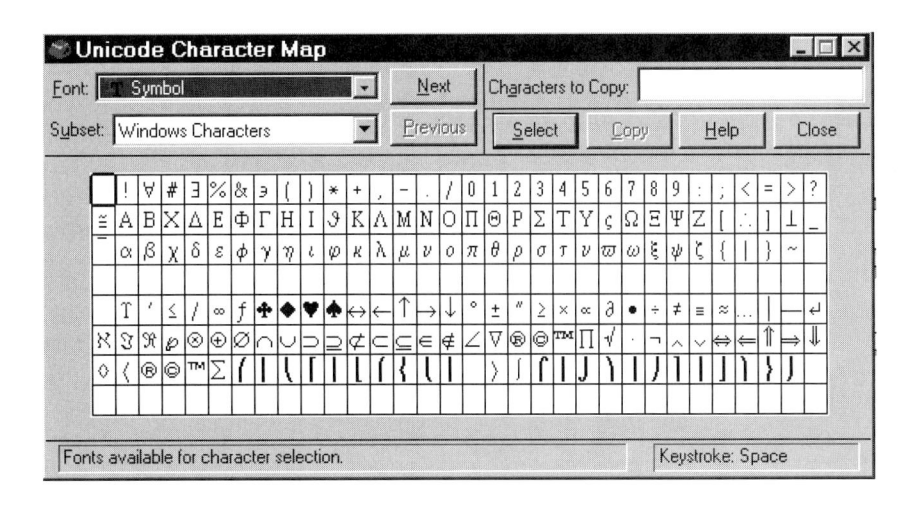

5. Move the screen cursor inside the text window and press the right mouse button to open the Edit Text popup menu shown in Figure 9.21.
6. Pick the <u>P</u>aste option to have the symbol inserted in the document. The term *document* refers to the text you are entering in the Multiline Text Editor. A document, in general, is any text or drawing that you are working with on the screen or what you print.

Field Notes

- Using the Unicode Character Map dialog box requires a few steps, but it becomes easy after a little practice. The Unicode Character Map dialog box provides you with many optional symbols and a visual place to select the symbols. You can also enter the same symbols in your document by using the Unicode value that matches the desired symbol. Notice the lower right corner of the Unicode Character Map dialog box in Figure 9.23. When a symbol is picked, this displays the Unicode number. In many cases, this number can be used to enter the same symbol at the text cursor location by typing \u+number. For example, if the number is 00b1, you type \u+00b1. The actual symbol appears in your document when you pick OK to complete the multiline text. This method might work if you use a few symbols commonly and remember the Unicode values.
- If you need to insert the same symbol many times, you can speed up the process by using the Unicode Character Map dialog box to insert the first symbol, followed by copying and pasting the symbol in the document as needed.

Import Te<u>x</u>t...: Pick this button to import text into the Multiline Text Editor from an existing text file. This button accesses the Open dialog box, where you can find an existing text file. Select the desired file to have it imported into the current document. If you pick a text file that is too large, AutoCAD LT gives you this message: This file is too large to import as an MTEXT entity. Maximum size is 16k. To import text that is in a file greater than 16k, go directly to the program where the document is located and copy the desired material to the Clipboard. Then, return to the Multiline Text Editor in AutoCAD LT and paste the material into your document.

Line and Column location: Notice in the lower right corner of Figure 9.19B, there is a box that says Ln11Col11. This constantly updates the location of the text cursor location as it moves. Ln11 refers to the vertical-text cursor location, which is the eleventh line down from the beginning of the document. Col11 refers to the horizontal-text cursor location, which is eleven characters to the right of the left margin.

Exercise 9.6

1. Open EX9.5.
2. Use the Multiline Text Editor to type the paragraph shown in Figure 9.20.
3. Save the drawing as EX9.6.

Adjusting Multiline Text Properties

The Properties tab of the Multiline Text Editor allows you to change features such as the text style, justification, boundary width, and text rotation angle. See Figure 9.24. The Properties tab options are explained in the following:

<u>S</u>tyle: This is a drop-down list that contains the created text styles.

<u>J</u>ustification: The tooltip calls this Object Orientation, which is the justification of the current paragraph. There are several options shown in Figure 9.25. The options are identified in the <u>J</u>ustification list, with an icon representing the appearance of the justification format, the name, and the abbreviation. The following explains each of the options:

CHAPTER 9 ||| Placing Text on a Drawing   361

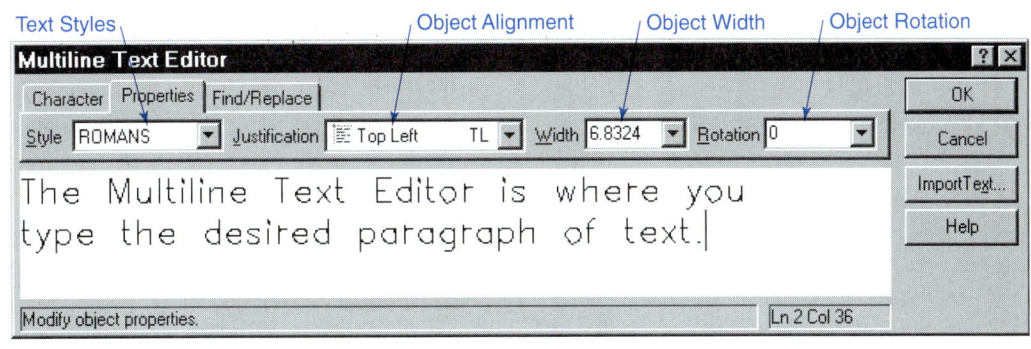

FIGURE 9.24 The Properties tab of the Multiline Text Editor.

Top Left	This is the default justification, which places the insertion point at the left of the top line and justifies the paragraph along the left edge.
Top Center	The insertion point is centered on the first line and the paragraph is justified along the center of each line of text.
Top Right	This option places the insertion point at the right of the top line and justifies the paragraph along the right edge.
Middle Left	The insertion point is located at the middle left edge of the text boundary and the text is justified along the left edge.
Middle Center	The insertion point is centered at the middle of the paragraph and the paragraph is justified along the center of each line of text.
Middle Right	The insertion point is located at the middle of the right edge of the text boundary and the text is justified along the right edge.
Bottom Left	Places the insertion point at the left of the bottom line and justifies the paragraph along the left edge.
Bottom Center	The insertion point is centered on the bottom line and the paragraph is justified along the center of each line of text.
Bottom Right	This option places the insertion point at the right of the bottom line and justifies the paragraph along the right edge.

The MTEXT justification options can also be entered at the keyboard by using the Justify option:

Command: **T, MT** or **MTEXT**↵
Current text style: ROMANS.
Text height: 0.2000
Specify first corner: ⟨*pick the first text boundary corner*⟩
Specify opposite corner or [Height/Justify/Rotate/Style/Width]:**J**↵
Enter justification [TL/TC/TR/ML/MC/MR/BL/BC/BR]<TL>:

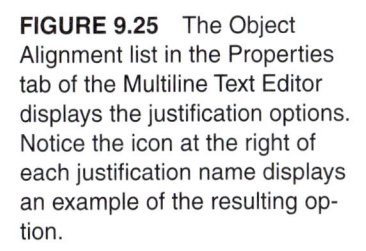

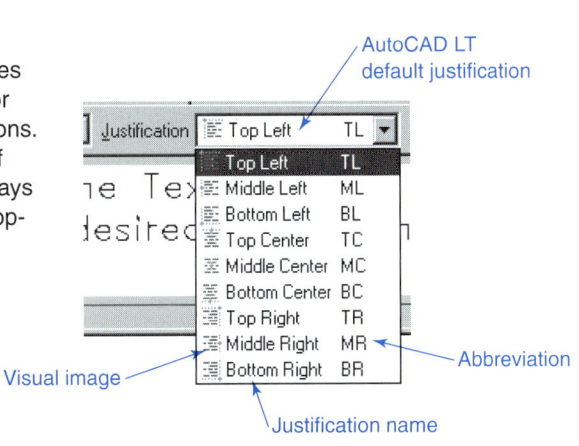

FIGURE 9.25 The Object Alignment list in the Properties tab of the Multiline Text Editor displays the justification options. Notice the icon at the right of each justification name displays an example of the resulting option.

These options are shown as the abbreviation of the MTEXT justification options that were previously discussed with the Multiline Text Editor. To set a justification option at the keyboard, type the letters representing the desired option and press Enter. The following list matches the abbreviation with the related option:

TL = Top Left	ML = Middle Left	BL = Bottom Left
TC = Top Center	MC = Middle Center	BC = Bottom Center
TR = Top Right	MR = Middle Right	BR = Bottom Right

Width: Use this text box to conveniently change the text boundary width. Double-click in the text box to highlight the current value and then type a new value. The previously used boundary widths are available in the list for your reference and use. There is also a no-wrap option, which allows you to type text beyond the text boundary.

Rotation: This text box allows you to enter any desired text rotation angle. The entire multiline text object is rotated at the specified angle. Zero rotation is the default, and the list gives you optional rotation angles in 15° increments.

Exercise 9.7

1. Open EX9.6.
2. Use the Multiline Text Editor to do each of the following: (the exact selections are up to you)

   Change the font of selected text.

   Change the text height of selected text.

   Type new text and make a selection bold and another selection italic.

   Underline a selection of text.

   Type a fraction and stack it.

   Change the color of selected text.

   Enter each of the following symbols directly from the Symbol list: degrees, plus/minus, and diameter.

   Insert the following symbols from the Unicode Character Map dialog box: ©, π, and ≥.
3. Save the drawing as EX9.7.

Finding and Replacing Multiline Text Items

The Multiline Text Editor has a Find/Replace tab, which allows you to conveniently find specific text within the document and replace it with other text. The Find/Replace tab is shown in Figure 9.26, and its features are explained in the following:

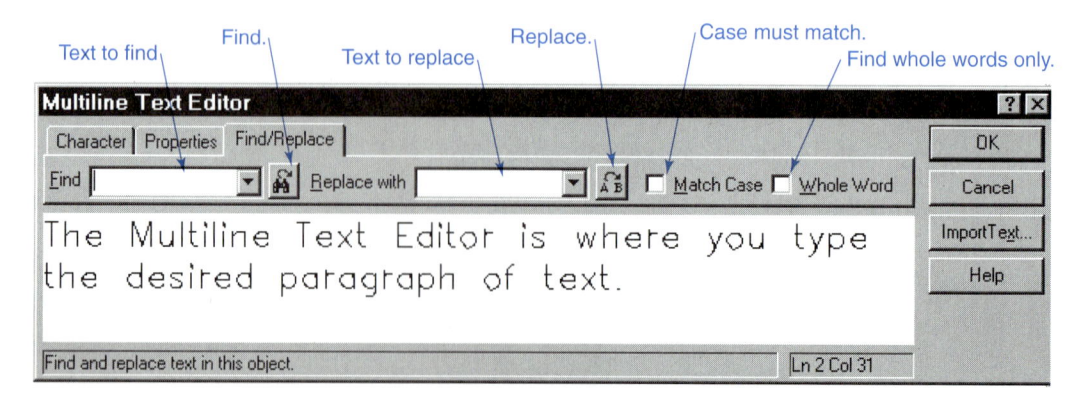

FIGURE 9.26 The Find/Replace tab of the Multiline Text Editor.

CHAPTER 9 ||| Placing Text on a Drawing   **363**

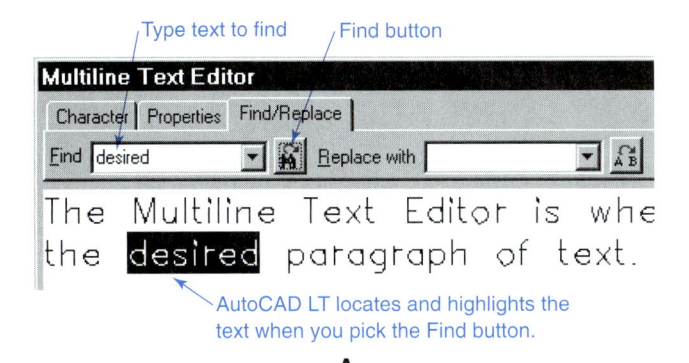

FIGURE 9.27 (A) Type the text that you want to find in the Find box and then pick the Find button. (B) Type the text that you want to replace in the Replace with box and then pick the Replace button. (C) The word that you typed in the Find box is replaced with the word that you typed in the Replace with box.

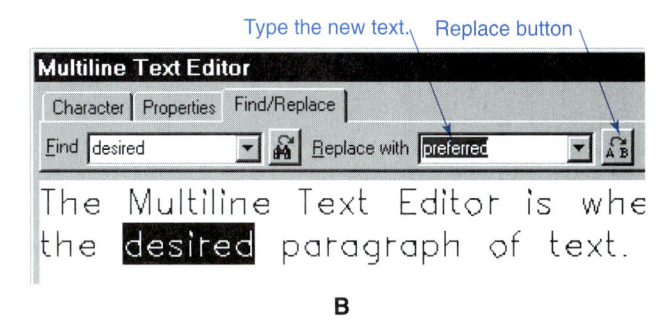

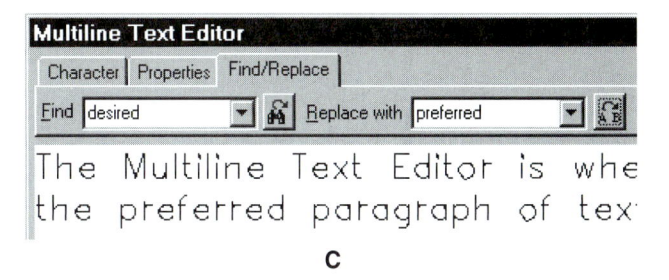

Find: This is a text box where you type the text that you want to find. For example, type *desired* in this text box if you want to find this word in the document. Pick the Find button to have the entered text located and highlighted, as shown in Figure 9.27A.

Replace with: This is a text box where you type the text you want to replace with the text you entered in the Find box. Figure 9.27B shows the word *preferred* typed in the Replace with box. Pick the Replace button to have the current word replaced with the new word, as shown in Figure 9.27C. Words that were used previously in the Find and Replace with boxes are stored in the list of each box for your convenience in selecting them later, if you wish.

Match Case: This check box is off by default, which forces AutoCAD LT to find a match for the specified word regardless of the text case. The term *character case* refers to the use of uppercase and lowercase text. For example, if Match Case is off and you want to find the word drill, AutoCAD LT will find it if it is entered as drill, Drill, or DRILL. If Match Case is on, the word is found only if it is entered exactly as you have it typed in the Find box.

Whole Word: This check box is off by default, which locates the word in the Find box even if it is part of another word. That is, if you type bore in the Find box, AutoCAD LT finds it even if it is part of the word counterbore, for instance. If this check box is on, AutoCAD LT finds only the single word that matches the word in the Find box.

Exercise 9.8

1. Open EX9.6.
2. Use the Multiline Text Editor to find the desired word and replace it with the preferred text as shown in Figure 9.27.
3. Type the new word DRILL. Type drill in the Find box. With the Match Case option on, pick the Find button. Turn Match Case off and pick the Find button again. Notice the difference.
4. Type the new word counterbore. Type bore in the Find box. With Whole Word on, pick the Find button. Turn Whole Word off and pick the find button again. Notice the difference.
5. Save the drawing as EX9.8.

Placing Paragraph Text at the Prompt Line

The Multiline Text Editor provides a screen for entering paragraph text within the text boundary, but multiline text can also be typed at the prompt line. Use the -MT or -MTEXT command to enter paragraph text at the prompt. This is a hyphen (-) typed before MT or MTEXT. All prompts and options are the same as those for using MTEXT and accessing the Multiline Text Editor, except they are all used at the prompt line like this:

> Command: **-MT** or **-MTEXT**↵
> Current text style: MECH.
> Text height: 0.1250
> Specify first corner: ⟨*pick the first text boundary corner*⟩
> Specify opposite corner or [Height/Justify/Rotation/Style/Width]: ⟨*pick the opposite corner*⟩
> MText: **The desired paragraph text is typed at the prompt line rather than in the Multiline Text Editor. You keep typing without concern for the end of the text line. AutoCAD LT automatically inserts the text within the text boundary when you are finished and have exited the command.**↵
> MText: ↵
> Command:

When using the -MTEXT command, type the desired paragraph text at the prompt line rather than in the Multiline Text Editor. Keep typing without concern for the end of the text line, or press the Enter key to go to the next line. AutoCAD LT automatically inserts the text within the text boundary when you are finished and have exited the command.

Exercise 9.9

1. Open EX9.5.
2. Use the MECH text style with all of the design options set to default values.
3. Use the -MTEXT command to type the paragraph shown with this command in the previous discussion.
4. Save the drawing as EX9.9.

✓ LEARNING CHECKPOINT

☐ Define the term *paragraph text*.
☐ What is the difference between line and paragraph text?
☐ Describe the text boundary and its purpose.
☐ Explain three ways to establish a text boundary.
☐ Discuss how text is typed and edited within the Multiline Text Editor.
☐ What is the command for and how do you type paragraph text at the prompt line?

Additional Line and Paragraph Text Applications

You can create special symbols, paste text from the Clipboard, and drag a text file into AutoCAD LT. **Control codes** allow you to insert special drafting symbols such as diameter (∅), degree (°), and plus-or-minus (±). Codes are also used to format paragraph text with features such as underline or text height changes within the paragraph. Additional applications include pasting text from the Clipboard and dragging a text file into AutoCAD LT.

Using Special Characters and Symbols

Drafting symbols such as diameter (∅), degree (°), plus-or-minus (±), and underline require special codes when used with the TEXT, DTEXT, or MTEXT commands. The code used to draw symbols with the TEXT or DTEXT commands is a pair of percent signs (%%) and a key letter or symbol typed where the symbol is needed. Table 9.2 lists the codes as applied to drawing different features. Notice that the overline and underline examples require that you enter the code *before* and *after* where you want the overline or underline to happen. You can overline and underline at the same time by typing both codes before and after the desired text, like this: %%o%%uSAMPLE%%o%%u = SAMPLE.

TABLE 9.2 Control codes for symbols used with the TEXT and DTEXT commands

Code	Result	Type This:	Result
%%c	∅	%%c1.75	∅1.75
%%d	°	45%%d	45°
%%p	±	%%p.625	±.625
%%o	Overline	%%oSAMPLE%%o	SAMPLE
%%u	Underline	%%uSAMPLE%%u	SAMPLE
%%%	%	50%%%	50%

Exercise 9.10

1. Open EX9.5.
2. Use the text style of your choice.
3. Use the DTEXT command to type the following:

    ∅1.75

    45°

    ±.625

    SAMPLE

    SAMPLE

    SAMPLE

4. Save the drawing as EX9.10.

Special control codes can also be used when placing drafting symbols with the MTEXT command. These codes were introduced with the Multiline Text Editor earlier in the chapter. The %%c = ∅, %%d = °, and %%p = ± codes can be used with the MTEXT command, but %%o and %%u cannot be used. In addition to these codes, special Unicode characters can be used to draw the symbols listed in Table 9.3. The Unicode characters can also be used to draw the same symbols with TEXT, DTEXT, and -MTEXT commands.

TABLE 9.3 Control codes for symbols used with the MTEXT, TEXT, DTEXT, and -MTEXT commands

Unicode	Result	Type This:	Result
\U+2205	∅	\U+22051.75	∅1.75
\U+00B0	°	45\U+00B0	45°
\U+00B1	±	\U+00B1.625	±.625

The Unicodes and %% codes can be used to draw symbols as previously shown, but other codes are required to do special formatting of paragraph text when using the -MTEXT command. Table 9.4 shows the format codes and the results you can expect. When using the format codes, use opening braces ({) before and closing braces (}) after the intended feature to apply a format to the text items that are enclosed within other text items.

TABLE 9.4 Formatting codes

Format Code	Result	Type This:	Result
\O	Overline on		
\o	Overline off	\OSAMPLE\o	$\overline{\text{SAMPLE}}$
\L	Underline on		
\l	Underline off	\LSAMPLE\l	$\underline{\text{SAMPLE}}$
\~	Nonbreaking space at line end	Do\~not\~break\~these\~words	Do not break these words
\\	Backslash	INCH\\METRIC	INCH\METRIC
\{	Open brace		
\}	Close brace	\{SAMPLE\}	{SAMPLE}
\Hx;	Change height	SAMPLE \H.25;TEXT	SAMPLE TEXT
\Cx;	Change color	SAMPLE \C1;COLOR	SAMPLE COLOR
\Ffont;	Change font	SAMPLE \Fromans;TEXT	SAMPLE TEXT
\Sx^x;	Stacks text	SAMPLE \SOVER^UNDER;	SAMPLE $\begin{smallmatrix}\text{OVER}\\\text{UNDER}\end{smallmatrix}$
\Sx/x;	Stacks text with dividing line	SAMPLE\SOVER\UNDER;	SAMPLE $\frac{\text{OVER};}{\text{UNDER}}$
\Tx;	Adjusts width	\T2;SAMPLE	SAMPLE
\Ax;	Aligns fractions 0 = bottom (\A0;) 1 = center (\A1;) 2 = top (\A2;)		
\S	Stacks	\A1;SAMPLE \S5/8	SAMPLE $\frac{1}{2}$
\P	End paragraph	paragraph\Pparagraph	paragraph paragraph

Note: The x given in the format code refers to the variable value, such as text height factor, color, width, or font.

Exercise 9.11

1. Open EX9.10.
2. Use the -MTEXT command and Unicodes or Format codes to type the following:

   ⌀1.75   SAMPLE TEXT
   45°   SAMPLE TEXT
   ±.625   SAMPLE $\frac{5}{8}$
   $\overline{\text{SAMPLE}}$
   $\underline{\text{SAMPLE}}$

3. Save the drawing as EX9.11.

Pasting Text from the Clipboard

Text that is copied from a Windows word processing program such as Microsoft Word or WordPerfect can be pasted into an AutoCAD LT drawing. The contents of the Clipboard can be inserted in the drawing by picking Paste from the Edit pull-down menu or by typing Ctrl+V. The text can only be pasted into the MTEXT editor using this method. To enter the text at the command line for TEXT, DTEXT, or -MTEXT, use the text window Edit menu and pick Paste or do a right click with the cursor in the command or text window and pick Paste.

Field Notes

Any word processor text formatting, such as colors, bold, italic, and size, are lost when the text is brought into an AutoCAD LT drawing.

CHAPTER 9 ||| Placing Text on a Drawing 367

> ### Through the Window...
>
> The drag and drop method of inserting text from another file into an AutoCAD LT drawing works with Windows95, Windows98, and Windows NT.
>
> The drag-and-drop method of inserting text from another file works with Windows Explorer. The files to be accessed must be ASCII (American Standard Code for Information Interchange) files. ASCII files contain text characters only. When you save the text file from your word processor, save it as a "text only" file with the .TXT extension. The process for inserting the text file is to open Windows Explorer and move it to the side enough to see the AutoCAD LT drawing. Move your cursor to the desired text file in Windows Explorer and pick. While holding down the pick button, drag the file to the AutoCAD LT drawing and release (drop) the pick button. The text file is now in the drawing and can be moved or edited as with any AutoCAD LT text.

✓ LEARNING CHECKPOINT

- ☐ What are control codes?
- ☐ Give the %% control codes for these applications: diameter, degrees, plus-or-minus, overline, and underline.
- ☐ Give the Unicode for these applications: diameter, degrees, and plus-or-minus.
- ☐ How does the Unicode presentation differ between MTEXT, -MTEXT, and DTEXT command use?
- ☐ Describe how to place text from the Clipboard into the drawing.
- ☐ Briefly describe how drag and drop works for inserting a text file into an AutoCAD LT drawing.

Editing Existing Text

AutoCAD LT provides you with many options for editing text. Editing commands such as MOVE, COPY, SCALE, and ROTATE can be used on text objects. You can enter the command first and then select the text or select the text and use the grips for the desired editing operation. You can also mirror text. When mirroring text, you can decide to have the text mirrored in reverse image or readable. Other text editing commands allow you to change the content, font, and other features. You can also check your spelling.

Using the DDEDIT Command

You can change the content of line text and you can change the content and justification of paragraph text with the DDEDIT command. This command is accessed by picking the Edit Text button in the Modify II toolbar, by picking Text ... in the Object cascade of the Modify pull-down menu, or by typing either **ED** or **DDEDIT** at the Command: prompt. When using this command, AutoCAD LT asks you to select an annotation. An *annotation* is anything that has to do with text, such as notes, dimensions, and text symbols. The command works like this:

Command: **ED** or **DDEDIT**
<Select an annotation object>/Undo:

Modify II
A̸
Edit Text
Modify
└ Object
  └ Text...
DDEDIT
ED

The Undo option allows you to undo the previous edit while still inside of the DDEDIT command.

Editing Line Text with DDEDIT
You can select one line of line text at a time for editing with the DDEDIT command. This allows you to change the content as needed. When you select the line of text, you get the Edit Text dialog box shown in Figure 9.28. When the Edit Text dialog box is first displayed, the text inside is highlighted. You can work with this text in one of the following ways:

- Begin typing. Everything that was highlighted is gone, allowing you to type a new line of text.
- Press the space bar, Delete key, or the Backspace key to have the text removed and then type the new text line.

FIGURE 9.28 Using the DDEDIT command to edit a single line of text. (A) The existing text is displayed in the Edit Text dialog box. (B) The text is edited as needed.

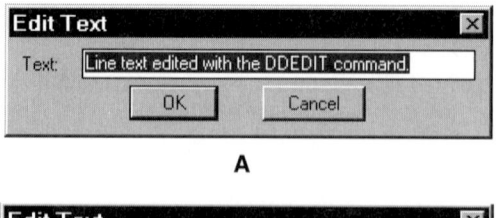

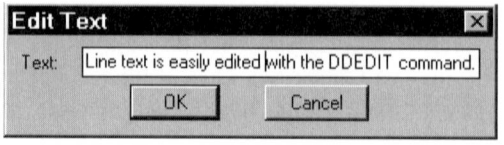

- Move the cursor to a desired place within the text line and pick. This removes the highlighting but keeps the existing text. There is now a text cursor at the place you picked.
- Use the text cursor to backspace or go forward as needed.
- Type any desired text at the location of the text cursor. Notice the revised text that has been typed in Figure 9.28B.
- If the line of text is too long to see both ends in the Edit Text dialog box, press the Ctrl key and the right arrow key to move the cursor to the right or the left arrow key to move the cursor to the left. The line is fully exposed when you move the cursor all the way to the desired end. The arrow key can be used alone to move one character at a time or with the Ctrl key to move to the start of the next word in the direction the arrow key points. The Home key can be used to go directly to the start of the text and the End key to go to the end of the text line. Also, the Ctrl+C, Ctrl+X, and Ctrl+V combinations can be used in the Edit Text dialog box as previously discussed.
- You can pick and hold while dragging the cursor to highlight specific text. Then just press the space bar, Delete key, or the Backspace key to have the text removed; or begin typing new text to automatically remove the highlighted text while entering new text.

After you are done editing the line of text, pick the OK button or press Enter to return to the screen. The text is changed and the select annotation prompt remains for further editing of the same line or other lines of text. The complete command sequence works like this:

Command: **ED** or **DDEDIT**↵
<Select an annotation object>/Undo: ⟨*pick the line of text to open the Edit Text dialog box. Pick the OK button when done.*⟩
<Select an annotation object>/Undo: ↵
Command:

Editing Paragraph Text with DDEDIT

The DDEDIT command can be used to change both content and justification of paragraph text. When you enter the DDEDIT command and select paragraph text, the familiar Multiline Text Editor appears. This works just like a word processor, as previously discussed. In addition to changing the text content you can easily change the other options, as previously explained. Refer back to Figure 9.19B. The command sequence works like this:

Command: **ED** or **DDEDIT**↵
<Select an annotation object>/Undo: ⟨*pick the paragraph text to open the Multiline Text Editor. Pick the OK button when done.*⟩
<Select an annotation object>/Undo: ↵
Command:

CHAPTER 9 ||| Placing Text on a Drawing 369

Exercise 9.12

1. Open EX9.5.
2. Use the MECH text style.
3. Use the DTEXT command to type the following:

    Line text edited with the DDEDIT command.

4. Use the DDEDIT command to change the text to read:

    Line text is easily edited by using the DDEDIT command to access the Edit Text dialog box.

5. Use the MTEXT command to type the following inside of a 3-in.-wide text boundary:

    The DDEDIT command can be used to change the content of paragraph text.

6. Use the DDEDIT command to change the text to read:

    The DDEDIT command can be used to edit the content of paragraph text and change the justification.

7. Change the Justification to Top Center before picking OK.
8. Save the drawing as EX9.12.

Using the DDMODIFY Command

The DDMODIFY command allows you to change text content just like the DDEDIT command, but it also lets you change many other features of both line and paragraph text. This command is accessed by typing DDMODIFY. The Properties button on the Object Properties toolbar also starts this command when only one object is selected. The DDMODIFY command asks you to select an object to modify because it can be used to edit many different individual objects:

    Command: **DDMODIFY**↵
    Select object to modify: ⟨*select either a line or paragraph of text*⟩

The Modify Text dialog box is opened if you select either line or paragraph text. Many of the features found in the Modify Text dialog box are the same for line text and paragraph text, but there is a major difference.

Object Properties
Properties
Modify
  └ Properties
AI_PROPCHK
DDMODIFY
MO

Editing Line Text with DDMODIFY

When you select line text to edit with the DDMODIFY command, the Modify Text dialog box shown in Figure 9.29 is displayed. The Modify Text dialog box is very convenient for changing many features of the text in addition to editing the content. The following explains each of the Modify Text dialog box options:

Properties	Pick the Color … button to access the Select Color dialog box where you can change the text color. Pick the Layer … button to get the select layer dialog box. The Linetype … button and Linetype Scale: box are for changing linetype. The Thickness: box is for 3-D drawings.
Text	This is where you can edit the text content. The Text: box works exactly the same as the Edit Text dialog box that was explained with the DDEDIT command.
Origin	This compartment is used to change the text insertion point. You can enter new coordinates in the X: and Y: boxes. The Z: button is for 3-D applications. Use the Pick Point< button if you want to return to the graphics screen where a rubberband cursor is connected to the text insertion point. Move the cursor and pick a new point.

FIGURE 9.29 Use the DDMODIFY command to select line text for editing in the Modify Text dialog box.

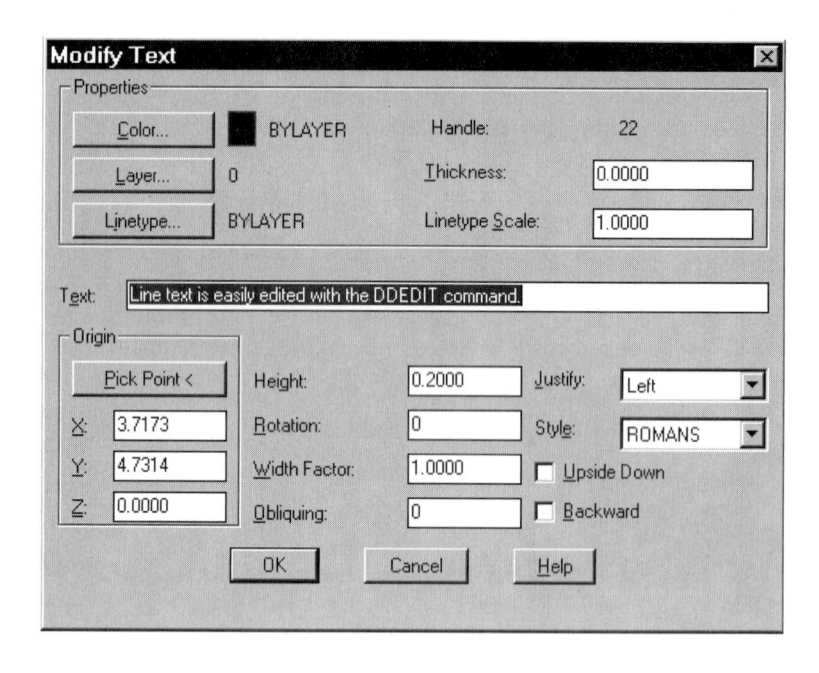

Height	Change the text height.
Rotation	Set a new rotation angle.
Width Factor	Enter a new text width factor.
Obliquing	Change the obliquing angle of the text.
Justify	Pick the down arrow to access the list of justification options. This list provides justification options in addition to the options that are available in the TEXT and DTEXT commands. All of the MTEXT justification options are available, as well as the standard line text options. Figure 9.7 displays each of the justification options in relationship to their locations on text.
Style	Pick the down arrow to access the list of available text styles. Change the style of the selected text by picking one of the options in the list.
Upside Down	Pick this toggle to make the selected text read upside down.
Backward	Check this toggle to make the selected text backward.

Pick the OK button when done.

Editing Paragraph Text with DDMODIFY

When editing paragraph text with the DDMODIFY command, the Modify MText dialog box shown in Figure 9.30 appears. The Modify MText dialog box has many of the same features as the Modify Text dialog box previously discussed. The items in the Properties and Insertion Point compartments are the same. Also the Height: and Rotation, boxes, and Style: list work the same. The Direction: list is used to orient text horizontally, vertically, or by the current style, which is theByStyle default. Vertical is available only for fonts that allow this orientation. The Justify: list provides the same MTEXT justification options that were previously discussed. The Width: box allows you to change the text boundary width. The big difference is in the way the text content is edited. Look at the Contents compartment in Figure 9.30. This displays part of the text you selected. To the right of this compartment is the Full editor ... button. Pick this button to open the familiar Multiline Text Editor. Refer back to Figure 9.19B to see text in the Multiline Text Editor. Use this to change the content of the selected text and modify the characteristics if desired.

FIGURE 9.30 Use the DDMODIFY command to select paragraph text for editing in the Modify MText dialog box.

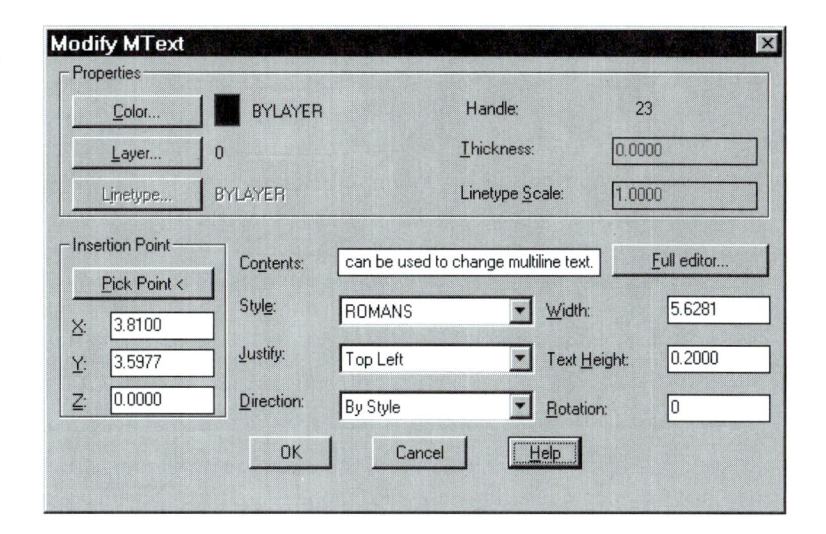

Exercise 9.13

1. Open EX9.12.
2. Use the DDMODIFY command to change the line text to read:

    Line text is easy to edit by using the DDMODIFY command.

3. Experiment on the line text by making the following changes. Pick the OK button and use the DDMODIFY command again to select the line text between each change to observe the effects:
    - Change the insertion point with the Pick Point < button.
    - Change the height to .188.
    - Change the rotation to 45.
    - Change the width to 1.5.
    - Change the obliquing angle to 15.
    - Use a variety of justification options of your own choosing.
    - Change the style.
    - Try the Upside down and Backward options if you wish.
4. Use the DDMODIFY command to change the paragraph text to read:

    The DDMODIFY command is used to open the Modify MText dialog box. You can then edit the content and change the justification.

5. Pick OK.
6. Back in the Modify MText dialog box, do experimentation on the line text by making the following changes. Pick the OK button and use the DDMODIFY command again to select the paragraph text between each change to observe the effects:
    - Change the insertion point.
    - Change the text height to 0.25.
    - Change the style.
7. Save the drawing as EX9.13.

Using the CHANGE Command on Text

The CHANGE command can be used to make a few basic changes to text. You can change the insertion point of line text but you cannot change the insertion point of paragraph text. You can change properties such as layer and color of line and paragraph text. You can change the style of line text but not of paragraph text. Enter this command by typing either **-CH** or **CHANGE** at the Command: prompt. This is a hyphen (-) typed before the CH. The command works like this:

    Command: **-CH** or **CHANGE**↵
    Select objects: ⟨*select one or more lines of line or paragraph text*⟩
    Select objects: ↵
    Properties/<Change point>: ⟨*pick a new insertion point for line text*⟩

If you try to pick a new insertion point for paragraph text, AutoCAD LT gives this message:

    No changeable object selected.

After changing the line text insertion point, you get prompts that allow you to change the text style, height, rotation angle, and text content. The text content is changed by typing the revised text at the last prompt. This sequence keeps the existing text:

    Text style: **ROMANS**
    New style or press ENTER for no change: **ROMAND**↵
    New height <0.2>: **.125**↵
    New rotation angle <0>: ↵
    New text <Line text is easily edited with the DDEDIT command.>: ↵
    Command:

Press Enter for any prompt you want to ignore. If you press Enter at the Change point prompt, you get a prompt that allows you to drag the text and pick a new insertion point:

    Command: **-CH** or **CHANGE**↵
    Select objects: ⟨*select one or more lines of line or paragraph text*⟩
    Select objects: ↵
    Properties/<Change point>:
    Enter text insertion point: ⟨*drag the line text and pick a new insertion point*⟩

Press Enter to skip the insertion point prompt and go directly to the Text style: prompt.

If you type **P** and press Enter, you get the following Properties options:

    Command: **-CH** or **CHANGE**↵
    Select objects: ⟨*select one or more lines of line or paragraph text*⟩
    Select objects: ↵
    Properties/<Change point>: **P**↵
    Change what property (Color/Elev/LAyer/LType/ltScale/Thickness)?

Type the capital letter or letters of the desired option and press Enter. The likely options for text might be Layer and Color. To change the layer and color, do this:

    Change what property (Color/Elev/LAyer/LType/ltScale/Thickness)? **LA**↵
    New layer <0>: **NAME**↵
    Change what property (Color/Elev/LAyer/LType/ltScale/Thickness)? **C** ↵
    New Color <BYLAYER>: ↵
    Change what property (Color/Elev/LAyer/LType/ltScale/Thickness)? ↵
    Command:

Color and layer can also be changed in the Change Properties dialog box by typing **-CH** or **CHANGE** at the Command: prompt.

Exercise 9.14

1. Open EX9.13.
2. Use the CHANGE command and select one of the lines of text.
3. Change the insertion point and change the text style.
4. Save the drawing as EX9.14.

Mirroring Objects with Text

The MIRROR command was introduced in Chapter 7. This command is accessed by picking Mirror in the Modify pull-down menu, by picking the Mirror button in the Modify toolbar, or by typing **MI** or **MIRROR** at the Command: prompt. When mirroring text or objects with text, the text can be mirrored in reverse image or upside down depending on how the object is mirrored. You can also set the text to be readable when mirrored. The MIRRTEXT system variable controls how text is displayed when mirrored. The MIRRTEXT options are 1 (on), which reverses or places the mirrored text upside down, and 0 (off), which makes mirrored text readable. The system variable works like this:

Command: **MI** or **MIRRTEXT**↵
New value for MIRRTEXT <1>: **0**↵
Command:

Figure 9.31 shows the results of changing the MIRRTEXT variable.

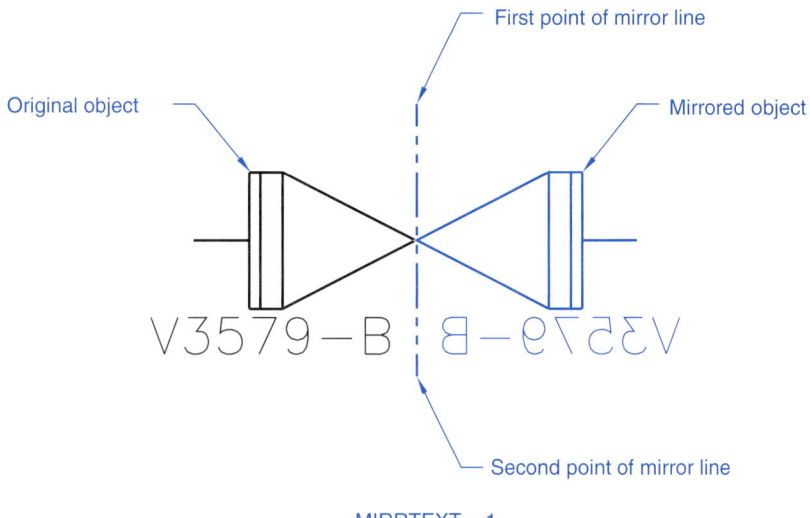

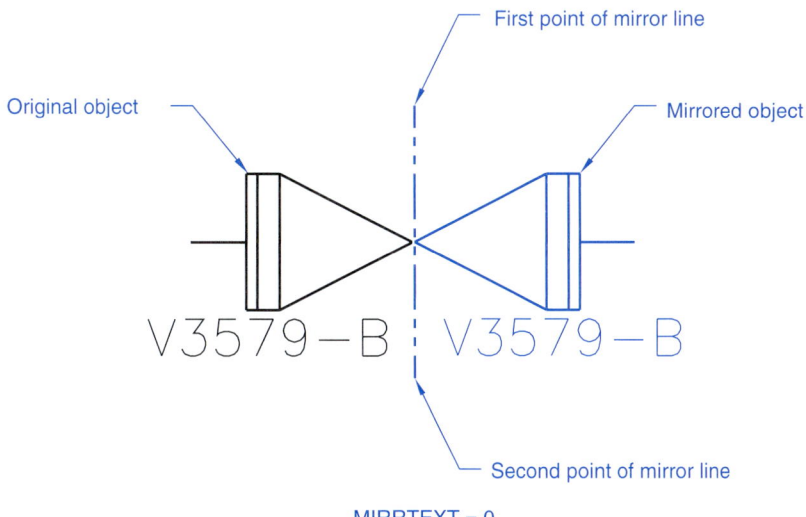

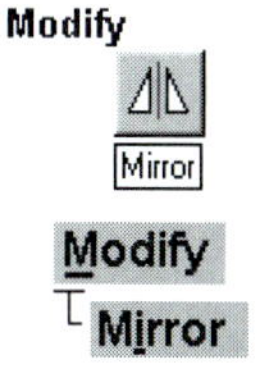

FIGURE 9.31 Using the MIRROR command with the MIRRTEXT system variable set to ON and OFF.

Making Quick Text

Quick text is used when you have a large drawing that contains a lot of text, and you want to increase display speed during a time when you do not plan to be drawing any text. Quick text changes the appearance of text to rectangles that represent only the frame of the text. To make this happen, use the QTEXT command by typing **QT** or **QTEXT** at the Command: prompt. The options are ON and OFF. OFF is the default that keeps the normal text display. Turn QTEXT on like this:

Command: **QT** or **QTEXT**↵
QTEXT ON/OFF <Off>: **ON**↵
Command:

To activate the quick text setting, type the REGEN command and press Enter. The difference between QTEXT ON and OFF is shown in Figure 9.32.

FIGURE 9.32 The difference between QTEXT OFF and ON.

ABCDEFGHIJKLM 123456

QTEXT = OFF

QTEXT = ON

Field Notes

- The Quick Text option can also be set within the Drawing Aids dialog box accessed through the RM or DDRMODES command.
- In a drawing that has many objects that use True Type Fonts, selecting objects can be much slower. Turning QTEXT on helps avoid this problem.

Exercise 9.15

1. Begin a new drawing, set a text style that has ROMANS font, and allow the text height to be adjustable each time you use the commands to draw text.
2. Make a drawing similar to the one shown in Figure 9.31, using MIRRTEXT ON and OFF.
3. Type something of your own choosing with technical content. For example, a general note from a textbook, drawing, or set of specifications.
4. Save the drawing as EX9.15.

Checking Your Spelling

Standard
Spelling

Tools
Spelling

SPELL
SP

AutoCAD LT provides you with a spelling checker that has dictionaries available in several different languages. Each dictionary contains a standard word list. You can also create a custom dictionary by adding your own words, abbreviations, or commonly used text. The AutoCAD LT spell checker is accessed by picking the Spelling button in the Standard toolbar, by picking Spelling in the Tools pull-down menu, or by typing **SP** or **SPELL** at the Command: prompt. You get the Select objects: prompt when you enter the SPELL command. You can select any number of lines or paragraphs of text, or you can type ALL to select all of the text on the drawing. If you select text that has no spelling errors, an AutoCAD LT Message tells you "Spelling check complete." Pick the OK button or press Enter to return to the Command: prompt. You also get this message when there are spelling problems and you have successfully completed checking. You get the Check Spelling dialog box shown in Figure 9.33 when you select text that has spelling problems. The command works like this:

Command: **SPELL**↵
Select objects: ⟨*select the text or type ALL and press Enter for all text*⟩
Select objects: ↵

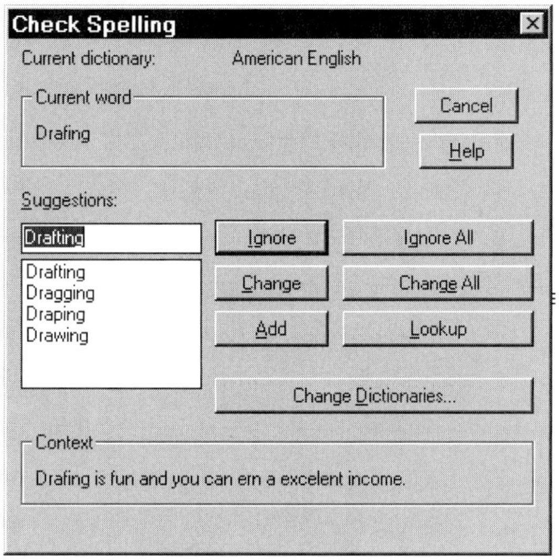

FIGURE 9.33 Using the SPELL command to select text and access the Check Spelling dialog box.

The AutoCAD LT spelling checker has many features. Look at the Check Spelling dialog box in Figure 9.33 as you review these features:

Context
: First look at the bottom of the Check Spelling dialog box and notice the Context compartment. This displays all or part of the text that you selected. If part of the text is displayed, it is the text that surrounds the current word Auto-CAD LT has identified as being misspelled.

Current dictionary:
: This identifies the current dictionary that is being used. The current dictionary in Figure 9.33 is identified as American English at the top of the Check Spelling dialog box.

Current word
: In this compartment, AutoCAD LT displays the current word that is misspelled or is not in the dictionary.

Suggestions:
: This is a list of words that AutoCAD LT thinks might be the correct spelling of the current word. The first word is in a text box and is AutoCAD LT's best suggestion. These are the options allowed with the Suggestions:

- Keep AutoCAD LT's best suggestion in the text box or pick one of the other words in the list to substitute. If you do not like the best suggestion or any of the other words in the list, you can change the word in the text box to a word that you like better.
- Continue this process until all words have been checked and AutoCAD LT issues the "Spelling check complete" message where you pick the OK button or press Enter to return to the drawing editor.

Ignore
: Pick this button if you want to accept this word as is and go on to the next word.

Ignore All
: Pick this button if you want AutoCAD LT to ignore this word each time it is found in the selected text.

Change
: Pick this button if you want AutoCAD LT to change the Current word to the word that is highlighted in the Suggestions: text box.

Change All
: Pick this button if you want AutoCAD LT to change the Current word, each time it is found in the selected text, for the word that is highlighted in the Suggestions: text box.

Add
: This button is active if there is a custom dictionary. Pick this button if you want to leave the suggested word unchanged and have it added to the custom dictionary.

Lookup
: Pick this button if you want AutoCAD LT to list additional words that are similar to the word in the Suggestions: box.

Change Dictionaries …
: Pick this button to open the Change Dictionaries dialog box.

FIGURE 9.34 The Change Dictionaries dialog box.

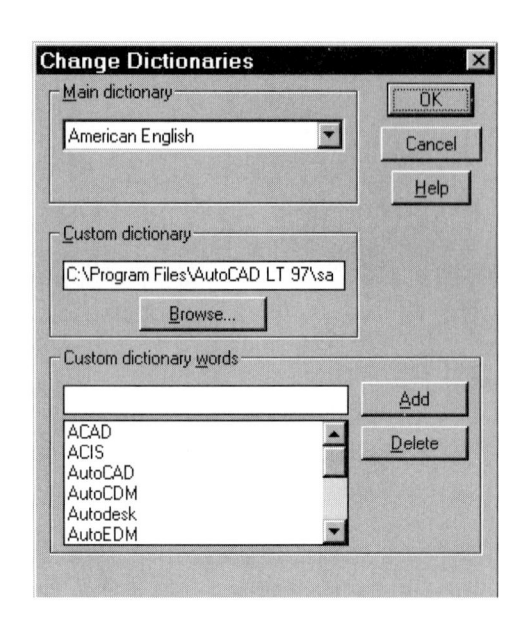

Changing, Using, and Creating Dictionaries

The Change Dictionaries ... button in the Check Spelling dialog box (Figure 9.33) is used to access the Change Dictionaries dialog box shown in Figure 9.34. The features of the Change Dictionaries dialog box are explained in the following:

Main dictionary — This list box displays the available dictionary options. Pick the down arrow and select a new current dictionary for your spell checking.

Custom dictionary — Use the text box to type the drive, directory, and file name of a custom dictionary that you want to use for spell checking. Custom dictionaries have the file extension .CUS. If no custom dictionaries have been created, you can create one. Custom dictionaries are designed by you and your company to include words that are not in the main dictionary. The custom dictionary has words, abbreviations, and technical terms that are used in your drafting field or business.

Follow these steps to create a custom dictionary:

- Check the spelling of text entered in your drawing.

- For this example, you are doing a civil (mapping) drawing, and the Spell Checker picks up the word cadastral as a misspelled word. You know it is spelled correctly. Therefore, the word is not in the Main Dictionary. You want to add it to a custom dictionary.

- Pick the Change Dictionaries ... button.

- Enter a name in the Custom dictionary text box and then pick the OK button. The name CIVIL is entered in Figure 9.35 to create a custom dictionary for words used in map drawings and civil engineering projects. AutoCAD LT has a sample custom dictionary called C:\Program Files\AutoCAD LT 98\sample.cus. You can have your custom dictionaries saved in the same directory by substituting your dictionary name, CIVIL, for the word sample, like this: C:\Program Files\AutoCAD LT 98\CIVIL.cus.

- The Check Spelling dialog box returns and the Add button is active to accept words to be added to the custom dictionary. If AutoCAD LT displays a current word that is correctly spelled, then it is not in the main dictionary.

- If this is a word that you want in the custom dictionary, pick the Add button. The Current word, cadastral, is shown in Figure 9.36 and the Add button is being picked.

FIGURE 9.35 Adding a custom dictionary.

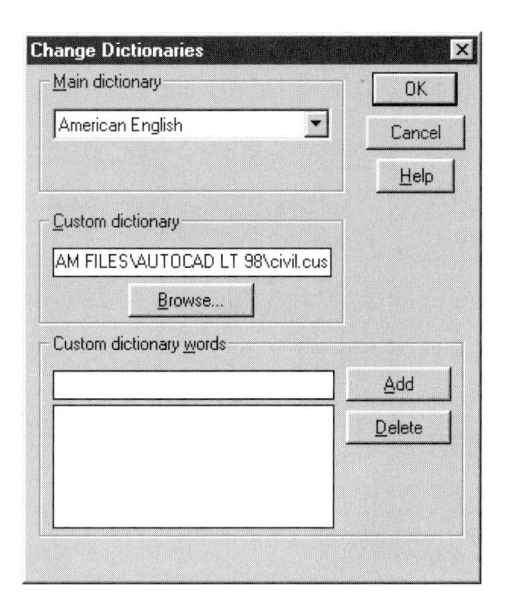

FIGURE 9.36 Adding words to the custom dictionary while in the Check Spelling dialog box.

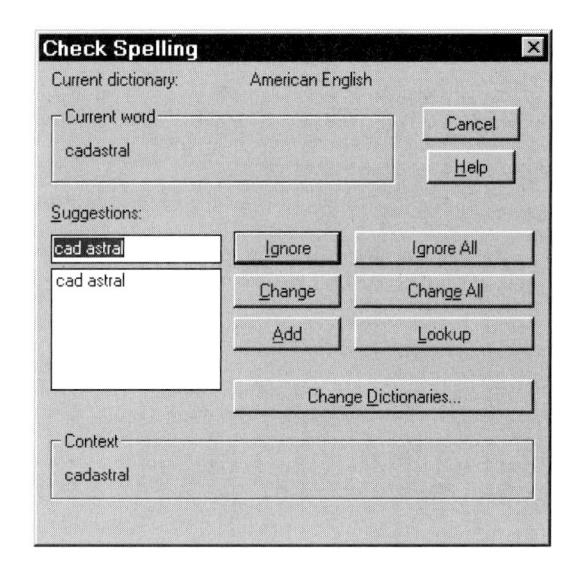

Follow these steps if a custom dictionary is already created and you want to add words to it:

- Pick the Change Dictionaries … button. The Change Dictionaries dialog box shown in Figure 9.37 is displayed with the Custom dictionary specified as C:\Program Files\AutoCAD LT 98\civil.cus. If the desired custom dictionary is not active, type a new dictionary drive, directory, and file name or pick the Browse … button to get the Select Custom Dictionary dialog box.
- The Custom dictionary words compartment has a text box and list of words found in the civil dictionary.
- Continue placing words in the CIVIL custom dictionary by typing each word in the Custom dictionary words box and pick the Add button after each entry. The word quadrangle is being added in Figure 9.37. When the Custom dictionary words list gets long, arrows and an elevator bar are available to help you find words. The spell checker is not case sensitive, so you can enter words using upper- or lowercase.
- To remove a word from the custom dictionary, highlight the word in the custom dictionary words list and pick the Delete button.

FIGURE 9.37 Adding words to the custom dictionary while in the Change Dictionaries dialog box.

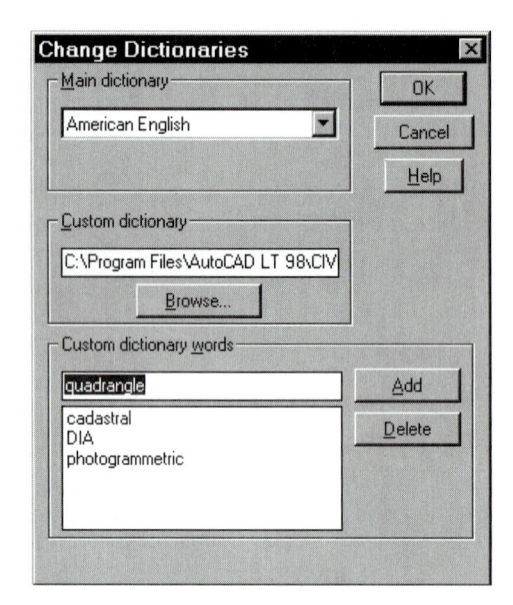

Exercise 9.16

1. Open EX9.15.
2. Check the spelling of the text in this drawing.
3. If no spelling errors exist, use the DDEDIT or DDMODIFY command to add some spelling errors to the text.
4. Check the spelling again and correct the errors.
5. Create a custom dictionary with the name of your favorite drafting discipline or that of the type of drafting you currently perform.
6. Return to the drawing and type several words that you feel are unique to your field of drafting.
7. Use the spell checker on the words, and place any words not found in the main dictionary into your custom dictionary.
8. Save the drawing as EX9.16.

✓ LEARNING CHECKPOINT

- ☐ Explain the difference between using the DDEDIT command on line and on paragraph text.
- ☐ Explain the difference between using the DDMODIFY command on line and on paragraph text.
- ☐ What are the key differences between the DDEDIT and DDMODIFY commands?
- ☐ Describe how the CHANGE command can be used to edit text.
- ☐ How do you mirror objects with text and get the text to be readable?
- ☐ What is the result and purpose of using quick text?
- ☐ Identify at least three ways to access the Check Spelling dialog box.
- ☐ Briefly explain how to create a custom dictionary.

MULTIPLE CHOICE

Circle the choice or enter your response on an answer sheet by selecting the option that most closely completes or answers the given statements.

1. A complete set of characters made up of letters, numbers, marks, and symbols all of unique proportion and design:
   a. characters
   b. font
   c. style
   d. text

2. This command places text on the screen while you type:
   a. DTEXT
   b. TEXT
   c. MTEXT
   d. STYLE

3. Determines how lines of text are aligned:
   a. alignment
   b. rotation
   c. position
   d. justify

4. This option allows you to place text between two points with control over height:
   a. Align
   b. Left
   c. Fit
   d. Right

5. This command opens the Text Style dialog box:
   a. STYLE
   b. DDSTYLE
   c. DDEDIT
   d. DDMODIFY

6. Multiline text is entered in the:
   a. Multiline Text Editor
   b. Mtext dialog box
   c. Edit MText dialog box
   d. Edit Text dialog box

7. Use this control code to draw a diameter symbol with your text:
   a. %%c
   b. %%d
   c. %%p
   d. %%u

8. Change the content of line text and the content and justification of paragraph text with:
   a. DDEDIT
   b. DDMODIFY
   c. CHANGE
   d. EDIT

9. Type this to access the Modify MText dialog box:
   a. ED
   b. DDMODIFY
   c. TE
   d. all of the above

10. Use this command to check your spelling:
    a. SPELLCHK
    b. SPELLING
    c. SP
    d. SPELL

MATCHING

Match each term to the correct description by writing the appropriate number in each box at the left.

- ☐ Annotation
- ☐ DDEDIT
- ☐ DDMODIFY
- ☐ DDSTYLE
- ☐ DTEXT
- ☐ Font
- ☐ Justify
- ☐ MTEXT
- ☐ -MTEXT
- ☐ %%c
- ☐ %%d
- ☐ Rotation
- ☐ SPELL
- ☐ Style
- ☐ Width

1. Complete set of characters, made up of letters, numbers, marks, and symbols of unique proportion and design.
2. Used to place paragraph text at the prompt line.
3. Used to change the content, justification, and other features of line and paragraph text.
4. Used to check the spelling.
5. Any text.
6. Determines how lines of text are aligned.
7. Stretches or compresses text characters.
8. Used to change the content of line text and the content and justification of paragraph text.
9. Control code for degree symbol.
10. Used to draw line text.
11. Used to draw paragraph text in a dialog box.
12. Settings that determine the appearance of text characters.
13. Load and customize text styles.
14. Control code for diameter symbol.
15. Text angle from horizontal.

CHAPTER 9 ||| Placing Text on a Drawing

WORD SCRAMBLE

Unscramble the seven scrambled words below, one letter to each square, to form seven AutoCAD LT–related words:

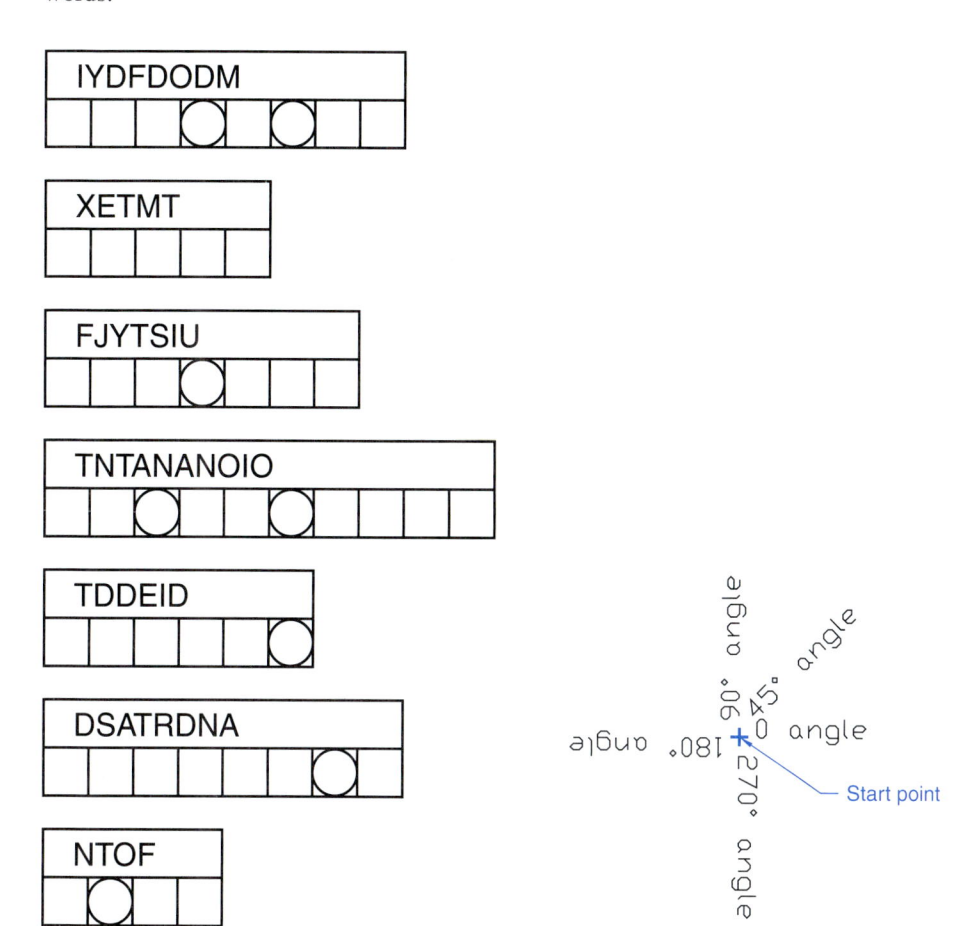

IYDFDODM

XETMT

FJYTSIU

TNTANANOIO

TDDEID

DSATRDNA

NTOF

Unscramble the circled letters above to form the special answer, as suggested by the illustration.

PROJECTS

Set up the following drawing projects with layers that relate to the type of drawing as outlined and discussed in Chapter 5.

9.1 Open P2.9 and add text. Use ROMANS font. Save as P9.1.

9.2 Open P3.9 and add text. Use ROMANS font. Save as P9.2.

9.3 Open P5.1 and add text. Use ROMANS font. Save as P9.3.

9.4 Open P6.4 and add text. Use ROMANS font. Save as P9.4.

9.5 Open P7.7 and add text. Use ROMANS font. Save as P9.5.

9.6 Open P7.5 and add text. Use ROMANS font. Save as P9.6.

9.7 Open P7.6 and add text. Use ROMANS font. Save as P9.7.

9.8 Open P8.9 and add text. Use CIBT font. Save as P9.8.

9.9 Open P8.10 and add text. Use CIBT font. Save as P9.9.

9.10 Clock
Open P8.7 and add text as shown below. Use GOTHICE and ROMAND fonts. Save as P9.10.

CHAPTER 10

Drawing Patterns and Section Lines

LEARNING GOALS

- Use the BHATCH and HATCH commands to draw hatch patterns.
- Select and draw several different pattern types.
- Change the pattern scale and angle.
- Create user-defined hatch patterns.
- Remove islands from a hatch pattern.
- Define the boundary set in a complex drawing.
- Use the style options.
- Have a new hatch pattern inherit the properties of an existing pattern.
- Perform and observe the difference between editing an associative and nonassociative hatch pattern.
- Use direct hatching.
- Hatch around text.
- Edit hatch patterns.

Introduction to Drawing Patterns and Section Lines

AutoCAD LT provides you with a library of 68 hatch patterns. The term *hatch* is used to describe the various patterns that can be used to fill in areas of your drawing. The AutoCAD LT standard hatch patterns are defined in the AutoCAD LT aclt.pat and acltiso.pat files and are displayed in Appendix C of this text. Hatch patterns are often used when drawing sectional views. AutoCAD LT provides the common material section line patterns for mechanical drafting. In mechanical drafting, standard hatch patterns are used to represent different materials, such as cast iron, brass, and aluminum. These standard hatch patterns are identified with ANSI numbers. For example, ANSI31 is the standard section symbol used to represent cast iron or general material in section. The American National Standard Institute document that recommends section line practice is ANSI Y14.3, *Multi and Sectional View Drawings*. AutoCAD LT also provides hatch patterns for materials such as concrete and earth for architectural sections. Drawing architectural elevations is made easier with material patterns for items such as brick and roofing. Hatch patterns can be used as an effective aid if you are designing charts and graphs. The uses are unlimited and can be applied to any drafting discipline, engineering field, or artistic design.

Hatch patterns are drawn in AutoCAD LT with the BHATCH and HATCH commands. The BHATCH command allows you to prepare hatch patterns using the Boundary Hatch dialog box and automatically hatches any enclosed area. BHATCH patterns can be *associative hatch patterns,* which means that the pattern is automatically revised if the boundary is changed. The *hatch boundary* is the shape that encloses the hatch pattern. The hatch boundary can be various objects that make up a shape or shapes. The HATCH command is used to draw hatch patterns using keyboard entry. Hatch patterns drawn with the HATCH command are *nonassociative hatch patterns,* which means that they are not revised when the hatch boundary is edited. The HATCH command can be used to hatch selected objects, or you can define a hatch boundary without selecting objects.

383

Hatch patterns can be edited using the HATCHEDIT command. This command allows you to change an existing associative hatch pattern.

Using the BHATCH Command

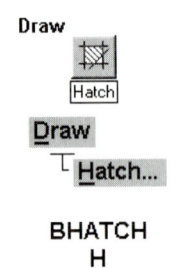

The BHATCH command allows you to automatically hatch any enclosed area using the Boundary Hatch dialog box shown in Figure 10.1. The BHATCH command is accessed by picking Hatch . . . from the Draw pull-down menu, by picking the Hatch button in the Draw toolbar, or by typing **H** or **BHATCH** at the Command: prompt.

The Boundary Hatch dialog box provides a convenient way to set up hatch pattern properties and draw hatch patterns. As you look at Figure 10.1, notice that some of the Boundary Hatch dialog box features are inactive. These items become active during certain applications, which are discussed later in this chapter. The following explanations discuss the various features of the Boundary Hatch dialog box.

Selecting a Pattern Type

The Pattern Type area of the Boundary Hatch dialog box allows you to visually select the desired hatch pattern for your drawing. The default pattern type is listed as Predefined. This refers to AutoCAD LT's standard hatch patterns, which are available in the aclt.pat and acltiso.pat files. Each predefined hatch pattern has a name and an example is shown in the image tile on the right side of the Pattern Type area. Look at the pattern image in Figure 10.1. This is the default AutoCAD LT hatch pattern named ANSI31. The ANSI31 hatch pattern is typically used for general section lines in mechanical drafting and is also the material designation for cast iron. Notice the name, ANSI31, displayed in the Patter_n_: box in the Pattern Properties area. If you want to change the pattern type, move the cursor to the image tile and pick. Every time you pick, another pattern is displayed in the image tile and its name is shown in the Pattern: box.

Figure 10.2A shows the ANSI32 pattern, which is a material symbol for steel in a mechanical drawing section. Figure 10.2B shows one of the available brick patterns. You can choose from 66 predefined patterns. Some of the patterns displayed in the image tile have a small box with an asterisk in the upper left corner. The asterisk indicates that the pattern sample is not shown to scale. The patterns without asterisk are shown at approximately 1:1 or FULL scale when the limits fill the screen. For example, look at pattern AR-B816 shown in Figure 10.3A. The AR-B816 pattern is one of the available brick representations. When displayed as shown, AR-B816 has a single line joint between the bricks. Move the cursor to the box and pick to get a new image of the bricks with double lines representing the mortar joints between the bricks. This is the AR-B816C pattern shown in Figure 10.3B. The AR-B816C pattern provides you with additional realism, but also increases file size. Several of the standard hatch patterns have this option.

FIGURE 10.1 The Boundary Hatch dialog box is accessed with the BHATCH command.

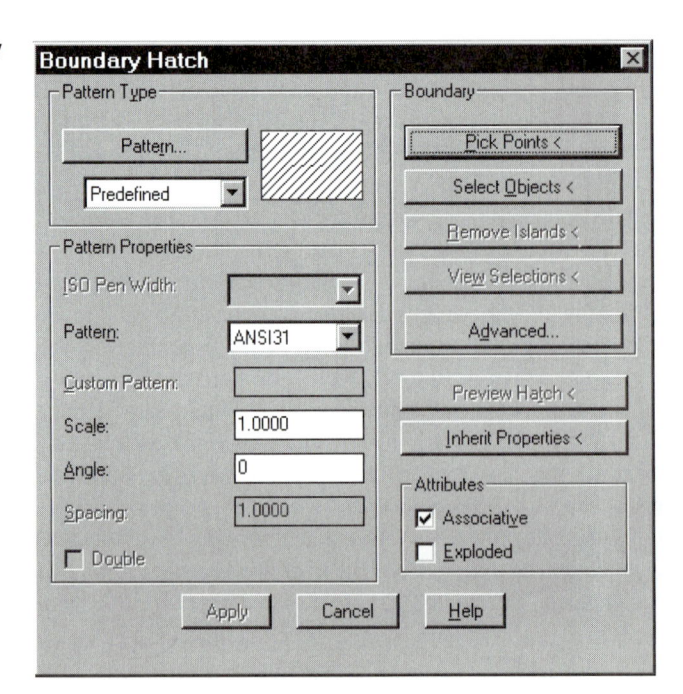

CHAPTER 10 ||| Drawing Patterns and Section Lines 385

FIGURE 10.2 (A) Picking on the image tile to access the predefined patterns in the Pattern Type area of the Boundary Hatch dialog box. The ANSI32 pattern represents steel in mechanical drafting. (B) The image tile displays the BRICK pattern.

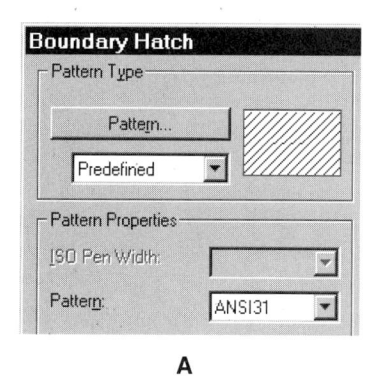

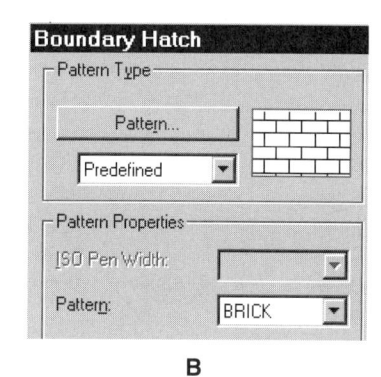

FIGURE 10.3 (A) AR-B816 is one of the available concrete block patterns for use in architectural elevations. Pick on the asterisk to access the AR-B816C pattern. (B) The image tile displays the concrete block AR-B816C, with mortar joints.

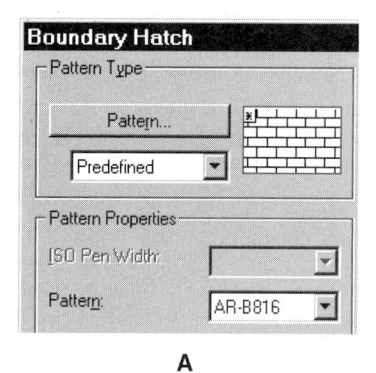

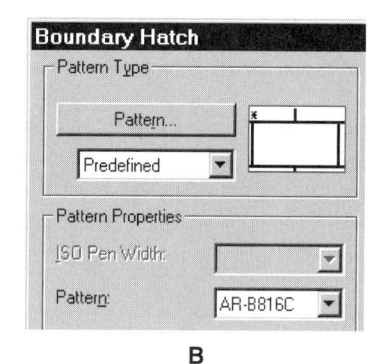

Another way to select a hatch pattern is to pick the Pattern... button in the Pattern Type area. This opens the Hatch pattern palette shown in Figure 10.4. The Hatch pattern palette is convenient because it shows you a visual image of each hatch pattern and a list of the pattern names. When a pattern name is highlighted in the list, the same corresponding pattern image is highlighted in the palette. Pick the Next button to access the next display of pattern images. Pick on a pattern image to automatically have the list changed to match. Each time you pick the Next button, another set of images is displayed until you get to the end. Pick the Previous button to review previous image palettes.

Notice the SOLID hatch pattern option selected in Figure 10.5. This is used to fill in areas solid.

The Pattern Type list contains two other options. These are User-defined and Custom. These options are fully explained later in this chapter, after you have learned about the additional features of the Boundary Hatch dialog box.

FIGURE 10.4 The Hatch pattern palette displays the image and name of each standard hatch pattern. Open the Hatch pattern palette by picking the Pattern... button in the Boundary hatch dialog box.

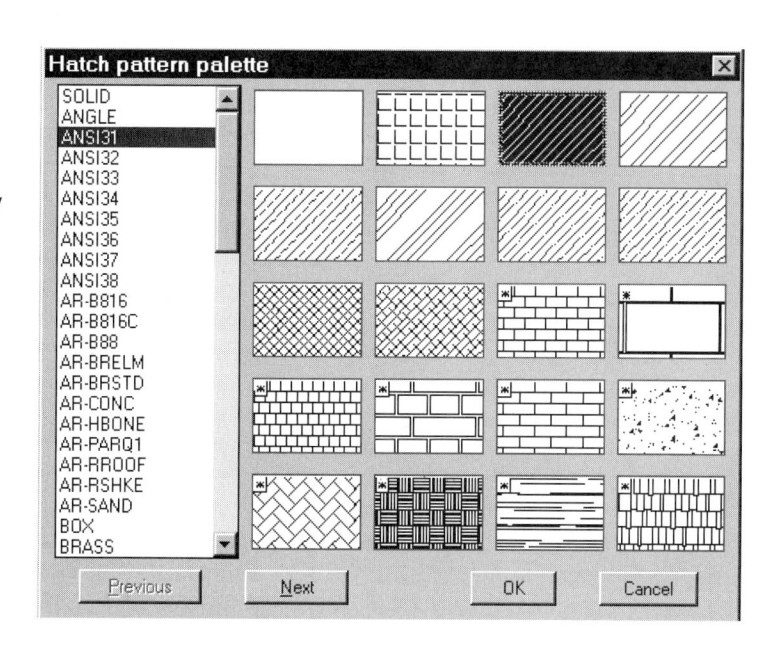

FIGURE 10.5 The SOLID pattern allows you to fill objects in solid.

Field Notes

The pattern type and values displayed in Figure 10.1 are the initial AutoCAD LT defaults. The values depend on the drawing area specified in the AutoCAD LT setup. When you make changes in the Boundary hatch dialog box, these changes remain active in the current drawing, until they are changed again.

Exercise 10.1

1. Begin a new drawing, or open one of your own prototypes.
2. Open the Boundary Hatch dialog box.
3. Pick on the image tile in the Pattern Type area. Notice how the Pattern: name changes with each different image tile display.
4. Exit the drawing without saving, or leave AutoCAD LT active for future exercises.

Changing Pattern Properties

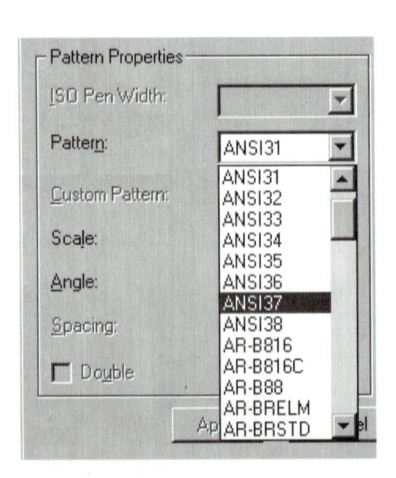

The Pattern Properties area of the Boundary Hatch dialog box is where you can modify the hatch pattern to fit your own specifications. Notice in Figure 10.1 that only the Pattern:, Scale:, and Angle: boxes are active.

Changing the Pattern

Earlier, you learned that the hatch pattern can be changed by picking on the image tile in the Pattern Type area of the Boundary Hatch dialog box. Changing the pattern in this manner also changes the name in the Pattern: box to match the representation in the image tile. You can also change the pattern name and image tile display by picking the desired name from the Pattern: list. To do this, use the down arrow and pick the desired pattern name, as shown in Figure 10.6.

FIGURE 10.6 Selecting a pattern name from the Pattern: list.

CHAPTER 10 ||| Drawing Patterns and Section Lines

FIGURE 10.7 The Pattern Properties compartment displays the Sca<u>l</u>e: box.

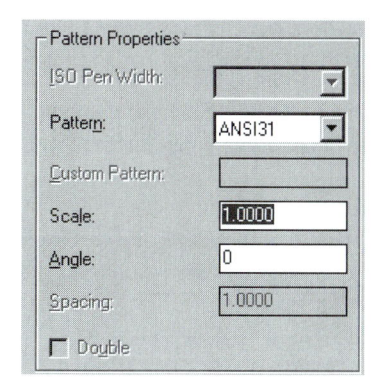

Changing the Pattern Scale

The default pattern scale is 1.0000 unit as shown in the Sca<u>l</u>e: box in Figure 10.7. The 1 unit scale represents full scale. You can set the scale to any desired value depending on your drawing requirements. Figure 10.8 displays the same hatch pattern drawn using several different scale factors.

Field Notes

When you start AutoCAD LT with a Wizard, the hatch pattern scale factor is automatically set based on the information you provide. The adjusted settings are related to the full scale of the objects you draw. You can leave the settings as established by AutoCAD LT or you can change them.

If you are using a template or starting AutoCAD LT from scratch, you can set the hatch pattern scale factor to match the drawing size. You can also set the hatch pattern scale to be based on the drawing to be plotted by relating the scale to paper space units. A scale can be set to paper space units by entering the scale value followed by XP. XP tells AutoCAD LT that the scale is related to paper space units. Entering a value of 1XP tells AutoCAD LT that the desired scale factor is related to 1 unit in paper space. The use of paper space is discussed in Chapter 13.

Changing the Pattern Angle

The default pattern angle is 0 as shown in the <u>A</u>ngle: box in Figure 10.7. This default angle displays the hatch pattern as represented in the image tile and in the symbol library shown in Appendix C. You can adjust the hatch pattern angle by entering a new value in the <u>A</u>ngle: box. Various hatch pattern angles are provided in Figure 10.9, using the ANSI31 pattern as an example.

FIGURE 10.8 A hatch pattern drawn using different scale factors.

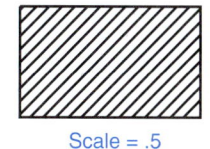

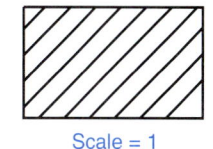

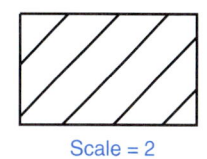

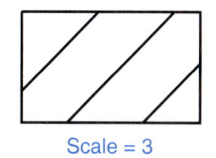

Scale = .5   Scale = 1   Scale = 2   Scale = 3

FIGURE 10.9 A hatch pattern drawn using different angle values.

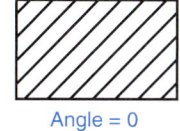

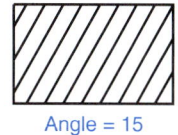

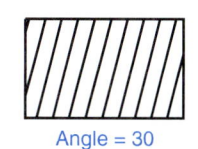

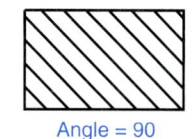

Angle = 0   Angle = 15   Angle = 30   Angle = 45   Angle = 90

> **Field Notes**
>
> The default pattern angle of 0 used on the ANSI31 pattern type actually draws lines at 45°. Be careful when using hatch patterns because the actual angle of the hatch lines and the rotation angle may be different as they are with the ANSI31 hatch pattern.
>
> The recommended angle for section lines in mechanical drawings is 45°. In mechanical drafting, it is recommended that section lines not be drawn parallel or perpendicular to other adjacent lines on the drawing. To avoid this, you may need to set the hatch pattern so the actual angle of the hatch lines is between 15° and 75°. Vertical and horizontal section lines should be avoided in mechanical drawings.

Accessing the ISO Pattern Types

AutoCAD LT provides you with 14 standard ISO hatch pattern types. ISO stands for the International Organization for Standardization. When you select one of the ISO patterns, the ISO Pen Width: box is activated in the Pattern Properties area as shown in Figure 10.10A. Pick the down arrow to access the list of available ISO pen widths. Select the desired pen width as shown in Figure 10.10B. Selecting a pen width from this list establishes the scale for an ISO hatch pattern. Setting the number shown in the ISO Pen Width list updates the Scale value to match. Both the ISO Pen Width and Scale options set the value of the HPSCALE system variable and therefore affect the appearance of the pattern in the same manner.

FIGURE 10.10 (A) Selecting an ISO pattern type. (B) The ISO Pen Width: list.

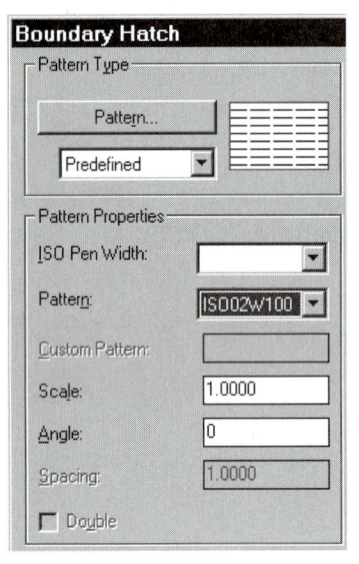

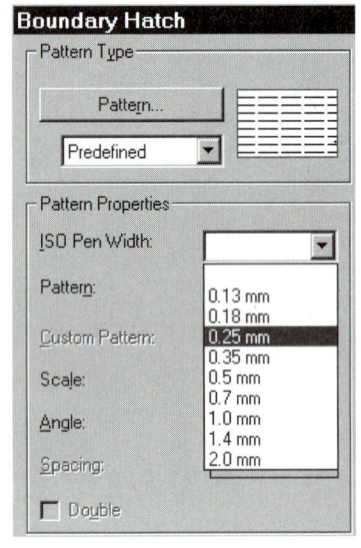

> **Field Notes**
>
> When the Measurement field on the User page of the Preferences dialog box is set to metric, the acltiso.pat file is used. This automatically scales hatch pattern definitions for metric equivalency.

The Other Pattern Type List Options

Earlier, you were introduced to the Predefined option in the Pattern Type list. Two other options are also available in the list. Pick the down arrow to access the User-defined and Custom options. Pick the User-defined option as shown in Figure 10.11A if you want to create your own simple hatch pattern. When the User-defined option is selected, the Spacing: and Double options are now active for the first time as you can see in Figure 10.11B. Notice also in Figure 10.11B that the image tile is no longer active. This is because the image tile displays only the standard patterns.

CHAPTER 10 ||| Drawing Patterns and Section Lines

FIGURE 10.11 (A) Pick the User-defined option in the Pattern Type list to create your own simple hatch pattern. (B) When the User-defined option is selected, the Spacing: box and Double toggle check box become active.

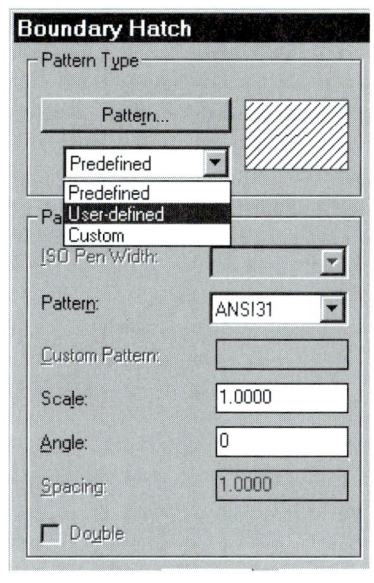

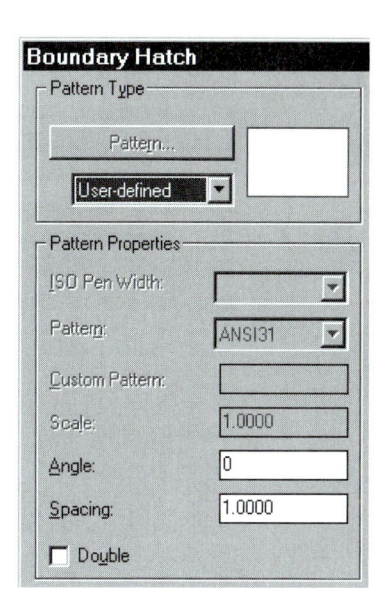

A

B

To define your own simple hatch pattern, set the angle, spacing between pattern lines, and the display of single or double lines. The Angle: box works just as previously described to set the desired angle for your pattern. In the User-defined application, pattern angles are measured from 0 (zero) as horizontal. The Spacing: box allows you to set the spacing between pattern lines. The 1.0000 default provides 1 unit of spacing between lines. The amount of spacing depends on your drawing size. A spacing of 0.125 might be good for an inch mechanical drawing, whereas 6 might be a valid setting for a metric mechanical drawing. An architectural drawing might use a setting of 2, depending on the application. The Double toggle should be off if you want a pattern with single lines. Check this toggle if you want double lines in your pattern. Double lines are created by placing two sets of lines that intersect at 90°. Figure 10.12 shows the results of a variety of user-defined hatch pattern designs.

The Custom option in the Pattern Type list is used to access third-party hatch pattern files that can be used with AutoCAD LT. When you pick the Custom option, the Custom Pattern: box becomes active. If you have other hatch pattern files available, enter the pattern name here for access. The hatch pattern name and file name must be the same.

Field Notes

Custom pattern definition files can contain only a single definition that defines a pattern having the same name as the file. Custom definitions can be added to the aclt.pat or acltiso.pat files as desired and are then available using the predefined option.

Drawing a Hatch Pattern

So far you have learned how to set up hatch pattern types. Now, you can either draw standard AutoCAD LT hatch patterns or create the simple user-defined hatch patterns. Follow these steps to draw one of the standard hatch patterns:

FIGURE 10.12 Examples of several different user-defined hatch patterns.

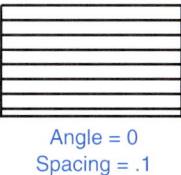

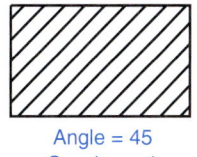

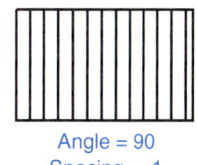

Angle = 0
Spacing = .1
Double = off

Angle = 45
Spacing =.1
Double = off

Angle = 90
Spacing = .1
Double = off

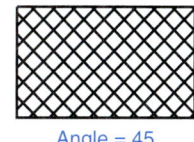

Angle = 45
Spacing = .1
Double = on

- Draw objects that you want to place hatch patterns within. For starters, consider drawing a closed rectangle with the LINE or PLINE command.
- Enter the BHATCH command to open the Boundary Hatch dialog box.
- Pick on the image tile until you find the desired hatch pattern, go to the Patter<u>n</u>: list and select the pattern by name, or pick the Pattern … button to open the <u>H</u>atch pattern palette..
- Adjust the scale and angle as desired.
- Go to the Boundary area, of the Boundary Hatch dialog box, and pick the <u>P</u>ick Points< button. Look back at Figure 10.1 or see Figure 10.14. The screen returns with the crosshairs present and the prompt asks you to select an internal point:

    Command: **H** or **BHATCH**↵
    ⟨*The Boundary Hatch dialog box opens. Pick the <u>P</u>ick Points< button.*⟩
    Select internal point: ⟨*move the crosshairs within the object and pick*⟩
    Selecting everything . . .
    Selecting everything visible . . .
    Analyzing the selected data . . .
    Analyzing internal islands . . .
    Select internal point: ↵

- AutoCAD LT gives you several messages as it evaluates the hatch boundary. You then press Enter to return to the Boundary Hatch dialog box.
- When back in the Boundary Hatch dialog box, pick the Preview Ha<u>t</u>ch< button. This is a great AutoCAD LT feature that lets you preview the results of your hatch drawing before the hatch is applied. After picking the Preview Ha<u>t</u>ch< button, the screen returns with the hatch pattern temporarily placed and the Boundary Hatch message box shown in Figure 10.13. Pick the <u>C</u>ontinue button to return to the Boundary Hatch dialog box. The advantage of using preview is that if you do not like the way the preview looks, you can return to the Boundary Hatch dialog box and try again without starting over. You do not have to use the preview, and it may not be very important in a simple drawing like this. However, it might save you considerable time when hatching in a complex drawing.
- If you are satisfied with the results of the preview, pick the Apply button at the bottom of the Boundary Hatch dialog box. This removes the dialog box and applies the hatch as you intended.

Through the Window...

There are some easy ways to use list boxes in Windows. For example, after popping the list down, you can use the keyboard cursor keys to move up or down through the list, and even use the Page Up, Page Down, Home, and End keys. The most convenient option is to press an alphabetic character key, which moves up or down the list to highlight the first item in the list beginning with the character you type.

FIGURE 10.13 After previewing the hatch, pick the <u>C</u>ontinue button to return to the Boundary Hatch dialog box.

CHAPTER 10 ||| Drawing Patterns and Section Lines

Field Notes

- If the hatch boundary is not properly closed, using the Pick Points< option results in an error message. This happens if there are any gaps in the hatch boundary. If you get this error message, carefully check the hatch boundary to be sure the perimeter is closed.
- When you are inside the BHATCH command at the Select internal point: prompt, you can type U to undo the previous pick if you decide it was not what you wanted.
- If you use Pick Points< and accidentally select the wrong location and do not undo it prior to pressing Enter and returning to the dialog box, you cannot deselect the area and must exit the BHATCH command to start over.
- If you complete the BHATCH command, and decide the results are not what you want, you can type U at the Command: prompt to undo the previous hatch.
- The Preview Hatch< button is an excellent way to look at an object that you have hatched before you accept it. If you discover that the hatch properties are not what you expected, you can change them and try again. However, when you pick the same object again, you get a Boundary Definition Error alert box. The message in the box reads "Boundary duplicates an existing boundary." Pick the OK button and continue the process.

Exercise 10.2

1. Open a new drawing, one of your prototypes, or use Exercise 10.1.
2. Use the LINE or PLINE command to draw a closed rectangle, similar to one of the rectangles shown in Figure 10.8. Copy the rectangle three times. You should have four rectangles similar to those shown in Figure 10.8.
3. Hatch inside the four rectangles using the ANSI31 pattern type and change the scale for each application, as was done in Figure 10.8. Be sure to use the Preview Hatch< button to preview each hatch before applying.
4. Make five more rectangles and use the ANSI31 pattern to hatch each rectangle with a different angle, as was done in Figure 10.9.
5. Draw four more rectangles and create a different user-defined hatch pattern for each rectangle. The results should look like Figure 10.12.
6. Draw as many more rectangles as you desire and experiment by placing a different standard hatch pattern in each rectangle. This gives you a chance to see what some of the other patterns look like.
7. Save the drawing as EX10.2.

Using the Additional Features of the Boundary Hatch Dialog Box

The Boundary area of the Boundary Hatch dialog box has several buttons, as shown in Figure 10.14. The purpose of these buttons is explained in the following:

FIGURE 10.14 The Boundary area of the Boundary Hatch dialog box.

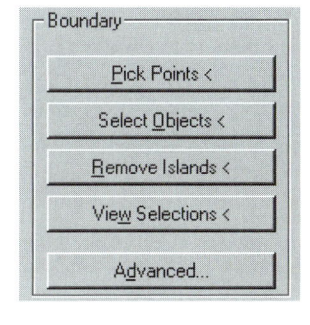

Using the Pick Points< Button

The Pick Points< button was explained in the previous discussion. This button is used to hatch a closed area by picking a point inside that area.

Using the Select Objects< Button

The Select Objects< button is used if you want to use one of the AutoCAD LT selection methods to select objects for hatching. Rather than the Select internal point: prompt that you get when using the Pick Points< button, you get the Select objects: prompt. This is what the command sequence looks like when using the Select Objects< button:

Command: **H** or **BHATCH**↵
⟨*The Boundary Hatch dialog box opens. Pick the Select Objects< button.*⟩
Select objects: ⟨*pick the objects to hatch*⟩
Select objects: ↵

The Boundary Hatch dialog box returns for you to complete the hatching process. Now, use the Preview Hatch< button to see if the defined hatch is okay. Pick the Apply button if you are satisfied with the preview.

In addition to providing you with another way to draw hatches, the Select Objects< button is useful when hatching multiple objects or an area that is separated by other objects. For example, the rectangle and circle in Figure 10.15 are divided by line objects and the plan is to hatch the entire circle and rectangle. The Select Objects< option works well in this example, because it is easier to pick the rectangle and the circle to have the hatch drawn through the entire object. The rectangle must have been drawn with the PLINE or RECTANG command to use one pick. If the LINE command is used to draw the rectangle, each line object must be selected.

FIGURE 10.15 Using the Select Objects< button to hatch objects.

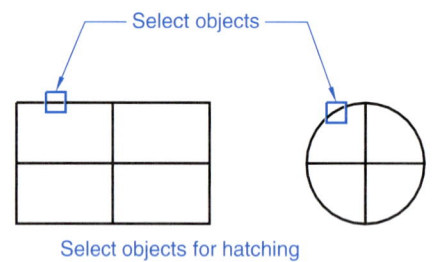

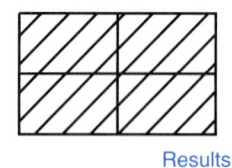

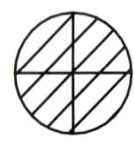

Select objects for hatching — Results

Exercise 10.3

1. Open a new drawing or one of your prototypes.
2. Draw a rectangle and circle with a horizontal and vertical line crossing each, similar to the original objects shown in Figure 10.15. Use the PLINE or RECTANG command to draw the rectangle.
3. Enter the Boundary Hatch dialog box and use the Pick Points< button to pick a point within the rectangle and circle. Return to the Boundary Hatch dialog box and preview the results. Notice that only one quarter of each object is hatched.
4. Pick the Select Objects< button, and this time pick the rectangle and the circle at the places shown in Figure 10.15. Return to the Boundary Hatch dialog box and preview the results. The entire rectangle and circle should be hatched as in Figure 10.15. If you are satisfied with the preview, pick the Apply button.
5. Save the drawing as EX10.3.

CHAPTER 10 ||| Drawing Patterns and Section Lines 393

Using the Remove Islands< Button

The Remove Islands< button is used to select islands to hatch within a hatch area. AutoCAD LT defines an *island* as an enclosed area within the hatch area as shown in Figure 10.16A. The Remove Islands< button is inactive until you use the Pick Points< button. If you use the Pick Points< button, and pick between the hatch boundary and the island, the island is automatically left unhatched as shown in Figure 10.16B. If you want to hatch through the island, you can do the following:

- Enter the BHATCH command and use the Pick Points< button to pick between the hatch boundary and the island as shown in Figure 10.16C. The following command sequence is used:

    Command: **H** or **BHATCH.**↵

The Boundary Hatch dialog box opens. Pick the Pick Points< button.

    Select internal point: ⟨*pick between the boundary and the island*⟩
    Selecting everything . . .
    Selecting everything visible . . .
    Analyzing the selected data . . .
    Analyzing internal islands . . .
    Select internal point: ↵

- The Boundary Hatch dialog box returns. Pick the Remove Islands< button. The screen returns and you get this prompt:

    Select island to remove: ⟨*pick the island as shown in Figure 10.16D*⟩
    <Select island to remove>/Undo: ↵

- The Boundary Hatch dialog box returns again. Preview the hatch and if it is what you expect, pick the Apply button. The result is shown in Figure 10.16E.

FIGURE 10.16 (A) An island is an enclosed area within a hatch boundary. (B) Using the Pick Points< button to hatch between the hatch boundary and the island. (C)–(E) Hatching through an island by using the Remove Islands< button. (F) and (G) Hatching inside an island by picking inside the island.

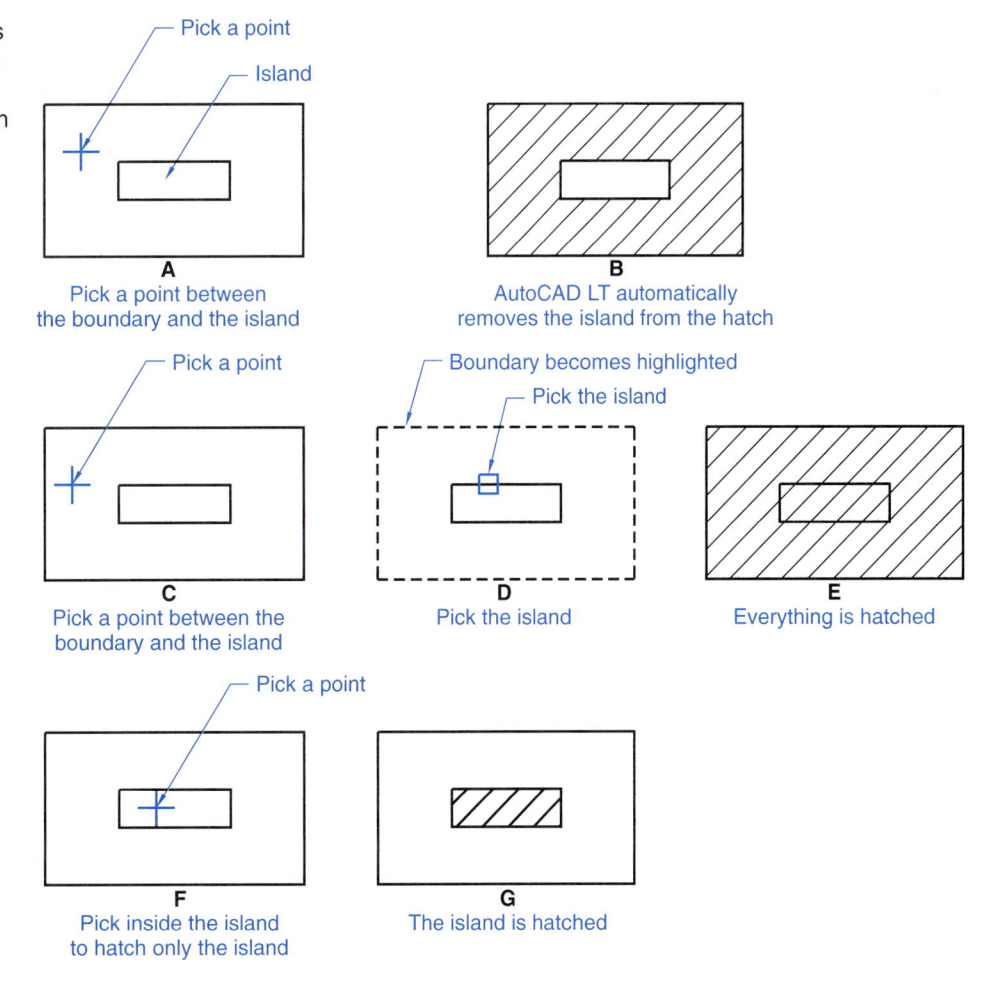

A — Pick a point between the boundary and the island
B — AutoCAD LT automatically removes the island from the hatch
C — Pick a point between the boundary and the island
D — Pick the island
E — Everything is hatched
F — Pick inside the island to hatch only the island
G — The island is hatched

If you want to hatch only within the island, use the Pick Points< button and pick inside the island as shown in Figures 10.16F and G.

> ### Exercise 10.4
>
> 1. Open a new drawing or one of your prototypes.
> 2. Draw an object similar to that shown in Figure 10.16A using the PLINE command.
> 3. Make two copies of the object.
> 4. Hatch the first object in a manner similar to Figure 10.16B.
> 5. Hatch the second object in a manner similar to Figure 10.16E.
> 6. Hatch the third object in a manner similar to Figure 10.16G.
> 7. Save the drawing as EX10.4.

Using the View Selection< Button

The View Selection< button is active only after you have used the Pick Points< or Select Objects< button to establish a hatch boundary. When you pick the View Selection< button, the screen returns and the hatch boundaries are highlighted for you to see. This just gives you a chance to see the selected hatch boundaries to confirm if they are what you intended. The Boundary Hatch Continue button, shown in Figure 10.13, is displayed. Pick this button when you are ready to go back to the Boundary Hatch dialog box.

Using the Advanced ... Button

Picking the Advanced ... button opens the Advanced Options dialog box shown in Figure 10.17. The features of the Advanced Options dialog box are explained in the following discussion.

FIGURE 10.17 The Advanced Options dialog box is opened when you pick the Advanced ... button in the Boundary Hatch dialog box.

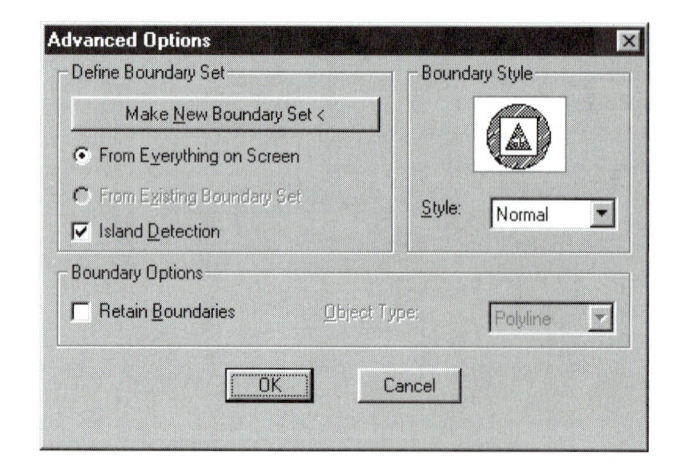

Using the Define Boundary Set Area

The Define Boundary Set area allows you to decide how AutoCAD LT analyzes the boundary to be used for hatching based on the internal point selected. The From Everything on Screen radio button is active by default. This forces AutoCAD LT to search everything on the screen until a suitable boundary is found. This process works well in many drawings, but can be time consuming in a very complex drawing. You can specify the area that you want AutoCAD LT to analyze. Doing this can produce the boundary faster, because AutoCAD LT must look at fewer objects. The From Existing Boundary Set radio button is not active until you specify the boundary set for AutoCAD LT to examine. A ***boundary set*** is a group of objects that AutoCAD LT analyzes for the boundary definition when you specify a point on the drawing. You can limit the boundary set by picking the Make New Boundary Set< button. Picking this button allows you to select the objects in the drawing that you want AutoCAD LT to examine when looking for the desired boundary. When you pick this button, the screen returns and the Select objects: prompt is issued. You place either a Window or Crossing box around the objects that define the boundary set. For example, if you want to hatch a small area in the structural drawing shown in Figure 10.18, pick the Make New Boundary Set< button and follow this sequence:

Command: **H** or **BHATCH**↵

CHAPTER 10 ||| Drawing Patterns and Section Lines   **395**

FIGURE 10.18 Using the Make New Boundary Set< button to hatch a small area in a complex drawing.

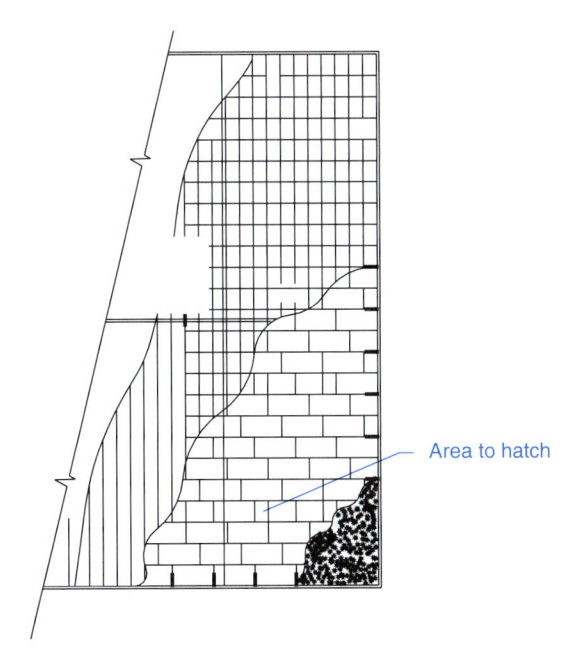

— Area to hatch

The Boundary Hatch dialog box opens. Pick the Advanced ... button. The Advanced Options dialog box opens. Pick the Make New Boundary Set< button and you get the Select objects: prompt. Use a Window or Crossing box to select the objects to be used for a boundary set. Any selection option works, but a Crossing box selects all of the objects the box encloses or crosses:

    Select objects: ⟨*use a Crossing box as shown in Figure 10.19*⟩
    Select objects: ↵

FIGURE 10.19 Using a Crossing selection box to select the area for a new boundary set.

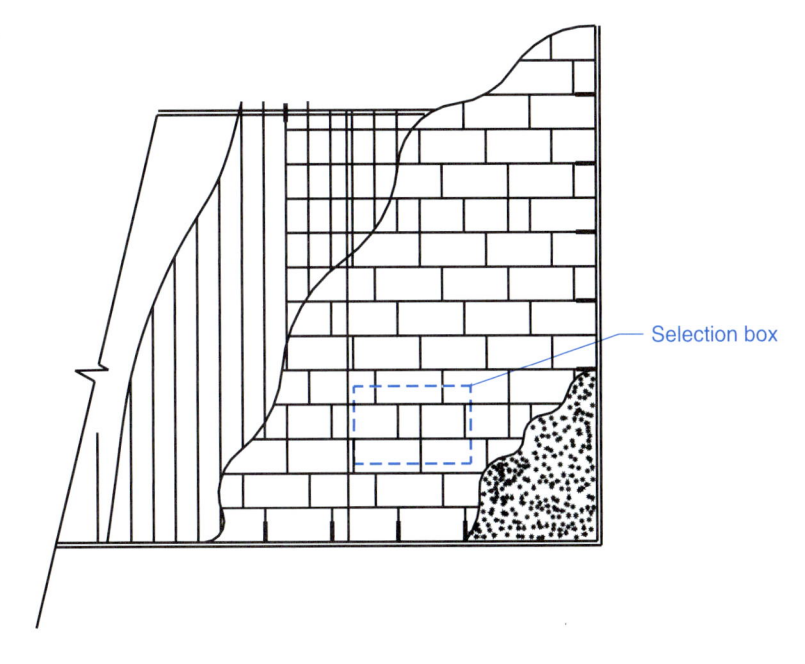

— Selection box

The Advanced Options dialog box returns. Pick the OK button. The Boundary Hatch dialog box returns. Pick the Pick Points< button and then pick a point inside the area to be hatched:

    Analyzing the selected data . . .
    Select internal point: ⟨*pick a point*⟩
    Analyzing internal islands . . .
    Select internal point: ↵

The Boundary Hatch dialog box returns. Preview the hatch and if it is fine, pick the Apply button. The hatch is complete as shown in Figure 10.20.

FIGURE 10.20 Hatching within the small area of the complex drawing shown in Figures 10.18 and 10.19.

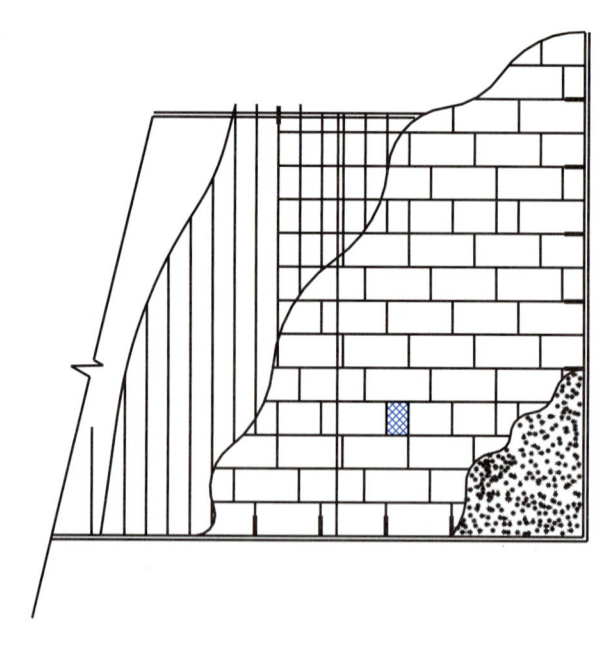

Using the Island Detection Toggle

Islands were explained in an earlier discussion. You need to be sure this toggle is on if you want AutoCAD LT to see the islands within the hatch area when you use the Pick Points < option. This toggle is on by default. If the Island Detection toggle is off, islands are hatched through unless you select them for removal using the Select Objects< button.

Using the Boundary Style Options

The Style: box of the Advanced Options dialog box provides you with three options. These options control how features within a hatch boundary are treated. The options are accessed by picking the name in the Style: list. The Style: names are Normal, Outer, and Ignore. When you pick one of the names in the Style: list, the image tile at the right changes to represent the result of the option. You can also pick on the image tile to conveniently change between options. Normal is the initial default style. This option hatches every other interior feature, as displayed in the image tile in Figure 10.21A. The Outer option hatches only the outer feature, leaving all other interior features unhatched, as shown in Figure 10.21B. The Ignore option ignores all interior features and hatches everything, as shown in Figure 10.21C.

FIGURE 10.21 (A) The Normal style option hatches every other feature in the object as shown in the image tile. (B) The Outer style option hatches only the outer feature in the object as shown in the image tile. (C) The Ignore style option hatches through everything in the object as shown in the image tile.

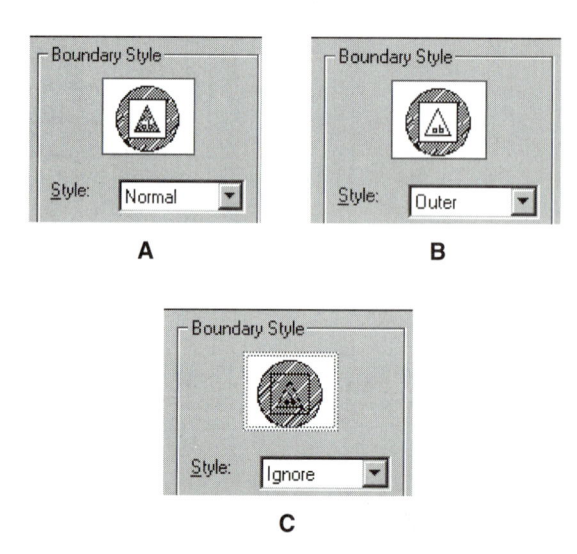

CHAPTER 10 ||| Drawing Patterns and Section Lines

Exercise 10.5

1. Open a new drawing or use one of your prototypes.
2. Draw an object similar to the representation in the image tile in Figure 10.21A, without hatching.
3. Make two copies of the object.
4. Hatch the first object using the Normal style. The results should be similar to the image tile shown in Figure 10.21A.
5. Hatch the second object using the Outer style. The results should be similar to the image tile shown in Figure 10.21B.
6. Hatch the third object using the Ignore style. The results should be similar to the image tile shown in Figure 10.21C.
7. Save the drawing as EX10.5.

Using the Retain Boundaries Toggle

The Retain Boundaries toggle is off by default. The hatch boundaries that are created to establish a hatch pattern are temporary if this toggle is off. This means that the hatch boundary does not remain as part of the drawing when the hatching process is over. As soon as the hatch pattern is drawn, the boundary is removed. Turning the Retain Boundaries toggle on keeps each hatch boundary as a polyline or a region. This stacks a new polyline or region on top of the existing boundary objects. This new object can be edited or erased if desired. You might want to do this if the original boundary is made up of line objects and you want a polyline or region boundary that you can use for purposes such as calculating the area.

Specifying the Boundary Object Type

The boundary objects created by the Retain Boundaries option are created as either regions or polylines, based on the setting in the Object Type list. Regions are discussed in Chapter 6, and polylines in Chapter 8. Using a region allows access to some data not available from a polyline object.

Using the Inherit Properties< Button

The Inherit Properties< button allows you to pick a hatch pattern that already exists on your drawing and use it as the pattern for hatching other areas. Doing this allows you to quickly and accurately duplicate an existing hatch pattern that is already in your drawing. This can save you time and maintain consistency in your drawing. To use this option, enter the BHATCH command and follow these steps:

Command: **H** or **BHATCH**⏎

The Boundary Hatch dialog box opens. Pick the Inherit Properties< button to get this prompt:

Select hatch object: ⟨*pick an existing hatch pattern on your drawing*⟩

The Boundary Hatch dialog box returns with the selected hatch displayed in the Pattern Type image tile and with its characteristics identified in the Pattern Properties area. Use the Pick Points< button or the Select Objects< button to select the object to hatch with the inherited pattern. If the Pick Points< button is used, the prompts continue like this:

Select internal point: ⟨*pick a point inside the desired area*⟩
Selecting everything . . .
Selecting everything visible . . .
Analyzing the selected data . . .
Analyzing internal islands . . .
Select internal point: ⏎

The Boundary Hatch dialog box returns. Preview the hatch and pick the Apply button, if satisfied.

> ### Exercise 10.6
>
> 1. Open a new drawing or use one of your prototypes.
> 2. Draw a circle and hatch it with the AR-HBONE pattern using a scale of 0.75 and an angle of 0.
> 3. Draw another circle the same size as the first. Hatch this circle with AR-PARQ1, using a scale of 0.75 and an angle of 0.
> 4. Draw another circle the same size as the first two. Go to the Boundary Hatch dialog box and pick the Inherit Properties< button. Select the hatch pattern in the first circle and apply it to the third circle.
> 5. Save the drawing as EX10.6.

Using the Associative Toggle

Earlier, you learned that hatch patterns drawn with the BHATCH command are associative. This means that the pattern is automatically revised if the boundary is changed. An associative hatch pattern is treated as a block. The Associative toggle in the Attributes area of the Boundary Hatch dialog box is on by initial default. See the lower right corner of Figure 10.1. For most applications, the associative feature is left on, but you can turn it off with this toggle. While the Associative toggle is turned off, all hatch patterns drawn with the BHATCH command are nonassociative. This means that each element of the pattern is an individual object. Figure 10.22A shows the results of stretching a hatched object with the associative feature on and off. You can use any of the available editing commands, such as ROTATE and SCALE, to modify objects with associative hatch patterns and have the pattern automatically change with the edit to the boundary. If you have an associative hatched object with an island, moving the island outside the boundary causes the boundary to be fully hatched and the moved island to also become hatched, as shown in Figure 10.22B. The area where the

FIGURE 10.22 (A) The results of using the STRETCH command to edit a hatched object with associative hatching on and off. (B) The results of using the MOVE command to move an island outside the boundary of an associatively hatched area.

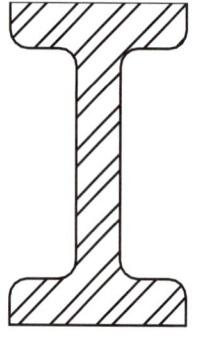

The original hatched object

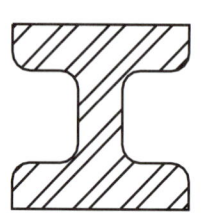

The object edited using the STRETCH command with associative hatch on

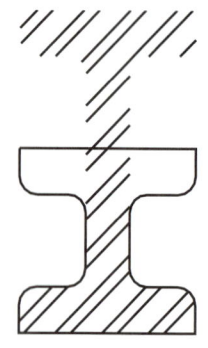

The object edited using the STRETCH command with associative hatch off

A

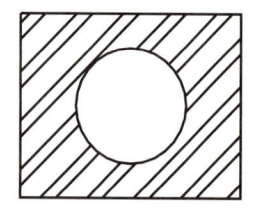

The original associative hatched object with an island

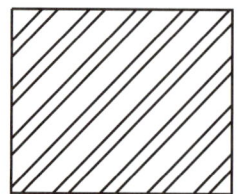

The results of using the MOVE command to move the island outside of the hatch boundary

B

CHAPTER 10 ||| Drawing Patterns and Section Lines

island in Figure 10.22B was moved became filled in with the hatch pattern. This also happens with an associative hatch pattern if you erase an island. This process is referred to as **healing**. As you can see with these examples, associative hatch patterns have the advantages of being able to edit the hatch boundary and having the hatch pattern automatically updated to match.

> ### Field Notes
>
> - When you are editing objects with hatch patterns, be sure that you select *only* the hatch boundary; do not select the hatch pattern.
> - Be careful with edits that open a hatch boundary, such as the BREAK command. These types of edits can cause the associativity to be removed.
> - Edits that add objects to the boundary, such as those occurring when using the FILLET or CHAMFER commands, may not properly update the pattern.

Exploded Hatch Pattern

Notice the Exploded toggle check box in Figure 10.1. Exploded is off by default. This means that the hatch pattern you draw is drawn as a block. A ***block*** is a special symbol or shape designed for multiple use. Blocks are discussed in detail in Chapter 12. In this condition, the entire hatch pattern is edited as one unit. If you place a check in the Exploded toggle check box, the elements of the hatch pattern are drawn as individual objects. Be sure to turn Exploded back off if you want to draw associative hatch patterns again.

You can explode an existing associative hatch pattern if you want to edit the individual elements of the pattern. Avoid exploding the hatch pattern if you want all elements of the pattern to act as one unit. The EXPLODE command is accessed by typing X or EXPLODE, by picking the Explode button in the Modify toolbar, or by picking Explode in the Modify pull-down menu. The EXPLODE command asks you to select objects.

Exercise 10.7

1. Open a new drawing or use one of your prototypes.
2. Draw an object similar to the original hatched object shown in Figure 10.22A without hatching.
3. Make a copy of the object.
4. Use the BHATCH command to hatch the first object with the ANSI32 pattern. Be sure the Associative toggle is on.
5. Turn the Associative toggle off and hatch the second object with the same pattern.
6. Use the STRETCH command on both objects and observe the results.
7. Turn the Associative toggle is on.
8. Draw and hatch the object shown at the left in Figure 10.22B.
9. Make two copies of the object to the right.
10. Use the MOVE command on one new object to move the island outside of the hatch boundary as shown on the right side of Figure 10.22B. Use transparent ZOOM to help as needed.
11. Erase the island from the other new object. Notice how the hatch pattern is "healed" where the island is erased.
12. Save the drawing as EX10.7.

✓ LEARNING CHECKPOINT

- ☐ List three ways to access the BHATCH command.
- ☐ Discuss two ways to change the Pattern Type in the Boundary Hatch dialog box.
- ☐ What does it mean when a hatch scale is set at 1XP?
- ☐ Briefly discuss the user-defined pattern type.
- ☐ Explain the purpose and importance of the hatch preview.

- Describe the difference between using the <u>P</u>ick Points< and the Select <u>O</u>bjects< buttons.
- What is an island?
- How does the <u>R</u>emove Islands< button work?
- Discuss the purpose of the Make <u>N</u>ew Boundary Set< button.
- List and describe the style options.
- What is the purpose of the Island <u>D</u>etection toggle?
- How does the <u>I</u>nherit Properties< button work?
- Define associative hatch pattern.
- Identify at least one major advantage of using associative hatching.

Drag-and-Drop Hatching with the Content Explorer

The Content Explorer provides a simple drag-and-drop interface for inserting hatch patterns into a drawing. In addition to inserting hatch patterns, the Content Explorer can also be used to insert symbols and externally referenced files into the current drawing. These topics are discussed in Chapters 12 and 13.

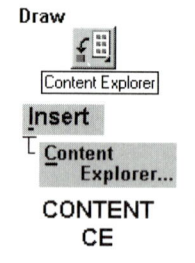

Draw
Content Explorer

Insert
Content Explorer...

CONTENT
CE

Accessing Hatch Patterns in the Content Explorer

To access the Content Explorer, pick Content Explorer ... from the Insert pulldown menu, pick the Content Explorer button on the Draw toolbar, or type CE or CONTENT at the Command: prompt. The CONTENT command displays the Content Explorer window on the right side of the screen, as shown in Figure 10.23.

FIGURE 10.23 The CONTENT command displays the Content Explorer window.

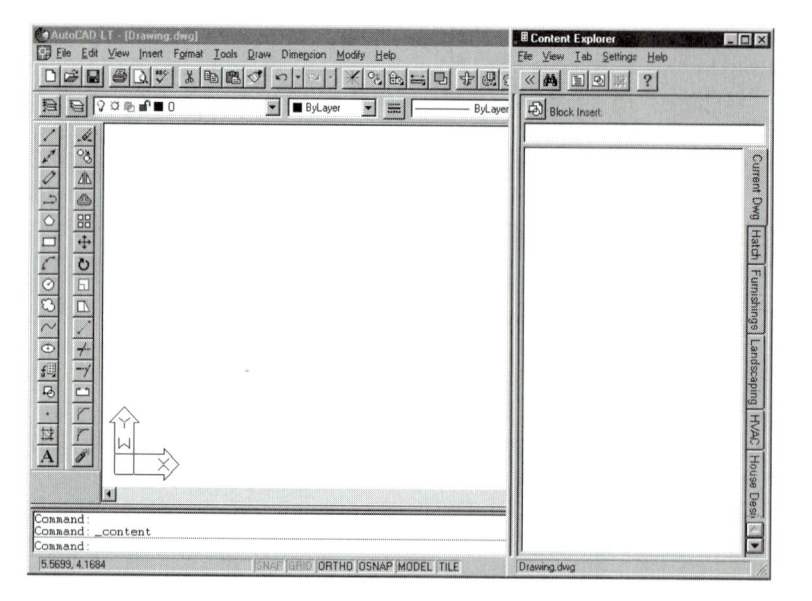

The Content Explorer displays a series of tabs along the right side that determine what type of content is displayed. To view the available hatch patterns, pick the tab labeled Hatch. Figure 10.24 shows the Content Explorer with the Hatch tab selected. You can use the scroll bar to view more patterns, or you can change the size of the Content Explorer window just as with any other program window. Notice that the current hatch pattern definition file is displayed on the status bar at the bottom. If the current drawing settings are for metric settings, the ACLTISO.PAT file definitions are used instead.

FIGURE 10.24 The Hatch tab of the Content Explorer window.

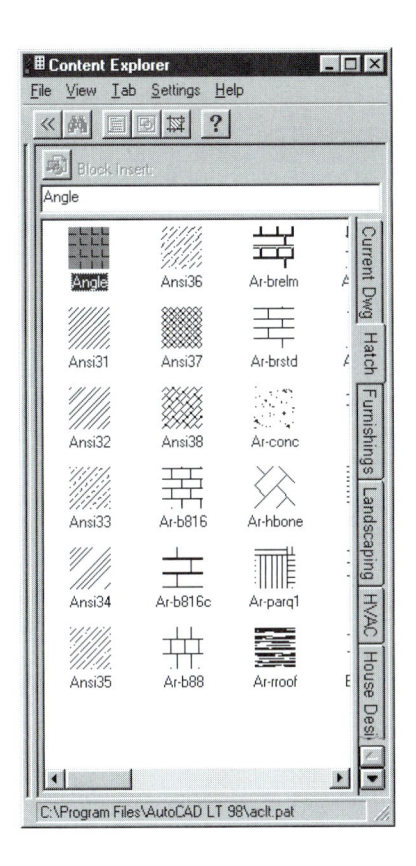

> ### Field Notes
>
> The current system of measurement is stored as the MEASUREMENT system variable. A setting of 0 means English measurements are being used, and a setting of 1 indicates metric settings. This variable controls which hatch pattern and linetype definition files are used for the current drawing. You can use any system variable just like a command. Type it at the Command: prompt to change its value.

To insert a hatch pattern in your drawing using the Content Explorer, find the pattern you want and do a standard Windows *drag-and-drop* operation. This means that you will point at the desired pattern, then press and hold the pick button. While holding the pick button, move the cursor to the location in your drawing where you want to *drop* the hatch pattern. When you move the cursor inside the AutoCAD LT program window, it is brought to the front of the display. Just as when hatching using the Pick Points option in the BHATCH command, you must pick your insertion point inside a closed boundary. Release the pick button to apply the hatch pattern using the current settings. Figure 10.25 shows a hatch pattern being dragged into position. The Content Explorer window has automatically been moved behind the AutoCAD LT window to allow access to the full drawing area. The prompt sequence is as follows:

```
Command: _.drginsert
Insertion point: ⟨release pick button inside boundary⟩
Selecting everything...
Selecting everything visible...
Analyzing the selected data...
Analyzing internal islands...
Command:
```

FIGURE 10.25 Dragging a hatch pattern into a drawing from the Content Explorer.

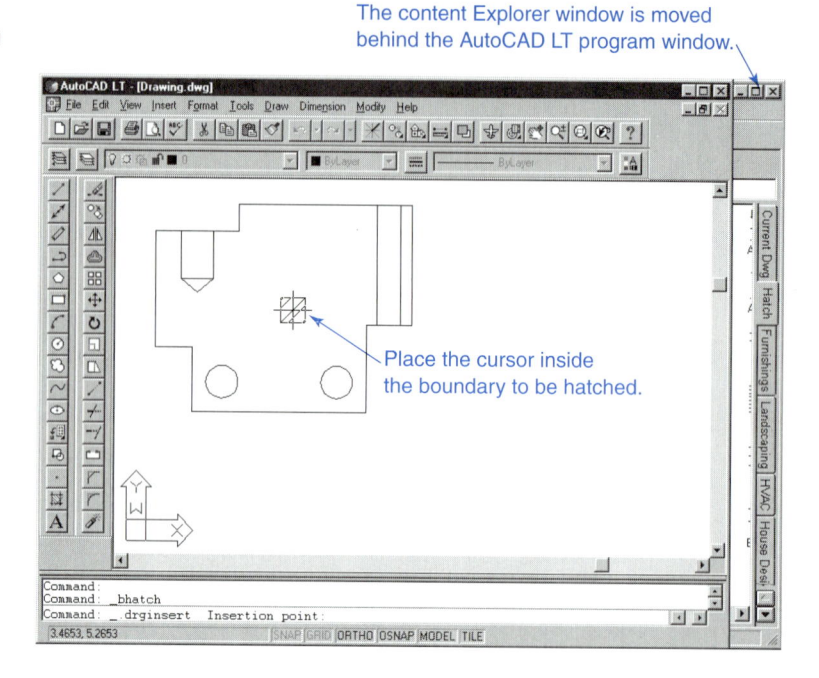

The content Explorer window is moved behind the AutoCAD LT program window.

Place the cursor inside the boundary to be hatched.

The command displayed on the command line is the DRGINSERT command. This command cannot be typed, nor can it be repeated by pressing Enter. If you press Enter, you will get whatever command you used just prior to the drag and drop. The only way to start this command is to drag an item out of the Content Explorer window.

When using the Content Explorer to insert hatch patterns, it is best to change the display so that the boundary for the new hatch pattern is visible on screen. Because this is a drag-and-drop style operation, the default behavior is to drop the pattern when you release the pick button. If the mouse button is released after a keyboard entry and before pressing Enter, the hatch pattern is not dropped. In this case, you must press the pick button to insert the pattern into the drawing. Therefore, if you want to enter a ZOOM command option, type the **'z** while still holding the pick button, and after you finish the display change, press the pick button to apply the hatch.

The section view in Figure 10.25 has two boundary areas that must be hatched to complete the view. In applications where you have multiple boundaries, you will need to repeat the drag and drop for each area that requires hatching. Optionally, you can set up the Content Explorer to allow multiple picks. This topic is discussed in the next section.

Setting Up Hatch Pattern Defaults in the Content Explorer

When you insert a hatch pattern from the Content Explorer, you are not prompted for the scale or rotation of the hatch pattern. These and other options must be set up prior to dragging the pattern into your drawing. To set up the Hatch defaults, pick the Hatch Properties… option from the Settings menu in Content Explorer, select the Hatch Properties button on the Content Explorer toolbar, or right-click on a hatch icon and pick the Hatch Properties… option. This displays the Hatch Settings dialog box, shown in Figure 10.26.

You have already been introduced to setting up the properties of a hatch pattern using the BHATCH command. Most of the options found in this dialog box are discussed earlier in this chapter. The options that are unique to this dialog box are as follows:

- **Multiple Pick Points**   When this option is checked, the hatching operation continues after you drop the first item. Each subsequent location must be picked individually. If this option is active, you will need to press Escape to return to the Command: prompt. This option can also be set on the popup cursor menu displayed when you right-click on a hatch pattern icon.

- **Regenerate Hatch Icons**   The icons displayed in the Content Explorer are, by default, regenerated each time you change the default hatch settings. They are updated to show changes in scale and rotation angle, so that you know what the pattern will look like before you apply it. Very large and very small scale factors will not be accurately displayed.

FIGURE 10.26 Setting up hatching defaults before hatching using the Hatch Settings dialog box.

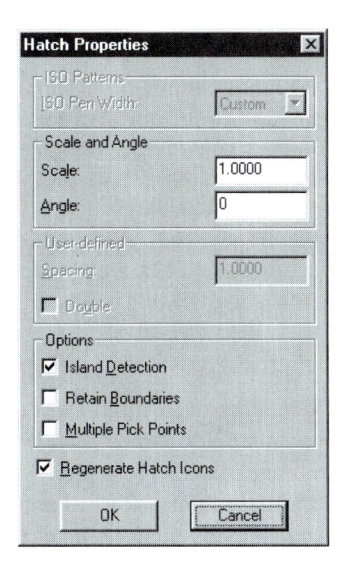

The popup cursor menu also provides an option to display the hatch pattern icons and names, or just the names. When just the names are displayed, regeneration of the icons is not required, and you will have fewer delays when hatching or adjusting hatch settings.

Another option for setting up your hatch pattern properties is to double-click on any pattern icon. This starts the BHATCH command with the selected pattern current. You can now make any adjustments desired and use the BHATCH command normally. Using this option does not allow the drag-and-drop method to be used.

Field Notes

The Content Explorer can also use custom hatch pattern definition files by accessing the Tree View. Accessing custom hatch patterns is discussed further in Chapter 17.

Exercise 10.8

1. Open EX10.7 for editing.
2. Erase the existing hatch pattern objects.
3. Rehatch the objects using the Content Explorer to drag and drop your patterns into place. Be sure to make the proper settings in the Hatch properties dialog box.
4. Save the drawing as EX10.8.

LEARNING CHECKPOINT

☐ Name the options for accessing the Content Explorer

☐ What is the command name displayed when dragging a hatch pattern into a drawing? What is unique about this command?

☐ How can you access the BHATCH command from the Content Explorer?

☐ What option allows for fewer delays when using the Content Explorer to access hatch patterns?

Using the HATCH Command

HATCH
-H

The HATCH command does not use a dialog box. Instead, its prompts are issued in the floating command window and the responses are entered at the keyboard. Hatch patterns drawn using the HATCH command are nonassociative. The HATCH command is less intuitive than BHATCH because its prompts are issued one at a time. You also cannot preview with the HATCH command and then go back and change values as you can with the BHATCH command. As you follow through the HATCH command prompts, you will see many of the same features identified earlier when using the BHATCH command. However, the HATCH command offers certain features that are not available when using BHATCH. The HATCH command can be accessed by typing **HATCH** or **-H**. This is a hyphen (-) typed before H. The HATCH command provides the following sequence of prompts:

Command: **-H** or **HATCH**↵
Enter pattern name or [?/Solid/User defined] <ANSI31>:

Notice that ANSI31 is the initial default hatch pattern type. You can accept this pattern type by pressing Enter or you can type one of the other pattern names. Appendix C shows the available standard hatch patterns and their names. You can also type **?** to specify particular pattern names, or press Enter again to accept the <*> wild card and get a list of the available patterns in a text window:

Enter pattern name or [?/Solid/User defined] <ANSI32>: **?**↵
Pattern(s) to list <*>: ↵

The AutoCAD LT Text Window is displayed with a listing of the names and short descriptions of all available standard hatch patterns. Close the text window when finished looking at the list. The Command: prompt returns after you look through the list of available pattern options. Reenter the HATCH command by pressing Enter and accept the default pattern, or type another pattern name and press Enter:

Command: ↵
Enter pattern name or [?/Solid/User defined]

The next prompt asks you for the pattern scale. Look back at Figure 10.8 and its related discussion on scale. Accept the default scale or enter a new value:

Scale for pattern <1.0000>: ↵

The next prompt requests a pattern angle. Review Figure 10.9 and the explanation about pattern angle:

Angle for pattern <0>: ↵

Next, you get the familiar Select objects: prompt. Use any of the AutoCAD LT selection options to select objects for hatching as shown in Figure 10.27:

Select hatch boundaries or press Enter for direct hatch options.
Select objects: ⟨*pick or select the objects for hatching*⟩
Select objects: ↵
Command:

CHAPTER 10 || Drawing Patterns and Section Lines   **405**

FIGURE 10.27 Selecting objects to hatch using the HATCH command.

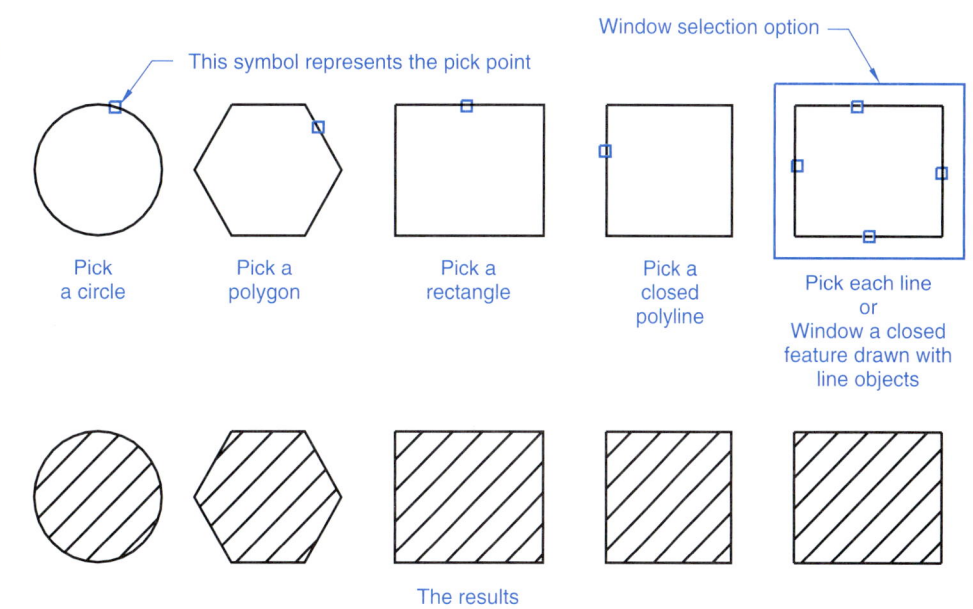

Pick a circle   Pick a polygon   Pick a rectangle   Pick a closed polyline   Pick each line or Window a closed feature drawn with line objects

This symbol represents the pick point

Window selection option

The results

Hatching Objects Solid

The Solid option of the HATCH command allows you to fill objects in solid. The results are the same as using the SOLID hatch pattern shown in the Hatch pattern palette in Figure 10.5. You can solid-hatch any closed object, such as those shown in Figure 10.27. You can also solid-hatch irregular-shaped objects such as the slot or polyline curves shown in Figure 10.28. The Solid option works like this:

> Command: **-H** or **HATCH** ↵
> Enter pattern name or [?/Solid/User defined] <ANSI31>: **S** ↵
> Select hatch boundaries or press Enter for direct hatch options.
> Select objects: ⟨*select the objects to hatch*⟩
> Select objects: ↵
> Command:

FIGURE 10.28 Using the Solid hatching pattern.

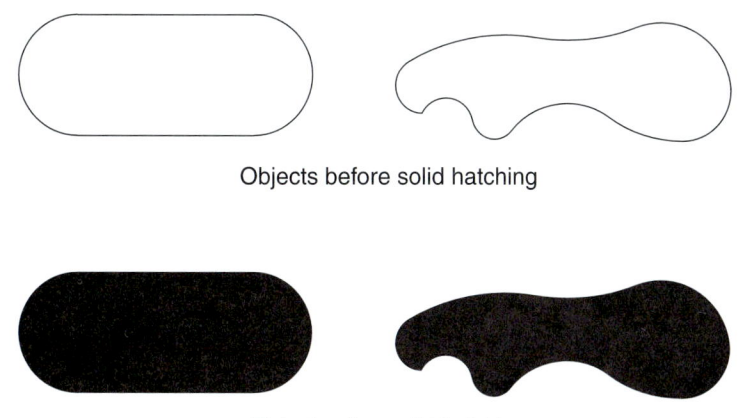

Objects before solid hatching

Objects after solid hatching

> ### Field Notes
>
> - When using the HATCH command, you should select individual objects such as circles, polygons drawn with the POLYGON command, rectangles drawn with the RECTANG command, or closed polylines. Any of these objects can be picked for hatching. Closed objects drawn with the LINE command require that you use one of the selection options such as Window or Crossing. Unexpected results can happen when selecting connected objects that are drawn with the LINE command. For example, if you try to hatch one side of two or more connected objects, the hatch lines can extend partly into the adjacent area. Do not worry if this happens. Undo the command and use the BHATCH command's Pick Points< button to hatch the desired area.
> - If you draw a hatch pattern and then immediately access the HATCH command by pressing Enter at the Command: prompt, AutoCAD LT takes you directly to the Select objects: prompt using the same hatch pattern from the previous command sequence.
> - If you hatch more than one separate object while inside the HATCH command, the hatch pattern for all the objects are modified together when using editing commands. To avoid this, hatch each object separately with its own HATCH command.

Exercise 10.9

1. Open a new drawing or use one of your prototypes.
2. Draw a circle, a hexagon, a rectangle using the RECTANG command, a closed polyline, and a closed rectangle using the LINE command. These should be similar to the objects shown at the top of Figure 10.27.
3. Hatch each object using the HATCH command. The results should be similar to those shown in the bottom part of Figure 10.27
4. Draw objects similar to the objects before hatching in Figure 10.28. Use arcs and lines to draw the slot, and use polyline arcs to draw the shape on the right. Be sure the objects are closed. Copy the objects below the original objects.
5. Use the Solid option of the HATCH command to solid-hatch the original two objects.
6. Use the BHATCH command SOLID pattern to hatch the other two objects.
7. Save the drawing as EX10.9.

Drawing User-Defined Hatch Patterns with the HATCH Command

The User-defined option in the Pattern Type area of the Boundary Hatch dialog box allows you to draw simple hatch pattern designs like those shown in Figure 10.12. You can also do this in the HATCH command with the User-defined option. The User-defined option allows you to establish a simple hatch pattern with hatch lines at a specified angle and spacing, and either single or double. These are the prompts:

Command: **-H** or **HATCH**↵
Enter pattern name or [?/Solid/User defined] <ANSI31>: **U**↵
Angle for crosshatch lines <0>: **45**↵
Spacing between lines <1.0000>: **.125**↵
Double hatch area? <N>: **Y**↵
Select hatch boundaries or press Enter for direct hatch options.
Select objects: ⟨select the objects to hatch⟩
Select objects: ↵
Command:

The results of the previous sequence are shown in Figure 10.29.

FIGURE 10.29 Creating a simple user-defined hatch pattern with the HATCH command.

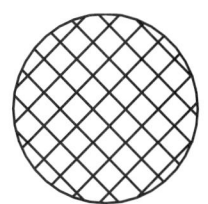

Using Direct Hatching with the HATCH Command

The HATCH command allows you to skip the Select objects: prompt and perform what is referred to as direct hatching. *Direct hatching* is used when you want to define a hatch boundary where the hatch pattern is to be placed, and then either keep the boundary or have it removed during the hatching process. You can use direct hatching to hatch individual areas within interconnected areas or for hatching where no boundary exists. AutoCAD LT reminds you that direct hatching is available by providing this message: "Select hatch boundaries or press Enter for direct hatch options." Press Enter at the Select objects: prompt to use the direct hatching feature. Any valid point entry method is acceptable, including osnap points, polar and relative coordinates, or direct distance entry:

> Command: **-H** or **HATCH**↵
> Enter pattern name or [?/Solid/User defined] <ANSI31>: ↵
> Scale for pattern <1.0000>: ↵
> Angle for pattern <0>: ↵
> Select hatch boundaries or press Enter for direct hatch options.
> Select objects: ↵

Next, AutoCAD LT asks if you want to keep the polyline boundary. Answer Y or N:

> Retain polyline? <N>: **Y**↵

Now you get prompts that allow you to draw a polyline boundary:

> From point: ⟨*pick the first point*⟩
> Arc/Close/Length/Undo/<Next point>: ⟨*pick the next point*⟩
> Arc/Close/Length/Undo/<Next point>: ⟨*pick the next point*⟩
> Arc/Close/Length/Undo/<Next point>: ⟨*pick the next point*⟩
> Arc/Close/Length/Undo/<Next point>: **C**↵

The Close option is used in the previous sequence to close the polyline boundary. Next, AutoCAD LT gives you a prompt that allows you to continue drawing additional polyline boundaries or to press Enter to apply the hatch:

> From point or press Enter to apply hatch: ↵
> Command:

The hatch is applied and the polyline boundary is kept as shown in Figure 10.30A. Figure 10.30B shows a footing detail with the earth hatch pattern drawn using direct hatch and without keeping the polyline boundary.

The other options found in direct hatching are described as follows:

Arc: This option allows you to draw a polyline arc using one of the PLINE arc options. Continue drawing arcs by picking the arc endpoints or by using one of the other options, or change to drawing straight polyline segments by entering the Line option. The prompts read like this when using the Arc option:

> From point: ⟨*pick the first point*⟩
> Arc/Close/Length/Undo/<Next point>: **A**↵
> Angle/CEnter/CLose/Direction/Line/Radius/Second pt/Undo/<Endpoint of arc>: ⟨*pick an arc endpoint or use another option*⟩
> Angle/CEnter/CLose/Direction/Line/Radius/Second pt/Undo/<Endpoint of arc>: **L**↵
> Arc/Close/Length/Undo/<Next point>: ⟨*pick a point*⟩
> Arc/Close/Length/Undo/<Next point>: **C**↵
> From point or RETURN to apply hatch: ↵
> Command:

FIGURE 10.30 (A) Using direct hatching with the polyline boundary. (B) Using direct hatching without the polyline boundary.

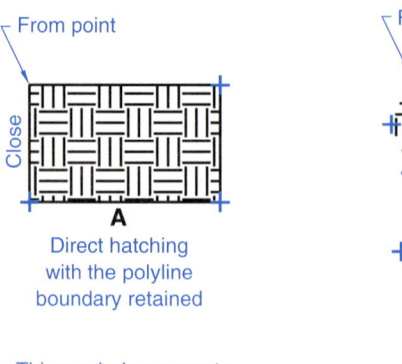

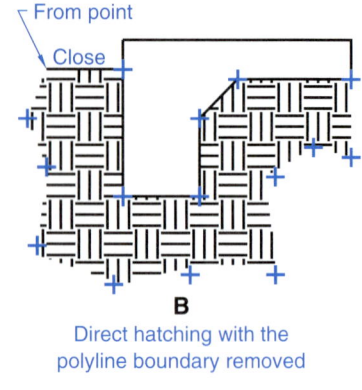

Refer to Chapter 8 for a complete review of the PLINE Arc options.

Close: The Close option is used by typing C and pressing Enter to close a polyline boundary.

Length: The Length option is used if you want to specify the length of a line in the last angle selected. If the previous segment was a line segment, the segment created using Length continues in the same direction. If the previous segment was an arc, the line segment drawn using Length continues at an angle tangent to the end of the arc segment. If the Length option is used on the first segment, the value stored in the LASTANGLE system variable is used.

Undo: The Undo option is available to let you undo the previous polyline element.

Exercise 10.10

1. Open a new drawing or use one of your prototypes.
2. Use direct hatching to draw the earth pattern inside of a polyline boundary similar to the one shown in Figure 10.30A.
3. Draw a footing detail without hatching similar to that shown in Figure 10.30B. Use direct hatching to hatch the earth symbol around the footing without the boundary displayed. The results should look like Figure 10.30B.
4. Save the drawing as EX10.10.

Field Notes

- If you draw more than one separate direct hatched area using the same HATCH command, all areas are treated as one when editing.
- You can draw a hatch pattern without a boundary using the direct hatching option of the HATCH command. You can also draw a hatch pattern within a boundary using either the HATCH or BHATCH command, and then erase the boundary if you want a pattern without a boundary displayed.

Drawing a Hatch Pattern with Individual Elements

When you use the HATCH command, the entire hatch pattern is a single block. You can also draw a hatch pattern where every element within the pattern is an individual object. This might be useful if you want to edit parts of the hatch pattern without affecting the entire pattern. To do this, enter the pattern name after an asterisk (*) like this:

Command: **-H** or **HATCH**↵
Enter pattern name or [?/Solid/User defined] <ANSI31>: ***ANSI31**↵

Now, continue drawing the hatch pattern as usual.

Existing hatch patterns can also be made into individual elements using the EXPLODE command. The EXPLODE command, which was introduced earlier, is accessed by typing **X** or **EXPLODE**, by picking Explode in the Modify pull-down menu, or by picking the Explode toolbar button. The command works like this:

Command: **X** or **EXPLODE**↵
Select objects: ⟨*pick the hatch pattern*⟩
Select objects: ↵
Command:

Modify

Explode

EXPLODE
X

When exploded, the hatch pattern loses its layer and color characteristics. The exploded hatch pattern is found on layer 0 and color BYBLOCK. Use Undo if you want to undo a previously used EXPLODE command.

Exercise 10.11

1. Open EX10.9.
2. Use the EXPLODE command on one of your hatch patterns.
3. Use the ERASE command by picking the exploded hatch pattern. Notice that each line of the hatch pattern is now an individual object.
4. Exit the drawing without saving, or save the drawing as EX10.11 if preferred by your instructor or supervisor.

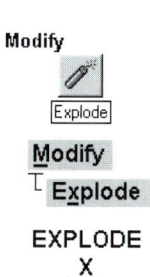

Hatching around Text

Text may be placed in an area that requires hatching. In these situations, you probably do not want the hatch pattern to run through the text. Text is hatched around when using the BHATCH command if the Style: is set to Normal or Outer and you use the Pick Points< button to pick between the boundary and the text. You can also use the Select Objects< button and select both the hatch boundary and the text. See Figure 10.31.

When using the HATCH command, you can hatch around text if you pick the object to be hatched then pick the text like this:

Command: **-H** or **HATCH**↵
Enter pattern name or [?/Solid/User defined] <ANSI31>: ↵
Scale for pattern <1.0000>: ↵
Angle for pattern <0>: ↵
Select hatch boundaries or press Enter for direct hatch options.
Select objects: ⟨*pick the object to hatch*⟩
Select objects: ⟨*pick the text*⟩
Select objects: ↵
Command:

Figure 10.31 illustrates the use of the BHATCH and HATCH commands to hatch around text.

FIGURE 10.31 Hatching around text.

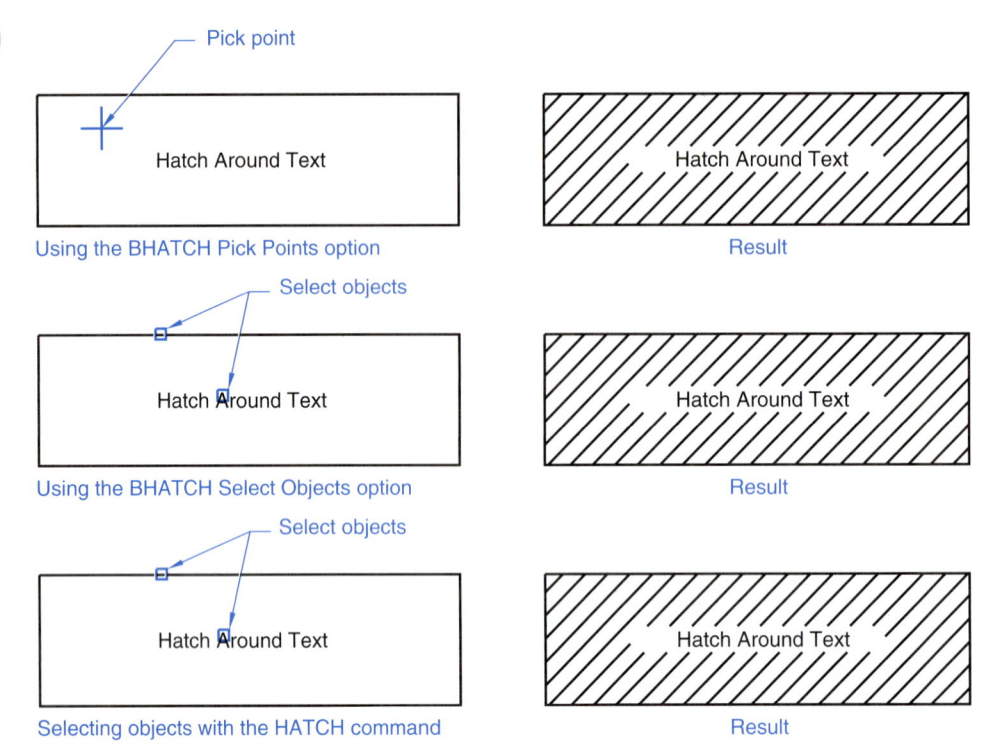

Pick point

Hatch Around Text

Using the BHATCH Pick Points option

Hatch Around Text

Result

Select objects

Hatch Around Text

Using the BHATCH Select Objects option

Hatch Around Text

Result

Select objects

Hatch Around Text

Selecting objects with the HATCH command

Hatch Around Text

Result

Field Notes

Now that you have learned how to use the BHATCH and HATCH commands, you might want to become familiar with the MaxHatch setting. This can be of value to help avoid exhausting your system resources by creating extremely large hatch patterns, or by specifying an extremely small scale for a complex hatch pattern in a very large area. This variable limits the number of objects that can be created by a single HATCH or BHATCH command. The value of this variable is used as the maximum number of objects that can be created to form a hatch pattern. If the hatch pattern parameters specified require more objects than indicated in MaxHatch, an error message is displayed and the pattern is not created. This variable can be set between 100 and 10,000,000. The default is 10,000. To change the value of the MaxHatch registry variable, use the SETENV command. Note that when you type the name of the variable to change, the variable is *case sensitive* and must be typed as MaxHatch.

Exercise 10.12

1. Open a new drawing or use one of your prototypes.
2. Draw three rectangles with the text "Hatch Around Text" in the middle of each rectangle. The drawings should be similar to the objects shown on the left side of Figure 10.31.
3. Hatch the first object using the BHATCH Pick Points< option.
4. Hatch the second object using the BHATCH Select Objects< option.
5. Hatch the third object using the HATCH command.
6. The results should be similar to the objects shown at the right in Figure 10.31.
7. Save the drawing as EX10.12.

☑ LEARNING CHECKPOINT

- ☐ List at least two key differences between the BHATCH and HATCH commands.
- ☐ How do you set a style option in the HATCH command?
- ☐ What is direct hatching?
- ☐ How do you tell AutoCAD LT to perform direct hatching with or without leaving the polyline boundary?
- ☐ What is the method used to instruct the HATCH pattern command to draw a hatch with individual elements?
- ☐ Identify two ways to hatch around text with the BHATCH command and at least one way with the HATCH command.

Editing Hatch Patterns and Using the HATCHEDIT Command

Any associative hatch pattern drawn using the BHATCH command can be edited along with any changes you make to the hatch boundary. For this to be true, the hatch pattern must have been drawn with the Associative toggle on. You can edit associative hatched objects with any of the grip editing commands or enter the COPY, MOVE, ROTATE, SCALE, and STRETCH commands before selecting the objects. You saw the effects of the STRETCH command on an associative and nonassociative hatch pattern in Figure 10.22A and the results of moving an island in an associative hatch pattern in Figure 10.22B. You can erase any hatched object just as you can any other object. When you are editing objects with hatch patterns, be sure that you select *only* the hatch boundary; do not select the hatch pattern.

Associative hatch pattern properties can be edited using the HATCHEDIT command. The HATCHEDIT command is accessed by typing **HE** or **HATCHEDIT** at the Command: prompt, by picking the Edit Hatch button in the Modify II toolbar, or by picking Hatch … in the Objects cascade of the Modify pull-down menu. This command asks you to select a hatch object:

Modify II
Edit Hatch
Modify
└ Object
  └ HATCH...
HATCHEDIT
HE

Command: **HE** or **HATCHEDIT**↵
Select hatch object: <*pick a hatch object*>

Selecting a hatch object opens the Hatch Edit dialog box shown in Figure 10.32. The Hatch Edit dialog box should look familiar to you because it is the same as the Boundary Hatch dialog box. The only difference from the Boundary Hatch dialog box is that the Boundary area selection buttons are not available. Notice in Figure 10.32 that these buttons are inactive. After selecting a hatch pattern, you can use the Hatch Edit dialog box to do any of the following edits:

- Change Pattern Type.
- Change the Pattern Properties in the Scale: and Angle: boxes. If a User-defined hatch pattern is selected, the Spacing: box and Double toggle become active.
- Use the Exploded toggle to explode the hatch pattern.
- Use the Inherit Properties< button to pick an existing hatch pattern for your selected hatch pattern to match.
- Turn off the Associative toggle. Associative is inactive if you pick a pattern drawn with the HATCH command.
- Pick the Advanced … button to open the Advanced Options dialog box. The only active features in the Advanced Options dialog box are the Bounday Style options. You can change the style and then pick the OK button.

After making all the desired changes in the Hatch Edit dialog box, pick the Preview Hatch < button to see if the results are what you expected. Pick the Apply button to apply the changes. The changes are now represented in the selected hatch pattern.

FIGURE 10.32 The Hatch Edit dialog box is accessed with the HATCHEDIT command.

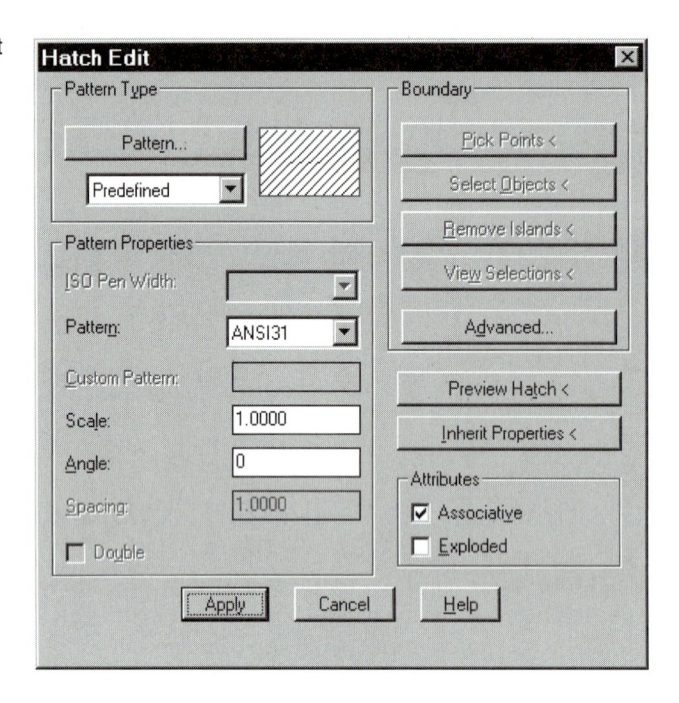

If you enter -HATCHEDIT at the Command: prompt, you get this:

Command: **-HATCHEDIT**↵
Select hatch object: ⟨*pick the hatch object to edit*⟩
Disassociate/Style/<Properties>**:**

The Disassociate option removes the associative quality from an associative hatch. The Style option allows you to change the hatch pattern style. Normal is the default, but you can use Ignore or Outer. Refer to Figure 10.21 for a review of these options. The Style prompt looks like this:

Disassociate/Style/<Properties>: **S** ↵
Ignore/Outer/<Normal>:

The Properties option allows you to specify new hatch properties using the keyboard. These are the familiar prompts when using the Properties option:

Enter pattern name or [?/Solid/User defined] <current pattern>**:** ↵
Scale for pattern <current>**:** ↵
Angle for pattern <current>**:** ↵
Command**:**

Exercise 10.13

1. Open EX10.5.
2. Use the HATCHEDIT command to change the pattern type to a different pattern for each object. Pick the Apply button.
3. Use the HATCHEDIT command to change the scale and angle of the pattern in each object to a different value. Pick the Apply button.
4. Use the HATCHEDIT command to change the object with the Ignore style to the Normal style. Pick the Apply button.
5. Save the drawing as EX10.13.

CHAPTER 10 ||| Drawing Patterns and Section Lines

☑ LEARNING CHECKPOINT

☐ What conditions must exist for a hatch pattern to change automatically when the hatch boundary is edited?

☐ Describe the difference between the Hatch Edit and Boundary Hatch dialog boxes.

☐ List at least six edits that can be made to a hatch pattern when using the HATCHEDIT command.

MULTIPLE CHOICE

Circle the choice or enter your response on an answer sheet by selecting the option that most closely completes or answers the given statements.

1. This term is used to describe the variety of patterns that can be used to fill in areas of your drawing:
   a. patterns
   b. symbols
   c. hatch
   d. library

2. These patterns are automatically changed when the boundary is edited:
   a. associative
   b. change
   c. update
   d. modify

3. The shape that encloses the hatch pattern:
   a. polyline
   b. boundary
   c. border
   d. outline

4. This command allows you to draw associative hatch patterns:
   a. HATCH
   b. BHATCH
   c. BHAT
   d. STYLE

5. Use this button if you want to look at the hatch pattern before applying it to the drawing:
   a. Inherit Properties<
   b. Preview Hatch<
   c. View Selections<
   d. Select Objects<

6. This is an enclosed area within a hatch area:
   a. island
   b. object
   c. boundary
   d. space

7. When this command is used, the hatch pattern is nonassociative:
   a. BHATCH
   b. EXPLODE
   c. HATCH
   d. DETACH

8. This terminology is used to describe the process of placing a hatch pattern by defining the boundary and either keeping or removing the boundary:
   a. direct hatch
   b. boundary definition
   c. boundary hatch
   d. polyline boundary

9. Use the HATCH command to draw a hatch pattern with its individual elements displayed by entering the hatch name like this:
   a. -ANSI31
   b. +ANSI31
   c. <ANSI31>
   d. *ANSI31

10. This command is used to edit existing hatch patterns:
    a. HEDIT
    b. HATCHEDIT
    c. EDITHATCH
    d. HATCHED

MATCHING

Match each term to the correct description by writing the appropriate number in each box at the left.

- ☐ Associative
- ☐ BHATCH
- ☐ Boundary
- ☐ Boundary set
- ☐ Direct
- ☐ HATCH
- ☐ HATCHEDIT
- ☐ Island
- ☐ Preview
- ☐ Solid
- ☐ Style
- ☐ User-defined

1. This hatch pattern allows you to fill objects.
2. This command is used to draw associative hatch patterns.
3. This command is used to change existing hatch patterns.
4. This option allows you to create simple hatch patterns.
5. These hatch patterns are automatically changed when the hatch boundary is edited.
6. This allows you to look at the hatch pattern before it is applied to the drawing.
7. This command is used to draw hatch patterns at the keyboard.
8. This is a closed feature within a hatch boundary.
9. This is the shape that encloses the hatch pattern.
10. This hatch option is used when you want to define a hatch boundary and either keep or remove the boundary when done.
11. This option is used to determine how internal features are hatched.
12. This is the object that AutoCAD LT analyzes when you pick a point.

WORD SCRAMBLE

Unscramble the five scrambled words below, one letter to each square, to form five AutoCAD LT–related words:

RBYODUAN

TAHHC

EIVPWER

AESLC

ADINLS

Unscramble the circled letters to the left to form the special answer, as suggested by the illustration.

PROJECTS

Set up the following drawing projects with layers that relate to the type of drawing as outlined and discussed in Chapter 5.

10.1 Collar

Given the pictorial drawing of the object below, draw a front view and half sectional view. Do not draw dimensions. Save as P10.1.

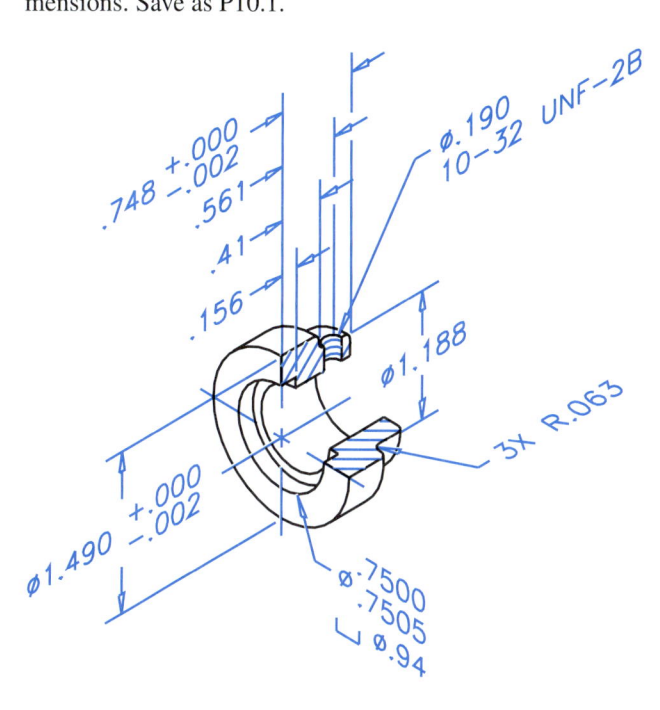

10.2 Pipe Connector

Given the pictorial drawing of the object below, draw a front and top view and a full sectional view. Do not draw dimensions. Save as P10.2. (Note: Only half of the object is shown in the pictorial.)

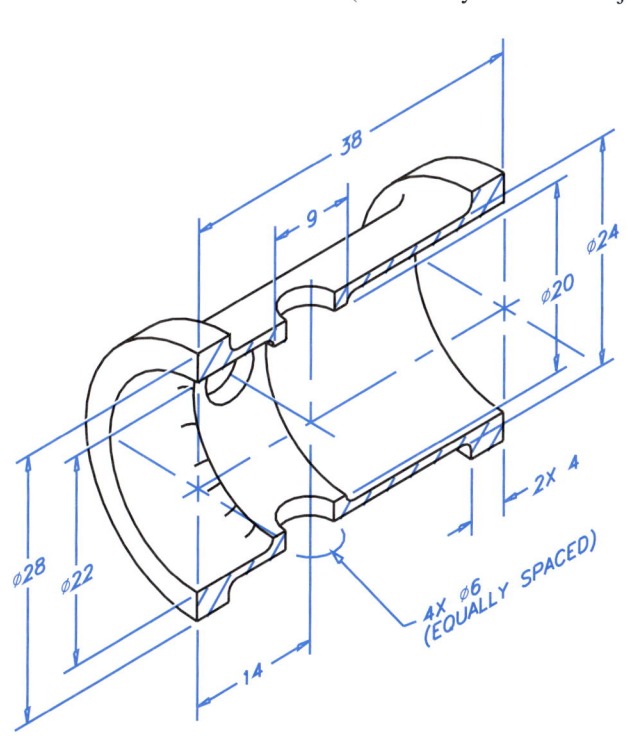

10.3 Arm

Given the pictorial drawing of the object below, draw a front and side view and a revolved section. Do not draw dimensions. Save as P10.3.

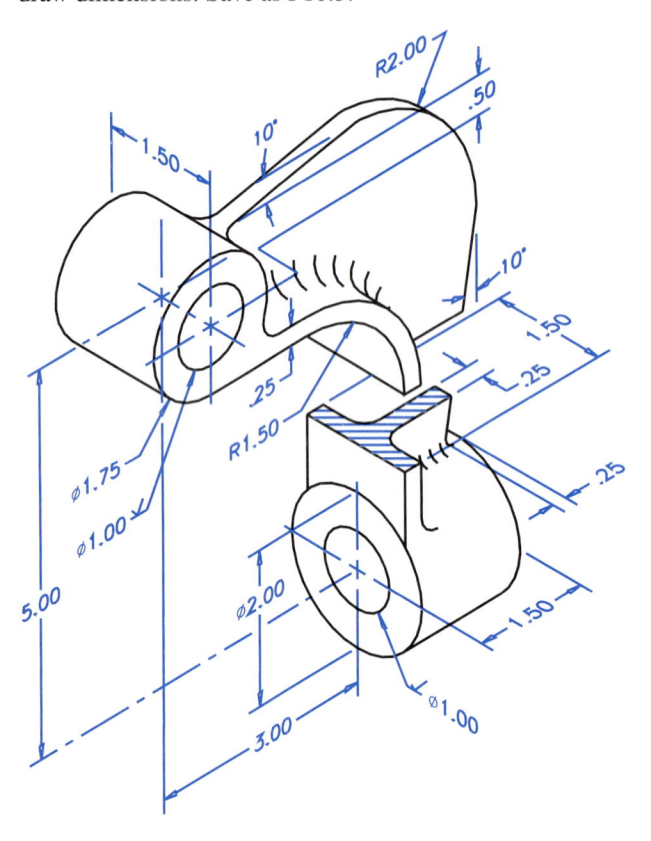

CHAPTER 10 ||| Drawing Patterns and Section Lines 417

10.4 Spur Gear
Draw the views of the gear and provide the spur gear data chart. Do not draw dimensions. Save as P10.4.
Note: Make undimensioned features approximate for students who have not studied gears and gear formulas.

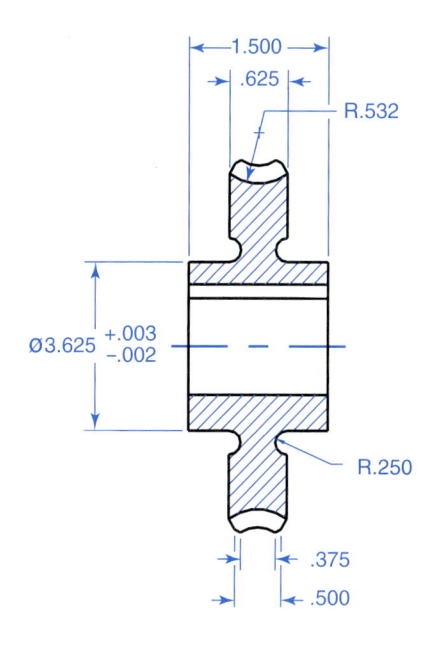

INCH

SECTION A–A

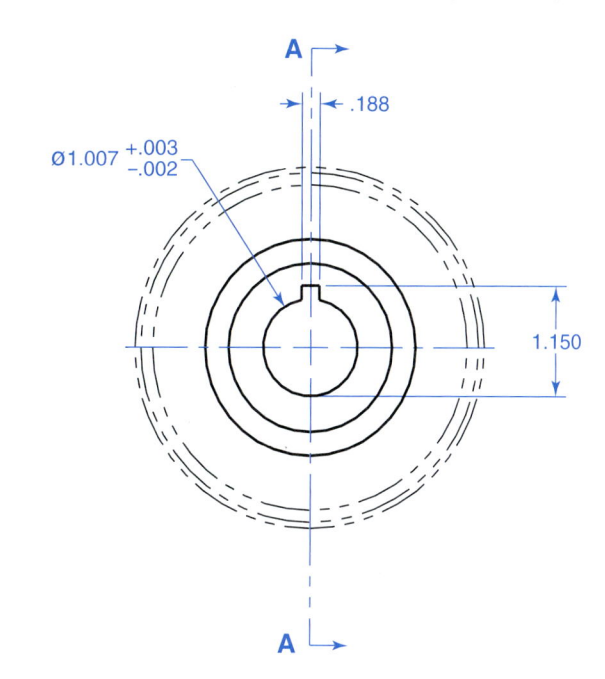

SPUR GEAR DATA	
DIAMETRAL PITCH	8
NUMBER OF TEETH	27
PRESSURE ANGLE	20°
PITCH DIAMETER	3.375
BASE CIRCLE DIAMETER	3.6187
CIRCULAR PITCH	.3927
CIRCULAR THICKNESS	.1964
ROOT DIAMETER	3.125

10.5 Draw the structural detail without dimensions and notes. Save as P10.5.

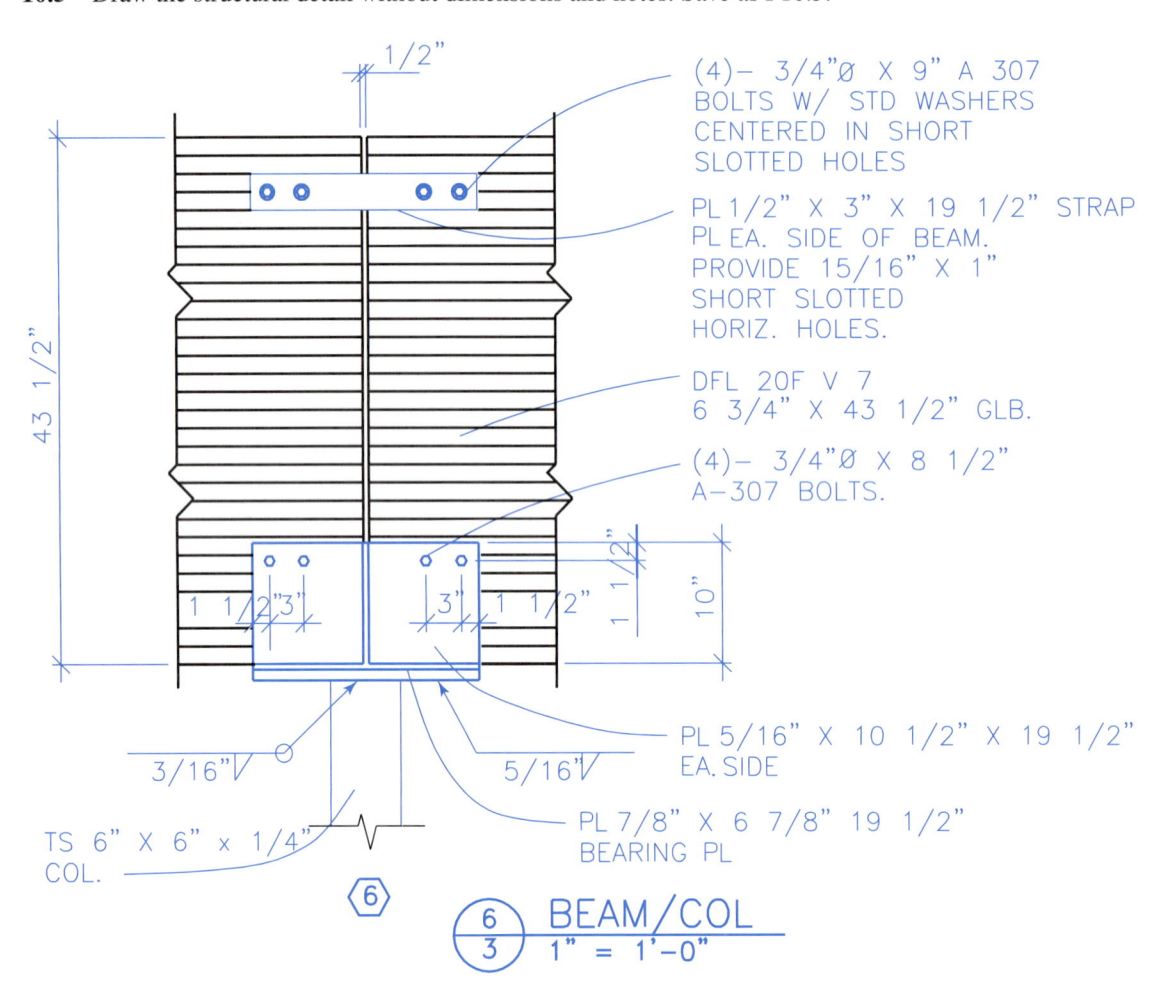

10.6 Draw the floor plan symbols without notes. Save as P10.6. (Note: Use similar symbols if the exact representation is not available.)

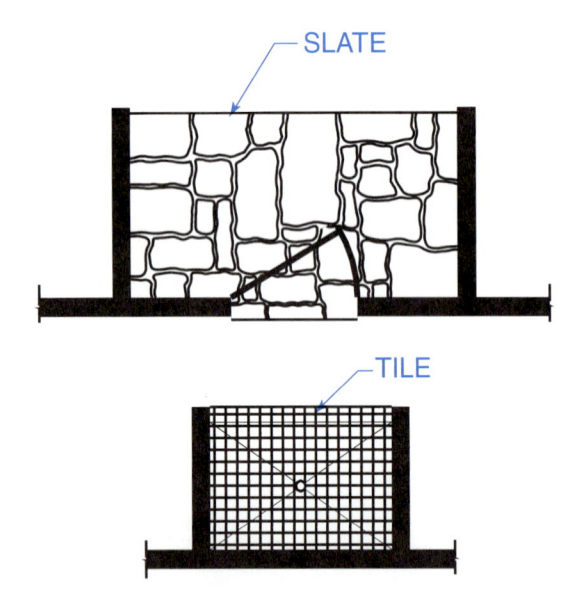

10.7 Draw the floor plan fireplace without notes or dimensions. Save as P10.7.

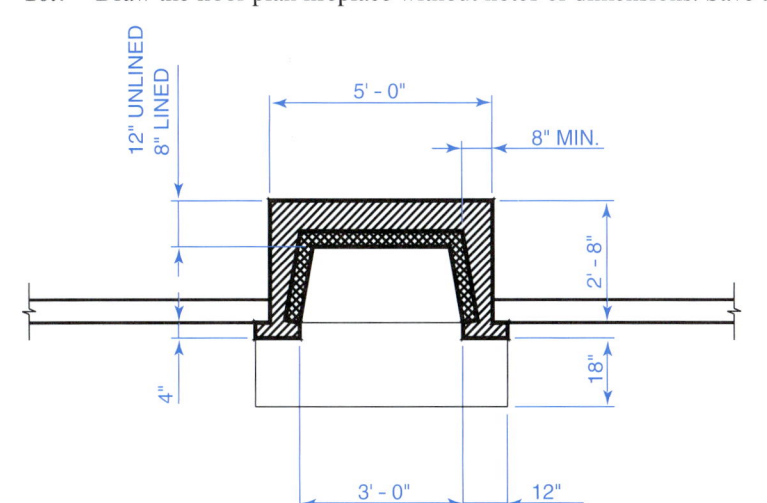

10.8 Draw the elevation shown below. The exact dimensions are up to you. Save as P10.8.

10.9 Design a company logo similar to the one shown below. Use the CityBlueprint or Stylus BT font. Save as P10.9.

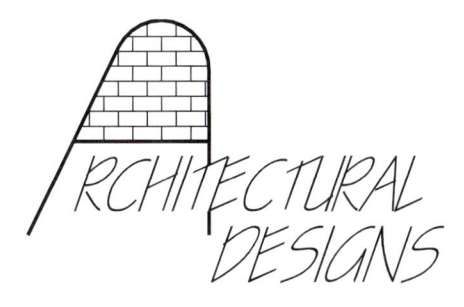

10.10 Draw the bar graph shown below. Use the ROMANS and ROMAND fonts. Save as P10.10.

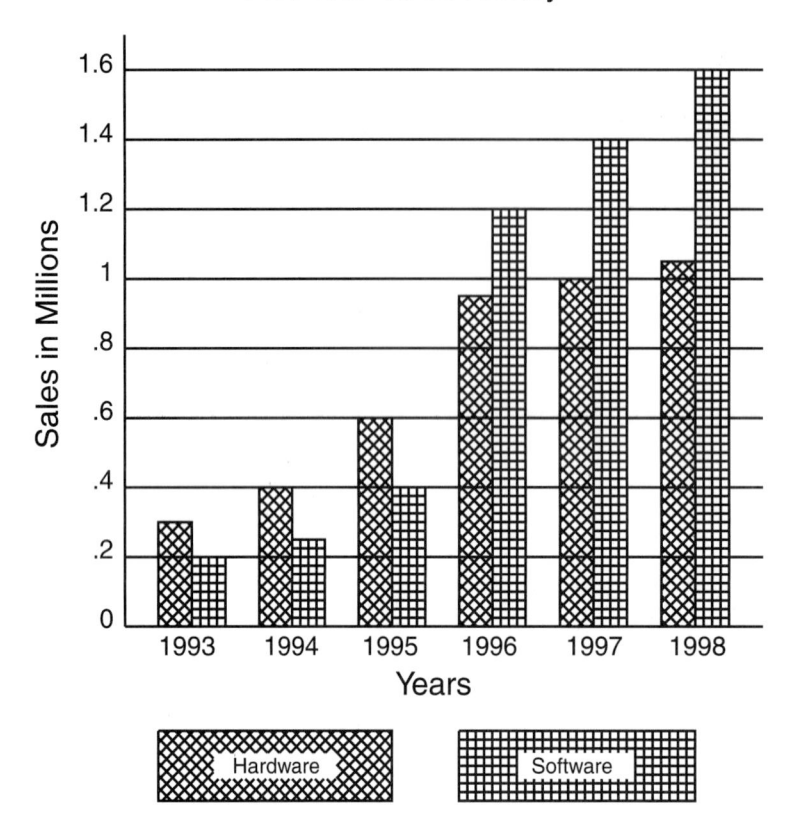

10.11 Design one of the holes for a golf course. Include the same features shown in the following proposal. Label each area with CityBlueprint or Stylus BT font. Be sure the hatch patterns do not cross the text. Save the drawing as P10.11.

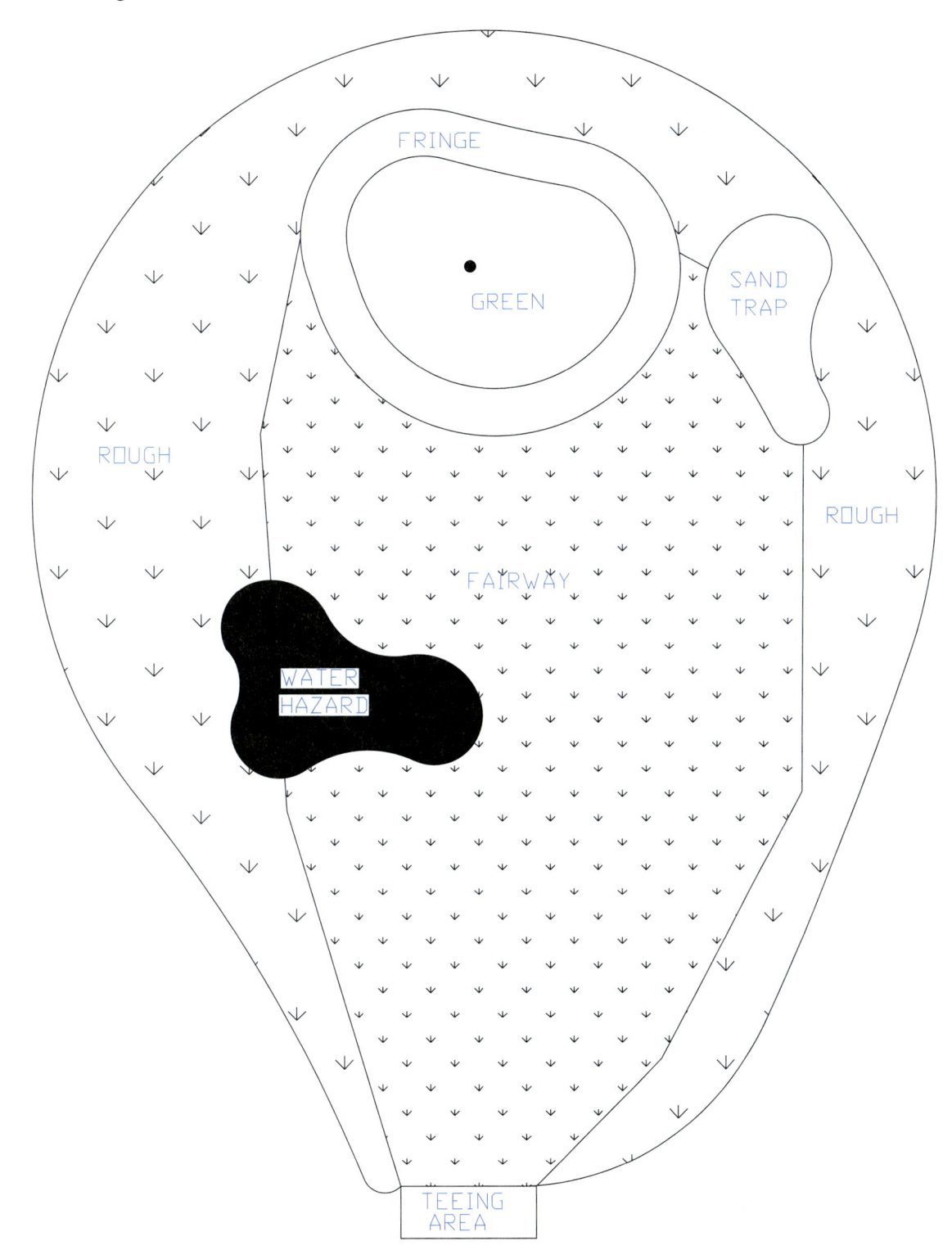

10.12 Design a landscaping plan similar to the following example. Include all the same characteristics, linetypes, hatch patterns, and shapes. Include the legend and display all text. Use CityBlueprint or Stylus BT font. Save the drawing as P10.12.

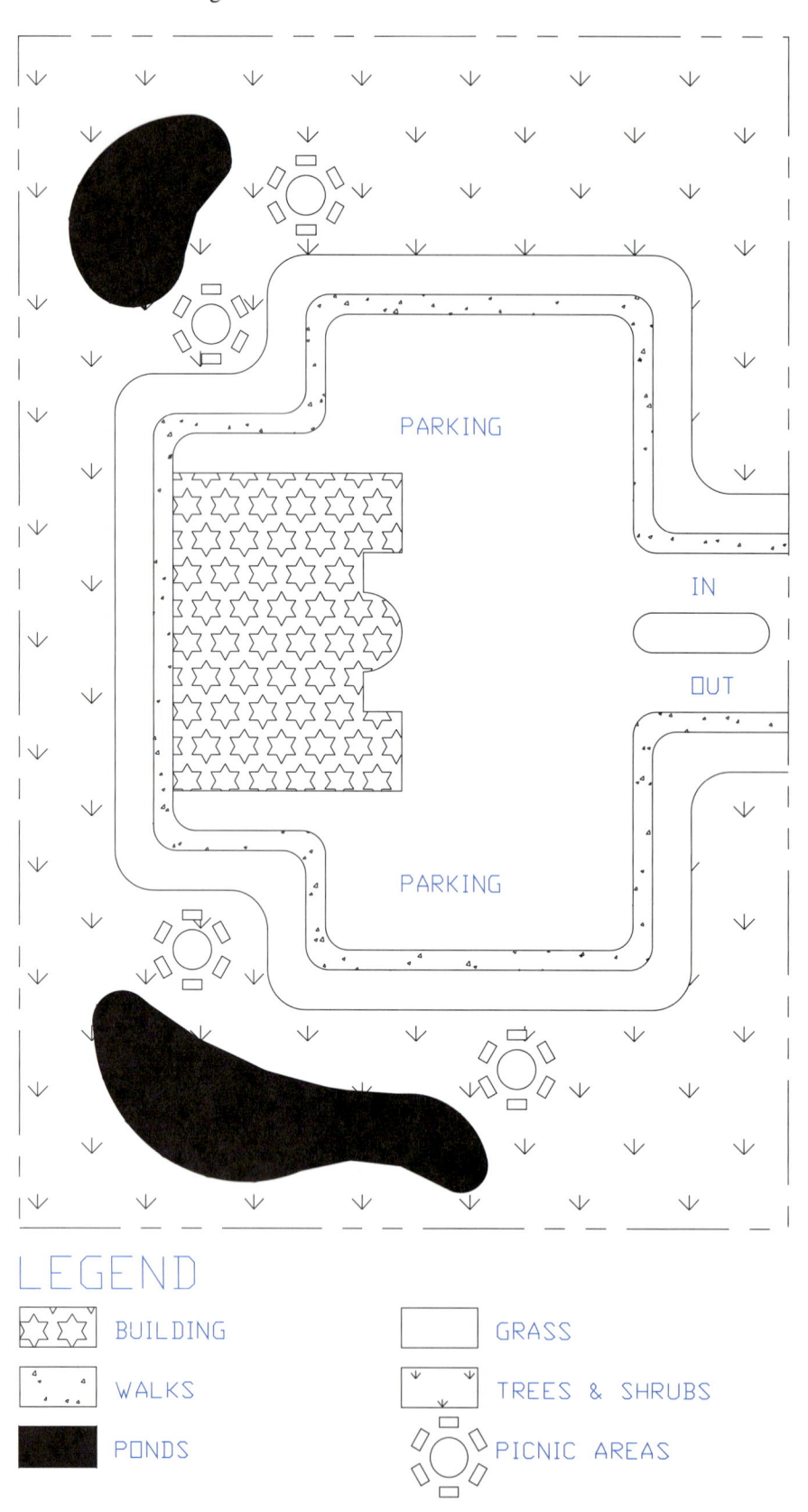

CHAPTER 11

Dimensioning a Drawing

LEARNING GOALS

- Draw linear dimensions.
- Select objects for direct dimensioning.
- Create chain and datum dimensions.
- Draw dimensions on slanted objects and angles.
- Dimension circles and arcs.
- Create arrowless (ordinate) dimensions.
- Manage dimension styles for your applications.
- Change dimension variables.
- Set tolerance values with dimension text.
- Draw a geometric tolerance symbol.
- Establish prefixes and suffixes with dimension text.
- Draw leader lines and notes.
- Edit existing dimensions.
- Change the variables of existing dimensions.
- Perform dimensioning at the command line.

So far, you have learned how to draw and edit objects, place text on a drawing, and prepare sections and other graphic designs. Drawings for manufacturing, architecture, construction, and other fields are usually incomplete without dimensions. *Dimensions* are defined as numerical values expressed in appropriate units of measure and indicated on a drawing and in other documents. Dimension numerals are placed along with lines, symbols, and notes to define the size and geometric or construction characteristics of a feature, part, or construction process or building component. Dimension numerals in mechanical manufacturing drafting are given in decimal inches or in metric units of millimeters. Mechanical drafting usually uses *unidirectional dimensioning,* in which all of the dimension numerals are placed horizontally and read from the bottom of the sheet. Dimensions in architectural drafting are given in feet and inches or in millimeters or meters. Civil drafting projects for mapping often use feet and decimal feet or metric units in millimeters, meters, and kilometers. Architectural, structural, and civil drafting usually use *aligned dimensioning,* in which text for horizontal dimensions is placed horizontally and reads from the bottom of the sheet, text for vertical dimensions is placed vertically and reads from the right side of the sheet, and dimensions placed at an angle have the text placed at the same angle. Electronic drafting projects use either decimal inches or millimeters and use either unidirectional or aligned dimensioning.

Dimensions fall into two types, size dimensions and location dimensions. *Size dimensions* are used to provide the measurements for the size of features and objects. *Location dimensions* are used to locate features and objects. Notes are also placed on drawings. *Notes* are not normally part of the dimensions but they may contain dimensional information. The two types of notes are general notes and specific notes. *General notes* supply information that applies to the entire drawing. *Specific notes,* also known as local notes, apply to specific features on the drawing and may be connected to the feature with a leader line.

Dimensioning standards for mechanical manufacturing drafting are recommended by the American Society of Mechanical Engineers in the document ASME Y14.5M-1994, *Dimensioning and Tolerancing.* Examples of many dimensioning standards and practices are displayed in Appendix B of this text. Dimensioning practices for architectural, structural, electronic, and precision sheet metal drafting applications are different from mechanical drafting and all practices are discussed throughout this chapter.

AutoCAD LT provides powerful dimensioning capabilities for two-dimensional drawings. AutoCAD LT allows you to dimension linear and angular features as well as circles and arcs with diameter and radius dimensions. AutoCAD LT also lets you draw ordinate dimensions that are sometimes referred to as *arrowless dimensions.* Ordinate dimensions are drawn without the traditional dimension lines and arrowheads. Figure 11.1A shows dimension elements using traditional dimensioning, and Figure 11.1B is an example of ordinate dimensioning.

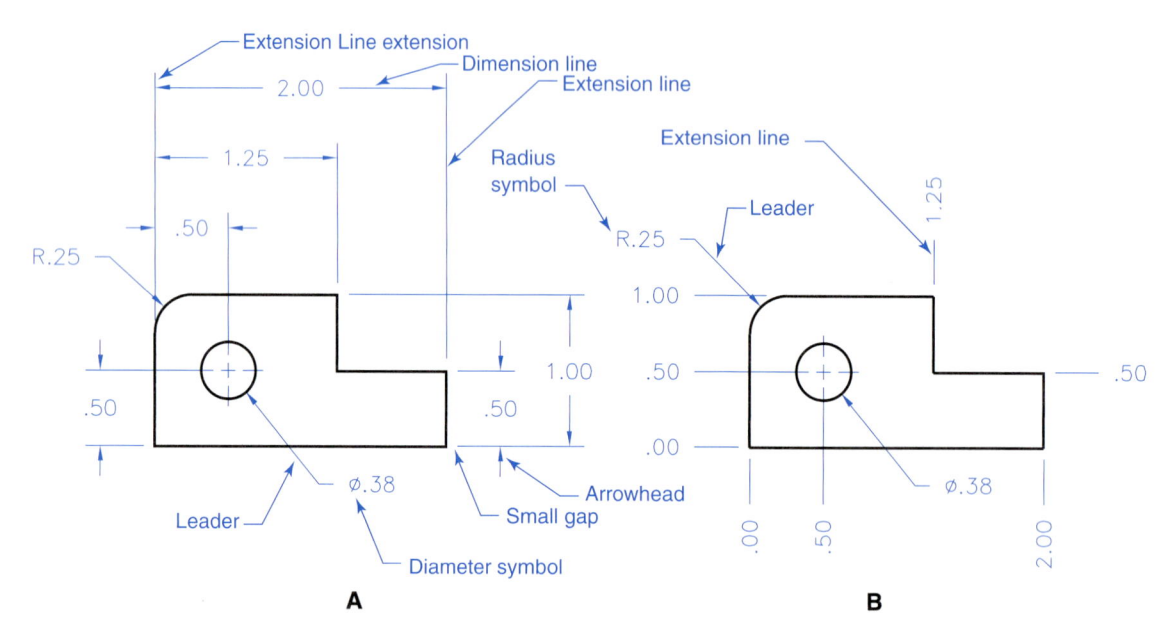

FIGURE 11.1 Basic dimensioning elements and practices. (A) Traditional dimension placement with extension and dimension lines having arrowheads. (B) Ordinate dimensioning, also known as arrowless dimensioning because there are no dimension lines and arrowheads.

The dimensioning variables can be set to control the way dimensions are presented. For example, you can control the size of the gap where the extension line meets the object, the arrowhead size and type, and the text style, height, and position.

This chapter shows you how to create dimension styles which contain the settings that are used on the types of drawings done at your school or company.

Field Notes

- When you dimension objects with AutoCAD LT, the objects are automatically measured exactly as you have drawn them. This makes it important for you to draw the original geometry accurately.
- Use the object snaps to your best advantage when dimensioning. AutoCAD LT dimensioning practices require that you locate features such as the extension line origin. This is accurately accomplished if you use an object snap such as INTersection. Setting the appropriate object snaps is a good idea when dimensioning.
- You should organize dimensions on a specific layer with an appropriate name and color suitable to your industry application.

Creating Dimensions

AutoCAD LT has a large variety of dimensioning capabilities that fall into five basic categories: linear, angular, diameter, radius, and ordinate.

> **Field Notes**
>
> Loading and docking toolbars was covered in Chapter 1. As a reminder, display the Dimension toolbar by picking T_oolbars... from the _V_iew pull-down menu. This opens the Toolbars dialog box. Check the Dimension box and pick the _C_lose button.

Drawing Linear Dimensions

Linear dimensions are placed in a straight line that can be horizontal, vertical, or at an angle. Linear dimensions can be drawn by picking the Linear button in the Dimension toolbar, picking _L_inear from the Dime_n_sion pull-down menu, or by typing **DLI** or **DIMLINEAR** at the Command: prompt. When drawing linear dimensions, AutoCAD LT asks you to pick the first and second extension line origins followed by the dimension line location as shown in Figure 11.2. The command sequence works like this:

Command: **DLI** or **DIMLINEAR** ↵
First extension line origin or press Enter to select: ⟨*pick the first extension line origin*⟩
Second extension line origin: ⟨*pick the second extension line origin*⟩
Dimension line location (Mtext/Text/Angle/Horizontal/Vertical/Rotated): ⟨*pick the dimension line location*⟩
Dimension text = 2.25
Command:

Dimension

Linear Dimension

Dimension
└ Linear

DIMLINEAR
DLI

FIGURE 11.2 Placing linear dimensions with the DIMLINEAR command.

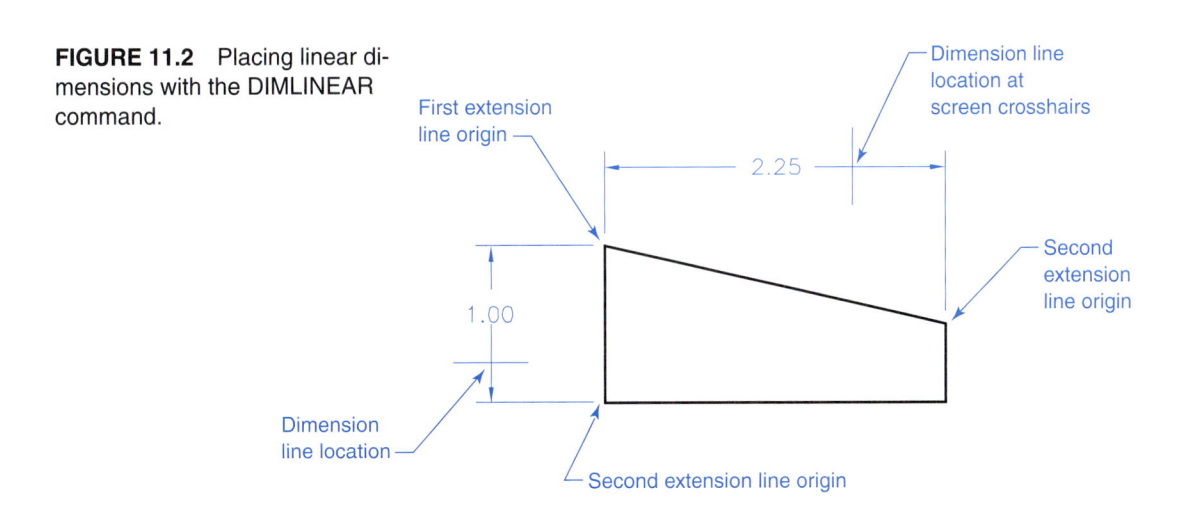

When you select the dimension line location, AutoCAD LT automatically centers the dimension text in a space provided in the dimension line. Later in this chapter you will learn how to place the text offset from center or above the dimension line for specific applications.

The First extension line origin can be on either end of a horizontal or vertical dimension. This is true unless the space between the extension lines is too small to accept the numeral with dimension line and arrowheads. When this happens, the First extension line origin establishes where the text is placed, as shown in Figure 11.3.

FIGURE 11.3 Placing linear dimensions in limited places. The First extension line origin determines the location of the dimension text.

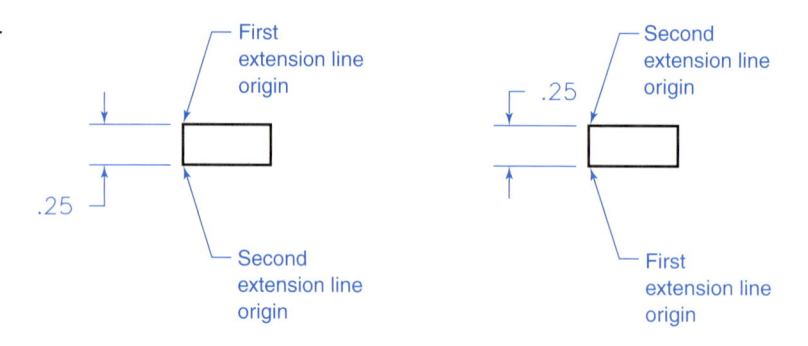

Exercise 11.1

1. Begin a new drawing or use one of your prototypes.
2. Draw an object and place a horizontal and vertical linear dimension similar to Figure 11.2.
3. Draw and dimension two objects similar to Figure 11.3.
4. Save the drawing as EX11.1.

Selecting Objects to Dimension

The DIMLINEAR command can also be used to select objects for automatic dimensioning without picking the extension line origins. To do this, press the Enter key when you see the "First extension line origin or press Enter to select:" prompt. You then get a Select objects prompt and a pick box for you to select the desired object on which to locate the dimension line and approve the dimension text or enter a new dimension numeral. Figure 11.4 shows this method being used to quickly dimension objects. The command sequence works like this:

Command: **DLI** or **DIMLINEAR**↵
First extension line origin or press Enter to select: ↵
Select object to dimension: ⟨pick the object⟩
Dimension line location (Mtext/Text/Angle/Horizontal/Vertical/Rotated): ⟨pick the dimension line location⟩
Dimension text = 1.00 ↵
Command:

FIGURE 11.4 Dimensioning objects directly by pressing Enter to select objects to dimension option of the DIMLINEAR command.

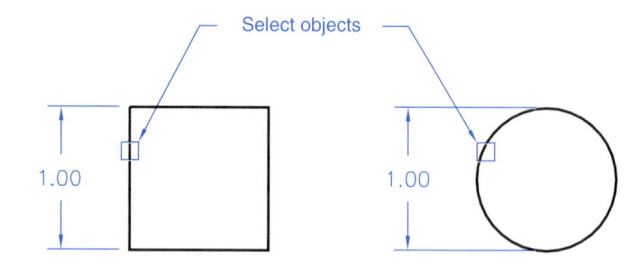

Exercise 11.2

1. Begin a new drawing or use one of your prototypes.
2. Draw two objects and place a horizontal or vertical linear dimension similar to that shown in Figure 11.4 by pressing Enter to select object option of the DIMLINEAR command.
3. Save the drawing as EX11.2.

Using the Other DIMLINEAR Options

The DIMLINEAR command has options that allow you to change the dimension text value, change the text angle, place the dimension either only horizontally or vertically, or place the dimension line at a desired angle other than horizontal or vertical. The options are found in the "Dimension line location (Mtext/Text/Angle/Horizontal/Vertical/Rotated):" prompt. The following discussion explains each of the DIMLINEAR options:

Mtext—Type **M** and press Enter to use the Mtext option. Doing this opens the Multiline Text Editor shown in Figure 11.5. When this dialog box opens, the text cursor is in front of angle bracket (<>) symbols, which represent the default text. The default text is the actual distance between the extension lines. If you want to place a diameter symbol in front of the current text, open the Symbol list and pick Diameter or type the symbol code %%c. If you want to add the abbreviation MAX after the current text, move the text cursor following the angle brackets and type MAX. If you want to change the value, remove the angle brackets and type a new text value. You can also make any other changes available in the Multiline Text Editor. Pick the OK button when done. Figure 11.6 shows the objects from Figure 11.4 with text changes. Refer to Chapter 9 for additional information about using the Multiline Text Editor.

FIGURE 11.5 The Multiline Text Editor is accessed when using the Mtext option of the DIMLINEAR command. Use the cursor to enter additional text or change the current text. The angle brackets (<>) represent the current text.

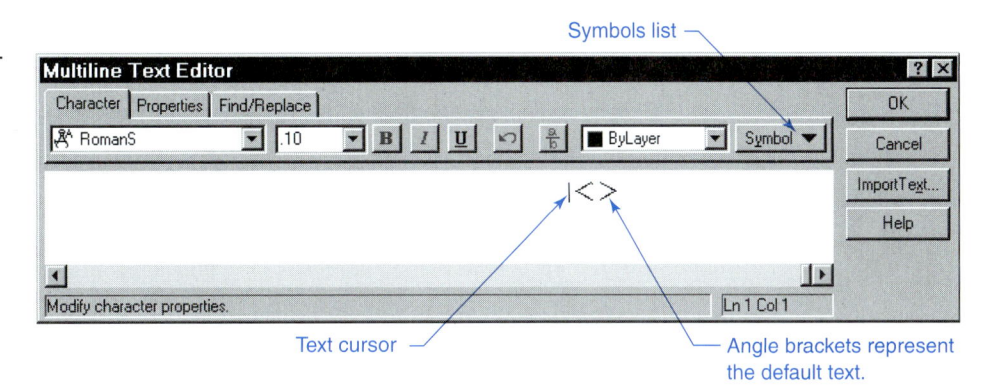

Text—Type **T** and press Enter to change dimension text at the prompt line. When you do this, AutoCAD LT identifies the current measurement in angle brackets. You can accept this value by pressing Enter, or you can type something else. For example, you can type angle brackets followed by MAX to have the current value placed in the drawing with the abbreviation MAX. Typing angle brackets keeps the current value, as shown in the following sequence:

Command: **DLI** or **DIMLINEAR** ↵
First extension line origin or press Enter to select: ⟨*pick the first extension line origin*⟩
Second extension line origin: ⟨*pick the second extension line origin*⟩
Dimension line location (Mtext/Text/Angle/Horizontal/Vertical/Rotated): **T** ↵
Dimension text <1.00>: **MAX** ↵
Dimension line location (Mtext/Text/Angle/Horizontal/Vertical/Rotated): ⟨*pick the dimension line location*⟩
Dimension text = 1.00
Command:

Type a different value if desired. To enter a symbol, such as diameter, type the control code. The control code for diameter is %%c. Refer to Chapter 9 for a refresher.

FIGURE 11.6 Using the Mtext option of the DIMLINEAR command to add text to the current value. The diameter symbol is added to the circle dimension.

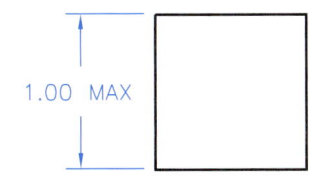

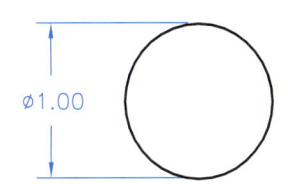

Field Notes

It is a good idea to leave the angle brackets as part of the dimension text when using the Mtext or Text options, because the angle brackets represent the default text. This is what maintains the associative nature of the dimension. If you want the flexibility of being able to edit dimensioned objects later, then they need to remain associative. Associative dimensions are automatically updated to match the change. Editing dimensions is discussed later in this chapter.

Angle—Type **A** and press Enter to use the Angle option. This option allows you to change the text angle as shown in Figure 11.7. For example, if you want to change the text angle from the horizontal default to 45°, type **45** when asked for the text angle and press Enter like this:

  Dimension line location (Mtext/Text/Angle/Horizontal/Vertical/Rotated): **A**↵
  Enter text angle: **45**↵
  Dimension line location (Mtext/Text/Angle/Horizontal/Vertical/Rotated): ↵
  Command:

A 45° text angle might not be commonly used, but rotating the text 90° is a typical application.

FIGURE 11.7 Using the Angle option of the DIMLINEAR command to place the text at an angle.

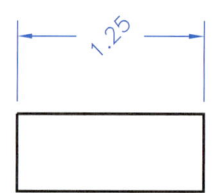

Horizontal or Vertical—AutoCAD LT interprets linear dimensions as being either vertical or horizontal by the distance from the origin to the dimension line. If the distance from the origin to the dimension line location is greatest on the Y axis, the dimension is interpreted to be horizontal. If the X axis distance is farther, the dimension is interpreted as vertical. You can see this work by moving the cursor to different locations as you drag the dimension line. If the default interpretation does not represent the type of dimension that you want to create, the Horizontal or Vertical option can be used to specify the type of dimension you want. To do this, type either **H** or **V**, as desired, and press Enter. AutoCAD LT then asks you to pick the dimension line location and also provides the Text and Angle options again in case you need them:

  Dimension line location (Mtext/Text/Angle/Horizontal/Vertical/Rotated): **H** or **V**↵
  Dimension line location (Mtext/Text/Angle): ⟨*pick the dimension line location or use the M, T, or A option, as desired*⟩

Rotated—This option lets you rotate the dimension line to any desired angle. This is used for situations when the object is at an angle and you want the dimension line parallel to the object. The command sequence for the dimension placed in Figure 11.8 is as follows:

  Dimension line location (Mtext/Text/Angle/Horizontal/Vertical/Rotated): **R**↵
  Dimension line angle <0>: **45**↵
  Dimension line location (Text/Angle/Horizontal/Vertical/Rotated): ↵
  Dimension text = 1.41
  Command:

FIGURE 11.8 Using the Rotated option of the DIMLINEAR command to place the dimension line at a desired angle.

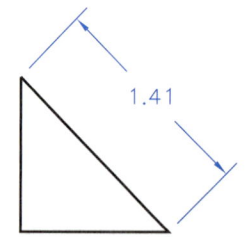

CHAPTER 11 ||| Dimensioning a Drawing 429

> **Exercise 11.3**
>
> 1. Begin a new drawing or use one of your prototypes.
> 2. Draw two objects and place vertical linear dimensions using the Text option to change the dimension text similar to that shown in Figure 11.5.
> 3. Draw an object and dimension it with text at an angle similar to that of Figure 11.7.
> 4. Draw an object and dimension it similar to that of Figure 11.8.
> 5. Save the drawing as EX11.3.

Drawing Chain and Datum Dimensions

Chain dimensioning is where the next dimension continues from the previous dimension. This is also referred to as *point-to-point dimensioning* and is called *continuous dimensioning* by AutoCAD LT. Chain dimensioning is commonly used in architectural drafting but can be used in mechanical drafting depending on the design factors. The initial dimension must be placed before drawing the attached chain dimensions. After placing the first dimension, AutoCAD LT automatically connects the next dimensions as you pick the second extension line origin. You can perform chain dimensioning by picking the Continue Dimension button in the Dimension toolbar, by picking Continue in the Dimension pull-down menu, or by typing **DCO** or **DIMCONTINUE** at the Command: prompt. The command sequence works like this and is displayed in Figure 11.9:

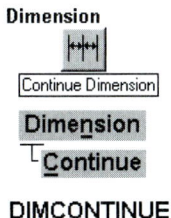

```
Command: DLI or DIMLINEAR↵
First extension line origin or press Enter to select: ⟨pick the first extension line origin⟩
Second extension line origin: ⟨pick the second extension line origin⟩
Dimension line location (Mtext/Text/Angle/Horizontal/Vertical/Rotated): ⟨pick the dimension line
    location⟩
Dimension text = 1.50
Command: DCO or DIMCONTINUE↵
Specify a second extension line origin or (Undo/<Select>): ⟨pick the next extension line origin⟩
Dimension text = 1.25
Specify a second extension line origin or (Undo/<Select>): ⟨pick the next extension line origin⟩
Dimension text = 1.25
Specify a second extension line origin or (Undo/<Select>): ↵
Select continued dimension: ↵
Command:
```

The previous command sequence placed chain dimensions immediately after placing the first linear dimension. You can also come back and place chain dimensions any time by using the Select continued dimension: option of the DIMCONTINUE command. The Select continued dimension: option is automatically

FIGURE 11.9 Creating chain dimensions with the DIMCONTINUE command.

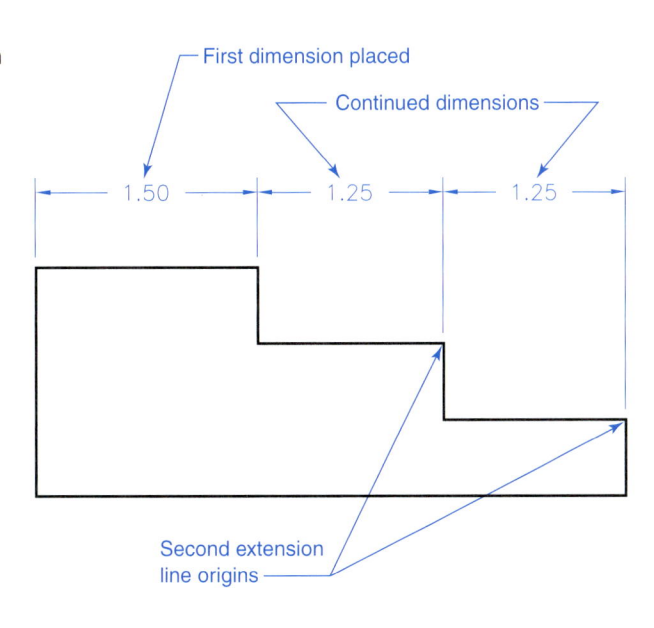

issued at the end of the DIMCONTINUE command sequence, as you can see in the previous example. This prompt wants you to select an existing dimension to continue dimensions from. You can also use the Select option to get the Select continued dimension: prompt immediately:

Comand: **DCO** or **DIMCONTINUE** ↵
Specify a second extension line origin or (Undo/<Select>): **S** ↵
Select continued dimension: ⟨*pick the dimension to continue from*⟩
Specify a second extension line origin or (Undo/<Select>): ⟨*pick the next extension line origin*⟩
Dimension text = 1.25
Specify a second extension line origin or (Undo/<Select>): ↵
Select continued dimension: ↵
Command:

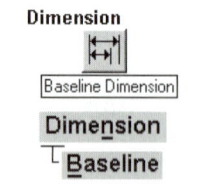

The Undo option allows you to undo the previously placed continue dimension. Just type **U** and press Enter:

Specify a second extension line origin or (Undo/<Select>): **U** ↵
Command has been completely undone.
Specify a second extension line origin or (Undo/<Select>):⟨*pick the next extension line origin*⟩

In *datum dimensioning* every dimension begins at the same starting place. AutoCAD LT calls this *baseline dimensioning.* Datum dimensioning is commonly used in mechanical drafting when the dimensions of a particular feature or features must be independent of other dimensions. Datum dimensioning is similar to chain dimensioning in the way it is created. The initial dimension must be placed before additional datum dimensions can be established. After placing the first dimension, AutoCAD LT automatically connects the next dimensions as you pick the second extension line origin. You can perform datum dimensioning by picking the Baseline Dimension button in the Dimension toolbar, by picking Baseline in the Dimension pull-down menu, or by typing **DBA** or **DIMBASELINE** at the Command: prompt. The command sequence works like this after placing the first dimension. Figure 11.10 illustrates the process:

Comand: **DBA** or **DIMBASELINE** ↵
Specify a second extension line origin or (Undo/<Select>): ⟨*pick the next extension line origin*⟩
Dimension text = 2.75
Specify a second extension line origin or (Undo/<Select>):⟨*pick the next extension line origin*⟩
Dimension text = 4.00
Specify a second extension line origin or (Undo/<Select>): ↵
Select base dimension: ↵
Command:

FIGURE 11.10 Creating datum dimensions with the DIMBASE command.

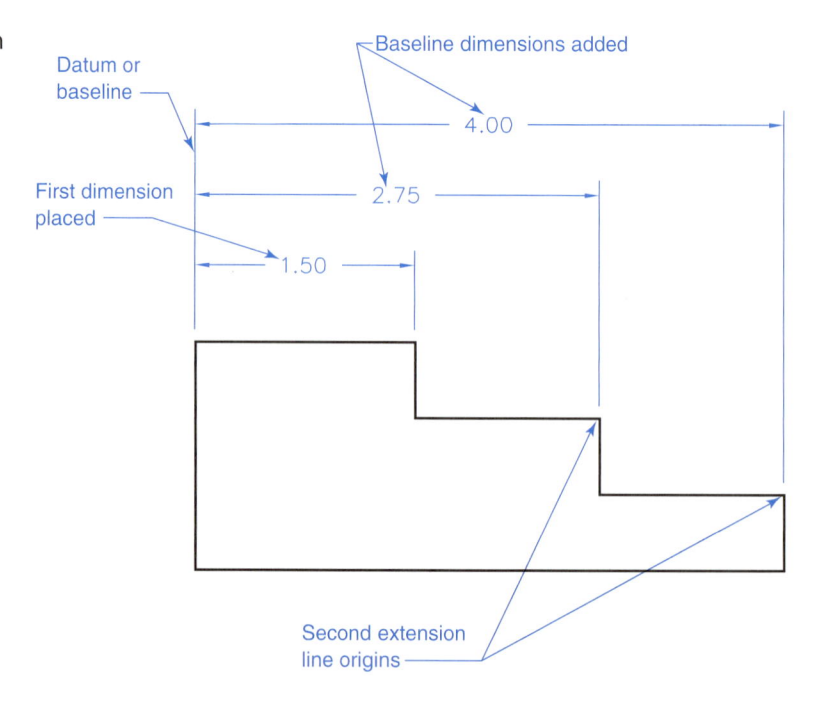

CHAPTER 11 ||| Dimensioning a Drawing

If you want to come back later and add datum dimensions to an existing dimension, you can use the Select base dimension: prompt or the Select option in the same manner as was demonstrated with chain dimensioning in the previous discussion. The Undo option also works, as previously described.

Exercise 11.4

1. Begin a new drawing or use one of your prototypes.
2. Draw an object and place chain dimensions as shown in Figure 11.9.
3. Draw an object and place datum dimensions as shown in Figure 11.10.
4. Save the drawing as EX11.4.

Drawing Dimensions Aligned with an Angled Object

Dimensions can be drawn aligned to a slanted object by using the Rotated option of the DIMLINEAR command as previously explained, or by using the DIMALIGNED command. With the Rotated option, you must specify the angle, but with DIMALIGNED the dimension line is automatically aligned with the extension line origin points. These dimensions are placed by picking the Aligned Dimension button in the Dimension toolbar, by picking Aligned in the Dimension pull-down menu, or by typing **DAL** or **DIMALIGNED** at the Command: prompt. Look at Figure 11.11 as you follow this command sequence:

Command: **DAL** or **DIMALIGNED**↵
First extension line origin or press Enter to select: ⟨*pick the first extension line origin*⟩
Second extension line origin: ⟨*pick the second extension line origin*⟩
Dimension line location (Mtext/Text/Angle): ⟨*pick the dimension line location*⟩
Dimension text = 1.41
Command:

FIGURE 11.11 Placing dimensions at an angle with the DIMALIGNED command.

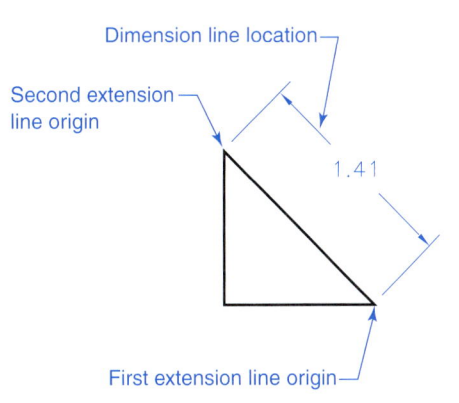

As with the other dimensioning commands, you can press Enter to pick objects directly for dimensioning when you see the press Enter to select prompt. You can also change the text value or the text angle by using the Mtext/Text/Angle options, as previously explained.

Exercise 11.5

1. Begin a new drawing or use one of your prototypes.
2. Draw an object and place an aligned dimension as shown in Figure 11.11.
3. Save the drawing as EX11.5.

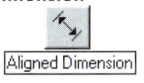

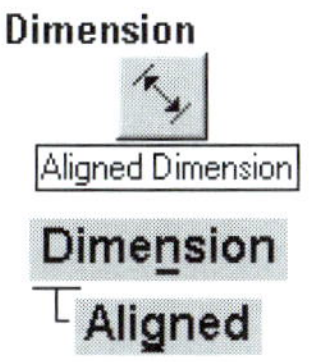

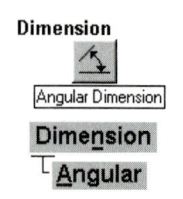

Dimensioning Angles

Angles are dimensioned in degrees with an arc-shaped dimension line. This is done by picking the Angular Dimension button in the Dimension toolbar, by picking Angular in the Dimension pull-down menu, or by typing **DAN** or **DIMANGULAR** at the Command: prompt. When entering this command, AutoCAD LT asks you to select an arc, circle, or line. After selecting the objects, you move the cursor to dynamically place the desired dimension line and text location. As you look at Figure 11.12, follow this command sequence for creating an angular dimension to line objects:

```
Command: DAN or DIMANGULAR↵
Select arc, circle, line, or press Enter: ⟨pick the first line⟩
Second line: ⟨pick the second line⟩
Dimension arc line location (Mtext/Text/Angle): ⟨pick the dimension line location⟩
Dimension text =45.00
Command:
```

FIGURE 11.12 Drawing angular dimensions with the DIMANGULAR command. (A) Dimension numeral placed within the dimension line. (B) Dimension numeral placed outside the dimension line due to the limited space inside the dimension line.

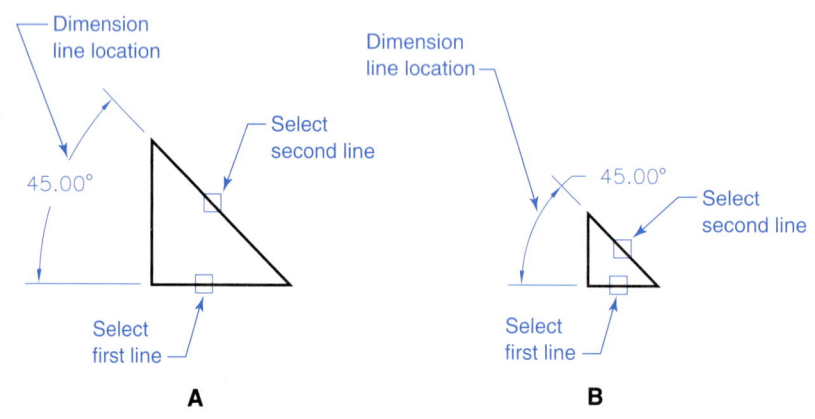

You can also apply an angular dimension to an arc or circle. When selecting an arc, the angle vertex is at the arc center and the angular measurement is to the arc endpoints. When selecting a circle, the angle vertex is at the center of the circle and the angle is established where you pick on the circle. Figure 11.13 shows an angle dimensioned to an arc and circle.

FIGURE 11.13 Using the DIMANGULAR command to dimension to an arc and circle.

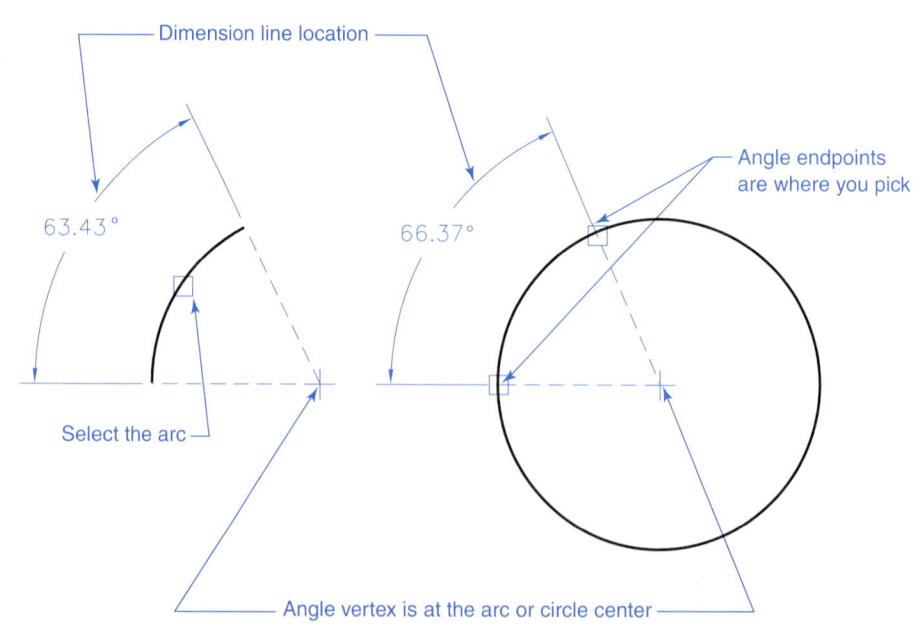

CHAPTER 11 ||| Dimensioning a Drawing

When you press Enter at the first DIMANGULAR prompt, you are asked to pick the angle vertex and the angle endpoints. This gives you the flexibility to pick these points on an object or to place an angle dimension without an object. The command sequence works like this and is displayed in Figure 11.14:

Command: **DAN** or **DIMANGULAR**↵
Select arc, circle, line, or press Enter: ↵
Angle vertex: ⟨*pick the vertex location*⟩
First angle endpoint: ⟨*pick the first endpoint of the angle*⟩
Second angle endpoint: ⟨*pick the next angle endpoint*⟩
Dimension arc line location (Mtext/Text/Angle): ⟨*pick the dimension line location*⟩
Dimension text = 45.00
Command:

FIGURE 11.14 Using the DIMANGULAR command's RETURN option to dimension an angle based on selecting the vertex and angle endpoints.

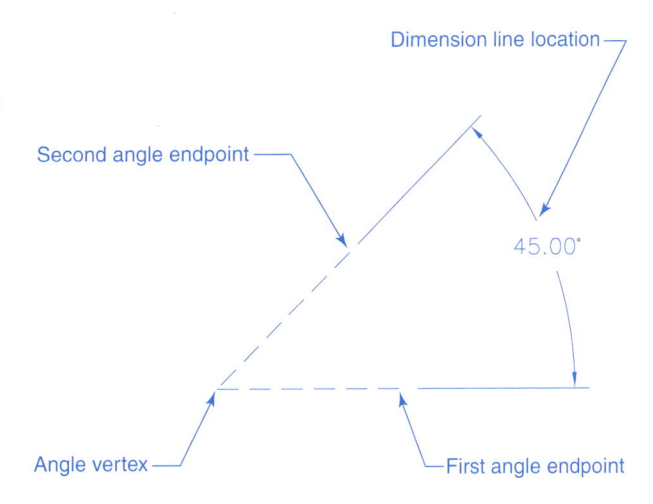

Exercise 11.6

1. Begin a new drawing or use one of your prototypes.
2. Draw objects and place angular dimensions as shown in Figure 11.12.
3. Draw objects and place angular dimensions as shown in Figure 11.13.
4. Draw an angular dimension similar to that shown in Figure 11.14.
5. Save the drawing as EX11.6.

Dimensioning Circles and Arcs

The American National Standards Institute (ANSI) and the American Society of Mechanical Engineers (ASME) recommend that a circle be dimensioned with a diameter and an arc be dimensioned with a radius. AutoCAD LT makes this practice easy by automatically placing a diameter symbol (∅) in front of the numeral when dimensioning a circle and a radius symbol (R) in front of the numeral when dimensioning an arc. You can dimension an arc or circle with a diameter or radius dimension, but the ANSI/ASME recommendation is the normal practice.

Circles are dimensioned by picking Diameter in the Dimension pull-down menu, by picking the Diameter Dimension button on the Dimension toolbar, or by typing **DDI** or **DIMDIAMETER** at the Command: prompt. Look at Figure 11.15 as you follow this command sequence:

Command: **DDI** or **DIMDIAMETER**↵
Select arc or circle: ⟨*pick the circle*⟩
Dimension text = 1.50
Dimension line location (Mtext/Text/Angle): ⟨*pick the leader location*⟩
Command:

Dimension

Diameter Dimension

Dimension
Diameter

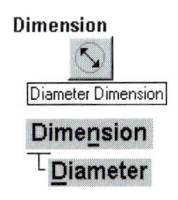

DIMDIAMETER
DDI

FIGURE 11.15 Dimensioning circles with the DIMDIAMETER command.

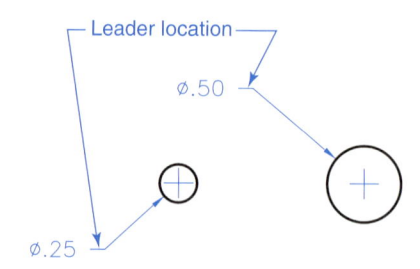

The previous command sequence allows you to change the dimension text. AutoCAD LT automatically places the diameter symbol with the default value. If you change the dimension text and want to keep the diameter symbol, you need to type the code %%c before the number. When asked for the dimension line location, you can drag the leader and pick the desired location. A leader and the diameter value are placed outside and a center mark is placed inside the circle. The leader automatically points to the center, as recommended by the ANSI/ASME standard. See Figure 11.15. Dimension variables that allow you more flexibility in the placement of the diameter dimension are used later in this chapter. The Mtext/Text/Angle options are available, as previously discussed.

Arcs are dimensioned by picking Radius in the Dimension pull-down menu, by picking the Radius Dimension button in the Dimension toolbar, or by typing **DRA** or **DIMRADIUS**. Look at Figure 11.16 as you follow this command sequence:

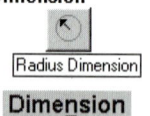

Command: **DRA** or **DIMRADIUS**↵
Select arc or circle: ⟨*pick the arc*⟩
Dimension text = .75
Dimension line location (Mtext/Text/Angle): ⟨*pick the leader location*⟩
Command:

FIGURE 11.16 Dimensioning arcs with the DIMRADIUS command.

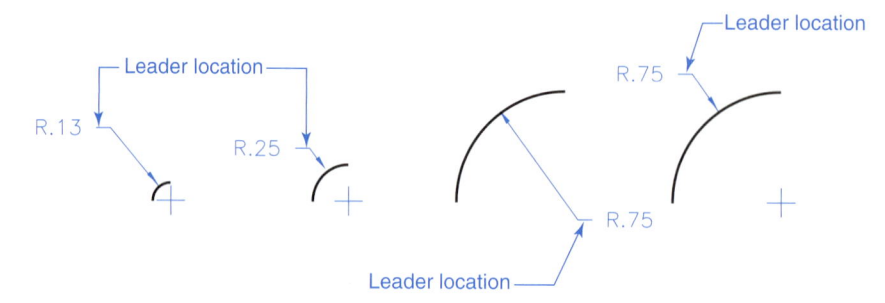

Dimensioning an arc is similar to dimensioning a circle. The size of the arc and the movement of your cursor determine the position of the dimension leader and text. AutoCAD LT automatically places the leader line pointing toward or through the arc or circle center as recommended by the ANSI/ASME standard. The Mtext/Text/Angle options are available, as previously discussed.

Exercise 11.7

1. Begin a new drawing or use one of your prototypes.
2. Draw objects and place diameter dimensions as shown in Figure 11.15.
3. Draw objects and place radius dimensions as shown in Figure 11.16.
4. Save the drawing as EX11.7.

CHAPTER 11 ||| Dimensioning a Drawing   435

Creating Ordinate Dimensions

Ordinate dimensions are drawn without the traditional dimension lines and arrowheads. Ordinate dimensions are sometimes referred to as *arrowless dimensions* and are also called *arrowless tabular dimensions* when a table is used to give the size and specifications of features such as holes. (Figure 11.1 shows a comparison between traditional dimensioning and ordinate dimensioning.) Ordinate dimensions are drawn by picking the Ordinate Dimension button in the Dimension toolbar, by picking Ordinate in the Dimension pull-down menu, or by typing **DOR** or **DIMORDINATE** at the Command: prompt.

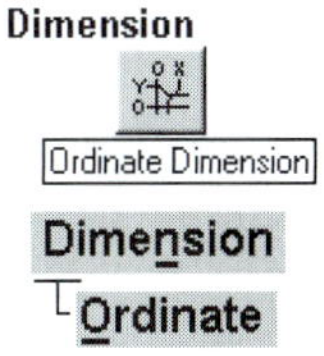

AutoCAD LT automatically places the ordinate dimension numeral at the end of an extension line from the feature you select. With ordinate dimensioning, the dimensions originate from datums. ***Datums*** are planes, points, surfaces, lines, or axes from which measurements are made. The datums on a part are usually zero, and dimensions to features on the part increase or decrease depending on their distance from the datums in the X and Y axes. Everything you draw originates from the World Coordinate System (WCS), which is the 0,0 coordinate. The WCS is in the lower left corner of the screen for most applications. When doing ordinate dimensioning, it is necessary to temporarily move the WCS to the corner of the object where the dimensions originate because this places the 0,0 coordinate origin in relationship to the object you are dimensioning. The Origin option of the UCS (User Coordinate System) command is used to move the WCS to the corner of the object as shown in Figure 11.17A. Use this command sequence:

Command: **UCS**↵
Origin/ZAxis/3point/OBject/View/X/Y/ZPrev/Restore/Save/Del/?/<World>: **O**↵
Origin point <0,0,0>: ⟨*enter the coordinates or pick the object corner*⟩
Command:

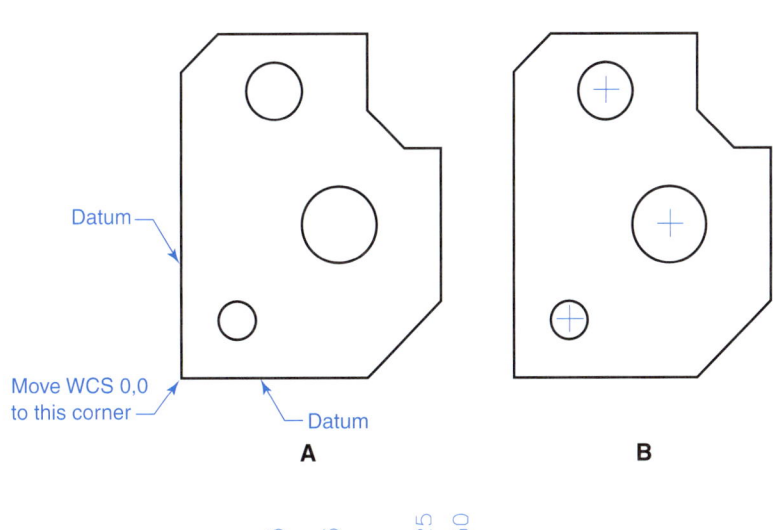

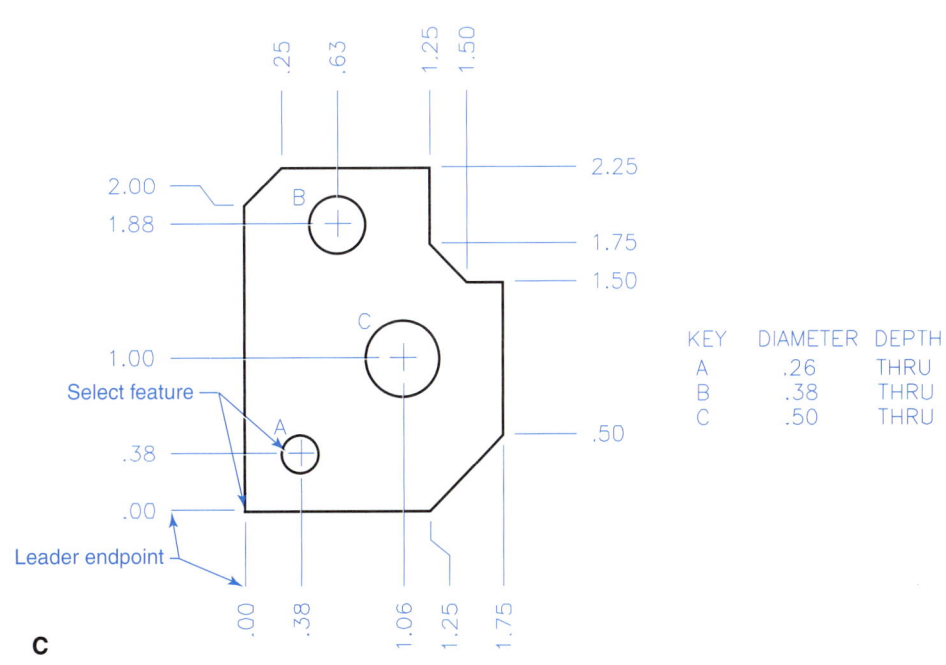

Dimension

Ordinate Dimension

Dimension
└ **Ordinate**

DIMORDINATE
DOR

FIGURE 11.17 Datum dimensioning with the DIMORDINATE command. (A) The object to be dimensioned is shown with the datums identified and the WCS (0,0) moved to the intersection of the two datum surfaces. (B) The center marks are placed in the circle using the DIMCENTER command. (C) The object is completely dimensioned using the DIMORDINATE command. The hole key and table were added using the DTEXT command.

KEY	DIAMETER	DEPTH
A	.26	THRU
B	.38	THRU
C	.50	THRU

436   CHAPTER 11 ||| Dimensioning a Drawing

Dimension
[Center Mark]

Dimension
└ **Center Mark**

DIMCENTER
DCE

Now you are ready to dimension the features of the object unless the features are circles and arcs. For circles and arcs, you should dimension from a center mark, which needs to be drawn first. Center marks are drawn by picking the Center Mark button in the Dimension toolbar, by picking Center Mark in the Dimension pull-down menu, or by typing **DCE** or **DIMCENTER** at the Command: prompt. Figure 11.17B shows the center marks placed using this command:

    Command: **DCE** or **DIMCENTER** ↵
    Select arc or circle: ⟨*pick the arc or circle*⟩
    Command:

Now you are really ready to use the DIMORDINATE command. When using the DIMORDINATE command, you are asked to select the feature to dimension. You should use the object snaps for best advantage. For example, use the ENDpoint or INTersect object snap for corners and use the ENDpoint to snap to the center marks of circles and arcs. AutoCAD LT automatically offsets the extension line a short distance from the point you pick. This leaves the desired extension line gap between the object and the start of the extension line. During the ordinate dimensioning process, you select the feature to dimension and then move the screen cursor to pick the extension line endpoint. AutoCAD LT refers to the extension line endpoint as a *leader endpoint*. The extension line is dragged into place as you move the cursor. Look at Figure 11.17C as you follow this command sequence:

    Command: **DOR** or **DIMORDINATE**↵
    Select feature: ⟨*pick the feature to dimension*⟩
    Leader endpoint (Xdatum/Ydatum/Mtext/Text): ⟨*pick the leader endpoint*⟩
    Dimension text = .38
    Command:

In Figure 11.17C the hole key and table are added using the MTEXT command.

    Mechanical drafting practices often use **unidirectional dimensioning,** in which all of the dimensions and notes read from the bottom of the sheet. AutoCAD LT automatically places ordinate dimensions in the aligned dimensioning format. *Aligned dimensioning* is used when you want to read the dimensions from the bottom of the sheet for horizontal dimensions and from the right side of the sheet for vertical dimensions. Notice that aligned dimensioning is used in Figure 11.17C, whereas unidirectional dimensioning is used in all previous figures.

    Sometimes a dimension might overlap another dimension if placed with a straight extension line from the object. This happens when the features are too close together. AutoCAD LT helps you with this problem by automatically offsetting the extension line between the feature and the extension line end that you pick. The result of this offset extension line is shown in Figure 11.17C and clarified in Figure 11.18. To create ordinate dimensions that use a straight line, turn ORTHO on while you are placing the dimension. ORTHO must be off to create an offset ordinate dimension.

FIGURE 11.18 AutoCAD LT automatically offsets the extension line when you pick an offset leader endpoint.

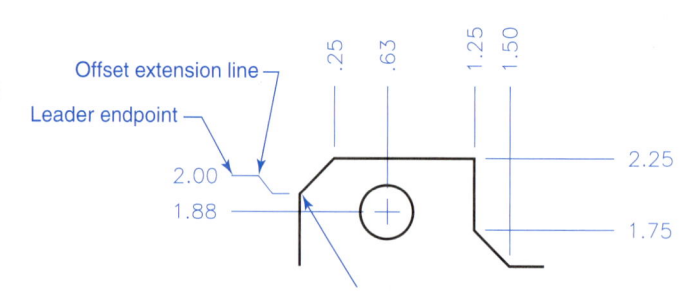

Exercise 11.8

1. Begin a new drawing or use one of your prototypes.
2. Draw and dimension the object shown in Figure 11.17C.
3. Save the drawing as EX11.8.

Creating Oblique Dimensions

An *oblique dimension* is one that has the extension lines placed at an angle from the feature being dimensioned. Oblique dimensions are sometimes used in situations where the dimension is crowded if the extension lines are projected horizontally or vertically from the object. This technique is sometimes used when dimensioning curves that are not defined by a radius. Oblique dimensions are placed by picking Oblique from the Dimension pull-down menu or by typing **DIMEDIT** at the Command: prompt and using the Oblique option. Before dimensions can be placed at an oblique angle, they need to be drawn as regular horizontal or vertical linear dimensions. The Oblique option is then used to rotate the dimension to the desired obliquing angle. Any positive angle from 1° to 179° can be entered. If an angle greater than 180° is entered, the 180° is subtracted and the resulting angle is used. Figure 11.19A shows dimensions place vertically and then changed to oblique as shown in Figure 11.19B. The DIMEDIT command sequence works like this:

> Command: **DIMEDIT**↵
> Dimension Edit (Home/New/Rotate/Oblique) <Home>: **O**↵
> Select objects: ⟨*pick the dimensions to oblique*⟩
> Select objects: ↵
> Enter obliqing angle (press Enter for none): **145**↵
> Command:

Dimension

Dimension Edit

Dime̱nsion
└ **Oblique**

DIMEDIT
DED

FIGURE 11.19 Drawing oblique dimensions with the DIM or DIMEDIT command's Oblique option.

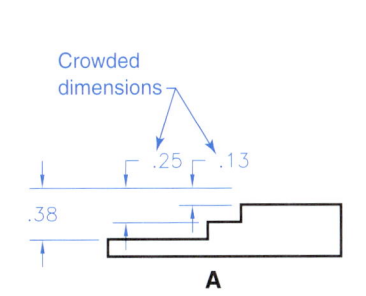

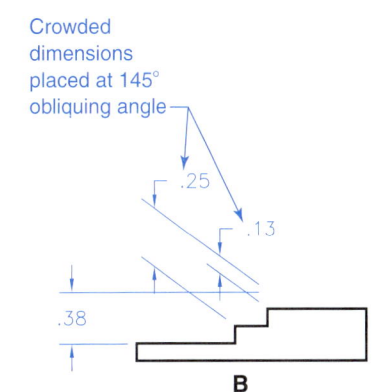

Oblique dimensions can also be created using the DIM command and the OBLIQUE option like this:

> Command: **DIM**↵
> Dim: **OBL** or **OBLIQUE**↵
> Select objects: ⟨*pick the dimensions to oblique*⟩
> Select objects: ↵
> Enter obliqing angle (press Enter for none): **145**↵
> Dim: ⟨*Press the Esc key*⟩
> Command:

Additional discussion about the DIMEDIT and DIM commands is provided later in this chapter.

Field Notes

The Oblique option of the DIMEDIT command is used in the creation of isometric dimensions as well. Instruction on creation of isometric dimensions is provided in Chapter 14.

Exercise 11.9

1. Begin a new drawing or use one of your prototypes.
2. Draw and dimension the object shown in Figure 11.19B.
3. Save the drawing as EX11.9.

☑ LEARNING CHECKPOINT

- ☐ Define the term *dimensions*.
- ☐ Explain the difference between size and location dimensions.
- ☐ List two types of notes.
- ☐ What are linear dimensions?
- ☐ How do you access the command used for drawing linear dimensions?
- ☐ Explain how to place linear dimensions by selecting the object directly.
- ☐ Describe how to change dimension text in the Edit MText dialog box.
- ☐ Explain two ways to rotate the dimension line to be aligned with a slanted object.
- ☐ How is chain dimensioning done?
- ☐ Describe the process for making datum dimensions.
- ☐ Name the command used to dimension angles.
- ☐ What command automatically places a diameter symbol when dimensioning circles and arcs?
- ☐ Name the command that automatically places a radius symbol when dimensioning arcs and circles.
- ☐ Name the command used to do arrowless dimensioning.
- ☐ Why is it important to move the WCS origin to the datum origin of the object when doing arrowless dimensioning?
- ☐ How do you offset the ordinate dimension extension line when needed to avoid crowding?
- ☐ Describe oblique dimensions.

Managing Dimension Styles

Dimension styles are saved sets of dimension variable settings that determine the appearance of the dimensions. Dimension styles are usually set up based on the type of drafting field for which they are used. ***Dimension variables*** are AutoCAD LT system variables that help you control the way dimensions look. A dimension style is established by changing the dimension variables as needed to accomplish the desired dimension appearance. For example, the dimension style for mechanical drafting probably has ROMANS text font placed in a break in the dimension line, and the dimension lines are capped with arrowheads. The dimension style for architectural drafting may use CityBlueprint text font placed above the dimension line, and dimension lines are terminated with slashes. See Figure 11.20. The dimension style can have dimensions based on national standards such as the ANSI/ASME or Architectural Graphic Standards, or set up to match company applications and standards. Dimension styles can also have a family of settings that allow you to assign different settings for each specific type of dimension if desired.

FIGURE 11.20 Dimensions drawn with two different dimension styles. (A) Mechanical drafting dimension. (B) Architectural drafting dimension.

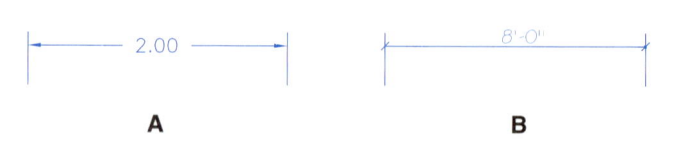

Creating New Dimension Styles

Dimension styles are created using the Dimension Styles dialog box shown in Figure 11.21. This dialog box is accessed by picking the Dimension Style button in the Dimension toolbar, by picking S̲tyle … in the Dime̲nsion pull-down menu, or by typing **D** or **DDIM** at the Command: prompt.

Saving and Renaming Dimension Styles

The Dimension Style area of the Dimension Style dialog box in Figure 11.21 displays STANDARD in the C̲urrent: text box. The C̲urrent: text box is where the active dimension style name is displayed. If additional text styles exist, they are accessed by picking the down arrow to open the list. Pick a name from the list to make another dimension style current. The STANDARD dimension style is the AutoCAD LT default. If you

CHAPTER 11 ||| Dimensioning a Drawing 439

FIGURE 11.21 The Dimension Styles dialog box. The STANDARD dimension style is the AutoCAD LT default.

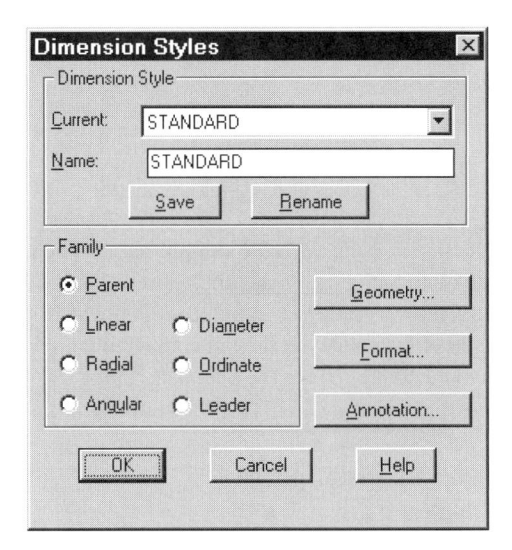

FIGURE 11.22 The Dimension Styles dialog box with the +STANDARD style displayed as current. The +STANDARD dimension style is automatically set by AutoCAD LT when you change any default dimension variables.

change any of the AutoCAD LT default dimension variables, the changes are automatically stored in a dimension style called +STANDARD as shown in Figure 11.22. The Name: text box is where you display a text style to be saved or renamed. When you have changed the dimension variables to match the desired drafting practice, the dimension style name is entered in the Name: text box. You then pick the Save button to save the new dimension style with the name given. If you want to rename a dimension style, you pick the style for display in the Current: text box. Then enter the new name in the Name: text box followed by picking the Rename button. In Figure 11.23A, a dimension style named MECHANICAL is entered in the Name: text box and the Save button is picked. This makes the MECHANICAL style current. Notice in Figure 11.23B how the list of dimension styles now includes three options.

Working with Dimension Style Families

Dimension style families allow you to create a dimension style that has variations depending on the type of dimension you are creating. As an example, you may want diameter dimensions to be created with center lines in the circle and radius dimensions to have only a center mark. Or you might want to display bilateral tolerances for linear dimensions but not for angular dimensions. Dimension style families offer this kind of flexibility. Dimension families are divided into two categories, parent styles and family members. A *parent style* is a general style that applies to all of the family members, or each type of dimension. A *family member* is one of the specific dimension types, including linear, radial, angular, diameter, ordinate, and leaders.

To create a parent style, make sure the Parent radio button on the Dimension Styles dialog box is selected while you define the general features of your dimensions. This includes text styles and sizes, arrowheads, and

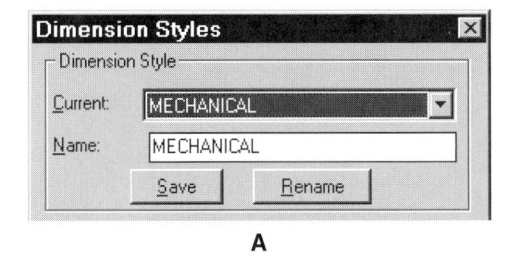

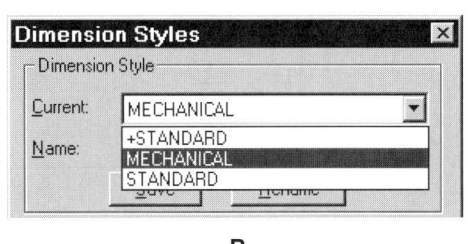

A

B

FIGURE 11.23 (A) Enter a new dimension style name in the Name: text box and pick the Save button. (B) The new dimension style name is now included in the list with the other styles.

FIGURE 11.24 The Save changes to current style Alert box.

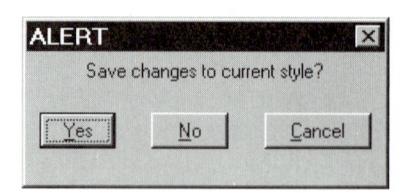

other general features. Save the parent style with the desired name. Then, to set specific variations for family members, select the appropriate radio button and make the desired changes. Each time you select a different family member after making changes, a prompt is issued asking if you want to save the changes to the current style, as shown in Figure 11.24. Changes to parent styles are not applied to family members after the style has been created, named, and saved. You should always create the parent style first and then modify each of the desired family members, saving your changes as you go. Modifying the features of dimension styles is covered next.

Changing Dimension Variables

The Dimension Styles dialog box has three buttons that access subdialog boxes for the purpose of changing dimension variables. These buttons are Geometry …, Format …, and Annotation …. Dimension variables, also called *dimvars,* can be changed intuitively in the dialog boxes or manually by typing at the command line. In this discussion, references to changing dimension variables at the *command line* include both the Command: prompt and the Dim: prompt. When typed at the Command: prompt, the entire dimension variable name must be typed. The DIM part of the dimension variable can be omitted when typing at the Dim: prompt. The following discussion explains both the dialog box and the command line methods of adjusting dimvars.

Changing Dimension Style Geometry

Pick the Geometry … button in the Dimension Styles dialog box to open the Geometry dialog box shown in Figure 11.25. This dialog box is used to change dimension features related to the dimension line, extension line, arrowheads, center mark, and scale. The following discussion explains how each of these adjustments works.

Changing the Dimension Line Presentation
The Dimension Line area of the Geometry dialog box is used to change the format of the dimension line with the following dimension variables:

Suppress:—*Suppress* means to keep from being displayed. The Suppress: option consists of two toggles that allow you to keep either the first or second or both dimension lines and their arrowheads from being displayed. The 1st and 2nd toggles refer to the first and second points picked when the dimension

FIGURE 11.25 Pick the Geometry … button in the Dimension Styles dialog box to open the Geometry dialog box.

CHAPTER 11 ||| Dimensioning a Drawing

was created. These are off by default, meaning that dimension lines and arrowheads *are* displayed. The command line equivalents for these dimension variables are DIMSD1 and DIMSD2 (**S**uppress **D**imension lines 1 and 2). When entering the value for variables that are either on or off, you can type **ON** or **OFF,** or you can use 0 and 1. A value of 0 means off, and 1 means on.

Extension:—This is a text box and is inactive unless you are using tick marks instead of arrowheads. Tick marks, also called *oblique arrowheads,* are often used when dimensioning architectural drawings. The different settings for arrowhead styles are explained later. In this style of dimensioning, the dimension lines often cross over the extension lines. The ***extension*** represents how far the dimension line extends beyond the extension line. When this text box is active, you can change the value from the .00 default. The command line dimension variable is DIMDLE (**D**imension **L**ine **E**xtension).

Spacing:—This text box allows you to change the spacing between dimension lines in baseline dimensions. The default spacing is .38 units. AutoCAD LT automatically spaces the dimension lines this distance when you use the DIMBASELINE command. Figure 11.26 shows the dimension line spacing. This setting may need to be changed, depending on the specified dimension text size, and whether the dimension is horizontal or vertical. The command line equivalent is DIMDLI (**D**imension **L**ine **I**ncrement), which asks you to enter a new value.

Color . . .—Picking this button opens the Select Color dialog box where you can assign a color to the dimension lines. The color is normally assigned BYBLOCK, which is the default, and indicates that the dimension assumes the currently active color setting. Different color settings are normally only used for pen width considerations when plotting the drawing. The command line equivalent is DIMCLRD (**C**o**L**o**R** of **D**imension line).

Changing the Extension Line Presentation
The Extension Line area of the Geometry dialog box is used to change the format of the extension lines with the following dimension variables:

Suppress:—This option is used to suppress either the first extension line or the second or both as desired. These toggles are off by default and all extension lines are displayed. You might want to suppress an extension line if it coincides with an object line or if you do not want it displayed for any reason. The command line entries are DIMSE1 and DIMSE2 (**S**uppress **E**xtension lines 1 and 2).

Extension:—This text box is used to set the extension line extension, which is the distance the extension line runs past the dimension line as shown in Figure 11.27. The default is .18, and the command line equivalent is DIMEXE (**EX**tension line **E**xtension). A common extension line extension is .125 in., but it depends on the type and size of drawing.

FIGURE 11.26 Using the Sp**a**cing**:** text box in the Geometry dialog box. The command line equivalent is DIMDLI.

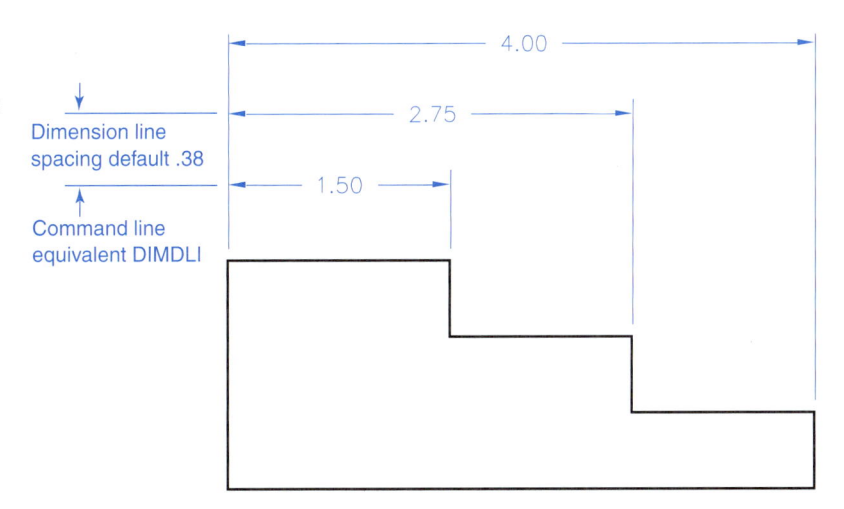

FIGURE 11.27 The extension line extension default is .18 and the command line dimension variable is DIMEXE.

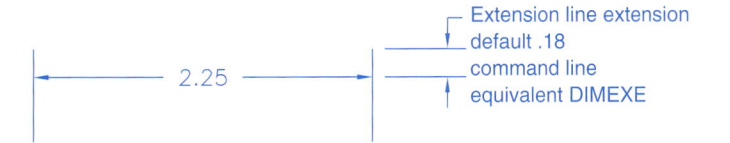

FIGURE 11.28 The extension line offset default is .0625 and the command line dimension variable is DIMEXO.

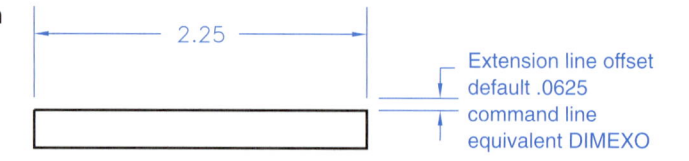

FIGURE 11.29 The extension line offset should be zero when an extension line meets a center line.

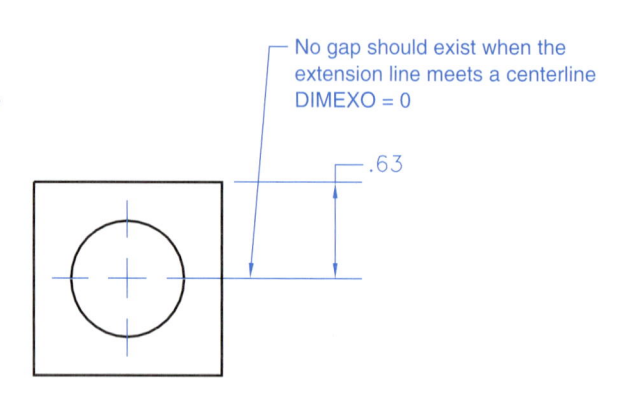

Origin Offset:—This text box is used to change the distance between the object and the beginning of the extension line as shown in Figure 11.28. Most applications require a small space, and the default is .06. It is recommended that no gap exist when an extension line meets a center line as shown in Figure 11.29. The command line equivalent is DIMEXO (**EX**tension line **O**ffset).

Color . . .—The color button is used to change the extension line color. The default is BYBLOCK, and the command line equivalent is DIMCLRE (**Co**Lo**R** of **E**xtension line).

Changing the Arrowhead Appearance

AutoCAD LT provides several different arrowhead options. These options are available in the Arrowheads area of the Geometry dialog box. The default arrowhead is Closed Filled as displayed in the 1st: and 2nd: list boxes and in the image tiles above the list boxes shown in Figure 11.30A. Open the list box to access the entire list of arrowhead options as shown in Figure 11.30B. If you pick a new arrowhead in the first list, AutoCAD LT automatically makes the same selection for the second list and the examples in the image tiles are changed to match. If you want a different arrowhead for each end of the dimension line, pick the desired first arrowhead and then open the second list and pick another. Figure 11.30C shows a different arrowhead selected for each end of the line.

You can also pick on the left image tile to have the image automatically changed, in both tiles, to the next arrowhead option in the list. Pick on the right image tile to make the second arrowhead different from the first. Eight different arrowhead options are provided by AutoCAD LT, or you can create your own arrow-

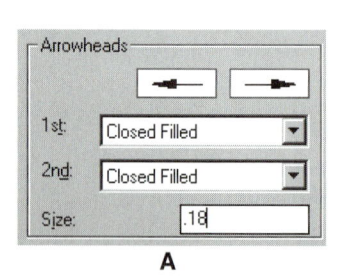

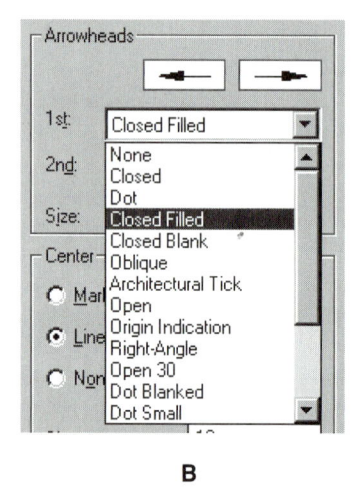

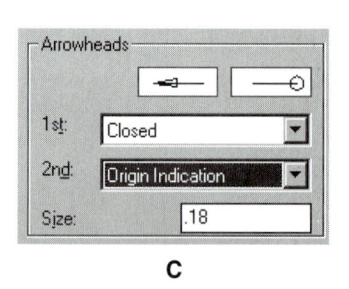

FIGURE 11.30 (A) The arrowhead area of the Geometry dialog box displays the first and second arrowhead name and image tile. (B) Access the list of optional arrowhead symbols. (C) Displaying different arrowhead symbols for each end of the dimension line.

CHAPTER 11 ||| Dimensioning a Drawing   443

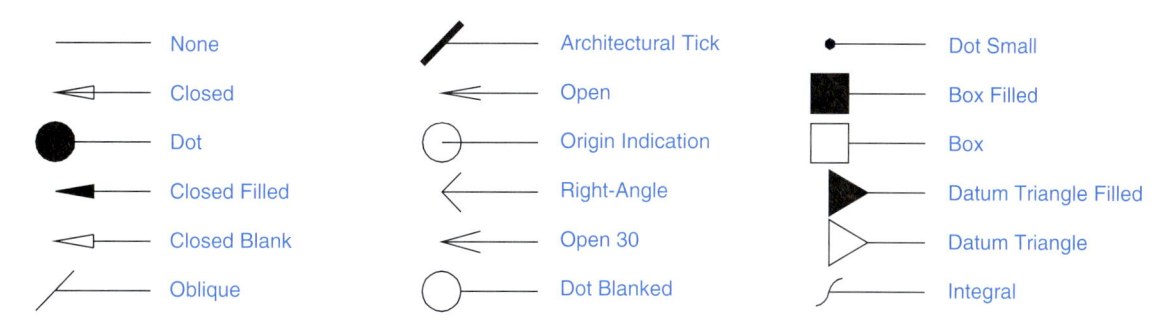

———	None	／———	Architectural Tick	•———	Dot Small
◁———	Closed	⇐———	Open	■———	Box Filled
●———	Dot	○———	Origin Indication	□———	Box
◀———	Closed Filled	⇐———	Right-Angle	▶———	Datum Triangle Filled
◁———	Closed Blank	⇐———	Open 30	▷———	Datum Triangle
／———	Oblique	○———	Dot Blanked	⌐———	Integral

FIGURE 11.31 The standard AutoCAD LT arrowhead options.

head design with the User Arrow … option. The Closed Filled default arrowhead is shown in the image tiles in Figures 11.30A and B. The other options are displayed in their related image tiles in Figure 11.31.

When changing arrowheads at the command line using dimvars, the variables used are DIMBLK, DIMBLK1, DIMBLK2, and DIMSAH. If both arrowheads are to be the same, the only variable that needs changed is the DIMBLK (**BL**oc**K**) variable. This accepts a text value that is the name of the arrowhead style you wish to use. Each of the names is listed in the arrowhead descriptions that follow. To set up separate arrowheads, first set DIMSAH (**S**eparate **A**rrow**H**eads) to on. The arrowheads that are used by the first and second dimension lines are set by using DIMBLK1 and DIMBLK2.

The various types of arrowheads are commonly used for the following applications, but you should check with your school, office, or appropriate national standards:

Architectural—Architectural Tick, Dot, Closed Filled, Oblique, Open, Right Angle, Open 30, or Dot Small. The Architectural Tick, Dot, and Closed Filled are the most commonly used.

Mechanical—Closed Filled, Closed, Closed Blank, or Open. The Closed Filled is the most commonly used and is represented in the ANSI/ASME standards. The Closed Filled is often used as the arrowhead for leaders in many drafting fields. The Small Dot symbol is used when a leader points to a surface.

Each of the AutoCAD LT arrowhead options are displayed and named in Figure 11.31. The arrowhead symbols are all displayed with the same size setting.

The User Arrow … option in the Arrowheads list requires that you create a block of the desired arrowhead design. A block is a commonly used symbol and the creation of blocks is discussed in Chapter 12. After a block is made and named, you can pick the User Arrow … option to open the User Arrow dialog box shown in Figure 11.32A. In this dialog box you enter an arrowhead name, in the Arrow <u>N</u>ame: box that matches the name of the arrowhead block that you created. Doing this activates the block to be used as the arrowheads for the dimension on your drawing. Figure 11.32B shows a variety of custom arrows that can be commonly used or can have special applications. The user arrow is controlled at the command line by the DIMBLK variable by typing the name of the block.

FIGURE 11.32 (A) The User Arrow dialog box. (B) Sample custom user arrows.

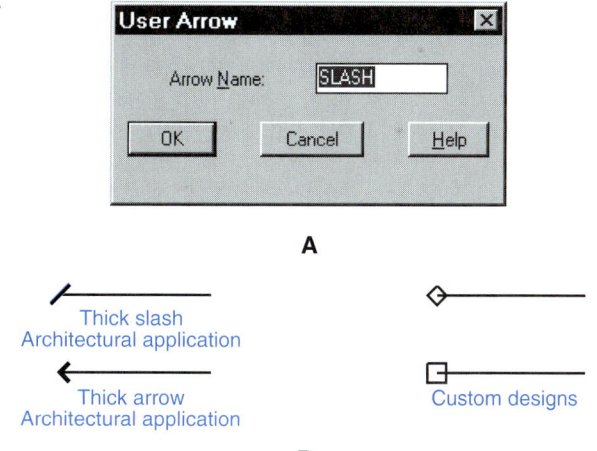

A

Thick slash
Architectural application

Thick arrow
Architectural application

Custom designs

B

FIGURE 11.33 The dimension line extension option is active when you pick the Oblique arrowhead option. This is the DIMDLE dimension variable.

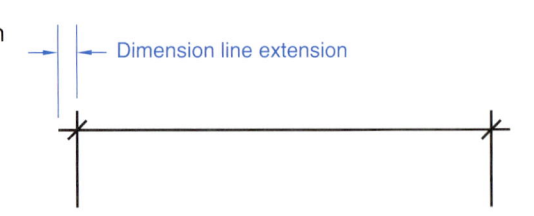

When you access the Oblique arrowhead option, the Extension: box in the Dimension Line area is activated. This allows you to enter a value for a dimension line projection beyond the extension line. The default value is zero, but some architectural companies like to project the dimension line past the extension line by setting this to a desired value as shown in Figure 11.33. This is controlled at the command line with the DIMDLE dimension variable.

Changing Arrowhead Size

The Size: box in the Arrowhead area of the Geometry dialog box allows you to change the size of any selected arrowhead. The default value is .18. Arrowheads are commonly .125 in. but vary depending on the drawing size. The arrowhead size can also be changed at the command line with the DIMASZ (Arrowhead SiZe) dimension variable.

Using Center Marks in Circles and Arcs

The Center area of the Geometry dialog box allows you to select the way center marks are placed in circles and arcs. The three radio buttons are identified as Mark, Line, and None. None is the default and provides for no center marks to be placed in circles and arcs. The image tile at the right of the radio buttons displays the effect of the currently selected radio button. The Mark option is used to place center marks only, and the Line option places center marks and center lines as displayed in the Figure 11.34 image tiles. The None option is used when no center marks are desired. You can also change the center mark option by picking directly on the image tile. After selecting either the Mark or Line center mark option, you can place center marks on circles and arcs by using the DIMCENTER command. This command is accessed by picking the Center Mark button in the Dimension toolbar, by picking Center Mark in the Dimension pull-down menu, or by typing **DCE** or **DIMCENTER** at the Command: prompt. The command asks you to select the arc or circle:

Command: **DCE** or **DIMCENTER**↵
Select the arc or circle: ⟨*pick the arc or circle*⟩
Command:

DIMCENTER
DCE

FIGURE 11.34 (A) The Mark option and the related tile image. (B) The Line option and the related tile image.

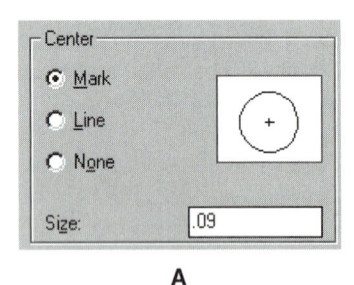

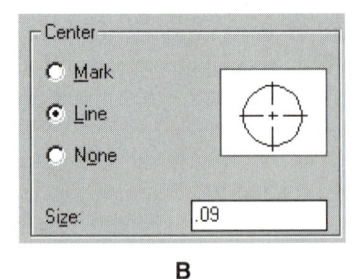

CHAPTER 11 ||| Dimensioning a Drawing

Changing the Center Mark Size

The Si*z*e: box in the Center area of the Geometry dialog box is used to change the size of the center mark presentation. The default size is .09. The size specification controls the *M*ark and *L*ine options in different ways, as shown in Figure 11.35.

The center mark option can also be changed at the Command: prompt by using the DIMCEN (**CEN**ter) dimension variable. Entering a positive value provides for the mark option as shown in Figure 11.35A. Entering a negative value provides for the line option as shown in Figure 11.35B. Keep in mind that only positive values need to be entered in the Si*z*e: box of the Geometry dialog box. The following shows a negative value used to provide for the line option to be used:

Command: **DIMCEN**↵
New value for DIMCEN <0.09>: **−.125**↵
Command:

FIGURE 11.35 (A) The size related to using the *M*ark option. (B) The size related to using the *L*ine option.

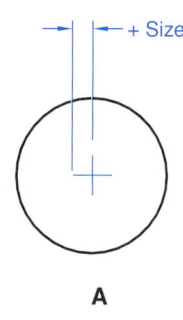

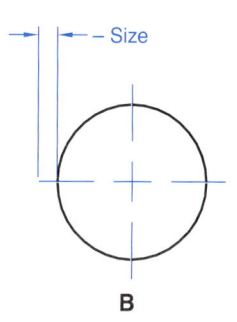

Remember that the DIMCENTER command is used to actually place the center marks after setting the dimension variable. Also, unlike most dimvars, the "DIM" prefix for DIMCEN cannot be omitted at the Dim: prompt. This is because typing **CEN** at the Dim: prompt starts the DIMCENTER dimensioning option.

Setting the Geometry Scale

The Scale area of the Geometry dialog box allows you to set the scale factor for all dimension features in the entire drawing by entering a value in the O*v*erall Scale: text box. AutoCAD LT automatically sets a scale factor based on the setup option that you use. If the scale factor is 1, then the dimension variables are equal to their designated settings. If the scale factor is 2, then the values of the dimension variables are doubled. For example, if the arrowhead size is .125, then a scale factor of 1 makes the arrowheads .125 and a scale factor of 2 makes the arrowheads .250. This value can also be set at the command line by using the DIMSCALE dimensioning variable. The Scale to *P*aper Space check box is used if you want the geometry scale factor to be related to paper space settings, or you can set DIMSCALE to 0 at the command line. The O*v*erall Scale is disabled when Scale to *P*aper Space is checked.

Exercise 11.10

1. Begin a new drawing or use one of your prototypes.
2. Open the Dimension Styles dialog box and notice STANDARD as the current dimension style.
3. Access the Geometry dialog box.
4. Look at the Dimension Line area as you refer to Figure 11.26 as a reference to dimension line spacing.
5. Look at the Extension Line area as you refer to Figure 11.27 as a reference to the extension line extension and Figure 11.28 for the extension line offset.
6. Look at the Arrowheads area and pick each of the arrowhead options; watch the example in the image tiles change to match your selection. Try picking on the image tile to see the results. Try making the first and second arrowheads the same and different. Notice when you pick the Oblique arrowhead that the Extension: box in the Dimension Line area becomes active. Look at Figure 11.33 to see the results of a value entered in this box.
7. Look at the Center area as you pick each of the radio buttons and see how the image tile changes to match the selection. Pick on the image tile to see what happens. Look at Figure 11.35 to see the results of changing the center mark size.
8. Use the Geometry dialog box to make the following settings based on your preferred drafting field:

Setting	Mechanical	Architectural
Dimension line spacing	.50	.75
Extension line extension	.125	.18
Extension line offset	.0625	.08
Arrowheads	Closed, Blank, Closed Filled, or Open	Dot, Closed Filled, or Architectural Tick
Arrowhead size	.125	.18
Center	Line	Mark
Center size	.25	.25

9. Pick the OK button. You are now back in the Dimension Style dialog box. Notice the +STANDARD dimension style added to the list.
10. Type MECHANICAL or ARCHITECTURAL in the Name: text box depending on the drafting field for which you made settings.
11. Pick the Save button. The dimension style you created should now be in the list.
12. Pick OK.
13. Save the drawing as EX11.10.

Changing the Dimension Format

The dimension format establishes the way dimension text appears on the drawing and the relationship with the positioning of the dimension lines and arrowheads. These controls are adjusted in the Format dialog box which is accessed by picking the Format ... button in the Dimension Styles dialog box. The default Format dialog box is shown in Figure 11.36.

Adjusting the Text Fit

The upper left area of the Format dialog box has several options for controlling the relationship between the placement of dimension text, dimension line, and arrowheads. The User Defined check box allows you to control the location of the dimension text. With User Defined off, as it is by default, AutoCAD LT decides where the text is placed relative to the dimension line or leader. For example, when placing linear dimensions, AutoCAD LT automatically centers the dimension text within the dimension line, as shown in Figure 11.2. You can have maximum control over text placement if you pick the User Defined check box. Figure 11.37 shows the difference in flexibility that can be achieved with User Defined off and on. As you look at Figure 11.37A, notice that the text is centered on the dimension line if the dimension is big enough. In Figure 11.37B, the text can be placed where you want it, such as moved to the side or placed outside of the extension lines. The User Defined check box acts the same as setting the DIMUPT (User Positioned Text) variable at the Command: prompt.

CHAPTER 11 ||| Dimensioning a Drawing   447

FIGURE 11.36 The Format dialog box is accessed by picking the Format ... button in the Geometry dialog box.

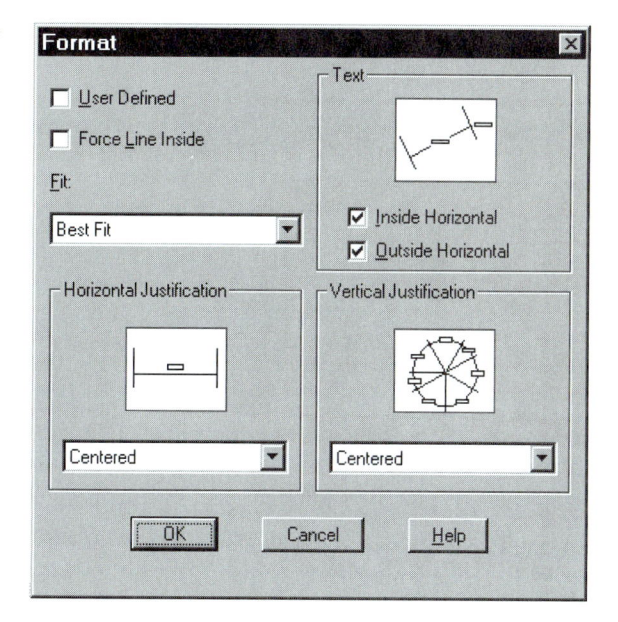

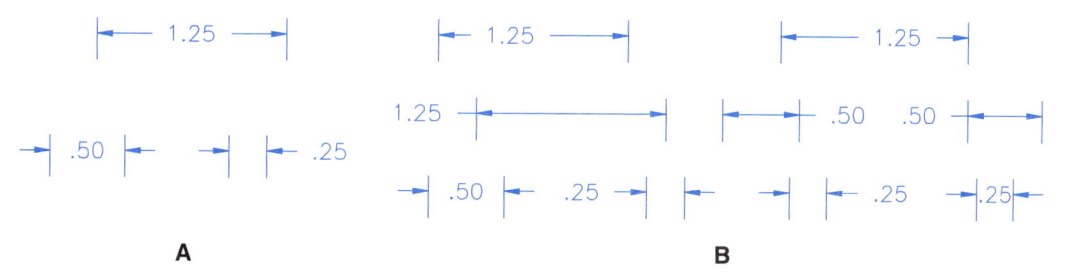

FIGURE 11.37 (A) These examples were created with the User Defined option off. AutoCAD LT automatically centers the dimension text on the dimension line. (B) These examples were created with the User Defined option on. This gives you control over placement of the dimension text.

The Force Line Inside check box causes AutoCAD LT to force the dimension line inside the extension lines even when the text and arrowheads are outside. The default application is with the dimension line and arrowheads outside the extension lines. Figure 11.38 shows the difference between Force Line Inside on and off. The practice used depends on the company preference. The command line dimension variable for this feature is DIMTOFL (**T**ext **O**utside, **F**orce **L**ine inside).

The Fit: list box provides several options that control the way the dimension line, text, and arrowheads are formatted. The default is Best Fit, which allows AutoCAD LT to place text and dimension lines with arrowheads inside of extension lines if space is available, or place the text inside and dimension line with arrowheads outside of extension lines, or place everything outside of extension lines depending on the amount of space between extension lines. Figure 11.39 shows the complete Fit: list. The DIMFIT variable has the same effect with a setting of 3 when typed at the Command: prompt. The other Fit: options are explained in the following list:

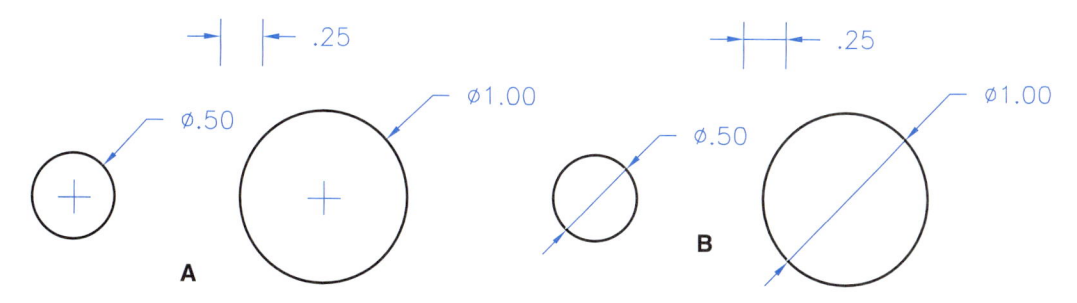

FIGURE 11.38 (A) Line representation with the Force Line Inside option off. (B) Line representation with the Force Line Inside option on. Notice the dimension line is forced between the extension lines and inside the circles.

FIGURE 11.39 The options available in the Fit: list of the Format dialog box.

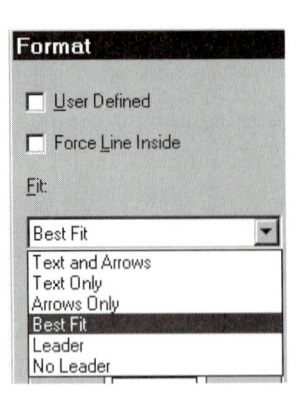

Text and Arrows—When this option is used, AutoCAD LT places the text, dimension line, and arrowheads inside the extension lines if there is enough space, or everything is placed outside the extensions if there is not enough space for everything inside. This is controlled by the DIMFIT variable set at 0.

Text Only—The text, dimension line, and arrowheads are placed inside the extension lines if there is enough space for everything. If there is enough space for only the text inside the extension lines, then the dimension lines and arrowheads are placed outside. Everything is placed outside if there is not enough room for the text inside. Use DIMFIT set at 1 for this option when using the command line.

Arrows Only—The text, dimension line, and arrowheads are placed inside the extension lines if there is enough space for everything. If there is enough space for only the arrowheads and dimension line inside the extension lines, then the text is placed outside. Everything is placed outside if there is not enough room for anything inside. This is a DIMFIT setting of 2.

Leader—AutoCAD LT places the text inside and the dimension line and arrowheads outside if space permits. If the text does not fit inside, the text is placed away from the dimension line and a leader line connects the text to the dimension line as shown in Figure 11.40A. This practice is not recommended by the ASME standard but can be used in crowded situations if all other options fail. This is the DIMFIT dimension variable set at 4.

No Leader—This is similar to the Leader option except the text is placed away from the dimension line with no leader connecting the dimension line as shown in Figure 11.40B. This is even more unusual than using the Leader option. The DIMFIT setting for this option is 5.

Setting the Horizontal Text Alignment

The Horizontal Justification area of the Format dialog box is used to align the placement of the dimension text horizontally with the dimension line or extension lines. The image tile provides a representation of the current option. The rectangle in the image tile represents the dimension text. The Center option is the AutoCAD LT default and is used to center text on the dimension line as shown by the image tile in Figure 11.36. Pick the down arrow to access the full list of options as shown in Figure 11.41. You can select the options by

FIGURE 11.40 (A) An example of the Leader option of the Fit: list in the Format dialog box.
(B) An example of the No Leader option of the Fit: list in the Format dialog box.

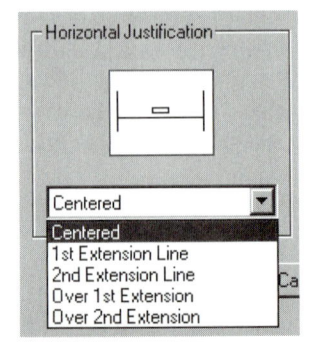

FIGURE 11.41 The list of options in the Horizontal Justification area of the Format dialog box.

FIGURE 11.42 The Horizontal Justification options and their related image tile representations found in the Format dialog box. The Centered default is shown in Figure 11.36. (A) The 1st Extension Line option. (B) The 2nd Extension Line option. (C) The Over 1st Extension option. (D) The Over 2nd Extension option.

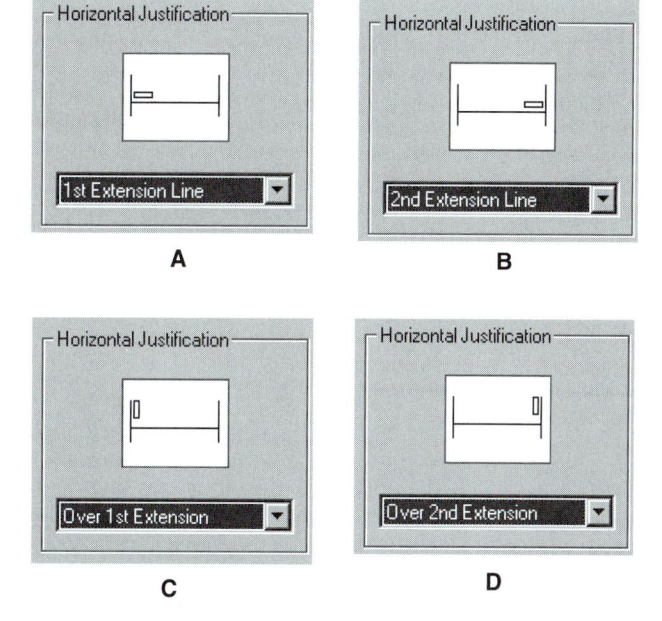

picking the desired name in the list or you can pick on the image tile to cycle through the options. The horizontal justification is controlled at the Command: prompt by using the DIMJUST (**JUST**ification) variable. The following list explains each of the options:

1st Extension Line—This option locates the text next to the extension line that is placed first. The image tile representation for this option is shown in Figure 11.42A. The DIMJUST setting is 1.

2nd Extension Line—This option locates the text next to the second extension line. The image tile representation for this option is shown in Figure 11.42B. The DIMJUST setting is 2.

Over 1st Extension—This option places the text aligned with and over the first extension line. The image tile is shown in Figure 11.42C. The DIMJUST setting is 3.

Over 2nd Extension—This option places the text aligned with and over the second extension line. The image tile is shown in Figure 11.42D. The DIMJUST setting is 4.

Field Notes

The Horizontal Justification options provide you with the ability to set the dimension text in a fixed position for all future dimension placement until you change to a different option. If these fixed settings do not give you enough flexibility, you might consider leaving horizontal justification at the Centered option and check the Under Defined box to give you flexibility when placing each dimension.

Setting the Vertical Text Alignment
The Vertical Justification area of the Format dialog box is used to set the vertical alignment of dimension text in relation to the dimension line. The Centered option is the default and places dimension text centered in a gap provided in the dimension line. Figure 11.36 displays this default option with its related image tile. This is the dimensioning practice that is commonly used in mechanical drafting and many other fields. The dimension variable used at the Command: prompt is DIMTAD (**T**ext **A**bove **D**imension line) turned off. To change the vertical justification, pick one of the options found in the list shown in Figure 11.43 or pick on the image tile to cycle through the options. The following list explains each of the other vertical justification options:

FIGURE 11.43 The list of Vertical Justification options found in the Format dialog box. The Centered option and its representative image tile are displayed.

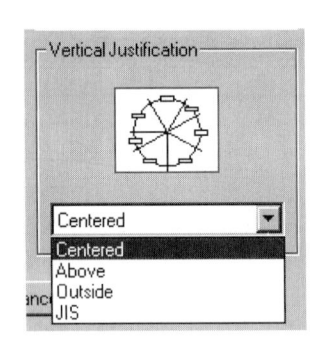

Above—This option is commonly used for architectural drafting and building construction. This option places the dimension text horizontally and above horizontal dimension lines and in a gap provided in vertical and angled dimension lines. Architectural drafting commonly uses *aligned dimensioning,* in which the dimension text is aligned with the dimension lines and all text either reads from the bottom or right side of the sheet. If the dimension text is to be placed above and aligned with vertical and angled dimension lines, the Inside Horizontal and Outside Horizontal check boxes must be off. This is explained in the next section. The Above option and its related image tile are shown in Figure 11.44A. When entered at the Command: prompt, the DIMTAD setting is on.

Outside—This option places the dimension text outside the dimension line and either above or below a horizontal dimension line or to the right or left of a vertical dimension line depending on which way you move the cursor. Figure 11.44B shows the related image tile.

JIS—Use this option when dimensioning for the Japanese Industry Standard. The related image tile is shown in Figure 11.44C.

FIGURE 11.44 The Vertical Justification options and their related image tile representations found in the Format dialog box. The Centered default is shown in Figure 11.43. (A) The Above option. (B) The Outside option. (C) The JIS (Japanese Industry Standard) option.

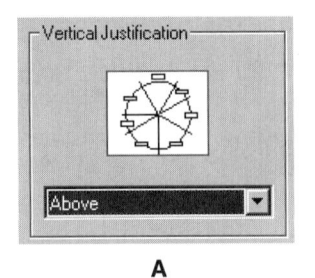

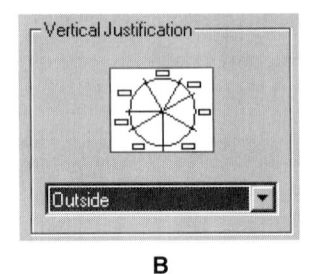

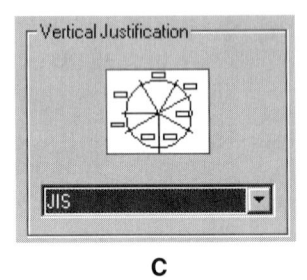

An actual example of each of the horizontal and vertical justification options is shown in Figure 11.45. Combinations of the horizontal and vertical options can be used to create different results.

FIGURE 11.45 Actual dimensions placed using Horizontal and Vertical Justifications from the Format dialog box. (A) Horizontal Justifications. (B) Vertical Justifications. Optional results are possible by combining the effects of horizontal and vertical justification in different ways.

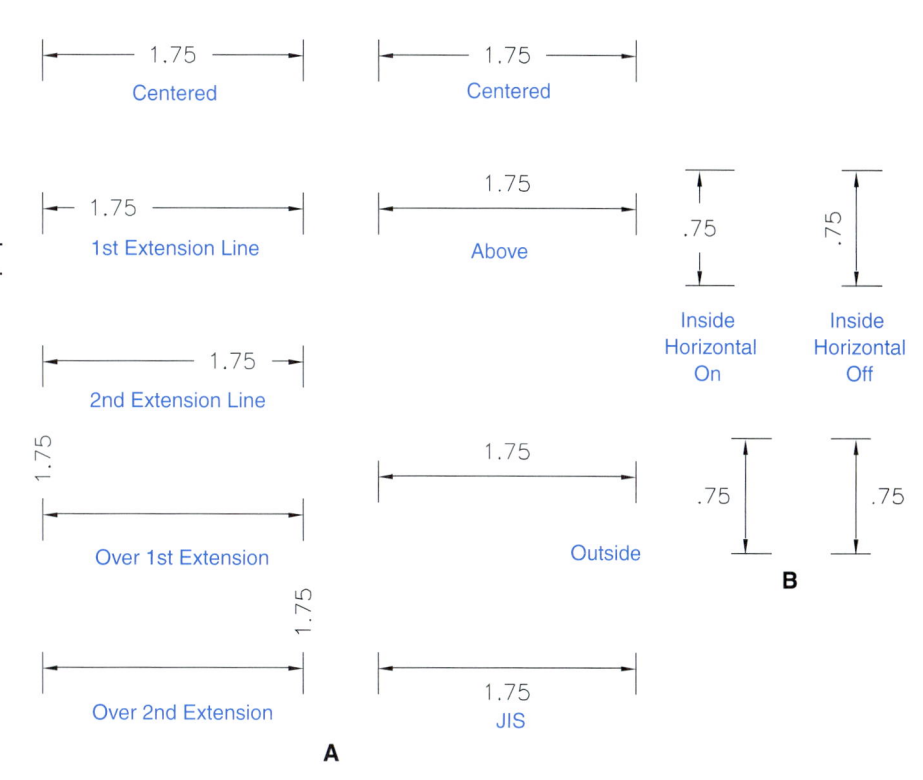

Dimension Text Alignment Inside or Outside the Extension Lines

The Text area of the Format dialog box allows you to control the alignment of dimension text inside and outside of the extension lines. This area is used when you want to draw unidirectional dimensions or aligned dimensions. These terms were defined early in this chapter. The default is for the Inside Horizontal and Outside Horizontal check boxes to be on, which draws the unidirectional dimensions that are common for mechanical drafting applications. The image tile represents the status of these check boxes. Inside Horizontal and Outside Horizontal are turned off when aligned dimensions are used. Aligned dimensions are typically used for architectural dimensioning. A combination can also be used, but normally these check boxes are either on or off. Inside Horizontal is controlled at the Command: prompt by the DIMTIH (**T**ext **I**nside is **H**orizontal) variable, and Outside Horizontal is controlled by the DIMTOH (**T**ext **O**utside is **H**orizontal) variable.

Figure 11.46 shows the image tile representation for Inside Horizontal and Outside Horizontal turned on and off. When doing dimensioning for mechanical drawing, it is common to have User Defined on, Horizontal and Vertical Justification Centered, and Inside Horizontal and Outside Horizontal on. For architectural drafting, it is typical to have User Defined on, Force Line Inside on, Horizontal Justification Centered, Vertical Justification Above, and Inside Horizontal and Outside Horizontal off. Figure 11.47 shows examples of these settings used for mechanical and architectural dimensioning applications. Both examples use the same objects with decimal dimensions; however, architectural drawings are usually dimensioned in feet and inches.

FIGURE 11.46 The Text area of the Format dialog box. (A) Inside Horizontal on and Outside Horizontal on. (B) Inside Horizontal off and Outside Horizontal off.

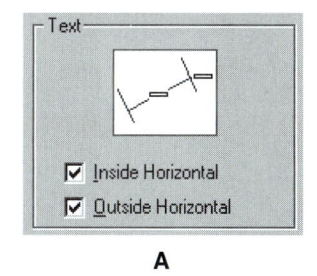

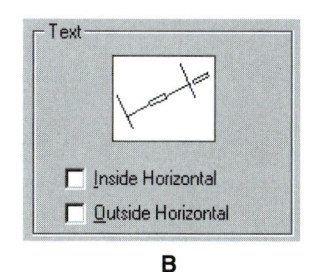

FIGURE 11.47 (A) Dimensioning for mechanical drafting using unidirectional dimensioning with text placed in a space in the dimension lines. (B) Dimensioning for architectural drafting using aligned dimensioning with text placed above the dimension lines.

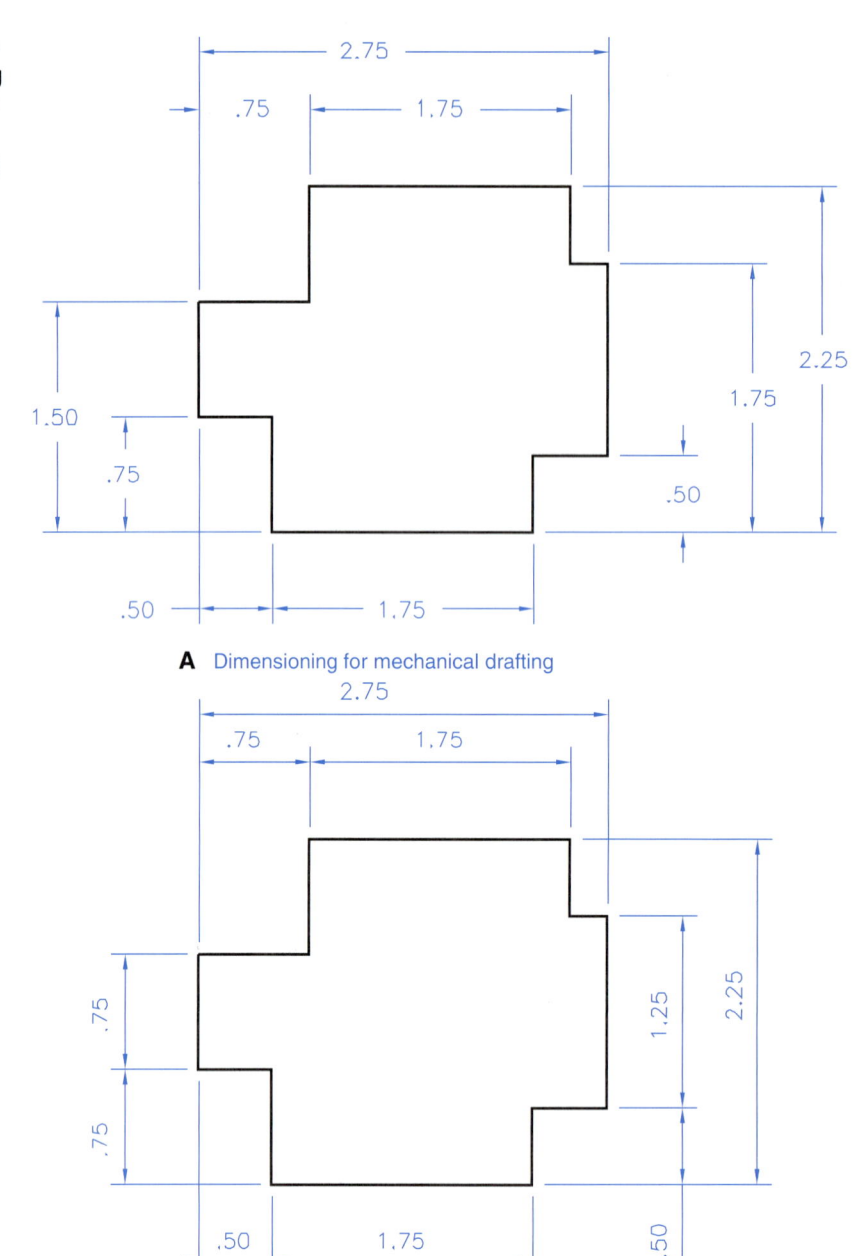

A Dimensioning for mechanical drafting

B Dimensioning for architectural drafting

CHAPTER 11 ||| Dimensioning a Drawing

Exercise 11.11

1. Begin a new drawing or use one of your prototypes.
2. Open the Dimension Styles dialog box and access the Format dialog box. Set the User Defined, Force Line Inside, and Fit options as needed to draw and dimension objects or place dimensions similar to those shown in Figures 11.37, 11.38, and 11.40.
3. Pick each of the Horizontal Justification options and watch how the image tile changes with each selection.
4. Pick each of the Vertical Justification options and watch how the image tile changes with each selection.
5. Set the Horizontal and Vertical Justification options as needed to place dimensions similar to those of Figure 11.45.
6. Turn Inside Horizontal and Outside Horizontal on and off and observe how the image tile changes.
7. Set the Inside Horizontal and Outside Horizontal options as needed to draw and dimension objects similar to those of Figure 11.47.
8. Save the drawing as EX11.11.

Changing the Dimension Text

A wide variety of changes can be made to dimension text by picking the Annotation ... button in the Dimension Styles dialog box. This opens the Annotation dialog box shown in Figure 11.48. AutoCAD LT defines an *annotation* as anything that has to do with dimensioning text.

Setting Primary Units

The ***primary units*** are the part of the dimension from which tolerances or other units are calculated or related. Tolerances are defined and explained later. The following paragraphs explain the functions of each of the options in the Primary Units area. Pick the Units ... button to access the Primary Units dialog box shown in Figure 11.49. The elements of the Primary Units dialog box are explained as follows:

Units—This area is where you select the type of units for use as dimension text. The default is Decimal units. Pick the down arrow to access the list shown in Figure 11.50. The purpose and examples of each type of unit were explained in Chapter 2 in the discussion of drawing setup and use of the UNITS command. Dimension units are controlled at the Command: prompt with the DIMUNIT variable.

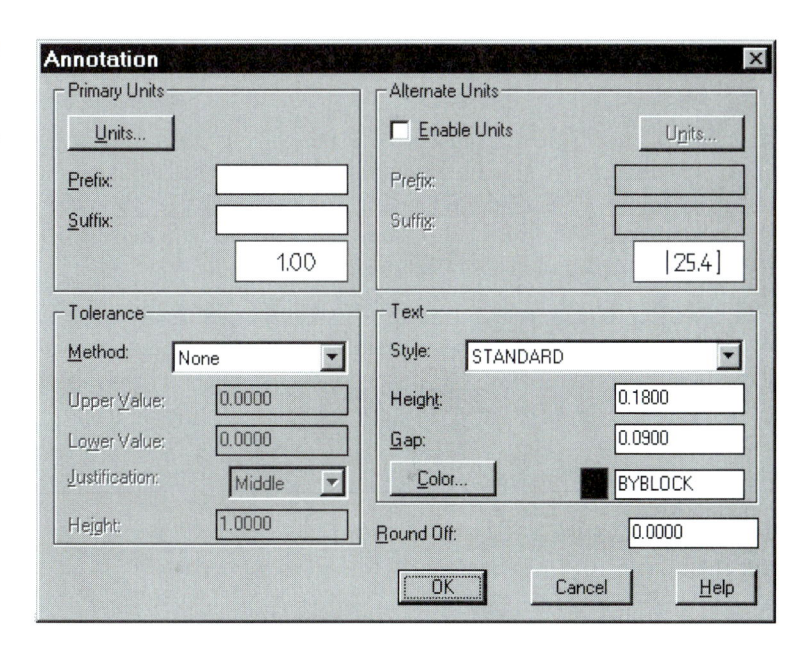

FIGURE 11.48 The Annotation dialog box is accessed by picking the Annotation ... button in the Dimension Styles dialog box.

FIGURE 11.49 The Primary Units dialog box is accessed by picking the Units ... button in the Primary Units area of the Annotation dialog box.

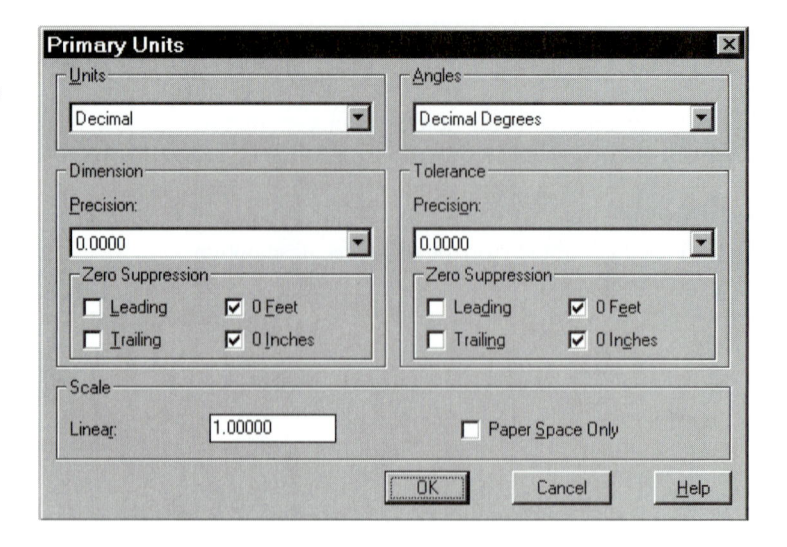

Dimension—The Dimension area controls the decimal place precision and the placement of leading and trailing zeros in dimension numerals. The Precision: list allows you to decide how many zeros follow the decimal place. This is important in mechanical drafting because adding zeros after the decimal point generally tightens the tolerance for unspecified tolerance dimensions. Tolerance terminology is defined later in this section. The default is 0.0000, although 0.00 and 0.000 settings are common in inch mechanical drafting depending on the desired tolerance. Varying degrees of dimension precision can be found on the same drawing. The list of Precision options is shown in Figure 11.51. Dimension unit precision is controlled at the Command: prompt with the DIMDEC variable.

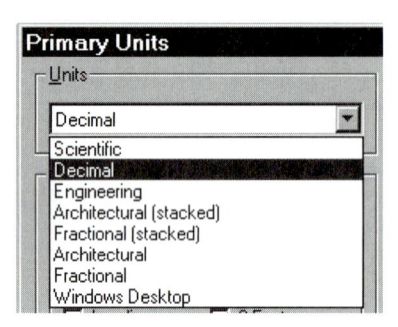

FIGURE 11.50 The list of Units options in the Primary Units dialog box.

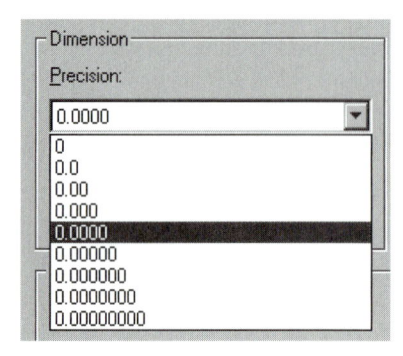

FIGURE 11.51 The list of Precision options in the Dimension area of the Primary Units dialog box.

Also found in the Dimension area of the Primary Units dialog box is the Zero Suppression area. Look at Figure 11.49, where you will see four check boxes that are used to control the display of leading and trailing zeros in the primary units. The Leading and Trailing check boxes are off by default, and the 0 Feet and 0 Inches are on by default. This is set at the Command: prompt with the DIMZIN (Zero INch display) variable. The following list explains the use of each option:

Leading—This check box is off by default, which leaves a zero on dimension numerals less than one. This complies with the ASME standard for metric dimensions. You should check this box if you are doing inch dimensioning. The results of each application are shown in Figure 11.52. The command line variable is DIMZIN set at 4.

FIGURE 11.52 (A) The recommended metric dimension text application with Leading Zero Suppression off. (B) The recommended inch dimension text application with Leading Zero Suppression on.

A Metric 0.5000
B Inch .5000

FIGURE 11.53 (A) The recommended metric dimension text application with Leading Zero Suppression off and Trailing Zero Suppression on. (B) The recommended inch dimension text application with Leading Zero Suppression on and Trailing Zero Suppression off.

Trailing—This is off by default, which leaves the number of zeros after the decimal point based on the precision setting. This is usually off for inch dimensioning because the trailing zeros often imply higher precision levels for the manufacturing process. However, the ASME standard recommends that zeros be removed following decimal metric dimensions, which means that you should check this box when doing metric dimensioning. The command line setting is DIMZIN at 8. Figure 11.53 shows an example with this option off and on.

0 Feet—This check box is on by default which removes the zero in feet and inch dimensions when there are zero inches. For example, when 0 Feet is on a measurement reads 8′. If 0 Feet is off the same dimension reads 8′-0″. This is the DIMZIN variable set at 0.

0 Inches—This check box is on by default, which removes the zero when the inch part of feet and inch dimensions is less than one inch, such as 8′-3/4″. If this check box is off, the same dimension reads 8′-0 3/4″. This is controlled at the Command: prompt with a DIMZIN setting of 3.

Continuing with our discussion of the Primary Units dialog box, these are the remaining options:

Angles—This area of the Primary Units dialog box is used to set the desired type of angular units for dimensioning. The angular unit options were discussed in Chapter 2 during the discussion of AutoCAD LT setup and the UNITS command. The UNITS command does not control the type of units used for dimensioning. These must be set here. The default is Decimal Degrees and the list of options is shown in Figure 11.54. Angular units for dimensions are set at the Command: prompt with the DIMAUNIT (Angular UNITs) dimension variable.

Tolerance—The Tolerance area of the Primary Units dialog box has the same settings as the Dimension area. A *tolerance* is the total amount by which a specific dimension is permitted to vary. Additional information and tolerance options are found later in this chapter. The Precision: list allows you to set the number of zeros displayed after the tolerance decimal place. The ANSI/ASME standard recommends that the precision for the tolerance and the dimension be the same. The dimension variable used for this setting at the Command: prompt is DIMTDEC (Tolerance DECimal).

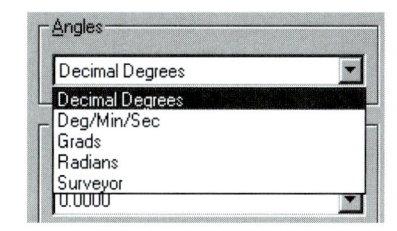

The Zero Suppression options in the Tolerance area have the same effect as previously discussed with the Dimension area. For example, Leading should be off and Trailing should be on for metric dimensions, and Leading should be on and Trailing should be off for inch dimensions. This option is controlled at the Command: prompt with the DIMTZIN (Tolerance Zero INch display) variable using the same settings as shown with the DIMZIN variable to obtain the same effect.

Scale—This area of the Primary Units dialog box is used to set the scale factor of linear dimensions. If the scale factor in the Linear: box is 1, then the dimension values are the same as their measured values. If the setting is 2, then the dimension values are twice as much as the measured amount. For example, an actual measurement of 1 in. is displayed as 1 with a linear scale of 1, but the same measurement is displayed as 2 when the linear scale is 2. This can also be set at the Command: prompt with the DIMLFAC (Linear units scale FACtor) variable.

FIGURE 11.54 The Angles options of the Primary Units dialog box.

FIGURE 11.55 The Methods: options in the Tolerance area of the Annotation dialog box.

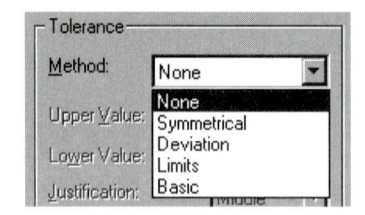

The Paper Space Only check box is off by default. Placing a check in this box makes the linear scale factor active only when dimensioning in paper space. To do this at the command line, set DIMLFAC to a negative value that represents the desired scale factor.

Setting Tolerance Methods

The concept of tolerances was mentioned in the discussion in the preceding section related to precision. A *tolerance* is the total amount a specific dimension is permitted to vary. Tolerance dimensions are typically used on mechanical drawings for manufacturing. The Tolerance area of the Annotation dialog box is where tolerance methods can be applied to your drawing. See Figure 11.48. The Method: list provides None as the default. This means that no tolerance method is used with your dimensions and the options in this area are disabled. The image tile in the Primary Units area displays 1.00. This is the image of a dimension without tolerance and corresponds to the None option in the Tolerance area. Pick the down arrow to see the other options in the Method: list as shown in Figure 11.55. The tolerance method options are explained in the following list:

Symmetrical: This option is used to draw dimension text displaying an equal bilateral tolerance. An *equal bilateral tolerance* is a tolerance for which the variation is permitted equally in both directions from the specified dimension. The *specified dimension* is the primary units part of the dimension with tolerance. When the Symmetrical option is selected, the Upper Value: box, Justification: list, and Height: box are active and the image tile in the Primary Units area displays an equal bilateral tolerance as shown in Figure 11.56A. Next, enter a value, such as .005, for the equal bilateral tolerance in the Upper Value: box, as shown in Figure 11.56B. Now, draw a dimension with the ±.005 tolerance applied. Figure 11.57 shows a sample dimension and its components. The Symmetrical option can be set at the Command: prompt by turning the DIMTOL (**TOL**erance) variable on and the DIMLIM (**LIM**its) variable off and setting the DIMTP (**T**olerance **P**lus) and DIMTM (**T**olerance **M**inus) variables to the same numerical value.

> ✏️ **Field Notes**
>
> If your dimension tolerances do not reflect the level of precision you want, check the setting of the DIMTDEC variable. Either type **DIMTDEC** at the command line, or use the Tolerance area of the Primary Units dialog box accessed by picking the Units … button in the Annotation dialog box.

FIGURE 11.56 (A) The Symmetrical tolerance method option. Notice the matching image tile in the Primary Units area. (B) Enter the desired value in the Upper Value: box.

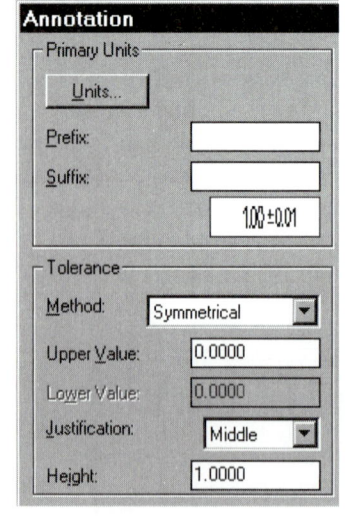

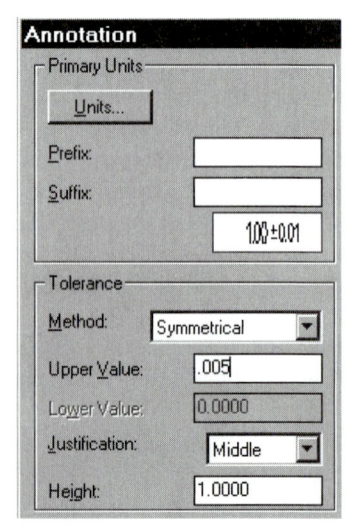

A   B

CHAPTER 11 ||| Dimensioning a Drawing   457

FIGURE 11.57 The elements of an equal bilateral tolerance dimension.

Specified dimension — Equal bilateral tolerance

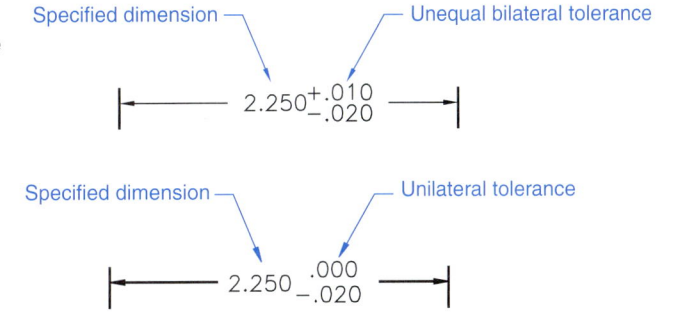

2.250±.005

FIGURE 11.58 The Deviation tolerance method option with values entered in the Upper Value: and Lower Value: boxes. Notice the matching image tile in the Primary Units area.

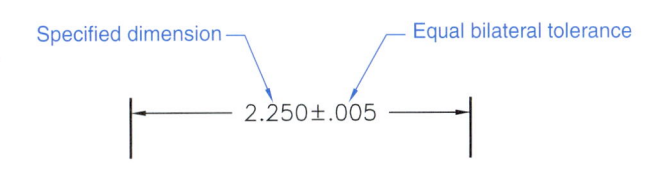

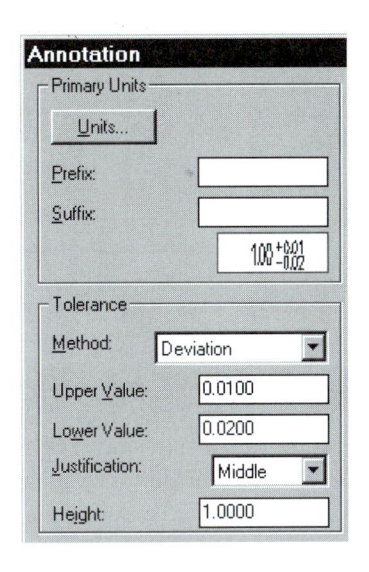

Deviation: AutoCAD refers to an unequal bilateral tolerance as *deviation.* An *unequal bilateral tolerance* is a tolerance for which the variation is permitted unequally in both directions from the specified dimension. When you select Deviation, the Upper Value: and Lower Value: text boxes are available to enter the desired upper and lower tolerance values as shown in Figure 11.58. Also, when you pick the Deviation option, the image tile in the Primary Units area changes to match a representation for this option. Figure 11.59 shows the results of drawing an unequal bilateral tolerance.

The Deviation option can also be used to draw unilateral tolerances. A *unilateral tolerance* is a tolerance for which the variation is permitted in only one direction from the specified dimension. If you want a unilateral tolerance, enter zero as either the Upper Value or the Lower Value. Figure 11.60 shows an example of a unilateral tolerance dimension. When you draw a unilateral tolerance, AutoCAD LT automatically drops the + or − value from the zero part of the tolerance. This is the preferred method for a metric tolerance but is not recommended by ASME for an inch tolerance. The Deviation option can be set at the Command: prompt by turning the DIMTOL variable on and the DIMLIM variable off, and then setting the DIMTP and DIMTM variables to different numerical values. When you turn DIMTOL on, DIMLIM is automatically turned off. Likewise, when you turn DIMLIM on, the DIMTOL variable is automatically turned off.

Limits: The types of dimension shown in Figures 11.57, 11.59, and 11.60 are referred to as *plus/minus tolerances.* This is where a specified dimension and tolerance values are given. A *limits tolerance* is a tolerance for which the plus and minus part of the tolerance is calculated with the specified dimension to provide tolerance limits. When you pick the Limits option, the Upper Value: and Lower Value: text boxes are available to enter the desired amount you want added and subtracted from the specified dimension to create the limits. The values can be the same or different—a choice that depends on the results you expect. The image tile in the Primary Units area is changed to represent tolerance limits as

FIGURE 11.59 The elements of an unequal bilateral tolerance dimension.

Specified dimension — Unequal bilateral tolerance

$2.250^{+.010}_{-.020}$

FIGURE 11.60 The elements of a unilateral tolerance dimension.

Specified dimension — Unilateral tolerance

$2.250^{\;.000}_{-.020}$

FIGURE 11.61 The Limits tolerance method option with values entered in the Upper Value: and Lower Value: boxes. Notice the matching image tile in the Primary Units area.

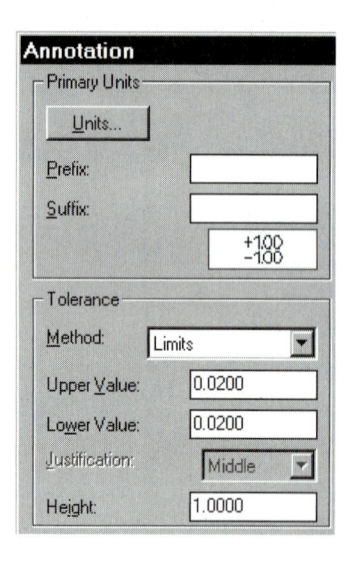

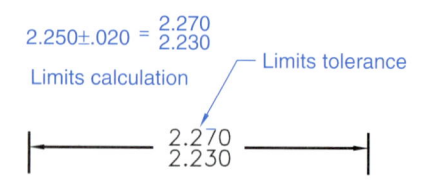

FIGURE 11.62 A sample limits tolerance dimension with the limits calculated automatically by AutoCAD LT based on the values you specify.

shown in Figure 11.61. A limits dimension is shown in Figure 11.62 using the values entered in Figure 11.61. The Limits option can be set at the Command: prompt by turning the DIMTOL variable off and the DIMLIM variable on, and set the DIMTP and DIMTM variables to the desired numerical values.

Basic: The Basic method option is used to draw basic dimensions. A ***basic dimension*** is used in geometric dimensioning and tolerancing and is used as a value that is considered a theoretically perfect size, profile, orientation, or location dimension. When you pick the Basic option from the Method: list, all other options in the Tolerance area are unavailable. A basic dimension has a box around it as displayed in the image tile in the Primary Units area shown in Figure 11.63. Figure 11.64 shows a sample basic dimension.

Field Notes

- With each tolerance method option you pick by name, the image tile in the Primary Units area changes to represent the selection. You can also pick on the image tile to automatically cycle through the tolerance method options.
- Inch tolerance dimensions should have the Leading Zero Suppression box checked in the Dimension and Tolerance areas of the Primary Units dialog box. This allows you to properly place inch tolerance dimensions based on ASME standards without the zero before the decimal point, such as .625±.005.
- Metric tolerance dimensions should have the Leading Zero Suppression box off (not checked) in the Dimension and Tolerance areas of the Primary Units dialog box. This allows you to properly place metric tolerance dimensions based on ASME standards with the zero before the decimal point; for example, 12±0.2.

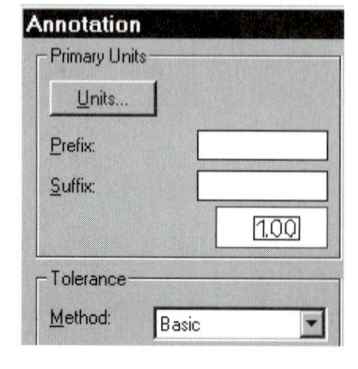

FIGURE 11.63 The Basic dimension tolerance method option. Notice the box around the dimension shown in the image tile in the Primary Units area.

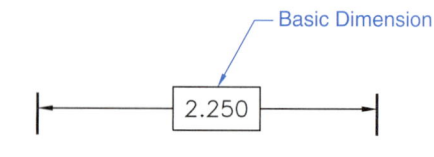

FIGURE 11.64 A sample basic dimension.

CHAPTER 11 ||| Dimensioning a Drawing

FIGURE 11.65 The Justification: list of the Tolerance area in the Annotation dialog box.

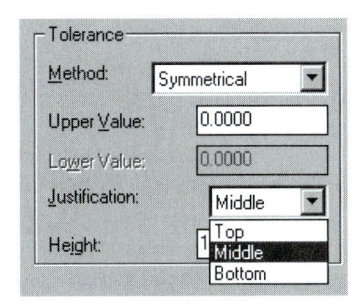

Tolerance Justification: The Justification: list in the Tolerance area is used to establish how the tolerance value is placed in alignment with the specified dimension. The Justification list is active when the Symmetrical and Deviation options are used. Middle justification is the default, and it centers the tolerance with the specified dimension. This is also the common ASME recommended practice. The other options are Top and Bottom as shown in Figure 11.65. The effect of using each of the justification methods is shown with tolerance dimensions in Figure 11.66. Tolerance justification is controlled at the Command: prompt with the DIMTOLJ variable.

Tolerance Height: The Height: box in the Tolerance area is used to set the text height of the tolerance in relationship to the text height of the specified dimension. The default is 1.00, which makes the tolerance text the same height as the specified dimension text. This is the recommended ASME practice. If you want the tolerance height three-quarters as high as the specified dimension height, enter .75 in the Height: box. Some companies prefer this practice when using unequal bilateral tolerances. Figure 11.67 shows an example of dimensions with different tolerance text heights. The tolerance height is set at the Command: prompt with the DIMTFAC variable.

FIGURE 11.66 Examples of the different tolerance justification options. The Middle option is recommended by the ASME standard.

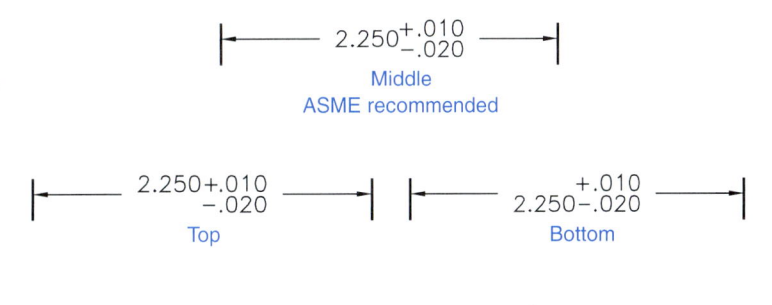

FIGURE 11.67 Examples of using different tolerance height options. (A) Tolerance height value of 1 is the default and makes the tolerance text the same height as the specified dimension text. This is the ASME recommended practice. (B) Tolerance height value of .75 makes the tolerance text height three-quarters the height of the specified dimension text height.

> ### Exercise 11.12
>
> 1. Begin a new drawing or use one of your prototypes.
> 2. Open the Dimension Styles dialog box and access the Annotation dialog box.
> 3. Open the Primary Units dialog box and open the Units list. Look at the options and pick Decimal.
> 4. Open the Dimension Precision: list and pick the four-place decimal.
> 5. Set the Dimension Zero Suppression as needed to draw the dimensions shown in Figures 11.52 and 11.53.
> 6. Open the Angles list in the Primary Units dialog box and look at the options before selecting Decimal Degrees.
> 7. Open the Method: list in the Tolerance area of the Annotation dialog box and pick each of the options and watch the image tile in the Primary Units area change to match the selections.
> 8. Make the necessary tolerance settings to draw the tolerance dimensions shown in Figures 11.57, 11.59, 11.60, 11.62, and 11.64.
> 9. Use the tolerance Justification: options to draw the dimensions shown in Figure 11.66. Reset to the default value when finished.
> 10. Set the tolerance Height: option as needed to draw the dimensions shown in Figure 11.67. Reset to the default value when finished.
> 11. Save the drawing as EX11.12.

Setting Dimension Text Options

The Text area of the Annotation dialog box is used to set the dimension text style, height, gap, and color. These options are explained as follows:

Style:—The dimension text style uses the STANDARD text style by default. Text styles must be defined in the current drawing before they are available for use in dimension text. You can access the list of loaded text styles by clicking the down arrow of the Style: list as shown in Figure 11.68. Dimension text styles are changed at the Command: prompt by using the DIMTXSTY variable.

Height:—The dimension text height is set by entering the desired value in the Height: box. Dimension text height is generally the same as the rest of the text height found on the drawing. The text height for other drawing text is set using the STYLE command. The default dimension text height is .18, which is an acceptable standard. Many companies use a text height of .125 in. The ASME standard recommends text heights between .125 and .188 in. Dimension text height can be set at the Command: prompt with the DIMTXT variable.

Gap:—The Gap: box is used to set the gap between the dimension line and the dimension text, and the gap between the basic dimension box and the text. The default gap is .09. Figure 11.69 shows the gap related to different applications. The gap is changed at the Command: prompt by using the DIMGAP dimension variable.

Color ...—Pick the Color ... button to access the Select Color dialog box if you want to change the color of dimension text. The dimension color default is BYBLOCK. The dimension text color is changed at the Command: prompt with the DIMCLRT (**CoLoR** of **T**ext) variable.

FIGURE 11.68 Open the Text Style: list to determine which dimension text styles have been loaded.

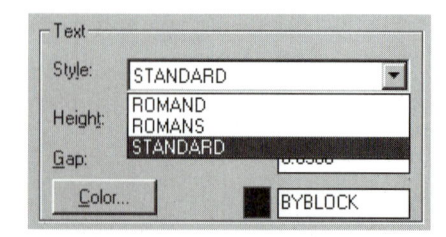

CHAPTER 11 ||| Dimensioning a Drawing   461

FIGURE 11.69 The effect of the dimension Gap option on different dimension applications. (A) Typical mechanical drafting dimension with dimension text placed in a space provided in the dimension line. (B) Typical architectural drafting dimension with the dimension text placed above the dimension line. (C) Basic dimension application.

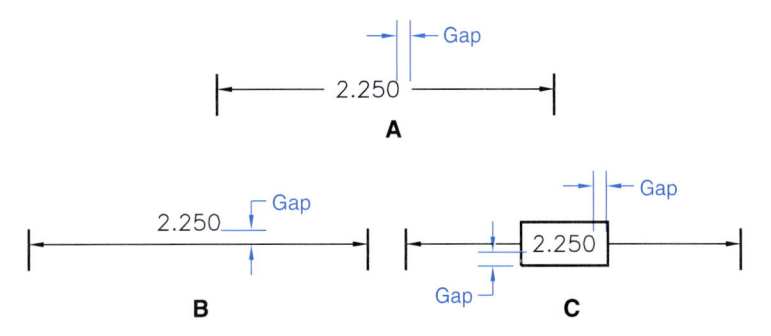

Setting Alternate Units Dimensioning

Alternate units have been referred to as dual dimensioning, which is the process of showing inch measurements followed by millimeters measurements in brackets or millimeters followed by inches in brackets. Dual dimensioning practice is no longer a recommended ASME standard. ASME recommends that drawings be dimensioned using inch or metric units only. Alternate units are activated by picking the Enable Units check box in the Alternate Units area of the Annotation dialog box as shown in Figure 11.70. This feature is set at the Command: prompt with the DIMALT variable.

Pick the Units ... button to access the Alternate Units dialog box. This dialog box looks similar to the Primary Units dialog box and its features work in the same manner. The related dimension variables when entered at the Command: prompt are Units, DIMALTU; Dimension Precision, DIMALTD; Dimension Zero Suppression, DIMALTZ; Tolerance Precision, DIMALTTD; Tolerance Zero Suppression, DIMALTTZ; and Scale, DIMALTF.

The Angles area of the Alternate Units dialog box is disabled because there are no alternate unit options for angular measurements. The image tile in the Alternate Units area serves the same function as the image tile in the Primary Units area except it displays the representation when changing alternate units settings for tolerance values.

Setting Prefixes and Suffixes

Prefixes are special notes or applications that are placed in front of the dimension text, and ***suffixes*** are special notes or applications that are placed after the dimension text. A typical prefix might be SØ2.5, where SØ means spherical diameter. A typical suffix might be 2.5 MAX, where MAX is the abbreviation for maximum, or 2.5 MIN, where MIN is the abbreviation for minimum. The abbreviation IN. can also be used when one or more inch dimensions are placed on a metric dimensioned drawing, or a suffix of MM can be used on one or more millimeter dimensions on an inch drawing.

The desired prefix is entered in the Prefix: box and the desired suffix is entered in the Suffix: box of the Primary Units area of the Annotation dialog box. Figure 11.71A shows S%%C entered as a prefix and MAX en-

FIGURE 11.70 Check the Enable Units box to activate the Alternate Units area of the Annotation dialog box.

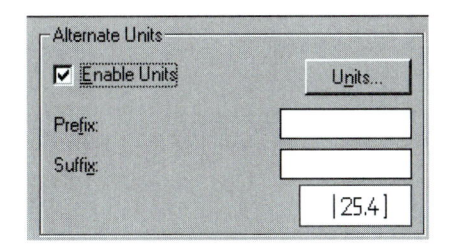

FIGURE 11.71 (A) Entering a prefix and suffix in the Primary Units area of the Annotation dialog box. (B) The S%%C value entered in the Prefix: box and the MAX value entered in the Suffix: box results in a dimension that looks like this.

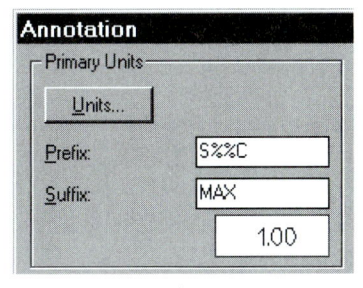

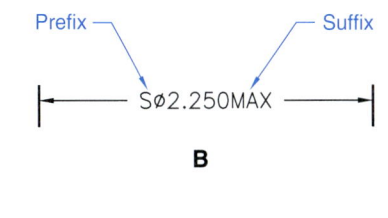

tered as a suffix. S%%C is the code that results in SØ. Figure 11.71B shows a dimension drawn with the SØ prefix and MAX suffix. The use of the Primary Units prefix and suffix options is controlled at the Command: prompt with the DIMPOST variable. You can also set prefixes and suffixes for Alternate Units as needed when the alternate units are enabled. These are controlled at the Command: prompt with the DIMAPOST variable.

> ### Field Notes
>
> Generally a prefix or suffix is not used on every dimension in the drawing. A prefix or suffix is normally a special specification and might be used in only a few cases. Because of this, you might set up a special dimension style for these applications or just enter them when needed by using the Mtext or Text option of the related dimensioning command.

Rounding Off Dimension Numerals

The Annotation dialog box has a Round Off: box where you can have AutoCAD LT round off all numbers to a designated value. The default is zero as shown in Figure 11.48. Zero in the Round Off: box means that no rounding takes place and all dimensions are placed exactly as measured. If you enter a value of .1, then all dimensions are rounded to the closest .1 unit. For example, an actual measurement of 4.188 is rounded to 4.2. The Command: prompt control for this variable is DIMRND.

Exercise 11.13

1. Begin a new drawing or use one of your prototypes.
2. Open the Dimension Styles dialog box and access the Annotation dialog box.
3. Load the ROMANS and Stylus BT text fonts. Open the Annotation dialog box and notice the options in the Text Style: list.
4. Set text height at .125 and the gap at .05.
5. Draw a dimension similar to that of Figure 11.69A using ROMANS font, and draw a dimension similar to that of Figure 11.69B using Stylus BT font.
6. Set the prefix and suffix needed to draw the dimension shown in Figure 11.71B.
7. Remove the prefix and suffix from the dialog box when finished.
8. Save the drawing as EX11.13.

Drawing Leader Lines and Notes

Dimension
Leader

Dimension
Leader

**LEADER
LE**

Leader lines were introduced earlier when drawing dimensions for circles and arcs using the DIMRADIUS and DIMDIAMETER commands. AutoCAD LT automatically draws a leader line connected to a circle or arc when using these commands. In certain situations, you may want to draw a leader line connected to a note other than a radius or diameter dimension. These types of notes apply to specific features or processes on the drawing and are referred to as *specific* or *local notes*. When you want to use a leader for an application like this, pick the Leader button in the Dimension toolbar, pick Leader in the Dimension pull-down menu, or type **LE** or **LEADER** at the Command: prompt. The LEADER command asks you to pick a point to start and end the leader and then add the desired text. AutoCAD LT refers to text with a leader as an ***annotation***. An arrowhead that matches the current dimension style is added at the start and a shoulder is automatically placed at the note. The following command sequence draws the leader and note shown in Figure 11.72 with the different elements labeled:

Command: **LE** or **LEADER**↵
From point: ⟨*pick the leader start point*⟩
To point: ⟨*pick the leader endpoint*⟩
To point (Format/Annotation/Undo) <Annotation>: ↵
Annotation (or press Enter for options): **2 × 10 JOISTS 16″ OC**↵
MText: ↵
Command:

FIGURE 11.72 The leader and its related elements drawn using the LEADER command.

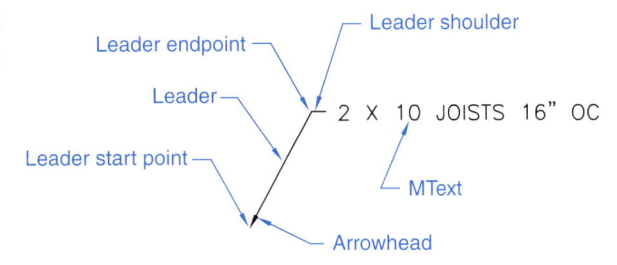

A leader in mechanical drafting normally has one line segment from the arrowhead to the shoulder. Although this is also true with architectural drafting, architectural leaders can be more flexible. Architectural leaders can have more than one segment if needed. To accomplish this, keep picking points at the To point: prompt. Leader text is multiline text. Keep entering as many lines of text as needed to complete the note. When there is more than one line of text, the leader shoulder is centered on the lines of the note. An example of a multi-segment leader with more than one line of text is shown in Figure 11.73.

FIGURE 11.73 Leaders can have multiple line segments, but a single straight segment is recommended for mechanical drawings by the ASME standard.

The LEADER command has three options with the second To point: prompt. The Annotation option is the default and was already discussed. The second option is Format and the third option is Undo, which removes the previously drawn leader line. The Format option works as follows. Type **F** and press Enter, as shown, to get the Format options:

To point (Format/Annotation/Undo) <Annotation>: **F**↵
Spline/STraight/Arrow/None/<Exit>:

The Format options allow you to decide how the leader line looks on the drawing. The different Format options are explained next:

Spline: This option allows you to draw leader lines that are curved. Curved leader lines are commonly used in architectural drafting. Use the following sequence to draw the leader shown in Figure 11.74:

Command: **LE** or **LEADER** ↵
From point: ⟨*pick the leader start point*⟩
To point: ⟨*pick the leader endpoint*⟩
To point (Format/Annotation/Undo) <Annotation>: **F**↵
Spline/STraight/Arrow/None/<Exit>: **S**↵
To point (Format/Annotation/Undo) <Annotation>: ⟨*pick another point if desired*⟩
To point (Format/Annotation/Undo) <Annotation>: ↵
Annotation (or press Enter for options): **2 × 10 JOISTS 16″ OC**↵
MText: ↵
Command:

FIGURE 11.74 The Spline option of the LEADER command is used to draw curved leader lines, which are often used in architectural drafting.

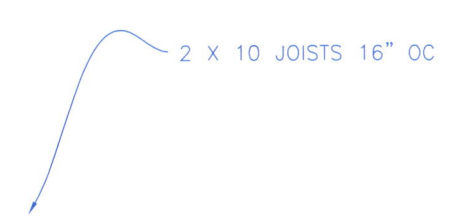

STraight: This option is the default that draws straight leader line segments as shown in Figures 11.72 and 11.73. Type **ST** and press Enter if you want to go from one of the other options back to drawing straight leaders. The LEADER command automatically goes back to the STraight option default when you leave the command.

Arrow: The LEADER command draws an arrowhead at the end by default. If you use the None option to remove the arrowhead, you need to use the Arrow option to place arrowheads on leaders again.

None: The None option is explained before the Arrow option, because the None option draws a leader without an arrowhead and the Arrow option is used to resume drawing leaders with arrowheads.

Exit: Press Enter to exit the Format options and return to the To point: prompt.

The LEADER command also has four options associated with the Annotation prompt. Press the Enter key as instructed in the following prompt to access these options:

To point (Format/Annotation/Undo) <Annotation>: ↵
Annotation (or press Enter for options): ↵
Tolerance/Copy/Block/None/<Mtext>:

The LEADER command's Annotation options are explained in the following list:

Tolerance: This option is used if you want to draw a geometric tolerancing feature control frame with the leader. A study of geometric tolerancing is recommended for this application. When you type **T** and press Enter, you get the Symbol dialog box shown in Figure 11.75. Pick one of the symbols and pick the OK button to get the Geometric Tolerance dialog box. Enter the desired geometric tolerancing values as shown in Figure 11.76 and pick the OK button. Although a full study of geometric tolerancing is recommended for accurate use of this feature, the following is a brief explanation of the items in Figure 11.76. The Sym area is where the geometric characteristic symbol is located from the Symbol dialog box. In the Tolerance 1 and 2 areas there is a Dia pick box for the insertion of a diameter symbol. The Value box is where the geometric tolerance is placed. Picking on the MC box opens the Material Condition dialog box where you can select one of the material condition symbols. There are three Datum areas where you enter the datum reference and related material condition for the feature control frame. The Height box is where you enter the value for a projected tolerance zone and then pick the box to the right of Projected Tolerance Zone to insert the related symbol. The Datum Identifier box is used to establish the letter for a datum feature symbol. The results of the values entered in Figure 11.76 are shown in Figure 11.77.

FIGURE 11.75 The Symbol dialog box is accessed when using the Tolerance option of the LEADER command.

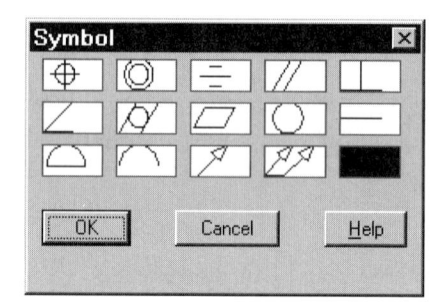

FIGURE 11.76 The Geometric Tolerance dialog box is opened when you select a symbol from the Symbol dialog box of the Tolerance option of the LEADER command.

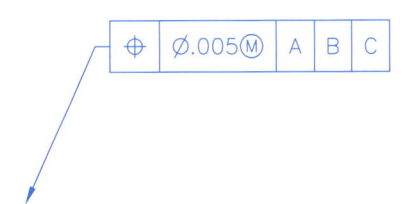

FIGURE 11.77 The results of drawing a geometric tolerance feature control frame on a leader when using the Tolerance option of the LEADER command.

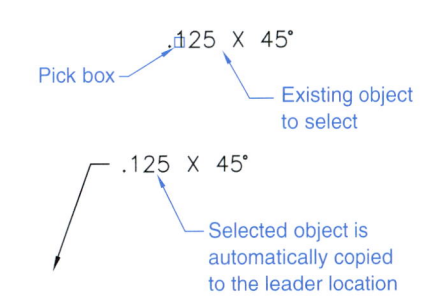

FIGURE 11.78 Using the Copy option of the LEADER command.

Copy: This option is used to copy an object, such as text or a block, from the current drawing and have it attached to the leader. Figure 11.78 shows the results of copying existing text for the leader using the following sequence:

Annotation (or press Enter for options): ↵
Tolerance/Copy/Block/None/<Mtext>: **C**↵
Select an object: ⟨select the object to copy⟩
Command:

Block: This option is used to insert a block at the leader location. A block is a symbol made for multiple insertions. Blocks are discussed in Chapter 12.

None: This option draws a leader line without any text.

Drawing Geometric Tolerancing Symbols without a Leader

The TOLERANCE command works in the same manner as the Tolerance option in the LEADER command except that it places a geometric tolerancing symbol without a leader. This command is accessed by picking the Tolerance button in the Dimension toolbar, by picking Tolerance … in the Dime_n_sion pull-down menu, or by typing **TOL** or **TOLERANCE** at the Command: prompt. When you enter the TOLERANCE command, you get the Symbol dialog box shown in Figure 11.75. Pick the desired geometric characteristic symbol and pick the OK button. This opens the Geometric Tolerance dialog box shown in Figure 11.76. Enter the desired values in the Tolerance and Datum areas as needed. Enter the Height and Projected Tolerance Zone symbol, if used. Establish a Datum Identifier, if appropriate. Pick the OK button when ready. AutoCAD LT then asks you to:

Enter tolerance location: ⟨pick the location for the symbol placement⟩
Command:

Dimension
Tolerance

Dimension
Tolerance...

TOLERANCE
TOL

The geometric tolerancing symbol is placed on your drawing in the location you pick. You can move it or copy it if needed. A complete introduction to geometric tolerancing is available in *Geometric Dimensioning and Tolerancing Basic Fundamentals,* by David Madsen, 1-800-323-0440.

Exercise 11.14

1. Begin a new drawing or use one of your prototypes.
2. Draw a note with leaders similar to those shown in Figures 11.72, 11.73, 11.74, and 11.77.
3. Use the LEADER command Copy option to draw a leader using an existing note from the drawing. Use Figure 11.78 as an example.
4. Save the drawing as EX11.14.

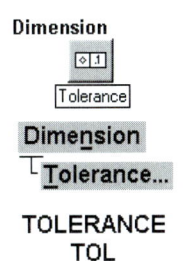

Creating a Dimension Style for Use with Mechanical Drafting Symbols

AutoCAD LT automatically draws the diameter symbol when you use the DIMDIAMETER command and the radius symbol when using the DIMRADIUS command. However, certain symbols, such as the counterbore, countersink, and depth symbols, are not directly available for mechanical drafting applications. You can create these symbols as blocks and insert them with your dimensioning text when needed, but this is extra work. Also, symbols inserted as blocks are not part of the dimension text and cannot be edited together with the dimension text. Creating and using blocks is discussed in Chapter 12.

If you commonly use these types of symbols, you can set up a dimension style that uses one of the standard AutoCAD LT fonts to place these symbols when needed. The AutoCAD LT font that contains these symbols is gdt.shx. The symbols are drawn when you press the lowercase letter keys. The uppercase letters are displayed as normal text in a romans font, which is good for mechanical drafting. All mechanical drafting text is drawn with uppercase letters, so when you need to insert a symbol, you just press the lowercase key that matches the desired symbol. Each of the symbols, the related keyboard letters, and the symbol descriptions are given in Figure 11.79. Follow these steps when setting up a dimension style of this type:

- Use the STYLE command to create a new text style named SYMBOLS. When the Text Style dialog box opens, pick the New... button and type SYMBOLS in the Style Name: text box. Pick OK. In the Font Name: list pick the gdt.shx font and then pick the Apply or Close button.

- Open the Dimension Styles dialog box and make all of the needed settings for mechanical drafting applications. Set SYMBOLS in the Text Style: list in the Annotation dialog box. Pick OK to accept each group of settings. Back in the Dimension Styles dialog box, create a new dimension style named SYMBOLS, or MECHANICAL SYMBOLS as you desire. Pick the OK button.

- Now, you are ready to place dimension text with the symbols you need. The note shown in Figure 11.80 was drawn using this LEADER command sequence:

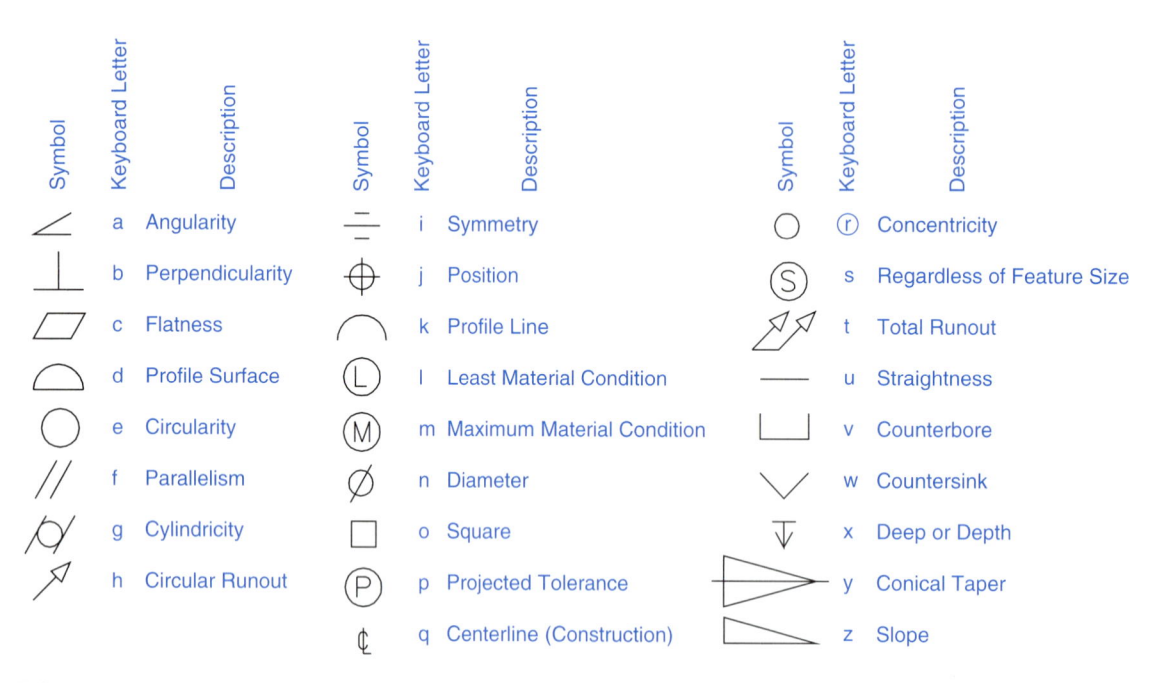

Symbol	Keyboard Letter	Description	Symbol	Keyboard Letter	Description	Symbol	Keyboard Letter	Description
∠	a	Angularity	=	i	Symmetry	○	r	Concentricity
⊥	b	Perpendicularity	⊕	j	Position	Ⓢ	s	Regardless of Feature Size
▱	c	Flatness	⌒	k	Profile Line	⌮	t	Total Runout
⌓	d	Profile Surface	Ⓛ	l	Least Material Condition	—	u	Straightness
○	e	Circularity	Ⓜ	m	Maximum Material Condition	⊔	v	Counterbore
∥	f	Parallelism	⌀	n	Diameter	∨	w	Countersink
⌭	g	Cylindricity	□	o	Square	↧	x	Deep or Depth
↗	h	Circular Runout	Ⓟ	p	Projected Tolerance	◁	y	Conical Taper
			℄	q	Centerline (Construction)	◁	z	Slope

FIGURE 11.79 The keyboard letter used to draw the symbols for the SYMBOLS dimension style with the gdt.shx font. Make a copy of this figure for reference while doing your mechanical drafting to use with this dimension style.

CHAPTER 11 ||| Dimensioning a Drawing

Command: **LE** or **LEADER** ↵
From point: ⟨*pick the leader start point*⟩
To point: ⟨*pick the second leader point*⟩
To point (Format/Annotation/Undo)<Annotation>: ↵
Annotation (or press Enter for options): **n.250 x1.750** ↵
MText: **vn.500 x.250** ↵
MText: ↵
Command:

FIGURE 11.80 Using the LEADER command to place a dimension note with the symbols from the SYMBOLS dimension style.

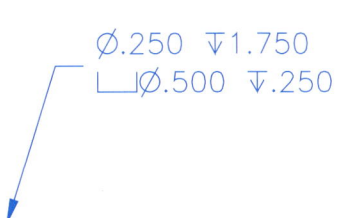

∅.250 ▽1.750
⌴∅.500 ▽.250

Field Notes

The following are some possible hazards to be aware of when using the SYMBOLS dimension style that was previously discussed:

- Be sure the SYMBOLS text style is current.
- AutoCAD LT automatically places a diameter symbol that is a little smaller than recommended when using the DIMDIAMETER command. However, the diameter symbol created with the SYMBOL dimension style is correctly sized in relation to the text height. When using the DIMDIAMETER command, use the Mtext or Text option to change the diameter symbol to match the SYMBOL dimension style.
- When using the Multiline Text Editor, be sure to set the text height at the current text height used in the drawing. A text height of .125 in. (3mm) is commonly used in mechanical drawings.

Exercise 11.15

1. Begin a new drawing or use one of your prototypes.
2. Create a text style using the gdt.shx font.
3. Create a dimensioning style for mechanical drafting with the gdt.shx text style.
4. Draw a dimension similar to Figure 11.80.
5. Save the drawing as EX11.15

✓ LEARNING CHECKPOINT

☐ Define dimension styles.
☐ Define dimension variables.
☐ What dimension style name is automatically used if you change any of the AutoCAD LT dimension variables?
☐ Discuss the function of dimension style families and family members.
☐ Name the dialog box where the dimension line and extension line appearance can be changed.
☐ Name the default arrowhead option that is also commonly used on mechanical drawings.
☐ Name the most common arrowhead option that is used for architectural dimensioning.

- Name the dialog box where the center marks can be changed.
- Explain the advantage of turning the User Defined check box on.
- Describe the recommended Format dialog box settings for mechanical drafting and architectural drafting applications.
- Define primary units.
- Give the recommended Zero Suppression settings for dimensioning in inches and in millimeters.
- Define tolerance.
- Name the tolerance method used for the following applications: specified dimension only, equal bilateral tolerance, unequal bilateral tolerance, unilateral tolerance, limits tolerance, and basic dimension.
- What tolerance justification option is recommended for use by the ASME standard?
- What tolerance height value is recommended by the ASME standard?
- Where is the gap measured when the dimension text is inserted in a space provided in the dimension line?
- Where is the gap measured when the dimension text is placed above the dimension line?
- Give an example of a dimension prefix and suffix on different dimension numerals.
- Name the command that can be used to place a leader line with a note on your drawing.
- Identify the option that can be used to draw curved leaders for architectural applications.
- Name the option used to place geometric tolerancing symbols with a leader line.
- What option is used to copy an existing note or object to a leader line?
- Name the command that is used to draw a geometric tolerancing symbol without a leader line.

Editing Existing Dimensions

AutoCAD LT dimensions are *associative dimensions.* This means that when a dimension object is edited, the dimension value automatically changes to match the edit. The automatic update is only applied when you accept the default value or keep the angle brackets, <>, as part of the text. This provides you with a big advantage when editing an AutoCAD LT drawing because any changes to the object are reflected in the dimensions without any extra work required of you. The STRETCH command is commonly used to either stretch or shrink an object. When using the STRETCH command, the associative dimensions are changed to match the measurement of the revised object. Figure 11.81 shows an example of an object being stretched and how the dimension changes to match. The STRETCH command used to edit the object and dimension in Figure 11.81 works like this:

Command: **S** or **STRETCH**↵
Select objects to stretch by crossing-window or crossing-polygon
Select objects: ⟨*select the object and dimension with a crossing*⟩
Select objects: ↵
Base point or displacement: ⟨*pick a base point*⟩
Second point or displacement: ⟨*pick a point to stretch the object*⟩
Command:

CHAPTER 11 ||| Dimensioning a Drawing

FIGURE 11.81 Using the STRETCH command to stretch an object and dimension. Notice how the dimension automatically changes to match the edit. This is referred to as an *associative dimension*.

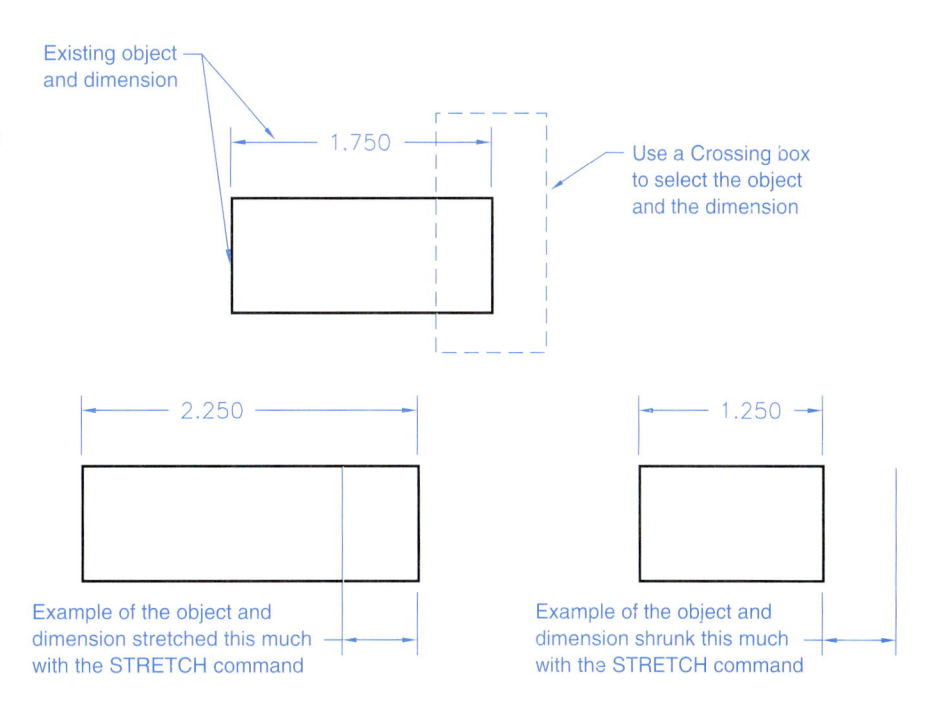

Other editing commands that result in automatic changes to dimensions include SCALE, TRIM, EXTEND, and LENGTHEN. The dimension variable that controls associative dimensioning is DIMASO. DIMASO is on by default, but you can turn it off if you want to disable associative dimensioning. When DIMASO is on, dimensions are created as single complex objects. When DIMASO is off, dimensions are drawn as individual component objects. This means that what is created is not a dimension object but is a collection of lines, solids, and text objects. Creating dimensions with DIMASO off is not recommended because the resulting dimensions are much more difficult to edit than associative dimensions.

The DIMSHO dimension variable allows you to watch dimensions change when being dragged during the editing process. DIMSHO is also on by default.

Field Notes

When you cannot get a dimension to appear as you want it to through working with dimension variables, you can use the EXPLODE command to break the dimension apart. This replaces the dimension object with the simpler objects used to create the dimension, including lines, solids, and text. These objects can then be edited freely, but an exploded dimension will no longer be automatically updated. Exploding dimensions should be avoided.

The objects that result from exploding a dimension are placed on layer 0, regardless of the layer on which the dimension was created. Also, the objects have the color BYBLOCK. To correct the appearance of these objects, use DDCHPROP to move them back to the proper layer and assign them a BYLAYER color.

Making Other Changes to Existing Dimensions

You can edit existing dimensions by changing the text value or location. You can also change dimension variables and then update existing dimensions to match the changed variables.

Aligning and Changing Dimension Text

Dimension text can be aligned to the left, right, at an angle, or moved to its original position. This is done by picking the Dimension Text Edit button in the Dimension toolbar, by picking one of the options in the Align Text cascade of the Dimension pull-down menu, or by typing **DIMTEDIT** at the Command: prompt. The Align Text cascade of the Dimension pull-down menu contains the Home, Rotate, Left, and Right options. These options are all available when entering the DIMTEDIT command like this:

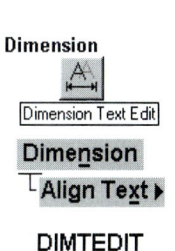

Dimension
Dimension Text Edit
Dimension
└ Align Text ▶

DIMTEDIT

Command: **DIMTEDIT**↵
Select dimension: ⟨*pick the dimension to edit*⟩
Enter text location (Left/Right/Home/Angle):

When you get the "Enter text location" prompt, the selected text is connected to the screen cursor for you to dynamically move the text and the entire dimension to any desired location. When the text and dimension are visually where you want, pick to keep that placement. If you prefer to use one of the options, they work like this:

Left: This option moves horizontal dimension text to the left or vertical text down.

Right: This option moves horizontal dimension text to the right or vertical text up.

Home: This option moves edited dimension text to its original position. For example, if you used the Left option to move dimension text to the left, the Home option moves it back to where it was. When you stretch an object and its dimension, the dimension value is updated to match the stretch, but the text may be moved to one side of the dimension line. The Home option moves the text back to be centered on the dimension line if it was originally centered.

Angle: This option allows you to place dimension text at an angle.

Figure 11.82 shows the effect of using the DIMTEDIT options.

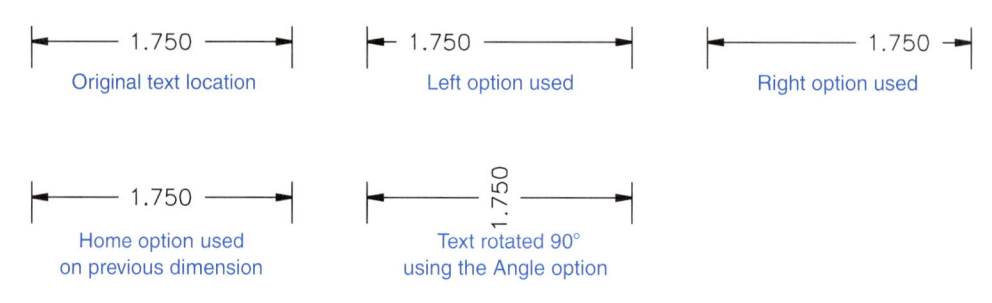

FIGURE 11.82 The results of using the DIMTEDIT options.

The DIMEDIT command can also be used to edit dimension text. This command is accessed by picking the Dimension Edit button in the Dimension toolbar or typing **DED** or **DIMEDIT** at the Command: prompt to get these options:

Command: **DED** or **DIMEDIT**↵
Dimension Edit (Home/New/Rotate/Oblique) <Home>:

The DIMEDIT options are explained next:

Home: This option works just like the DIMTEDIT Home option. Home moves previously edited dimension text back to its original place. Home is the default, so you can either press Enter or type **H** and press Enter. AutoCAD LT then asks you to "Select objects:" which are the dimensions you want to edit.

New: This option allows you to change dimension text values. The New option works like this:

Command: **DED** or **DIMEDIT**↵
Dimension Edit (Home/New/Rotate/Oblique) <Home>: **N**↵

The New option opens the Multiline Text Editor dialog box where you change the dimension text as desired and pick the OK button to get this prompt:

Select objects: ⟨*select the dimension or dimensions to edit*⟩
Select objects: ↵
Command:

Rotate: This option allows you to rotate existing dimension text to a designated angle.

Oblique: The Oblique option was discussed earlier in this chapter under the topic of creating oblique dimensions. See Figure 11.19.

Changing the Variables of Existing Dimensions

Situations might happen when you need to change dimension variables and have the changes take place on existing dimensions in a drawing. For example, maybe a drawing has dimension text set at a height of .188 in. and you want a height of .125 in. You can make a change like this on one or all dimensions. To do this, select the Dimension Update button in the Dimension toolbar, pick the Update option in the Dimension pull-down menu, or type **DST** or **DIMSTYLE**. Before using this command, you need to make changes to existing dimension variables. For example, enter the Dimension Styles dialog box and then change the arrowhead type in the Geometry dialog box. When you pick the Dimension Update button in the Dimension toolbar, or pick the Update option in the Dimension pull-down menu, AutoCAD LT automatically lists all the current dimension variable settings in the command window. Most of the variable listings are hidden behind the graphics window. You can see them by using the vertical command window scroll bars. You also get a series of options. The Apply option allows you to select the dimensions to update:

    Command: **DST** or **DIMSTYLE** ↵
      current dimension variable settings are listed
    Dimension Style Edit (Save/Restore/STatus/Variables/Apply/?) <Restore>: **A** ↵
    Select objects: ⟨*select the dimension or dimensions to change*⟩
    Select objects: ↵
    Command:

Each of the Dimension Style Edit options are explained in the following:

Apply: AutoCAD LT automatically issues this as _apply followed by the Select objects prompt when you pick the Dimension Update toolbar button or Update from the Dimension pull-down menu. If you type the command, then the Apply option is accessed by typing **A** and pressing Enter, as in the previous command sequence. This option updates the selected dimension or dimensions using the current dimension variables and any changes you have made to the dimension style.

> ### Field Notes
> - Dimensions that are changed in this manner lose reference to their dimension style.
> - You cannot change the spacing between dimension lines that were created with the DIMDLI variable.

Save: Type **S** and press Enter for this option. The Save option allows you to save the dimension style changes to a new dimension style name. These are the prompts:

    Dimension Style Edit (Save/Restore/STatus/Variables/Apply/?) <Restore>: **S** ↵
    ?/Name for new dimension style: **NEW NAME** ↵

The new dimension style becomes current. If you enter the name of an existing dimension style, AutoCAD LT issues this warning:

That name is already in use, redefine it? <N>:

No is the default, because you need to think carefully about renaming an existing dimension style. If you type Y, all associative dimensions are regenerated to use the redefined dimension style.
    If you want to display the difference between the current dimension style and the dimension style you name, type a tilde (~) followed by a style name, like this:

?/Name for new dimension style: **~STYLE NAME** ↵
Differences between STYLE NAME and the current settings:

AutoCAD LT gives you a list comparing the style you name with the current dimension style setting.
    The ? option inside the Save prompt and other prompts allows you to list the named dimension styles in the current drawing.

Restore: This option allows you to restore dimension variable to an existing named dimension style by specifying the name of the dimension style or picking a dimension on the drawing that represents the desired style:

    Dimension Style Edit (Save/Restore/STatus/Variables/Apply/?) <Restore>: **R** ↵
    ?/Enter dimension style name or ENTER to select dimension: ⟨*type an existing dimension style name or press ENTER to select an existing dimension*⟩

If you want to display the difference between the current dimension style and the dimension style you name, type a tilde (~) followed by a style name.

STatus: Type **ST** to access this option. This option lists the current values of all dimension styles in the current drawing by displaying the AutoCAD LT Text Window. Press the F2 key to return to the graphics window.

Variables: This option is used to list the dimension variables of a named dimension style or of a selected dimension. The following familiar prompt is issued:

Dimension Style Edit (Save/Restore/STatus/Variables/Apply/?) <Restore>: **V** ↵
?/Enter dimension style name or ENTER to select dimension: ⟨*type an existing dimension style name or press Enter to select an existing dimension*⟩

This lists the dimension variables of the specified or selected dimension style in the AutoCAD LT Text Window. Press the F2 key to return to the graphics window.

If you want to display the difference between the current dimension style and the dimension style you name, type a tilde (~) followed by a style name.

?: Type ? to list the dimension variables of a named dimension style or press Enter to accept the <*> wild-card default and list all dimension styles in the current drawing:

Dimension Style Edit (Save/Restore/STatus/Variables/Apply/?) <Restore>: **?** ↵
Dimension style(s) to list <*>: ⟨*type a dimension style name and press Enter or press Enter to list all current dimension styles*⟩

The dimension styles and their variables are displayed in the AutoCAD LT Text Window. Press the F2 key to return to the graphics window.

If you want to display the difference between the current dimension style and the dimension style you name, type a tilde (~) followed by a style name.

The DIM and DIM1 commands are introduced next in this chapter. The Update command can be issued through the DIM or DIM1 command. This allows you to change dimension variables and then select a dimension or dimensions to have the changes made. The command works like this:

Command: **DIM** ↵
Dim: **UPDATE** ↵
Select objects: ⟨*select the dimension or dimensions to change*⟩
Select objects: ↵
Command:

Exercise 11.16

1. Begin a new drawing or use one of your prototypes.
2. Draw an object with dimensions similar to the existing object and dimensions shown in Figure 11.81. Copy the object and dimensions to two new places below the existing object.
3. Use the STRETCH command on one of the copies to stretch the object and dimensions.
4. Use the STRETCH command on the other copy to shrink the object and dimensions. The results should look similar to those of Figure 11.81.
5. Draw a dimension similar to the original text location shown in Figure 11.82.
6. Copy the dimension to four places similar to the layout shown in Figure 11.82.
7. Use the DIMTEDIT command options to create results similar to the dimensions given in Figure 11.82.
8. Use the DIMEDIT command's Home option to place the previously rotated dimension back to its original position. Use the Undo command to undo this edit.
9. Draw a dimension of your own choosing. Use the DIMEDIT command's New option to change the dimension text.
10. Make a change to a couple of dimension variables. For example, change the arrowhead type and length, and change the dimension text height.
11. Update a few of the dimensions on this drawing to reflect the changes you just made to the variables. Observe the results and then Undo the effect if you wish.
12. Save the drawing as EX11.16.

CHAPTER 11 ||| Dimensioning a Drawing

Dimensioning at the Command Line

AutoCAD LT provides maximum flexibility by giving you command access with toolbar buttons and pull-down menus. Many commands open dialog boxes for you to have the most interaction with the process. You can also enter commands using the keyboard. The dimensioning practices that have been discussed throughout this chapter can be accessed at the command line by putting AutoCAD LT into the *dimensioning mode.* Many of the commands that have been introduced and commands from earlier AutoCAD LT releases can be entered while in the dimensioning mode. The dimensioning mode is used by typing either **DIM** or **DIM1** at the Command: prompt. The DIM command allows you to enter as many consecutive dimensioning commands as you want until you decide to exit the command. The DIM1 command allows you to use only one dimensioning command before automatically returning you to the Command: prompt. When you type the DIM or DIM1 command, you enter the dimensioning mode like this:

Command: **DIM** or **DIM1**↵
Dim:

If you want to leave the dimensioning mode, type **E** or **EXIT** and press Enter, or press the Esc key. Dimensioning commands, with names that are different from what you have already learned, are used at the Dim: prompt while you are in the dimensioning mode. The following list shows the AutoCAD LT commands and the same dimensioning mode commands:

AutoCAD LT Command	Dimensioning Mode Commands
DIMALIGNED	ALIGNED
DIMANGULAR	ANGULAR
DIMBASELINE	BASELINE
DIMCENTER	CENTER
DIMCONTINUE	CONTINUE
DIMDIAMETER	DIAMETER
DIMEDIT (Home)	HOMETEXT
DIMLINEAR (Horizontal)	HORIZONTAL
LEADER	LEADER
DIMEDIT (Text)	NEWTEXT
DIMEDIT (Oblique)	OBLIQUE
DIMORDINATE	ORDINATE
DIMOVERRIDE	OVERRIDE
DIMRADIUS	RADIUS
DIMSTYLE (Restore)	RESTORE
DIMLINEAR (Rotated)	ROTATED
DIMSTYLE (Save)	SAVE
DIMSTYLE (Status)	STATUS
DIMEDIT	TEDIT
DIMEDIT (Rotate)	TROTATE
DIMSTYLE (Apply)	UPDATE
DIMSTYLE (Variables)	VARIABLES
DIMLINEAR (Vertical)	VERTICAL

To give you an example of how the DIM command works, try drawing a horizontal linear dimension and a couple of datum dimensions similar to Figure 11.10 using this command sequence:

Command: **DIM**↵
Dim: **HORIZONTAL**↵
First extension line origin or press Enter to select: ⟨*pick the first extension line origin*⟩
Second extension line origin: ⟨*pick the second extension line origin*⟩
Dimension line location (Text/Angle): ⟨*pick the dimension line location*⟩
Dimension text <1.50>: ↵
Dim: **BASELINE**↵
Second extension line origin or press Enter to select: ⟨*pick the origin of the next dimension's second extension line*⟩
Dimension text <2.75>: ↵
Dim: **BASELINE**↵

Second extension line origin or press Enter to select: ⟨*pick the origin of the next dimension's second extension line*⟩
Dimension text <4.00>: ↵
Dim: ⟨*type* **E** *and press Enter, type* **EXIT** *and press Enter, or press the Esc key*⟩
Command:

Exercise 11.17

1. Begin a new drawing or use one of your prototypes.
2. Use the DIM command to draw an object with dimensions similar to those of Figure 11.10.
3. Save the drawing as EX11.17.

☑ LEARNING CHECKPOINT

- ☐ Define associative dimensions.
- ☐ Explain the advantage of having associative dimensions.
- ☐ What function does the Home option of the DIMTEDIT or DIMEDIT command perform?
- ☐ Name the DIMTEDIT options.
- ☐ What is the purpose of the DIMEDIT command's New option?
- ☐ How do you change the dimension variable on existing dimensions in a drawing?
- ☐ Name the command to use if you want to perform one dimensioning task in dimensioning mode.
- ☐ Name the command to use if you want to create several consecutive dimensions while in dimensioning mode.

MULTIPLE CHOICE

Instructions: Circle the choice or enter your response on an answer sheet by selecting the option that most closely completes or answers the given statements.

1. The command used for drawing straight line dimensions:
   a. DIMANGULAR
   b. DIMRADIUS
   c. DIMLINEAR
   d. DIMDIAMETER

2. The option used to select objects directly for dimensioning:
   a. Select
   b. Press Enter to select
   c. Object
   d. Linear

3. This command is used to draw arrowless dimensions:
   a. DIMARROWLESS
   b. DIMTABULAR
   c. DIMORDINATE
   d. DIMBASE

4. Saved sets of variables that determine the appearance of the dimensions:
   a. dimension variables
   b. dimension settings
   c. dimension styles
   d. dimension controls

5. This dialog box used to change the dimension line, extension line, arrowhead, and center mark presentation is called:
   a. Annotation
   b. Format
   c. Geometry
   d. Styles

6. Variables that control the way dimension text appears on the drawing and the relationship with the positioning of dimension lines and arrowheads are adjusted in this dialog box:
   a. Annotation
   b. Format
   c. Geometry
   d. Styles

7. The dimension variable that provides maximum flexibility in the placement of dimension text, dimension line location, extension line length, and arrowhead placement:
   a. DIMUPT
   b. DIMUD
   c. DIMUPC
   d. DIMUP

8. Architectural drafting applications typically use this Vertical Justification option:
   a. Centered
   b. Outside
   c. Above
   d. JIS

9. The type of dimension that results when a dimension object is edited and the dimension automatically changes to match the edit:
   a. Update
   b. DIMEDIT
   c. DIMTEDIT
   d. associative

10. This DIMEDIT option is used to change the value of dimension text:
    a. Home
    b. Change
    c. New
    d. Edit

MATCHING

Match each term to the correct description by writing the appropriate number in each box at the left.

- ☐ Associative
- ☐ DIMLINEAR
- ☐ DIMCONTINUE
- ☐ DIMBASE
- ☐ DIMANG
- ☐ DIMALIGNED
- ☐ DIMDIAMETER
- ☐ DIMRADIUS
- ☐ DIMORDINATE
- ☐ Geometry
- ☐ DIMCENTER
- ☐ Annotation

1. This dialog box is used to change the dimension line, extension line, arrowhead, and center mark presentation.
2. This command is used to draw straight line dimensions.
3. Circles should be dimensioned with this command.
4. Changes can be made to the appearance of dimension text in this dialog box.
5. Dimensions that automatically update when editing changes are made.
6. This command is used to draw arrowless dimensions.
7. This command is used to draw dimensions beside a slanted object.
8. Arcs should be dimensioned with this command.
9. Chain dimensioning is performed with this command.
10. This command is used to dimension angles in degrees.
11. Center marks are placed on arcs and circles with this command.
12. Datum dimensioning is performed with this command.

CHAPTER 11 ||| Dimensioning a Drawing   **477**

WORD SCRAMBLE

Unscramble the five scrambled words below, one letter to each square, to form five AutoCAD LT–related words:

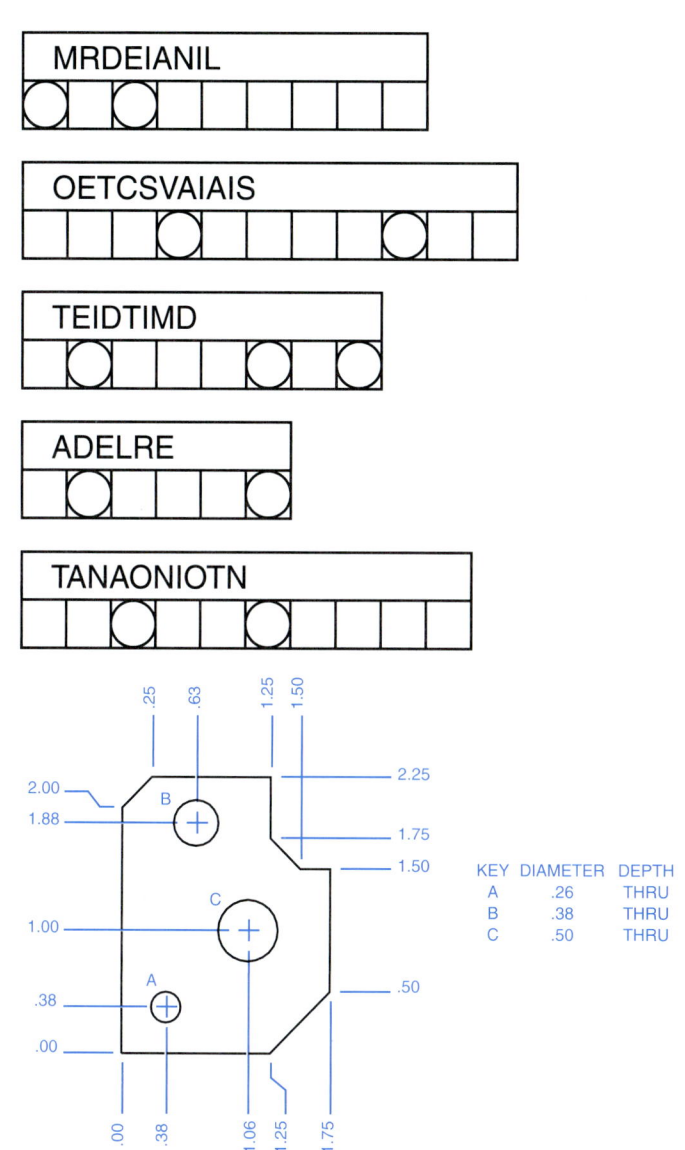

MRDEIANIL

OETCSVAIAIS

TEIDTIMD

ADELRE

TANAONIOTN

Unscramble the circled letters above to form the special answer, as suggested by the illustration.

PROJECTS

Set up the following drawing projects with the dimensions placed on a specific layer. Review Chapter 5 if needed. Establish dimension styles based on the type of drafting, such as mechanical, architectural, or electrical. Review this chapter and plan the dimension style to match the project before beginning work on the project. The following are some basic recommended guidelines to follow unless otherwise specified by your instructor or company (Values are given in inches. Convert to millimeters as needed):

Mechanical	Setting
Dimension line spacing	.50 minimum
Extension line offset	.0625
Extension line extension	.125
Arrowhead	Closed Filled
Dimension text height	.125 (should match balance of drawing)
Gap	.06
Dimension text style	ROMANS (should match balance of drawing)
Dimension text centered	
Unidirectional dimensioning	

Zero Suppression for inch or metric as outlined in this chapter and in compliance with ANSI/ASME dimensioning standards.

Architectural	Setting
Dimension line spacing	.50 minimum
Extension line offset	.0625
Extension line extension	.125
Arrowhead	Architectural Tick, Dot, or Closed Filled
Dimension text height	.125 (should match balance of drawing)
Gap	.06
Dimension text style	CityBlueprint or Stylus BT (should match balance of drawing)
Dimension text above	
Aligned dimensioning	

Zero Suppression for feet and inches as outlined in this chapter and in compliance with AIA dimensioning standards.

11.1 Open P3.4 and dimension as shown in the original layout. Save as P11.1. **[INCH]**

11.2 Open P3.5 and dimension as shown in the original layout. Save as P11.2. **[METRIC]**

11.3 Open P3.6 and dimension as shown in the original layout. Save as P11.3. **[INCH]**

11.4 Open P3.7 and dimension as shown in the original layout. Save as P11.4. **[METRIC]**

11.5 Open P5.2 and dimension as shown in the original layout. Save as P11.5. **[INCH]**

11.6 Open P5.3 and dimension as shown in the original layout. Save as P11.6.

11.7 Open P6.3 and dimension as shown in the original layout. Save as P11.7.

11.8 Open P6.4 and dimension as shown in the original layout. Save as P11.8. **[INCH]**

11.9 Open P6.5 and dimension as shown in the original layout. Save as P11.9. **[METRIC]**

CHAPTER 11 ||| Dimensioning a Drawing

11.10 Open P6.6 and dimension as shown in the original layout. Save as P11.10. [INCH]

11.11 Open P6.9 and completely dimension by placing the appropriate dimensions on the right side view. Save as P11.11. [INCH]

11.12 Open P6.8 and properly dimension the views. Save as P11.12. [INCH]

11.13 Open P6.9 and properly dimension the views. Save as P11.13. [INCH]

11.14 Open P6.12 and properly dimension the views. Save as P11.14. [INCH]

11.15 Open P7.3 and dimension as shown in the original layout. Save as P11.15. [INCH]

11.16 Open P7.7 and dimension the completed object. Save as P11.16. [INCH]

11.17 Open P7.8 and dimension as shown in the original layout. Save as P11.17. [INCH]

11.18 Open P8.9 and properly dimension the partial floor plan. Save as P11.18.

11.19 Open P8.10 and properly dimension the partial floor plan. Save as P11.19.

11.20 Open P10.1 and properly dimension the views. Save as P11.20. [INCH]

11.21 Open P10.2 and properly dimension the views. Save as P11.21. [METRIC]

11.22 Open P10.3 and properly dimension the views. Save as P11.22. [INCH]

11.23 Open P10.4 and properly dimension the views. Save as P11.23. [INCH]

11.24 Open P10.5 and dimension as shown in the original layout. Save as P11.24.

11.25 Open P10.5 and dimension as shown in the original layout. Save as P11.25.

CHAPTER 12

Designing and Using Your Own Symbols

LEARNING GOALS

- Group objects together for easier editing
- Use the BLOCK command to create reusable symbols
- Save blocks as individual drawing files for use in any drawing
- Use the Insert command to insert predrawn symbols
- Create and use a symbol library
- Use the Content Explorer to manage symbols and symbol libraries
- Use attributes to store additional information with symbols
- Extract attribute information to generate a bill of materials
- Import clip art into a drawing
- Access information contained in external drawing files
- Overlay multiple drawing files to create a combined drawing database

Grouping Objects

In most drawing applications, several objects in a drawing are used to represent a more complex shape. For example, in a multiview drawing, a collection of drawing objects is used to depict the front, top, or side view of an object. In a schematic application, several simpler objects are used to represent specific symbols. Many assembly drawings may consist of several smaller subassemblies. In each of these cases, your drawing contains sets of objects that you may need to select and edit as a unit. You may need to relocate a view or duplicate a symbol or subassembly. AutoCAD LT provides a way to group these objects together so that they can be selected and edited as though they were a single object. Objects within a group can also be edited individually if needed. The following section covers grouping and ungrouping objects, plus management of object groups.

The Group Manager

The GROUP command opens the Group Manager. You can access the GROUP command by selecting Group Manager … from the Tools pull-down menu, by picking the Group button from the Group toolbar or by typing **G** or **GROUP** at the Command: prompt. The Group Manager is similar to the AutoCAD LT toolbars; it can be docked at the top or bottom, or it can be placed in a floating position. The Group Manager cannot be docked on either side of the AutoCAD LT program window. Figure 12.1 shows the Group Manager in a floating position (A) and a docked position (B). The Group Manager can be closed by dragging it to a floating position and picking the Close button in the upper right corner.

When you first start the Group Manager in a drawing with no groups defined, only one of its radio buttons is selectable. Just below the row of control buttons on the right side of the Group Manager is the Group Manager status bar. This area provides supplementary information when you are working with groups. The initial message, "Select objects & click Create Group," refers to using the noun/verb selection method of grip-selecting the objects and then picking the Create Group button, as shown in Figure 12.2. No prompts are issued in the floating command window.

Group

Group Manager

Tools
└ Group
  Manager...
  GROUP
  G

481

FIGURE 12.1 The Group Manager can be placed in a floating position (A), or it can be docked at the top or bottom of the AutoCAD LT program window (B).

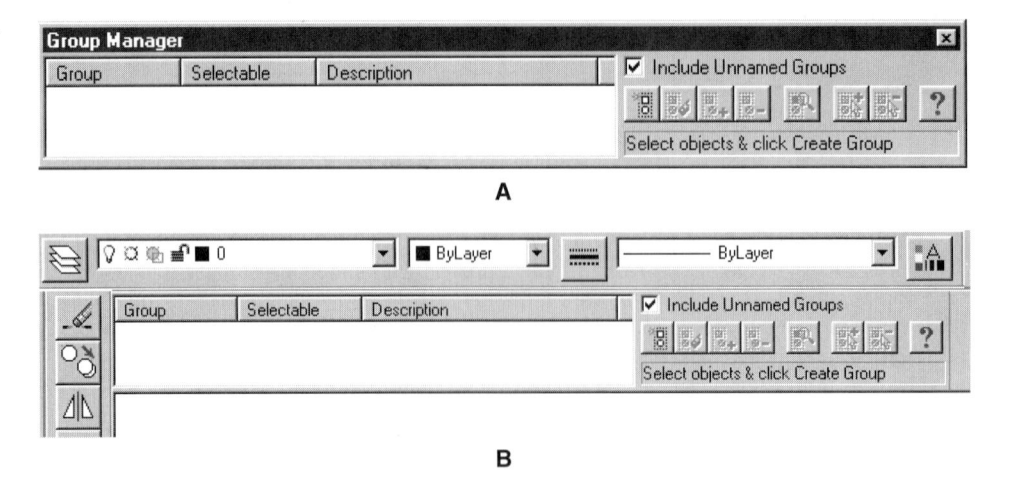

FIGURE 12.2 Grip-select the objects you want to group, then pick the Create Group button in the Group Manager.

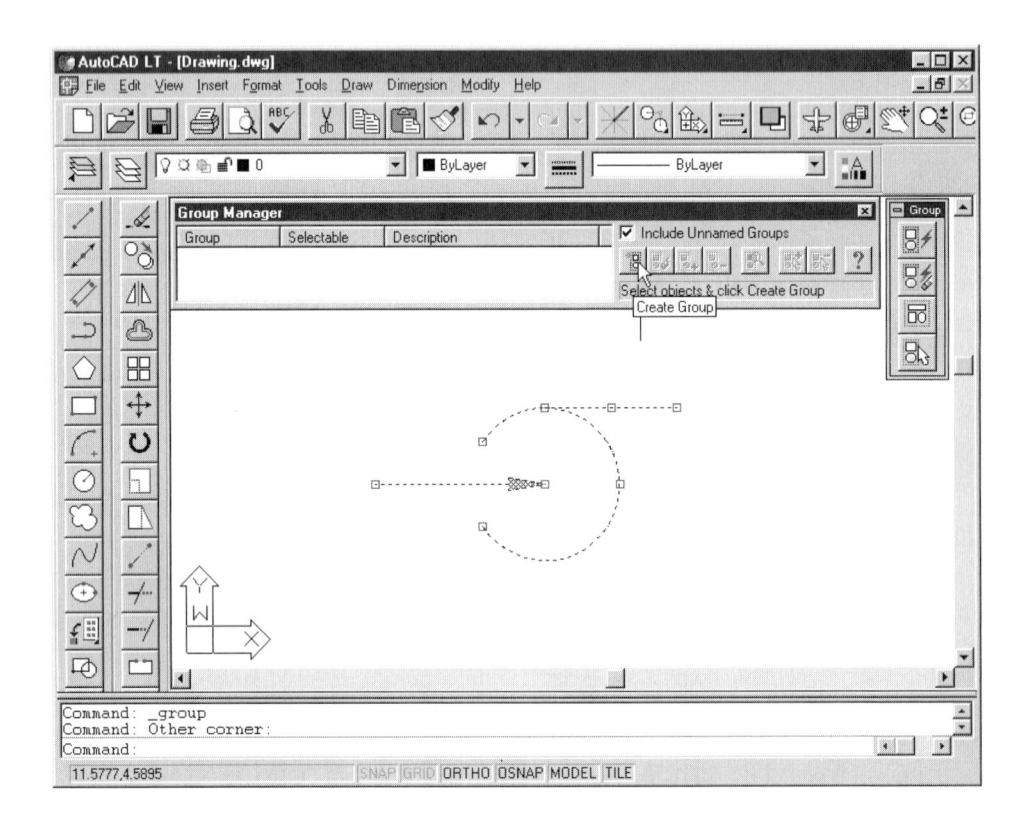

When items have been selected for grouping and the Create Group button is picked, the items are grouped and an active edit box appears in the Group column on the left side of the Group Manager. You may enter a group name that is up to 31 characters long. As in naming other objects such as layers and views, you can use dollar signs ($), hyphens (-), and underscores (_), but cannot use blank spaces or other restricted characters.

After you have named the new group, you can adjust other settings as needed. First, you can specify whether the group is selectable. When a group is selectable, picking any component of the group also selects all other objects that are part of the group. Objects in a group that is not selectable can be picked and edited individually without affecting the rest of the group. When the light bulb in the Selectable column is on (yellow), the group is selectable. Click on the light bulb icon itself to turn it on or off.

You can also enter a description of up to 64 characters to provide supplementary information about a group. This information can provide helpful reminders about the nature and content of your groups. The description can be entered, deleted, or edited at any time. Figure 12.3 shows a description being entered for a currently unselectable group containing three objects.

Every group requires a unique name. You cannot have multiple groups with the same name. If you copy an existing group with the COPY command, the new set of objects is assigned to an *unnamed* group. Unnamed groups are assigned a sequential name with the first unnamed group being named "*A1," the second

CHAPTER 12 ||| Designing and Using Your Own Symbols   483

FIGURE 12.3 The group description may contain up to a 64-character description for each group. The status bar provides additional information about the currently selected group in the group list.

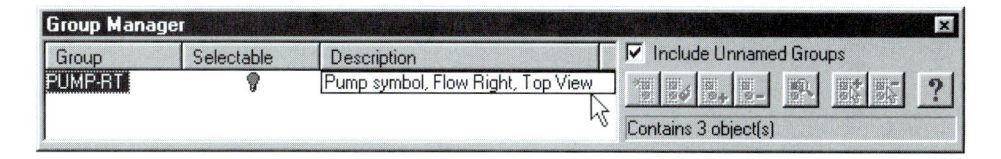

"*A2," and so on. These groups will appear in the Group Manager list only if the Include Unnamed Groups toggle is checked.

The group control buttons allow you to add new objects to a group, remove existing objects, ungroup, and more. The function of each of these buttons is as follows:

- **Create Group** If objects are currently grip-selected, they are added to a new group. You may enter a name for the new group or press Enter to create a new unnamed group. If no objects are currently selected, an empty group is created.
- **Ungroup** Discards the group definition and removes the association between the objects that composed the group. The objects remain in the drawing as they were before they were grouped.
- **Add to Group** Adds the currently selected objects to the highlighted group name in the group list. This button is available only when objects in the drawing are grip-selected.
- **Remove from Group** Removes the currently selected objects from the specified group. If the group is selectable, all objects are selected when you pick one component. You can use the Shift key to unselect components, but you may find it easier to simply turn off selectability while specifying which objects to remove.
- **Details** Displays the Group Manager - Details dialog box shown in Figure 12.4. The details for all highlighted group names appear in the listing. When a group name is selected, the number of objects it contains and the space they are in is displayed, along with the description field. Additionally, the group is highlighted on the screen to show its location. If the group is not entirely visible on screen, the Zoom Group Extents button is available.
- **Zoom Group Extents** Zooms to show the currently selected group as large as possible, centered on the screen.
- **Zoom Previous** Displays the area visible before Zoom Group Extents was selected.
- **Select Group** Selects the objects that compose the highlighted group name or names. You can use this button to find groups by highlighting them or to make noun/verb selections.
- **Deselect Group** Deselects any currently selected objects that are components of the highlighted group name. You can select objects by any standard means and then conveniently remove the grouped objects from the selection set.
- **Help** Displays context-sensitive help associated with the GROUP command.

Field Notes

Groups can be selected automatically at a Select objects: prompt by using the Group option. The following example shows the MOVE command being used, but most Select objects: prompts allow this option.

Command: **MOVE**↵
Select objects: **G**↵
Enter group name: **PUMP-RT**↵
3 found
Select objects:

FIGURE 12.4 The Group Manager - Details dialog box.

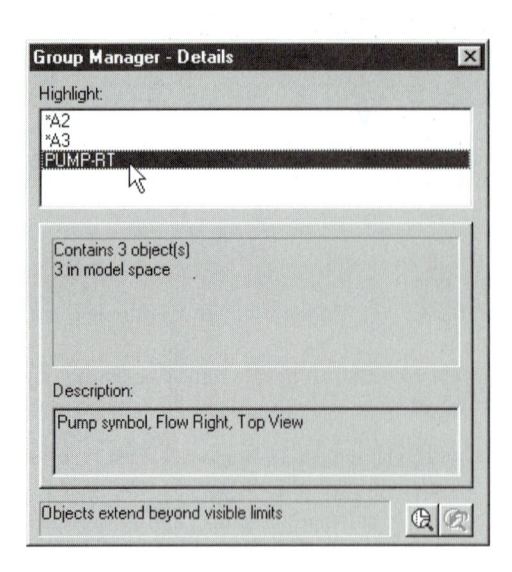

The Group Toolbar

In addition to the GROUP command, other options are also found on the Group toolbar. Using the group toolbar provides a fast and convenient means of using groups that do not require names and descriptions. In many cases, this is the most productive way to use object groups. Right-click on a currently visible toolbar button, then select Group from the popup cursor menu to display the Group toolbar.

Group
[Group]
Tools
└ Group
-GROUP
-G

The Group button on the Group toolbar automatically creates an unnamed group from the selected objects. This option is also found on the Tools menu. If it is picked when no objects have been selected, you are prompted to select the objects to group. The next sequential "*A_" name is used for the new unnamed group. This option provides a convenient way to group associated objects without having to name and describe the group. This toolbar button actually uses the command line version of the GROUP command. When objects are currently grip-selected, using this option displays the following at the command line:

Command: _-group
?/Add/Remove/Ungroup/REName/Selectable/<Create>:
? /* (unnamed group) / Group name: * Group description:
9 found
Command:

Group
[Ungroup]
Tools
└ Ungroup
-GROUP
-G

To ungroup objects without having to find the group name in the Group Manager, use the Ungroup tool from the Group toolbar or the Tools pull-down menu. If the group has been grip-selected, it is ungrouped with no further prompts. If no objects have been selected, you are prompted to select the group to ungroup.

Command: _-group
?/Add/Remove/Ungroup/REName/Selectable/<Create>: _un
? /* (unnamed group) / Group name: *
9 found

Group
[Group Selection On/Off]
PICKSTYLE
CTRL+H

The Group Selection On/Off option toggles the current setting for the PICKSTYLE system variable, which controls whether selecting a member of a group selects all objects within the group. You can also toggle this setting by pressing CTRL+H or by using the Object Selection Settings dialog box. This global setting overrides the Selectable setting for individual groups within the Group Manager.

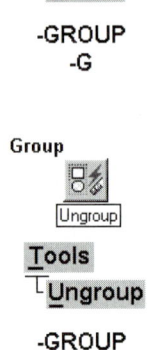

✎ Field Notes

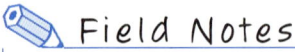

- Erasing the objects that make up a group does not remove the group from the drawing; rather, it results in an empty group. To remove the group name, you must use the Ungroup option.
- Groups can be nested, meaning that one set of grouped objects can be part of another group.

CHAPTER 12 ||| Designing and Using Your Own Symbols   485

> ### Exercise 12.1
>
> 1. If it is not already visible, display the Group toolbar.
> 2. Start the Group Manager using the GROUP command. Make sure that "Include Unnamed Groups" is checked.
> 3. Draw a symbol similar to the one shown in Figure 2.2.
> 4. Grip-select the objects in the symbol and pick the Create Group button.
> 5. Name the group PUMP-RT, make it selectable, and give it a description.
> 6. Start the MOVE command, and at the Select objects: prompt, pick the group using the pickbox. Complete or cancel the MOVE command.
> 7. Start the COPY command, and at the Select objects: prompt, type G for Group, then enter the group name. Complete the COPY command by placing one copy of the group. Notice the new group name that appears in the Group Manager.
> 8. Make the PUMP-RT group unselectable.
> 9. Grip-select the arc segment, then pick Remove from Group.
> 10. Make the group selectable again, and ERASE it. Notice that the Group Manager now reports this group as having 0 objects. Use OOPS to bring the group back.
> 11. Grip select the line segment you removed from the group, and pick Add to Group.
> 12. Zoom to an area where the PUMPT-RT group is no longer visible. Highlight the PUMP-RT group name in the Group Manager and pick the Details button.
> 13. Use the Zoom to Group Extents button to see the group. Use Zoom Previous to return to the previous view and dismiss this dialog box.
> 14. Use the Select Group button to select a group, then pick Deselect Group.
> 15. Draw a shape of your own design using several objects.
> 16. Use the Group button from the Group toolbar to group the new objects. Select the new group and pick the Ungroup button.
> 17. Save the drawing as EX12.1.dwg.

✓ LEARNING CHECKPOINT

- ☐ Why is it useful to group objects?
- ☐ What command starts the Group Manager?
- ☐ The Group Manager can be docked or floating. Where can you not dock the Group Manager?
- ☐ What limitations apply to Group names?
- ☐ Describe the features of the Group Manager - Details dialog box.
- ☐ How can the Group and Ungroup toolbar buttons on the Group toolbar be faster and more convenient than using the Group Manager?
- ☐ Group selection is controlled globally using what system variable? What is the shortcut key to toggle this variable?

Using Drafting Symbols in AutoCAD LT

In drafting, the term *symbol* refers to a simplified graphic image used to represent specific elements of a drawing. Most drafting disciplines make use of symbols in one form or another to illustrate many of the common features within a drawing. The use of standard symbols can clarify and simplify many types of technical drawings. For example, an architectural drawing uses many standard symbols to represent various features of a floor plan. To draw views of specific doors, windows, or other architectural features as they actually appear is a long and unnecessary process. Instead, simplified symbols are used to describe the style, position, and orientation of such features. This reduces drafting time, and the lower detail level helps to prevent overcrowding in complex drawings.

A manual drafter uses tools such as templates or sticky-backs to speed up the process of using symbols. ***Templates*** are plastic guides that provide an easy-to-follow outline, allowing the drafter to draw uniform symbols quickly wherever needed in a drawing. *Sticky-backs* are predrawn symbols printed on transparent media with an adhesive backing. When a symbol is needed, it is simply placed in the appropriate location and then held in place by the adhesive. This allows a manual drafter to insert symbols into a drawing without having to actually draw them in each location.

Using AutoCAD LT, you can use the concept of sticky-backs in an electronic format. Predrawn symbols are referred to as *blocks* within AutoCAD LT. Once a symbol is drawn, using its geometry to define a block allows the symbol to be used over and over again as needed within a drawing—without having to redraw it or copy the original to each new location. And, if you need to use the same symbol in more than one drawing, it can be saved to disk and inserted as desired in any subsequent drawing session. Frequently needed symbols can be incorporated into a standard symbol library for yourself or your company.

Typically, in a drawing that uses symbols, several of the symbols are likely to occur in many different locations within the drawing. However, some symbols can vary in what they represent. For example, electronic components, such as fixed-value resistors, can have properties that vary from one resistor to the next. Some resistors may come from different manufacturers and have varied resistance values. Even so, in an electronic schematic drawing, the same standard symbol is used to represent each fixed-value resistor. In AutoCAD LT, blocks can be assigned certain properties called *attributes*. These attributes can be assigned individually to each occurrence of the block to distinguish it from all of the others. The attributes can be displayed as visible text on the drawing, or they can be invisible and stored only within the block itself. Block attributes can even be extracted from a drawing and used to automate the creation of a bill of materials.

You should always remember that the primary productivity gain from using a CAD application comes from never having to draw the exact same thing twice. When you draw something that you are going to need again in the future, you can save it in a form that makes it easily accessible to all future drawing sessions. Mastering the use of drawing symbols, or blocks, in AutoCAD LT can greatly increase your drafting productivity. AutoCAD LT 98 provides a powerful tool called the Content Explorer for working with symbols and symbol libraries. It provides an easy "drag-and-drop" interface for use and management of your symbols. This chapter discusses the creation, management, and use of symbols and symbol libraries through the use of the Content Explorer and other AutoCAD LT tools.

Creating and Inserting Blocks in a Drawing

Creating Blocks

Draw
Make Block

Draw
˪ Block ▶
 ˪ Make...

BMAKE
B

A *block* is a collective representation of any number of regular AutoCAD LT objects that is stored and used as a single object. Blocks can be created within a specific drawing and used only in that drawing, or you can make a block available for use in other drawings. This section discusses the basics of defining a block.

The first step in creating any block definition is to draw the geometry that represents the required symbol or component. This is done using normal drawing and editing commands. If what you are drawing is to be used as a standard drafting symbol, you should always refer to the appropriate reference material to ensure that the symbol complies with accepted industry standards. When creating a block to represent a nonstandard symbol, such as a frequently used part or subassembly, be sure that the symbol complies with all applicable company standards.

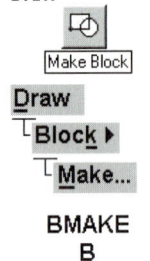

✎ Field Notes

The descriptions and definitions of accepted industry standard symbols can be found in documents published by a variety of organizations. Some of the most widely recognized standards organizations include these:

- **ASME**—American Society of Mechanical Engineers
- **AIA**—American Institute of Architects
- **IEEE**—Institute of Electrical and Electronics Engineers
- **ISO**—International Standards Organization
- **MIL-STD**—United States Military Standards
- **SAE**—Society of Automotive Engineers

All symbols should comply with pertinent drafting standards. The standards documents that you need to reference are usually based on the final destination of the drawing you are creating. Usually, it is your customer who will specify the standards by which a project is to be completed.

Depending on the scope of your business, it may be necessary to maintain multiple drawing templates and symbol libraries to meet the needs of a diverse customer base.

Additional information regarding standards documents and organizations is found in Appendix B.

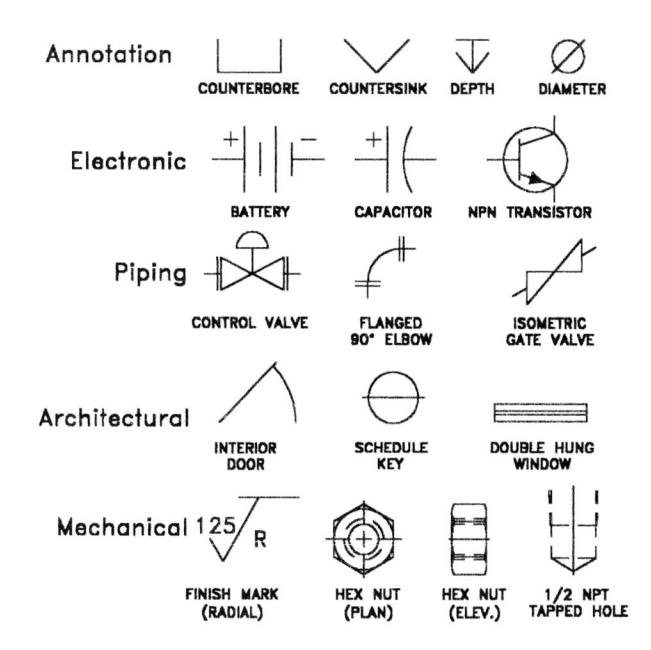

FIGURE 12.5 Standard drafting symbols are used in almost every drafting discipline.

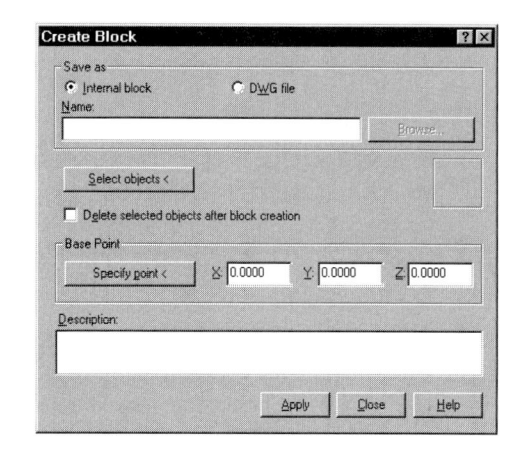

FIGURE 12.6 The Create Block dialog box is used for creating new block definitions.

In preparation for the following example, create a piece of geometry to represent the electronic schematic symbol for an NPN transistor like the one shown in Figure 12.5. Based on a standard symbol height of 0.125 units, the circle in this symbol is defined as being 0.375 units in diameter. The rest of the features are drawn proportionately to match the example in Figure 12.5.

Once you have completed the geometry that defines the new symbol, start the BMAKE command to display the Create Block dialog box. The BMAKE command is accessed by picking the Make Block button in the Draw toolbar, selecting Make ... from the Block cascade or the Draw pull-down menu, or by typing **B** or **BMAKE** at the Command: prompt. The Create Block dialog box is shown in Figure 12.6. This dialog box starts out with the Name: field active. You can enter this information first, or you can proceed to other areas of the dialog box and return to this field later if you wish.

The upper area of the Create Block dialog box is labeled Save As. This is where you tell AutoCAD LT what name to assign to the block and where to save it. Blocks can be created and saved internally or externally. Saved internally within a drawing, a block is then available only while working within the drawing that the block was created in. When saved externally, the block is saved as an individual drawing file. That file can then be inserted into other drawing files, and it can even be opened directly by AutoCAD LT in a subsequent editing session if desired. When you insert one drawing file into another drawing, it is brought in as a block object. Creating and using external blocks is covered later in this chapter.

In this example, the block Name: value is entered first. The name specified for a block is up to you, as long as it complies with the AutoCAD LT conventions for block names. First, the block name must be no more than 31 characters in length. The Block Definition dialog box does not allow you to enter a name that is longer than this. Second, the name can consist only of ***alphanumeric characters*** (letters and numbers) and the special characters $ (dollar sign), - (hyphen), and _ (underscore). This also means that spaces cannot be used in block names. When a block name is accepted by AutoCAD LT, all of the alphabetical characters are automatically converted to uppercase.

Although block names can be up to 31 characters in length, it is usually best to stay well below this maximum length. Extremely long block names can be cumbersome to work with, and can cause complications when creating permanent symbol libraries and using external references as discussed later in this chapter.

Another consideration when specifying block names is to use a clearly recognizable name. Keep in mind that you may not be the only person to edit this drawing. If a client or coworker opens this drawing at a later date, the block names you have defined should be easily recognizable to them as well.

Since the symbol in Figure 12.5 represents an NPN transistor, an acceptable option for a short, descriptive name might be NPNTRANS. Or, to make it easier to read, you can separate the individual parts of the description using an underscore character as in NPN_TRANS.

> ### Field Notes
>
> When using block names composed of multiple words or designations, readability is enhanced by separation of the individual naming components. Spaces cannot be used in block names, but you can use the hyphen and underscore characters to achieve the same result. For example, an appropriate name for the radial finish mark symbol shown in Figure 12.5 might be FINMARKRAD. Adding a hyphen, an underscore, or both makes the name much more readable:
>
> FIN_MARK-RAD
>
> In most cases, it is best to use the shortest possible name that effectively communicates the nature of the symbol. Avoid the use of long, descriptive sentences for block names. Use the separator characters only when readability is improved by doing so.

Once you have entered the name for the new block, you now need to tell AutoCAD LT which objects in your drawing are to be used to define the new block. Picking the Select Objects < button hides the dialog box and allows you to select the desired objects. Any standard object selection method can be used at the Select objects: prompt. When you are finished selecting the objects that define the new block, press Enter at the Select objects: prompt. The Create Block dialog box reappears and displays a preview of the block. If this image is not what you expected, you can discard the previous selection and start the selection process over by picking the Select Objects < button again.

Just below the Select Objects < button is a toggle labeled Delete selected objects after block creation. If this box is not checked, the geometry selected to define the new block remains in the drawing after the block is created. Placing a check mark in this field causes all the geometry used in the block definition to be erased. If you are in the process of defining more than one block, and the existing geometry can be easily modified to match the specification for the next symbol, you may wish to retain the selected objects. Otherwise it is usually a good idea to toggle this field on so the geometry is automatically erased. The primary reason to erase the selected geometry is because any use of the symbol in your drawing should be with the new block definition rather than the original geometry. An additional benefit is that erasing the selected geometry provides an obvious indicator as to whether any objects were missed in the selection process. Any block definition geometry that remains on screen was not used in the new block definition. If you do need to retain the objects and forget to set the toggle correctly, use the OOPS command at the Command: prompt to restore the erased objects.

> ### Field Notes
>
> It is recommended that you turn on the Delete selected objects after block creation toggle and use the OOPS command to restore the objects if you have further need for them. Seeing which objects disappear can be a helpful checkpoint in the block definition process, because otherwise it may not be obvious if any objects were missed in the selection process. The block preview image is very small and may not always provide an accurate enough image.
>
> One such situation is in a drawing where one or more layers are locked. During the selection process, surrounding the desired objects with a window or crossing can lead you to believe that all of the objects have been selected, when in fact, any objects on locked layers were not selected. If Delete selected objects after block creation is turned off, the objects not successfully selected are immediately obvious because they are still visible.

The next information you need to provide for the block definition is an insertion *base point*. The ***insertion base point*** represents a meaningful reference point that is used to position the symbol when you insert it into your drawing after the block definition has been created. Figure 12.7 shows a variety of symbols with an appropriate insertion base point for each symbol indicated by a filled circle. The rationale for the insertion base points shown in this figure becomes clear when you consider how each of the symbols is used. For example, electronic schematic symbols and single line piping diagram symbols are ordinarily connected to the end of a line object that designates a circuit pathway or a section of pipe. Looking at the electronic and pip-

CHAPTER 12 ||| Designing and Using Your Own Symbols

ing symbols, you can see that the defined insertion base point makes it a quick and easy process to connect the symbol to an existing line using an ENDPoint object snap setting. An insertion base point located somewhere in the middle of the symbol would make it more difficult to position accurately.

The mechanical symbols shown specify the most commonly referenced point for locating the feature as the insertion base point. For example, a finish mark is located by placing the bottom point directly on the surface being described. The insertion base point shown for the finish mark in Figure 12.7 makes this an easy process. The hex nut symbol is typically positioned by centering it on a bolt or stud—so the center of the nut is the insertion base point. The NPT thread symbol insertion base point is where the surface profile and the hole center line intersect. Doors and windows are typically dimensioned to the center line of the opening, so an insertion base point that corresponds to the dimensioned position may work best.

To specify the desired insertion base point for the new block, pick the Specify point < button in the Base Point area. The Create Block dialog box is temporarily hidden while you pick the desired point. For the transistor block, a simple pick using the ENDpoint object snap mode accurately sets the desired insertion point. The following sequence is displayed at the command line:

Command: _bmake
Insertion base point: **ENDP**↵
of ⟨*pick the line near the end as shown in Figure 12.7*⟩

FIGURE 12.7 The specified insertion point of a block should always reference the feature or location that is most commonly used as a base point when positioning the symbol in a drawing. The filled circles indicate appropriate insertion points for the symbols shown.

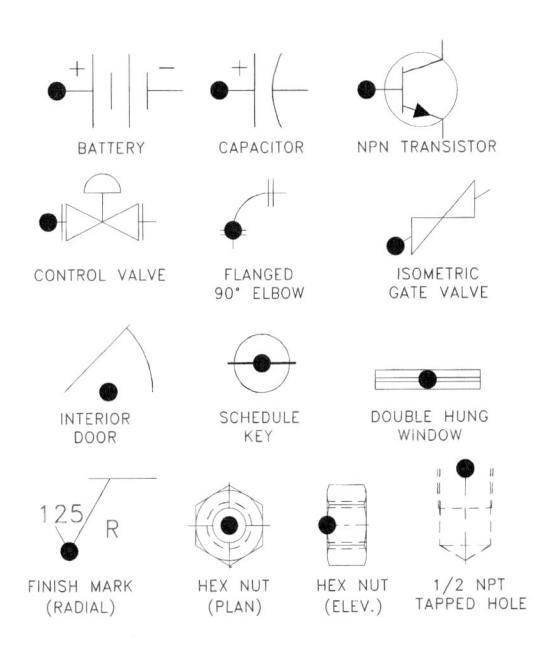

After selecting an insertion base point, the Create Block dialog box reappears and the coordinate location is displayed in the X:, Y:, and Z: text boxes. If you are not satisfied with the specified point, pick the Select Point < button again to specify a different insertion base point.

Alternately, if you already know the exact coordinate location of the desired insertion base point, you can directly enter the X, Y, and Z values in the appropriately labeled text boxes. Regardless of the method used to enter the coordinates for the insertion base point of a block, be certain that the specified point is completely accurate. If you are picking the point with your cursor, be sure to use a suitable precision drawing aid such as the snap grid or an applicable object snap mode.

The last field in this dialog box is the Description: text box. This optional field can be used to store a detailed description of the symbol, along with any other desired comments. Allowing a maximum of 256 characters, this field can be viewed when using the Content Explorer. The Content Explorer is discussed in the next section.

Figure 12.8 shows the appearance of the Create Block dialog box on completion of this block definition. The block name is set to NPN_TRANS, the coordinates for the endpoint of the transistor's base lead are displayed, eight selected objects are to be used in the definition, and the Delete selected objects after block creation toggle has been turned on. Pick the OK button to complete the block definition process.

FIGURE 12.8 The appearance of the Create Block dialog box on completion of the definition for the NPN_TRANS block.

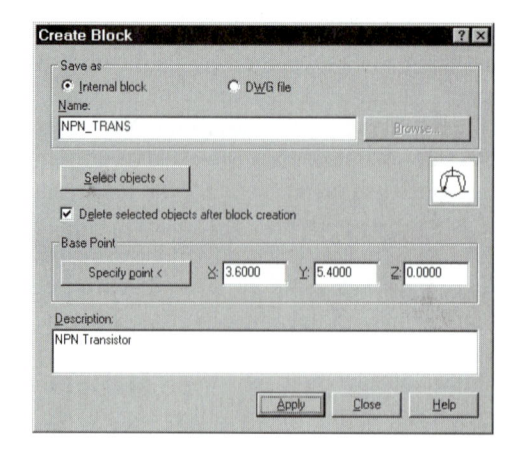

When you select the Apply button, the block definition data is checked for validity. If the block name you have specified duplicates an existing block name, a warning message is issued, as shown in Figure 12.9. To avoid redefining the existing symbol name with the new block definition, pick the Cancel button and specify a new block name. Redefining and renaming existing symbols is covered later in this chapter.

Once a symbol, or block, is defined in a drawing, it can be quickly and easily inserted into each desired location. Inserting symbols in a drawing is covered in the next section.

FIGURE 12.9 This warning is displayed if the specified block name duplicates an existing block name.

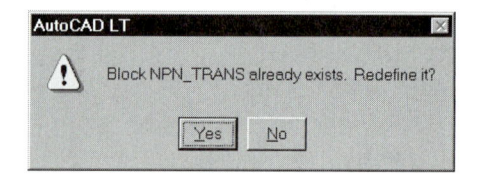

Field Notes

- For unique symbols that are particular to your business, you may need to simply create the required symbols on an "as-needed" basis. When a project requires a new symbol, create it and save it in your custom symbol library. Creating and managing custom symbol libraries is discussed later in this chapter.
- For standard drafting symbols, it can be advantageous to buy predrawn commercial symbol libraries to save yourself valuable drafting time. The Autodesk company markets symbol library packages designed specifically for use with AutoCAD LT, or you may find other companies that market a similar product.

Exercise 12.2

1. Start a new drawing using the Quick Setup defaults. Draw the geometry to describe an NPN transistor, as shown in Figure 12.7, and use it to define a block named NPN_TRANS specifying the insertion base point as shown in the illustration.
2. Draw four more symbols of your choice from Figure 12.7. Generate new block definitions for each symbol, and assign a short and descriptive name to each block. Use the insertion base points as shown in the illustration.
3. Save the drawing as EX12.2.

LEARNING CHECKPOINT

☐ What are the advantages of using drafting symbols?
☐ Describe the primary productivity gain from using a CAD application.

FIGURE 12.10 The Insert dialog box is accessed by using the DDINSERT command.

- What is the first step in creating any block definition?
- Detail the block name conventions required by AutoCAD LT.
- What should be considered when defining a block insertion base point?
- What is the function and significance of the D<u>e</u>lete selected objects after block creation toggle?
- What are the recommended guidelines for specifying block names?

Inserting Blocks

Once a block definition has been created, it remains available in the current drawing unless it is intentionally removed from the drawing database. To insert a block into a drawing, use the DDINSERT command. DDINSERT can be accessed by picking the Insert Block button on the Content Explorer flyout in the Draw toolbar, selecting <u>B</u>lock … from the <u>I</u>nsert pull-down menu, or by typing **I** or **DDINSERT** at the Command: prompt. The Insert dialog box is shown in Figure 12.10.

The Insert dialog box provides an easy interface for inserting blocks into a drawing. To insert a locally defined block, pick the <u>B</u>lock . . . button. A *locally defined block* refers to a block that is defined within the current drawing. For example, the sequence in the previous section creates the block NPN_TRANS as a locally defined block. The blocks that have been defined for the current drawing are listed in the Defined Blocks dialog box, as shown in Figure 12.11. Notice that the block named NPN_TRANS appears in the defined block name list.

To select a block name for insertion, pick the desired block name to highlight it and pick the OK button, or just double-click on the block name. The highlighted block name appears in the <u>S</u>election: text box. If your drawing has a long list of block names defined, you can use the <u>P</u>attern: text box to indicate specific block names to list or possibly a wild card specification to narrow down the listing. After accepting the selected name, you are returned to the Insert dialog box, and the selected block name appears in the text box to the right of the <u>B</u>lock … button. For this example, pick the NPN_TRANS block name for insertion.

FIGURE 12.11 All blocks defined for the current drawing are listed in the Defined Blocks dialog box.

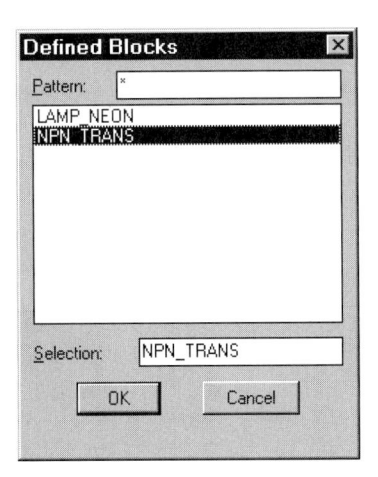

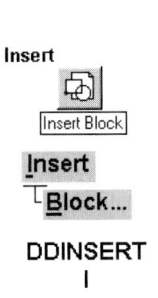

Insert
Insert Block

Insert
<u>B</u>lock...

DDINSERT
I

FIGURE 12.12 The block is dragged with the cursor by its defined insertion base point. Picking an insertion point attaches the block to the selected point—also by its defined insertion base point.

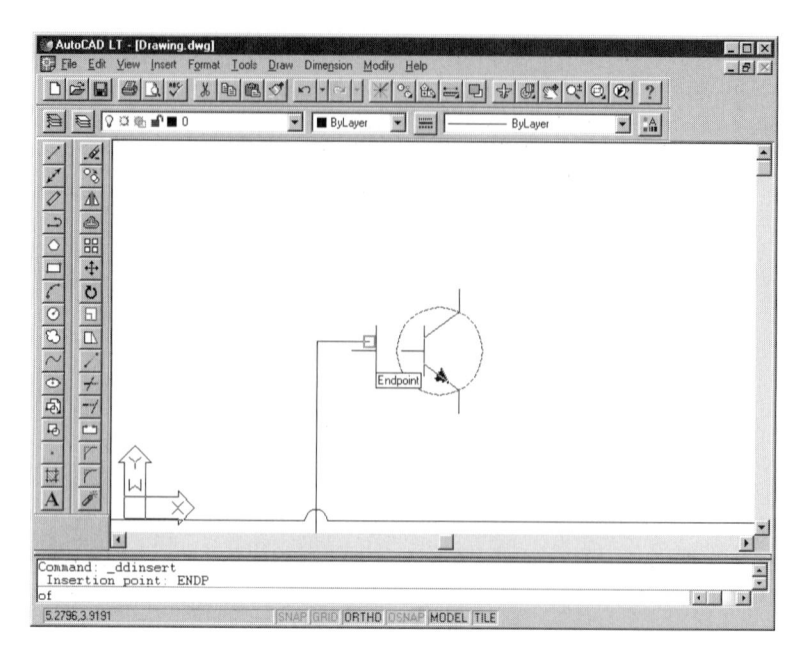

Indicating where and how to insert the block is done in the Options area of the Insert dialog box. By default, the Specify Parameters on Screen toggle is checked, and all of the other fields in this area are disabled. To continue with the block insertion process using this default option, pick the OK button. The Insert dialog box is dismissed and you will see the selected symbol attached to your cursor by its defined insertion base point. AutoCAD LT then issues the following prompt:

Command: _ddinsert
Insertion point: ⟨pick the location for the block insertion base point⟩

The NPN_TRANS block is attached to the specified insertion point by its insertion base point as specified in the block definition. Figure 12.12 shows the block attached to the cursor, with the ENDpoint object snap active, while picking an existing line. Using an applicable precision drawing aid, such as the snap grid or object snap, when inserting your block ensures that it is positioned accurately.

After specifying the location of the symbol within the drawing, you are prompted for an insertion scale factor. The insertion scale factor allows you to adjust the size of the symbol as needed for any specific application. Many symbols, such as those used in schematic diagrams, are drawn at a standard size and are typically inserted at the default scale factor of 1. Some symbols may vary in size depending on the application. Symbols that vary in size are often drawn based on a unit of 1, and the size is adjusted as needed during the insertion process. The example in Figure 12.13 uses a standard-sized schematic symbol, therefore the defined block is already the correct size. The following prompts are displayed at the command line to determine scale factors:

X scale factor <1> / Corner / XYZ: ↵
Y scale factor (default=X): ↵

Pressing Enter at the X scale factor prompt accepts the default of 1 as displayed in the angle brackets: <1>. The next prompt asks for the Y scale factor and defaults to the value used for the X scale factor. Pressing Enter at this prompt accepts the default scale factor of 1.

Finally, you are prompted for a rotation angle. This allows you to reorient the block as needed for each placement in your drawing. The prompt is as follows:

Rotation angle <0>: ↵

Again, pressing Enter accepts the default of zero degrees rotation. This is appropriate in this case, because the symbol is already oriented correctly for this application. The result of inserting the block NPN_TRANS using the default values for each of the insertion parameters is shown in Figure 12.13.

FIGURE 12.13 The NPN_TRANS block as it appears after being inserted at a specified point using the default values for insertion options.

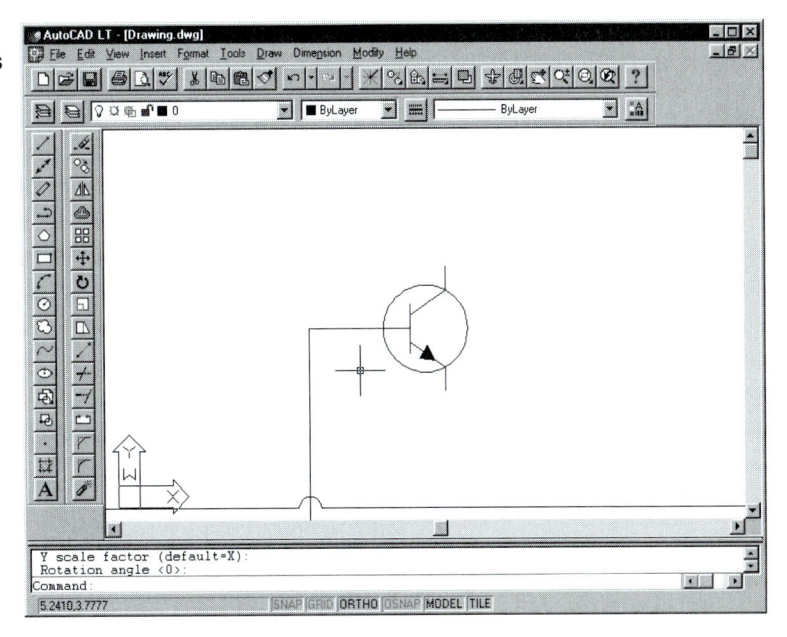

Field Notes

A distinct advantage to using blocks within a drawing is decreased drawing file size. A block definition is maintained as a singular record in the drawing database. Every insertion of the block in a drawing references the original definition and therefore does not duplicate information regardless of how many times the block is used in the drawing. Each individual block insertion stores only unique information such as its insertion point, scale factors, and rotation angle.

When working with schematic diagram drawings, inserted symbols often need to be rotated into the proper orientation. The rotation angle prompt can be used to adjust the orientation of a symbol when inserting it. To try this, use the DDINSERT command again. Notice that the last block inserted is presented as the default—the NPN_TRANS block name appears in the text box to the right of the Block ... button. Pick the OK button to accept the default and insert another copy of this block.

For the following example, pick any desired location on the screen for the insertion point and accept the default values for the X and Y scale factors. When prompted for the rotation angle, enter an angle of 90 degrees. Note that, similar to using the ROTATE command, a rotation angle can be specified by entering a numeric value using the keyboard or you can pick the angle using your cursor. If you enter the value using your keyboard, the prompt sequence looks like this:

Command: _ddinsert
Insertion point: ⟨*pick a point on the screen*⟩
X scale factor <1> / Corner / XYZ: ↵
Y scale factor (default=X): ↵
Rotation angle <0>: **90**↵

The inserted symbol is rotated 90 degrees and appears as shown in Figure 12.14. Notice that the insertion base point is also the rotation base point. For symbols that are frequently rotated when used, this can be an important consideration when defining the location of the block insertion base point.

Each of the previous examples shows a block inserted using the default values for the insertion scale factors. The insertion scale factors serve as direct multipliers for the sizes of the objects as they were drawn in the original block definition. By adjusting the values of the X and Y scale factor options, the size and aspect ratio of a symbol can be modified as needed, allowing for added flexibility when using symbols in your drawings. The term *aspect ratio* refers to the ratio of width to height, or in this case the ratio of X to Y scale factors.

FIGURE 12.14 The second insertion of the NPN_TRANS block is rotated about the insertion base point 90 degrees.

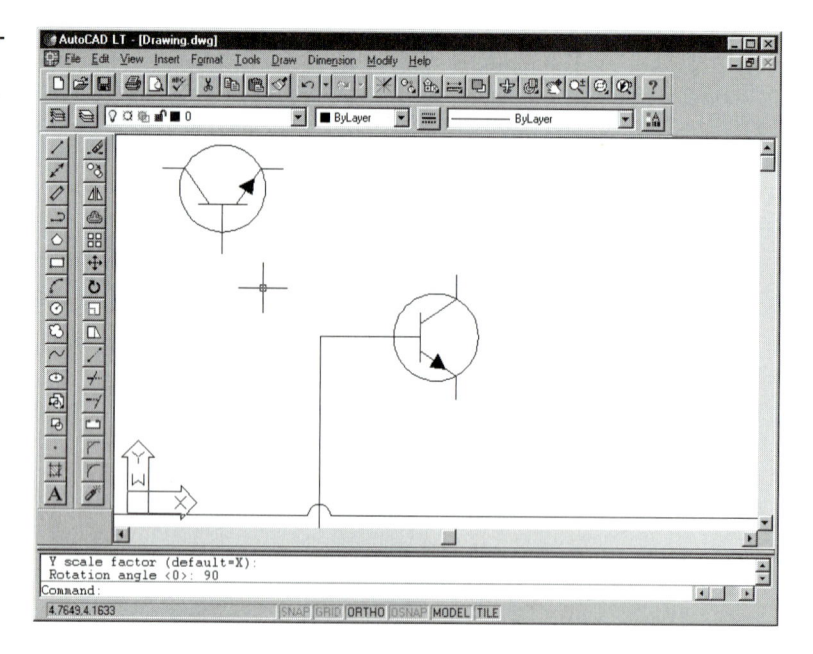

Changing the X scale factor resizes the block based on the X axis of the original block definition geometry. Likewise, the Y and Z scale factors resize the block based on the Y and Z axes of the objects used in the original block definition. Additionally, a block can be mirrored upon insertion by specifying a negative insertion scale factor value. To mirror the symbol horizontally, indicate an X scale factor of −1; to mirror vertically, specify a Y scale factor of −1. Figure 12.15 shows several examples of various X and Y scale factors. Notice the effects of the negative values and the positive values both greater than and less than one. The Z axis value has no effect unless the block being inserted contains 3-D objects that have a Z axis dimensional value. Drawing 3-D objects is covered in Chapter 14.

As stated earlier, some symbols are defined as being a specific size. These symbols are drawn full size for the block definition and then inserted at a scale factor of 1. Other symbols, however, may vary in size or aspect ratio from one application to the next.

One example of a symbol that can vary in overall size from one application to the next includes annotation symbols, as shown in Figure 12.5. An *annotation symbol* is a symbol used in combination with text. The definitions of annotation symbols change based on the height of the text with which they are being used. Figure 12.16 shows the definition of a depth symbol as specified in ASME Y14.5M-1994. The "h" used in the dimensions references the height of the text with which the symbol is being used. The dimensions are not part of the symbol.

FIGURE 12.15 Various insertion scale factors can be used to alter the overall size or the aspect ratio of an inserted block. Negative values can be used to mirror a symbol on one or both axes during insertion.

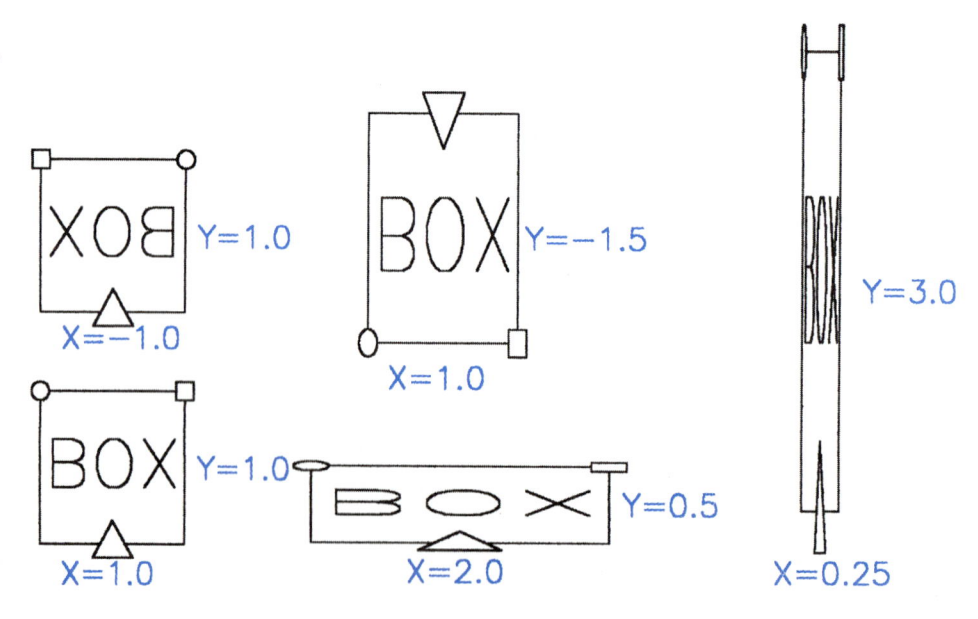

CHAPTER 12 ||| Designing and Using Your Own Symbols   495

FIGURE 12.16 Annotation symbols will vary in size depending on the height of the text with which they are used. The "h" in the specified dimensions is a reference to the height of the accompanying text.

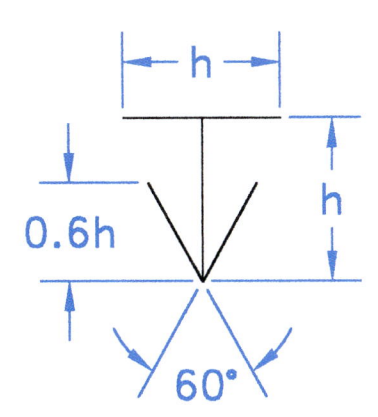

When creating a symbol that varies in size, the best approach is to create the block definition based on a unit of 1. This means that to create the definition for the annotation symbol shown in Figure 12.16, substitute a distance of 1 unit for the "h" dimension. Because the "h" dimension is drawn at 1 unit, the scale factor corresponds to the height of the text where the symbol is to be used. For example, in a mechanical drawing that uses 1/8-in. annotation text, the depth symbol is inserted using equal X and Y scale factors of 0.125. Because the scale factor is a multiplier, the defined symbol height of 1 unit is multiplied by 0.125, resulting in an inserted height of 0.125 units—the same as the text. If the text height is 5/32, use an insertion scale factor of 0.15625 (or 5/32). Whatever the text height is indicates what the insertion scale factor for the annotation symbol needs to be.

Field Notes

Remember that many of the most commonly accessed annotation symbols are available as part of the text when using the GDT.shx font. Even if you need to use a different font, using the MTEXT editor enables you to create text objects that use more than one font file. If the symbol you need is not available as part of the text, then use the methods described here to create the needed annotation symbol.

An example of using symbols that vary in aspect ratio could include different types of block diagrams, such as a simplified floor plan that uses appropriately sized rectangles to depict various furnishings. A possible application for this type of drawing is for space planning in a building or office, where floor space is the concern rather than furniture details. To prepare for this task, create a simple 1-unit square for a block definition and name it very generically. For example, you could name the block FURN as a nonspecific reference to furniture.

When inserting a symbol to represent a desk measuring 30 in. deep by 60 in. wide, set the X scale factor at 30 and the Y scale factor at 60 and indicate the desired rotation angle. The same symbol can then be used to represent a conference room table measuring 42 in. 3 96 in. by using X and Y scale factors of 42 and 96, respectively. This type of an application has one major disadvantage, which is the fact that all the symbols have the same name. So unless you insert some text labels, you may not remember what each insertion represents. A good solution for this problem is to use block attributes, which are discussed later in this chapter.

Other Insertion Scale Factor Options

When using the Specify Parameters on Screen option, two additional options are available for specifying insertion scale factors. To explore these options, use the DDINSERT command to insert the NPN_TRANS block. Pick any desired insertion point on screen and study the additional available options shown at the X scale factor prompt:

    Command: _ddinsert
    Insertion point: ⟨pick any point on the screen⟩
    X scale factor <1> / Corner / XYZ: C↵
    Other corner:

To use the corner option, type **C** and press Enter at the prompt, as shown above. The next prompt asks for the "Other corner:" of a user-specified rectangle. The implied First corner is automatically assigned to the block

FIGURE 12.17 Turning off the Specify Parameters on Screen toggle enables the text boxes located in the Options area of the Insert dialog box.

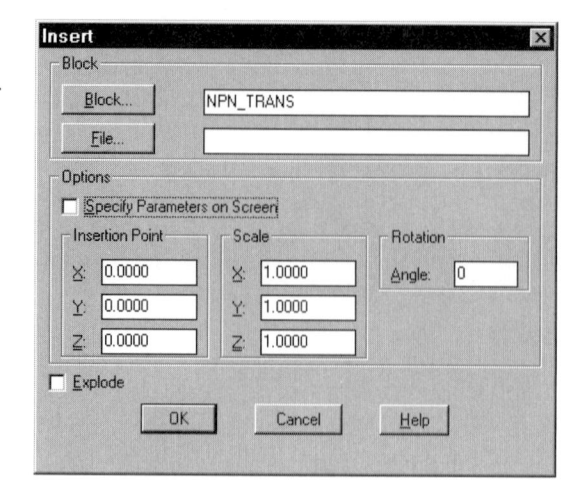

insertion point. The other corner can be an arbitrarily picked point, or specified using any valid coordinate entry method. AutoCAD LT then measures the X and Y axis distances between two corners of the rectangle. The distance on the X axis is used for the X scale factor and the distance on the Y axis is supplied for the Y scale factor. If the X coordinate of the second point is greater than that of the insertion point, the X scale factor is positive. An X axis value for the second corner that is less than the X axis value of the block insertion point results in a negative X scale factor. This is also true of the Y axis values. The Corner option is not very accurate when picking the other corner manually. This option can be more accurately controlled if you type a coordinate specification or use appropriate precision drawing aids.

After specifying the other corner, you are prompted for a rotation angle:

Rotation angle <0>: ↵

Typically, the Z scale factor is defaulted to the value of the X scale factor. If you need to use a specific Z scale factor that is not the same as the X scale factor, and you are Specifying Parameters on Screen, the XYZ option is used. This option allows specification of different scale factors for all three axes if desired. This is how it works:

Command: _ddinsert
Insertion point: ⟨pick any point on the screen⟩
X scale factor <1> / Corner / XYZ: **X** or **XYZ**↵
X scale factor <1> / Corner: ⟨enter the X scale factor⟩
Y scale factor (default=X): ⟨enter the Y scale factor⟩
Z scale factor (default=X): ⟨enter the Z scale factor⟩
Rotation angle <0>: ↵

Alternately, after activating the XYZ option, you can use the Corner option to indicate the X and Y scale factors and you are then prompted for the Z scale factor.

Regardless of the application, specifying block insertion parameters can also be done using the Options area of the Insert dialog box. After specifying the block name to insert, remove the check from the Specify Parameters on Screen toggle. The text boxes located in the Options area are now enabled and can be modified as needed, as shown in Figure 12.17.

To use the Options area of the Insert dialog box effectively, you must already know the correct coordinates for the block insertion point. After indicating the insertion point coordinates, you can specify individual or common X, Y, and Z scale factors and a rotation angle. Notice that when you set the X scale factor, the Y and Z default values are automatically set to match. If this is not correct, you then need to adjust the Y and Z values individually.

Presetting Block Insertion Parameters

When inserting a block, as you move the cursor, you drag along a representation of the block as it appears using the default insertion parameters. After picking an insertion point, the block is then stretched as you move your cursor to show the insertion scale factors indicated by the current X and Y distances from the selected point to the current cursor location. While entering the rotation angle, you can drag the cursor to point to any angle from the insertion point and the block representation is actively rotated to show the results.

CHAPTER 12 ||| Designing and Using Your Own Symbols

In some cases, it can be helpful to see the block representation in its final form, according to the scale factor or rotation angle (or both) that you intend to use. This can be done using block insertion parameter presets. Presetting any or all of the insertion parameters allows AutoCAD LT to display the dragged block representation according to actual values you specify. Depending on which preset options you use, AutoCAD LT can use the preset values for inserting the block with no further prompting, or you can give a temporary preset value for the display only and you are then presented with the normal prompts.

Presets can only be used on screen, using the INSERT command or the DDINSERT command with the Specify Parameters on Screen toggle turned on. To enter a preset scale factor, type **S** at the Insertion point: prompt.

Command: **INSERT**↵
Block name (or ?) <NPN_TRANS>: ↵
Insertion point: **S**↵
Scale factor: **2**↵
Insertion point: ⟨*specify the insertion point*⟩
Rotation angle <0>: ⟨*specify a rotation angle*⟩
Command:

When you are dragging the cursor at the second Insertion point: prompt, the block representation is displayed at a scale factor of 2. Notice that when using this method, only a single scale factor is requested and is used for both the X and Y values and no default values are given. Also, the preset value is automatically applied to the final inserted block reference with no further prompts. The rotation angle is then requested.

Another option is to preset the rotation angle:

Command: **INSERT**↵
Block name (or ?) < NPN_TRANS >: ↵
Insertion point: **R**↵
Rotation angle: **45**↵
Insertion point: ⟨*specify the insertion point*⟩
X scale factor <1> / Corner / XYZ: ↵
Y scale factor (default=X): ↵
Command:

And if desired, you can preset both the scale factor and the rotation angle:

Command: **INSERT**↵
Block name (or ?) <NPN_TRANS>: ↵
Insertion point: **S**↵
Scale factor: **2**↵
Insertion point: **R**↵
Rotation angle: **45**↵
Insertion point: ⟨*specify the insertion point*⟩
Command:

It is also possible to preset individual X, Y, and Z scale factors in the same manner by typing **X, Y,** or **Z** at the Insertion point: prompt.

If you want to use the presets as a reference only, but you also want an opportunity to enter a value different from the preset, you can use a temporary preset. Temporary presets are used in the same manner as the presets just described, but you are still issued the normal scale factor and rotation angle prompts after picking the insertion point. To make the preset temporary, precede the preset option with a P. For example, the next sequence is used to set a temporary preset scale factor:

Command: **INSERT**↵
Block name (or ?) <NPN_TRANS>: ↵
Insertion point: **PS**↵
Scale factor: **2**↵
Insertion point: ⟨*specify the insertion point*⟩
X scale factor <1> / Corner / XYZ: ⟨*specify a scale factor*⟩
Y scale factor (default=X): ⟨*specify a scale factor*⟩
Rotation angle <0>: ⟨*specify a rotation angle*⟩
Command:

> ✏️ **Field Notes**
>
> AutoCAD LT also provides command line versions of the BMAKE and DDINSERT commands for making and inserting blocks.
>
> - The BLOCK command is used to create new block definitions using text entry at the command line.
> - The INSERT command (alias = IN) is used to insert blocks using text entry at the command line.
>
> The BMAKE and DDINSERT commands provide a more effective interface for creating and using blocks than these command line versions. Additionally, blocks created using the BLOCK command do not display a preview image in the Content Explorer. However, the command line versions are necessary when employing advanced automation techniques such as command scripts. The use of command scripts is detailed in Chapter 17.

> ### Exercise 12.3
>
> 1. Open the drawing EX12.2.
> 2. Use the DDINSERT command to insert the NPN_TRANS block using default insertion options.
> 3. Insert additional copies of NPN_TRANS and experiment with changing the values for the X and Y scale factors and rotation angles. Try both positive and negative values.
> 4. Create the geometry for the DEPTH symbol, as shown in Figure 12.16, substituting a distance of 1 unit for the "h" dimension.
> 5. Insert the DEPTH symbol in conjunction with a text object to create a note specifying a 0.25 diameter by a depth of 1.75 units.
> 6. Save the drawing as EX12.3.

☑ LEARNING CHECKPOINT

- ☐ To what does the term *locally defined block* refer?
- ☐ How can you display a list of the blocks defined for the current drawing?
- ☐ What are the advantages of using the Specify Parameters on Screen option?
- ☐ Describe each of the prompts issued when specifying parameters on screen.
- ☐ How does the definition process differ for a symbol that may vary in size?
- ☐ Name the command line versions of BMAKE and DDINSERT.
- ☐ What is meant by defining a block based on a unit of 1?
- ☐ Describe the use of the Corner option for specifying insertion scale factors.

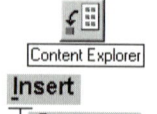

Using the Content Explorer to Insert Blocks

AutoCAD LT 98 provides a powerful tool for managing symbols and symbol libraries, known as the Content Explorer. The Content Explorer provides a variety of tools that help you to more intuitively manage and use symbols. Throughout this chapter, applications for the Content Explorer are discussed in each area where they apply. One of the most fundamental uses of the Content Explorer is for drag-and-drop block insertion. To activate the Content Explorer, pick Content Explorer... from the Insert pull-down menu, select the Content Explorer button from the Draw or Insert toolbar, or enter **CE** or **CONTENT** at the Command: prompt. The Content Explorer is launched if it is not already running, and then it is made the current window. The default

CHAPTER 12 ||| Designing and Using Your Own Symbols 499

FIGURE 12.18 The default appearance of the Content Explorer window with the default tab set.

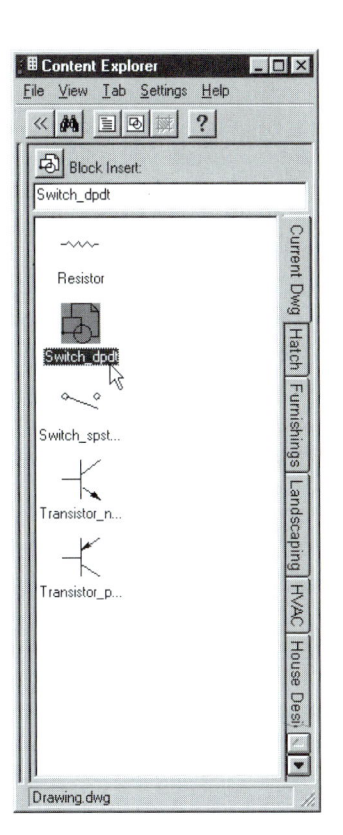

FIGURE 12.19 Blocks created using the BLOCK command do not display a preview in the Content Explorer window.

appearance is shown in Figure 12.18, where the current drawing has no blocks defined and the default tab set is loaded. The default tab set was specified when you installed AutoCAD LT 98. Changing the default tab set is discussed later.

The Current Dwg tab shows all blocks defined in the current drawing. If the block was created using the Create Block dialog box, it will also display an icon representation of the block for easy recognition. Blocks that have been created using the BLOCK command or blocks from drawings created in earlier versions of AUTOCAD LT display only a generic block icon. Both types of representations are shown in Figure 12.19; the block named Switch_dpdt was created using the BLOCK command.

To insert a block from this listing into the current drawing, simply point your cursor at the desired block; then press and hold the pick button to drag the icon. When you drag the icon into the AutoCAD LT graphics screen area, the drawing window moves to the top to give you access to all the currently displayed drawing area. If you release the pick button, the block is inserted at the current cursor location. You are not prompted for the insertion parameters; the default scale factor of 1 is used with a rotation angle of 0:

Command: _.drginsert Insertion point: <*Release the pick button*>

Field Notes

Using the drag-and-drop method to insert a block issues the _.drginsert command. Unlike other commands in AutoCAD LT, this one is not repeated when you press Enter at the Command: prompt. Additionally, typing DRGINSERT at the command line returns an "Unknown command" error message.

This drag-and-drop insertion method makes certain assumptions that do not always apply. Although the scale factor of 1 will match most applications, the required rotation angle often differs from 0. If you do need to change the insertion scale factors or rotation angles, you must double-click on the icon rather than use drag-and-drop. When you double-click, the AutoCAD LT 98 drawing window is made current and the INSERT command is issued, using all the normal prompts. This method allows you to specify scale factors and a rotation angle.

It is also possible to use the previously discussed preset options. However, you must enter the first preset option before you release the pick button. Releasing the pick button before your keyboard entry causes the block to be inserted at the current cursor location using the default insertion parameters. In the following example, the block is inserted using a scale factor of 2 and a rotation angle of 45°:

Command: _.drginsert Insertion point: **S**↵
Scale factor: **2**↵
Insertion point: **R**↵
Rotation angle: **45**↵
Insertion point: **ENDP**↵
of *Point to insertion point and release pick button*
Command:

Field Notes

- If the mouse pick button is released after a keyboard entry and before the Enter key is pressed, the block is not released. In this case you must press the pick button again when locating the block insertion point
- You can access object snap overrides at the Insertion point: prompt either by typing the three-character abbreviation, pressing SHIFT+RIGHT-CLICK, or by picking the appropriate toolbar osnap button. When using this method, you must release the pick button when the cursor menu appears and then press it to pick the desired option from the cursor menu and press it again to locate the block insertion point.
- If you accidentally release the pick button before you specify insertion factors and rotation angle, it is easy to use the grip editing methods you learned in Chapter 7 to adjust the block as needed. By immediately grip selecting the inserted block, making the insertion point grip hot, and then right-clicking, you can easily scale and rotate the block.

The Content Explorer can also be used to access symbol libraries and symbols contained in other drawings. These applications are discussed later in this chapter.

LEARNING CHECKPOINT

☐ What is the Content Explorer?
☐ How is the Content Explorer used for inserting blocks?
☐ What things are unusual about the DRGINSERT command?
☐ How can the default scale and rotation of a block be set when using the Content Explorer?

Working with Blocks

A block that has been inserted into a drawing is known as a block reference. It is called a ***block reference*** because that is exactly what it does—it references a block definition. Each insertion of a specific block references the same stored block definition data, and has no actual definition of its own. Relevant information that is specific to a block reference includes its insertion point, scale factors, and rotation angle, plus a reference to the layer on which it was inserted.

CHAPTER 12 ||| Designing and Using Your Own Symbols

Editing a Block

Blocks are not like other objects in an AutoCAD LT drawing. A block is a complex object, meaning that regardless of how many objects are used in the block definition, a block is still handled like a single object. Selecting a block reference at a Select objects: prompt highlights all of the component objects, but the prompt reports only one object found. This is similar to a polyline object, which can be composed of multiple line and arc segments, but is still handled as a single object.

Block editing capabilities are very limited. The only editing commands that can be used are those that affect the entire block rather than individual components within the block reference. For example, duplication commands can be used with a block reference, including COPY, MIRROR, and ARRAY. Commands that change the size, position, or orientation of the block can be used, such as MOVE, SCALE, and ROTATE. Certain properties associated with a block reference can be changed using DDMODIFY and DDCHPROP. Additionally, any block reference can be removed from a drawing using the ERASE command.

When editing block references, object snap modes can be used to increase accuracy. The INSert object snap mode snaps to the block's defined insertion base point. All object snap modes work the same on objects that are components of a block reference as they do with individual objects.

When you need to change the location, scale factors, or rotation angle of a block reference, the DDMODIFY command provides a one-step method to change any or all of the block insertion parameters. DDMODIFY is accessed by picking the Properties button from the Object Properties toolbar, by right-clicking and picking Properties …, by selecting Properties … from the Modify pull-down menu, or by typing **MO** or **DDMODIFY** at the Command: prompt.

Select a single block reference at the prompt to display the Modify Block Insertion dialog box, as shown in Figure 12.20. Several of the properties of block references can be modified using this dialog box. Of the items in the area labeled Properties at the top of the dialog box, the only option that is likely to have any noticeable effect is changing the Layer … setting. The color, linetype, and individual object linetype scale properties of a block are dependent on how the original block definition was created. Techniques for controlling these properties within block references are detailed later in this section.

The lower area of the Modify Block Insertion dialog box provides options for modifying the insertion point, the X, Y, and Z scale factors, and the block rotation angle. The insertion point can be picked on screen or entered directly as individual X, Y, and Z coordinate values. Alternately, the CHANGE command can be used to quickly modify the insertion point and rotation angle of a block reference using the command line. Note that any changes to scale factors and rotation angles in this manner use the insertion point as the base point for the scaling or rotation.

As mentioned earlier, any command that attempts to edit individual components within the block reference cannot be used. Commands such as BREAK, TRIM, LENGTHEN, FILLET, and CHAMFER have no effect on blocks. For example, in the NPN_TRANS block, it is not possible to separately modify the circle, lines, or the polyline object that comprise the block reference. To do this type of editing, the block reference must first be exploded.

FIGURE 12.20 The Modify Block Insertion dialog box provides a convenient means to change the insertion parameters of an existing block reference.

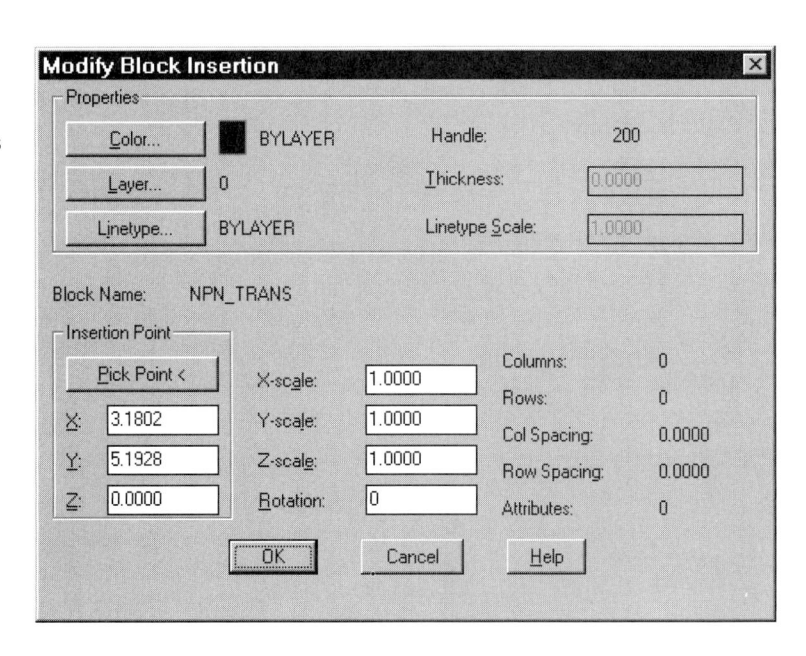

Object Properties
Properties
Modify
Properties
AI_PROPCHK
DDMODIFY
MO

Exercise 12.4

1. Open the drawing EX12.3.
2. Use the DDINSERT command to insert the NPN_TRANS block using default insertion options.
3. Try using editing commands, such as TRIM, EXTEND, or FILLET to modify the component geometry of the block reference. Notice the messages issued by AutoCAD LT.
4. Edit the block using editing commands such as COPY, MOVE, and ROTATE to duplicate, reposition, and reorient the block reference.
5. Use the DDMODIFY command to change the scale factors, insertion point, and rotation angle of the block reference.
6. Save the drawing as EX12.4.

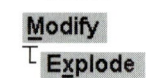

Exploding a Block

When you need to edit individual elements of a block in your drawing, you can disassemble the block reference using the EXPLODE command:

Command: **X** or **EXPLODE**.↵
Select objects: ⟨select a block reference⟩
Select objects: ↵
Command:

Exploding a block reduces it to its component objects. This means that the block reference is replaced with individual objects that represent the block definition. AutoCAD LT modifies these individual objects to match the exploded block's scale factors and rotation angle so that the size, position, and orientation of the displayed geometry remain the same.

Once a block reference has been exploded, it is no longer a complex object, and it loses all association with the original block definition. For example, exploding the NPN_TRANS block replaces the singular block reference object with one circle, six lines, and one polyline. Now the component objects can be freely edited with no effect on other NPN_TRANS block references in the drawing.

Field Notes

Exploding a block that was inserted using unequal scale factors can sometimes result in the creation of different object types than were used in the original block definition. For example, unequal insertion X and Y scale factors cause a circle object to appear elliptical in the inserted block reference. In order to preserve the appearance of the geometry when the block is exploded, AutoCAD LT substitutes an appropriate ellipse in place of the circle used in the original definition. Additionally, arc objects within such a block reference are converted to elliptical arcs when the block is exploded.

Inserting an Exploded Block

If you know prior to inserting a block that you are going to need to edit the geometry, you can turn on the Explode toggle in the Insert dialog box. The Explode toggle is located below the Options area of the Insert dialog box. Toggling this on causes a block to be inserted as component objects and not as a block reference. Essentially, the block is automatically exploded while it is being inserted. To do this using the INSERT command, precede the specified block name with an asterisk. For example:

Command: **INSERT**↵
Block name (or ?) <NPN_TRANS>: ***NPN_TRANS**↵
Insertion point: ⟨pick an insertion point⟩
Scale factor <1>: ↵
Rotation angle <0>: ↵

CHAPTER 12 ||| Designing and Using Your Own Symbols

When a block is exploded during insertion, unequal scale factors cannot be specified. Notice that the prompt is for a single scale factor, which is then applied equally to the X, Y, and Z axes. Similarly, if the Specify Parameters on Screen toggle is off when the Explode toggle is on, you will notice that the Y and Z scale factor options are disabled, allowing you to enter only a single scale factor that is applied to X, Y, and Z.

> **Exercise 12.5**
>
> 1. Open the drawing EX12.4.
> 2. Before beginning, ensure that inserted block references exist using both equal and unequal X and Y scale factors.
> 3. Use the EXPLODE command to explode several of the blocks.
> 4. Insert a new copy of a block using DDINSERT with the Explode toggle on and the Specify Parameters on Screen toggle off.
> 5. Insert a new copy of a block using INSERT and precede the block name with an asterisk.
> 6. Using the LIST command, list the properties of the component circle objects of the exploded blocks. Notice the difference in object type, depending on the insertion scale factors of the original block reference.
> 7. Save the drawing as EX12.5.

Redefining a Locally Defined Block

One very powerful aspect of using blocks in your drawings comes from the ability to revise every copy of a specific block in a drawing by simply revising the block definition. Inserted block references have no actual definition of their own. All insertions of a block reference within a drawing display the geometry described in the current block definition.

To redefine a symbol, first insert an exploded block reference of the block you are redefining. Alternately, you can insert the block reference and then explode it prior to editing. Which method you use is not important, but it is crucial that the block be exploded before you do any editing.

After exploding the block, perform all of your desired edits. Once you are finished editing the block and are satisfied with the new symbol, start the BMAKE command. In the Block Name: field, enter the same name that the block used previously. Specify the insertion base point and select the objects to use for the block definition. When you pick OK, AutoCAD LT warns you that the block name you specified already exists. This warning dialog box, shown in Figure 12.21, presents a yes-or-no option: pick the Yes button to redefine the block or No to cancel.

Block Redefinition Problems

If you forget to explode a block reference before revising it, you may encounter some unexpected difficulties when trying to redefine the existing block definition. If you need to remove or change some of the objects that comprise the definition, you will find that you cannot edit the individual components of a block reference prior to exploding it. Even if all you need to do is add some new objects to the definition, you are still required to explode the reference in order to use its component geometry in the revised definition. Otherwise, as shown in Figure 12.22, the message "Block references itself." is displayed in an alert box when you pick the OK button to complete the redefinition.

AutoCAD LT permits existing block references to be used in the creation of *other* block definitions. This practice is called **nesting** and is discussed in the next section. However, AutoCAD LT does not allow an inserted block reference to be used as part of the block definition that has the same name as the reference. To demonstrate this concept, the following example shows the definition of a block named SIGN, followed by

FIGURE 12.21 Picking the Yes button revises the block definition and, on exiting the Block Definition dialog box, updates all previously inserted block references using the new definition.

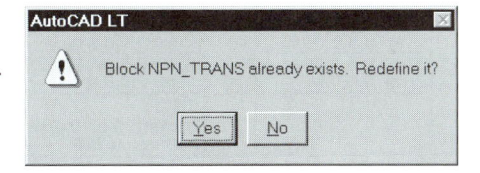

FIGURE 12.22 An error message is displayed when a block is specified as part of its own definition.

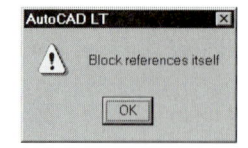

one successful and one unsuccessful attempt to redefine it using the component geometry of the block reference as part of the new definition.

All block definitions consist of a descriptive listing of the objects selected to represent the block geometry. As an example, in Figure 12.23A, the block named SIGN has been created using the three listed line objects to comprise the block definition. Each of the lines selected is clearly defined in the drawing database, and AutoCAD LT uses this information in the definition for the block named SIGN.

As with any block reference, an inserted SIGN block simply reads the source definition in order to know what component geometry to display. The source definition of SIGN lists the descriptions of the three component lines.

In Figure 12.23B, the block is successfully redefined. To use the geometry comprising the current definition as part of the new definition, an insertion of the block reference SIGN is placed in the drawing. Explode the block during insertion as practiced in Exercise 12.5, or after insertion, use the EXPLODE command. This removes the block reference and replaces it with individual objects that represent the existing block definition. Edits can now be made to the existing geometry, and in this example, a circle is placed inside of the triangle formed by the three lines.

Now that the revisions to the symbol are complete, use the BMAKE command to change the block definition. The objects selected as the definition are three line objects and a circle object. As with the previous definition of SIGN, these objects are clearly defined in the drawing database and AutoCAD LT uses this information in the new definition for the block named SIGN. Additionally, any other occurrences of a reference to this block definition are immediately updated.

An error situation is produced in Figure 12.23C, where an attempt is made to revise the definition of the block named SIGN using an existing reference to the block as part of its new definition. In this case, the block reference has not been exploded and is therefore still just a reference to the block definition of SIGN. As in Figure 12.23B, the revision edit consists of a circle being placed in the triangle. When the BMAKE command is used and the descriptive geometry is selected, this time only two objects are found: the circle and an inserted reference to the definition of the block named SIGN. To determine how to display a representation of the component objects, AutoCAD LT finds the drawing database records of the selected objects. The circle is clearly defined, but the block reference SIGN is now defined as comprising two objects, a circle and the block named SIGN. At this point, the block named SIGN does not have a complete definition. It is defined as being comprised of an inserted reference to itself and a circle.

The final result is that when the inserted block *reference* named SIGN looks to the new block *definition* to find out what geometry to display, it finds that the *definition* of the block SIGN contains an inserted block *reference* named SIGN. Any attempts to resolve the definition of the SIGN block result in another reference to a block named SIGN. This creates an endless loop and prevents AutoCAD LT from being able to determine what geometry to use to display the new definition. A block definition that uses an inserted reference to

FIGURE 12.23 (A) The original SIGN block is defined using three line objects. (B) The correct approach is to explode the block reference before trying to redefine a block. This example successfully redefines the block SIGN as being comprised of three line objects and a circle. (C) An error is produced when the existing block SIGN is used as part of the definition for the new SIGN block.

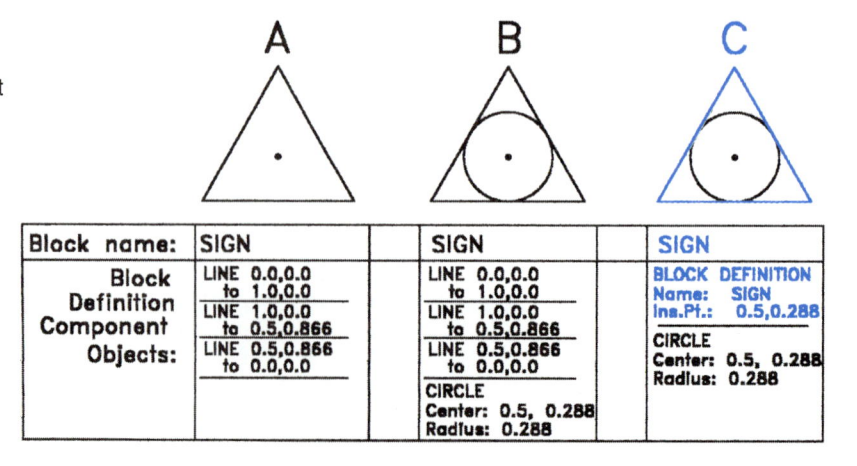

Block name:	SIGN	SIGN	SIGN
Block Definition Component Objects:	LINE 0,0,0.0 to 1,0,0.0 LINE 1,0,0.0 to 0.5,0.866 LINE 0.5,0.866 to 0,0,0.0	LINE 0,0,0.0 to 1,0,0.0 LINE 1,0,0.0 to 0.5,0.866 LINE 0.5,0.866 to 0,0,0.0 CIRCLE Center: 0.5, 0.288 Radius: 0.288	BLOCK DEFINITION Name: SIGN Ins.Pt.: 0.5,0.288 CIRCLE Center: 0.5, 0.288 Radius: 0.288

itself as part of its own definition is what is referred to by the message "Error—this block references itself." So if you see this message while redefining a locally defined block, exit the Block Definition dialog box and explode the existing block reference. Now you should be able to proceed without any further problems.

Renaming a Block

To change the name of a block definition, use the DDRENAME command. You can access the DDRENAME command by typing **REN** or **DDRENAME** at the Command: prompt or by picking Rename … from the Format menu. To rename a block, pick Block from the Named Objects list and highlight the name of the block you want to rename. The old name then appears in the Old Name: text box. Enter the new name in the Rename To: text box and pick the Rename To: button. Now pick OK. If you forget to pick the Rename To: button before picking OK, the block will not be renamed.

Format
└ Rename...

DDRENAME
REN

Exercise 12.6

1. Start a new drawing session.
2. Create a 1-unit square using LINE objects. Use these four lines as a definition for a block named TILE, using the lower left corner as the insertion base point.
3. Insert one TILE block reference using default values. Insert four others using any desired insertion parameters.
4. Draw a circle within the first inserted TILE block reference.
5. Using the BMAKE command, try to redefine the block TILE. When selecting objects, pick both the inserted block reference and the circle. Notice the message issued by AutoCAD LT when you pick the OK button.
6. Cancel the BMAKE command and use the EXPLODE command to explode the block reference. Try using BMAKE again to redefine the block TILE, and select all four lines from the exploded block and the circle object.
7. Notice the changes made to the other inserted TILE block references.
8. Save the drawing as EX12.6.

✓ LEARNING CHECKPOINT

☐ What are the limitations regarding editing inserted block references?
☐ Which properties of a block reference can be changed with DDMODIFY?
☐ Name the command that reduces a block to its components.
☐ What two methods can be used to explode a block while inserting it?
☐ What happens to block references when the block definition is modified?
☐ What is meant by a block referencing itself?
☐ How can you avoid a block referencing itself when redefining it?

Nesting Blocks

Block references can be used as needed in other block definitions, this practice is called *nesting.* One situation for which a nested block is useful is within a subassembly that occurs in multiple locations within a drawing or within multiple drawings. In many cases, the parts of the subassembly may be represented as symbols that were created using blocks. For example, in the piping subassembly shown in Figure 12.24A, several individual blocks representing valves, tanks, gauges, and other components were inserted and connected by lines as appropriate to form the subassembly representation. The resulting geometry is then used as the definition for another block that represents the full subassembly. This procedure allows you to insert the entire subassembly as needed, rather than constructing it from individual blocks in each required location. Figure 12.24B shows the use of the subassembly in a piping diagram. Notice that the block on the right has been inserted using a negative X scale factor, and therefore appears mirrored.

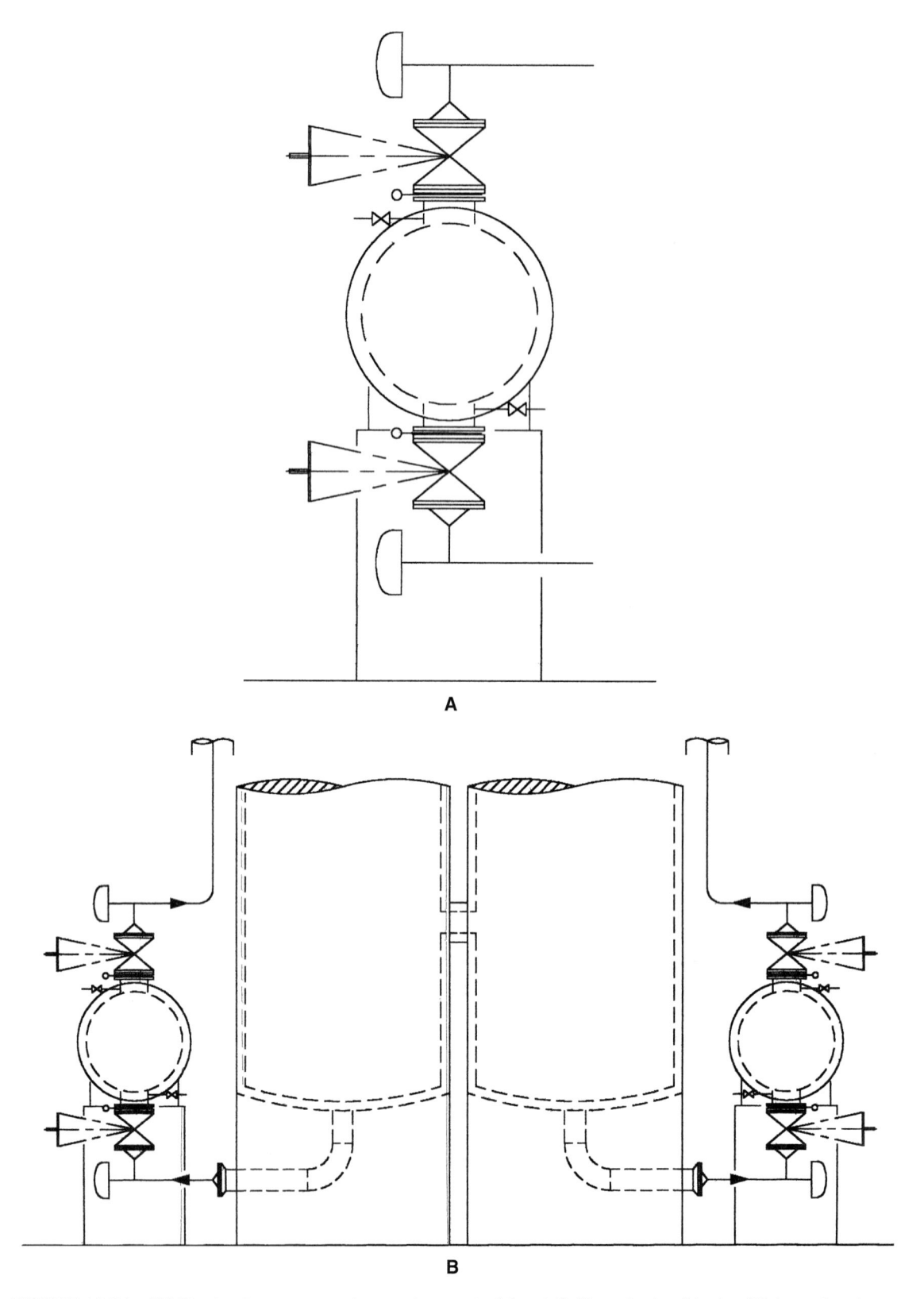

FIGURE 12.24 (A) Block references can be used as part of the definition of other blocks. (B) Inserting the block representing the subassembly can save a great deal of time if the subassembly is a commonly used feature.

FIGURE 12.25 (A) These objects were created on varying layers using a bylayer setting. (B) Objects created on layer 0, using bylayer settings, take on the properties of the layer on which the block reference is inserted. Objects created on other layers, using bylayer settings, are displayed according to their individual layer settings.

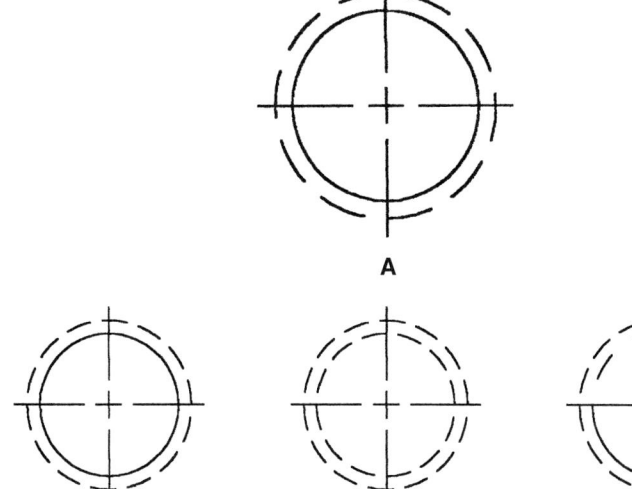

Blocks and Layers

Blocks have a special relationship with layers in an AutoCAD LT drawing, and certain considerations need to be made both when creating and when inserting block references. The objects that are used in the block definition can be created on any desired layer, or can even have any desired color and linetype assignments apart from layer settings. The most appropriate layer, color, and linetype settings for the component geometry of a block definition are determined by the desired appearance of the actual inserted block reference.

Objects created using "bylayer" color and linetype settings ignore any absolute color and linetype settings that are active when the block reference is inserted. These bylayer objects behave differently in the actual inserted block reference depending on whether they were created on layer 0 or on a user-defined layer. If created on layer 0, an object acquires the properties of the layer on which the block reference exists. This means that the objects initially take on the properties that the block reference is inserted on, but if the block reference is moved to a different layer these objects are updated to the settings for the new layer. However, if the object is created on any user-defined layer, they maintain the properties associated with that layer regardless of what layer the block reference exists on. This concept is demonstrated in Figure 12.25. The objects used to define the threaded hole symbol shown in Figure 12.25A were created using the settings listed in Table 12.1.

In Figure 12.25B, the block reference has been inserted on each of the three layers 0, HID, and CEN as indicated. Notice that the primary circle, which was created on layer 0, has taken on the properties of the layer on which the block reference was inserted. The objects that were created on layers other than layer 0 are displayed according to the current settings of that layer, regardless of the layer on which the block reference is inserted.

TABLE 12.1 Threaded hole settings

	Solid Circle	**Dashed Circle**	**Center Lines**
Current layer setting	"0"	"HID"	"CEN"
Current layer color	BYLAYER	CYAN	GREEN
Current layer linetype	BYLAYER	HIDDEN	CENTER
Current color setting	BYLAYER	BYLAYER	BYLAYER
Current linetype setting	BYLAYER	BYLAYER	BYLAYER

If you need the inserted block always to maintain the exact same appearance with regard to colors and linetypes, you can assign permanent settings to some or all of the objects within a block definition. Using the DDEMODES command (or DDCOLOR, COLOR, DDLTYPE, or LINETYPE as appropriate), you can set an absolute color or linetype setting for all new objects. Any objects used in a block definition that are created using absolute settings for color or linetype (or both) maintain those same settings regardless of the layer on which the block reference is inserted. When absolute settings are used, it does not matter on which layer the objects were created.

A specialized setting exists, for both the color and linetype options, called *byblock.* This can be set using the DDEMODES command, or any of the available commands for changing absolute color and linetype settings. When the byblock setting is active, any objects drawn are displayed using color number 7 and continuous lines. But when these objects are used in a block definition, they are treated like any other newly created object when the block reference is inserted. If the currently active color or linetype is bylayer, the objects are displayed according to the settings of the layer on which the block reference is inserted. When an absolute color or linetype is set, the objects are displayed accordingly. All byblock objects respond in this manner, regardless of the layer on which they were created.

Note that the color and linetype of component objects created using byblock settings can also be changed within the inserted block reference. You can use the DDMODIFY or DDCHPROP (or CHPROP) commands to change the layer, the absolute color, or even the linetype of the block reference. Remember that only the objects in the block definition that were created using byblock settings are affected by these changes.

Field Notes

- When a block reference is exploded, each component object reverts to the layer on which the same object in the original block definition was created. This means that component objects created on layer 0, using bylayer settings, no longer use the color and linetype settings of the layer on which the block reference was inserted. If this is not desirable, you can easily move the objects back to the appropriate layer. A simple way to do this is to pick the Properties toolbar button to start either the DDMODIFY or DDCHPROP command and make the required changes.
- Objects created as "byblock," when the block reference is exploded, revert to continuous white (or black) lines and are placed on the layer on which they were created.

Block References and Layer Controls

When you insert a block reference, it is always inserted on the current layer. This means that the block reference is affected by the visibility controls and other settings for the layer on which it is inserted. As an example, in Figure 12.25, a block definition of a threaded hole was created using objects on layers 0, CEN, and HID, and the resulting block has been inserted while layer 0 is current. Although the component geometry references other layers in the drawing, the block reference is created on layer 0. This means that freezing layer 0 makes the entire inserted block invisible, regardless of the status of the layers referenced by the component geometry. Likewise, if layer 0 is visible, but the layer named HID is frozen, all objects in the block referencing layer HID are invisible. However, even if some of the components of a block reference are currently invisible, they are still affected by edits made to the visible geometry.

In the Figure 12.25 example, if layer 0 is locked the block cannot be edited regardless of the current status of layers CEN and HID. Since component geometry cannot be directly edited without exploding the block reference, locking one or more layers referenced by the component geometry does not limit your editing options for the block reference itself.

CHAPTER 12 ||| Designing and Using Your Own Symbols

Exercise 12.7

1. Start a new drawing session using the Quick Setup default options.
2. Set up a layer system as follows:

0	Color—7	Linetype—Continuous
OBJ	Color—5	Linetype—Continuous
HID	Color—4	Linetype—Hidden
CEN	Color—3	Linetype—Center

3. Create a block definition of a threaded hole, as shown in Figure 12.25, according to the following parameters:

Primary circle	Layer—0	⌀0.865
Hidden circle	Layer—HID	⌀1.0
Center lines	Layer—CEN	DIMCEN=−0.09

   The block insertion base point should be at the center of the circles, and name the block 1-8UNC-2B_P to indicate a ⌀1-in. hole, 8 threads per inch, internal thread, and a plan view.
4. Insert one copy of this block on each layer. Notice the display of the primary circle on each layer.
5. Change the color of layer HID to color 2 and layer 0 to color 6. Study the effects on each insertion of the block reference.
6. Draw three ⌀1.0 circles and create new block definitions as indicated:

Name—C-BYL	Color—Bylayer	Linetype—Bylayer
Name—C-ABS	Color—Blue	Linetype—Phantom
Name—C-BYB	Color—Byblock	Linetype—Byblock

7. Using current color and linetype settings of bylayer, insert each of the three blocks created in Step 6 on each layer in your drawing.
8. Change the current color and linetype to absolute settings of your choice, and insert each of the blocks again as in Step 7. Compare the results with the settings used for drawing the circles in the block definitions.
9. Save the drawing as EX12.7.

☑ LEARNING CHECKPOINT

- ☐ What is meant by the term *nesting blocks?*
- ☐ Describe the behavior of bylayer block components when inserted.
- ☐ What is the effect of using absolute properties in block components?
- ☐ How are byblock objects displayed when inserted in a block?
- ☐ How does layer visibility affect the display of inserted blocks?

Creating and Managing a Symbol Library

A block definition created within any specific drawing is available only within that drawing or through the Content Explorer. To save your individual blocks permanently for use in other drawings, you can save the block definitions as separate AutoCAD LT drawing files on disk, and insert them into any other drawing as needed.

As you create blocks to represent commonly used symbols, establish a standard procedure for saving them in a symbol library. The term **symbol library** is used to describe an organized collection of drafting symbols and other commonly used drawing elements saved as individual AutoCAD LT drawing files. A procedure for symbol library development should include correctly and accurately drawing each symbol conforming to drafting standards. Additionally, it is important to provide adequate documentation. Professionally developed symbol libraries include documentation with a graphic representation of each symbol, its file name, and the directory where the drawing file is located.

The Content Explorer provides many tools for creating and using symbol libraries as well. First, however, you should have a good understanding of the basic processes for saving symbols as individual AutoCAD LT drawing files.

Saving a Block as a Separate Drawing File

To begin saving your blocks as AutoCAD LT drawing files, you first need to decide where the drawing files are to be saved. You should not save the files in any of the directories used by the AutoCAD LT program. Otherwise you are likely to have files in that directory that are not part of the symbol library, and this can make file management much more difficult.

Creating directories on your hard disk cannot be done in any file dialog box in the AutoCAD LT program, or you can use the appropriate file management tools as provided by your particular operating system to create the desired directories. The directory names and structure that you use for the symbol library are completely up to you, but the best results are often obtained following a few basic guidelines.

> **Through the Window...**
>
> Creating new directories can be accomplished using various methods available in Windows. A simple and commonly used technique is given here using the Windows Explorer.
>
> From the Start menu on the Windows Taskbar, pick Programs and select the Windows Explorer program. In the Windows Explorer window, you will see icons representing the disk drives on your computer, folder icons representing the existing directories, and other icons representing files.
>
> To create a new folder, or directory, under the AutoCAD LT 98 directory, double-click the \Program Files\AutoCAD LT 98 folder to open it. Now pick the File menu and select New; then pick the Folder option. A new folder is placed and your cursor is positioned in the name field with the default folder name—usually similar to "New Folder." Change the name as appropriate and press Enter. If you enter the name incorrectly and want to change it, highlight the folder then select Rename from the File menu.
>
> When you are finished, exit the Windows Explorer by picking the Close button in the upper right corner of the program window.

A common practice is to create the new drawing files in a directory that has been created to store specific types of symbols and is appropriately named. Whether you are creating the symbol library for your own personal use or as a permanent, shared resource for your company, the directory structure that you use should be as simple as possible. Complex directory structures can be difficult to navigate through and can make finding a needed symbol a long and involved process.

In Windows, directory and file names can be extremely long and descriptive if desired. Even so, shorter names are often easier to work with. It is sometimes helpful to use descriptive names, but you should avoid using an entire sentence as a directory name. Other considerations are covered later in this section.

One possible directory structure is shown in Figure 12.26. It is simple, easy to understand, and allows for organized storage of varied symbols associated with different areas of drafting.

FIGURE 12.26 A symbol library directory structure should be easy to find, simple in nature, and use short, descriptive names.

CHAPTER 12 ||| Designing and Using Your Own Symbols 511

Using the WBLOCK Command

The command used to save a block as a separate drawing file is the WBLOCK command. WBLOCK stands for Write-BLOCK, and it writes a specified block definition as a separate drawing file. The WBLOCK command is accessed by typing **W** or **WBLOCK** at the Command: prompt. When you start the WBLOCK command, the Create Drawing File dialog box is displayed, as shown in Figure 12.27. Using this dialog box, go to the desired directory location and enter an appropriate file name in the File Name: text box. The file name specified should be in accordance with standards, and the file name should be the same as the standard symbol name to avoid confusion. In Figure 12.27, the block that is to be written to disk is named 1-8UNC-2B_P, so the file uses the same name. It is not necessary to include the .DWG file extension. AutoCAD LT automatically adds the file extension for you.

WBLOCK
W

After you pick OK, you are returned to the command line and prompted to enter the block name to write to file.

Command: **W** or **WBLOCK**↵
Block name: **1-8UNC-2B_P**↵
Command:

FIGURE 12.27 The Create Drawing File dialog box is used to specify the drawing file name to create from the specified block definition.

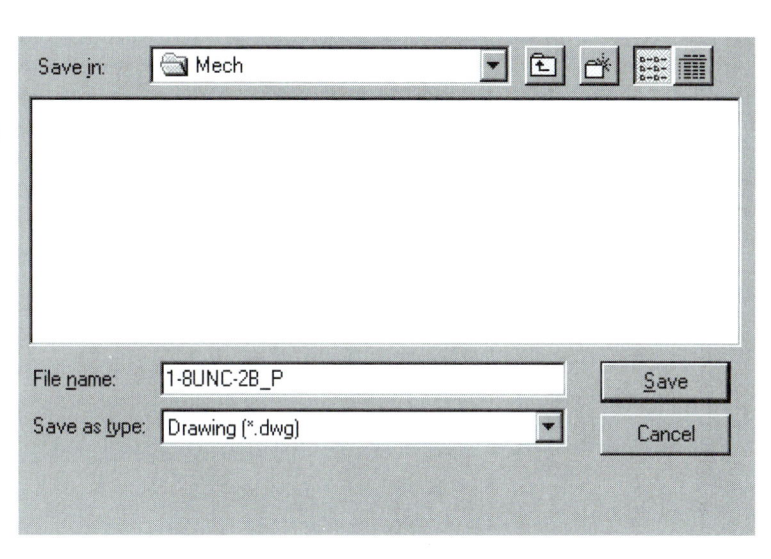

If the block name is found in the current drawing, its definition is used to create the specified drawing file. Depending on the amount of geometry contained in the block definition and the speed of your workstation, you may see the message "Saving:" on the status bar along with the percentage complete meter.

If you enter a block name that has not been defined in the current drawing, AutoCAD LT issues an appropriate message and reissues the prompt.

Command: **W** or **WBLOCK**↵
⟨specify the path and file name using the Create Drawing File dialog box⟩
Block name: **NO_SUCH**↵
Block NO_SUCH not found.
Block name:

✏️ Field Notes

- When the drawing file name and the block name are the same, a quick and easy shortcut can be used at the Block name: prompt by typing the equals sign (=). This tells AutoCAD LT that the block name matches the specified drawing file name. If you enter the equals sign and the specified file name does not match a defined block, a message is issued and you are again prompted for the block name.
- The AutoCAD LT 98 document often refers to drawing files as being "Wblocks," which can be somewhat confusing at first, because it seems to imply a difference between Wblocks and drawing files. However, a Wblock is simply an AutoCAD LT drawing file without a preview, nothing more and nothing less.

When you are creating a symbol that you are going to save to disk, you do not need to use the BMAKE or BLOCK command prior to using WBLOCK. The WBLOCK command allows you to pick geometry in your drawing and specify an insertion base point. It then writes the information directly to disk just as if you had specified a block name. To select objects instead of specifying a block name, press Enter at the Block name: prompt:

Command: **W** or **WBLOCK**↵
⟨*specify the path and file name using the Create Drawing File dialog box*⟩
Block name: ↵
Insertion base point: ⟨*specify a coordinate point*⟩
Select objects: ⟨*select the objects that define the symbol*⟩
Select objects: ↵

You are prompted to specify an insertion base point and select the objects to include in the new drawing file. These options work exactly the same as when you are using the BLOCK command.

Since the WBLOCK command creates a drawing file, the SAVE or SAVEAS commands are also options when saving symbols to a symbol library. If the current drawing is a symbol or another commonly used drawing element, you can save the entire file in your symbol library to make it available for insertion in other drawings. However, some special considerations must be made when using this approach.

When you insert a drawing into another drawing, AutoCAD LT uses the value stored by a system variable named INSBASE as the insertion base point. The default value for this variable is 0,0. If you used WBLOCK to create the file, the value for INSBASE was set to the insertion base point of the specified block, or the point you picked at the Insertion base point: prompt if you selected individual objects in your drawing.

You have two choices for resolving the base point of a symbol created using SAVE or SAVEAS. One option is to move all of the geometry so the desired insertion point is located at the 0,0 coordinate point. An easier approach is to use the BASE command. The BASE command allows you to specify an insertion point that is not located at 0,0. To use the BASE command, type **BA** or **BASE** at the Command: prompt.

Command: **BA** or **BASE**↵
Base point <0.0000,0.0000,0.0000>: ⟨*specify desired insertion point*⟩

When you insert a drawing file, everything that is defined in that drawing comes with it. This means that any block definitions existing in the inserted drawing are now defined in the current drawing, along with any layer names, text styles, dimstyles, or other named data. This can work to make a drawing file much larger than necessary, which can slow down drawing productivity.

To avoid this situation, you can use another option of the WBLOCK command instead of the SAVE or SAVEAS commands. Start the WBLOCK command, and indicate the desired file name and path. If the specified file name is the same as the current name or another existing drawing, AutoCAD LT asks you if you really want to replace the existing drawing. Pick Yes if the current drawing name is the desired file name.

At the block name prompt, type an asterisk (*) and press Enter:

Command: **W** or **WBLOCK**↵
⟨*specify the path and file name using the Create Drawing File dialog box*⟩
Block name: *↵
Command:

This has the effect of stripping out all unused information from the current drawing and writing what is left to the specified drawing file. The removed data include block definitions that have no inserted block references, any text styles that are not referenced by existing text, any layers that contain no objects, and any other unused information. All that remains is the information that is actually used in the drawing. This can reduce file size for the saved file and file size for any drawings in which it is subsequently inserted. Additional information on reducing file size is found in Chapter 15.

CHAPTER 12 ||| Designing and Using Your Own Symbols 513

> ### Field Notes
>
> *Self-referencing drawing files:* A drawing that contains a block definition with the same name as the drawing file cannot be inserted into another drawing because AutoCAD LT converts the data in the drawing file into a block definition when it is inserted. In the previous discussion regarding self-referencing blocks, we explained that a block definition that contains a reference to itself cannot be resolved.
>
> When you try to insert a drawing file containing a block reference with the same name as the drawing file, AutoCAD LT issues the message:
>
> Block ⟨*filename*⟩ references itself
> *Invalid*
>
> (The drawing name you specified is displayed in place of ⟨*filename*⟩.)

Exercise 12.8

1. Using the appropriate file management tools, create the directory \SYM-LIB\MECH. If you need assistance, ask your instructor or refer to the Windows documentation.
2. Open the drawing file EX12.7 for editing in AutoCAD LT.
3. Using the WBLOCK command, write the block definition for the block named 1-8UNC-2B_P to a drawing file of the same name in the directory created in step 1.
4. Draw a 1-unit square with a circle inside of it. Using the WBLOCK command, create a new drawing file using these two objects to define it. Specify the lower left corner as the insertion point.
5. Use the WBLOCK command once again and specify the file name EX12.8. At the Block name: prompt, enter an asterisk.
6. Open the drawing file EX12.8 for editing in AutoCAD LT. Using the appropriate commands, check the status of the layers, linetypes, and defined block names.
7. Save the drawing as EX12.8.

Inserting a Drawing File

Inserting a drawing file works much the same as inserting any other block. The DDINSERT command provides a flexible way of finding and inserting other drawing files in the current drawing. Using the DDINSERT command displays the Insert dialog box as shown in Figure 12.10. To insert a drawing file, pick the File ... button. This displays the Select Drawing File dialog box shown in Figure 12.26. Use this file dialog box to locate the drawing file you want to insert. The Select Drawing File dialog box works the same as the Select File dialog box when using the OPEN command.

When you pick a file name and select the OK button, you are returned to the Insert dialog box and the selected file name appears to the right of the File ... button. Notice also that the file name appears in the Block Name: text box, but does not display a path or a drawing file extension. After specifying any other desired options in the Insert dialog box, pick the OK button. You can now insert the selected file the same as any other block, specifying any desired insertion point, scale factors, and rotation angle.

Once you insert a drawing file, that block name is now defined in the current drawing. The drawing is available from the defined block list by picking the Block ... button in the Insert dialog box.

If the selected file name is too long or contains characters that cannot be used in a block name, or if you just want the name of the block to be different than the drawing name, you can use the Block Name: text box to edit the block name as needed. When the block is inserted, it is renamed accordingly and added to the block list with the specified name.

> ### ✏️ Field Notes
>
> - The INSERT command can be used from the command line to start an automated search for a block name. If the specified block name is found in the current drawing, it is inserted without looking further. If the specified block name is not found in the current drawing, then the AutoCAD LT *library search path* is scanned for a drawing file matching the specified block name. The library search path includes the current working directory, the drawing directory, all directories specified in the *support path,* and the directory containing the AutoCAD LT program file (aclt.exe). As soon as a matching file name is found, the search stops and the file is inserted into the current drawing.
> - The support path is specified using the Files page of the Preferences dialog box and can be edited to include any desired directories. The easiest way to add a new directory is to pick Add... and then pick the Browse button. In the Browse for Folder dialog box, go to the desired directory, highlight the appropriate folder, then select the OK button. Unneeded directories can be deleted from the path if desired. Placing your symbol library directories on the support path forces AutoCAD LT to search the specified directories automatically if the block name specified is not yet defined in the current drawing.

Inserting a Drawing File using the Content Explorer

The Content Explorer provides an intuitive interface for accessing and inserting other drawing files into the current drawing. If the Content Explorer is already started, you can bring it to the top by picking the Content Explorer button, selecting it from your pull-down menu, typing **CE** or **CONTENT** at the Command: prompt, or pressing ALT-TAB and then selecting the Content Explorer program. To browse through the available drawing files, press the Tree View button located on the toolbar below the Content Explorer menu bar. See Figure 12.28A. When you select the Tree View button, the Content Explorer opens a window to display a tree view of your computer system. In the tree view, you can see and access all disk drives connected to your computer as well as all network drives to which you have access. Figure 12.28B shows the Content Explorer in tree view mode.

In tree view, you can move through the directory structure the same as in when using the Windows Explorer. Simply double-click on a drive or folder to display its contents. Note that the Current Dwg is also dis-

FIGURE 12.28 (A) The Tree View button in the Content Explorer and (B) the Content Explorer in Tree View mode.

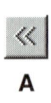

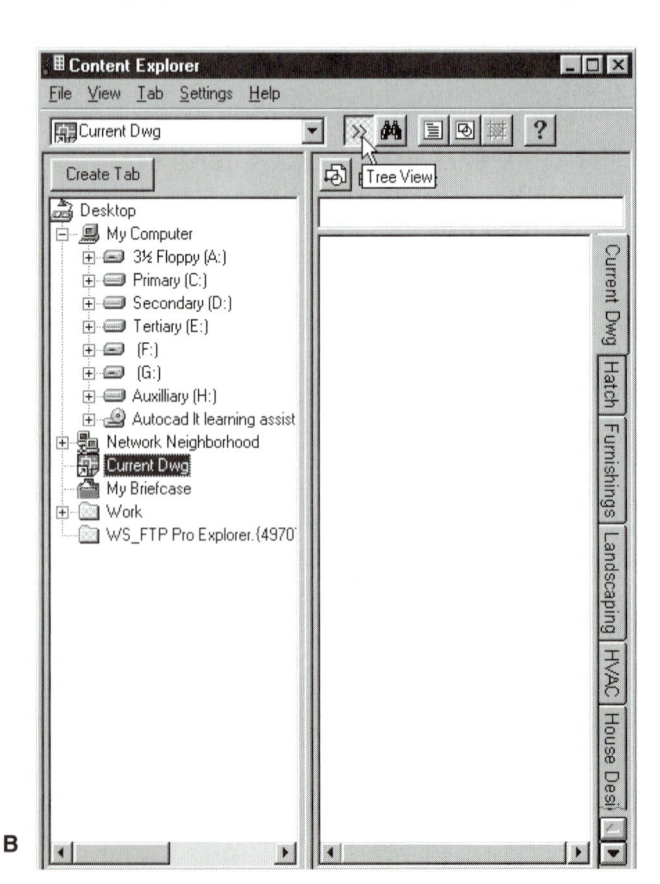

CHAPTER 12 ||| Designing and Using Your Own Symbols

played in Tree View as a drawing file icon in the tree window. Clicking on the Current Dwg icon shows the symbols defined in the current drawing. To access the drawings in a specific folder, double-click on the drive letter where the folder is. Next, find the folder where the drawings are stored. When you find the folder you are looking for, do not double-click on the folder icon—instead, just pick it once. The Content Explorer will then create a symbol library view, as shown in Figure 12.29. If you do double-click, all the drawing icons are also displayed in the Tree View window. This in itself is not a problem, but when the drawing icons are not displayed, more of the drives and folders are visible in the tree view, making it easier to navigate. Now, you can drag-and-drop or double-click on any of the visible icons to insert the associated symbol.

When you insert a drawing using the Content Explorer, the same insertion methods are used as if you were inserting a block. Using a drag-and-drop method involves the default scale factor of 1 and rotation of 0. Double-click on the files if you need to use alternative insertion parameters. Also, as with DDINSERT, the inserted drawing is then used to create a new block definition of the same name within the current drawing. To hide the Tree View, pick the Tree View button again.

Field Notes

- When inserting a file that uses a long file name containing spaces, the Content Explorer automatically modifies the name of the block, substituting an underscore character (_) for each space and each unusable character in the file name (e.g., ", " or "#"). If the file name is too long, it is truncated to use the first 29 characters and a two-digit numeric designation. For example, the file name **A #file name far, far too long to be 31 Characters.dwg** is inserted using the block name **A__FILE_NAME_FAR__FAR_TOO_LON01**.
- You can select multiple files or blocks within the Content Explorer; however, you cannot insert multiple blocks in a single operation.
- AutoCAD LT 98 creates a temporary file named TMP.CE in each folder for which it displays the preview images. AutoCAD LT 98 uses this file to store the preview images for the files in that directory. This allows for a faster display time the next time you select the folder. If you delete this file, AutoCAD LT 98 automatically recreates it the next time you view the contents of the folder.

FIGURE 12.29 Content Explorer displays all the drawings in a selected folder as icons that you can drag-and-drop, like blocks, into the current drawing.

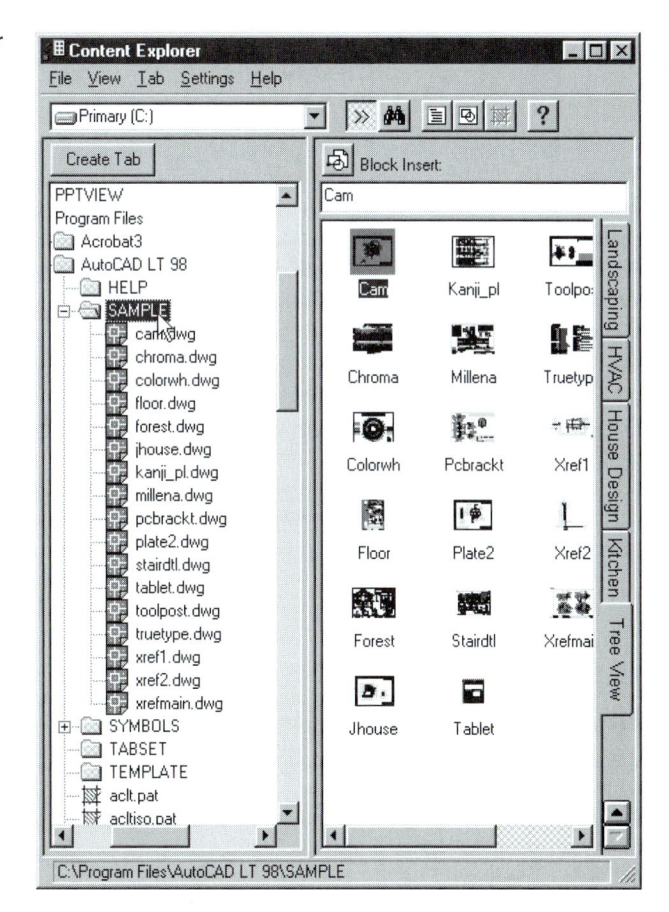

☑ LEARNING CHECKPOINT

- ☐ List the methods available for viewing the Content Explorer when it is has already been started but is not currently visible.
- ☐ How is Tree View turned on and off in the Content Explorer?
- ☐ What is the difference between picking once on a folder and double-clicking?
- ☐ How are long file names and invalid block name characters handled by the Content Explorer?

Defining or Redefining Block Definitions from the Symbol Library

If a symbol has been revised and you need to update the block references in the current drawing, you can force a quick and easy redefinition at the command line using the INSERT command. When prompted for the block name to insert, enter the block name, an equals sign, and the name of the file to read for the updated information. In a case where the existing block name is the same as the file name, and the block name is G-VALVE, the prompts appears as follows:

Command: **IN** or **INSERT**↵
Block name: **G-VALVE=G-VALVE**↵
Block G-VALVE redefined
Regenerating drawing.
Insertion point:

If you need another copy of the specified block in your drawing, you can continue with the INSERT command. Otherwise you can press the Esc key to cancel the insertion because the block definition has already been updated. All inserted references to the specified block are automatically revised according to the new definition.

The preceding example shows the block name and file name as being the same, but this is not necessary. This technique works exactly the same even if the block name is different from the file name.

Exercise 12.9

1. Using the PR or PREFERENCES command, update the support path to include the \SYM-LIB\MECH directory you created in Exercise 12.8.
2. Start a new drawing using the Quick Setup defaults.
3. Use the INSERT command and type the block name 1-8UNC-2B_P. Notice that AutoCAD LT automatically searched your symbol library path to find the drawing file.
4. Save the current drawing as EX12.9.
5. Open the file 1-8UNC-2B_P.DWG for editing. Change the primary circle to the layer named OBJ and then save the file.
6. Open EX12.9 for editing.
7. Insert several copies of 1-8UNC-2B_P on various layers in the drawing. At this time you may notice that the layers defined in the 1-8UNC-2B_P drawing were brought in when it was inserted.
8. Use the INSERT command and specify the block name as 1-8UNC-2B_P=1-8UNC-2B_P.
9. Notice the effects of the block redefinition.
10. Save the drawing as EX12.9.

☑ LEARNING CHECKPOINT

- ☐ When should you consider developing a symbol library?
- ☐ What methods can be used to save a block as a drawing file?
- ☐ Describe some basic guidelines for a symbol library directory structure.
- ☐ How can one drawing be inserted into another?

CHAPTER 12 ||| Designing and Using Your Own Symbols

- List three ways to use the WBLOCK command.
- How can a block be updated to match an existing drawing file?

Using the Content Explorer to Create and Manage Symbol Libraries

The Content Explorer provides simple ways to turn any drawing or folder containing drawings into a symbol library. As discussed previously, using the Tree View allows you to open any directory as an accessible symbol library simply by picking it. AutoCAD LT 98 comes with a series of drawings that are defined as Tab Sets. A *Tab Set* is a series of shortcuts to drawings containing blocks or to folders containing drawings. Picking the appropriate tab on the right side of the Content Explorer window then displays the available symbols in the drawing or folder to which it points. AutoCAD LT 98 prompts on installation for which of the supplied Tab Sets should be displayed by default. The three available options are Architectural, Mechanical, and Electronic. Figure 12.30 shows the Content Explorer with the Architectural Tab Set loaded and the Furnishings Tab currently displayed. Regardless of which option was indicated during the installation process, any of the Tab Sets can be viewed at any time. Additionally, you can create custom Tab Sets using your own symbols.

To create a Tab from an existing folder that contains drawings, use the Tree View to go to that folder and display the drawings it contains. Then, select Create... from the Tab menu in Content Explorer. The Create Tab dialog box is displayed, with the folder name displayed in the Tab name: field. The Tab location is shown below. In Figure 12.31, a folder named Welding was selected. Because the current Tab Set already contains a tab named Welding, the Content Explorer appends the number 1 to the end.

To create a Tab that accesses the symbols in an existing drawing file, use the Tree View to find the drawing file that contains the blocks you need to access. Select the drawing file icon in the Tree View window to display the blocks it contains. Again, select Create... from the Tab menu and name the new Tab. It is not necessary to create a Tab in order to access blocks or drawing files through the Content Explorer, but doing so allows you to easily access the same files at a later time with a single pick.

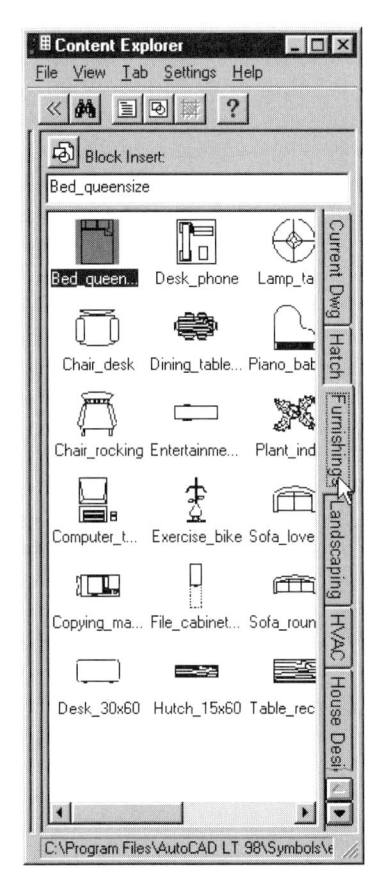

FIGURE 12.30 Predefined Tab Sets in Content Explorer give you ready access to a variety of industry standard symbols.

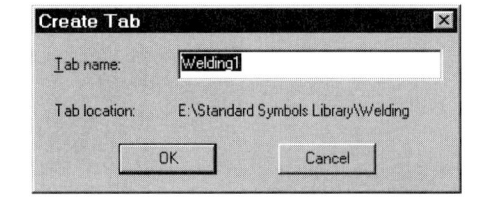

FIGURE 12.31 The Create Tab dialog box allows you to add new tabs to the current tab set.

FIGURE 12.32 New Tab Sets can be created and saved permanently for use at any time.

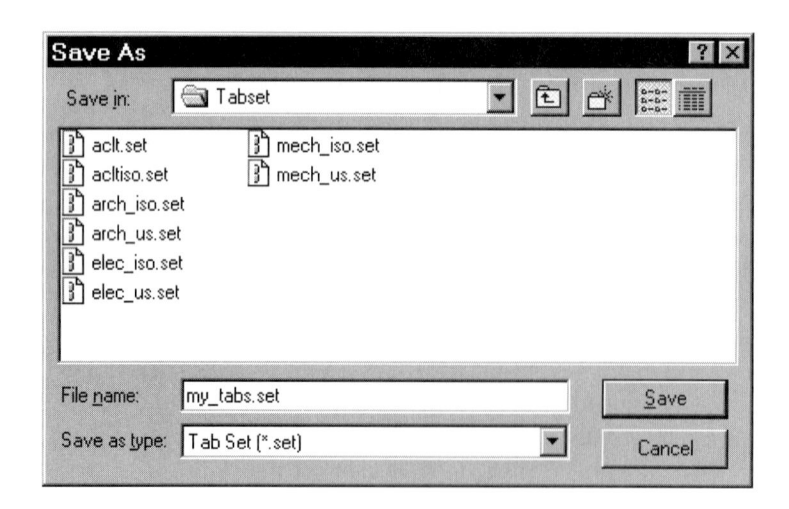

All created Tabs are added to the current Tab Set but are not permanently saved unless you select Save As Tab Set... from the Tab menu and overwrite the original Tab Set file. To create a completely new Tab Set, select Delete All from the Tab menu and delete all current tabs. The Content Explorer asks if you really want to delete all of the tabs. Select Yes, but don't worry, the Tab Set file is not changed by doing this. You will be able to restore all these tabs any time you need to. Now, create all of the new tabs that you want to be included in the new Tab Set. Finally, select Save As Tab Set... from the Tab menu and specify a name for the new Tab Set. In Figure 12.32, the new tab set is being saved as "my_tabs.set." The default location for saving Tab Set files is in the Tabset folder, found under the AutoCAD LT 98 folder. It is recommended that you save your Tab Set files here for easy access.

To merge, or combine, another Tab Set with the current Tab Set, select Merge Tab Set... from the Tab menu. You can then select another Tab Set file to combine its tabs with the tabs currently displayed. Neither the current Tab Set nor the merged Tab Set are permanently affected unless you save and overwrite the existing Tab Set files. This gives access to symbols from multiple Tab Sets. Note that if the Tab Set being merged has a Tab name that matches one of the existing names, a message is displayed indicating that it was not loaded.

To move, rename, or delete an existing Tab, right-click on the tab and a popup menu is displayed. From this menu select the Move... option to display the Move Tab dialog box. See Figure 12.33. This dialog box is then used to move the selected Tab up or down relative to other Tabs in the current Tab Set. Selecting Rename... or Delete allows you to change the name of a Tab or remove it from the current set. These options are also available on the Tab menu.

Changing the View in the Content Explorer

When creating blocks, AutoCAD LT 98 allows you to add a description to each symbol you create. This description can be viewed by picking Description from the View menu in the Content Explorer. As shown in Figure 12.34A, a small window opens above the symbol display area to display the description for the currently selected symbol icon. To display a larger version of the symbol preview image (see Figure 12.34B) select Preview from the View menu. This can be very useful for previewing large or complex symbols that are not adequately represented in the preview icon.

FIGURE 12.33 Tabs can be relocated so that your most frequently used symbols are the most easily accessible.

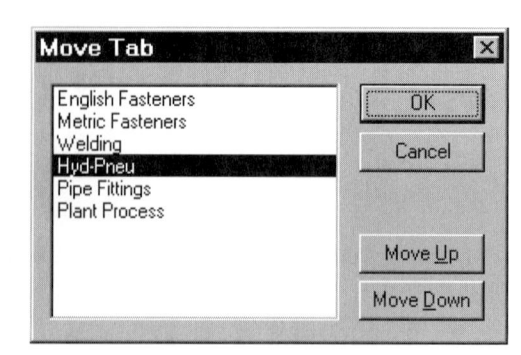

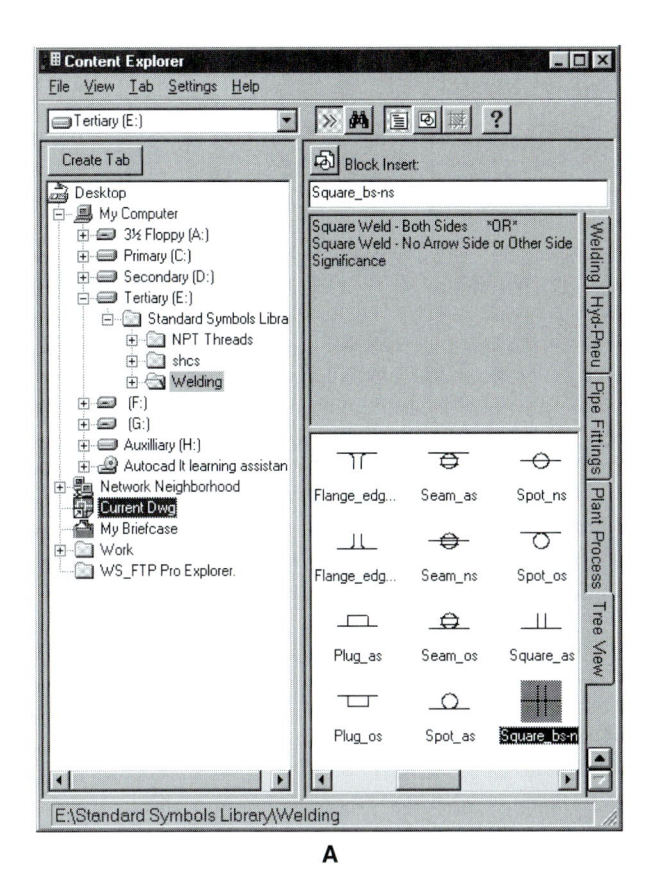

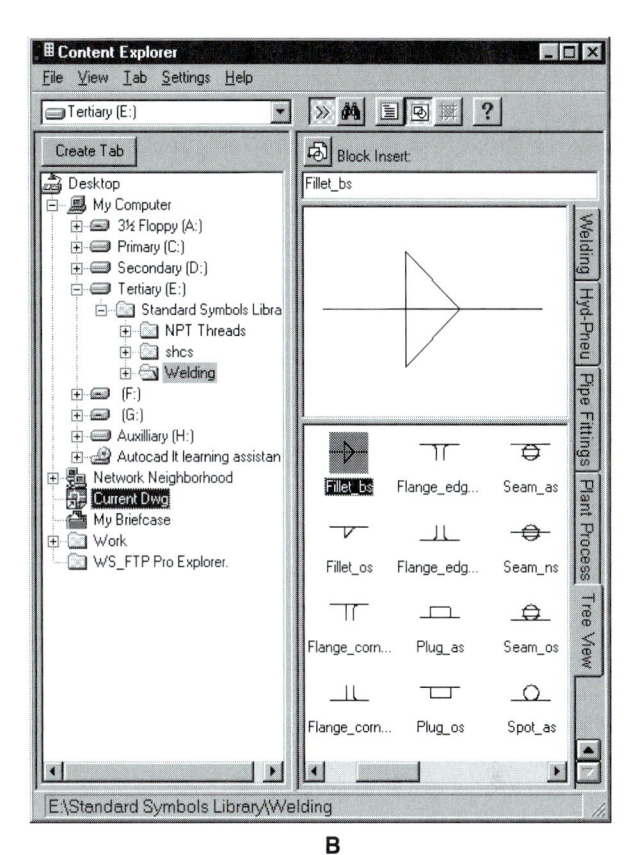

CHAPTER 12 ||| Designing and Using Your Own Symbols

FIGURE 12.34 A small window can be opened to display either (A) the symbol description or (B) the symbol preview image.

In a drawing with many symbols or when the symbol previews are not needed, the listing can be modified to display only the block or file names. To do this, right-click in the symbol preview area; then select Names Only. Picking Icons and Names restores the symbol previews.

It is also possible to make the Content Explorer stay on top of the AutoCAD LT 98 window, even when it is not current, by picking Always on Top from the View menu. This can be distracting because it covers part of the AutoCAD LT screen, so you may want to leave this option turned off.

Field Notes

The Content Explorer provides two options on the File menu for moving or copying content. This enables you to copy or move objects from the current folder to any tab that points to another folder. You cannot copy content to or from a tab that points to a drawing.

Because this capability may affect other users in your department or class, it is recommended that you check with your system administrator or instructor before using these tools.

Using Block Attributes

Blocks are complex objects that can be defined using many different object types. Any desired information can be stored as part of a block reference. The term *attributes* is used to describe information stored within a block reference.

Visible block attributes can be used to generate simple text labels to identify specific information regarding a symbol. For example, a resistor symbol on an electronic schematic diagram is often labeled with a resistor number, such as R1 or R27. Another visible label on a resistor symbol might include the resistance value.

Other information about these components is often required, but is not frequently used as part of a text label. This information is stored as *invisible block attributes* and might include the manufacturer, part number, and price. Invisible block attributes can be used to store data associated with a component when you do not want the information to be displayed on the drawing.

Defining Attributes

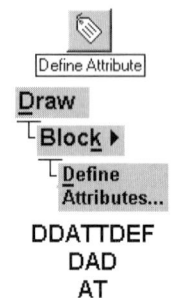

An *attribute definition* is a special type of object that is included as part of a block definition. The properties you set up in an attribute definition determine how the attribute acts when it is inserted as part of a block reference. Use the DDATTDEF command to create new attribute definitions. DDATTDEF is accessed by typing **AT**, **DAD** or **DDATTDEF** at the Command: prompt, by picking the Define Attribute button, or by picking Define Attribute … from the Block cascade of the Draw pull-down menu. Optionally, you can use the command line version ATTDEF by typing -**AT** or **ATTDEF,** but the DDATTDEF command provides an easy-to-use dialog interface and is usually preferred.

Command: **DAD** or **DDATTDEF**↵

The Attribute Definition dialog box is shown in Figure 12.35. This dialog box is used to define the characteristics of an attribute. A leader bubble provides a simple example of a block with an attribute. A *leader bubble* is a circle attached to a leader and with a numeric value inside. They are often used to reference an item in a bill of materials listing or parts list. An example of a leader bubble is shown in Figure 12.36. To create this symbol from scratch each time it is needed, you have to first draw the circle, then specify the desired text properties, and finally enter the appropriate text for each occurrence of the bubble in your drawing. Creating a block that uses an attribute automates the process, making it fast and simple.

FIGURE 12.35 The Attribute Definition dialog box is used to create an attribute definition and specify the desired characteristics of the inserted attribute.

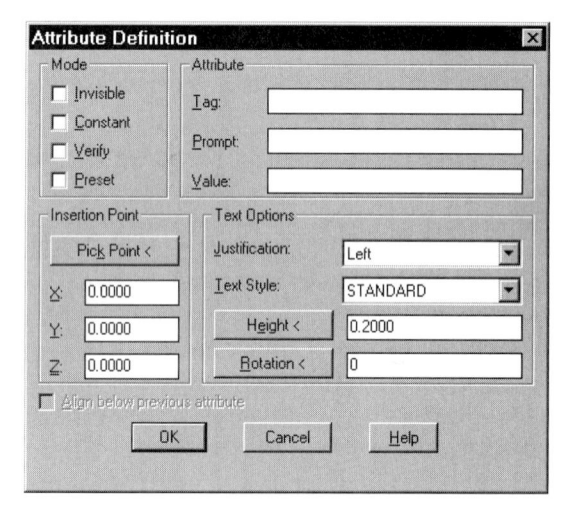

FIGURE 12.36 By creating a block from a circle and an attribute definition, the process of creating a leader bubble is greatly simplified.

The first step in defining a block with attributes is to create the actual geometry that represents the symbol. In this case, a circle is drawn with a 5/16-in. diameter. Now, it is time to create the attribute definition using the DDATTDEF command.

An attribute can act in many different ways when inserted, depending on what settings you use in this dialog box. The settings you use typically depend on the nature of the attribute you are defining. First, look at the options in the Mode area of the Figure 12.37 Attribute Definition dialog box.

Invisible: If this toggle is checked, the inserted attribute is not displayed in the drawing. It does not appear on screen and it is not plotted.

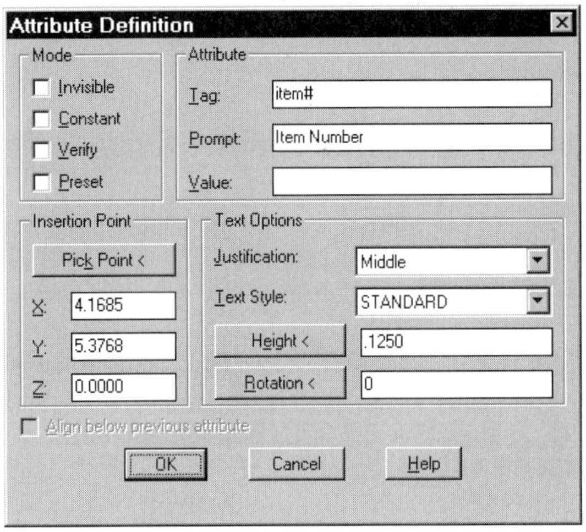

FIGURE 12.37 The Attribute Definition for the leader bubble attribute.

Constant: Turning on this toggle forces the attribute to use the default value and does not prompt you for a new value. A constant attribute cannot be edited later.

Verify: After the initial prompts for attributes are entered, the values are verified by prompting the user again and presenting the entered value as a default.

Preset: A preset attribute accepts the default value without prompting, but can be edited later if necessary.

A leader bubble with an invisible number would not be of much use, so this attribute should be visible. The value changes with each bubble so it should not be constant or preset. And since the value is only one to three characters in length and is not a particularly critical feature of the drawing, verification is not necessary.

The next critical data fields are found in the area labeled Attribute. The items that are defined here include the following:

Tag: The tag is a dual-purpose feature. First, the text entered here is used to represent the attribute definition so that you have an object to select when you are defining the block. Second, it provides a means of access for extracting attribute values from a drawing. The tag can consist of any numbers or characters but cannot include spaces. Although a tag can be almost any length, it is recommended that they be short and descriptive.

Prompt: This is the text prompt that appears to the user each time a block is inserted, if the constant or preset modes are not set. This should be a clear message to the user that communicates the exact nature of the information to be entered. A colon (:) is automatically attached to the end of the prompt you enter when the block is inserted. If you do not provide a prompt for a nonconstant attribute, the tag text is used as the prompt.

Value: This is a standard default value that is offered with the prompt. As with other default values in AutoCAD LT, the default is offered in angle brackets: ⟨*default value*⟩.

The tag should be unique and clearly related to the attribute definition it represents. A prompt should be simple and clear, and a default value should be supplied if a specific value is commonly used. Because the leader bubble has a different value for each insertion in a given drawing, there is no appropriate default value.

Now it is time to set the properties for the attribute text. Attribute text is displayed like any other text in AutoCAD LT, referencing a defined text style and allowing you to specify the insertion point, height, rotation angle, and justification method. These values must be specified even if the attribute is to be invisible. The properties you give to the text are based on the desired appearance of the inserted symbol. For example, with the leader bubble block, the numeric value should be middle justified at the center point of the circle with a 0.125 text height and 0 rotation angle.

The completed attribute definition for the leader bubble is shown in the Attribute Definition dialog box of Figure 12.36.

When you pick OK, the tag for the newly defined attribute appears on screen at the specified location. To define the block named BUBBLE, use the BMAKE command and select both the circle and attribute definition. Now you can insert the block and see how the attribute works. One special note is that attribute definitions act like any other component object of a block with regard to layers and color settings.

```
Command: I or DDINSERT↵
⟨use the dialog box to specify the block name⟩
Insertion point: ⟨specify an insertion point⟩
X scale factor <1> / Corner / XYZ: ⟨specify a scale factor⟩
Y scale factor (default=X): ⟨specify a scale factor⟩
Rotation angle <0>: ⟨specify a rotation angle⟩
Enter attribute values
Item number: 15↵
```

The block appears at the insertion point and displays the specified attribute text. When you work with symbols that require more than one text label, you can create as many attribute definitions as you need. Additionally, each individual attribute definition can be assigned appropriate characteristics depending on the requirements for the symbol. In Figure 12.38, the resistor symbol is supplied with various attributes, some used for labels and some to store information that is not displayed on the drawing. Study each of the attribute definition properties shown in the table in Figure 12.38.

FIGURE 12.38 Attribute definition properties that might be used for a resistor symbol.

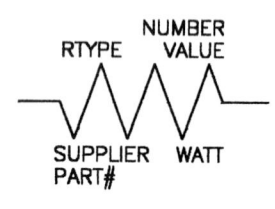

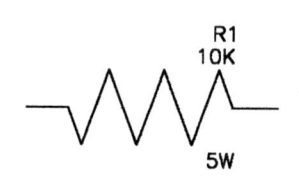

TAG	PROMPT	DEFAULT	MODE
RTYPE		FIXED	INVISIBLE, CONSTANT
NUMBER	Resistor designation		
VALUE	Resistance value	1K	
WATT	Wattage rating	5W	
SUPPLIER	Supplier name	ACME	INVISIBLE, PRESET
PART#	Part Number		INVISIBLE, VERIFY

The symbol attributes defined for the resistor symbol shown in Figure 12.38 can be used to demonstrate the reasoning for when it is appropriate to use each of the available attribute modes.

Whether an attribute is defined as visible or invisible depends completely on how the attribute information is to be used. Attributes defined as invisible for a block typically represent pieces of information that are not needed within the drawing but are useful outside of the drawing. For example, the supplier name and part number of a resistor is not necessary to understand the content or nature of the schematic diagram. The geometry used in the symbol clearly shows that it is a fixed-value resistor, so the RTYPE attribute is also nonessential information within the drawing. After the drawing is complete, however, this information can be useful in scheduling and planning or in the creation of an accurate bill of material.

If a value never changes, it should be set as constant. A constant attribute does not prompt when inserted and always uses the default value. The symbol geometry used to define the block in this example represents a fixed-value resistor; if a variable resistor is needed then a different resistor is used. Therefore, the RTYPE attribute can be set to constant.

A preset attribute, like one that is constant, does not prompt when inserted. The difference between preset and constant is that a preset attribute value can be easily changed if necessary, providing added flexibility. Use the preset mode when an attribute almost always uses a particular value, but you want to reserve the option of editing it at a later date. Presetting the supplier in this example implies that these parts are typically ordered from Acme, Inc., but that another supplier can be used if desired.

Attribute values that vary frequently should not be constant or preset. If you can identify one value that is used very frequently, you can set a default value. This saves you a little time in each case where the default is applicable.

CHAPTER 12 ||| Designing and Using Your Own Symbols

Verification can be useful in some cases, but if used too often it can slow down your drawing productivity. An attribute value should be verified if the value represents a critical feature in the drawing, or has a long or complex value where a mistake can easily be made. The part number for the resistor is fairly critical, since ordering an incorrect part number means that the wrong part is installed and the integrity of the design is compromised. Verifying the part number allows the drafter to quickly double-check that the number was entered correctly.

The prompt sequence when inserting the resistor block is as follows:

Command: **I** or **DDINSERT**↵
⟨*use the dialog box to specify the block name*⟩
Insertion point: ⟨*specify an insertion point*⟩
X scale factor <1> / Corner / XYZ: ⟨*specify a scale factor*⟩
Y scale factor (default=X): ⟨*specify a scale factor*⟩
Rotation angle <0>: ⟨*specify a rotation angle*⟩
Enter attribute values
Resistor designation: **R1**↵
Resistance value <1K>: **10K**↵
Wattage rating <5W>: ↵
Catalog number: **R17N10-5**↵
Verify attribute values
Catalog number <R17N10-5>: ↵
Command:

Field Notes

- Carefully designing a prompt and offering an appropriate default value can greatly simplify the insertion process. One aspect of designing a prompt is capitalization. The prompts issued by AutoCAD LT are never displayed as all capital letters. Look at the following prompts. Notice that the sentence case prompt looks more like a standard AutoCAD LT prompt:

    RESISTANCE VALUE:
    Resistance value <1K>:

Another consideration is the wording. A concise prompt is best, but it must be completely clear as to what the user is expected to enter. Study the following three prompts. The first does not offer a default, and the second may not be clear enough. The third prompt is clear, offers a default value, and appears to be the best choice.

    What's the resistance?:
    Value <1>:
    Resistance value <1K>:

Always keep in mind that the symbols you create may be part of a symbol library for many years to come. Thoughtfully designed symbols and attributes present a professional appearance and work very effectively.

- The order of presentation of attribute prompts depends on the selection method used when creating the block. If you pick the attributes one at a time, the order in which you select them is the order in which the prompts are issued. If you use a window selection, the attribute definitions are selected in the order of their closeness to the 0,0 point, with the closest one selected first, and the farthest selected last. Because the prompts are issued in the order in which the attribute definitions are selected, window selections can result in attribute prompts being presented out of order.

> ### Exercise 12.10
>
> 1. Start a new drawing using the Quick Setup defaults.
> 2. Use the example shown in Figure 12.38 to define a block named RES-F_H that uses the attribute definitions shown in the table.
> 3. Insert RESIST in three separate locations in your drawing, supplying as varied values as possible for attributes.
> 4. Save the drawing as EX12.10.

Automating Drawing Procedures Using Attributes

Certain text-based features are common to most technical drawings. One such item is a drawing title block. An engineering drawing title block usually has many different data fields that are often unique values in each drawing you create. Here, the term *data field* refers to the individual areas that are filled in with information in a drawing title block. Creating, positioning, sizing, and justifying a large number of text objects can take a significant amount of time. If you have to repeat this task in every drawing you create, it can lower your drafting productivity level considerably.

An effective way to handle your title block is to place appropriate attribute definitions in each of the areas where text information is required and then save the title block as a separate drawing file. Now, when you insert the title block into another drawing the attributes will prompt you for the appropriate values and automatically position, justify, and size the text according to the characteristics you assigned to the attribute definitions. In addition to simplifying the process of filling in the title block, this method ensures that the title block will maintain the same standard appearance from one drawing to the next.

Some other features that can be automated using blocks and attributes include revision blocks, parts lists, item schedules, general notes, and any other text-based information systems in your drawings.

Modifying Attribute Definitions

Modifying an attribute definition before you create the block is a simple process. You can use the DDEDIT command to edit the tag, prompt, and default values. Figure 12.39 shows the DDEDIT dialog box after selecting an attribute definition. It is important to note that an attribute *definition* has been selected, as opposed to an attribute that is part of an inserted block reference.

If you need to change other characteristics of the attribute definition, such as the text size, insertion point, or mode settings, use the DDMODIFY command. The DDMODIFY dialog box is shown, after picking an attribute definition, in Figure 12.40. Note that the Justify: drop-down list in the DDMODIFY dialog box provides many more options than the Justification: list in the Attribute Definition dialog box.

After you have defined a block, you cannot directly edit the attribute definitions. If you want to modify the characteristics or behavior of the attributes associated with a defined block, you must redefine the block. As with any other block, exploding a block reference replaces it with the component objects of the current block definition. Any attribute values in the block are replaced by the attribute definitions, and the tags are visible again. Now you can use either DDEDIT or DDMODIFY to make the required changes and then redefine the block. Any future insertions of the block reflect the modifications made to the attribute characteristics.

Unfortunately, when redefining a block in AutoCAD LT, only the geometry is updated in any existing block references. Attributes in the existing blocks are unaffected by any changes you make to the block definition.

FIGURE 12.39 Some attribute definition properties can be changed using the DDEDIT command.

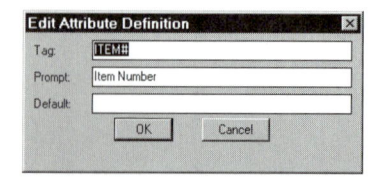

CHAPTER 12 ||| Designing and Using Your Own Symbols

FIGURE 12.40 The DDMODIFY command allows you to change any characteristic of an attribute definition.

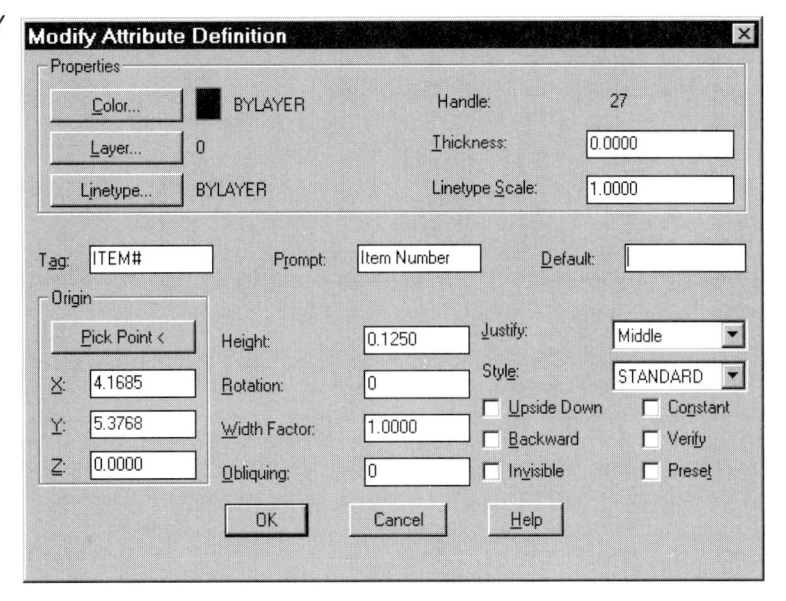

Editing Attribute Values in a Single Block Reference

The values of the attributes in an inserted block reference can be modified as long as the attribute was not defined as a constant. You can edit individual attribute values or, if needed, you can edit many attribute values at one time. To edit the attribute values within a single block, you can use the DDATTE command by typing **ATE** or **DDATTE** at the Command: prompt, picking the Edit Attribute button from the Modify II toolbar, or by selecting Attribute from the Object cascade of the Modify pull-down menu and then picking the Single ... option. At the Select block: prompt, pick the block containing the attributes you need to edit. You can pick anywhere on the block or pick any visible attribute. When you select a block that has one or more nonconstant attributes, the Edit Attributes dialog box is displayed as shown in Figure 12.41.

The name of the block you select appears in the upper left corner of the dialog box, and all of the attribute prompts are displayed along with their current values. This dialog box also displays all preset attributes. The preset values can be changed as needed. Pick any text box to edit the displayed value. If the block contains more than eight attributes, the Next button is enabled. Pick Next to see the next page of attributes, or Previous to go back. When you are finished editing the attributes, pick OK to complete the operation. Be aware that if you pick Cancel, all of the changes you made in the dialog box are discarded and the attributes are not modified.

Modify II
Edit Attribute
Modify
└ Object ▶
  └ Attribute ▶
    └ Single...
DDATTE
ATE

FIGURE 12.41 The Edit Attributes dialog box.

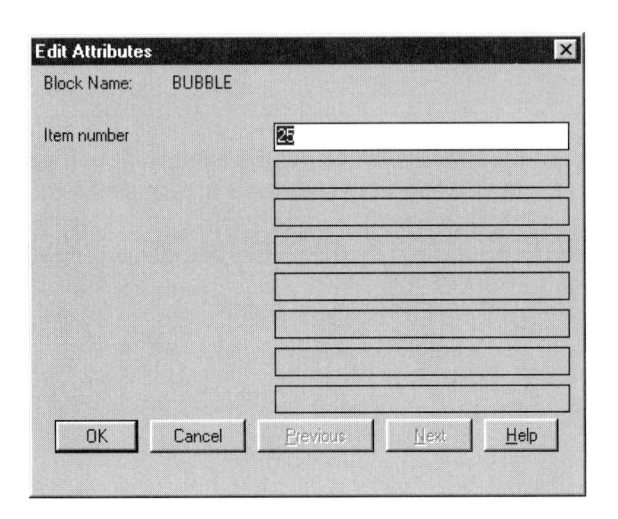

Editing Attribute Values Globally

Sometimes, you may need to do a global edit on specific attribute values. Doing a *global edit* means that you are changing every occurrence of a specific attribute value in the current drawing. As an example, if you completed an electronic schematic drawing and then determined that you were going to buy fixed-value resistors from a different supplier than ACME, you would need to change every attribute value that referenced ACME

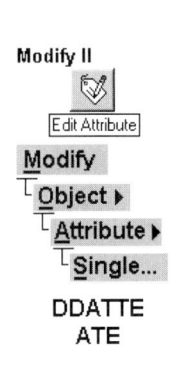

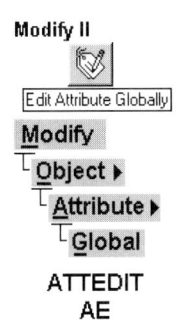

Modify II
Edit Attribute Globally
Modify
└ Object ▶
  └ Attribute ▶
    └ Global
ATTEDIT
AE

to the name of the new supplier. The ATTEDIT command is used to edit attribute values globally, and can be accessed by typing **AE** or **ATTEDIT** at the Command: prompt, by picking the Edit Attribute Globally button, or by selecting Attribute from the Objects cascade of the Modify pull-down menu and then picking the Global option. The ATTEDIT command displays the following prompts:

> Command: **AE** or **ATTEDIT**↵
> Edit attributes one at a time? <Y> **N**↵

Answering "No" to editing attributes one at a time allows global editing. Now you can edit every attribute contained in every block reference in the drawing, or you can use the next prompts to limit editing to specific blocks, tags, or even to attributes having a specified value:

> Global edit of attribute values.
> Edit only attributes visible on screen? <Y> **N**↵
> Drawing must be regenerated afterwards.

By entering a "No" to editing only attributes visible on screen, you can force AutoCAD LT to automatically select and edit every attribute in the drawing that matches the values entered at the subsequent prompts. You can force the search for matching values to be limited to a specific block name by typing that name as shown here:

> Block name specification <*>: **RES-F_H**↵

This limits the search to only blocks with the name RES-F_H. To limit the search to two or more specific block names, enter the block names separated by commas. Additionally, wild card parameters can be used for convenience. The default is an asterisk wild card, which means *all* block names.

The search can also be limited to particular tag names for attributes found in the previously specified blocks. As with the block names, a single tag name can be entered, or you can specify multiple tag names and wild cards. Refer back to Chapter 8 if you need to review the use of wild card characters. The following entry limits the search to attributes with a tag name of SUPPLIER:

> Attribute tag specification <*>: **SUPPLIER**↵

You can further limit the selection of the specified attributes found in the designated blocks to only those attributes with a particular value. Again, single values, multiple values, and wild cards can be used. This example specifies only attributes whose value is ACME:

> Attribute value specification <*>: **ACME**↵

The drawing database is now searched, and every insertion of RES-F_H is checked for an attribute with the tag name SUPPLIER and a value of ACME. In this example, three matching attributes are found in the drawing:

> 3 attributes selected.
> String to change: **ACME**↵
> New string: **Zenith**↵

After reporting the number of matching attributes, the prompt asks you to enter the text string that you want to change. In the previous example, the entire string is replaced. If you only want to change part of an attribute value you can enter just the text to change. For example, to change an attribute string of "Logn Attribute Text" to "Long Attribute Text," the string to change would be "gn" and the new string is "ng." In this way, you can avoid having to completely retype long text values. If the specified string to change occurs more than once in the selected attribute, only the first occurrence is modified.

Each string that is changed is now shown on the text screen as it appears after the modifications, the drawing is regenerated, and all of the modified attributes are updated:

> Zenith
> Zenith
> Zenith
> Regenerating drawing.

As you might imagine, this is a terrific time saver in a drawing where you need to change 50, 60, or even 100 or more existing attribute values.

You can also edit attributes one at a time. A common way of using this option is to accept the default values for each of the prompts. This leaves you at a Select Attributes: prompt with the freedom to pick any desired attribute. You can window a group of blocks or you can pick individual attributes. When you pick individual attributes, the selection process is like the "multiple" selection option because nothing is highlighted

CHAPTER 12 ||| Designing and Using Your Own Symbols

until you finish the selection process by pressing Enter at the Select Attributes: prompt. Regardless of how you select attributes, the following prompt is displayed:

Value/Position/Height/Angle/Style/Layer/Color/Next <N>:

Looking at the selected attributes on your screen, you see that one is highlighted and has a small X-shaped marker. Changing the position, rotation angle, text style, layer, and color work just as you would expect them to. However, when changing the value of an attribute, you have the option to replace the existing text or to just change specific parts:

Change or Replace? <R>: **R**↵
New attribute value: **10W**↵
Value/Position/Height/Angle/Style/Layer/Color/Next <N>: **V**↵
Change or Replace? <R>: **C**↵
String to change: **10W**↵
New string: **5W**↵
Value/Position/Height/Angle/Style/Layer/Color/Next <N>: ↵
Command:

The default option Next moves the X marker to the next attribute if more than one was selected. Any modifications that you make are applied only to the currently marked attribute.

Field Notes

When selecting attributes to edit using the ATTEDIT command, it is important to be aware that invisible attributes cannot be selected. If the attribute you need to edit is currently invisible, you can force AutoCAD LT to display all attributes whether they are defined as visible or invisible. To do this, use the ATTDISP command as follows:

Command: **ATTDISP**↵
Normal/ON/OFF <Normal>: **ON**↵

Turn the attribute display on to see invisible attributes. Turn it off to hide all attributes, and use the Normal setting to display visible attributes but not invisible ones.

Exercise 12.11

1. Open the drawing EX12.10.
2. Insert additional copies of RES-F_H until you have a total of 10 occurrences in your drawing. Use any available default values while inserting the blocks.
3. Turn ATTDISP on.
4. Use the DDATTE command to edit the attributes in three of the resistor blocks.
5. Change the wattage rating of each of the three blocks to 10W.
6. Start the ATTEDIT command, select global editing, enter NO to editing only visible attributes, and specify a block name of RES-F_H, a tag of SUPPLIER, and a value of ACME.
7. Change the string "ACME" to "Zenith."
8. Set ATTDISP back to Normal.
9. Save the drawing as EX12.11.

LEARNING CHECKPOINT

- ☐ What is an attribute?
- ☐ Describe applications for each of the four modes for an attribute.
- ☐ What is an attribute tag? prompt? default value?
- ☐ How are attributes included in a block?
- ☐ What is the purpose of invisible attributes?

- What commands can be used to modify an attribute definition?
- What commands are used to edit an attribute?
- Describe the procedure for global editing.
- How can invisible attributes be made temporarily visible for selection?

Suppressing Attribute Prompts

In some situations, you may not want to answer attribute prompts when inserting blocks. During the initial phases of a design, you may not be ready to assign final attribute values. Having to repeatedly divert your attention away from the design process to answer unnecessary prompts can interrupt your concentration and adversely affect your creativity. At such a time, it may be more convenient simply to insert symbols where they go and then come back and fill in the specific attributes later.

To turn off all attribute prompts, set the ATTREQ system variable to 0 by typing **ATTREQ** at the Command: prompt as follows:

Command: **ATTREQ**↵
New value for ATTREQ <1>: **0**↵

ATTREQ is short for ATTribute REQuest, and controls whether or not AutoCAD LT issues attribute prompts when they are inserted. When ATTREQ is set to 0 no prompts are issued, and if a default value was specified in the attribute definition, that value is automatically used.

Set ATTREQ back to 1 when you are ready for attribute prompts to once again be issued normally. Any blocks that were inserted at default values can then be edited as needed to assign the appropriate values.

Extracting Attribute Values from a Drawing

Using AutoCAD LT, you can gather any or all of the available information regarding blocks and attributes in a drawing and save it in a text file. Before the attributes can be extracted from a file, some preparations are required. First, a special kind of text file, called a ***template file,*** is created to specify what information AutoCAD LT is to extract from the blocks and attributes. This makes it possible to extract only specific information as required for particular uses.

Field Notes

> Accessing the values of attributes is termed *attribute extraction.* The word *extract* implies that the attributes are being removed from the drawing, but this is not the case. The drawing and the attributes it contains are in no way affected by the attribute extraction process.

A template file can be created using any normal text editor program. Windows provides a basic text editor called *Notepad.* This program creates what is known as an ASCII file (American Standard Code for Information Interchange), which means that the file contains text characters only. Files created with a word processing program such as Microsoft Word or Word Perfect often contain special printer codes that AutoCAD LT does not understand. If you use a word processor to generate a template file, be sure to save the file as "text only."

A template file uses special types of notations that tell AutoCAD LT which information to extract and the format in which to present it. The tag name for the attribute to extract is used, along with the formatting information. As an example, to extract the value associated with the attribute whose tag is SUPPLIER, the following specification could be used in the template file:

SUPPLIER   C008000

The tag name is indicated followed by formatting codes for the extracted information. All values assigned to attributes are stored as text-based information in the drawing. This can be inconvenient when importing the information into a spreadsheet application because text and numbers are handled differently. You can control whether the extracted information is stored as text or as numerical data with the first character in the formatting code. In the preceding example, the supplier information is expected to be text so a "C" is used to specify "Character" data. If the value is numerical data, the formatting code is preceded with an "N" for "Numerical." In the following example, the value for the WATT attribute is specified:

CHAPTER 12 ||| Designing and Using Your Own Symbols

WATT   N006002

The rest of the formatting code is comprised of two three-digit numbers that determine the appearance and content of the data extracted. The first three digits are used to specify the total field width for the extracted value. The term *field width* indicates the number of character positions used. So, the previously shown specification for the SUPPLIER attribute extracts up to eight characters. The last three digits are always required, but their value is ignored if the attribute value is specified as being character data.

If the extracted data are specified as numeric data, the first three digits are still used for field width and the second three digits of the formatting code indicate how many decimal places to use in the number. Note that the field width indicates the total number of character positions including the decimal numbers and the decimal point. Therefore, the WATT specification given earlier indicates that two decimal places are to be used in a number that can use up to six character positions. Since two decimals are specified, and the decimal point takes one position, only three positions are left for numbers to the left of the decimal point. Figure 12.42 shows an illustrated explanation of the formatting code options.

In addition, you can extract information specific to the block references. This can include the block names, insertion points, scale factors, rotation angles, and more. An information code is used, preceded by a "BL:" designation, but the formatting codes are exactly the same as for attribute data. The BL: designation stands for "Block." The table in Figure 12.43 shows each information category available for extraction, the specification method, and whether it is character or numeric data.

FIGURE 12.42 Attribute extraction field formatting codes.

```
Attribute Tag Names
                      C for Character data
                      12 Characters total field width
                      No decimal places required

  TAGNAME1            C012000

  TAGNAME2            N009003
                      N for Numeric data
                      9 positions total field width
                      3 decimal places
```

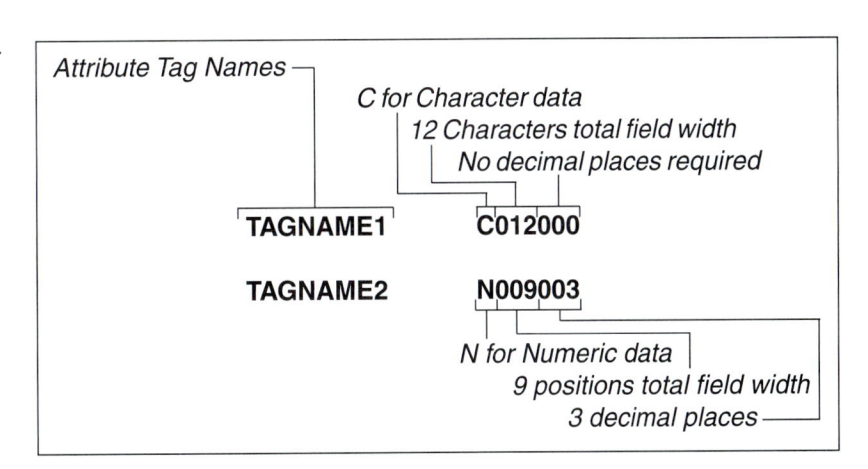

FIGURE 12.43 Useful block information can also be extracted.

Template Specification	Type	Description
BL:NAME	C	Block name
BL:X	N	X coordinate of block insertion point
BL:Y	N	Y coordinate of block insertion point
BL:Z	N	Z coordinate of block insertion point
BL:NUMBER	N	Block counter (Incremented for each block found)
BL:HANDLE	C	Block Handle (Unique object name)
BL:LAYER	C	Block insertion layer
BL:ORIENT	N	Block rotation angle
BL:XSCALE	N	Block insertion X scale factor
BL:YSCALE	N	Block insertion Y scale factor
BL:ZSCALE	N	Block insertion Z scale factor
BL:XEXTRUDE	N	Block extrusion direction X value
BL:YEXTRUDE	N	Block extrusion direction Y value
BL:ZEXTRUDE	N	Block extrusion direction Z value
BL:LEVEL	N	Block nesting level

Some of these options are of little use for most applications, but information such as the block name, location, rotation, and scale can frequently be useful. These items are listed in the template file in the same manner as attribute extraction designations, substituting the item listed in the Template Specification column instead of an attribute tag name. For example, the following listing might be useful for the drawing created in Exercise 12.11 to extract the information regarding each of the attributes and to select block information:

```
RTYPE       C008000
NUMBER      C004000
VALUE       C006000
WATT        C004000
SUPPLIER    C008000
PART#       C016000
BL:NAME     C012000
BL:X        N006003
BL:Y        N006003
BL:NUMBER   N004000
BL:LAYER    C032000
```

This template file listing provides each of the attribute values, the block name and location, and the layer on which the block is located. Additionally, using the NUMBER field provides a quick count of the total number of blocks with attributes in the drawing. Figure 12.44 shows this template being created in the Windows Notepad program.

FIGURE 12.44 Notepad is an easy-to-use text editor that can be used to create attribute extraction template files.

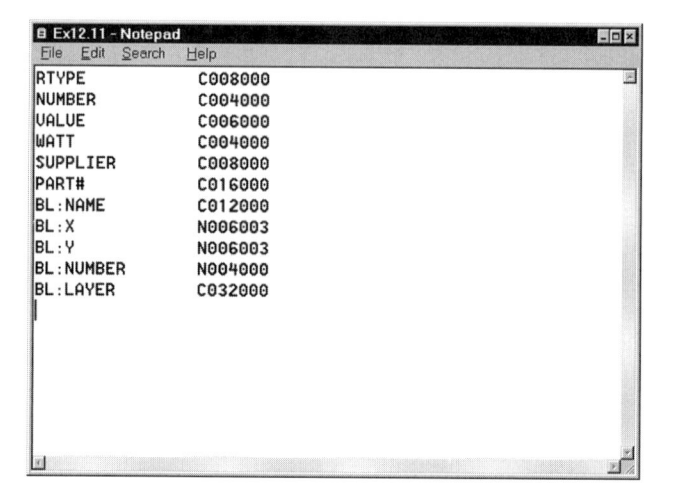

CHAPTER 12 ||| Designing and Using Your Own Symbols

Through the Window...

Creating template files is easy to do using the Notepad text editor available in Windows. Finding and starting this application is done somewhat differently in each operating system. From the Start menu on the Taskbar, pick Programs, then Accessories, and select the Notepad program. Once the editor has opened, you can begin typing and enter all of the information required in your template file.

Once you save the file and exit the Notepad program, it is very easy to reopen the file if you need to edit it. From the Start menu on the Taskbar, pick Documents. The name of your template file should appear in the cascading submenu that appears. Picking the file name automatically starts Notepad and preloads the template file.

Field Notes

- You can only place one extraction specification per line in the template file.
- Although the sample template files show the field formatting codes as all beginning in the same column, this is not necessary. This is done in the text examples for readability, and for that same reason, it is recommended that you format your files in this manner. When each of the fields is aligned, it is easier to spot any errors.
- One easy mistake to make when creating a template file is to use an uppercase "O" instead of a 0 (zero) in the formatting code. They are not always easy to spot, but they do appear slightly wider and should be visible under close inspection.
- The AutoCAD LT User's Guide recommends that you always include at least one space (using the space bar) between the field or attribute name and the field formatting code rather than using the [TAB] key.
- The most common mistake made when creating a template file is forgetting to press Enter at the end of the last line in the file. Forgetting to do this causes an error during the attribute extraction process.

Exercise 12.12

1. Start the Windows Notepad Program.
2. In Notepad, enter the following template file information as shown:

        RTYPE   C008000
        NUMBER   C004000
        VALUE   C006000
        WATT   C004000
        SUPPLIER   C008000
        PART#   C016000
        BL:NAME   C012000
        BL:X   N006003
        BL:Y   N006003
        BL:NUMBER   N004000
        BL:LAYER   C032000

3. Be sure to press Enter at the end of the last line (the BL:LAYER line).
4. Save the file as EX12.12.TXT.

Tools
└ **Attribute Extraction...**

DDATTEXT

After creating the template file, you are ready to proceed with extracting the attributes from a drawing. The primary command used to extract attributes is the DDATTEXT command. To access DDATTEXT you can type **DDATTEXT** at the Command: prompt or pick Attribute Extraction... from the Tools pull-down menu.

Command: **DDATTEXT**↵
⟨the Attribute Extraction dialog box is displayed . . .⟩

Starting the DDATTEXT command displays the Attribute Extraction dialog box as shown in Figure 12.45. The File Format area of the Attribute Extraction dialog box allows you to specify how the attribute information is formatted in the output file. The format used depends primarily on how you intend to use the output file. The most common use of attribute extraction files is as input to spreadsheet or database programs. Many such applications can read the CDF, or Comma Delimited File format. The term *delimit* means "to establish the limits of," and indicates that individual fields within each record are separated from each other. This ensures that the application you are importing into knows where one field ends and the next begins. In a CDF file the fields are each separated by commas inserted in the output file as it is written. The second option is SDF, or Space Delimited File format. This format does not actually insert any characters, spaces or otherwise, into the file. When using an SDF format, you must specify field widths containing more characters than the values actually require. Any character positions not filled in by the value are left as empty spaces and are considered the field delimiters. Most applications, such as the Microsoft Excel spreadsheet program, are very flexible with regard to the types of files they can read and can import files of either type. Database applications such as dBase IV can easily read SDF formats. Regardless of which of these formats you use, each block occurrence and all of its attributes is considered a single record and is written on a single line. Each individual data item extracted from the block and each attribute make up separate fields within a record.

The Drawing Interchange File (DXF) setting writes a very unique file with a .DXX file extension, which is a subset of the DXF file format discussed in Chapter 15. This selection does not utilize a template file, and automatically writes all block and attribute data to the output file. This setting is only for very specialized needs, and is not commonly used for exporting data to spreadsheets or databases.

The Select Objects < button allows you to select only specific blocks for the extraction process. The number of objects selected appears to the right of the button. If the Number found: value is 0, the specified data is extracted from all of the blocks within the drawing that contain attributes. In a drawing with many different blocks defined, you can limit the extract file output by selecting the blocks to use. As a special note, if you have inserted different symbols on specific layers, the selection process is made easier by freezing the unneeded layers.

Enter the name of the template file in the Attribute Template File ... field. A file extension of .TXT is expected and is the default. When no file extension is entered AutoCAD LT automatically looks for the specified file name with a .TXT extension. If an extension other than .TXT is entered, it is automatically changed when you pick the OK button. To use a file dialog box to select the template file, pick the Attribute Template File ... button.

The Output File ... field works the same with regard to the file extension. Only .TXT can be used here as well. And again, to use the file dialog box for specification of the output file name, select the Output File ... button. If you specify the same name for both the template and the output, you are requested to change the name of one of the files.

FIGURE 12.45 The Attribute Extraction dialog box provides an intuitive interface for extracting attribute values from a drawing.

Picking OK will then start the attribute extraction process, and any errors encountered are listed on the screen. If the error is not too serious, the extract file is still created, but may not be as you expect. Always be sure to press the F2 key to examine your text screen and read any messages after doing an attribute extraction. A completely successful extraction results in a message that specifies how many records were created in the output file:

Command: **DDATTEXT**↵
10 records in extract file.

The command line version of this command is the ATTEXT command, also available at the Command: prompt only, by typing either **AX** or **ATTEXT.** The command line version does not provide the same convenience or safeguards as the dialog version.

Error messages you may encounter can be caused by any of several possible problems in your template file. If, for example, a specification in a template file does not allow enough characters to hold the value assigned to an attribute, an error message is displayed. This situation is reported as a field overflow, and the message is repeated for each time the problem is encountered:

**Field overflow in record 1
**Field overflow in record 2
**Field overflow in record 3
**Field overflow in record 4
**Field overflow in record 5
**Field overflow in record 6
**Field overflow in record 7
**Field overflow in record 8
**Field overflow in record 9
**Field overflow in record 10
10 records in extract file.

This error situation does not halt the creation of the output file. To correct this problem, check that each listing in the template file includes the correct field width and look in the output file to see what field appears incomplete.

Another possible problem is when a duplicate field definition exists in the template file. Each field can be defined only once, so this produces an error and the output file is not created. This message is produced when trying to write an extract file named C:\CHAP_12.TXT using a template containing a duplicate definition:

Command: **DDATTEXT**↵
**Duplicate field specification:
RTYPE C009000
Unknown command "C:\CHAP_12.TXT". Press F1 for help.

This can be corrected by removing the duplicate definition from the Template file and saving it again.

Specifying a field that does not exist creates no problems, but if a field listing is not constructed correctly, then no output file is created and an error message is issued. In the next example, the formatting code is not entered completely and an error message is produced:

Command: **DDATTEXT**↵
**Invalid field specification:
BL:NUMBER   N004
Unknown command "C:\CHAP_12". Press F1 for help.

When you get this message, check each item in the template file carefully to ensure that each field specification is complete and correct. Also, another reason this message might appear is if you forgot to press Enter at the end of the last line in the template file. After correcting the problem, save the updated template file and try the extraction again.

If a field is specified as numeric but actually contains text characters, you may get two possible results. If a number is in the first character position, then the text that follows is not extracted. A text character in the first position causes the field value to be entered as 0 (zero) or another inappropriate numeric value. Either way, an error message is issued for each incorrect item encountered:

**Bad numeric value for field RTYPE, record 1
**Bad numeric value for field RTYPE, record 2
**Bad numeric value for field RTYPE, record 3

```
**Bad numeric value for field RTYPE, record 4
**Bad numeric value for field RTYPE, record 5
**Bad numeric value for field RTYPE, record 6
**Bad numeric value for field RTYPE, record 7
**Bad numeric value for field RTYPE, record 8
**Bad numeric value for field RTYPE, record 9
**Bad numeric value for field RTYPE, record 10
10 records in extract file.
```

> ### Field Notes
>
> - Any tag names listed in the template file that do not exist are still written to the output file. If the listing indicates a character field, it is written as an empty field. A numeric specification results in a value of 0 (zero) being written to the output file. When you are using an SDF file, this can be used to your advantage.
>   One problem with a space delimited file is that the numeric entries are right justified and the character entries are left justified. Because no delimiting characters are inserted in an SDF file, this means that a numeric field followed directly by a character field has no separation. To fix this problem, enter the name of a nonexistent attribute tag and specify it as character data with a width of 1. Now the nonexistent tag is written as a single blank space, which separates the fields.
> - If any tag name appears more than once in a template file, only the first listing is recognized. When you need more than one blank field, be sure to specify different names in each location in the template file.

Once you have successfully created an extract file, it should look similar to one of the files shown in Figures 12.46 and 12.47. One shows a CDF file and the other, an SDF file.

FIGURE 12.46 An attribute extract file created using CDF format and opened using Notepad.

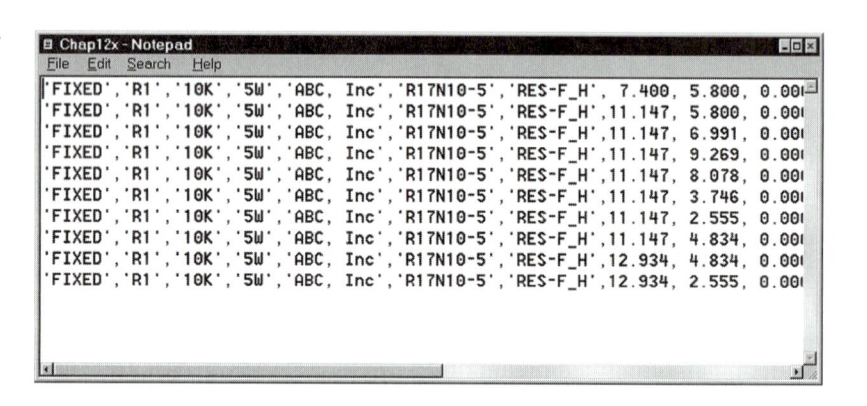

FIGURE 12.47 An attribute extract file created using SDF format and opened using Notepad.

CHAPTER 12 ||| Designing and Using Your Own Symbols

Special Extract File Formats

Some database applications may require specific file formats other than CDF or SDF. If you are using such an application, you can customize your extract files using two special template file modifiers. As an example, all character fields written to the output file are surrounded with single quote (') characters by default. Some applications, like Microsoft Excel, import these characters as part of the text string in character fields. However, text surrounded in double quotes (") is brought in without the surrounding quotes, reducing the amount of editing that must be done. You can force AutoCAD LT to surround text in the output file with whatever character you wish by specifying a C:QUOTE field. This field is followed by the character you want used, so to specify the use of double quotes, the following line is included in the template file:

C:QUOTE "

You may also wish to use a special character as a delimiter, depending on which application you are taking your data into. This is done using the C:DELIM field specification. For example, to use a forward slash as a field delimiter, enter the following line into the template:

C:DELIM /

These specifications are entered on a line by themselves, anywhere in the template file. Before using these fields, you should be certain of the requirements for importing information into the spreadsheet or database application you are using.

Exercise 12.13

1. Open drawing EX12.11 There should still be 10 occurrences of the block RES-F_H present in your drawing. If not, insert them now using the attribute values as specified in Exercise 12.10.
2. Start the DDATTEXT command, and specify a comma delimited file format.
3. Specify a global attribute extraction (by not using the Select Objects < button).
4. Use the template file 12.12.TXT.
5. Specify the output file as EX12.13C.TXT and start the extraction.
6. Check your text screen for error messages. If you see any error messages, make the necessary corrections as described earlier in this section and run the extraction again.
7. Use Notepad to open and view the output file EX12.13C.TXT.
8. Start the DDATTEXT command again, specifying a space delimited file format.
9. Using the Select Objects < button, pick five occurrences of the RES-F_H block.
10. Use the template file 12.12.TXT again.
11. Specify the output file as EX12.13S.TXT and start the extraction.
12. Check your text screen for error messages. If you see any error messages, make the necessary corrections as described earlier in this section and run the extraction again.
13. Use Notepad to open and view the output file EX12.13S.TXT.

LEARNING CHECKPOINT

- ☐ How can attribute prompts be suppressed? Why is suppression sometimes desirable?
- ☐ What is meant by the term *attribute extraction?*
- ☐ What is the purpose of a template file?
- ☐ Detail the use of the field formatting codes used in a template file.
- ☐ What are some of the most common BL: codes used in a template file?
- ☐ Describe the use of the DDATTEXT command.
- ☐ What file extension is required for template and extract files?
- ☐ Define the CDF and SDF extract file formats.
- ☐ List the causes and fixes for some common attribute extraction errors.
- ☐ What are the purposes of C:QUOTE and C:DELIM in a template file?

Using Clip Art

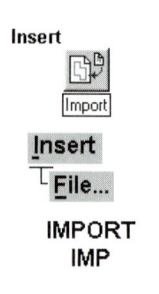

Insert

[Import]

Insert
└ File...

IMPORT
IMP

Technical images such as drafting symbols are usually constructed in AutoCAD LT using standard drawing geometry, such as lines, arcs, circles, and polylines. AutoCAD LT provides precision drawing tools necessary for creating these technically accurate images.

Some applications may require the use of nontechnical images within a drawing project, or you may have other uses for drawings that use artistic symbols or images. These artistic symbols and images are called *clip art.* You can import these images into AutoCAD LT in a manner similar to that of inserting blocks in a drawing.

Clip art takes many forms, and a very commonly used format is the .WMF file—or Windows MetaFile. These files, unlike bitmap images used by paint programs, support both raster and vector information. ***Raster information*** is a record of the assigned colors of pixels within a defined area. Although it can be imported, this type of information cannot be directly edited in AutoCAD LT. ***Vector information*** is a record of distances, angles, and properties associated with distinct drawing objects.

As an example, a line recorded in a paint program is raster information. This means that the entire line cannot be selected as a single object and edited. The only record kept is a listing of which pixels are colored and what color they are. The fact that they look like a line is not recognized by a raster-based program. Changing the appearance of the line is done by changing the color assigned to the pixels.

On the other hand, a line recorded in AutoCAD LT is vector information. The line can be selected and modified as a unit. It has two defined endpoints with a single vector drawn between them. The appearance of this object can be changed by modifying its properties. Its location can be changed by moving the endpoints.

A Windows MetaFile can store both raster and vector information. If it does contain raster information, the only way it can be directly edited once it has been imported is to be resized. A Windows MetaFile that contains only vector information comes in as a block, and can therefore be exploded. The actual object type used for the vectors within an exploded .WMF file is polylines.

A Windows MetaFile can be imported into any AutoCAD LT drawing using either the IMPORT command or the WMFIN command. The IMPORT command is accessed by typing **IMP** or **IMPORT** at the Command: prompt, picking the Import button from the Insert toolbar, or picking File... from the Insert pulldown menu. The Import File dialog box is shown in Figure 12.48. The List Files of type: pull-down list offers the options to import either a DXF file or a WMF file. The DXF option is discussed further in Chapter 15.

When you select the .WMF option, any existing WMF file names are shown in the file name area. The Preview area on the right displays a preview of the currently highlighted .WMF file name. As with many file dialog boxes, this one also offers a Find File ... option that allows you to search your local disk drive or network drives for available files.

When a .WMF file is imported using this dialog box, the insertion point, scale factors, and rotation angle are entered automatically. After insertion, however, you can edit the image as you would any block. The insertion point, scale factors, and rotation angle can be changed, or you can explode it and edit it further.

More control is available when you import clip art using the WMFIN command. You can specify the insertion point, scale factors, and rotation angle. This command is accessed by typing **WI** or **WMFIN** at the Command: prompt, and it starts the Import WMF dialog box. This dialog box works just like the Import File dialog box except that it will only import .WMF and .CLP files. CLP files can be either .WMF style art or text and are saved by the Clipboard or Clipbook Viewer program. The Import WMF dialog box is shown in Figure 12.49.

Importing .WMF files can bring a significant amount of overhead into a drawing. AutoCAD LT offers certain controls that can be set to control the display of wide lines and fill areas in an imported .WMF file.

FIGURE 12.48 The Import File dialog box can be used to import .WMF files.

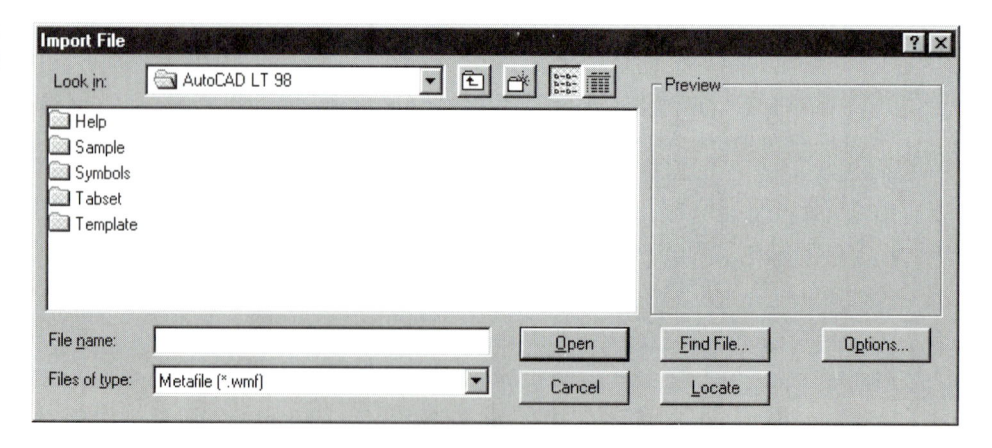

CHAPTER 12 ||| Designing and Using Your Own Symbols 537

FIGURE 12.49 The WMFIN command starts the Import WMF dialog box and offers more flexibility when importing .WMF files.

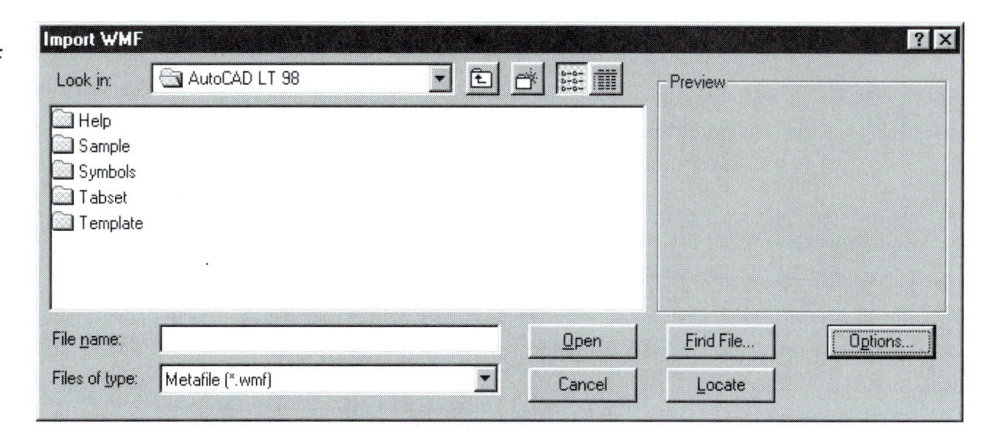

FIGURE 12.50 The WMF Import Options dialog box provides controls for how imported .WMF files are displayed.

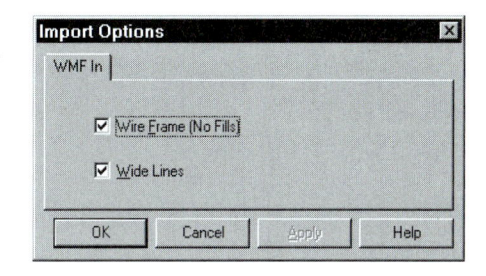

The WMF options are set using the WMFOPTS command. You can type **WMFOPTS** at the Command: prompt or select Options … from the Import File dialog box to display the WMF Import Options dialog box as shown in Figure 12.50.

Two toggles are available under WMF Import Options: Wire Frame (No Fills) and Wide Lines. If Wire Frame (No Fills) is set, all .WMF files are imported as outlines and all filled areas are left empty. When Wide Lines is set, the width of wide lines within the .WMF file is maintained when the file is imported.

Exercise 12.14

1. Start a new drawing using the default options for Quick Setup.
2. Set Wire Frame (No Fills) to ON using the WMF Import Options dialog box, and Wide Lines to OFF.
3. Start the IMPORT command and import a .WMF file from the CLIPART directory.
4. Explode the new object and LIST one of its components.
5. Set Wire Frame (No Fills) to OFF using the WMF Import Options dialog box, and Wide Lines to ON.
6. Start the IMPORT command and import a .WMF file from the CLIPART directory.
7. Explode the new object and LIST one of its components.
8. Save the drawing as EX12.14.

✓ LEARNING CHECKPOINT

- ☐ What is clip art?
- ☐ Where can the AutoCAD LT sample clip art be found?
- ☐ What are the differences between using IMPORT and WMFIN?
- ☐ What is a .WMF file?
- ☐ In what ways can a .WMF file be edited inside of AutoCAD LT?
- ☐ When can a .WMF file not be exploded?
- ☐ Name the command that helps limit the overhead of .WMF files.

MULTIPLE CHOICE

1. A collective representation of any number of regular AutoCAD LT objects that is stored and used as a single object is called a:
   - **a.** file
   - **b.** symbol
   - **c.** block
   - **d.** shape

2. The command used to insert a block into a drawing is:
   - **a.** symbol
   - **b.** block
   - **c.** DDINSERT
   - **d.** XREF

3. The point referenced when inserting a block into a drawing is called the:
   - **a.** insertion base point
   - **b.** origin point
   - **c.** grip point
   - **d.** reference point

4. A symbol used in combination with text is often referred to as a:
   - **a.** text symbol
   - **b.** annotation symbol
   - **c.** dimension
   - **d.** character

5. To simplify the process of inserting annotation symbols whose scale factor matches the text height, the block definitions should be based on:
   - **a.** a unit of one
   - **b.** ASME standards
   - **c.** a unit of 10
   - **d.** your intuition

6. A specialized setting for color and linetype that provides the greatest flexibility when constructing blocks is called:
   - **a.** BYBLOCK
   - **b.** BYLAYER
   - **c.** BYGOSH
   - **d.** BYCOLOR

7. Saving a block as a separate drawing file is done using this command:
   - **a.** MAKEBLOCK
   - **b.** WRITEBLOCK
   - **c.** WBLOCK
   - **d.** MBLOCK

8. This is not an available option in the Mode area of the Attribute Definition dialog box:
   - **a.** invisible
   - **b.** constant
   - **c.** off
   - **d.** preset

9. This command allows attribute values to be edited using a dialog box:
   - **a.** ATTEDIT
   - **b.** ATTDIA
   - **c.** DDATTE
   - **d.** ATTDLG

10. Nontechnical, artistic symbols and images are called:
    - **a.** blocks
    - **b.** clip art
    - **c.** bitmaps
    - **d.** sketches

MATCHING

Match each term to the correct description by writing the appropriate number in each box at the left.

- ☐ Byblock
- ☐ ATTREQ
- ☐ ATTDIA
- ☐ INSBASE
- ☐ Complex linetype
- ☐ Simple linetype
- ☐ WBLOCK
- ☐ Constant
- ☐ Verify
- ☐ Preset
- ☐ Tag
- ☐ Nesting

1. Using a block as part of the definition of another block.
2. System variable that controls the insertion base point.
3. An attribute with this property does not prompt, but can be edited later.
4. Creates a drawing file from a block definition.
5. An attribute with this property prompts twice.
6. A "handle" to select attribute definitions with.
7. Controls whether or not any attribute prompts the user.
8. When set to 1, attributes prompt using a dialog box.
9. Consists only of dots, dashes, and gaps.
10. A special color and linetype setting that is useful when creating blocks.
11. An attribute with this property does not prompt and cannot be edited later.
12. May use text or shapes, along with dots, dashes, and gaps in its definition.

WORD SCRAMBLE

Unscramble the six scrambled words below, one letter to each square, to form six AutoCAD LT–related words:

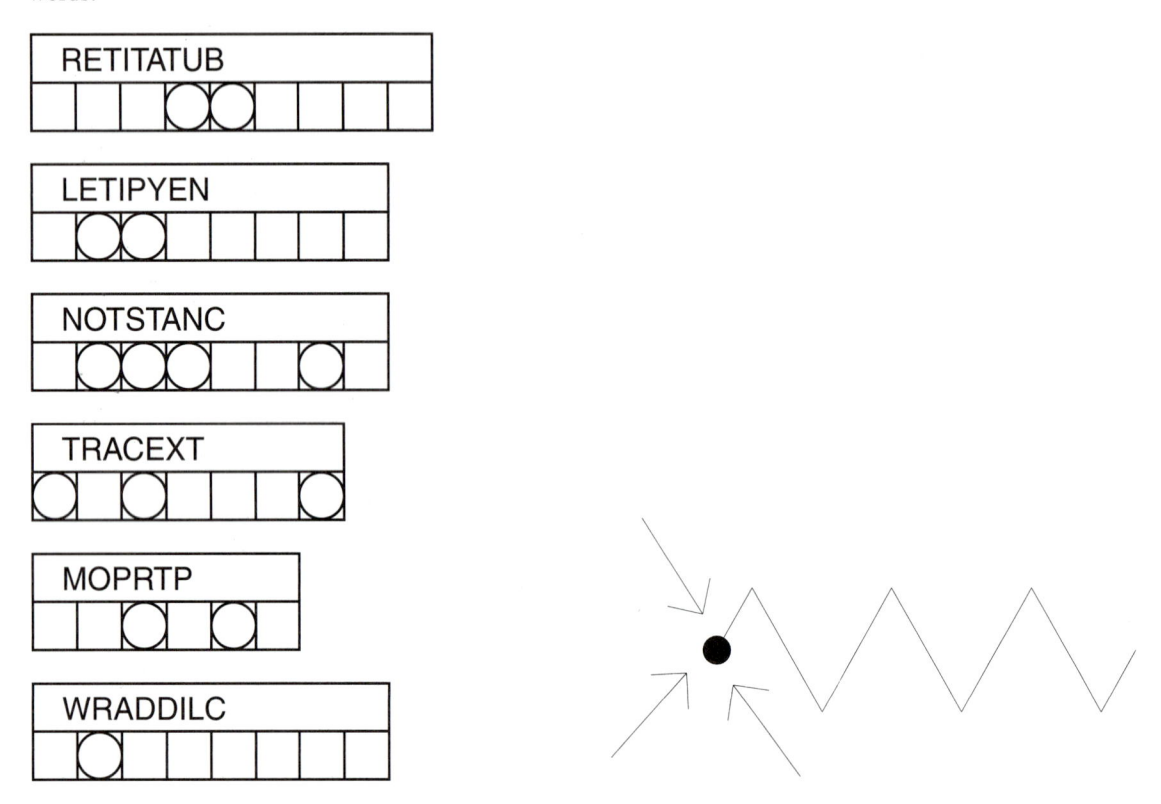

RETITATUB

LETIPYEN

NOTSTANC

TRACEXT

MOPRTP

WRADDILC

Unscramble the circled letters above to form the special answer as suggested by the illustration.

PROJECTS

12.1 Draw the figure below. Create two block definitions as shown, one named BOX and the other ARROW, and create the figure below. Save the drawing as P12.1.

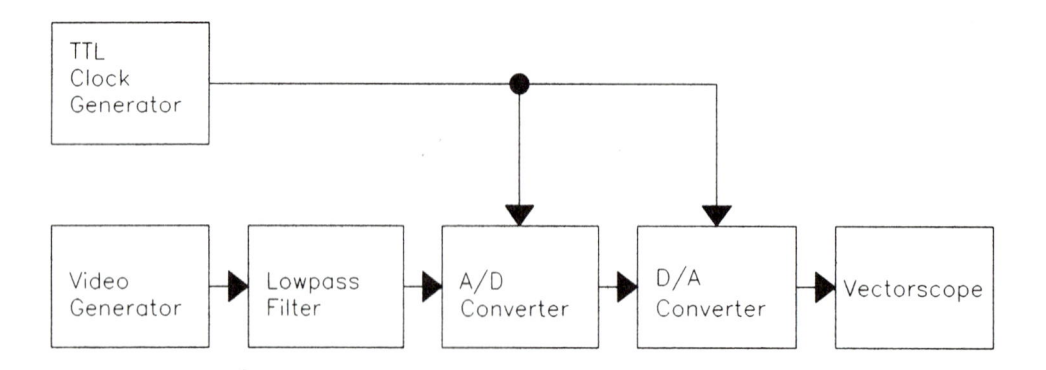

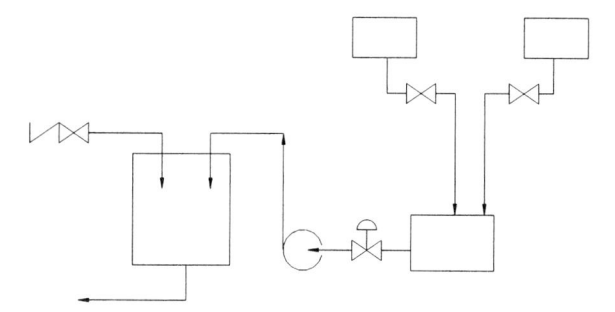

CHAPTER 12 ||| Designing and Using Your Own Symbols   541

12.2 Create blocks for each of the symbols in the figure below and draw the figure using the new blocks. Save the drawing as P12.2.

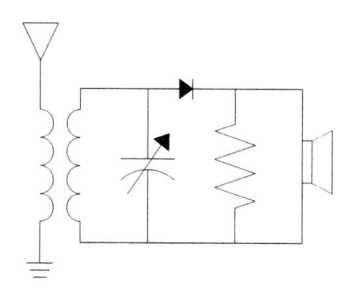

12.3 Create blocks for the doors and each of the legend symbols in the figure below and draw the figure using the new blocks. Save the drawing as P12.3.

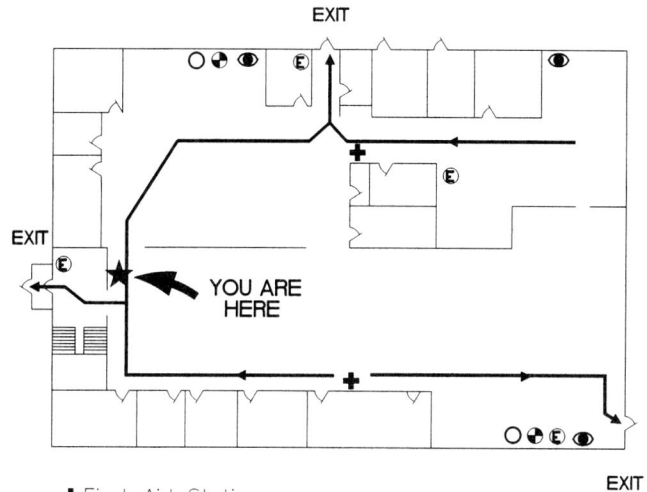

+ First Aid Station
O Self Contained Breathing Apparatus (SCBA)
● Respirator, Chemical Cartridge (protection for Ammonia Gas)
Ⓔ Fire Extinguisher
◉ Eye Wash Station
MEETING AREA: SW CORNER EMPLOYEE PARKING LOT

12.4 Create blocks for each of the symbols in the figure below and draw the figure using the new blocks. Save the drawing as P12.4.

12.5 Create blocks for each of the symbols shown in the figure below using attribute definitions to prompt the user for the appropriate labeling. Use attribute editing to change the orientation of the text, where required. Save the drawing as P12.5.

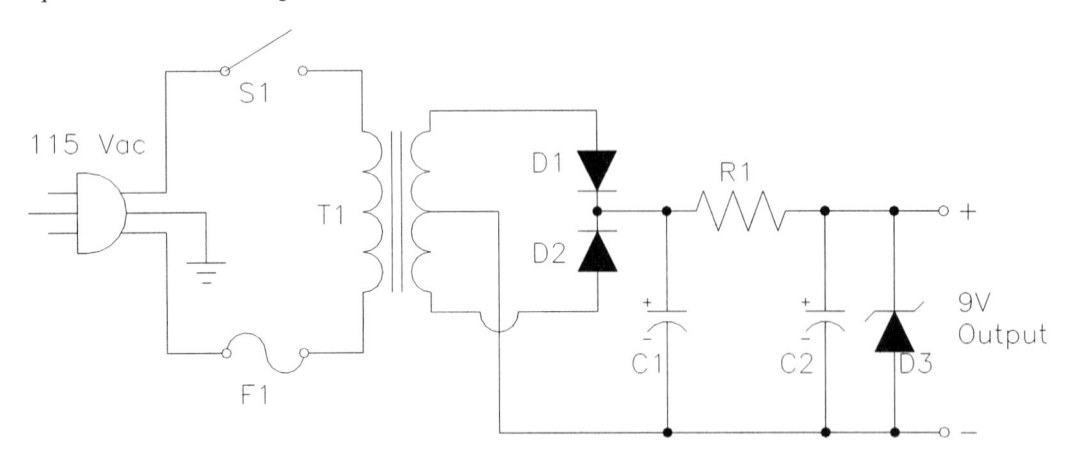

12.6 Create proportionately sized blocks representing office furniture. The symbols you create are to include a standard desk, corner desk, office chair, house plant, 4′ × 8′ table, a computer workstation, printer, and office telephone. Using the blocks, design an office layout suitable for four workstations and a receptionist. Save the drawing as P12.6.

12.7 Create the following block definition with attribute definitions as shown. The block name should be VALVE. When defining the attributes, use the table below as a guide. Save the drawing as P12.7.

TAG	DEFAULT	VERIFY	INVISIBLE	PRESET	CONSTANT
MFGR	ACME				Y
PARTNO	SV112-10	Y			
SIZE	4″		Y	Y	
PRICE	72.00		Y		

12.8 Open a suitable text editor for creating an attribute extraction template file. Use the following as a guide for creating the template file, and save it as P12.8.TXT.

FIELD	CHARACTERS	DECIMAL PLACES
MFGR	8	0
PARTNO	8	0
SIZE	6	0
PRICE	6	2

12.9 Open the drawing P12.7 for editing. Insert the block VALVE in 10 locations within the drawing using differing values in some of the insertions. Extract the attribute values to both a CDF and an SDF file using the template file P12.8. Name the output files P12.9C.TXT and P12.9S.TXT.

12.10 In a new drawing, import 4 of the WMF images found in the CLIPART directory. Save the drawing as P12.10.

CHAPTER 13

External References and Multiview Drawing Layout

LEARNING GOALS

- Reference external drawing files in the current drawing session
- Use each of the XREF command options
- Incorporate information contained in externally referenced drawing files
- Establish multiple drawing views with tiled model space viewports
- Set up model space viewports from within paper space
- Control individual viewport layer visibility
- Control linetype, associative hatch pattern, and linetype scaling in paper space
- Plot multiview drawings from paper space

Externally Referenced Drawings

In Chapter 12 you learned that any drawing can be inserted into any other drawing by using the INSERT command. One disadvantage to inserting another drawing into the current drawing is that the inserted drawing becomes a locally defined block and no longer maintains any connection with the original drawing. This can cause problems when it is time to update a design.

Consider the drawing update process required by a design change on a particular subassembly that is used in many different drawings. If in each case, the subassembly drawing had been inserted into another drawing, you would have to open and update the original drawing, and then open and update every other drawing where the subassembly had been used. This can be a long and time-consuming process.

An alternative exists that is known as *referencing* an external drawing. A drawing database that is stored outside of the current drawing is called an ***external drawing.*** The term ***referencing*** means that AutoCAD LT refers to the source file for the information, rather than storing it in the current drawing. Therefore, an ***external reference*** is a source drawing outside of the current drawing that AutoCAD LT refers to for information displayed in the current drawing. Using an external reference works much like inserting drawings, except that the information is not added to the current drawing database. Instead, each time you open a drawing, AutoCAD LT reads the source file for each external reference and displays the geometry in the current drawing.

Using external references has many advantages over inserting drawings. One advantage is that the information is not permanently added to the current drawing and the drawing file size can be kept from getting unnecessarily large. Another advantage of external references is that any number of drawings can reference a specific drawing file. Also, AutoCAD LT reads the source drawing file for each external reference every time you open a drawing that uses external references. So, all drawings that reference external drawings automatically reflect the latest state of the referenced drawing files.

In addition to external references, this chapter discusses the concepts of and techniques for using paper space. With a proper understanding of paper space, you can easily create standard drawing layouts that display model space geometry at any desired scale. Also, paper space simplifies the process of producing a hardcopy drawing by allowing you to plot at a scale of 1 to 1 on any size sheet of paper—regardless of the true size of your model.

FIGURE 13.1 The External Reference dialog box provides an intuitive interface for working with Xrefs.

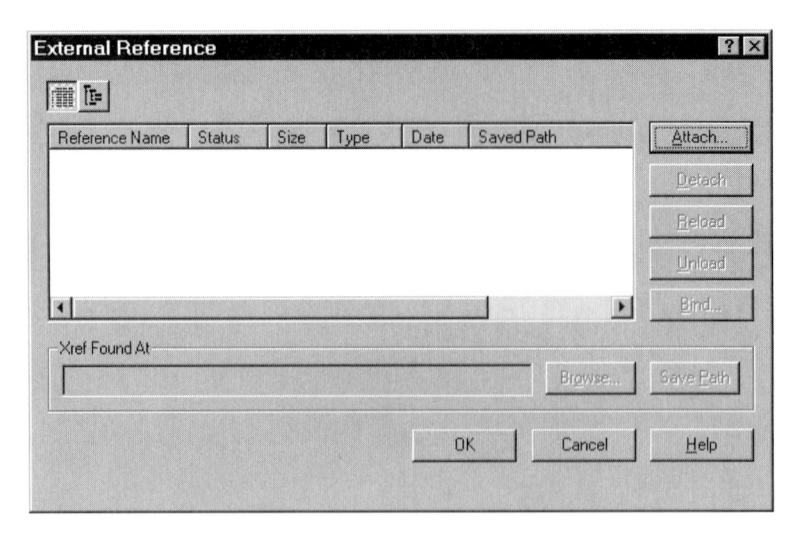

Attaching an External Reference

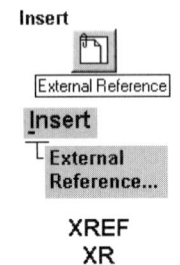

Insert
— External Reference...

XREF
XR

The primary command used for working with externally referenced drawing files is the XREF command. In fact, an external reference is most commonly referred to as an *"Xref."* The External Reference dialog box is accessed by picking External Reference ... from the Insert pull-down menu, from the Insert toolbar, or by typing **XR** or **XREF** at the Command: prompt. The External Reference dialog box is shown in Figure 13.1.

The basic XREF option is the Attach ... option. This option attaches an Xref to the current drawing. When an Xref is attached, it is displayed in the current drawing at each specified location. The definition of the Xref is automatically updated each time you open the current drawing. Additionally, an attached Xref can be nested. The term *nested* means that an Xref can contain other Xrefs. So if an Xref is attached to a drawing, and that drawing is then referenced by another drawing, the nested Xref is also displayed.

Your first step when using Xrefs is to create the drawing that will be referenced. Next, open the drawing that is to reference it and use the XREF Attach option. This is accessed by picking Attach ... in the External Reference dialog box.

Picking the Attach ... button in a drawing that currently has no externally referenced files displays the Select file to attach dialog box. See Figure 13.2. Use this dialog box as you do any file dialog to go to the desired folder, preview, and select an existing drawing file. When you pick the Open button, the Attach Xref dialog box is displayed, where you specify the insertion parameters for the referenced file. In Figure 13.2, the file named XREF1 found in the SAMPLE folder is selected.

In a drawing that already contains one or more externally referenced files, picking the Attach ... button in the External Reference dialog box displays the Attach Xref dialog box. The Attach Xref dialog box, after selecting the file named XREF1, is shown in Figure 13.3.

FIGURE 13.2 The Select file to attach dialog box allows you to preview and select a file to reference.

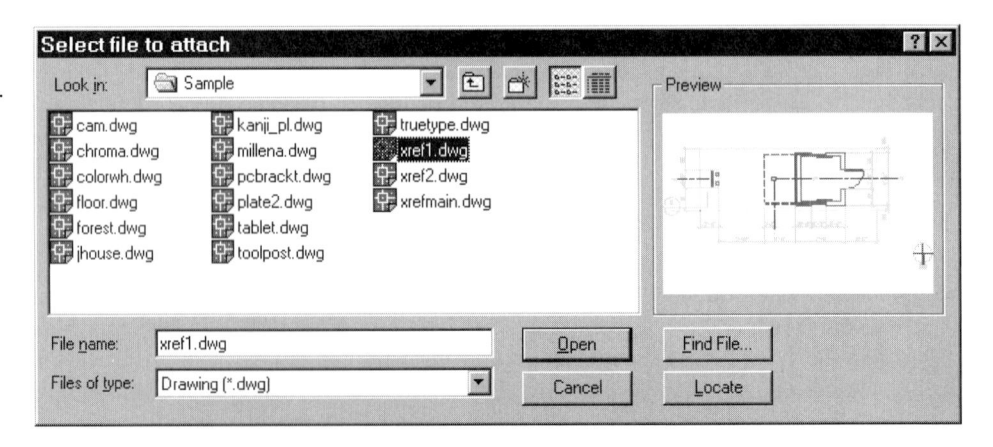

FIGURE 13.3 The Attach Xref dialog box is used to specify the insertion parameters for the referenced file.

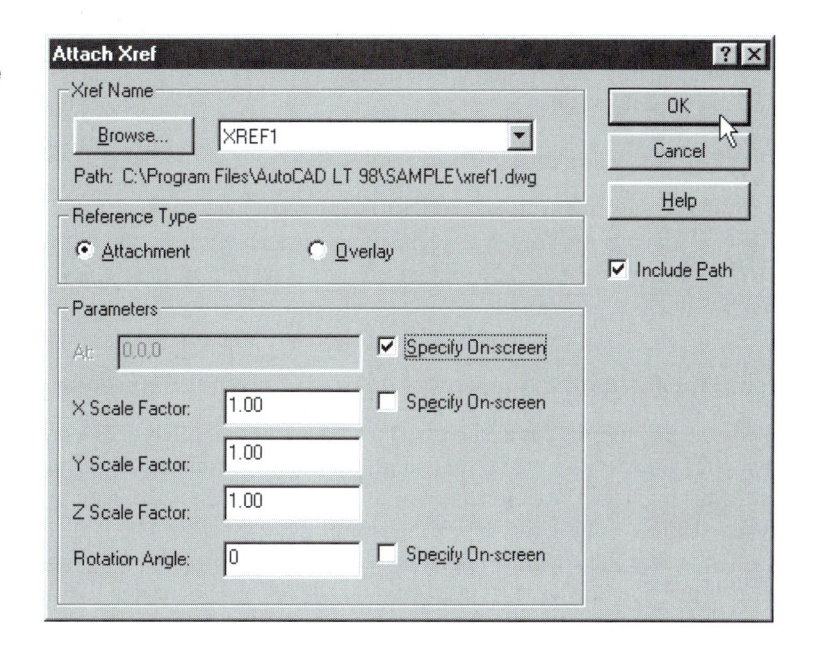

Field Notes

The XATTACH command provides greater convenience for attaching external references. For the first XREF in a drawing, XATTACH automatically displays the Select file to attach dialog box. All subsequent uses of this command display the Attach Xref dialog box. XATTACH is accessed by typing **XA** or **XATTACH**.

The Attach Xref dialog box displays the name and path of the currently selected file in the Xref Name area. If you need to return to the Select file to attach dialog box, pick the Browse ... button.

In the area labeled Reference Type, select the Attachment option. External Reference Attachments and Overlays are handled differently and have different applications. Xref overlays are discussed later in this chapter.

Typically, the toggle labeled Include Path is checked. This option controls whether the full path to the Xref is saved in the current drawing. If the path is not saved, the next time the current drawing file is opened, AutoCAD LT will look for the referenced file only in the AutoCAD LT Support File Search Path, as set in the Files tab of the Preferences dialog box.

The insertion parameters are specified in the Parameters area. When an externally referenced file is brought into a drawing, its placement, sizing, and orientation are handled similar to when you use the DDINSERT command. To be prompted for the insertion location, scale factors, or rotation angle at the command line, pick the Specify On-screen toggle next to the option. Otherwise, indicate the desired values in this dialog. When all parameters are specified, pick the OK button. In this example, the insertion point is specified on-screen, and the scale and rotation are specified in the dialog. The following appears at the command line:

Command: **XR**↵
XREF
Attach Xref XREF1: C:\Program Files\AutoCAD LT 98\SAMPLE\xref1.dwg
XREF1 loaded.

Insertion point: 0,0,0

The result is that a representation of the drawing named XREF1 appears in the current drawing. To place additional copies of an Xref in a drawing, you can duplicate an existing copy using any duplication command or you can use XREF Attach again. When the XREF Attach option is used to place a second copy, a message is displayed on the command line as follows:

Command: **XR** or **XREF**↵
Xref XREF1 has already been defined.
Using existing definition.

Insertion point: ⟨*specify a point*⟩

The second time you use the XREF command, picking the Attach ... button displays the Attach Xref dialog box. You can then select any already referenced file from the drop-down list in the Xref Name area. To select a file that is not already referenced, you need to pick the Browse ... button to display the Select file to attach dialog box.

Using the Content Explorer to Attach an External Reference

The Content Explorer can also be used to attach external references using its simple drag-and-drop interface. Pick Xref Attach from the File menu in the Content Explorer, or select the Block Insert button to toggle to Xref Attach mode. The tabs that point to drawings are disabled, leaving access only to the tabs that point to folders. Unless you already have a tab pointing to the folder where the file to be referenced is, you will need to activate Tree View mode to get to the desired folder.

When you find the file you want to attach, either drag it into the drawing window or double-click on it. This works the same as when inserting a drawing—if you drag-and-drop, a scale of 1 and rotation of 0 is used.

Currently attached xrefs do not appear in the Current Drawing tab. To reinsert an existing xref using Content Explorer, you have to use tree view to go to the folder where it is found. Then, simply drag it into your drawing again.

Field Notes

- When using the Xref Attach option to reference a file that uses a long file name or certain characters that are not allowed in block names, AutoCAD LT 98 displays the dialog box shown in Figure 13.4.

  FIGURE 13.4 The Substitute Block Name dialog box.

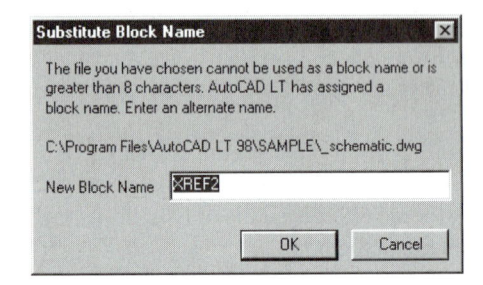

- If the file name contains spaces, commas, or other disallowed characters, you must replace them with characters that AutoCAD LT 98 can use in block names. This dialog box also indicates that the Xref name cannot be more than eight characters. However, if you reenter the name without any illegal characters, AutoCAD LT accepts it and allows you to attach the drawing without changing the name, even if it exceeds eight characters.
- When using the Content Explorer, illegal characters are automatically replaced with underscores in the Xref name. Even so, AutoCAD LT remembers the actual name of the Xref file and maintains the link between the Xref insertion and the source file.

Dependent Symbols

Xrefs are very different from blocks. When you insert a block, all the named objects are then defined in the current drawing. A ***named object*** is anything that is assigned a name, such as layers, blocks, linetypes, and text styles. The named objects defined in an Xref are brought in as dependent symbols. The term ***dependent symbol*** is used to describe any named object defined in an externally referenced drawing.

The previous example attached the external drawing named "XREF1" into an otherwise new drawing. No layers, linetypes, or any other named objects had been previously defined. However, all the dependent symbols are now present in the current drawing. For example, the Layer Control dialog box shown in Figure 13.5 shows a variety of layer names defined in the current drawing. Notice that the layer names are all preceded by the name of the externally referenced drawing file that they are dependent on, which is the drawing they were defined in. The symbol used to separate the dependent symbol name from the Xref it is dependent on is the "|" symbol, called a *vertical bar*. Experienced DOS users may also call this the *pipe* symbol.

FIGURE 13.5 The shown layer names are dependent symbols, defined in the externally referenced drawing named XREF1.

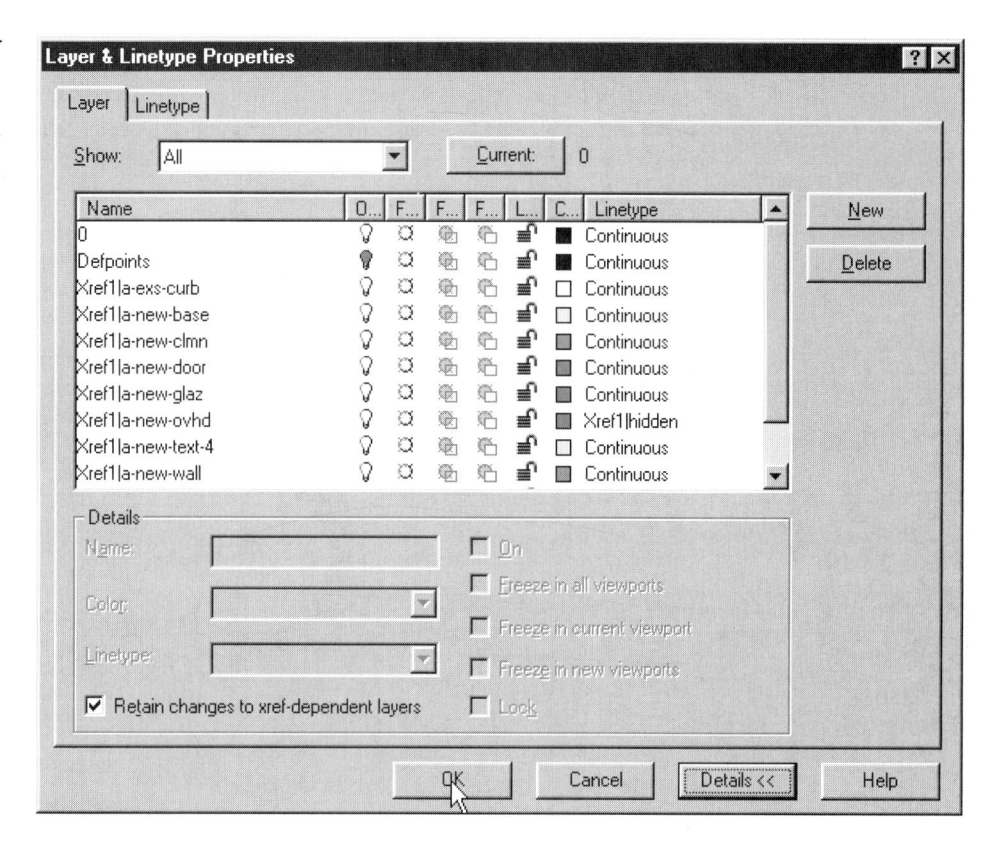

Attaching this particular external drawing has created many different dependent layer names, linetypes, text styles, and even a new dimstyle. Many of these dependent symbols can be brought permanently into the current drawing, as discussed later. Note that dependent symbols are not considered named objects in the current drawing and, therefore, do not appear in the Rename dialog box.

AutoCAD LT uses this type of naming system for dependent symbols to ensure that no conflicts are produced by duplicate named objects. For example, a text style named STANDARD exists in the current drawing and a style of the same name exists in the drawing file XREF1. If the STANDARD style in the current drawing is modified to reference the ROMANS.SHX font file, then a conflict exists because the STANDARD style in XREF1 uses the font file TXT.SHX. By naming the dependent style XREF1|STANDARD, the two separate definitions can coexist with no problems. Notice that the DEFPOINTS layer is not named in this manner, as well as layer 0 and the continuous linetype.

Because dependent symbols may change, or even disappear the next time the Xref is loaded, you cannot directly use dependent symbols. You cannot make a dependent layer current, nor can you rename a dependent layer. Additionally, you cannot rename or delete any dependent symbol.

Visibility changes can be made to dependent layers as desired, but by default, all of those changes are discarded the next time you load the Xref that the layers are dependent on. For example, if the layer TEXT is thawed in the drawing XREF1 and you freeze the layer XREF1|TEXT in the current drawing, it is thawed again the next time you open the current drawing and the Xref is reloaded.

To retain the visibility settings of dependent layers, you can set an AutoCAD LT system variable named VISRETAIN (VISibility RETAIN). The default setting for this variable is 0, which means OFF. To turn it on, type **VISRETAIN** at the Command: prompt and enter a value of 1. Set it to zero again to turn this variable back off:

Command: **VISRETAIN**↵
New value for VISRETAIN <0>: **1**↵

The effects of VISRETAIN become apparent the next time you load the Xref, because any visibility changes you have made to dependent layer names are preserved. This option can also be accessed by placing a check in the Retain changes to xref-dependent layers toggle in the Details section under the layer tab of the Layer & Linetype Properties dialog box. See Figure 13.5.

> ### Field Notes
>
> - The word *resolve* is frequently used with regard to external references. It refers to the process of finding the referenced file and reading the drawing information it contains.
> - When a drawing that has external references is opened, if an XREF cannot be *resolved* it is displayed as a text item in the drawing. The text shows the drive letter, directory path, and drawing file name for the Xref.

Exercise 13.1

1. Begin a new drawing, starting from scratch.
2. Use the XREF Attach option to attach the drawing \AutoCAD LT 98\SAMPLE\XREF1 to the current drawing. Use 0,0 for the insertion point and default scale and rotation values, use ZOOM ALL to see the entire drawing.
3. Open the Layer Control dialog box and try to set a dependent layer to be current. Then try to rename a dependent layer. Close the Layer Control dialog box.
4. Copy the Xref to a new location.
5. Use the XREF command again to insert another copy of XREF1.
6. Use the Layer Control dialog box to freeze the layer XREF1|TEXT in the current drawing.
7. Save the current drawing as EX13.1.
8. Use the OPEN command to reopen EX13.1.
9. Check the visibility of the XREF1|TEXT layer.
10. Freeze the XREF1|TEXT again, and set VISRETAIN to 1.
11. Repeat Steps 7, 8, and 9.
12. Turn VISRETAIN off and save the current drawing as EX13.1.

✓ LEARNING CHECKPOINT

☐ What are the advantages of Xrefs compared to inserting drawings?
☐ Describe three ways in which the XREF command is accessed.
☐ What is a dependent symbol?
☐ What limitations apply to dependent symbols?
☐ What is the function of the VISRETAIN system variable?

Overlaying an External Reference

One potential problem with Xrefs comes from what is called ***circular referencing.*** This is what happens when two drawings reference each other. Consider the possibility in which a floor plan of an office is created in order to do office layout planning and maintenance of records. To plan for placement of equipment, the electrical layout for the building is attached as an external reference. Then at a later date, the electrical wiring of the building is revised. To plan the electrical layout to match the needs of the office, the office floor plan is attached to the electrical drawing as an external reference.

When attaching an external reference that references the current drawing, AutoCAD LT 98 displays the warning dialog box shown in Figure 13.6 and allows you to continue or cancel the operation.

CHAPTER 13 ||| External References and Multiview Drawing Layout   549

FIGURE 13.6 Attaching a reference file that references the current drawing creates what is called a circular reference.

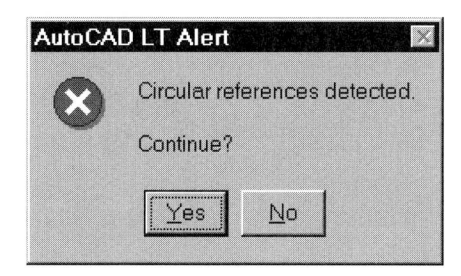

Selecting Yes to continue attaches the Xref and produces the following message:

Command: **XR**↵
XREF
Attach Xref _XR2: C:\Program Files\AutoCAD LT 98\Floorplan.dwg
Floorplan loaded.

Breaking circular reference from Floorplan to current drawing.

This indicates that the actual data from this drawing are being used, not the data referenced by the attached file. Although this method can be used, there is a much better way to handle this type of situation.

The way to avoid this situation is to overlay external references instead of attaching them. An attached Xref travels with the drawing it is attached to, but when the Overlay option is used, the external reference is not attached to the current drawing and does not travel with it as a nested Xref. This prevents the problem of circular referencing from occurring. The Overlay option can be accessed by picking the Overlay radio button from the Reference Type area of the Xref Attach dialog box, as shown in Figure 13.7.

FIGURE 13.7 Using the overlay option prevents circular referencing between referenced files.

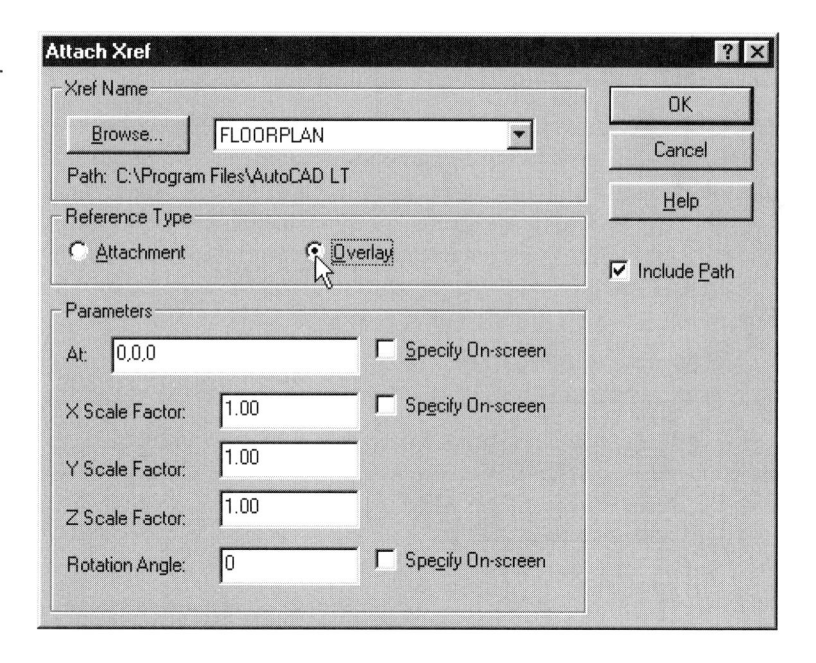

In this example, even when overlaying Floorplan into Elecplan, the circular referencing alert will still be displayed, because Elecplan is *attached* to Floorplan. However, when the Floorplan drawing is again opened, it does not have a circular reference back to itself, because the overlaid copy of Floorplan does not travel with the attached Elecplan reference.

> **Exercise 13.2**
>
> 1. Begin a new drawing.
> 2. Use the XREF Attach option to attach the drawing \AutoCAD LT 98\SAMPLE\XREF1 to the current drawing. Use 0,0 for the insertion point and default scale and rotation values. Use ZOOM ALL to see the entire drawing.
> 3. Save the drawing as EX13.2-ATTACH.
> 4. Open the drawing \AutoCAD LT 98\SAMPLE\XREF1.
> 5. Use the XREF command, and attempt to attach the drawing EX13.2-ATTACH. Notice the error message.
> 6. Begin a new drawing. *DO NOT* save changes to \AutoCAD LT 98\SAMPLE\XREF1.
> 7. Use the XREF Overlay option to overlay the drawing \AutoCAD LT 98\SAMPLE\XREF1 in the current drawing. Use 0,0 for the insertion point and default scale and rotation values. Use ZOOM ALL to see the entire drawing.
> 8. Save the drawing as EX13.2-OVERLAY.
> 9. Open the drawing \AutoCAD LT 98\SAMPLE\XREF1.
> 10. Use the XREF command, and attach the drawing EX13.2-OVERLAY. Use the default insertion parameters.
> 11. Begin a new drawing. *DO NOT* save changes to \AutoCAD LT 98\SAMPLE\XREF1.

Detaching an External Reference

Although you can erase an external reference, doing so does not remove the actual reference from the current drawing. All dependent symbol names remain defined even after erasing all copies of an Xref. The XREF Detach option is used to remove completely an Xref and all its dependent symbols. This is accessed by picking Detach in the External Reference dialog box. The currently highlighted Xref names are then detached.

External References and Demand Loading

AutoCAD LT 98 provides an Xref feature called demand loading. **Demand loading** increases the performance of AutoCAD LT by loading only the portion of a referenced drawing that is required to regenerate the current drawing. This means that information on layers that are frozen in the referenced drawing is not loaded with the xref.

In order to benefit from demand loading, the referenced drawing must first be saved with a layer index. To save a drawing with a layer index, the system variable named INDEXCTL is set to 1. As discussed in earlier chapters, any AutoCAD LT system variable can be adjusted by typing the variable name at the command line, as follows:

Command: **INDEXCTL**↵
New value for INDEXCTL <0>: **1**↵

This variable can also be set by using the SAVEAS command when saving the drawing. Select Save As ... from the File menu; then in the Save Drawing As dialog box, pick the Options ... button. From the Export Options dialog box, shown in Figure 13.8, pick the Index type: drop-down list to specify what type of indexing is to be saved with the drawing.

FIGURE 13.8 The INDEXCTL system variable can be set using the Export Options dialog box.

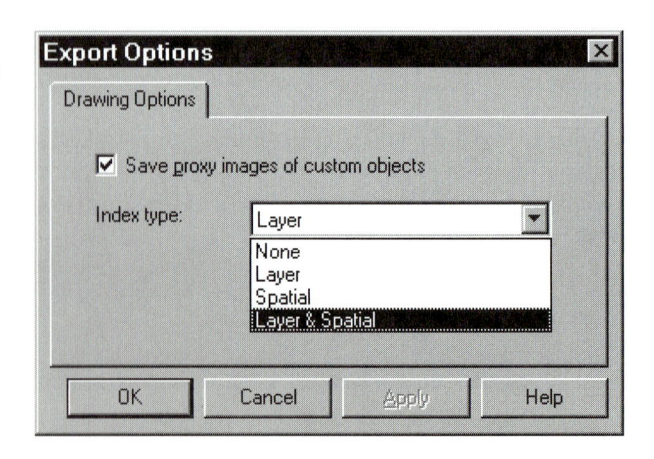

CHAPTER 13 ||| External References and Multiview Drawing Layout

The available settings for INDEXCTL are as follows:

Value	Index Type	Effect
0	None	No indexes are saved.
1	Layer	Layer states are indexed.
2	Spatial	Xref Clipping data are saved.
3	Layer and Spatial	Layer states and Xref Clipping data are saved.

> **Field Notes**
>
> Drawings created in AutoCAD Release 14 are able to create clipping boundaries so that only a specified portion of an externally referenced file is visible. AutoCAD LT 98 cannot create these boundaries, but if you are working with AutoCAD Release 14 drawings using AutoCAD LT 98, you should set INDEXCTL to save a spatial index.
>
> When working in an AutoCAD R14 drawing that contains clipped xrefs, set the XCLIPFRAME variable to 1 if you want to see the clipping boundaries.

Once INDEXCTL has been set in the referenced drawing, demand loading must be enabled in the drawing you are bringing the referenced file into. Demand loading is enabled under the System tab in the Preferences dialog box or by directly setting the XLOADCTL system variable. The settings for XLOADCTL are as follows:

Value	Effect
0	Demand load disabled.
1	Demand load enabled. Referenced file is kept open.
2	Demand load enabled. Copy of referenced file is opened.

When demand loading is disabled, AutoCAD LT 98 opens the referenced drawing, reads the entire file, and then closes it. With demand loading enabled, AutoCAD LT reads the file and loads the necessary information. However, the drawing is kept open in case more data must be loaded from the referenced file. While the drawing is kept open, it cannot be edited by anyone else. A setting of 2 forces AutoCAD LT to make a copy of the referenced file and keep the copy open. Thus, the original referenced file can be opened and edited by another user if necessary. This situation is often required in a networked environment where several CAD drafters are working on a single project and, therefore, sharing files.

Updating an External Reference

Each time you open a drawing with external references, the source files are read and the referenced drawing is displayed in its latest state. However, depending on your demand load settings, it may be possible for someone else to modify the referenced drawing while you are working in your current drawing. This is possible in a networked environment, where computers are interconnected and drawing files are shared. However, even on a stand-alone workstation, it is possible for you to have more than one session of AutoCAD LT active at once, so you could possibly change the definition of an Xref being referenced by a currently open drawing.

If an externally referenced drawing has been changed and you want to update the reference without having to reopen the current drawing, you can reload the referenced file by picking the Reload button in the External Reference dialog box. Highlight the files that you want to reload and pick reload. The file is not actually reloaded until you pick OK in the External Reference dialog box. The dependent symbols are automatically updated along with any changed drawing geometry or visibility adjustments to layers. All instances of this XREF in the current drawing are updated when the definition is reloaded.

The External Reference Directory Path

If the Include Path toggle in the Attach Xref dialog box is checked when referencing, an external reference is remembered by the drawing to which it is referenced by using the drive letter, directory path, and drawing file name of the Xref. If your directory structure changes or you move or rename the externally referenced file, any drawings referencing it cannot find the file where it is expected and AutoCAD LT is unable to resolve the Xref. As discussed earlier, when an Xref cannot be resolved, a text object representing the drive path and name of the Xref is displayed at the insertion point of the Xref to show that it exists in the drawing but was not resolved.

When this happens, you can change the path associated with an external reference by using the Save Path button in the Xref Found At area in the External Reference dialog box. If you know the path for the new location, you can simply type it in the text box. Otherwise, use the Browse ... button to display the Select New Path dialog box. Go to the new folder and select the file name to use for the referenced file. Note that this can be a completely new file name, or it can even be a completely different file if desired. Pick the Open button and you are returned to the External Reference dialog box. Pick the Save Path button; then pick OK. The drawing is then updated using the new reference file.

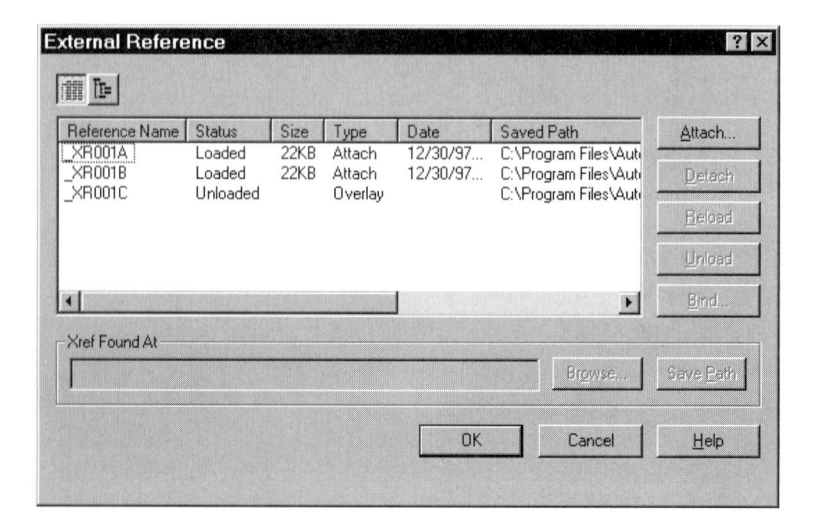

Although the original Xref is given the same name as the file referenced, if you change the path of an Xref, the name stays the same. Even when the name of the source file has changed, the name of the Xref in the drawing does not change in the current or in any future session. Once the path of an Xref is successfully changed, the new definition is immediately displayed in the drawing.

If the new path and file name cannot be resolved, the AutoCAD LT message dialog box is displayed, as shown in Figure 13.9.

FIGURE 13.9 This warning appears when AutoCAD LT cannot find the specified external drawing file.

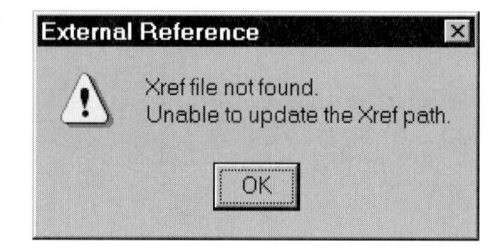

Unloading External References

The Unload button in the External Reference dialog box allows you to suppress the display and regeneration of the Xref definition. It does not remove it from the drawing, as with the Detach option. This is used primarily to speed up performance by reducing the amount of drawing information that needs to be regenerated. To restore the Xref in the drawing, use the Reload option.

Obtaining Information About External References

The External Reference dialog box has two display modes. The default display mode is the List View, which displays text information about the referenced files. Figure 13.10 shows an example of the External Reference dialog box in List View. The text information displayed includes the Reference Name, Status, file Size, attachment Type, Date modified, and the Saved Path. Similar to other Windows dialog boxes, the category buttons at the top of the list can be selected to sort the listing based on the information in that column.

FIGURE 13.10 The External Reference dialog box in List View.

CHAPTER 13 ||| External References and Multiview Drawing Layout 553

Alternatively, the listing can be shown as a Tree View. This is very useful for quickly identifying the status and relationships of the Xrefs in your drawing. Figure 13.11 shows the same dialog box as Figure 13.10, with Tree View active. Using this mode, you can quickly determine the nesting levels of your Xrefs, plus their current status. Note that _XR001B is a nested attachment to _XR001A, and _XR001C is a currently unloaded overlay. An arrow is displayed on the icon if an Xref is to be reloaded (up arrow) or unloaded (down arrow). If a question mark is displayed on an icon, it indicates that the Xref has been orphaned. An Xref is orphaned if the Xref it is nested in is unloaded.

FIGURE 13.11 The External Reference dialog box in Tree View.

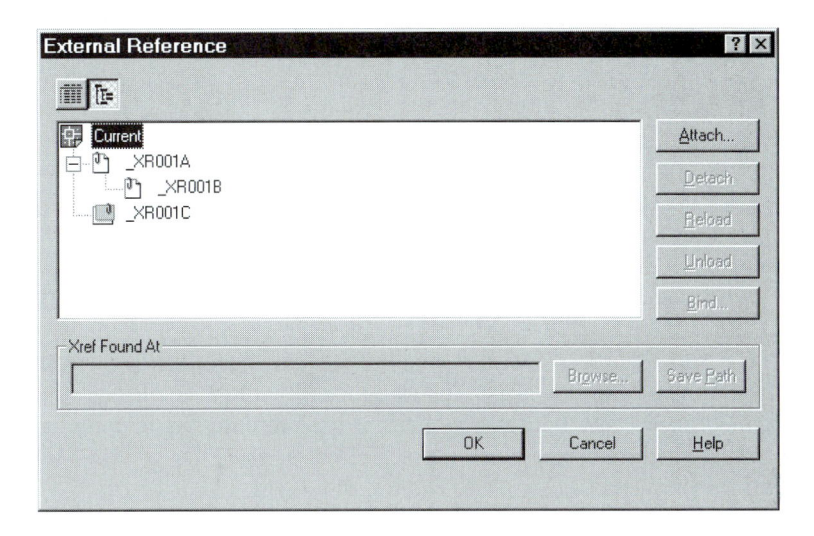

Field Notes

When sharing a drawing that has external references, it is necessary to include all of the Xref files as well as the actual drawing. Otherwise, any of the Xrefs that are not available will be unresolved when the drawing is opened, which may leave the drawing incomplete.

Using the Xref Log File

To assist you in keeping track of Xrefs, AutoCAD LT can generate an Xref log file. To turn this feature on, set the system variable XREFCTL to 1. By default, this variable is set to 0 and no log file is maintained. When this feature is activated, it is then active for all drawings—not just the one in which it is activated.

The file that is created is a standard ASCII text file that is given the same name as the drawing, but has an .XLG file extension. The Xref log file is created in the same directory location where the drawing file is found.

To set the XREFCTL variable, type **XREFCTL** at the Command: prompt:

Command: **XREFCTL**↵
New value for XREFCTL <0>: **1**↵

To turn this feature back off, set XREFCTL to 0 again. When you need to view or print this file, it can be opened with the Notepad text editing program. Figure 13.12 shows the Notepad program with an Xref log file loaded.

When XREFCTL is on, the Xref log file for any given drawing is updated each time an Xref command option is used to attach, overlay, reload, or detach an Xref, and each time the Xrefs in a drawing are resolved. A title block is written to the file as it is updated. For example, the following is a title block from the Xref log file shown in Figure 13.12:

```
==============================
Drawing: C:\Program Files\AutoCAD LT 98\Floorplan.dwg
Date/Time: 12/30/98 11:38:49
Operation: Attach Xref
==============================
```

FIGURE 13.12 The Notepad text editor program can be used to open the Xref log file for viewing or printing.

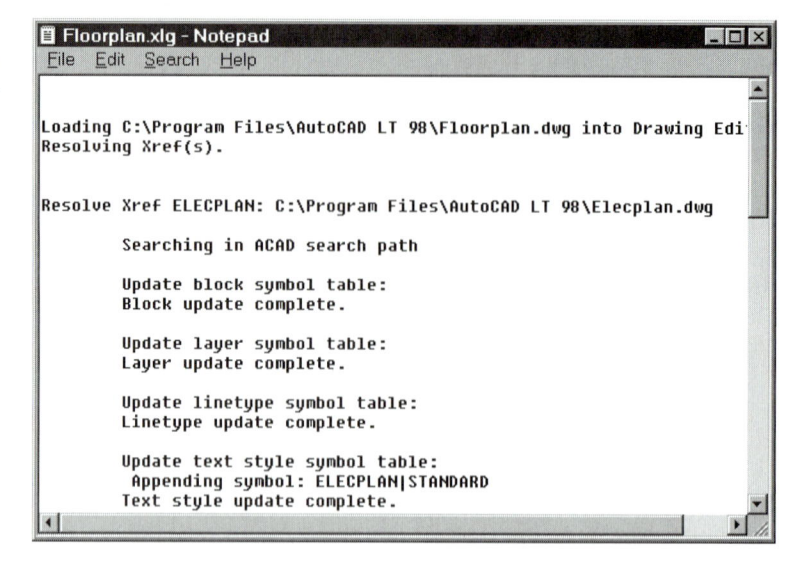

This title block confirms the drawing file name, provides a time and date stamp, and indicates what type of operation took place. Following this title block is a listing of the updates performed to each of the symbol tables. The term *symbol table* is used to describe the information stored regarding named objects such as blocks, linetypes, and text styles. Additionally, the Xref log indicates the nesting level of all Xrefs.

Field Notes

If XREFCTL is ON, and a drawing that is opened contains no external references, the .XLG file is written with the following information:

Loading C:\⟨*name of drawing*⟩ into Drawing Editor.
Resolving Xref(s)

But no actual information is entered regarding Xrefs, since none exists.

Exercise 13.3

1. Open the drawing EX13.2-OVERLAY for editing.
2. Set the XREFCTL variable to a value of 1.
3. Use the open command again to open EX13.2-OVERLAY.
4. Enter the XREF command and the Reload option.
5. Access the Path option of the XREF command, and change the XREF1 external reference path to \AutoCAD LT 98\SAMPLE\XREF2.DWG.
6. Use the Detach option of XREF to detach the Xref named XREF1.
7. Use the NOTEPAD program to open and view the Xref log file named EX13.2-OVERLAY.XLG.
8. Set XREFCTL to a value of 0.
9. Save the current drawing file as EX13.3.

LEARNING CHECKPOINT

☐ What are the advantages of an Xref Overlay compared to an Attached Xref?

☐ Which option is used to list the current external references in a drawing?

☐ How can an Xref be updated without reopening your drawing?

☐ Describe the purpose and use of the XREF Detach option.

CHAPTER 13 ||| External References and Multiview Drawing Layout   555

- What is an Xref log file?
- What variable controls the creation of Xref log files?
- What program can be used to open an Xref log file?
- How is an Xref log file named and where is it stored?
- What system variables control demand loading features?

Binding Xrefs

Sometimes, you might want to make an Xref a permanent part of the current drawing. This is a convenient way to share your drawings with others. Rather than including a base drawing and the source drawings for several different Xrefs, you can simply bind the Xrefs to make them a permanent part of the current drawing. This way, anyone else who needs to use your drawing has only one file to deal with instead of several. The process of permanently adding an Xref to the current drawing is called ***binding.*** Whether an Xref is attached or is an overlay, the Bind option can be used to bind it to the current drawing.

When you bind an Xref, all of the external drawing's dependent symbols also become part of the current drawing. The XREF Bind option is used when you want to bind an entire drawing. This option is accessed in the External Reference dialog box by highlighting the names of the Xrefs you want to bind and picking the Bind ... button. Note that when nested Xrefs are selected without their parent drawing, the Bind ... button is disabled and a message is displayed in the lower left area of the dialog box. If you bind an Xref that has nested Xrefs attached, the nested Xrefs are also bound to the current drawing. You can bind both attached and overlaid Xrefs.

When you select references to bind, the Bind Xrefs dialog box is displayed. See Figure 13.13. Here you must specify how the Xrefs are to be bound. The two options are Bind and Insert.

FIGURE 13.13 The Bind Xrefs dialog box allows you to specify how the Xref is brought in to the current drawing.

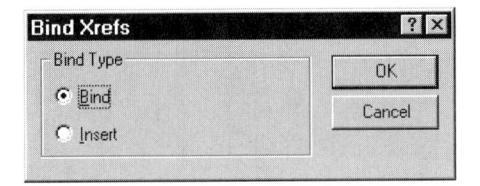

When an Xref is bound to the current drawing using the Bind option, all its dependent symbols are brought in also. To prevent possible conflicts, the names use a format similar to that used when they are dependent. The vertical bar character is replaced with a "0" (dollar sign, zero, dollar sign) sequence. So the dependent layer named XREF1|TEXT is renamed to XREF1$0$TEXT when it is permanently added to the current drawing. This is true of all dependent symbols; however, once added to the current drawing these items can be renamed as desired. The easiest way to rename named objects is to use the Rename dialog box accessed with RN or DDRENAME. The Layer Control dialog box shown in Figure 13.14 shows a list of layer names added to the current drawing as part of an XREF command Bind option.

FIGURE 13.14 The Layer & Linetype Control dialog box displays the new names of the bound layers.

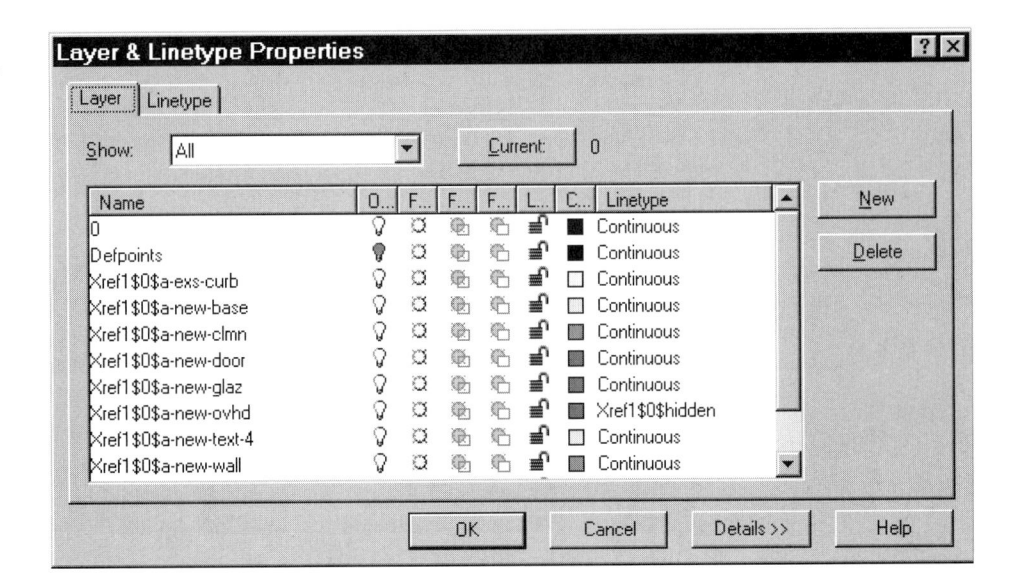

Once bound to the current drawing, the external reference is removed and the source geometry is added to the current drawing as a new block definition. Using the list option after binding an Xref shows that the external reference name does not show up anymore. However, the externally referenced drawing is now a block definition and acts like one in every way. Additional copies can be freely inserted using the INSERT or DDINSERT commands and, if needed, it can be exploded.

Using the Insert option in the Bind Xrefs dialog box brings in the geometry and dependent symbols but maintains no reference to the original Xref file. The results are similar to what would happen if you detached the Xref and inserted the file using DDINSERT. The primary difference is that an inserted drawing creates a block definition for the inserted drawing, and binding a reference with the Insert option does not. What this means is that the dependent symbols are stripped of the Xref name. When symbol names match, then the definition in the current drawing overrides that of the incoming definition.

Binding Dependent Symbols

Modify
 Object ▶
  External
  Reference
  Bind...
  XBIND
  XB

Oftentimes, a text style, dimension style, layer, linetype, or a block that you want to use exists in the current drawing as an Xref dependent symbol. As discussed earlier, dependent symbols cannot be used while they are dependent on an Xref. Rather than bind an entire Xref when you only need one or two items from it, you can bind dependent symbols into the current drawing on an individual basis. Doing this helps to decrease drawing file size. Binding an entire drawing brings all named objects with it and can also define the Xref as a block in the current drawing just as if you used the INSERT command. The XBIND command allows you to pick specific elements from an external reference drawing to import into the current drawing.

The XBIND command can be accessed by typing XB or XBIND at the Command: prompt. Optionally, you can select External Reference Bind ... from the Object cascade of the Modify menu. The XBIND command displays the Xbind dialog box, as shown in Figure 13.15. All Xrefs, whether attached or overlaid, are displayed in a tree view in the Xrefs list on the left side of the dialog box. Expand and collapse the branches of the Xrefs and Symbol Tables Categories by double-clicking or picking the "+" or "–" symbol. Empty categories cannot be expanded. Use the Add and Remove buttons to build your list of Definitions to Bind, and pick OK when you are finished.

In Figure 13.15, a block named XREF1|TAG-SECT was added to the Definitions to Bind list.

FIGURE 13.15 The Xbind dialog box provides an intuitive interface for making Xref dependent symbols available in the current drawing session.

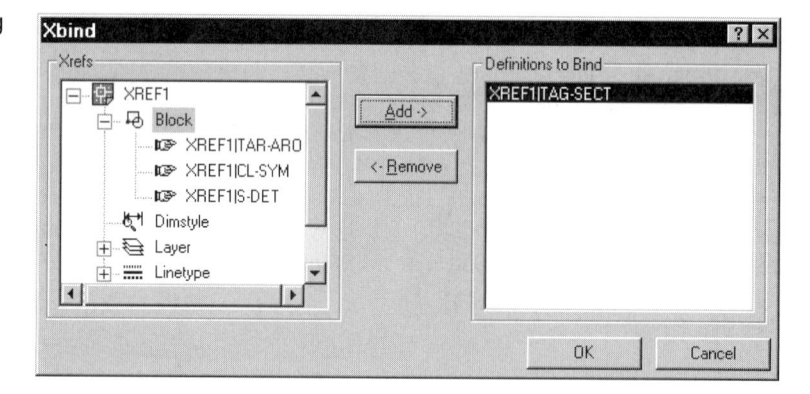

The binding process makes a dependent symbol a permanent part of the current drawing, even if the Xref is later detached. If the bound symbol is a layer, that layer becomes available for use. If the bound symbol is a block, the block becomes defined in the current drawing and is then available for insertion. Text styles, dimension styles, and linetypes can be made current and used as needed.

The previously dependent block is now renamed XREF1$0$TAG-SECT in the current drawing. This does not affect the source file for the external reference. Additionally, the next time you resolve the Xref by either opening the current drawing or reloading the Xref, the previously assigned name is again listed in any inquiries you make. So, for example, after binding the layer as just shown and reloading the Xref, both block names XREF1|TAG-SECT and XREF1$0$TAG-SECT now exist.

Figure 13.16 shows the text screen of AutoCAD LT with a listing of the defined blocks displayed. The listing shows that the Xref named XREF1 is still externally referenced, and the dependent symbols are appropriately labeled. In this case, the entire external reference named XREF2 has been bound and all of its dependent symbols have been defined in the current drawing. Any of the items not listed as Xref (External Ref-

CHAPTER 13 ||| External References and Multiview Drawing Layout   557

FIGURE 13.16 Once a dependent symbol is bound, AutoCAD LT changes its name and makes it available in the drawing in which it is bound.

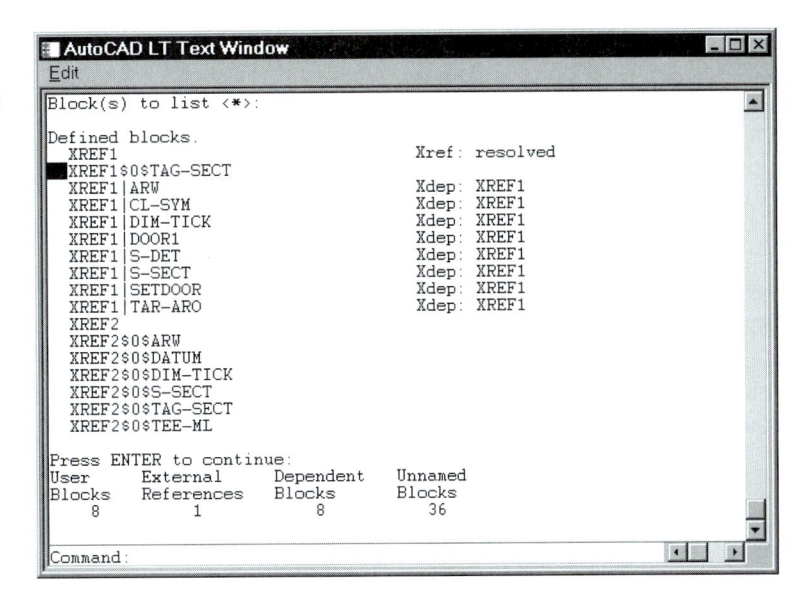

```
AutoCAD LT Text Window
Edit
Block(s) to list <*>:
Defined blocks.
    XREF1                        Xref: resolved
    XREF1$0$TAG-SECT
    XREF1|ARW                    Xdep: XREF1
    XREF1|CL-SYM                 Xdep: XREF1
    XREF1|DIM-TICK               Xdep: XREF1
    XREF1|DOOR1                  Xdep: XREF1
    XREF1|S-DET                  Xdep: XREF1
    XREF1|S-SECT                 Xdep: XREF1
    XREF1|SETDOOR                Xdep: XREF1
    XREF1|TAR-ARO                Xdep: XREF1
    XREF2
    XREF2$0$ARW
    XREF2$0$DATUM
    XREF2$0$DIM-TICK
    XREF2$0$S-SECT
    XREF2$0$TAG-SECT
    XREF2$0$TEE-ML

Press ENTER to continue:
User      External      Dependent    Unnamed
Blocks    References    Blocks       Blocks
  8           1            8           36

Command:
```

erence) or Xdep (Externally dependent) are now defined as blocks in the current drawing. Notice that the block name XREF1$0$TAG-SECT is not shown as an Xref-dependent symbol.

Field Notes

- When a particular dimension style, layering convention, text style, linetype, or block definition exists in another drawing, it can be quickly and easily defined in the current drawing even if you do not need to reference the drawing for any other reason. Here's how:

    1. XREF (Attach <u>OR</u> Overlay) the source drawing. Use the default settings.
    2. XBIND the needed items into the current drawing.
    3. XREF Detach the drawing.

    Now, the items you need are defined in the current drawing without unneeded overhead generated by inserting drawings.

- Whether listing blocks, text styles, or another dependent symbol, you can focus your search by specifying a pattern using the Xref name followed by an asterisk. For example, to list dependent symbols of XREF1, at the search prompt or in the Pattern text box, use the following search pattern:

    XREF1|*

- Binding dependent symbols leaves them with long and cumbersome names. The RENAME or DDRENAME command can be used to remove the unnecessary part of the name.

Exercise 13.4

1. Start a new drawing.
2. Examine the current setup layers, text styles, dimension styles, blocks, and linetypes.
3. Use XREF Attach to \AutoCAD LT 98\SAMPLE\XREF1.DWG.
4. Reexamine the layers, text styles, dimension styles, blocks, and linetypes.
5. Bind the entire XREF1 drawing to the current drawing using XREF Bind.
6. Reexamine the layers, text styles, dimension styles, blocks, and linetypes.
7. Use XREF Overlay to overlay \AutoCAD LT 98\SAMPLE\XREF2.DWG.
8. Use XBIND to bind the XREF2|TAG-SECT dependent block.
9. Rename XREF2|TAG-SECT to TAG-SECT2.
10. Save the drawing as EX13.4.

✓ LEARNING CHECKPOINT

- ☐ Explain the use of the XREF Bind option.
- ☐ How does XREF Bind differ from XBIND?
- ☐ What is an advantage of selectively binding dependent symbols?
- ☐ Describe the naming convention for bound symbols.

Multiview Drawing Layout

While a drawing is being created onscreen, the layout is very flexible because you can use display change options such as Pan and Zoom to view any portion of the drawing you need to see. All of the geometry you create in a CAD drawing is always drawn on a 1-1 scale. This means that one AutoCAD LT drawing unit represents one real-world measurement unit. You may frequently be drawing objects that are much larger than the paper you will be producing your final plotted drawing on, particularly if you are doing architectural drafting or any other large-format drawings.

Engineering and architectural drawings often require several views of the part or building you are drawing, and these views are usually presented at varying scale factors for the best clarity. For example, on a small mechanical part, an enlarged detail, for example, a 4:1 scale may be needed in order to dimension the part adequately. In an architectural drawing, the floor plan is presented at a specific scale (for example, 1/4″ = 1′0″). The stair and footer details look better when plotted at a slightly larger scale, such as 1/2″ = 1′0″. Finally, a title block and border are placed around the completed views and the composite image is plotted at a scale of 1″ = 1″. The term *composite* refers to the combination of views, border, and title block. In a manual drawing, producing the final composite image is easy because each view is drawn at varied scales. In a CAD drawing all of the geometry is created at full size, but it can be displayed at different scale factors when creating the final multiview layout. The term *multiview layout* is used to describe a drawing that shows more than one view of the object drawn. Multiview layouts are commonly used in most drafting disciplines to communicate all of the required information.

Presenting varied views of a drawing at differing scales, all on the same sheet, is achieved using an AutoCAD LT feature known as paper space. *Paper space* is a special drawing environment intended only for creating a final layout of your drawing for plotting purposes.

This section discusses the differences in concepts and applications of paper space and model space. The term *model space* refers to space where you create the geometry that defines your model, or drawing. Regardless of whether the drawing you are working on is a two-dimensional or a three-dimensional representation of an object, the geometry you create to define the object is referred to as the *model*.

Model Space Concepts

There are two named spaces in which AutoCAD LT objects can exist, model space and paper space. Model space provides a three-dimensional coordinate system and a practically unlimited area for the construction of two- and three-dimensional drawings of objects that can be virtually any size. Although you can draw many types of objects in paper space, the drawing model should be created within model space. In addition to allowing for more flexibility when generating the final drawing layout, model space offers some distinct advantages when creating a drawing.

When working in model space, you have access to some commands and options that are not available in paper space. For example, AutoCAD LT does not allow three-dimensional display change commands to be used in paper space. Three-dimensional display changes are discussed in Chapter 14. The UCSFOLLOW system variable is ignored when paper space is active.

All of the drawing exercises and problems you have done so far have been done in model space. When you start a new drawing from scratch, using quick setup or any of the supplied drawing templates, you automatically start out in model space. This makes sense, because your first task is usually to draw the model; then you annotate and plot it later.

One setup is available to start you out in a way that allows you to see the drawing layout (paper space) while you work in model space. This is accomplished by using the Advanced Setup Wizard, and setting up your model and paper space preferences on Step 7: Layout, as shown in Figure 13.17. The Advanced Setup Wizard was introduced in Chapter 3.

FIGURE 13.17 The Advanced Setup Wizard allows you to start out being able to view the final layout by starting in paper space.

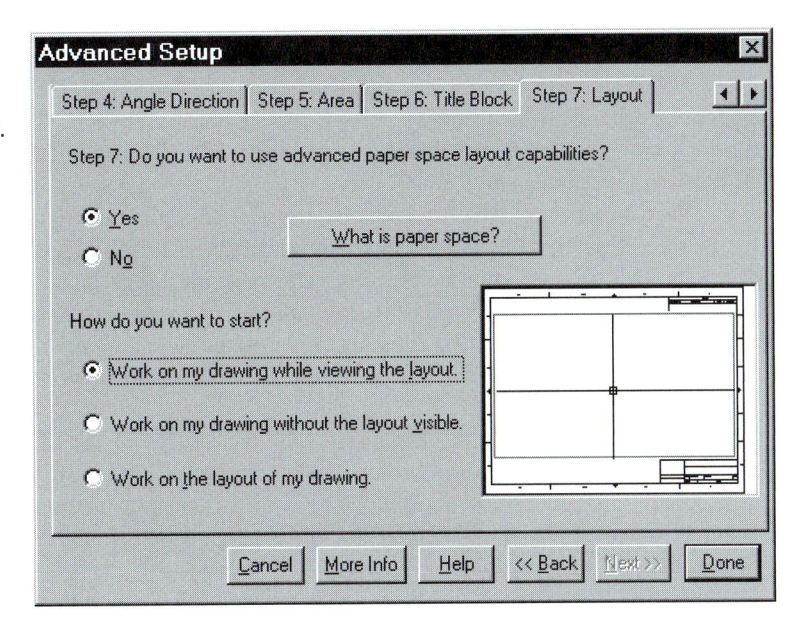

You can select each of the setup options in Step 7 to see an immediate display in the preview window. This display represents the results of the current settings. Although it is possible to have both model and paper space visible at once, it can waste valuable screen space to have paper space visible while you are still creating your model. It is recommended that you simply work in model space until it is time to work on the final layout of your drawing, or time to create a hardcopy image.

Paper Space Concepts

When the model is complete, it is time to enter paper space and do the drawing layout. Because AutoCAD LT provides automatic scaling features for dimensions, it is usually a good idea to wait until after you complete the layout to finish dimensioning the part.

As previously discussed, the primary function of paper space is to provide an area to set up the drawing layout and generate a plotted hardcopy. Essentially, paper space is used to represent the "paper" on which you lay out your views, set up a title block, and provide the appropriate annotation after completing the actual model. Consider placing an object on your desk and then holding a sheet of paper in front of the object. You would not be able to see the object through the paper. This is the case with paper space also. When you enter paper space, you can no longer see your model, because you have placed a sheet of "paper" between you and the drawing. To see the object on your desk you need to cut a hole in the paper that you can look through to see the model. In paper space, you can create "holes" called *floating model space viewports* that look through the "paper" into model space. Figure 13.18 demonstrates this concept.

FIGURE 13.18 Paper space is used to create a drawing layout for plotting purposes. To see through the "paper" into model space, "holes" called *floating model space viewports* are cut from the paper.

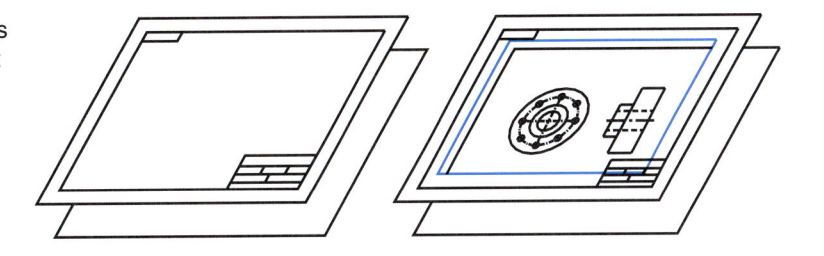

Each viewport can display the same or different views of model space. Varied scale factors can be used. In the case of a 3-D drawing, you can even set up each viewport to look at the model from a different 3-D viewing angle. Additionally, layer visibility can be controlled for individual viewports so that some viewports only display objects on specific layers. Understanding the use and control of floating model space viewports is necessary to effectively use the paper space drawing environment.

Switching to Paper Space

The TILEMODE system variable controls whether viewports created in your drawing are displayed as nonoverlapping display areas known as tiled model space viewports, or as movable, resizable display elements referred to as floating model space viewports. When TILEMODE is set to 1 (on), the active area of your drawing is known as *tiled model space.* By default, model space is displayed as a single viewport tile that fills the entire display area. The creation and use of multiple tiled viewports is discussed later.

Setting TILEMODE to 0 makes paper space active. The TILEMODE setting can be changed by typing **TM** or **TILEMODE** and entering the new value. Picking Model Space (Floating) or Model Space (Tiled) from the View pull-down menu sets TILEMODE to 0 or 1, respectively. Additionally, you can toggle TILEMODE by double-clicking the TILE button on the status bar. One easy way to determine the current value of TILEMODE is by the appearance of the text on the TILE button. The text is dark when TILEMODE is on, and gray when it is off.

Another unique feature in each space is the appearance of the UCS icon. To see the difference, with TILEMODE on, use the UCSICON command to activate the icon in model space. Then go to paper space by setting TILEMODE to 0. Now use the UCSICON command to activate the icon in paper space. Refer to Chapter 11 if you need to review the UCSICON command. The model space and paper space UCS icons are shown in Figure 13.19.

Setting TILEMODE to 0 activates paper space. It may help to think of paper space as being a sheet of paper that is placed between you and the drawing. To see into model space it is necessary to cut a "hole," or model space viewport, in the paper. As mentioned previously, a model space viewport allows you to see through the paper into model space. Changing the value of TILEMODE using either the keyboard or the status bar toggle places you in paper space, but does not create any model space viewports. As indicated by the prompt issued when TILEMODE is set to 0, the MVIEW command is used to create floating model space viewports. The TILE button on the status bar is double-clicked in the following sequence:

```
Command: _tilemode
New value for TILEMODE <1>: 0
Entering paper space. Use MVIEW to insert model space viewports.
Regenerating drawing.
```

FIGURE 13.19 (A) The UCS icon in model space and (B) the UCS icon in paper space.

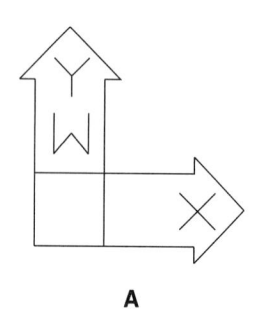

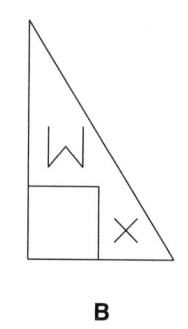

Floating Model Space Viewports

View
Floating
Viewports
MVIEW
MV

If you enter paper space by picking Model Space (Floating) from the View menu or toolbar, AutoCAD LT checks to see if a model space viewport has already been created in paper space. If no model space viewports exist yet, the MVIEW command is started automatically. To start the MVIEW command after you are already in paper space, type **MV** or **MVIEW,** pick Model Space (Floating) or one of the options from the Floating Viewports cascade of the View menu, or pick the Model Space (Floating) button from the Space flyout on the Standard toolbar. The MVIEW command can only be used in paper space. MVIEW offers a wide variety of command options for setting up a model space viewport layout. In addition to these initial setup options, you can use MVIEW at a later time to create additional viewports as needed.

The default option of MVIEW is a single viewport defined by picking two opposite corners, similar to using the RECTANG command. This allows you to draw a single viewport placed anywhere in the drawing area. Using this option allows the greatest flexibility because you can place and size the view as desired, and then repeat the command to draw additional viewports. The MVIEW command works like this:

CHAPTER 13 ||| External References and Multiview Drawing Layout   561

Command: **MV** or **MVIEW**↵
ON/OFF/Hideplot/Fit/2/3/4/Restore/<First Point>: ⟨enter a point⟩
Other corner: ⟨enter another point⟩
Regenerating drawing.

After specifying the two corners of the floating model space viewport, the rectangle opens a hole through the "paper" to display the currently active view of the model space work area centered within the floating viewport. The view of your drawing that was displayed in the active tiled viewport before you entered paper space is the active model space view. This same view is redisplayed when you return to tiled model space by setting TILEMODE to 1.

If you need to work with one viewport and you want it to fill your screen, use the Fit option of the MVIEW command. This creates a new floating model space viewport the same size as the current view:

Command: **MV** or **MVIEW**↵
ON/OFF/Hideplot/Fit/2/3/4/Restore/<First Point>: **F**↵
Regenerating drawing.

Other options of the MVIEW command can be used to create more than one floating viewport at a time. Look at Figure 13.20 as you review the following uses of the MVIEW command. The numeric options of MVIEW create the indicated number of viewports. For example, to create two viewports at the same time, the following approach can be used:

Command: **MV** or **MVIEW**↵
ON/OFF/Hideplot/Fit/2/3/4/Restore/<First Point>: **2**↵
Horizontal/<Vertical>: ↵
Fit/<First Point>: **F**↵
Regenerating drawing.

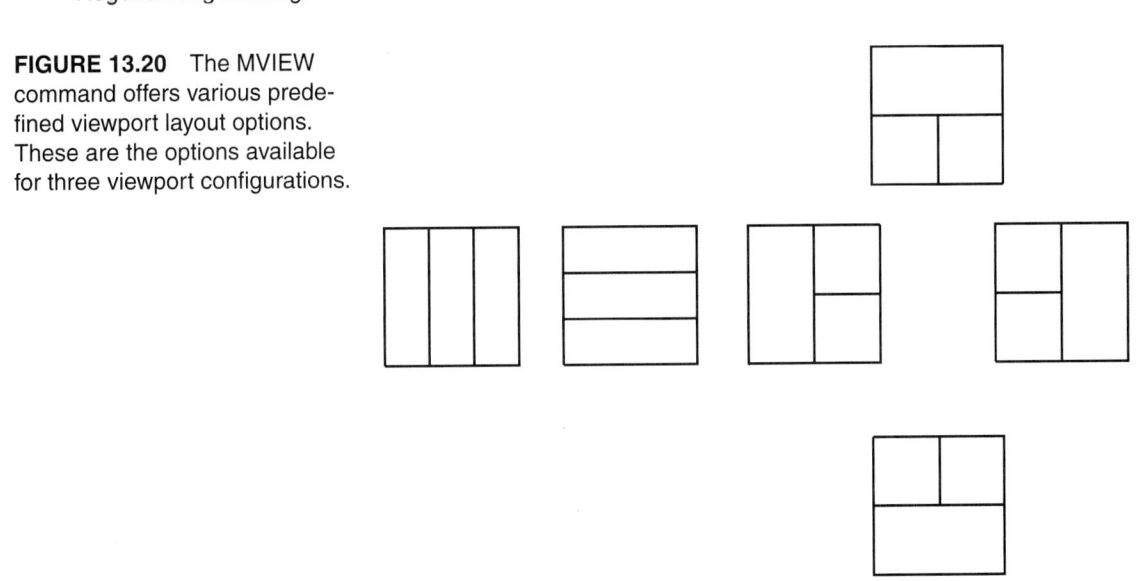

FIGURE 13.20 The MVIEW command offers various predefined viewport layout options. These are the options available for three viewport configurations.

Two viewports are placed within the described area, just as with the previously demonstrated single-viewport option. The Horizontal or Vertical option controls whether the viewports have the same horizontal or vertical dimension as the area specified in the following prompt. The default Vertical option places two viewports side by side that have the same vertical dimension as the specified window, or of the current view if Fit was specified. The Horizontal option places one viewport above the other, each with the same horizontal dimension as the window or Fit area.

The 3 Viewport option provides additional choices for viewport layout. With most of the three viewport layouts, one viewport fills half of the specified area and the other two viewports fill the remaining half. The choice of Right, Left, Above, or Below determines the placement of the large viewport. Optionally, you can specify a column of three by entering Horizontal or a row of three viewports using the Vertical option. The following sequence creates the viewport configuration shown in Figure 13.21:

Command: **MV** or **MVIEW**⏎
ON/OFF/Hideplot/Fit/2/3/4/Restore/<First Point>: **3**⏎
Horizontal/Vertical/Above/Below/Left/<Right>: ⏎
Fit/<First Point>: **F**⏎
Regenerating drawing.

FIGURE 13.21 When using the Fit option, the viewports fill the currently visible area in the paper space.

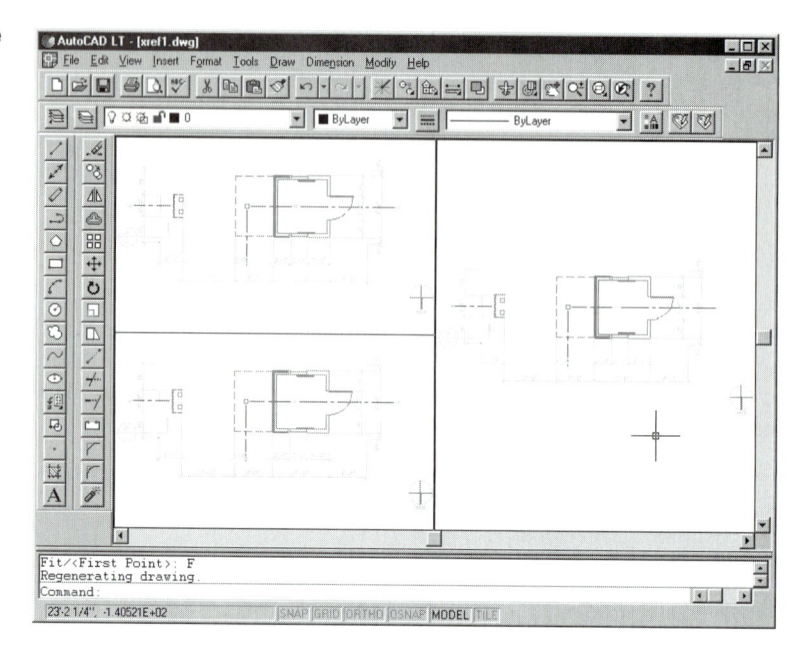

The 4 Viewport choice offers only the window or Fit options and fills the specified area with an arrangement of viewports that is two viewports high and two viewports wide.

Command: **MV** or **MVIEW**⏎
ON/OFF/Hideplot/Fit/2/3/4/Restore/<First Point>: **4**⏎
Fit/<First Point>: ⟨*pick first point*⟩
Second point: ⟨*pick second point*⟩
Regenerating drawing.

Exercise 13.5

1. Open an existing drawing containing geometry created in model space.
2. From model space, pick Paper Space from the View pull-down menu.
3. Observe the results. Notice that a single viewport was automatically created because no viewport previously existed.
4. Use the U command to undo the viewport and return to model space.
5. Double-click on the TILE button on the status bar. Using this method, no viewports are created.
6. Try each of the viewport creation options on the Floating Viewports cascade on the View menu, using the U command to undo each one before trying the next.
7. Set up the final viewport configuration to be 3 Viewports using the Right and Fit options.
8. Save the drawing as EX13.5.

After creating model space viewports, you are still in paper space. The floating model space viewport allows you to see the objects in model space, but you cannot select, edit, or directly dimension them while you are in paper space. You cannot select a model space object from paper space by picking or any other means. If you use the selection option "ALL" at a Select objects: prompt, only the items found in the current space are found. In the following sequence, a single floating viewport exists in paper space:

Command: **SE** or **SELECT**↵
Select objects: **ALL**↵
385 found
383 were not in current space.
1 was the paper space viewport.
Command: **SE** or **SELECT**↵
Select objects: **PREVIOUS**↵
1 found
Select objects: ↵
Command:

Study the prompts in the previous example carefully. Although there are 385 objects in the drawing, 383 of those objects are in model space and cannot be selected. One of the objects found is the actual paper space viewport, but this cannot be selected either. As a verification to see what was actually selected, the SELECT command that follows uses the PREVIOUS option. This shows that the only object selected by the ALL specification in this example was the floating model space viewport.

Floating model space viewports are AutoCAD LT drawing objects, similar to lines, arcs, and circles. Therefore, floating model space viewports can be freely edited, with a few limitations. You can move them about in paper space using the MOVE command or GRIP editing to position them as desired. Floating viewports can be resized horizontally or vertically using the STRETCH and SCALE commands, or through GRIP editing. You can move or resize a viewport regardless of which MVIEW option was used to create the layout. In a multiple-viewport layout, each viewport is a separate object and can be edited independent of the others. Resizing a viewport does not affect the size of the model, nor does it change the apparent size of the geometry displayed within the viewport (Figure 13.22).

A floating model space viewport can be duplicated with many of the standard AutoCAD LT duplication commands. Floating viewports can be copied, mirrored, and even arrayed, but they cannot be rotated. Trying to rotate a floating viewport simply moves it around the selected base point, but does not change its actual orientation.

FIGURE 13.22 Resizing viewports is very easy using grips.

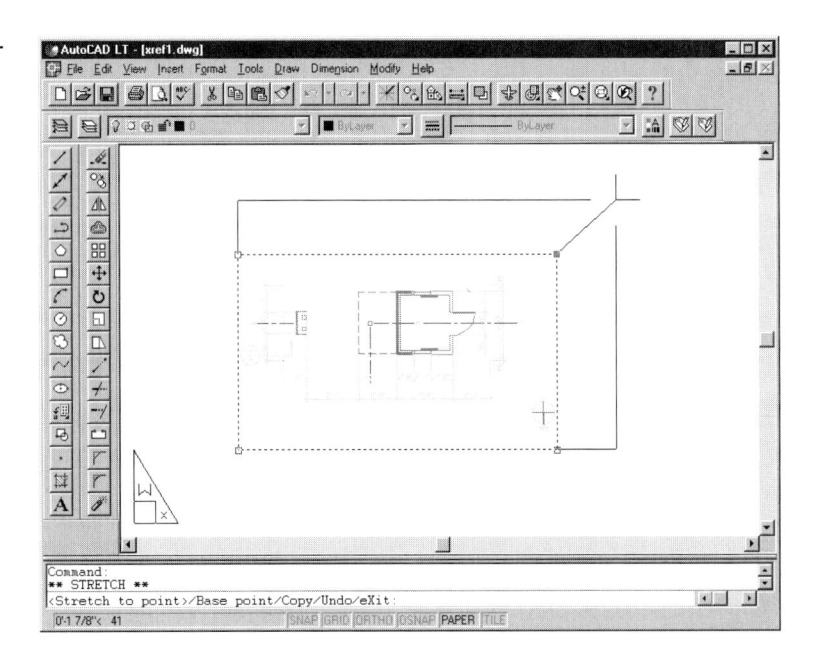

Field Notes

- Grip selecting a single corner grip on a floating viewport provides a fast and easy way to resize viewports. With ORTHO off, you can freely move the corner to resize the viewport both vertically and horizontally at the same time. Toggling ORTHO on restricts the movement of the corner to vertical or horizontal movements, or the current polar snap angle increment.
- Editing floating model space viewports does not affect the model space objects in any way.
- Irregularly shaped viewports can be simulated by copying a viewport and locating the copy in the exact same location as the original. Now use grip editing to move the corners of the copy to the new desired location. Using this technique keeps the model in the same apparent position, and allows you to create L-shaped viewports. With additional copies you can make even more complex shapes when required to show a specific view.

Floating model space viewports can be erased when they are no longer needed in the drawing. Regardless of what kind of edit you perform on a floating model space viewport, the model space drawing objects displayed in it are completely unaffected. To help you understand, think of the viewport simply as an opening that you look through to see objects in model space. Closing or moving the opening has no effect on the objects you see through the viewport. Additionally, any objects created in paper space are not visible in model space, including the floating viewports. You can draw or insert a title block and border and add any desired notation in paper space, all without affecting the model.

Virtually any number of floating model space viewports can be created in a drawing. Although there is no specific limit to the number of viewports that can be created in a drawing, there is a limit to the number that can be active at the same time. A viewport is referred to as *active* when it is on and displaying an area of model space.

The maximum number of viewports that can be active at the same time is determined by your operating system and display driver. The maximum number of active viewports can also be controlled by the setting of the AutoCAD LT system variable named MAXACTVP. The default for MAXACTVP is 16, which is a commonly used value because you will seldom need to display more than 16 viewports in a drawing. As with most system variables, MAXACTVP can be set by typing its name at the Command: prompt:

Command: **MAXACTVP**↵
New value for MAXACTVP <16>: **20**↵
Command:

The MAXACTVP variable does not accept any value that is beyond the capabilities of your system. If you try to set a value that is too high, you get this message:

Command: **MAXACTVP**↵
New value for MAXACTVP <16>: **49**↵
Requires an integer between 2 and 48.
New value for MAXACTVP <16>: **48**↵
Command:

Field Notes

- The MAXACTVP variable can be set to a low value to increase your system performance. Inactive viewports are left blank, and their contents are not regenerated.
- The paper space viewport is counted in the number of active viewports. This means that if MAXACTVP is 16, only 15 model space viewports can be active at once.

The MVIEW command also provides options for turning viewports on and off. When a viewport is off, it is left blank and is not regenerated. It is a common practice to turn off viewports that are needed for the final layout, but not for the current drawing task. The MVIEW command also provides an option to turn viewports on.

The Hideplot option is used to force viewports to remove hidden lines when plotting from paper space. This is used more commonly in 3-D work, where some objects may be behind others in the drawing.

The MVIEW command also allows the use of saved named tiled Vport configurations as a model for setting up the floating model space viewports. The term *Vport* is used in reference to tiled model space viewports. These options are discussed later in this chapter.

> ### Exercise 13.6
> 1. Open EX13.5 for editing.
> 2. While in paper space, try selecting a model space object that is visible through the model space viewport.
> 3. Grip select a viewport and resize it using the grip points with the Ortho setting off.
> 4. Grip select a viewport and resize it using the grip points with the Ortho setting on.
> 5. Set MAXACTVP to 3. Use ZOOM Extents to force a regeneration and observe the results.
> 6. Notice that one viewport has been deactivated. Paper space counts as the first viewport and the three floating model space viewports make a total of four viewports, but MAXACTVP only allows three to be active.
> 7. Use the MVIEW command and the On option to turn the blank viewport on and observe the results. Another viewport is deactivated to respect the MAXACTVP setting.
> 8. Save the drawing as EX13.6.

Working with Floating Model Space Viewports

The fundamental use of a model space viewport is to display different areas of a drawing at the same time and at various scale factors in order to generate the desired plotted drawing. AutoCAD LT allows you to specify the viewing area and set up a specific scale for each viewport, giving you real flexibility for generating complex multiview layouts of your drawings.

To make your control of what is displayed in each model space viewport easier, AutoCAD LT provides a way of controlling layer visibility for individual viewports. This allows for the reduction of unnecessary detail, and for the same areas to be shown in more than one viewport and dimensioned at varied scales without interfering with each other.

It is possible to access the drawing model from inside of a floating model space viewport. Most of the work you do on your drawing model is done while TILEMODE is on. This gives you the greatest amount of display area in which to work. If needed, however, you can work on your model inside of any of the active floating model space viewports.

Grid and snap settings are also local to individual viewports, which means that these drawing aids can be on or off in different viewports and they can each have different settings.

Changing the Scale of a Viewport

As with model space, objects created in paper space are drawn at a scale factor of 1 to 1. Also, to maximize the benefit of paper space, your final plots are made in paper space at a scale of 1 to 1. All changes to the apparent scale of geometry displayed in the final plot are made within the individual floating model space viewports.

To make any adjustments or do any editing within a floating model space viewport, you must first enter model space. To enter model space through a viewport, the MSPACE command is used instead of changing the value of TILEMODE, which would return you to tiled model space. The MSPACE command can only be used in paper space, meaning that TILEMODE must already be set to 0 and at least one active model space viewport defined.

The MSPACE command is activated by typing **MS** or **MSPACE** at the Command: prompt, picking the Model Space (Floating) button from the Space flyout on the Standard toolbar, or by picking Model Space (Floating) from the View menu. Another way to toggle the current space is by using the space button on the status bar. The current space is reported by this button reading either Paper or Model. If you are currently in paper space and one or more model space viewports are available, double-click the space button to move to Model space.

When you first enter model space, the border of the current viewport is highlighted and the cursor appears only within the boundaries of that viewport. When the cursor is moved outside of the viewport boundary, it changes from crosshairs into a system cursor, or arrow. Figure 13.23 shows the appearance of the cursor both inside and outside of the model space viewport while model space is active. You are now in model space again, and any changes made to the drawing in the viewport directly affect your model.

To change the apparent scale of the area of the drawing displayed in the viewport, the ZOOM XP option is used. The designation *XP* means *times paper space*. Using the XP option displays model space at a scale directly relative to paper space, and paper space is representative of the real-world size since it will be plotted at 1:1. Therefore, to display the drawing geometry at 1/2 scale, use the ZOOM command and specify .5XP or 1/2XP. Displaying the model at double scale or 2:1 is done using ZOOM 2XP. The ability to use direct fractions makes it easy to set up the scale. For example, to set up 1/4″=1′0″ scale, use 1/48XP. This is because there are four 1/4″ in 1″ and there are twelve 1″ in 1′, so the equation is $4 \times 12 = 48$ and the resultant XP factor is 1/48. To present another example, consider setting a viewport to display at 1/8″=1′0″: There are eight 1/8″ in 1″ and again 12″ in 1′, the equation is $8 \times 12 = 96$, so the resultant XP factor is 1/96.

FIGURE 13.23 (A) When model space is active, the crosshairs are shown only within the boundaries of the viewport. (B) Moving the pointer outside of the viewport boundary displays the system cursor.

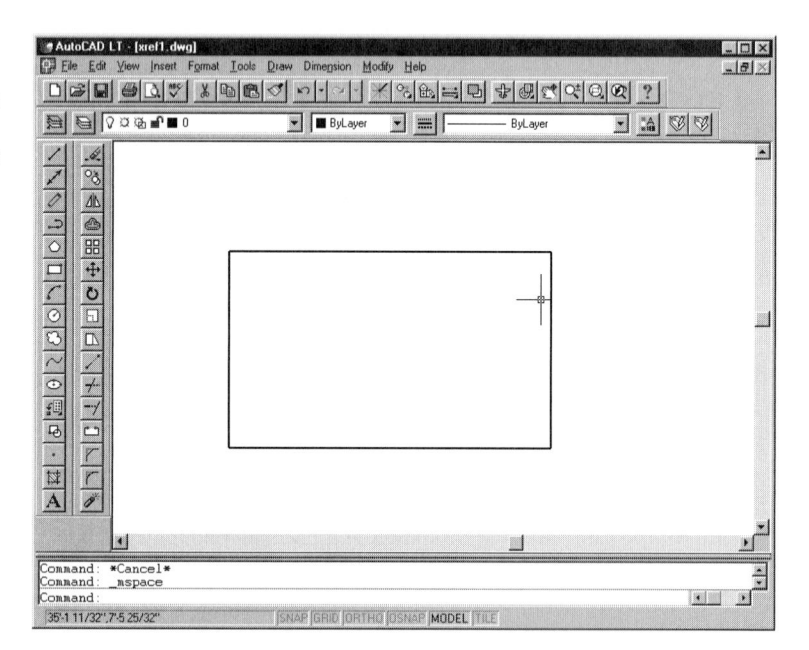

A

B

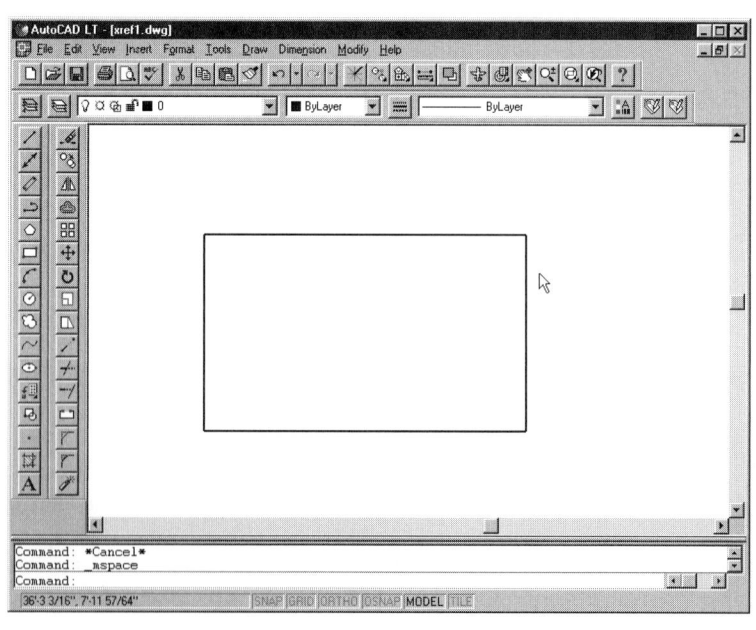

CHAPTER 13 ||| External References and Multiview Drawing Layout

A model space viewport acts the same as tiled model space with regards to most display change tools. To change the view displayed within the viewport, you must first switch to model space within the viewport you want to change. You can use the ZOOM, PAN, or VIEW commands with the same results as in tiled model space. ZOOM Extents displays the model space geometry as large as possible in the viewport, ZOOM All displays the drawing limits or extents, and a ZOOM Window displays the selected window within the viewport. When using the View Control dialog box, you will notice that the views have the space they belong to listed to the right of the name. You can restore only views made in the current space.

Field Notes

Sometimes, you may simply wish to display the model space geometry at the largest possible scale. If you are not sure what scale to use, you can use the ZOOM Extents option. Then, after zooming to the extents in the viewport, switch to paper space and use the LIST command to list the properties of the viewport. One of the items displayed in the listing is the *Scale relative to Paper space;* which tells you the currently displayed XP value. If, for example, the reported scale was .1317XP, this is very close to .125 or 1/8. Using a ZOOM .125XP option sets the viewport to display at a scale of 1:8.

To make a different model space viewport active, move the pointing device until the cursor points at the desired viewport and press the pick button. The crosshairs are moved to the selected viewport and its border is highlighted.

Exercise 13.7

1. Open EX13.6 for editing.
2. Set MAXACTVP to allow all three of the viewports to be displayed at one time.
3. In paper space, use the ZOOM Extents option to force a drawing regeneration and update the display.
4. In model space, use the ZOOM XP option to set up different scale factors in each of the three viewports.
5. Save the drawing as EX13.7.

Changing Layer Visibility in a Floating Model Space Viewport

The capability to control layer visibility in specific viewports provides tremendous flexibility for setting up your multiview layout. One situation where this will help is when a model has very small features that must be dimensioned in a separate viewport from the main model. For example, in Figure 13.24 a section view is shown in tiled model space that has a very small feature. The small feature cannot be dimensioned at the same scale as the rest of the drawing without crowding the dimensions, so it has been dimensioned with DIMSCALE set to .25. To facilitate the use of viewport-specific layer control, the full size dimensions are on one layer, and the 1/4 size dimensions are on another.

After completing the model, paper space is entered and two viewports are created. In the first viewport, ZOOM 1XP and adjust the viewport boundaries from paper space appropriately to display the entire view. Make the second viewport active, zoom in to the desired display area, and then ZOOM 4XP. Now, use the appropriate panning commands to center the view and adjust the viewport size and shape from paper space, if necessary. The resulting view looks like the view shown in Figure 13.25, and is not yet complete because all of the dimensions are still visible in both viewports.

To control the visibility of layers in specific viewports, use the VPLAYER command. This command is accessed by typing **VL** or **VPLAYER** at the Command: prompt. The VPLAYER command offers options to freeze, thaw, freeze new layers, control the visibility of layers in viewports yet to be created, reset changes to defaults, or even list the names of all of the layers currently frozen in a particular viewport.

VPLAYER
VL

FIGURE 13.24 Two different scales of dimensioning are required on this drawing. The dimensioning has been completed in model space, and the visibility control is to be established after setting up model space viewports from paper space.

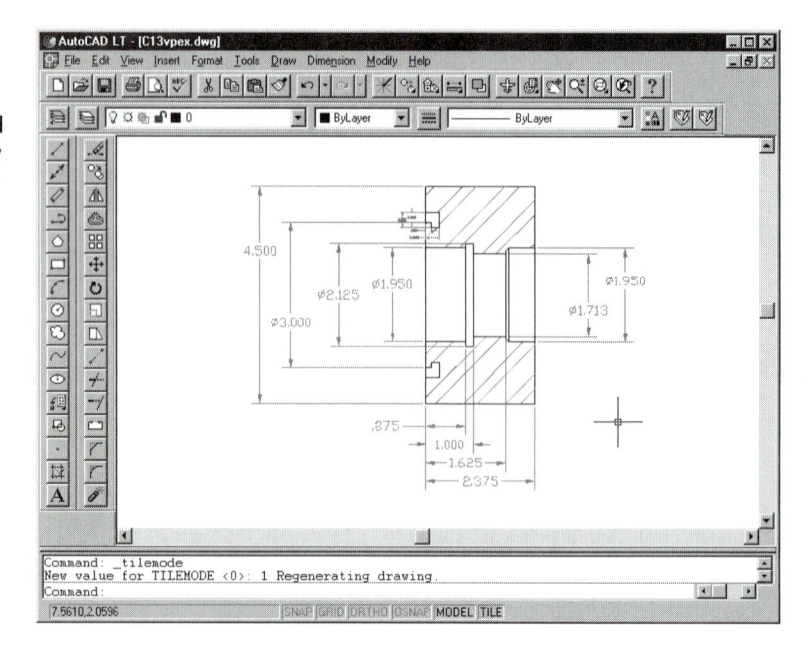

FIGURE 13.25 The two viewports are set up at different scales, but all of the dimensions are still visible in both viewports.

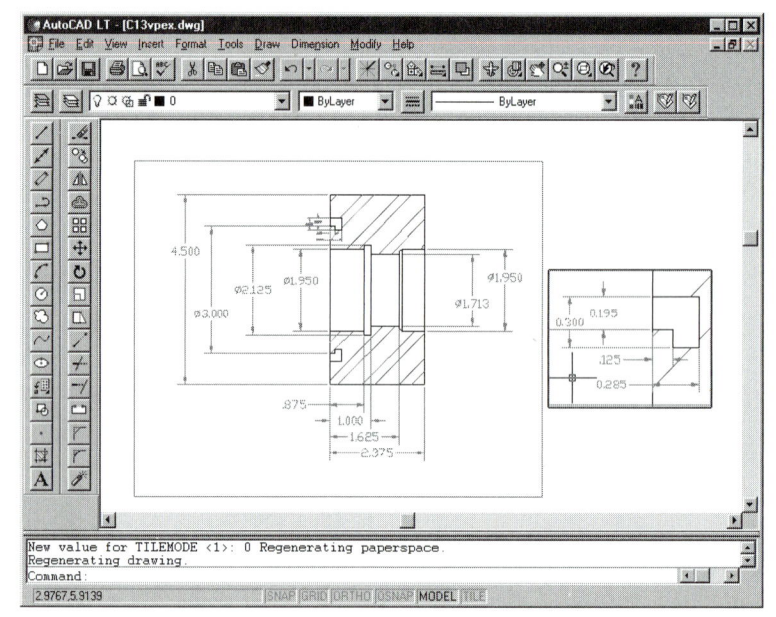

> ### Field Notes
>
> - When specifying layer names for the VPLAYER command, you can simplify matters by using wild cards for designation of multiple layer names.
> - To use a VPLAYER option on all layers introduced by a particular Xref, use the wild card XREFNAME|*, substituting the actual name of the Xref for XREFNAME. For example, all dependent layers in the Xref named XREF1.DWG can be specified as XREF1|*.

The Freeze option is used to freeze layers within specific viewports. A single layer name or multiple layer names can be specified for the Freeze option. In this example, the full-size dimensions are created on a layer named DIM-1 and the 1/4 scale dimensions are created on layer DIM-4. The current viewport is the full-scale view. Here is the command sequence to freeze the DIM-4 layer in the current viewport:

CHAPTER 13 ||| External References and Multiview Drawing Layout

Command: **VL** or **VPLAYER**↵
?/Freeze/Thaw/Reset/Newfrz/Vpvisdflt: **F**↵
Layer(s) to Freeze: **DIM-4**↵
All/Select/<Current>: ↵
?/Freeze/Thaw/Reset/Newfrz/Vpvisdflt: ↵
Regenerating drawing.

The drawing is regenerated, and layer DIM-4 is no longer visible in the full-scale viewport. Although the previous example shows the operation being performed in the current viewport, this is not necessary. The following example shows the Select option being used to freeze the DIM-1 layer in the 4X scale viewport:

Command: **VL** or **VPLAYER**↵
?/Freeze/Thaw/Reset/Newfrz/Vpvisdflt: **F**↵
Layer(s) to Freeze: **DIM-1**↵
All/Select/<Current>: **S**↵
Switching to Paper space.
Select objects: ⟨select the viewport⟩
1 found
Select objects:
Switching to Model space.
?/Freeze/Thaw/Reset/Newfrz/Vpvisdflt: ↵
Regenerating drawing.

Notice that paper space is made current so that you can select any desired viewports for the specified operation. The result of freezing these layers is shown in Figure 13.26.

FIGURE 13.26 Freezing layers in specific viewports allows unnecessary details to be removed from those viewports. These two viewports now show only the dimensions pertinent to the displayed view.

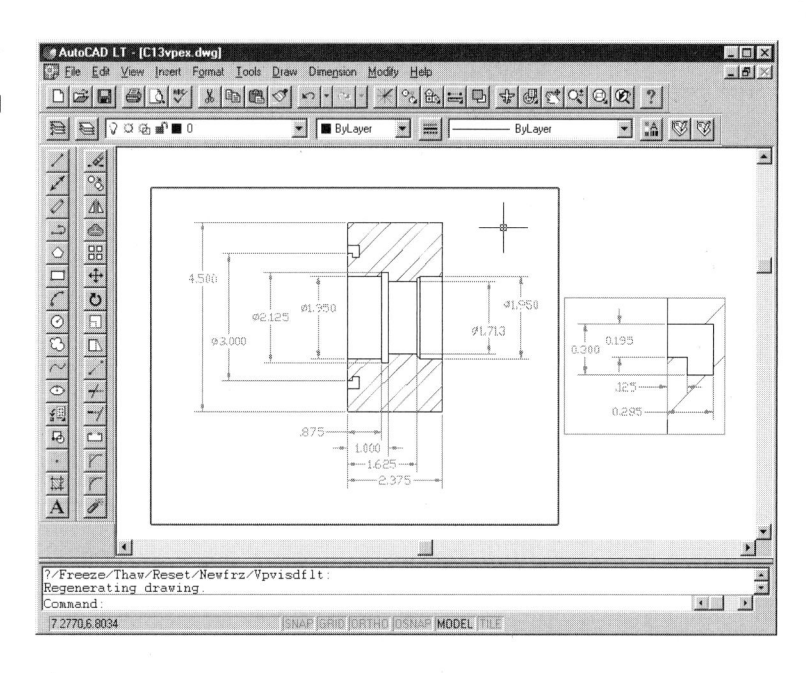

If the All selection option is used, the specified operation affects all viewports, whether they are on or off, active or inactive. The current layer can be frozen in a *floating* model space viewport, but it cannot be frozen in *tiled* model space. If the current layer is frozen, the geometry associated with that layer is no longer visible, and any objects drawn while the frozen layer is active disappear immediately after they are drawn.

The Thaw option of VPLAYER works the same as the Freeze option. Layers in the current viewport, selected viewports, or even all viewports can be thawed. The following example shows all layers being thawed in all viewports:

Command: **VL** or **VPLAYER**↵
?/Freeze/Thaw/Reset/Newfrz/Vpvisdflt: **T**↵
Layer(s) to Thaw: *****↵
All/Select/<Current>: **ALL**↵
?/Freeze/Thaw/Reset/Newfrz/Vpvisdflt: ↵
Regenerating drawing.

The VPLAYER command offers a simple shortcut for creating new layers that are visible only in specific viewports. The Newfrz option of VPLAYER creates a new layer that is frozen in all viewports. By following with the Thaw option, the new and frozen layer can be made visible in the desired viewports.

Command: **VL** or **VPLAYER**↵
?/Freeze/Thaw/Reset/Newfrz/Vpvisdflt: **N**↵
New Viewport frozen layer name(s): **DETAIL-A**↵
?/Freeze/Thaw/Reset/Newfrz/Vpvisdflt: ↵

This approach is very useful when you have several viewports visible on your drawing and you want the new geometry to be visible only in one or two. Rather than having to freeze the new layer in all viewports where you do not want it visible, simply thaw the layer in viewports where you do want it shown. Also, it is often easier to see where needed geometry is missing in a viewport than it is to see where too much geometry exists.

When the Newfrz option is used, the created layers are also frozen by default in all newly created viewports. If you need to change this default visibility setting, the Vpvisdflt option of VPLAYER is used:

Command: **VL** or **VPLAYER**↵
?/Freeze/Thaw/Reset/Newfrz/Vpvisdflt: **V**↵
Layer name(s) to change default viewport visibility: **DETAIL-A**↵
Change default viewport visibility to Frozen/<Thawed>: ↵
?/Freeze/Thaw/Reset/Newfrz/Vpvisdflt: ↵

After adjusting the layer visibility within a viewport, you can easily set all of the layers back to their default visibility settings by using the Reset option of the VPLAYER command:

Command: **VL** or **VPLAYER**↵
?/Freeze/Thaw/Reset/Newfrz/Vpvisdflt: **R**↵
Layer(s) to Reset: *↵
All/Select/<Current>: ↵
?/Freeze/Thaw/Reset/Newfrz/Vpvisdflt: ↵
Regenerating drawing.

The ? option allows you to list the layers that are currently frozen in a selected viewport:

Command: **VL** or **VPLAYER**↵
?/Freeze/Thaw/Reset/Newfrz/Vpvisdflt: **?**↵
Switching to Paper space.
Select a viewport: ⟨pick a viewport⟩
Layers currently frozen in viewport 2:

DIM-4
DETAIL-A

Switching to Model space.
?/Freeze/Thaw/Reset/Newfrz/Vpvisdflt: ↵

Note that the listing provides a number for the viewport selected. The first number available for a model space viewport is 2, because viewport number 1 is the paper space viewport. All others are numbered sequentially as they are created.

Viewport layer visibility can also be controlled easily from the Layer Control dialog box and the Layer Control drop-down list on the Object Properties toolbar. In the Layer Control dialog box, the Thw and Frz buttons to the right of the Cur VP and New VP labels are used. Highlight the layers you want to change, and then pick the appropriate icon to thaw or freeze the layer in either the current viewport or in all new viewports. This is similar to the Newfrz and Vpvisdflt options of VPLAYER. To adjust viewport layer visibility in the current layer, pick the drop-down list and select the icon in the third column from the left. When the rectangle shows a sun next to it, it is thawed in the current viewport. When frozen it shows a snowflake. See Figure 13.27.

FIGURE 13.27 The layers named DOORS and FURNITURE are frozen in the current viewport. Using this drop-down list is often the quickest and easiest method for controlling layer visibility on the fly.

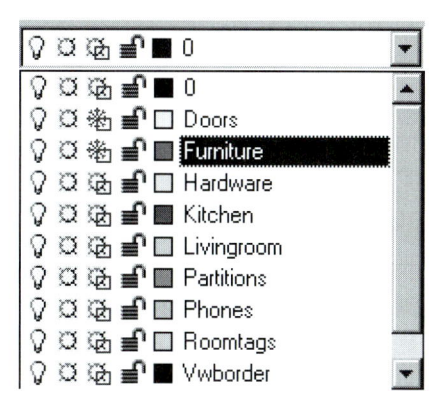

Field Notes

- Selecting the Scale to Paper Space option in the Geometry dialog box of the DDIM command allows you to move between model space viewports while dimensioning without having to adjust the DIMSCALE value. When dimensions are scaled to paper space, the dimensions are automatically scaled to appear correct with respect to the scale of the display in the viewport.
- If the zoom factor of a viewport is changed after dimensioning, use the DIM UPDATE command to update the dimensions to the new scale of the viewport display. Alternately, select and move a grip point on the dimension slightly to cause it to update.
- Be careful not to select dimensions in other viewports when updating dimensions, because updating changes all selected dimensions to the scale of the *current* viewport.
- Setting Object Linetype Scale (CELTSCALE) to −1 causes the linetype scale to match the display scale of the viewport you are drawing in.
- When the PSLTSCALE variable is set to 1, the global linetype scale is displayed relative to paper space.
- Hatch patterns can be set to adjust their scale to the current viewport by setting a scale factor using an XP designation. For example, to retain a scale of 1 in any viewport, specify 1XP as the scale factor. This applies to both the HATCH and the BHATCH commands. The same hatch pattern cannot be displayed differently in different viewports at the same time.

Exercise 13.8

1. Start a new drawing using the Quick Setup defaults.
2. Using the XREF Attach option with TILEMODE set to 1, attach the following three drawings into the current drawing: XREF1.DWG, XREF2.DWG, and XREF3.DWG. These drawings are found in the \AutoCAD LT 98\SAMPLE subdirectory.
3. Insert the drawings each at 0,0 using default insertion scale factors and rotation angle.
4. Using the MVIEW command in paper space, create three floating model space viewports. Place the first viewport (#2) corners at 0.0, 13.5 and 36.0, 24.0. Place viewport #3 corners at 0.0,0.0 and 12.5,13.5. Place viewport #4 corners at 12.5,0.0 and 36.0,13.5.
5. In viewport #2, use VPLAYER to freeze the layers associated with XREF2 and XREF3. In viewport #3, freeze the layers associated with XREF1 and XREF3, and in viewport #4, freeze the layers associated with XREF1 and XREF2.
6. Using ZOOM XP in floating model space, set viewport #2 to display at 1/2″=1′, viewport #3 at 1″=36″ and viewport #4 at 1″=1′.
7. Using the appropriate display, change commands to center each view at the display scale shown in item #6. Viewport #4 should be centered on Detail G.
8. Set TILEMODE to 1 and use the ZOOM Extents option and observe placement of the XREF drawings.
9. Return to paper space.
10. Save the drawing as EX13.8.

LEARNING CHECKPOINT

- ☐ What is the purpose of paper space?
- ☐ What is a floating model space viewport?
- ☐ Which space is the model typically drawn in?
- ☐ Explain the significance of TILEMODE settings.
- ☐ How can the Advanced Setup Wizard be used to set up paper space?
- ☐ What command is used to create model space viewports?
- ☐ What types of editing commands can be used on viewports?
- ☐ Are grid and snap settings required to be uniform in all viewports?
- ☐ How are standard display changes made inside of a viewport?
- ☐ Explain the use of ZOOM XP to set the desired display scale.
- ☐ Name the variable that controls the maximum number of active viewports.
- ☐ Describe the options of the VPLAYER command.
- ☐ Besides VPLAYER, what can be used to change viewport layer visibility?

Using Tiled Model Space

Tiled model space, as described earlier, is a configuration of viewports in model space that do not overlap and cannot be moved or resized through conventional object editing commands. The default number of tiled viewports is one. When there is one tiled viewport, it fills the entire drawing area of the AutoCAD LT window.

Options for setting up tiled model space viewports are easiest to use when selected from the Tiled Viewports cascade of the View menu. These options work very much like the floating model space options for two, three, and four viewports, except that the entire drawing window is filled with no other option presented. For example, picking 2 Viewports offers the Horizontal and Vertical options. The 3 Viewports option offers Above, Below, Left, and Right for the placement of the third viewport and 4 Viewports makes four even areas. Using one of these options inside of a tiled viewport further divides it into smaller areas, but there is a limit as to how small the viewports can be divided. Picking 1 Viewport at any time reverts to a single viewport filling the entire screen. See Figure 13.28.

Other options on this menu include Save, Restore, Delete, Join, and Layout .... The Join option is used to join two separate viewports into a single viewport. To be joined, the two viewports must form a rectangular shape when put together.

FIGURE 13.28 This is the result of selecting 2 Viewports and using the Vertical option.

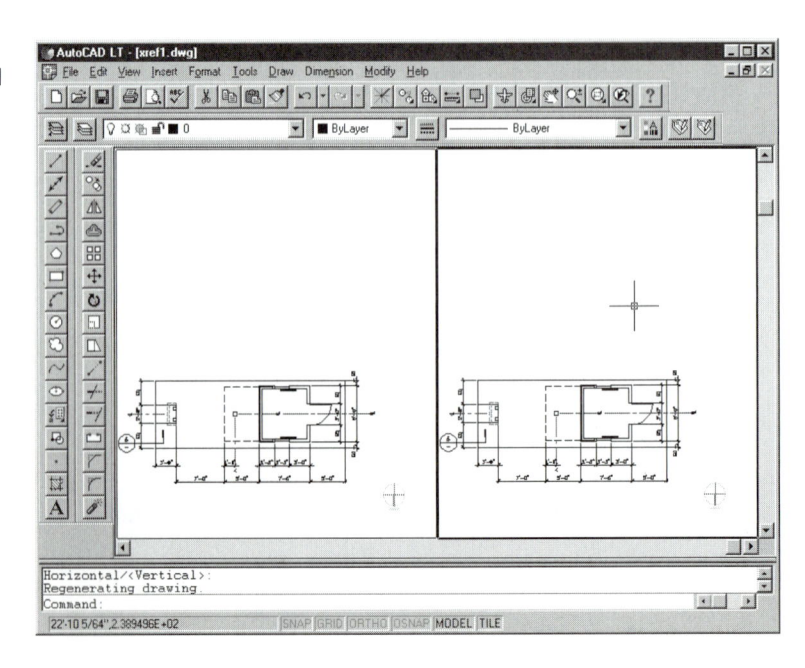

The Save option is used to save the current tiled viewport configuration with a name so it can later be restored using Restore. The Delete option allows you to delete previously saved named viewport configurations. The Layout ... option provides an easy way to lay out the tiled viewports. When selected, this option displays an image tile menu of predefined viewport layouts that you can access with one pick. This menu is shown in Figure 13.29.

Tiled viewports can be used to display two or more separate areas of the drawing when it is helpful. Typically, tiled viewports are used for 3D drawing applications. Examples of the use of tiled viewports are shown in Chapter 14.

FIGURE 13.29 The Layout ... option on the Tiled Viewports cascade displays an image tile menu with a number of predefined tiled viewport layouts available.

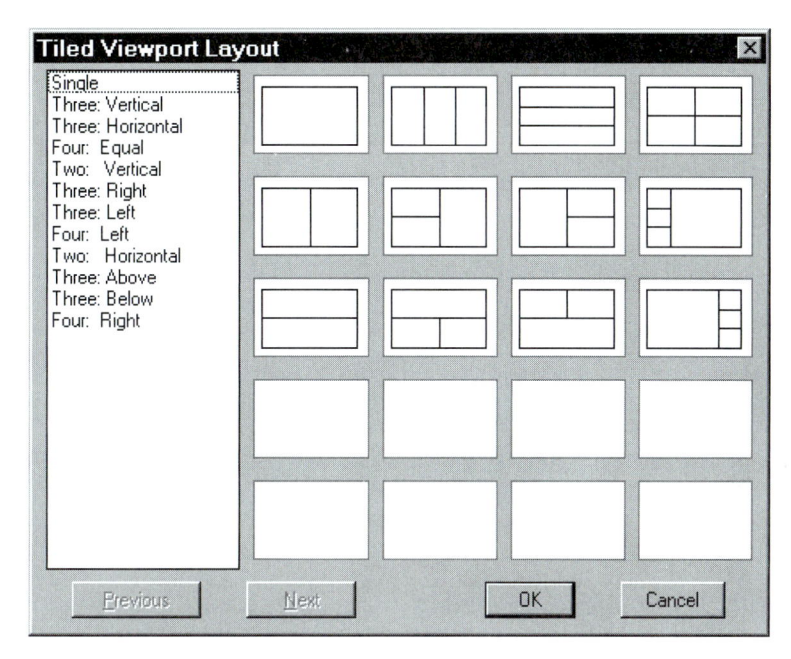

Exercise 13.9

1. Open a drawing from a previous chapter.
2. Use each of the options presented on the Tiled Viewports cascade on the View pull-down menu.
3. Set up the tiled viewports so that three viewports are created with the large viewport on the left.
4. Save the drawing as EX13.9.

Plotting a Multiview Layout

Once you have finished creating a multiview layout, you are ready to plot the drawing. Plotting from paper space is done in the same way as in Chapter 3, where you were shown how to plot from model space. The primary difference is that there are no scale factors to calculate; the plotted scale is 1:1.

However, you may wish to hide the boundary lines for the viewports prior to creating a final plot. Boundary lines, like other objects, can be placed on a specific layer and frozen. Freezing a layer that contains floating model space viewports does not remove the viewport itself, just the lines representing the boundary. The hole through model space is still there and the model remains visible. One popular approach is to create a layer named VIEWPORT and place all of the viewport objects on that layer. When you are working in the drawing and want the borders visible, thaw the VIEWPORT layer. Once it is time to plot, just freeze the VIEWPORT layer and proceed normally.

An alternate approach is to place the viewports on the DEFPOINTS layer. This allows the viewports to stay visible, but does not allow them to plot. Remember that any drawing objects on the DEFPOINTS layer will not plot. Any object type can be stored on this layer. This makes a useful tool for keeping the viewports, notes, or reference objects visible in the drawing without having them also appear on the plot. To change the layer that a viewport or any other object is on, use the DDMODIFY or DDCHPROP commands.

If you are doing a partial plot and do not need all of the views that are currently defined, use the MVIEW command to turn off the unnecessary viewports.

> ### Field Notes
>
> When you prepare to plot, be sure that you are in paper space. If you plot from within a model space viewport, you are plotting from model space and you may get unexpected results.

☑ LEARNING CHECKPOINT

- ☐ What happens when a layer containing a viewport is frozen?
- ☐ What is the advantage of placing viewports on the DEFPOINTS layer?
- ☐ Why should you be certain that paper space is active before plotting?

Exercise 13.10

1. Open EX13.8.
2. Change all viewports to be on the DEFPOINTS layer.
3. Set up a C size sheet and plot your drawing at 1:1 from paper space.

MULTIPLE CHOICE

Circle the choice or enter your response on an answer sheet by selecting the option that most accurately completes or answers the statements.

1. One primary advantage to using external references is:
   a. shorter layer names   c. faster insertion
   b. smaller file sizes   d. easier insertion

2. Named objects brought in with an external reference are called:
   a. reference symbols   c. dependent symbols
   b. dependent objects   d. external symbols

3. Visibility changes to dependent layer names are remembered when this variable is set to 1:
   a. visretain   c. xreflayervis
   b. vpvisdflt   d. viewres

4. An Xref that cannot be resolved is:
   a. displayed as a block   c. discarded
   b. displayed as text   d. detached

5. An external reference option that does not result in nested Xrefs is:
   a. Overlay   c. Attach
   b. Access   d. Insert

6. To permanently attach an entire externally referenced file, use:
   a. XREF Attach   c. XREF Bind
   b. WBLOCK   d. BLOCK

7. The model should always be created:
   a. in the drawing extents   c. in the drawing limits
   b. in model space   d. in paper space

8. Drawings should always be plotted from paper space at:
   a. To FIT   c. 1:1
   b. Not to Scale   d. 1:2

CHAPTER 13 ||| External References and Multiview Drawing Layout

9. A "hole" in paper space is called a:
   a. floating model space viewport
   b. plot window
   c. tiled model space viewport
   d. Vport
10. The option of the ZOOM command used to set the viewport scale is:
    a. X
    b. VMAX
    c. XP
    d. VP

MATCHING

Match each term to the correct description by writing the appropriate number in each box at the left.

☐ XREF Attach
☐ XREF Overlay
☐ XREF Detach
☐ XREF Bind
☐ XREF Path
☐ XREF Reload
☐ XBIND
☐ VPLAYER Newfrz
☐ VPLAYER Vpvisdflt
☐ |
☐ 0
☐ MAXACTVP
☐ VISRETAIN
☐ FLOATING
☐ TILED

1. Freezes layers in new viewports.
2. Sets the maximum number of active viewports.
3. Used to prevent circular references.
4. Basic Xref option.
5. Character used in dependent symbol names.
6. Updates an external reference.
7. Sets visibility default for viewport layers.
8. Removes external reference data.
9. Permanently attaches Xref data.
10. Characters in bound dependent symbol names.
11. Controls Xref layer visibility settings between drawing sessions.
12. Used when Xref location changes.
13. This type of viewport is created in model space.
14. Binds <u>all</u> data from an Xref.
15. This type of viewport is created in paper space.

WORD SCRAMBLE

Unscramble the six scrambled words below, one letter to each square, to form six AutoCAD LT-related words:

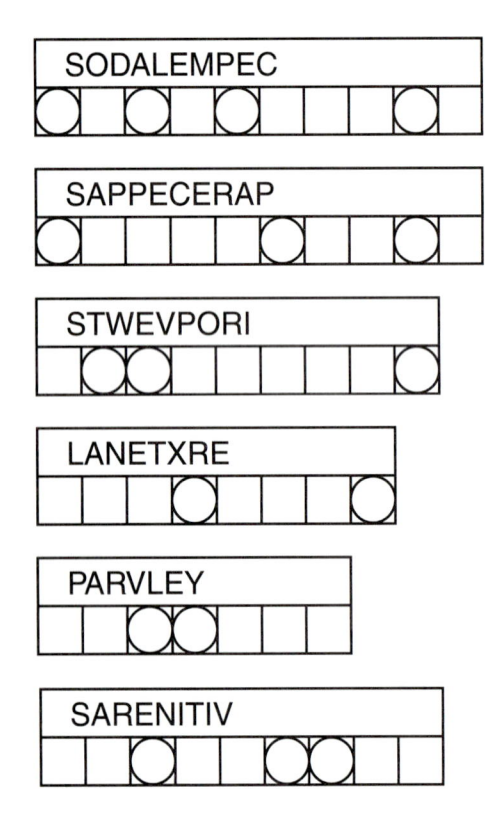

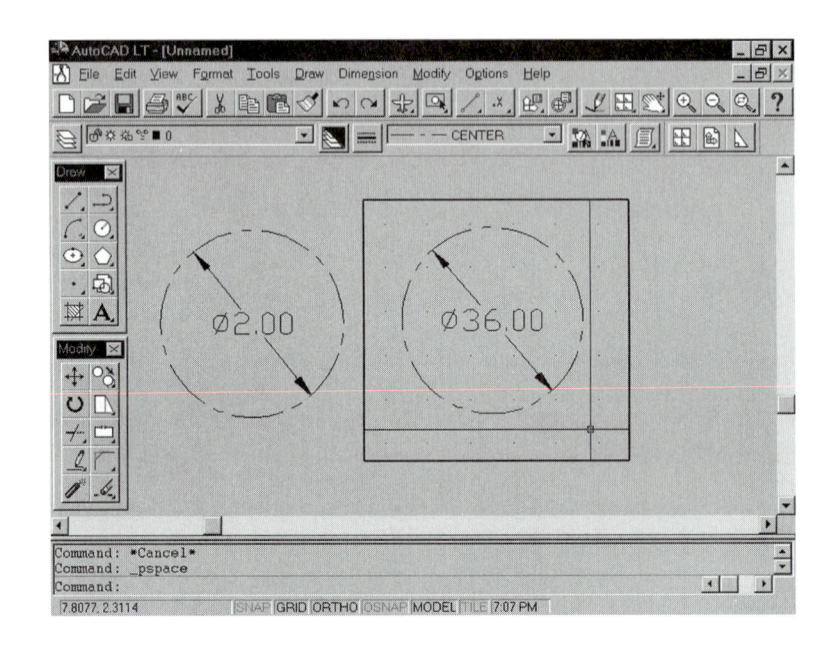

SODALEMPEC

SAPPECERAP

STWEVPORI

LANETXRE

PARVLEY

SARENITIV

Unscramble the circled letters above to form the special answer, as suggested by the illustration.

PROJECTS

13.1 Start a new drawing, using the Start from Scratch option. Set up the drawing with the following settings:

Layer Name	Color	Linetype
0	BLUE	Continuous
OBJ	WHITE	Continuous
CEN	50	Center
HID	CYAN	Hidden
DIM	RED	Continuous

Text Styles	Properties
Standard	Use three different font files. Assign
Annotation	properties as desired.
Label	

Dimension Styles	Properties
Standard	Default properties.
Mechanical	Assign properties as appropriate for
Architectural	the specific dimension style.

Save the drawing file as P13.1.

13.2 Start a new drawing, using the Start from Scratch option. Using the XREF Attach option, create a reference to P13.1. When prompted to supply a block name, enter **P13-1**. Use the XBIND command to bind all of the named objects shown in the tables in Project 13.1. Use the DDRENAME command to remove the **P13-1$0$** from each symbol name if possible. Save the drawing as P13.2.

13.3 Start a new drawing, using the Start from Scratch option. Attach an external reference to the drawing file P13.1. When prompted to supply a block name, enter **P13-1**. Using XBIND, bind the "Architectural" dimension style. Detach the external reference to P13.1. Use DDRENAME to remove the **P13-1$0$** from the dimension style name. Save this drawing as P13.3.

13.4 Start a new drawing, using the Start from Scratch option. Attach an external reference to the drawing file P13.1. When prompted to supply a block name, enter **P13-1**. Using Layer Control, freeze the layers named P13-1|DIM and P13-1|HID. Set VISRETAIN to 1, and save the drawing as P13.4. Reopen the drawing file to be sure that the visibility changes have been retained.

13.5 Start a new drawing, using the Start from Scratch option. Save the drawing as P13.5. Now, set the variable XREFCTL to 1, in order to generate an Xref log file. Repeat the steps listed in Project 13.2. Turn the Xref log file off by setting XREFCTL to 0. Open the file named P13.5.XLG using Notepad. Exit the XLG file without saving, and save the drawing file as P13.5.

13.6 Start a new drawing using the Advanced Setup Wizard. In Step 7: Layout, answer Yes to working with *Advanced paper space layout capabilities,* and select the option labeled *Work on my drawing while viewing the layout.* In the model space viewport, draw several shapes of your choice. Move to paper space and create or insert a title block at a scale of 1:1. Save the drawing file as P13.6.

13.7 Open a drawing file, from the previous chapter problems, that has drawing geometry visible. Use the Tilemode variable to move to paper space, and the 3 Viewport option of the MVIEW command to create a layout with three different views. Display a different, but specific, scale in each viewport by using the ZOOM XP option. Save the drawing file as P13.7.

13.8 Open the drawing file P13.7. Using VPLAYER, freeze one layer in each of the two smaller viewports. Save the drawing as P13.8.

13.9 Start a new drawing, using the Start from Scratch option. Using the VPORTS command in tiled model space, set up tiled viewports using the 4 Viewports option. Next, use the Single option to go back to one viewport. Finally, use the 3 Viewport option with the large viewport on the left side of the screen. Save the drawing as P13.9.

13.10 Start a new drawing, using the Start from Scratch option. Using the VPORTS command in tiled model space, set up six or more tiled viewports using a layout of your choice.

CHAPTER 14

3-D Drafting with AutoCAD LT

LEARNING GOALS

- Apply the right-hand rule to determine three-dimensional fundamentals
- Utilize three-dimensional coordinate systems
- Utilize the User Coordinate System (UCS) when working in three dimensions
- Use Elevation and Thickness values to simulate surfaces
- Effectively use tiled viewports for 3-D display options
- Change 3-D views dynamically
- Create automatic perspective views of 3-D models
- Remove hidden lines and display shaded views
- Simulate 3-D models using isometric drawing tools

3-D Drafting

Creating three-dimensional, or 3-D, drawings can be a very effective way to communicate an idea. A complete 3-D object is often much easier to visualize than two-dimensional, or 2-D, views of an object. When you look at a multiview drawing, you must then assemble each of the separate 2-D views in your mind to visualize the final 3-D shape. Seeing objects already constructed in 3-D can help you to better visualize the finished product.

AutoCAD LT 98 is primarily a 2-D drafting program. This means that it is used principally for producing flat drawings, similar to those drawn on a sheet of paper. However, AutoCAD LT software is capable of basic 3-D functions. Most of the applications earlier in this text use 2-D coordinates that represent values on the X and Y axes of the Cartesian coordinate system. In this chapter, you will learn to work with the 3-D coordinate system by specifying X, Y, and Z axis values. An illustration of the three axes of the Cartesian coordinate system is shown in Figure 14.1.

Both 2-D and 3-D objects can be placed anywhere in three-dimensional space by supplying a Z coordinate location. The Z coordinate location is called the *elevation.* Although AutoCAD LT does allow some objects to be either drawn with or to be given a ***thickness*** to simulate 3-D surfaces, it does not allow the creation of true 3-D solid objects. The 3-D objects you can create in AutoCAD LT give the appearance of being 3-D. It is even possible to produce a view that looks like a solid model and has shading to make the object appear more realistic. Although these objects can be used to determine spatial information and better visualize a final product, they do not contain information such as mass, center of gravity, or surface area.

AutoCAD LT can directly share drawings with AutoCAD Release 14, which is a full-featured package that can create 3-D solid objects. When such objects are present in a drawing, AutoCAD LT can be used to do simple editing, and even make copies of existing solid objects—but no new solid objects can be defined.

Whether sharing an AutoCAD Release 14 drawing or creating a simple 3-D drawing of your own, it is important to understand the use of the 3-D coordinate system. The coordinate system in AutoCAD LT is extremely powerful and provides you with a great deal of flexibility for working in two or three dimensions. You were introduced to the concept of modifying the User Coordinate System, for creating ordinate dimensions, in Chapter 11. In this chapter, you will learn new ways to use the UCS to make working in 3-D much easier.

FIGURE 14.1 The Z axis adds elevation and depth concepts to the drafting process. The Z axis is perpendicular to the X,Y plane.

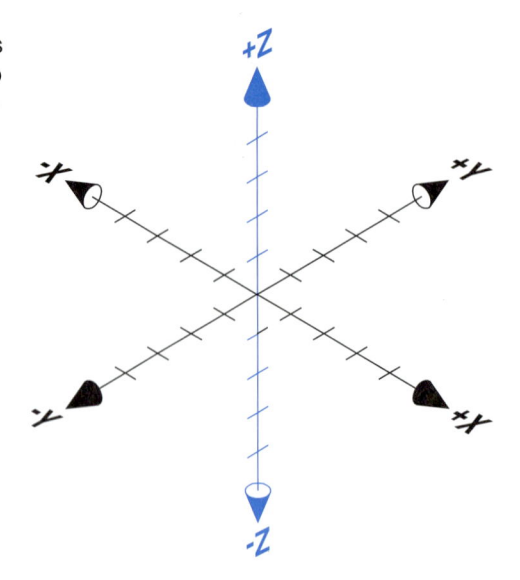

Another effective way of communicating 3-D information is by creating an *isometric* view of your drawing. *Isometric drawings* create a 3-D pictorial in which the three axes are true measurements of the object and form equal angles. Isometric drawings are commonly used when the creation of an actual 3-D model is not practical. Sometimes an isometric drawing is combined with a standard orthographic drawing to assist in the visualization process. A very common use for isometric drawings is in the field of technical illustration. AutoCAD LT provides several powerful tools for use in creating isometric drawings.

Using X,Y,Z Point Coordinates

The coordinate systems presented up to this point in the text have been 2-D coordinates, specifying point coordinate locations on the X,Y plane of the World Coordinate System. The World Coordinate System, or WCS, was defined in Chapter 11 as a fixed coordinate system used by default in AutoCAD LT. You were also introduced to the concept of the movable User Coordinate System, or UCS, which is covered in greater detail in this chapter.

In the WCS, the X axis is horizontal, the Y axis is vertical, and the Z axis is perpendicular to the X,Y plane. Specifying a 2-D absolute point coordinate is done by supplying an X,Y value. A 2-D coordinate specification defaults to a 0 value for the Z axis. This means that the coordinate specification 6,4 is interpreted as 6,4,0. To specify a 3-D point coordinate that does not lie on the X,Y plane, a nonzero Z axis value is supplied. Figure 14.2 shows a representation of the point coordinate 6,4,2. Notice that the point is found 6 units along the positive X axis, 4 units along the positive Y axis, and 2 units on the positive Z axis.

The X,Y,Z coordinate specifications work the same as standard X,Y coordinates with regard to absolute and relative specifications. This means that a coordinate point entered as X,Y,Z indicates an absolute location in 3-D space. When the coordinate point is preceded by the "@" symbol, the coordinate entry is interpreted as being relative to the last point entered. The first example in the following sequence uses absolute coordinate entry. The results are shown in Figure 14.3A. The second example uses relative coordinate entry, and its results are shown in Figure 14.3B:

```
Command: L↵
From point: 6,4,2↵
To point: −2,0,3↵
To point: ↵

Command: L↵
From point: 6,4,2↵
To point: @−2,0,3↵
To point: ↵
```

CHAPTER 14 ∭ 3-D Drafting with AutoCAD LT

FIGURE 14.2 A 3-D point coordinate uses a Z value that indicates its elevation. The elevation is the distance of the point from the X,Y plane of the current UCS.

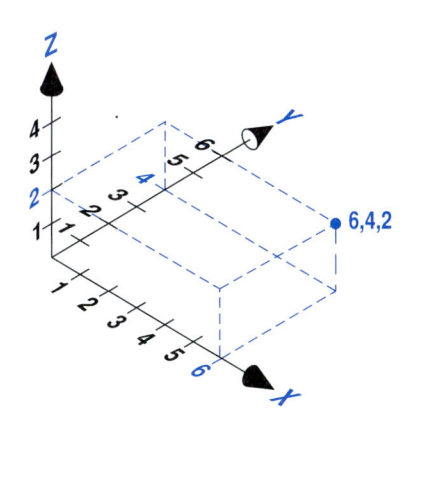

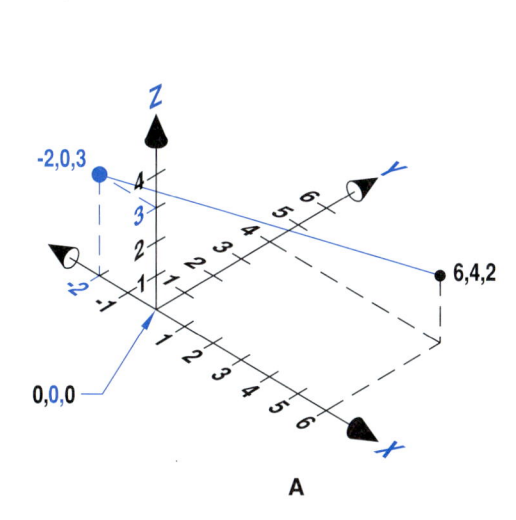

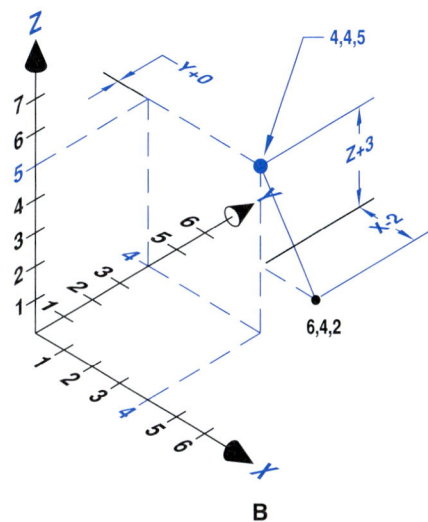

FIGURE 14.3 As with 2-D coordinate entry, preceding a 3-D coordinate with the "@" symbol makes it relative to the last point entered. In this figure, a line is drawn from the point 6,4,2. (A) An entry of –2,0,3 indicates an absolute coordinate location. (B) An entry of **@-2,0,3** indicates a point that is relative to the current location, resulting in a line drawn to 4,4,5.

Field Notes

Even when you are working with 3-D objects in a drawing, many operations are completed in the current X,Y plane. For these tasks, it is not necessary to specify 3-D coordinates. For example, to move a 3-D object 2 units in the positive X direction and 1 unit in the negative Y direction with no change in the Z axis, you do not need to specify the Z coordinate:

> Command: **MOVE**↵
> Select objects: ⟨*pick object*⟩
> Select objects: ↵
> Base point or displacement: **@2,–1**↵
> Second point of displacement: ↵

In such a situation, any acceptable method of 2-D coordinate entry can be used, including absolute, relative, polar, or even direct distance entry.

The Right-Hand Rule

The *right-hand rule* provides an easy-to-understand reference to determine the positive and negative directions of the X, Y, and Z axes. Knowing how to use this simple reference makes it easier to visualize the relationships of the X, Y, and Z axes in 3-D space. This helps to ensure that objects you create and edit are placed in the correct location in your drawing. But don't worry, if you do place something incorrectly, you can always *undo* it!

Figure 14.4 shows the first point of the right-hand rule. Hold your right hand so your thumb points in the positive direction of the X axis and your index finger points in the positive direction of the Y axis. When you are using the default WCS, the back of your hand is toward the screen, your thumb points right, and your index finger points up. Now, extending your middle finger as shown in Figure 14.4 shows you the positive direction of the Z axis. In the WCS, the positive direction of the Z axis is toward you. This method still works when you are using a UCS; rotate your hand appropriately to match the setting of the UCS.

The second point of the right-hand rule allows you to determine the direction of positive rotation around each axis. Figure 14.5 illustrates this concept. Point your right thumb in the positive direction of any axis, then curl your fingers as shown. The direction in which your fingers curl indicates the positive rotation angle. For example, using the example shown in Figure 14.4, you know that the positive direction of the Z axis of the WCS points toward you. With your right hand, point your thumb toward yourself. The curl of your fingers is in the counterclockwise direction, which is the positive rotation direction around the Z axis. This agrees with what you have already learned about rotating objects in the X,Y plane.

FIGURE 14.4 The right-hand rule helps you to better visualize the positive and negative directions of the X, Y, and Z axes.

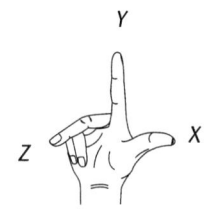

FIGURE 14.5 Point your right thumb in the positive direction of any axis. The curl of your fingers shows the positive rotation angle.

3-D Polar Coordinate Entry

The 2-D coordinate entry system in AutoCAD LT provides a flexible interface for indicating distances and directions for creating and editing objects. Rather than requiring just absolute or relative coordinate entry, the polar method is provided for use when you know a distance and an angle rather than an X and Y location or displacement value. AutoCAD LT also provides similar options for working in a 3-D drawing environment. There are two variations of the polar coordinate entry system that provide much greater flexibility when entering 3-D point coordinates. These variations are called *cylindrical* coordinates and *spherical* coordinates.

Cylindrical coordinates are a simple variation of polar coordinate entry that use a standard polar coordinate entry followed by a Z axis value. A cylindrical coordinate entry looks like this:

2<90,6

This coordinate entry is interpreted as *Distance<Angle,Z-axis.* The *Distance<Angle* entry of 2<90 is measured in the X,Y plane of the current UCS and the *,Z-axis* value of **,6** is the Z coordinate. In this form, the coordinate entry is relative to the 0,0,0 origin point. It is more often used in the following form:

@2<90,6

Preceding the coordinate entry with the "@" symbol makes it relative to the last point entered. An example of entering a cylindrical coordinate is shown in the following example:

```
Command: L↵
From point: 2,2↵
To point: @2<90,6↵
To point: ↵
```

In this example, the line object is started at 2,2 in the current X,Y plane. Because no Z coordinate is specified, the point is interpreted as 2,2,0. The first part of the *To point:* coordinate entry, **@2<90**, works in the X,Y plane, just like its 2-D equivalent. The **,6** value that follows indicates a Z axis value. Because this is preceded by the "@" symbol, all of the values are calculated from the last point entered: 2,2,0. The resulting point location is 2 units at 90° in the X,Y plane, or **2,4,0,** and 6 units in the positive Z direction for a result of **2,4,6.** Figure 14.6 demonstrates the results of this example.

CHAPTER 14 ▕▏▏ 3-D Drafting with AutoCAD LT   583

FIGURE 14.6 The cylindrical coordinate entry specifies a polar value in the X,Y plane and a Z axis distance.

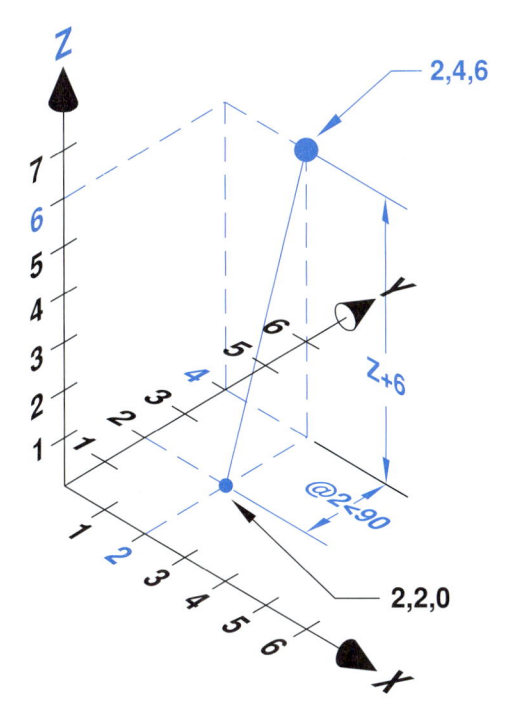

The spherical coordinate system provides a true 3-D polar coordinate entry option. This coordinate entry method allows you to specify the distance from the point of origin followed by the angle *in* the X,Y plane and the angle *from* the X,Y plane. A spherical coordinate specification looks like this:

2<45<60

This entry is defined as *Distance<Angle from X axis<Angle from X,Y plane*. The specification indicates a point that is 2 units from the origin at an angle of 45° in the X,Y plane and 60° from the X,Y plane. This format establishes the point relative to 0,0,0. The following format is more commonly used:

@2<45<60

This format establishes the new point relative to the last point entered. For example, the following sequence creates the line shown in Figure 14.7:

Command: **L↵**
From point: **2,2↵**
To point: **@2<45<60↵**
To point: ↵

FIGURE 14.7 The spherical coordinate entry specifies a polar value both in and from the X,Y plane.

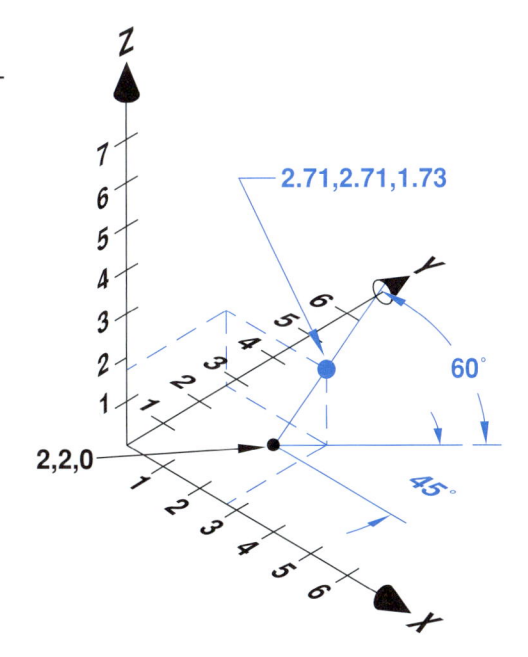

> ✎ **Field Notes**
> - When using cylindrical or spherical coordinates, the individual values can be specified as either positive or negative to get the desired results.
> - Point filters can be very valuable in any 3-D application. By entering **.XY** at a point prompt, you can select a point in the drawing and then type or pick a separate Z value. These filters include .XY, .XZ, .YZ, .X, .Y and .Z.

Applying 3-D Coordinates

AutoCAD LT does not provide a great deal of 3-D functionality. The 3-D coordinate system allows you to place objects anywhere you want in the drawing; however, AutoCAD LT does not provide the capability to create any true 3-D solid objects. A common application for working with advanced 3-D coordinate systems such as cylindrical and spherical coordinates is found when AutoCAD LT is used in an office to supplement an installation of AutoCAD Release 14. In such a case, AutoCAD LT may be used to edit 3-D drawings created in AutoCAD. 3-D drawings created in AutoCAD LT are typically of 2-D objects that have been assigned a thickness. Placement of these objects is best handled through working with the User Coordinate System. How to work with User Coordinate Systems and assign thickness are covered later in this chapter.

Similar to 2-D coordinate entry, deciding which 3-D coordinate entry method to use depends on what information is available and what is most effective. For example, the next sequence uses a variety of coordinate entry methods to draw a simple wire frame shape. The term *wire frame* is used to describe a 3-D shape that uses lines and curves to describe its outline. The linetype of the objects is set so that the finished shape is easier to understand. The final command in this sequence is VPOINT, which is described later, and is used to view the final shape from a 3-D viewing angle.

Command: **L**↵
From point: **2,2**↵
To point: **@2<0**↵
To point: **@2<90**↵
To point: **C**↵

At this point, you have drawn a simple triangle using continuous lines. Because this triangle is drawn on the WCS, no Z coordinates are required. Next, the linetype is changed and two more lines are drawn to create an apex, or top point:

Command: **-LT**↵
-LINETYPE
?/Create/Load/Set: **S**↵
New object linetype (or ?) <BYLAYER>: **CENTER**↵
?/Create/Load/Set: ↵
Command: **L**↵
From point: **2,2**↵
To point: **@2<0,3**↵
To point: **@2<90,−3**↵
To point: ↵

Notice the use of cylindrical coordinates. The polar point specifications are the same as the horizontal and vertical legs of the triangle created in the previous segment, but a Z coordinate is supplied. The first cylindrical coordinate brings the Z coordinate up by using a positive value and the second one brings it back down using a negative Z value.

The following sequence draws a blue line from the red base triangle to the yellow apex:

Command: **-LT**↵
-LINETYPE
?/Create/Load/Set: **S**↵
New object linetype (or ?) <BYLAYER>: **HIDDEN**↵
?/Create/Load/Set: ↵
Command: **L**↵
From point: **4,2**↵
To point: **@0,0,3**↵
To point: ↵

Notice that a relative 3-D coordinate is used here. There is no change in the X or Y coordinates, but the Z value changes by positive 3. The next example uses a command covered later in this chapter to display a 3-D viewpoint:

Command: **VP**↵
VPOINT Rotate/<View point> <0.0000,0.0000,1.0000>: **−1,1,1**↵
Regenerating drawing.

The resulting display should look like the illustration shown in Figure 14.8. Study the figure and review the coordinate entries used to make each line.

FIGURE 14.8 Using the appropriate coordinate entry methods for each task can simplify 3-D drafting requirements.

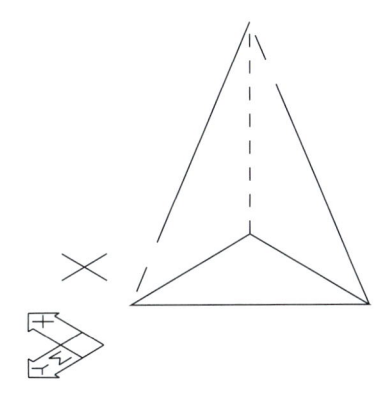

Exercise 14.1

1. Begin a new drawing.
2. Using the appropriate 3-D coordinate entry methods, draw a 3-D wire frame cube that is 2 units on each side. Begin the lower left corner at 2,2,0.
3. Now draw a 3-D wire frame pyramid that is 3 units tall and has a 2-unit square base.
4. Use the VP or VPOINT command as shown in the previous example to set a 3-D viewpoint using −1,1,1.
5. Save the drawing as EX14.1.

✓ LEARNING CHECKPOINT

- ☐ Why do 3-D drawings present an idea more effectively than 2-D drawings?
- ☐ Where is the Z axis found in the Cartesian coordinate system?
- ☐ How can a 3-D coordinate be specified as relative to the last point entered?
- ☐ Describe the WCS.
- ☐ What are the two points of the right-hand rule?
- ☐ Describe how cylindrical and spherical coordinates are used.
- ☐ Give a summary of the 3-D capabilities of AutoCAD LT.

Customizing the User Coordinate System

The World Coordinate System, or WCS, and User Coordinate System, or UCS, were introduced in Chapter 11. The WCS is the default coordinate system used by AutoCAD LT. This coordinate system is based on Cartesian coordinates. It exists on the plane parallel to the X and Y axis at the zero point of the Z axis, as shown in Figure 14.9.

FIGURE 14.9 The World Coordinate System is the default coordinate system on which all User Coordinate Systems are based.

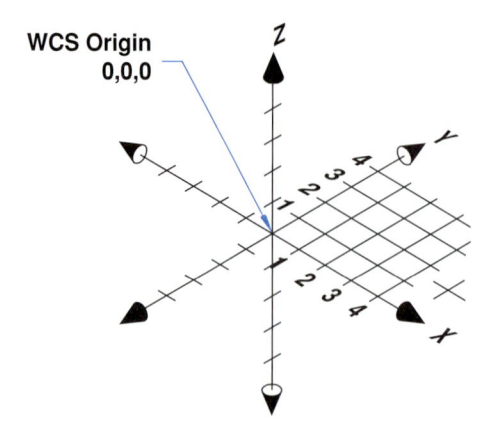

The UCS is a custom coordinate system that can be relocated as needed in 3-D space. All User Coordinate Systems are based on the WCS. Defining a new UCS to meet your needs can greatly simplify your work, whether you are drawing in two or three dimensions.

When you relocate the UCS, the 0,0 location can be placed anywhere in your drawing and the current UCS plane can be rotated to any desired angle. The uses that were explored earlier included placement of the 0,0 point for use in ordinate dimensioning and rotating it to match the orientation of an auxiliary view. 3-D applications for customizing the UCS are discussed in this section.

Controlling the UCS Icon

Also discussed briefly in Chapter 10 was the UCSICON command. You learned to use the ON and OFF options, as well as Origin and Noorigin. It is very important to understand the use of the UCS icon when working in 3-D. The UCS icon helps you to keep track of where you are in 3-D space. Figure 14.10 shows the various ways in which the UCS icon is displayed.

Descriptions for each of the UCS icon configurations are given here:

A   The W in the icon indicates that the WCS is active and this is displaying its current orientation.

B   When the W is not present, a UCS is currently active.

C   The UCS icon appears deformed when the current 3-D viewing angle is not perpendicular to the active UCS.

D   When the UCS is rotated, the icon shows the positive directions for the X and Y axes.

E   The plus sign (+) means that the icon is displayed at the origin (0,0 point) of the current UCS. If the origin is not visible in the current view, the icon will be displayed in the lower left corner of the viewport without the plus sign.

F   This icon is intended to look like a broken pencil. The broken pencil is used to indicate that the viewing angle is almost parallel to the X,Y plane of the current UCS. When this icon is displayed, specifying point locations with your cursor may produce unexpected results.

FIGURE 14.10 The UCSICON is used to help keep track of where you are in a 3-D drawing.

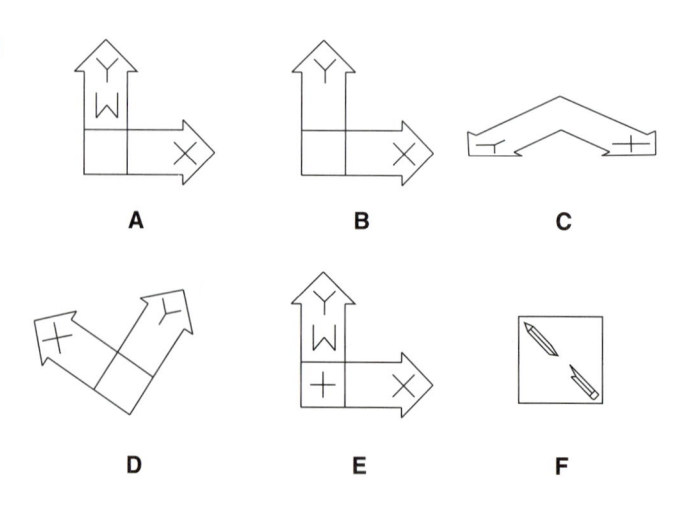

The options for the UCS icon are set using the UCSICON command. To use the UCSICON command, pick the desired option from the UCS Icon cascade on the Display cascade on the View pull-down menu, or type **UCSICON** at the Command: prompt. When used this way, any settings you change affect only the current viewport.

The two primary options available for the UCS icon are turning it on and off, and controlling whether or not it is displayed at the UCS origin. When you access the pull-down menu, a check mark is displayed next to the option if it is currently active. One advantage to typing UCSICON is that the settings can be applied to all viewports at the same time. The following example turns the UCS icon on and places it at the origin in all viewports:

Command: **UCSICON**↵
ON/OFF/All/Noorigin/ORigin <OFF>: **A**↵
ON/OFF/Noorigin/ORigin <OFF>: **ON**↵
Command: **UCSICON**↵
ON/OFF/All/Noorigin/ORigin <ON>: **A**↵
ON/OFF/Noorigin/ORigin <ON>: **OR**↵
Command:

View
└ Display ▶
  └ UCS Icon ▶
UCSICON

Field Notes

The UCS icon is off, by default, in AutoCAD LT. When you are using the WCS, it is often considered to be unnecessary clutter on the screen. However, it should always be turned on when you are working with a UCS. This helps to keep you properly oriented in your drawing.

Relocating the UCS

Any coordinate system that is not the WCS is called a UCS. The current UCS controls the placement of objects that you create in your drawing, because coordinates that you enter are interpreted based on the current UCS, not the WCS. Also, the location and orientation of the current UCS affects operations performed by pointing with the cursor.

Several tools are available for relocating the UCS. The coordinate system can be rotated, its origin can be changed, it can even be set to match the UCS of an object in your drawing or to match the current 3-D viewing angle. After creating a new UCS, it can be named and saved and restored as desired. If a saved UCS is no longer needed, it can be deleted from the named UCS list. AutoCAD LT even provides dialog boxes that allow you to select a predefined UCS.

Most of the available options are provided in the UCS command. The UCS command options can be accessed from the UCS toolbar found on the Standard toolbar, by picking the UCS cascade on the Tools pull-down menu, or by typing **UCS** at the Command: prompt.

The default option for the UCS command is World, which restores the World Coordinate System. Although you can type W to access this option, it is not necessary because World is the default:

Command: **UCS**↵
Origin/ZAxis/3point/OBject/View/X/Y/Z/Prev/Restore/Save/Del/?/<World>: ↵

UCS
[icon]
UCS
Tools
└ UCS ▶
UCS

The Origin option of the UCS command sets a new UCS origin point. No rotation is applied to the UCS using this option; rather the X,Y origin point (0,0) is moved to a new location. This movement can be in the current X,Y plane, or it can be used to move the current UCS up or down the Z axis while maintaining the current rotation. The Origin option is used in the following sequence to move the UCS from the front face to the back face of the wire frame box as shown in Figure 14.11:

Command: **UCS**↵
Origin/ZAxis/3point/OBject/View/X/Y/Z/Prev/Restore/Save/Del/?/<World>: **O**↵
Origin point <0,0,0>: **@0,0,3**↵
Command:

UCS
[icon]
Origin UCS
Tools
└ UCS ▶
  └ Origin
UCS
└ Origin

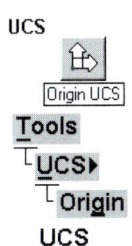

The UCS orientation is maintained, but the origin point is moved 3 units in the positive Z axis direction. When setting UCS options, you can use either absolute or relative coordinates. The definition for the WCS given earlier states that it is the basis for all User Coordinate Systems. However, all coordinate specifications given for drawing or editing objects, as well as relocating the UCS are relative to the *current* UCS. Preceding the coordinate specification with the @ symbol makes it relative to the last point entered. Alternately, absolute coordinate points can be entered.

The ZAxis option of the UCS command allows you to select a new origin point and specify the direction for the new Z axis. The UCS is automatically rotated as necessary around both the X and Y axis as necessary to place the Z axis in the specified direction from the origin points. The following example shows the ZAxis option being used. The results are illustrated in Figure 14.12:

Command: **UCS**↵
Origin/ZAxis/3point/OBject/View/X/Y/Z/Prev/Restore/Save/Del/?/<World>: **ZA**↵
Origin point <0,0,0>: ⟨specify a point⟩
Point on positive portion of Z-axis <0.0000,0.0000,1.0000>: ⟨specify a point⟩

The UCS icon indicates the new origin and orientation of the UCS. If you discover that the new UCS is not what you actually want, simply undo the change using the UNDO command.

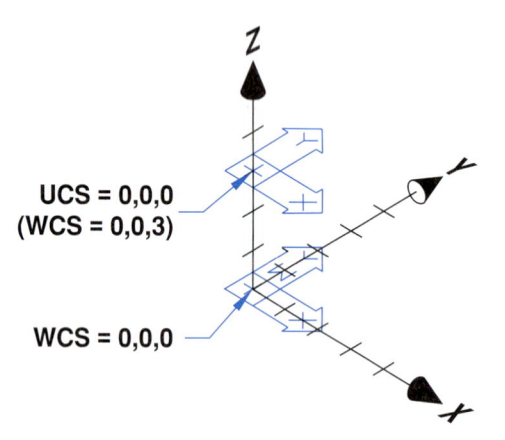

FIGURE 14.11 The Origin option of the UCS command sets the location of the 0,0,0 point while maintaining the current rotation and orientation. This example shows the UCS origin point being moved 3 units in the positive Z axis direction.

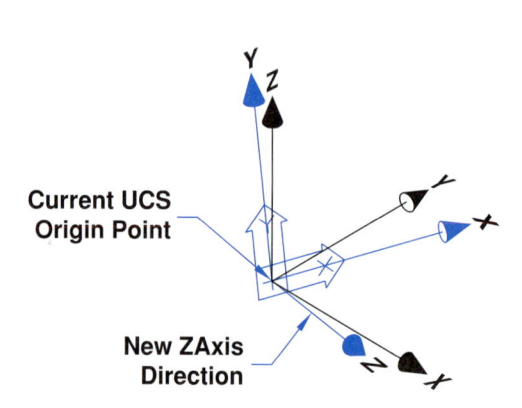

FIGURE 14.12 The ZAxis option of the UCS command sets the location of the 0,0 point and allows you to change the current rotation and orientation by specifying a new Z axis direction. This example shows a new UCS origin and Z axis direction being specified.

The 3point option provides a flexible UCS tool for setting up a coordinate system that aligns with existing features in the drawing. Similar to the ZAxis option, you are prompted to enter an origin point. The difference is that with this option you are prompted for the positive directions for both the X and Y axes.

The following sequence shows the prompts issued when using the 3point option:

Command: **UCS**↵
Origin/ZAxis/3point/OBject/View/X/Y/Z/Prev/Restore/Save/Del/?/<World>: **3**↵
Origin point <0,0,0>: **2,2,0**↵
of ⟨pick origin point⟩
Point on positive portion of the X-axis <3.000,2.000,0.000>: **ENDP**↵
of ⟨pick point on positive X axis⟩
Point on positive-Y portion of the UCS XY plane <2.000,3.000,0.000>: **ENDP**↵
of ⟨pick point on positive X axis⟩

This example shows object snap modes being used for point selection for accuracy. Any valid point entry is acceptable, including relative, polar, spherical or cylindrical coordinates, or direct distance entry. Figure 14.13 illustrates the three points that would be picked to create a UCS on the inclined plane shown.

The Object option provides a convenient way to establish a UCS that matches an existing object in the drawing. Simply select an object and the UCS is set to match:

Command: **UCS**↵
Origin/ZAxis/3point/OBject/View/X/Y/Z/Prev/Restore/Save/Del/?/<World>: **OB**↵
Select object to align UCS: ⟨pick an object⟩

The determination of how the UCS is interpreted depends on the type of objects selected. The following explains how different objects are used to set up the UCS. Note that the following applies to each object as viewed from the positive side of the X,Y plane.

CHAPTER 14 ▪ 3-D Drafting with AutoCAD LT   589

FIGURE 14.13 The 3point option of the UCS command sets the location of the 0,0 point and allows you to change the current rotation and orientation by specifying both a new X axis and Y axis direction. This example shows the new UCS based on the three points selected.

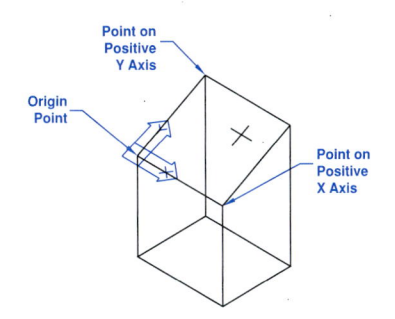

LINE	The endpoint nearest the pick point becomes the origin. The line direction defines the X axis.
CIRCLE	The center of the circle is the new origin. The point where you pick the circle determines the X axis direction.
POLYLINE	The first vertex is the origin. The direction of the first segment is the X axis.
ARC	The center is the origin. The end nearest the pick point determines the X axis direction.
POINT	Sets the origin only.

Some objects, such as splines, ellipses, and elliptical arcs cannot be used to define a coordinate system.

Using the View option of the UCS command sets the X,Y plane of the UCS parallel to the current view of the drawing. The current origin point is maintained. This method is simple and effective when you establish a 3-D view that you wish to use to define your UCS.

    Command: **UCS**↵
    Origin/ZAxis/3point/OBject/View/X/Y/Z/Prev/Restore/Save/Del/?/<World>: **V**↵

The X, Y, and Z options are commonly used options that allow you to rotate the UCS around the specified axis. For example, Figure 14.14 shows the beginning of the construction of a 3-D wire frame box. The first rectangle is drawn in the WCS, then the UCS is rotated 90° around the X axis for the construction of the next rectangle. When using these options, refer to the second step of the right-hand rule to determine whether the angle should be specified as positive or negative. The following sequence illustrates the procedure used in Figure 14.14:

    Command: **RC**↵
    First corner: **0,0**↵
    Other corner: **4,4**↵
    Command: **UCS**↵
    Origin/ZAxis/3point/OBject/View/X/Y/Z/Prev/Restore/Save/Del/?/<World>: **X**↵
    Rotation angle about X axis <0>: **90**↵
    Command: **RC**↵
    First corner: **0,0**↵
    Other corner: **4,4**↵

FIGURE 14.14 With the UCS rotated, 2-D objects can be drawn in 3-D space.

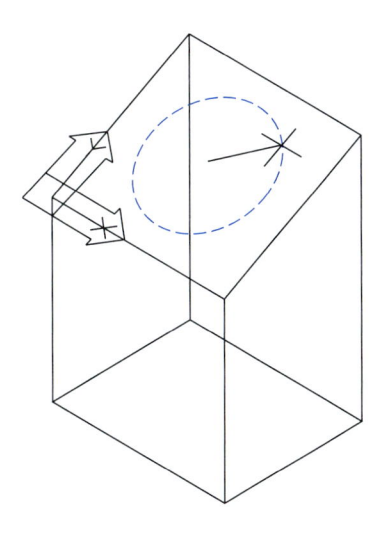

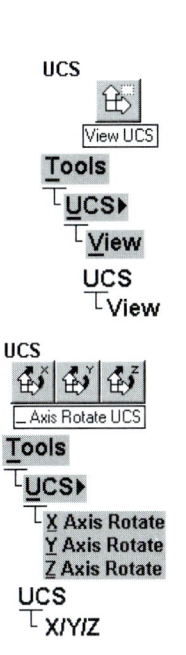

Displaying the Current UCS

When you change the UCS, your current viewing angle does not automatically change to match. Sometimes it is helpful to view your work from a 3-D angle, rather than a flat plan view. Therefore, the UCS and viewing angle are handled separately. When you want to view your drawing from a plan view of either the WCS or any existing UCS, use the PLAN command. The PLAN command is accessed by typing **PLAN** at the Command: prompt, or by picking an option from the Plan View cascade under the 3D Viewpoint cascade on the View pull-down menu. A very common use of the PLAN command is to quickly set your view to the plan view of the current UCS. The following example shows how this is done:

    Command: **PLAN**↵
    <Current UCS>/Ucs/World: ↵
    Regenerating drawing.

The default option is Current UCS. Pressing Enter at the prompt displays its plan view. Typing **W** displays the plan view of the WCS. The UCS option allows you to enter the name of a saved UCS to view. Working with named User Coordinate Systems is discussed in the next section.

> **Field Notes**
>
> - To specify a point in the WCS without making it the current coordinate system, precede the point coordinate with an asterisk. For example, the following entry specifies a coordinate in the WCS:
>
>   To point: ***2,4,0**↵
>
>   All coordinate entry methods can be used this way. For example, an absolute cylindrical coordinate would be:
>
>   ***2<30,4**
>
>   When the coordinates are relative to the last point entered, the asterisk follows the @ symbol:
>
>   **@*2.25<60** or **@*3<45<60** or **@*2<30,4**
>
> - Paper space does not allow the use of certain commands discussed in this chapter. The PLAN command is one of the commands that can only be used in model space.

Working with Named UCSs

The basic philosophy behind any CAD software is that if you are going to need something again, save it. If you have done it once, there is no need to do it again. This is true of blocks, named views, layering systems, and any other feature of a drawing that can be saved. It is also possible to assign a name to a UCS so that you can immediately restore it at any time in the future. This keeps you from having to define the UCS each time you need it.

The first step in this process is to create a needed UCS. After creating it, if you feel you may need to use it again, it should be saved with a recognizable name. To name and save a UCS, use the Save option of the UCS command or pick the Save option from the UCS cascade menu:

    Command: **UCS**↵
    Origin/ZAxis/3point/OBject/View/X/Y/Z/Prev/Restore/Save/Del/?/<World>: **S**↵
    ?/Desired UCS name: **FRONT**↵

To get a listing of the currently saved coordinate systems, use the question mark option of the UCS command or pick the List option from the UCS cascade menu. Similar to listing most named objects, AutoCAD LT prompts for a search string, where a specific name can be entered, or wild card characters can be used. In the following example, the default asterisk wild card is accepted to get a listing of all saved coordinate systems:

    UCS name(s) to list <*>: ↵
    Current UCS: FRONT
    Saved coordinate systems:

CHAPTER 14 ▬ 3-D Drafting with AutoCAD LT

```
FRONT
    Origin = <0.0000,0.0000,0.0000>, X Axis = <1.0000,0.0000,0.0000>
    Y Axis = <0.0000,1.0000,0.0000>, Z Axis = <0.0000,0.0000,1.0000>

Origin/ZAxis/3point/OBject/View/X/Y/Z/Prev/Restore/Save/Del/?/<World>:
```

The numbers displayed will be more familiar to you as you become accustomed to working in 3-D. The Origin coordinate, as implied, indicates the location of the UCS origin with respect to the current UCS. The X, Y, and Z axes coordinates indicate a point, based on the current UCS, that the specified axis passes through in its positive direction. When a UCS is current, it always shows the same description found in the preceding example. In the next listing, a new UCS has been defined and is now current:

```
UCS name(s) to list <*>: ↵
Current UCS: NEW-UCS
Saved coordinate systems:
FRONT
    Origin = <2.2825,−1.0166,1.3254>, X Axis = <−0.2923,0.0673,−0.9539>
    Y Axis = <0.4403,0.8950,−0.0718>, Z Axis = <0.8489,−0.4410,−0.2913>
NEW-UCS
    Origin = <0.0000,0.0000,0.0000>, X Axis = <1.0000,0.0000,0.0000>
    Y Axis = <0.0000,1.0000,0.0000>, Z Axis = <0.0000,0.0000,1.0000>
```

To make a saved UCS current, use the Restore option. The Restore option is accessed by typing **R** or by picking the Restore option from the UCS cascade on the Tools pull-down menu.

```
Command: UCS↵
Origin/ZAxis/3point/OBject/View/X/Y/Z/Prev/Restore/Save/Del/?/<World>: R↵
?/Name of UCS to restore: ⟨type name of UCS to restore⟩
```

✎ Field Notes

> When you restore a saved UCS, remember that even though the UCS is restored, your view may not be parallel to the X,Y plane of the UCS. Be sure to check your UCS Icon, and use the PLAN command if necessary.

If you have incorrectly created a saved UCS, or simply no longer need it, use the Delete option of the UCS command to remove it. You can also select Delete from the UCS cascade menu. Wild card characters can also be used at the UCS name prompt when you need to delete more than one UCS. If you accidentally delete the wrong UCS name, you can use the U command to undo the deletion. The following example shows the prompts issued when deleting a UCS:

```
Command: UCS
Origin/ZAxis/3point/OBject/View/X/Y/Z/Prev/Restore/Save/Del/?/<World>: D↵
UCS name(s) to delete <none>: NEW-UCS
Deleted 1 UCS name.
```

The UCS Previous option provides the same kind of convenience as the ZOOM PREVIOUS command. This allows you to step back through the last 10 coordinate systems created in the current space. Also like ZOOM PREVIOUS, this movement through coordinate systems is one way only. This option can be accessed through the Previous option of the UCS command, by picking the Previous UCS button on the UCS toolbar, or by picking Previous from the UCS cascade menu:

```
Command: UCS↵
Origin/ZAxis/3point/OBject/View/X/Y/Z/Prev/Restore/Save/Del/?/<World>: P↵
```

The DDUCS command displays the UCS Control dialog box. This provides an easy way to work with named coordinate systems. The DDUCS command is accessed by typing **UC** or **DDUCS** at the Command:

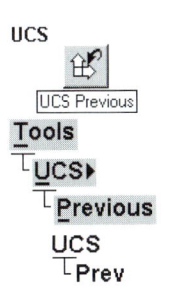

prompt, by picking Named U<u>C</u>S ... from the <u>U</u>CS cascade menu, or by picking the Named UCS button from the UCS toolbar. The UCS Control dialog box is shown in Figure 14.15.

The UCS functions provided in this dialog box are limited to the following:

<u>C</u>urrent   Makes the highlighted UCS name the current UCS.

<u>D</u>elete   Removes the highlighted UCS name from the list of defined coordinate systems.

List ...   Displays the descriptive information for the highlighted UCS in the dialog box shown in Figure 14.16.

<u>R</u>ename To: Renames the highlighted UCS to the current contents of the edit box.

FIGURE 14.15 The UCS Control dialog box offers limited functionality when working with named coordinate systems.

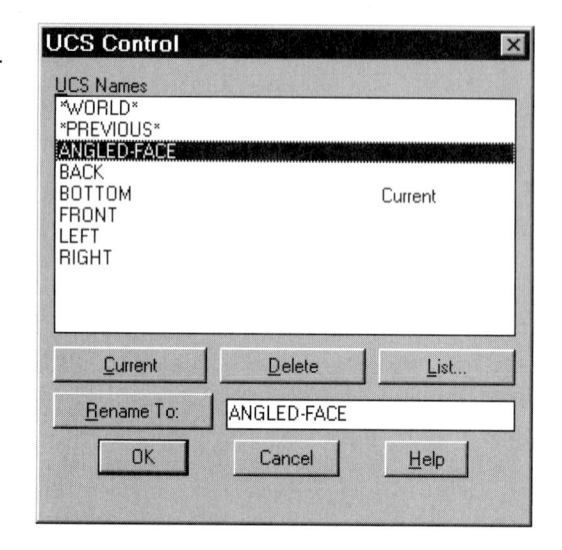

FIGURE 14.16 The UCS dialog box displays information about the highlighted UCS name.

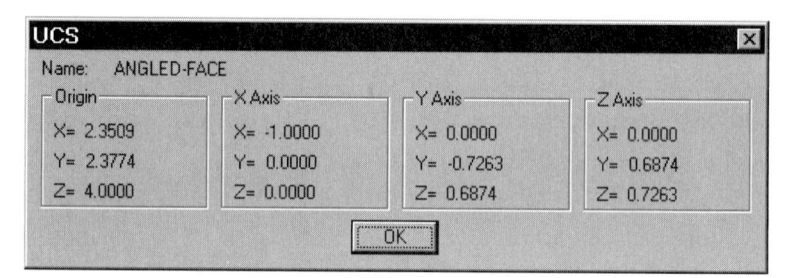

UCS Presets

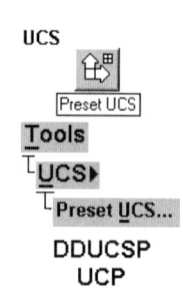

Several preset UCS settings are available by using the UCS Orientation dialog box. This dialog is displayed by using the DDUCSP command. To access this command, type **UCP** or **DDUCSP** at the Command: prompt, pick Preset <u>U</u>CS ... from the <u>U</u>CS cascade of the <u>T</u>ools pull-down menu, or pick the Preset UCS button on the UCS toolbar.

The preset UCS selection provides six coordinate system orientations that match the six sides of a cube. This includes front, back, top, bottom, left, and right. Just like when you set the UCS by any other means, the view does not change. To switch to the plan view of any current UCS, use the PLAN command and accept the default of *Current UCS*.

The images in the UCS Orientation dialog box show grid patterns on the side of the cube that describe each of the available UCS options. This dialog box is shown in Figure 14.17.

There are two ways to use these presets, absolute and relative. The absolute method works in reference to the WCS, and is specified by selecting the radio button labeled <u>A</u>bsolute to WCS. With this method, the Top is the default WCS, and the other five options rotate the UCS around the appropriate axes to generate the described view. The WCS option, indicated by the UCS Icon with the W, and the current view options are automatically established by this method and the <u>A</u>bsolute to WCS button is activated.

The <u>R</u>elative to Current UCS method is easier to understand if you picture holding a cube in your hand and a sheet of paper on the face representing the current UCS. The current UCS is always the top face of this cube. So, to move the UCS to the front face, you rotate your paper 90° on the X axis. However, the face you have moved your paper to, the new current UCS, is now considered to be the top for the next use of this dialog box.

CHAPTER 14 ⋅ 3-D Drafting with AutoCAD LT

FIGURE 14.17 The UCS Orientation dialog box provides an easy-to-understand method of relocating the UCS.

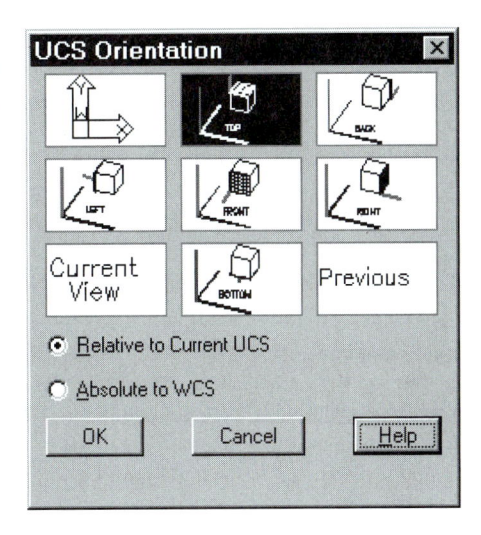

The Previous option works the same as the command line version. It simply restores the previously active coordinate system.

> **Field Notes**
>
> When using a preset UCS, all rotations are made with respect to the current UCS origin point (0,0,0). Use the UCS Origin option to move the origin point to a more appropriate location, if necessary.

Exercise 14.2

1. Open EX14.1.
2. Use the PLAN command to restore the WCS.
3. Set the UCS Origin to 4,2,0.
4. Use the Y option of the UCS command, and rotate the UCS 90°.
5. Save the Current UCS as R-SIDE.
6. Use the BHATCH command to apply a hatch pattern within the shape.
7. Use the VPOINT command, and set the viewpoint at −1,1,1.
8. Save the drawing as EX14.2A.DWG.
9. Begin a new drawing.
10. Set UCSICON to Origin.
11. Draw two lines, two arcs and two circles any size and location, and a rectangle from 0,0 to 4,2.
12. Use the OBject option of the UCS command to create varied UCSs by picking different points on the objects. Use the UCS Previous option to go back through several UCS settings.
13. Set the UCS to World. Save this UCS as "FRONT."
14. Using the UCS Rotate option, rotate 90° around the X axis. Use the PLAN command to view the current UCS.
15. Draw another rectangle the same as the first, but in the new UCS.
16. Save this UCS as "TOP."
17. Set the UCS Origin to the upper left corner of the rectangle, and rotate 90° around the X axis. Repeat Step 15. Save this UCS as "BACK."
18. Repeat Step 17, saving the UCS as "BOTTOM."
19. Restore each UCS in turn, hatching each rectangle with a pattern of your choice.
20. Use VIEWPOINT to set the viewpoint to 1,−1,1.
21. Save the Drawing as EX14.2B.

✓ LEARNING CHECKPOINT

- ☐ Where and what is the WCS?
- ☐ What is a UCS?
- ☐ How can using UCSs make 3-D drafting tasks easier?
- ☐ Describe the use and value of named coordinate systems.
- ☐ In the preset UCS options, which face of a cube is the current UCS?

Setting Up 3-D Viewing Angles

<u>T</u>ools
└ <u>3D Viewpoint</u>
　└ <u>V</u>ector
VPOINT
VP

In the previous sections you used the VPOINT command to establish a 3-D viewing angle to be able to better see the results of your 3-D drawing efforts. When your view is parallel to the plane in which the objects you are viewing were created, you can only see two of the available three dimensions. The PLAN command allows you to set your viewing angle parallel to any available UCS, but allows no real flexibility for viewing from different angles. 3-D viewing angles are easiest to create using the VPOINT command. The VPOINT command cannot be used in paper space.

To access the VPOINT command, type **VP** or **VPOINT** at the Command: prompt, or pick <u>V</u>ector from the <u>3</u>D Viewpoint cascade on the <u>V</u>iew pull-down menu. When this command is activated while the WCS is current, the following prompt sequence is displayed:

Command: **VP** or **VPOINT**↵
VPOINT Rotate/<View point> <0.0000,0.0000,1.0000>:

This prompt awaits a direction vector. A *vector* is a line describing distance and direction. The vector is described as a line from the 3-D coordinate point that you enter to the 0,0,0 point of the UCS. You might understand this concept better if you picture looking at the drawing through a camera. The camera is positioned at the coordinate location you specify and pointed directly at 0,0,0. Figure 14.18 shows an illustration of this concept using the settings specified in the following sequence:

Command: **VP** or **VPOINT**↵
VPOINT Rotate/<View point> <0.0000,0.0000,1.0000>: **−1.5,−1.5,3.47**↵
Regenerating drawing.

The viewpoint is always set in reference to the WCS. Any time you specify a vector to describe the viewpoint, the coordinates and origin point always reference the WCS. If the WCS is not current, the prompt sequence tells you that it is switching to the WCS to apply the specified setting. After adjusting the viewpoint, the UCS is then restored, as shown in the following example:

Command: **VPOINT**↵
*** Switching to the WCS ***
Rotate/<View point> <−1.5000,−1.5000,3.4787>: **2,2,5**↵
*** Returning to the UCS ***
Regenerating drawing.

FIGURE 14.18 The vector determines the distance and direction of the viewing plane from the WCS origin.

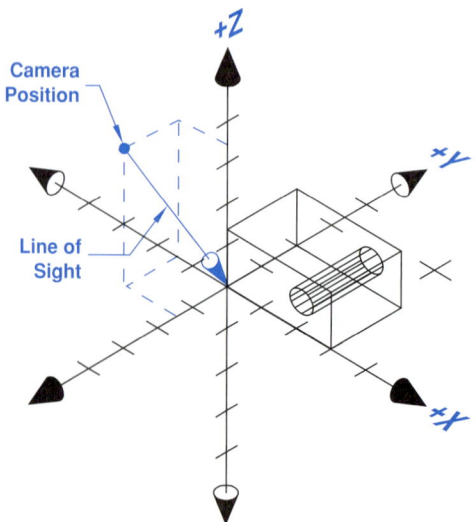

CHAPTER 14 ■ 3-D Drafting with AutoCAD LT 595

> **Field Notes**
>
> - When specifying the vector point, running object snap modes can affect the point you specify. Although the difference in the current X,Y plane may be small, the difference in elevation can be significant.
> - Once you have a clear understanding of 3-D views, you may wish to specify your viewpoints with respect to the current UCS instead of the WCS. To make this possible, you need to set the WORLDVIEW system variable to 0. When WORLDVIEW is set to 0, the WCS is not made current during the VPOINT and DVIEW commands. DVIEW is discussed later in this chapter. To change the value of WORLDVIEW, just like any other system variable, type it at the Command: prompt:
>
>   Command: **WORLDVIEW**↵
>   New value for WORLDVIEW <1>: **0**↵
>
> **Important:** The examples in this chapter all use the WORLDVIEW default value of 1.

This method works very well once you have a solid understanding of 3-D coordinate systems and can visualize 3-D viewpoints accurately. Another method that can be used is the Axis Tripod, accessed by picking Tripod from the 3D Viewpoint cascade on the View pull-down menu, or by pressing Enter at the Rotate/<View point> prompt:

Command: **VP** or **VPOINT**↵
Rotate/<View point> <2.0000,2.0000,5.0000>: ↵
⟨specify the new 3D viewpoint⟩
Regenerating drawing.

The Axis Tripod is a visual display of the current orientation of the X, Y, and Z axes. Use this, combined with the Compass, to define a 3-D viewing angle. See Figure 14.19. This provides additional visual clues to the resulting 3-D viewpoint. As you move your cursor, you will see a small set of crosshairs moving within the compass circles. The resulting viewpoint is further demonstrated by the position of the Axis Tripod.

FIGURE 14.19 The Axis Tripod and Compass can be used to help visualize the desired viewing angle.

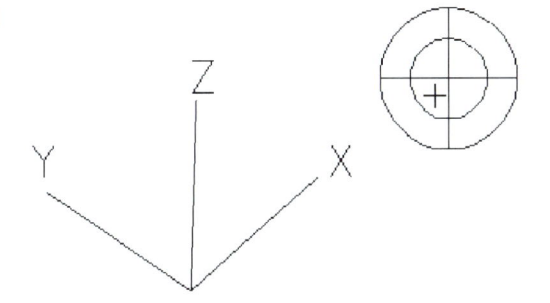

The compass represents a globe, flattened out so that you can see all of it. The center point is the North Pole, the inner circle is the Equator, and the outer circle is the South Pole. Pointing directly at the North Pole represents the Top view in the WCS. Keep this in mind as you adjust the viewpoint.

The compass is very sensitive to cursor movements. You can point more accurately by turning Snap on while adjusting the viewpoint. Do this by pressing the F9 key, Ctrl+B, or by double-clicking the SNAP button on the status bar.

Although the Axis Tripod shows the relative positions of the X, Y, and Z axes, it is still a two-dimensional display and may not be completely clear. For example, with Snap on, move the cursor to the North Pole and then downward and to the left a couple of clicks. The Z axis appears shorter than the rest to imply that it is now pointing either toward you or away from you. Without the compass display, it would be impossible to tell which way it is actually pointing. Since you know that it is pointing directly at you when the cursor was on the North Pole, it can be determined that it is still pointing toward you, but not directly toward you. Continue to move the cursor downward and to the left, at approximately 225° from the North Pole. When you reach the equator, the Z axis is at its full length. As you continue movement beyond the Equator, the Z axis again becomes shorter. Now it is pointing away from you. By using both of these visual aids, it is easier to determine the results of the display change you are describing.

Because the Z axis is inclined toward you while it is within the inner circle, this indicates that the viewpoint you are describing is looking from above the X,Y plane of the WCS. When the cursor is between the Equator and the South Pole, the viewing angle you are describing is looking from below the X,Y plane.

Using the Rotate Option

An alternate method of adjusting the 3-D viewing angle using VPOINT is the Rotate option. This allows you to specify a relative rotation both *in* the X,Y plane and *from* the X,Y plane of the WCS. To fully understand this option, it is helpful to know that the angle specifications are the same as they are for spherical coordinate specifications. Figure 14.20 shows the results from the following example:

Command: **VP** or **VPOINT**↵
Rotate/<View point> <0.0000,0.0000,1.0000>: **R**↵
Enter angle in XY plane from X axis <270>: **225**↵
Enter angle from XY plane <90>: **45**↵
Regenerating drawing.

FIGURE 14.20 The Rotate option allows specification of the viewing angle in terms of the rotation angle both in and from the X,Y plane. The angles used are the same as those used when specifying spherical coordinates.

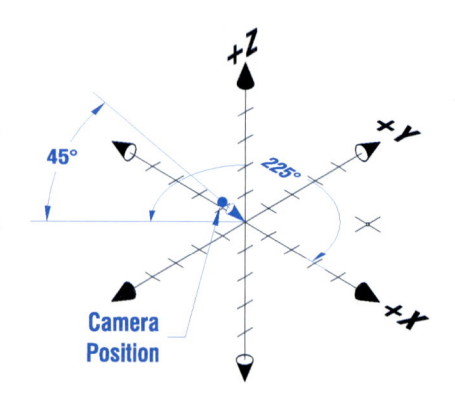

Exercise 14.3

1. Open EX14.2B.
2. Using the VPOINT vector option, set the current viewpoint to −1,−1,1. Use ZOOM PREVIOUS to return to the previous view and the U command to undo the ZOOM PREVIOUS. Using these two commands, switch back and forth to compare the views.
3. Use the Axis Tripod and Compass to change the viewpoint again.
4. Use the Rotate option, set the viewpoint rotation angle to be 225° in the X,Y plane and 45° from the X,Y plane.
5. Save the drawing as EX14.3.

Field Notes

When working with 3-D viewpoints, you can work more effectively by saving viewpoints that you need to work with again. Named views, as discussed in Chapter 4, can also be used to save 3-D viewpoints. Always use names that are clearly recognizable to avoid confusion in later drawing sessions.

3-D Viewpoint Presets

Similar to the UCS presets, AutoCAD LT also provides 3-D viewpoint presets. These are predefined views that are commonly used and are already defined to allow you to switch immediately to the desired view. To see the available 3-D viewpoint options, look at the 3D Viewpoint cascade on the View pull-down menu or use the View toolbar.

The top, bottom, left, right, front, and back views are the same as the UCS options when specified as absolute to the UCS. The isometric options provide 3-D vantage points that are not parallel to any of the cube faces. Although it is often easier to work with your view parallel to the current UCS, the isometric options can sometimes provide a better perspective for viewing the results of your efforts. Table 14.1 shows the available isometric view toolbar buttons and their corresponding VPOINT vector and rotation.

When using the preset viewpoints, the vector entries are specified with an asterisk preceding them. This indicates that the coordinate entries are in the WCS. However, this is unnecessary, because the VPOINT command automatically switches to the WCS before applying the viewpoint change. After the viewpoint change is made, if a UCS was active when the command was used, it is then restored.

TABLE 14.1 Isometric view toolbar buttons

Toolbar Button	View Name	Vector	Rotation *IN* X,Y Plane	Rotation *FROM* X,Y Plane
	SW Isometric	−1,−1,1	225°0′	35°16′
	SE Isometric	1,−1,1	315°0′	35°16′
	NE Isometric	1,1,1	45°0′	35°16′
	NW Isometric	−1,1,1	135°0′	35°16′

Field Notes

- The term *isometric* is used to describe two different drafting techniques. One is an isometric projection, and the other is an isometric drawing. The preset isometric views in AutoCAD correspond to an isometric projection.

    Isometric projection: This method is seldom used for 2-D drafting in industry because it represents the *true appearance* of the model as though it were tilted 35°16′ toward you, and thus requires the drafter to scale each line correctly.

    Isometric drawing: This method is commonly used for 2-D drafting in industry because the isometric lines are drawn actual length and require no scaling.

- When using the VPOINT command options or presets, the extents of the drawing are displayed when the viewpoint is changed. Depending on the desired view, you may need to zoom in or out. To still see the drawing as large as possible, without touching the edges of your display area, use a ZOOM scale option such as 0.9X.

Exercise 14.4

1. Begin a new drawing.
2. Set the UCS Icon to ON and ORigin.
3. Draw a 2-unit square using the RECTANG command. The lower left corner should be at 0,0,0.
4. Use each of the 3D Viewpoint Presets to look at the drawing from each available preset.
5. Set the SW Isometric viewpoint to be current and set the UCS to the current view.
6. Draw a horizontal line from 0,0 to 2,0.
7. Create an angular dimension that shows the 30° angle of projection.
8. Rotate the UCS 90° around the Y axis and use the PLAN command to view the new UCS.
9. Draw a horizontal line from 0,0 to 2,0.
10. Set angular dimension units to Degrees/Minutes/Seconds, and Precision to 1 place. Create an angular dimension that shows the 35°16′ incline.
11. Save the drawing as EX14.4.

Giving Objects Thickness

In a 2-D environment, objects have two dimensions, height and width. The third dimension is thickness, or depth. AutoCAD LT 98 allows you to simulate 3-D objects by giving 2-D objects a thickness property. In a true 3-D system, an object is solid and has properties such as mass. Some 3-D systems allow the creation of surface models. A *surface model* is a visual representation of a 3-D object created by describing the surfaces only. Such objects do not have the same properties as solid objects. 3-D objects in AutoCAD LT simulate 3-D surface models. There are no true 3-D surface objects in AutoCAD LT, but an object with thickness can present the appearance of a 3-D surface model. With a bit of creativity and imagination, fairly complex 3-D drawings can be created with the available tools.

Format
└ **Thickness**

THICKNESS
TH

There are two ways to give objects thickness in AutoCAD LT. The first is to set the current object thickness using the THICKNESS command. This is just like setting the current object linetype or color—all objects drawn will use the specified value, if applicable. The THICKNESS command is accessed by typing **TH** or **THICKNESS** at the Command: prompt. For example:

Command: **TH** or **THICKNESS**.↵
New value for THICKNESS <0.0000>: **1.25**↵

Figure 14.21 shows different object types drawn with the thickness at 1.25 as set previously. Notice that some objects do not observe the thickness setting. Objects that can be drawn with thickness include lines, arcs, circles, polylines, 2-D solids, hatches, and points. Shapes created using polylines can also be drawn with thickness, including rectangles, spline-fit polylines, polygons, boundaries, and donuts. The viewpoint setting used in Figure 14.21 is the SW Isometric view.

Text objects are automatically drawn at zero thickness regardless of the current object thickness setting. The thickness property of text objects can be changed after they are drawn, in order to create 3-D text. This can be done using any of the commands for changing object properties. Figure 14.22 shows a text object after changing the thickness with the following sequence:

Command: **CHPROP**↵
Select objects: ⟨*select text*⟩
1 found
Select objects:
Change what property (Color/LAyer/LType/ltScale/Thickness) ? **T**↵
New thickness <0.0000>: **1**↵
Change what property (Color/LAyer/LType/ltScale/Thickness) ? ↵

Some objects cannot be given a thickness at any time. These objects may reflect a nonzero thickness property but still do not appear thick. Others may show the thickness property edit box disabled in the DDMODIFY dialog box.

CHAPTER 14 ▮▮▮ 3-D Drafting with AutoCAD LT   599

FIGURE 14.21 The current object thickness setting determines the thickness for newly drawn objects. Not all object types observe the thickness setting.

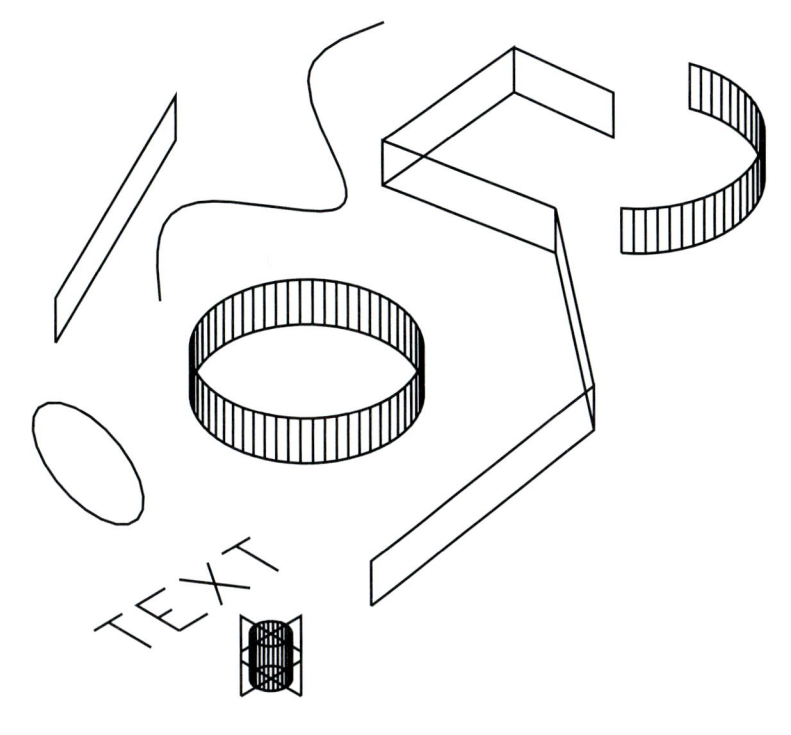

FIGURE 14.22 Text is drawn with a thickness of zero even when the current object thickness setting is nonzero. The thickness property can be changed to create 3-D text.

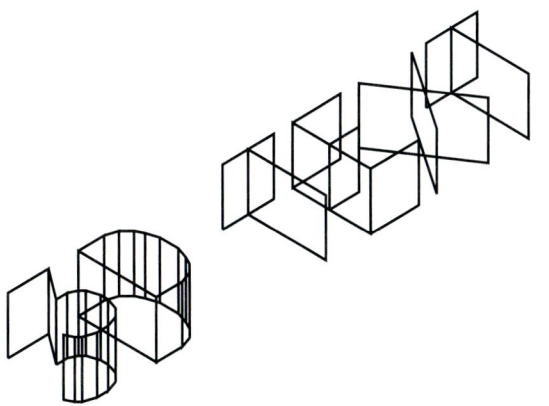

Field Notes

The current object thickness can be set to either a positive or negative value. When set to positive, the thickness extends in the positive Z axis direction. When set to negative, the thickness extends in the negative Z axis direction.

Exercise 14.5

1. Begin a new drawing.
2. Set the current viewpoint to SW Isometric.
3. Set the current object thickness to 1.5.
4. Draw each of the object types shown in Figure 14.22.
5. Save the drawing as EX14.5.

Using Elevation

ELEV

The term *elevation* refers to the Z axis value of the current drawing plane. For example, if the elevation is zero, then you are drawing *on* the X,Y plane of the current UCS. If the elevation is 2, then you are drawing 2 units *above* the X,Y plane of the current UCS. Essentially, the elevation is simply the current Z axis value. The elevation can be positive or negative.

The current elevation is set using the ELEV command. This command can be accessed by typing **ELEV** at the Command: prompt. The following example sets the current elevation to 2.5:

Command: **ELEV**↵
New current elevation <0.0000>: **2.5**↵
New current thickness <1.2500>: ↵

When accessed using the ELEV command, an opportunity is presented to set the current thickness also. The result is the same as that produced using the THICKNESS command.

Setting the elevation is an alternative to moving objects on the Z axis or defining a new UCS origin. A very important note is that the elevation setting defines the current construction plane in reference to the current coordinate system. The elevation setting remains in effect even when you change to a different UCS, which can cause confusion. Such confusion can be avoided by leaving the elevation at zero and setting a new UCS origin when you need to draw at a new elevation.

Because the UCS is a more reliable and straightforward method of controlling your current construction plane, it is recommended that the UCS Origin option be used rather than the ELEV command.

Exercise 14.6

1. Begin a new drawing.
2. Set the current viewpoint to SW Isometric.
3. Set the current object thickness to 0.15.
4. Draw a hexagon, with the center at 2,2 and a .25 radius.
5. Make two copies of the hexagon, one centered at 3,2 and the other at 4,2.
6. Zoom in a little closer to your work.
7. Set the elevation to 0.15, and the thickness to .75. Draw a circle at the center of the first hexagon, using the point coordinate 2,2 and a .15 radius.
8. Set the UCS Origin to 0,0,0.15. Draw a circle at the center of the second hexagon, using the point coordinate 3,2 and a .15 radius.
9. Set the elevation to 0. Draw a circle at the center of the third hexagon, using the point coordinate 4,2 and a .15 radius.
10. Save the drawing as EX14.6.

✓ LEARNING CHECKPOINT

- ☐ What primary command is used to change the 3-D viewing angle?
- ☐ By default, what coordinate system is used when changing 3-D viewpoints?
- ☐ Describe the function of the Axis Tripod and Compass.
- ☐ How does the Rotate option work to change the 3-D viewing angle?
- ☐ Describe each 3-D viewpoint preset option.
- ☐ What is thickness?
- ☐ What is the effect of thickness on text objects?
- ☐ What object types does thickness affect?
- ☐ What are the disadvantages of using ELEV instead of UCS?

Simulating 3-D Surfaces

In a true 3-D CAD environment, AutoCAD Release 14 for example, a 3-D surface is a 2-D solid object. This means that it has height and width but no thickness. A 3-D surface can be located and oriented anywhere in 3-D space. These objects are used to define the "skin" of a 3-D object, also known as a surface model.

AutoCAD LT does not have a 3-D surface object type. However, 2-D objects that have been given a thickness property can be used to simulate 3-D surfaces. The term *simulate* means to look like, or give the appearance of.

When objects are drawn on screen, whether using 2-D coordinates or 3-D coordinates, they do not appear to be truly three dimensional. This is because the objects are represented as a wire frame. A wire frame drawing does not appear to be actually 3-D because you can see lines that would not normally be visible because they are on the back side of the object. For example, in Figure 14.23, two circles have been drawn with thickness to give the appearance of cylinders. However, while they are displayed as wire frame objects, all of the lines used to define them are completely visible. This does not give a true 3-D appearance. Additionally, it is difficult to be sure of the orientation of the cylinders—are they vertical or horizontal?

FIGURE 14.23 Objects shown as wire frame do not give a clear 3-D appearance.

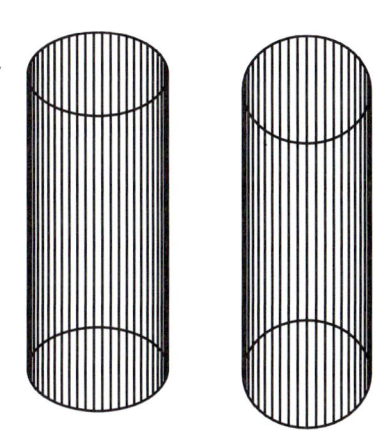

Removing Hidden Lines

In drafting, lines that would not be seen in the view being drawn are called *hidden lines*. Hidden lines are drawn in a different linetype to avoid confusion. To make a 3-D drawing easier to understand, you can view it with the hidden lines removed from the view. The HIDE command is used to remove these hidden lines. After removing the hidden lines, you can continue to work or you can restore the previous appearance of your drawing by using the REGEN command. The HIDE command is accessed by picking Hide from the View pull-down menu or type **HI** or **HIDE** at the Command: prompt. Depending on how many 3-D objects are in your drawing and the speed of your computer, this may take only a moment or it can take several minutes. The current status of the hide operation is displayed while AutoCAD LT works out the calculations:

View
└ Hide

HIDE
HI

    Command: **HIDE**↵
    Regenerating drawing.
    Hiding lines 100% done.

The HIDE operation affects only the current viewport. The percentage starts at 0% and dynamically indicates the progress of the operation. If you feel the operation is going to take too long, you can cancel by pressing the Escape key.

Figure 14.24 shows the circles drawn previously, this time with the hidden lines removed. With the hidden lines removed, the circles appear to be a solid cylinder. The orientation of the cylinder in 3-D space also becomes obvious.

Another point that becomes obvious only after hidden lines are removed is the relative position of objects in 3-D space. In Figure 14.25A, the relative positioning of each of the objects is difficult to determine. The removal of the hidden lines in Figure 14.25B clears up any confusion.

The hidden image remains visible until the next regeneration occurs in that viewport. Notice that in Figure 14.25B the circles simulate surfaces not only on the thickness, but also on the ends—in the X,Y plane. The polyline object, however, only simulates a surface along its thickness. This is true also of lines, arcs, and

FIGURE 14.24 With the hidden lines removed, the true nature of the 3-D objects becomes apparent.

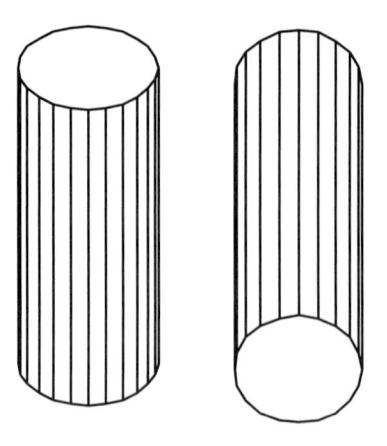

FIGURE 14.25 Removing hidden lines clarifies both the orientation and the relative positioning of objects in 3-D space.

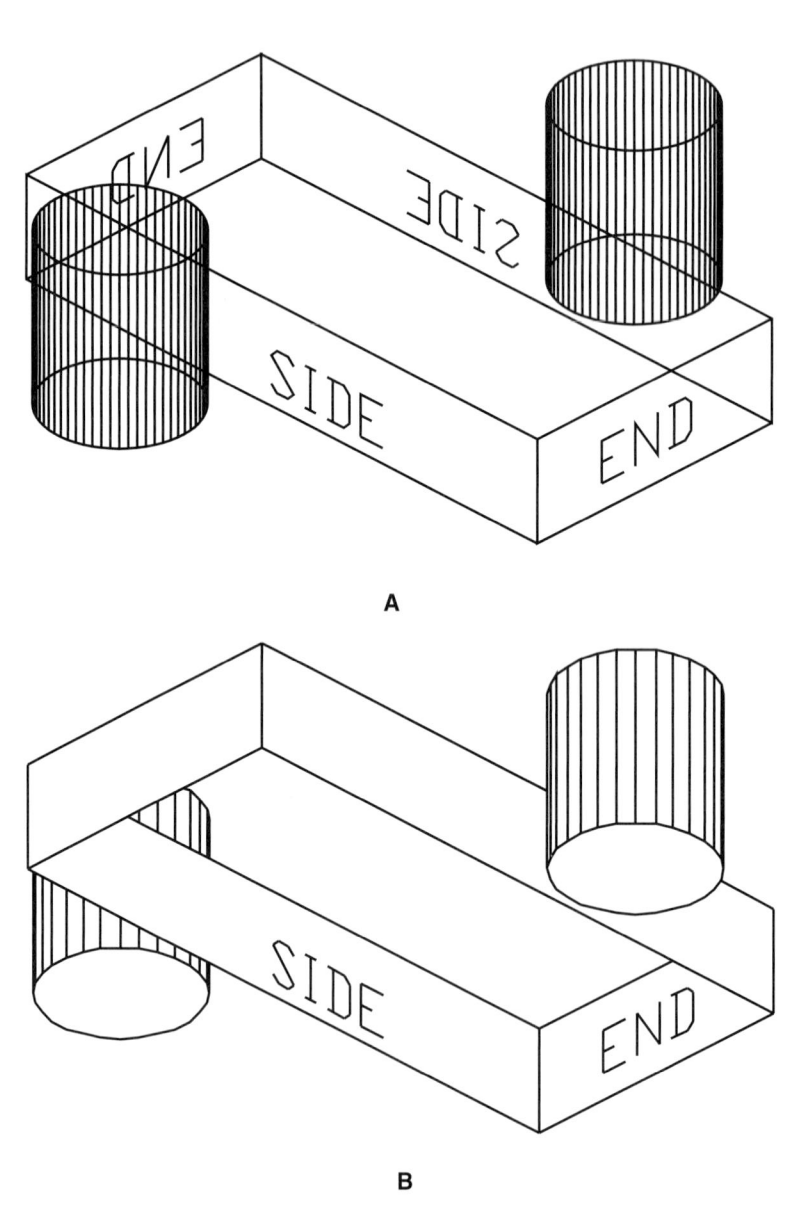

A

B

spline-fit polylines. Therefore, a complete box cannot be made by simply giving a rectangle a thickness value. This means that in order to create a convincing 3-D image, you must exercise some creative imagination.

The following example creates a surfaced cube using line objects. First, the four sides are drawn, then the UCS is rotated and the top and bottom are added. The results are shown in Figure 14.26:

CHAPTER 14 ▌ 3-D Drafting with AutoCAD LT 603

```
Command: TH↵
New value for THICKNESS <0.0000>: 2↵
Command: L↵
From point: 0,0↵
To point: 2,0↵
To point: 2,2↵
To point: 0,2↵
To point: C↵
Command: UCS↵
Origin/ZAxis/3point/OBject/View/X/Y/Z/Prev/Restore/Save/Del/?/<World>: X↵
Rotation angle about X axis <0>: −90↵
Command: PLAN↵

<Current UCS>/Ucs/World: ↵
Regenerating drawing.
Command: L↵
From point: 0,0↵
To point: 2,0↵
To point: ↵
Command: L↵
From point: 0,−2↵
To point: 2,−2↵
To point: ↵
```
⟨set the current viewpoint to SW Isometric⟩
```
Command: HIDE↵
Regenerating drawing.
Hiding lines 100% done.
```

FIGURE 14.26 This cube appears to be a complete surface model. Each face is covered by a line object with a thickness property.

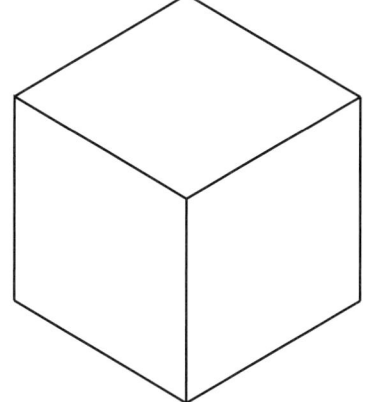

Very complex models can be created using a combination of thick objects created in varied coordinate systems. In the model shown in Figure 14.27, lines were created using varied coordinate systems and thickness values. Next, the direct hatch option was used because the thickness of an object is not hatchable by selecting the area or the object. Prior to creating each hatch pattern, the UCS was set to match the plane of the objects being hatched.

FIGURE 14.27 Creativity and imagination can be valuable when constructing a 3-D model. Even with AutoCAD LT's limited 3-D tool set, complex 3-D floor plans and other 3-D models can be simulated.

> **Field Notes**
>
> Although AutoCAD cannot create true 3-D surfaces, one of its object types can be used in a similar manner. When viewed from a 3-D angle, the SOLID object type does not appear filled in, but when the HIDE command is used, any lines behind the solid are not visible.

Adding Color to Surfaces

View
└ Shade

SHADE
SHA
SH

The term *rendering* is used to describe the process of applying colors to the surfaces in a drawing. The simplest form of rendering is called *shading.* This applies simple colors to all of the surfaces, without allowing for lighting, shadows, or reflections. See Figure 14.28.

AutoCAD LT shades all simulated surfaces, such as thick objects and solids. Shading can be applied to any object that responds to the HIDE command. The SHADE command is accessed by typing **SH** or **SHADE** at the Command: prompt, or by picking an option from the Shade cascade on the View pull-down menu:

Command: **SH** or **SHADE**↵
Regenerating drawing.
Shading complete.

FIGURE 14.28 A shaded drawing applies simple colors to the surfaces in the drawing.

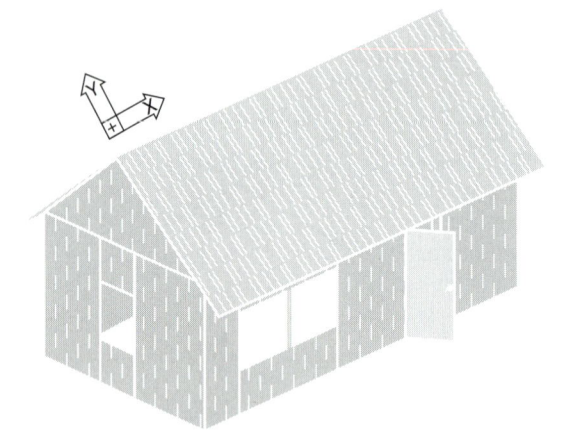

Similar to the HIDE command, there are no prompts to answer. The shaded image remains until a regeneration occurs in that viewport. Shaded objects cannot be selected for editing, so you need to regenerate the viewport to continue working. Shaded images can only be displayed on screen; they cannot be plotted.

The SHADE command uses the current settings for two system variables, SHADEDGE and SHADEDIF, to determine the final appearance of the shaded image. The SHADEDGE variable controls the shading of edges and can be adjusted by typing **SD** or **SHADEDGE** at the Command: prompt. The four SHADEDGE settings are available automatically from the Shade cascade on the View pull-down menu. These four options, a brief explanation, and the SHADEDGE value used are shown in Table 14.2. A sample shaded image, using each of these settings, is shown in Figure 14.29. Looking at these images, you can see

TABLE 14.2 The SHADEDGE options

Option	Description	SHADEDGE setting
256 Color	Shades faces using a 256-color palette; does not show face edges.	0
256 Color Edge Highlight	Shades faces using a 256-color palette; highlights edges using background color.	1
16 Color Hidden Line	Shades the edges, not the faces. Looks similar to results obtained when using the HIDE command.	2
16 Color Filled	Fills faces using object color; highlights edges using background color.	3

CHAPTER 14 ‖ 3-D Drafting with AutoCAD LT 605

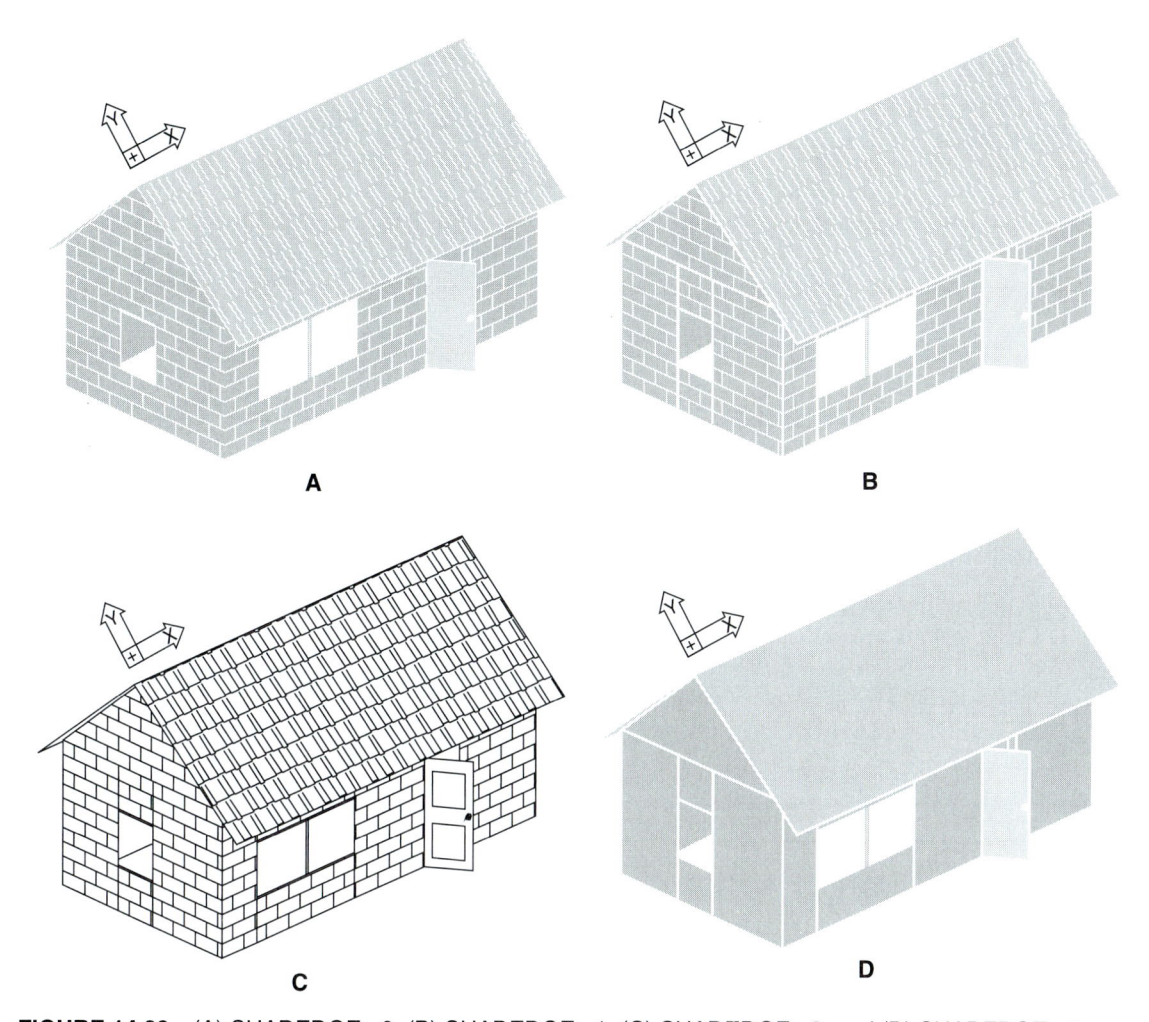

FIGURE 14.29 (A) SHADEDGE=0, (B) SHADEDGE=1, (C) SHADEDGE=2, and (D) SHADEDGE=3.

that the 256-color shade with highlighted edges, where SHADEDGE=1, shows the most accurate representation of the model being shaded. This model relies on the display of edges as well as faces to show the most detail. To achieve more refined results, you can adjust the value of the SHADEDIF variable.

SHADEDIF controls the way AutoCAD LT uses lighting in the shaded image. Two different types of lighting are used, ambient and diffuse reflective. *Ambient light* refers to the surrounding light, which produces a uniform light reflection level. *Diffuse reflective light* produces varied reflection levels. The light source is always considered to be a single source from directly behind your eye. SHADEDIF controls the percentage of light used in the shading process that is considered to be diffuse reflective, and can be set between 0% and 100%. The default is 70%, which means that the other 30% is ambient light. Figure 14.28 used the default value for SHADEDIF. In Figure 14.30, the SHADEDIF value has been set to 85% so the edges show up better.

Field Notes

- In order for SHADEDIF to have an effect, the SHADEDGE value must be set to 0 or 1.
- Hatch lines in an image are considered to be edges, and will only be visible when viewed from a suitable viewing angle with an appropriate SHADEDIF value.

FIGURE 14.30 The SHADEDIF value and the viewing angle affect the appearance of edges in a shaded image.

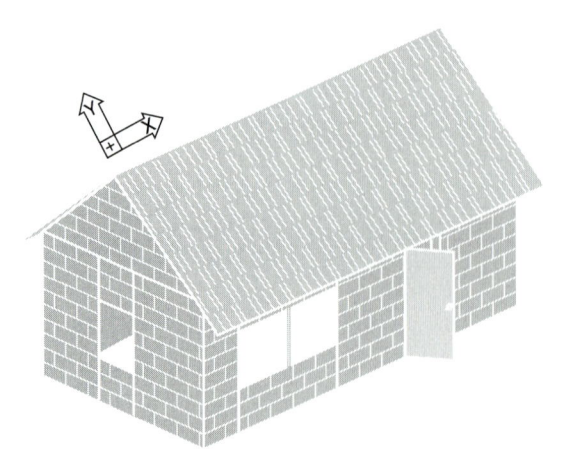

Exercise 14.7

1. Start a new drawing from scratch.
2. Create a simulated solid cube, as shown in Figure 14.26.
3. Set up a SE Isometric viewpoint.
4. Shade the image using each of the available shading options, by adjusting the value of SHADEDIF and SHADEDGE.
5. Save the drawing as EX14.7.

✓ LEARNING CHECKPOINT

☐ What part of a 2-D object can be used like a surface?
☐ Describe the effects of SHADEDGE and SHADEDIF.

Dynamic 3-D Viewing Options

View
⌐ 3D Dynamic View
   DVIEW
   DV

With standard 3-D viewpoint options, it may be necessary to try several various settings until you find one that suits your needs. AutoCAD LT offers a way to change the view dynamically. This means that you can see the results as you change the settings, similar to RTPAN and RTZOOM. The DVIEW command, short for Dynamic VIEW, is accessed by typing DV or DVIEW at the Command: prompt, or by picking 3D Dynamic View from the View pull-down menu.

The DVIEW command offers a number of options. You can define a viewing angle as with other 3-D viewing options, termed a *parallel projection.* You can also create perspective views. In drafting, a *perspective view* is defined as the most realistic form of pictorial illustration. It presents objects as though they were being viewed in the real world, with closer objects being larger and distant objects being smaller.

There are two primary ways to use the DVIEW command. When this command is started, a Select objects: prompt is displayed. Because the DVIEW command is dynamic, it needs a way to display the results of the view changes as you make them. You can select objects in your drawing for AutoCAD LT to use for this purpose. A word of caution: Selecting too many objects can cause the dynamic display to be very slow. Also, too many selected objects can make the resulting display difficult to interpret. It is best to select as few objects as possible, as long as the selected objects present a clear representation of the current view. Alternately, pressing Enter without selecting any objects displays a simple wire frame model of a house to represent the current view results. Figure 14.31 shows this image.

FIGURE 14.31 The default image used by DVIEW is a simple wire frame house. This is used when you press Enter instead of selecting objects in your drawing.

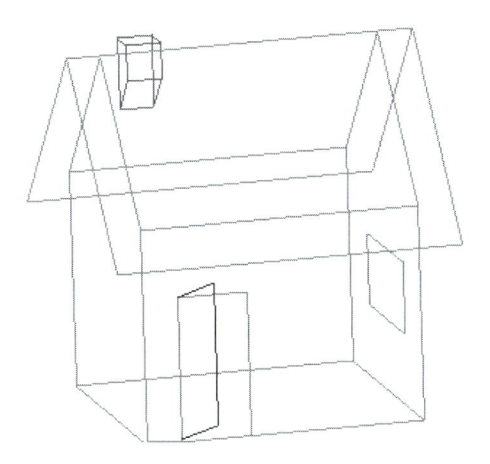

Field Notes

> The wire frame house used by the DVIEW command is actually a block named DVIEWBLOCK. You can create your own customized DVIEWBLOCK. Create the geometry you want to use, then use the BLOCK command and specify the block name as DVIEWBLOCK. When asked if you want to redefine it, pick Yes. The geometry you create should fit within a $1 \times 1 \times 1$ cube.

After specifying what the DVIEW command is to display at the Select objects: prompt, you are returned to the WCS to begin making your adjustments. Both parallel projections and perspective views require that you set up an appropriate viewing angle. The following describes the options that are used to define your viewing angle.

At the DVIEW option line prompt, you can select an option or simply pick a point on screen. The point you select becomes the base point for a dragging operation. As you move your cursor, the view onscreen updates continuously. The first point you pick becomes the base point for the drag line. Use the status line display as a reference for your next pick. The items listed Dir: and Mag:, for Direction and Magnitude, represent the direction of rotation (Dir:) and how far (Mag:) to rotate the viewing angle. For example, dragging your cursor upward, you can see that the apparent position of the model is rotated the same direction. If you continue to drag until the Mag: value is 180 and pick, the view is now from the back of the model and it appears to be upside-down.

The Dir: value can be confusing at first, because the camera is actually rotated in the opposite direction. For example, if you are looking at the front of a house and you specify Dir:270 and Mag:90, the resulting view is from the top instead of the bottom as you might expect.

Another means of entering the Dir: and Mag: values is by simply typing them in, separated by a comma. This is shown in the following example:

Command: **DV** or **DVIEW**↵
Select objects: ↵
*** Switching to the WCS ***
CAmera/TArget/Distance/POints/PAn/Zoom/TWist/CLip/Hide/Off/Undo/<eXit>: ↵
Enter direction and magnitude angles: **270,90**↵
CAmera/TArget/Distance/POints/PAn/Zoom/TWist/CLip/Hide/Off/Undo/<eXit>: ↵
*** Returning to the UCS ***
Regenerating drawing.

Field Notes

> The AutoCAD LT on-line Help states that, when using the Dir: and Mag: values, you are *rolling the view under the camera*. It is important to understand that the objects in a drawing are not reoriented, rather the camera position is changed. Therefore, rolling the view 90° downward is actually accomplished by rotating the camera 90° upward.

Using the CAmera Option

This adjusts the position of the camera by rotation around the target point. The *target point* defines an anchor point in the drawing and is set using the Target option. The CAmera option does not alter the distance from the target point. When CAmera is selected, the following prompt is displayed:

Command: **DVIEW**↵
Select objects: ↵
CAmera/TArget/Distance/POints/PAn/Zoom/TWist/CLip/Hide/Off/Undo/<eXit>: **CA**↵
Toggle angle in/Enter angle from XY plane <90.0000>: **45**↵
Toggle angle from/Enter angle in XY plane from X axis <−90.0000>: **45**↵
CAmera/TArget/Distance/POints/PAn/Zoom/TWist/CLip/Hide/Off/Undo/<eXit>: ↵
Regenerating drawing.

The option line for the DVIEW command is repeated until the EXIT option is used or the command is canceled. The Toggle angle option allows you to switch between the two angle input modes. Similar to entering spherical coordinates, you are specifying angles either *in* or *from* the X,Y plane. Typing **T,** for Toggle, at the prompt toggles you between these two input modes.

When entering the angle, you can either move the cursor and pick, or you can type an angle value. If you pick a point at the first prompt, AutoCAD LT accepts the input and rotates the camera in the appropriate plane. The Toggle option allows you to switch between entering angles *in* the X,Y plane and *from* the X,Y plane. If an angle is typed at the first prompt, you are then prompted for the other angle.

All adjustments in the DVIEW command are made with respect to the WCS. If the WCS is not active when you use DVIEW, it will be made current while your view adjustments are made:

Command: **DV**↵
Select objects: ↵
*** Switching to the WCS ***
CAmera/TArget/Distance/POints/PAn/Zoom/TWist/CLip/Hide/Off/Undo/<eXit>: **CA**↵
Toggle angle in/Enter angle from XY plane <45.0000>: **T**↵
Toggle angle from/Enter angle in XY plane from X axis <45.0000>: **T**↵
Toggle angle in/Enter angle from XY plane <45.0000>: ⟨*pick an angle*⟩
CAmera/TArget/Distance/POints/PAn/Zoom/TWist/CLip/Hide/Off/Undo/<eXit>: ↵
*** Returning to the UCS ***
Regenerating drawing.

The previous UCS is restored when you exit the DVIEW command and the drawing is regenerated. Figure 14.32 illustrates the concept of rotating the camera around the target.

FIGURE 14.32 Adjusting the camera changes the direction from which you are looking; the target position remains the same.

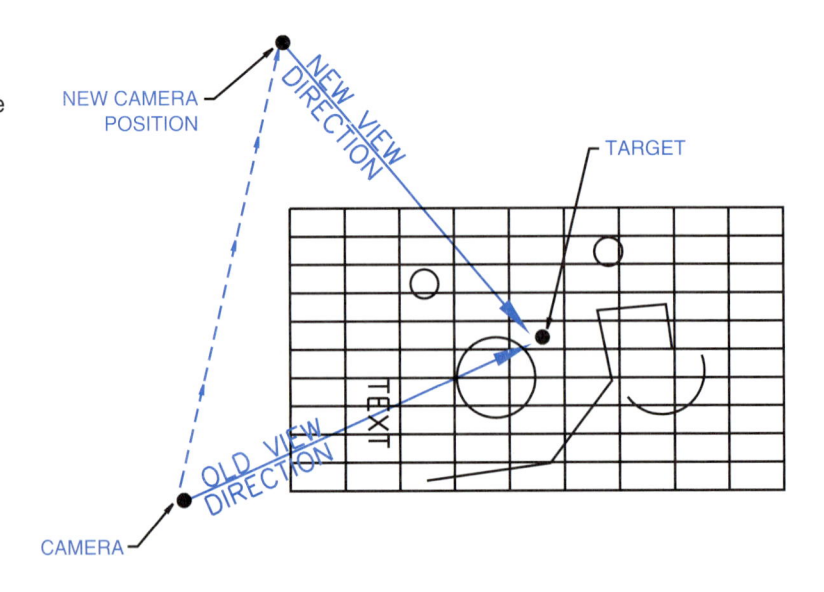

Using the TArget Option

The TArget option allows you to change the rotation angle of the target point in reference to the camera position. The target indicates the point at which your camera is looking. This point is used as the base point for DVIEW options. The position of the target is adjusted by specifying the angles of rotation in and from the X,Y plane:

Command: **DV**↵
Select objects:
*** Switching to the WCS ***
CAmera/TArget/Distance/POints/PAn/Zoom/TWist/CLip/Hide/Off/Undo/<eXit>: **TA**↵
Toggle angle in/Enter angle from XY plane <45.0000>:
Toggle angle from/Enter angle in XY plane from X axis <0.0000>:
CAmera/TArget/Distance/POints/PAn/Zoom/TWist/CLip/Hide/Off/Undo/<eXit>: ↵
*** Returning to the UCS ***
Regenerating drawing.

This option also allows you to pick the angle and toggle the input mode, as with the CAmera option. Figure 14.33 shows the effect of rotating the target point.

FIGURE 14.33 Adjusting the target changes the location at which the camera is looking. The camera position stays the same and the distance from camera to target does not change.

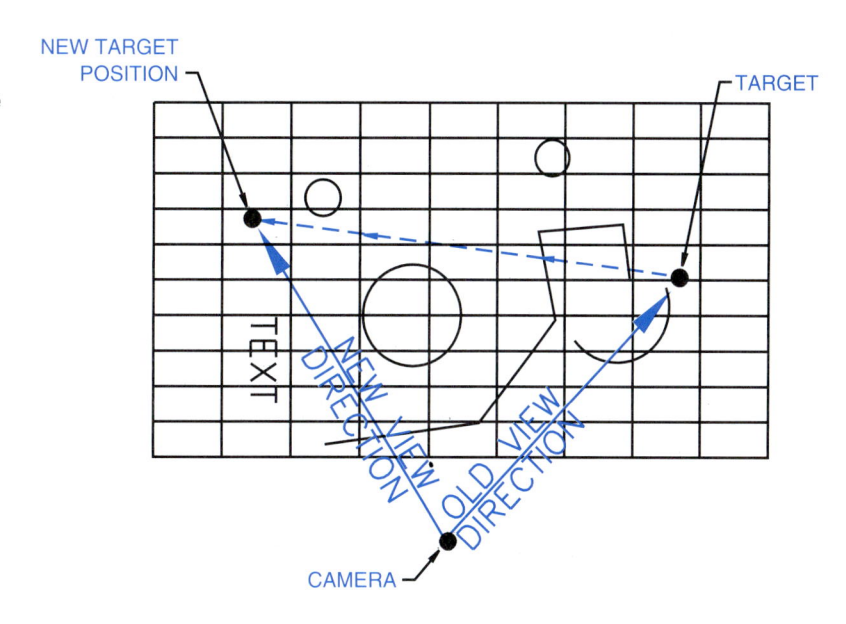

Using the Distance Option

This option turns perspective viewing mode on, and allows you to adjust the distance between the camera and the target along the line of sight. The term *line of sight* refers to an imaginary line of infinite length that passes through the camera location and the target point. When this option is used, AutoCAD LT displays a ***slider bar*** at the top of the graphics screen area. This feature is shown in Figure 14.34. Moving your cursor to the right or left will increase or decrease the distance between the camera and the target by the multiple shown.

Often, when you start the Distance option, only part of the drawing is visible. To correct this, increase the distance between camera and target. The numbers on the slider are used as multiplier values, so anything over 1 increases the distance and anything under 1 decreases the distance. Sometimes it is more convenient to simply type in a number. When typed, a number is taken as an absolute distance, not a multiplier.

When the current view is in perspective, AutoCAD LT replaces the UCS icon with a special perspective icon, shown in Figure 14.35. If the UCS icon is turned off, this icon is not visible. Figure 14.36 shows a perspective view defined using the Distance option.

FIGURE 14.34 The slider bar allows you to change your distance dynamically.

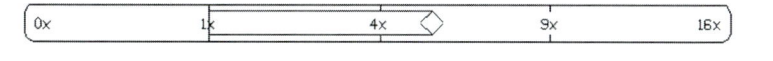

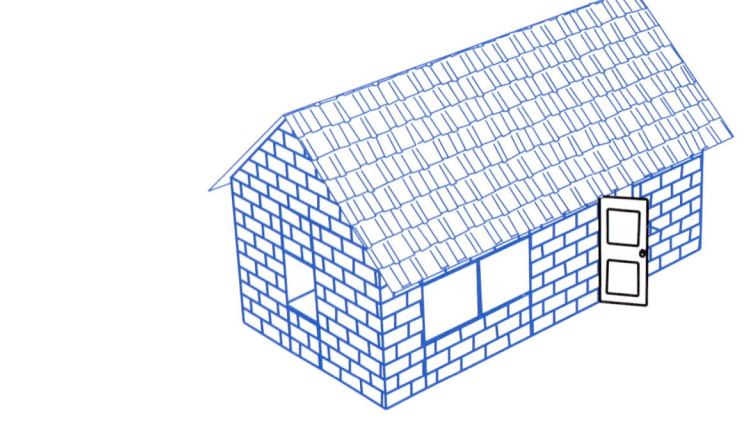

FIGURE 14.35 This icon indicates that your view is currently in a perspective view.

FIGURE 14.36 Perspective views look more realistic than parallel projections.

> ✏️ **Field Notes**
>
> - Many standard AutoCAD LT options are disabled when perspective view is active. These include zooming, panning, and sketching. Additionally, picking points using your pointing device is not allowed in some cases.
> - When in perspective view, you cannot ZOOM PREVIOUS. Using the DVIEW OFF option does not help, because a ZOOM PREVIOUS restores the dynamic view and, again, you cannot restore previous views. Be sure to save the current view as a named view prior to creating the perspective, so you can easily restore that view.
> - When working with the DVIEW command, it is best to make adequate use of named views. Saving unique viewpoints allows you to restore them immediately without having to remember all of the settings for that view.

Using the POints Option

This option allows you to locate the camera and target points using absolute X,Y,Z coordinates. The current locations are displayed as default values and can be used as a reference point. You can specify the new point through any acceptable coordinate entry method. Polar and relative coordinates are in reference to the current location. The prompt sequence looks like this:

    Command: **DV**↵
    Select objects: ↵
    *** Switching to the WCS ***
    CAmera/TArget/Distance/POints/PAn/Zoom/TWist/CLip/Hide/Off/Undo/<eXit>: **PO**↵
    Enter target point <14.3493, −11.4063, 6.9002>: **4,2,7**↵
    Enter camera point <−10.9996, −36.7553, 24.6445>: **@4<30<15**↵
     CAmera/TArget/Distance/POints/PAn/Zoom/TWist/CLip/Hide/Off/Undo/<eXit>: ↵
    *** Returning to the UCS ***
    Regenerating drawing.

Using the PAn Option

The PAn option moves the image without changing the magnification. This command actually moves the target and camera points, but maintains the same distance and angle between them. In a perspective view, the image will change as the angles of perspective change. The actual image does not change in a parallel projection view, it is simply relocated.

The movement is similar to a PAN command, requiring a base point and second point of displacement. This option is performed with respect to the current view. The following example shows the prompt sequence:

Command: **DV**↵
Select objects: ↵
*** Switching to the WCS ***
CAmera/TArget/Distance/POints/PAn/Zoom/TWist/CLip/Hide/Off/Undo/<eXit>: **P**↵
Ambiguous response, please clarify. . .
PAn or POints? **PA**↵
Displacement base point: ⟨*pick first point*⟩
Second point: ⟨*pick next point*⟩
CAmera/TArget/Distance/POints/PAn/Zoom/TWist/CLip/Hide/Off/Undo/<eXit>: ↵
*** Returning to the UCS ***
Regenerating drawing.

Several of the DVIEW options share the same first character with another option and therefore require that the first two characters be typed to access them. As with all option prompts in AutoCAD LT, the required entry is shown in uppercase characters.

Using the Zoom Option

When the current view is a parallel projection, this option works similar to the scale option of the ZOOM command. The value typed represents the scale factor to be applied to the current magnification. It can be entered as a simple number, or it can be followed by an **X.** Both methods produce the same results. The slider bar can also be used to specify the zoom scale factor. The slider bar is the same as the one shown in Figure 14.34.

If a perspective view is currently displayed, the Zoom option adjusts the lens length of the camera. This is similar to changing the length of a lens on a real camera; the distance between the camera and the object does not change but the field of view does. The default setting is 50mm, which displays the drawing as though it were being viewed using a 35mm camera and a 50mm lens. A longer lens, similar to a telephoto lens, displays the model larger but narrows the field of vision. Shorter lens lengths widen the field of vision, similar to a wide-angle lens on a real camera.

Through working with a combination of the Distance setting and the lens length using Zoom, you can display a drawing using varied lines of perspective. Be careful to avoid displaying extreme lines of perspective, as shown in Figure 14.37. To return to a more conventional perspective view, increase both the lens length and distance values.

Using the TWist Option

The TWist option rotates the view around the line of sight. This means that the axis of rotation is the line between the camera and the target point. The twist angle is absolute, relative to zero, and is not cumulative. Therefore, specifying a twist angle of 15° twice in a row leaves the twist at 15°, not 30°. The angle can be specified by dragging the cursor and picking, or by typing the angle directly at the prompt.

FIGURE 14.37 Too short of a distance and lens length can produce extreme angles of perspective, resulting in a drawing that appears distorted.

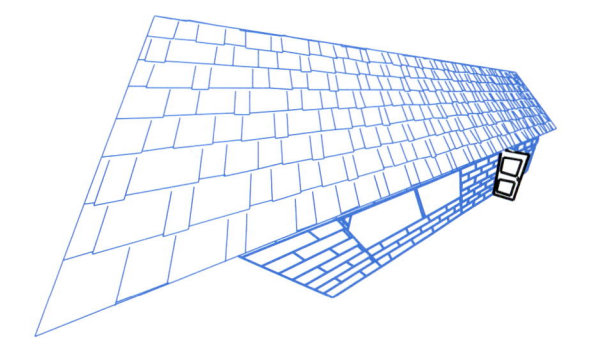

Using the CLip Option

To view only part of the model, clipping planes can be positioned in the drawing. A ***clipping plane*** is an imaginary plane that hides part of the drawing. There are two clipping planes, the front and the back. Objects and parts of objects that occur in front of the front clipping plane or behind the back clipping plane are not drawn. These options are used to create cutaway sections or simply to reduce drawing clutter. Clipping planes are parallel to the current view, and they move when the view is changed. Figure 14.38 shows an illustration of the function of clipping planes.

Selecting the CLip option presents the following option line:

Back/Front/<Off>:

FIGURE 14.38 The front and back clipping planes control which objects in a view are drawn.

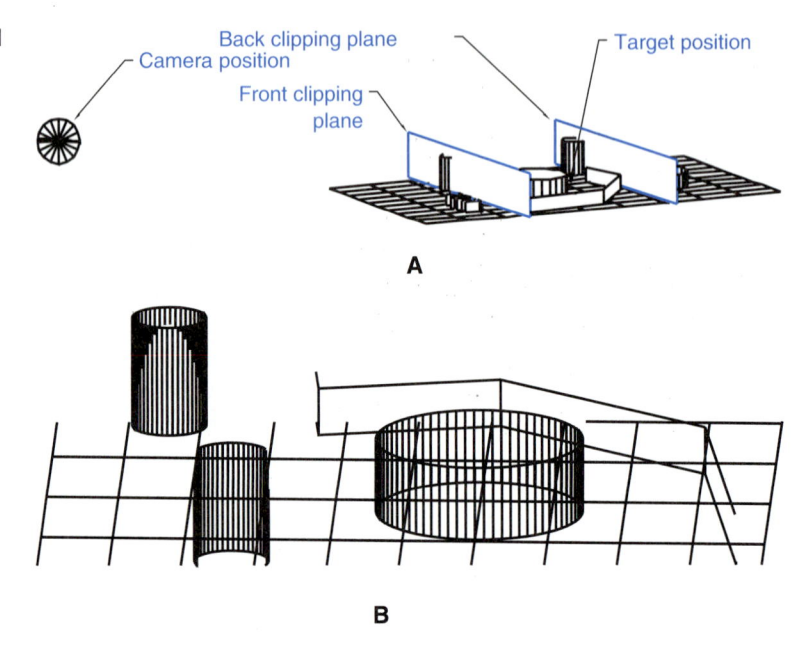

The default option, Off, turns both clipping planes off. The Back and Front options access additional options for the selected plane. The following options are the same for both the front and back clipping planes:

ON	Turns on clipping in the current clipping plane location.
OFF	Turns off the clipping for the specified plane.
Distance from target	Positions the clipping plane at the specified distance from the target point, along the line of sight.

The Front plane provides an additional option:

Eye   Sets the front clipping plane to its default location, at the camera point.

Using the Hide Option

This option works just like the HIDE command. Hidden lines are removed from the display to provide a clear and understandable image of the model. This option works whether you have selected objects with DVIEW or the DVIEWBLOCK is being used.

Using the Off Option

The Off option is used to turn perspective viewing off, which restores the model to a parallel projection. Perspective viewing is turned on when the Distance option is used.

CHAPTER 14 ▕▕▕ 3-D Drafting with AutoCAD LT   **613**

Using the Undo Option

This is very valuable when working with DVIEW. You can undo one option at a time, all the way back to the beginning of this DVIEW command.

Exiting the DVIEW Command

The eXit option exits the DVIEW command and implements the view changes made within the DVIEW command. The entire drawing is regenerated according to the viewpoint and camera options specified.

> ✎ Field Notes
>
> - If you have made several adjustments to the view using DVIEW and do not wish to save them, you can press the Esc key at any time to cancel the effects of the DVIEW command.
> - As discussed at the beginning of this chapter, you cannot create 3-D surface objects in Auto-CAD LT. However, you can import, duplicate, and edit 3-D surfaces. The object type in Auto-CAD R14 for a 3-D surface is called a 3DFACE. By opening or inserting a drawing containing 3DFACE objects, you have the opportunity to experiment with these object types in AutoCAD LT. Inserting and exploding the block named DVIEWBLOCK leaves its component objects in your drawing. Because this block definition uses 3DFACEs, it is now possible to duplicate and grip edit these objects for your own project.

Exercise 14.8

1. Open EX14.27 for editing.
2. Use each of the DVIEW command options. Be sure to use the HIDE option frequently to clarify the results.
3. Produce a perspective view.
4. Save the drawing as EX14.8.

☑ LEARNING CHECKPOINT

☐ What does the term *camera* refer to?

☐ Define the term *target*.

☐ Which DVIEW option creates a perspective view?

☐ What are clipping planes?

Tiled Viewports and 3-D Drawings

Tiled viewports, introduced in Chapter 13, can be very useful for 3-D drafting. The biggest problem in 3-D drafting is visualization. Designers and drafters must be able to visualize what they are drawing in order to create accurate drawings. The problem comes from viewing 3-D objects through a 2-D screen. This gets back to the same concept of communicating 3-D ideas on 2-D paper. The most effective way to do this is by using several different views from various angles.

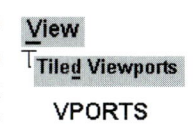

    When tiled viewports are used, each viewport can be set to view the model from different angles and at any desired scale factors. Additionally, various grid and snap settings can be used. Some views can show hidden lines removed or even shaded images. Figure 14.39 shows an example of a working tiled viewport layout.

    The primary functions for creating viewports can be accessed from the Tiled Viewports cascade on the View pull-down menu, or they can be accessed at the Command: prompt using the VPORTS command. The available VPORTS command options are discussed in Chapter 13.

<u>V</u>iew
└ Tile<u>d</u> Viewports
   VPORTS

Creative use of the VPORTS command allows you great flexibility in designing your working layout. The basic guideline for generating viewport layouts is not to make viewports so small that you cannot easily edit objects within them.

The following sequence is used to create the layout shown in Figure 14.39:

Command: **VPORTS**↵
Save/Restore/Delete/Join/SIngle/?/2/<3>/4: **2**↵
Horizontal/Vertical/Above/Below/Left/<Right>: **V**↵
Regenerating drawing.
⟨pick in the left viewport to make it current⟩
Command: **VPORTS**↵
Save/Restore/Delete/Join/SIngle/?/2/<3>/4: **2**↵
Horizontal/Vertical/Above/Below/Left/<Right>: **V**↵
Regenerating drawing.

FIGURE 14.39 Tiled viewports can be used to create a versatile environment for working in 3-D drawings.

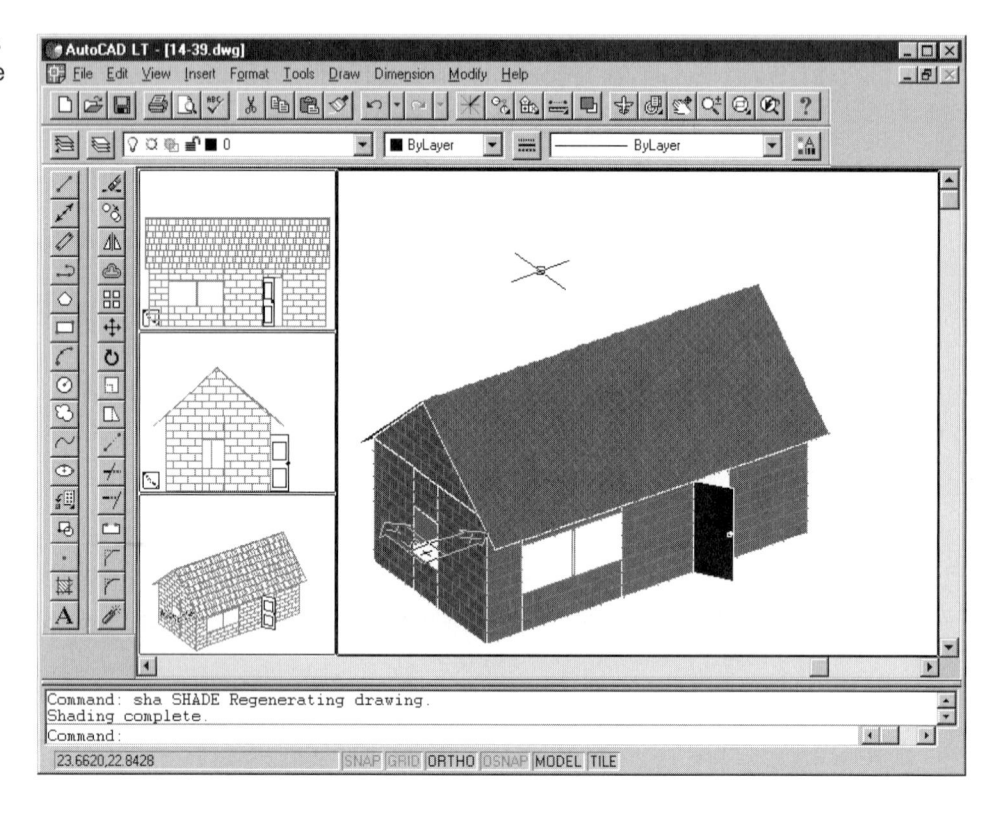

This results in the configuration shown in Figure 14.40.

Command: **VPORTS**↵
Save/Restore/Delete/Join/SIngle/?/2/<3>/4: **J**↵
Select dominant viewport <current>: ⟨pick right viewport⟩
Select viewport to join: ⟨pick middle viewport⟩
Regenerating drawing.

CHAPTER 14 ■ 3-D Drafting with AutoCAD LT   615

FIGURE 14.40 The primary display is divided into two viewports. Then the viewport on the left is further divided into two vertical viewports.

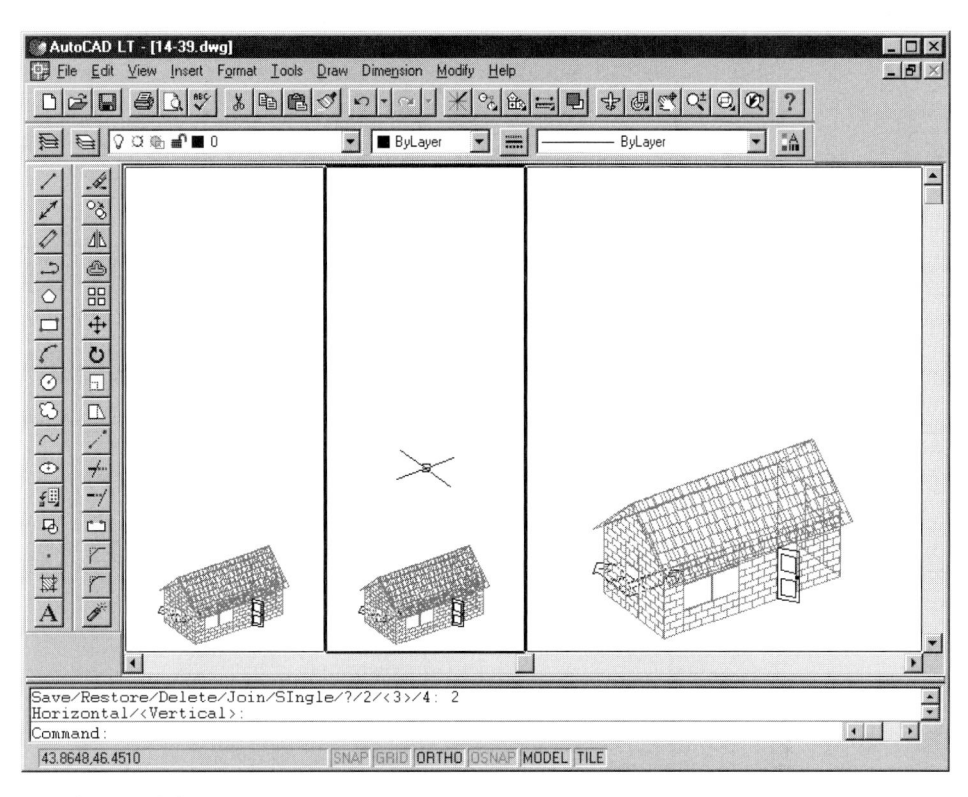

Now, two viewports exist as shown in Figure 14.41:

⟨*pick in the left viewport to make it current*⟩
Command: **VPORTS**↵
Save/Restore/Delete/Join/SIngle/?/2/<3>/4: **3**↵
Horizontal/Vertical/Above/Below/Left/<Right>: **H**↵
Regenerating drawing.

FIGURE 14.41 Now, one viewport fills 75% of the display, and the second fills the other 25%.

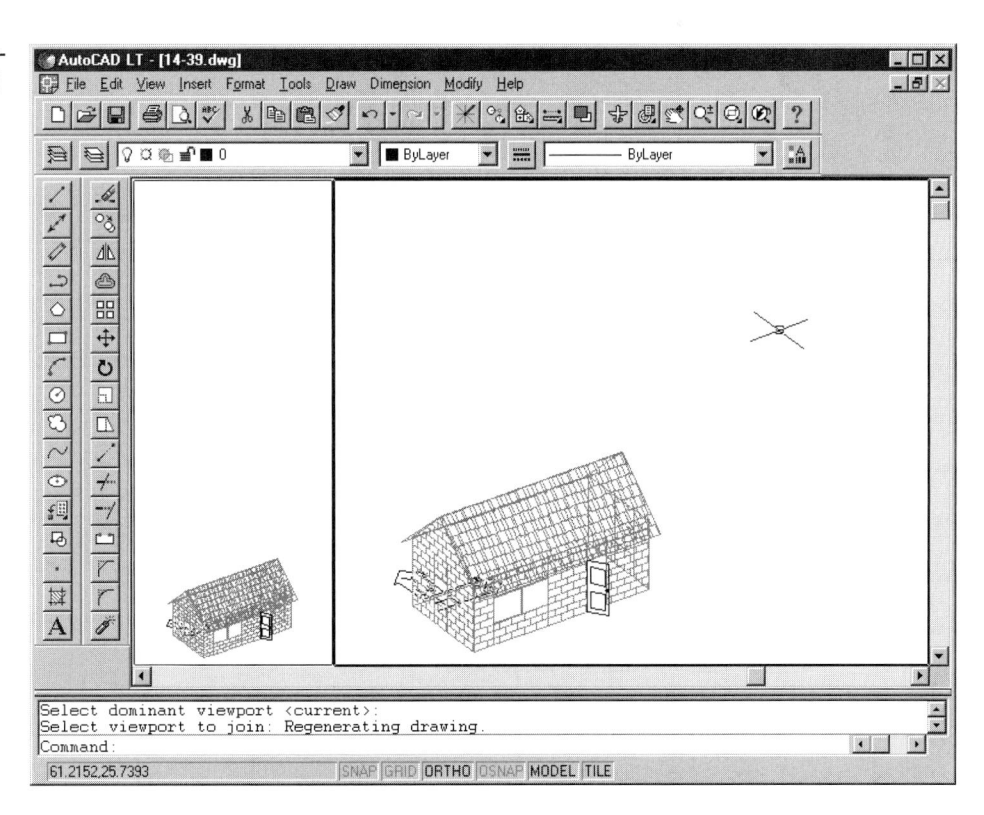

Finally, the display is divided as shown in Figure 14.39. This represents one possible configuration, but many other configuration possibilities exist. Using tiled viewports to your advantage can greatly enhance productivity when working with 3-D drawings.

> ### Exercise 14.9
>
> 1. Open EX14.8.
> 2. Create the viewport layout shown in Figure 14.39.
> 3. Save the drawing as EX14.9.

☑ LEARNING CHECKPOINT

☐ What is the basic guideline for creating tiled viewports?

Creating Isometric Drawings

An isometric drawing can be used to simulate a 3-D view of an object. In some cases, this may be much quicker than actually creating a full 3-D drawing. Because true 3-D solids cannot be created in AutoCAD LT, drawings created in 3-D are simulations and are primarily useful for visualization only. Therefore, it is often more productive to generate an isometric representation of a part.

AutoCAD LT provides some basic isometric drawing tools to assist you when creating isometric views. The first of these tools is the isometric snap grid. The SNAP command is used to enable this feature, or you can access the DDRMODES command by picking Drawing Aids … from the Tools pull-down menu. In the lower right corner of the Drawing Aids dialog box are the options for the isometric snap modes. Figure 14.42 shows this dialog box.

FIGURE 14.42 The isometric snap/grid options can be set in the Drawing Aids dialog box.

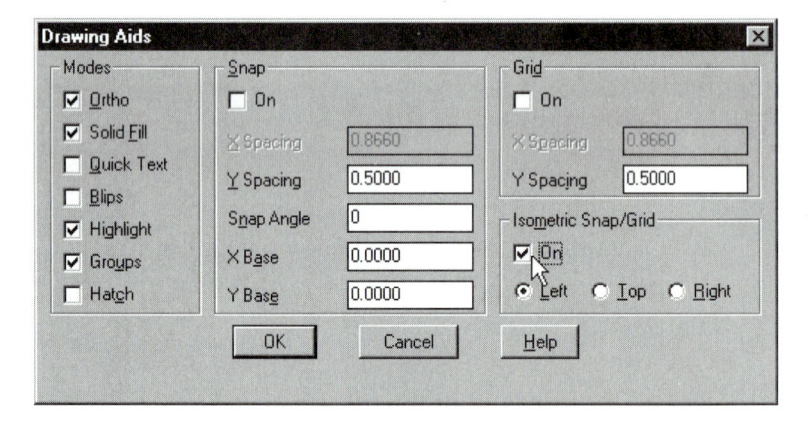

ISOPLANE
IS

Enabling the isometric snap/grid mode changes the cursor into an isometric cursor. A one-unit cube is shown in Figure 14.43, with the three isometric planes labeled. While isometric mode is on, the cursor can be set to the correct configuration for each of these isometric planes as needed. The Left, Top, and Right radio buttons can be used, or the F5 or Ctrl+E keystroke toggles through the three settings. The IS or ISOPLANE command can also be used, but this is the long way around. Each of the plane toggling options can be used transparently. An example of using ISOPLANE is shown here:

Command: **IS** or **ISOPLANE** ↵
Left/Top/Right/<Toggle>: ↵
Current Isometric plane is: **Top**

Ortho mode restricts some movement to be parallel to the cursor. This is also true in isometric mode. Figure 14.44 shows the third segment of a line sequence being drawn using an isometric snap/grid mode, with Ortho on.

CHAPTER 14 ▌ 3-D Drafting with AutoCAD LT 617

FIGURE 14.43 The three isometric planes are Left, Right, and Top. The cursor is modified for each of these planes when working in isometric mode.

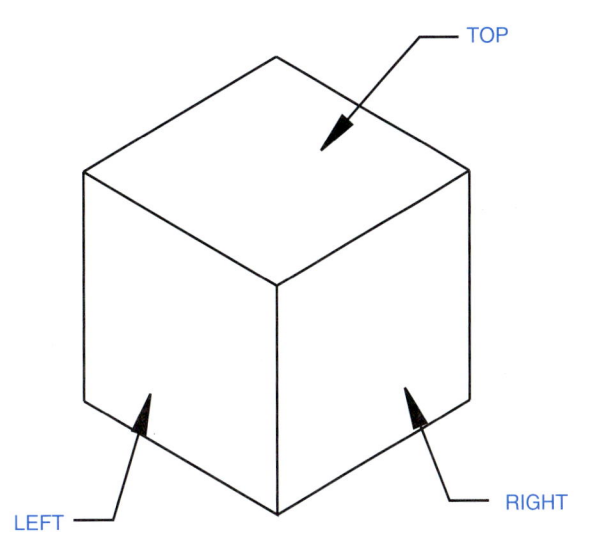

FIGURE 14.44 The isometric cursor also responds to Ortho settings.

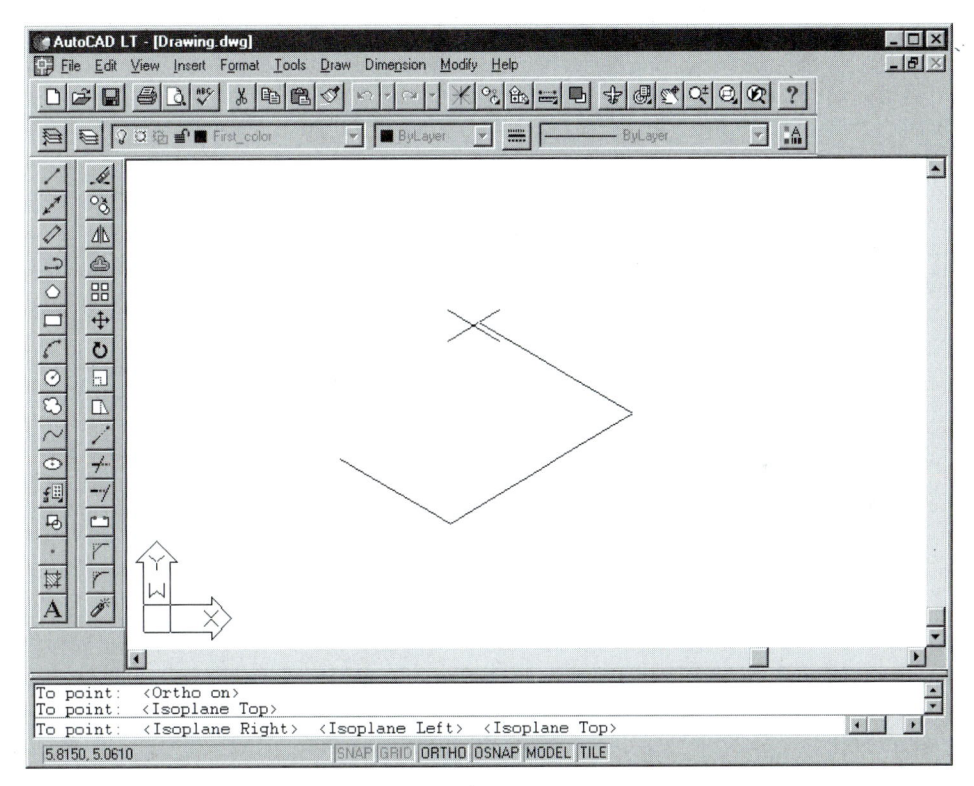

Although the snap and grid orientation changes in isometric mode, the coordinate system is not changed. You can define a new UCS at any time, but you cannot create a UCS that matches a 2-D isometric snap/grid. Figure 14.45 shows an isometric drawing environment with Grid turned on and example coordinate locations labeled.

Drawing Isometric Circles and Arcs

Because an isometric plane is rotated and not viewed flat, an isometric circle appears as an ellipse. When in isometric mode, the ELLIPSE command offers the Isocircle option to assist in drawing isometric circles and arcs:

   Command: **EL** or **ELLIPSE**.↵
   Arc/Center/Isocircle/<Axis endpoint 1>: I↵
   Center of circle: ⟨*pick a point*⟩
   <Circle radius>/Diameter: ⟨*specify radius or D for diameter*⟩

Isometric arcs can be created either by editing isometric circles or they can be drawn directly with the ELLIPSE command. The ELLIPSE Arc option line also presents an option for isometric mode:

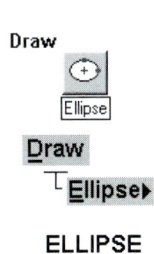

Draw
Ellipse

Draw
└ **E**llipse▸

ELLIPSE
EL

FIGURE 14.45 The isometric snap/grid mode does not affect the UCS.

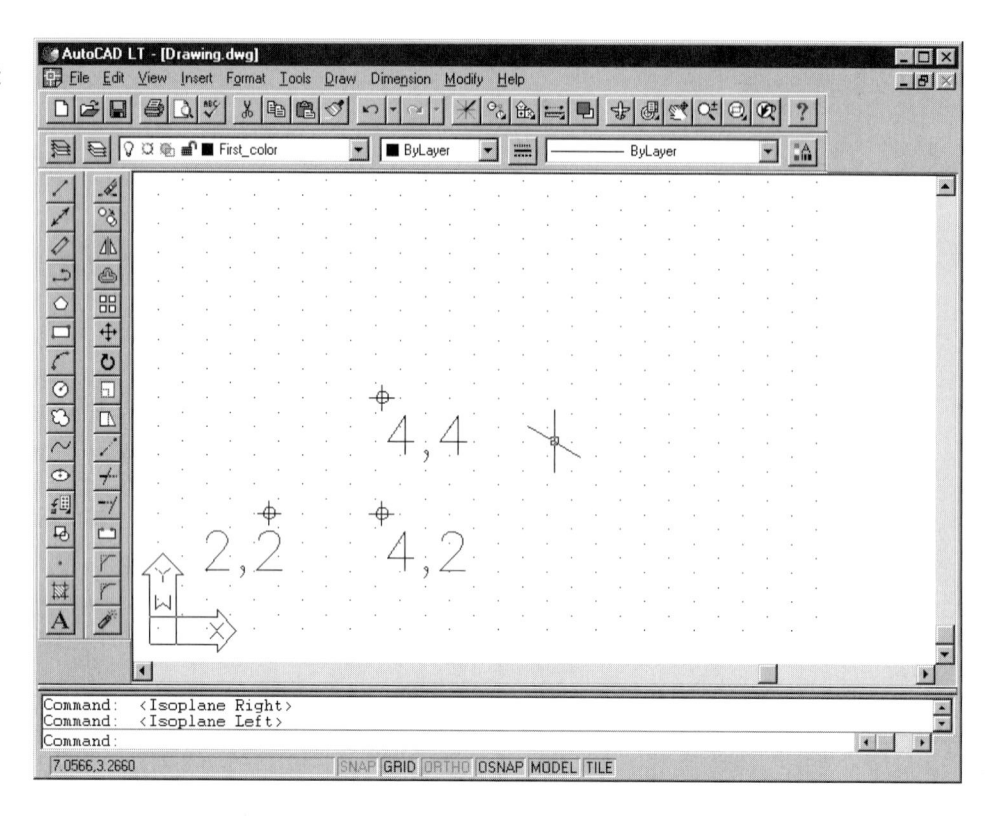

```
Command: EL↵
Arc/Center/Isocircle/<Axis endpoint 1>: A↵
<Axis endpoint 1>/Center/Isocircle: I↵
Center of circle: ⟨pick a point⟩
<Circle radius>/Diameter: .25↵
Parameter/<start angle>: ⟨specify an angle or option⟩
Parameter/Included/<end angle>: ⟨specify angle or option⟩
```

The isometric circle or arc is automatically created as it should appear in the currently active isometric plane. Figure 14.46 shows an isometric circle in each of the isometric planes.

FIGURE 14.46 Isometric circles are automatically drawn to appear correct in the currently active isometric plane.

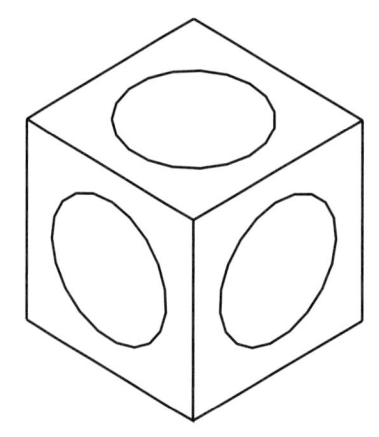

Isometric Text

Using the text obliquing angle within the STYLE command, and rotation angle when creating text, text can easily be made to appear to be drawn on any isometric plane. The cube in Figure 14.47 shows the settings for the text shown on each face. The obliquing angle is defined in the text style, but the rotation can be specified for each line of text. If you create two text styles, one obliqued +30° and the other −30°, the rotation angle can be specified as you create text to create it on the desired isometric plane.

CHAPTER 14 ⫶ 3-D Drafting with AutoCAD LT   **619**

FIGURE 14.47 Settings for isometric text.

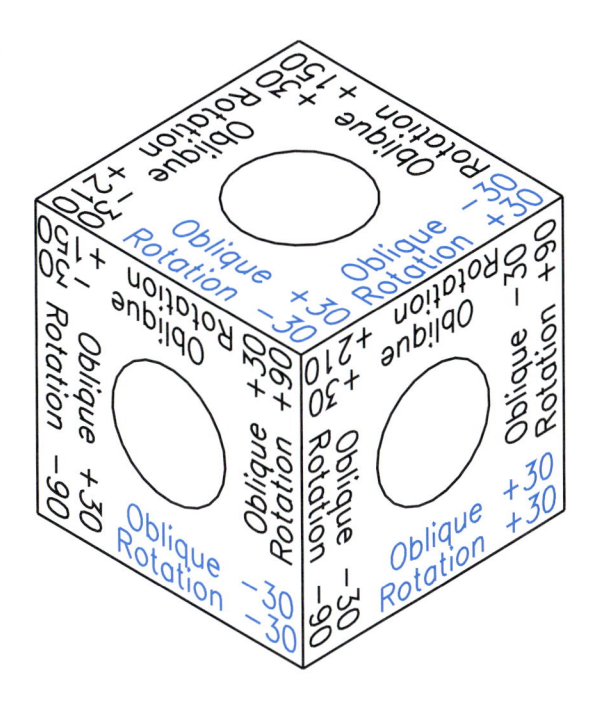

Isometric Arrowheads

It is not a common practice to fully dimension isometric drawings. However, it is sometimes necessary to dimension specific features or use a leader for pointing in an isometric drawing. AutoCAD LT does not have any isometric arrowheads available in its standard dimensioning features. You can, however, create your own and AutoCAD LT can use them while dimensioning.

Isometric arrowheads can be created using the SOLID command. It may be helpful to draw an outline for the arrowhead first as a guide for the SOLID command. In Figure 14.48, all of the isometric arrowheads are shown.

As you create isometric arrowheads, keep in mind that the DIMASZ setting is a multiplier for the *length*. In order for DIMASZ to have the correct effect, the original geometry must be drawn at one unit long. That way, a DIMASZ value of 0.125 creates a 1/8″-long arrowhead because 0.125 × 1″ = 0.125″ (1/8″).

After creating the arrowheads, you must then make them into blocks. Use a simple, yet effective naming system. For example, the left horizontal arrowhead on the right plane could be named RHL, the one on

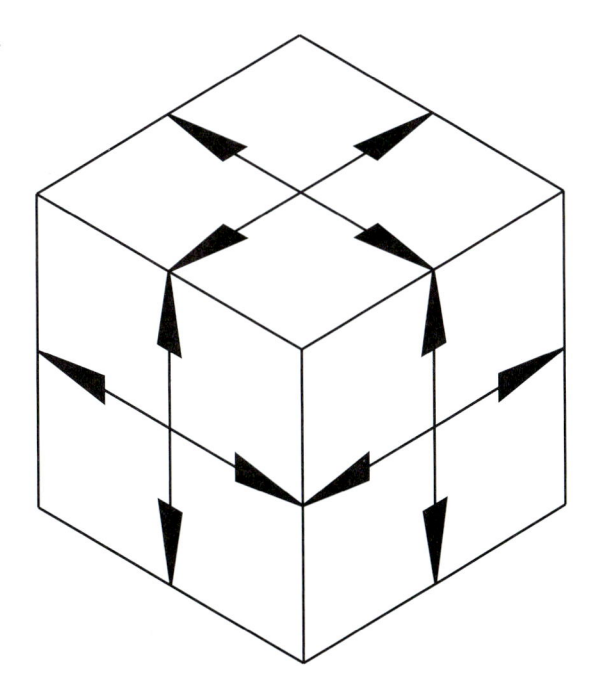

FIGURE 14.48 Isometric arrowheads.

the right might be RHR. The vertical arrowheads could be RVB and RVT for Right-Vertical-Bottom and Right-Vertical-Top. Any naming system that makes sense to you can be used.

To use isometric arrowheads in AutoCAD LT dimension objects, it is necessary to adjust the DIMBLK1 and DIMBLK2 settings according to the isometric plane you are working on. Additionally, you need to set the DIMTXSTY variable to the appropriate setting for the plane and direction of the dimensions. A more effective means would be to define an individual dimension style for vertical and horizontal dimensions on each plane. This way you only need to change one setting rather than three when you need a different type of dimension.

When drawing the dimensions, the DIMALIGNED option can be used because most isometric lines are drawn true length. DIMVERTICAL can be used for the vertical lines. To adjust the dimensions to appear to be in an isometric plane, the OBLIQUE option is used. Figure 14.49A shows an isometric drawing dimensioned using DIMALIGNED and DIMVERTICAL. In Figure 14.49B, the OBLIQUE command has been used to make the dimensions appear correctly. The obliquing angle used appears next to each dimension.

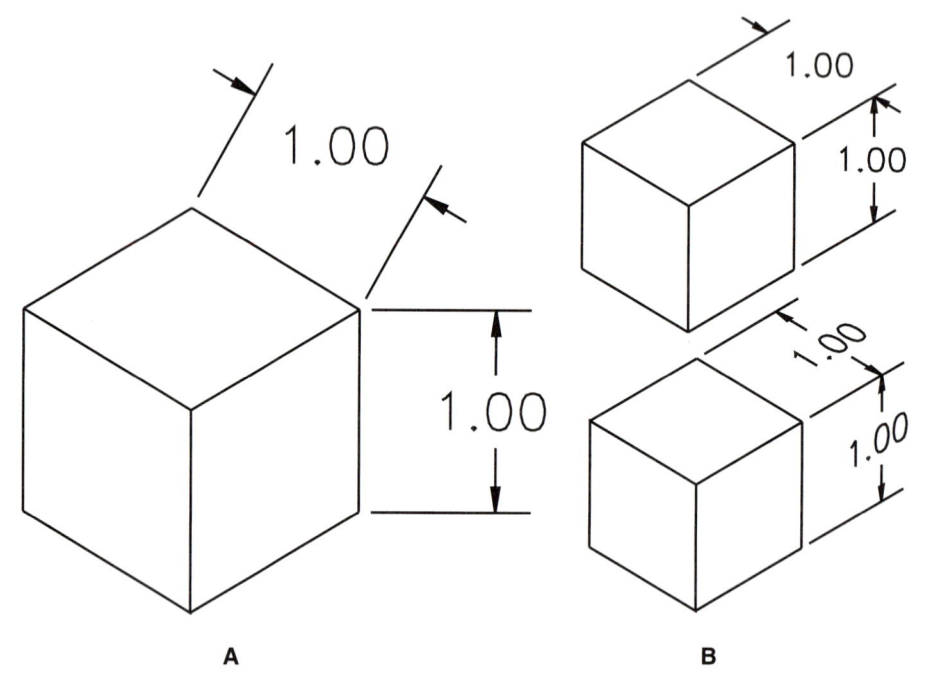

FIGURE 14.49 (A) Dimensions before obliquing. (B) Dimensions after obliquing.

Field Notes

If you plan to do more than one isometric drawing in your career, it is best to define all your isometric options in an isometric template, or prototype drawing. This template should have all of the appropriate text styles, arrowhead blocks, and dimension styles already defined.

Exercise 14.10

1. Start a new drawing.
2. Draw an isometric cube using the appropriate isometric environmental settings.
3. Place an isometric circle at the center of each face of the cube.
4. Place an isometric fillet at each corner using the ELLIPSE Arc Isometric option.
5. Save the drawing as EX14.10.

CHAPTER 14 ▍ 3-D Drafting with AutoCAD LT

☑ LEARNING CHECKPOINT

☐ What are the ways to change the current isometric plane? Which is best?

☐ How does Ortho respond to isometric settings?

☐ What is the effect of isometric snap on the coordinate system?

☐ How is isometric text created?

☐ Describe how isometric dimensions are created.

☐ Why is an isometric template valuable?

MULTIPLE CHOICE

Circle the choice or enter your response on an answer sheet by selecting the option that most closely completes or answers the given statement.

1. The fixed coordinate system used by default in AutoCAD LT is called the:
   a. default coordinate system
   b. user coordinate system
   c. world coordinate system
   d. object coordinate system

2. This simple reference makes it easier to visualize the relationships of the X, Y, and Z axes in 3-D space:
   a. the coordinate display
   b. the right-hand rule
   c. object snap
   d. the status bar

3. This variation of polar coordinate entry uses a standard polar coordinate followed by a Z axis value:
   a. relative coordinates
   b. absolute coordinates
   c. spherical coordinates
   d. cylindrical coordinates

4. 2<45<60 represents an example of:
   a. relative coordinates
   b. absolute coordinates
   c. spherical coordinates
   d. cylindrical coordinates

5. A custom coordinate system that can be relocated as needed in 3-D space is called:
   a. default coordinate system
   b. user coordinate system
   c. world coordinate system
   d. object court system

6. This command is used to set up 3-D viewing angles:
   a. VIEW
   b. ZOOM dynamic
   c. VPOINT
   d. RTZOOM

7. This term refers to the Z axis value of the current drawing plane:
   a. elevation
   b. height
   c. UCS origin
   d. thickness

8. This system variable controls the way that AutoCAD LT uses lighting in the shaded image:
   a. SHADEDGE
   b. SHADEDIF
   c. LIGHTS
   d. SHADELIGHT

9. Which keystroke is used to toggle the isometric plane?
   a. Ctrl+A
   b. Ctrl+E
   c. Ctrl+B
   d. Ctrl+P

10. What is the name of the command used to draw an isometric circle?
    a. ISOCIRCLE
    b. ELLIPSE
    c. ISOELLIPSE
    d. CIRCLE

MATCHING

Match each term to the correct description by writing the appropriate number in each box at the left.

- ☐ SHADEDGE
- ☐ VPOINT
- ☐ HIDE
- ☐ SHADE
- ☐ SHADEDIF
- ☐ Camera
- ☐ Target
- ☐ THICKNESS
- ☐ ELEVATION
- ☐ DVIEW
- ☐ UCS
- ☐ WCS
- ☐ PLAN
- ☐ VPORTS
- ☐ CLIPPING

1. Coordinate system defined by the user.
2. Removes hidden lines.
3. Where the camera looks.
4. Can be used to create a perspective view.
5. Applies color to 3-D objects.
6. The default coordinate system.
7. The variable that controls edge shading.
8. The variable that controls lighting in a shaded image.
9. Command to change your viewpoint.
10. Command to change your view dynamically.
11. Front and back planes control what part of the drawing is displayed.
12. Command to set up tiled viewports.
13. View perpendicular to a coordinate system.
14. The Z axis coordinate.
15. The Z axis dimension.

WORD SCRAMBLE

Unscramble the six scrambled words below, one letter to each square, to form six AutoCAD–LT related words:

VOSTRIPEW

PREALLLA

EPCORTINOJ

MECIRITOS

EINVALETO

EDVWI

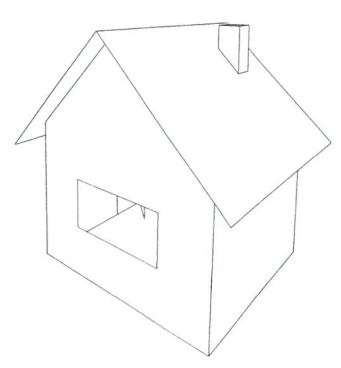

Unscramble the circled letters above to form the special answer, as suggested by the illustration.

PROJECTS

14.1 Start a new drawing using the Start from Scratch option. Construct a 3-D wire frame cube, two units per side, with the bottom-left corner at the 0,0,0 origin. Use the LINE command, and supply only *absolute* coordinates. Construct two more cubes, one using *spherical* coordinates with a bottom-left corner at 3,0,0, and the other using *cylindrical* coordinates and a bottom-left corner at 0,3,0. Use the VPOINT command to setup a 3-D viewing angle of your choice. Save the drawing as P14.1.

14.2 Open P14.1 for editing. Using the UCS command, create and save two user coordinate systems. Create one on the Y,Z plane with an origin of 0,0,0 in the World Coordinate System and assign a name of YZ. Create the other on the X,Z plane, with an origin of 4,2,9 in the WCS and name it XZ. Restore the WCS and save the drawing file as P14.2.

14.3 Start a new drawing using the Start from Scratch option. Create a cube that simulates a surface model by drawing lines and giving them a thickness. The cube should be one unit on a side and the bottom-left corner at 2,2,0. Save the drawing as P14.3.

14.4 Open P14.3 for editing. Create five named views, with the viewing angle being appropriate for the view name. The views should be TOP, FRONT, RIGHT, SW-ISO, and SE-ISO. Restore the SW-ISO view, use the HIDE command, and save the drawing file as P14.4.

14.5 Start a new drawing using the Start from Scratch option. Set the current THICKNESS value to 2.0. Draw a circle, an arc, a line, a polyline, a spline, and a line of text. Each should be appropriately sized within an area of about 12 × 9 units. Change the current view to a SW Isometric view. Use the HIDE command and save the drawing as P14.5.

14.6 Open P14.5 for editing. Change the properties of the text object so that the thickness is 0.5 units. Use the HIDE command and save the drawing as P14.6.

14.7 Open P14.4 for editing. Create six named user coordinate systems: TOP, BOTTOM, LEFT, RIGHT, FRONT, and BACK. Each UCS should have an origin and alignment on the appropriate face of the cube. Now, place a different hatch pattern on each face of the cube. Change the view to SW Isometric and use the HIDE command. Save the drawing as P14.7.

14.8 Open P14.7 for editing. Adjust the value of the SHADEDIF and SHADEDGE system variables to produce the best image when using the SHADE command. Try different values and use the one you think looks best. Use the SHADE command and save the drawing as P14.8.

14.9 Draw the figure below. Use standard drawing tools for the orthographic portion, and use isometric tools to create the isometric view. Save the drawing as P14.9.

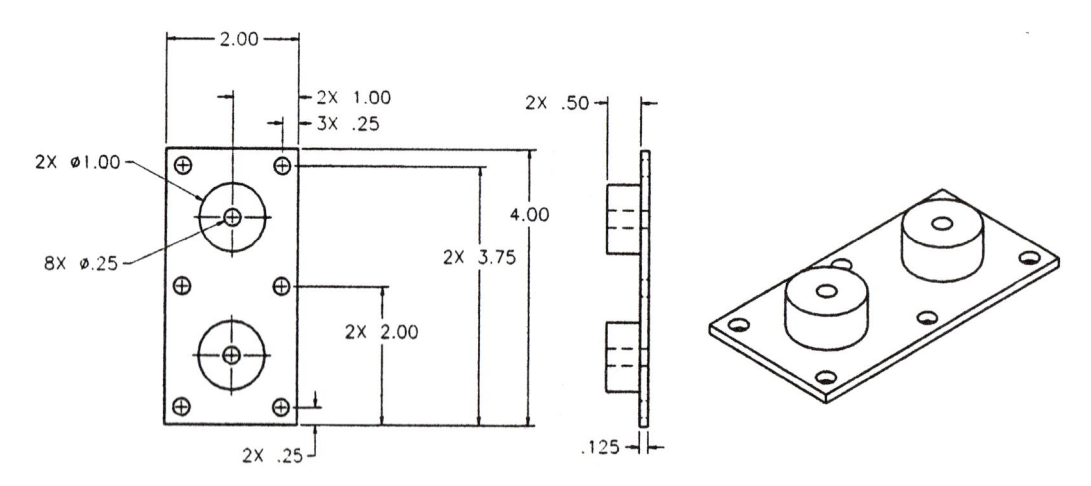

14.10 Create an isometric view of the figure below. Save the drawing as P14.10.

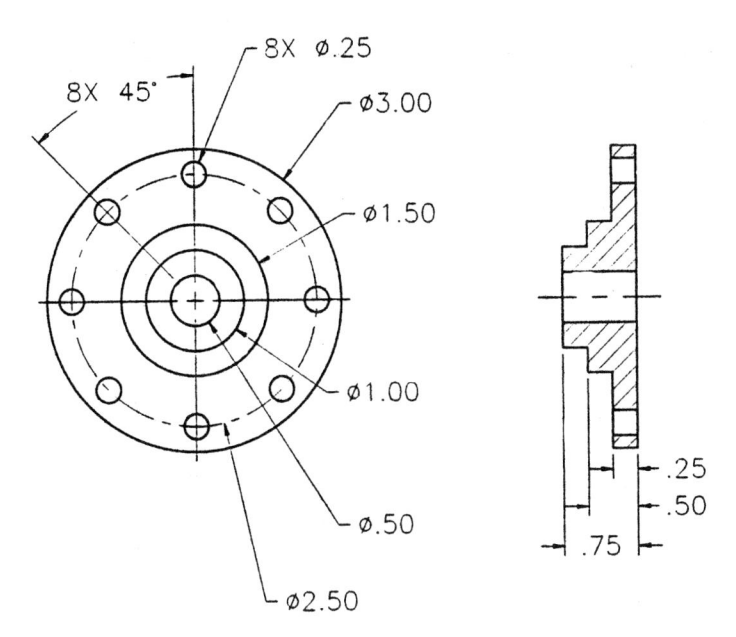

CHAPTER 15

File Management and Data Exchange

LEARNING GOALS

- Optimize drawing files for minimum size.
- Manage AutoCAD LT files in a networked environment.
- Import and export AutoCAD LT drawing information.
- Print drawings to a file.
- Create live documents using OLE.
- Use the Windows Clipboard for data exchange.

AutoCAD LT Files

In a CAD environment, computer files are at the very heart of everything you do. The programs you use rely on information stored in files that the computer evaluates and executes. Many of the features of AutoCAD LT such as linetype and hatch pattern definition are also stored in files. Most importantly, the drawings you create in AutoCAD LT are stored as drawing files. Understanding proper file management techniques allows you to maximize the potential of your workstation and saves you time when working in AutoCAD LT.

Managing Drawing File Size

The size of the drawing you are working in can affect the speed of your workstation. Used in this sense, the term *size* does not refer to the area displayed within the drawing; rather, it reflects the amount of information contained in the drawing. Recall from Chapter 1 that computer files are measured in size by the number of *bytes* required to store all of the information in the file. A byte is approximately equal to one character. A single line object needs to store a record of its coordinate locations, layer, color, linetype, elevation, thickness, linetype scale, and more. Therefore, this simple line object can require several hundred bytes of storage space within the drawing. Considering the number of lines, arcs, circles, and other objects in a typical drawing, it is easy to see how files can become large in a short time.

In addition to the objects on the screen that you can see, other types of information within drawings can add unnecessarily to the overall file size. For example, block definitions are not visible on your drawing—just the block reference. If a block definition exists within your drawing, but has not been inserted anywhere, that definition is consuming valuable space for no reason. Some drafters will load all of the linetype definitions for convenience when working. When the drawing is complete, however, the unused linetype definitions are also unnecessary. All unnecessary information in a drawing makes the file larger than it needs to be.

Earlier chapters discussed the value of using blocks and Xrefs to help keep drawing file size at a minimum. Another technique for maintaining efficient drawing sizes is through purging unnecessary data out of the drawing.

Removing Unused Data from a Drawing

File
└ Drawing Utilities
  └ Purge...
PURGE
PU

AutoCAD LT 98 provides an easy dialog interface for purging unreferenced drawing data. The term *unreferenced* indicates data that defines something that is not used within the drawing. For example, when a block definition exists in a drawing but the block has not been inserted anywhere, that block definition is unreferenced. A layer that contains no objects and is not associated with existing block definitions is another example of unreferenced data. Use the PURGE command to remove unreferenced data from a drawing.

Using the PURGE Command

You can access the PURGE command by picking Purge ... from the Drawing Utilities cascade on the File pull-down menu or by typing **PU** or **PURGE** at the Command: prompt. The PURGE command displays the Purge dialog box, as shown in Figure 15.1.

The graphic list in the center of the Purge dialog box displays icons and labels representing the types of information that can be purged from a drawing. The categories are as follows:

- **All items** This category represents the whole drawing. Picking Purge with this option highlighted will purge all unused information listed in each of the categories below it.
- **Blocks** Block definitions can be purged when they define blocks that are not currently inserted anywhere in the drawing, are not referenced by a dimension style, and are not referenced by other block definitions.
- **Dimension styles** Dimension styles can be purged when they are not referenced by existing dimension objects and are not referenced in any block definitions. The STANDARD dimension style cannot be purged.
- **Layers** A layer can be purged when it is not the current layer, contains no objects, and is not referenced by objects that comprise existing block definitions. Layer 0 cannot be purged.
- **Linetypes** A currently loaded linetype definition can be purged when it is not used by any objects in the drawing and is not referenced by objects that are part of an existing block definition. The linetypes named CONTINUOUS, BYLAYER, and BYBLOCK cannot be purged.
- **Mline styles** Multiline styles can be purged when they are not referenced by existing multilines. AutoCAD LT cannot create multilines or multiline styles, so this category will contain only items other than STANDARD if the drawing has been edited using AutoCAD. The style named STANDARD cannot be purged.

FIGURE 15.1 The Purge dialog box.

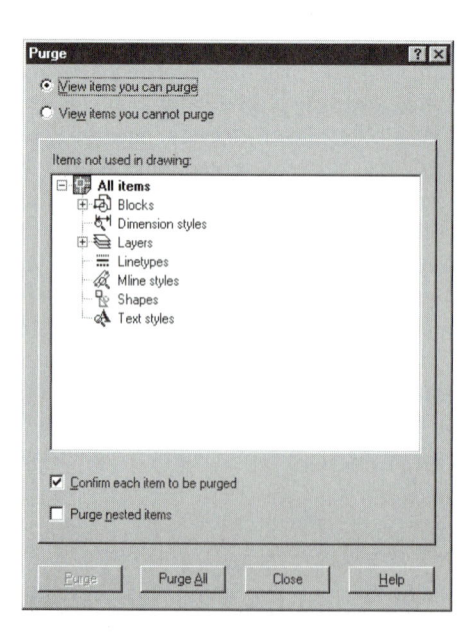

- **Shapes**   Shape definition files (.shx) can be purged when no shapes defined by the file are used in the current drawing, and the shape definitions are not referenced by any linetype definitions. In AutoCAD LT, shape definitions are used only as part of complex linetype definitions (such as Fenceline1 and Tracks). A drawing edited previously in AutoCAD may contain additional shape definitions.
- **Text styles**   A text style definition can be purged when it is not used by any existing text, mtext, or attribute object and is not referenced by any block definition, dimension style, or complex linetype. The text style named STANDARD cannot be purged.

The radio buttons at the top of the Purge dialog box control whether the list displays items that can be purged from the drawing. When you select the *View items you can purge* button, the list title reads "Items not used in drawing:" and the appropriate items are listed.

The list appears in a tree-style view that shows the drawing at the root of the tree and branches into categories of data. A category with a plus sign next to it indicates that the category contains items that can be purged. Categories without a plus sign have no items available for purging. In some drawings you may find no listing of unused data, which means that nothing can be purged.

Purging Selectively

The Purge dialog box allows you to select specific items for purging. In Figure 15.1, a plus sign is displayed next to the icons of categories that have unused data. The drawing used in this example is Xrefmain.dwg, found in the Sample folder. Notice that this drawing currently contains unused blocks and layers. Expanding the Blocks category shows two block definitions that are not used in the drawing. To remove one of the definitions, pick that definition and select the Purge button. By default, the *Confirm each item to be purged* option is active, and the Confirm Purge dialog box is displayed for each item to be purged.

To suppress this confirmation, remove the check next to this option. The Confirm Purge dialog box is shown in Figure 15.2, asking for confirmation before purging the block definition named "24X36."

FIGURE 15.2 The Confirm Purge dialog box.

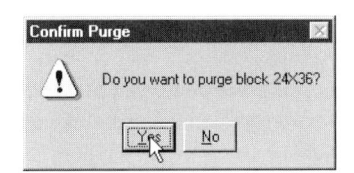

The list in the Purge dialog box has standard Windows functionality, and allows you to select multiple items in different categories by using the Shift and Ctrl keys in combination with picking. Alternatively, you can purge all items within a specific category by highlighting its icon and picking Purge. To select multiple categories, use the Shift or Ctrl keys when picking.

Purging All Unused Data

To purge all unused elements from your drawing, either select the Purge All button at the bottom of the dialog box or highlight the drawing icon labeled **All items** and pick the Purge button. It is best to purge all unused data when a drawing project is finished.

When you select the Purge All button, the Confirm Purge dialog box is displayed even if you have not checked the Confirm each item to be purged option. The Confirm Purge dialog box allows you to pick Yes to purge the item or Yes to All to purge all remaining items with no further confirmations. Picking No skips the listed item and continues to the next item. The default button is Cancel, which stops the purging operation and returns you to the Purge dialog box.

Checking the *Purge nested items* toggle allows removal of definitions that are nested, or contained as part of the definition of other items. This option works only when you pick the Purge button when *All items* or *Blocks* is selected, or when you select the Purge All button. A nested item is available for purging only after the definition in which it is nested has been purged. For example, when the block named 24X36 is purged from the drawing Xrefmain as shown previously, a new layer and a new text style are available for purging.

If you want to find out why a particular item cannot be purged, select the *View items you cannot purge* radio button at the top of the Purge dialog box. This changes the list title to "Items currently used in drawing:" and displays named items that cannot be purged. Picking any item displays a possible reason why it cannot be purged.

> ### Field Notes
>
> Drawing files can become unexpectedly large when inserting other drawings. Objects such as dimensions are created as *unnamed blocks.* This means that they have a block definition stored within the drawing. Even if the insertion of the block has been erased, the definition remains. Unnamed blocks are named with an asterisk preceding them. For example:
>
> Purge block *D0? <N>:
>
> When an unnamed block is presented for purging, it means that the definition is no longer needed and that it is safe to purge the definition.

The Power Purge

The purge command is flexible and allows careful selection of what information is purged and what is not. This is very valuable when the drawing you are purging from is a working drawing and you may need some of the currently unreferenced information in a later drawing session. When the drawing is complete and ready to be transferred to another location, you should reduce the file size to the absolute minimum. Although the PURGE command can do this, another option is available.

To wrap up a drawing project and reduce the file size to the bare minimum in a single step, the WBLOCK command can be used. WBLOCK writes drawing information to disk, and it is usually used to write a single block as an individual drawing file. WBLOCK can also be used to write the entire drawing to disk, minus any and all unreferenced information. To do this, enter an asterisk at the Block name: prompt, as shown in this example:

Command: **WBLOCK**↵
⟨*select the original drawing file name using the displayed file dialog box*⟩
⟨*when prompted, pick Yes to overwrite the original (or you may wish to create a backup first!)*⟩
Block name: *↵

The current drawing is written to a file with all unreferenced data fully purged. As noted in the example, it is never a bad idea to create a backup of any critical file before overwriting it.

> ### Field Notes
>
> AutoCAD LT practices incremental saves. This means that each time you save, the current drawing information is added to the end of the file. The reason for this is to speed up the saving operation. This can sometimes, however, make a drawing appear to be nearly twice as large as it actually is. Once the wasted space passes 50% of the file size, AutoCAD LT rewrites the entire file and it drops back to its true size. If you watch the status line during the save, you can tell whether an incremental save or a full save has been performed by watching for the Saving: message and status bar. This information is only displayed during a full save.

Deleting Other Nonessential Files

If the amount of free hard disk space on your system is very low, it can cause problems. A "disk full" error can result in loss of important data files. Be careful to ensure that you do not run out of space. If you are reaching a state where there is little free space left on your hard disk, it is time to do some file management. If replacement with a larger drive or adding on another drive is an option, this is usually the best choice. If not, it may be time to delete noncritical files.

CHAPTER 15 ||| File Management and Data Exchange

Always take care never to delete a file unless you know what it is and you also know that it is OK to delete. This type of work is usually best left to your system administrator. Also, take care when deleting AutoCAD LT drawing backup files (.BAK file extension). If the primary drawing has problems, the backup drawing may save you many hours of redoing your drawing.

Networked Environments and File Sharing

In a networked environment, the drawing files are typically stored on a central computer known as a *file server*. These files may be accessible from many different workstations. This can create a problem if the same file is accessed by more than one user at the same time. Imagine what could happen, for example, if the same drawing were opened by two different users. When the first user decided to save, the changes this user made would then be saved. Now, when the second user saved, the changes made by this user would overwrite the changes made by the first user. The last user to save the file would write the last version of the drawing according to the changes made on that workstation. This means that all of the changes made by the other user would be completely lost. To prevent multiple user file access with AutoCAD LT, the Windows file locking system is used.

A write-locked drawing can still be opened for reading by another user. A drawing opened in read-only mode can be edited normally, but the changes cannot be saved to the original file. Attempting to do so displays the message shown in Figure 15.3. The SAVEAS command can, however, be used to save the drawing under a different name.

FIGURE 15.3 This message is displayed when trying to save a file opened in read-only mode.

☑ LEARNING CHECKPOINT

- ☐ Why is it important to manage file sizes for AutoCAD LT drawings?
- ☐ What command removes unreferenced data from a drawing file?
- ☐ Describe how WBLOCK can be used to "power purge" drawings.

Exchanging Drawing Information with Other Applications

Drawing data can be imported into or exported from AutoCAD LT in order to share data with other applications. Several file formats are supported, including both vector and raster formats. In earlier chapters you learned that vector information is composed of actual objects, such as lines or polylines. A raster file is a record of pixels, and each pixel is separate from all of the others. The type of file used depends on the type of application. CAD-based applications usually create vector files, and paint programs usually create raster files.

Exchanging Drawing Files

AutoCAD LT can read files directly from many other Autodesk software programs. For example, drawing files (.DWG extension) created using AutoCAD Release 12, 13, or 14 or AutoCAD LT Release 2, AutoCAD LT for Windows 95 and AutoCAD LT 97 can be read directly by AutoCAD LT 98. A drawing file created in an older version of AutoCAD LT or AutoCAD is automatically converted to AutoCAD LT 98 format when it is opened, but the original file does not change unless you save the file using the same name. Once it has been converted and saved, it can no longer be read by the older application.

Drawing files can be exchanged freely among AutoCAD Release 14, AutoCAD LT 97 and AutoCAD LT 98. This means that if you open an AutoCAD Release 14 drawing using AutoCAD LT and then save the drawing, it can still be opened and edited using AutoCAD Release 14.

If you need to communicate back and forth with earlier software versions, you can use the SAVEAS command to save your drawings in a compatible format. The SAVEAS command can be typed at the Command: prompt or it can be selected from the File menu. When the Save Drawing As dialog box appears, select the desired drawing file format from the Save as type: drop-down list, as shown in Figure 15.4.

When working with DWG files, regardless of the software version they are created with, the OPEN command is used to open the drawing with AutoCAD LT.

FIGURE 15.4 AutoCAD LT 98 can save drawings in a format readable by earlier software versions by using the SAVEAS command.

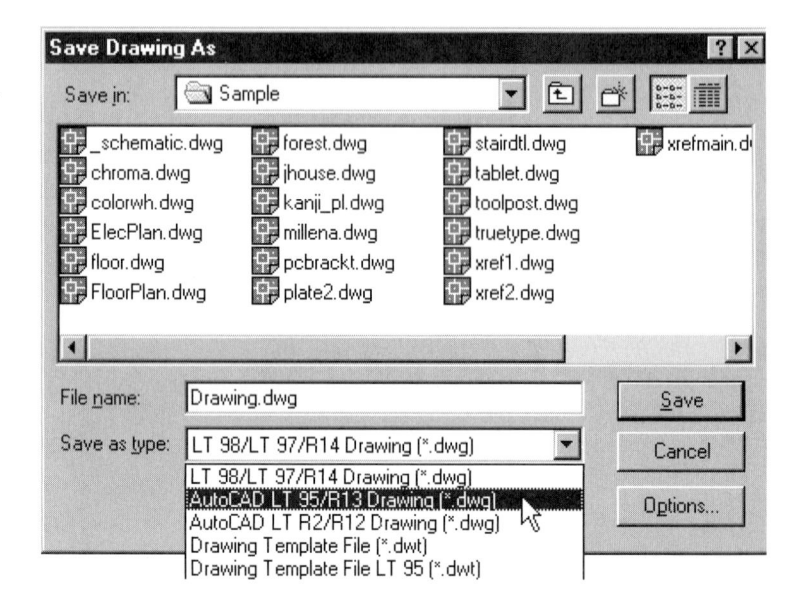

Importing Drawing Interchange File Information

DXFIN
DN

The Drawing Interchange File (.DXF extension) is a proprietary file format created by Autodesk for exchanging drawing file information. Many applications can read DXF files and convert them to their own format. Most applications that can read a DXF file can also create DXF files.

DXF files are imported into AutoCAD LT by using the OPEN command. The OPEN command can be accessed by picking Open ... from the File pull-down menu, and specifying DXF (*.DXF) in the Files of type drop-down list (see Fig. 15.5). You can also type **DN** or **DXFIN** at the Command: prompt. If you use the OPEN command, the Select File dialog box is displayed. However, no preview is shown for a DXF file. The DXFIN command displays the Select DXF File dialog box. Using DXFIN displays the Select DXF file dialog box. Both dialog boxes are used the same way: Navigate to the appropriate directory, select the desired file, and pick the Open button.

When a DXF file is imported, two results are possible, depending on the state of the current drawing and how the DXF file was created. A DXF file can be created to store only the definition of selected objects or it can store all of the drawing information, as discussed further in the section on exporting DXF files. When only selected objects are stored in the DXF file, importing it results in the definition of those objects in the current drawing with no changes to the system variable settings. However, in AutoCAD LT 98, DXF files can be imported only into a new, and blank, drawing file. An exception is DXF files that were created with AutoCAD Release 12 or earlier versions. These files can be imported into existing AutoCAD LT drawings. To access a DXF file created with R13 or R14, you must use the OPEN (or DXFIN) command in a new drawing file created using the Start from Scratch option.

CHAPTER 15 ||| File Management and Data Exchange 633

FIGURE 15.5 The Select File dialog box displayed by the Open command allows DXF files to be opened directly.

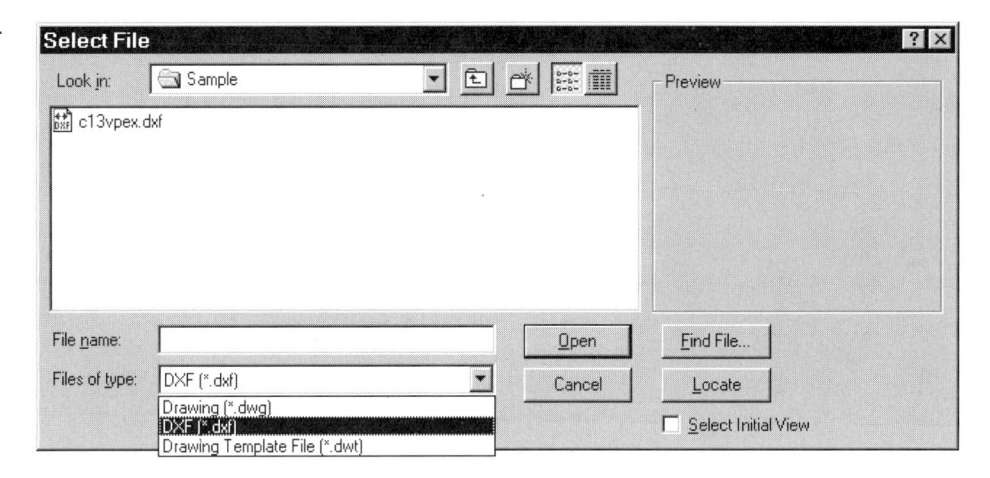

Creating DXF Files

Many applications can read DXF files, so this is a common format to use when transferring your AutoCAD LT drawings into another application. The DXFOUT command is used to create a DXF file. This command is accessed by picking Export ... from the File pull-down menu, then picking DXF (*.DXF) from the Save File as type drop-down list in the Export Data dialog box. You can also type **DX** or **DXFOUT** at the Command: prompt. Using the EXPORT command displays the Export Data dialog box (see Figure 15.6), and the DXFOUT command displays the Create DXF File dialog box. Both of these dialog boxes are used in the same way; navigate to the desired directory and specify the desired file name. A DXF file uses the .DXF file extension.

Selecting the Options ... button displays the Export Options dialog box, where you can specify the desired file format, the precision level, and what is to be written to the exported file. The Export Options dialog box is shown in Figure 15.7.

If you want to want to select objects in your drawing to save in the DXF file, place a check mark in the Select Objects toggle. If this is not checked, the entire drawing file is exported to the DXF file.

DXFOUT
DX

FIGURE 15.6 The Export Data dialog box allows DXF files to be saved in formats compatible with either current or older AutoCAD releases.

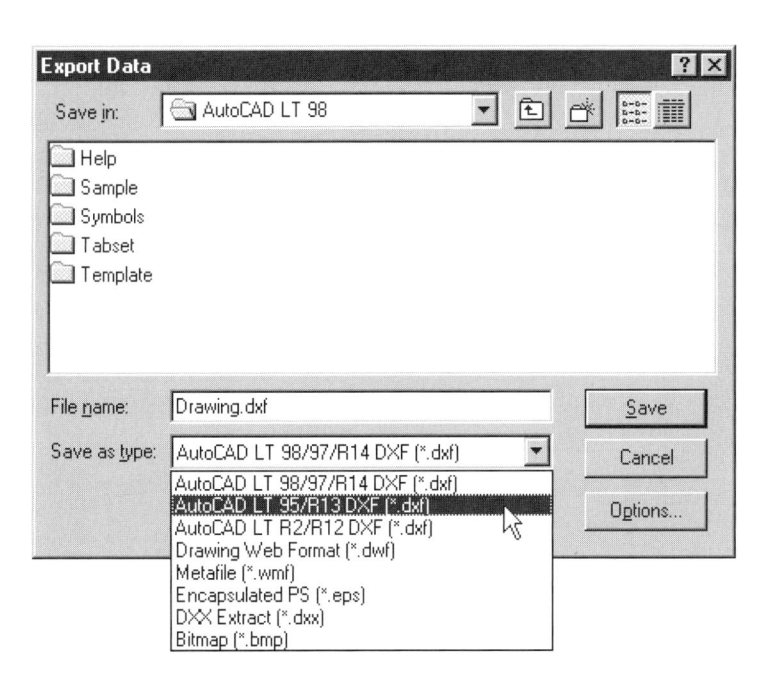

FIGURE 15.7 Use the Export Options dialog box to specify format and precision level for the DXF file being created.

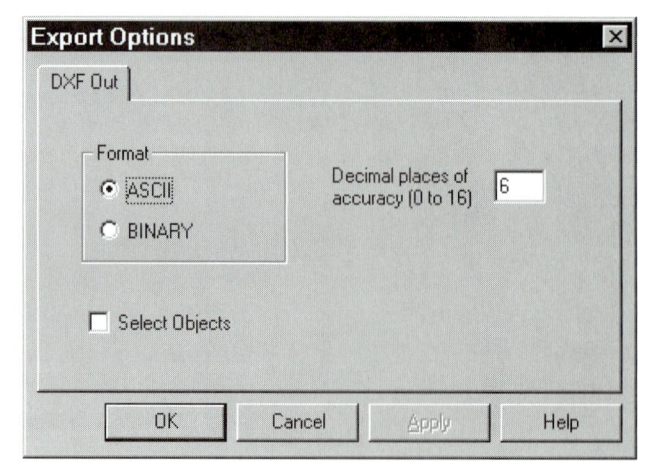

The next step is to specify the accuracy level of the DXF file. The number of decimal places of accuracy should be set no higher than needed. The default of 6 is sufficient for most applications, but AutoCAD LT accepts values from 0 to 16. The number of decimal places you specify can significantly affect the final DXF file size. To demonstrate this, the drawing named FOREST in the SAMPLE folder was saved as a DXF file using 3 decimal places and then using 16 decimal places. The 16-decimal-place version was 23% larger than the 3-decimal place version (1.7 MB versus 2.1 MB). Typical applications for this drawing would not apply accuracy beyond 3 decimal places, so a more accurate version is of no additional benefit. After you specify the number of decimal places, the DXF file is created and you are returned to the Command: prompt.

The default option for creating a DXF file generates an ASCII file. The term *ASCII* (pronounced "askee") stands for American Standard Code for Information Interchange, and refers to alphabetical characters and numbers. The other possible file format is **binary**, in which information is stored as 1's and 0's. A binary DXF file can be significantly smaller than its ASCII equivalent and can be read faster. To create a binary DXF, pick the Binary option from the Format area of the Export Options dialog box.

Notice that the Binary option disables the accuracy level setting. This is because the binary option always uses the maximum accuracy level. Even so, using the binary option on the FOREST drawing results in a file size of 1.23 MB. When compared to the ASCII equivalent, which uses 16-decimal-place accuracy, the resulting binary file is just over half the size of the ASCII file. Therefore, in an application requiring the highest level of precision, a binary DXF file is smaller and, therefore, may be preferred.

Field Notes

DXF files are often much larger than the original DWG file and, therefore, should only be used when taking the drawing information to an application that cannot read DWG files. To provide a contrast, the DWG file for the FOREST drawing referenced in the previous examples was only 677K in size. The smallest DXF file was created by the binary option, which was still nearly double the size of the original drawing file.

CHAPTER 15 ||| File Management and Data Exchange   635

Exercise 15.1

1. Open a drawing, from a previous chapter, that contains drawing objects.
2. Create three DXF files as follows:
3. Create one from the whole drawing, using 3-decimal-place precision.
4. Create one by selecting all of the objects in the drawing, and specify 16-decimal-place precision.
5. Create the third using the binary option.
6. Open the Windows Explorer (or File Manager) and check the relative sizes of the three DXF files.
7. Start a new drawing.
8. Import the DXF file created in Step 3.
9. Save the drawing as EX15.1

☑ LEARNING CHECKPOINT

- When transferring drawing files between CAD systems, what is the best file format to use?
- Describe how DWG files can be shared between different versions of AutoCAD and AutoCAD LT.
- Explain each of the DXFIN and DXFOUT option settings.

Exchanging Windows MetaFiles

The Windows MetaFile (WMF) format can be read and edited by many different applications, including CAD software, painting programs, and word processors. WMF files are vector files, meaning that the object is object based. This file format is used by many applications as clip art, because the vector format means that it can be scaled up and down as desired without loss of resolution or detail. The term *clip art* refers to nontechnical images that can be imported into a document or drawing as needed. Many Windows-based programs come with a variety of sample clip art in WMF format. The Import WMF File dialog box is shown in Figure 15.8.

FIGURE 15.8 The WMFIN command displays the Import WMF File dialog box and provides a preview of the highlighted file name.

Using the WMFIN Command

WMFIN
WI

WMF files are imported using either the WMFIN or the IMPORT commands. After the File … option is selected from the Insert pull-down menu, specify Metafile (*.WMF) in the Files of type: drop-down list. To access the WMFIN command, type **WI** or **WMFIN** at the Command: prompt. When WMFIN is used, the Select WMF File dialog box is displayed as shown in Figure 15.8. These files have a .WMF extension. The highlighted file name can be previewed in the Preview area.

Once the file name has been specified, the prompt sequence is the same as that used by the INSERT command. If you used the IMPORT command rather than WMFIN, each prompt is answered automatically using the default options. The insertion point is 0,0, the X,Y,Z scale factors are 1, and the rotation angle is 0 degrees.

Command: **WMFIN**↵
⟨specify the file name using the file dialog box⟩
Insertion point: ⟨specify point⟩
X scale factor <1>/Corner/XYZ: ⟨specify scale⟩
Y scale factor (default=X): ⟨specify scale⟩
Rotation angle <0>: ⟨specify rotation⟩

The WMF file is brought in as a block object. Because it is a block, it can be exploded if you need to edit the component objects. If it is a raster WMF file, it cannot be exploded. Exploding a vector WMF file reduces all of the component objects to solids, polylines, and polyline segments. Text objects in the WMF file are also reduced to polyline objects.

> **Field Notes**
>
> When WMF files are brought in, they are scaled based on the Windows desktop screen size. This means that the AutoCAD LT units system is ignored when importing a WMF file. So, the same WMF file is imported at the same apparent size regardless of the drawing area displayed by AutoCAD LT, meaning that the actual size of the image in AutoCAD LT's units varies depending on the size of the area displayed when the file is imported.
>
> To scale accurately the WMF file drawing information, use the Reference option of the SCALE command, after insertion is complete.

Using the WMFOPTS Command

The WMFOPTS command controls how WMF files are brought in to AutoCAD LT. **WMFOPTS** can be typed at the Command: prompt, or select the Options … button from the Import WMF File dialog box. The Import Options dialog box is shown in Figure 15.9. Turning on the Wire Frame (No Fills) option brings the file in with filled areas shown only as outlines. The Wide lines option controls the display of wide lines.

Using the WMFOUT Command

When you want to use drawing information in a document, or you have other applications for AutoCAD LT drawing information, the WMFOUT command creates a WMF format file from any selected objects visible in the graphics area of your drawing window. The WMFOPTS settings do not affect the appearance of a file that is being exported.

FIGURE 15.9 The WMF Import Options dialog box.

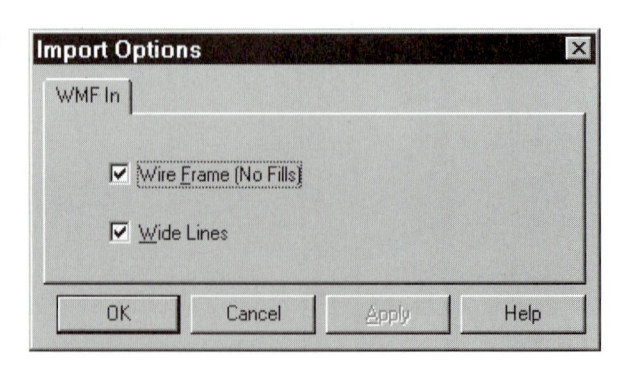

CHAPTER 15 ||| File Management and Data Exchange   637

The WMFOUT command can be accessed by selecting Export … from the File pull-down menu and then selecting Metafile (*.WMF) from the Save file as type: drop-down list. You can also start WMFOUT by typing **WO** or **WMFOUT** at the Command: prompt, which displays the Create WMF File dialog box.

WMFOUT
WO

Both means of creating WMF files work the same from this point. Navigate to the desired directory and specify the file name. The dialog box disappears and a Select objects: prompt is issued. Any valid selection method can be used; however, objects or parts of objects that are not currently displayed are not included in the file. Objects that are only partially displayed are trimmed and saved with only the visible portion. The WMF file created can then be imported into AutoCAD LT or any other application that uses WMF files.

Field Notes

> Many graphics files use what is termed as a bounding box. A ***bounding box*** defines the size of the area in which the image is contained. When a WMF file is created in AutoCAD LT, the bounding box is defined by the edges of the graphics screen area. This means that actual image size is the size of the graphics screen. Therefore, before creating a WMF file, it is often best to zoom in so the selected geometry fills the graphics area.
>
> The graphics screen area not only defines the image size, it also defines the image shape. This means that you can resize the AutoCAD LT program window until the graphics screen area is the size and shape you want, then zoom the image to an appropriate size, to avoid padding your image with a lot of empty space.

Exchanging Bitmap Files

Bitmap files (.BMP extension) are the simplest sort of graphics files. A ***bitmap*** is a record of pixel colors that comprises an image. This is the type of file used by non-object-oriented programs such as paintbrush-style applications. An image is recorded as a number of small rectangles arranged in rows and columns, with the color being listed for each. Bitmap files, by nature, produce a very coarse image in any application. Bitmaps are seldom used for detailed or accurate graphics applications. AutoCAD LT is an object-oriented program, and does not have a means to directly edit a bitmap image. AutoCAD LT does not directly import bitmap files, but the image displayed in the graphics screen area can be saved as a bitmap file.

The command used in AutoCAD LT to export a BMP file is the BMPOUT command. This command can be accessed by selecting Export … from the File pull-down menu and specifying Bitmap (*.BMP) in the Save file as type: drop-down list, or it is accessed directly by typing **BMPOUT** at the Command: prompt. AutoCAD LT creates what is called a *device-independent bitmap.* The file name has an extension of .BMP. This type of file can be used by almost any Windows software that imports or exports graphics.

As with creating a WMF file, the screen determines the size and shape of the bounding box, and only the selected objects are included in the exported image. After specifying the name and location of the new BMP file, a Select objects: prompt is issued. Also similar to the WMF file, only the visible portions of the objects are saved in the exported file.

Exercise 15.3

1. Open EX15.2.
2. Create a BMP file named EX15.3.BMP using all of the objects visible on the screen.

Exporting PostScript Files

The EXPORT command allows EPS formats for exporting drawing data. EPS format is an *encapsulated PostScript* file. When the contents of your drawing are to be imported into an application such as a desktop publishing, presentation, or illustration program, this is often the best choice. The EPS format offers high-resolution print capability utilizing the same language that PostScript printers use. Rather than communicating pixel information, an EPS file communicates in an object-oriented manner. A PostScript file has descriptions for Post-

Script objects such as ***path objects***, text that references PostScript fonts, and fill patterns. This allows PostScript printers to print at resolutions of 600 dpi and higher, for a crisp, clean print.

An EPS file is produced using the PSOUT command. The PSOUT command can be accessed by picking Export ... from the File pull-down menu and then specifying Encapsulated PS (*.EPS) or by typing **PSOUT** at the Command: prompt. Use the file dialog box to specify the directory folder and file name. The name will use an .EPS file extension.

Because an EPS file is written in the PostScript printer language, the PSOUT command works much like plotting a drawing. Producing a PostScript file is considered *plotting to a file,* because the drawing information is the same as would be sent to the printer, but it is being stored in a file instead. PostScript is object oriented, and drawing data to be exported does not have to be visible on the screen. Like plotting, rather than select objects to export, you specify an area of the drawing, and objects or portions of objects that are outside of the area to export are not included.

Select the Option ... button to display the Export Options dialog box for PostScript output, as shown in Figure 15.10.

The first field is for specification of the prolog section name. This is for specialized printing needs and can be left blank for most applications. The What to plot area allows specification of what part of the drawing is to be included in the PostScript file. If you select Window ... and use the Pick option, a message appears indicating that you will be prompted for the window after all other specifications have been made.

The user-defined window exports all drawing information contained within the window. You may also choose to export the currently displayed area, the drawing extents, the preset limits, or even an area previously saved as a named view. Many graphics applications offer an option to preview graphics files just like AutoCAD LT displays previews of drawing files. If the destination of the file is to be a printer, there is no need to increase the size of the file by including a preview image. A PostScript printer cannot use a file that has been given a TIFF preview. TIFF stands for tagged image file format, and is a widely used graphics file format. The TIFF format for image previews is used by applications such as Microsoft Word.

The size units and scale determine the size of the final image. If you need a specific scale, it should be entered appropriately. When a specific scale is not required, using the Fit to paper option ensures that the selected area will fit within the printed area.

Select the appropriate paper size to indicate the final output. When the final output is intended to fill an entire sheet, the appropriate sheet size can be specified. If the image you wish to generate does not match one of the listed options, you can enter a custom width and height. For example, to specify an area 6 units wide by 4 units high, enter these values in the Width and Height fields. Pick OK when you are finished, and the EPS file is created.

FIGURE 15.10 Exporting an .EPS file is very similar to using the PLOT command to plot to a file.

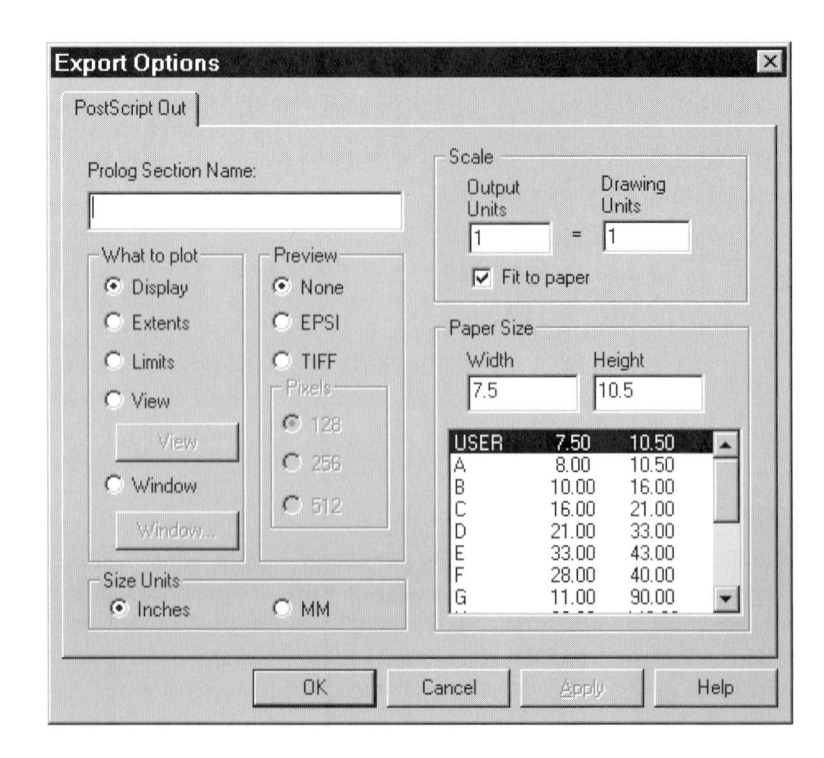

CHAPTER 15 ||| File Management and Data Exchange   639

FIGURE 15.11 Select the File Name ... button to specify the name and location of your plot file.

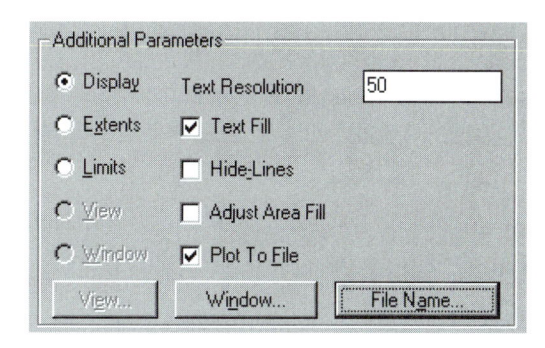

Plotting to a File

One of the options for producing a plot is plotting to a file. Instead of sending the output from the PLOT command directly to a printer or plotter, it is stored in a file. A plot file can be easily transported or stored for later use.

If you need to get a hardcopy of a drawing produced at home and wish to use a large-format plotter or high-resolution printer at work or school, a plot file can be more convenient to take than the actual drawing file. Plot files can be sent out to a plotting service, and many plot spoolers use plot files. A ***plot spooler*** is a piece of hardware or software that sends plot files to a plotting device. A spooler can be set up to run overnight or during weekends and holidays for unattended plotting.

There are two different ways to plot to a file using the PLOT command. The first is to plot to a PLT file. To create a PLT file, use the Print/Plot Configuration dialog box, displayed by the PLOT command. Under the Additional Parameters section, set the Plot to File ... toggle ON by placing a check in the box. Just below, the File Name ... button is enabled, as shown in Figure 15.11.

A PLT file uses a .PLT file extension. Use the Create Plot File dialog box to specify the location and file name. All of the other features of the Plot Configuration dialog box are used exactly in the same way as when you are plotting to a file. When you select OK, the plot information is written to disk and given the specified name.

Exercise 15.4

1. Open EX15.2 for editing.
2. Plot to a file to produce a .PLT file of the current display.
3. Save the drawing as EX15.4.BMP.

☑ LEARNING CHECKPOINT

☐ What file formats can AutoCAD LT exchange with other applications?
☐ What is meant by "plotting to a file"?
☐ In what ways can a PLT file be used? An EPS?

Using Object Linking and Embedding

Object Linking and Embedding, or OLE, is a feature of the Windows operating systems that allows information from different applications to be combined into a single document or drawing. OLE is often used to produce technical documents that combine descriptive text with technical drawings or illustrations. Most Windows applications support object linking and embedding. The term ***object application*** is used to describe the source application, and the destination is called the ***container application***. The terms ***server application*** and ***client application*** are also used in some references to describe the source and destination.

The AutoCAD LT software provides powerful drafting tools, but like most drafting programs, it provides few tools for creating complex or artistic style graphic images. Additionally, AutoCAD LT does not handle large quantities of text as well as a word processor. OLE provides great flexibility, however, allowing you to share data created in two or more different applications.

The shared information is handled differently, depending on whether it has been linked or embedded. The difference between linking and embedding is much like the difference between the XREF and the INSERT commands in AutoCAD LT. Similar to the results of the INSERT command, the *embedding* of information makes a copy of the external information but maintains no further connection with the original data. Similar to external references made using XREF, a *linked object* is connected to the original data and is updated when the source file changes.

Embedding Objects in AutoCAD LT Drawings

When it is not necessary to maintain a link to a separate original data file, information can be embedded within a drawing. In the following example, a bitmap image is embedded into an AutoCAD LT drawing. The bitmap is a logo graphic designed in the Paint program, which is found in the Accessories group of Windows. This software is included with the Windows operating system. In this case, the object application is Paint, and the container application is AutoCAD LT. Figure 15.12A shows the Paint program being selected from the Accessories group on the Windows Start menu. In Figure 15.12B, a logo graphic has been designed.

The Windows Clipboard can be easily used to embed objects. After selecting the desired area of the graphic, press Ctrl+C or pick Copy from the Edit pull-down menu. The selected objects are copied to the Clipboard. Now they can be pasted into another application, such as AutoCAD LT.

The PASTECLIP command is used to paste the contents of the Clipboard into the current drawing. To access the PASTECLIP command, press Ctrl+V or pick Paste from the Edit pull-down menu. The contents of the Clipboard are placed in the upper left corner of the drawing area. See Figure 15.13.

The INSERTOBJ command can be used to embed an object, but PASTECLIP is faster and easier. If the INSERTOBJ command is used, the Link toggle should be turned off to embed an object. The Insert Object dialog box is detailed later in this chapter in the discussion on creating links.

Once it is embedded, a limited number of ways are available in which AutoCAD LT can edit an object, including deleting, repositioning, and resizing. To change the content of an embedded object, the source application must be used, but the very nature of an embedded object simplifies this process. An embedded object maintains no link to the original source data, but it does maintain an association with the source application. This means that when you need to edit the embedded object, the source application can be started automatically.

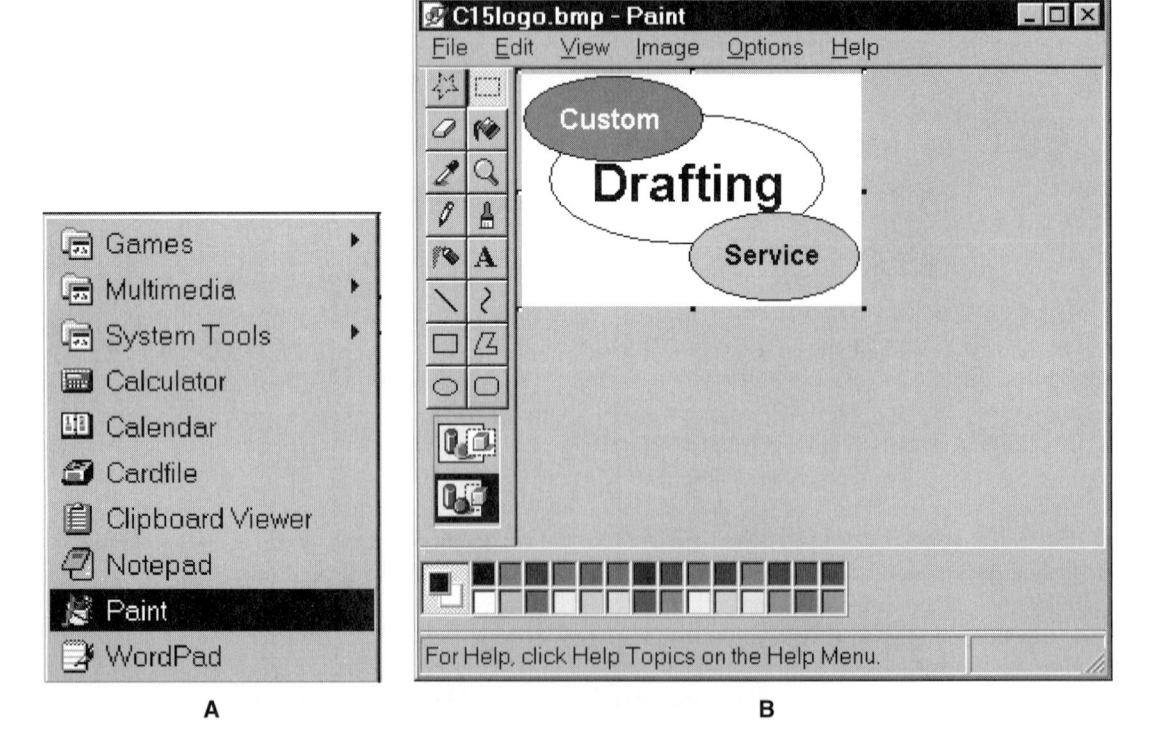

FIGURE 15.12 (A) The Paint program is started from the Accessories group. (B) Bitmap editors can be used to make colorful graphic images.

CHAPTER 15 ||| File Management and Data Exchange 641

FIGURE 15.13 The embedded object is placed in the upper left corner of the drawing area by default.

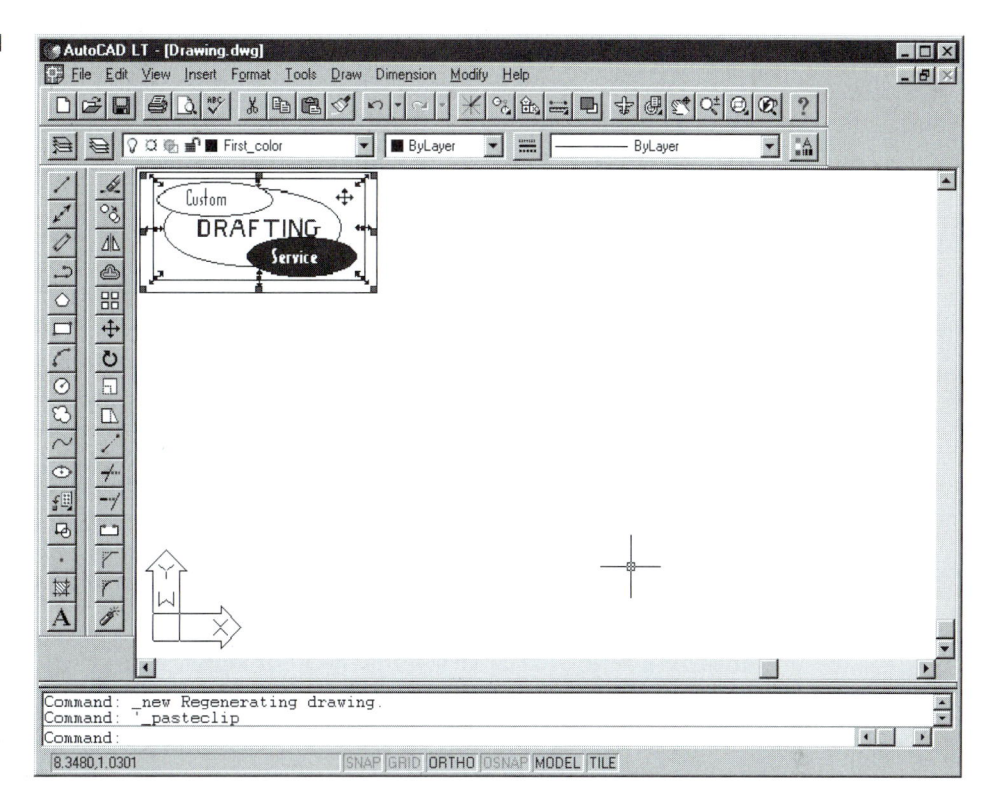

The grip selection technique is used to select an embedded object. At the Command: prompt, point to the object with the cursor and pick. When selected, the object shows a boundary line and eight squares around the border. The cursor changes to an appropriate system arrow, depending on what feature of the object you point to. Pointing within the image displays the move cursor. With this cursor visible, press and hold the pick button to drag the image to a new position. Pointing to the squares at the four corners displays the diagonal resize button. Press and hold the pick button to resize the object. The top, bottom, and side squares allow vertical and horizontal resizing. Figure 15.14 shows these features. To start the application associated with the object, double-click on it. The application is automatically started with the object already open for editing.

Another option is to display a cursor menu by right-clicking on the embedded object. This allows you to conveniently select from the available options. The options on this menu, shown in Figure 15.15, are as follows:

Cut	Copies the image to the clipboard and removes it from the drawing.
Copy	Copies the image to the clipboard.
Clear	Removes the image from the drawing.
Undo	The standard AutoCAD LT UNDO command has no effect on embedded objects. This allows you to undo the last actions performed on the image. Each image stores its own Undo record and the Undo option can be used repetitively, as with the AutoCAD LT UNDO command. All actions after the object was embedded can be undone. However, there is no Redo option.
Selectable	Turns the object's frame on or off to control selection options.

FIGURE 15.14 Embedded objects are resized and repositioned in a manner similar to that used for program windows.

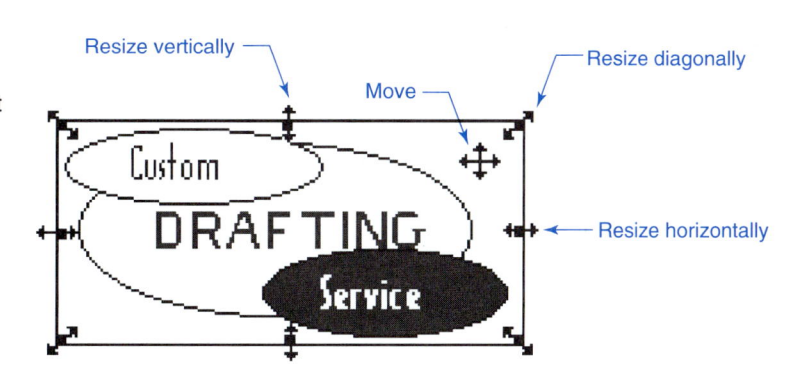

FIGURE 15.15 The OLE cursor menu.

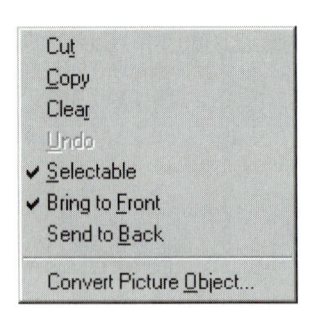

Bring to Front	Brings object to the front of the display.
Send to Back	Sends the object to the back of the display.
Convert Picture Object	This option allows you to convert the object from an embedded OLE object to an AutoCAD LT object. For example, with a Paint image, the Convert dialog box offers you the option of converting a file to a device-independent bitmap. Doing this removes all OLE associations.

Embedding AutoCAD LT Drawings in Other Applications

As with embedding objects in AutoCAD LT drawings, the primary advantage over importing is that the object maintains an association with the source application. This makes it easy to edit the object at a later time. The simplest way to embed an AutoCAD LT drawing in another application is to use the Clipboard. In AutoCAD LT, select the objects to embed, and then use the COPYCLIP command by pressing Ctrl+C. The AutoCAD LT objects are copied to the Clipboard.

In the destination application, use the PASTE option to embed the AutoCAD LT drawing. In most Windows applications, this is done by pressing Ctrl+V or by picking Paste from the Edit pull-down menu. Once it is embedded, the object can be edited in AutoCAD LT by double-clicking on it. Because no connection is maintained to the original source file, if there is one, editing the object has no effect on the source data.

> **Field Notes**
>
> When AutoCAD LT is used as an object application, the current display size and shape control the appearance of the image brought into the container application. If a selected object is only partially visible, this is how it is displayed in the OLE object. Additionally, all of the empty space around the selected objects is also displayed in the OLE object.
>
> For the best final image quality, use the program window resizing options to shape the drawing area as desired and zoom so that the objects to be selected fill the drawing area.

One very common application for embedding AutoCAD LT drawings is placing them within a technical document created in a word processor. Figure 15.16 shows an AutoCAD LT drawing embedded in a WordPad document.

Linking Objects in AutoCAD LT Drawings Using the Clipboard

When it is necessary to maintain a continued relationship between the object and the original source data file, a link can be established. The link can only be made to a file, so the data must first be saved to a file on disk. Linking is most useful when more than one document uses the same information, and that information may change in the future. Each time a container application opens a document with links, the original object data file is read to get the latest version of the data. This means that when the information changes, editing the source data file automatically updates all documents and applications that are linked to that file.

CHAPTER 15 ||| File Management and Data Exchange 643

FIGURE 15.16 Embedding drawings within a word processor document is a common use of OLE.

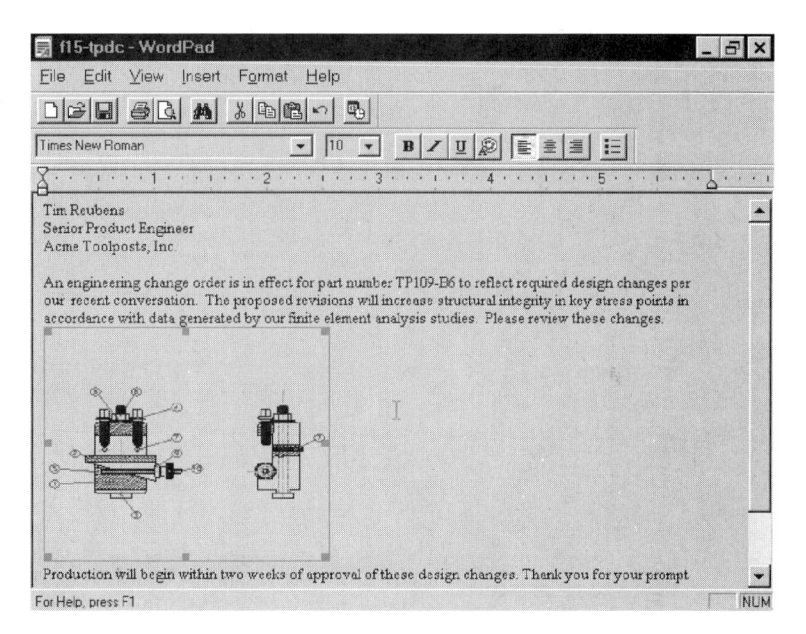

It is not a common practice to link word processing documents in drawings. However, other types of data, such as spreadsheets and graphic images can be very useful in an AutoCAD LT drawing. Spreadsheet applications, such as Microsoft Excel, are powerful tools for managing table data. In Figure 15.17, a dimension table has been created that specifies the dimensional values for different configurations of the same design. After saving the file to disk, it can be linked within an AutoCAD LT drawing.

Each piece of information in a spreadsheet is stored in a box called a *cell*. Using the standard features of the spreadsheet, the desired cells can be selected and the information can be copied to the clipboard by pressing Ctrl+C. After switching to AutoCAD LT, the link can be established by using the PASTESPEC command. PASTESPEC is an abbreviation for Paste Special, and allows objects to be either embedded or linked. The PASTESPEC command is accessed by selecting Paste Special … from the Edit pull-down menu.

The options in the Paste Special dialog box vary depending on the source of the information currently held in the Clipboard. Because the contents of the Clipboard are from Excel, the options in the Paste Special dialog box in this example are as shown in Figure 15.18.

The default option in the Paste Special dialog box is to embed the object into the drawing. To ensure that a link is established, the Paste Link toggle must be checked as shown in Figure 15.19.

Once the linked object is placed into the drawing, it appears just like an embedded object does. The difference is that a connection is kept between the source data and the OLE object. Figure 15.20 shows the linked spreadsheet cells in an AutoCAD LT drawing.

FIGURE 15.17 Table data is easily managed within spreadsheet programs.

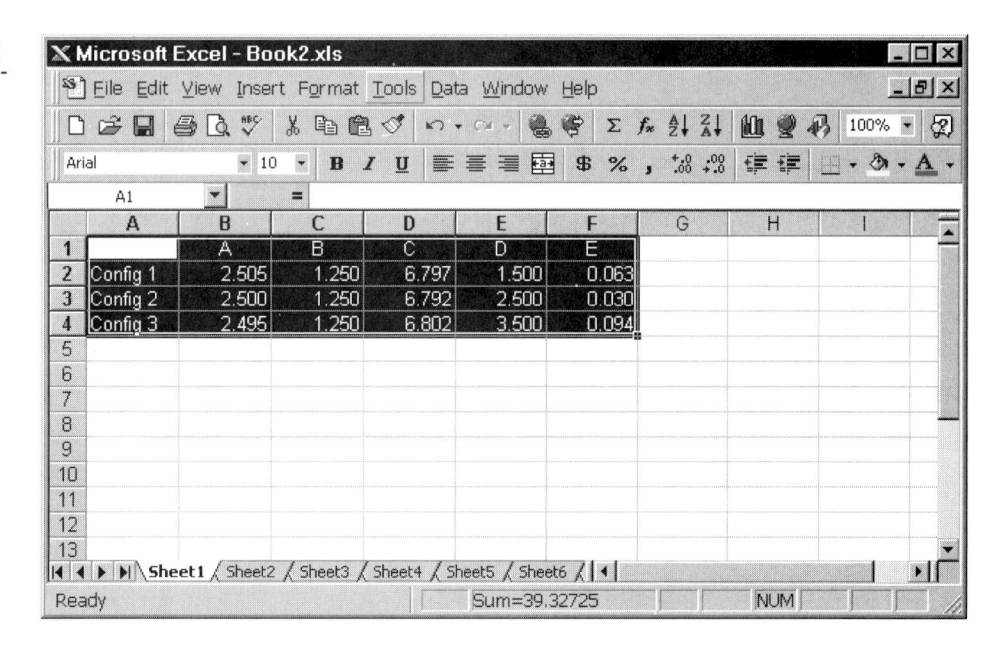

FIGURE 15.18 The Paste Special dialog box offers different options depending on the source of the Clipboard data.

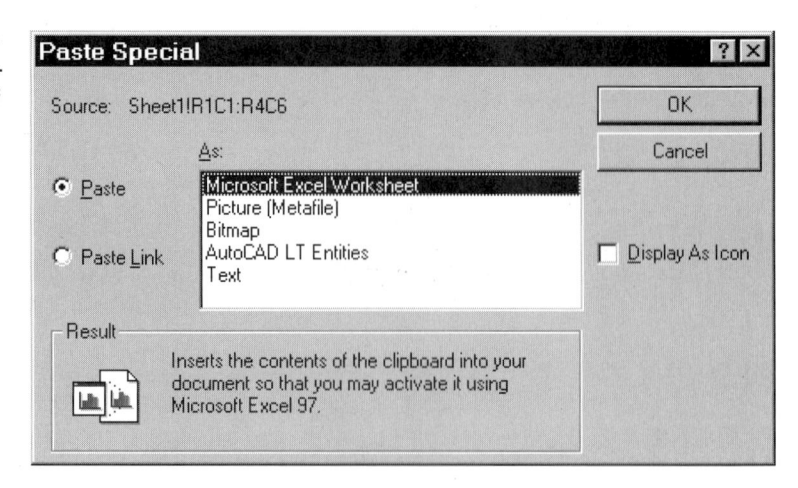

FIGURE 15.19 Selecting Paste Link allows a link to be established to the source data file.

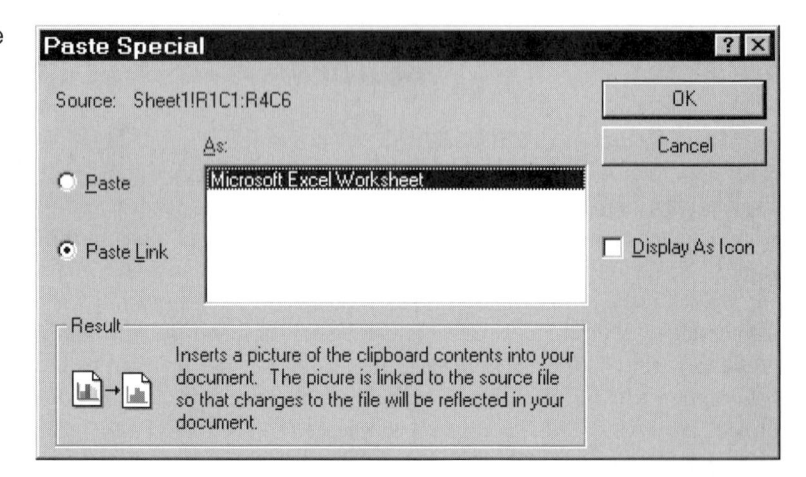

FIGURE 15.20 Linked and embedded objects appear the same but are much different functionally.

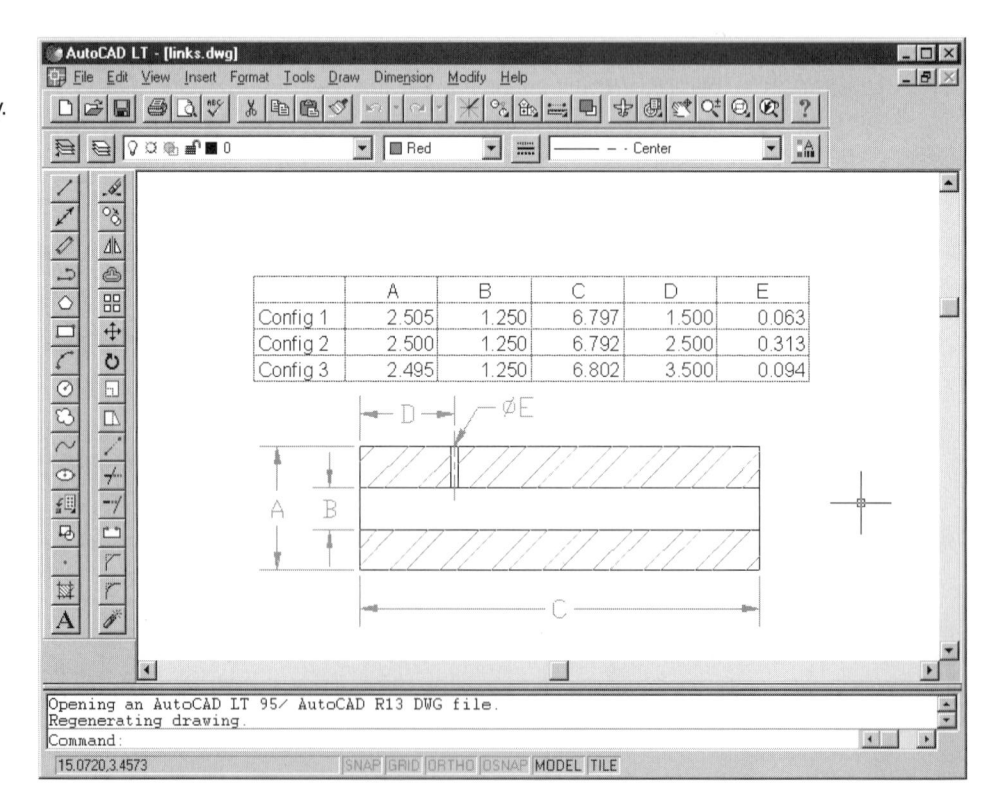

Now that a link has been established, any changes made in the source spreadsheet data are immediately reflected in the linked object. For example, in Figure 15.21, a change has been made to one cell in the spreadsheet. When both the object application and the container application are active at the same time, linked object status is polled, or checked every few seconds, to determine if changes have been made. Within a matter of seconds, the drawing file is updated to match the changes made in the spreadsheet.

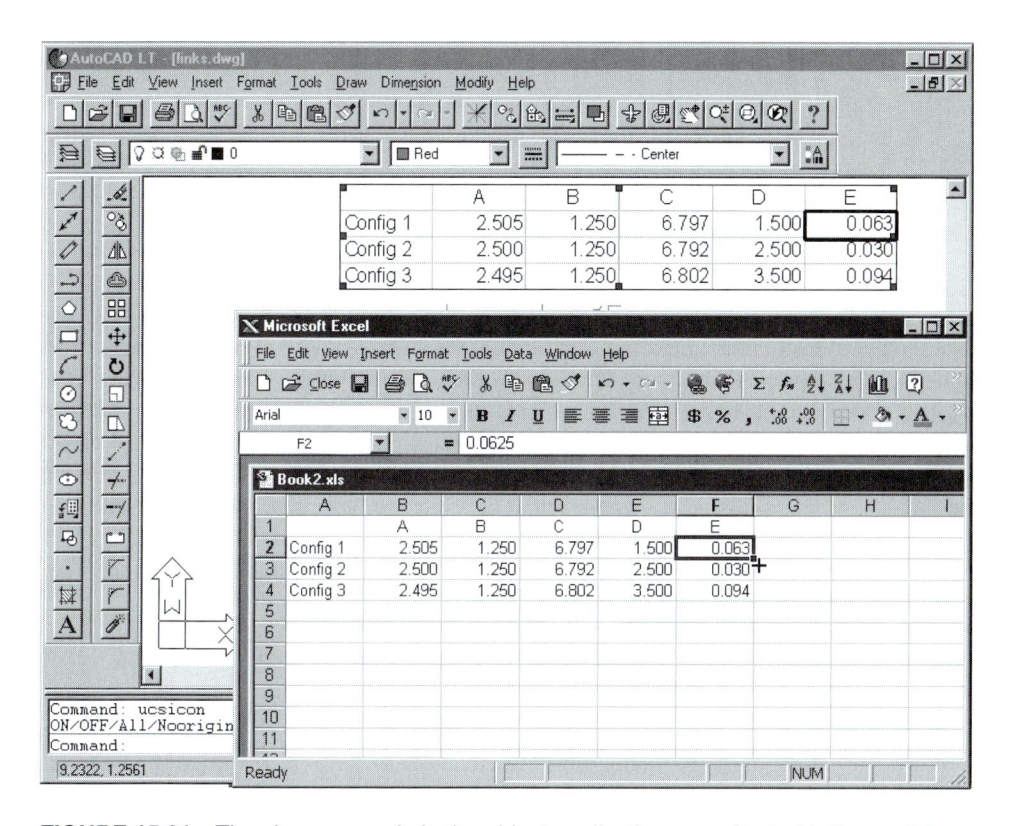

FIGURE 15.21 The changes made in the object application are reflected in the container application.

Field Notes

Links require that a file exists to link to. If the data copied to the Clipboard have not yet been saved as a file, the Paste Link … option in the Paste Special dialog box is not enabled. To correct this, save the file in the source application and again copy the data to the Clipboard.

Linking Objects in AutoCAD LT Drawings Using Data Files

When the data you need to link do not yet exist or exist in a file but the object application is not open, then the Clipboard cannot be used to transfer the data using PASTESPEC. Instead, the INSERTOBJ command is used to insert a new or existing object into the drawing. The INSERTOBJ command is accessed by picking PLE Object … from the Insert pull-down menu or by typing **INSERTOBJ** at the Command: prompt.

The INSERTOBJ command displays the Insert Object dialog box, as shown in Figure 15.22. By default, the selected option is Create New, which is used to start the appropriate source application in order to generate the OLE object. The options displayed in the Object Type list box show the applications and object types currently registered on your system. Most software *registers* the type of files that it uses during the installation process. The listing that appears in the Object Type list box depends on the software and system drivers currently installed on your computer.

FIGURE 15.22 The Insert Object dialog box with the Create New toggle checked.

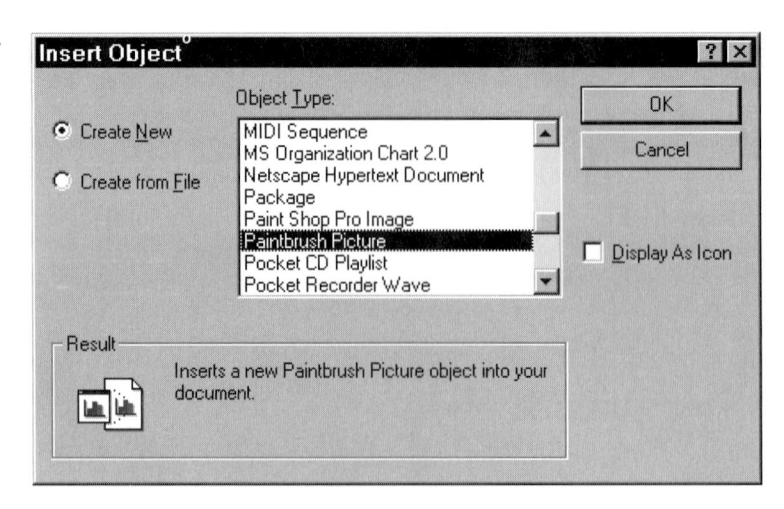

In Figure 15.22, the Paintbrush Picture option is highlighted. Selecting this option starts the Paintbrush program with a temporary file listed as "Paintbrush Picture in *drawingname* drawing." Because this is a temporary file, and no longer exists after exiting the Paintbrush program, there is no option to link to this object. The Create New option can, therefore, only be used to create embedded objects; it cannot be used to establish a link.

Selecting the Create from File option changes the layout of the Insert Object dialog box, as shown in Figure 15.23. This can also be used to embed an object, or the Link toggle can be checked to establish a link to the original data file. If you know the directory folder location and file name, it can be typed in the File: text box. To find a file, use the Browse ... button to display the Browse File dialog box.

Any type of file that is a registered object type can be linked using INSERTOBJ. If the contents of the file can be displayed, such as text or a graphic image, a picture of the file is displayed appropriately in the drawing. Some objects, such as multimedia sound recordings, can be linked or embedded, but cannot be displayed. In this case, the icon representing the object application is displayed instead.

Multimedia features are becoming more widely used to enhance drawings now that most computer systems are sold as multimedia capable. If your system has a sound card, you can record and play sounds. Voice messages can be used to help clarify information in a drawing. Figure 15.24 shows a drawing with a sound file placed within it. Double-clicking on the icon causes the object application to start and the sound file to play.

FIGURE 15.23 When creating an object from a file, a link can be established.

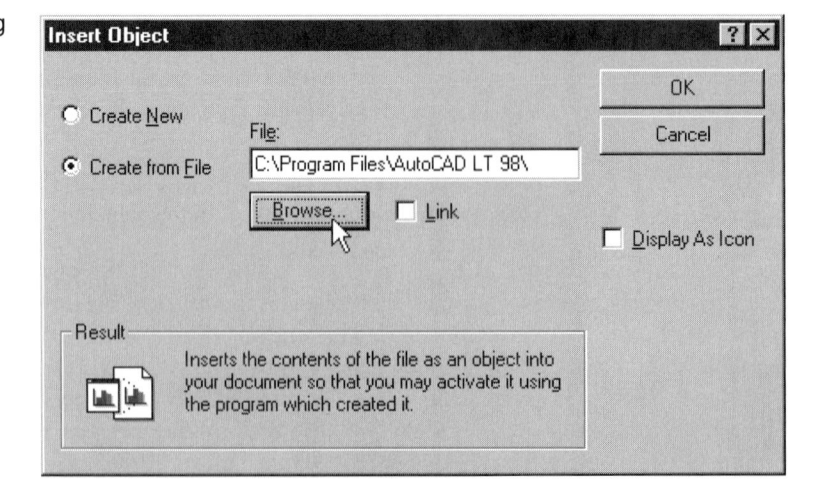

CHAPTER 15 ||| File Management and Data Exchange 647

FIGURE 15.24 An embedded sound file is displayed as an icon within the drawing.

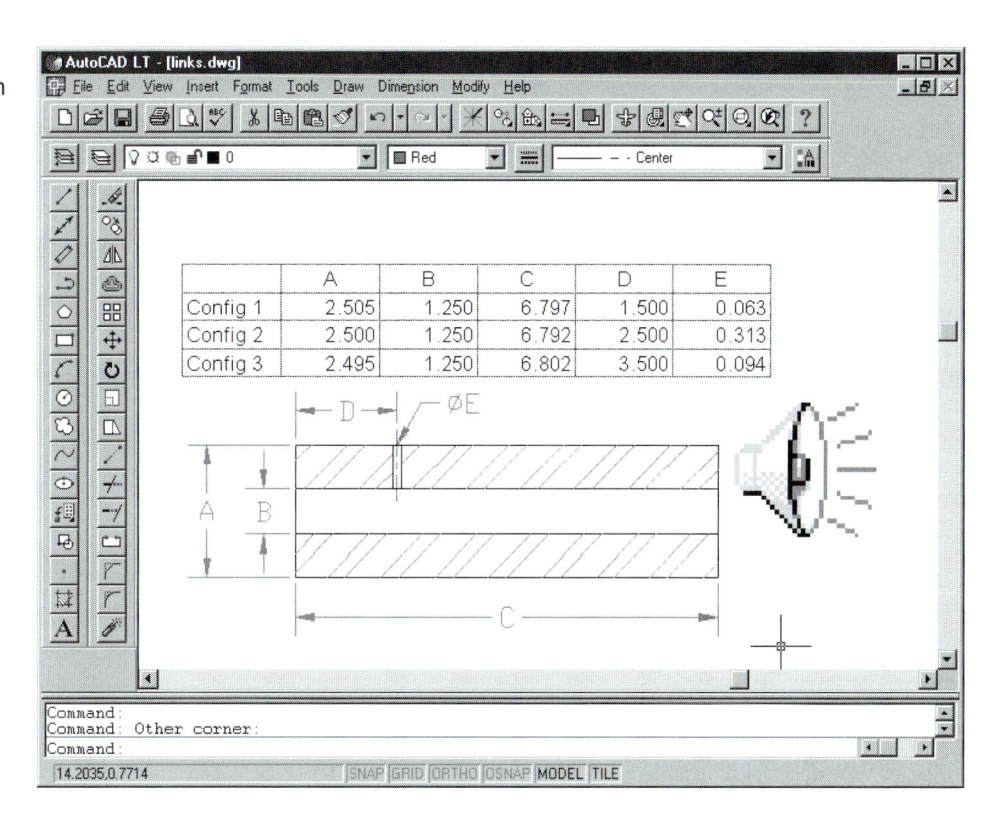

Field Notes

When using sound files in a drawing, the file size can be significantly increased. To keep drawing size manageable, keep voice messages short and to the point. Additionally, your sound recording software provides settings to control sound quality. A sound that is recorded using a CD Quality setting will result in a much larger file than the same recording using the Telephone Quality setting.

Also, sound files are unlikely to be used in multiple locations requiring synchronized updates. It is usually unnecessary to maintain a link with a sound file in a drawing.

Linking AutoCAD LT Drawings in Other Applications

The COPYLINK command is accessed by picking Copy Link from the Edit pull-down menu. This option is not available in an unnamed drawing, because links can only be established with a file. This command copies the current view to the clipboard, with all visible objects selected. To place this in another application, use the Paste Special … option on the Edit pull-down menu, or whatever method is normally used to establish a link in the software you are using. When the drawing object in the container application is double-clicked, Auto-CAD LT is started and the drawing object is loaded automatically.

Managing Links in AutoCAD LT

Once a link has been established, it may occasionally require maintenance in special circumstances. If a link is disconnected because the original file was relocated or renamed, it must be updated and reconnected. Or, if a link is no longer necessary, it can be broken. The Links dialog box is displayed by the OLELINKS command, which is accessed by picking Links … from the Edit pull-down menu.

All links associated with this drawing are displayed in the Links: list box. Picking a link enables the option buttons, shown in Figure 15.25, and described as follows:

Update Now   This reads the file and updates the linked object according to the current information.
Open Source   Opens the source file using the object application.

FIGURE 15.25 Selecting a link enables the option buttons.

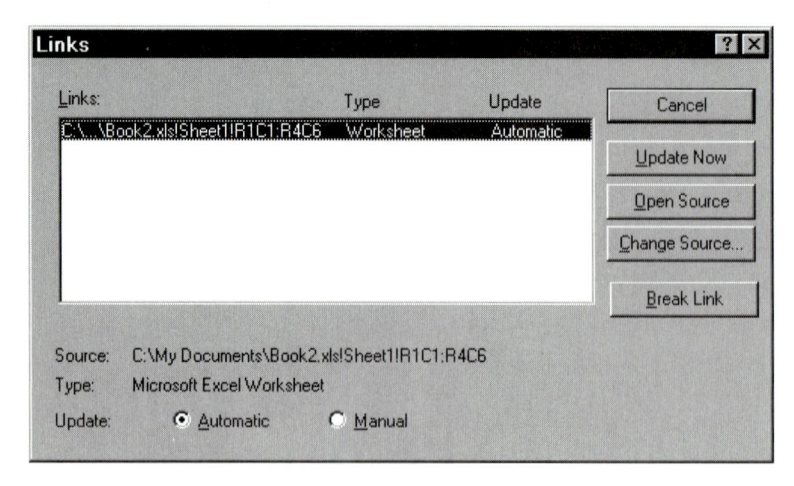

Change Source ... Allows the link to be changed to reference a new file. This option is also used when the source file has been relocated or renamed.

Break Link Removes link information from an OLE object, converting it to an embedded object.

Field Notes

> OLE objects cannot be plotted using non-Windows drivers. This includes plotting devices that utilize HPGL, HPGL/2, PCX, GIF, TIFF, and BMP plot data formats. If your printer or plotter is set as the system printer by Windows, and you are configured to plot to the system printer, then OLE objects are also plotted.

Exercise 15.5

1. Using the Paintbrush program, create a simple graphic and name it EX15.5.BMP.
2. Start a new AutoCAD LT drawing from scratch.
3. Use the INSERTOBJ command with Create from File specified, and do not check the Link: option.
4. Use the Browse dialog box to find the file named EX15.5.BMP.
5. After the object has been embedded, use the cursor to resize and reposition the object.
6. Double-click on the object to start the Paintbrush program. Edit the object, save it, and exit Paintbrush.
7. Save the drawing as EX15.5E.
8. Open Paintbrush and create a simple graphic. Save it to a file named EX15.5L.BMP and copy the image to the Clipboard.
9. Use the PASTESPEC command to insert the object with a link to the original file.
10. Arrange your desktop so that both Paintbrush and AutoCAD LT are visible.
11. Edit the paintbrush image and observe the automatic updates.
12. Save the drawing file as EX15.5L.
13. Start the WordPad program to create a simple word processor document.
14. Start a new drawing from scratch in AutoCAD LT.
15. Create a simple drawing in AutoCAD LT and save it as EX15.5O.
16. In AutoCAD LT, use the COPYLINK command.
17. From WordPad, use Paste Special ... option from the Edit pull-down menu to paste the AutoCAD LT drawing link.
18. Save the WordPad file as EX15.5.

CHAPTER 15 ||| File Management and Data Exchange   649

☑ LEARNING CHECKPOINT

- How can OLE be used with AutoCAD LT for technical documentation?
- What is the difference between linking and embedding?
- What are some other useful applications for OLE?

Working with Slide Files

In AutoCAD LT, a *slide* is a "picture" of a drawing. This is a special type of file that records the current drawing display so it can be viewed later. Slide files (.SLD extension) contain no geometry and cannot be edited. Slide files have different applications, from drawing management to presentation portfolios. In drawing management applications, slides can be used to create and view full-screen previews of drawings. Viewing a slide file is much faster than opening a drawing file. Slide files can be used to create a portfolio to show to prospective employers. Slide files are much smaller than the original drawing files. Where 20 or 30 large drawings might not fit on a diskette, the same number of slides fits very easily on a single diskette.

To make a slide file, use the MSLIDE command. The MSLIDE command is accessed by typing **MSLIDE** at the Command: prompt. Use the Create Slide File dialog box, shown in Figure 15.26, to specify the name and location of the slide file.

To view a slide file, the VSLIDE command is used. Access the VSLIDE command by typing **VS** or **VSLIDE** at the Command: prompt. Use the Select Slide File dialog box, shown in Figure 15.27, to select the slide file.

You can view a slide at any time, even while you are editing a drawing. Viewing a slide replaces the current display with the contents of the slide file, but does not actually affect the geometry in your drawing. To remove the slide from your display and restore the view of the current drawing, use the REDRAW command.

FIGURE 15.26 The Create Slide File dialog box.

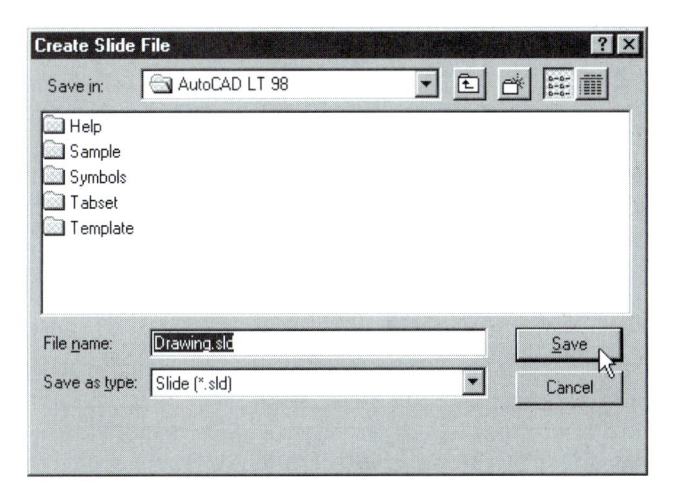

FIGURE 15.27 The Select Slide File dialog box.

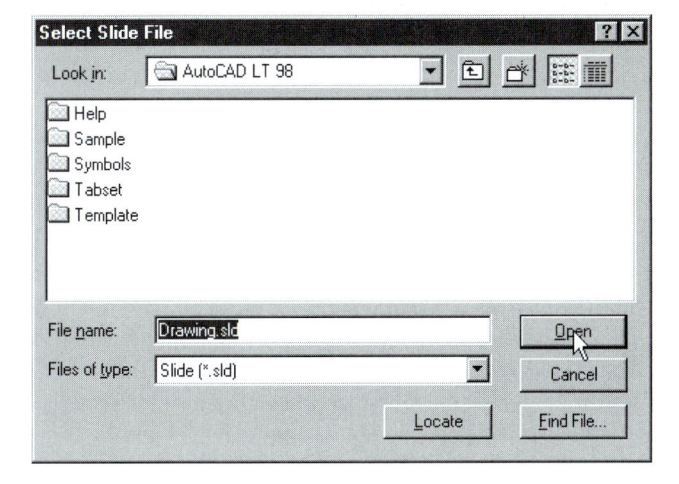

> **Exercise 15.6**
>
> 1. Open a drawing from a previous problem or exercise.
> 2. Create a slide file named EX15.6 using MSLIDE.
> 3. Open a different drawing file.
> 4. View the EX15.6 slide file using VSLIDE.
> 5. Use the REDRAW command to remove the slide.

Creating a Slide Library

Slide files that are used in a group, such as for a portfolio demonstration or other purposes, are easier to manage if they are combined into a single slide library file. A slide library is a special type of tile that stores any number of individual slide files in it. This allows you to work with a single file even when your particular application requires a large number of slides.

To create a slide library, you must first create the individual slides that you want to incorporate into the library. This is done using the MSLIDE command as discussed earlier. Next, use Notepad to create a text file listing of the name of each slide file you intend to use, placing only one slide name on each line. Save this file, using any desired name, in the same directory location as the slide files.

Now, you need to use the SLIDELIB command at the OS prompt. The *OS prompt* refers to the MS DOS prompt available by opening an MS DOS window by picking MS DOS Prompt from the Start menu.

Once at the MS DOS prompt, navigate to the directory where the slide files are that you want to put into the library file. Ask your instructor or system administrator or consult the appropriate documentation if you need assistance. From within the directory location where the slide files are located, you need to access the SLIDELIB.EXE file found in the AutoCAD LT folder. This is done by typing the following at the OS prompt:

C:\AutoCAD LT 98\SLIDELIB *LibraryName* < *SlideListFileName*

If your installation of AutoCAD LT is on a different drive letter or in a different directory folder name, change the drive and path name to match. The *LibraryName* is the file name you want to assign to the new slide library. Used in this manner at the OS prompt, the less than symbol is called a *redirection* symbol. The *SlideListFileName* entry refers to the name and file extension you assigned to the list of slides created in Notepad.

To put this into effect, the following example creates a slide library file named LIB001. The slide list file name in this example is SLDLIST.TXT.

C:\AutoCAD LT 98\SLIDELIB LIB001 < SLDLIST.TXT

This creates a file named LIB001.SLB. If any errors are reported, no slide library is created and you must correct the error and try again. The most common error encountered is an improperly spelled slide file name or a nonexistent file.

Viewing slides from a slide library is somewhat different than using a standard slide file. For example, to view a slide named SLIDE01 that is in the LIB001 slide library, a slide name is entered as:

LIB001(SLIDE01)

The slide library name is entered first, followed by the slide name in parentheses. There are no spaces in this entry.

> **Field Notes**
>
> Slides that are in slide libraries cannot be viewed using the Select Slide File dialog box displayed by the VSLIDE command. The entry is only accepted at the command line, so prior to using VSLIDE, the system variable CMDDIA must be set to 0. This is only true when viewing the slides manually; most standard applications for slide files are not affected by the CMDDIA setting. Remember to set CMDDIA back to 1 before continuing with other tasks.
>
> If, at a later time, you wish to add, remove or change a slide from the library, you cannot do so. Instead, the slide library must be recreated. Therefore, it is advisable to keep the slides and the slide list on file for such a need.

CHAPTER 15 ||| File Management and Data Exchange 651

> **Exercise 15.7**
>
> 1. Create four different slide files. Name them SLIDE01 through SLIDE04.
> 2. Using Notepad, create a text file that lists the names of each of the slides, one name per line, and save it in the directory that holds the slide files.
> 3. Open a DOS window and go to the directory folder that holds the slides.
> 4. Use the SLIDELIB command to create a slide library named EX15.7.SLB.
> 5. Close the DOS window and return to AutoCAD LT.
> 6. Turn CMDDIA off by setting it to 0, and view each of the slides in the slide library.
> 7. Turn CMDDIA back on.

MULTIPLE CHOICE

Circle the choice or enter your response on an answer sheet by selecting the option that most closely completes or answers the given statement.

1. What is the name of the command that allows you to remove unreferenced data from a drawing?
   a. REDUCE   c. COMPRESS
   b. PURGE   d. REMOVE

2. In addition to other uses, this command can be used to perform what is called a *power purge*:
   a. POWERPURGE   c. WBLOCK
   b. PURGEALL   d. COMPRESS

3. When using the command referenced in Question 2, the response given at the Block name: prompt should be:
   a. all   c. (the current drawing name)
   b. *   d. purge

4. A drawing interchange file, or DXF file, is created using this command:
   a. MAKEDXF   c. DXFOUT
   b. MDXF   d. EXCHANGE

5. A Windows MetaFile is brought into AutoCAD LT as this type of object:
   a. image   c. xref
   b. graphic   d. block

6. This feature of the Windows operating system allows information from different applications to be combined into a single document or drawings:
   a. cut and paste   c. object linking and embedding
   b. multitasking   d. external references

7. In OLE, this term describes the source application:
   a. source document   c. container application
   b. object application   d. clipboard

8. The destination application, in OLE, is called the:
   a. destination document   c. container application
   b. object application   d. clipboard

9. To create a link to external data as it is brought into AutoCAD LT, this command is used:
   a. PASTESPEC   c. LINKOBJ
   b. PASTELINK   d. NEWLINK

10. This command is used to manage links in an AutoCAD LT drawing:
    a. LINKEDIT   c. OLELINKS
    b. LINKS   d. EDITLINK

MATCHING

Match each term to the correct description by writing the appropriate number in each box at the left.

- [ ] PURGE
- [ ] WBLOCK
- [ ] WMFOPTS
- [ ] WMFOUT
- [ ] DXF
- [ ] Object application
- [ ] PSOUT
- [ ] Slide
- [ ] BMPOUT
- [ ] .GIF, .BMP, .TIF, .PCX
- [ ] Link
- [ ] OLELINKS
- [ ] Clipboard
- [ ] IMPORT
- [ ] EXPORT

1. Command to output a drawing in an alternate format.
2. Drawing Interchange File extension.
3. Outputs a Windows MetaFile.
4. Sets options for WMF files.
5. The "power purge" command.
6. These file types can be created by plotting to a file.
7. This command lets you manage linked objects in a drawing.
8. Command to input data into a drawing that is not in DWG format.
9. Storage place for cut data.
10. Removes unreferenced data from a drawing.
11. A connection to the object application.
12. The source application for an OLE object.
13. A "picture" of a drawing file.
14. Creates a PostScript output file.
15. Creates a bitmap (.BMP) file.

CHAPTER 15 ||| File Management and Data Exchange   653

WORD SCRAMBLE

Unscramble the six scrambled words below, one letter to each square, to form six AutoCAD LT–related words:

RUGEP

PORPSTICTS

ANINORECT

LEDIS

BOETJC

PIMTAB

Unscramble the circled letters above to form the special answer, as suggested by the illustration.

PROJECTS

15.1 Open a project drawing file from Chapter 13. Use the PURGE command as many times as necessary to remove all unreferenced data from the file. Save the drawing as P15.1.

15.2 Open the same project drawing file from Chapter 13 that was used in Project 15.1. Use the WBLOCK command to perform a "power purge," saving the new file as P15.2. Use a file management utility, such as Windows Explorer, to compare the file sizes for P15.1 and P15.2.

15.3 Open two simultaneous AutoCAD LT sessions. Open P15.2 in the first AutoCAD LT session. Now, attempt to open the same file in the second AutoCAD LT session. In Using the File Management options in the second session, remove the lock file from the drawing and open the drawing. Close the first AutoCAD LT session, answering the prompts and error messages appropriately.

15.4 Open P15.2 for editing. Create a DXF file named P15.4.DXF.

15.5 Start a new drawing using the Start from Scratch option. Import the file P15.4.DXF. Save the drawing as P15.5.

15.6 Start a new drawing using the Start from Scratch option. Draw an object such as a line or a circle. Import the file P15.4.DXF. Note the message on the command line. Save the drawing as P15.6.

15.7 Open P15.2 for editing. Using the Plot to File options, create the following Plot files: P15.7.BMP, P15.7.TIF, P15.7.GIF, and P15.7.PCX.

15.8 Open a word processing application such as WordPad, Write, or Word. Write a paragraph describing the drawing file P15.2, and embed the drawing in the document with no links. Save the document as P15.8.

15.9 Open a word processing application such as WordPad, Write, or Word. Write a paragraph describing the drawing file P15.2, and embed the drawing in the document with a link to the original file. Save the document as P15.9.

15.10 Use the Paint Brush program to create a small bitmap image. Select and copy the image. Start a new drawing in AutoCAD LT and paste the image in with no links. Save the drawing as P15.10.

CHAPTER 16

AutoCAD LT and the Internet

LEARNING GOALS

- Identify Internet-related terminology.
- Utilize the WWW to access valuable resources.
- Create drawings designed for use in Web pages.
- Transmit and receive drawing data to and from remote sites.
- Place a DWF file in a Web page.

New technologies are rapidly changing the way things are done in industry. One of the most influential technologies in today's design industry is the Internet. The *Internet* is a worldwide network of computers connected to one another through telecommunication lines. One of the more popular uses of the Internet is for fast and convenient communications through the medium of e-mail. *E-mail*, or electronic mail, uses the Internet to transmit messages and computer files anywhere in the world in a matter of minutes.

The *World Wide Web* is probably the most widely known application of Internet technologies. The World Wide Web, or WWW, provides an easy-to-understand interface for the Internet. You may also see the WWW referred to as W3, or just the Web. This powerful medium uses HyperText Markup Language (HTML) files to present information. When viewed with a piece of software known as a Web browser, HTML files provide a graphical user interface (GUI) to the Internet, similar to the way that the Windows operating system simplifies complex computer processes using buttons, icons, and menus. The term *HyperText* describes text items that are *linked* to other resources, but links are often attached to images, icons, and menus as well. Items in HTML documents that are *linked* to other Web resources are called *hyperlinks*.

Web technologies are now widely used in the design industry. Because this industry is driven by information, the Web is a perfect medium for presenting and accessing information quickly and easily. AutoCAD LT 98 provides a powerful tool set, called the Internet Utilities, for incorporating Web-based technologies into your design process. Using the Internet Utilities, you can share your drawings with anyone, anywhere in the world. AutoCAD LT 98 can save drawing files in a special format that can be viewed using just a Web browser. This means that clients or coworkers can now view your AutoCAD LT drawings in an electronic format even if they do not have AutoCAD or AutoCAD LT software.

This chapter covers the AutoCAD LT 98 Internet Utilities and how to integrate Internet and Web-based technologies into your design process. Maximum benefit from this chapter will require Internet access and a Web browser.

The Internet Connection

Conceived in 1969 by the Advanced Research Projects Agency of the U.S. government, the Internet began as a network consisting of four computers. Today, the Internet is a publicly accessible communications system that consists of literally millions of computers worldwide that are interconnected through the use of existing public telecommunications networks—in other words, standard telephone lines.

Many large companies, schools, and governmental agencies use a high-speed connection to the Internet known as the *T-Carrier* digital transmission system. The two types of T-Carrier connections commonly used are referred to as T-1 and T-3 lines, with T-3 being much faster than T-1. Another common means of accessing the Internet is through the use of a modem and a standard telephone line. A *modem* is a translation device that allows a computer to transmit and receive digital information through telephone lines. A modem modulates, or converts, digital computer data into sounds. The sounds are transmitted through your telephone lines to another modem that then demodulates the sound back into digital computer information.

If you are using a computer at work or school, ask your instructor or system administrator how to gain access to the Internet. If you are working at home or in a company not yet connected to the Internet, a telephone line and a modem may be a workable solution.

When selecting a modem, speed is the primary concern. Web pages consist not only of text, but also graphic images, sounds, and many other large data files. All these files must be sent to your computer through your modem, and a slower modem means more time spent waiting for files to be downloaded to your system. The term *download* refers to the process of receiving files from a remote site through your modem or network connection. As a rule, you should not consider anything less than a 28.8-Kbps modem. A 56-Kbps (*kilobits per second*) modem is a better option for a standard telephone line connection.

For faster transmission speeds at an affordable rate for home and small businesses, you may wish to consider an ISDN line. Offering transmission speeds of up to 128 Kbps, the Integrated Services Digital Network requires an ISDN adapter rather than a modem. Not yet available in all areas, an ISDN connection requires installation of a special ISDN line and is subject to an installation charge and monthly fee. This cost can quickly be recovered in reduced wait times when accessing Web resources or transmitting and receiving large data files.

Once you have established a means for connecting your computer system to the Internet, you will need to contact an Internet Service Provider, or ISP. You can select an ISP from your phone book, but it is usually the best idea to ask for a recommendation from a friend or associate who already has Internet access. Another option is an on-line service provider such as CompuServe® or America On-Line®, who also provide Internet access. Most ISPs will provide you with the required software and instructions for accessing the Internet and the Web. Additionally, your ISP typically provides you with e-mail access and assigns a personal e-mail address.

Included with your Windows operating system is an Internet browser package called Internet Explorer. A popular alternative is the Netscape Communicator software, which is a powerful and versatile Web browser package. This inexpensive package can be purchased at a local software store or even on-line. Additionally, you can download an evaluation version of Netscape to try it before you decide to purchase it. Whatever your browser software choice is, be certain that it is the latest version available and that it is Java-enabled.

> **Field Notes**
>
> The latest versions of Netscape and Internet Explorer fully support the HTML 3.0 standard used to design many of the Web sites you will encounter. Some on-line service providers, however, may use proprietary browsers that are not capable of viewing these sites correctly.

Accessing Web Resources

Your Web browser can be launched from within AutoCAD LT 98 by selecting Connect to Internet from the Help menu or by picking the Browser button from the Internet Utilities toolbar. This menu selection launches your default browser and takes you directly to your currently specified Internet location. Alternatively, you can enter the BROWSER command directly at the Command: prompt. When entered at the Command: prompt, the BROWSER command allows you to specify an alternate URL. A *URL* (uniform resource locator) is the term that describes the location, or *address*, of a file found on the Internet. The default URL takes you to the Home Page of Autodesk's AutoCAD LT 98 Web site:

Command: **BROWSER**↵
Location <http://www.autodesk.com/acltuser>: *Enter URL or press Enter*

If you enter a different location, AutoCAD LT launches the browser and opens the specified location, but this does not change the default URL. This deafult should be set to the Web locations that you most frequently access when you start your browser. This could be your company Web site, a client's Web site, a Web Search engine, or any other site that you access frequently. The system variable named INETLOCATION is used to store the value for the default URL. If you would like your browser to start at a different location, you can change the value of this variable at the command line:

CHAPTER 16 ||| AutoCAD LT and the Internet 657

```
Command: INETLOCATION
New value for INETLOCATION <"http://www.autodesk.com/acltuser">:
http://www.cadnet1.com.↵
Command:
```

The AutoCAD LT 98 Web site is a dual-purpose site. It offers sales-oriented information for prospective customers as well as technical assistance for current users. Figure 16.1 shows the AutoCAD LT 98 Home Page in the Netscape Communicator Web browser.

FIGURE 16.1 The AutoCAD LT 98 Home Page is the initial default location accessed when launching your Web browser from within AutoCAD LT.

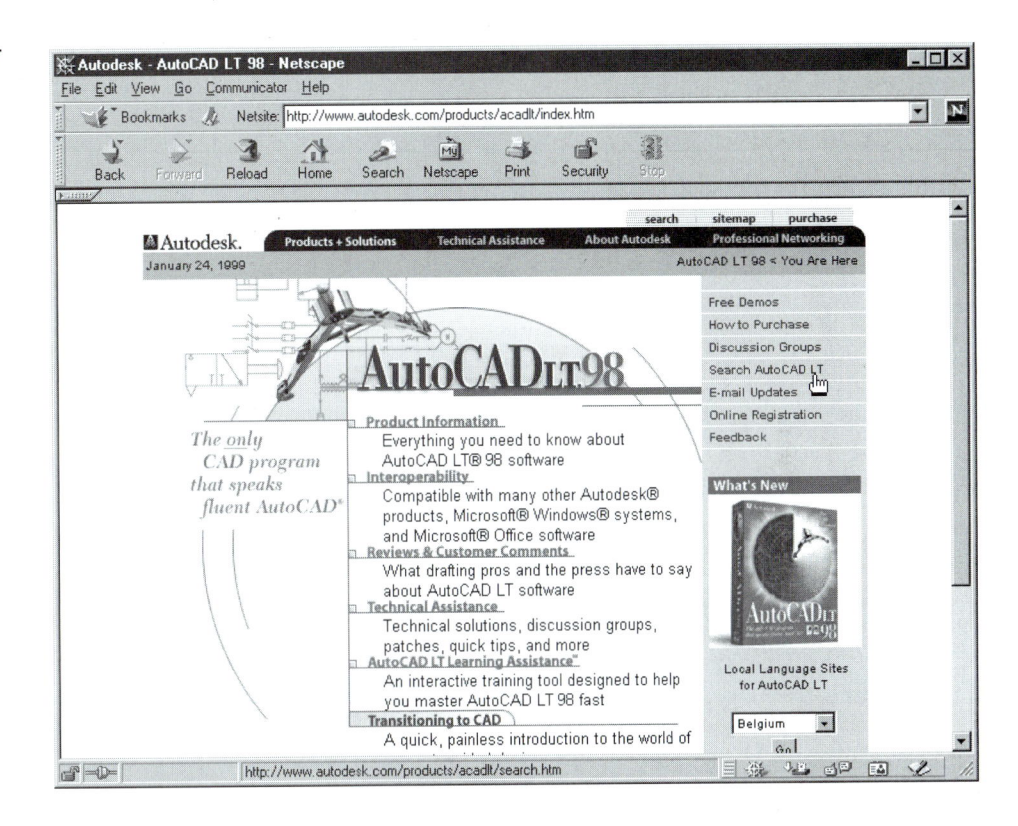

Field Notes

As with most professionally maintained Web sites, the AutoCAD LT 98 Web site is frequently revised and updated. Therefore, the current appearance may differ from that shown in the illustrations found in this chapter.

There are several categories of information shown on the AutoCAD LT 98 home page. As you move your cursor around the page, it will change to a hand and pointing finger as you move across various images and text items. This indicates the presence of a hyperlink, and picking the item will take you to a new location or document with related information.

Although most of the information on this site is concise and well organized, it is still very easy to get lost within any large Web site. The most effective selection you can make from the AutoCAD LT 98 home page is the SEARCH AutoCAD LT link. Using a search tool, or *search engine*, to find the specific information you are looking for can greatly reduce the amount of time spent at a Web site. Figure 16.2 shows the Search page for the AutoCAD LT 98 Web site.

In the example in Figure 16.2, a search is entered for documents related to the Internet. For valuable tips and instructions on using the search engine, pick the link labeled Search Tips. When you enter the search, the entire Web site is searched for documents related to the words you indicate. A listing is then provided, as shown in Figure 16.3. Each item is presented as a link, which can then be picked to display the listed page.

FIGURE 16.2 Using search engines will reduce the amount of time spent browsing a Web site.

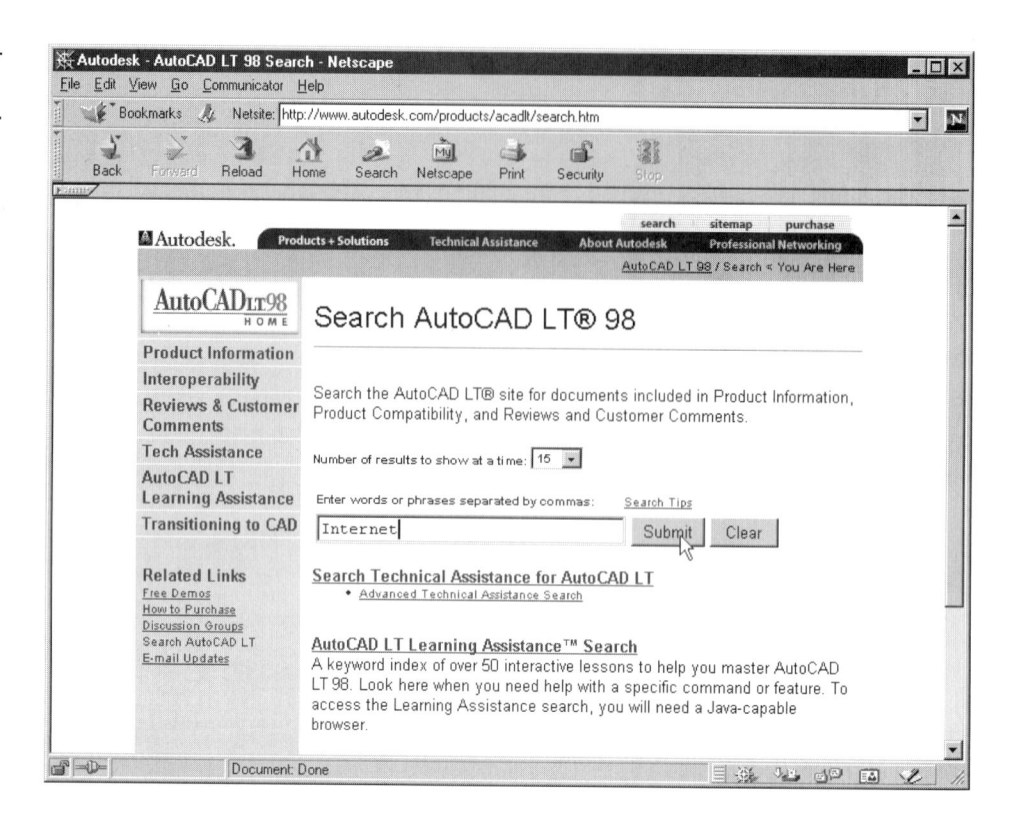

FIGURE 16.3 Search Results are displayed as links that can be picked to display Web pages related to the information you are searching for.

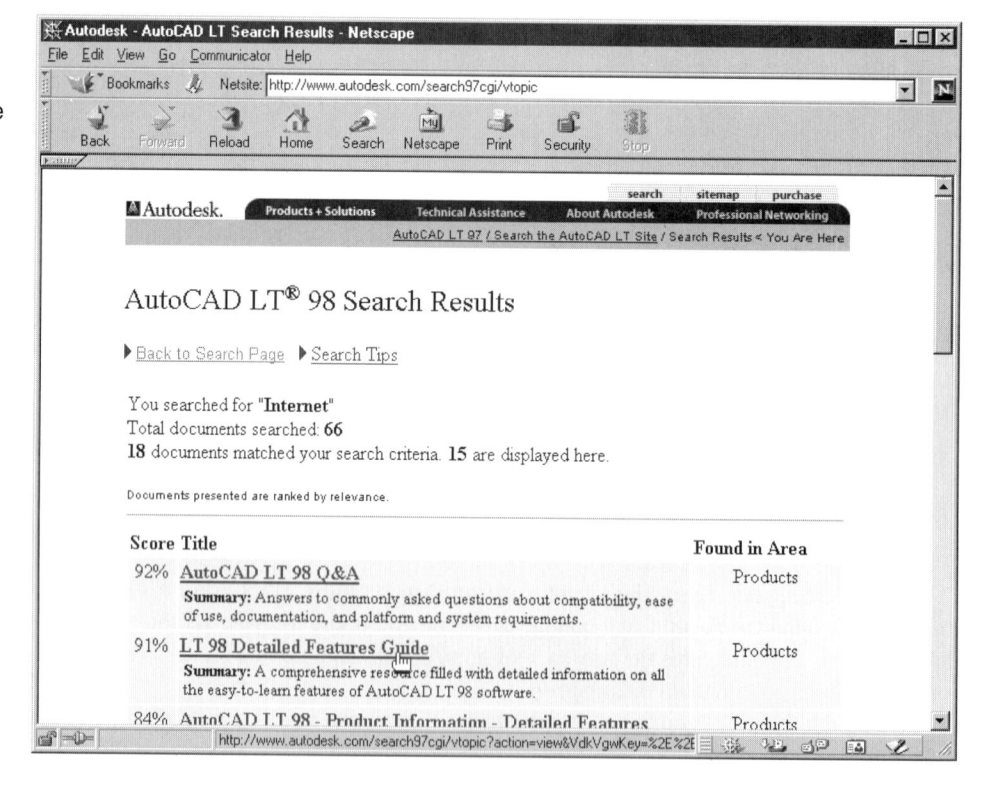

FIGURE 16.4 The Autodesk Newsgroups offer fast answers and lots of valuable information.

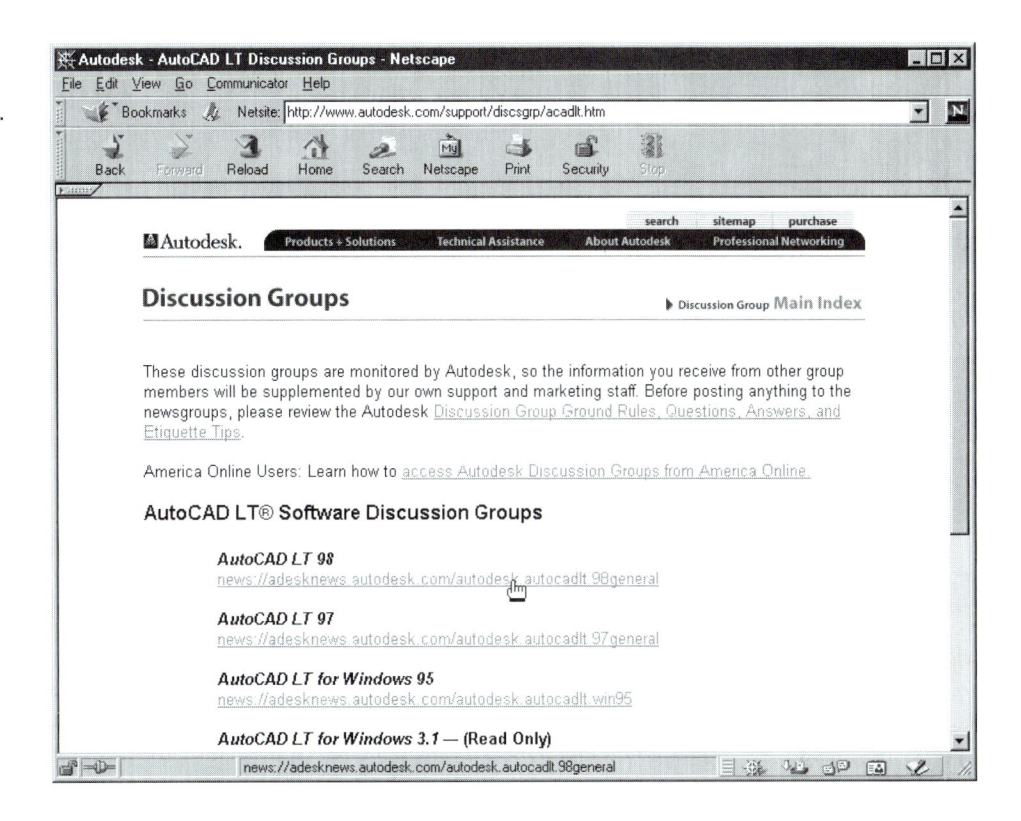

Another valuable resource that is accessible through the AutoCAD LT 98 Web site is the discussion groups. The Autodesk *Discussion Groups* are open-forum areas where you can post questions or messages for others to read and respond to. This forum is read by many AutoCAD LT 98 users as well as Autodesk staff members. If you have an unexplained software problem or have a question on using the software effectively, posting your questions in these forums can often get you a fast solution. To access the Autodesk News Groups, select the link labeled DISCUSSION GROUPS on the AutoCAD LT 98 Home Page (see Figure 16.1). This takes you to the Discussion Groups page, shown in Figure 16.4, where you can select the news group that you want to participate in.

Field Notes

Netscape Communicator has a built-in discussion group viewer that is activated by picking a discussion group link. If you are unable to access the news groups, ask your system administrator or instructor for assistance.

✓ LEARNING CHECKPOINT

☐ What are the most widespread uses of the Internet?
☐ Define the terms *HyperText* and *hyperlink*.
☐ Name three ways to connect to the Internet.
☐ Where is the default Internet location in AutoCAD LT 98?
☐ What is a discussion group?

> **Exercise 16.1**
>
> 1. If you are using a computer at work or at school, ask your system administrator or instructor for assistance in gaining Web access.
> 2. Determine what your default Web browser software is.
> 3. Use the BROWSER command to start your browser and go to the AutoCAD LT 98 Home Page.
> 4 Use the search engine to search for documents on two or more topics.

The Internet Utilities

AutoCAD LT 98 incorporates a powerful tool set called the Internet Utilities. These utilities provide advanced tools for utilizing Web-based technologies to maximize your information-exchange capabilities. One of the most basic of these capabilities is for sending a drawing as an e-mail attachment. You can also save drawings to or open drawings from a location on the Internet, or you can insert a drawing from the Internet. This section covers the AutoCAD LT 98 Internet Utilities.

Sending Drawings as E-mail Attachments

If you currently have a system e-mail tool, such as Microsoft Outlook®, the Send... option on the File pulldown menu in AutoCAD LT 98 can be selected. Otherwise, it appears grayed out and cannot be selected. Picking this option starts your e-mail tool and automatically attaches the current drawing to the e-mail. In Figure 16.5, the drawing file icon shows up in the e-mail message composer to indicate that the file has been attached.

Although this option represents a simple and convenient method for sending drawings to another location, it does have one major disadvantage. This option sends the drawing file as is, meaning at full size. Usually, when sending a drawing electronically, it is best to compress the file using some type of file compression utility. A good file compression tool can reduce the file size for a drawing to less than half of the actual size. This is especially valuable when sending larger drawings.

FIGURE 16.5 The Send... option on the File menu starts your e-mail tool and attaches the current drawing to the message.

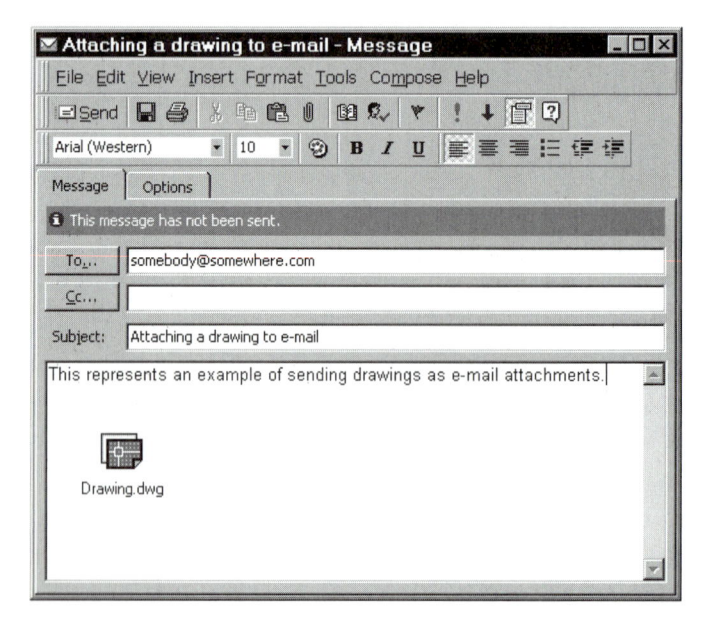

FIGURE 16.6 The Internet Utilities toolbar provides a convenient means of using the AutoCAD LT 98 Internet tools.

Field Notes

Many file compression utilities are available in today's market. Many, such as WinZip, can be tested before they are purchased. This powerful, yet inexpensive, utility can create self-extracting archive files for the convenience of the recipient. To try the shareware version of WinZip, you can visit their Web site at WWW.WINZIP.COM.

The Internet Utilities Toolbar

If the Internet Utilities toolbar is not currently visible, use the toolbars popup cursor menu to make it visible. Right-click on any toolbar button and pick Internet Utilities. The Internet Utilities toolbar is shown in Figure 16.6.

Saving a Drawing to a URL

The AutoCAD LT 98 Internet Utilities allow you to save a drawing file to a URL. Remember that the term URL (Uniform Resource Locator) refers to the location of a document on the Internet. When you save a drawing to a URL, you are specifying a location on the Internet to store the drawing file.

Saving a drawing to the Internet is typically used for communication of drawing data to clients or colleagues. By storing the file on the Internet, the other users can access the data if and when needed. The base URL, which is the save location without the drawing file name included, is typically a location on a Web site. This means that the drawing gets stored on the computer system used for the Web server. A *Web server* is a computer system that stores and sends requested files on the World Wide Web.

The command used to save a drawing to a URL is SAVEURL. The SAVEURL command can be typed at the Command: prompt, you can select the Save to URL button from the Internet Utilities toolbar, or you can pick Save to Internet... from the File pull-down menu. This displays the Save DWG to URL dialog box, as shown in Figure 16.7.

The first time you use this dialog box in a drawing session, you will need to configure the Internet Host information. Selecting the Options... button displays the Internet Configuration dialog box. See Figure 16.8. Or, you can go directly to this dialog box by picking the Configure Internet Host button from the Internet Utilities toolbar.

The FTP Login option is used to specify the location to which you want to save the drawing. FTP stands for file transfer protocol, and an FTP site is a location on the Internet from and to which you can copy files. The process of copying a file to the Internet is called *uploading*, and copying files from the Internet is called *downloading*. An FTP site requires a login, or an identification to authorize the file transfer process. Some public sites may allow what is called an *anonymous login*. This means that no secure user name or password is required. If the site you are saving to allows anonymous logins, you can check the Anonymous Login toggle; otherwise, you must supply a user name and password. Note that the password you enter here is remembered only during the current AutoCAD LT session. If you close AutoCAD LT, the password is reset to be blank. This prevents others from using a stored password to access files while you are away from your workstation.

Internet Utilities
Save to URL
File
Save to Internet
SAVEURL

FIGURE 16.7 The Save DWG to URL dialog box allows specification of the URL to which the drawing is to be saved.

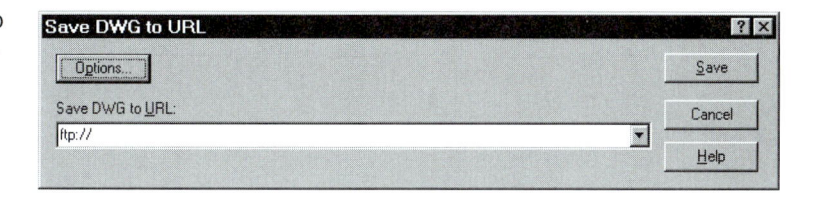

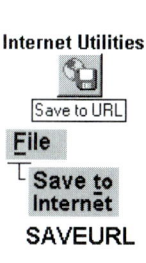

FIGURE 16.8 Use the Internet Configuration dialog box to specify required login information, such as user names, passwords, and connection information.

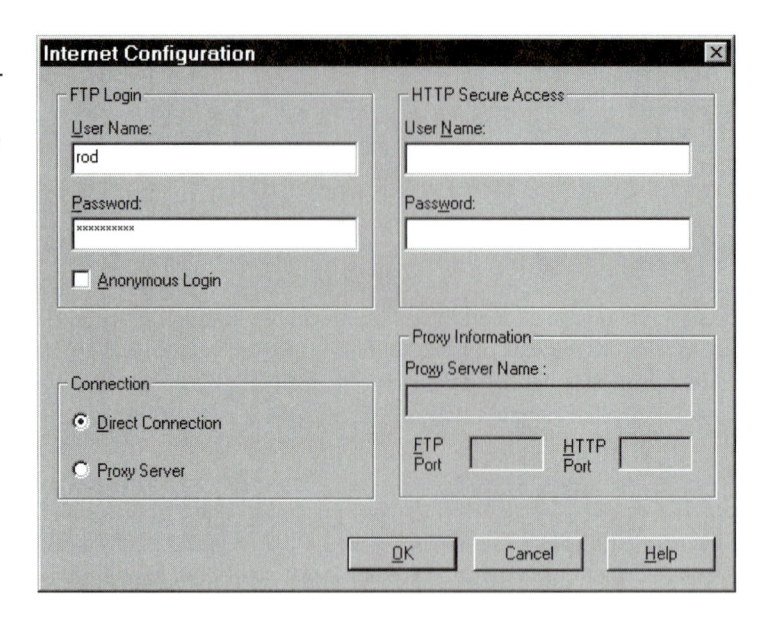

Other configuration details include HTTP Secure Access, which deals with opening drawing files from the Internet, Connection information, and Proxy information. The HTTP Secure Access login data are required when opening drawings from the Internet, which is discussed later in this chapter. Your connection information indicates whether you have a direct connection to the Internet or if you are routed through a proxy server. Check with your system administrator or your instructor for this information. If you are routed through a proxy server, you will also need to complete the fields in the Proxy Information area. Again, check with your system administrator or instructor for this information. Once you have configured your Internet Host information, pick OK and you are returned to the Save DWG to URL dialog box. Specify the desired location for saving the drawing in the Save DWG to URL: text box and pick the OK button. AutoCAD LT now displays the Remote Transfer in Progress dialog box to indicate the status of the transfer. See Figure 16.9.

Field Notes

You cannot save an unnamed drawing to the Internet. Be sure to use SAVE or SAVEAS before using SAVEURL.

FIGURE 16.9 The Remote Transfer in Progress dialog box indicates the status of the file transfer.

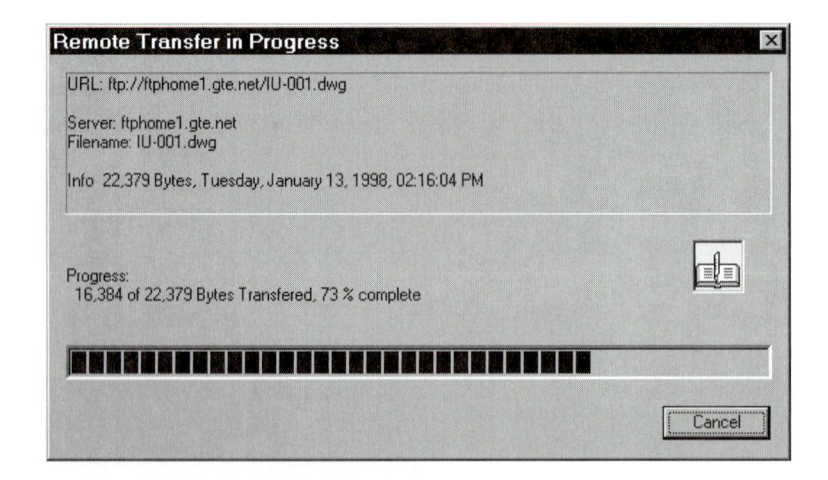

CHAPTER 16 ||| AutoCAD LT and the Internet   663

FIGURE 16.10 Use the Open a DWG from URL dialog box to specify a URL to open a drawing from.

Opening a Drawing from a URL

AutoCAD LT 98 can open a drawing directly from a URL. The OPENURL command is accessed by typing OPENURL at the Command: prompt, by picking Open from Internet... on the File menu, or by picking the Open from URL button in the Internet Utilities toolbar. The OPENURL command displays the Open DWG from URL dialog box (Figure 16.10).

You may also need to first configure the Internet host, which is similar to saving to a URL, and you will need to specify the exact URL in the text box. When you open a drawing from the Internet, a copy of it is made in your local temporary directory (usually C:\TEMP). If a drawing has previously been opened from the Internet, you will get a dialog box with a message asking if you really want to overwrite the existing file, as shown in Figure 16.11.

Internet Utilities
Open from URL
File
└ **Open from Internet**
OPENURL

Inserting a Drawing from a URL

Drawing files for symbols can be inserted from a URL to provide easy access to entire symbol libraries, even when working at remote locations. To insert a drawing from a URL, type INSERTURL at the Command: prompt, pick File from Internet... from the Insert menu, or pick the Insert from URL button on the Internet Utilities toolbar. The INSERTURL command works much like OPENURL, except that instead of actually opening the drawing, it is simply inserted into the current drawing. As with opening from a URL, you may first need to configure your Internet host. Also, as with opening, a local copy of the file is made in your temporary file directory. After this, the command works just like inserting a local drawing file and prompts for an insertion point, scale factors, and rotation angle.

Internet Utilities
Insert from URL
Insert
└ **File from Internet...**
INSERTURL

Working with Drawing Web Format Files

AutoCAD LT 98 can save drawings in a special drawing file format known as Drawing Web Format (DWF) files. These files are simple, vector-based proxy representations of actual drawings, similar in many ways to the output sent to plotters. DWF files can be viewed using a Web browser and, therefore, do not require the viewer to have the AutoCAD LT 98 software. Because they are vector format files and not raster images, they are much more flexible and accurate for presenting CAD drawings. Although a user can view and print a DWF file, it cannot be opened or edited. Additionally, no data can be extracted from these files. Essentially, they are for viewing only.

The EXPORT command is used to create DWF files. Type EXPORT at the Command: prompt or pick Export... from the File menu to display the Export Data dialog box. See Figure 16.12. From the Save as type: drop-down list, pick the Drawing Web Format (*.dwf) option. Alternatively, you can use the DWFOUT command. You cannot export a DWF file from a paper space view.

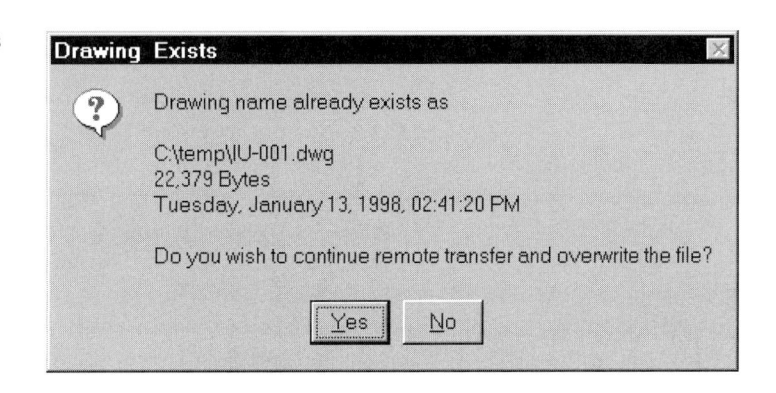

FIGURE 16.11 If a drawing has been opened from the Internet previously, you must tell AutoCAD LT whether or not to overwrite the existing copy.

FIGURE 16.12 Any drawing can be saved in the Drawing Web Format (dwf).

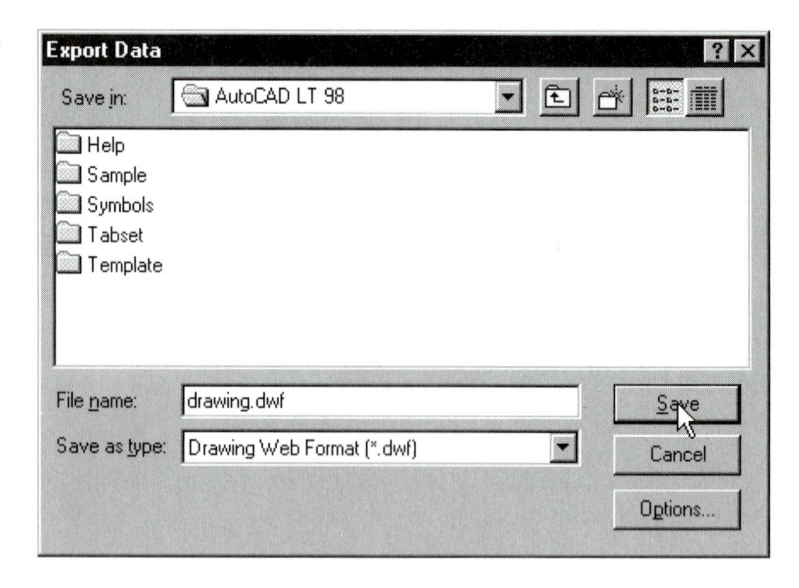

Before saving the DWF file, you need to set the options for this type of file. Picking the Options... button displays the DWF Export Options dialog box, as shown in Figure 16.13. The Precision area allows you to specify the precision level to use with the saved DWF file. This controls the number of decimal places of accuracy used when saving the drawing. Low precision saves 16-bit numbers, Medium precision saves 20-bit numbers, and High precision saves 32-bit numbers. If your drawing is large and complex, a higher precision level ensures that the drawing looks correct even when you zoom in very closely. In smaller drawings, the low-precision settings should be more than sufficient. A low-precision DWF file can be about one-eighth the size of the original drawing file. Using higher precision results in larger drawings, so you should typically use the lowest acceptable precision level. The option to Use File Compression produces a file that is about 25% or less of the size of a file generated without using this option.

The format options available are Compressed Binary, Binary, and ASCII, which control how the file is created. Compressed Binary is the default and the most commonly used option. There are very few reasons why you would not want the binary file to be compressed. Use the ASCII option if you need to be able to modify the file using an external process, such as PERL scripting.

The toggle at the bottom lets you choose whether or not to include layer information. If you do not include layer information, viewers will not be able to change layer visibility when viewing the drawing in a browser.

> **Field Notes**
>
> Only layers that are visible when the DWF file is created are included in the resulting file. This provides a simple way to control what information is available in the DWF file.

FIGURE 16.13 The DWF Export Options dialog box.

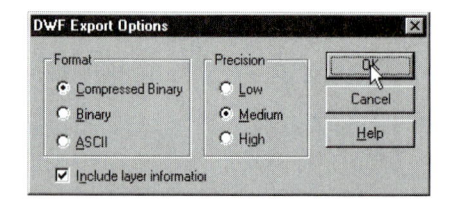

It is beyond the scope of this text to discuss the creation of Web sites or Web pages; however, a great deal of information on incorporating DWF drawing files into Web pages is provided on the Autodesk Web site.

To view a DWF format file with either Netscape or Internet Explorer, you will require the Whip® driver from Autodesk. This is a free downloadable file available on the Autodesk Web site. Be sure to check the *system requirements* pages to see which version of the Whip driver you should download. After you have downloaded the necessary files, follow the instructions on the Web site for installing the Whip driver. At the time of this writing, the URL for Whip information was http://www.autodesk.com/products/whip/index.htm.

CHAPTER 16 ||| AutoCAD LT and the Internet 665

Using Hyperlinks in DWG and DWF Files

Using the Internet Utilities, you can place hyperlinks in a drawing that can take the viewer to other drawings or other pertinent Web-based documents. The process of placing hyperlinks in a drawing file is the same whether you are creating standard drawings (.dwg) or Drawing Web Format (.dwf) files.

The primary command for placing a link in a drawing is ATTACHURL. To use this feature, type ATTACHURL at the Command: prompt, pick Attach URL from the Internet cascade on the Tools menu, or pick the Attach URL button from the Internet Utilities toolbar. The following prompt is displayed:

Command: _attachurl
URL by (Area/<Objects>):

Internet Utilities
Attach URL
Tools
└ Internet ▶
    └ Attach URL
ATTACHURL

A hyperlink can be attached to an object or to an area of the drawing. The default option is Objects, which allows you to select one or more objects to which you can attach the link:

Command: _attachurl
URL by (Area/<Objects>): ↵
Select objects: *Select one or more objects*
Select objects: ↵
Enter URL: **http://www.cadnet1.com/resources.html**↵
Command:

The area option places a rectangle in the drawing that is associated with a URL. This rectangle is created on a layer called URLLAYER. Do not rename this layer. When using the Area option, you are prompted to select the two corners of the rectangular area:

Command: _attachurl
URL by (Area/<Objects>): **A**↵
First corner: *Pick first corner*
Other corner: *Pick other corner*
Enter URL: **http://www.cadnet1.com/resources.html**↵

Once a link is placed in a drawing, you can access it directly in AutoCAD LT 98 by right-clicking on the object the URL is attached to or in the case of a URL specified by area, by right-clicking on the representative rectangle. This produces a popup menu with a Go to URL... option listed. See Figure 16.14. Picking this option starts your default system browser and the attached URL is opened.

In a DWF drawing viewed in a Web browser, pointing at a hyperlinked object or area produces the link cursor, the hand with a pointing finger. Note that the rectangles defining a linked area of the drawing do not display in a DWF drawing file.

FIGURE 16.14 Right-clicking on a hyperlinked object or area in an AutoCAD LT drawing produces a popup menu with an option to go to the specified URL.

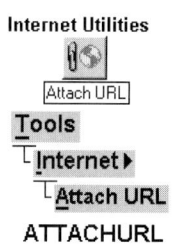

Removing a Link in a Drawing

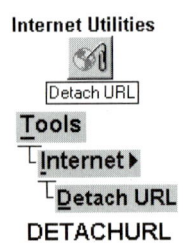

Internet Utilities
[Detach URL]
Tools
└ Internet ▶
  └ Detach URL
DETACHURL

The DETACHURL command removes hyperlink information from an object or area. To remove a link, type DETACHURL at the Command: prompt, pick Detach URL from the Internet cascade on the Tools menu, or pick the Detach URL button from the Internet Utilities toolbar. You are then given a standard Select objects: prompt. AutoCAD LT does not confirm the link removal when selecting a linked object, but when nonlinked objects are selected, a message is displayed indicating that the objects without links were filtered out of the selection:

```
Command: _detachurl
Select objects: 2 found
1 was filtered out.
Select objects:
```

Selecting the red rectangle representing a URL attached to an area deletes the rectangle, removes the link, and then displays the following message:

```
Command: _detachurl
Select objects: 1 found
Select objects: ↵
DetachURL, deleting the Area
```

Locating Links in a Drawing

Internet Utilities
[Select URLs]
SELECTURL

The Internet Utilities also provide a tool for finding any existing links in a drawing. The SELECTURL command can be typed at the Command: prompt, or you can pick the Select URL button from the Internet Utilities toolbar. This command simply grip-selects and highlights any objects or areas that have attached hyperlinks. This command issued no prompts and has no options. Once the objects are grip-selected, you can then activate any desired editing command to work with the selected objects, just as you would with any noun-verb selection process.

Listing Link Information

Internet Utilities
[List URLs]
Tools
└ Internet ▶
  └ List URLs
LISTURL

To list the link information attached to an object, use the LISTURL command. This command can be typed at the Command: prompt, you can pick List URLs from the Internet cascade of the Tools menu, or select the List URLs button from the Internet Utilities toolbar. The LISTURL command produces a Select objects: prompt and then displays any attached link information. Any objects not having attached links are filtered out of the selection set:

```
Command: _listurl
Select objects: Other corner: 3 found
1 was filtered out.
Select objects: ↵
```

URL for selected object is: WWW.Autodesk.com
URL for selected object is: WWW.CADNET1.COM

✓ LEARNING CHECKPOINT

- ☐ Name the most fundamental of tools for communicating drawings via the Internet.
- ☐ How is the Internet Utilities toolbar displayed?
- ☐ Name the command used to save a drawing to an Internet location.
- ☐ Define the term *anonymous login*.
- ☐ When a drawing is opened from the Internet, where is the local copy stored?
- ☐ What is a DWF file?
- ☐ Define the term *hyperlink*.
- ☐ Describe the DWF Export options.
- ☐ What commands are used to create and manage hyperlinks in a drawing?

CHAPTER 16 ||| AutoCAD LT and the Internet 667

> ### Exercise 16.2
>
> 1. Send a drawing to an associate using the Sen<u>d</u>... option on the <u>F</u>ile menu.
> 2. Use the Toolbars dialog box to display the Internet Utilities toolbar.
> 3. If you have access to an FTP site, do Exercises 4, 5, and 6.
> 4. Save a drawing to your FTP site using SAVEURL.
> 5. Reopen the same drawing using the OPENURL command.
> 6. Start a new drawing, and use INSERTURL to insert the saved drawing into the current drawing. Note the messages and warnings displayed.
> 7. Open a drawing from a previous chapter. Use the Internet Utilities to attach hyperlinks to one or more objects and an area in the drawing.
> 8. Right-click on one of the links and use the <u>G</u>o to URL... option.
> 9. Return to AutoCAD LT 98 and remove one of the links.
> 10. Use the SELECTURL option to highlight each of the links you have attached. Now pick LISTURL to list out the link information.
> 11. Save the drawing as a DWF file, using each of the DWF Export Options. Compare file sizes.

MULTIPLE CHOICE

1. Which term is not an acronym or term used to describe the World Wide Web?
   a. WWWeb
   b. WWW
   c. W3
   d. the Web

2. Which term does not describe an Internet connection?
   a. modem
   b. ISDN
   c. coaxial
   d. T-1

3. The term ISP stands for:
   a. Information Services Protocol
   b. Internet Service Provider
   c. Intranet Systems Project
   d. Internet System Protocol

4. A software package used to view World Wide Web documents is called a(n):
   a. Browser
   b. Web viewer
   c. CAD Package
   d. Internet editor

5. The AutoCAD LT command used to start the software described in Question 4 is:
   a. GotoURL
   b. INETLOCATION
   c. BROWSER
   d. OPENURL

6. The command used to set the default Internet location is:
   a. SETURL
   b. INETLOCATION
   c. DEFAULTURL
   d. OPENURL

7. The initial default Internet location is:
   a. Autodesk Home Page
   b. http://www.yahoo.com/www.Yahoo.com
   c. AutoCAD LT 98 Home Page
   d. Netscape Home

8. The tool used to quickly find the information you are looking for on a Web site is called a:
   a. QuickFinder
   b. Internet locator
   c. search engine
   d. thesaurus

9. An open forum area where questions and messages can be posted for others to read is called a:
   a. chat room
   b. FTP site
   c. Web site
   d. discussion group

10. In order to use the Sen<u>d</u>... option on the <u>F</u>ile menu, you must first have a(n):
    a. e-mail tool
    b. ISDN line
    c. Web browser
    d. recycle bin

11. The command used to save a drawing file to an FTP site is:
    a. SAVEURL
    b. SAVETOURL
    c. SEND
    d. ATTACHURL

12. To open a drawing from a Web site, this command is used:
    a. OPENURL
    b. OPENFROMURL
    c. GOTOURL
    d. INSERTURL

13. The command used to insert a drawing from a remote location on the Internet is:
    a. OPENURL
    b. OPENFROMURL
    c. GOTOURL
    d. INSERTURL

14. DWF stands for:
    a. dynamic Web file
    b. drawing Web format
    c. drawing With flair
    d. drawing Web file

15. Using file compression when creating a DWF file often results in files about this percentage of the size of files created without compression:
    a. 15%
    b. 20%
    c. 25%
    d. 50%

16. To attach a link to an object or area, this command is used:
    a. ATTACHLINK
    b. ATTACHURL
    c. INSERTURL
    d. OPENURL

17. To remove a link from an object or area, use this command:
    a. DETACH
    b. UNDO
    c. DETACHURL
    d. DELETEURL

18. To access the URL attached to an object or area in an AutoCAD LT drawing file:
    a. right-click on the object
    b. type the GOTOURL command
    c. use the OPENURL command.
    d. highlight the object and press Enter

19. This command is used to find the linked objects and areas in a drawing:
    a. FINDURL
    b. FINDLINK
    c. GETURL
    d. SELECTURL

20. To display link information, this command is used:
    a. GETURL
    b. SHOWLINK
    c. OPENURL
    d. LISTURL

MATCHING

Match each term to the correct description by writing the appropriate number in each box at the left.

- ☐ URL
- ☐ HTTP
- ☐ HTML
- ☐ WWW
- ☐ FTP
- ☐ ISDN
- ☐ ISP
- ☐ DWF
- ☐ Kbps
- ☐ T-1/T-3
- ☐ Modem
- ☐ dwg

1. Standard drawing file extension.
2. World Wide Web.
3. T—Carrier connections.
4. Internet Service Provider.
5. Kilobytes per second.
6. HyperText Transfer Protocol.
7. Modulator/Demodulator.
8. Hypertext Markup Language.
9. Integrated Services Digital Network.
10. Uniform Resource Locator.
11. Drawing Web Format.
12. File Transfer Protocol.

CHAPTER 16 ||| AutoCAD LT and the Internet **669**

WORD SCRAMBLE

Unscramble the six scrambled words below, one letter to each square, to form six AutoCAD LT–related words:

WIERDWELDBO

NINETRE

THYEXPER

PERKYNIHL

DEMOM

Unscramble the circled letters above to form the special answer as suggested by the illustration.

CHAPTER 17

Customizing AutoCAD LT

LEARNING GOALS

- Create custom command alias definitions.
- Automate AutoCAD LT using command scripts.
- Create and modify toolbars and toolbar buttons.
- Modify the AutoCAD LT pull-down menu system.
- Incorporate DIESEL strings in custom menu entries.
- Define custom linetypes and hatch patterns.

Why Customize?

One very important reason for the popularity of the AutoCAD and AutoCAD LT software packages is ease of customization. Within the technical drafting and design area there are many different methods and standards. Technical drawing fields include mechanical, architectural, electronic, civil, and other categories, with many highly specialized applications in each category. Some CAD software packages are very specialized, working most effectively within one specific discipline. AutoCAD LT is capable of working productively in each of these fields to meet almost any technical drawing need. This is because the AutoCAD LT software allows custom tools to be developed to meet specific needs. These custom tools automate repetitive tasks and can quickly finish even very complex tasks.

There are many ways to customize the AutoCAD LT software package to help you be more productive. You have already done simple customization of the interface by placing and positioning toolbars and setting up the drawing environment. Screen layout and drawing setup are two very important aspects of customizing your drafting environment; however, many other aspects of this software can be customized as well. You can customize the initialization files to control how AutoCAD LT starts up. Command scripts can be written and used for automating procedures. Custom menus can be built from scratch or the existing menu system can be modified to meet your needs. Your menu picks can be made "intelligent" through the use of DIESEL strings. You can create new command aliases for frequently used commands, and even design new linetype and hatch pattern definitions.

When you learn to customize AutoCAD LT, you are learning how to get the most out of your software. This chapter shows you how to be more productive and meet specialized needs through customizing the AutoCAD LT software.

Creating Your Own Command Aliases

Command aliases are shortened names for commands that allow you to access commands more easily from the keyboard. All command alias definitions are created and stored in an AutoCAD LT support file called ACLT.PGP. The term *support file* refers to files that are not part of the core program that are used to enhance or modify the way AutoCAD LT works. The ACLT.PGP file is used to modify the way AutoCAD LT works, but because it is not a part of the core program, it is not required in order for AutoCAD LT to run. The file extension PGP stands for ProGram Parameters.

All the existing command aliases you have learned so far are defined in the ACLT.PGP file. For example, the alias L for the LINE command, C for the CIRCLE command, and E for ERASE are all command aliases that are set up in the ACLT.PGP file.

The ACLT.PGP file is found in the \AutoCAD LT 98 folder. It is a standard ASCII text file and can be edited using the Notepad text editing software. Notepad is a simple text editing program that comes with the Windows operating system. To open the ACLT.PGP file using Notepad, start Notepad from the Accessories group and pick Open … from the File pull-down menu. Using the Open dialog box, go to the AutoCAD LT 98 folder and select the ACLT.PGP file. Figure 17.1 shows the ACLT.PGP file loaded in the Notepad text editor.

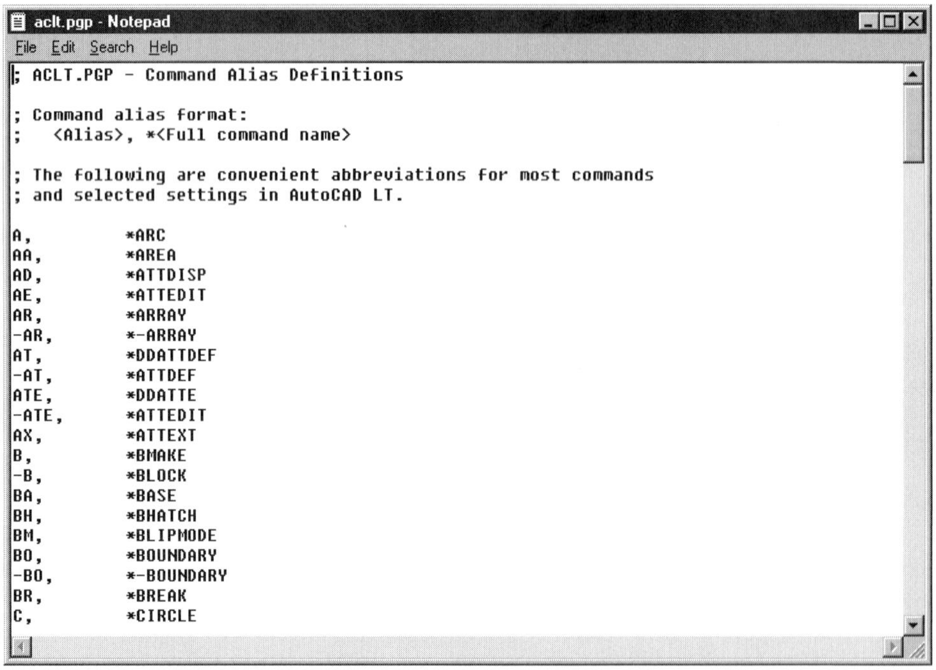

FIGURE 17.1 Notepad can be used to edit the ACLT.PGP file.

```
; ACLT.PGP - Command Alias Definitions

; Command alias format:
;   <Alias>, *<Full command name>

; The following are convenient abbreviations for most commands
; and selected settings in AutoCAD LT.

A,       *ARC
AA,      *AREA
AD,      *ATTDISP
AE,      *ATTEDIT
AR,      *ARRAY
-AR,     *-ARRAY
AT,      *DDATTDEF
-AT,     *ATTDEF
ATE,     *DDATTE
-ATE,    *ATTEDIT
AX,      *ATTEXT
B,       *BMAKE
-B,      *BLOCK
BA,      *BASE
BH,      *BHATCH
BM,      *BLIPMODE
BO,      *BOUNDARY
-BO,     *-BOUNDARY
BR,      *BREAK
C,       *CIRCLE
```

The introductory text at the top of the ACLT.PGP file explains how to create a command alias. Notice that the informative lines begin with a semicolon (;). Any line in the ACLT.PGP file that starts with a semicolon is considered a comment. Comments in files are ignored by AutoCAD LT. Comments in files are typically used for informative purposes and can be placed anywhere in the file as long as the first character on the comment line is a semicolon.

The introductory statement shows that the listing that defines a command alias is in this format:

<Alias>, *<Full command name>

This means that the alias, or shortened command name, is listed first, separated by a comma from the full command name. The full command name is preceded by an asterisk (*). The command alias can be any combination of alphanumeric characters. The term *alphanumeric* refers to any letters of the alphabet and the numbers 0 through 9. For example, a command alias could be named "1," "A," or even "A1." Any number of characters can be used in a command alias, but the purpose of an alias is to reduce typing requirements so the name should typically be shorter than the full command name. Another guideline that can be helpful is to stick with a shortened version of the actual command name. This makes the alias easier to remember. For example, the MSLIDE command does not have an alias listed in the ACLT.PGP file. If you were to create one, a logical choice for an alias name might be MSL. The choice of MS might be preferred, but this has already been assigned to MSPACE. It is best to avoid redefining existing aliases. An unrelated alias, M7 for example, could be used, but might not be as easy to remember.

When adding a new alias, it is a good idea to place your custom alias listings in the appropriate alphabetical position with the existing alias definitions. This helps you avoid accidentally redefining an existing command alias. If more than one listing is present in the PGP file for a single alias name, the last one encountered is the one that is used. If you prefer to do so, you can group your custom alias definitions in a separate area of the PGP file.

CHAPTER 17 ||| Customizing AutoCAD LT 673

To use Notepad to add the alias MSL for MSLIDE, move the cursor to the line where you wish to enter the new definition. If there is already an entry on that line, press the Enter key to move it down one line and then use the arrow keys to move back up to the new blank line. Now, enter the following:

MSL, *MSLIDE

The modified ACLT.PGP file is shown in Figure 17.2. The number of spaces between the comma and the asterisk does not matter. You can have no spaces, one space, or any number of spaces. The primary factor is keeping the file neat and easy to read. Next, save the file by picking Save … from the File pull-down menu.

FIGURE 17.2 The new line in the ACLT.PGP file is highlighted. This creates a command alias named MSL for the MSLIDE command.

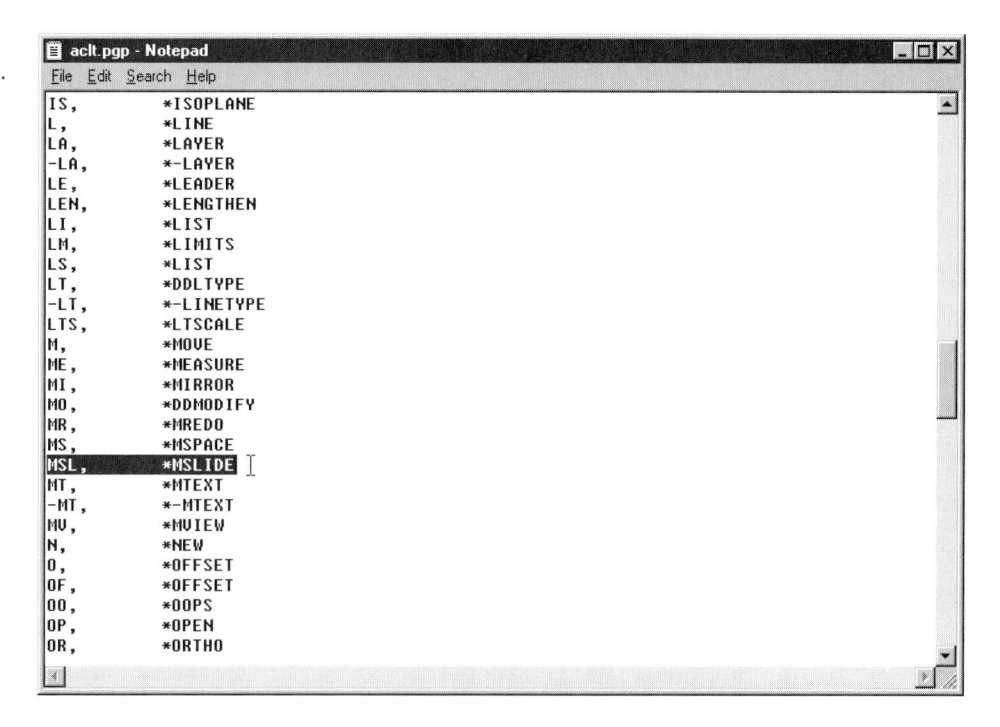

If AutoCAD LT has not already been started, the new PGP file is automatically loaded when you do start it. If AutoCAD LT is already active, you need to use the REINIT command to *reinitialize,* or reload, the PGP file. This command is started by typing **RI** or **REINIT** at the Command: prompt. The REINIT command displays the dialog box shown in Figure 17.3.

REINIT
RI

After reloading the PGP file, the new command alias is ready to use:

Command: **MSL**↵
MSLIDE
⟨*the Create Slide File dialog box is displayed*⟩

FIGURE 17.3 The REINIT command displays the Reinitialize dialog box. This allows you to reload the PGP file after making changes.

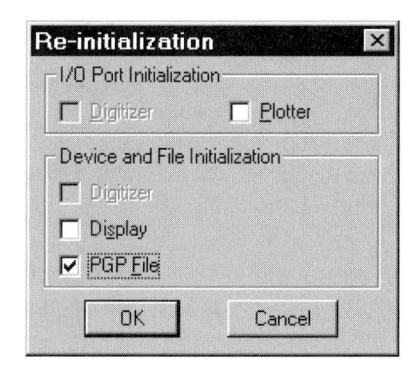

Command aliases can be defined only for starting commands, and they cannot access any of the options of that command. This means that although the Z alias can start the ZOOM command, it is not possible to define a command alias that automatically does a ZOOM Window or ZOOM Previous. Although command aliases have this limitation, you may still find that an effectively designed command alias list can help you be much more productive. Once you learn to use the keyboard effectively, it can be much faster than picking commands from the menus.

Field Notes

Existing command aliases can be redefined as desired. However, if your workstation is also used by others, you should not change the existing alias definitions.

When editing a support file, it is often a good idea to first create a backup version of the file you are editing. For example, before editing the PGP file you may wish to copy it to a file such as ACLT.PGP.BACKUP. This way, if you make changes that you do not like, you can always refer back to the original file.

Through the Window ...

When AutoCAD LT is installed, it automatically associates the PGP file with the Notepad text editing program. This means that if you double-click on the PGP file from Windows Explorer or File Manager, the Notepad program is automatically started with the PGP file loaded.

Exercise 17.1

1. Using your file management application, make a copy of ACLT.PGP and name it ACLT.PGP.BACKUP.
2. Using the Notepad editor, open the ACLT.PGP file for editing.
3. Add three custom command alias definitions to the PGP file.
4. Save the ACLT.PGP file.

✓ LEARNING CHECKPOINT

☐ Define the term *command alias*.
☐ In what file are command alias definitions created?
☐ What type of software application is used to edit the command alias file?
☐ Show how the alias DXI could be defined to start the DXFIN command.
☐ What command reloads the command alias file?

Automating AutoCAD LT Using Command Scripts

A simple, yet effective means of customizing the AutoCAD LT software is through the use of command scripts. A **command script** is a text file that contains a list of commands and options that AutoCAD LT reads and performs. It is called a script because the file tells AutoCAD LT what to do and what sequence to do it in. In essence, a script is a plain English programming language for AutoCAD LT.

A script file is an ASCII text file with a .SCR file extension. You can create a script file with any text editing software, but if you use a word processor, be certain to save the file as a *text* file. One easy way to create a script file is by using the Notepad program, found in the Accessories group. Within the script file, there are a few things you need to keep in mind as you create a script. First, any blank spaces in the file are interpreted as an Enter keystroke—just like when you press the space bar at the AutoCAD LT Command: prompt. Additionally, the end of each line is considered an Enter keystroke.

If the command script has any errors, it will run to the point where the error is encountered and then stop. Possible command script errors include misspelled commands or options, and incorrectly answering an AutoCAD LT prompt. Also, the use of spaces should be kept to a minimum, because spaces are not easy to count, and if you have one too many or one too few, it can cause your script file to produce an error.

Applications for script files vary widely. They can be used for doing drawing setups, unattended plotting, or even for running automated script shows using slide files. Creating and viewing slide files was discussed in Chapter 15. The following example shows a simple script file that does a brief setup procedure:

```
LIMITS
0,0
36,24
GRID
.5
SNAP
.25
ZOOM
ALL
```

The file can have any valid file name but must have a file extension of .SCR. A reasonable name for this might be SETUP-D.SCR because it performs a setup sequence for a D size sheet. Loading a script file into AutoCAD LT is done using the SCRIPT command. The SCRIPT command is accessed by Run Script … from the Tools pull-down menu or by typing **SCR** or **SCRIPT** at the Command: prompt. The SCRIPT command displays the Select Script File dialog box. Use this file dialog box to go to the correct directory and select the desired script file name. The Select Script File dialog box is shown in Figure 17.4.

Tools
Run Script...
SCRIPT
SCR

FIGURE 17.4 The Select Script File dialog box.

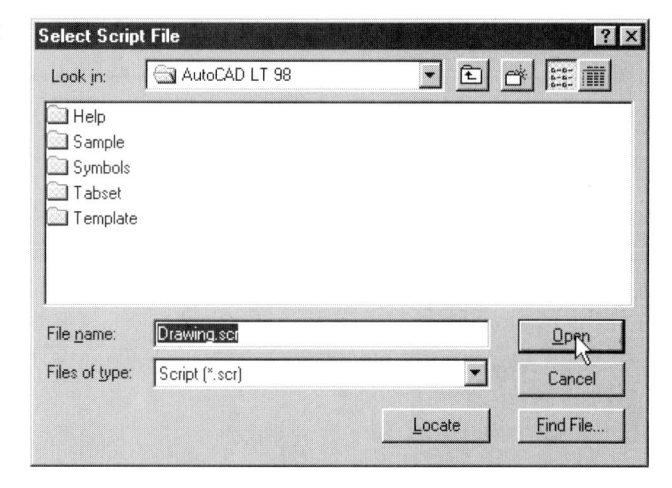

As the script file is processed, each entry is shown at the command line. This is useful for troubleshooting the script if it malfunctions. The term *troubleshooting* is used to describe the process of figuring out what went wrong. The command line entries for the SETUP-D script file are shown in the following example as they appear on the text screen:

```
Command: SCRIPT
Command: LIMITS
Reset Model space limits:
ON/OFF/<Lower left corner> <0.0000,0.0000>: 0,0
Upper right corner <12.0000,9.0000>: 36,24
Command: GRID
Grid spacing(X) or ON/OFF/Snap/Aspect <0.0000>: .5
Command: SNAP
Snap spacing or ON/OFF/Aspect/Rotate/Style <1.0000>: .25
Command: ZOOM
All/Center/Dynamic/Extents/Left/Previous/Vmax/Window/<Scale (X/XP)>: ALL
Regenerating drawing.
```

A more complex script file might set up layers, insert title sheets, or automate almost any desired task. Keep in mind, however, that the best and easiest way for setup procedures is often through the use of drawing template files. Another common use for script files is to create a running "slide show" for any number of purposes. A *slide show* in AutoCAD LT, similar to a presentation given using standard slides and a projector, displays a sequence of graphic images. An AutoCAD LT slide show can display a comprehensive portfolio or proposal to a prospective client, and slide shows are often used at trade shows and product demonstrations.

To create a portfolio using a slide show, you first need to create all of the slides you wish to display. These slide files might be of various drawing projects on which you have worked. Unless you have a laptop computer to run the show, it is likely that you will be transporting the slide show files on a floppy diskette. With this in mind, the following example assumes that the slide files have been placed on a floppy diskette that occupies the A: drive.

Once you have created and stored your slide files, it is time to write the script file. In this example, four slide files have been created using a simple naming system of PFS001.SLD through PFS004.SLD. The command used to view a slide file is VSLIDE, so this is the first command, followed by a space for an Enter and then the file name entry. This example shows the use of spaces, but it also works the same with each entry on its own line. It is not necessary to specify the .SLD file extension. When running a script file, the command line versions of commands are used, with no dialog boxes being displayed. Here is how the script file starts:

VSLIDE A:\PFS001

At this point, it is necessary to pause the script file for a short time. Allowed to run unchecked, the slides are displayed as quickly as AutoCAD LT can process the script file. This does not allow any viewing time for the slides being viewed. For this purpose, AutoCAD LT provides the DELAY command. The DELAY command does just as its name suggests—it delays before processing the next command. The DELAY command prompts for the amount of time to delay, and the input is read as *milliseconds,* or thousandths of a second. So, a delay time of 500 is 500/1000 s, or 1/2 s. A delay time of 4000 produces a 4-s delay. The DELAY command accepts delay times up to 32,767 ms, which is just over 30 s.

Before placing the DELAY command in the script, the next slide file to be viewed can be preloaded. This causes the next script file to be read from disk and stored in memory while the previous slide is being viewed. This helps the script file to run smoother. To preload a slide file, use the VSLIDE command and precede the slide file name with an asterisk:

VSLIDE A:\PSF001
VSLIDE *A:\PSF002
DELAY 2000

Now, the slide show starts by displaying PSF001, then it preloads PSF002 and delays for 2 s of viewing time. When a slide file has been preloaded, it is viewed by entering the VSLIDE command again without specifying a file name. So for the script to continue after the delay, another VSLIDE command is necessary:

VSLIDE A:\PSF001
VSLIDE *A:\PSF002
DELAY 2000
VSLIDE

The preload and delay sequence is now repeated. The completed script file is shown here with comments to clarify the purpose of each line:

;Display PSF001.SLD
VSLIDE A:\PSF001
;Preload PSF002.SLD
VSLIDE *A:\PSF002
;Delay 2 seconds for viewing time of PSF001.SLD
DELAY 2000
;Display the preloaded PSF002.SLD
VSLIDE
;Preload PSF003.SLD
VSLIDE *A:\PSF003
;Delay 1.5 seconds for viewing time of PSF002.SLD
DELAY 1500
;Display the preloaded PSF003.SLD
VSLIDE
;Preload PSF004.SLD

VSLIDE *A:\PSF004
;Delay 4 seconds for viewing time of PSF003.SLD
DELAY 4000
;Display the preloaded PSF004.SLD
VSLIDE

Comments can be placed in a script file on a line that begins with a semicolon, similar to the PGP file. Each comment listed in the preceding script example explains the function of the line that follows.

The previous example shows one run-through of the script file. The delay times you set up in your slide show should be based on how much viewing time is necessary for the viewer to absorb the intent of each slide. A simple introductory slide, such as a lead-in title slide, might require only a second or two. A more complex slide that shows many important details might require four or five seconds or even longer.

If you want to interrupt a script without canceling the command, press the Backspace key. The Esc key can also be used, but the Backspace key does not print *CANCEL* on the command line. To resume the script processing where it left off, enter the RESUME command at the Command: prompt.

There are also specialized commands available for your script files that allow added flexibility. Here is a listing of those commands:

RSCRIPT   This command can be placed at the end of a script file to repeat the script. This creates a self-running script file that runs until interrupted.

TEXTSCR   The TEXTSCR command displays the AutoCAD LT text window.

GRAPHSCR   This displays the AutoCAD LT graphics window.

Field Notes

- In a script file, you must press Enter after the final entry on the last line or the entry will not be processed.
- When creating a script file, the best technique is to walk through the commands and options manually and write down each command and option as you go. This helps you to avoid errors that can occur from not addressing a prompt sequence correctly.

Exercise 17.2

1. Create a selection of four slide files from drawings you have completed so far.
2. Create a script file that runs a *repeating* slide show of these four slides.
3. Be sure to preload slides when appropriate and allow for sufficient viewing time for each slide.
4. Save the script file as EX17.2.SCR.

LEARNING CHECKPOINT

- What is a script file?
- How can script files be used to increase drafting productivity?
- Describe how slide shows can be created using script files.
- What special commands are available in script files? What do they do?

Customizing Toolbars and Toolbar Buttons

Toolbar buttons provide top-level access to many frequently used commands and options. Rather than having to first pick a menu and then pick an option from the menu, many toolbar buttons can access the same options with a single pick. In addition to providing a wide variety of toolbars and toolbar buttons for you to use, AutoCAD LT also allows you to modify the existing tools or even to create your own completely new tools.

Having a custom tool set for different types of drafting needs can greatly enhance your productivity levels. Using toolbars and toolbar buttons, you can create buttons that start commands and create menu macros. A *macro* is a set of multiple commands and options that runs automatically when started. For example, a selection that starts the ZOOM command is not considered a macro. A selection that starts the ZOOM command and then enters the Previous option is a macro because it does more than one thing.

The simplest way to work with toolbars is to control toolbar visibility and location. Right-clicking on any existing toolbar button accesses the Toolbars cursor menu. As shown in Figure 17.5, the toolbars menu shows a checkmark by the names of the toolbars that are currently visible. To change the current visibility of any toolbar listed, just pick its name. The next time you display this menu, the toolbar name displays a checkmark, indicating that it is currently visible.

FIGURE 17.5 Right-click on any toolbar button to display the Toolbar cursor menu.

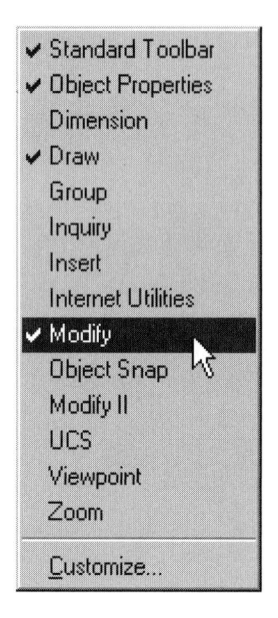

You can place toolbars anywhere on the screen in either a floating or a docked state. A docked toolbar appears as though it were part of the program window, attached near the top, bottom, or sides of the window. By default, the Standard and Object Properties toolbars are docked at the top of the screen; the Draw and Modify toolbars are docked on the left side of the screen. To change the Modify toolbar to a floating state, point to any location on the toolbar that is not a button; then press and hold the pick button on your mouse. When you move your cursor, you will see the outline of a toolbar. A bold outline indicates that if you release the pick button, the toolbar will drop into a floating state. When your cursor approaches the edge of the window, the outline becomes thin and may change shape or orientation, which indicates that the toolbar will be docked on the edge to which you are pointing. Figure 17.6 illustrates the differences in the dragged outline. While you are dragging a toolbar the helpstring displayed on the status bar at the bottom of the AutoCAD LT window indicates that you can prevent docking by holding the Ctrl key as you drag the toolbar. This is useful when you want to move a toolbar near an edge but you do not want it to be docked.

A docked toolbar defaults to a single row or column and cannot be resized. When a toolbar is floating, it can be resized as desired. Resizing toolbars is limited to adjusting the number of rows or columns in which the buttons are displayed. Toolbars are resized just like program windows. Move your cursor to an edge and when you see the resizing cursor, press and hold the pick button. Drag the toolbar into the desired shape and release the pick button. Toolbars can be resized only horizontally and vertically, not diagonally.

To begin working with toolbars, select T̲oolbars … from the V̲iew pull-down menu or right-click on any toolbar button and select C̲ustomize…from the cursor menu. Both of these methods results in the display of the Customize dialog box, which is shown in Figure 17.7.

The toolbar listings in the T̲oolbars list show the names of the toolbars preceded by a check box used to display or hide the toolbar.

CHAPTER 17 ||| Customizing AutoCAD LT   **679**

FIGURE 17.6 The outline of the toolbar indicates whether the toolbar will be (A) Floating or (B) Docked when the button is released.

A

B

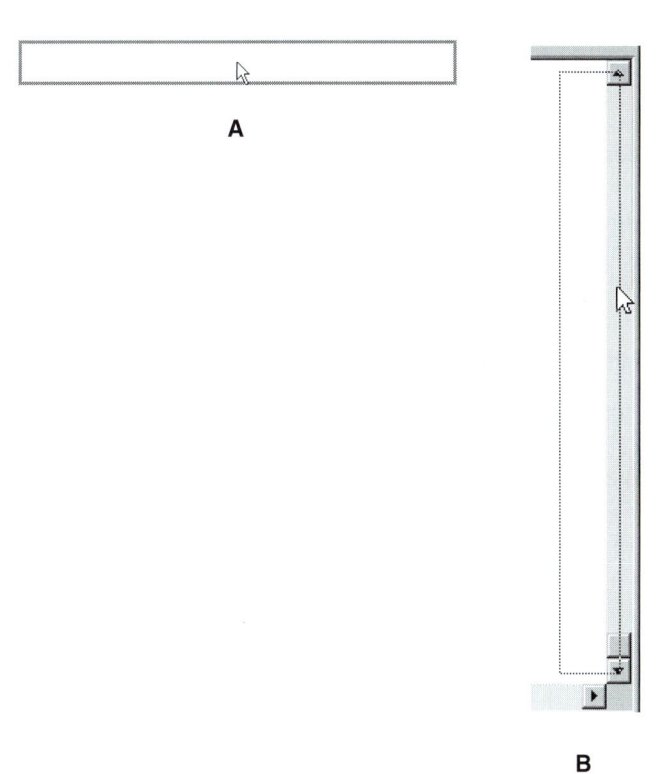

FIGURE 17.7 The Customize Toolbars dialog box.

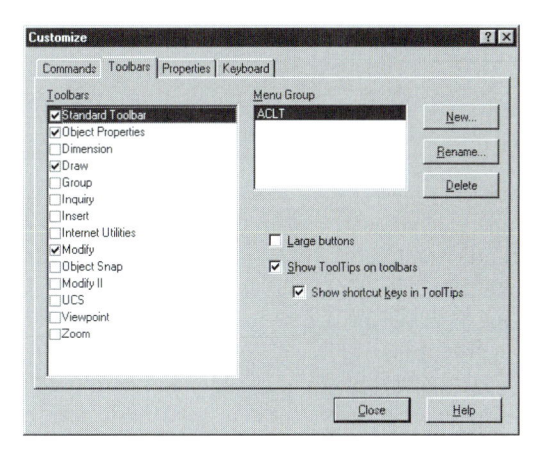

Field Notes

> As you customize the AutoCAD LT tools, it is usually a good idea to maintain the standard tool set unchanged. Place your new and modified tools in new toolbars. This keeps the basic AutoCAD LT interface in the same condition as described in the documentation and reduces relearning requirements for the drafters using the new tool set.

The Customize Dialog Box

AutoCAD LT 98 provides an easy-to-use interface for creating and modifying toolbars and toolbar buttons. Figure 17.7 shows the Customize dialog box with the Toolbars tab in front. This dialog box has four tabs. The Toolbars tab is displayed by default when you pick Toolbars… from the View pull-down menu. As indicated previously, the checkboxes next to the names in the Toolbars list allow you to control toolbar visibility. The Menu Group field selection determines the menu file whose toolbars are displayed in the Toolbars list. Loading multiple menus and using menu groups is covered later in this chapter.

The settings in the lower right area control the appearance and functionality of the toolbar buttons. The default size of toolbar buttons is 16 pixels wide by 15 pixels high. You can increase the size of the toolbar buttons to 24×22 pixels by checking the Large buttons checkbox. You will need to have your screen resolution set higher than 800×600 to use this setting effectively, because some of your toolbars will be too long to fit vertically on the screen. This means that the buttons at the bottom of these toolbars will not be visible when they are docked on the sides of the window.

It is highly recommended that you leave the Show ToolTips on toolbars option active. Even experienced users will benefit from having ToolTips displayed when using unfamiliar toolbars. The Show shortcut keys in ToolTips option helps you become familiar with all the shortcut keys available in AutoCAD LT.

The three buttons on the right side allow you to create new toolbars and rename or delete existing toolbars. These options are detailed in the next section.

Creating a New Toolbar

To create a new toolbar, pick the New… button from the Toolbars tab in the Customize dialog box. The New Toolbar dialog box, shown in Figure 17.8, prompts you for the name and menu group of the new toolbar. The toolbar name can contain spaces and a maximum of 128 characters. It is usually best to use shorter, descriptive names for your new toolbars. If you do not provide a specific name for the toolbar, it is named Toolbar1. A second unnamed toolbar defaults to the name Toolbar2, and so on. Unless you have more than one menu loaded already, the Save toolbar in menu group: list shows only the default ACLT menu group.

FIGURE 17.8 The New Toolbar dialog box.

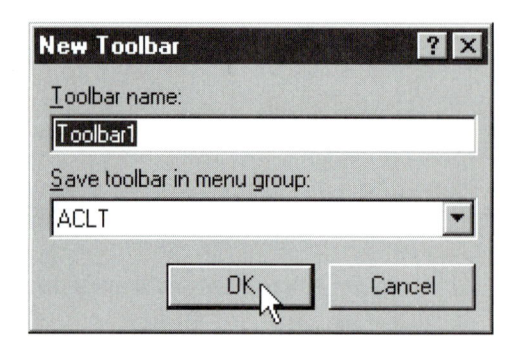

After specifying the new toolbar name and group information, pick OK and the new toolbar will appear on the screen near the top of the AutoCAD LT window. Because the new toolbar is empty, it may not be wide enough to display the assigned name on its title bar. Figure 17.9 shows a new toolbar named Custom Tools as it appears when first created.

FIGURE 17.9 The new toolbar appears without any buttons in it.

> **Field Notes**
>
> Unneeded toolbars can be deleted using the Toolbars dialog box. Highlight the name of the toolbar to delete and pick the Delete button. Before you delete any toolbar, be absolutely certain that you have selected the correct toolbar name and be sure that you actually want to delete it. There is no OOPS command for toolbars, and the UNDO command does not affect any changes made to toolbars, so ***deleted toolbars cannot be automatically restored!***

Adding Buttons to a Toolbar

Existing toolbar buttons can be placed in the new toolbar to form your own specific grouping of existing AutoCAD LT tools, or you can create completely new buttons. To place an existing AutoCAD LT toolbar button on the toolbar, pick the Commands tab in the Customize dialog box. The Commands tab is shown in Figure 17.10.

FIGURE 17.10 The Customize dialog box.

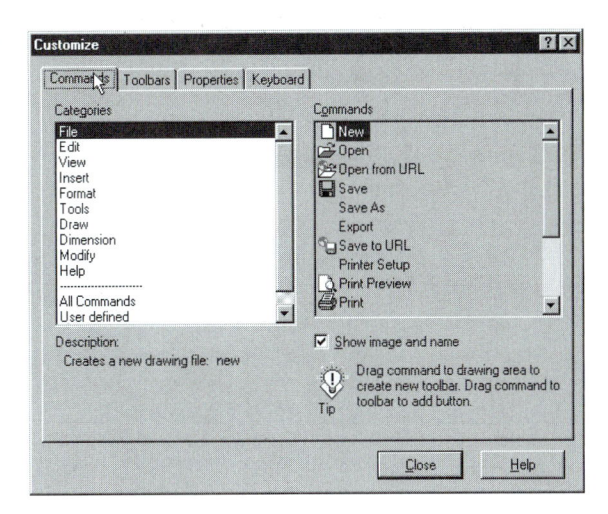

When adding components to the new toolbar, you can select from any existing toolbar buttons or define completely new buttons. Two lists are displayed on this tab, labeled Categories and Commands. The Commands list displays the existing toolbar button definitions based on the current specification in the Categories list. The commands that do not display a button icon do not have a corresponding toolbar button defined.

The command categories are the same as the pull-down menus, which makes it easier to find the button you are looking for. Optionally, you can select All Commands from the category list to display all the AutoCAD LT commands. The User Defined category is discussed later in this chapter. Scrolling the list downward displays the Flyouts category, which contains all the existing flyout button definitions. In all categories, when you highlight a command, a short text description appears below the Categories list.

To select a command to place on the new toolbar, point to it with the cursor; then press and hold the pick button. When the cursor is moved away from the selected tool, an outline appears that is then dragged to the desired toolbar. Drag the toolbar button inside of the toolbar where you want it and then release the pick button. Figure 17.11 shows the toolbar button for the Real-Time Zoom tool being selected, dragged, and then dropped into the new toolbar.

When placing additional buttons into a toolbar, they are added on the side where they are dropped. Once placed, the toolbar buttons can be relocated by picking and dragging them to the desired new location.

When dragging buttons from the Modify Toolbars dialog box to a toolbar, be sure that the dragging image is within the boundary of the toolbar before dropping it. If it is not within the boundary, it automatically creates a new toolbar. The new toolbar is given a generic name using the format "Toolbar1." Each time you create a toolbar using this method, the number is increased by one, so the second one is named "Toolbar2." If you do accidentally create a toolbar, it can be deleted using the Delete button on the Toolbars tab in the Customize dialog box, or you can pick Rename… and change the name.

In addition to placing buttons from the Customize dialog box, you can copy buttons from other toolbars. This works similar to other drag-and-drop type operations in Windows. Select the button from one toolbar, press and hold the pick button, then press and hold the Ctrl key on the keyboard. A small "+" sign appears on the image being dragged to let you know that you are not just moving the button, but that it is being copied. Figure 17.12 shows the appearance of the plus sign on the dragged image.

To remove a button from a toolbar, drag it away from the toolbar it is on and release it in the drawing area. Make sure the dragged button is not over a different toolbar, or it is simply moved to the toolbar whose boundaries it falls within.

Field Notes

One common application for creating new toolbars is to group commonly used commands into one convenient location. You may have several tools that you use very frequently that are located across several different toolbars. Having all of these toolbars visible at the same time can take up too much valuable screen space. The solution is to create a new toolbar and place each of the desired tools within that single toolbar.

FIGURE 17.11 The drag-and-drop method is used to place toolbar buttons in a toolbar. (A) Select the desired tool, (B) press and drag to the new toolbar, and (C) drop it into the new toolbar.

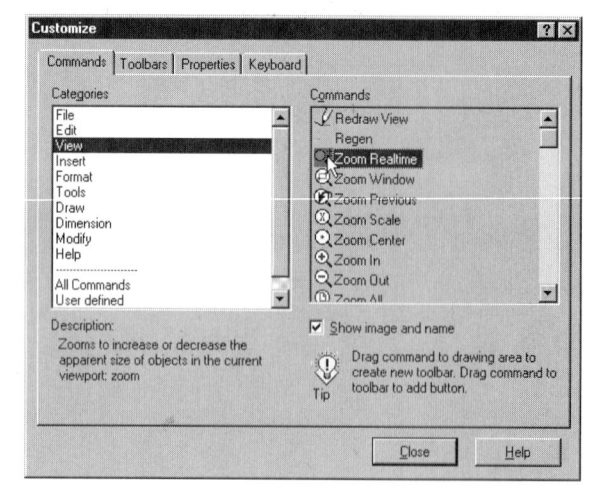

A

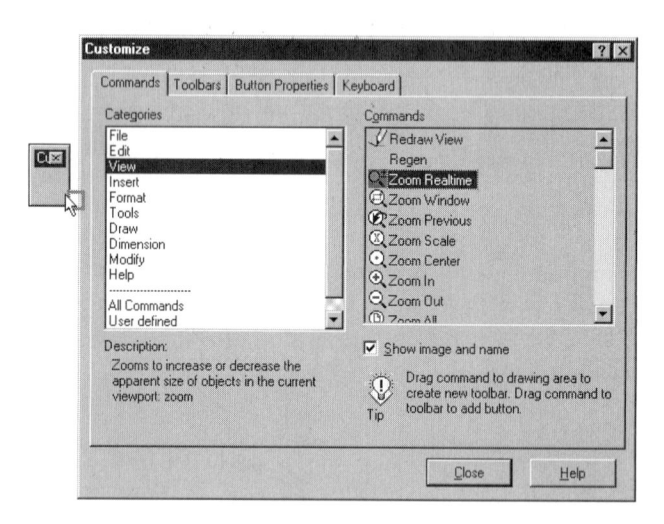

B

C

FIGURE 17.12 To copy a button from one toolbar to another, press the Ctrl key while dragging the image.

CHAPTER 17 ||| Customizing AutoCAD LT

Exercise 17.3

1. Create a new toolbar using the New ... button in the Toolbars tab of the Customize dialog box.
2. In the New Toolbar dialog box, name the new toolbar Custom Tools and pick OK.
3. Display the Commands tab.
4. Think about five toolbar buttons that you use frequently. Place these five buttons on the new toolbar.
5. Remove a button from the toolbar by dragging it off of the toolbar.
6. Drag a button out of the Customize dialog box and drop it on the graphics screen area, outside of any toolbar boundaries.
7. Find the item "Toolbar1" on the Toolbars: listing or the Toolbars tab.
8. Remove the unwanted toolbar by highlighting its name and picking the Delete button. Be sure that the correct name is highlighted before picking the Delete button.

Working with Toolbar Buttons

Toolbar buttons can be created and modified as desired, to do any specific set of tasks available within the AutoCAD LT command structure. Most of the existing tools either start a command or supply one or two options to the command. This is just the tip of the iceberg with regard to the powerful tools you can create using menu macros.

To begin working with toolbar buttons, you need to learn a few special codes that are used within the menu system, but the rest is all plain English. Once you have become familiar with these special codes, menu customization can be very easy to master. One of the best ways to begin learning is by looking at what is already there. Once the Customize dialog box is visible, you can use the Button Properties tab by picking any button. Optionally, you can right-click on the button and pick Properties... from the pop-up cursor menu. Figure 17.13 shows the Button Properties tab with the Line toolbar button properties displayed. The Name: text box shows the name of the toolbar button. This text is displayed in the tooltip when you point at the button with the cursor and the text in the Description: text box is displayed on the status bar. The entry in the Macro associated with this button: area shows the menu code that is activated when you select the button. Finally, the Button Image area shows the graphic image that is displayed on the button.

The content and function of the button name and help are self-explanatory. In the Macro associated with this button: area is the actual functionality of the button. In the case of the Line tool, the function is fairly simple. The entry is as follows:

FIGURE 17.13 The Button Properties for the Line toolbar button.

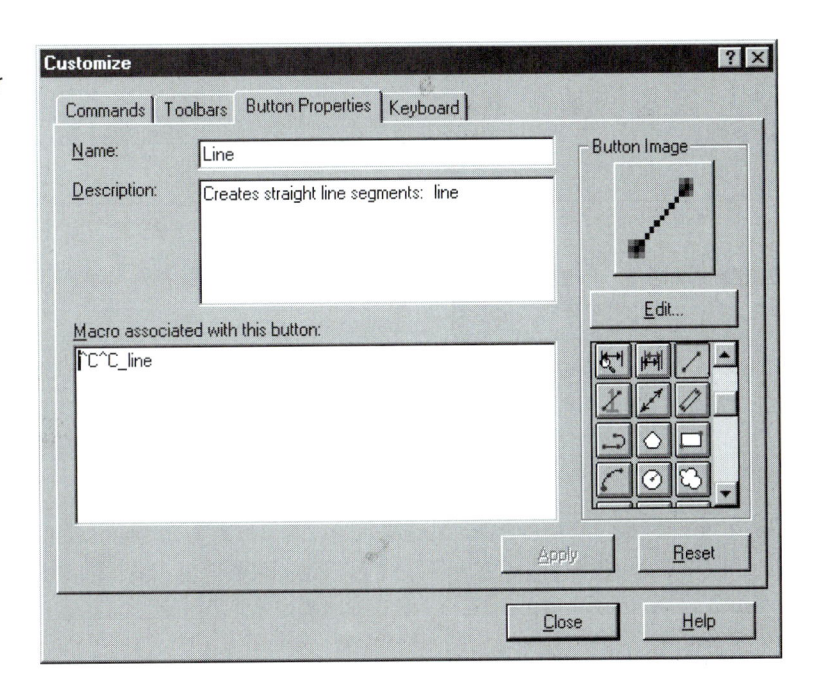

```
^C^C_line
```

The function of the ^C is a cancel, as if you pressed the Esc (Escape) key. If you have configured AutoCAD LT to recognize AutoCAD Classic keystrokes using the Preferences dialog box, then the Ctrl+C keystroke is a cancel also. In the menu file, the ^ character is known as a *caret,* and it indicates the use of the Ctrl key. So, the ^C code is called *Control C,* which is simply a cancel. This is true regardless of any settings in the Preferences dialog box.

Notice that there are two ^C's in sequence in the preceding entry. This ensures that the rest of the code starts at the Command: prompt. If, for example, you are in Dim: mode and start a Horizontal subcommand, the first ^C returns you to the Dim: prompt and the next ^C returns you to the Command: prompt before issuing the LINE command. Unless a menu macro is intended to be transparent, it should always begin with ^C^C.

Next is the actual command. In this case, the command is preceded with an underscore character (_). The underscore character is not necessary unless you are producing menu that may be used on non-English versions of AutoCAD LT. The underscore character causes the commands and options to be translated automatically so they can work on any foreign language version of AutoCAD LT. The actual command text is entered the same as it would be at the Command: prompt. AutoCAD LT automatically adds an Enter to the end of the menu macro in most cases. The exceptions are discussed later. This is the simplest form of menu macro, and represents the type of content for most of the toolbar buttons.

> **Field Notes**
>
> Do not use command aliases in toolbar or menu macros. Always use the full command name.

More complex macros require some additional special codes. The next example is of the Break 1 Point Select button found in the All Commands category in the Commands tab. The Button Properties dialog box for this tool is shown in Figure 17.14.

The menu code entered in the macro listing for the Break 1 Point Select tool is:

```
^C^C_break \_f \@
```

FIGURE 17.14 The Button Properties for the Break 1 Point Select tool.

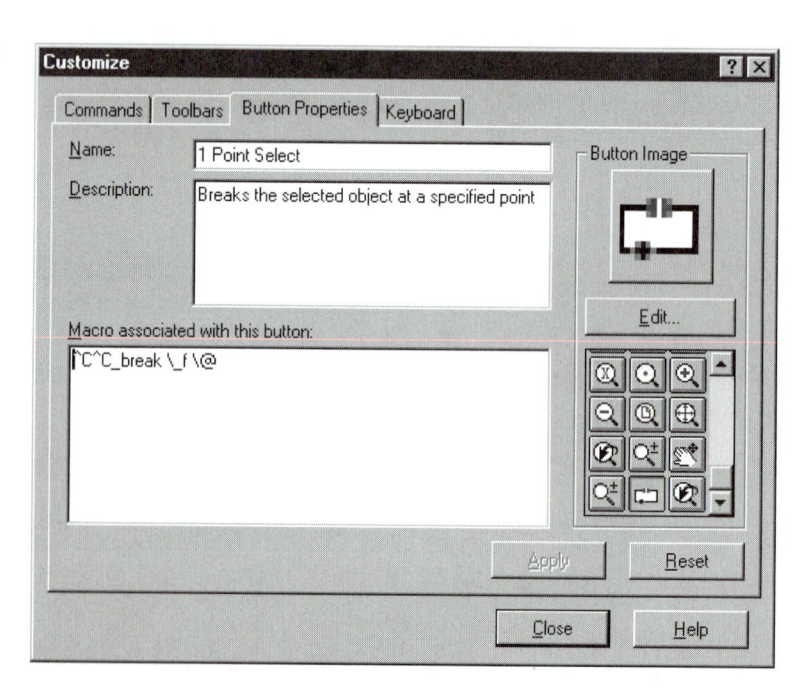

Again, to ensure that the Command: prompt is available, ^C^C is the first entry. The underscore characters are for international versions and do not affect the basic functionality of the macro.

Field Notes

A *transparent* command or macro is one that can be processed without canceling the currently active command. If a macro is to be transparent, do not use the ^C^C characters. Any commands used in the macro should start with an apostrophe. For example, to do a transparent ZOOM Previous, the macro appears as:

'ZOOM;P

A macro can only be transparent if all of its commands are commands that can be used transparently.

Although this macro works normally when an object is properly selected at the prompt, it can have unexpected results if no object is selected. First, let's take a look at how it works and then explore how to make it work better.

As it is written now, the first command in the macro after the double cancel is the BREAK command, followed by a single space. As when entering commands at the Command: prompt, a space is used as an Enter keystroke. Optionally, you may use a semicolon character to indicate an Enter keystroke in a menu macro. It is strongly recommended that you use semicolons instead of spaces, because it is much easier to count semicolons than it is to count spaces. If your macro has an extra space or is missing one, your macro may not function properly. Trying to find the source of the problem can be much easier when you can see and count the Enter keystrokes in your macro.

The next item encountered after issuing the BREAK command is a backslash character. The backslash pauses the macro and allows user input—in this case, a pick point. Once the user picks a point, the BREAK command issues the prompt

Enter second point (or F for first point:):

The macro supplies an F and a space (Enter) to the prompt to use the first point option and then follows with another backslash to allow the user to pick a point for the first break point. The final prompt for this command is

Enter second point:

The macro uses the last point variable by supplying the "@" symbol, indicating that the first and second break points are the same. An automatic Enter is issued at the end of the macro. The result is the object is broken at a single point. Although this macro works when an object is properly picked by the user, it can produce unexpected prompts if you accidentally miss the object on your first pick attempt. Here is an example:

Pick the menu button
Command: _break Select object: *Pick a point not on an object*
No object found
Select object: _f
First fence point: *If you try again to pick the object...*
Undo/<Endpoint of line>: @
Invalid point, polygon segment is zero length.
Undo/<Endpoint of line>: *Press Escape to cancel*

Because the anticipated object was not selected, this macro fails and issues unexpected prompts and error messages. This next example shows a simple, yet effective, means of preventing this problem. The improved version of the macro looks like this:

^C^C_select;_single;_break;@;_f;\@

The first command issued in this macro is the SELECT command, which is used to create a selection set. The character following the SELECT command is a semicolon. As previously discussed, the semicolon is the same as an Enter keystroke. Spaces can also be used as an Enter, but spaces are not as easy to count. The use of semicolons makes it easier to design and troubleshoot menu macros.

The SELECT command issues the Select objects: prompt, and the option entered is SINGLE. The SINGLE selection mode is commonly used in menu macros because it limits the selection set to a single selection. The BREAK command can only break a single object, so this helps to ensure that a single object is selected. This is also followed by an Enter (semicolon).

A backslash character is placed next. In a menu macro, the backslash pauses for user input. In this macro, after SINGLE is entered at the Select objects: prompt, the Select objects: prompt is issued again. Here is where the menu macro pauses for user input, allowing the user to select the object to be broken. However, if no object is picked, the SELECT command reissues the Select objects: prompt. Additionally, if the user presses Enter at the prompt, the macro halts, instead of starting the FILLET command (as does the first version). Because SINGLE selection mode is being used, the SELECT command is complete and the Command: prompt is returned. The rest of this macro works in the same way as the first version.

This macro provides an excellent example of combining automated procedures with user input to accomplish a complex task. Using AutoCAD LT's existing tools as examples helps you to learn valuable techniques like this.

> ### Field Notes
>
> The BREAK command requires a point selection. You can prevent the user from using an implied window or crossing at the selection by setting the PICKAUTO variable to a value of 0. This can be part of the menu macro. The following example temporarily disables PICKAUTO for the selection sequence:
>
> ^C^C_**pickauto**;0;select;_single;_**pickauto**;1;_break;@;_f;\\@

When you begin to create macros for toolbar buttons, it is important to be certain that you address each prompt as it occurs at the command line. If you provide an incorrect response to a prompt, the macro will not work properly. The best way to ensure that each prompt is answered correctly is to walk through the entire procedure one step at a time, writing down the appropriate command or option entries as you go. Then, reference this listing as you develop the macro.

The next step in creating a custom toolbar button is to place a blank button on the toolbar. A blank button can be found in the User Defined category. Two buttons are available in this category; one is a blank button, the other is a *flyout* button and is discussed later. Figure 17.15 shows a blank button placed within the new toolbar.

FIGURE 17.15 Blank buttons can be used to create completely new toolbar buttons.

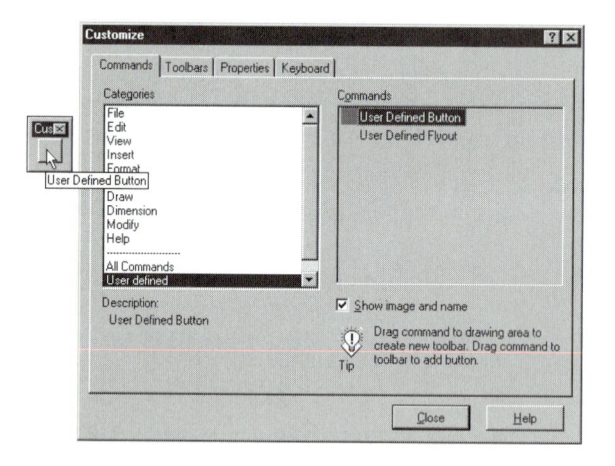

After placing the button, pick it to access the Button Properties. The Button Properties fields reads "User Defined Button," and the macro area displays the familiar ^C^C , as shown in Figure 17.16. This example creates a macro designed to perform basic setup procedures for a mechanical E size sheet. The intent is that after creating a drawing, this macro will move into paper space, set up the snap, grid and display, create a model space viewport, and insert an E size border and title block. As suggested earlier, it is best to walk through the process step by step first in order to determine the required command and option entries. The command sequence is shown here:

CHAPTER 17 ||| Customizing AutoCAD LT

FIGURE 17.16 The default Button Properties for a User Defined Button.

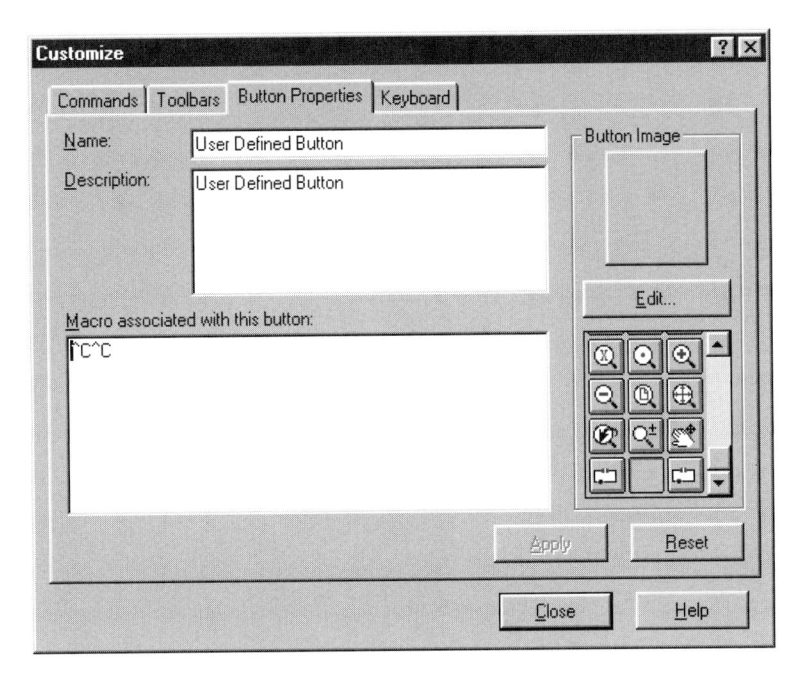

```
Command: TILEMODE↵
New value for TILEMODE <1>: 0↵
Regenerating drawing.
Command: LIMITS↵
Reset Paper space limits:
ON/OFF/<Lower left corner> <0.0000,0.0000>: 0,0↵
Upper right corner <12.0000,9.0000>: 48,36↵
Command: GRID↵
Grid spacing(X) or ON/OFF/Snap/Aspect <0.5000>: 0.5↵
Command: SNAP↵
Snap spacing or ON/OFF/Aspect/Rotate/Style <0.5000>: 0.25↵
Command: ZOOM↵
All/Center/Extents/Previous/Window/<Scale(X/XP)>: ALL↵
Regenerating drawing.
Command: MVIEW↵
ON/OFF/Hideplot/Fit/2/3/4/Restore/<First Point>: 0,0↵
Other corner: 48,36↵
Regenerating drawing.
Command: INSERT↵
Block name (or ?): TITLE-E↵
Insertion point: 0,0↵
X scale factor <1> / Corner / XYZ: 1↵
Y scale factor (default=X): 1↵
Rotation angle <0>: 0↵
```

Using the AutoCAD LT text screen is an easy way to reference the step-at-a-time procedure. Now, with this information, a macro can be constructed by simply entering the command sequence in as a macro and substituting semicolons where Enter was pressed:

```
^C^Ctilemode;0;limits;0,0;48,36;grid;0.5;snap;0.25;zoom;all;mview;0,0;48,36;
insert;title-e;0,0;1;1;0
```

Other elements to define include the name and help text for the button. Figure 17.17 shows the Button Properties dialog box with all of the entries completed.

FIGURE 17.17 The custom E-Size Setup toolbar button properties.

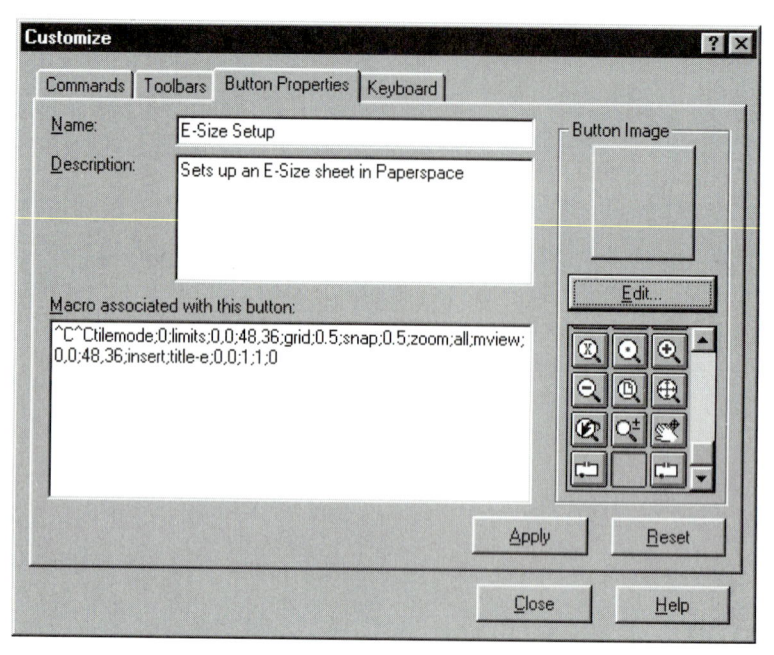

Field Notes

At the end of a macro, AutoCAD LT issues an automatic Enter. If, however, the last character of the macro is a semicolon, this is not true. Therefore, if you want more than one Enter at the end of the macro, it is necessary to place one semicolon for each Enter needed. For example, when using an option of the LAYER command, an Enter is required for the option, and another is used to return to the Command: prompt:

^C^CLAYER;MAKE;DIM;;

where the DIM; returns you to the Layer option line, and the next Enter returns the Command: prompt.

The final property to define is the icon, or graphic image, for the button. The Button Image area of the Button Properties tab offers three options for defining the appearance of a button. First, the scrolling image list displays all of the currently defined buttons. Although you are free to select any existing button, this can cause confusion if the icon looks the same as a familiar icon that starts a different command or macro. The next option is to select an existing button and then pick the Edit ... button to alter its appearance. Or, you can select a blank button image and pick the Edit ... button to define the button image from scratch. In this case, a blank button image is selected and the Edit ... button is picked. This displays the Button Editor dialog box, shown with its features labeled in Figure 17.18.

The drawing area of the editor is in the center of the dialog box and is composed of a grid of squares, or pixels. If the AutoCAD LT buttons are currently displayed at the small size, this grid is 16×15 pixels. If the Large buttons toggle has been set in the Toolbars tab, the image is displayed at 24×22 pixels. To see this grid visibly displayed, select the Grid toggle in the Button Editor dialog box.

The four basic drawing tools are in a row across the top of the dialog box. The current color used by these tools is set by picking the desired color swatch from the Colors column on the right side of the Button Editor dialog box. The available drawing tools include Pencil, Line, Circle, and Erase and are used as follows:

Pencil: The Pencil tool colors one pixel at a time in the current color by pressing the pick button on your pointing device. Holding the pick button down while you move the Pencil colors each grid that is touched.

Line: The Line tool draws straight lines in the current color. To draw a line, move the cursor to the location where the line is to start, then press and hold the pick button while moving the cursor to the other end of the desired line. Similar to drawing lines in AutoCAD LT, a rubberband line is displayed to show where the line is to be drawn. Releasing the pick button causes the line to be drawn.

FIGURE 17.18 The Button Editor dialog box can be used to create or modify button icon images.

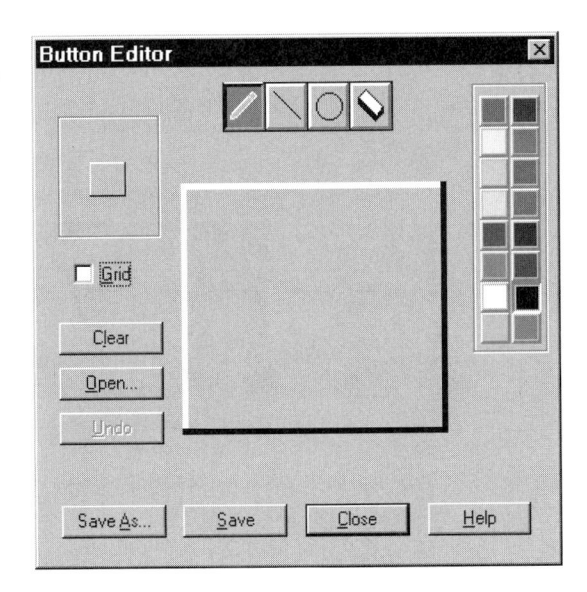

Circle: Although the AutoCAD LT documentation refers to this as a Circle tool, it would be more accurate to call it an Ellipse tool. The first point picked is the center of the circle or ellipse. Then the final shape of the object is determined by the second pick. Both circles and ellipses can be created, but it may take some practice to create truly round circles.

Erase: The Erase tool returns pixels back to the background color. The functionality is much like the Pencil tool; individual pixels can be erased or you can hold the pick button and move the eraser to affect each pixel it touches.

A preview of the image being created is displayed actual size in the upper left corner of the Button Editor dialog box. This changes size depending on the currently configured size of the toolbar buttons in AutoCAD LT. The other options available in the Button Editor dialog box are as follows:

Clear: This is used to completely clear the image from the drawing area. This is your basic "start over" button.

Open: The Open button allows you to open an existing bitmap file. You can only open files that are the appropriate size, either 16×15 or 24×22 pixels. The Paintbrush program and other software that produces bitmaps can be used to create button images, but the image size must be correct.

Undo: This works like the U command in AutoCAD LT, but you can only undo one operation. You can even undo a Clear.

Save As . . .: This allows you to save the created image as bitmap files.

Save: This button saves the current image using the current file name if it has been named. If the image has not been saved to a file, then it is saved in the menu resource file, which is discussed later.

Close: The Close option closes the Button Editor. If you have unsaved changes, a prompt is issued to allow you to save changes before exiting.

Help: This offers help for the dialog box.

Figure 17.19A shows an image created in the Button Editor for the E-Size Setup tool. After picking the Save and then the Close buttons, the Button Properties dialog box now displays the newly created icon, as shown in Figure 17.19B.

The Apply button must be selected before any of the changes are actually applied to the button being edited. If you dismiss this dialog box without picking Apply, all of your changes are lost and cannot be recovered. Any time that the Apply button is enabled, it means that you currently have unsaved changes. After picking the Apply button, it is again disabled until further changes need to be saved. Once the changes have been applied, the new image appears on the toolbar button and the macro is associated with it.

To complete the process, close the Customize dialog box. A message then appears on the status line telling you that AutoCAD LT is compiling menu files, and lists various file names. The term *compiling* refers to a process in which the menu files are rewritten, with the latest changes, in a way that provides the fastest access to the information by AutoCAD LT. Once the menu is compiled and the Command: prompt reappears, the new toolbar button is ready to use.

FIGURE 17.19 (A) After an image has been designed for the toolbar button, (B) it appears in the Button Properties dialog box where it can be applied to the button.

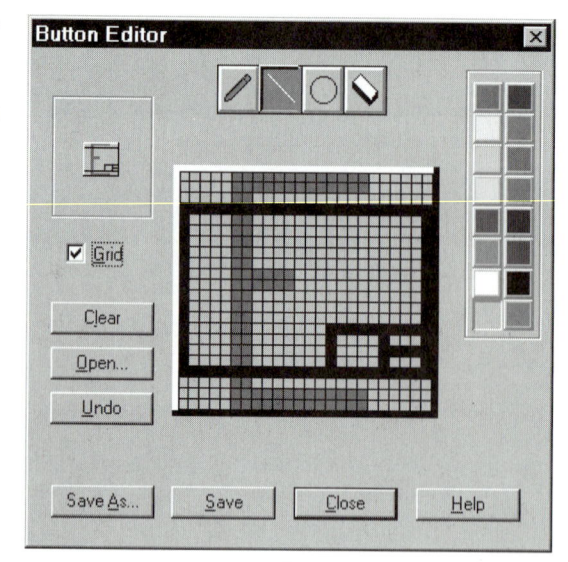

A

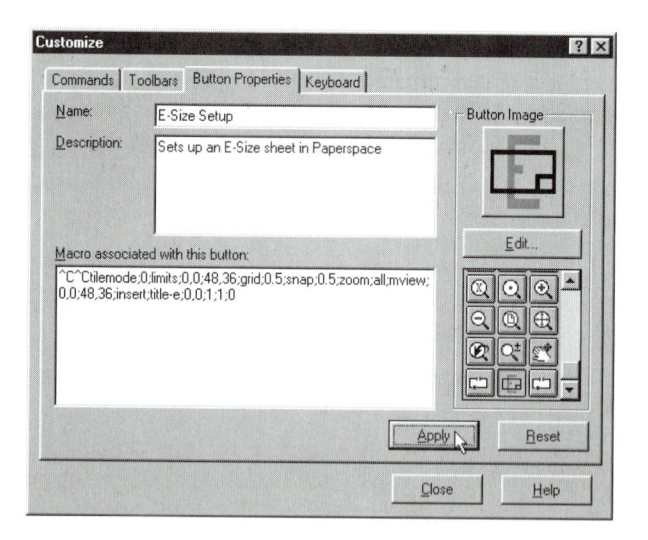

B

Field Notes

When a macro is finished processing, control reverts back to the command line. This means that you can use a macro to start a command, or even supply some of the options, and then return control to the user. When inserting a block with attributes using a macro, the attribute prompts can be answered in the macro or control can be returned to the user after the block is placed. In the E-Size Setup macro, the macro ends after placing the block so any attribute prompts are issued to the user normally.

Exercise 17.4

1. Place a blank button from the Custom category on the Custom Tools toolbar.
2. Create a custom macro, similar to E-Size Setup, that does a setup routine for an A size sheet. Assign an appropriate name and help text.
3. Create an image in the Button Editor that somehow communicates the intent of the button.
4. Apply the changes to the button and test it to be certain it works properly.

CHAPTER 17 ||| Customizing AutoCAD LT   691

☑ LEARNING CHECKPOINT

- ☐ What should all macros start with if they are not intended to be transparent?
- ☐ What character pauses a macro for user input?
- ☐ Which two characters can be used for an Enter keystroke? Which is best?
- ☐ How is a new toolbar created?
- ☐ Describe how a new toolbar button is created.
- ☐ How is the Button Editor used?
- ☐ What is the requirement for using bitmap files not created with the Button Editor?
- ☐ Why must two images be created for each new button?
- ☐ How are toolbar buttons moved and copied?
- ☐ What happens if you forget to pick the Apply button after making changes?

Creating Toolbar Flyouts

Toolbar flyouts allow you to hide an entire toolbar behind a single toolbar button. As an example, when you open the Insert flyout from the Draw toolbar, what you are actually seeing is the Insert toolbar. To see the contents of a toolbar associated with a flyout, pick the flyout button when the Customize dislog box is visible. This displays the Flyout Properties tab. To see the actual toolbar, place a check next to the toolbar name in the list on the Toolbars tab. The insert toolbar is shown with the insert flyout on the Draw toolbar in Figure 17.20.

The advantage of flyouts is that you can conserve valuable screen space while keeping the maximum number of tools immediately available. This is why there are several flyouts within the built-in AutoCAD LT tool set.

To create a flyout, you must first have a toolbar created that the flyout is to display. Figure 17.21A shows a toolbar with the E-Size Setup and buttons for A, B, C, and D sizes as well. To assign a toolbar to a flyout button, you must know the name of the toolbar. This toolbar has been named Setups, and the name is highlighted in the Toolbars listing on the Toolbars tab in Figure 17.21B.

FIGURE 17.20 The Insert toolbar.

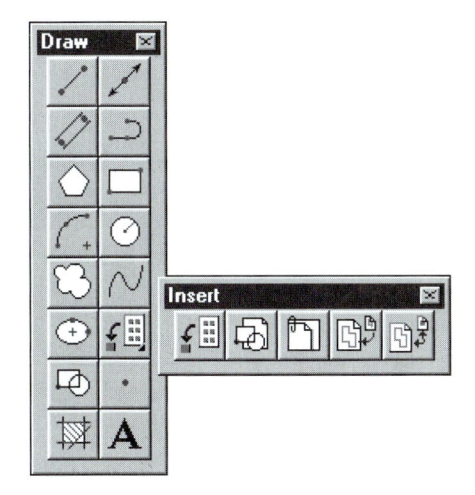

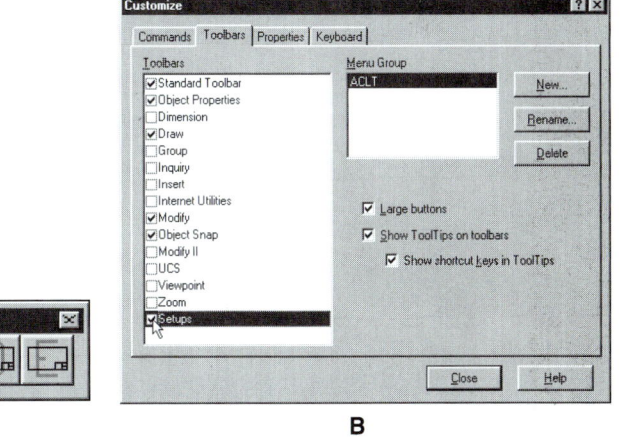

FIGURE 17.21 (A) To create a flyout, you must have a toolbar available to assign to the flyout. (B) Toolbar names are displayed in the Customize dialog box.

The next step is to have a toolbar in which to place the flyout button. Do not place a flyout button *in* the toolbar that it displays, this creates what is called a ***recursive toolbar.*** Once you have a toolbar to place the flyout in and a toolbar for the flyout to display, you are ready to create the flyout button.

From the User defined category in the Commands tab, drag a blank flyout button to its destination toolbar. Next, pick the new flyout button. A warning dialog box is displayed indicating that the associated toolbar cannot be found. Pick the OK button to continue. The Flyout Properties tab is shown in Figure 17.22.

FIGURE 17.22 The Flyout Properties dialog box.

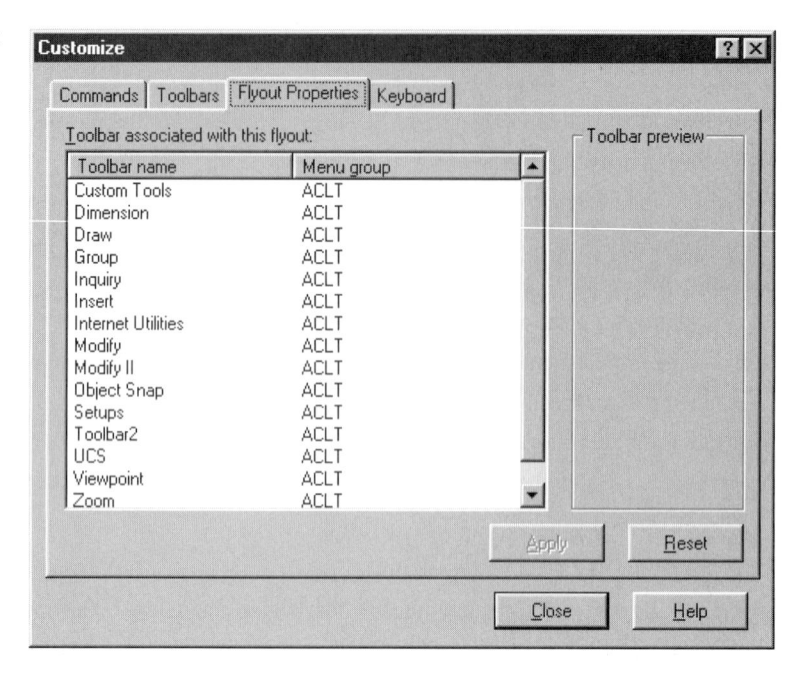

To associate the desired toolbar with the flyout button, the toolbar's name must be highlighted in the Toolbar associated with this flyout list box, as shown in Figure 17.23. To complete this operation, pick the Apply button and close the Customize dialog boxes.

When the changes are applied to the flyout button, it then displays the first button from the toolbar it is associated with. When you press and hold the pick button while pointing at the flyout button, it expands to show the entire toolbar. If one of the tools is picked, that button's icon is then displayed by the flyout. Figure 17.24 shows the Setups toolbar as an expanded flyout.

FIGURE 17.23 The completed Flyout Properties dialog box for the Setups flyout.

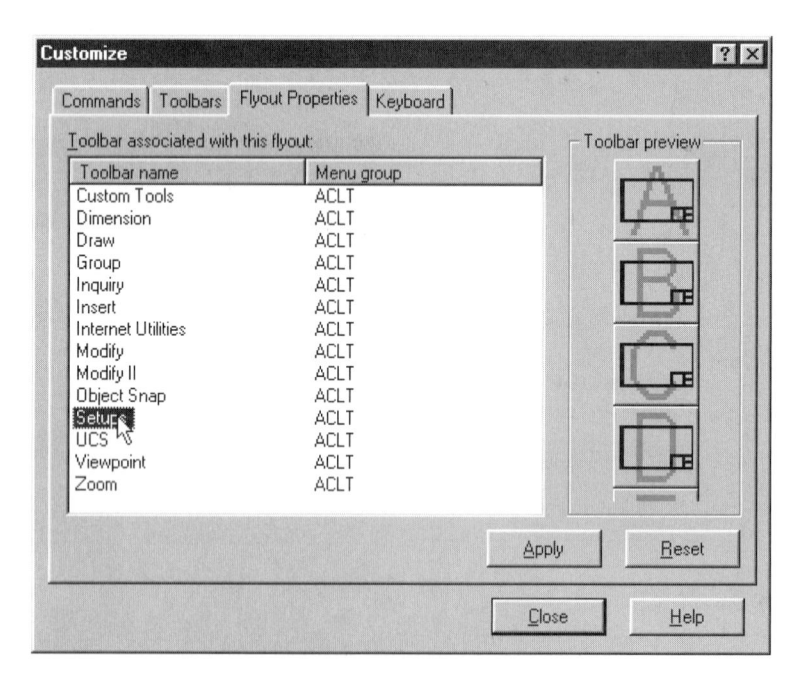

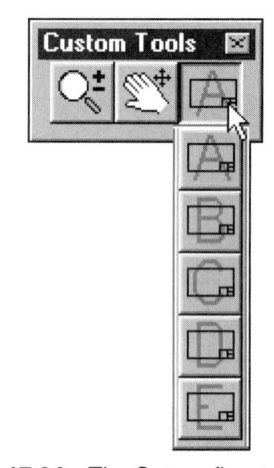

FIGURE 17.24 The Setups flyout.

CHAPTER 17 ||| Customizing AutoCAD LT 693

> **Exercise 17.5**
>
> 1. Create a new toolbar named Setups.
> 2. Using the E-Size Setup button as a template, create setup macros for A, B, C, and D size sheets also, and place them on the Setups toolbar.
> 3. Create a new toolbar named Custom Tools.
> 4. Place a flyout button on the Custom Tools toolbar.
> 5. Set the properties of the flyout button so it displays the Setups toolbar.

✓ LEARNING CHECKPOINT

- ☐ What is a flyout?
- ☐ How are toolbars associated with flyout buttons?
- ☐ What image is displayed on the flyout button?
- ☐ How do flyout buttons work when displaying their own icons?
- ☐ What happens if you forget to pick the Apply button after making changes?

Customizing the AutoCAD LT Menu System

The AutoCAD LT menu system is a combination of several different interfaces. You have already worked with toolbars and toolbar buttons, which are also part of the menu system. Other features of the menu system include digitizer button menus, pull-down and cursor menus, image tile menus, keyboard accelerators, help strings, and the tablet menu.

Menus are defined using ASCII text files that associate a particular menu action with a command or macro, in the same way that commands and macros are associated with toolbar buttons. Several different files are used by the AutoCAD LT menu system, with each one serving a special function. The default menu files included with AutoCAD LT are named ACLT, with various file extensions depending on what the file does. Each of the menu file types and their purpose is listed in the following list by file extension:

.MNU: The .MNU file is called a *template* file. It is referred to as a template because it is what the actual menu source file is based on. The ACLT.MNU file contains menu code and comments that can be referenced when you are learning to work with the menu system. The .MNU file is typically only edited when it is desirable to make your changes a permanent part of the menu system.

.MNS: This is the menu *source* file. The .MNS file is the primary file that you edit when making changes to the AutoCAD LT menu system. Any changes you make to the toolbar menus are stored in this file.

.MNC: The .MNC file is the *compiled* version of the source file. This file cannot be read and edited directly, but it is a much faster file for AutoCAD LT to work with than the ASCII version (.MNS).

.MNR: This file is the menu *resource* file. All bitmap images for toolbars and image tile menus are stored in this file for easy access and fast retrieval. This helps to avoid unnecessary delays when displaying graphic menus.

To edit the menu source file, you must use a text editor that can edit larger files. When trying to open the .MNS file with Notepad, you may get the message that the file is too large to open with Notepad. The prompt asks if you would like to open the file with WordPad instead. It is OK to open the file and edit it using WordPad, but you need to be certain that if you save the file, you save it as a text-only file. Similar to script files, discussed earlier, a menu source file must be saved in ASCII format. If you use any word processor to edit your menu, be sure that you save it as a text-only file.

It is not recommended that you directly edit the ACLT menu files. It is not necessary to edit these files when adding new features to the menu system; edit them only if you wish to change something about the built-in menus. If you do edit the ACLT menu files, be sure that you create a backup copy of the menu to refer back to if you have problems. You can do this using Windows Explorer.

Menus in the Workplace

When modifying a menu system in a professional environment, certain considerations must be made. With any new interface, the users will need time to learn to use it effectively. This process is often referred to as a *learning curve*. In the workplace, time is money, so it is important to keep the learning curve as short as possible. One of the best methods for assisting users in this process is to maintain a base menu that is common to each workstation. It is also easier for new employees to integrate into a department when the AutoCAD LT default menu is used as the base menu system.

Frequently, the menu system is modified only by adding to it rather than by removing or relocating existing features. The best approach for making these additions is to start a completely new menu file where your additions will be stored. You can then load the new menu file in addition to the existing base menu and even specify which elements of any currently loaded menus are visible. Loading and unloading of menu files is covered later in this chapter.

Another aspect of menus in the workplace is usability. All the new elements should be easy to recognize and to use. Graphic images, labels, and helpstrings should be clear and concise. Always keep in mind that users of varied experience levels may use your custom menus. If your menu is designed to meet the needs of less experienced users, then it will be usable by all.

Menu Sections

When you open the .MNS file, you see that it is divided into several sections. Figure 17.25 shows the ACLT.MNS file opened using WordPad. Each section can be identified easily because the section names have three asterisks in front of them. For example, the first group in the menu file is listed as:

***MENUGROUP=ACLT

FIGURE 17.25 The ACLT.MNS file can be edited using WordPad.

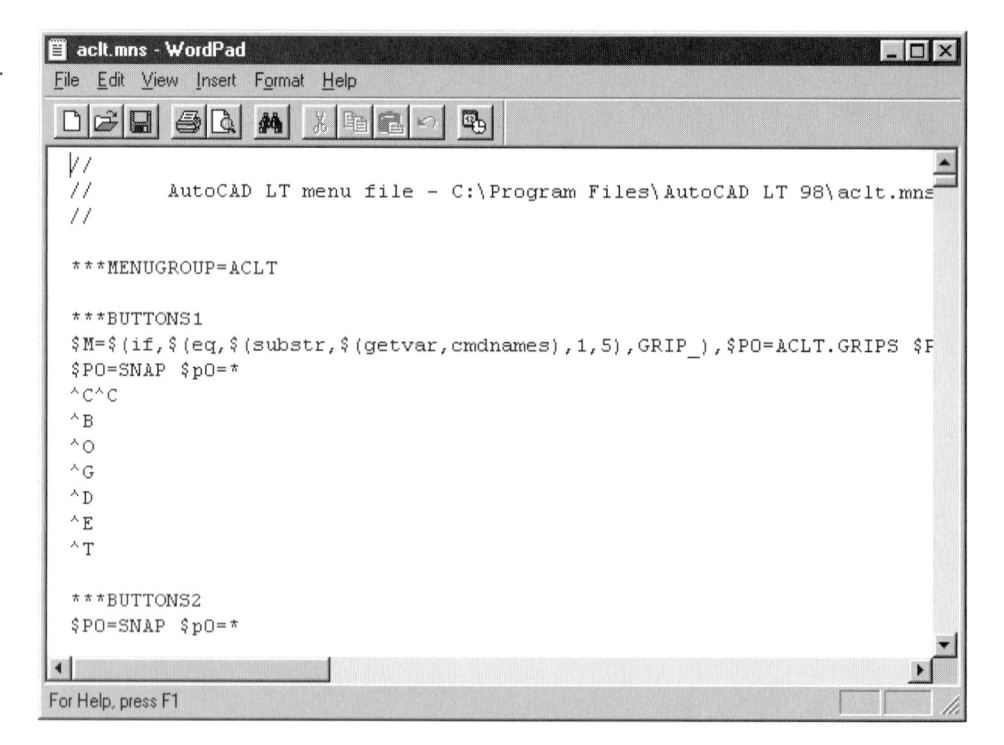

Group names are used when loading partial menu files, which is discussed later in this section. The MENUGROUP section supplies the group name, but does nothing else. Prior to this first group listing are three lines that start with the characters //. The double-slash indicates that the line is a comment line and is ignored by AutoCAD LT.

The next section in the menu file is listed as:

***BUTTONS

The BUTTONS section describes the function of each button on your pointing device, with the exception of the pick button. Although you can use this section to redefine your second and third mouse buttons, it is actually intended for multibutton pointing devices such as digitizers. Many digitizers have anywhere from 4 to 16 buttons. Editing this section allows you to assign special functions to each of these buttons.

Using the text search feature in your editor, searching for three asterisks is an easy way to locate menu sections within the menu file. The following listing provides a brief description of each of the sections found in the menu:

***BUTTONS1 and ***BUTTONS2**: These sections are used if your computer does not use a system pointing device, such as the system mouse in Windows. The term *system mouse* can refer to either a mouse or a digitizer and indicates that the pointing device is used not only by AutoCAD LT but also by the operating system. Although there are only two buttons sections in the default menu, you can have up to four buttons menu sections. The purpose of each section is detailed later.

***AUX1 and ***AUX2**: These menus are equivalent to the buttons sections when you are using a system mouse. Windows uses a system mouse by default, but can be configured to use another pointing device. There can also be up to four AUX sections.

***POP0**: This defines the cursor menu, which is accessed by using the middle button on a three-button mouse, or by pressing the Shift key and right-clicking. The default cursor menu displays the object snap override menu.

POP1–POP10**: These are the standard pull-down menus. AutoCAD LT can support POP menus up to POP16 within a single menu file. Additional POP menus are used by the system.

***TOOLBARS**: Toolbars can be edited manually from the menu file, but it is much easier to edit them as explained previously in this chapter.

***IMAGE:** This section defines your image tile menus.

***ACCELERATORS**: If Keystrokes Accelerators is set to Customizable in the Preferences dialog box, you are able to use keystrokes like Ctrl+C for COPYCLIP and Ctrl+V for PASTECLIP. These are referred to as accelerator keystrokes and are defined in this section.

***HELPSTRINGS**: Help strings, also referred to as help text, for toolbars are defined in the Help: text box within the Button Properties dialog box. For pull-down menus, the help strings are defined here.

TABLET1–TABLET4**: These sections define a menu system for use with a digitizer tablet. The default configuration allows for four menu areas and a screen pointing area.

Exercise 17.6

1. Open the ACLT.MNS file using WordPad.
2. Using the Find option, locate each of the menu sections.
3. Using the Save As … option, save the menu file with the name CHAP17.MNS.
4. Close the text editor.

MENUGROUP Names and Partial Menus

AutoCAD LT supports the use of multiple menus, allowing you to combine menu elements from different menu source files. Whether you load all elements of an additional menu file or just some elements, it is referred to as a *partial* menu. Each partial menu file to be loaded must have a unique menu group name. As shown previously, the menu group name for a menu file is specified in the main menu section labeled ***MENUGROUP. A menu group name cannot have spaces or punctuation marks and can be up to 32 characters in length. The menu group name for the default AutoCAD LT menu is ACLT.

There are different ways to start a menu project. In many cases, the best way is to create a new menu file and assign it a menu group name. You can do this by opening any text editor application and creating a new file. As the first line of text in the file, enter the following:

***MENUGROUP=MYMENU

Be certain to press the Enter key after entering this line, otherwise AutoCAD LT may not be able to read the file correctly. This menu group uses the name MYMENU, but you can specify any desired named as long as it complies with the naming conventions indicated earlier.

Save the file in a *text only* format and name it as desired, but you must specify a file extension of **.MNS**. This menu file is now ready to load and use in AutoCAD LT. Once loaded, any new toolbar additions can be added to this menu file by selecting the menu group name in the New Toolbar dialog box (refer to Figure 17.8).

If you choose to, you can begin editing a copy of the existing menu file rather than creating a brand new file. This enables you to work within the existing menu structure, which can be very helpful for learning how the menu works. For working through the pull-down menu discussion later in this chapter, it is recommended that you use this method. To update the menu group information within the new menu file, you will need to do two things. First, change the entry in the MENUGROUP field to a new menu group name. This example uses the menu group name **CHAP17**. The second step is to replace all references to the menu group name in the menu from ACLT to match the CHAP17 specification in the MENUGROUP field. Menu calls are discussed later in this chapter, but for now you should know that menu calls within the menu file specify a menu group name, period, and then the actual menu name. So all menu calls in this file will currently read ACLT.*menuname*. To update this file, you need to change the "ACLT." into "CHAP17." in each occurrence within the menu. The easiest way to do this is to use your editor's Find & Replace tool to find the text **ACLT.** and replace it with **CHAP17.** Selecting a Replace All option makes all the replacements in a single operation. Be certain to include the period for both the find and replace values.

Exercise 17.7

1. Use Wordpad to open the file CHAP17.mns you created in Exercise 17.6 for editing.
2. Use the Find & Replace tool to update all menu group references in the menu file by placing "ACLT." in the *Find what:* field, and "CHAP17." in the *Replace with:* field. Use the Replace All option to make all the replacements in a single operation.
3. Save the menu file and close the text editor.

Loading the Menu

Once a menu file has been created or modified, it must be loaded into AutoCAD LT before it can be used. The command used to load menus is MENULOAD. The MENULOAD command can be accessed by picking Menus… from Customize cascade on the Tools pull-down menu, or by typing MENULOAD at the Command: prompt. The MENULOAD command displays the Menu Customization dialog box, as shown in Figure 17.26.

To load a menu file, either type the full directory path and file name in the File Name: text box, or select the Browse… button to use a file dialog box. It is usually easier to use the file dialog box, which is displayed in Figure 17.27.

FIGURE 17.26 The Menu Customization dialog box is used to load menu files.

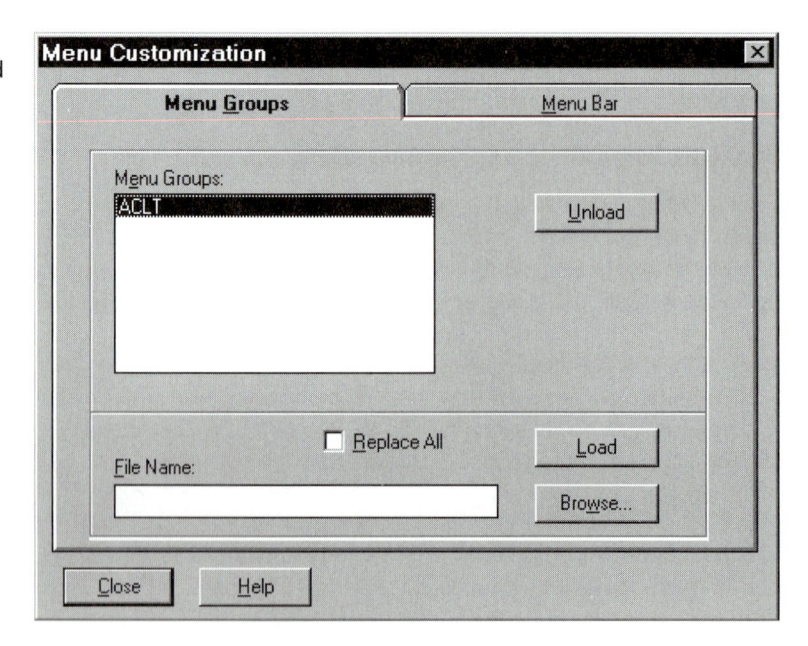

CHAPTER 17 ||| Customizing AutoCAD LT   697

FIGURE 17.27 The Select Menu File dialog box provides an easy way to specify the name and location of a menu file to load.

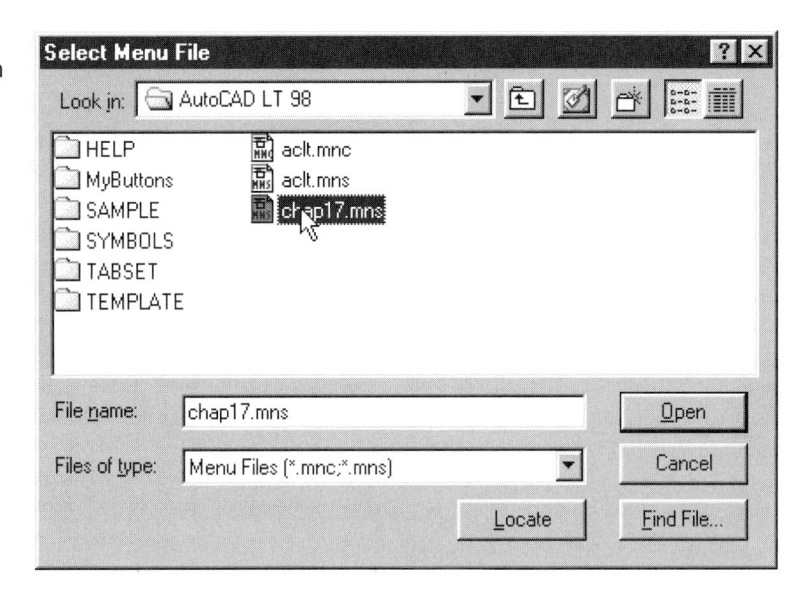

Notice that the Files of type: list defaults to *Menu Files (*.mns, *.mnc)*. This is the correct setting, and should not be changed unless you intend to load a template file (.MNU). Be aware that loading a menu template file automatically overwrites any changes you have made to the toolbars, because toolbar changes and additions are stored in the .MNS file. Loading an .MNU file creates a new .MNS file, thereby discarding all of your toolbar modifications. If you do try to load a menu template file, a strong warning is issued to ensure that you really want to go through with it before the file is actually loaded. The warning dialog box is shown in Figure 17.28.

FIGURE 17.28 Loading a menu template file overwrites any changes you have made to the toolbar menu system. If loaded by accident, it can destroy many hours of toolbar modification work in just a few short seconds.

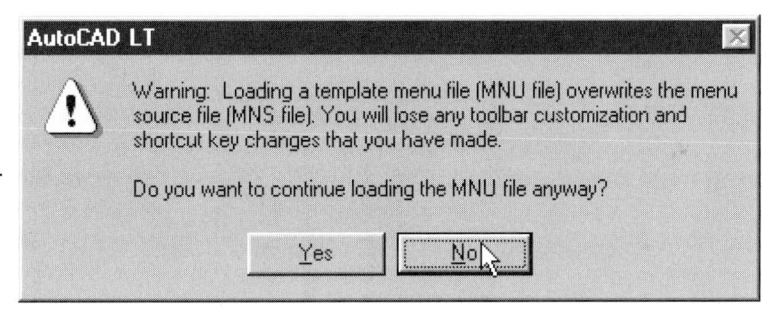

Once you find and select the .MNS file to be loaded, you are returned to the Menu Customization dialog box. AutoCAD LT cannot load multiple menus that use the same MENUGROUP name. If you attempt to reload the ACLT.MNS file, an error message is displayed, as shown here:

Unable to load menu: C:\Program Files\AutoCAD LT 98\aclt.mns
A menu with that MENUGROUP name already exists.

To reload an existing menu regardless of the MENUGROUP name, check the Replace All toggle. This causes the menu currently loaded in memory to be redefined based on the newly loaded menu.

When loading a menu with a different MENUGROUP name, the toolbars and pull-down menus from both menus are then available. This allows you to continue using your standard menu while being able to use tools from other menu files also. Figure 17.29 shows the Menu Customization dialog box with both the ACLT menu and the CHAP17 menu loaded.

When more than one MENUGROUP name is currently loaded, you can specify which features you want available from each menu system. To set up the toolbars, select Toolbars … from the View pull-down menu. Specify the MENUGROUP name for which you want to adjust the toolbars by selecting it from the Menu Group list as shown in Figure 17.30.

To adjust the pull-down menus, use the Menu Customization dialog box. The Menu Bar page of this dialog box, shown in Figure 17.31, allows you to insert, remove, and relocate pull-down menus from the currently loaded MENUGROUP names.

FIGURE 17.29 More than one menu can be loaded at a time using MENULOAD.

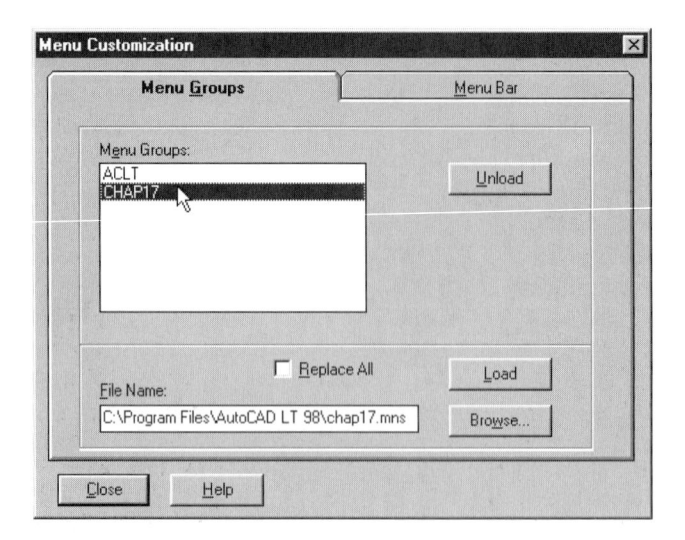

FIGURE 17.30 All the currently available MENUGROUP names are listed in the Toolbars tab. You can select the toolbars from each menu that you want to be visible.

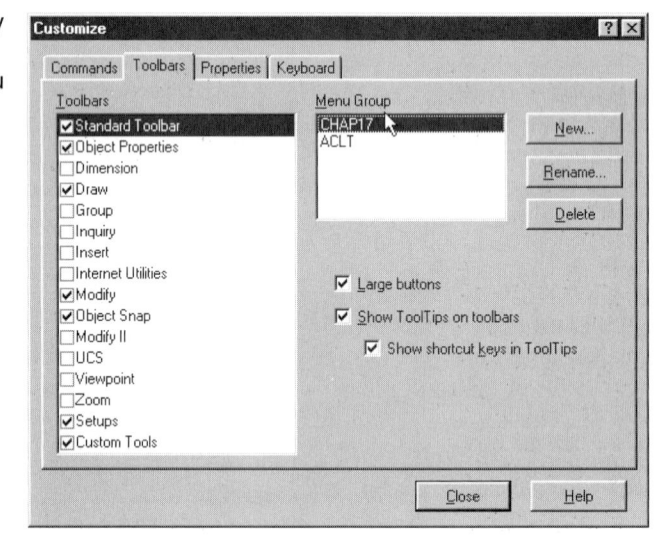

FIGURE 17.31 Pull-down menus from more than one menu can be made available on your menu bar.

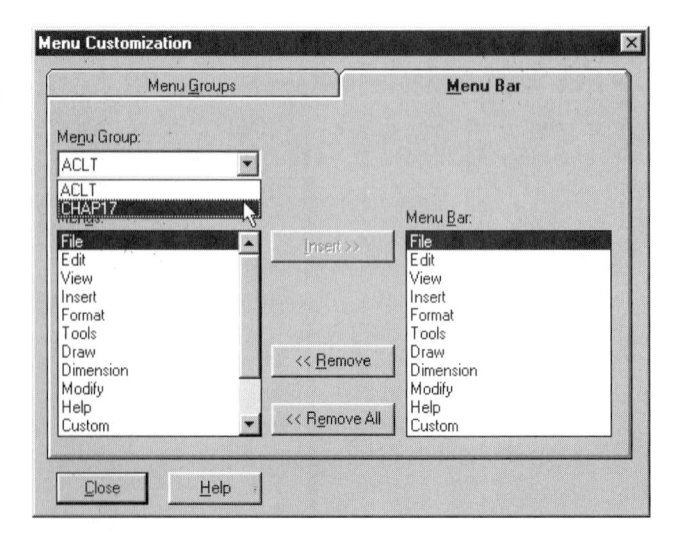

To insert a new pull-down menu, first select the appropriate MENUGROUP name from the Menu Group: drop-down list. Next, highlight the name of the menu to insert in the Menus: list box. Finally, select the name of the menu that you want it inserted to the left of, from the Menu Bar: list box, and pick the Insert>> button. Repeat this procedure for each menu that you need to insert.

Removing a menu from the menu bar is even easier. Pick the appropriate name from the Menu Bar: list and pick the <<Remove button. Removing a menu does not delete it from the menu file; it simply removes it from the menu bar. Picking the <<Remove All button clears the menu bar of all menus.

When a menu is no longer needed, it should be unloaded. This reduces the amount of memory required by AutoCAD LT and speeds up your menu system. To unload a menu, go to the Menu Groups page of the Menu Customization dialog box. In the Menu Groups: list, highlight the MENUGROUP name that you wish to remove and pick the Unload button.

Field Notes

- The buttons menus, accelerators, and tablet menus are not changed when loading additional menus, unless the Replace All toggle is checked.
- The MENUUNLOAD command also displays the Customize Menus dialog box.
- The UNDO and U commands have no effect on menu changes made using MENULOAD or MENUUNLOAD.

Exercise 17.8

1. Use MENULOAD to load the CHAP17.MNS file. Do not check Replace All.
2. Use the Menu Bar page to insert pull-down menus from the CHAP17 menu group and remove one or two existing pull-down menus.
3. In the Toolbars dialog box, adjust the visibility of various toolbars from each menu group.
4. Use MENULOAD to load CHAP17.MNS. This time, check the Replace All toggle and see how the results differ from previously.
5. Use the Unload option to remove CHAP17.MNS and reload ACLT.MNS.

Working with Buttons Menus

The default buttons menu section provides preset functions for 9 buttons. Therefore, if you have a 10-button pointing device, the pick button remains unchanged, and the second through tenth buttons are given the appropriate function assignments as listed, and in the order provided, in the menu. You can freely edit these to change the default assignments, and you can add additional functions if you have a 12- or 16-button pointing device.

To show how the buttons menu system works, this example references the AUX1 menu as used by the Windows system mouse. Because the first button on the mouse is the pick button, the first listing in the menu section is applied to the second button. This means the rightmost button, unless you are using a left-handed mouse. The buttons are reversed on a left-handed mouse. In the AutoCAD LT environment, the right-click is an Enter. Looking at the AUX1 menu section, you see a complex-looking macro that controls the function performed when you right-click through the use of something called DIESEL code. An introduction to DIESEL code is provided later in this chapter. This code determines the current drawing status before determining what to do on a right-click. For example, when a grip is currently hot, right-clicking displays the grips cursor menu. When no command is active, the standard popup menu is displayed. If a command is active but a grip is not hot, right-clicking is equivalent to an Enter keystroke. Although it is not visible on this page, if you look at this line in the menu file, you will see that the rightmost character is a semicolon. Just as when working with toolbars, a semicolon in the menu file is an Enter. Also like the toolbar buttons, an automatic Enter is issued by AutoCAD LT at the end of each menu pick, unless the last character is a semicolon. The AUX1, AUX2, AUX3 and AUX4 menu sections are listed here:

```
***AUX1
$M=$(if,$(eq,$(substr,$(getvar,cmdnames),1,5),GRIP_),$P0=CHAP17.GRIPS
  $P0=*,$(if,$(and,$(and,$(and,$(=,$(getv…
$P0=SNAP $p0=*
^C^C
^B
^O
^G
^D
^E
^T

***AUX2
$P0=SNAP $p0=*

***AUX3
$P0=SNAP $p0=*

***AUX4
$P0=SNAP $p0=*
```

Take a close look at the second listing in AUX1. The $P0=SNAP $p0=* is a menu call. A ***menu call*** is a special code that displays a menu or makes it active. All menu calls start with a dollar sign ($). In this menu call, the "p0" tells AutoCAD LT that it is referring to the ***POP0 menu, which is the cursor menu. The "=*" part tells AutoCAD LT to display the menu on screen *now*.

If you are using a three-button mouse, the middle button displays the object snap cursor menu. This makes sense, because the second listing in the menu is applied to the third button. However, to display the cursor menu using a two-button mouse, it is necessary to press the Shift key while right-clicking. The Shift key modifier tells AutoCAD LT to use AUX2 instead of AUX1. Notice that the listing for the second button in the AUX2 menu is the cursor menu call. The AUX3 and AUX4 menus use other modifiers. Figure 17.32 shows a table with the available key and button combinations and their effects listed.

FIGURE 17.32 Available button and key combinations and their effect.

Key and Button Sequence	Menu Used
Button only	AUX1 (or BUTTONS1)
Shift + Button	AUX2 (or BUTTONS2)
Ctrl + Button	AUX3 (or BUTTONS3)
Shift + Ctrl + Button	AUX4 (or BUTTONS4)

Therefore, it is possible to get four separate functions from the second button of the mouse if the AUX3 and AUX4 sections are added to the menu. With a three-button mouse, this provides for up to eight different functions besides picking.

The added items in the default AUX and BUTTONS menus include the ^C^C, which is a cancel, and several other control codes. These control codes are only available at the keyboard if you are configured for AutoCAD classic keystrokes in the Preferences dialog box, but they work from the menu file regardless of this setting. The function of these codes is as follows:

^B	SNAP Toggle
^O	ORTHO Toggle
^G	GRID Toggle
^D	COORDS Toggle
^E	IsoPlane Toggle
^T	Tabletmode Toggle

Any or all of these codes can be changed to a command or macro, as desired. The rules for working within menu files is much the same as working with toolbar buttons. To assign the LINE command to a Shift+RightClick, modify the AUX2 menu section to read as follows:

```
***AUX2
^C^CLINE
```

> ### Field Notes
>
> In the BUTTONS and AUX menu sections, the first backslash character accepts the current screen coordinates of the cursor location rather than waiting for user input. This can be used to begin a command at the current location, for example:
>
> ^C^CLINE;\
>
> When this macro is accessed, the LINE command is started using the current cursor location as the first input item. The first prompt for the LINE command is From point;, so the line is started at the cursor location.

Exercise 17.9

1. Open CHAP17.MNS with WordPad.
2. Find the third and fourth buttons menu sections (AUX3 and 4 or BUTTONS3 and 4, as appropriate).
3. Edit your menu so CTRL + right-click starts the U command transparently and CTRL + SHIFT + right-click starts the REDO command.
4. Close the file and save your changes.

Customizing Pull-Down Menus

Pull-down menus can be modified as desired, removed, and new ones added. In a single menu file, AutoCAD LT supports up to 16 pull-down menus. The default ACLT menu defines 10 pull-down menus. It is generally recommended that the primary menu system remain as is, and that any modified menus be additions from a partial menu file. This keeps the AutoCAD LT documentation accurate, and ensures that all levels of AutoCAD LT users can function productively with the menu system.

To avoid the need to write an entire menu file from start to finish, AutoCAD LT allows the use of partial menu files. A ***partial menu file*** is one that has only specific items in it, such as a set of specialized pull-down menus or toolbars. All that is required in a partial menu file is a unique MENUGROUP name and the definitions for the items you want included.

To begin constructing pull-down menus, whether in a full menu file or a partial one, you need to understand what the necessary elements of a pull-down menu are. This example builds a partial menu file, one step at a time, that has a single pull-down menu in it. Except for the requirement for a unique MENUGROUP name in the partial menu file, the procedures and techniques are exactly the same.

Because it is a partial menu file and will be loaded separately from the primary menu, the menu must have its own unique menu group name. This name is placed in the MENUGROUP section as follows:

   ***MENUGROUP=Example

If you wish to place comments in the file, they can go on any blank line, as long as they are preceded with two forward slashes. The top of your partial menu file might look like this:

   //
   // Partial menu file name: Chap17A.mns
   // This file holds custom drafting macros in a single pull-down menu.
   //

   ***MENUGROUP=Example

Comments are not required, but they can be useful to help explain the intent of specific items, or to record information such as revision dates and author's name. The next required element is a POP menu name assignment. Even though there are already 10 pull-down menus in the default menu file, this is a unique file and its pull-down menu sequence should begin at POP1. POP1 is a main menu section, so it is preceded by three asterisks:

   ***POP1

The first line below the pull-down menu name is for the label that is to appear on the menu bar. The term *label,* as used here, refers to an item of text that is visible to the user on a given menu feature. The labels on the menu bar are the only means of accessing the menu underneath, so this is a required element. Labels are enclosed in square brackets and should be 14 characters or less. The following example assigns the label "Custom" to this new pull-down menu:

***POP1
[Custom]

All menu bar items in the default menu have a menu shortcut key associated with them. A ***menu shortcut key*** is the underlined character that gives keyboard access to the menu item. For example, in the File menu, the F is the menu shortcut key, so the File menu can be accessed by pressing Alt+F. To assign a menu shotcut key to a menu label, place an ampersand (&) in front of the character to use. For example, to make the Custom label appear as Custom on the menu bar, the label is written as:

***POP1
[&Custom]

All shortcut keys should be unique in the area of the menu that they are a part of, whenever possible. Ideally, the menu bar and each individual menu or cascade should not have duplicate shortcut keys. This helps prevent unnecessary conflicts when trying to access a menu item. The shortcut key C does not conflict with any of the mnemonics in the default ACLT menu. If, however, you want to make the "u" the mnemonic, as in Custom, the ampersand is placed in front of the "u" like this:

[C&ustom]

The next step is to place the new menu selections in the pull-down menu. Unlike toolbar buttons, pull-down menus do not display graphics and so they require a text label to pick when activating the desired menu selection. The menu item labels are created just like the menu bar label. The first item on this menu is a macro that erases the last object drawn. Pull-down menus expand to match the width of the widest label they contain, but as a rule of thumb, label names should be no longer than needed. If additional information is required, it can be supplied as a help string, which is discussed later.

This next menu macro erases the last object drawn, so a suitable label might be "Erase Last," so this is now added to the menu:

***POP1
[&Custom]
[Erase &Last]

The menu code for an Erase Last macro is fairly simple, but all menu codes should be checked and verified at the command line to avoid errors. At the command line, erasing the last object looks like this:

Command: **Erase**↵
Select objects: **L**↵
1 found
Select objects: ↵
Command:

To write this as a menu macro, simply duplicate the keystrokes, substituting semicolons for Enters, like this:

erase;l;;

The actual macro needs to begin with ^C^C to ensure that the macro always starts at the Command: prompt. So far, the custom pull-down menu looks like this:

***POP1
[&Custom]
[Erase &Last]^C^Cerase;l;;

It is possible to make menu items automatically repeat, working until the user cancels the macro. This is done by placing an asterisk in the first position within the actual macro code. For example, the following defines a macro that draws single line objects by starting the line command, asking the user for two input points, canceling the LINE command, and repeating:

[&1 LINE]*^C^CLINE;\\;

The label uses the "1" for the shortcut key character. An asterisk as the first character of the macro code tells AutoCAD LT to repeat the macro until the user cancels. The ^C^C ensures that the macro starts at the Command: prompt, and LINE; starts the LINE command. Two backslashes allow for two items of user input, which in this case is a From point: and a To point: for the line. Finally, the last semicolon serves the same purpose as pressing Enter at the To point: prompt, which returns you to the Command: prompt.

```
***POP1
[&Custom]
[Erase &Last]^C^Cerase;l;;
[&1 LINE]*^C^CLINE;\\;
```

Another use for the SINGLE selection mode in menus comes with specialized functions that are only intended to work with one selection. Placed in a repeating command, this option allows the command to execute as soon as you make a selection. For example, the next macro is an Erase 1 macro that erases objects as they are picked:

```
[&Erase 1]*^C^Cerase;si;
```

When the repeating macro starts, the ERASE command is issued, followed by the SINGLE selection option. When an object is selected, the command executes with no further input. The effect is that when you pick an object, it is immediately erased without the need to press Enter to finalize the selection set.

This macro, however, ignores the current setting of PICKAUTO. That means that you cannot select objects using an implied window. To allow for implied windowing, add the AUTO selection mode as follows:

```
[&Erase 1]*^C^Cerase;si;au;
```

Field Notes

> When using repeating macros, do not use a ^C^C sequence other than in the initial *^C^C. Doing so causes the repeating macro to be canceled.

The current partial menu file, with each of the edits in this example, now looks like this:

```
***MENUGROUP=EXAMPLE
***POP1
[&Custom]
[Erase &Last]^C^Cerase;l;;
[&1 LINE]*^C^CLINE;\\;
[&Erase 1]*^C^Cerase;si;au;
```

One very important aspect of creating menus is to keep the menu selections organized and easy to use. Most of the built-in menus group similar commands together, often separating them from other groups with dividing lines. This example menu is presented in a more logical fashion if the Erase macros are grouped and separated from the other items on the menu. The following listing reorganizes the menu selections and incorporates a dividing line. The dividing line is placed in a menu using a label of two hyphens, or dashes, as shown in this sequence:

```
***MENUGROUP=EXAMPLE

***POP1
[&Custom]
[Erase &Last]^C^Cerase;l;;
[&Erase 1]*^C^Cerase;si;au;
[--]
[&1 LINE]*^C^CLINE;\\;
```

To load the partial menu, the Menu Customization dialog box is used. After browsing and locating the file, the Load button is picked and the new MENUGROUP appears in the Menu Groups: listing. On the Menu Bar page, the Example menu group is selected, and the Custom pull-down menu is inserted into the menu bar, as shown in Figure 17.33A. The actual pull-down menu is shown in Figure 17.33B.

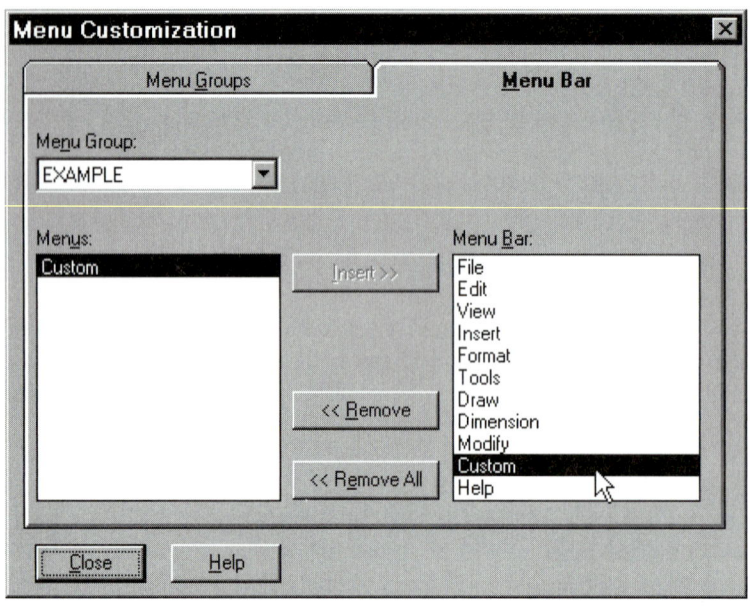

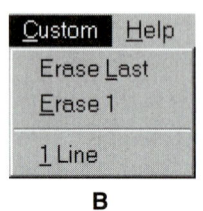

FIGURE 17.33 (A) Pull-down menus from partial menu files can be inserted into the menu bar using the Menu Customization dialog box. (B) The Custom pull-down menu.

> ### Field Notes
>
> Modifying the menu system is not covered within the AutoCAD LT User's Guide. The only built-in documentation is found using the on-line help system.

Exercise 17.10

1. Start a new file with Notepad or WordPad.
2. Create a partial menu, using the previous examples as a guideline. The menu group name should be CHAP17A and the pull-down menu name should be Custom.
3. Design a pull-down menu that has two drawing commands or macros, two editing commands or macros, and two display commands or macros.
4. Use separator lines to group similar menu selections.
5. Save the file as CHAP17A.MNS and use MENULOAD to load the partial menu file and place it on the menu bar.
6. Check your menu to ensure that everything works properly.

✓ LEARNING CHECKPOINT

- ☐ What is a partial menu file?
- ☐ How are comments separated from menu code in the menu file?
- ☐ What is the maximum number of pull-down menus that can be defined in a single menu file?
- ☐ How is a label specified in a pull-down menu?
- ☐ What is a mnemonic and how is it specified?
- ☐ Describe the creation of a repeating menu macro.
- ☐ How is a separator line placed in a menu?

Creating Cascading Submenus

Similar to the concept of a Toolbar Flyout, a cascading submenu allows mode menu items to be accessible from the same menu. Because using a cascading submenu requires an additional pick, these menus are often reserved for macros as opposed to simple commands. Menu selections that simply start a command are generally kept at the top level; otherwise it is quicker and easier to use the keyboard. Figure 17.34 shows the Arc cascading submenu on the Draw menu. Notice that commands on the top level are those such as Line, Polyline, and others that simply start a command. The options on these cascades run macros of varying complexity.

FIGURE 17.34 Cascading submenus require an additional pick, and therefore are most frequently used for macro items that do more than simply start a command.

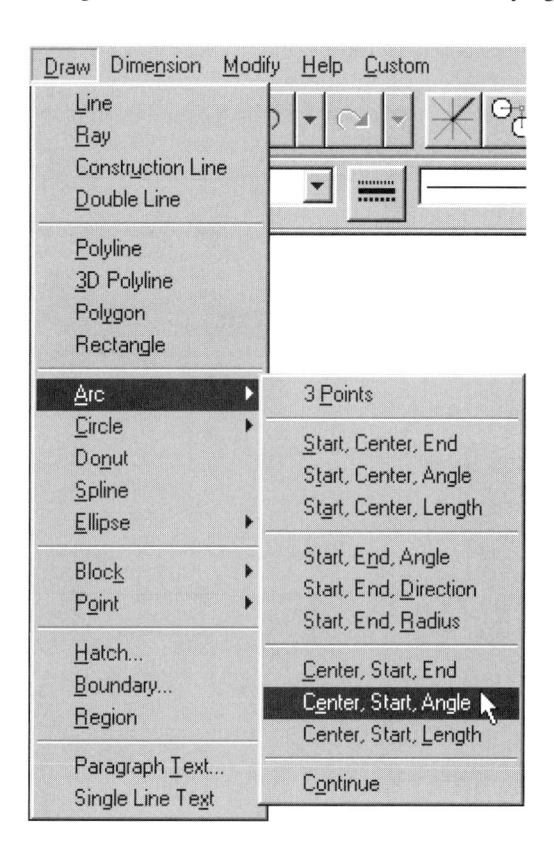

Cascade sections are created by inserting special labels into the menu. The label that opens a cascading submenu cannot be assigned its own macro. Picking it only displays the cascading menu underneath. The characters used in the label to begin and end cascade sections are the *less than* (<) and *greater than* (>) symbols combined with a hyphen to form an arrow shape (-> <-). The *begin cascade* symbol is ->, an arrow that points to the right, the *end cascade* symbol <- points to the left. As you use these symbols in labels to define cascades, it may help to think of these symbols as directional arrows. The following listing shows the format used for cascade menu sections:

```
[->Begin Cascade]
[Submenu Item 1] macro code . . .
[Submenu Item 2] macro code . . .
[Submenu Item 3] macro code . . .
[etc. . . .] . . .
[<-Last Submenu Item on cascade] macro code . . .
```

The last item on the cascade has the End Cascade character placed in the label. To put this technique into use with the Custom pull-down menu, the next example groups the two Erase macros together in a cascading submenu. The first step is to insert a new label with the Begin Cascade character and then place the End Cascade character in the label of the last item on the cascade, like this:

```
***MENUGROUP=EXAMPLE

***POP1
[&Custom]
[->&Erase Macros]
  [Erase &Last]^C^Cerase;l;;
  [<-&Erase 1]*^C^Cerase;si;au;
[- -]
[&1 LINE]*^C^CLINE;\\;
```

As you study this example, notice that the Begin Cascade label can also have a shortcut key, and that the last cascade item is not changed except for the placement of the End Cascade character as the first character in the label. Figure 17.35 shows the Custom menu with the cascading submenu expanded.

A cascading submenu can also be placed on another cascading submenu. This practice, called **nesting,** should be avoided, when possible, to keep menu picks as close to the top level as possible. When nesting must be done, you should never nest more than two cascades.

FIGURE 17.35 The cascading submenu for the Custom menu.

> ### Exercise 17.11
> 1. Open CHAP17A.MNS for editing using a text editor.
> 2. Define three cascading submenus, one for the drawing commands, one for the editing commands, and one for the display commands.
> 3. Using MENULOAD, unload the previous version of CHAP17A, and load the new version.
> 4. Check each of the menu features to see if they work.

Working with Image Tile Menus

The default ACLT menu does not utilize any image tile menus, but AutoCAD LT still supports their use. An image tile menu is similar to a dialog box, and it can display graphic items for menu picks. These graphic images are created using the MSLIDE command, and are stored in slide libraries created using SLIDELIB. Creating slide libraries is detailed in Chapter 15. Figure 17.36 shows an example of an image tile menu.

An image tile menu offers the capability to display up to 20 images. All 20 boxes are displayed regardless of how many are actually used in any given application. The unused boxes remain blank. If more than 20 are specified, the Next button is enabled and the images tiles are continued on the next page. Because it displays slide images, an image tile menu is often a preferred method of presenting symbol libraries to the user for easy selection.

All image tile menus are actually submenus found in the IMAGE section. The default ACLT menu has an IMAGE section, but you can place another one in a partial menu file. The IMAGE section uses three asterisks, because it is the main section name. Each of the actual image tile menus is a submenu of the IMAGE section, and submenus are designated using only two asterisks. An IMAGE section and a title for a submenu named SYMBOLS1 are shown in the following listing, placed in the EXAMPLE partial menu:

```
***MENUGROUP=EXAMPLE

***POP1
[&Custom]
[->&Erase Macros]
  [Erase &Last]^C^Cerase;l;;
  [<-&Erase 1]*^C^Cerase;si;au;
[- -]
[&1 LINE]*^C^CLINE;\\;

***IMAGE
**SYMBOL1
```

CHAPTER 17 ||| Customizing AutoCAD LT   707

FIGURE 17.36 An image tile menu displays custom graphics images as menu selections, and offers a text-based version of the menu in the list on the left.

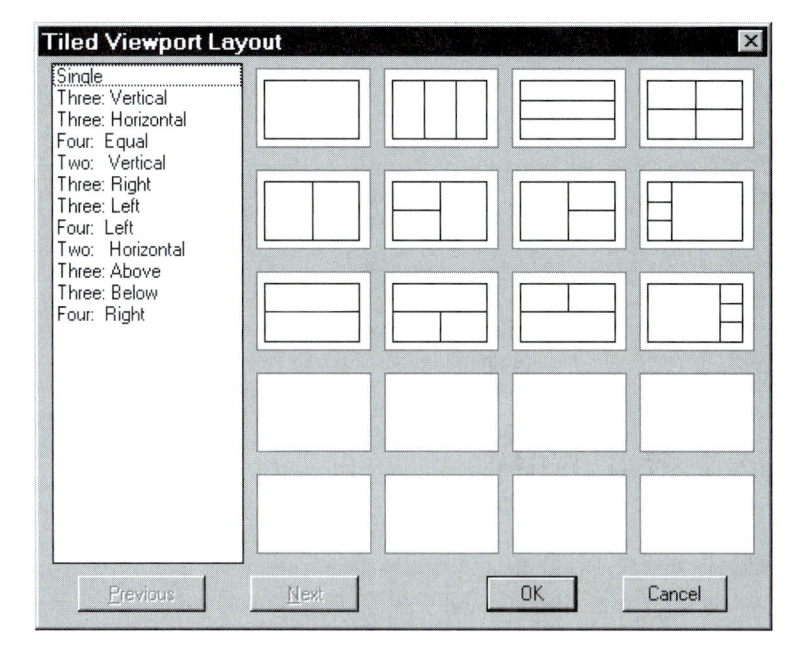

The first item in an image tile menu description is the text that appears at the top of the image tile menu. Each subsequent listing describes one of the image tile options. The description of an individual image tile is done in the label, and the menu code that follows the label is executed when either the image or the corresponding text listing in the list box is selected.

The actual image tile is described by naming the slide image that is to be used in the tile. A slide *may* be part of a slide library, or you can use individual slide files in an image tile menu. The label determines what is displayed both in the image tile and in the text list. The four ways to set up the image tile label depend on the slide name, library name and the text that you want displayed in the list box, and are as follows:

[SlideName]: The name of the slide file that is to be displayed. When used this way, the slide file name also appears in the text listing.

[SlideName,Label Text]: The name of the slide file to display and a custom text label to appear in the text listing.

[LibName(SlideName)]: The slide SlideName, found in the LibName slide library, is displayed, and the text SlideName is displayed in the text listing.

[LibName(SlideName,Label Text)]: The slide SlideName, found in the LibName slide library, is displayed, and the text Label Text is displayed in the text listing.

Although it is acceptable to use individual slide files in your image tile menus, it is highly recommended that you use the slide library method instead. A slide library provides a single file that stores all the image tiles associated with your menu. Managing a multitude of individual slide files can be a formidable challenge. The examples in this text use the slide library method.

Field Notes

When creating slides to use in an image tile menu, be certain to optimize the space on the screen. Image tile menus are very small, and can be difficult to see if the image is small when you make the slide. A good rule of thumb is to zoom the geometry so that it is centered and completely fills the screen, then ZOOM .95X. In this way, the geometry is centered and fills the screen without touching the very edges.

Wide polylines and solid objects are displayed as outlines on image tiles. To create an area that appears filled, create a dense hatch pattern in the area, but be careful not to do this too often, because these patterns can slow down the display of the image tile menu.

For the purposes of this example, three symbols have been defined, and slides were made of each symbol and incorporated into a slide library named SYMBOLS. The symbols are annotation symbols used in mechanical drafting, including the depth symbol, and symbols for countersinks and counterbores. The slide and symbol names are the same as follows: DEPTH, CSINK, and CBORE. The next example shows the construction of the labels for this image tile menu, and the menu code inserts the appropriate defined symbol. The first label is for the text that appears at the top, and then each of the three image tiles is defined:

```
***IMAGE
**SYMBOL1
[Select a Symbol to Insert:]
[symbols(depth,Depth)]^C^Cinsert;depth;
[symbols(csink,CounterSink)]^C^Cinsert;csink;
[symbols(cbore,CounterBore)]^C^Cinsert;cbore;
```

This code has sufficiently defined an image tile menu, but there is not yet a way to display this menu. Unlike the toolbars and pull-downs, there are no buttons or menu bars that activate image tile menus. An image tile menu is displayed by a menu call activated by a menu pick on an accessible menu system, such as a toolbar or a pull-down menu. A menu call always begins with a dollar sign, followed by the type of menu to display, an equals sign, and the menu specification. For example, the next listing makes an image tile menu named SYMBOL1 active. Notice the required placement of the MENUGROUP name in front of the menu name, separated by a period in the following:

```
$i=EXAMPLE.SYMBOL1
```

The act of making an image tile menu current does not actually display the menu. An image tile menu is displayed, similar to the display of pull-down and cursor menus, using an asterisk as the menu specification like this:

```
$i=SYMBOL1 $i=*
```

Sequential menu calls are separated by a single space. Placing a semicolon between menu calls makes them unusable, and an extra space reactivates the last command used. This menu call must now be placed on an accessible menu, such as the Custom pull-down menu as follows:

```
***POP1
[&Custom]
[->&Erase Macros]
   [Erase &Last]^C^Cerase;l;;
   [<-&Erase 1]*^C^Cerase;si;au;
[- -]
[&1 LINE]*^C^CLINE;\\;
[- -]
[&Symbols]$i=EXAMPLE.SYMBOL1 $i=*
```

Now, when the menu is reloaded, the new selection makes SYMBOL1 the current image tile menu and causes it to be displayed. This image tile menu appears as shown in Figure 17.37.

Field Notes

Image tile menu selections can issue menu calls that display other image tile menus.

FIGURE 17.37 An image tile menu is useful for insertion of symbols.

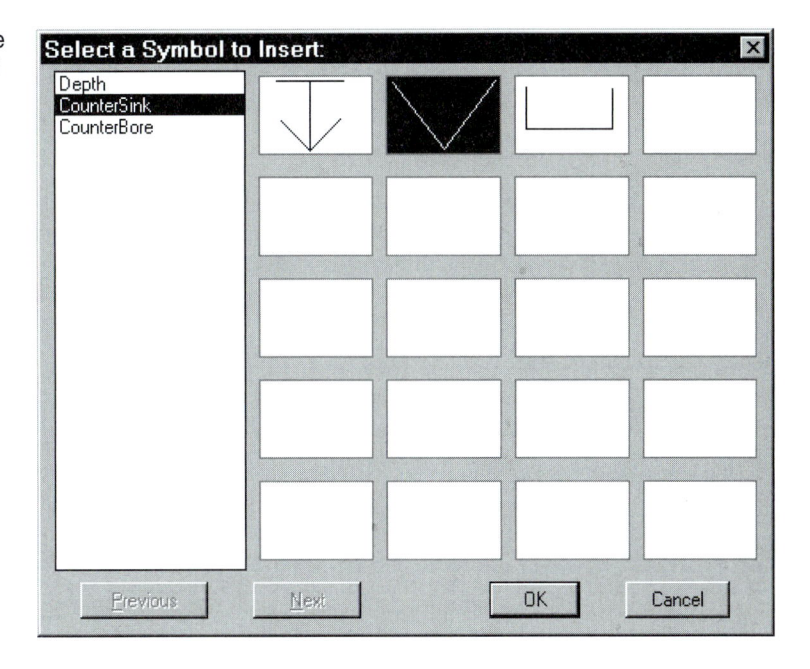

Exercise 17.12

1. Define three symbols, create slides of each of the symbols, and store them in a slide library named EX17-11.SLB.
2. Open CHAP17A.MNS for editing and create an IMAGE section.
3. Place a definition for an image tile menu named EX17-11 in the menu. Each image tile should insert one of the symbols.
4. Save CHAP17A.MNS and reload it into AutoCAD LT.
5. Check your new image tiles to be sure they work.

☑ LEARNING CHECKPOINT

- ☐ Describe an image tile menu. Why is it often used for inserting blocks?
- ☐ How many tiles are available in one menu?
- ☐ What happens when there are more or less tile listings than the image tile menu displays?
- ☐ Can individual slides be used in creating image tile menus? What method is preferred?
- ☐ Where is the title text for an image tile menu defined?
- ☐ How are image tile menus displayed? Show an example.
- ☐ What must be in front of the image tile menu name in the actual menu call?

Defining Help Strings

Help strings, the text items that appear on the status line when a menu selection is pointed to or highlighted, help users of all levels to be certain of what action is to be performed. There are many different toolbar button images and menu picks, and new ones can be defined at any time. It would not be an easy task to memorize every button image and menu pick so that they are all instantly recognized. Help strings, however, can help avoid this obstacle by providing quick descriptions of the menu items on the status line.

Help strings are defined in the HELPSTRINGS section. To create a help string, you must define an ID Tag, plus the actual help text. An *ID Tag* is a unique name that begins with ID_, and allows menu items to reference the help string. For example, the following listing is found in the ACLT.MNS file:

     ID_PEDIT   [Edits polylines]

The actual text displayed by this help string is placed in square brackets, much like menu labels. The ID Tag is the unique identifier referenced by menu items that are to display this particular help string. The Edit Polyline option in the Modify pull-down menu looks like this:

ID_Pedit   [Edit &Polyline]^C^C_pedit

The help string reference is placed prior to the label. Now, whenever this menu item is highlighted, the associated help string is displayed on the status line. The text in a help string should be as concise as possible. A short and clear message is understood at a glance, and this is the goal for all help strings.

Field Notes

Help strings can be referenced only if they are defined in the same menu file. For example, a partial menu cannot reference help strings defined in the base menu. The help strings must also be defined in the partial menu. Also, ID Tags cannot be duplicated in the same file, but an ID Tag in a partial menu file can have the same ID Tag as a help string listed in the base menu—even if the actual help text is different. Each menu item knows which help string to use.

If a help string is duplicated in the same menu file, the last definition encountered in the file is the one that is used.

Exercise 17.13

1. Open CHAP17A.MNS for editing.
2. Create help strings for each menu item on the pull-down menu.
3. Create and place ID Tags so that each menu pick references its help string.
4. Save and exit. Then reload the menu in AutoCAD LT.
5. Test your help strings.

☑ LEARNING CHECKPOINT

- ☐ Why are help strings such a vital part of any menu file?
- ☐ What section are help strings defined in?
- ☐ Describe an ID Tag and its function.
- ☐ Why should help strings be as clear and concise as possible?

Defining Custom Accelerator Keys

Accelerator keystrokes are key combinations that activate a command or macro. For example, the Ctrl+C keystroke accesses the COPYCLIP command and Ctrl+V accesses PASTECLIP. These keys can be redefined or new keystrokes can be added. Accelerators are defined only in the base menu, and are not affected by any listings in a partial menu.

Accelerator keys can be defined in either of two ways, through supplying a macro or through referencing an ID Tag. The first method is much like the construction of a pull-down menu item. The difference is that the label specifies the accelerator keystroke. For example, the next listing, placed in the ***ACCELERATORS section, defines the Ctrl+M keystroke as the MOVE command:

[CONTROL+"M"]^C^Cmove

Accelerator macros cannot pause for user input; any backslash characters are passed directly to the command line and do not cause the macro to pause. You can, however, create longer macros as long as they do not require user input.

The next way to define accelerator keys is called mapping to a command. By placing an ID Tag in front of the accelerator key label, the keystroke is mapped to the command or macro in the menu file that references that ID Tag. For example, the following accelerator definition maps the Ctrl+W keystroke to the macro in the menu file that uses the ID Tag ID_UCSWORLD:

CHAPTER 17 ||| Customizing AutoCAD LT 711

ID_UCSWorld   [CONTROL+"W"]

The following listing within the POP6 menu is accessed now by a Ctrl+W keystroke:

ID_UCSWorld   [&World]^C^C_ucs_w

Accelerator keys cannot use Alt key combinations, because the Alt key accesses Windows system functions. They can, however, use Ctrl, Shift, and Ctrl+Shift combinations. All of the letter keys are used by placing the letter of the key in quotation marks as shown in the previous examples. Any of the function keys can be used in the same manner. The following example makes the Shift+F7 key run a macro that sets up your grid and snap:

[SHIFT+"F7"]^C^Cgrid;.5;snap;.25

To use a numeric keypad number, use "NUMPAD0" for the 0 key, "NUMPAD1" for the 1 key and so on. The following accelerator definition sets a Ctrl+2 on the numeric keypad to zoom using a 2X option:

[CONTROL+"NUMPAD2"]'ZOOM;2X

If you want to access the "2" key found above the alphabetical keys on your keyboard, leave out the "NUMPAD" part and just specify which number like this:

[CONTROL+"2"]'ZOOM;2X

Other keys that can be referenced are listed here:

"HOME"	HOME key	"UP"	UP ARROW key
"END"	END key	"DOWN"	DOWN ARROW key
"INSERT"	INS key	"LEFT"	LEFT ARROW key
"DELETE"	DEL key	"RIGHT"	RIGHT ARROW key
		"ESCAPE"	ESC key

The Ctrl and Shift keys are called modifiers. To use two modifiers, place a plus sign between them as follows:

[CONTROL+SHIFT+"M"]

You can add accelerator keys directly to the menu or use the Keyboard tab of the Customize dialog box. You can access the Customize dialog box as you have previously by picking the Keyboard tab or by selecting Keyboard… from the Customize cascade on the Tools pull-down menu. The Customize dialog box provides a simpler method for working with your keyboard macros, but it has some limitations. The Keyboard tab is shown in Figure 17.38 with a menu group named EXAMPLE.

The Categories drop-down list shows a listing of the names of the pull-down menus in the current menu group as specified in the Menu Group list. At the bottom of the Categories list is the AutoCAD LT Commands option, where you can select the built-in AutoCAD LT Commands option. This allows you to assign keyboard shortcuts to any existing AutoCAD LT pull-down menu selection.

FIGURE 17.38 The Keyboard tab on the Customize dialog box provides an easy way to create, edit, and remove accelerator key definitions.

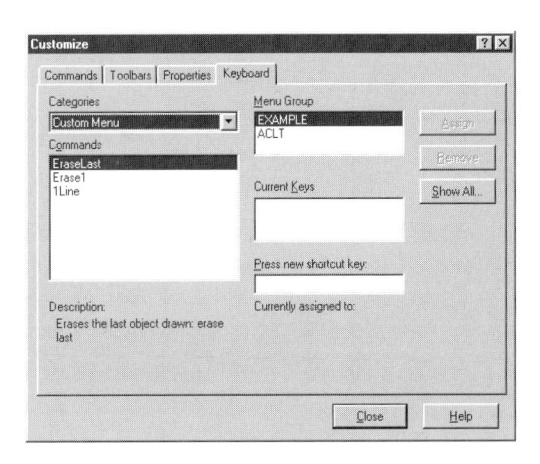

The labels for each of the menu options are displayed in the Commands category. The contents of the EXAMPLE menu group used in Figure 17.38 are shown here:

```
***MENUGROUP=EXAMPLE

***POP1
                [&Custom]
ID_ERASELAST    [Erase &Last]^C^Cerase;l;;
                [&Erase 1]*^C^Cerase;si;
                [--]
                [&1 Line]*^C^Cline;\\;

***HELPSTRINGS
ID_ERASELAST    [Erases the last object drawn: erase last]
```

To assign a new menu short-cut key to one of the commands in the Commands list, first highlight its name. Below the Commands list, the helpstring for the highlighted command will appear if one has been defined. Any existing accelerator keystrokes associated with that command are shown in the Current Keys category. Pick the edit box labeled Press new shortcut key: to make it active. Now, press the keystroke combination you want to assign to this command. If you select a keystroke that is already being used, this is indicated in the Currently assigned to: area. For example, in Figure 17.39 the keystroke CTRL+E has been selected for the Erase Last command. A message indicates that this is currently assigned to *Cycles through isometric planes*. Selecting the Assign button makes the new assignment and places a description of the keystroke in the Current Keys list. Keep in mind that if you use a previously assigned keystroke, AutoCAD LT recognizes the one whose menu group was loaded first. Also, AutoCAD LT and Windows both have certain key assignments that cannot be changed. In the previous assignment of CTRL+E to the Erase Last tool, testing the keystroke after leaving the Customize dialog box reveals that it still activates the Isoplane toggle. If the keystroke that you want is already in use, try adding a Shift key to the combination. Instead of CTRL+E,. try CTRL+Shift+E or maybe something totally different, like Shift+F2. To remove an unwanted shortcut key definition, highlight the key in the Current Keys list and pick the Remove button. Figure 17.40 illustrates this procedure.

FIGURE 17.39 If a selected keystroke has already been defined, its current assignment is shown below the Currently assigned to: label.

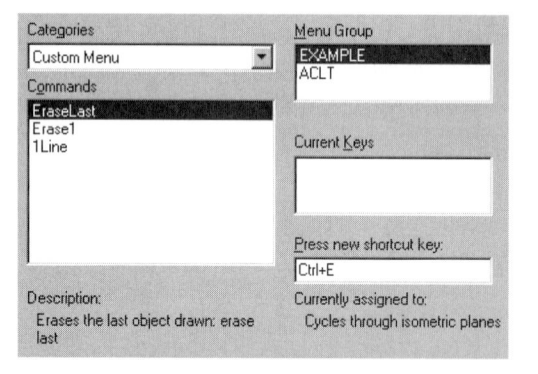

FIGURE 17.40 Unwanted shortcut key definitions can be removed from a menu group.

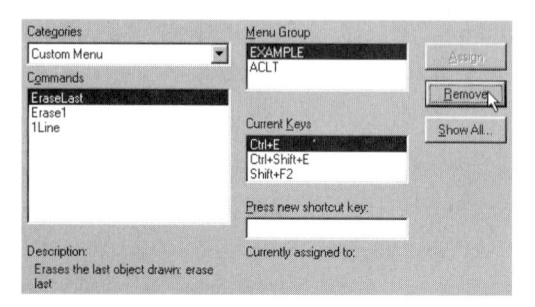

When the changes are applied, you can reopen the MNS file to see the changes that AutoCAD LT has added to your ***ACCELERATORS menu section. You will also find that any menu items that did not previously have ID tags now have a tag that relates to the label for the menu item:

CHAPTER 17 ||| Customizing AutoCAD LT

```
***MENUGROUP=EXAMPLE

***POP1
                    [&Custom]
ID_ERASELAST        [Erase &Last]^C^Cerase;l;;
ID_Erase1_0         [&Erase 1]
                    [--]
ID_1Line_0          [&1 Line]*^C^Cline;\\;

***TOOLBARS

***ACCELERATORS
ID_ERASELAST        [CONTROL+SHIFT+"E"]
ID_ERASELAST        [SHIFT+"F2"]

***HELPSTRINGS
ID_ERASELAST        [Erases the last object drawn: erase last]
```

Field Notes

Always be very careful when editing a menu file from a text editor and within AutoCAD LT at the same time. If you are not careful, you can lose all the changes you have made in one of the two processes. For example, if you currently have the MNS file open in a text editor and you make some changes in AutoCAD LT, then the version that is open in the text editor is no longer up to date. AutoCAD LT has rewritten the menu file on disk, but those changes are not automatically made in the text editor. You must close the file and reopen the new version to see the changes. An easy way to avoid this type of problem is to simply close the MNS file in your text editing application while you are making changes from within AutoCAD LT.

Similarly, each time you save the file with the text editor, you must unload the menu and reload it to see the changes. If you forget to unload and reload the menu and then make changes in AutoCAD LT, the saved changes are not incorporated in the new version of the file that AutoCAD LT creates. Always be sure that the first thing you do after editing your menu file in a text editor is to unload and reload the menu. For your convenience, you can even make a toolbar button that does this with a simple pick. The following example provides the menu macro for unloading and reloading a menu file named Chap17.mns that uses the menugroup name EXAMPLE.

^C^Cmenuunload;EXAMPLE;menuload;CHAP17

Exercise 17.14

1. Open the CHAP17.MNS file for editing.
2. Add three new accelerator keystroke definitions.
3. Save and exit the menu file.
4. Reload the menu file in AutoCAD LT.
5. Check the functionality of the new accelerators.
6. Use the Keyboard tab on the Customize dialog box to define two new keyboard shortcuts.
7. Close the Customize dialog box and test your new keystrokes.
8. Open your menu file to see the changes entered by AutoCAD.

✓ LEARNING CHECKPOINT

- ☐ What is an accelerator keystroke?
- ☐ Describe the two ways to define an accelerator.
- ☐ Can accelerators be defined in partial menu files?
- ☐ What is a modifier?

Customizing Tablet Menus

A tablet menu is a menu that is accessed using a digitizer tablet. Because of the many difficulties often associated with getting a reliable WinTab driver, fewer companies are using digitizer menus today. A *WinTab driver* is a piece of software that allows AutoCAD LT to utilize a tablet while working in the Windows environment. With all of the toolbars available, plus pull-down menus and accelerator keys, digitizer tablets are often unnecessary. If you are using a tablet and a tablet menu, and you would like to modify it, the process is much the same as modifying any other area of the menu system with regard to actual menu code. Like the Buttons menus, labels are not displayable and are not required. However, placing your menu macros in the proper location requires an understanding of the structure of the tablet menu section.

The tablet menu is very large and has many repeated items. This is because the tablet itself is divided into grid squares whose position is reported to the system as a set of X,Y coordinates. The menu itself is also divided into grid squares that tell AutoCAD LT what menu item you have selected based on the X,Y coordinates returned to the system.

Configuring the tablet is detailed in the AutoCAD LT 98 on-line help. The default row and column settings can be changed, but the ACLT menu system is set up for the default configuration. If you have a tablet, you can print the tablet menu template that has been supplied in the Sample directory folder in the drawing named TABLET.DWG. This drawing is shown in Figure 17.41.

Although any area of the tablet menu is subject to modification as desired, the area that is actually intended for user modification is the top menu area defined on the template. This area is set up in the default menu as a group of rectangular areas, called cells, defined as 25 columns by 9 rows. This means that you could have as many as 225 separate menu items placed in this area. The section of the menu file that represents this menu area is:

```
***TABLET1
**TABLET1STD
```

In the default menu, each cell is provided with a semicolon, which issues an Enter. Cells can be modified as desired to hold menu macros of your choice. If you have a menu template, you will see that the rows are labeled alphabetically and the columns are labeled numerically. This helps you to reference the cell position in the menu file. For example, the first entry under TABLET1STD is for cell A1, the next is for A2 and so on. After getting to A25, the next menu listing is assigned to cell B1 and the cycle continues.

Additionally, multiple cells can be set to the same macro to create larger selection areas. For example, setting cells A1, A2, B1, and B2 to the same macro creates a square selection area that is four times the area of a single cell.

Finally, using the TABLET drawing as a guide, you can draw the upper area menu template using AutoCAD LT. Then, plot the entire drawing, including your additions. Place this template on your tablet and use the TABLET command to configure the tablet menu areas. Use Appendix H in the User's Guide as a reference for setting up the tablet menu.

An Introduction to DIESEL Code

The term *DIESEL* stands for Direct Interpretively Evaluated String Expression Language. DIESEL allows menu macros to be given decision-making abilities, effectively creating "smart" menu picks. Using DIESEL, you can determine the current settings of system variables and act based on this information. DIESEL code greatly increases the capabilities of your menu macros.

A DIESEL code expression is preceded by a dollar sign ($) similar to a menu call. If compared with a menu call, the menu specification is "M"; on the other side of the equals sign is the actual macro code. For example, the following DIESEL expression could be added to an image tile macro created earlier to get the current values for the DIMSCALE and TEXTSIZE variables, multiply them, and supply the product as the scale factor for the insertion of the symbol:

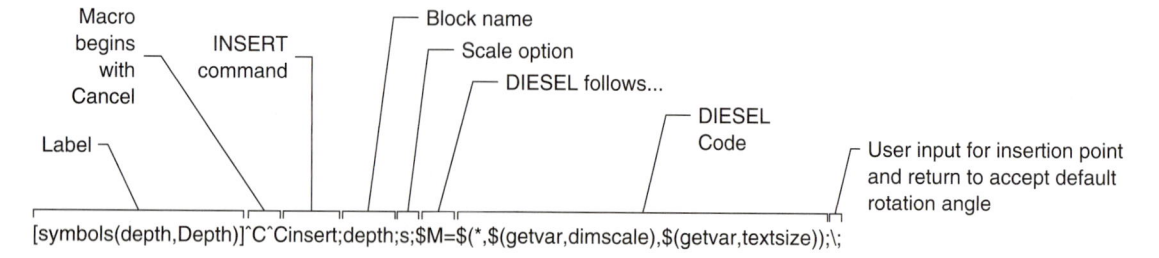

```
[symbols(depth,Depth)]^C^Cinsert;depth;s;$M=$(*,$(getvar,dimscale),$(getvar,textsize));\;
```

- Label
- Macro begins with Cancel
- INSERT command
- Block name
- Scale option
- DIESEL follows...
- DIESEL Code
- User input for insertion point and return to accept default rotation angle

CHAPTER 17 ||| Customizing AutoCAD LT

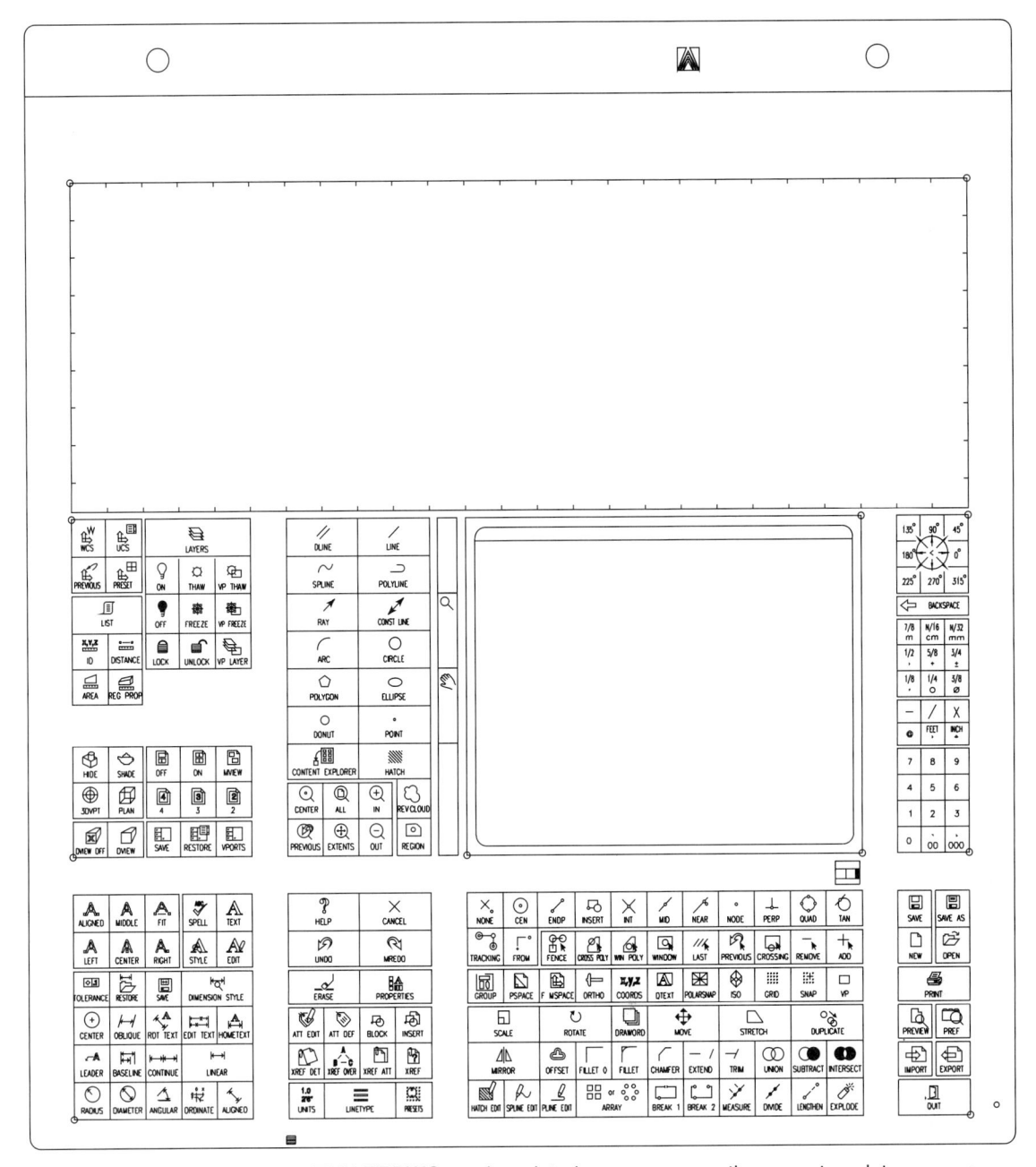

FIGURE 17.41 The drawing TABLET.DWG can be printed so you can use the menu template on your tablet.

To prepare for this insertion method, the original symbol is drawn 1 unit tall, so if DIMSCALE is 1.0, and TEXTSIZE is 0.125, the symbol is also 0.125 units tall, because 1.0 × 0.125 = 0.125.

The label specifies the image tile appearance, and the actual macro begins here with the ^C^C. The INSERT command is issued, the block name specified, and the Insertion point is answered with the S option to preset the scale factor. When the command line prompts for the scale factor, the macro evaluates the DIESEL expression and returns the result to the prompt. The $M= tells AutoCAD LT that the information to follow is a DIESEL macro. Each individual DIESEL expression, even nested expressions, is preceded by a dollar sign. The first expression in this macro is multiplication, indicated by the asterisk. The syntax, or correct layout, for any DIESEL expression is for the function to be listed, followed by any required arguments, with each item separated with a comma. The term *argument* refers to data provided for the function to operate on or with. For example, the arguments for a multiplication expression are the numbers to multiply. Therefore, a multiplication expression is always written as:

(*, *arg1*[, *arg2*, . . ., *arg9*])

In this listing, the items shown in square brackets are optional. All DIESEL expressions have a maximum limit of 10 parameters, including the function name. The term ***parameter,*** as used here, refers to any item in the DIESEL expression—functions and arguments alike. According to this limit, a multiplication function can be supplied with one, two, three, or more arguments up to a total of nine. If only one argument is provided, that same value is returned. The expression in the previous example provided two arguments, which are also DIESEL expressions. A DIESEL expression inside of another expression is a nested expression. The nested expressions are evaluated first and the values they return are used by the upper level expression. In this example, the GETVAR expression is used to get the value of the two variables that are used to determine the insertion scale factor for the symbol, DIMSCALE and TEXTSIZE. The GETVAR expression accepts a single argument, which is the variable name to get. So, the values returned by these two expressions are multiplied and the returned value is used by the INSERT command as a preset scale factor:

$(getvar,dimscale)
$(getvar,textsize)

Exercise 17.15

1. Create two block definitions for annotation symbols, such as a depth symbol, and a countersink or counterbore symbol.
2. Open the partial menu file CHAP17A.MNS for editing.
3. Set up the appropriate menu picks on either an image tile menu or on the pull-down menu.
4. Use DIESEL code to preset the scale factors for insertion to match the current dimensioning text size by referencing the DIMSCALE and TEXTSIZE variables.
5. Save and exit the file. Reload the partial menu and test your menu entries.

In addition to modifying specific macros, a DIESEL expression can be used to make decisions in a macro. For example, the DIESEL language provides an IF function. The classic IF-THEN-ELSE model is a fundamental of all programming languages, allowing one course of action to be taken if a condition exists, and a different course if not. In the DIESEL language, the IF expression syntax is as follows:

$(if,*test*,*do-if-true*[, *do-if-false*])

The IF function requires a test and an expression to perform if the test is positive (the THEN item). The expression to do if the test fails (the ELSE item) is optional. If no value or zero is returned by the test expression, then the test has failed. If a nonzero value is returned, the test has passed. As a sample implementation, the next set of code uses DIESEL to construct a toggle for the Blipmode system variable as a pull-down menu item:

[Blip&mode]$M=$(if,$(getvar,blipmode),blipmode;0;,blipmode;1;)

The test expression is $(getvar,blipmode), which returns 1 if Blipmode is on and 0 if Blipmode is off. A positive result, meaning that Blipmode is on, causes the *do-if-true* expression to be evaluated. The *do-if-true* expression is blipmode;0, which turns Blipmode off. The *do-if-false* expression is blipmode;1, which turns Blipmode on. Notice that the setting is not followed with an Enter because an automatic Enter is issued at the end of the macro. This sample represents but one minor example of decision making using DIESEL code.

Exercise 17.16

1. Open the partial menu file CHAP17A.MNS for editing.
2. Create a cascading submenu on the Custom pull-down menu. Label it "Toggles."
3. Place three menu selections on the cascade that toggle any three variables of your choice. These variables must have 0 and 1 values to apply this technique.
4. Save and exit the menu file. Reload the menu and test your new menu entries.

While making decisions about what to do, the DIESEL codes can also decide how to display the menu selection itself. Menu displays can be modified in simple ways to more effectively communicate with the user. For example, items that are not available at the current time can be "grayed out," or settings that are currently active can have check marks placed by them.

Using DIESEL code within the actual label allows testing for conditions and modification of the display based on the results. The two most common sequences used to modify menu labels are the tilde (~) and an exclamation point–period combination (!.). The tilde character, placed in the first position in the label, grays out the menu item. The !. sequence places a check mark in front of the item.

As a working example of graying items out, the View pull-down menu grays out items specific to paper space when model space is active, and grays out model space items when paper space is active. It does this by checking the value of the TILEMODE system variable and implementing the tilde using DIESEL. Study the label in the following menu macro:

[$(if,$(getvar,tilemode),~)MView]^C^Cmview

Because the DIESEL code here is part of the label, and not part of the macro, the $M= prefix is not required. The test expression gets the value of tilemode and returns it to the IF function. When TILEMODE is set to 1, the MVIEW command cannot be used. Therefore, the *do-if-true* expression supplies a tilde as the first character when TILEMODE is 1. This has the effect of graying out the item, which disables it so that it cannot be picked.

Exercise 17.17

1. Open the partial menu file CHAP17A.MNS for editing.
2. Create a menu entry for the VPORTS command.
3. Using DIESEL code, gray out the menu item when Tilemode is 0; enable the item when Tilemode is 1.
4. Save and exit. Reload the menu and test your entries.

Placing a check mark in front of a menu item is done in exactly the same way as graying an item out, except that the !. is used instead of the ~. A test is performed to find the appropriate course of action and it is executed using DIESEL. In the next example, the entry made earlier for the Blipmode toggle is modified so that if Blipmode is on, a check mark is displayed in front of the label:

[$(if,(getvar,blipmode),!.)Blip&mode]$M=$(if,$(getvar,blipmode),'blipmode;0,'blipmode;1)

The test returns 1 if Blipmode is on, which places the !. at the beginning of the label, causing a check mark to be displayed. The remainder of the code does not change; it still toggles the current setting. Figure 17.42 shows a pull-down menu with a grayed out item and a check mark placed in front of another item.

FIGURE 17.42 DIESEL code can be used to control both the function and the appearance of menu items.

Exercise 17.18

1. Open the partial menu file CHAP17A.MNS for editing.
2. Edit each of the menu picks on the Toggles cascade on the Custom pull-down menu so that a check mark is displayed when the current setting is 1, or ON.
3. Save and exit. Reload the menu and check your entries.

Creating Custom Linetypes

AutoCAD LT provides a wide variety of linetypes, but this represents only a small portion of the many different linetypes used in technical drawings. The linetypes included with AutoCAD LT include the ASME and ISO standard linetypes. Additionally, a number of complex linetypes are included to represent fencing, batting, water lines, and more. Still, there are many other linetypes used in industry that are not included with AutoCAD LT. To allow the greatest degree of flexibility possible, AutoCAD LT allows you to create your own custom linetypes as desired.

The two basic categories of linetypes in AutoCAD LT are simple linetypes and complex linetypes. A *simple linetype* is one that is made up only of lines and spaces, like CENTER lines and HIDDEN lines. A *complex linetype* often incorporates text or symbols into the line pattern to supply additional information or to be instantly recognizable.

Simple linetypes can be created directly at the Command: prompt using the -LINETYPE command. When the -LINETYPE command is entered, the following prompt is displayed:

Command: **-LINETYPE**↵
?/Create/Load/Set:

The Create option allows new linetypes to be defined. When accessed, the Create option asks you to name the new linetype that you are about to create. This option can be used to your advantage to see how existing linetypes are defined. Reviewing the definitions for the existing linetypes can help you to better understand how to create the new linetype you need. For example, the linetype to be created in this example is very similar to the DIVIDE2 linetype, which displays a long dash, two dots and then repeats. The new linetype is to have a long dash, one dot, a short dash, another dot and then repeat. Looking first at the definition of DIVIDE2 can be very helpful, as shown in the following example:

?/Create/Load/Set: **C**↵
⟨use the Create or Append Linetype File dialog box to pick the ACLT.LIN file⟩
Wait, checking if linetype already defined ...
DIVIDE2 already exists in this file. Current definition is:
    *DIVIDE2,__..__..__..__..__..__..__..__..__..
    A,0.25,−0.125,0,−0.125,0,−0.125
Overwrite? <N> ↵
Name of linetype to create:

All the built-in simple linetypes are defined in the file named ACLT.LIN. New linetypes can be stored here also or placed in a different file. The ACLT.LIN file must be specified here in order to get the current definition of DIVIDE2 to be displayed. The current definition is listed as:

    *DIVIDE2,__..__..__..__..__..__..__..__..__..
    A,0.25,−0.125,0,−0.125,0,−0.125

The first line of the definition is the name of the linetype followed by a keyboard-generated approximation of the appearance of the linetype. This approach is optional; you can use a simple text description instead if you wish. A reasonable description might be "Long dash, two dots, long dash," or something along these lines. Any description should stay under 47 characters in length.

The second line is the actual descriptive code for the linetype. Every linetype definition starts with the "A," which specifies the alignment style. AutoCAD LT only supports A type alignment. This ensures that lines and arcs made using noncontinuous lines both start and end on a dash sequence, and not on an empty space. When constructing linetypes at the command line, A type alignment is automatically entered. The sequence of numbers in the description represents the PEN DOWN and PEN UP distances used as a model for the linetype. Positive numbers are Pen Down, and negative numbers are Pen Up distances. The terms Pen Down and Pen Up may be easier to understand by observing a pen plotter. *Pen Down* means that your pen is in contact with the media and you are drawing. *Pen Up* indicates that the pen is not in contact with the paper, so it is moving but not drawing. To put it in simple terms, pen down distance is dash length, and pen up distance is gap length.

A careful look at the DIVIDE2 linetype shows that the specification indicates a 0.25 dash, a 0.125 gap, a 0 length dash (dot), another 0.125 gap, another dot, and finally a 0.125 gap before the sequence repeats. Using this information as a model, this example places a short dash between the two dots in a new linetype named SAMPLE:

Name of linetype to create: **SAMPLE**↵

CHAPTER 17 ||| Customizing AutoCAD LT

Wait, checking if linetype already defined …
Descriptive text: An example of creating simple linetypes.
Enter pattern (on next line):
   A,0.25,−.125,0,−.125,.125,−.125,0,−.125↵
New definition written to file.
?/Create/Load/Set: ↵
Command:

Figure 17.43 shows the two linetypes side by side for an easy comparison. Study this figure, along with the actual linetype definitions shown above.

FIGURE 17.43 A comparison between the DIVIDE2 and SAMPLE linetypes.

Once a linetype has been defined, it is saved in a linetype file and can be loaded in any drawing as desired.

Field Notes

- Linetype definition files are simple ASCII text files and can be directly edited using Notepad or any other text editor.
- The ACLT.LIN file is the primary linetype definition file, and the ACLTISO.LIN file is provided for those using ISO drafting standards.

Exercise 17.19

1. Use the LINETYPE command to create a new linetype that has a long dash, short dash, dot, short dash and repeats, as follows:

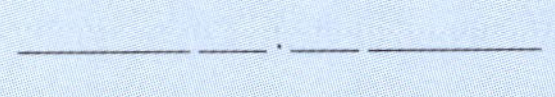

   _____ ___ . ___ _____

2. Find a linetype to use as a template and list its definition for reference.
3. Call the new linetype EX17.19, and save it in a linetype definition file named CHAP17.LIN.

Complex linetypes are not quite as easy to create as simple linetypes, but the Pen Up/Pen Down information is handled exactly the same. To work with complex linetypes, you must open the linetype definition file with a text editor. The complex linetype section of the ACLT.LIN file is shown here:

```
;; Complex linetypes
;;
;; Complex linetypes have been added to this file.
;; These linetypes were defined in LTYPESHP.LIN in
;; Release 13, and are incorporated in ACAD.LIN in
;; Release 14.
;;
;; These linetype definitions use LTYPESHP.SHX.
;;
*FENCELINE1,Fenceline circle ,----0,----0,----0,----0,----0,----0,----
A,.25,-.1,[CIRC1,ltypeshp.shx,x=-.1,s=.1],-.1,1
*FENCELINE2,Fenceline square ,----[],----[],----[],----[],----[],----
A,.25,-.1,[BOX,ltypeshp.shx,x=-.1,s=.1],-.1,1
*TRACKS,Tracks -|-|-|-|-|-|-|-|-|-|-|-|-|-|-|-|-|-|-|-|-|-
A,.15,[TRACK1,ltypeshp.shx,s=.25],.15
```

```
*BATTING,Batting
SSSSSSSSSSSSSSSSSSSSSSSSSSSSSSSSSSSSSSSSSSS
A,.0001,–.1,[BAT,ltypeshp.shx,x=–.1,s=.1],–.2,[BAT,ltypeshp.shx,r=180,x=.1,s=.1],–.1
*HOT_WATER_SUPPLY,Hot water supply —— HW —— HW —— HW ——
A,.5,–.2,["HW",STANDARD,S=.1,R=0.0,X=–0.1,Y=–.05],–.2
*GAS_LINE,Gas line ,----GAS,----GAS,----GAS,----GAS,----GAS,----
A,.5,–.2,["GAS",STANDARD,S=.1,R=0.0,X=–0.1,Y=–.05],–.25
*ZIGZAG,Zig zag /\/\/\/\/\/\/\/\/\/\/\/\/\/\
A,.0001,–.2,[ZIG,ltypeshp.shx,x=–.2,s=.2],–.4,[ZIG,ltypeshp.shx,r=180,x=.2,s=.2],–.2
```

In addition to simple Pen Up/Pen Down information, complex linetypes also allow for text elements and shapes from shape definition files. Shapes and the shape definition file are discussed later.

The easiest way to begin creating your own complex linetypes is to start by modifying existing linetypes. The following example helps to explain the various elements of a complex linetype definition:

```
*HOT_WATER_SUPPLY,----HW----HW----HW----HW----HW----
A,.5,−.2,["HW",STANDARD,S=.1,R=0.0,X=−0.1,Y=−.05],−.2
```

The first line is exactly the same as in a simple linetype definition. The linetype name and a text description. When creating a linetype at the command line, some of the entries are made automatically by AutoCAD LT. The asterisk in front of the linetype name, for example. This, along with the A specification for alignment, is one of the required elements that is automatically entered in the definition for you when you define the linetype at the command line. When you are directly editing the definition file, none of these entries is made automatically. Pay special attention to each detail to make sure that nothing is overlooked as you define new complex linetypes.

The second line starts out with the A for the alignment specification, and then defines the appearance of the linetype. A 0.5 pen down is followed by a 0.2 pen up. Within the square brackets is the text item definition, followed by another gap of 0.2 before the pattern repeats. The required elements within the text definition are the actual text, in quotation marks, and the text style name to use. Five additional parameters can be used to assign the desired properties to the text, as follows:

S=   Specifies a scale factor.
R=   Specifies a relative rotation angle.
A=   Specifies an absolute rotation angle.
X=   Specifies an offset distance in the X axis to aid in locating the text. The text is inserted lower-left justified, and the offsets are used to center the text within a gap.
Y=   Specifies an offset distance in the Y axis.

Based on this format, the text defined in the Hot_Water_Supply linetype places the text "HW" using the STANDARD text style. The text height is 0.1 times the height described in the style definition. If a height of 0 is used for the style definition, the scale value becomes an absolute height. Whether relative or absolute, text size is scaled using the current object and global linetype scales. The relative rotation of 0 degrees ensures that the text maintains its orientation relative to the line direction. The X and Y offset values help to center the text properly.

```
["HW",STANDARD,S=.1,R=0.0,X=−0.1,Y=−.05]
```

To create a similar linetype that can be used for the cold water lines, the first step is to copy the existing HW linetype definition. For this example, the rest is easy. Simply change the H to a C. However, few modifications are this simple. To demonstrate a more challenging example, the next sequence creates a linetype to represent sewage lines. This new linetype is to use the text SEWER in the line gaps. If the HW line is modified by simply changing the HW to SEWER, the resulting linetype does not look correct, as shown in Figure 17.44. Two adjustments need to be made to this linetype. First, the gap is widened to fit the longer text string, and the dash length is increased proportionally so as not to change the appearance of the line too much. Next, the text offsets must be adjusted to center the longer text string. The new linetype definition looks like this:

```
*SEWER_LINES,----SEWER----SEWER----SEWER----SEWER----
A,.7,−.3,["SEWER",STANDARD,S=.1,R=0.0,X=−0.25,Y=−.05],−.3
```

Compare this with the definition of the Hot_Water_Supply linetype. Figure 17.45 shows the Sewer_Lines linetype after the changes are made to accommodate the longer text string. Almost any requirements can be met for creating new linetypes by using an existing linetype as a template and adjusting it as needed to make the necessary changes.

FIGURE 17.44 Some modifications require more work than simply changing the text value.

FIGURE 17.45 Adjusting the parameters of existing linetype definitions is the fastest and easiest way to create new linetypes.

Exercise 17.20

1. Using the GAS linetype as a template, create a new linetype by substituting the text string "CABLE" for "GAS."
2. Make the necessary adjustments to the gap and modify the dashes to maintain the correct appearance for the linetype.
3. Adjust the X and Y offset values to center the text in the gap.
4. Load the new linetype and draw several objects using it.
5. Save the drawing as EX17.20.

A shape is a special type of object that is defined using the same system used to define text fonts. AutoCAD LT comes with a shape definition file named LTYPESHP.SHX, which defines the shapes used by some of the complex linetypes. This shape file contains only five shapes, named as follows:

TRACK1
ZIG
BOX
CIRC1
BAT

This does not allow for a large number of options for creating linetypes using shapes. The following example creates a third fence line linetype, using both the BOX and the CIRC1 shapes. Because the existing parameters work well in the other two fence line linetypes, they are reused here:

```
*FENCELINE3,----0----[]----0----[]----
A,.25,[CIRC1,ltypeshp.shx,s=.1],-.2,1.25,[BOX,ltypeshp.shx,s=.1],-.2,1
```

The first entry in the shape specification is the name of the shape followed by the name of the shape file that contains its definition. Shapes use the same type of modifiers as text strings, including Scale, Rotation, X-Offset, and Y-Offset. Figure 17.46 shows the appearance of this linetype.

FIGURE 17.46 The FENCELINE3 linetype uses elements of both the FENCELINE1 and FENCELINE2 linetype definitions.

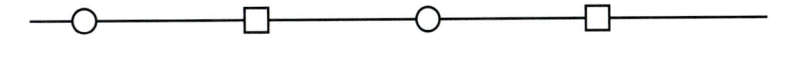

> ✏️ **Field Notes**
>
> If your office or school also has installations of AutoCAD, you can design new shapes and compile new shape definition files. Check the AutoCAD documentation regarding creating shapes, and look into these commands: SHAPE, LOAD, and COMPILE.

Exercise 17.21

1. Open the file ACLT.LIN for editing using Notepad.
2. Using the FENCELINE1 and 2 definitions as a reference, create a new linetype named FENCELINE3 that uses a pattern of dash, circle, dash, circle, dash, square, and repeats:

   ——o——o——[]——o——o——[]——

3. Save the linetype in a new linetype definition file named CHAP17C.LIN.
4. Load the new linetype and draw several objects. Save the drawing as EX17.21.

☑ LEARNING CHECKPOINT

- ☐ What is the difference between simple and complex linetypes?
- ☐ Explain what PEN UP and PEN DOWN distances refer to and how they are specified in a linetype definition.
- ☐ What are the two primary linetype definition files?
- ☐ What parameters are available to control the appearance of text and shapes in a complex linetype?
- ☐ Define A type alignment.
- ☐ What is a shape and where are they found?

Defining Custom Hatch Patterns

AutoCAD LT comes with an extensive library of hatch patterns but, like linetypes, a multitude of applications exist that require specialized applications. The capability to create new hatch patterns is just one additional way in which AutoCAD LT can be customized to meet almost any need. AutoCAD LT's default hatch patterns are stored in the file ACLT.PAT. The .PAT file extension is used for all hatch pattern definition files. Custom patterns can be defined within the ACLT.PAT file or in a separate file. A .PAT file is an ASCII text file and can be edited with your text editor. If defined in a separate file, only a single pattern is defined in each file and the pattern name and file name must match. As an example, a pattern named TESTPAT needs to be defined in a file named TESTPAT.PAT.

The format for a hatch pattern listing is similar to a linetype definition file: The name is preceded by an asterisk, and a text-based description follows. One of the simplest pattern definitions in the ACLT.PAT file is for the following ANSI31 pattern:

*ANSI31, ANSI Iron, Brick, Stone masonry
45, 0,0, 0,.125

where the *ANSI31 entry indicates the pattern name, and the ANSI Iron, Brick, Stone masonry provides a brief text description of what the pattern represents. The additional lines represent that actual pattern definition, which in this case fits all on one line. Each line of the definition for a pattern describes one of its vectors. The ANSI31 pattern has only one vector, which is repeated as needed to fill a specified area.

The first entry in the pattern definition (45,) specifies the angle for drawing the vector being described. The next entry is an X,Y coordinate, in this case 0,0. The snap base setting is what AutoCAD LT uses to determine where the pattern fill should begin, and this determines where this particular vector is drawn from in relationship to the snap base. Finally, the third entry in this definition is another X,Y coordinate value

CHAPTER 17 ||| Customizing AutoCAD LT   **723**

that determines the offset for the next instance of this vector. In other words, with a setting of 0,0.125, the next vector begins at the same X coordinate as the previous vector, but the Y axis distance is 0.125 units from the start point of the previous instance. For this offset calculation, the direction of the line is considered to be the X axis. Therefore, the Y offset specifies the distance between parallel copies of the vector, and the X offset is meaningful only when working with dashed hatch lines. Figure 17.47 demonstrates this concept.

FIGURE 17.47 The starting point for the vector and the offset distance for a hatch pattern control its final appearance.

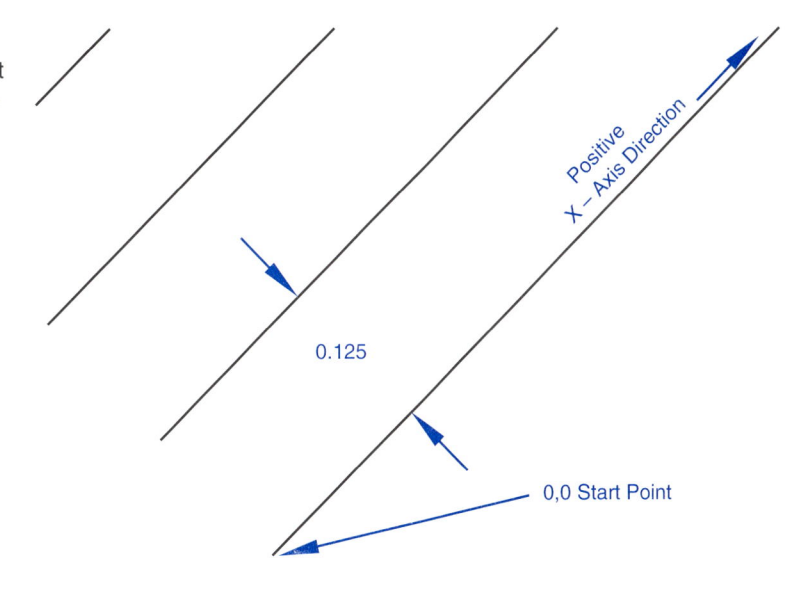

All hatch patterns are defined as vectors. A *vector* is a distance and angle that describe a straight line. By combining lines of various lengths at the appropriate angles, virtually any pattern can be created. Most patterns, however, do not have only continuous lines as with the ANSI31 pattern. Most patterns require a Pen Down and Pen Up style description to allow for dashed hatch lines. The dash length specifications are appended to the pattern definition after the offset values. For example, to draw a dashed version of the ANSI31 pattern that is the same angle and spacing but has 0.75 dashes separated by 0.25 gaps, the following is added to the pattern definition:

*45D, A 45 degree dashed pattern
45, 0,0, 0,.125, **0.75,−0.25**

The circle in Figure 17.48 is hatched using the 45D pattern defined. Notice that, like linetype definitions, Pen Down is a positive number and Pen Up is a negative number. A maximum of six dash length specifications can be used in a single line of the pattern definition.

FIGURE 17.48 Adding a Pen Up and Pen Down specification to the ANSI31 pattern creates a dashed pattern.

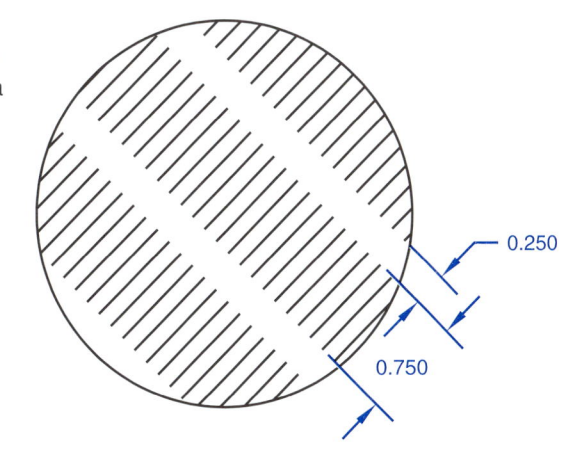

The pattern name is specified as 45D, so the definition is saved in a file named 45D.PAT that has been placed in one of the AutoCAD LT support directories.

Now that a dashed pattern is being used, the effect of an X offset value can be seen. The 45D pattern definition is changed as follows to produce the pattern shown in Figure 17.49.

*45D, A 45 degree dashed pattern
45, 0,0, **0.5**,.125, 0.75, −0.25

By using X and Y offset distances, Pen Up and Pen Down specifications, and a combination of lines at different angles, very complex hatch patterns can be created. The easiest way to get started creating a hatch pattern is to first draw the intended pattern in AutoCAD LT. Using AutoCAD LT inquiry commands, the lengths, angles, and distances can be easily determined and placed in a pattern file.

For example, using the POLYGON command, the hexagon shown in Figure 17.50 can easily be constructed as the basis for a tiled hexagonal like the standard pattern named "Honeycomb." After drawing it, use the EXPLODE command to reduce it to individual line objects for easier inquiries.

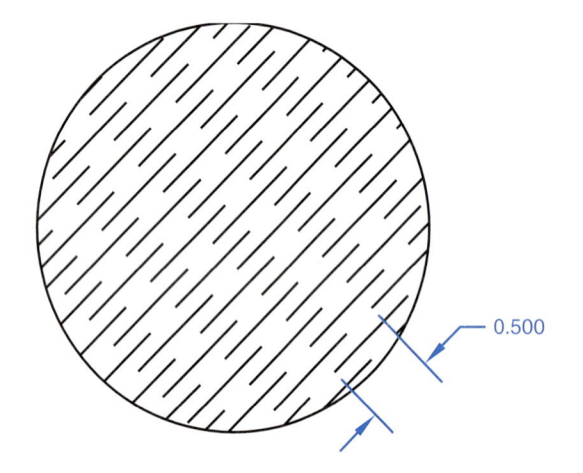

FIGURE 17.49 The X offset values can be used in dashed line pattern definitions.

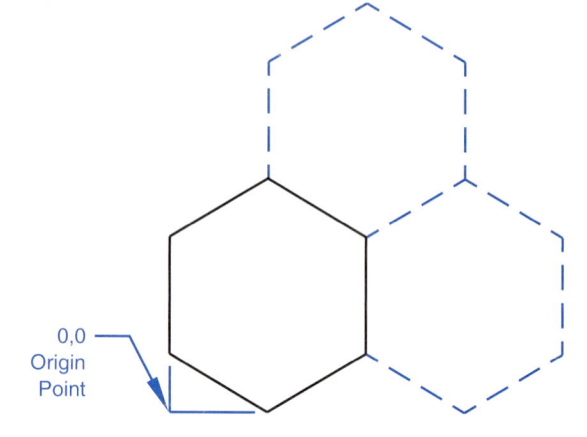

FIGURE 17.50 Drawing the hatch pattern first makes it easier to create because you can use the AutoCAD LT inquiry tools instead of a calculator to determine the required data for the pattern.

In the following example, a file named HEXAGON.PAT is to be created with a definition for a hatch pattern also named HEXAGON. The first line of the pattern definition names the pattern and provides a brief description. The description should be 80 characters or less in length:

*HEXAGON, A tiled hexagon pattern.

The order in which the lines are listed in a pattern definition is not critical. The important factor is to be sure that all of the data are entered and entered correctly. In Figure 17.50, notice the placement of the hexagon in relationship to the 0,0 origin point. This makes it easier to work with the numbers received from inquiry commands. The added hexagons are shown to help determine offsets and dash lengths, but it is only necessary to define the first hexagon. The rest are automatically calculated based on offsets and dash length.

The first objective in this example is to define the vertical line on the left. Using the LIST command in AutoCAD LT, the following information is provided:

LINE Layer: 0
Space: Model space
Handle = 3BB
from point, X= 0.0000 Y= 0.8660 Z= 0.0000
to point, X= 0.0000 Y= 0.2887 Z= 0.0000
Length = 0.5774, Angle in XY Plane = 270
Delta X = 0.0000, Delta Y = −0.5774, Delta Z = 0.0000

The information needed in the hatch pattern definition is shown in bold text, and includes the start point, length, and angle of the line. So, the first part of the definition looks like this:

*HEXAGON, A tiled hexagon pattern.
270, 0,0.866,

CHAPTER 17 ||| Customizing AutoCAD LT

The next entries in the pattern definition are for the offsets. Figure 17.51 shows how the offsets for this line are determined. After adding the X and Y offsets to the pattern definition, the dash lengths are specified. From the previous LIST command, it is known that the Pen Down length for this line is .5774. Using the DIST command, the Pen Up distance can be determined. Figure 17.52 shows where the 1.1547 measurement for the Pen Up distance was determined.

Completing the definition for this line, the pattern definition now appears as follows:

*HEXAGON, A tiled hexagon pattern.
270, 0,0.866, 0.866,0.5, 0.5774,−1.1547

Because of the combination of offsets and dashes, this first line definition actually creates two of the parallel lines for the hexagon. To see what the pattern looks like so far, it can be saved and used as is. Figure 17.53 shows the partial hatch pattern created by this definition.

FIGURE 17.51 To determine offsets, find the position where this line is repeated in the pattern and measure the X and Y offset values.

FIGURE 17.52 Use the DIST command to determine the Pen Up distances.

FIGURE 17.53 It can be helpful to check hatch pattern definitions one line at a time, in order to avoid errors. This is the effect of the first line of the HEXAGON pattern definition.

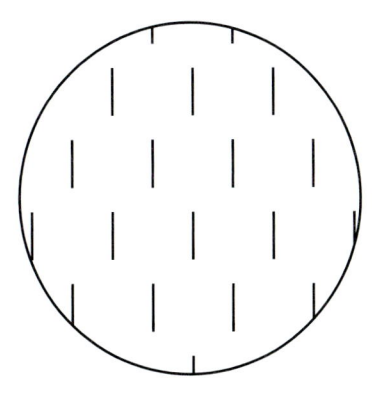

> **Field Notes**
>
> When constructing a hatch pattern, testing as you go is a good idea. Hatch a simple shape in the drawing editor using the new pattern definition and specifying an *associative* hatch. Each time you make a modification and save the definition file, return to AutoCAD LT and pick a grip point to make a minor adjustment in the boundary. When AutoCAD LT updates the pattern, it reads the definition file again and automatically implements your latest changes.

Using the LIST command for the next line provides this information:

LINE   Layer: 0
Space: Model space
Handle = 3BA
from point, X= 0.5000 Y= 1.1547 Z= 0.0000
to point, X= 0.0000 Y= 0.8660 Z= 0.0000
Length = 0.5774, **Angle in XY Plane= 210**
Delta X = −0.5000, Delta Y = −0.2887, Delta Z = 0.0000

Each line in a hexagon is the same length, and all of the offsets and dash lengths are the same. The necessary information from this listing is the start point and the angle of the line. Modifying the pattern definition as follows produces the pattern shown in Figure 17.54.

*HEXAGON, A tiled hexagon pattern.
270, 0,0.866, 0.866,0.5, 0.5774,−1.1547
210, 0.5,1.1547, 0.866,0.5, 0.5774,−1.1547

FIGURE 17.54 Updating the hatch pattern in the drawing produces this result.

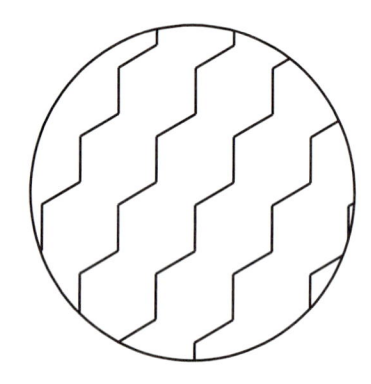

Finally, listing the third line provides the information needed to complete the pattern definition as shown here:

*HEXAGON, A tiled hexagon pattern.
270, 0,0.866, 0.866,0.5, 0.5774,−1.1547
210, 0.5,1.1547, 0.866,0.5, 0.5774,−1.1547
330, 0,0.2887, 0.866,0.5, 0.5774,−1.1547

Saving the pattern file and updating the pattern in the drawing produces the results shown in Figure 17.55.

FIGURE 17.55 The final appearance of the HEXAGON hatch pattern definition.

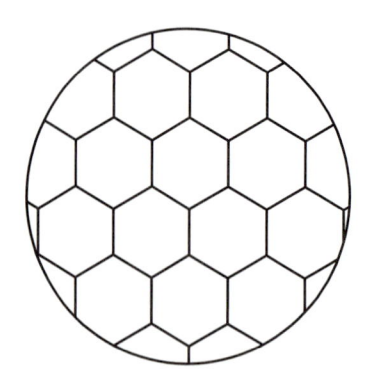

CHAPTER 17 ||| Customizing AutoCAD LT   727

Exercise 17.22

1. Create a hatch pattern definition called OFFSQR in a file of the same name.
2. The pattern will be of a 1-unit by 1-unit square, offset by .5 units, as shown in the following illustration:

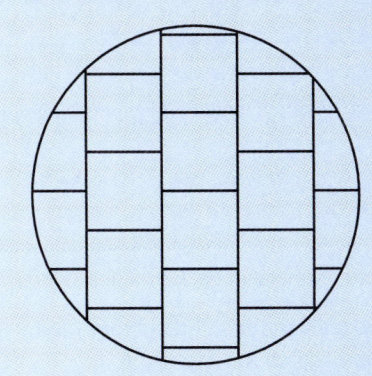

3. Save the file and text the new hatch pattern.

MULTIPLE CHOICE

Circle the choice or enter your response on an answer sheet by selecting the option that most closely completes or answers the given statements.

1. Files that are not part of the core program, which are used to enhance or modify the way AutoCAD LT works, are called:
   a. support files
   b. drawing files
   c. initialization files
   d. backup files grid

2. The PGP file stores definitions for:
   a. pull-down menus
   b. toolbar buttons
   c. command aliases
   d. hatch patterns

3. A text file that contains a list of commands and options that AutoCAD LT reads and performs is called a(n):
   a. menu file
   b. option list
   c. command script
   d. text file

4. This is the file extension for the primary file that is edited when making changes to the AutoCAD LT menu system:
   a. MNU
   b. MNS
   c. MNC
   d. MNR

5. This command is used in AutoCAD LT to load menu files:
   a. MENU
   b. MENULOAD
   c. LOADMENU
   d. LOAD

6. When loading menus, the menu file with this file extension is typically avoided:
   a. MNU
   b. MNS
   c. MNC
   d. MNR

7. AutoCAD LT cannot load multiple menus that use the same:
   a. file name
   b. MENUGROUP name
   c. buttons menu
   d. icon images

8. The menu section named POP0 contains the code for which menu?
   a. the buttons menu
   b. the cursor menu
   c. the first pull-down menu
   d. the help menu

9. The characters used in the menu label to begin and end cascade sections are:
   a. -/ /-
   b. >> <<
   c. ( )
   d. -> <-

10. A linetype definition file has this file extension:
    a. .ltd
    b. .lin
    c. .ldf
    d. .lts

MATCHING

Match each term to the correct description by writing the appropriate number in each box at the left.

☐ DIESEL
☐ Cascade
☐ Macro
☐ .MNR
☐ .MNU
☐ .MNC
☐ .MNS
☐ Partial menu
☐ POP
☐ IMAGE
☐ .LIN
☐ .PAT
☐ .SCR
☐ .SLD
☐ .SLB

1. File extension for a slide library file.
2. Menu resource file extension.
3. Menu template file extension.
4. Compiled menu file extension.
5. A supplementary menu file.
6. Menu section for pull-down menus.
7. Menu section for image tile menus.
8. File extension for a linetype definition file.
9. File extension for a menu source file.
10. File extension for a script file.
11. A pull-down menu feature.
12. A menu selection that does more than one task.
13. File extension for a slide file.
14. Direct Interpretively Evaluated String Expression Language.
15. Hatch pattern definition file extension.

CHAPTER 17 ||| Customizing AutoCAD LT

WORD SCRAMBLE

Unscramble the six scrambled words below, one letter to each square, to form six AutoCAD LT–related words:

ZITUSCOME

CROMA

EIZNITRIALIE

TEGPSHLIRN

DESCACA

FOULTY

Ctrl + O

Unscramble the circled letters above to form the special answer as suggested by the illustration.

PROJECTS

17.1 Open the ACLT.PGP file with Notepad. Add six new command aliases of your choice to the file. As you consider your options for the alias definitions, select the options that will best benefit you in your day-to-day drafting needs. Save the PGP file and use the REINIT command to reinitialize the PGP file. Test each of your alias definitions and make any necessary corrections.

17.2 Using Notepad, create a script file for a C size drawing setup. The script file should set units, limits, grid, snap, all layer settings, and any other settings that you think should be included. Then it should insert the correct title block in paper space. Save the script file as P17.2.SCR and test it in a new drawing. Make any necessary corrections and save the file again.

17.3 Create block definitions for the symbols shown in the figure below. Now, create a toolbar with a button for each of the symbols. Use a value of 1.0 for "h." When selected, the toolbar button should insert the symbol, allowing the user to specify the insertion point, scale factors, and rotation angle. Create an appropriate graphic on the toolbar buttons for both large and small buttons. Name the toolbar P17–3.

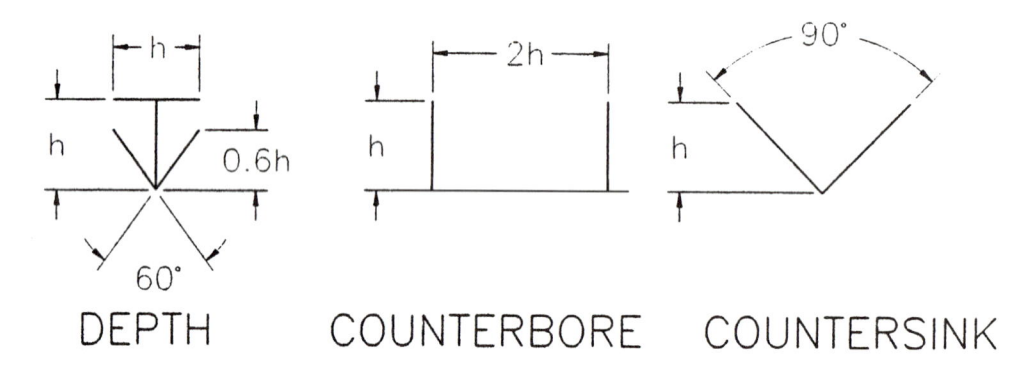

17.4 Create a flyout button and place it on the Dimensioning toolbar. When picked, it should display the P17–3 toolbar you created in Project 17.3.

17.5 Create a partial menu file named P17.MNS using Notepad. The MENUGROUP name should be P17. Create a new pull-down menu named CUSTOM. On the new menu, place four drawing options and four editing options. Include at least one macro in each category. Set up appropriate labeling and mnemonics for each item. Load the partial menu file in a drawing and test each menu option. Make any necessary corrections and save the file again as P17.MNS.

17.6 Open the file P17.MNS for editing in Notepad. Place an IMAGE section in the file, and create appropriate image tiles for at least four common architectural symbols. You will need to create both the geometry and slide images for each of the symbols. Place a menu call in your Custom pull-down menu that displays the image tile menu. Save the file as P17.MNS. Load the partial menu file in a drawing and test each menu option. Make any necessary corrections and save the file again as P17.MNS.

17.7 Using a file manager such as Windows Explorer, make a backup copy of the file ACLT.MNS named ACLT.MNS.BAK. If you need assistance, ask your instructor or system administrator. Open the file ACLT.MNS for editing. Create two new accelerator keystroke definitions in the ACCELERATORS section. Save the file and test the accelerator keystrokes. Make any necessary corrections and save the file again.

17.8 Using Notepad, create a new file named P17–8.LIN. Create a simple linetype definition in this file that has three dashes then three dots. Test the linetype and make any necessary corrections.

17.9 Using Notepad, open P17–8.LIN. Create a complex linetype definition in this file that has a text entry of "P17." Test the linetype and make any necessary corrections.

17.10 Using Notepad, create a file named P17.PAT. Enter a hatch pattern definition for a hexagon pattern. Test the pattern and make any necessary corrections.

APPENDIX A

Installing AutoCAD LT 98

As with most programs designed for the Windows operating system, the installation of AutoCAD LT 98 is automated. This means that the transfer of files from the CD and diskette to your hard disk is done automatically. The Install application creates all of the appropriate directory folders and places the necessary files in the proper locations. However, before you begin installation of the AutoCAD LT 98 software, you should check the system requirements listing to be certain that your system meets the specified requirements.

Checking Your System Requirements

To run AutoCAD LT 98, you need the following software and hardware:

- Windows 95, Windows 98, or Windows NT4
- 486DX/66 (minimum) or Pentium®-based PC
- Mouse/pointer (Microsoft IntelliMouse recommended)
- VGA display or better (800 x 600 display recommended)
- CD-ROM drive
- 16 megabytes of RAM
- 55MB free hard-disk space for full installation
- 32MB free hard-disk space for swap file
- Wintab digitizer (optional)
- 45MB Hard disk space for Internet Explorer (required for on-line help)

Optional Hardware

- Printer or plotter
- Digitizer tablet

Special Requirements

- Microsoft Internet Explorer 4.0 or later is required for on-line help. Internet Explorer will be automatically installed or updated during AutoCAD LT 98 installation if required (an additional 45MB of hard disk space needed). Although Internet Explorer is required, you can still use your existing Web browser for accessing the Internet.

- To view DWF files with Netscape Navigator or Internet Explorer you will need to download and install Release 2 or later of the *Whip!*® browser plug-in. For information on downloading and using *Whip!*, you can visit the Autodesk web site at www.autodesk.com.

731

Before You Begin...

AutoCAD LT is shipped on a single CD-ROM disk. The packaging has a label containing your serial number and the CD key. Be sure to transcribe this information to a safe location for a permanent record copy.

Installing AutoCAD LT 98

The installation CD contains an application named SETUP.EXE. This is the application that installs Auto-CAD LT on your system. To begin the installation:

1. Exit from any applications that are currently running.

2. Place the CD-ROM disk in your CD-ROM drive. This CD has an AutoRun feature that automatically starts the installation program when you load the CD. If it does not automatically start, pick the Run... option from the Start menu on your Windows task bar, use the browse option to navigate to your CD-ROM drive, and run the file named Setup.exe.

3. As the installation begins, the InstallShield® Wizard installation status is reported:

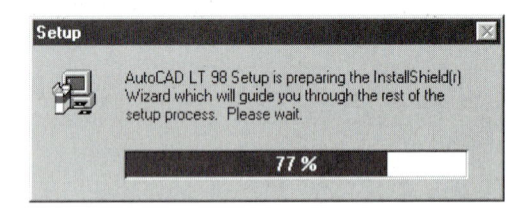

4. The Welcome dialog box reminds you to exit any currently running applications and gives some additional information, as well as copyright warnings. Pick Next > to continue.

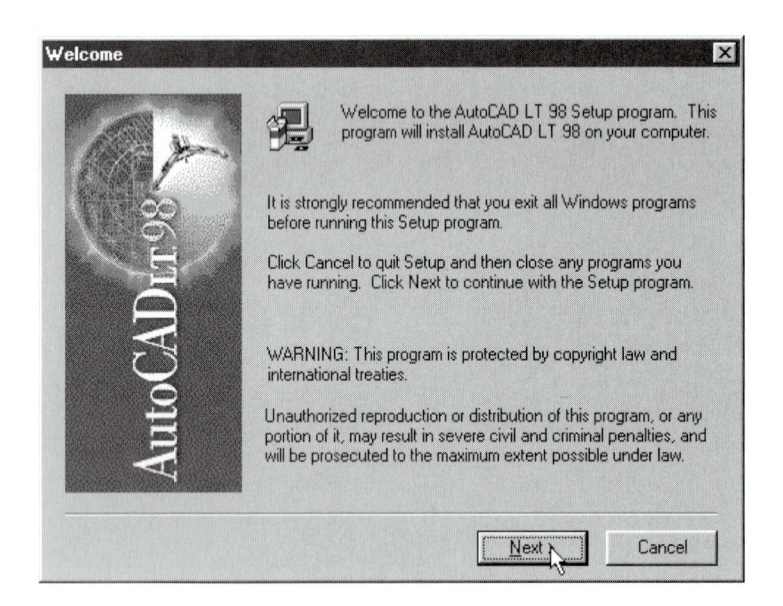

APPENDIX A ||| Installing AutoCAD LT 98

5. Find the serial number and CD Key information on the CD package to complete the next dialog box.

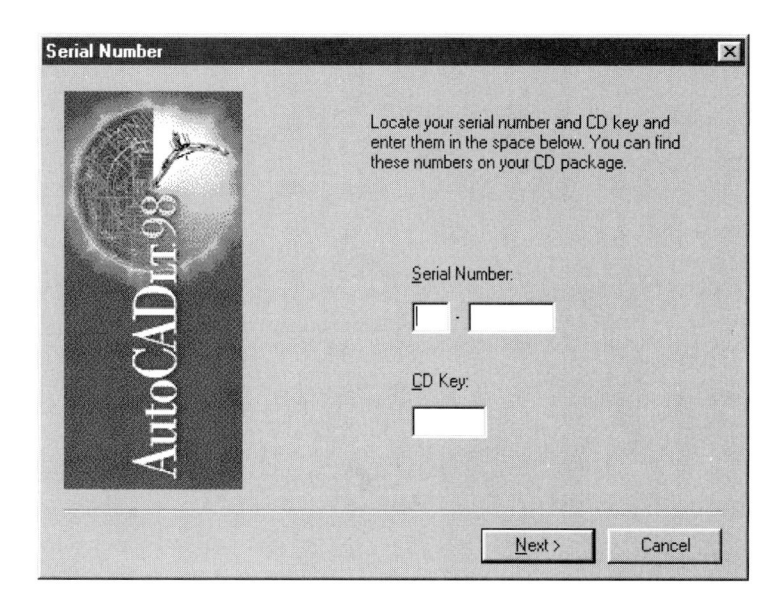

6. The Personal Information dialog box allows you to personalize the installation information.

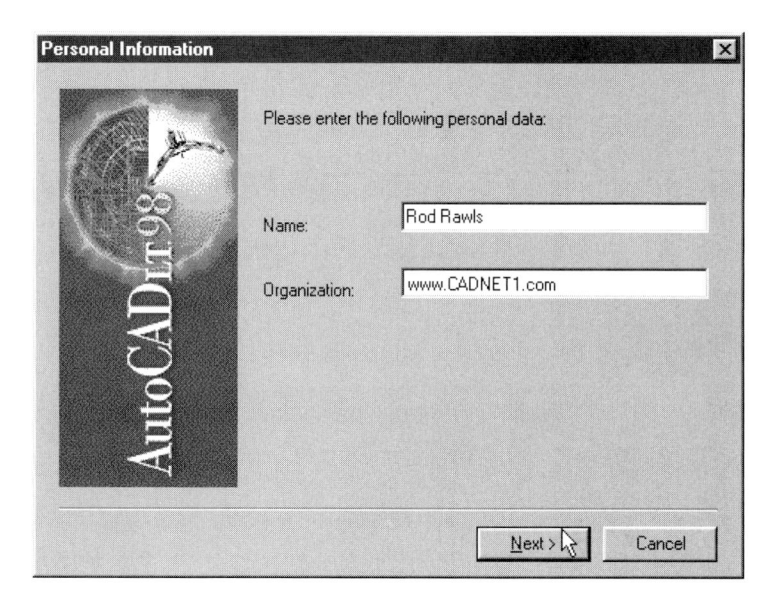

7. If you wish to change the personalization information, pick the < Back button. Otherwise, select Next > to proceed.

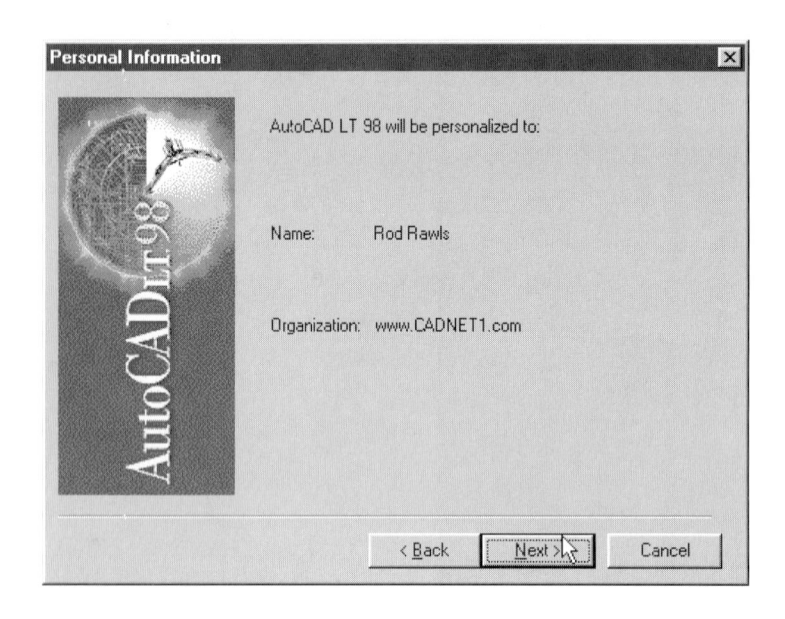

8. You can select the location where AutoCAD LT 98 is installed. Be sure that you select a drive with sufficient disk space available.

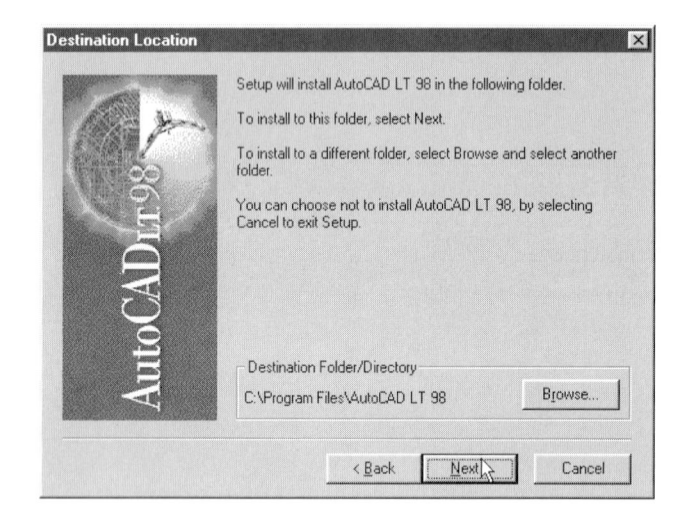

To complete the installation process, the currently logged-in user must have write permission for the folder where AutoCAD LT 98 is to be installed, for the Windows system folder, and for the System Registry. If you need assistance, check with your system administrator or instructor. It is always the best practice to close any programs that are currently running before starting the installation process for any new software application.

APPENDIX A ||| Installing AutoCAD LT 98

9. AutoCAD LT 98 confirms the path specification, asking if the directory location should be created if it does not currently exist:

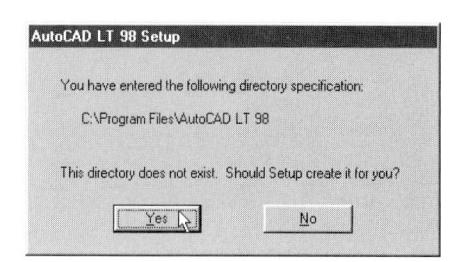

10. Then Specify the type of installation desired. The Typical installation meets the needs of most AutoCAD LT users. The Compact installation is commonly used on laptop computers when available disk space is low and only basic functionality is required. A compact installation does not install tutorials, sample files or dictionary files. Advanced users may wish to explicitly specify what files to install. To do this, select Custom.

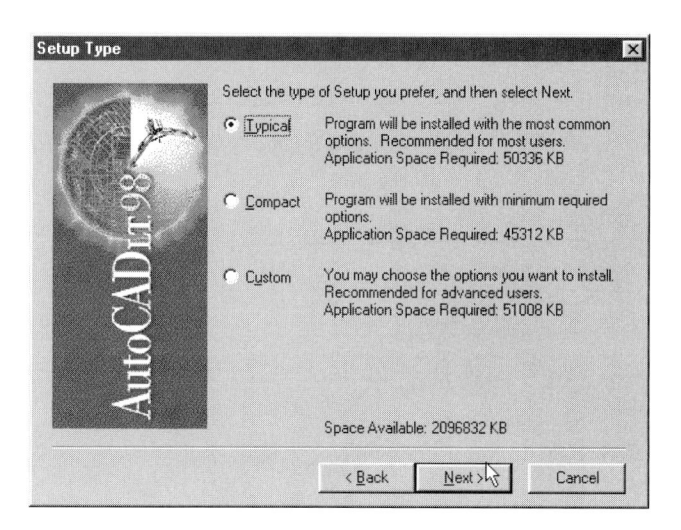

11. The AutoCAD LT 98 installation program verifies that there is sufficient disk space in the selected location:

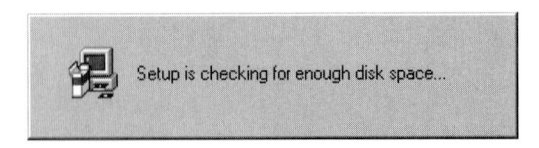

12. By default, AutoCAD LT creates a new program group named AutoCAD LT 98. You can specify a different name for the new group or you can select an existing group for the program icons to be placed in.

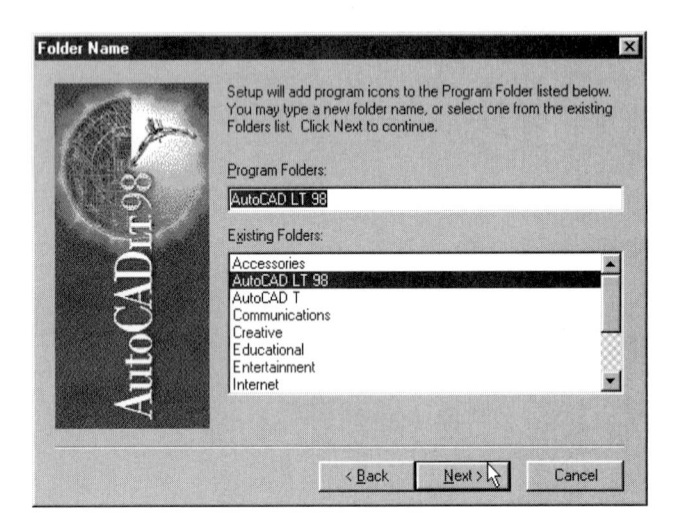

APPENDIX A ||| Installing AutoCAD LT 98

13. You are now prompted for selection of which set of predefined symbols to use as the default symbol set. You can change this later if you choose to, and no matter which selection you make, all the symbol sets are installed. The one that you select will be made the default symbols in the Content Explorer:

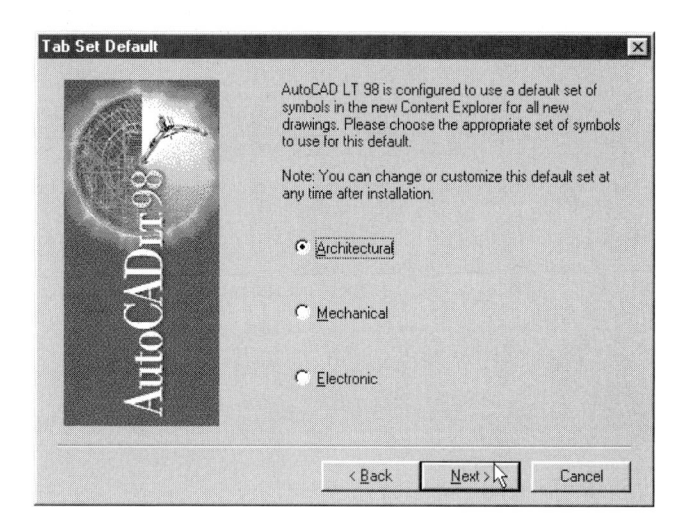

14. This dialog box displays a summary of the installation options you have specified. Select Next > to accept these options and continue, or pick the < Back button to go back and change any desired settings:

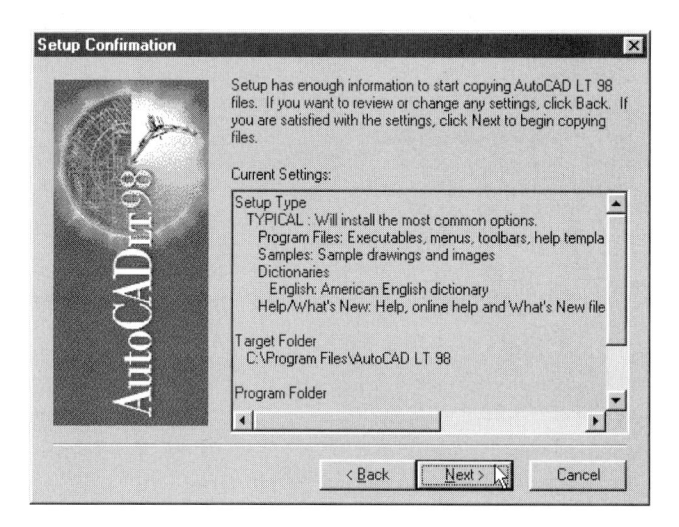

15. The installation process is now underway. A progress meter shows the current percentage towards completion of the setup process. Various banners are displayed that tell you about features found in AutoCAD LT.

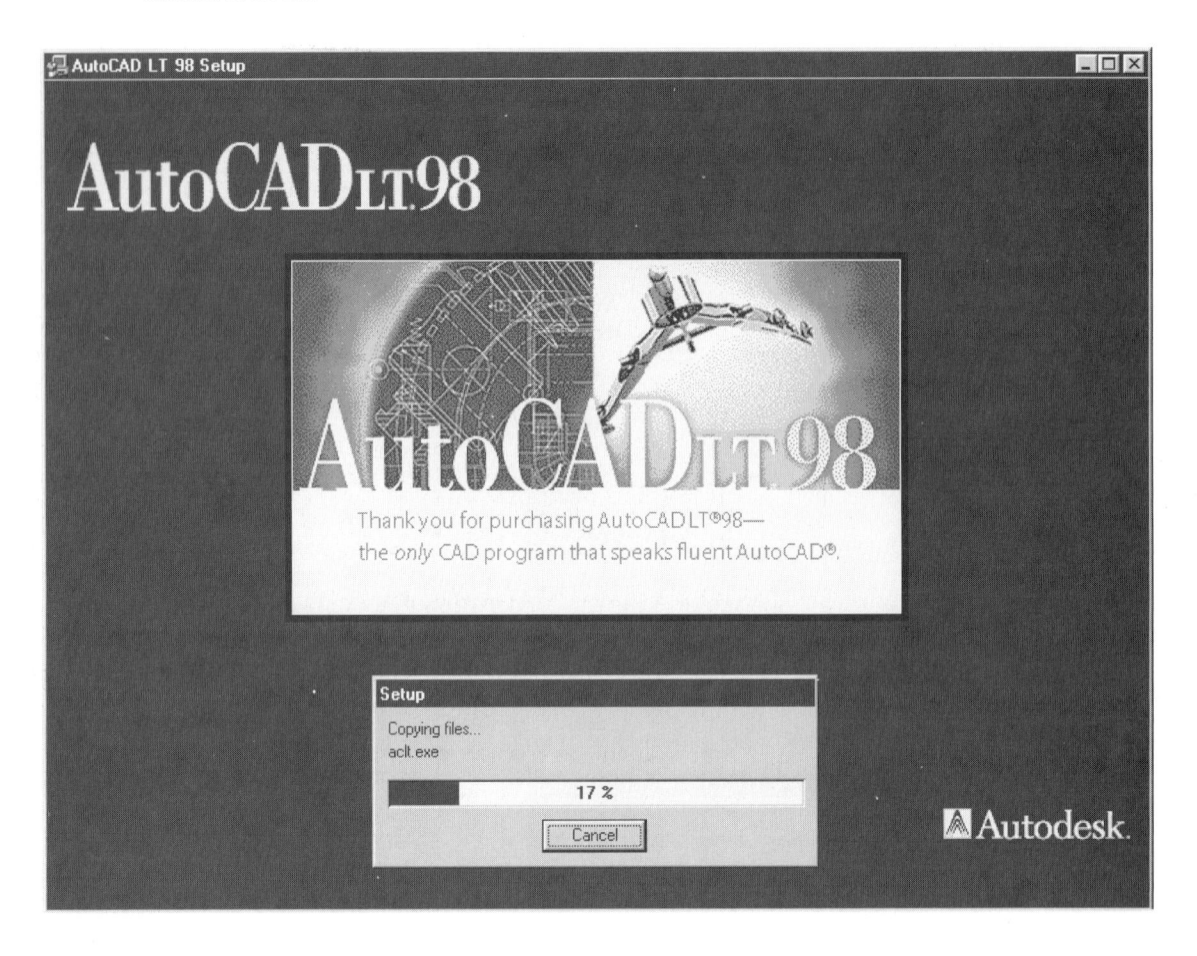

APPENDIX A ||| Installing AutoCAD LT 98

16. The final banner urges you to register your software, which is highly recommended. This enables you to receive any incremental upgrades that are issued and also allows you to receive occasional product information mailings.

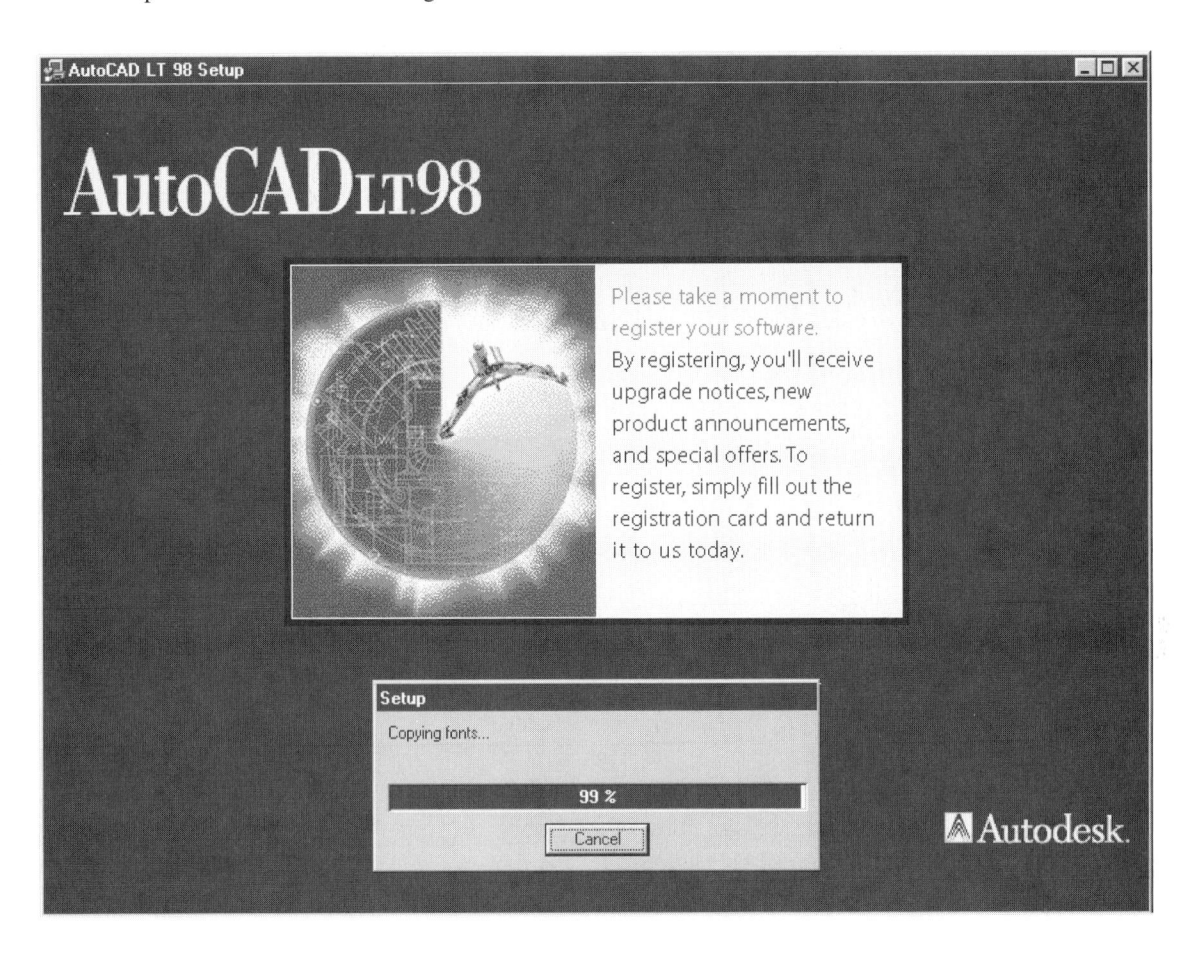

17. When installation is complete, AutoCAD LT asks for permission to restart your system. If you opt to restart your system later, you are offered an opportunity to view the README file. A *README* file contains important information that may not be included in the printed documentation. It is recommended that you look through the README file before using your software.

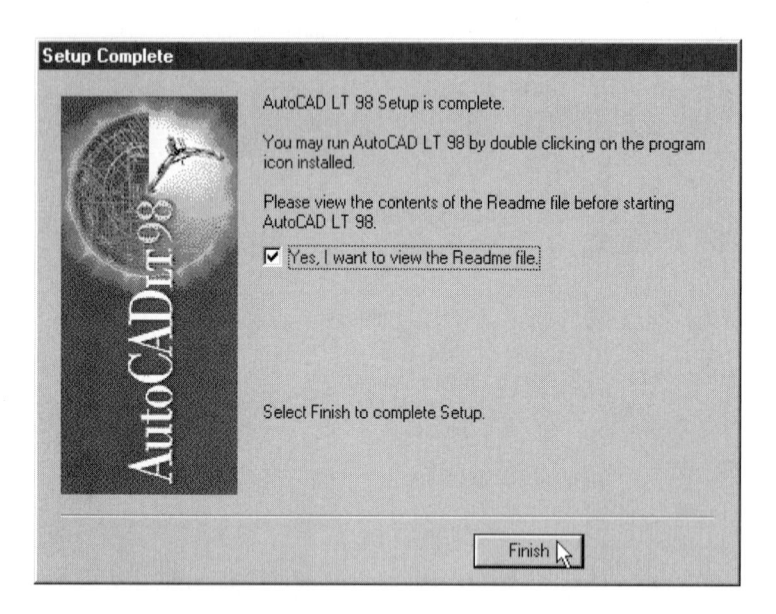

APPENDIX B

Drafting Standards

The following lists provide some of the national drafting standards that are recommended for a variety of disciplines:

Architectural

Architectural Graphic Standards, American Institute of Architects (AIA), John Wiley and Sons, New York.

CAD Layer Guidelines, AIA Press, 1735 New York Avenue, NW, Washington D.C. 20006

Mechanical

American National Standards Institute (ANSI)
11 West 42nd Street
New York, NY 10036

American Society of Mechanical Engineers (ASME)
345 East 47th Street
New York, NY 10017

ANSI Y14.1	*Drawing Sheet Size and Format*
ASME Y14.1M	*Metric Drawing Sheet Size and Format*
ASME Y14.2M	*Line Conventions and Lettering*
ANSI Y14.3	*Multi and Sectional View Drawings*
ASME Y14.5M	*Dimensioning and Tolerancing*
ANSI Y14.6	*Screw Thread Representation*
ANSI Y14.6aM	*Screw Thread Representation Metric Supplement*
ANSI Y14.13M	*Mechanical Spring Representation*
ASME Y14.35M	*Revision of Engineering Drawings and Associated Documents*
ANSI Y14.36	*Surface Texture Symbols*
ANSI/AWS A2.4	*Standard Symbols for Welding, Brazing and Nondestructive Examination*

Technical Illustration

ASME Y14.4M	*Pictorial Drawing*

Electrical and Electronic

ANSI Y14.15	*Electrical and Electronic Diagrams*
ANSI Y31.9	*Graphical Symbols for Electrical Wiring and Layout Diagrams Used in Architecture and Building Construction*

Piping

ASME Y32.2.3	*Graphical Symbols for Pipe Fittings, Valves and Piping*

The following illustrations display the standard inch sheet sizes based on ANSI Y14.1, Drawing Sheet Size and Format, and metric sheet sizes based on ASME Y14.1M, Metric Drawing Sheet Size and Format.

Standard ANSI inch sheet sizes

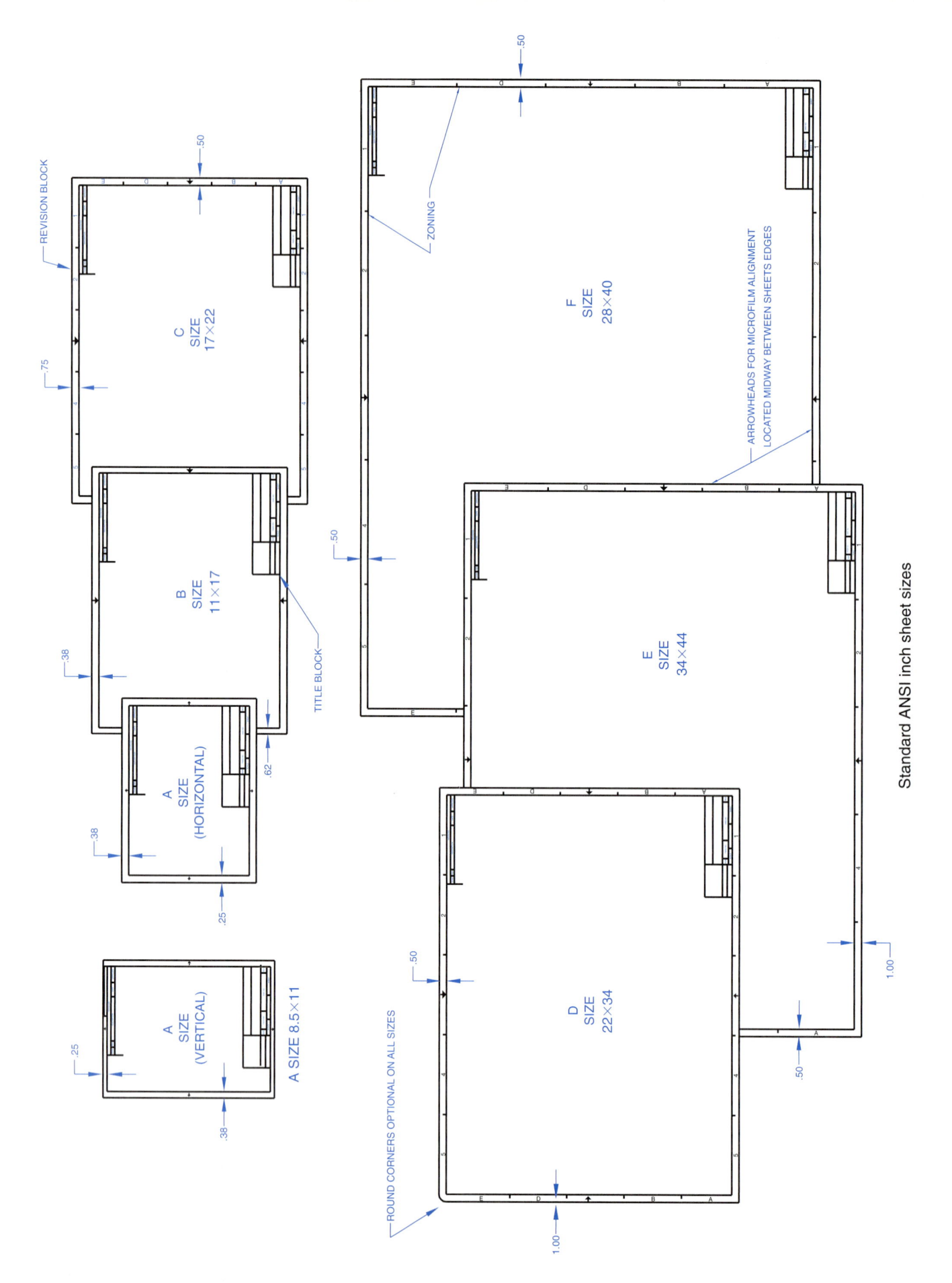

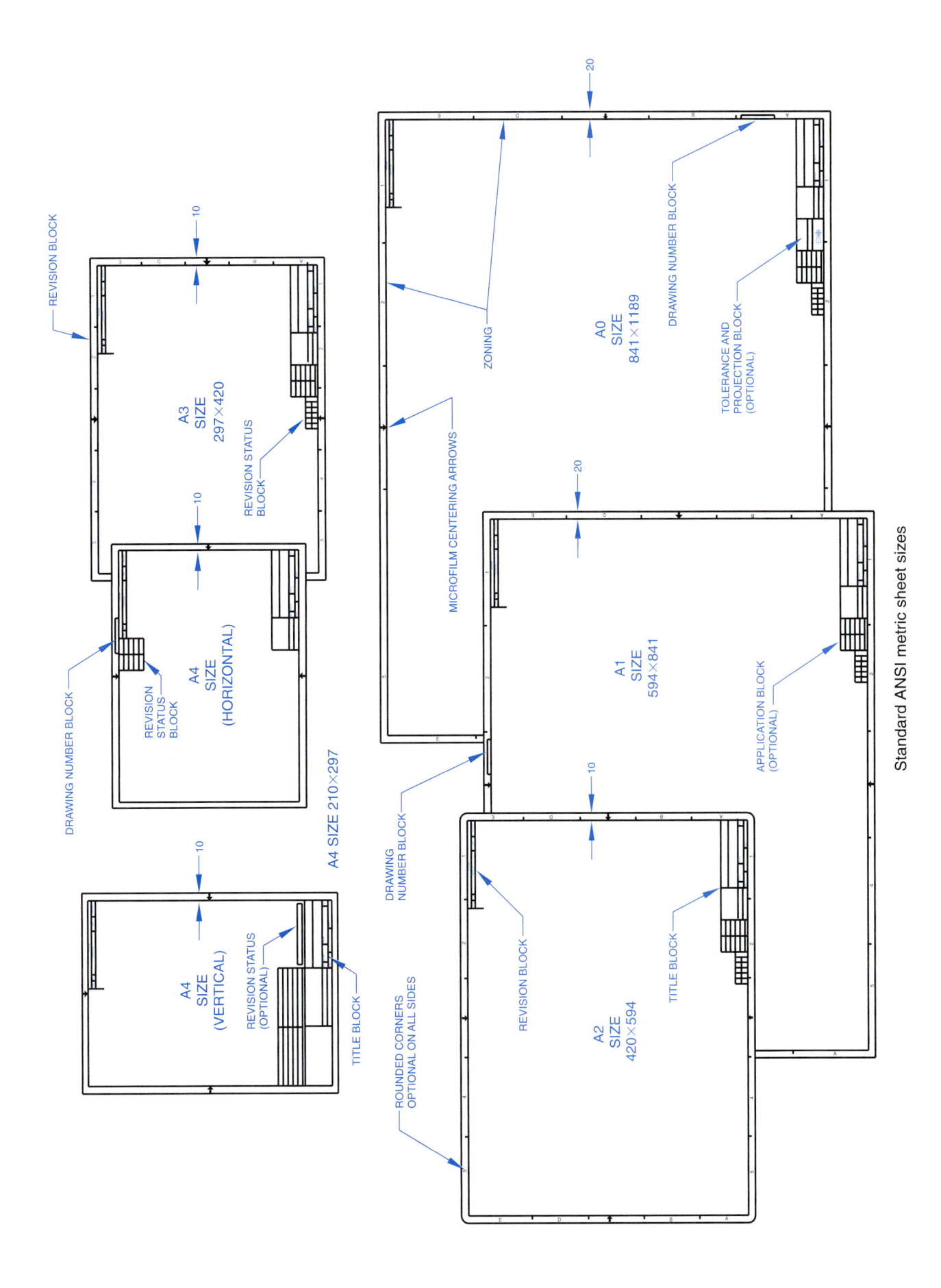

Standard ANSI metric sheet sizes

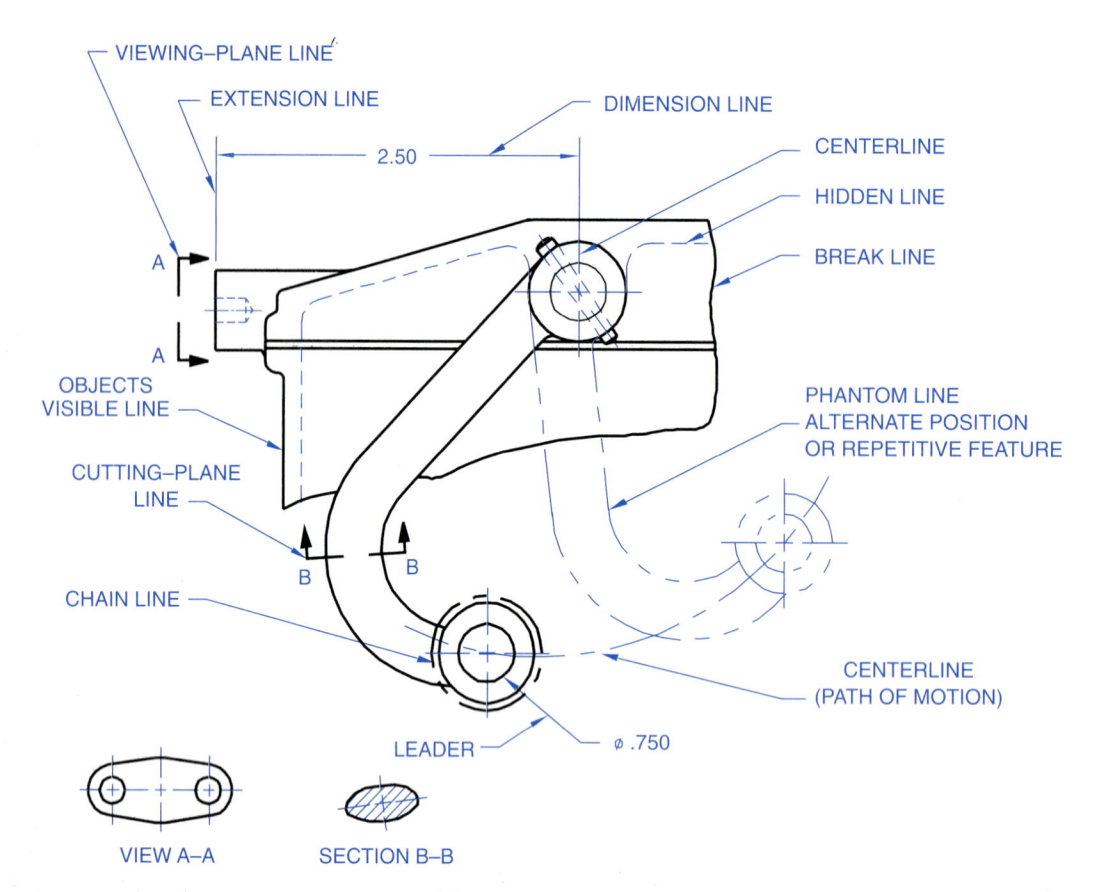

Applications of lines

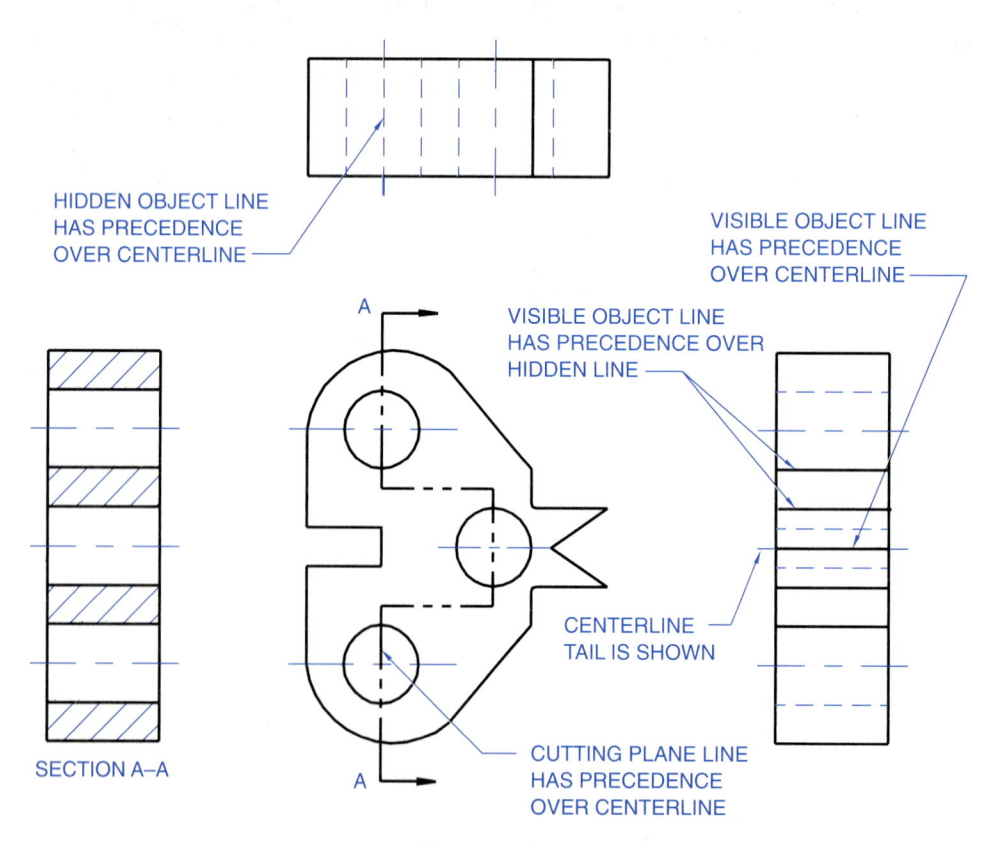

Line precedence

APPENDIX B   Drafting Standards   **745**

Symmetry line applications

Hidden line techniques

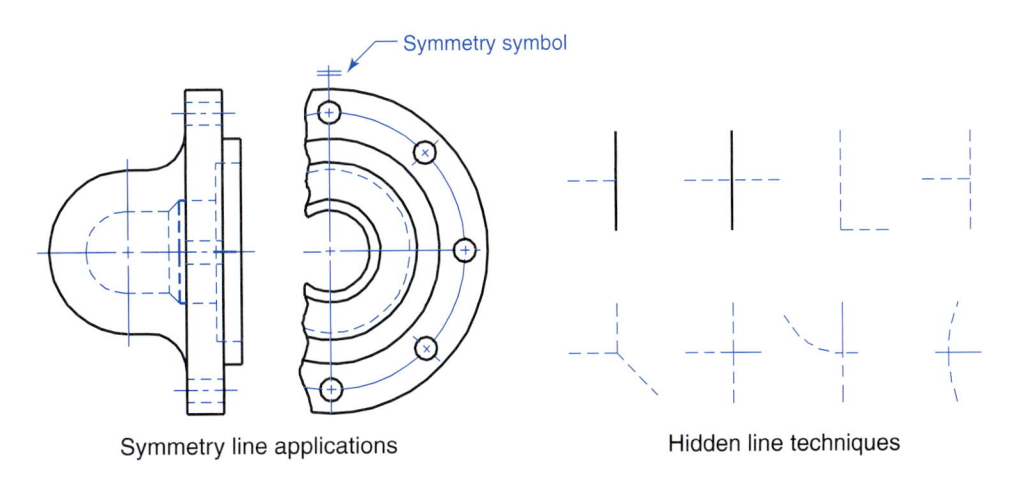

(Some preferred hidden line techniques are difficult to obtain with AutoCAD LT.)

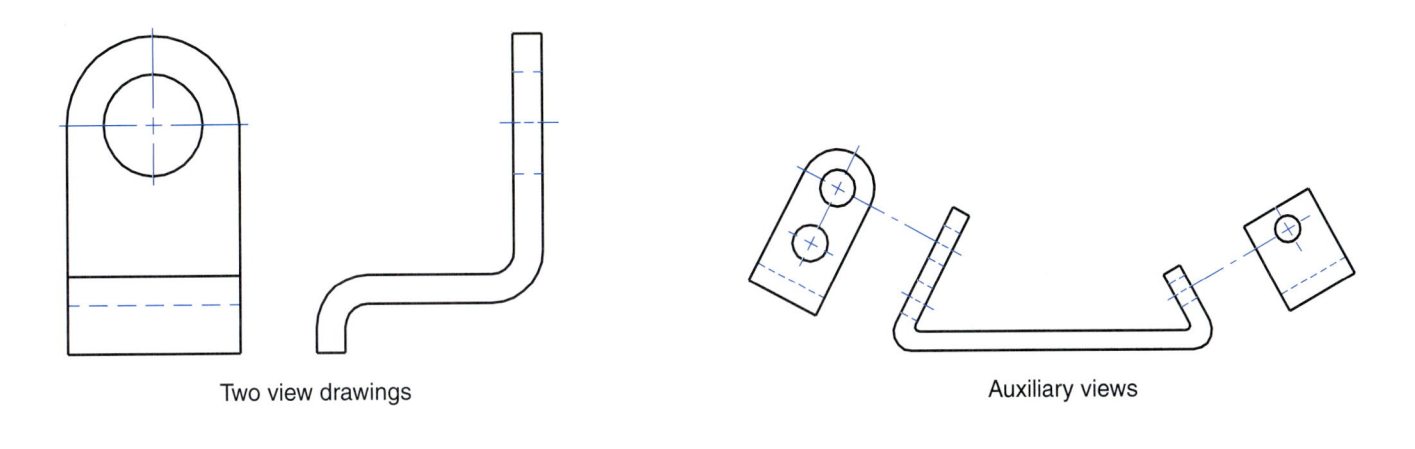

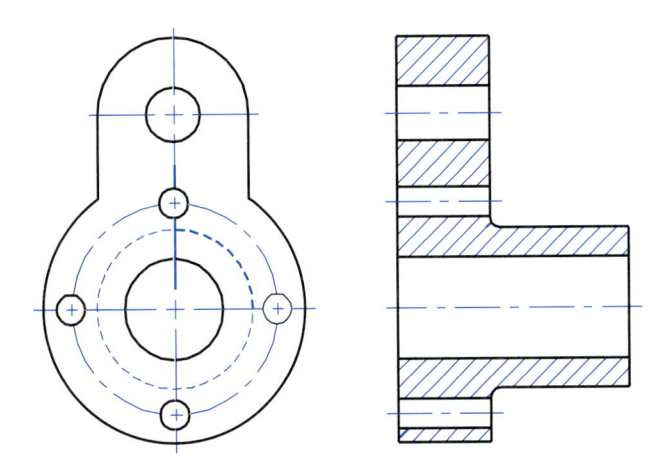

Two view drawings

Auxiliary views

Full section
(Cutting plane line not required if section is obvious.)

SECTION B–B

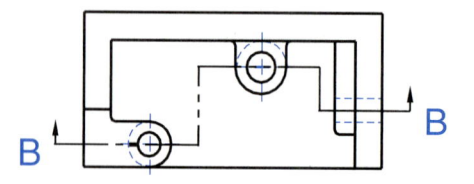

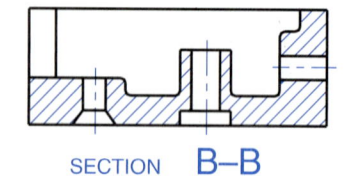

Offset section

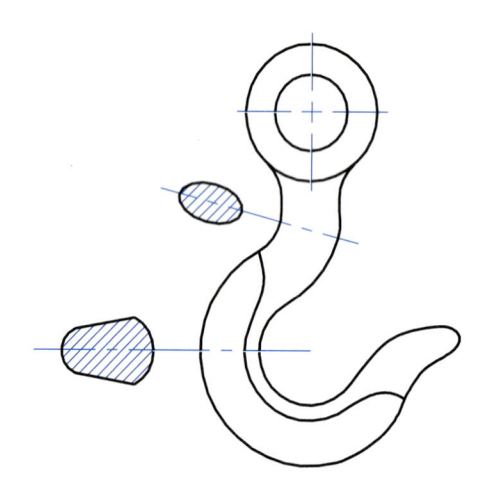

Alternate removed section method

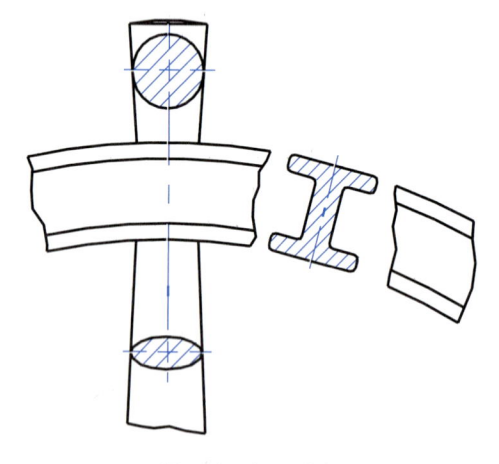

Revolved sections

APPENDIX B ||| Drafting Standards 747

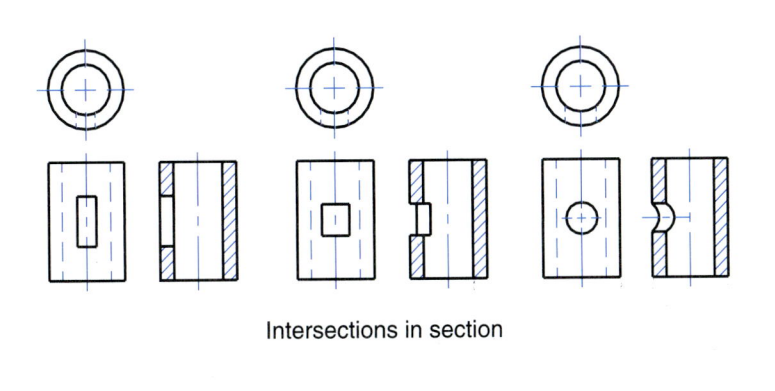

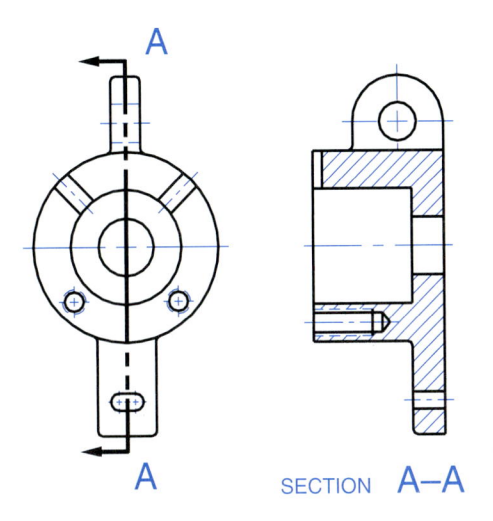

Intersections in section

SECTION A–A

Conventional representation of ribs and rotated details

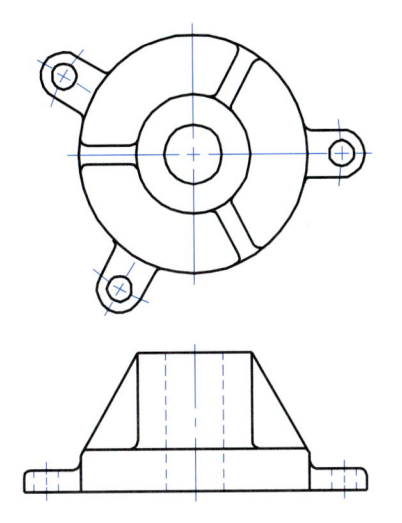

Rotated features conventional practices

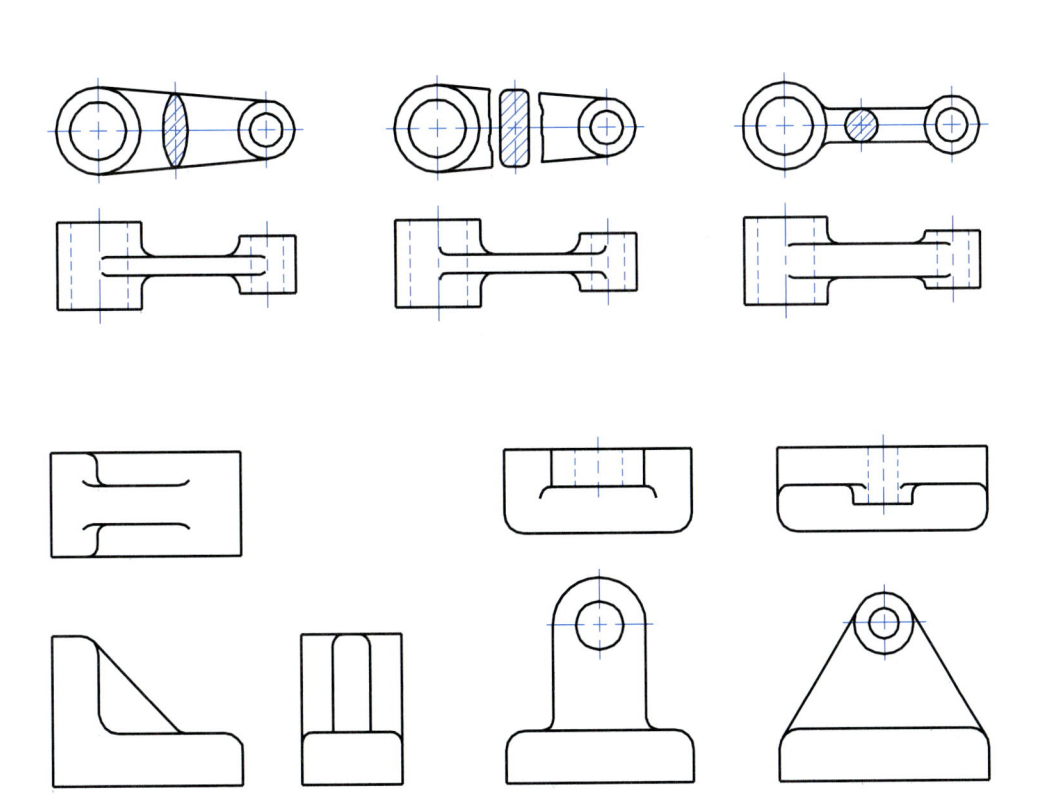

Conventional representation of fillets and runouts

Decimal inch dimensions

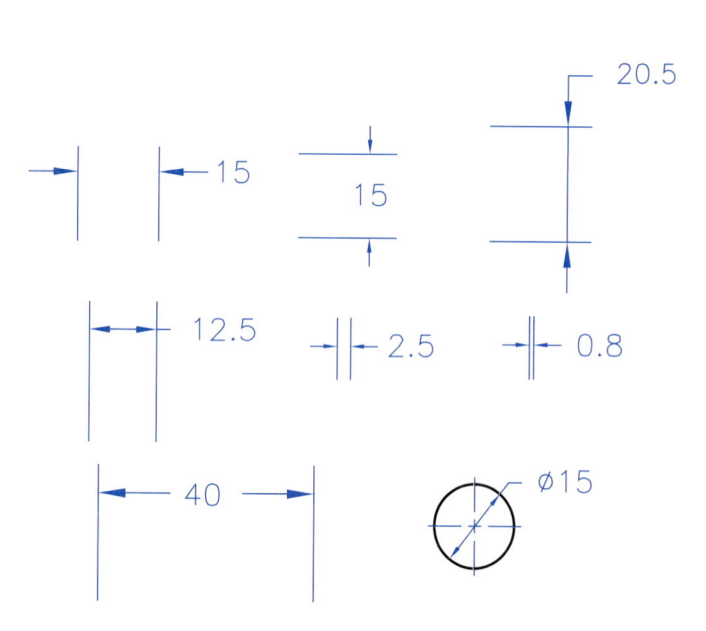

Millimeter dimensions

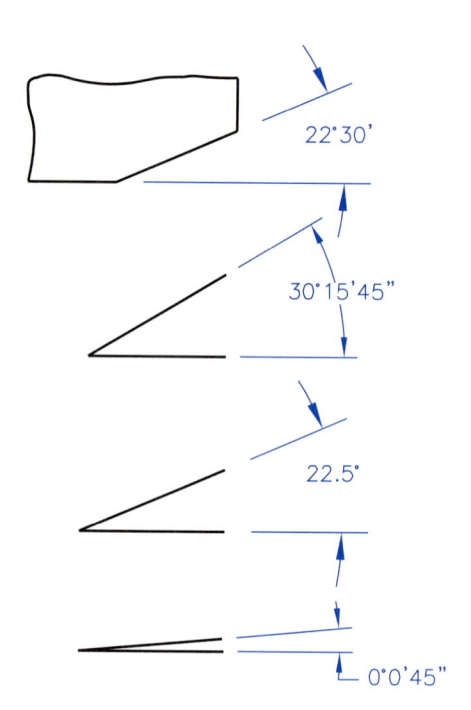

Angular dimensions

APPENDIX B ||| Drafting Standards

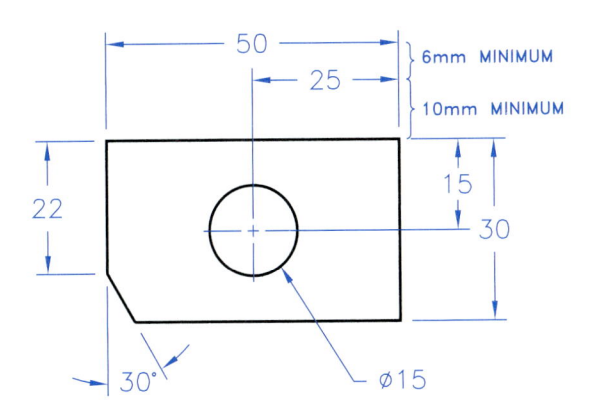

Applications of dimensions

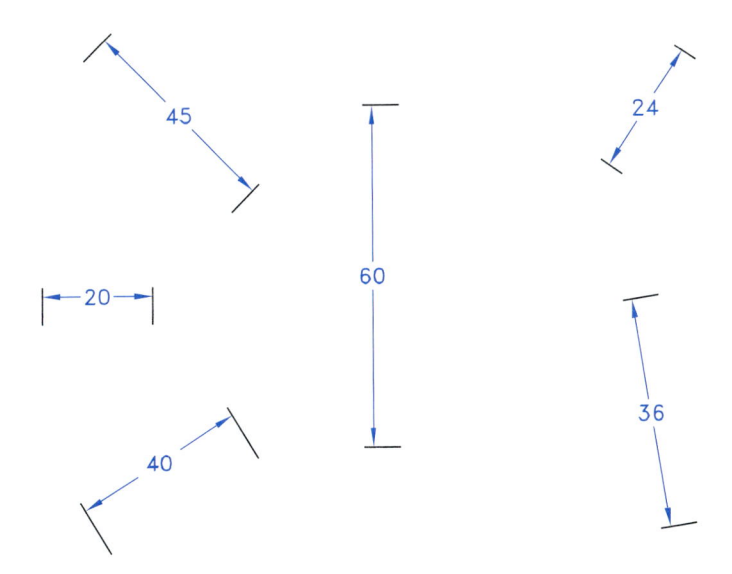

Reading direction for unidirectional dimensions

APPENDIX B ||| Drafting Standards

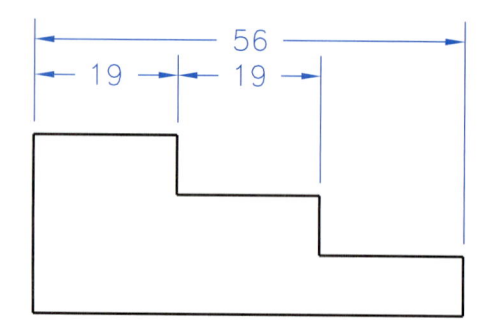

Grouping of dimensions

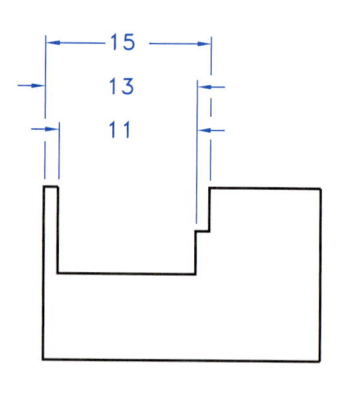

Breaks in extension lines

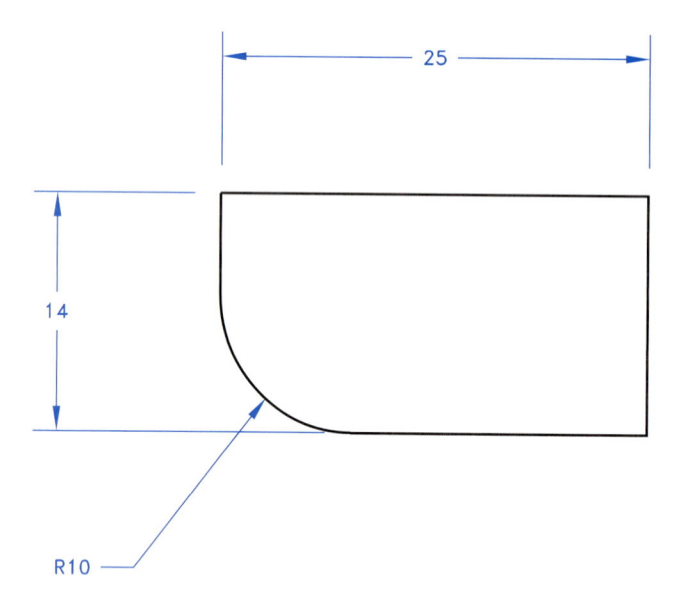

Rounded corners

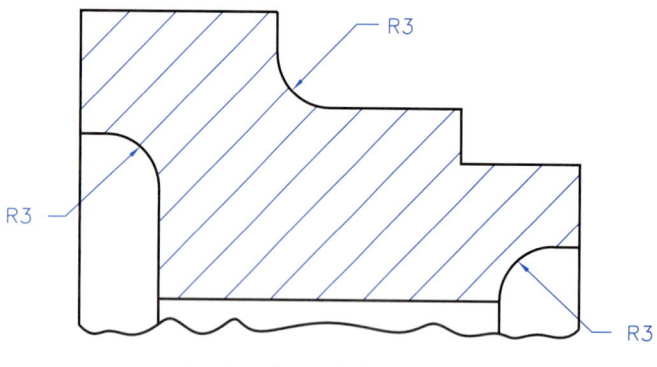

Leader-directed dimensions

APPENDIX B ||| Drafting Standards

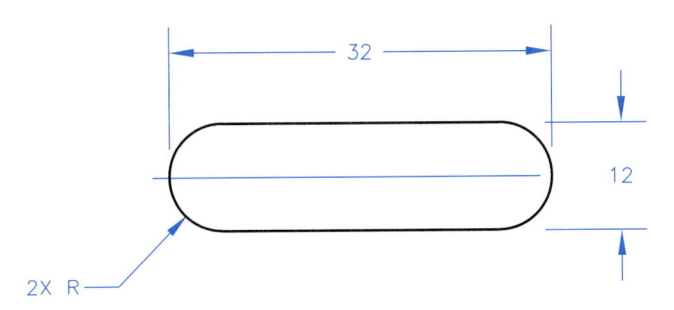

32

12

2X R

Fully rounded ends

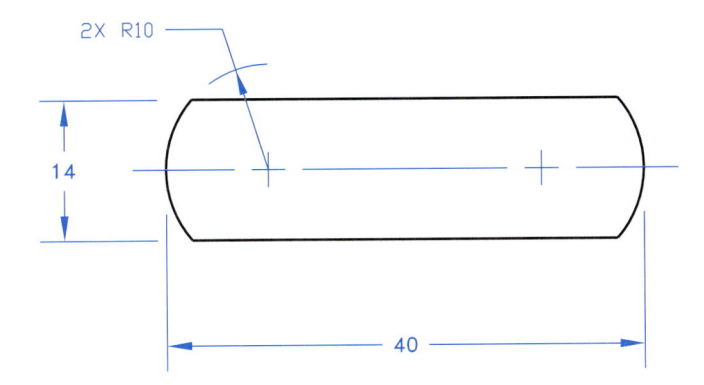

2X R10

14

40

Partially rounded ends

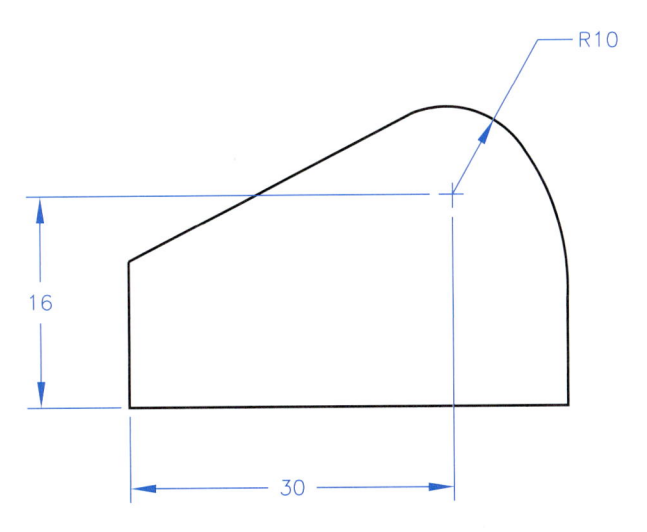

R10

16

30

Radius with located center

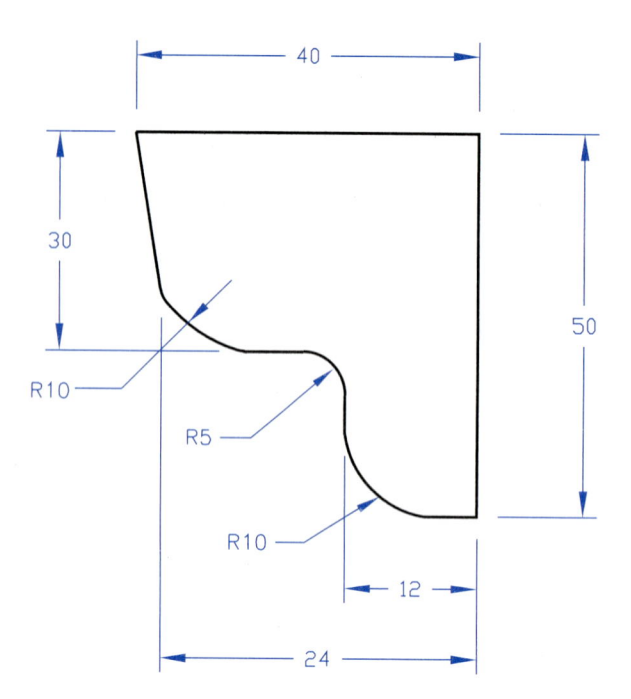

752 APPENDIX B ||| Drafting Standards

Radii with located centers

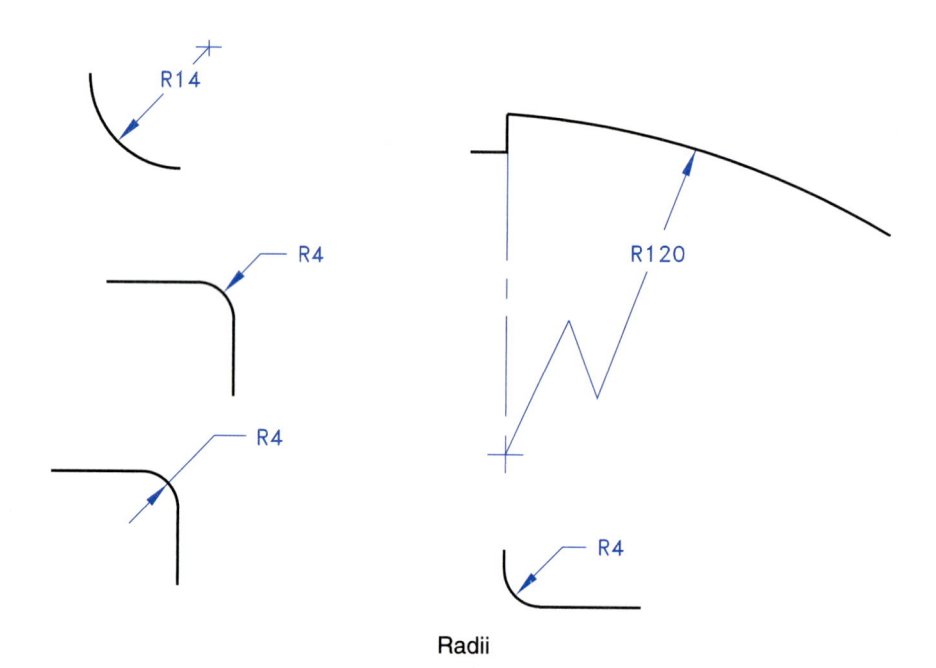

Radii

APPENDIX B ||| Drafting Standards   **753**

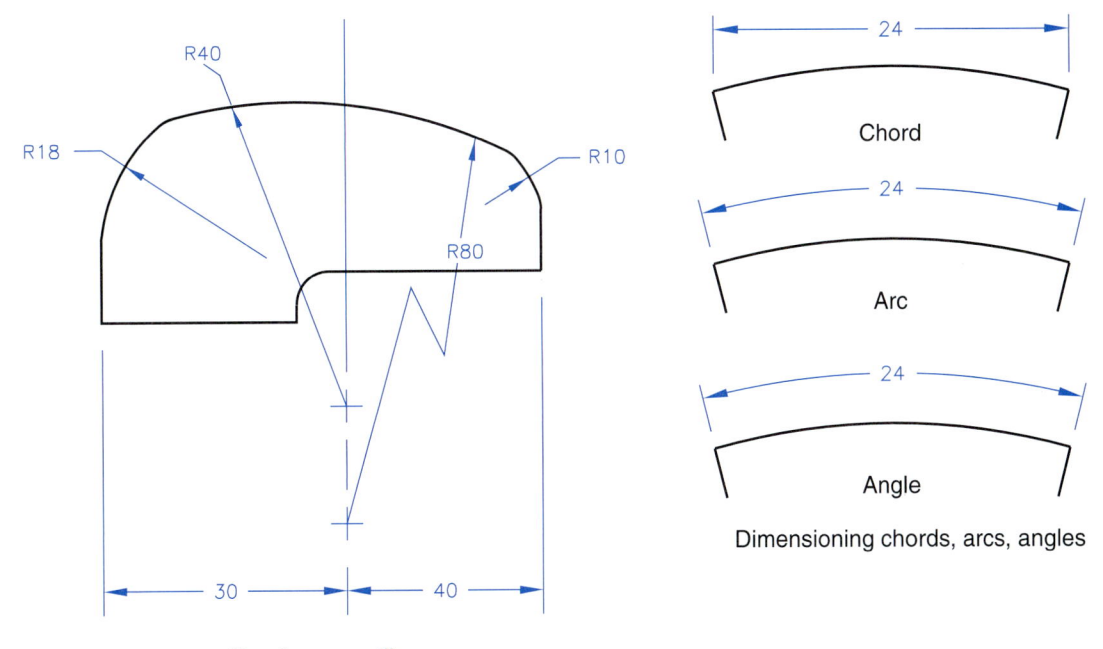

Circular arc outline

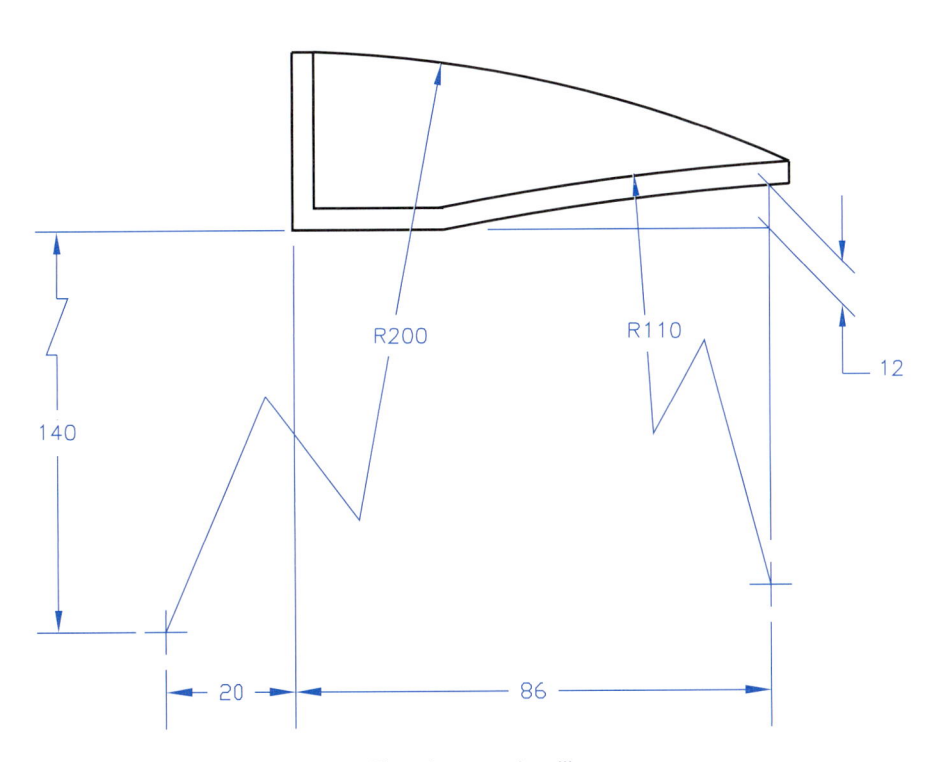

Dimensioning chords, arcs, angles
- Chord — 24
- Arc — 24
- Angle — 24

Foreshortened radii

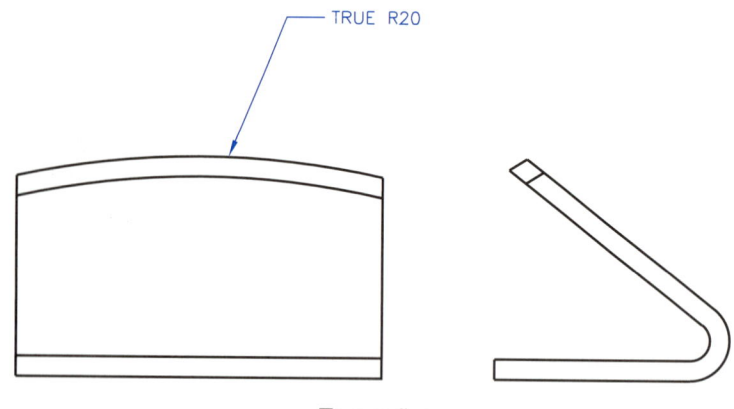

True radius

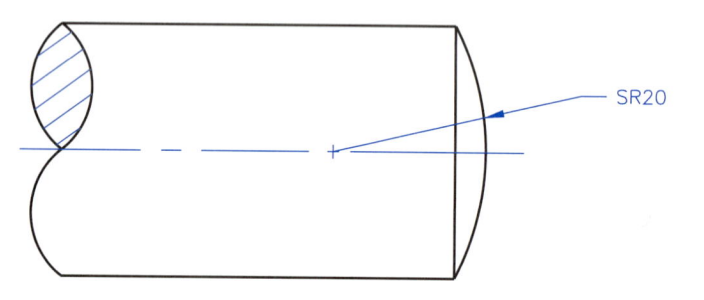

Spherical radius

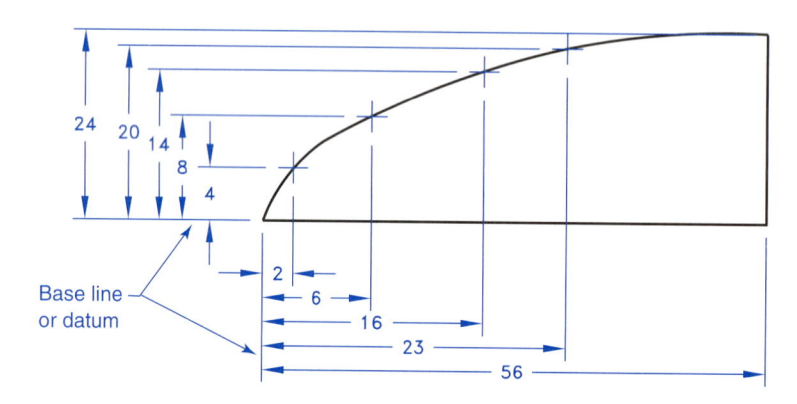

Coordinates of offset outline

APPENDIX B ||| Drafting Standards 755

Base line or datum

Arrowless tabular dimensioning of offset outline

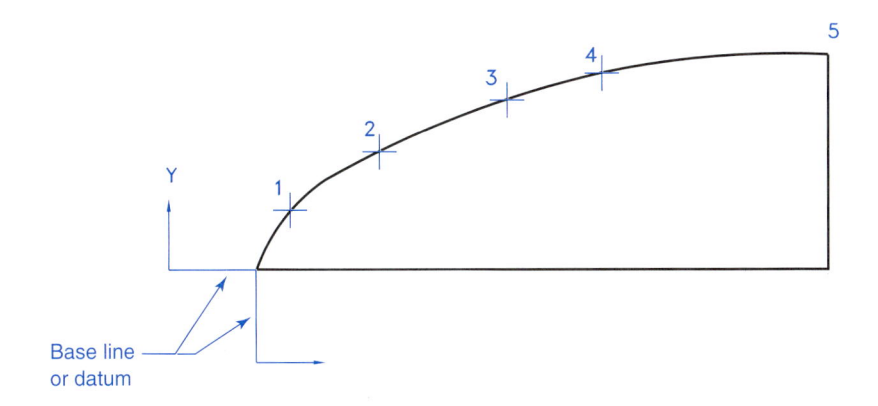

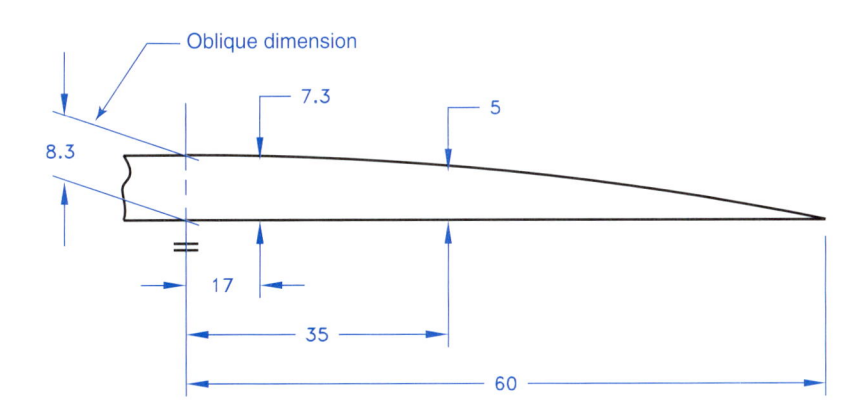

STATION	1	2	3	4	5
X	2	5	15	25	55
Y	4	8	15	20	24

Oblique dimension

8.3
7.3
5
17
35
60

Symmetrical outlines

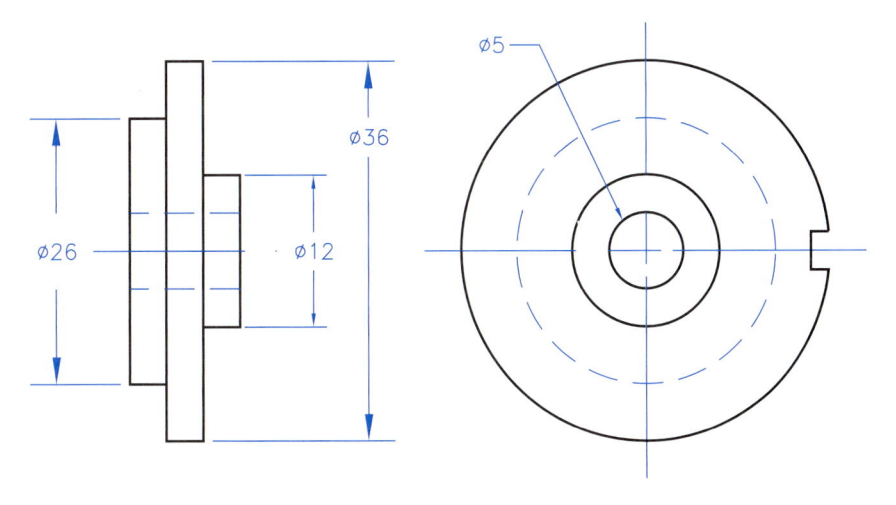

Ø5
Ø36
Ø26
Ø12

Diameters of cylindrical features and holes

756 APPENDIX B ||| Drafting Standards

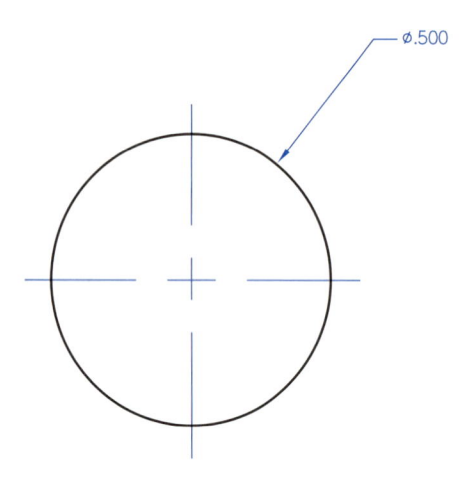

⌀.500

Leader direction

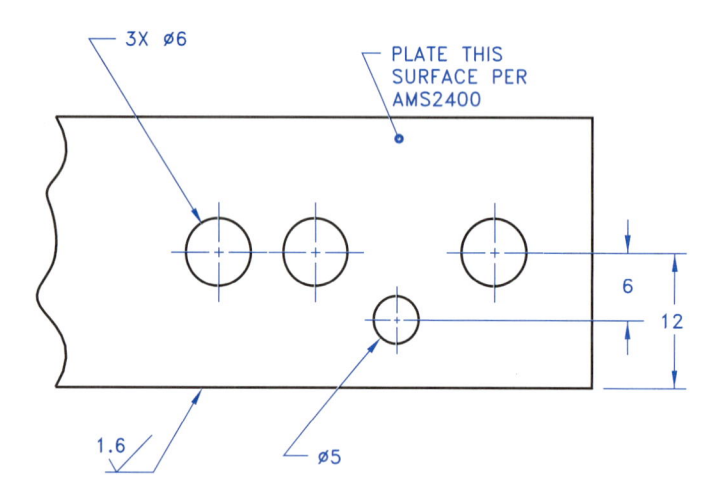

3X ⌀6

PLATE THIS
SURFACE PER
AMS2400

6

12

1.6

⌀5

Leader usage

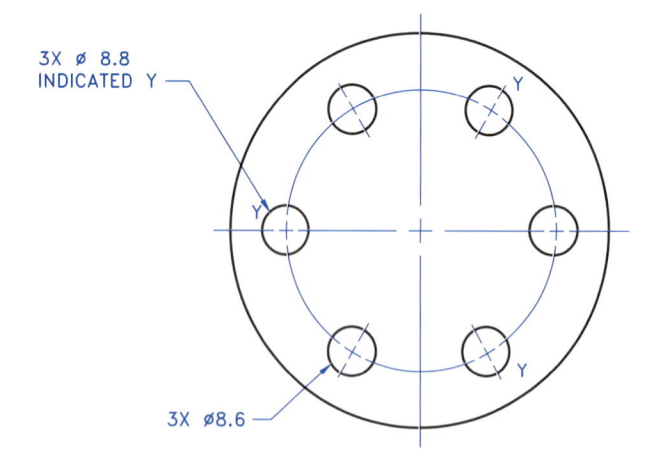

3X ⌀ 8.8
INDICATED Y

3X ⌀8.6

Minimizing leaders

APPENDIX B ||| Drafting Standards

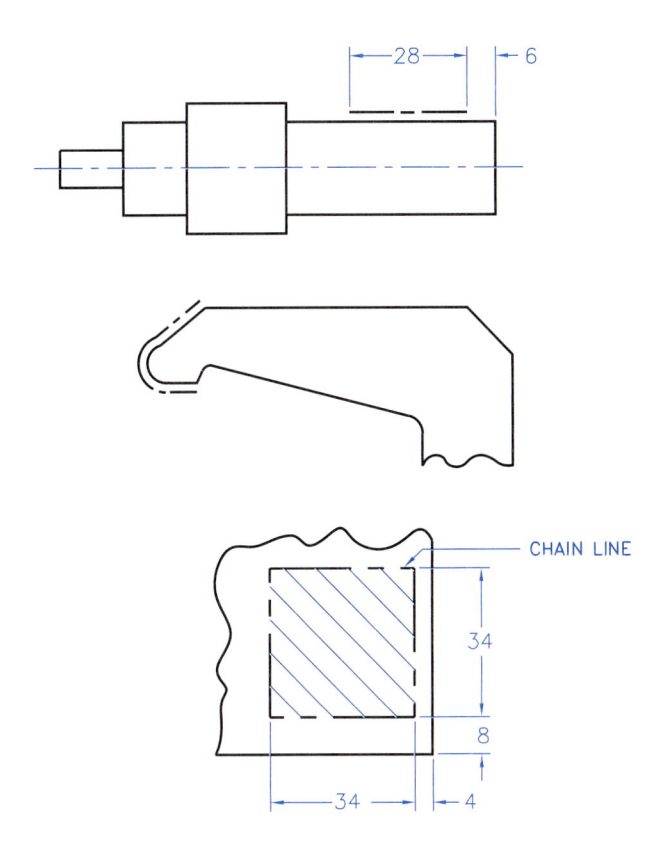

Limited length or area indication

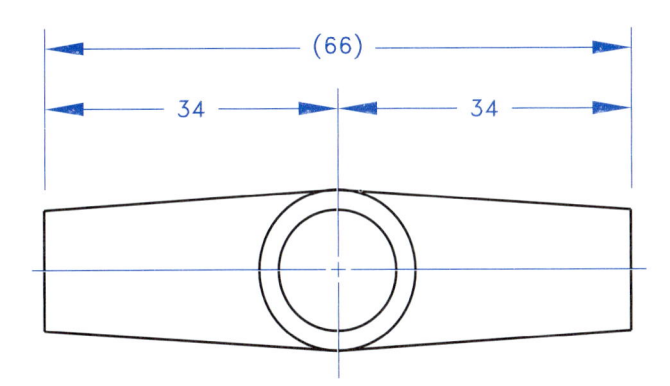

Overall reference dimension

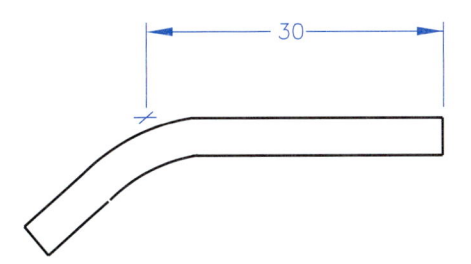

Point location

APPENDIX C

Standard Support Libraries

AutoCAD LT provides standard library files for you to define linetypes, hatch patterns, text fonts, and symbols for dimensioning. This appendix illustrates or describes

- Linetypes included in the *aclt.lin* file
- Standard hatch patterns included in the *aclt.pat* file
- Standard text and symbol fonts *(.shx)*
- TrueType fonts *(.ttf)*
- Geometric characteristic symbols

*Courtesy of Autodesk, Inc.

Standard Linetypes

AutoCAD LT provides a library of standard linetypes in the *aclt.lin* file.

Name	Pattern
Acad_iso02w100	—— —— —— —— ——
Acad_iso03w100	—— —— —— ——
Acad_iso04w100	—— · —— · —— ·
Acad_iso05w100	—— · · —— · · ——
Acad_iso06w100	—— · · · —— · · ·
Acad_iso07w100	· · · · · · · · · · · ·
Acad_iso08w100	——— — ——— — ———
Acad_iso09w100	——— — — ——— — —
Acad_iso10w100	—— · —— · —— ·
Acad_iso11w100	—— — —— — —— —
Acad_iso12w100	—— · · —— · · ——
Acad_iso13w100	——— — · · ——— · ·
Acad_iso14w100	——— · · · ——— · · ·
Acad_iso15w100	——— — · · · ———
Batting	⧖⧖⧖⧖⧖⧖⧖⧖⧖⧖⧖⧖⧖⧖⧖⧖
Border	— — · — — · — — ·
Border2	- - · - - · - - ·
Borderx2	—— —— · —— ——
Center	——— — ——— — ———
Center2	— - — — - — — -
Centerx2	———— —— ————
Continuous	————————————
Dashdot	— · — · — · — · — ·
Dashdot2	- · - · - · - · - ·
Dashdotx2	—— · —— · —— ·
Dashed	— — — — — — — —
Dashed2	- - - - - - - - - -
Dashedx2	—— —— —— —— ——
Divide	— · · — · · — · ·
Divide2	- · · - · · - · ·
Dividex2	—— · · —— · · ——
Dot	· · · · · · · · · · · ·
Dot2	·············
Dotx2	· · · · · ·

APPENDIX C ||| Standard Support Libraries   **761**

FenceLine1
FenceLine2
Gas_Line
Hidden
Hidden2
Hiddenx2
Hot_water_supply
Phantom
Phantom2
Phantomx2
Tracks
Zigzag

Standard Hatch Patterns

AutoCAD LT provides a library of standard hatch patterns in the *aclt.pat* file.

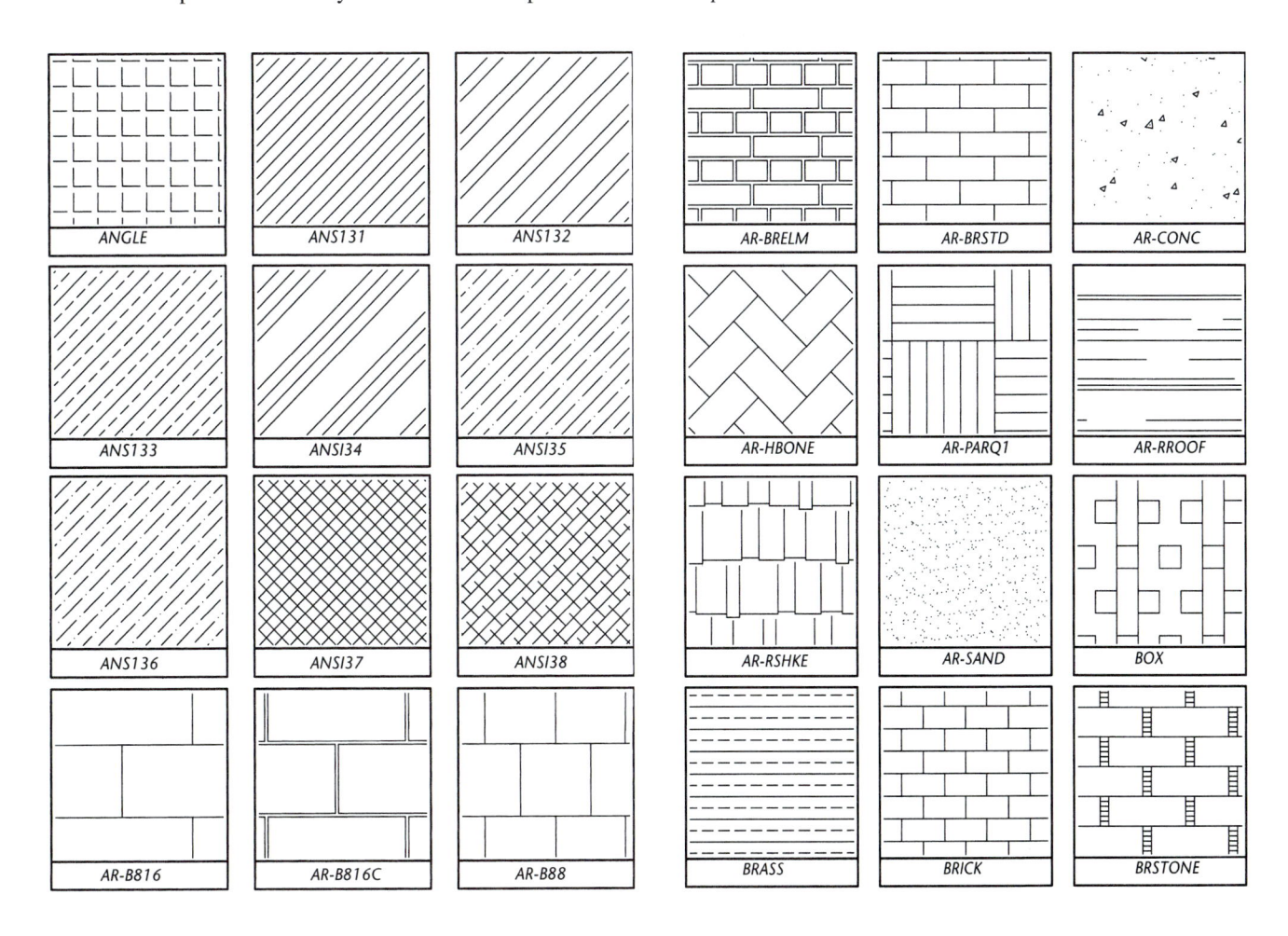

ANGLE	ANSI31	ANSI32	AR-BRELM	AR-BRSTD	AR-CONC
ANSI33	ANSI34	ANSI35	AR-HBONE	AR-PARQ1	AR-RROOF
ANSI36	ANSI37	ANSI38	AR-RSHKE	AR-SAND	BOX
AR-B816	AR-B816C	AR-B88	BRASS	BRICK	BRSTONE

APPENDIX C ||| Standard Support Libraries

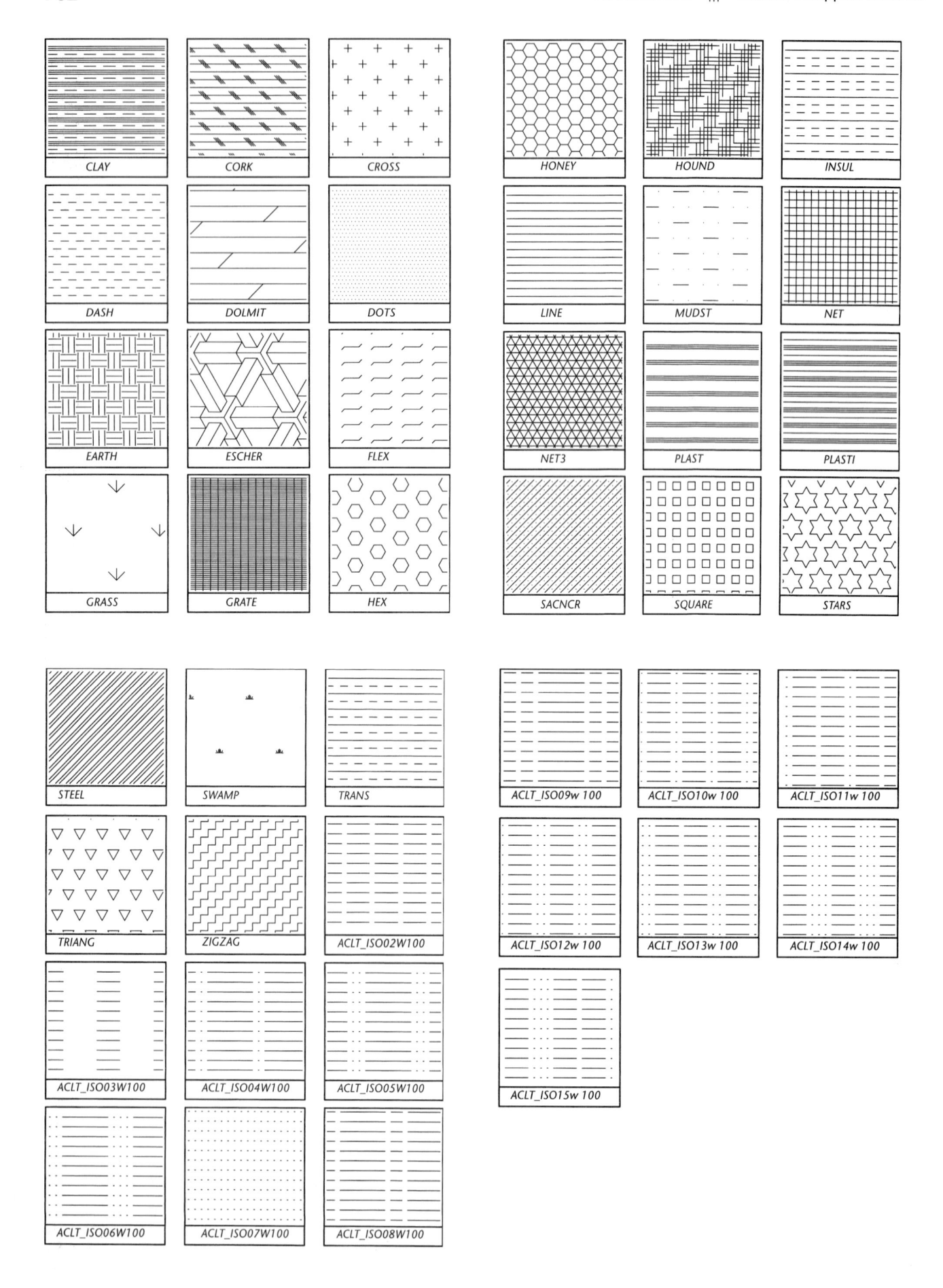

CLAY	CORK	CROSS	HONEY	HOUND	INSUL
DASH	DOLMIT	DOTS	LINE	MUDST	NET
EARTH	ESCHER	FLEX	NET3	PLAST	PLASTI
GRASS	GRATE	HEX	SACNCR	SQUARE	STARS
STEEL	SWAMP	TRANS	ACLT_ISO09w 100	ACLT_ISO10w 100	ACLT_ISO11w 100
TRIANG	ZIGZAG	ACLT_ISO02W100	ACLT_ISO12w 100	ACLT_ISO13w 100	ACLT_ISO14w 100
ACLT_ISO03W100	ACLT_ISO04W100	ACLT_ISO05W100	ACLT_ISO15w 100		
ACLT_ISO06W100	ACLT_ISO07W100	ACLT_ISO08W100			

APPENDIX C ||| Standard Support Libraries **763**

Standard Text and Symbol Fonts

AutoCAD LT provides a variety of text and symbol fonts available for use in your drawings. Using commands and techniques discussed in Chapter 9, you can customize the appearance of these text fonts to meet specialized needs. The width factor of text can be adjusted, you can slant the text to the right or left, and you can even apply horizontal or vertical orientation. Text creation commands allow further controls, such as text height and baseline rotation angle.

In all but the monospaced text font (monotxt), characters are proportionally spaced; that is, the space needed for the letter *l* is narrower than that for the letter *m*. AutoCAD LT 98 supports the use of compiled shape/font files as well as standard Windows TrueType® fonts. Compiled shape/font files have a .shx file extension, and are unique to AutoCAD products.

The following table lists the font names and samples of the AutoCAD LT compiled shape (.shx) fonts, and the Windows TrueType fonts that ship with AutoCAD LT 98. Most of the .shx fonts are also available as TrueType fonts, for increased flexibility while working within AutoCAD LT 98 or within other Windows applications.

AutoCAD LT 98 (.SHX) Shape/Font Listing

✓ - A checkmark in the TT column indicates the font is also available as a True Type font.

Font Name	TT	Font Sample
gdt	✓	ABCD ... 1234567890
gothicg	✓	𝔄𝔅ℭ𝔇𝔈𝔉𝔊ℌ𝔍𝔎𝔏𝔐𝔑𝔒𝔓𝔔ℜ𝔖𝔗𝔘𝔙𝔚𝔛𝔜ℨ abcd 1234567890
gothici	✓	ABCDEFGHIJKLMNOPQRSTUVWXYZ abcd 1234567890
greekc	✓	ΑΒΧΔΕΦΓΗΙϑΚΛΜΝΟΠΘΡΣΤΥΩΞΨΖ αβχδ 1234567890
greeks	✓	ΑΒΧΔΕΦΓΗΙϑΚΛΜΝΟΠΘΡΣΤΥΩΞΨΖ αβχδ 1234567890
isoct	✓	ABCDEFGHIJKLMNOPQRSTUVWXYZ abcd 1234567890
isocp	✓	ABCDEFGHIJKLMNOPQRSTUVWXYZ abcd 1234567890
isocp2	✓	ABCDEFGHIJKLMNOPQRSTUVWXYZ abcd 1234567890
isocp3	✓	ABCDEFGHIJKLMNOPQRSTUVWXYZ abcd 1234567890
isoct2	✓	ABCDEFGHIJKLMNOPQRSTUVWXYZ abcd 1234567890
isoct3	✓	ABCDEFGHIJKLMNOPQRSTUVWXYZ abcd 1234567890
italict	✓	*ABCDEFGHIJKLMNOPQRSTUVWXYZ abcd 1234567890*
italicc	✓	*ABCDEFGHIJKLMNOPQRSTUVWXYZ abcd 1234567890*
italic	✓	*ABCDEFGHIJKLMNOPQRSTUVWXYZ abcd 1234567890*
ltypeshp		Not a text font file. Contains shapes used in complex linetypes.
monotxt	✓	ABCDEFGHIJKLMNOPQRSTUVWXYZ abcd 1234567890
romanc	✓	ABCDEFGHIJKLMNOPQRSTUVWXYZ abcd 1234567890
romand	✓	ABCDEFGHIJKLMNOPQRSTUVWXYZ abcd 1234567890
romans	✓	ABCDEFGHIJKLMNOPQRSTUVWXYZ abcd 1234567890
romant	✓	ABCDEFGHIJKLMNOPQRSTUVWXYZ abcd 1234567890
scriptc	✓	*ABCDEFGHIJKLMNOPQRSTUVWXYZ abcd 1234567890*
scripts	✓	*ABCDEFGHIJKLMNOPQRSTUVWXYZ abcd 1234567890*
simplex	✓	ABCDEFGHIJKLMNOPQRSTUVWXYZ abcd 1234567890
syastro	✓	... 1234567890
symap	✓	... 1234567890
symath	✓	... 1234567890
symeteo	✓	... 1234567890
symusic	✓	... 1234567890
txt	✓	ABCDEFGHIJKLMNOPQRSTUVWXYZ abcd 1234567890

AutoCAD LT 98 TrueType Font Listing

Font Name	Font Sample
BankGothic Lt BT	ABCDEFGHIJKLMNOPQRSTUVWXYZ ABCD 12345
BankGothic Md BT	ABCDEFGHIJKLMNOPQRSTUVWXYZ ABCD 1234
CityBlueprint	ABCDEFGHIJKL-MNOPQRSTUVWXYZ abcd 1234567890
CommercialPi BT	±°′″∅+−×÷=±°′″ . ….. ℞♀♂• ©®©® ●●■■○○□★
Complex	ABCDEFGHIJKLMNOPQRSTUVWXYZ abcd 1234567890
CommercialScript BT	ABCDEFGHIJKLMNOPQRSTUVWXYZ abcd 1234567890
CountryBlueprint	ABCDEFGHIJKLMNOPQRSTUVWXYZ abcd 1234567890
Dutch801 Rm BT	ABCDEFGHIJKLOMNOPQRSTUVWXYZ abcd 1234567890
Dutch801 Bd BT	ABCDEFGHIJKLMNOPQRSTUVWXYZ abcd 1234567890
Dutch801 Bi BT	ABCDEFGHIJKLMNOPQRSTUVWXYZ abcd 1234567890
Dutch801 XBd BT	ABCDEFGHIJKLMNOPQRSTUVWXYZ abcd 1234567890
EuroRoman	ABCDEFGHIJKLMNOPQRSTUVWXYZ abcd 1234567890
GothicE	ABCDEFGHIJKLMNOPQRSTUVWXYZ abcd 1234567890
Monospac821 BT	ABCDEFGHIJKLMNOPQRSTUVWXYZ abcd 1234567890
Proxy 1	ABCDEFGHIJKLMNOPQRSTUVWXYZ abcd 1234567890
Proxy 2	ABCDEFGHIJKLMNOPQRSTUVWXYZ abcd 1234567890
Proxy 3	ABCDEFGHIJKLMNOPQRSTUVWXYZ abcd 1234567890
Proxy 4	ABCDEFGHIJKLMNOPQRSTUVWXYZ abcd 1234567890
Proxy 5	ABCDEFGHIJKLMNOPQRSTUVWXYZ abcd 1234567890
Proxy 6	ABCDEFGHIJKLMNOPQRSTUVWXYZ abcd 1234567890
Proxy 7	ABCDEFGHIJKLMNOPQRSTUVWXYZ abcd 1234567890
Proxy 8	ABCDEFGHIJKLMNOPQRSTUVWXYZ abcd 1234567890
Proxy 9	ABCDEFGHIJKLMNOPQRSTUVWXYZ abcd 1234567890
PanRoman	ABCDEFGHIJKLMNOPQRSTUVWXYZ abcd 1234567890
Romantic	ABCDEFGHIJKLMNOPQRSTUVWXYZ abcd 1234567890
SanSerif	ABCDEFGHIJKLMNOPQRSTUVWXYZ abcd 1234567890
Stylus BT	ABCDEFGHIJKLMNOPQRSTUVWXYZ abcd 1234567890
SuperFrench	ABCDEFGHIJKLMNOPQRSTUVWXYZ abcd 1234567890
Swis721 BT	ABCDEFGHIJKLMNOPQRSTUVWXYZ abcd 1234567890
Swis721 BdOul BT	ABCDEFGHIJKLMNOPQRSTUVWXYZ abcd 1234567890
Swis721 BdCnOul BT	ABCDEFGHIJKLMNOPQRSTUVWXYZ abcd 1234567890
Swis721 Cn BT	ABCDEFGHIJKLMNOPQRSTUVWXYZ abcd 1234567890
Swis721 BlkCn BT	ABCDEFGHIJKLMNOPQRSTUVWXYZ abcd 1234567890
Swis721 LtCn BT	ABCDEFGHIJKLMNOPQRSTUVWXYZ abcd 1234567890
Swis721 Ex BT	ABCDEFGHIJKLMNOPQRSTUVWXYZ abcd 1234567890
Swis721 BlkEx BT	ABCDEFGHIJKLMNOPQRSTUVWXYZ abcd 1234567890
Swis721 LtEx BT	ABCDEFGHIJKLMNOPQRSTUVWXYZ abcd 1234567890
Swis721 Blk BT	ABCDEFGHIJKLMNOPQRSTUVWXYZ abcd 1234567890
Swis721 BlkOul BT	ABCDEFGHIJKLMNOPQRSTUVWXYZ abcd 1234567890
Swis721 Lt BT	ABCDEFGHIJKLMNOPQRSTUVWXYZ abcd 1234567890
TechnicBold	ABCDEFGHIJKLMNOPQRSTUVWXYZ ABCD 1234567890
TechnicLite	ABCDEFGHIJKLMNOPQRSTUVWXYZ ABCD 1234567890
Technic	ABCDEFGHIJKLMNOPQRSTUVWXYZ ABCD 1234567890
UniversalMath1 BT	ΑΒΨΔΕΦΓΗΙΞΚΛΜΝΟΠΘΡΣΤΘΩ6ΧΥΖ αβψδ +−×÷=±∓°′″
Vineta BT	ABCDEFGHIJKLMNOPQRSTUVWXYZ abcd 1234567890

Geometric Characteristic Symbols

The following table shows the geometric characteristic symbols used in geometric tolerancing. Unless otherwise stated, these symbols adhere to ANSI standards. AutoCAD LT 98 automatically creates and places these symbols within feature control frames when using the TOL (Tolerence) command. These symbols can be accessed directly by entering lower-case characters while using the GDT.shx font file (or GDT .ttf).

Geometric characteristic symbols

Symbol	Name
⊕	Position
◎	Concentricity/coaxiality
=	Symmetry
//	Parallelism
⊥	Perpendicularity
∠	Angularity
/⌒/	Cylindricity
▱	Flatness
○	Circularity or roundness
—	Straightness
⌒	Profile of a surface
⌒	Profile of a line
↗	Circular runout
↗↗	Total runout
⌀	Diameter
Ⓜ	Maximum material condition (MMC)
Ⓛ	Least material condition (LMC)
Ⓢ	Regardless of feature size (RFS)
Ⓟ	Projected tolerance

Using the GDT Font

The GDT font file provided with AutoCAD LT 98 gives you the capability to create text objects that use symbols such as countersink, counterbore, depth, or geometric characteristic symbols. This font file is provided both as a .shx file and as a TrueType font file (.ttf).

Uppercase character entries using this font produce standard uppercase text characters that resemble the RomanS font (which is highly suited for a variety of drafting applications). All lowercase character entries produce GDT and drafting-related symbols. The following table lists the results obtained for both upper- and lowercase keystrokes.

Key Entry	GDT Font Character	Key Entry	GDT Font Character	Key Entry	GDT Font Character
A	A	S	S	k	⌒
B	B	T	T	l	Ⓛ
C	C	U	U	m	Ⓜ
D	D	V	V	n	⌀
E	E	W	W	o	□
F	F	X	X	p	Ⓟ
G	G	Y	Y	q	¢
H	H	Z	Z	r	⊚
I	I	a	∠	s	Ⓢ
J	J	b	⊥	t	
K	K	c	▱	u	—
L	L	d	⌒	v	⊔
M	M	e	○	w	∨
N	N	f	∥	x	⊽
O	O	g	⌰	y	▷
P	P	h	↗	z	▷
Q	Q	i	≡		
R	R	j	⌖		

APPENDIX D

Accessibility Features

Effective use of a CAD workstation can present significant challenges to users with impaired vision or hearing, or with restricted physical mobility. Both AutoCAD LT 98 and the Windows operating systems provide options for customizing the user interface to meet specialized needs. Additionally, the availability of adaptive technologies such as voice input, magnified displays, specialized keyboards, and alternative pointing devices create many new possibilities for all computer users. This appendix introduces many of the available options for increasing computer accessibility, both in the Windows operating systems and in the area of adaptive technologies.

Windows Accessibility Options

The Windows NT 4, Windows 95, and Windows 98 operating systems have built-in accessibility options that can make it easier to work in the Windows environment. In Windows 98, the Accessibility Wizard provides a simple guided process for adjusting the system appearance and behavior to meet individual needs. To access this feature, select the Start button on the task bar, pick Programs > Accessories > Accessibility, and then pick the Accessibility Wizard option. If you do not have Windows 98, or if you prefer not to use the wizard, you can use the Control Panel to make adjustments. To access the Control Panel, pick the Start button on the task bar, then select Settings and Control panel. The following section discusses both methods of setting up your system accessibility.

Display Options

The Welcome page is displayed when you start the Accessibility Wizard. Here, the first settings you make are for the text size used in window titles and menus. Three sizes of text are presented and you are asked to select the smallest size of text that you can read (see Figure D.1).

FIGURE D.1

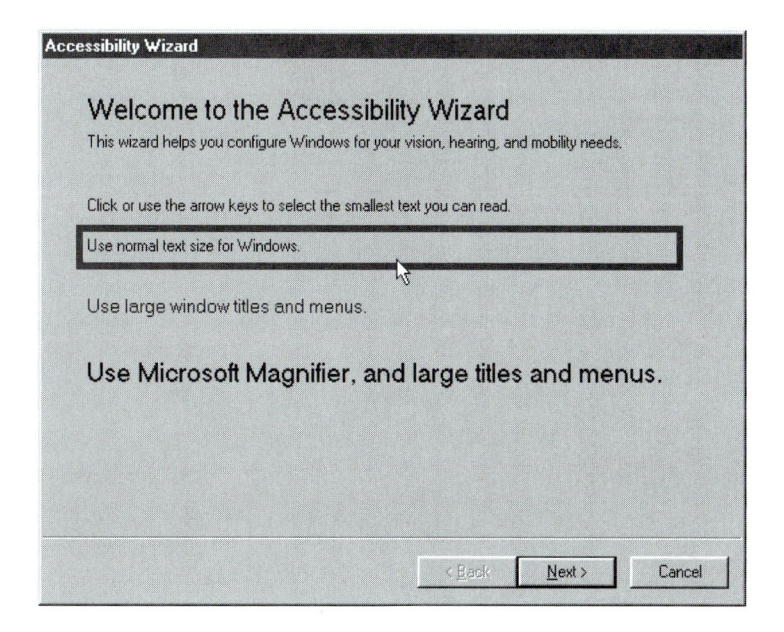

767

Based on the default Windows system settings, if you select the smallest size of text displayed, then no changes are made to the text size. Selecting the larger text increases the size of text used in window titles and menus. If you select the largest of the text sizes displayed, the *Microsoft Magnifier* is used. The Microsoft Magnifier displays an area of your desktop based on the current settings and lets you specify a magnification factor of up to nine times the standard display size. Also, title and menu sizes are increased for greater visibility. Figure D.2 shows the Microsoft Magnifier being used at a magnification of 4X, with the Magnifier dialog box visible. You can adjust the behavior and appearance of this feature in the Magnifier dialog box. One of these options is a high-contrast color scheme. The Microsoft Magnifier is not available in Windows 95 or Windows NT4.

FIGURE D.2

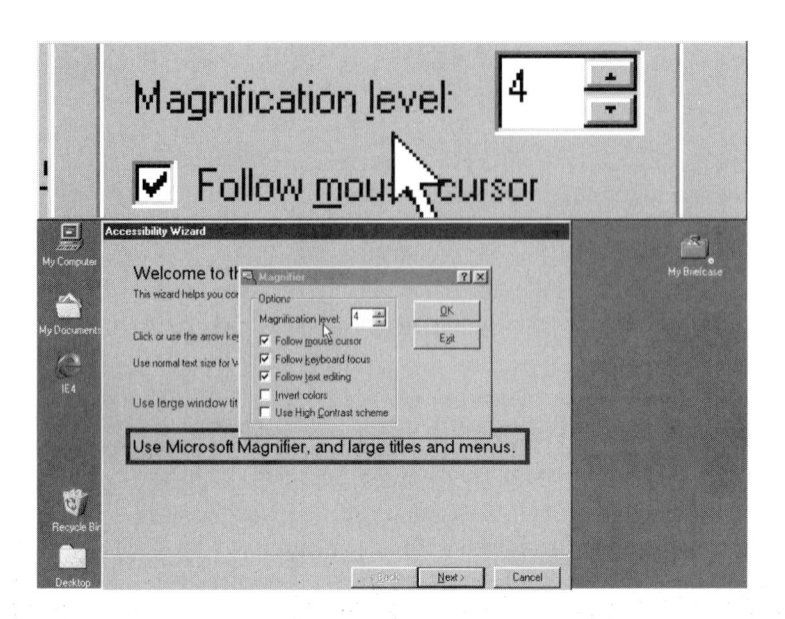

The next step in the wizard is the Text Size page in which you specify whether you want to increase the standard font size, switch to a lower screen resolution, or use the Microsoft Magnifier. The settings will be preset to recommended values based on the font size you selected on the previous screen. You can keep these values or specify new settings if desired.

The Set Wizard Options page of the wizard is displayed next. The settings you make here control what accessibility options are offered through the remainder of the Accessibility Wizard. Select each applicable option in the list. In this discussion of the Accessibility Wizard, each of the available options has been selected so that all features are presented.

The next few pages of the wizard allow you to set desired sizes for scroll bars, window borders, and program icons as well as to set your desired color scheme. If you indicated that you have difficulty hearing sounds from the computer, you are offered options that supplement system sounds with visual cues. The SoundSentry allows you to set up the system to display visual warnings of system events that normally produce a sound. The ShowSounds feature can be set to display captions for speech and sounds in applications that support this option. Some multimedia programs have the capability to display captions when playing speech or other sound files.

With the exception of the Microsoft Magnifier, each of these options is available in Windows 95 and Windows NT4. The Control Panel is used to make the appropriate settings, using the Display and Accessibility Options applications. Figure D.3 shows these icons within the Control Panel.

Pick the icon labeled Display, as shown in Figure D.3, to change the display settings. The first step is typically to set the display resolution, which controls the overall size of on-screen features. Keep in mind that a resolution of 800×600 is the minimum recommended resolution for using AutoCAD LT 98. To set the resolution, pick the tab labeled Display as shown in Figure D.4.

The area labeled Desktop Area provides a slider bar that allows you to choose from the available resolution settings. **Never apply any changes to this setting until you have successfully tested it.** Lower reso-

FIGURE D.3

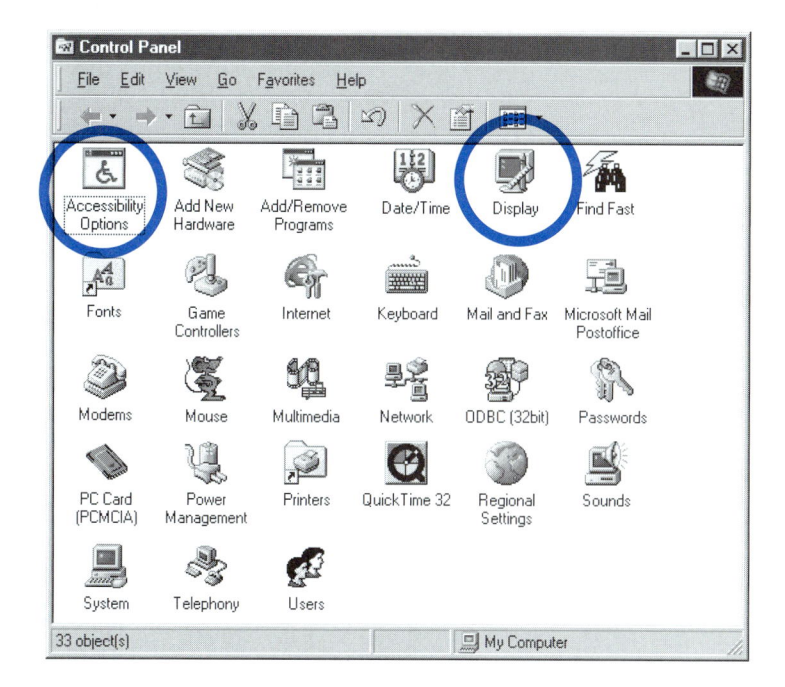

FIGURE D.4

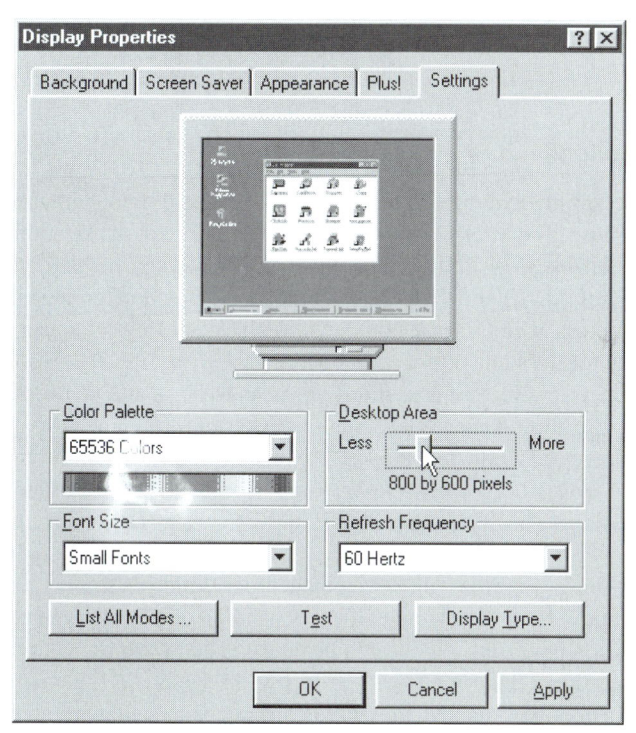

lution settings result in larger on-screen features. As you adjust the resolution you may also need to change the number of colors in the Color Palette settings or the Refresh Frequency rate. Again, as you make adjustments always test each setting before trying to use it. Incorrect settings can disable your display, requiring you to reboot your system in "safe mode." The primary font size can also be adjusted using the Font Size list. If you do adjust the font size, you may be required to restart your system before the changes take effect

To adjust the size of individual screen features and text elements, pick the Appearance tab. The Appearance tab of the Display Properties dialog box is shown in Figure D.5 with the Scheme: list open. Although you can adjust each element on the screen individually, you may find it more convenient to select a predesigned scheme from this list. The display area at the top of this tab shows the results of any settings you make. Schemes are available for both size and color adjustments. Finally, you can adjust the sizes of desktop icons from the tab labeled "Plus!"

FIGURE D.5

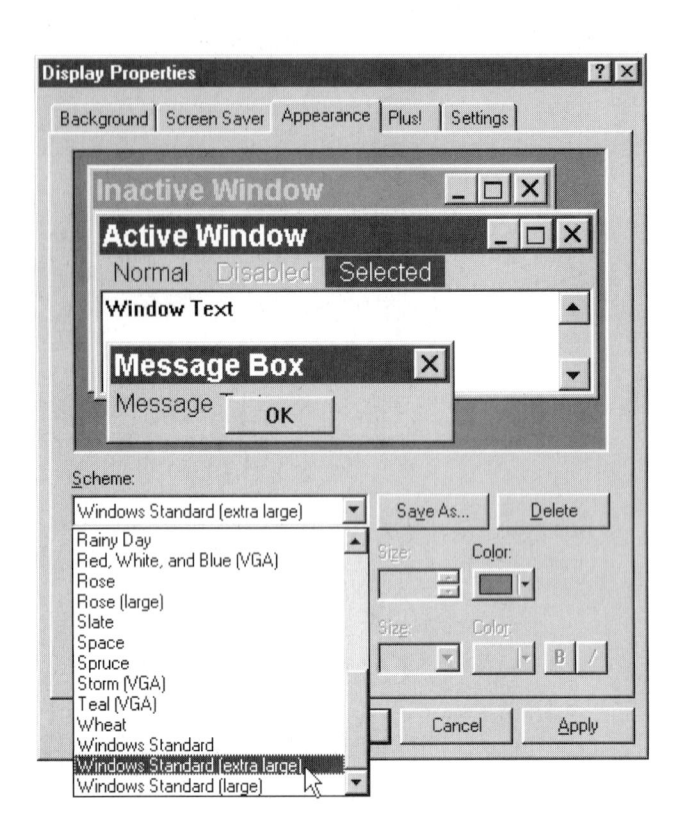

Keyboard Options

Keyboard accessibility features are presented by the wizard if you indicated that you have difficulty using the keyboard or mouse. The Sticky Keys feature is helpful for keystroke combinations that you need to use, such as Ctrl+(key), Alt+(key) or Shift+(key). When Sticky Keys is enabled, you can press one key at a time. For example, in AutoCAD LT the Ctrl+N keystroke starts the NEW command. Normally, you have to press and hold Ctrl, then press N and release both keys. With Sticky Keys, you can press and release the Ctrl key, then press the N key for the same effect.

The BounceKeys feature is useful if your hands shake and you sometimes press a key more times than you intend to. Enabling BounceKeys causes the system to ignore repeated keystrokes. In the BounceKeys settings you can specify how fast the keystrokes must be repeated in order to be ignored, and you can also have Windows play a beep when the keys are accepted. A test area is provided where you can test your BounceKey settings. This feature is called FilterKeys when accessed from the Accessibility Properties dialog box.

The ToggleKeys options allow you to instruct Windows to play a sound when you press Caps Lock, NumLock, or Scroll Lock. The sound differs depending on whether you are turning the toggle on or off. Keep in mind that if you have told Windows to display a visual warning, your screen will also flash.

The MouseKeys feature allows you to use the keyboard numeric keypad instead of your mouse for pointing. If this option is enabled, you will be prompted to set the speed of the pointer.

You can select a custom mouse cursor for better visibility and you can specify both its size and colors. Other mouse settings you can choose include the button to be used for the pick button, the speed of the cursor on screen, and mouse trails. When mouse trails are enabled, moving the cursor leaves behind a temporary trail to make it easier to locate the cursor.

Finally, Windows allows you to configure your system for a multiple-user environment by setting automatic time-outs for the accessibility features and specifying whether the current settings are automatically applied to all new user accounts on the workstation. Windows also allows you to save your settings in a file so you can restore them at any time or even take them with you to other workstations.

If you are using Windows 95 or NT4, all these settings can be made in the Accessibility Options dialog box. The Windows 98 Accessibility Properties dialog box is shown in Figure D.6.

FIGURE D.6

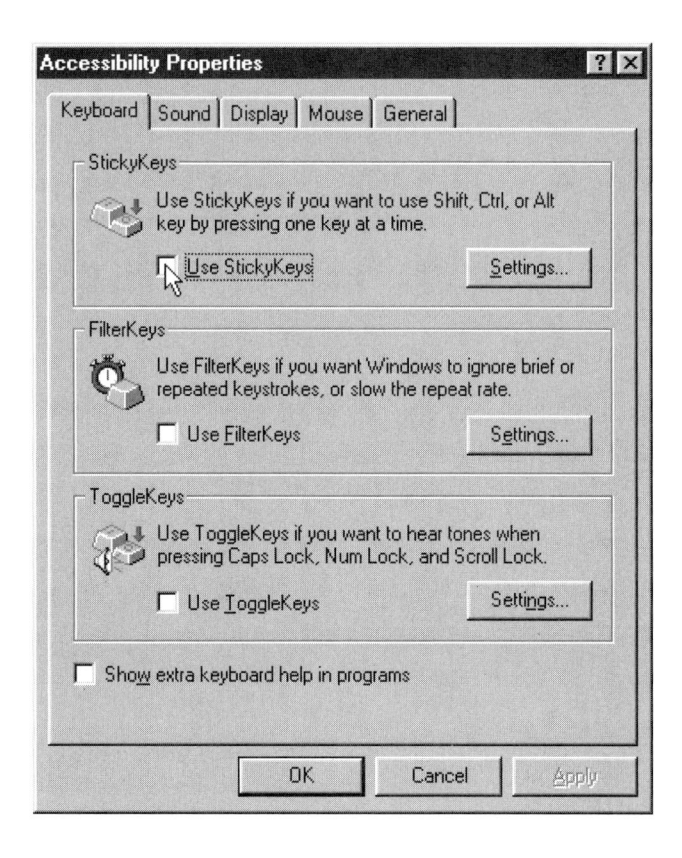

Adaptive Technology

Adaptive technology refers to equipment used in conjunction with a computer to assist people with disabilities in the use of the computer. Adaptive technology includes devices that are designed to assist those with impaired vision, hearing, or motor skills.

The purpose of the following discussion is to increase your awareness of the types of adaptive technology devices that are currently available. You should always consult with your physician, physical therapist, or other appropriate medical professional prior to making decisions regarding the use of such devices.

Display Options

In addition to the Windows Accessibility Options discussed previously, different display technologies are available to assist visually impaired users. Common solutions include larger display areas, audible feedback, and even tactile output using a Braille system.

Depending on the severity of the visual impairment, a simple increase in the size of the display may be a workable solution. The most common size for display monitors used in modern CAD industry is between 17″ and 19″. Larger display sizes are available from many different manufacturers. A 21″ monitor provides more than 1½ times the area of a 17″ monitor and monitor sizes up to 35″ are now available, providing more than four times the area of a 17″ monitor.

Very large computer monitors can be very expensive and so may be cost-prohibitive. One alternative is to use a dual monitor system. If your video adapter supports multiple display monitors, you can place two smaller monitors side by side to increase the display area at a much more affordable price.

Audible feedback systems can augment the display through tools such as *screen readers*. A screen reader converts text on your screen into speech, but it has no option for displaying geometric information such as a CAD drawing.

Braille output systems can also output text in a nonvisual format, typically one to four lines of up to 80 characters per line, but like audible feedback systems, cannot yet display geometric or graphical information.

Keyboard Options

A variety of adaptive technology options are available to provide enhanced accessibility to computer keyboards. One of the simplest options is to configure your keyboard to match your style of use. Earlier discussion introduced many of the options for keyboards that are set using the Accessibility Wizard (or Accessibility Options). Other options are available from the Keyboard Properties dialog box. For example, if you tend

FIGURE D.7

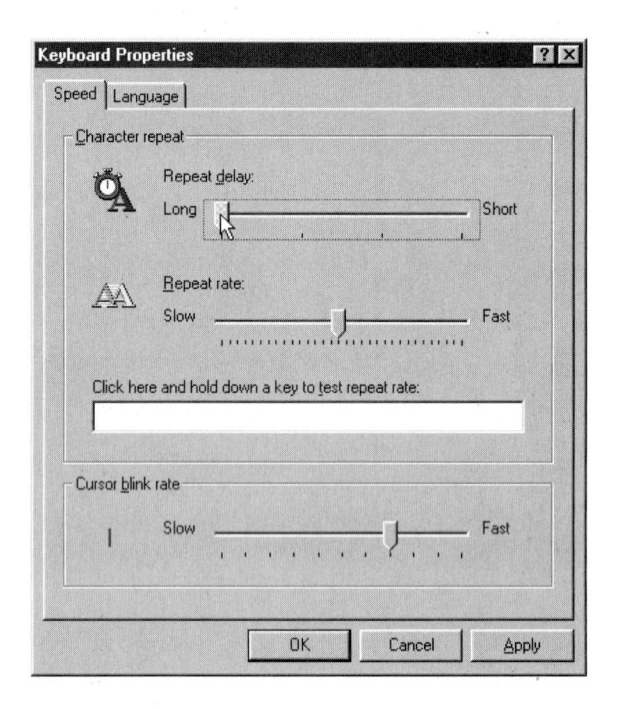

to press keys too slowly, the keyboard may switch into repeat mode and enter multiple characters when you intended to enter only one. To modify the behavior of your keyboard, pick the Start button from your task bar, then pick Settings Control Panel. In the Control Panel window, pick the Keyboard icon to display the Keyboard Properties dialog box, as shown in Figure D.7.

The Repeat Delay slider controls how long you must continue to press a key before it begins to repeat. Four incremental settings are shown along the slider bar. When the slider is moved all the way to Short, the delay is one-half second; all the way toward Long sets the delay at 2 seconds. The Repeat Rate slider controls how fast Windows enters the repetitive characters. If the slider is moved all the way to Fast, approximately 40 characters per second are printed when repeating; the Slowest speed prints out about 2 or 3 characters per second.

If this option does not work or does not produce consistent results, a *key guard* may be a better choice. A key guard is a plastic or metal overlay that covers the keyboard and has holes in it that allow only the keys positioned directly below them to be pressed. This device helps prevent accidental pressing of more than one key at a time with either a finger or a typing stick. This cover also helps improve accuracy and minimizes accidental keystrokes. Additionally, it allows users to rest their hands on the key guard without fear of accidentally pressing keys. These features make the keyboard much more accessible to users with stress injuries or motor coordination impairments.

For those users with very minor difficulties using the keyboard, a good solution might be to use an ergonomic keyboard. The Keyboard Properties dialog box also allows the keyboard to be reconfigured for the DVORAK keyboard layout. The DVORAK keyboard layout is a much more efficient layout that requires significantly fewer motions than the standard (or QWERTY) keyboard. To make this change, pick the Language tab in the Keyboard Properties dialog box. Highlight the English (United States) selection in the list and pick the Properties button. In the Language Properties dialog box, pick the United States — Dvorak option. Changing the function of specific keys on the keyboard is referred to as *remapping* the keys. Keep in mind that remapping the keys does not change the letters that appear on the keyboard; it changes only which characters appear on screen when you press the keys. You will need to learn the DVORAK keyboard layout before you can begin to use this configuration effectively.

Some companies currently manufacture single-handed keyboards, which are designed to provide quick and comfortable access to all the available keys. Figure D.8 shows an example of single-handed keyboards for right- and left-handed users. Notice the curved design that keeps all the keys within reach at the same time, allowing easier access for users who have limited mobility or who are able to use only a single hand. The manufacturer of the keyboard shown in this illustration indicates that experienced users have demonstrated the ability to input up to 60 words per minute in word-processing applications. Other considerations made for single-handed users include "Push-On" and "Push-Off" functions for the Shift, Ctrl, and Alt keys to assist with pressing key combinations with one hand. Another unique product for single-handed users implements a foot pedal that allows one-finger input for combined keystrokes.

APPENDIX D ||| Accessibility Features

FIGURE D.8 For computer users who are only able to use one hand for keyboarding, adaptive single-handed keyboards provide easier and faster access than conventional keyboards. [Photos courtesy of PCD Maltron, Ltd. (www.Maltron.com)]

Other keyboard designs are available for users who can use only a one-finger pointing method or who cannot use their hands to operate a keyboard. These keyboards use a gently curved profile that helps minimize motion requirements for better accessibility. Figure D.9 shows an example of this style of keyboard and shows a user working with a mouth stick to access the keys. Users working with a mouth stick need to minimize motions to prevent neck and shoulder fatigue.

FIGURE D.9 The mouth stick style keyboard provides easy access for users who cannot use their hands to operate a keyboard. [Photo courtesy of PCD Maltron, Ltd. (www.Maltron.com)]

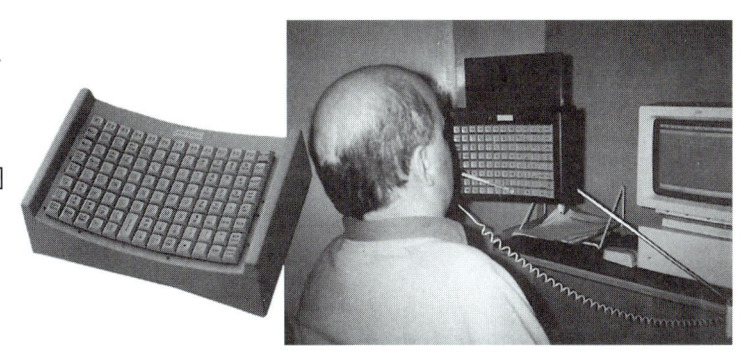

Expanded keyboards are oversized keyboards with larger keys, "sticky" buttons, and other accessibility features. Some expanded keyboards use slightly recessed keys to help prevent entry errors due to convulsive movement or muscular spasms.

Software applications can be used to manage a *virtual keyboard* — a simulated keyboard that is displayed on the monitor and accessed with a pointing device or speech recognition system. Many of these applications assist the user through *word prediction*, which reduces typing requirements by automatically finishing many of the words or commands being typed.

Some systems provide a comprehensive speech recognition interface that allows the user to input software commands by speaking. Speech recognition systems are much better today than they were a few years ago, but they still present certain challenges to working effectively. Inconsistencies in speech patterns, background noises, and the system's difficulty in understanding contiguous speech can increase the possibilities that voice commands will be misunderstood. Modern speech recognition systems may have a 30,000- to more than a 50,000-word vocabulary. Software can be "trained" to recognize new commands or words, such as technical terms or even vendor names. Optionally, custom voice command libraries containing many words specific to specific trades or industries can be purchased.

Pointing Devices Options

Pointing devices come in many different configurations. Users who have difficulty working with a mouse can find a variety of alternative pointing devices. One of the most common mouse alternatives is the trackball. Both the mouse and the trackball translate the movement of a ball into cursor movement on screen. When using a mouse, you must continually move your hand, rotate your wrist, and extend your arm. A trackball, however, allows you to rest your hand and arm in a comfortable position and roll the ball with your fingers or thumb to move the cursor. Many different sizes and styles of trackballs have been designed to assist with a diverse range of needs.

Joysticks are frequently thought of primarily as a gaming accessory; however, many companies manufacture joystick and software combinations that provide all the functionality of a two- or three- button mouse.

Many computer users who experience difficulty using a mouse are able to use a joystick effectively. Much like a trackball, a joystick allows you to rest your arm and hand comfortably in a set position.

Some of the additional adaptive technologies that address pointing device accessibility include touch screens and touch tablets. With a touch screen, users can point to what they want directly on the display and tap it to pick. A touch tablet works according to the same principle, but rather than a display monitor, a flat tablet device is used. The tablet can lie flat or it can be inclined as needed. Some of these devices, though, require as much or more motion than even a mouse.

Users who require a hands-free-style interface may be able to utilize eye-control technology as their primary interface option. Some systems are able to track the motion of the eyes and apply that motion to the on-screen cursor. Others track head movement to guide the cursor. An intentional blink is used to specify a cursor pick. Blinking twice signifies a double-click. Because text input is fundamental to much of what we do with computers, these types of adaptive technologies are often used in conjunction with an on-screen keyboard and integrated word prediction.

Earlier, we described how a mouth-stick can provide keyboard accessibility. This same type of interface can be applied as a pointing device and used with a virtual (on-screen) keyboard. Many mouth stick pointing device systems use a breath switch system referred to as sip and puff. A "sip" (drawing air in) through the mouth stick activates one mouse button function, such as a pick. A "puff" (pushing air out) through the mouth stick activates the second mouse button function. Some sip-and-puff systems have additional control features that respond to lip pressure or other user actions.

Resources for Further Study

The following is a list of some available resources on the World Wide Web for gathering further information on accessibility features and adaptive technology.

Center for Information Technology Accommodation (CITA)
http://www.itpolicy.gsa.gov/cita

Alliance For Technology Access
http://www.ataccess.org

Vendor Members of the Alliance for Technology Access
http://www.ataccess.org/atavendors.html

The National Institute on Disability and Rehabilitation Research —
U.S. Department of Education "AbleData" Website
http://www.abledata.com

Center for Applied Special Technology
http://www.cast.org

Equal Access to Software and Information
http://www.isc.rit.edu/~easi

Family Guide to Assistive Technology
http://www.pluk.org/AT1.html

Glossary

absolute coordinates A point specification method based on the Cartesian coordinate system that indicates locations in a drawing relative to the origin, 0,0. Absolute coordinates are entered as X axis and Y axis values separated by a comma (X,Y) or, in a 3D point specification, X,Y, and Z axis values (X,Y,Z).

accelerator keystrokes Key combinations provided for easy access to commonly used functions and commands.

actual size When referring to an AutoCAD LT drawing, the scale is 100% or full size. The AutoCAD term for this is *World Size*.

alert box Used to display an error or warning message.

aligned dimensioning Type of dimensioning in which text for horizontal dimensions is placed horizontally and reads from the bottom of the sheet, text for vertical dimensions is placed vertically and reads from the right side of the sheet, and dimensions placed at an angle have the text placed at the same angle.

alphanumeric character Letters and numbers.

alternate units The second set of units shown when dual dimensioning is used. Dual dimensioning shows inch measurements followed by millimeter measurements in brackets or vice versa. Dual dimensioning is no longer a recommended ASME standard.

annotation Any text, notes, dimensions, and text symbols on a drawing.

annotation symbol A symbol used in combination with text.

aperture A box on the screen cursor that allows the user to easily pick an object. Also known as a *target box*.

approximation point A point that a curve or surface follows, but might not pass through. Compare with *interpolation point*.

argument Data provided to a function that operates on the data.

ASCII American Standard Code for Information Interchange. Refers to a set of standard alphabetical characters and numbers.

aspect ratio The ratio of width to height.

associative dimensions Dimensions whose values automatically change to match those of an edit.

associative hatch pattern A hatch that is automatically revised to fit a new boundary if the hatch boundary is changed.

attribute Information stored within a block reference the describe the characteristics of the block. See also *invisible block attributes* and *visible block attributes*.

attribute definition Special type of object that is included as part of a block definition.

Autosnap A feature of AutoCAD that works with object snaps to display a marker at the object snap location when you move the cursor to indicate the desired object or snap point.

baseline dimensioning See *datum dimensioning*.

basic dimension Value that is considered a theoretically perfect size, profile, orientation, or location dimension.

bearing The direction of a line with respect to one of the quadrants of a compass. Bearings are measured either clockwise or counterclockwise depending on the quadrant and beginning from either north or south.

big font An Asian or other large-format font. A big font cannot be specified as a primary font file.

binary file format Format in which information is stored as a series of 1's and 0's.

binding The process of permanently adding an Xref to the current drawing.

bitmap A record of colors that comprises an image.

blip Temporary screen marks that are displayed when you pick a point.

block A collective representation of any number of regular AutoCAD LT objects that is stored and used as a single object. Predrawn symbols. See also *locally defined block*.

block reference A block that has been inserted into a drawing.

boundary set A group of objects that AutoCAD LT analyzes for the boundary definition when you specify a point on the drawing.

bounding box Defines the size of the area in which a drawing is contained.

B-spline An approximate curve. Also known as a *nonuniform rational B-spline (NURBS)*.

byblock A specialized linetype and color setting that allows objects that are part of a block to reflect current drawing or layer settings.

byte The approximate space required by a computer to store one text character. A byte is eight bits, which are electronic on/off signals that are put together to make a message for the computer to interpret.

Cartesian coordinate system Coordinate system used to locate points within a drawing relative to two intersecting axes (2D), or three intersecting axes (3D). In 2D coordinate specifications, the X and Y axes are used, and in 3D coordinates the third Z axis is also referenced.

cascading menu Groups of selected commands that are accessed by picking a pull-down menu item.

central processing unit (CPU) Primary component of computer that processes the data and numerical calculations needed to run software applications.

775

chain dimensioning Type of dimensioning in which the next dimension continues from the previous dimension. Also called *continuous dimensioning* and *point-to-point dimensioning*.

chamfer In mechanical drafting for manufacturing, chamfers are slightly angled corners. AutoCAD LT lets you make any desired angled corner using the CHAMFER command.

circular referencing The situation that occurs when a drawing is externally referenced that, in turn, externally references the current drawing.

circumference Perimeter line of a circle.

client application See *container application*.

clip art A collection of artistic symbols and images.

clipping plane An imaginary plane that hides part of a drawing.

command Instructions given by the user of a computer program.

command alias A shortened version of a command name that allows you to enter commands more quickly at the keyboard.

command script A text file that contains a list of commands and options that AutoCAD LT reads and performs.

compact disk See *optical disk*.

compile The process by which menu files are rewritten, with the latest changes, in a way that provides the fastest access by AutoCAD LT to the information.

complex linetype A linetype that incorporates text or symbols into the basic line pattern to supply additional information.

composite The final drawing that is a combination of views, border, and title block.

computer-aided design (CAD) Area of CADD that is associated with the creation and editing of technical drawings.

computer-aided design and drafting (CADD) Computer technology that provides powerful engineering tools used for the creation and analysis of precision technical drawings.

construction lines Lines that extend into infinity in one or two directions. Also referred to as *xlines* and *rays*.

container application The destination application, or software package, for an OLE object. Also called *client application*.

continuous dimensioning See *chain dimensioning*.

control code Combinations of text characters used to add special characters to a text object, such as a degree or diameter symbol.

coordinate Numbers assigned to points so they can be located on a grid in the Cartesian coordinate system.

coordinate display Indicates where the cursor is in relation to the drawing origin.

crosshairs Vertical and horizontal line combination cursor.

cubic curve An extremely smooth curve with the elements of the curve passing through the first and last control points and close to the other control points. Compare with *quadratic curve*.

cursor Computer onscreen symbol to indicate location on the screen. It moves with the movement of the mouse or arrow keys.

cylindrical coordinate A coordinate specification that uses a standard polar coordinate entry followed by a Z axis value.

data field Individual areas that are filled in with information in a drawing title block.

datum dimensioning Dimensioning in which every dimension begins at the same starting place. Also called *baseline dimensioning*.

Default Command prompt options and values that are set by AutoCAD LT until changed. The changed option or value is then used.

delimit To separate individual objects or fields within a group or series; some text files use spaces or commas to separate and identify each field.

demand loading A feature that increases the performance of AutoCAD LT by loading only the portion of a referenced drawing that is required to regenerate the current drawing.

dependent symbol Any named object defined in an externally referenced drawing.

desktop Refers to the layout of icons and features on the operating system screen.

deviation See *unequal bilateral tolerance*.

dialog box Provides the means for entering instructions or settings for a software program.

diameter The distance across a circle that passes through the center of a circle.

digitizer tablet Device used to track the position of the pointing device on its surface.

dimension styles Saved sets of dimension variable settings that determine the appearance of the dimensions.

dimension variables AutoCAD LT system variables that help you control the way dimensions look. Also called *dimvars*.

dimensioning Measurements given on a drawing. See also *aligned dimensioning, chain dimensioning, datum dimensioning,* and *unidirectional dimensioning*.

dimensioning mode AutoCAD LT dimensioning at the command line using the DIM or DIM1 commands.

dimensions Numerical values expressed in appropriate units of measure and indicated on a drawing and in other documents. See also *associative dimensions, linear dimensions, location dimensions, oblique dimensions, ordinate dimensions,* and *size dimensions*.

dimvar See *dimension variable*.

direct distance entry Feature that allows the user to point the cursor in the direction in which the next point should be placed and simply specify the distance.

direct hatching Used to define a hatch boundary and hatch pattern placement. The user then instructs AutoCAD to remove or retain the hatch boundary during the hatching process.

docked Placement of a toolbar that removes the title bar and embeds it in the program window.

donut In AutoCAD LT, a filled circle or ring. Also known as a *doughnut*.

dot matrix printer Low-quality printer often used for check prints rather than final drawings.

double line Pairs of parallel lines and arcs.

double-click Mouse action of clicking a mouse button twice very quickly.

download The process of receiving files from a remote site through your modem or network connection.

drawing aids Help make drawing easy and accurate; examples are Grid, Snap, and Ortho.

drawing database The information stored by AutoCAD LT to define the objects in a drawing file.

drawing extents The area of a drawing that contains objects.

drawing origin Located at coordinates 0.0000,0.0000 and found at the lower left corner of the screen when you start AutoCAD. Also referred to simply as *origin*.

edit The process of erasing, moving, copying, or altering objects.

edit box A box that provides a means for entering text or number values into a dialog box. Also referred to as a *text box*.

electrophotographic plotter A plotter used for large-volume plots. The process uses a line of closely spaced, electrically charged wire nibs to produce dots on coated paper. Pressure or heat is then used to attach ink to the charged dots. It is much faster than a pen plotter. Also known as an *electrostatic plotter*.

elevation The Z coordinate location.

ellipse An object drawn by a curve that has a constant value equal to the sum of its distance from two fixed points.

e-mail Shortened version of *electronic mail*, this is a means of communication via computer.

embedding The process of placing an OLE object in a container application.

equal bilateral tolerance Tolerance for which variation is permitted equally in both directions from the specified dimension. Compare with *unequal bilateral tolerance*.

ergonomic With reference to computers, refers to the science of adapting a workstation to fit the user's body comfortably.

extended intersection The point at which one object would intersect another if both objects were extended far enough along their natural paths of extension.

extension The distance a dimension line extends beyond the extension line.

external reference A source drawing outside of the current drawing that AutoCAD LT refers to when information is needed. Referred to as an *Xref*.

family member In terms of dimensions, this is one of the specific dimension types, including linear, radial, angular, diameter, ordinate, and leaders.

fast font A font that can be drawn and regenerated very quickly.

field width Number of character positions used in a field.

file server A central computer with a large amount of storage space that is used for storing files from many workstations within a network.

fillet In mechanical drafting for manufacturing, fillets are slightly rounded inside corners, and rounds are slightly rounded outside corners. AutoCAD LT lets you make any desired rounded corner using the FILLET command.

filters Used to remove or combine certain values to create a new value.

floating model space viewports "Holes" through which the viewer can see through the paper to the drawing in model space.

flyout A toolbar button that displays additional related commands. This is like a toolbar within a toolbar.

font See *text font*.

font file A font definition resource in which a complete font is available for use.

From An option that allows you to specify a point that is a specific location from a given point.

general notes Notes that supply information that applies to the entire drawing.

global edit The process of changing every occurrence of a specific attribute value in the current drawing.

global setting A type of setting that affects an entire drawing. Compare to *individual setting*, which affects a single object or group of objects.

gradient A unit of angular measure. A circle has 400 grads.

grid A pattern of dots displayed on the screen in increments established by the user.

grips Squares that are automatically displayed on a line when you move the cursor to the line and pick it.

hard disk Magnetic drive for storage of computer programs and files. Also referred to as a *nonremovable drive*.

hardcopy A printed version of a computer file.

hardware Physical computer equipment.

hatch A pattern used to fill in areas of a drawing.

hatch boundary The shape that encloses a hatch pattern.

hatchable Capable of being hatched. An object must be closed to be hatchable, or be part of a set of objects that form a closed boundary.

healing A situation in which an area becomes filled with a hatch pattern.

help strings The items that appear on the status line when a menu selection is pointed to or highlighted. They allow users to be certain of what action is to be performed.

hyperlink Items in HTML documents that are linked to other Web resources.

HyperText Text items that are linked to other resources.

implied windowing The ability to automatically place a window around an object or objects to select by picking and moving the mouse.

included angle The angle formed between the start point, endpoint, and center of an arc.

individual setting A type of setting that affects only an individually drawn object or group of objects without changing the entire drawing. Compare to *global setting*, which affects the entire drawing.

ink-jet printer Printer that is capable of producing a high-quality image, but at slower rates than a laser printer, by spraying ink droplets onto paper to produce dot matrix images.

insertion base point A meaningful reference point that is used to position a symbol when it is inserted into a drawing after a block definition has been created.

interactive layer A logical grouping of data; akin to transparent overlays on a mechanical drawing.

interface The method by which users communicate with a computer program, which is referred to as the user interface. The hardware interface is where the computer works with other parts of the system. The software interface is the programming that allows the computer applications to work with the operating system.

Internet A worldwide network of computers connected to one another through telecommunication lines.

interpolation point A point through which a curve or surface passes to define the curve or surface. Compare with *approximation point*.

intuitive interface A method by which users communicate with a computer program in a clear, easy-to-understand manner. Also see *interface*.

invisible block attribute Attribute that is part of the block reference but not displayed on the drawing as part of a text label. Compare with *visible block attributes*.

island An enclosed area within a hatch pattern.

isometric drawing A 3-D pictorial in which the three axes are true measurements of the object and form equal angles.

isometric projection The true appearance of the model as though it were tilted toward the viewer.

justification Determines how text is aligned with the insertion point.

keyboard Input device for a computer, with keys that are similar to a typewriter and additional keys such as numeric keys and function keys.

label An item of text that is visible to the user on a given menu.

laser printer Printer capable of producing high-quality images using a laser, which draws lines on a revolving plate that is charged with high voltage. The laser light causes the plate to discharge as an ink toner adheres to the images and ink is bonded to paper by pressure or heat.

layer visibility The property that determines if an object that has been drawn on a layer is visible or invisible.

leader bubble A circle attached to a leader and with a numeric value inside.

limits tolerance Tolerance for which the plus and minus part of the tolerance is calculated with the specified dimension to provide tolerance limits. Compare to *plus/minus tolerance*.

line of sight An imaginary line of infinite length that passes through the camera location and the target point.

line text See *single-line text*.

linear dimensions Dimensions that are placed in a straight line that is either horizontal, vertical, or at an angle.

linetype Types of drafting lines. Recommended linetypes have been identified by the American National Standards Institute. See Appendix B for examples.

linetype scale Scale used to determine the length of dashes in linetypes such as hidden and center lines.

linked object An object that is connected to the original data and is updated when the source file changes.

list box A box that provides several options from which to choose.

locally defined block A block that is defined within the current drawing.

location dimensions Used to locate features and objects.

lock file When a file is being edited, AutoCAD LT creates a lock file to prevent the file from being simultaneously opened and edited by another user. Drawing lock files have a .DWK file extension.

logical extents The area of the drawing that AutoCAD LT is currently keeping within video memory.

macro A set of multiple commands and options that runs automatically once started.

major axis The length of an ellipse.

marker A special symbol used to indicate the correct object snap mode and point on an object on screen.

memory Temporary storage space in a computer.

menu List of available options and commands from which to choose.

menu call A special code that displays a menu or makes it active. All menu calls start with a dollar sign ($).

minor axis The width of an ellipse.

mnemonic Underlined character in a menu bar and each menu option that provides keyboard access to the pull-down menus and menu items, rather than use of a mouse pick item.

mode A setting or operating condition controlled by the user.

model AutoCAD LT name for a drawing. The geometry that is created to define the object drawn.

model space The space in which the geometry is created that defines your model, or drawing.

modem A translation device that allows a computer to transmit and receive digital information through telephone lines.

monitor Display device for a computer.

mouse Pointing device used to control the onscreen movement of the cursor.

multiline text Letters and numbers on a drawing that are entered and edited in paragraph form. Compare to *single-line text*. Also called *paragraph text*.

multiview layout A drawing that shows more than one view of the object drawn.

named object Any item that is assigned a name, such as layers, blocks, linetypes, and text styles.

nested Xref Any Xref contained within another Xref.

nesting The practice of permitting existing block references to be used in the creation of other block definitions.

node A point object.

nonassociative hatch pattern A hatch that is not automatically revised to fit a new boundary if the hatch boundary is changed.

notes Information provided on a drawing. See also *general notes* and *specific notes*.

noun/verb selection The process of picking objects to be edited prior to selecting the editing command.

NURBS See *B-spline*.

object application The source application, or software package, for an OLE object. Also called *server application*.

object snaps Allow commonly referenced points on an object to be selected easily and accurately.

oblique dimensions Dimensions that have the extension lines placed at an angle from the feature being dimensioned.

on-line help Help supplied by a computer program while a user is working.

operating system Software that controls the basic operation of a computer.

optical disk Storage device for computer program files that has large amounts of storage, typically 4 GB or more. Also referred to as a *compact disk*.

option line The available options for the currently active command.

ordinate dimensions Dimensions drawn without the traditional dimension lines and arrowheads. Also called *arrowless dimensions*.

orphaned The situation describing an Xref when the Xref in which it is nested is unloaded.

pan Changing the location of a view without changing its size.

paper space A special drawing environment intended only for creating a final layout of your drawing for plotting purposes.

paragraph text See *multiline text*.

parallel projection A 3-D view that does not show perspective.

parameter A value, name, option, or characteristic. Also defines the boundaries of an object when used as part of an AutoCAD LT command.

parent style In terms of dimensions, this is a general style that applies to all of the family members, or each type of dimension.

partial menu file One that has only specific items in it, such as a set of specialized pull-down menus or toolbars.

path objects An object type used in the creation of PostScript files.

peripherals Computer input and output devices.

perpendicular At right (90-degree) angles.

perspective view View of objects that makes them appear as if they are being viewed in the real world, with closer objects being larger and distant objects being smaller.

pick box A small box to which the cursor changes when you get the Select objects: prompt.

pick button Button on a mouse, puck, or stylus that is used to cause an action.

picture elements See *pixels*.

pipe symbol. See *vertical bar*.

pixels An acronym for *picture elements*, these are the small discrete elements that together make up an image on a monitor.

pline See *polyline*.

plot spooler A piece of hardware or software that sends plot files to a plotting device.

plotter Output device used to print large-format drawings. *Pen plotters* and *pencil plotters* are available. Plotters use a liquid ink, felt tip, or pencil to place images on paper by traversing. Also see *electrophotographic plotter*.

plus/minus tolerance Tolerance for which a specified dimension and tolerance values are given. Compare to *limits tolerance*.

point filter Used to extract the X, Y, and Z coordinate values from individual points in order to create a new combined point. Also referred to as *coordinate filters*.

point-to-point dimensioning See *chain dimensioning*.

polar coordinates A point specification method based on the Cartesian coordinate system that indicates locations in a drawing relative to the current location. Polar coordinates are entered as a distance and angle preceded by the @ symbol and separated by the < symbol (@distance<angle).

Polarsnap A feature that allows you to draw or edit objects using specific angles and increments without typing values at the keyboard.

Polar tooltip An AutoCAD LT feature that tells you the distance and angle being entered.

polygon A planar geometric object with three or more sides.

polyline An object composed of one or more line segments or circular arcs that are treated as a single object. Also referred to as a *pline*.

prefix A special note or application that is placed in front of the dimension text.

primary units That part of the dimension from which tolerances or other units are calculated or related.

printer Output device for a computer that provides hard copy.

prompt A request by a program for input.

puck Specialized type of pointing device for cursor control. Used with a digitizer tablet.

pull-down menu A menu that is accessed by picking a menu name. The menu displayed appears to be pulled down from the menu bar.

quadrant One quarter of the circle in the polar coordinate system.

quadratic curve Not as smooth as a cubic curve because the curve passes through the first and last control points but the rest of the curve is tangent to the polyline segments at intermediate control points. Compare with *cubic curve*.

radian An angular unit, arc, or rotational measure in which pi radians equals 180 degrees.

radius The distance from the center of a circle to its circumference.

raster information A record of the assigned colors of pixels within a defined area.

ray casting The process of sending out an invisible ray. When the ray hits an object, it turns counterclockwise and follows the object to trace the hatch boundary.

read-only memory (ROM) Memory that allows files to be read, but not changed and no additional data can be added.

rectangle A geometric figure with four sides and four right angles.

recursive toolbar Used when a flyout toolbar button displays the toolbar that the flyout is on.

referencing The process by which AutoCAD LT refers to the source file to obtain information, rather than storing it in the current drawing.

regenerate The process of reading the current drawing database and redefining the virtual screen.

regular polygon A plane geometric object with three or more equal length sides and equal included angles.

reinitialize To reload a support file or restart a device driver.

relative coordinates A point specification method based on the Cartesian coordinate system that indicates locations in a drawing relative to the current location. Relative coordinates are entered as the total change in X and Y axis values preceded by the @ symbol and separated by a comma (@change in X, change in Y).

rendering The process of applying shape and color to the surfaces in a drawing.

resolution Term used to indicate display quality. The more pixels, the higher the resolution and sharper the image. Also refers to the quality of a printed image.

rewritable Capable of storing, erasing, and replacing files.

right-hand rule Provides an easy-to-understand reference to determine the positive and negative directions of the X, Y, and Z axes.

rubberband cursor Temporary dashed line between a chosen point and the current cursor location; shows the user how the line will be placed if a particular point is chosen in relation to the preceding point.

running object snap An object snap option or group of options that is set to run continuously.

scale factor Determines the final size of characteristics such as text height, dimension features, and linetype appearance for a plotted drawing.

search area The area searched by AutoCAD's DLINE Snap option when attempting to snap to another object.

selection set The objects selected for editing become part of a selection set.

serifs Fine artistic lines projecting from, generally, the top and bottom of a letter.

server application See *object application*.

shading The process of applying simple colors to all drawing surfaces without consideration being given to lighting, shadows, or reflections.

sheet size The size of the paper on which a drawing is printed or plotted. When printed or plotted, units are scaled to fit the sheet size. Appendix B shows standard ANSI/ASME inch and metric sheet sizes.

simple linetype A linetype that is made up only of lines and spaces.

single-line text Short text entries of letters and numbers on a drawing. Each line of text can be edited individually. Compare to *multiline text*. Also called *line text*.

size dimensions Used to provide the measurements for the size of features and objects.

slide A special type of file that records the current drawing display so it can be viewed later. A "picture" of a drawing.

slide show Displays a sequence of graphic images created from slide files.

slider Used to change values interactively by picking the arrows at either end of a bar and moving them along the bar.

snap An invisible grid that forces the cursor to move in exact increments as established by the user.

Snaptip A feature that identifies the name of the object snap that has been activated.

software Computer programs.

spec Abbreviation for *specification*.

specific notes Notes that apply to specific features on a drawing and may be connected to the features with a leader line. Also known as *local notes*.

specified dimension Primary units part of the dimension being toleranced.

spherical coordinate A coordinate specification that uses a standard polar coordinate entry to specify distance and angle *in* the X,Y plane, followed by an angle specification *from* the X,Y plane.

spline-fit curve The curve created when using the Fit and Spline options of the PEDIT command.

sticky-back Predrawn symbol that is printed on a transparent media that has an adhesive backing. When a symbol is needed, it is simply placed in the appropriate location on the drawing and held in place by the adhesive.

stylus Specialized type of pointing device for cursor control. Used with a digitizer tablet.

subdialog box A box that is displayed and made active without hiding or ending the previous dialog box.

suffix A special note or application that is placed behind the dimension text.

support file A file that is not part of the core program that is used to enhance or modify the way AutoCAD LT works.

surface model A visual representation of a 3-D object created by describing the surfaces only. Such objects do not have the same properties as solid objects.

symbol A simplified graphic image used to represent specific elements of a drawing.

symbol library An organized collection of drafting symbols and other commonly used drawing elements that is saved as an individual AutoCAD LT drawing file.

symbol table The information stored regarding named objects such as blocks, linetypes, and text styles.

system mouse Refers to either a mouse or digitizer and indicates that the pointing device is used by AutoCAD LT as well as the operating system.

2-D Two-dimensional; a flat drawing method where objects are drawn on the X,Y plane and have no Z axis value (thickness).

3-D Three-dimensional; a drawing that represents objects on the X, Y, and Z axes to give a real-world appearance. Three-dimensional objects have height, width, and thickness.

Tab Set A series of shortcuts to drawings containing blocks or to folders containing drawings.

tangent The characteristic of a line, arc, or circle touching another arc or circle at only one point without intersecting or crossing each other and a line from the center of the arc or circle is 90° to a line at the point of tangency, or a line between the centers of tangent arcs or circles passes through the point of tangency.

target box See *aperture*.

target option An anchor point in a drawing; used with the CAmera option.

template A drawing file with preestablished settings. Also referred to as a *prototype*.

text The AutoCAD LT term for letters and numbers.

text boundary Establishes the width of the paragraph text.

text font A complete set of characters, including letters, numbers, marks, and symbols, that is of unique proportion and design.

text style The settings that determine the appearance of text characters. The user controls what the computer does by sending it commands via keyboard or other input device.

thermal plotter A plotter that uses tiny heat elements to burn dot matrix characters into treated paper. Produces high-quality hardcopy.

thickness A property assigned to drawing objects or the drawing environment that controls the Z axis dimension.

tiled model space The active area of a drawing when TILE-MODE is set to 1 (on).

title bar Area across the top or bottom of a program window that lists the program and name of the currently opened file.

tolerance Total amount by which a specific dimension is permitted to vary. See also *equal bilateral tolerance, limits tolerance, plus/minus tolerance, unequal bilateral tolerance,* and *unilateral tolerance.*

tooltip A small text box displayed next to the cursor that shows the name of the button at which the cursor is pointing.

tracking A process in which a point is located relative to other points on the drawing.

transparent command A transparent command can be used without interrupting a currently active command as long as it does not require a drawing regeneration and it does not change the drawing database. Transparent commands are entered by typing an apostrophe (') before the command name.

troubleshooting The process of trying to figure out what went wrong, for example, if a script file does not execute properly.

undo To return to the condition a drawing was in prior to execution of the last command.

unequal bilateral tolerance Tolerance for which variation is permitted unequally in both directions from the specified dimension. Compare with *equal bilateral tolerance.* Also known as *deviation.*

ungraceful exit An unplanned exit from AutoCAD LT that is caused by system crashes and power failures.

unidirectional dimensioning Type of dimensioning in which all of the dimension numbers are placed horizontally on the drawing and read from the bottom of the sheet.

unilateral tolerance Tolerance for which variation is permitted in only one direction from the specified dimension.

unreferenced data Data that defines something that does not exist or is not used in a drawing.

URL Uniform resource locator; a feature that describes the location, or address, of a file found on the internet.

variable A text item that represents a value which is stored for later use.

vector A line that describes distance and direction.

vector information A record of the distances, angles, and properties associated with distinct drawing objects.

vertex The point at which polyline segments meet. Plural: *vertices.*

vertical bar Symbol (|) used to separate the dependent symbol name from the Xref on which it is dependent. Also called the *pipe symbol.*

video adapter card One of a computer's printed circuit boards that controls the graphic display on a monitor.

viewport Window or windows in which the model space of a drawing in paper space is displayed.

virtual screen An area of memory in which AutoCAD LT stores the current drawing so the user can change the display area without having to read the drawing from the hard disk.

visible block attribute Attribute that is used to generate simple text labels to identify specific information regarding a symbol. Compare with *invisible block attributes.*

Web server A computer system that stores and sends requested files on the World Wide Web.

wild card An asterisk (*) symbol which is used to match anything that is similar.

window Graphical user interface-type operating system in which a rectangular frame or frames on the screen allow the user to work on applications or files. Allows the user to run different applications at the same time, each in its own window.

WinTab driver A piece of software that allows AutoCAD LT to utilize a tablet while working in the Windows environment.

wire frame A 3-D shape that uses lines and curves to describe its outline.

word wrapping The process by which words that exceed the boundary width are automatically moved, or "wrapped," to the next line.

workstation Powerful personal computer set up to do work applications. Provides quality graphics and has high-capacity hard drive and can be networked.

World Wide Web An easy-to-understand interface to the Internet.

Xref See *external reference.*

zoom To change the apparent size of an object for viewing.

Index

A

A (*See* ARC command)
AA (*See* AREA command)
Absolute coordinates, 52
Accelerator keys, 19, 710–13
Add option, 65–66, 236, 323
Advanced Options dialog box, 394, 395
Advanced Setup, 85–95
Advanced Setup dialog box, 85–95, 559
AE (*See* ATTEDIT command)
Aerial View window:
   adjusting display, 143
   controlling updating, 143–44
   panning with, 143
   role of, 141
   toggling between, 141, 144
   zooming with, 142–43
Alert box, 15–16
Aligned dimensioning, 423, 431, 436, 450
Alignment/justification options, 344–46
Alphanumeric characters, 487, 672
Alternate units dimensioning, 461
Ambient light, 605
Angle(s) (*See also* 3-D viewing angles):
   bearing, 87
   calculating, 207
   decimal degrees, 86
   degrees/minutes/seconds, 86
   dimensioning, 432–34
   direction, 88
   drawing bisector of, 218
   drawing construction lines at an, 217–18
   gradient (grads), 87
   hatch patterns, 387–88
   included, 105, 110–11, 255

   measure tab, 87–88
   radians, 87
   rotating with a reference, 251–52
   rotating with a relative, 251
   rotation, 109
   setting, 86–88
   Snap, 220–22
   surveyor, 87
Angle options, drawing chamfers with, 283
Annotation, 367, 453, 462
Annotation dialog box, 453–62
Annotation symbol, 494–95
Anonymous login, 661
APERTURE (AP) command, 193
Aperture size, adjusting, 193
Approximation point, 322
AR (*See* ARRAY command)
ARC (A) command, 103–7
Architectural units, 40, 41, 58
Arcs, dimensioning, 432–34
Arcs, drawing:
   angle options, 105
   direction option, 106
   double line, 331–32
   elliptical, 109–11
   isometric, 617–18
   length of chord option, 105–6
   polyline, 301–3
   from previously drawn line of arc, 106–7
   radius option, 106
   start, center, end options, 104–5
   three-point specification, 104
Area:
   calculating, 207–9, 308
   drawing size, 41–43, 88
AREA (AA) command, 207–9, 210
Argument, 715
Array(s):
   defined, 246

   polar, creating, 248–49
   rectangular, creating, 246–48
ARRAY (AR) command, 246–49
Arrowheads, isometric, 619–20
Arrowless dimensioning, 424, 435–36
Arrowless tabular dimensions, 435–36
Aspect ratio, 493
Associative dimensions, 468
Associative hatch patterns, 383
ATTACHURL command, 665
Attach Xref dialog box, 545
ATTDISP command, 527
ATTEDIT (AE) command, 89, 526
ATTEXT (AX) command, 533
ATTREQ system variable, 528
Attribute definition:
   defining, 191, 520–23
   modifying, 524–25
Attribute Definition dialog box, 520–23
Attribute extraction, 528–35
Attribute Extraction dialog box, 532
Attributes, block (*See* Block attributes)
AutoCAD LT (*See also* Customizing AutoCAD LT):
   discussion groups, 659
   installing, 11–12, 731–40
   role of, 11
   starting, 11–19
   Website/home page, 656–59
AutoSnap:
   changing settings, 193–94
   role of, 182, 183
AX (*See* ATTEXT command)

B

BASE (BA) command, 512
Base grips, 240

783

Baseline dimensioning, 430–31
Base point option, 242, 250
   for mirror line, 268
Basic dimension, 458
Bearings, 87
BHATCH (H) command:
   accessing ISO pattern types, 388
   changing pattern properties, 386–88
   drawing a hatch pattern, 389–91
   pattern type list options, 388–89
   role of, 383
   selecting pattern type, 384–86
Big fonts, 350
Binary files, 634
Binding:
   defined, 555
   dependent symbols, 556–57
   Xrefs, 555–56
Bitmap files, 637
BLIPMODE command, 61
Blips, 59, 61
Block(s):
   Content Explorer used to insert, 498–500
   defined, 191, 399, 486
   defining/redefining block definitions from symbol library, 516
   drag-and-drop insertion, 498–99
   creating, 486–90
   editing, 501
   exploding, 502–3
   inserting, 491–98
   inserting drawing files, 513–15
   inserting exploded, 502–3
   insertion base point, 488–89
   layers and, 507–8
   locally defined, 491, 503–5
   naming, 487–88
   nesting, 503, 505–6
   presetting insertion parameters, 496–97
   redefining locally defined, 503–5
   reference, defined, 500
   references and layer controls, 508
   renaming, 505
   saving, as separate drawing files, 510–13
   unnamed, 630
Block attributes:
   attribute definitions;
     defining, 520–23
     modifying, 524–25
   automating drawing procedures using, 524

   defined, 519
   editing individual values, 525–27
   error messages, 533–34
   extracting values from a drawing, 528–35
   invisible, 520
   role of, 486
   suppressing prompts, 528
   visible, 519
BLOCK command, 498, 499
Block Definition dialog box, 487
BMAKE command, 487
BMPOUT command, 637
Boolean operations, 210
   INTERSECT, 212
   SUBTRACT, 211–12
   UNION, 211
Boundary edges, 278
Boundary hatch, defined, 383
Boundary Hatch dialog box, 365, 366–81, 383, 384–99
   Advanced ... button, 394
   Associative toggle, 398–99
   Define Boundary Set area, 394–95
   Exploded toggle, 399
   Inherit Properties < button, 397
   Island Detection toggle, 396
   Pick Points < button, 392
   Remove Islands < button, 393–94
   Retain Boundaries toggle, 397
   Select Objects < button, 392
   specifying boundary object type, 397
   style options, 396
   View Selection < button, 394
Boundary set, 394–95
Bounding box, 637
BREAK (BR) command, 271–72, 685, 686
Break option:
   double lines and, 333
   PEDIT (PE) command, 308–9
BROWSER command, 656
B-spline, 313–14
   nonuniform rational, 318
Button Editor dialog box, 688–90
Button Properties dialog box, 683, 684, 686–88
Buttons (*See also* Toolbar buttons):
   dialog box, 13
   flyout, 21
   image, 15
   radio, 14
   window control, 17

BYBLOCK, 167
Byblock setting, 508
ByLayer, 160, 166–67
Bytes, 2, 627

C

C (*See* CIRCLE command)
CAD (*See* Computer-aided drafting)
CADD (*See* Computer-aided design and drafting)
CAmera option, 608
Canceling:
   commands, 18
   object snaps, 187
Cards, 2–3
Caret (^), use of, 684
Carpal tunnel syndrome, 3, 9
Cartesian coordinate system, 51
Cascading submenu, 19, 705–6
CDF (Comma Delimited File format), 532, 535
CD-ROM, 6
CE (*See* CONTENT command)
Cell, 643
Center Justify option, 345
Center object snap, 187–88
Central processing unit (CPU), 2
CH (*See* CHANGE command)
CHA (*See* CHAMFER command)
Chain dimensioning, 429–30
CHAMFER (CHA) command, 282–84, 316
Chamfer option, 114–15
Chamfers:
   defined, 279
   distance and angle method, 283
   distance method, 282–83
   drawing, 282–84
   on polylines, 316
   Trim option, 284
CHANGE (CH) command, 372
Change Dictionaries dialog box, 376–78
Change Properties dialog box, 170–71
Characters, setting special, 364–66
Check Spelling dialog box, 375–76
CHPROP (CH) command, 170, 598
CIRCLE (C) command, 100–3, 189–90, 198
Circles, dimensioning, 433–34
Circles, drawing:
   with center and diameter, 100–1
   with center and radius, 100

INDEX

isometric, 617–18
tangent to two objects, 102–3
with three-point option, 101–2
with two-point option, 101
Circles, drawing polygons based on, 112–13
Circular referencing, 548
Circumference, circle, 101
Client application, 639
Clip art, 536–37, 635
Clipboard:
  defined, 285
  editing with, 285–86
  linking objects using, 642–45
  pasting text from, 366
CLip option, 612
Clipping plane, 612
Clones, 2
Closing:
  polygons, 55–56
  polylines with PEDIT (PE) command, 306
  polylines with PLINE (PL) command, 300
  a spline, 320–21
  SPLINEDIT command, 323, 325
COLOR command, 167–68
Color to surfaces, adding, 604–6
Comma Delimited File (CDF) format, 532, 535
Command(s):
  accessing, 16–18
  aliases, 22, 671–74
  apostrophe preceding, 140–41
  canceling, 18
  dimensioning, 473–74
  repeating previous, quickly, 56
  scripts, 674–77
  transparent, 60–61, 140–41, 146–47, 168, 685
  underscore in, 48
  undoing and redoing, 63, 69–70
Commands, types of (*See also under name of*):
  APERTURE (AP), 193
  ARC (A), 103–107
  AREA (AA), 207–9, 210
  ARRAY (AR), 246–49
  ATTACHURL, 665
  ATTDISP, 527
  ATTEDIT (AE), 89, 526
  ATTEXT (AX), 533
  BASE (BA), 512
  BHATCH (H), 383, 384–91

BLIPMODE, 61
BLOCK, 498, 499
BMAKE, 487
BMPOUT, 637
BREAK (BR), 271–72, 685, 686
BROWSER, 656
CHAMFER (CHA), 282–84, 316
CHANGE (CH), 372
CHPROP (CH), 170, 598
CIRCLE (C), 100–3, 189–90, 198
COLOR, 167–68
CONTENT (CE), 400
COPY (CP), 242–43
COPYCLIP, 286, 642
COPYLINK, 647
CUTCLIP, 285
DDATTDEF (DAD), 520
DDATTE (DE), 89, 525
DDATTEXT (DAX), 532–34
DDCHPROP, 170, 508
DDCOLOR, 167, 168
DDEDIT (ED), 367–68
DDEMODES, 508
DDGRIPS, 241
DDIM (DM), 438
DDINSERT (I), 491–97, 513, 522, 523
DDLMODES, 152, 164
DDLTYPE, 159, 165
DDMODIFY, 284–85, 369–71, 501, 524–25
DDOSNAP, 192
DDPTYPE, 196
DDRENAME, 169, 349, 505
DDRMODES, 44, 59, 60, 204, 616
DDSELECT, 238, 239
DDSTYLE, 348, 354
DDUCS (UC), 591–92
DDUCSP (UCP), 592
DDUNITS, 93, 94
DDVIEW (V), 144
DELAY, 676–77
DETACHURL, 666
DIM, 437, 472, 473–74
DIMALIGNED (DAL), 431
DIMANGULAR (DAN), 432–33
DIMBASELINE (DBA), 430
DIMCENTER (DCE), 436, 444–45
DIMCONTINUE (DCO), 429–30
DIMDIAMETER (DDI), 433–34
DIMEDIT (DED), 437, 470
DIMLINEAR (DLI), 425–28
DIMORDINATE (DOR), 435, 436
DIMRADIUS (DRA), 434
DIMSTYLE (DST), 471

DIMTEDIT, 469–70
DIST (DI), 207
DIVIDE (DIV), 197
DLINE (DL), 299, 328–33
DONUT (DO or DOUGHNUT), 116–17
DRGINSERT, 402
_.drginsert Insertion point, 499–500
DSVIEWER (DS), 141, 143
DTEXT (DT), 342–53, 364–65
DVIEW (DV), 606–11
DXFIN (DN), 632
DXFOUT (DX), 633
ELEV, 600
ELLIPSE (EL), 108–11, 617–18
END, 183–84
ENDP, 184
ERASE (E), 62–67
EXPLODE (X), 286, 313, 316–17, 399, 409, 502
EXPORT, 663
EXTEND (EX), 278–79, 313
FILL, 118
FILLET (F), 279–81, 316, 686
GRAPHSCR, 677
GRID, 44–45, 60
GROUP, 248, 481, 484
HATCH (-H), 383, 404–10
HATCHEDIT (HE), 384, 411–12
HELP, 31
HIDE (HI), 601, 604
ID, 206
IMPORT (IMP), 536
INDEXCTL, 550–51
INSERT, 497, 498, 502, 516
INSERTOBJ, 640, 645–46
INSERTURL, 663
INTERSECT (IN), 212
ISOPLANE (IS), 616
–LAYER (-LA), 163–66
LEADER (LE), 462–65
LENGTHEN (LEN), 255–58
LIMITS (LM), 95
LINE (L), 47–48
LINETYPE (LT), 159, 163–66, 168
LIST (LS), 209
LISTURL, 666
LTSCALE (LTS), 164, 165, 166
MASSPROP, 212
MEASURE (ME), 198
MENULOAD, 699
MENUUNLOAD, 699
MIRROR (MI), 244–45, 261, 268–69, 373

Commands, types of, *continued*:
 MOVE (M), 249–50, 261, 264–66
 MREDO, 70
 MSLIDE, 240, 649, 650
 MSPACE (MS), 565
 MTEXT (MT), 355–67
 MVIEW (MV), 560–62
 NEW, 28–29
 OFFSET (OF), 243–44
 OLELINKS, 647
 OOPS, 68
 OP, 50
 OPEN, 29, 50
 OPENURL, 663
 ORTHO, 59–60, 200–1
 OSNAP (O), 192–93
 PAINTER, 287–88
 PAN (P), 137–40
 PASTECLIP, 285, 286, 640
 PASTESPEC, 643
 PEDIT (PE), 305–17
 PICKBOX, 68, 239, 333
 PICKFIRST, 67
 PLAN, 590
 PLINE (PL), 299–305
 PLOT, 71, 240
 POINT (PO), 191, 196
 POLYGON (PG), 112–16
 PREFERENCES (PR), 137
 PRINT, 71
 PSOUT, 240, 638
 PURGE (PU), 628–29
 QTEXT (QT), 374
 QUIT, 30–31
 RAY, 219–20
 RECTANG (REC), 114–16
 REDO, 69–70
 REDRAW (R), 61, 240
 REGEN (RE), 118, 240
 REGION (REG), 210
 REINIT (RI), 673
 RENAME (REN), 169
 RESUME, 677
 REVCLOUD, 299, 334–35
 ROTATE (RO), 250–52 , 261, 266–67
 RSCRIPT, 677
 RTZOOM, 136
 SAVE, 49
 SAVEAS, 48–49, 97
 SAVEURL, 661
 SCALE (SC), 253–55, 261, 267–68
 SCRIPT (SCR), 674
 SELECT (SE), 237, 563, 685–86
 SELECTURL, 666
 SHADE (SH), 604
 SLIDELIB, 650
 SNAP, 44–45, 60
 SOLID (SO), 117
 SPELL (SP), 374
 SPLINE (SPL), 313, 318–22
 SPLINEDIT, 322–27
 STRETCH (S), 259–60, 261, 262–64, 313, 468–69
 STYLE (ST), 348, 354, 618
 SUBTRACT (SU), 211–12
 TEXT (T), 342–53
 TEXTSCR, 677
 THICKNESS (TH), 598
 TILEMODE (TM), 560
 TIME (TI), 209–10
 TOLERANCE (TOL), 465
 TRIM (TR), 273–77, 313
 UCS, 587–93
 UCSICON, 560, 586–87
 UNDO (U), 69–70
 UNION (UNI), 211
 UNITS (UT), 93–95
 'VIEW, 146–47
 VPLAYER (VL), 567–70
 VPOINT (VP), 594–96
 VPORTS, 613–16
 VSLIDE (VS), 240, 649, 650, 676–77
 WBLOCK (W), 511–12, 630
 WMFIN (WI), 536, 636
 WMFOPTS, 537, 636
 WMFOUT (WO), 636–37
 XATTACH (XA), 545
 XBIND (XB), 556
 XLINE (XL), 214–20
 XREF (XR), 544–46, 549, 555–57
 ZOOM (Z), 127–37
Command window, 18
 how to use, 22–23
 scroll bars, 18
Compact disks (CDs), 6
Compatibles, 2
Compiling, 689
Complex linetype, 718, 719
Composite, defined, 558
Computer-aided design and drafting (CADD), role of, 1
Computer-aided drafting (CAD), role of, 1
Computers/computer equipment:
 accessibility options for people with disabilities, 10
 central processing unit, 2
 data storage devices, 6
 keyboards, 3–4
 memory, 2
 monitors, 3
 networks, 7–8
 operating systems, 8
 plotters, 6–7
 pointing devices, 4–6
 printers, 6
 terminology, 2
 types of, 2–3
Construction lines:
 at an angle, 217–18
 between two points, 214–15
 bisector of an angle, 218
 defined, 214
 horizontal and vertical, 215–16
 offset from another line, 218–19
 RAY command used to draw, 219–20
 role of, 214
 XLINE (XL) command used to draw, 214–20
Container application, 639
CONTENT (CE) command, 400
Content Explorer, 17, 486
 changing views in, 518–19
 creating symbol libraries with, 517–18
 drag-and-drop hatching and, 400–3
 external references attached with, 546
 inserting blocks with, 498–500
 inserting drawing files with, 514–16
Continuous dimensioning, 429–30
Control codes, 364–66
Coordinate display, 47
Coordinate filters, 200
Coordinates:
 absolute, 52
 Cartesian, 51
 changing from one display to another, 55
 combining, 57–58
 cylindrical, 582–84
 defined, 51
 drawing lines using, 51–55
 polar, 54–55
 relative, 53–54
 spherical, 582–84
 3-D drafting:
  applying, 584–85
  cylindrical, 582–84
  polar coordinate entry, 582–83
  right-hand rule, 82
  spherical, 582–84
  using X, Y, Z point, 580–81
COPY (CP) command, 242–43
COPYCLIP command, 286, 642
Copying objects:
 ARRAY (AR) command, 246–49
 COPY (CP) command, 242–43

INDEX

COPYCLIP command, 286
MIRROR (MI) command, 244–45
OFFSET (OF) command, 243–44
properties of, 287–88
Copying with grips:
  MOVE command, 264–66
  STRETCH command, 264
COPYLINK command, 647
CP (*See* COPY command)
Create Block dialog box, 486–90
Create Drawing File dialog box, 511
Create New Drawing dialog box, 29, 85, 92–93
Create Slide File dialog box, 649
Create Tab dialog box, 517
Crosshairs, 4
Crossing box, erasing objects with, 64–65
Crossing Polygon option, 234–35
Cubic curve, 314
Current layer, 160–61
Cursor, 4
Customize Toolbars dialog box, 679–80
Customizing AutoCAD LT:
  command aliases, 671–74
  command scripts, 674–77
  DIESEL (Direct Interpretively Evaluated String Expression Language), 714–17
  hatch patterns, 722–27
  linetypes, 718–22
  menus, 693–714
  reasons for, 671
  toolbars and toolbar buttons, 677–93
CUTCLIP command, 285
Cutting edges, 273
Cutting objects, 285
Cycling, 236
Cylindrical coordinates, 582–84

D

DAD (*See* DDATTDEF command)
DAL (*See* DIMALIGNED command)
DAN (*See* DIMANGULAR command)
Data:
  field, 524
  storage devices, 6
  unreferenced, 628
Data files, linking objects using, 645–47
Date stamp, 89
Datum, defined, 435
Datum/baseline dimensioning, 430–31
DAX (*See* DDATTEXT command)

DBA (*See* DIMBASELINE command)
DCE (*See* DIMCENTER command)
DCO (*See* DIMCONTINUE command)
DDATTDEF (DAD) command, 520
DDATTE (DE) command, 89, 525
DDATTEXT (DAX) command, 532–34
DDCHPROP command, 170, 508
DDCOLOR command, 167, 168
DDEDIT (ED) command, 367–68
DDEMODES command, 508
DDGRIPS command, 241
DDI (*See* DIMDIAMETER command)
DDIM (DM) command, 438
DDINSERT (I) command, 491–97, 513, 522, 523
DDLMODES command, 152, 164
DDLTYPE command, 159, 165
DDMODIFY command, 284–85, 369–71, 501, 524–25
DDOSNAP command, 192
DDPTYPE command, 196
DDRENAME command, 169, 349, 505
DDRMODES command, 44, 59, 60, 204, 616
DDSELECT command, 238, 239
DDSTYLE command, 348, 354
DDUCS (UC) command, 591–92
DDUCSP (UCP) command, 592
DDUNITS command, 93, 94
DDVIEW (V) command, 144
DE (*See* DDATTE command)
Decimal degrees, 86
Decimal units, 40, 41, 58
Decurve option, PEDIT (PE) command, 314–15
DED (*See* DIMEDIT command)
Define Boundary Set area, 394–95
Define New View dialog box, 145
Degrees/minutes/seconds, 86
DELAY command, 676–677
Deleting:
  files, 628–31
  Named Views, 146
  toolbars, 680
Delimit, defined, 532
DELOBJ system variable, 320
Delta option, 255–56, 258
Demand loading, 551–52
Dependent symbols, 546–47, 556–57
Desktop, 9
DETACHURL command, 666
Deviation/unequal bilateral tolerance, 457

Device-independent bitmap, 637
DI (*See* DIST command)
Dialog boxes:
  buttons, 13
  editing with, 284–85
  edit/text, 14
  error messages, 15–16
  image buttons, 15
  keyboard shortcuts, 16
  list, 13
  popup list, 13–14
  radio buttons, 14
  role of, 12–13
  sliders, 15
  sub-, 13
  toggles, 15
  types of:
    Advanced Options, 394, 395
    Advanced Setup, 85–95, 559
    Annotation, 453–62
    Attach Xref, 545
    Attribute Definition, 520–23
    Attribute Extraction, 532
    Block Definition, 487
    Boundary Hatch, 383, 384–99
    Button Editor, 688–90
    Button Properties, 683, 684, 686–88
    Change Dictionaries, 376–78
    Change Properties, 170–71
    Check Spelling, 374–75
    Create Block, 486–90
    Create Drawing File, 511
    Create New Drawing, 29, 85, 92–93
    Create Slide File, 649
    Create Tab, 517
    Customize Toolbars, 679–80
    Define New View, 145
    Dimension Style, 438–40
    Direction Control, 94
    Drawing Aids, 44, 220, 221, 616
    Edit Attribute Definition, 524, 525
    Edit Text, 367–68
    Export Data, 663, 664
    Export Options, 550
    External Reference, 544, 552–53
    Flyout Properties, 691–92
    Format, 446–52
    Geometry, 440–45
    Grips, 241
    Import File, 536
    Import WMF, 536–37, 635
    Insert, 491–96
    Insert Object, 646
    Internet Configuration, 661, 662

Dialog boxes, types of, *continued:*
   Layer & Linetype Properties, 152–54, 157–59, 161, 162, 165, 170, 172, 174
   Links, 647–48
   Load or Reload Linetypes, 157, 158
   Menu Customization, 696–99
   Modify Arc, 170, 270
   Modify Attribute Definition, 524–25
   Modify Block Insertion, 501
   Modify Circle, 170, 270, 284–85
   Modify Line, 170, 270
   Modify MText, 370–71
   Modify Text, 369–70
   Modify Toolbars, 683–84
   New Text Style, 349
   New Toolbar, 680
   Object Selection Settings, 67, 68, 238
   Object Sort Method, 239
   Open DWG from URL, 663
   Ortho/Polar Settings, 204–5
   Osnap Settings, 192, 194
   Paste Special, 643–45
   Pen Assignments, 174, 175
   Plot Rotation and Origin, 73
   Point Style, 196
   Preferences, 137
   Preview, 30
   Preview Effective Plotting Area, 74
   Primary Units, 453–56
   Print/Plot Configuration, 71–76
   Property Settings, 288
   Purge, 628, 629
   Quick Setup, 39–40
   Re-initialization, 673
   Remote Transfer in Progress, 662
   Rename, 169
   Rename Text Style, 349
   Save Drawing As, 29, 48–49, 97–98
   Save DWG to URL, 661
   Select Color, 155–56, 167
   Select Drawing File, 510, 513
   Select File, 29, 50
   Select File to Attach, 544
   Select Layer, 170
   Select Linetype, 157, 158
   Select Linetype File, 159
   Select Menu File, 697
   Select Script File, 675
   Select Slide File, 649
   Set Layer Filters, 172–73
   Start Up, 39, 85
   Substitute Block Name, 546
   Symbol, 464
   Text Style, 348–52
   UCS Control, 591–92
   UCS Orientation, 593
   Unicode Character Map, 360
   Units Control, 94
   User Arrow, 443
   View Control, 144–45
   Window Selection, 72
Diameter:
   circle, 100–1
   dimensioning, 433–34
Dictionaries, 376–78
DIESEL (Direct Interpretively Evaluated String Expression Language), 714–17
Diffuse reflective light, 605
Digitizer tablet, 5
DIMALIGNED (DAL) command, 431
DIMANGULAR (DAN) command, 432–33
DIMASO dimension variable, 469
DIMBASELINE (DBA) command, 430
DIMCENTER (DCE) command, 436, 444–45
DIM command, 437, 472, 473–74
DIMCONTINUE (DCO) command, 429–30
DIMDIAMETER (DDI) command, 433–34
DIMEDIT (DED) command, 437
Dimensions/dimensioning:
   aligned, 423, 431, 436, 450
   angular, 431
   arcs, 432–34
   arrowless/ordinate, 424, 435–36
   associative, 468
   basic, 458
   chain, 429–30
   circles, 433–34
   at command line, 473–74
   datum/baseline, 430–31
   defined, 423
   diameter, 433–34
   dual, 461
   editing existing, 468–72
   linear, 425–28
   location, 423
   notes, 423, 462–65
   oblique, 437
   ordinate/arrowless, 424, 435–36
   prefixes and suffixes, setting, 461–62
   primary units, 453–56
   radius, 434
   rounding off dimension numerals, 462
   size, 423
   specified, 456
   standards, 424
   tolerances, 456–59
   unidirectional, 423, 436
Dimension Style dialog box, 438–40
Dimension styles:
   creating, for use with mechanical drafting symbols, 466–67
   defined, 438
   families, working with, 439–40
   saving and renaming, 438–39
Dimension variables (dimvars), changing:
   defined, 438, 440
   format, 446–52
   geometry, 440–45
   text, 453–62
DIMLINEAR (DLI) command, 425–28
DIMORDINATE (DOR) command, 435, 436
DIMRADIUS (DRA) command, 434
DIMSHO dimension variable, 469
DIMSTYLE (DST) command, 471
DIMTEDIT command, 469–70
Dimvars (*See* Dimension variables, changing)
Direct distance entry, 200–1
Direct hatching, 407–8
Direct Interpretively Evaluated String Expression Language (DIESEL), 714–17
Direction, drawing arcs using, 106
Direction Control dialog box, 94
Directory folders:
   creating, 510
   looking in, 30
Disabilities, accessibility options for people with, 10
Discussion groups, 659
Diskettes, 6
Disks:
   compact, 6
   hard, 6
Displacement option, 243, 250

INDEX

Distance option:
   drawing chamfers with, 282–83
     and angle method, 283
   DVIEW (DV) command and, 609–10
Distances, calculating, 207
DIST (DI) command, 207
DIVIDE (DIV) command, 197
DL (*See* DLINE command)
DLI (*See* DIMLINEAR command)
DLINE (DL) command, 299, 328–33
DM (*See* DDIM command)
DN (*See* DXFIN command)
Docking toolbars, 28
DONUT (DO or DOUGHNUT) command, 116–17
Donuts, drawing, 116–17
DOR (*See* DIMORDINATE command)
Dot matrix printers, 6
Double-clicking, 11, 12
Double lines:
   Break option, 333
   defined, 299
   dragline, setting, 329
   drawing, 328–33
   drawing arcs, 331–32
   offsetting start of, 330–31
   placing caps on, 330
   snapping to other objects, 332–33
   width, setting, 328–29
DOUGHNUT (DO or DONUT) command, 116–17
Download, 656, 661
DRA (*See* DIMRADIUS command)
Drag-and-drop hatching, Content Explorer and, 400–3
Drag-and-drop insertion:
   of adding buttons, 680–82
   of blocks, 491–98
   of exploded blocks, 502–3
   of text, 367
Dragline options, 329
Drawing(s):
   arcs, 103–7
   chamfers, 282–84
   circles, 100–3
   construction lines, 214–20
   database, 140
   donuts, 116–17
   double lines, 328–33
   ellipses, 108–9
   elliptical arcs, 109–11
   ending, 30–31
   environment, 39
   extents, 72, 139
   external, 543
   external reference, 543–57
   file extension .dwg, 29–30
   fillets, 279–81
   limits, 42, 43, 72
   lines, 46–59
   naming, 48–49
   opening, 50, 663
   origin, 47, 51
   polygons, 112–16
   polylines, 299–305
   printing, 71–76
   rays, 219–20
   rectangles, 112, 114–16
   revision clouds, 334–35
   saving changes, 30, 48–49, 663–64
   setting size of, 41–43
   solids, 117–18
   spline curves, 318–27
   starting a session, 28–30
   time, 209–10
Drawing aids:
   Blips, 59, 61
   factors to consider when setting values, 45–46
   Grid, 44–45
   Ortho, 59–62
   Snap, 44–45
Drawing Aids dialog box, 44, 220, 221, 616
Drawing display area, changing, scroll bars for, 139–140 (*See also* Aerial View window; Named Views; Pan/panning; Zoom/zooming; ZOOM command)
Drawing extents, 139
Drawing files:
   exchanging, 631–39
   hyperlinks in, 665
   inserting, 513–15
   managing size of, 627
   networked environments and sharing, 631
   purging, 628–31
   saving blocks as separate, 510–13
   self-referencing, 513
Drawing Interchange File (.DXF), 532, 632–34
Drawing setup options:
   Advanced Setup for, 85–95
   changing, 93–95
   model and paper space, 43
   Quick Setup for, 39–40
   from scratch, 92–93
   setting limits, 42, 43
   setting size of drawings, 41–43
   setting units of measure, 40–41, 85
   templates for, 93, 96–99
Drawing Web Format (DWF) files, 663–64
   hyperlinks in, 665
Draw toolbar, 17, 20
DRGINSERT command, 402
_.drginsert Insertion point command, 499–500
DS (*See* DSVIEWER command)
DST (*See* DIMSTYLE command)
DSVIEWER (DS) command, 141, 143
DTEXT (DT) command:
   alignment/justification options, 344–46
   setting and creating text styles with, 348–52
   special characters and symbols, using, 364–66
   use of, 342–43
Dual dimensioning, 461
DVIEWBLOCK, 607
DVIEW (DV) command:
   CAmera option, 608
   CLip option, 612
   Distance option, 609–10
   exiting, 613
   Hide option, 612
   Off option, 612
   PAn option, 610–11
   POints option, 610
   role of, 606–7
   TArget option, 609
   TWist option, 611
   Undo option, 613
   Zoom option, 611
DWF (Drawing Web Format) files, 663–64
   hyperlinks in, 665
.DWG files, 631
   hyperlinks in, 665
DX (*See* DXFOUT command)
.DXF (*See* Drawing Interchange File)
DXFIN (DN) command, 632
DXFOUT (DX) command, 633
Dynamic option, 257–58

E

E command (*See* ERASE command/erasing)
ED (*See* DDEDIT command)
EDGEMODE system variable, 276, 278
Edge option, drawing polygons using, 113
Edit Attribute Definition dialog box, 524, 525
Edit boxes, 14
Editing (*See also* ERASE command/erasing):
  block attributes, 525–27
  blocks, 501
  changing objects from original position, 249–61
  copying methods, 242–49
  existing dimensions, 468–72
  existing text, 367–72
  global, 525–27
  grips for, 261–70
  hatch patterns, 411–12
  Modify Circle dialog box for, 284–85
  polylines, 305–17
  polyline vertices, 308–11
  selection methods, 233–41
  splines, 318–27
  trimming and extending objects, 271–79
  Windows Clipboard for, 285–86
Edit Text dialog box, 367–68
EL (*See* ELLIPSE command)
Electrophotographic plotters, 7
Elevation, 115, 579, 600
ELEV command, 600
Ellipse:
  defined, 108
  parts of, 108
ELLIPSE (EL) command, 108–11, 617–18
Ellipses, drawing:
  axis endpoint option, 108
  center option, 108–9
  rotation angle, 109
Elliptical arcs, drawing:
  included angles, 110–11
  parameters, 111
  start and end angles, 109–10
E-mail (electronic mail), 8, 655, 660–61
Embedding files [*See* Object Linking and Embedding (OLE)]
Encapsulated PostScript (EPS) files, 637–38
END command, 183–84
Ending drawings, 30–31
ENDP command, 184
Endpoint:
  leader, 436
  object snap, 183–84
Engineering units, 40, 41, 58
Enter key, 28
EPS [*See* Encapsulated PostScript (EPS) files]
Equal bilateral tolerance/symmetrical tolerance, 456
ERASE (E) command/erasing:
  crossing box for, 64–65
  defined, 62
  entering the command, 62
  getting erased objects back, 60, 62
  grips for, 61
  implied windowing and, 63–64
  last object drawn, 63
  noun/verb selection, 66–67
  picking objects, 62–63
  removing objects from those to be erased, 65–66
  selecting objects for, 62–64
Ergonomic keyboards, 4
Ergonomics, in the workplace, 9–10
Error messages:
  attribute extraction, 533–34
  dialog box, 15–16
Esc (escape) key, 18
EX (*See* EXTEND command)
Exchanging files, 631–39
  bitmap files, 637
  Drawing Interchange File (.DXF), 532, 632–34
  .DWG files, 631
  plotting, 639
  PostScript files, 637–38
  Windows MetaFile (WMF), 635–37
Exiting programs, 30–31
EXPLODE (X) command, 286, 313, 316–17, 399, 409, 502
Exploding:
  blocks, 502–3
  polylines, 316–17
EXPORT command, 663
Export Data dialog box, 663, 664
Exporting PostScript files, 637–38
Export Options dialog box, 550
Extended intersection, trimming to, 275–76
EXTEND (EX) command, 278–79, 313
Extending objects, 278–79
External drawing, 543
External Reference dialog box, 544, 552–53
External references (Xrefs):
  attaching, 544–46
  binding, 555–57
  Content Explorer and, 546
  defined, 543
  demand loading and, 550–51
  dependent symbols, 546–48
  detaching, 550
  directory path, 551–52
  obtaining information on, 552–53
  overlaying, 548–49
  resolved, 548
  unloading, 552
  updating, 551
  Xref log file, 553–54

F

F (*See* FILLET command)
Family member dimension style, 439–40
Fast font, 347
Fence selection option, 235
Field width, 529
File(s) [*See also* Drawing files; Object Linking and Embedding (OLE)]:
  binary, 634
  bitmap, 637
  compression tools, 661
  Drawing Web Format (DWF) files, 663–64
  exchanging, 631–39
  linking objects using data, 639–48
  managing size, 627
  networked environments and sharing, 631
  plotting to, 639
  PostScript, 637–38
  purging, 628–30
  server, 8, 631
  slide, 649–50
  sound, 646–47
File transfer protocol (FTP), 661
File System page, 514
FILL command, 118
FILLET (F) command, 279–81, 316, 686

INDEX

Fillets:
  defined, 115, 279
  drawing, 279–81
  parallel lines, 281
  on polylines, 316
  setting radius, 279–80
  Trim option, 281
Filters:
  coordinate, 200
  defined, 200
  point, 200
Fit Data option, SPLINEDIT command, 322–24
Fit option:
  DTEXT command, 344–45
  PEDIT (PE) command, 312–13
Fit points:
  approximation, 322
  interpolation, 322
Fit Tolerance, adjusting spline, 321–22
Floating model space viewports:
  changing layer visibility, 567–71
  changing scale of viewport, 565–67
  defined, 559
  described, 560–65
Floating windows, 25
Flyout buttons, 21
Flyout Properties dialog box, 691–92
Flyouts, creating toolbar, 691–92
Font(s):
  big, 350
  defined, 341, 347
  fast, 347
  file, 347
  selecting, 349–50
  standard symbol, 763–64
Format, changing dimension
  adjusting text fit, 446–48
  alignment inside or outside extension lines, 451–52
  horizontal text alignment, 448–49
  vertical text alignment, 449–50
Format dialog box, 446–52
Fractional units, 40, 41, 58
From option, 198–99
FTP [*See* File transfer protocol (FTP)]

G

GDT font, 766
General notes, 423
Geometric characteristic symbols, 765
Geometry, changing dimension style:
  arrowhead appearance, 442–44
  center mark size, 445
  dimension line presentation, 440–41
  extension line presentation, 441–42
  scale factor, setting, 445
  using center marks in circles and arcs, 444
Geometry dialog box, 440–45
Global editing, 525–27
Global scale factor, 165
Gradient (grads), 87
Graphical user interface (GUI), 655
Graphics card, 3
Graphics screen, 17
GRAPHSCR command, 677
Grid, 44–45
GRID command, 44–45, 60
Grip(s):
  base, 240
  changing object properties with, 270
  commands, 261–62
  defined, 67, 240
  editing with, 261–70
  mirroring with, 268–69
  moving with, 264–66
  resizing viewports using, 564
  rotating with, 266–67
  scaling with, 267–68
  selecting with, 240–41
  stretching with, 262–64
  unselected, 240
  used to change layers and linetypes, 171
Grips dialog box, 241
GROUP command, 248, 481, 484
Grouping objects, 481–84
Group Manager, 481–84
Group toolbar, 484

H

H (*See* BHATCH command)
-H (*See* HATCH command)
Hardcopy, 6
Hard disks, 6
Hardware, 2
Hatch:
  boundary, 383
  defined, 383
HATCHEDIT (HE) command, 384, 411–12
HATCH (-H) command
  direct hatching with, 407–8
  hatching around text, 409–10
  individual elements used to draw, 408–9
  role of, 383, 404
  Solid option, 405–6
  User-defined option, 406–7
Hatching, Content Explorer and drag-and-drop, 400–3
Hatch patterns:
  associative, 383
  boundary, 383
  Boundary Hatch dialog box, 383, 384–99
  customizing, 722–27
  direct, 407–8
  editing, 411–12
  nonassociative, 383
  role of, 383
  standard, 761–62
Hatch patterns, BHATCH (H) command and:
  accessing ISO pattern types, 388
  angles, 387–88
  changing pattern properties, 386–88
  Custom option, 389
  drawing a hatch pattern, 389–91
  error messages, 391
  pattern type list options, 388–89
  previewing, 391
  role of, 384
  scale factor, 387, 388
  selecting pattern type, 384–86
  User-defined option, 388–89
Hatch patterns, HATCHEDIT (HE) command and, 384, 411–12
Hatch patterns, HATCH (-H) command and:
  direct hatching with, 407–8
  hatching around text, 409–10
  individual elements used to draw, 408–9
  role of, 383, 404
  Solid option, 405–6
  User-defined option, 406–7
HE (*See* HATCHEDIT command)
Healing, 399
Help/HELP command:
  browsing Contents, 31–33
  context-sensitive, 35
  display controls, 33
  index, 34
  on-line, 12–13, 31–35
  searching, 34–35
  string, 18, 20, 709–10
HI (*See* HIDE command)

Hidden lines, removing, 601–4
HIDE (HI) command, 601, 604
Hide option, 612
Hierarchical menu, 19
HTTP Secure Access, 662
Hyperlinks, 33
   defined, 655
   in DWG and DWF files, 665
HyperText Markup Language (HTML), 655

I

I (*See* DDINSERT command)
IBM, 2
ID command, 206
ID Point, 206
Image buttons, 15
Image tile menus, 706–9
IMP (*See* IMPORT command)
Implied windowing, 63–64, 238
Import File dialog box, 536
IMPORT (IMP) command, 536
Import WMF dialog box, 536–37, 635
IN (*See* INTERSECT command)
Included angle, 105, 110–11, 255
INDEXCTL command, 550–51
Individual object linetype scale factor, 165
INETLOCATION system variable, 656–57
Ink-jet plotters, 6
Ink-jet printers, 6
INSERT command, 497, 498, 502, 516
Insert dialog box, 491–96
Inserting:
   drawing files, 513–16
   drawings from URL, 663
Insertion, drag-and-drop:
   of blocks, 491–98
   of exploded blocks, 502–3
   of text, 367
Insertion base point, 488–89
Insertion Point object snap, 191
INSERTOBJ command, 640, 645–46
Insert Object dialog box, 646
Insert option, PEDIT (PE) command, 309
INSERTURL command, 663
Installing AutoCAD LT, 11–12, 731–40
Integrated Services Digital Network (ISDN), 656

IntelliMouse, 5, 6
   zooming with, 137
Interface, 11
   intuitive, 12
Internet:
   accessing Web resources, 656–66
   applications, 655
   connections, 655–56
   development of, 655
   e-mail, 8, 655, 660–61
   Explorer, 656
   search engine, 657
   Service Provider (ISP), 656
Internet Configuration dialog box, 661, 662
Internet Utilities, 655
   Drawing Web Format (DWF) files, 663–64
   hyperlinks in DWG and DWF files, 665
   inserting a drawing from URL, 663
   opening a drawing from a URL, 663
   saving a drawing to a URL, 661–63
   sending drawings as e-mail attachments, 660–61
   toolbar, 661
Interpolation point, 322
INTERSECT (IN) command, 212
Intersection object snap, 185–86
Intuitive interface, 12
Invisible block attributes, 520
IS (*See* ISOPLANE command)
ISDN (Integrated Services Digital Network), 656
ISO (International Organization for Standardization), pattern types, 388
Isometric:
   defined, 597
   drawings, 580
      arrowheads, 619–20
      circles and arcs, 617–18
      defined, 597
      role of, 616–17
      text, 618–19
   projection, 597
Isometric view toolbar buttons, 597
ISOPLANE (IS) command, 616

J

Join option, PEDIT (PE) command, 306–7

Justification:
   options, 344–46
   tolerance, 459

K

Keyboards, 3–4
   options, 770, 771–72
Keyboard shortcuts, 16
Kilobyte, 2

L

L (*See* LINE command)
-LA (*See* -LAYER command)
Label, 702
Landscape printer orientation, 75
Laser printers, 6
Layer(s):
   blocks and, 507–8
   changing listings, 170–73
   changing objects to correct, 170–71
   colors, 155–56, 167–68, 171
   creating, 152–60
   current, making, 160–61
   defined, 151
   freezing/thawing versus turning off, 162, 163
   grips used to change, 171
   linetypes, 157–60, 163–66, 168
   locking and unlocking, 162
   managing with –LAYER and –LINETYPE commands, 163–66
   naming, 151–52, 155
   overriding settings, 160–68
   plotting line widths assigned to, 174–75
   prefixes, 152
   renaming, 169–70
   visibility, controlling, 162
   visibility in floating model space viewports, 567–71
Layer & Linetype Properties dialog box, 152–54, 157–59, 161, 162, 165, 170, 172, 174
-LAYER (-LA) command, 163–66
Layout tab, 89, 91
LE (*See* LEADER command)
Leader bubble, 520
Leader endpoint, 436
LEADER (LE) command, 462–65
Leader lines, 462–65
LENGTHEN (LEN) command, 255–58

Lengthening objects:
  Delta option, 255–56, 258
  Dynamic option, 257–58
  Percent option, 256–57
  Select object option, 255
  Total option, 257, 258
Length of chord option, 105–6
Length option, PLINE, 304–5
Less than symbol (<), 13
Lettering, defined, 341
Libraries (*See also* Symbol libraries):
  search path, 488
  slide, 650
  standard support, 759–66
LIMITS (LM) command, 95
Limits of drawings, setting, 42, 43
Limits (plus/minus) tolerances, 457–58
Linear dimensions, 425–28
LINE (L) command:
  closing polygons, 55–56
  coordinates used for, 51–55, 57–58
  picking points with, 47–48
Line of sight, 609
Lines, drawing (*See also* Construction lines; Double lines; Polylines, PEDIT command and):
  closing polygons, 55–56
  coordinates used for, 51–55, 57–58
  picking points with LINE command, 47–48
  standards for, 46–47
Line text (*See* Single-line text)
Linetype(s):
  changing listings, 171–74
  complex, 718, 719
  controlling appearance of polyline, 315–16
  customizing, 718–22
  defined, 157
  grips used to change, 171
  overriding, 168
  renaming, 169–70
  scale, 164–66
  simple, 718–19
  standard, 760–61
  using layer, 157–60
LINETYPE (LT) command, 159, 163–66, 168
Linking files [*See* Object Linking and Embedding (OLE)]
Links dialog box, 647–48
List boxes, 13

Listing object properties, 209
Listing physical properties of regions, 212–13
LIST (LS) command, 209
LISTURL command, 666
LM (*See* LIMITS command)
Load or Reload Linetypes dialog box, 157, 158
Local area networks (LANs), 8
Locally defined blocks, 491, 503–5
Local notes, 462–65
Location dimensions, 423
Logical extents, 136, 140
Login, anonymous, 661
LS (*See* List command)
LT (*See* LINETYPE command)
LTSCALE (LTS) command, 164, 165, 166
Ltype gen option, 315–16

M

M (*See* MOVE command)
Macro, 678, 685
Major axis of ellipse, 108
Markers, AutoSnap, 182, 183
MASSPROP command, 212
MAXACTVP system variable, 564
MaxHatch setting, 410
Maximizing windows, 25
MEASURE (ME) command, 198
Measurements, setting, 40–41, 58–59, 85
MEASUREMENT system variable, 401
Megabyte (MB), 2
Memory, 2
Menu(s):
  accelerator keys, 19, 710–13
  access keys, 18
  call, 700
  cascading submenu, 19, 705–6
  compiled, 693
  customizing, 693–714
  files, 693
  help strings, 18, 20, 709–10
  hierarchical, 19
  how to use, 16–18
  image tile, 706–9
  loading, 696–99
  partial menu file, 695–96, 701
  pull-down, 18–19, 701–4
  resource, 693
  sections, 694–95

  shortcut key, 702
  source file, 693
  tablet, 714
  template, 6, 693
  walking, 19
  working with buttons, 694–95, 699–701
Menu Customization dialog box, 696–99
MENUGROUP name, 695–96
MENULOAD command, 699
MENUUNLOAD command, 699
MI (*See* MIRROR command)
Microcomputers, 2
Middle Justify option, 345–46
Midpoint object snap, 184
Minimizing windows, 25
Minor axis of ellipse, 108
Mirroring:
  with grips, 268–369
  objects with text, 373
Mirror line, 245, 268
MIRROR (MI) command, 244–45, 261, 268–69, 373
MIRRTEXT system variable, 373
Mode, defined, 59, 89
Model, defined, 558
Model space:
  concepts, 91, 558–59
  defined, 43, 89, 558
  floating viewports, 559, 560–71
  tiled, 560, 572–573
Modems, 656
Modify Arc dialog box, 170, 270
Modify Attribute Definition dialog box, 524–25
Modify Block Insertion dialog box, 501
Modify Circle dialog box, 170, 270, 284–85
Modify Line dialog box, 170, 270
Modify Mtext dialog box, 370–71
Modify Text dialog box, 369–70
Modify toolbar, 17, 20
Modify Toolbars dialog box, 683–84
Monitors, 3
Mouse, 4–5
  system, 695
  zooming with IntelliMouse, 137
MOVE (M) command, 249–50, 261, 264–66
Move option:
  PEDIT (PE) command, 309–10
  SPLINEDIT command, 323–24, 325

Moving:
  grips and, 264–66
  objects, 249–50
MREDO command, 70
MSLIDE command, 240, 649, 650
MSPACE (MS) command, 565
MTEXT (MT) command:
  multiline text created with, 355–64
  role of, 347
  setting and creating text styles with, 348–53
  special characters and symbols, using, 364–66
Multiline text/Multiline Text Editor:
  Character tab, 358–61
  creating, 355–64
  editing with DDEDIT, 368
  editing with DDMODIFY, 370
  Find/Replace tabs, 362–63
  keystroke options, 356
  placing text at prompt line, 364
  popup menu for, 357–58
  Properties tab, 360–62
Multiple selection option, 237, 242
Multiview layout:
  defined, 558
  floating model space viewports, 559, 560–71
  model space, 558–59
  paper space, 559–60
  plotting, 573–74
MVIEW (MV) command, 560–62

N

Named object, 546
Named Views:
  defining, 145–46
  deleting, 146
  getting descriptions, 146
  restoring, 146
  role of, 144
  transparent management of, 146–47
Naming:
  blocks, 487–88
  drawings/files, 49
Nearest Point object snap, 191
Nested Xrefs, 544
Nesting blocks, 503, 505–6
Netscape Communicator, 656
Networked environments, sharing files and, 631
Networks, computer, 7–8
NEW command, 28–29

New Text Style dialog box, 349
New Toolbar dialog box, 680
Node object snap, 191
Nonassociative hatch patterns, 383
None object snap, 191
Nonremovable drives, 6
Nonuniform rational B-spline (NURBS), 318
Notepad text editor, 528, 530, 531, 672, 673, 674
Notes, general and specific, 423, 462–65
Noun/verb selection, 66–67
NURBS (*See* Nonuniform rational B-spline)

O

O (*See* OSNAP command)
Object application, 639
Object Linking and Embedding (OLE):
  defined, 639–40
  embedding AutoCAD LT drawings in other applications, 642
  embedding objects in AutoCAD LT drawings, 640–42
  linking AutoCAD LT drawings in other applications, 647
  linking objects in AutoCAD LT drawings using Clipboard, 642–45
  linking objects in AutoCAD LT drawings using data files, 645–47
  managing links in AutoCAD LT, 647–48
  slide files, 649–50
Object Properties toolbar, 17, 20
Object selection methods, 233
  customizing, 238–40
  Fence option, 235
  grips for, 240–41
  SELECT command, 237
  for stacked objects, 236–37
  Window and Crossing Polygon option, 234–35
Object Selection Settings dialog box, 67, 68, 238
Object snaps (*See also* AutoSnap):
  aperture size, adjusting, 193
  canceling, 187
  Center, 187–88
  disabling, 191

Endpoint, 183–84
Insertion Point, 191
Intersection, 185–86
Midpoint, 184
Nearest Point, 191
Node, 191
None, 180
Perpendicular, 186–87
Quadrant, 188
role of, 181–82
running, 191–93
Tangent, 189–90
Object Sort Method dialog box, 239
Oblique dimensioning, 437
Off option, 612
OFFSET (OF) command, 243–44
Offset options, double line, 330–31
Offset snap locations, 266
OLE (*See* Object Linking and Embedding)
OLELINKS command, 647
On-line help, 12–13, 31–35
OOPS command, 68
OP command, 50
OPEN command, 29, 50
Open DWG from URL dialog box, 663
Opening:
  drawings, 50
  drawings from a URL, 663
  polylines with PEDIT (PE) command, 306
  SPLINEDIT command, 325
OPENURL command, 663
Operating systems, 9
Optical disk drives, 6
Optical mouse, 5
Option line, 22
Ordinate dimensioning, 424, 435–36
Origin:
  coordinate, 51
  drawing, 47
Ortho, 59–62
ORTHO command, 59–60, 200–1
Ortho/Polar Settings dialog box, 204–5
OSNAP (O) command, 191–92
Osnap Settings dialog box, 192, 194
OS prompt, 650

P

P (*See* PAN command)
PAINTER command, 287–88

INDEX

Pan/panning:
    with Aerial View, 143
    defined, 127
    Pan Point tool, 138–39
    Real-Time Pan tool, 137
PAn option, 610–11
PAN (P) command, 137–40
Paper space:
    concepts, 91, 559
    defined, 43, 89, 558
    switching to, 560
Paragraph text (*See* Multiline text/Multiline Text Editor)
Parallel lines, filleting, 281
Parallel projection, 606
Parameters:
    defined, 716
    drawing elliptical arcs using, 111
Parent member dimension style, 439–40
Partial menu file, 701
PASTECLIP command, 285, 286, 640
PASTESPEC command, 643
Paste Special dialog box, 643–45
Pasting:
    defined, 286
    drawings, 286
    text from Clipboard, 36
Path objects, 638
Patterns, drawing (*See* Hatch patterns)
PEDIT (PE) command, polylines and:
    adding curve options, 314
    Break option, 308–9
    calculating area, 307
    closing and opening, 306
    command options, 306–16
    controlling appearance of linetypes, 315–16
    creating spline curves, 313–14
    editing, 305–17
    editing vertices, 308–11
    fitting curves to vertices, 312–13
    Insert option, 309
    joining objects to, 306–07
    Move option, 309–10
    Regen option, 310
    removing curve from a fit or spline curve, 314–15
    Straighten option, 310
    Tangent option, 310–11
    width, adjusting, 307
    Width option, 311
PEDIT (PE) command, spline curves and:
    adding curve options, 314
    creating, 313–14
    effects on editing commands, 314
    removing curve from, 314–15
Pen Assignments dialog box, 174, 175
Pencil plotters, 7
Pen parameters, 72, 174
Pen plotters, 7
Pentium processors, 2
Percent option, 256–57
Peripherals, 2
Perpendicular object snap, 186–187
Perspective view, 606
PG (*See* POLYGON command)
PGP (*See* ProGram Parameters)
PICKAUTO system variable, 686
Pick button, 5
Pick box, 62, 68
PICKBOX command, 68, 239, 333
PICKFIRST command, 67
Pipe, 547
Pixels, 3, 193
PLAN command, 590
PLINE (PL) command, polylines and:
    arcs, drawing, 301–3
    closing and undoing, 300
    command options, 300–5
    defined, 299
    drawing, 299–305
    length, adjusting, 304–5
    width, adjusting, 303–4
    vertices, 305–6
PLOT command, 71, 240 (*See also* Print/Plot Configuration dialog box):
    plotting line widths assigned to layer colors, 174–75
Plot Preview, 74–75
Plot Rotation and Origin dialog box, 73
Plot spooler, 639
Plotters, 6–7
Plotting to a file, 639
Plus/minus (limits) tolerances, 457–58
Point filters, use of, 200
Pointing devices, 4–6, 773–74
POINT (PO) command, 191, 196
Points and reference points:
    direct distance entry, 200–1
    dividing and measuring, 197–98
    From option, 198–99
    identifying, 206
    LINE command to pick, 47–48
    options, 196–97
    point filters, use of, 200
    tracking, 201–3
POints option, 610
Point Style dialog box, 196
Point-to-point dimensioning, 429–30
Polar arrays, creating, 248–49
Polar coordinates, 54–55
PolarSnap, 204–5
POLYGON (PG) command, 112–16
Polygons
    based on a circle, 112–13
    closing, 55–56
    defined, 55, 112
    drawing, 112–16
    edge option, 113
    regular, 112
    Window and Crossing Polygon option, 234–35
Polyline, defined, 208, 299
Polylines, PEDIT (PE) command and:
    adding curve options, 314
    Break option, 308–9
    calculating area, 307
    closing and opening, 306
    command options, 306–16
    controlling appearance of linetypes, 315–16
    converting spline, to true splines, 319–20
    creating spline curves, 313–14
    drawing fillets and chamfers on, 316–17
    editing, 305–17
    editing vertices, 308–11
    exploding, 316–17
    fitting curves to vertices, 312–13
    Insert option, 309
    joining objects to, 306–7
    Move option, 309–10
    Regen option, 310
    removing curve from a fit or spline curve, 314–15
    Straighten option, 310
    Tangent option, 310–11
    width, adjusting, 307
    Width option, 311
Polylines, PLINE (PL) command and:
    arcs, drawing, 301–3
    closing and undoing, 300
    command options, 300–5
    defined, 299
    drawing, 299–305
    length, adjusting, 304–5
    width, adjusting, 303–4

Polylines, PLINE (PL) command and, *continued*:
   vertices, 305–6
Popup list boxes, 13–14
Portrait printer orientation, 75
Positioning:
   toolbars, 27–28
   windows, 24–27
PostScript files, 637–38
Preferences dialog box, 137
PREFERENCES (PR) command, 137
Prefixes, setting, 461–62
Presets, 592–93, 597
Preview dialog box, 30
Preview Effective Plotting Area dialog box, 74
Previous selection option, 237
PRINT command, 71
Primary units:
   defined, 453
   setting, 453–56
Primary Units dialog box, 453–56
Printed circuit boards, 2–3
Printers:
   orientation of, 75
   types of, 6
Printing drawings, Print/Plot Configuration dialog box, 71–76
Print/Plot Configuration dialog box:
   additional parameters, 72–73
   paper size and orientation, 72, 75
   pen parameters, 72
   plot preview, 74–75
   plotting line widths assigned to layer colors, 174–75
   scale, rotation, and origin, 73–74
   setup and default information, 71
ProGram Parameters (PGP), 671–74
Project option, 278
Prompt, 22
Property Painter, 287
Property Settings dialog box, 288
Prototype [*See* Template(s)]
PSOUT command, 240, 638
PU (*See* PURGE command)
Puck, 5
Pull-down menu, 18–19
   customizing, 701–4
Pull-down menu bar, 17
Purge dialog box, 628, 629
PURGE (PU) command, 628–29
Purging files, 628–31

Q

QTEXT (QT) command, 374
Quadrant, defined, 54, 188
Quadrant object snap, 188
Quadratic curve, 314
Quick Setup, 39–40
Quick Setup dialog box, 39–40
Quick text, making, 374
QUIT command, 30–31

R

R (*See* REDRAW command)
Radians, 87
Radio buttons, 14
Radius:
   circle, 100
   dimensioning, 434
   drawing arcs using, 106
   fillet, 279–80
Raster file, 631
Raster information, 536
RAY command, 219–20
Rays (*See* Construction lines)
RE (*See* REGEN command)
Read-only memory (ROM), 6
Real-Time Pan tool, 137
Real-Time Zoom tool, 135–36
Rectangles, drawing, 112, 114–16
RECTANG (REC) command, 114–16
Rectangular arrays, creating, 246–48
Recursive toolbar, 691
REDO command, 63
REDRAW (R) command, 69–70, 240
Reference angle, rotating with, 251–52
Reference option, 252
   grip rotation, 267
   to scale objects, 254–55
Reference points (*See* Points and reference points)
Referencing, defined, 543 [*See also* External references(XREFs)]
Refining spline curves, 325–27
REG (*See* REGION)
Regenerate option, PEDIT (PE) command, 310
Regenerating, 118, 140
REGEN (RE) command, 118, 240
REGION (REG) command, 210
Regions, listing physical properties of, 212–13
Regular polygons, 112
Re-initialization dialog box, 673
REINIT (RI) command, 673
Relative angle, rotating with, 251
Relative coordinates, 53–54
Remote Transfer in Progress dialog box, 662
Remove option, 65–66, 236, 271

Rename dialog box, 169
RENAME (REN) command, 169
Rename Text Style dialog box, 349
Renaming:
   blocks, 505
   dimension styles, 438–39
   layers and linetypes, 169–70
Rendering, 604
Repetitive stress, 9
Resolution:
   monitor display, 3
   printer/plotter, 6
Resolve, defined, 548
RESUME command, 677
REVCLOUD command, 299, 334–35
rEverse option, SPLINEDIT command, 327
Revision clouds, drawing, 334–35
Rewritable disks, 6
RI (*See* REINIT command)
Right-hand rule, 582
ROTATE (RO) command, 250–52, 261, 266–67
Rotating:
   grips and, 266–67
   objects, 250–52
   3-D viewing angle, 596
Rotation angle, 109
RSCRIPT command, 677
Rubberband line, 47
Running object snap, 191–93
RTZOOM command, 136

S

S (*See* STRETCH command)
SAVEAS command, 48–49, 97
SAVE command, 49
Save Drawing As dialog box, 29, 48–49, 97–98
Save DWG to URL dialog box, 661
SAVEURL command, 661
Saving:
   blocks as separate drawing files, 510–12
   dimension styles, 438–39
   drawings, 30, 48–49
   a drawing to a URL, 661–63
   templates, 97–98
Scale factor:
   geometry, 445
   global, 165
   hatch patterns, 387
   individual object linetype, 165
   insertion options, 495–96
   linetype, 164–66
   to scale objects, 253–54

INDEX

SCALE (SC) command, 253–55, 261, 267–68
Scaling:
  grips and, 267–68
  objects, 253–55
Scientific units, 40, 41, 59
SCR (*See* SCRIPT command)
.SCR file extension, 674–77
Script file formats, 674–77
SCRIPT (SCR) command, 674
Scroll bars, 17, 18
  for changing display area, 139–40
  how to make, visible, 140
SDF (Space Delimited File format), 532, 535
SE (*See* SELECT command)
Search area, 332
Search engine, 657
Select Color dialog box, 155–56, 167
Select Drawing File dialog box, 510, 513
Selected grips, 240
Select File to Attach dialog box, 544
Select File dialog box, 29, 50
Selection , set, 62, 65–66, 233 (*See also* Object selection methods)
Select Layer dialog box, 170
Select Linetype dialog box, 157, 158
Select Linetype File dialog box, 159
Select Menu File dialog box, 697
Select object option, 255
Select Script File dialog box, 675
SELECT (SE) command, 237, 563, 685–86
Select Slide File dialog box, 649
SELECTURL command, 666
Self-referencing drawing files, 513
Serifs, 347
Server application, 639
Set Layer Filters dialog box, 172–73
Setting up/installing AutoCAD LT, 11–12, 731–40
SHADEDGE system variable, 604–5
SHADEDIF system variable, 605–6
SHADE (SH) command, 604
Shading, 604
Simple linetypes, 718–19
Simulation [*See* 3-D surfaces, DVIEW (DV) command and simulating; 3-D surfaces, simulating]
Single-line text:
  alignment/justification options, 344–46
  defined, 341
  DTEXT and TEXT commands, 342–43
  editing with DDEDIT, 367–68

editing with DDMODIFY, 369–70
Size dimensions, 423
Sizing:
  toolbars, 27–28
  windows, 24–27
Slide files, 649–50
SLIDELIB command, 650
Slide library, creating, 650
Slider bar, 609
Sliders, 15
Slide show, 676
Smart mode, 276, 278–79
Snap (*See also* AutoSnap; Object snaps):
  angle, 220–22
  double lines to other objects, 332–33
SNAP command, 44–45, 60
SnapTip(s), 103, 182, 183
SO (*See* SOLID command)
Software, 2
Solid option, 405–6
Solids, drawing, 117–18
SOLID (SO) command, 117, 619
Sound files, 646–47
Space Delimited File (SDF) format, 532, 535
Specific notes, 423, 462–65
Specified dimension, 456
Spelling checker, 374–78
SPELL (SP) command, 374
Spherical coordinates, 582–84
SPLFRAME system variable, 319
SPLINE (SPL) command, 313, 318–22
Spline curves:
  PEDIT (PE) command and:
    adding curve options, 314
    creating, 313–14
    effects on editing commands, 314
    removing curve from, 314–15
  SPLINE (SPL) command and:
    adjusting Fit Tolerance, 321–22
    closing a spline, 320–21
    converting spline polylines to true splines, 320
    difference between NURBS and spline-fit, 318
    displaying spline frame, 319
  SPLINEDIT command and:
    Close/Open option, 325
    Fit Data options, 322–24
    moving a vertex, 325
    refining curves, 325–27
    rEverse option, 327
SPLINEDIT command, 322–27
Spline-fit curves, 318
SPLINESEGS system variable, 314

SPLINETYPE system variable, 314
ST (*See* STYLE command)
Stacked objects, selecting, 236–37
Standards:
  dimensioning, 424
  drafting, 741–57
Standards organizations, list of, 486
STANDARD text style, 347–48
Standard toolbar, 17, 20
Starting AutoCAD LT:
  basics, 11–12
  using dialog boxes, 12–16
Starting drawings, 28–30
Start Up dialog box, 39, 85
Status bar, 18
Straighten option, PEDIT (PE) command, 310
Stretching:
  grips and, 262–64
  objects, 259–60
STRETCH (S) command, 259–60, 261, 262–64, 313, 468–69
Style option, role of, 347
STYLE (ST) command, 348, 354, 618
Stylus, 5
Subdialog box, 13
Submenu, cascading, 19, 705–6
Substitute Block Name dialog box, 546
SUBTRACT (SU) command, 211–12
Suffixes, setting, 461–62
Support file, 671
Support path, 514
Surface model, 598
Surveyor angles, 87
Symbol(s) [*See also* Block(s)]:
  annotation, 494–95
  defined, 485
  dependent, 546–47, 556–57
  geometric characteristic, 765
  not allowed in file names, 49
  redirection, 650
  setting special characters and, 364–66
  standard text and fonts, 763–64
  sticky-backs, 485
  table, 554
  tolerance, 465
Symbol dialog box, 464
Symbol libraries:
  creating, 509–10
  with Content Explorer, 517–18
  defined, 509
  defining/redefining block definitions from, 516
Symmetrical/equal bilateral tolerance, 456

System mouse, 695
System variables:
  ATTREQ, 528
  DELOBJ, 320
  EDGEMODE, 276, 278
  INETLOCATION, 656–57
  MAXACTVP, 564
  MEASUREMENT, 401
  MIRRTEXT, 373
  PICKAUTO, 686
  SHADEDGE, 604–5
  SHADEDIF, 605–6
  SPLFRAME, 319
  SPLINESEGS, 314
  SPLINETYPE, 314
  TILEMODE, 560
  TRIMMODE, 281
  UCSFollow, 558
  VISRETAIN, 547–48
  WORLDVIEW, 595
  XREFCTL, 553

T

T (*See* TEXT command)
Tablet menus, customizing, 714
Tab sets, 517–18
Tagged image file format (TIFF), 639
Tangent, circle, 102–3
Tangent object snap, 189–90
Tangent option, PEDIT (PE) command, 310–11
TArget option, 609
Target point, 608
T-Carrier digital transmission, 655
Template(s):
  customizing existing, 96–99
  defined, 93, 485
  drawing with, 96–99
  file, 528
  saving, 97–98
Tendinitis, 3, 9
Text:
  alignment/justification options, 344–46
  backwards, 350–51
  boundary, 355–56
  boxes, 14
  changing dimension:
    alternate units, setting, 461
    prefixes and suffixes, setting, 461–62
    primary units, setting, 453–56
  rounding off dimension numerals, 462
  text options, setting, 460
  tolerance methods, setting, 456–59
  defined, 341
  drag-and-drop insertion of, 367
  DTEXT and TEXT commands, 342–43
  editing:
    CHANGE (CH) command for, 372
    DDEDIT (ED) command for, 367–68
    DDMODIFY command for, 369–71
  font, 341, 347
  formatting codes, 365–66
  hatching around, 409–10
  isometric, 618–19
  mirroring objects with, 373
  multiline, 355–64
  pasting from Clipboard, 366
  quick, 374
  screen, 17, 22–23
  single-line, 341–46
  slant of characters (obliquing angles), 351
  special characters and symbols, using, 364–66
  spell checker, 374–78
  standard, and fonts, 763–64
  upside down/backward, 350
  vertical, 351
  width settings, 351
TEXTSCR command, 677
Text Style dialog box, 348–52
Text styles:
  creating and using, 347–54
  customizing, 353–54
  defined, 341–42, 347
  defined with DDSTYLE command, 348
  defined with –STYLE command in prompt line, 348, 354
  steps in creating, 352–53
TEXT (T) command:
  alignment/justification options, 344–46
  setting and creating text styles with, 348–53
  special characters and symbols, using, 364–66
  use of, 342–43
Thermal plotters, 7
Thickness, 115, 579, 598–99
THICKNESS (TH) command, 598
3-D drafting [*See also* Isometric drawings; User Coordinate System (UCS)]:
  applying 3-D coordinates, 584–85
  benefits of, 579
  polar coordinate entry, 582–83
  right-hand rule, 582
  tiled viewports and, 613–16
  using X, Y, Z point coordinates, 580–81
3-D surfaces;
  DVIEW (DV) command and simulating:
    CAmera option, 608
    CLip option, 612
    Distance option, 609–10
    exiting, 613
    Hide option, 612
    Off option, 612
    PAn option, 610–11
    POints option, 610
    role of, 606–7
    TArget option, 609
    TWist option, 611
    Undo option, 613
    Zoom option, 611
  simulating:
    adding color to surfaces, 604–6
    defined, 601
    removing hidden lines, 601–4
3-D viewing angles:
  elevation, using, 600
  giving objects thickness, 598–99
  presets, 597
  Rotate option, 596
  VPOINT (VP) command for setting up, 594–96
Three-point option, 101–2
Through option, 244
TI (*See* TIME command)
TIFF (tagged image file format), 638
Tiled model space, 560, 572–73
Tiled viewports, 3-D drawing and, 613–16
TILEMODE (TM) command, 560
TILEMODE system variable, 560
TIME (TI) command, 209–10
Title bar, 17, 24
Title Block, 88–89
TM (*See* TILEMODE command)
Toggles, 15
Tolerances:
  basic dimension, 458

INDEX

defined, 455, 456
deviation/unequal bilateral, 457
height, 459
justification, 459
limits (plus/minus), 457–58
symbols, 443
symmetrical/equal bilateral, 456
unilateral, 435
TOLERANCE (TOL) command, 465
Toolbar buttons, 20–22
   adding, 680–83
   customizing, 683–93
   isometric view, 597
Toolbars:
   adding buttons to, 680–83
   creating a new, 680
   customizing, 677–93
   deleting, 680
   docking/attaching, 28
   Draw, 17, 20
   flyouts, 691–92
   Group, 484
   hiding of floating, 22
   how to use, 20–22
   Internet Utilities, 660
   isometric view, 597
   Modify, 17, 20
   Object Properties, 17, 20
   recursive, 691
   sizing and moving, 27–28
   Standard, 17, 20
Tooltip, 20
Total option, 257, 258
TR (See TRIM command)
Trackball, 5
Tracking points, 201–3
Transparent commands, 60–61, 140–41, 146–47, 168, 685
Trimming objects:
   AutoCAD LT smart mode, 276
   to extended intersection, 275–76
   how to do, 273–74
   multiple, 274–75
TRIMMODE system variable, 281
Trim option:
   CHAMFER command and, 284
   FILLET command and, 281
TRIM (TR) command, 273–77, 313
Troubleshooting, 675
TTR option, 102
TWist option, 611
Two-point option, 101

U

U (See UNDO command)
UC (See DDUCS command)
UCP (See DDUCSP command)
UCS (See User Coordinate System)
UCS command, 587–93
UCS Control dialog box, 591–92
UCSFollow system variable, 558
UCSICON command, 560, 586–87
UCS Orientation dialog box, 593
Underscore in commands, 48
Undo option:
   DVIEW (DV) command and, 613
   polylines and, 300
UNDO (U) command, 69–70
Unequal bilateral/deviation tolerance, 457
Unicode Character Map dialog box, 360
Unidirectional dimensioning, 423, 436
Uniform resource locator [See URL (uniform resource locator)]
Unilateral tolerance, 457
UNION (UNI) command, 211
Units, primary, 453–56
Units Control dialog box, 94
Units of measure, setting, 40–41, 58–59, 85
UNITS (UT) command, 93–95
Unnamed blocks, 630
Unreferenced data, 628
Unselected grips, 240
URL (uniform resource locator), 656
   inserting a drawing from, 663
   opening a drawing from, 663
   saving a drawing to, 661–62
User Arrow dialog box, 443
User Coordinate System (UCS), 580, 585
   controlling UCS icon, (UCSICON), 586–87
   customizing, 585–93
   displaying current, 590
   presets, 592–93
   relocating, 587–89
   working with named, 590–92
User-defined option, 406–7
UT (See UNITS command)

V

V command (See DDVIEW command)
Vector, 594, 723
Vector information, 536
Vertical bar, 547
Vertices, polyline:
   defined, 305–6
   editing, 308–11
   fitting curves to, 312–13
Video adapter card, 3
Video graphics array (VGA), 3
'VIEW command, 146–47
View Control dialog box, 144–45
Viewports, 91
   floating model space, 559, 560–71
   resizing, using grips, 564
   tiled, 613–16
Views (See also Multiview layout; 3-D viewing angles):
   changing drawing display area, scroll bars for, 139–40 (See also Aerial View window; Named Views; Pan/panning; Zoom/zooming; ZOOM command)
   in Content Explorer, changing, 518–19
   creating named, 144–47
   perspective, 606
   rolling, under camera, 607
Visible block attributes, 519
VISRETAIN system variable, 547–48
VPLAYER (VL) command, 567–70
VPOINT (VP) command for setting up, 594–96
Vport, use of term, 565
VPORTS command, 613–16
VSLIDE (VS) command, 240, 649, 650, 676–77

W

Walking menu, 19
WBLOCK (W) command, 511–12, 630
WCS (See World Coordinate System)
Web server, 661
Web (World Wide Web) (WWW), 655 (See also Internet)
Whip driver, 664
WI (See WMFIN command)
Width, 115
   double line, 328–29
Width option:
   adjusting polyline, 303–4, 307

Width option, *continued:*
  PEDIT (PE) command, 311
Window and Crossing Polygon option, 234–35
Window Selection dialog box, 72
Windows:
  accessibility features, 767–74
  control buttons, 17
  defined, 24
  displaying multiple, 27
  floating, 25
  implied, 63–64, 238
  maximizing, 25
  MetaFile (WMF), 536–37, 635–37
  minimizing, 25
  sizing and positioning, 24–27
Windows Clipboard:
  defined, 285
  editing with, 285–86
  linking objects using, 642–45
  pasting text from, 366
Windows MetaFile (WMF), 536–37, 635–37
Windows 95:
  drag-and-drop insertion of text, 367
  paper size and orientation, 75
Windows 97, paper size and orientation, 75
Windows NT 4.0:
  drag-and-drop insertion of text, 367
  paper size and orientation, 75

WinTab driver, 714
WinZip, 661
Wire frame, 584
Wizard:
  Advanced Setup, 85–95
  Quick Setup, 39–40
.WMF file (Windows MetaFile), 536–37
WMFIN (WI) command, 536, 636
WMFOPTS command, 537, 636
WMFOUT (WO) command, 636–37
Word wrapping, 355, 356
Workstations, 2
World Coordinate System (WCS), 435, 580, 582, 585–86
World size, 42
WORLDVIEW system variable, 595
World Wide Web (WWW) (Web), 655 (*See also* Internet)

X

X (*See* EXPLODE command)
XATTACH (XA) command, 545
XBIND (XB) command, 556
XLINE (XL) command, 214–20
XREFCTL system variable, 553
XREF (XR) command:
  attaching external references, 544–46
  binding, 555–56

  detaching, 550
  directory path, 551–52
  overlaying, 548–49
  updating, 551

Z

Zoom option, 611
Zoom/zooming:
  Aerial View, 142–43
  defined, 127
  in and out, 127
  IntelliMouse, 137
  transparent, 140–41
ZOOM XP (times paper space) option, 566
ZOOM (Z) command:
  options, 127
  Real-Time Zoom tool, 135–36
  Zoom All tool, 130
  Zoom Center tool, 133–35
  Zoom Extents tool, 133
  Zoom In option, 128–29
  Zoom Out tool, 129
  Zoom Previous tool, 135, 143
  Zoom Scale tool, 129–30
  Zoom Window tool, 130